PANEL LAYOUT
for competition[1]

First Edition Published	March 2012
Compiler	DAMDI Publishing Co.
Publisher	Suh, Kyong won
Editor	Pyo, Mi young
Design	Choi, Ye ji
Photograph	Roh, Kyung young
Intern	Lee, Chang wook
Translator	Lee, Ji eun
Publishing	RHED Publishing
Address	50 Playfair Road # 07-02
	Noel Building, Singapore 367995
TEL	+ 65 62899208
FAX	+ 65 62899108
E-mail	info@rhedpublishing.com
webpage	www.rhedpublishing.com

March 2012 by Damdi Publishing Co, Seoul
August 2012 by RHED Publishing, Singapore

Printing: Tiger Printing (Hongkong) Co., Ltd.
ISBN 978-981-07-3145-8 (set)

new
PANEL
LAYOUT
for competition1

CONTENTS

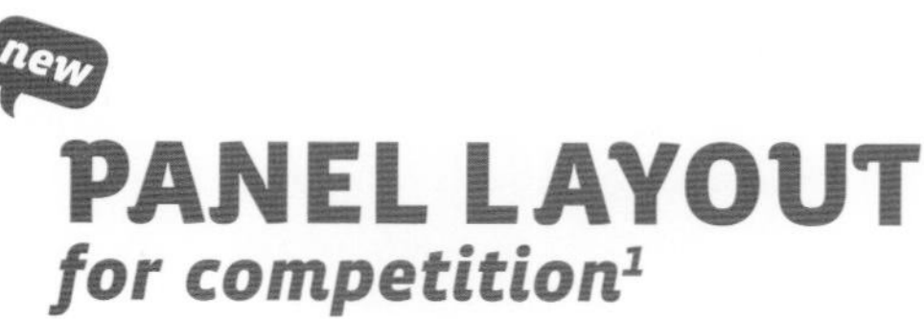
new
PANEL LAYOUT
for competition1

“ THE CLARITY OF THE LAYOUT IN THE ARCHITECTURAL PANEL IS BASIC FOR EASY UNDERSTANDING. THE REST IS LEFT TO THE IMAGINATION. ”

by Carloslampreia[x]arquitectos

Architecture in a communication era

"To say that architecture looks like nature and the nature looks artificial ...constitutes the highest stage we can reach." - Eduardo Souto de Moura visiting Machu Picchu

1 – Architecture is always the construction of an artificiality over the territory. The way it communicates through drawings and models is itself an artificiality, a desire. Nowadays, in a competition the desire is commonly passed on as panel containing the narrative of the project, bringing Architecture closer than ever to other forms of communication and expression.

Nowadays Architecture is getting closer to Film complexity. Panels seems to be made in the same way as one makes a movie; architects resemble film directors, image producers or photography directors, specialized technicians who pursue the dream of the virtual Architectural space.

In the early 20th Century, throughout the transition between silent and sound films, there was a loss of quality due the technical limitations...cameras had to remain static inside soundproof chambers resulting in a lack of movement in the action causing a retrograde towards theatre... Yet, actors spoke... there was sound.

Nowadays, something seems to be happening in the early stages of architectural creation and the way its expressed. We have computers at our disposal to achieve the desired virtual representation of space, the production of complex drawings and photomontages... and yet these images, based on the architecture, have a predominance that competes with basic architectural drawing, often pointing to the dyslexia between the dynamics of the project and dynamics of these images.

Architecture seems to be moving towards a new academicism searching only for its own image... I remember the time of Russian constructivism photo-collages... efforts of those who wanted to create the illusion of machines producing the dream... I remember architects drawing by hand plans and sections to look like those printed by plotters and made by computers, which at that time could not yet be produced... perhaps today, in the same way, we are seeking for new identities for our time.

Organizing a panel has become, for all these reasons, a complex matter, were it is necessary to have a strong composition and communication strategy based on the concept of the architectural project. There is a fusion between the project and its own communication, but not resulting in a basic advertizing strategy, weakening architecture itself.

As always the strength of Architecture comes from the quality of the project...of its own story and anxiety moments forcing magic to happen... trying to unify images and fragments of dreams... reinventing places... improving them and the way they are viewed.

For us, the confrontation with new places is very important, an they are always new... most of them far away, some known, others unknown.

2 – In the spring of 2004, we begun to work on our first international competition. A proposal for a mythical place, one of the wonders of the world, a place we had never visited, the city of Macchu Pichu in Perú.

Discovering how little we knew of this place, with its magical and rugged territory that rises towards the sky, was the quest and the engine of the whole project. We produced several models, in which the territory became the main actor of a project that could not compromise him... transforming himself in a sculptural mass... strategically pierced.

The final model was made of solid concrete, as a representation to the heavy character of the place, and the intervention was represented as absence of matter. Photographs were taken and sent to Peru.

The decision was to structure the only panel around the model as if it was the ultimate Inca icon in a museum window. This was the premise to structure the panel, leaving the remaining project elements to a second role, the whole narrative of drilling the mountain and arriving there in an cable car unveiling the immense view over Macchu Pichu, as well as the small hotel hidden inside the support platform of the viewpoint.

3 – In opposition, in the last competition we entered, six panels were produced which connected like puzzle pieces, in addition to several mandatory drawings. The project was meant to take place in a small city in the Norwegian Fjords, strains of occupied land which extend trough the water, geologicaly formed by the pressure of the ice sheets over time against the rocks.
The existence of a strong urban densification in the edge of the fjord brings a strong artificialisation of it.
The panels carried a graphic narrative based on the comparison between water represented in white and rocky matter represented in black, providing the panels horizontal structure.
This type of representation showed the history of the fjord occupation since the initial wooden constructions, through the jugenstil stone building reconstruction, after a fire which destroyed the whole city.
Modernity conflicted with this Historic city... so our approach strategy was based on the fundamental principles of Art Deco, the creation of an organic connection between the elements.
These elements: water, stone and ice redefined the city in its shape and outline... in the city center an old hill was replaced by stony buildings... in the port the new platform acquired the character of a newcomer wandering iceberg... one is the new central square, the other is the new cruise terminal.

• *by remote-controlled*

Function all one is absurd because it has no information beyond it

"If you want to build a ship, don't drum up the men to gather wood, divide the work and give orders. Instead, teach them to yearn for the vast and endless sea." - Antoine de Saint-Exupery

It is really hard to transfer an poetic idea into the mind of other people by just using images. The future is to make movies including sound and creating an environment which fits to the basic idea of the project.

Function all one is absurd because it has no information beyond it.

But in the end, there is no way to transport your visions like you have it in your mind. It is only a closed approach.

• *by blank studio architecture*

The board is never meant to distract nor entertain

How we do it. In a word – simplify. The board is never meant to distract nor entertain; it must contain the most important information, have a good eye path, and always have hierarchy. If a project has a strong organizing philosophy (Golden Section proportions, for example) that we will use that to subtly reinforce the scheme being presented but never in an overt or decorative way.

by PRAUD

How to make our Presentation Boards

PRAUD strictly focuses on projects that we can develop our own architectural language, which we call "TOPOLOGY ə TYPOLOGY". Therefore, when we develop the design of a project, it becomes a thorough process of developing the concept of Topology and Typology of the building.

A presentation board is a way of explaining this concept. We first try to present the process of the massing, which is relevant to "TOPOLOGY", in the early part of the presentation board. This is why we have broader pictures of the project in the first page of boards, such as site plan, bird's eye view, or perspective view from a distance.

These images are placed together with massing diagrams so that presentee can understand the project very easily from the first page.

As we move on to other pages, we try to put technical drawings and required renderings in the middle parts of boards, and present the systematical approach to the project, which is relevant to "TYPOLOGY".

As "TYPOLOGY" is more about a system, it mostly comes with structural diagrams and section drawings. Also, in over all boards, we try to balance between line drawings and solid renderings, 2D diagrams and axon diagrams, and texts and images. After all, we put the final rendering image on the last board so that it can work as a closing quote and also let a presentee see all the connections to diagrams, drawings and texts we showed previously.

by scandurrastudio

Reducing and synthesizing the information in order to make the proposal's hierarchy clear

Representation is a kind of multiple dream, a concentric series of meanings able to bring back to one's own idea of architecture.
It's a display where one represents himself through the representation of another subject: the project.

The incisiveness of a panel depends on the ability to powerfully represent the concept of a proposal. The form of the representation can leave out some details in order to evoke the main idea of the concept. We should reduce and synthesize the information in order to make the proposal's hierarchy clear.

The kind of representation we choose shows the language of the project. The graphic, the composition, all the visual elements should be part of the process of the project itself. The author/designer should create his own consistent, uniform language, should find the form of representation that better identify his own values, a solid structure liable to unexpected variations and exceptions.

I have a particular interest in exploring different established linguistic codes, in proceeding on the basis of quotations. Since the universe of imagery has exploded, we can put together pieces, like elements of excited representation, playing with references to a collective imagination.

by Jägnefält Milton

The panel is not the end, It is not even the beginning of the end

As soon as we feel comfortable that we have an idea that we will develop further for a competition we do a simple layout sketch of the panels. Usually the numbers of panels and the format is set by the competition organizers so the question is instead what material do, we need to produce to be able to present convincing arguments for our idea. The presentation of our ideas tend to be broken down into four or five basic types of materials; renderings, text, diagrams, drawings, and sometimes, but not always, a physical model.
The following is our view on how to use those types of materials in a competition presentation.

Our boards are often dominated by one rendering for each board. We use the rendering to create an interest for our idea, not for answer all the questions that our idea creates. A headline usually accompanies our rendering on the first board. Rather than saying what the idea is about or explaining the picture, the headline is there to create more impact. This can be done by saying something that provokes or is the seemingly opposite of what the picture shows.

We tend to put a lot of energy into the preface and the body text. That doesn't mean the scope of the text is extra long or set in a intricate typeface but instead made in such a way that it will be read and understood without making any noise itself. The preface is just one or two sentences that will explain our idea in a very condensed way and the following body text will do the job of explaining this idea in detail and hopefully make a good argument for it.

We use diagrams both in explaining the concept and also in describing details. We try to have an open mind when it comes to the style of the diagrams but, having said that, we very often end up in doing exploded axonometric projections. You could argue that such three dimensional and measurable diagrams have an advantage in explaining spatial ideas compared to free hand sketches, perspectives and two dimensional diagrams. But there is also the fact that we always been interested in the aesthetics of such illustrations probably originating in our childhood with the Lego manuals and books with cross sections of fires stations, planes, boats etc.

When it comes to our drawings we try to make them as simple and readable as possible. It is probably a lost cause to try to find any poetics in our drawings. But as in the case of our headlines that try to contrast the renderings we try to make the same clash between our sober drawings and our more subversive renderings.

If we are allowed to hand in a presentation model we will do that knowing a physical model is an excellent way to describe a project. During our process we also produce sketch-models but they are often just for us to help us understand and develop our idea and are more seldom exposed in the final presentation.

Even though each types of materials mentioned above gets different exposure on the panels we believe that all the types of material are important in making a convincing argument for our idea and therefore they deserve, and hopefully gets, the same amount of attention during our production of the materials. A brilliant rendering is not so brilliant any more if the headline under it is misspelled which by the way has happened to us.

by KLAIR Architecture

Our key words for PANEL presentation

Hierarchy: operate choices
Above all, it is about opting for clear choices, defining priorities in the reading of the project we present.
Some elements could be placed behind for the benefit of others, making visual "calls" and dynamic links between two principal components: text and image.

Communication of an Architectural project: specificity
From the connection between "sensible" part and "technical" one, two dimensions could be developed and mastered, to release a dynamic reading of presentation.
The "eye circulation" should be organized in this complementarity, to define how one of these dimensions invite and drive to another.

Invariants: Playing with codes
For each project, we establish a graphical charter based on invariants of different types: typographical code, color code, location code. We seek always to found a united form, at the same time diversity in a presentation.
A sharp balance must be founded and placed. If too many similitudes can motivate boring and monotony, too many diversities can disturb the readability, contradict comprehension and tend to disrupt the notion of a set.
A good balance allows creating homogeneity.
Panels should be sensed as a "whole", made of clearly identifiable elements, and not as a heterogeneous sum of independent elements.

A visual course
We are questioning often about the relation between text and image, to determine what status we allow to one and to another, in each presentation.
The text is mostly informative, and also sometimes questioning, when the image is illustrative, informative and questioning at the same time.
We should identify what are the essential informative contents, necessary questioning elements, and the optional void as a margin of "respiration".
If the content is unbreathable because it is too dense, there will be no focal point or attractive force. In addition, if the content is "floating" because of its poor density, it may lack substance and could not cause more attraction.

For us, balance, is the key word because it allows offering a real visual course at reading panels. It revolves around three fundamental concepts:
Interpellation : attract the interest of the viewer
Information : bring substance and comprehension
Respiration: induce a plurality of distances, release visual captivity.
The panel layout can involve more "spatial" and "physical" relation.
Visual impact of large size images calls viewer's eyes from distance, they can almost make magnetic effect.
Plans or details require more important physical proximity, call for less distance between the support and the viewer, requiring concentration.
Diagrams induce more freedom and fluidity, and release tension.

In the end, the aim is to promote a dynamic look, like an invitation, which calls for the density, responding to the desire to learn more, reaching the substance of the project, and also de-densify the information, to invite more liberty and give breath to the whole presentation.

by gutiérrez-delafuentearquitectos

They are attractive enough to persuade the jury in a few seconds

gutiérrez-delafuente arquitectos is an architecture office focused on the construction of public buildings as a result of winning national and international competitions. Then the office has to deal every day with the competition panels, "they" are capital for us.

The panels, They, are the only way to condense visits to the competition site, kilometers by car, internal debates, hours and hours of hard work, emails, sometimes good ideas...

They are attractive enough to persuade the jury in a few seconds, to have an impact with a simple glance and to pass the round, specially nowadays with the increase of the number of participants in all the competitions.

When starting a competition they are one of the first focuses to be addressed, due to each project needs to have its own layout. From the beginning the office establishes the content of the panels in order to focus the efforts on the exact content, no unneeded material. It's a very useful strategy.

They are constantly changing from each project to the next. Understanding that each project has a different identity, means that each project has a different style of panels.
Several strategies can be used in order to be as effective as possible depending on the type of competition:
- in competitions with several scales (from the city to the details), a high density of information, deep analysis and need for a lot of text, the office try to use "cards" or a series of vignettes which help to create a clear sequence of information.
(e.g.: the projects in Linz, Aigle, Forchheim, Asturias and Candás.)
- in competitions for a "simple" building, it's preferable to show the plans and the views or models in the clearest way possible, representing them in a large size and "isolated" from each other.
(e.g.: the projects in Madrid_kindergarden and Burgos.)
- in competitions for urban art-works and temporary installations, the concept has to catch attention from the beginning with "brave" panels, a strong identity, and using a sense of humor. Crossing the borders of the marketing and advertisement strategies.

by Figura Arquitetos

Pictures say much more than words

Making panels is always a difficult task. It is pure graphic design done by architects. The first goal is to produce nice 2d drawings, informative sketches and strong 3d renderings to have a beautiful visual in the end. Never discard the first sketches; they can help to explain the way that you reach the final design. Particularly, I don't like panels with a lot of texts. Pictures say much more than words. A good tip is generating the main image with a clean background (like a blue sky) to make it possible adding some texts or even cad drawings on it.

by franz zt gmbh

The first impression of the final presentation board is the most important thing

The first impression of the final presentation board is the most important thing you have to consider.
The Viewer has to be made curios in the first 10 seconds. There's no second chance to make a first impression.

For our strategy we think in four dimensions:
The first dimension is about the graphic design. Our plan has to be clearly structured, so that the clients don't get overstrained with overloaded panels.
The second dimension concerns the required content, such as floor plans, sections or elevation plans.
Pictograms and diagrams form the third dimension. Spatial representation is always the best way to support the viewer's imagination.
Photorealistic Renderings meet the current state of the art.
In the 4th dimension we think about the time, to spell it out, the already mentioned short term an idea has to be clear for the spectator.
Clear Statements and a simple readability make it easier for members of a jury to understand someone's concept.
Careful Use of Color is characteristic for our panels. Our Layouts always base on 3 rules, we determined.
The Title:
Pragmatic, bold and simple titles are the first tool to arouse attention
Pictograms and diagrams:
These are always usable to substantiate the intention of us, as author of an idea
Concept explanations:
Specified explanation with a few short sentences is the completing addition for pictograms.
To find the perfect panel it is always a process of trying things out and discussing them within the whole team.

by Sinestezia

It is always our aim to encourage people to ask for more.

Surely, it is important to make everything clear, understandable and obvious enough so anyone could like it. We learned and experienced that fonts should be big enough so that when you step back once or twice from a board it is just the right distance to catch the focal idea. As well as pictures, fonts ask for contrast and hierarchy, so our efforts are always directed toward the evaluation of information we are introducing to the audience.

On the other hand we find YouTube very supportive platform as there are people ready to share their knowledge. Here we have learned that the overall color scheme of renders and drawings should be maintained under the limits of HUE, but we experienced that many details are ready to be explored outside those limits. Following this is composition and it is always necessary to decide what will be "sacrificed" for the sake of context where ideas, which make a difference, will find their place and be noticed.

Finally, we came to ideas and point of breakthrough which will make people ask for more.

by Posad

Panels are also supposed to tell a story to a viewer without the designer aside

Panels serve as a communication tool for designers when presenting their design. Panels are also supposed to tell a story to a viewer without the designer aside.

Posad's main goal of visual communication is to create an understanding about the project, its method and strategy. Next to being a communication tool for a messenger, panels function to convince and seduce the viewer.

Regardless of scale, any design is influenced by the challenges of the physical and social context. Posad operates throughout a broad range of scales ranging from region, to city, to street and vice versa. Besides thinking and working on multiple scale-levels, Posad also organizes their panels in a certain rhythm. This rhythm of graphics is based on two things:

1. STORY TELLING - Hierarchy and location of images on a panel is created by the order of the project definition.
2. DISTANCE TOWARDS RECEIVER - The size and intensity of images is based on the importance of content.

These levels give the viewer the opportunity to scan the project from a meter distance, and get the message of the project. Hierarchy on panels with different image sizes and types of detail is key to reach this. By layering the panels, the viewer gets informed with small steps at a time.

Graphics which fill the Panels of Posad serve the design or data and not the other way around. If graphics take over a panel, difficulties to communicate your design appear. During the design process, translations of data and drawings are put into clean diagrams, schematic maps and rich visualizations. Also in graphics of Posad, the link between several scales, between user and plot should be clear and logical.

This strategy of organizing images on panels and our use of graphics to present a design in the best possible way has proven itself by winning several competitions. Multiple jury reports complement the projects of Posad, based on the clear and convincing visual communication on the panels.

by marchi_Architectes

We wanted that this idea to be transformed in one specific history told by a strong view

Our projects born out with one idea based on uses and applications and sometimes this idea awake with some intuition.
We wanted that this idea to be transformed in one specific history told by a strong view.
This image has to make people dream!
To support our idea we need:
References images creates a specific atmosphere
Plans, 3D models demonstrate project's feasibility
Definitive project ' views
All these elements have to create harmonious progression for "easy-looking-pictures"

Leon11 Architects

Collective Creativity As A Strategy For The Formal Representation

MODUS OPERANDIS
COLLECTIVE CREATIVITY AS A STRATEGY FOR THE FORMAL REPRESENTATION
LEON 11: THE CREATIVITY SUSTAINABLE

PANNEL DESIGN? Is it a real graphic representation of thoughts or is a manipulative tool?
When we noticed that DAMDI was working on a new publication about the way to make panels we felt very fortunate to participate in this discussion because we believe it to be, a very interesting and contemporary matter, both, in the field of architecture and of design.

From the beginning, we all had many ideas about what we would like to say and make clear on this subject. Certainly now, writing this little text is very difficult to express a clear position of what we think, as this issue is full of nuances. Therefore after a little internal debate among ourselves, we decided that instead of explaining about what we think should or should not be the design of the panels, we will explain how, until today, we make panels of our projects.
Honestly, we have never written or thought about how we design panels, because as we always say in Leon11 what we do always is survive pulling ahead in the best way possible what we have inside..
Following this opportunity to reflect on this issue we appreciate that there is an essential thing in our work that creates a special way to represent our thoughts and make projects. This clue is what we have defined as 'COLLECTIVE CREATIVITY'.

Leon11 consists in a team of 13 persons who are permanently working together in the same place and there are many others who are incorporated into our team depend on the project we do. The fact that we were, as a TEAMWORK, has built the way we have, to represented our ideas. It has shaped the fact that our goal is not to, has a personal style or a particular obsession, but rather that it has become a tool that has its own life and has helped us to learn continuously, new things. It shows that each of our projects is behind the trends and what interests us is the investigation of the creative processes and not the end of a formal representation.

Among the first questions that appear on the table at the start of a project is: What is the collective strategy what is the most optimal for this project?
This means that when developing a project, the fact that we utilise Teamwork which most of the time, is composed of different people, has the result that it is the team organization what really marks the aesthetic result of the proposal. By this we emphasize that what makes the aesthetics of the project definition, are not the people involved in it, but the team organization and the strategy we have to organize the job. Thus it is clear that discussions of whether something is ugly or pretty, whether red or white should not concern us, as the debate focuses on what the best strategy for working group work better if we have different schedules and even from different cities.

What most concerns us in this form of working in groups is the opportunity it affords us to always evolve and learn new things from others. As always in Zuloark say, "that the collective organizations have taught us much more than that Master degree that we could never afford". So far, this is the way of doing Architecture, design panels, or face any new challenge we have. It is an active tool that helps us learn and evolve trying to be different from any static trend or figurative obsession.

There are three main points between which you could frame our way of drawing, design, thinking...
- Collective creativity. The choice of a collective strategy will be incor-

porated as a fundamental part of the thinking process of the project. This adds a greater degree of plurality and complexity of the architectural and design goal.

- Document open. Sustain the potential energy.
- Every document, every idea, every drawing must be open to coexist and host other new concepts.

We try not to set records closed, but patterns of possibility, to generate more debate and more architecture. Essentially, to work in a team as we do implies a constant, reinterpretation of the different members about every idea in the project. This multiple approach, allows the implementation of documents for different hands, with different styles, and even different conceptual points of view.
The thought process is not linear. It is not going to get debugging an idea to its essentials, is about developing the branches of a tree of options without any pruning.

We are not seeking for a particular style which defines the way we have to make architecture, each project will generate a series of new questions.

by Donner Sorcinelli Architecture

The clarity of the layout in the architectural panel is basic for easy understanding. The rest is left to the imagination

Hitting the imagination of the jury and the customer, this is the goal. The panels are the consequence.
Explaining the concept, references and illustrating the project are the stages of this process to form the layouts of a competition or for a presentation.
The clarity of the layout is basic for easy understanding.
The rest is left to the imagination.

by Alessandro Console Studio

Panel is rather a synthetic and thoughtful work conceived as an integral part of the project itself

Making panels for an architectural competition is not a mere aesthetic operation aimed to wonder and to marvel through the fascinating power of the image. It is rather a synthetic and thoughtful work conceived as an integral part of the project itself.
Within the bounded white space of one or more panels, you need to rationalize your project through a selection process oriented to tell and to get understandable its genesis and development, from the concept idea to the final configuration.
A narrative process, then, that is not intended as merely ephemeral communication or as fast and diverted experience of images; but a process where the image itself is an ancillary tools, a device for building and showing the real complete meaning of the project.
In this way, patterns, diagrams, drawings, renderings are conceived and created to have a specific role within the general layout of the panel/s.: they are not outcomes of an a posteriori work, but rather the representation of the different steps of a journey, the journey of the project, that is knowledge and re-invention at the same time.

by LUIS ARREDONDO_ARCHITECT

Different strategies to compose a board

The presentation of a project is not just the accumulation of plans and sections but it is the generation of a summary document. The surface of the panels is the limitation of space we have and the building should be explained by interrelated documents. In our case the starting point is usually the description of the place on which we zoom in different levels so we could explain the decisions that have been taken in the design process. The partial documents do not have a casual position but are linked between them to express the main ideas. Each document is treated as an object that plays a role in the void so that the boundaries belong to what is represented and not the board. In this way the sites are cut out, the skies of the perspectives become floors of the sections or models and diagrams appear floating in the void.

by GEOTECTURA

You must make it to the final cut

you have an idea for a competition
you think it can make a difference
but the jury has 1 minute to go over your panel
one among hundreds
you must make it to the final cut
so you put the main issues upfront
you redirect the people to see what is important
and you hide the unnecessary for their first review
you put in small letters and drawings the required and more in-deep information
hoping that the project will deserve a second glimpse and be evaluated as it should be

by Slot.

The idea behind your project has to be understood in a few seconds

In competitions, the idea behind your project has to be understood in a few seconds; otherwise your project won't pass the first stage of evaluation.
We usually start with a strong render image, which shows the project as a whole. Right after, we explain the concept with sketches and simple diagrams. We then continue to place the information gradually from general information to details. The last board finishes with another strong render perspective.
Another characteristic of our boards is that we never put more than one render perspective per board and perspectives have a considerable size in order to reinforce the idea.

by b4architects

Making panels

One of the primary premise of the working method is that to specify a strong intention as starting point for every project able to begin an aesthetic "process of the intention". This aesthetic process is the background of every phase and then also in the making of a supporting layout, as object to transfer the content and the intent.
Generally the planning of a layout follows the focus of the concept that derives from the initial brainstorming. On the concept idea it starts directly the choice of the elements-materials that will be insert effectively in the panels. This is to permit the creative resources to focus on the final contents, cause of the shortage of time typical for a project competition. If the competition panels are more than one, as normally it happens, it states that there is a narrative guideline, a sort of storyboard of the project.
"Material elements" are also all the lettering operation that have the same importance of the images and drafts.
So a texture cames out, or better still a watermark that dislocates all the objects and their hierarchies.
The lettering has the role of bridge, of connecting between the different images, besides to carry out its normal role of communication of the contents.

The images are mostly drew near, rarely overlapping effects are foreseen. The preference is that to saturate the available space to the edge cutting boards. The picture don't have frames or borders. This choice reinforce the abstract contents of the project.
The chosen images are of different type, render, models photos until the sketches. Often the choice of an image position is direct consequence of the creative process of the project working on: for example the sketch can be the instant expression of a concept of the general synthesis more "representative", often it is a perspective sketch; the rendering pictures have the role to communicate, also from distance, immediately the atmosphere, the complex spatial sensation that is searched in some projects.
In the same way that in some urban projects there is an interest for the "space in-between", in the compositive graphics of the panels much interest is also on the "void space" between the different objects: these voids have the role to "put tension" of the graphic final composition.
In short we can say that there are three systems founding a layout:
1. the watermark, texture, formed by the continuous alignments on the different panels
2. the object-images drew near
3. the lettering operations working as general bracketing
On these founding systems we apply a reading approach for an observer, whether he is a member of the jury or a visitor of an exhibition where the project is showed. The layout have to work obviously whether from distance, perceiving the panels as a one coherent element from which it must be possible to understand the general concept, or from near, as if it is a fractal approach to the informations given from the smallware of the details in which a project can be analyzed.

by IaN+

The competition board is a story of the project, and not the project itself

To talk about competition boards means to retrace the story of IaN+ projects' representation. A story about the evolution and transformation of an architectural firm, the strategies and expectations of a group of architects accepting the challenge of competition as the only instrument that ensures the quality of architecture and, consequently, the continuous advancement of the International architectural debate.

We will talk about some key projects that can be considered the first in a series and that, more than others, are defining this story. The projects are: the extension of Mies Van der Rohe Foundation in Barcelona in 1998, the multi-storey car park in Rome in 2001, the ECB headquarters in 2003, the Tittot Glass Museum in 2004, the Cheongna City Tower in 2008, the Cà d'Oro Masterplan in 2010, the new Maribor Art Gallery in 2010 and the Serlachius museum expansion in 2011.

It is certainly reductive to try to summarize the complexity of a project representation in few lines, especially because, in a competition board all the different ways to communicate a project come together, from images to diagrams.

The competition board is a story of the project, and not the project itself. Through this tale we try to reach a balance between the different souls the architectural object represents.

In the project for the extension of the Mies Van der Rohe foundation we described a process rather than a project through the use of diagrams. Architecture is a system of spaces articulating in time rather than in space. The diagrams at the center of the boards tell exactly this process through the endless possible variations in shape of the architectural object and the architectonic image is resulting from the diagrams turning into volume.

In the boards for the multi-storey car park project in Rome the center of the representation is the image showing the architectural object in its definite and complete appearance. The colored concrete structure defining the front façade takes up an entire board; that image is in charge of the entire story, while the rest stays in the background. Structure and color in the center, then diagrams explaining the different uses of this facade which turns into a playground for the facing park.

In the competition boards for the new Tittot Glass Museum in Taipei the project is represented as the synthesis of a diagrammatic-narrative and formal process. Representation is complex and articulated. The starting point is the description of the way to live the museum different places, both in terms of space and time, and how this can shape the space. It goes from diagrams to the architectural object, up to the choice of materials and detailing definition.

Cheongna City Tower is 350 meters tall arch, the new landmark characterizing the Cheongna park in Incheon, South Korea. The arch is an archaic structure with strong symbolic and historical value, it is a "natural" and "primordial" structure. The boards describe this relationship between history and nature that finds its synthesis within a symbol turning into architecture.

In the boards for the Cà d'Oro Masterplan competition in Venice we focused our attention toward urban ecology concepts, what we have defined "New Ecology". Nowadays sustainability is an essential requirement for design, especially in certain urban interventions particularly complex and extensive. "Concreteness" is the motto of these boards, where the housing development operation is described through diagrams and details to explain that to design sustainability means to think about a sustainable society.

In the project for the new Art Gallery in Maribor the use of a single color intends to evoke the idea of a micro-city building suggesting a complex urban space. The micro city is represented both as a unique and recognizable element and as a system of separate parts.

In the Serlachius Museum extension competition the natural landscape is at the center of the representation, a rich and important background where the project is just a cut in the landscape. In the boards we represented the relationship between figure and background, between landscape and architecture, between mass and void.

by Keiichi Hayashi Architect

Panel is kind of a picture-card show

In my presentations, I draw illustrations as simply as possible when I am explaining something. Rather than read drawings and think about the meaning of the words, people should feel the contents of the illustrations instantly.
I try to draw many illustrations because continuous pictures help the story develop. It is kind of a picture-card show.

by Kevin Kennon Architects

The panels will be seen with hundreds of others and must stand out

The composition for good presentation panels contains minimal info, yet tells a story through a narrative with a beginning, middle, and end through graphic clarity and organization. The panels will be seen with hundreds of others and must stand out. It is important to have a clear and eye catching images that best describe the idea(s) of your project.

“ PANELS SERVE AS A COMMUNICATION TOOL FOR DESIGNERS WHEN PRESENTING THEIR DESIGN. PANELS ARE ALSO SUPPOSED TO TELL A STORY TO A VIEWER WITHOUT THE DESIGNER ASIDE. ”

001 [tamor] | *Alessandro Console Studio*

Location : Rome, Italy
Typology : Housing Tower

site: GRA (Grande Raccordo Anulare)
city: Rome
State: Italy
program: housing + pulic activities
elements: CORE + CLUSTERS
CORE
height: 180m
internal volume: 17900m³
CLUSTERS
dimension: 12X7X7m
internal volume: 390m³
number: 0 - 60
towers
GRA
river Tevere

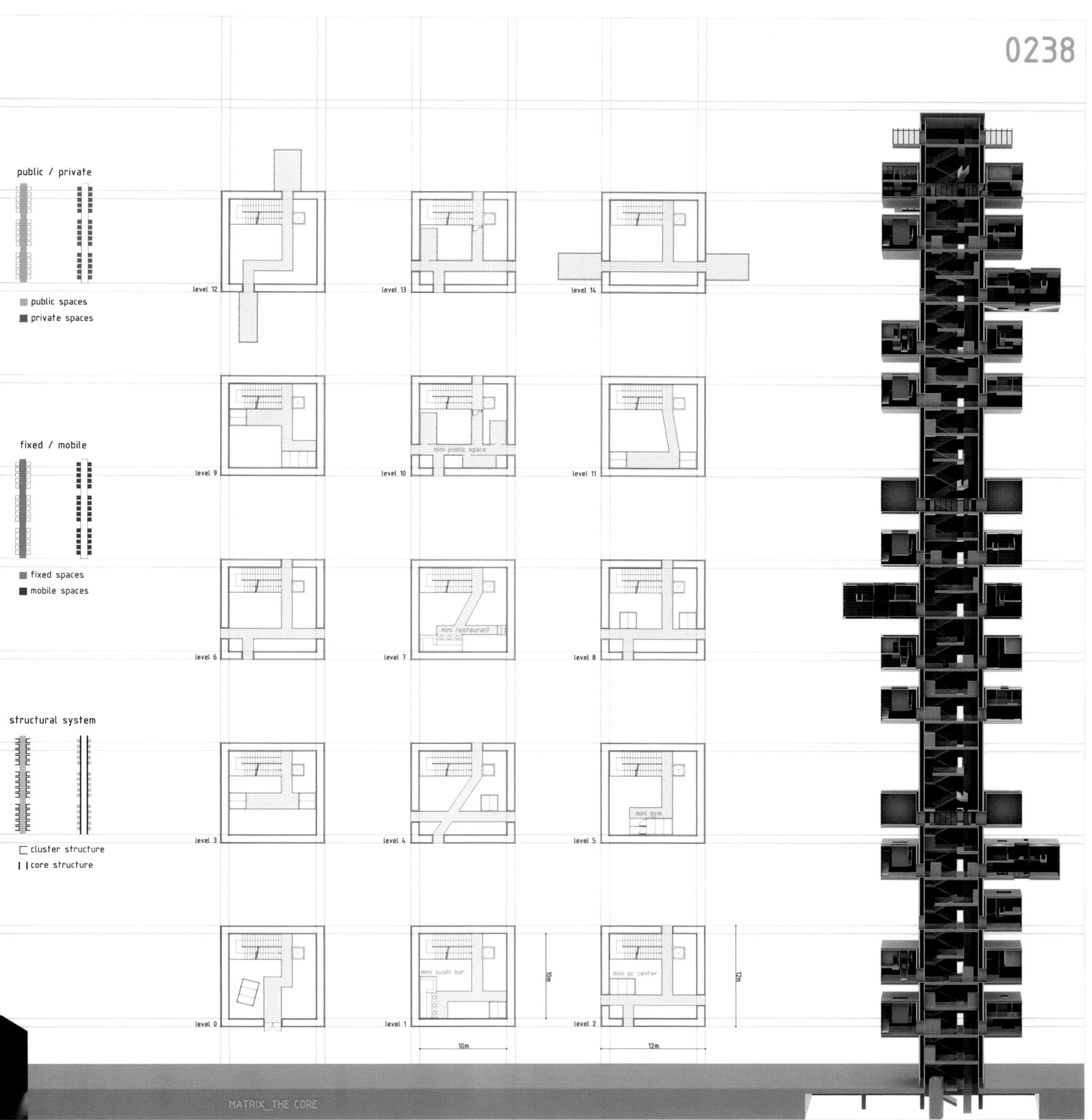
0238
public / private
public spaces
private spaces
fixed / mobile
fixed spaces
mobile spaces
structural system
cluster structure
core structure
level 12
level 13
level 14
level 9
level 10
mini public space
level 11
level 6
level 7
mini restaurant
level 8
level 3
level 4
level 5
mini gym
level 0
level 1
mini sushi bar
level 2
mini pc center
10m
12m
MATRIX_THE CORE

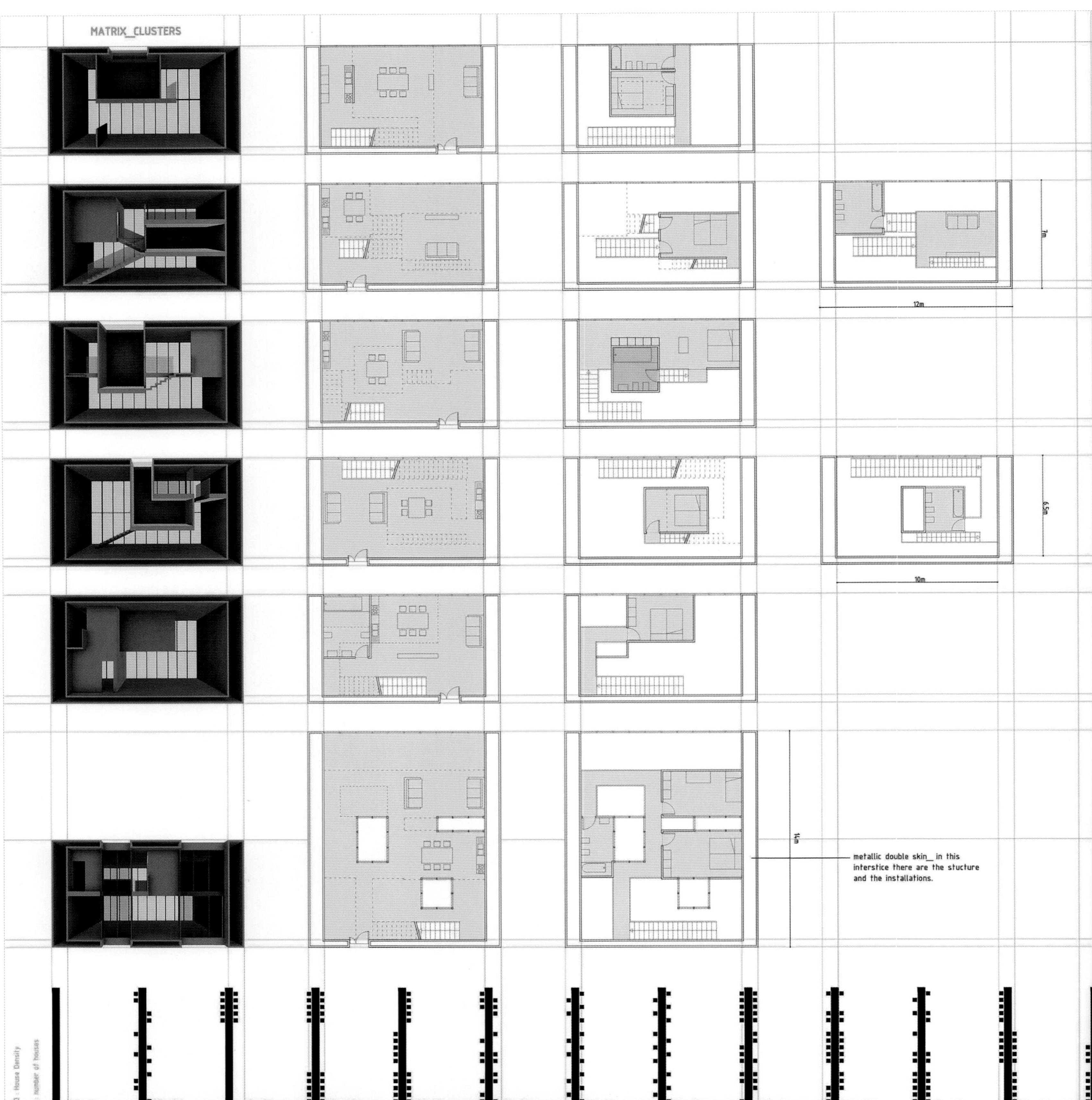

DIAGRAM OF POSSIBLE CONFIGURATIONS

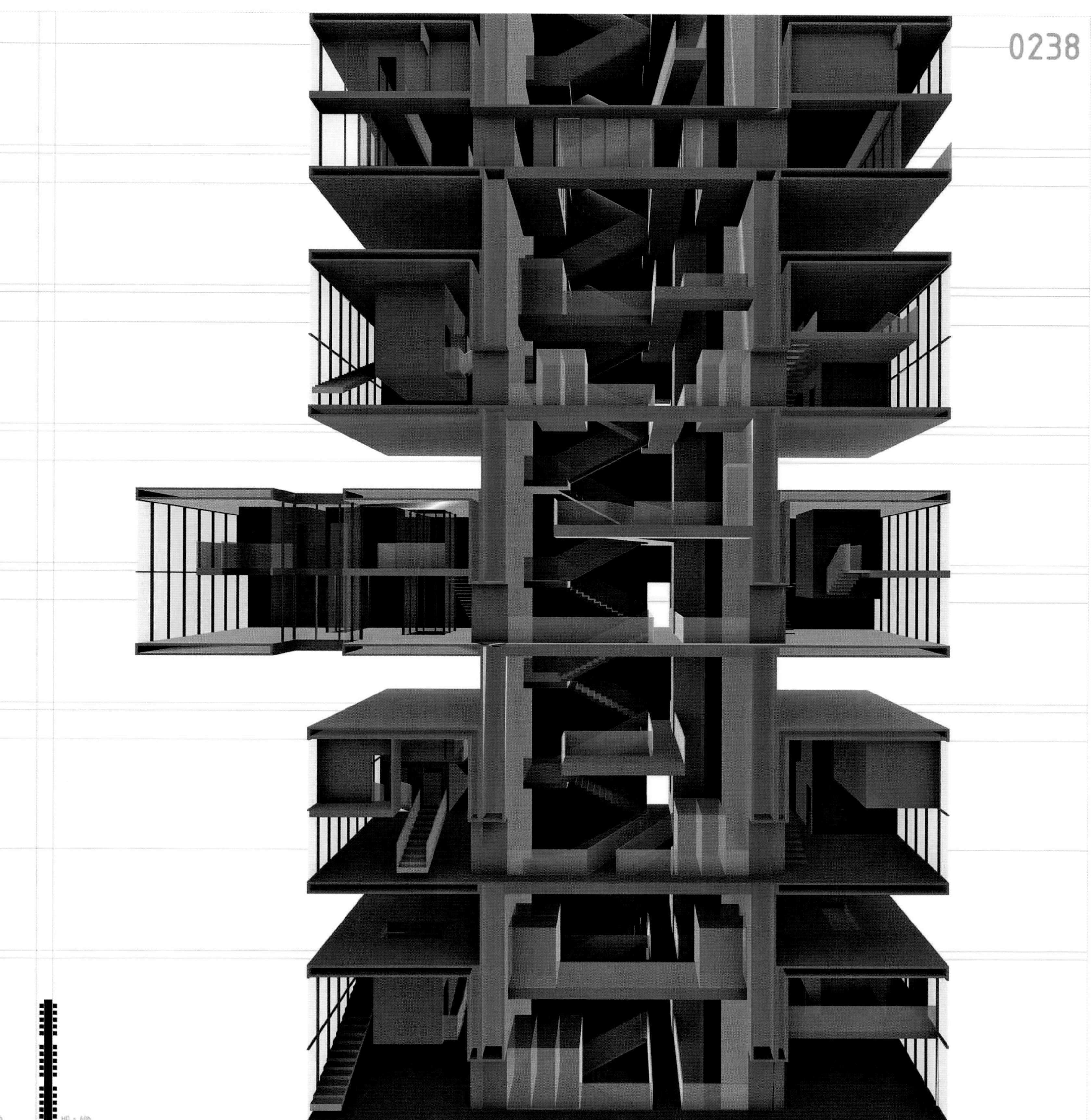
0238

400,000 Houses | *Thurlow Small Architecture*

Location : Amposta, Spain
Design Team : Andrew Thurlow, Maia Small, Grant Robinson
Competition Sponsor : Quaderns

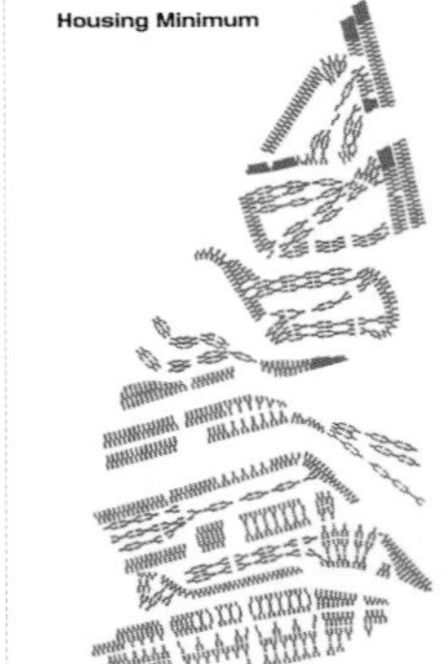

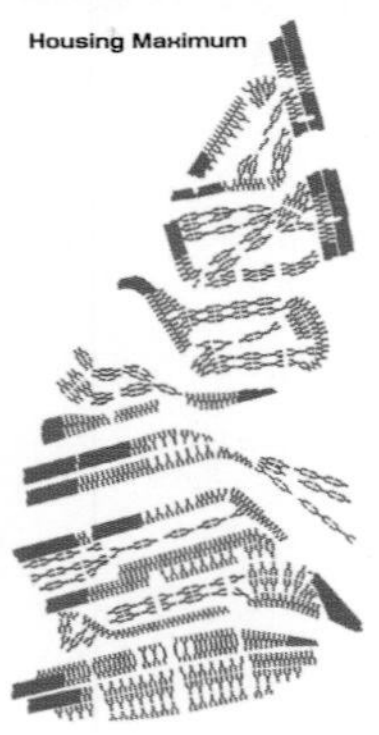

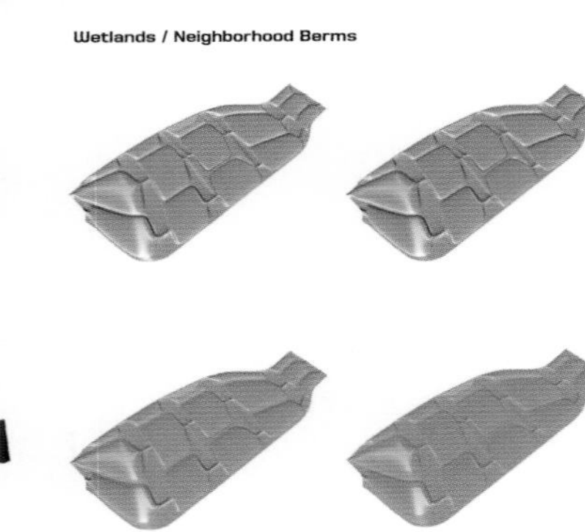

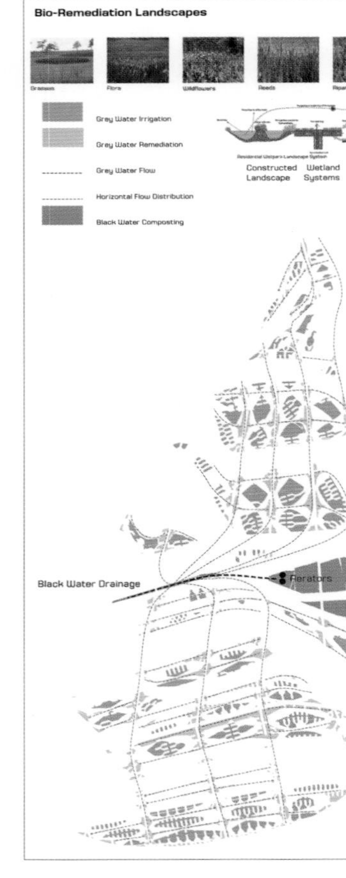

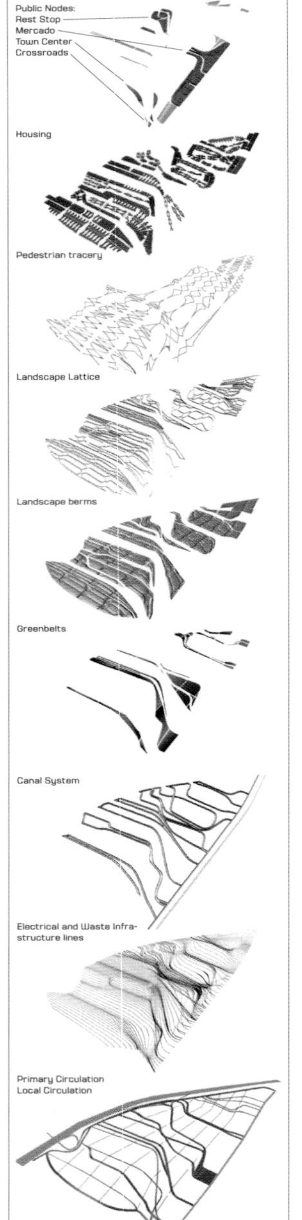

amposta

The Future is Open (Linux ad copy) Despite an intention by many current political forces to promote construction of more and more definite boundaries and market globalization to steer us towards homogeneity through consolidation of land and commercial ownership, global landscapes are growing into increasingly complex layered systems, composites of cultural, economic and temporal modalities. Due to patterns of life that offer more global and less local pressures and the ease of international travel and temporary migration, contemporary culture fosters new "families" that are not longer defined only by strict racial, typological or economic categories, but cross and flex as subsequent generations increasingly embrace interracial marriage, non-married or non-reproductive couples, varieties of sexual orientation, divorce, secularism, single parent households, roommates, co-habitating multi-generational families, adoption, etc.

To control these entropic environments we increasingly build gated communities, enclave business parks, privatized "public" space, viral quarantine and airport security checkpoints; we exert control over our edges, afraid of physical and psychic terrorism. We want free trade, as long as it isn't free. In reaction to this inherent contradiction, between the formation of loose social networks and the imposition of constricted spatial boundaries where existing political and economic powers quietly appropriate and coordinate public territory, our design proposes systems of variable boundary that reinforce both the natural organized blending and multiplicity of culture and natural environments. This multiplicity has the potential to create rich iterations and personal identity within common experience that requires a more variable relationship between time and space; thus, ownership, interior and exterior relationships, and neighborhood boundaries must become more flexible.

Paragenesis In reaction to both the failures of Modernism's closed compositions and Post-Modernism's praise of non-designed street life, we propose an open-ended paragenetic system, a strategy of restructuring and synchronizing surrounding settlement patterns to offer a new urban infrastructure with variable boundaries. Our intention is to vary the housing types and ownerships in order to seed the intentions of individual interconnected neighborhoods, dense nodes of central activity, and civic space fostered by both economic and public endeavors. Paragenesis develops from a mapping of the existing long lot configurations present already within the site and surrounding landscape. The long lot configuration, more than simply mute existing geometry, speaks about the delineation of land, land ownership and agricultural appropriation. They are markers,

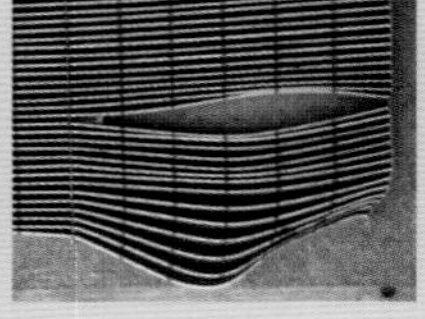

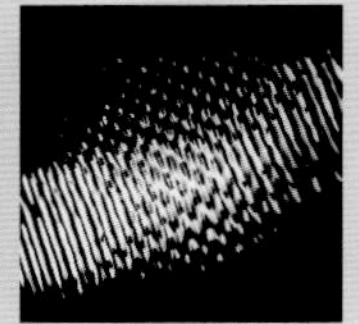

Site Perspective
C_0_8354

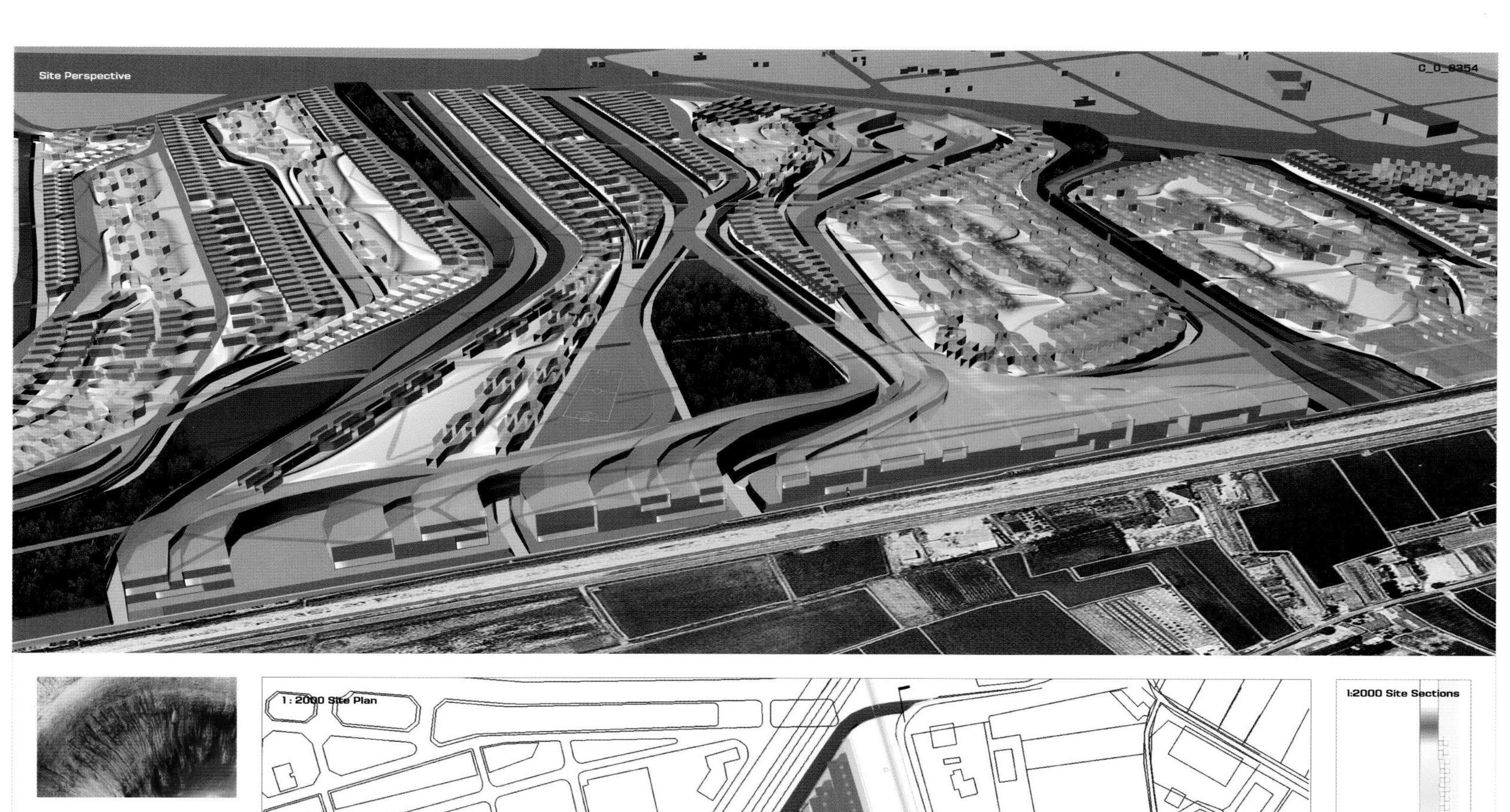

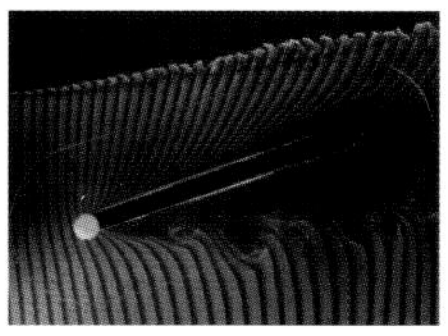

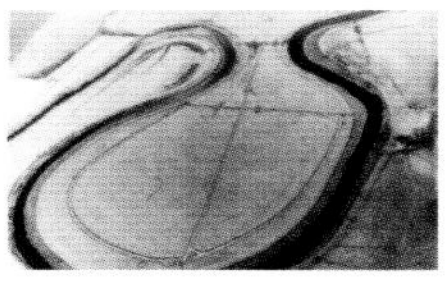

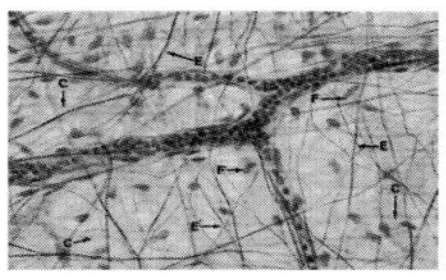

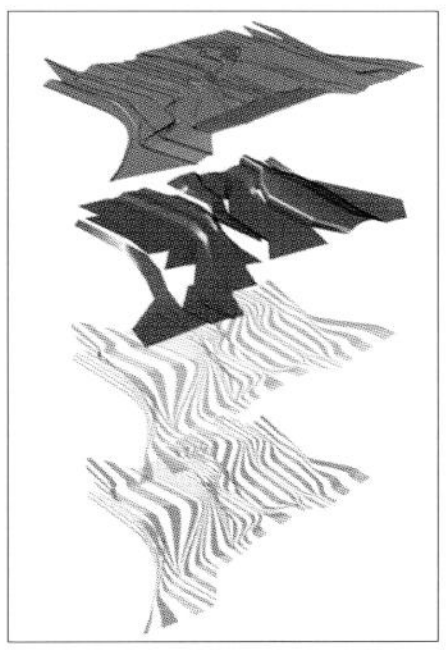

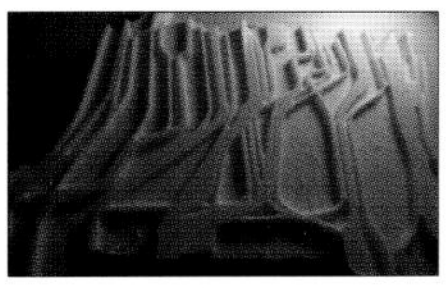

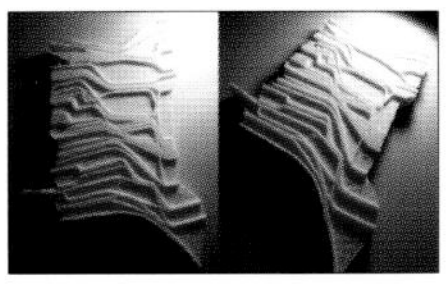

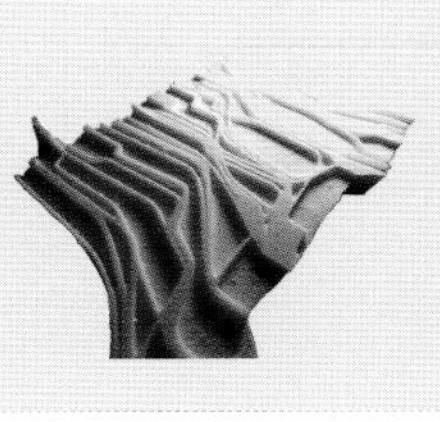

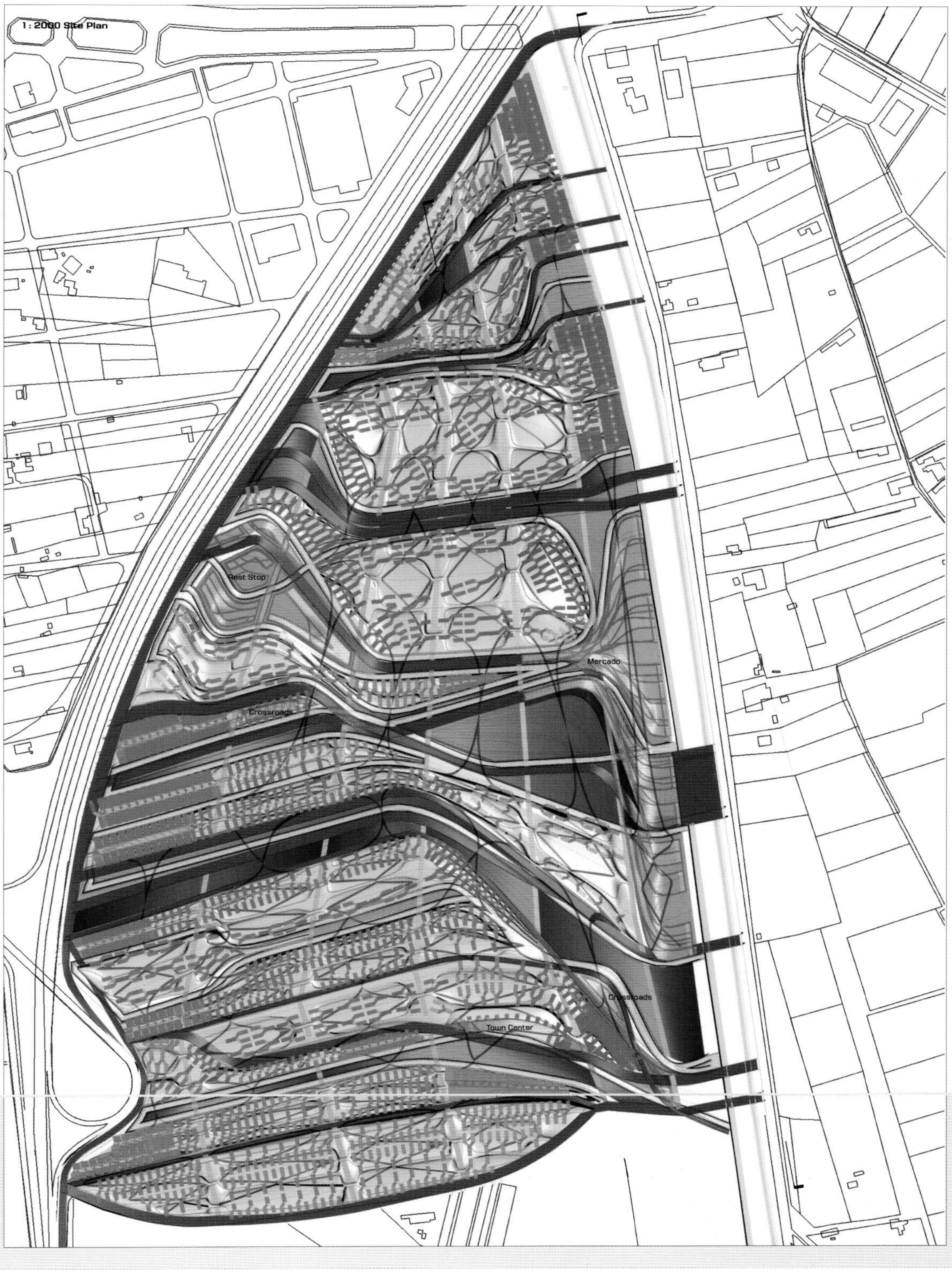

1 : 2000 Site Plan
Rest Stop
Mercado
Crossroads
Crossroads
Town Center

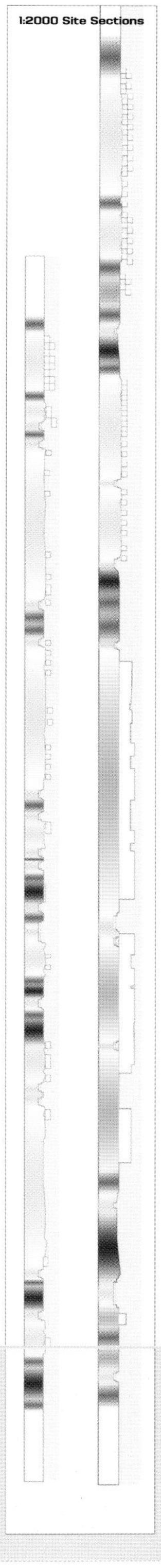

1:2000 Site Sections

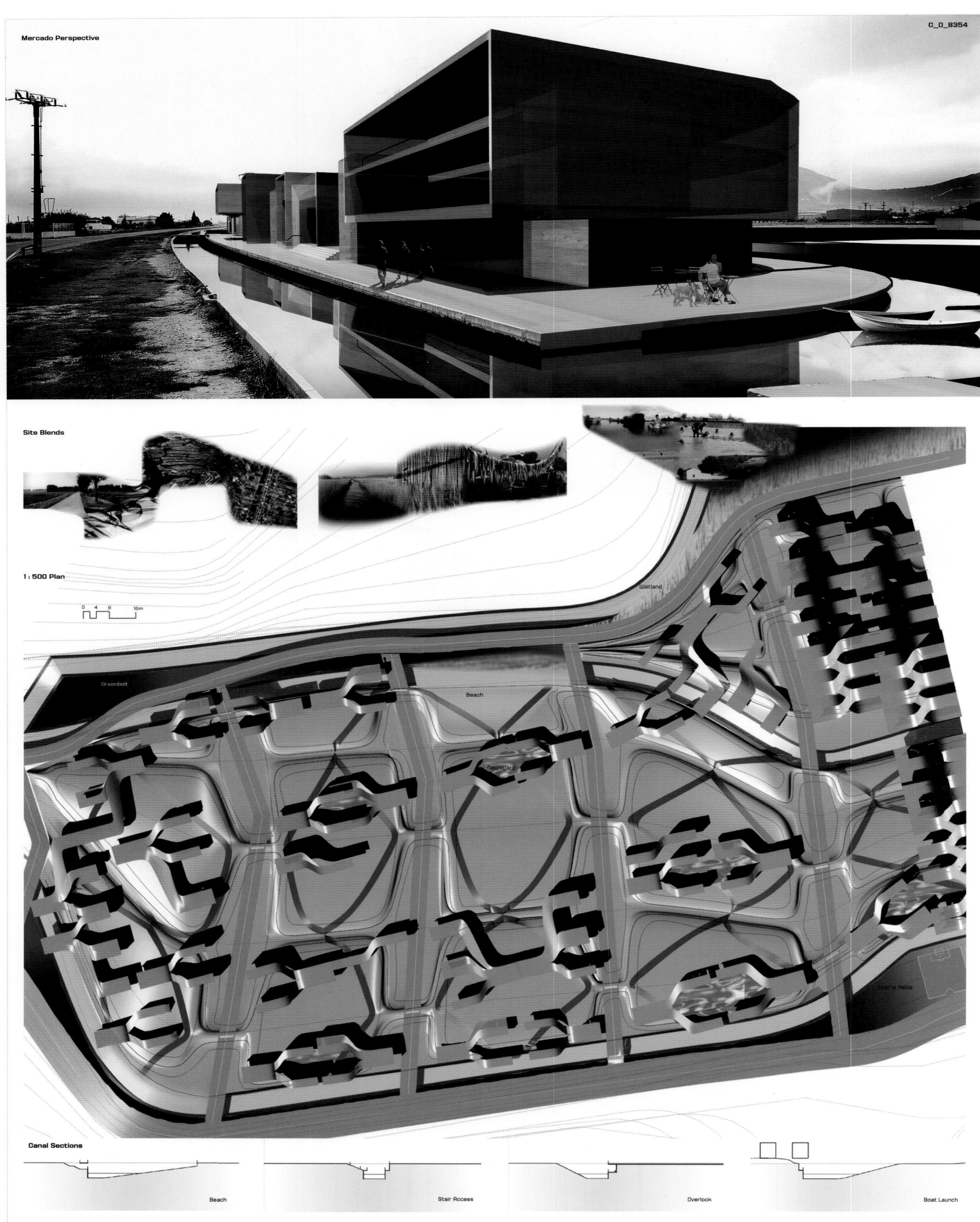

references and historical descriptions of ownership, use and land pragmatics. Thus if we seek to transform the land striations-- taking familiar dimensions of land-- and transform them into new widths based on the connection to the old ones, then we are re-appropriating the landscape, re-dimensioning it in terms of the possible multiplicity of configuration. The connections, however, not only imply major axis or circulation routes, begin to also organize the systems of land: ownership, densities of inhabitation, commercial nodes, public space, water infrastructure, etc.

Location, Location, Location This project proposes an economic and spatial organization that accounts for minimum and maximum conditions of spatial appropriation for housing, commerce and public space. It seeks to avoid the recent divisions that allow for both our desires of exclusivity and lifestyle as well as foster haunted divisions of elitism, ghettoism and real estate fashion. Rather than "location, location, location" to describe a triple intensity of site importance for one site (site³), this term is retermed to imply that the variable boundaries imply that there are actually three locations overlapped within one (site + site + site).

Critical systems

LANDSCAPE BERMS:	Flexible Land Territories
Y-WING HOUSING:	Expandable Housing Ownership
NODES:	Precipitant public space
MERCADO:	Public re-appropriation of the urban civic space
CANALS:	Movement Infrastructures
GREENBELTS:	Blended succession landscapes
LATTICE:	Pedestrian networks

LANDSCAPE BERMS: Flexible Land Territories The configurations of the berms stem from latent densities within the site of past infrastructures. Where the paragenetic lines overlap, nodes develop, where they part, they become electrical, water and waste infrastructural organization that organize the residential neighborhoods. The berms define site. Each site has flexible edges, defined by topographic changes, the rising and falling level of the canal overspill and possible expansion of ownership to neighboring housing wings. The Ebro Delta thus plays an integral role in the experience of each site. Weather, season, agricultural need all participate in a leveling of sites over time. Where the berms remain separate from the waterways, the topography itself defines gradations of ownership and responsibility. In some cases the berms push into the ground rather than protrude and therefore buffer the housing from the highway and denser noise zones.

Y-WING HOUSING: Expandable Housing Ownership The Y-Wing is less a specific architecture and more a system of spatial organization. It does not preference a specific form, technology, or material, but instead suggests a variable individual unit that connects with other around it to create either larger units for expanding families or extended spaces for necessary use. The extension of the two arms can create a courtyard space when conjoined with another unit or act as a house addition to provide for changing family needs. This open core functions similarly to the housing blocks currently found in Amposta. The Y-Wing also offers a system for creating four types of housing: the single family house, conjoined units, row house, and apartments. The system of housing across the site follows the logics of the circulatory networks, but primarily allows for dense edge and more open centers. Rather than cluster towards the center and leaving the edges vacant and growing, the housing first defines various edges to secure the nodes a strong economic base. We suggest three densities of housing-- the minimum, medium and maximum conditions that take the Amposta site from a garden city to thick neighborhoods.

Economies of (Variable) Scale In looking at the statistics of Catalonia, we noticed that the housing needs varied among family types. While 72% of dwellings house between 2 to 4 people, the 17% of the population lives alone and 11% lives in groups of 5 or more. Housing must be variable: it must allow for changes within the family unit, additions of children or the elderly, subtractions of the empty nest or through death. The key to allowing for minimum and maximum spatial boundaries is strategizing the economic system to allow for expandable and partial ownership. The Y-Wing configuration allows for the spatial expansion, but ownership models would need to follow this appropriation of neighboring territory. For example, a Tenants in Common agreement would allow for a series of structures to be owned together and distributed or redistributed among the various families. Co-operative housing structures would also allow for this variability.

NODES: Precipitant space While long lot dimensions are used to organize densities across the site-- the variations of relationships between one side and the other create dense zones for inhabitation and commerce. Where the variations overlap, commercial nodes evolve;

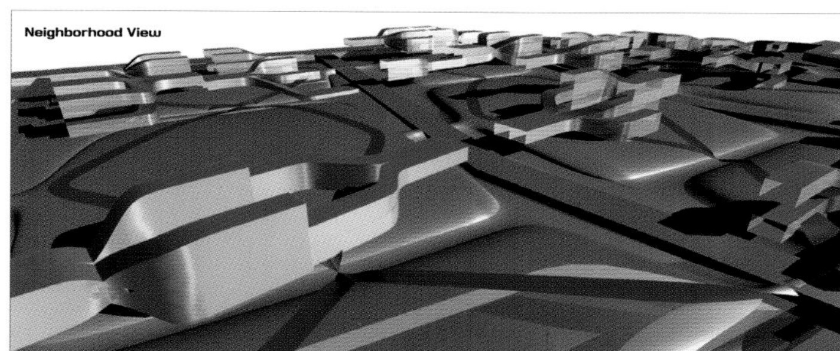

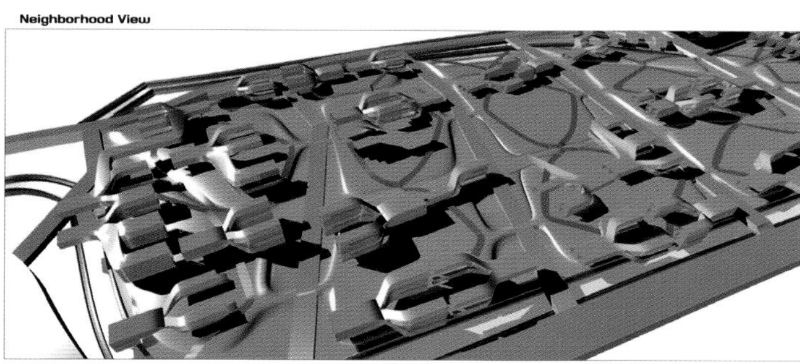

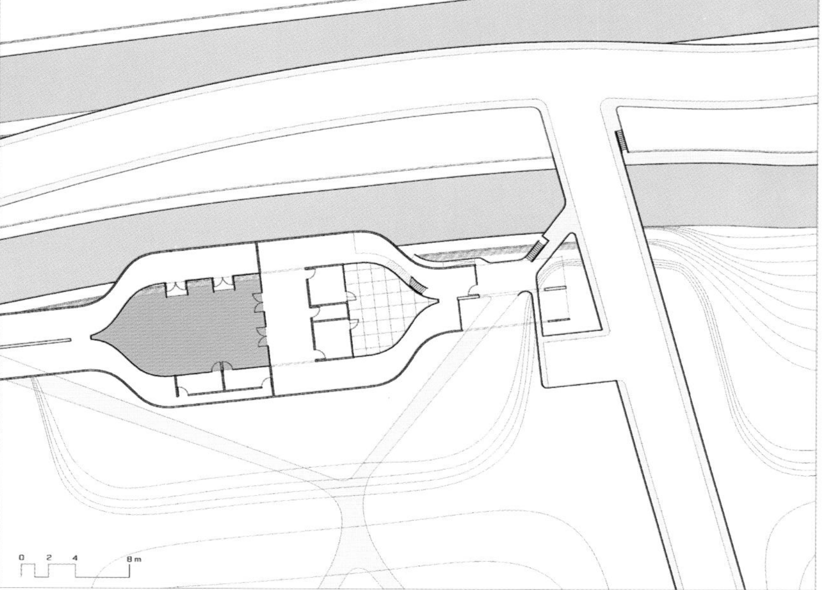

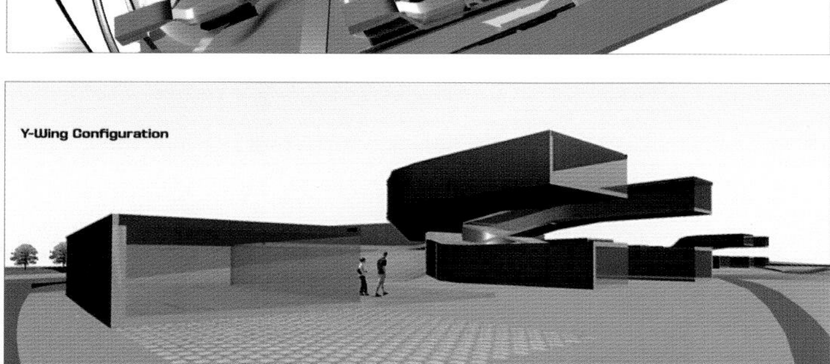

where there are more connections, denser housing evolves. The commercial nodes vary in scale from a "cross-road" configuration where an intersection can foster a corner store or small-scale market, to a "towncenter" which would offer a sampling of uses (restaurant, cafe, market, dry goods store, park, even a postal drop), to the Mercado that includes a multi-tiered, open air shopping zone, banks, public square, civic buildings, churches, and public library.

MERCADO: Public re-appropriation of the urban civic space The mercado is not simply an exterior mall or shopping strip, but rather a pedestrian civic space and transportation hub. A density of canals and roadways lead towards this edge that is also away from the highway. It is intended to be a distinctive civic space that also functions as a gateway between the Amposta site and whatever developments may occur along that exterior edge. The mercado also extends into the depth of the site transitioning seamlessly into housing. It is not intended to separate use, but rather to facilitate the blending of commerce, civic space and inhabitation.

CANALS: Movement infrastructure The Ebro Delta waterscape offers an alternative way to enter a housing landscape: by boat. While roadways enter the site both off of the highway and the local arteries, a new opportunity exists in the water systems that already line the site. The canal waterways act as both a reminder of the sea, the agricultural dependence on water, and offer the experience and program of active waterways. They are not fixed, but open up softly to the berm landscape creating changing border between houses and a constant re-appropriation of exterior land conditions. Your backyard is shared with your neighbor, but you can simultaneously know what is "yours" and what is "hers" even if that lines changes. Here, territory is more defined by time than space. The canals open up into different conditions of engagement: overlook, sidewalk promenade, boat launch, wetland, ramped "beach". These are related to specific house sites, but also offers blended outdoor experiences for the public.

GREENBELTS: Blended succession landscapes Blended natural landscape run along many of the canals and distributed throughout the site. They are a combination of four types of natural and artificial ecosystems: trees, grasslands, wetlands and cultivated fields. While the soil can not support extensive forest, this ecologically is important to help sustain a natural ecosystem as well as define the dense edges of housing and program. The grasslands lead to the wetlands, the heart of the health of the ecological systems on the site. The berms act as a water collection and organization system which separates black, grey and potable waterways. The cultivated fields can either be for gardening and agriculture or for organized parks and sports areas.

LATTICE: Pedestrian networks While the berms, canals, greenbelts and minor and major roadways layer across the site, it is the lattice pedestrian pathways knit them all together. These bikeways, walkways and trails weave through the residential neighborhoods, as well as the public spaces. They also connect to public bus routes on the major roadways and bring people via foot to the mercado and urban center. Inevitably, they are the most important thread to lead people across and over the waterscape into and through the variable topographic changes and create a diagonal network of experience on the site.

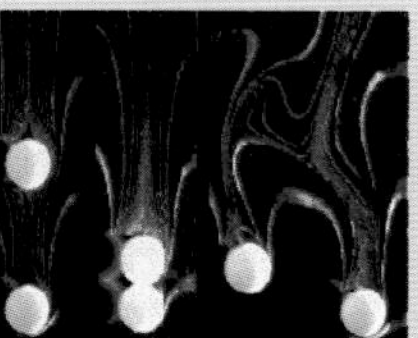

003

AIDS Mobile Unit | *Thurlow Small Architecture*

Location : Subsaharan Africa
Design Team : Andrew Thurlow, Maia Small; Eliza Higgins, Dianna Pozdniakov
Fabrication Team : Nathaniel Richards, Evan Richards
Fabrication Assistance : Joseph Lombari, Display World, Inc., Dani Lett, Z Corporation

Competition Sponsor : Architecture for Humanity
Awards : Selected for international traveling exhibition

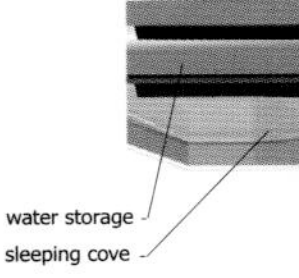

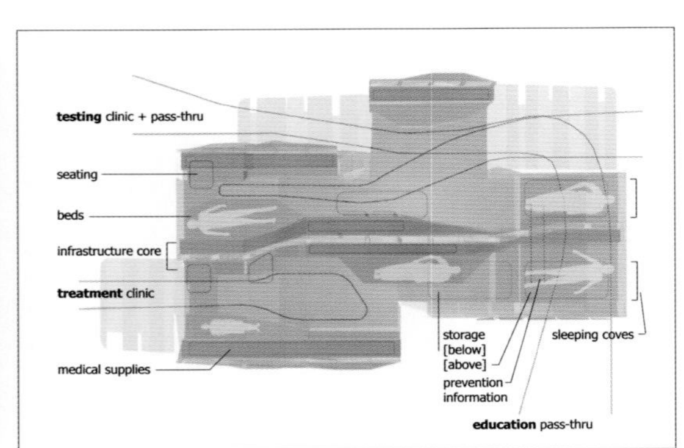

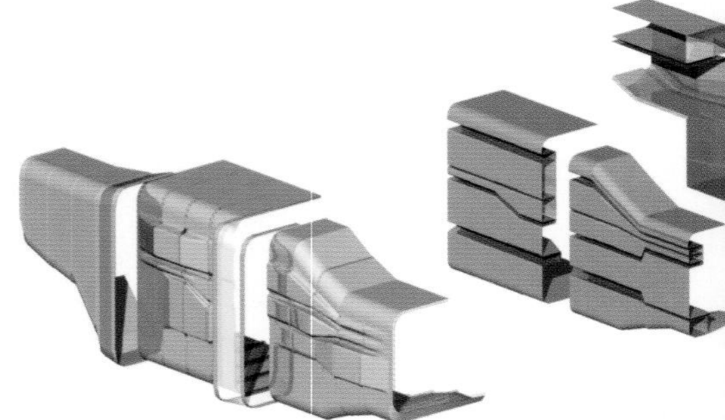

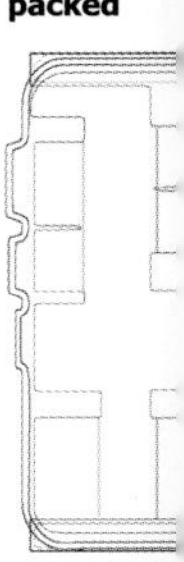

treatment

education pass-thru

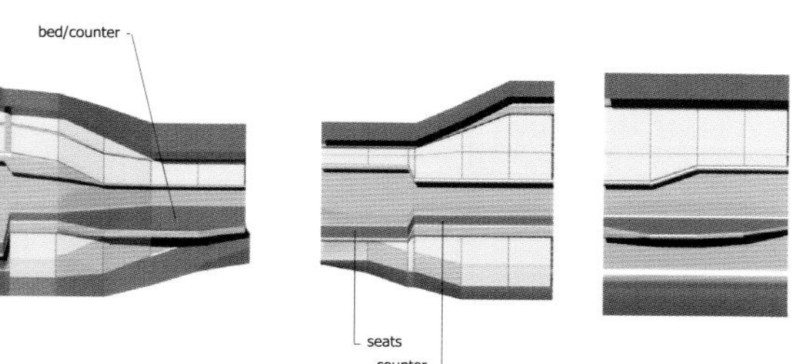

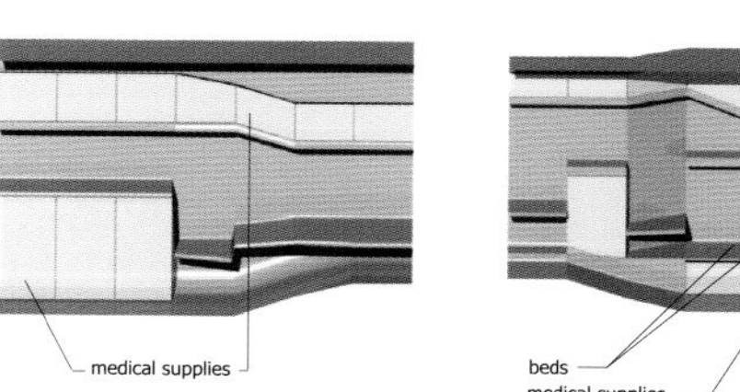

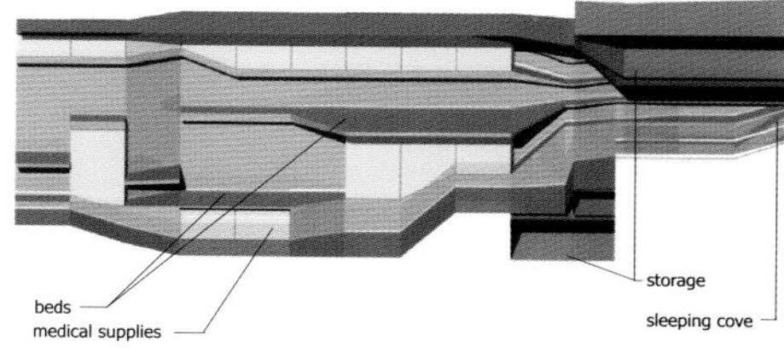

HIV/AIDS MOBILE CLINIC

"Modern life accustoms us to live with the intermittent awareness of monstrous, unthinkable-- but, we are told, quite probable-- disasters. Every major event is haunted, and not only by its representation as an image... Besides the photographic or electronic simulation of events there is also the calculation of their eventual outcome. Reality has bifurcated, into the real thing and an alternate version of it, twice over. **There is the event and its image.** And there is the event and its projection. But as real events often seem to have no more reality for people than images, so our reaction to events in the present seeks confirmation in a mental outline, with appropriate computation, of the event in its projected, ultimate form..."

"That even an apocalypse can be made to seem a part of the ordinary horizon of expectation constitutes an **unparalleled violence that is being done to our sense of reality**, to our humanity. But it is highly desirable for a specific dreaded illness to come to seem ordinary. Even the disease most fraught with meaning can become just an illness... It is bound to happen with AIDS, when the illness is much better understood and, above all, treatable. For the time being much in the way of individual experience and social policy depends on the struggle for rhetorical ownership of the illness: how it is possessed, assimilated in argument and in cliché... With this illness, one that elicits so much guilt and shame, the effort to detach it from these meanings, these metaphors, seems particularly liberating, even consoling. But the metaphors cannot be distanced just by abstaining from them. They have to be exposed, criticized, belabored, used up."

Susan Sontag, *AIDS and its Metaphors,* 1989

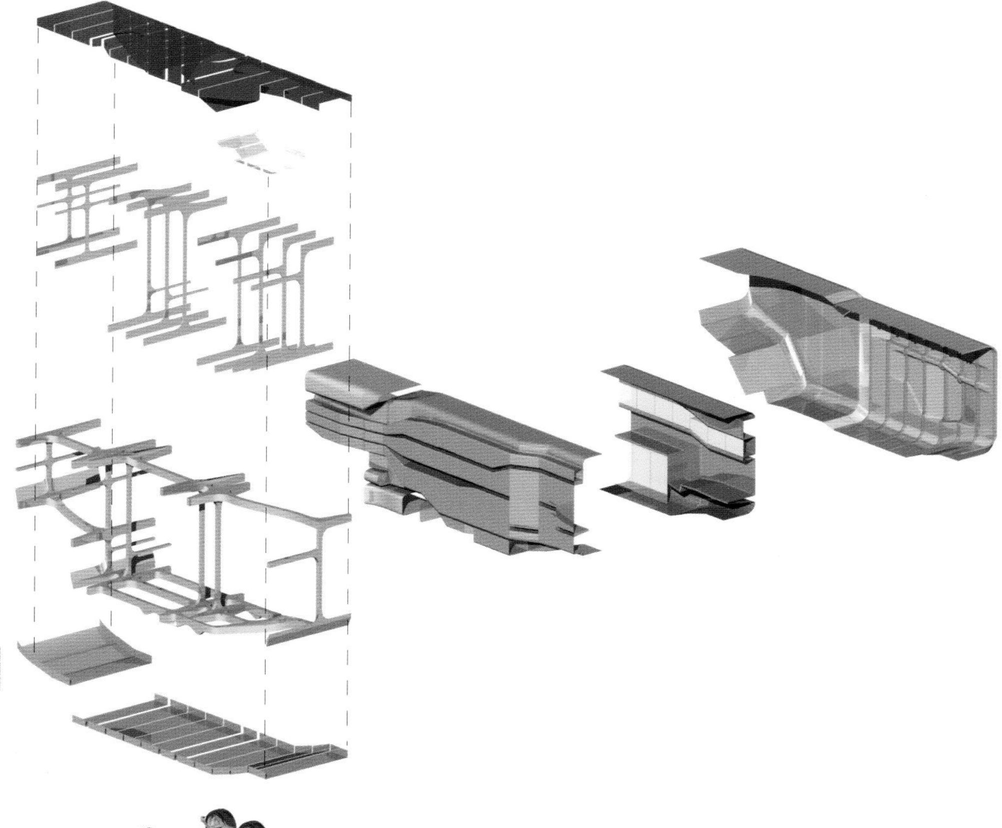

RHINO HIV in Africa is not only a crisis beyond words, but beyond images. The calamitous epidemic, caused by an unseen microscopic force, becomes apparent through absence-- it is the loss of community, parentage, future that unfolds through a slow disappearance of life. And it is **memory** that remains, our own images of connectivity and potential, of faces and cities. The RHINO project seeks to negotiate between the desire to give the reality of HIV a presence through image-- a mobile architectural icon-- and let the mobile object be a smooth and familiar part of the communities it serves. Thus, this is done through space and time. When arriving to a site, the unit is a distinct object, noticeable in its material difference and shape. It then begins a transformation which allows it to open up to the community, to **take shape** and connect to existing familiar networks and pathways. It **unpacks** and reveals three areas of engagement: space for **education**, **testing** and **treatment**. The first opening is at the front end, [where it detaches from its engine, a heavy duty truck], which can serve as a place to get information. The second is through one side that opens up allowing for easy access to HIV testing and minor medical assistance. The third is the clinic side, that limits access to patients in need of greater care, pregnant women needing exams or longer term help. It can become a center for multiple levels of activity, to engage anyone affected by HIV, to form new memories and spread information.

The mobile unit consists of a double-sided spatial configuration that pushes out into its site. The interior is defined by the activities within; specific profiles allow for storage, counter space, seating and bed surfaces to be pushed or pulled from the structural liners. In between the liners lies all of the infrastructure necessary for a medical unit including: water stored in tanks, medical supplies, miscellaneous storage, staff space, rigid structure and electrical systems. These are combined into a central spine in order to increase the area for circulation. The intent is to provide smooth access to internal spaces in order to maximize the number of contact hours between clinic staff and people.

unpacked

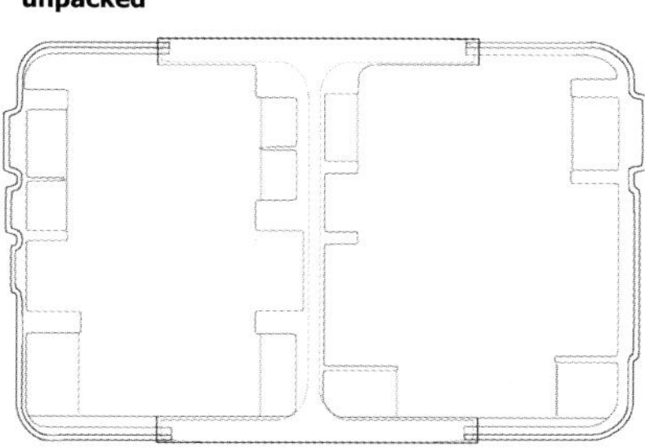

004 The Tomato Exchange | *CJ Lim / Studio 8 Architects*

Project : Community Gathering Place
Location : London, UK
Design Team : CJ Lim/Studio 8 Architects with Jen Wang, Yongzheng Li, Frank Fan, Barry Cho
Consultants : Techniker (structural engineers)

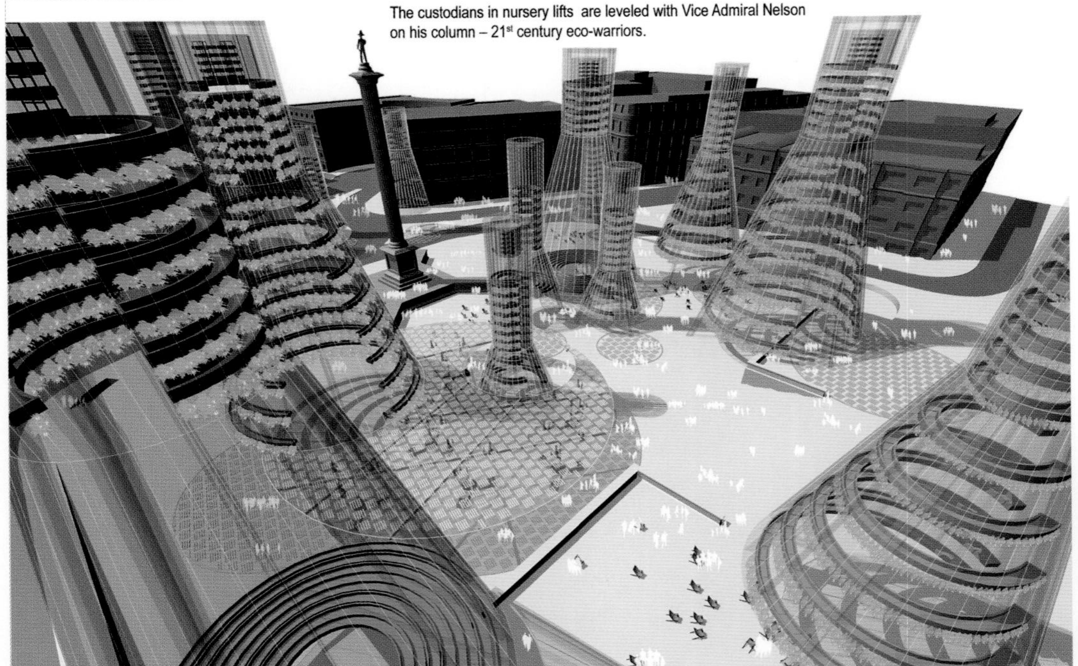
The custodians in nursery lifts are leveled with Vice Admiral Nelson on his column – 21st century eco-warriors.

The semi-enclosed glass skin traps the sun's energies to create an ideal microclimate.

Community Kitchen: Tomatoes are harvested by the local community, transforming into salsa, gazpacho, ketchup, ragu, borscht, chutney, relish, bloody mary, and jumabalaya under the supervision of the global citizens.

Growing and sharing food is a valuable resource for bringing people together - a new ecologically-friendly programme for the 21st century city square.

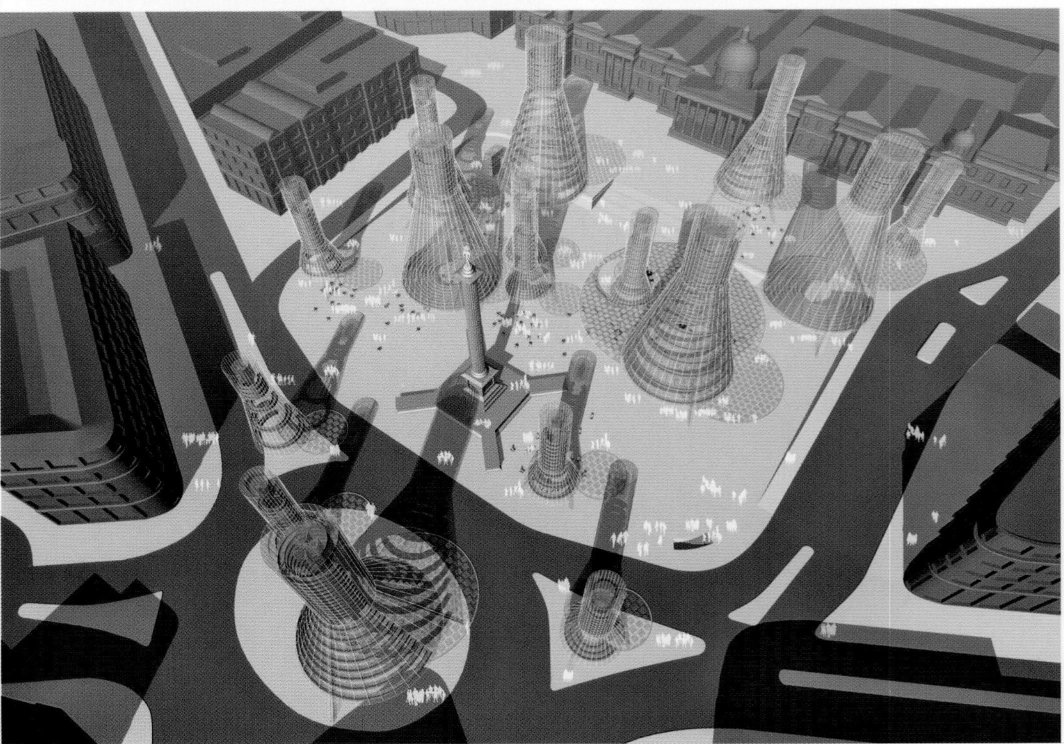

2009 Central Glass International Architectural Competition A Community Gathering Place: *THE TOMATO EXCHANGE*

London's *Tomato Exchange* in Trafalgar Square is a permanent forum for global intercultural exchange to encourage social integration and celebrate ethnic diversity. Sixteen glass bell-like structures display circular tiers of sprawling vines with scent and visual lushness, and also provide shelter for preparing and sharing tomato-based delicacies. Growing and sharing food is a precious resource for bringing people together and helps limit the huge environmental damage of the modern food industry. The exchange, with nurseries, disperses seeds to local suburban populace who in turn propagate and share knowledge with their own communities creating a secondary exchange network – an out-reaching community gathering place.

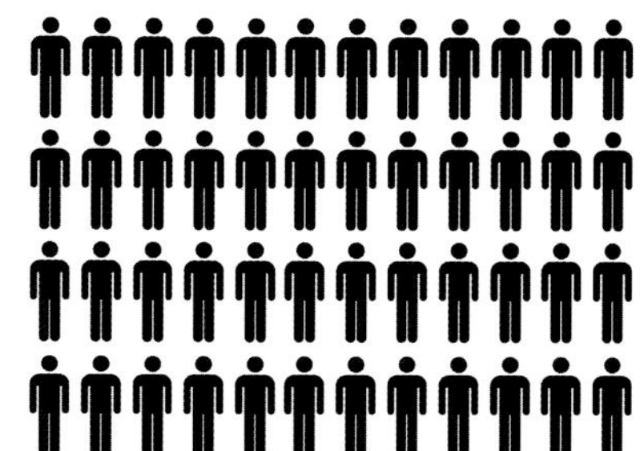

Global citizens + local communities

TIANANMEN SQUARE BEIJING	SAFRA SQUARE JERUSALEM	RED SQUARE MOSCOW	OLD TOWN SQUARE PRAGUE
DONEGALL SQUARE BELFAST	MARKET SQUARE KRAKÓW	RADHUSPLASSEN OSLO	AZADI SQUARE TEHRAN
PLAZA DE MAYO BUENOS AIRES	TRAFALGAR SQUARE LONDON	PLACE de la CONCORDE PARIS	NATHAN P. SQUARE TORONTO
TAKSIM SQUARE ISTANBUL	CITY SQUARE MELBOURNE	CHURCH SQUARE PRETORIA	MCPHERSON SQUARE WASHINGTON DC

Global communities gathering networks for social integration + ethnic diversity

Upside-down tomatoes

Tiananmen Square, Beijing

Red Square, Moscow

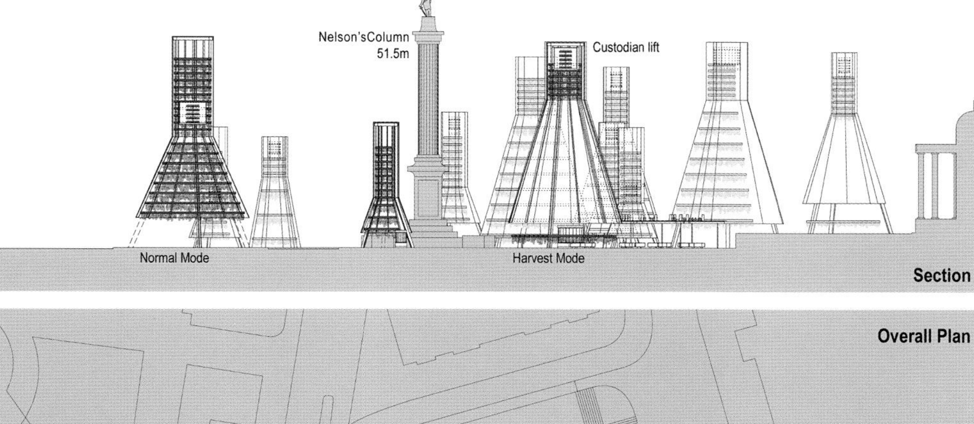

Section

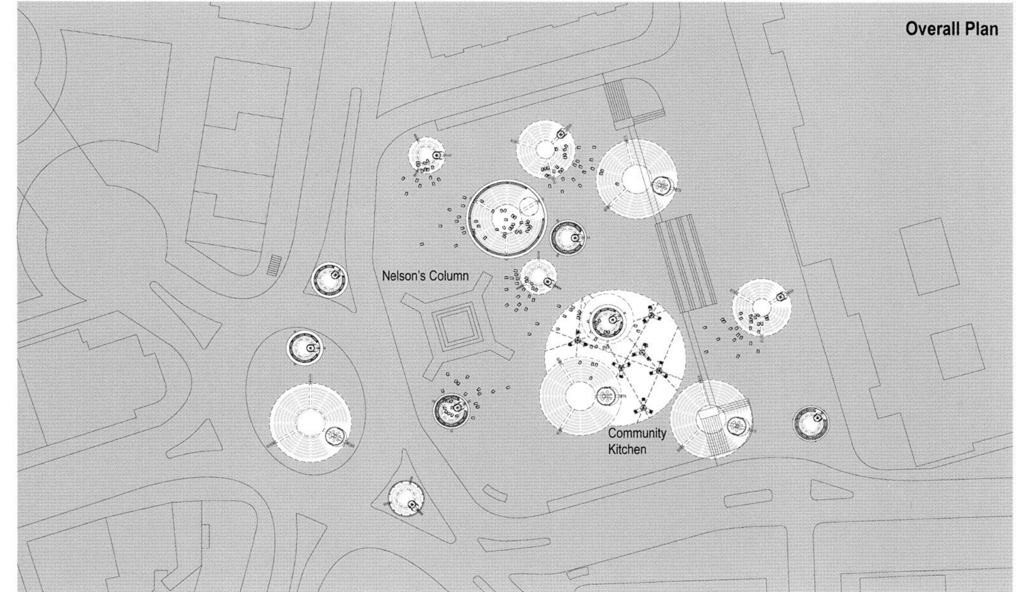

Overall Plan

005 Curtains | *2A+P/A*

Type : International Design Competition "Pass"
Program : Social Housing
Project : 2A+P/A with Greenville
Location : Rome, Italy

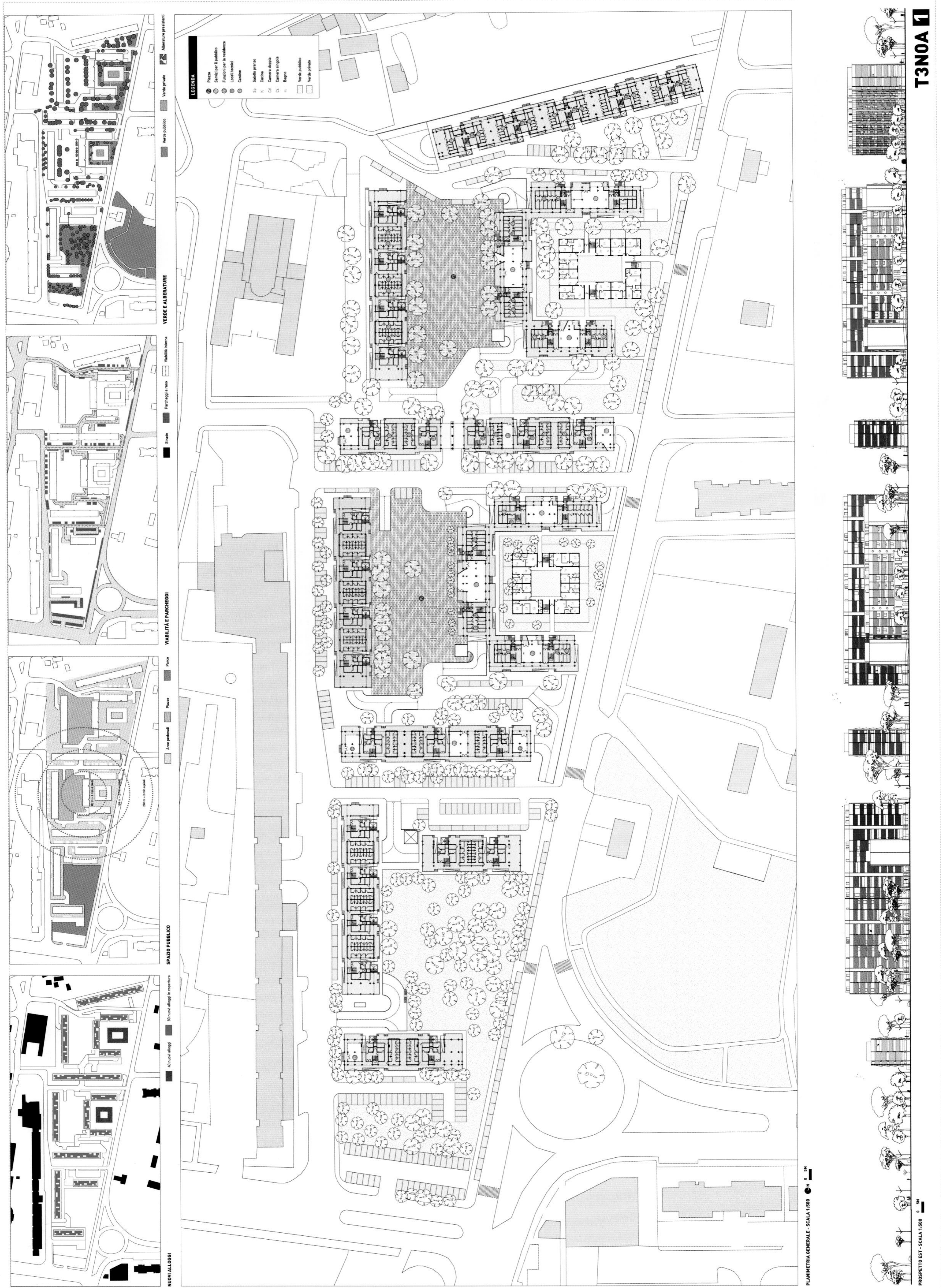

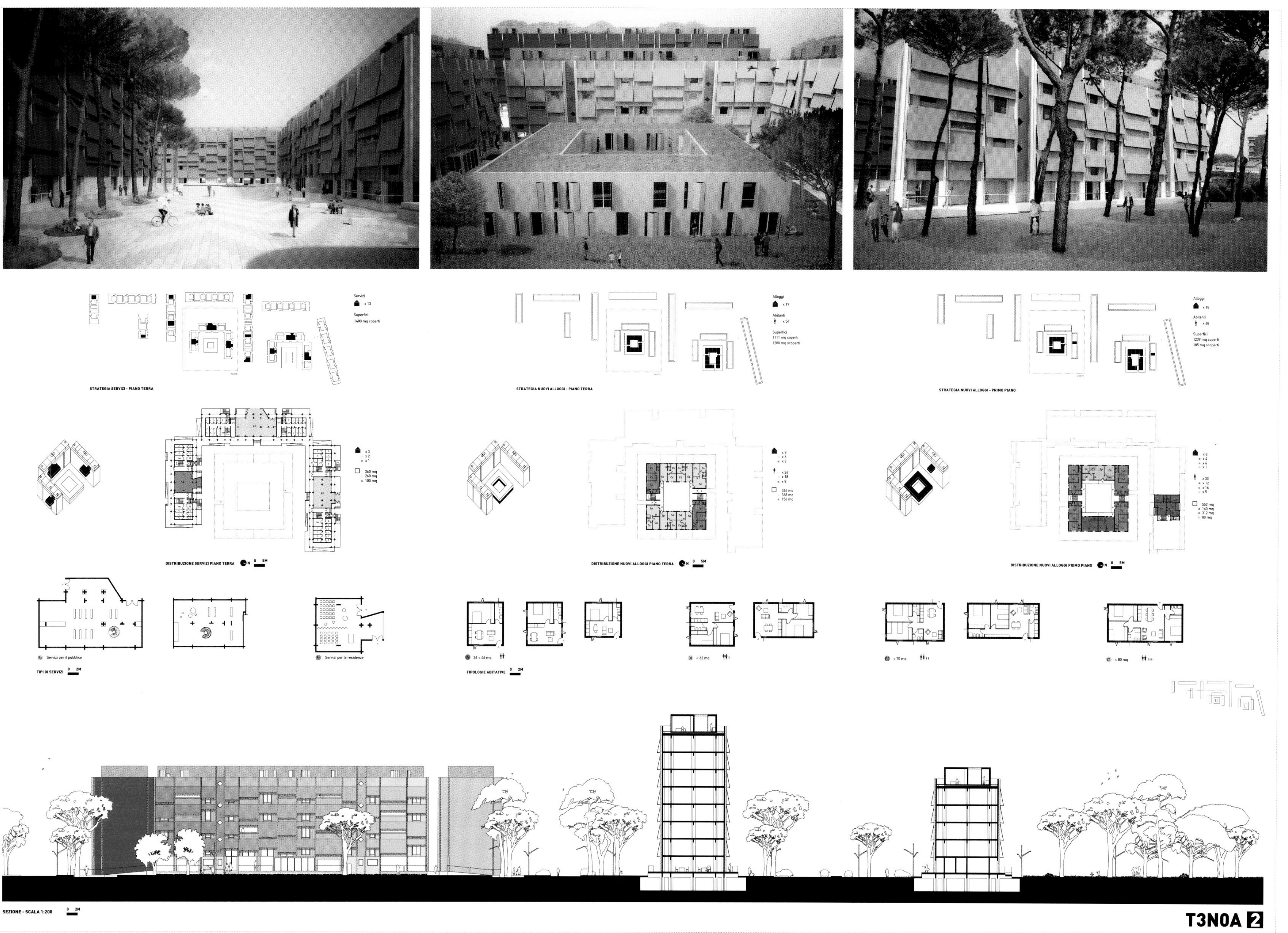
STRATEGIA SERVIZI - PIANO TERRA
STRATEGIA NUOVI ALLOGGI - PIANO TERRA
STRATEGIA NUOVI ALLOGGI - PRIMO PIANO
DISTRIBUZIONE SERVIZI PIANO TERRA
DISTRIBUZIONE NUOVI ALLOGGI PIANO TERRA
DISTRIBUZIONE NUOVI ALLOGGI PRIMO PIANO
TIPI DI SERVIZI
TIPOLOGIE ABITATIVE
SEZIONE - SCALA 1:200
T3N0A 2

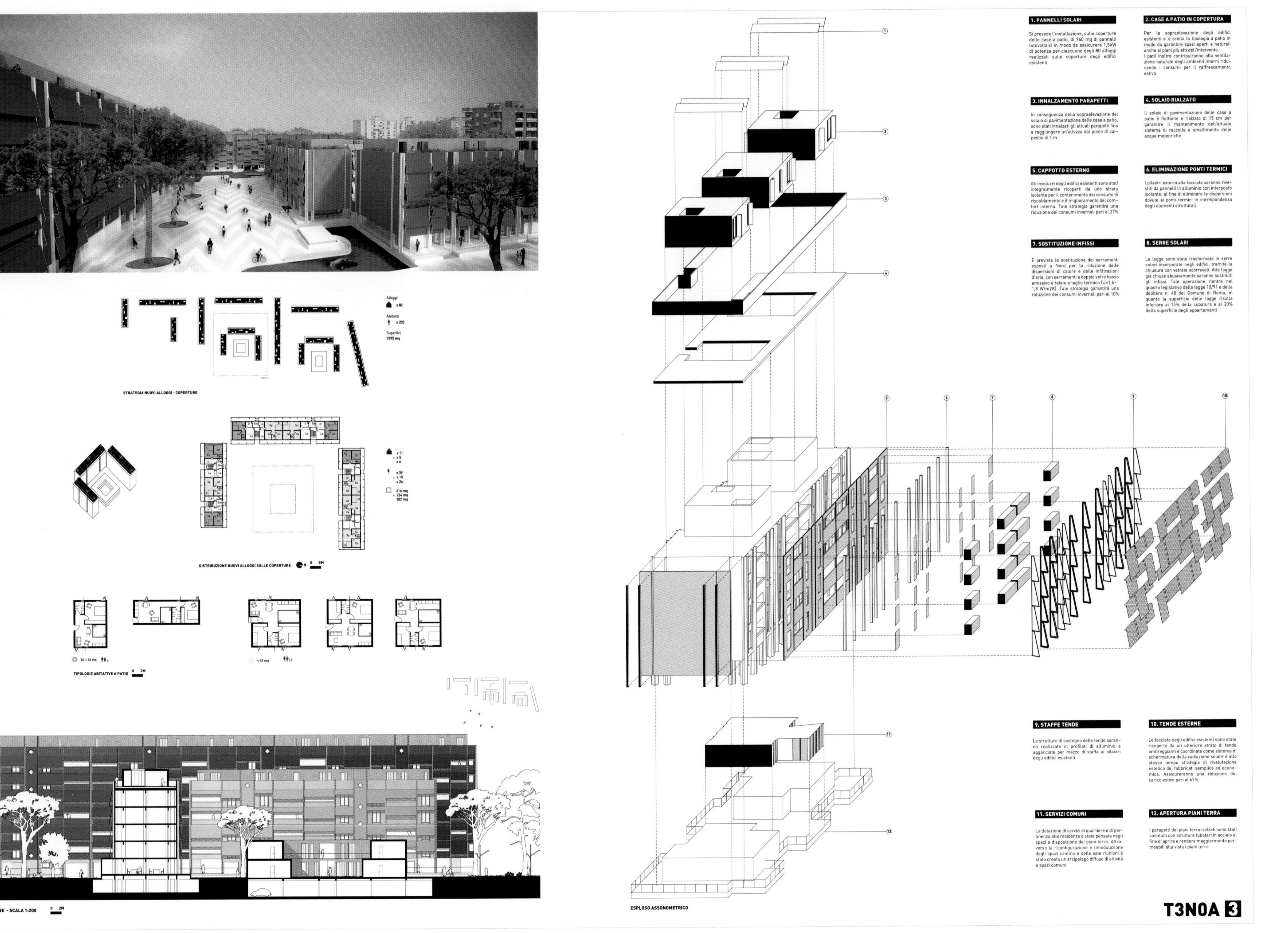
STRATEGIA NUOVI ALLOGGI - COPERTURE
Alloggi x 82
Abitanti x 203
Superfici 3995 mq
DISTRIBUZIONE NUOVI ALLOGGI SULLE COPERTURE
TIPOLOGIE ABITATIVE A PATIO
SEZIONE - SCALA 1:200
ESPLOSO ASSONOMETRICO
1. PANNELLI SOLARI
Si prevede l'installazione, sulle coperture delle case a patio, di 960 mq di pannelli fotovoltaici in modo da assicurare 1,5kW di potenza per ciascuno degli 80 alloggi realizzati sulle coperture degli edifici esistenti
2. CASE A PATIO IN COPERTURA
Per la sopraelevazione degli edifici esistenti si è scelta la tipologia a patio in modo da garantire spazi aperti e naturali anche ai piani più alti dell'intervento.
I patii inoltre contribuiranno alla ventilazione naturale degli ambienti interni riducendo i consumi per il raffrescamento estivo
3. INNALZAMENTO PARAPETTI
In conseguenza della sopraelevazione del solaio di pavimentazione delle case a patio, sono stati innalzati gli attuali parapetti fino a raggiungere un'altezza dal piano di calpestio di 1 m
4. SOLAIO RIALZATO
Il solaio di pavimentazione delle case a patio è flottante e rialzato di 15 cm per garantire il mantenimento dell'attuale sistema di raccolta e smaltimento delle acque meteoriche
5. CAPPOTTO ESTERNO
Gli involucri degli edifici esistenti sono stati integralmente ricoperti da uno strato isolante per il contenimento dei consumi di riscaldamento e il miglioramento del comfort interno. Tale strategia garantirà una riduzione dei consumi invernali pari al 27%
6. ELIMINAZIONE PONTI TERMICI
I pilastri esterni alla facciata saranno rivestiti da pannelli in alluminio con interposto isolante, al fine di eliminare le dispersioni dovute ai ponti termici in corrispondenza degli elementi strutturali
7. SOSTITUZIONE INFISSI
È prevista la sostituzione dei serramenti esposti a Nord per la riduzione delle dispersioni di calore e delle infiltrazioni d'aria, con serramenti a doppio vetro basso emissivo e telaio a taglio termico (U=1,6-1,8 W/m2K). Tale strategia garantirà una riduzione dei consumi invernali pari al 10%
8. SERRE SOLARI
Le logge sono state trasformate in serre solari incorporate negli edifici, tramite la chiusura con vetrate scorrevoli. Alle logge già chiuse abusivamente saranno sostituiti gli infissi. Tale operazione rientra nel quadro legislativo della legge 10/91 e della delibera n. 48 del Comune di Roma, in quanto la superficie delle logge risulta inferiore al 15% della cubatura e al 20% della superficie degli appartamenti
9. STAFFE TENDE
Le strutture di sostegno delle tende saranno realizzate in profilati di alluminio e agganciate per mezzo di staffe ai pilastri degli edifici esistenti
10. TENDE ESTERNE
Le facciate degli edifici esistenti sono state ricoperte da un ulteriore strato di tende ombreggianti e coordinate come sistema di schermatura della radiazione solare e allo stesso tempo strategia di rivalutazione estetica dei fabbricati semplice ed economica. Assicureranno una riduzione del carico estivo pari al 67%
11. SERVIZI COMUNI
La dotazione di servizi di quartiere e di pertinenza alle residenze è stata pensata negli spazi a disposizione dei piani terra. Attraverso la riconfigurazione e rimodulazione degli spazi cantina e delle sale riunioni è stato creato un arcipelago diffuso di attività e spazi comuni
12. APERTURA PIANI TERRA
I parapetti dei piani terra rialzati sono stati sostituiti con strutture tubolari in acciaio al fine di aprire e rendere maggiormente permeabili alla vista i piani terra
T3N0A 3

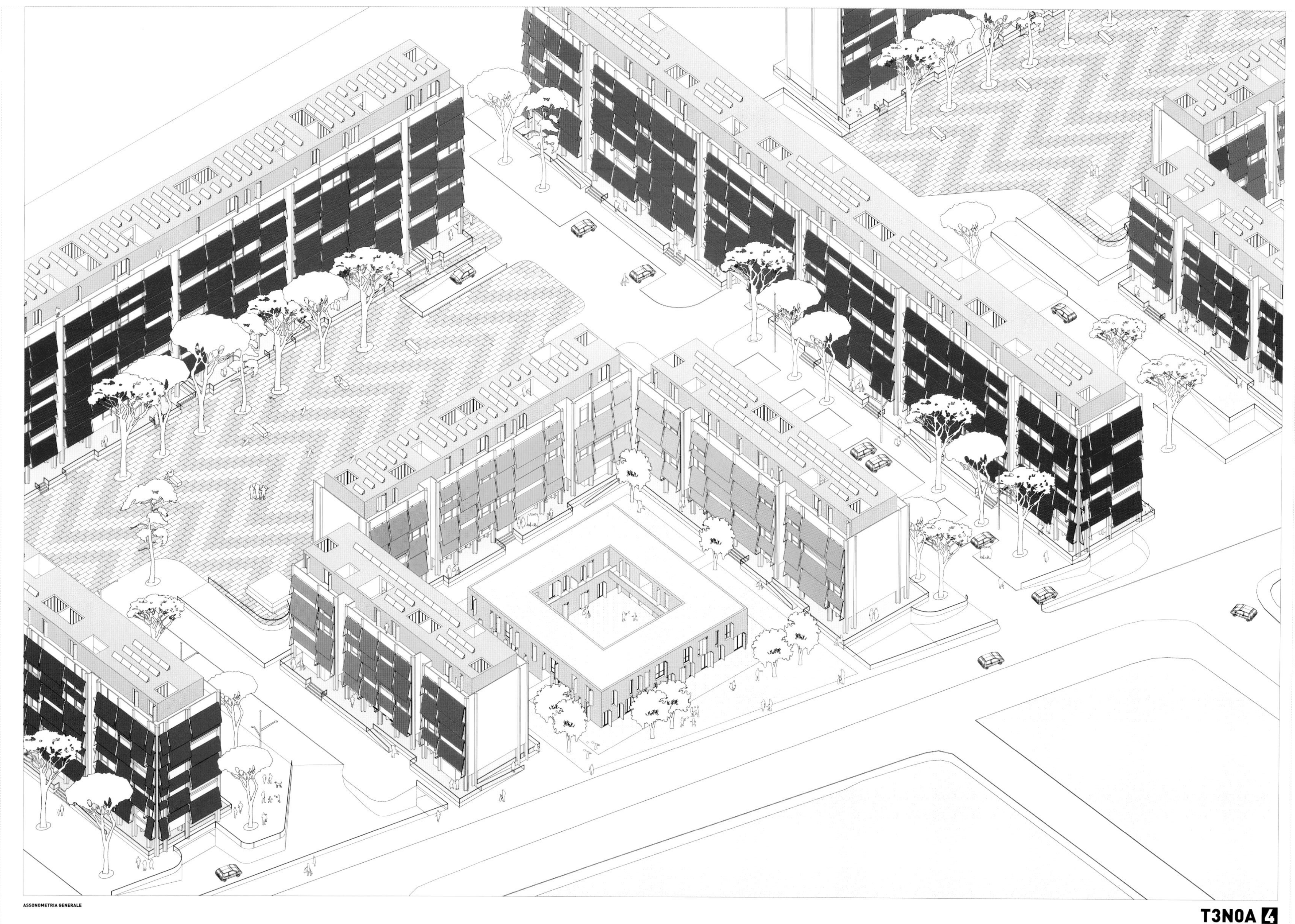
ASSONOMETRIA GENERALE
T3N0A 4

006 De Laanwoningen in Haagwijk | *XCOOP*

Type : Housing (Private Villa)
Size : 186 m²
Location : The Hague [The Netherlands]
Credits : Andrea Bertassi, Cristina C. Murphy, Jaap van Dijk and Raymond van den Broek

Paar
Kleine familie
Grote familie
Kunstenaar
Bewoner
Garage
Dienst
Slaap
Verblijf
Chill
Speel
Patio
Muziek
Kies je eigen programma
Keramisch
Chipwood
Metaal
Multiplex met goud print
Beton
Behang
Multiplex
Beton
Kies je eigen vormen en materialen
177m²
192m²
174m²
164m²
Kies je eigen samenstelling
Ca' Virginia
Ca' Nerino
Ca' Luigi
Ca' Anna
Binnen
Ca' Virginia
Ca' Nerino
Ca' Luigi
Ca' Anna
Buiten
De laanwoningen in Haagwijk:
soft **rock** wonen in de natuur
soft **rock** biedt de mogelijkheid een droomhuis te ontwerpen, verscholen in de bossen. Een strak omlijnde/gevormde woning tegen een serene achtergrond van weldadig groen.
soft **rock** is een open systeem dat harmonieus twee elementen combineert: een schil met een zadeldak (de traditionele vorm voor landelijke gebouwen) en functiedozen (efficiënt en makkelijk te combineren). De schil hecht het huis met haar omgeving.
Het programma wordt samengesteld naar behoefte zodat u uw huis kunt afstemmen op uw levensstijl.
soft **rock** biedt u grote flexibiliteit, een efficiënte bouwwijze en de mogelijkheid uw eigen luxe woonhuis te bouwen tegen concurrerende kosten.
soft **rock** biedt opgaan in de natuur en tegelijkertijd karakter, eigenheid en een lichtelijk moderne sensatie door het scala aan materialen, de samenstelling van de elementen, de gekozen maat en de oriëntatie van de compositie.
Het resultaat is een contrast aan kleuren tegen het bos erachter, een explosie van puur gedefinieerde vormen en het genot van de buitenruimte.
Uw eigen huis vormgeven is makkelijk! Alle modellen zijn recht voor de raap, ruim, elementair en open. Door een keuze voor een andere combinatie van materialen, schilvorm en samenstelling van dozen wordt de gebruiker een geweldige mogelijkheid geboden de ruimtelijkheid te voelen in al haar weidsheid, zichtrelaties en samengaan met de natuur.
soft **rock** streeft 3 keer respect voor de omgeving na: 1/ in de keuze voor duurzame/herbruikbare of recyclebare onderdelen 2/ in de bouwvorm ingepaste natuurlijke ventilatie, hoogwaardige isolatie en energieopslag 3/ softrock promoot een nieuwe manier om tot de natuur te staan en deze respectvol te gebruiken.
De bebossing omsluit de kavels en maakt ze afgeschermd en vredig: de kwaliteit die de huizen bieden is dat de bewoner de deur uitstapt de natuur in en zich thuis voelt! De vloeiende relatie tussen binnen en buiten van de architectuur verleidt tot het vormen van gezellige buitenruimtes die voelen als woonkamers buiten en natuur binnen. Bomen als geopende armen, majesteitelijke bomen, die de hemel raken... zelfs het huis raakt de hemel.
xcoop®
Stadhuisplein 13-u07 3012AR Rotterdam The Netherlands
+31 (0)10 786 37 38 | info@xcoo.org | www.xcoop.org

From Flower to Flower | *nodo17-architects*

Location : Las Margaritasneighbourhood, Getafe, Madrid, Spain
Design Team : Manuel Perez Romero, Felix Toledo Lerín, Birga Wingenfeld, Luis Del Rey Cristobal, Jaime Tarazona Lizarraga, Mercedes Peña Martín, Alegría Zorrilla Miras
Client : Getafe's Town Hall

Company / Firm Name_ nodo17-architects/ Manuel Pérez Romero
Country_ Spain

Project Name_ From Flowers to Flowers
Location of Site_ Las margaritas neighbourhood, Getafe. Madrid. Spain.
Design Team_ Felix Toledo Lerín_ Birga Wingenfeld_ Luis del Rey Cristóbal_ Jaime Tarazona Lizarraga Mercedes Peña Martín_ Alegría Zorrilla Miras

Project Type_ Remodelling and rehabilitation of the neighbourhood of Las Margaritas
Client_ Getafe's Town Hall
Built-up Area_ (160.000 sm housing to be rehabilitated (Density: 551,30 housing/hectare)

Site Area_ 46.000 sm
Public space_ 15.000 sm
New_ 16.000 sm parking area.
Date of completion_ State- Executive project

BUILDER FOREMAN_ Ignacio Delgado Conde
URBAN ACTION_ Boamistura

1.REVERSE TIMING_ First architecture_after urban planning

The traditional timing of the urban process has beed reversed: first the architecture, and after and the urban planning.
The reverse urban planning proposes the construction of tested architectural prototypes, and after develop the urban planning over these optimized models.
An architecture that is going to be first, out of order, but at the same time, it is going to be the base of the future order.
From this point of view, the architecture is in constant revision, and the architect should manage the information submitted.

BLOCK TYPES → STREET → ENVIRONMENTAL UNITS → NEIGHBOURHOOD → MARGARITAS COMMUNITY PLAN

ACTUAL BLOCK / BLOCK TYPE A / BLOCK TYPE B

ENVIRONMENTAL UNIT EXAMPLE

Lilac street / Chrysanthemum street / Gladiolus street

ENVIRONMENTAL UNITS

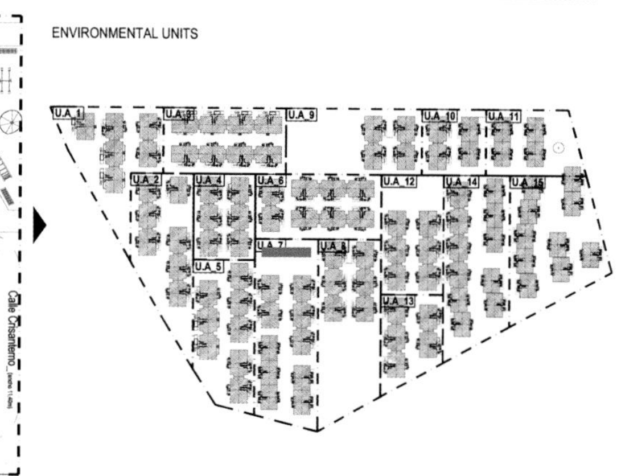

FOTO HABITACIÓN estado actual_ FOTO GENERAL DEL BARRIO estado actual_

2. FROM THE ROOM TO THE NEIGHBORHOOD_

¿How do you transform a room from a process of urban renovation? or, ¿how can a room condition the process of urban renovation?
The reverse urban planning propose re-project the room, and how this new renovation, will condition the steet, the environmental units, the neighbourhood....
It is a process from the private interior to the public exterior, but always from the point of view of joint responsability.

INTERIOR ROOM_Actual state → ROOM RENOVATION → NEW EXTERIOR ROOM → NEW TERRACE → NEW NEIGHBOURHOOD

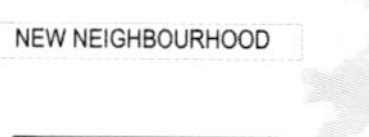

3. THE UNFINISHED AND EDUCATIONAL CITY_

The city has never been finished.
It is always in a continuous state of change.
The project consider every state of the construction of the city, like a city itself.
All the steps or phases have the same quality of the wrong called consolidated city.

INTERIOR HOUSING CONSTRUCTION PROCESS

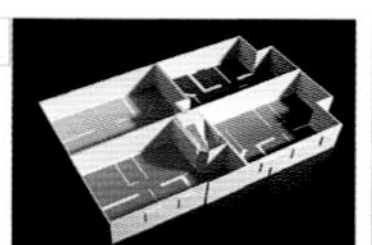
[1] ACTUAL STATE_

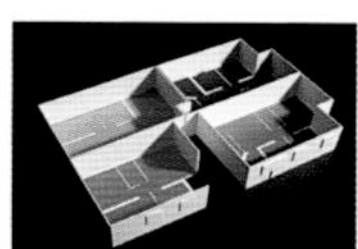
[2] ROOM AND STAIR DEMOLITION_

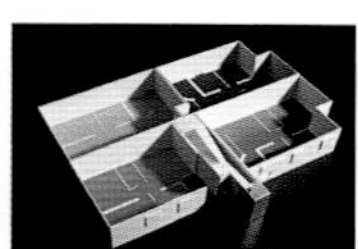
[3] NEW STAIR AND ELEVATOR_

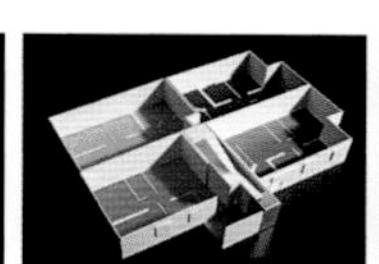
[4] NEW ROOM_

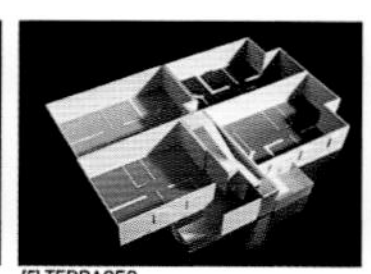
[5] TERRACES_

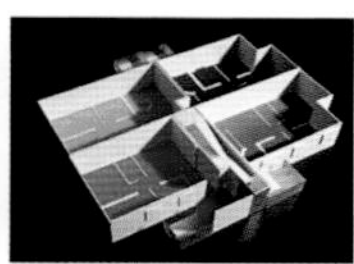
[6] TERRACES_

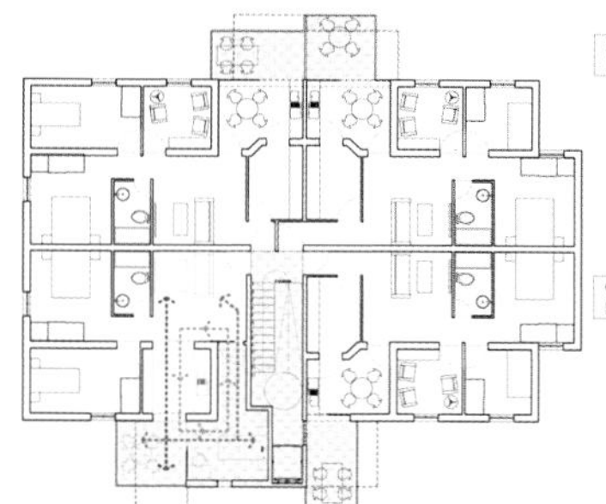

BUILDING CONSTRUCTION PROCESS

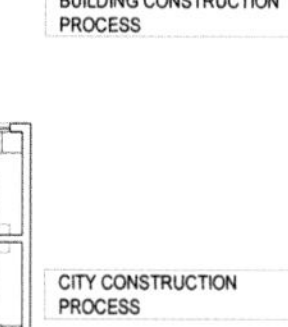

fase 1 FOUNDATION / fase 2 BELONGINGS TRANSPORT HOUSING ADAPTATION / fase 3 AUXILIARY STAIRS FOR TEMPORARY HOUSING ACCESS / fase 4 COMMON SPACES RENOVATION / fase 5 NEW STAIR AND ELEVATOR DESASEMBLE AUXILIARY STAIR / fase 6 ELEVATOR NEW TERRACES / FINAL FINAL CONSTRUCTION PHASE

CITY CONSTRUCTION PROCESS

4. UNDETERMINATE_

The reverse urban planning is undeterminate.
It is aproximate, not precise.
We use tools like probabilities, potential sections, movements areas...
A project that will focus on the future and his changing condition.

BUILDING LIMITS UPPER LEVELS
BUILDING LIMITS GROUND AND 1st LEVEL
REAL LIMIT BUILDING RENOVATION
VEGETATION LIMIT
PAVING AREAS

1960 [TYPE A] 1980 2012 2020

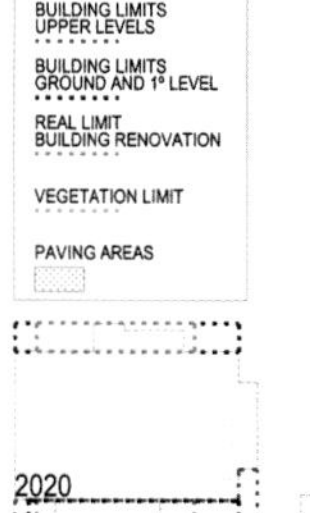

1960 [TYPE B] 1980 2012 2020

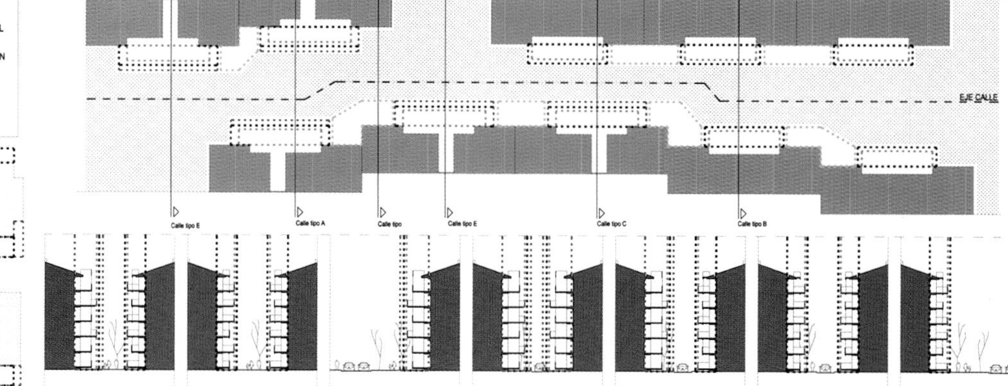

Fancy Fences | *arenas basabe palacios arquitectos*

Project : Housing development in Turku (Finland)
Team : arenas basabe palacios arquitectos
Authors : Enrique Arenas Laorga, Luis Basabe Montalvo, Luis Palacios Labrador
Collaborators : Almudena Cano, Helena de Sebastian

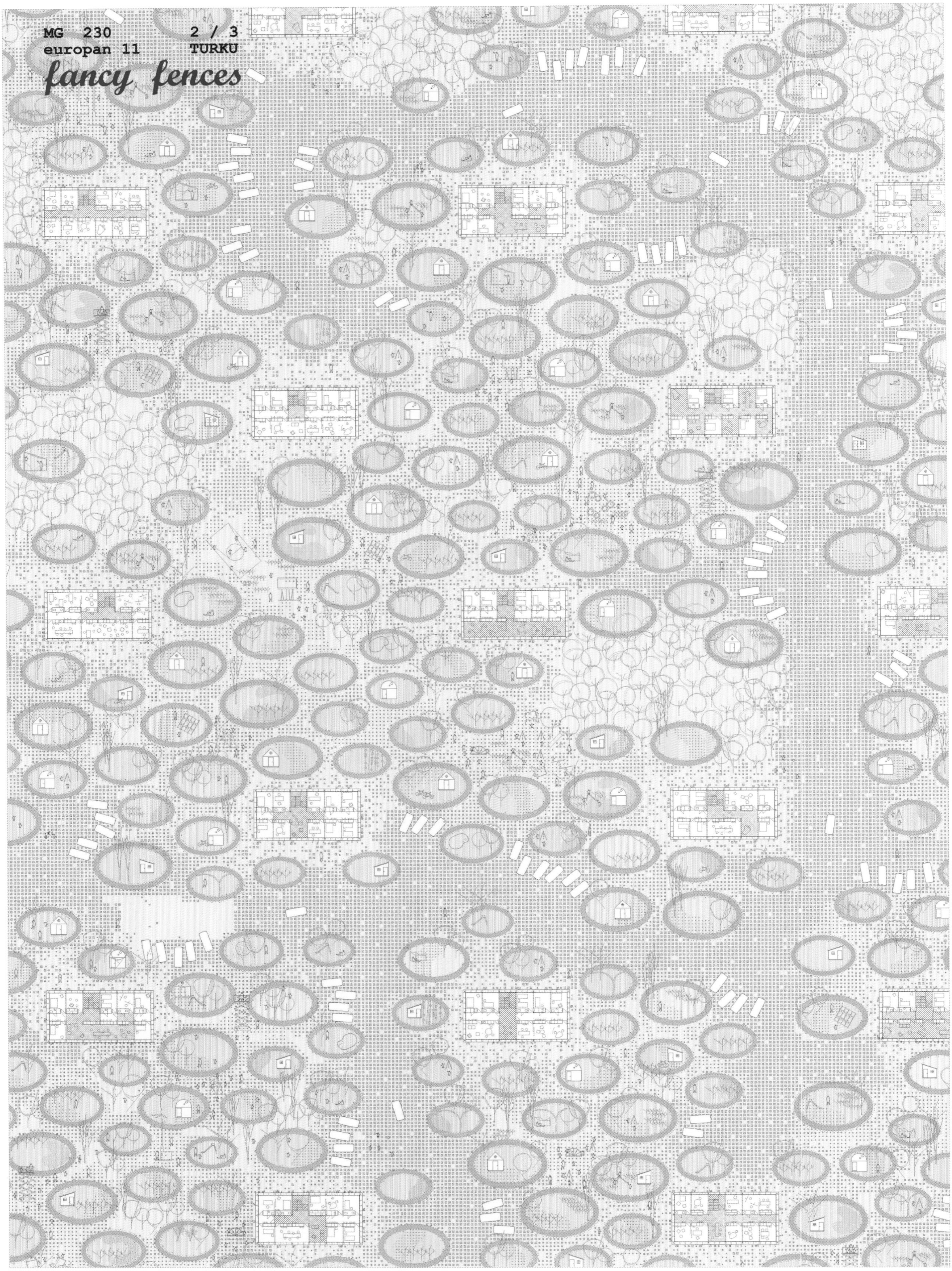

MG 230 2 / 3
europan 11 TURKU
fancy fences

MG 230 3 / 3
europan 11 TURKU

fancy fences

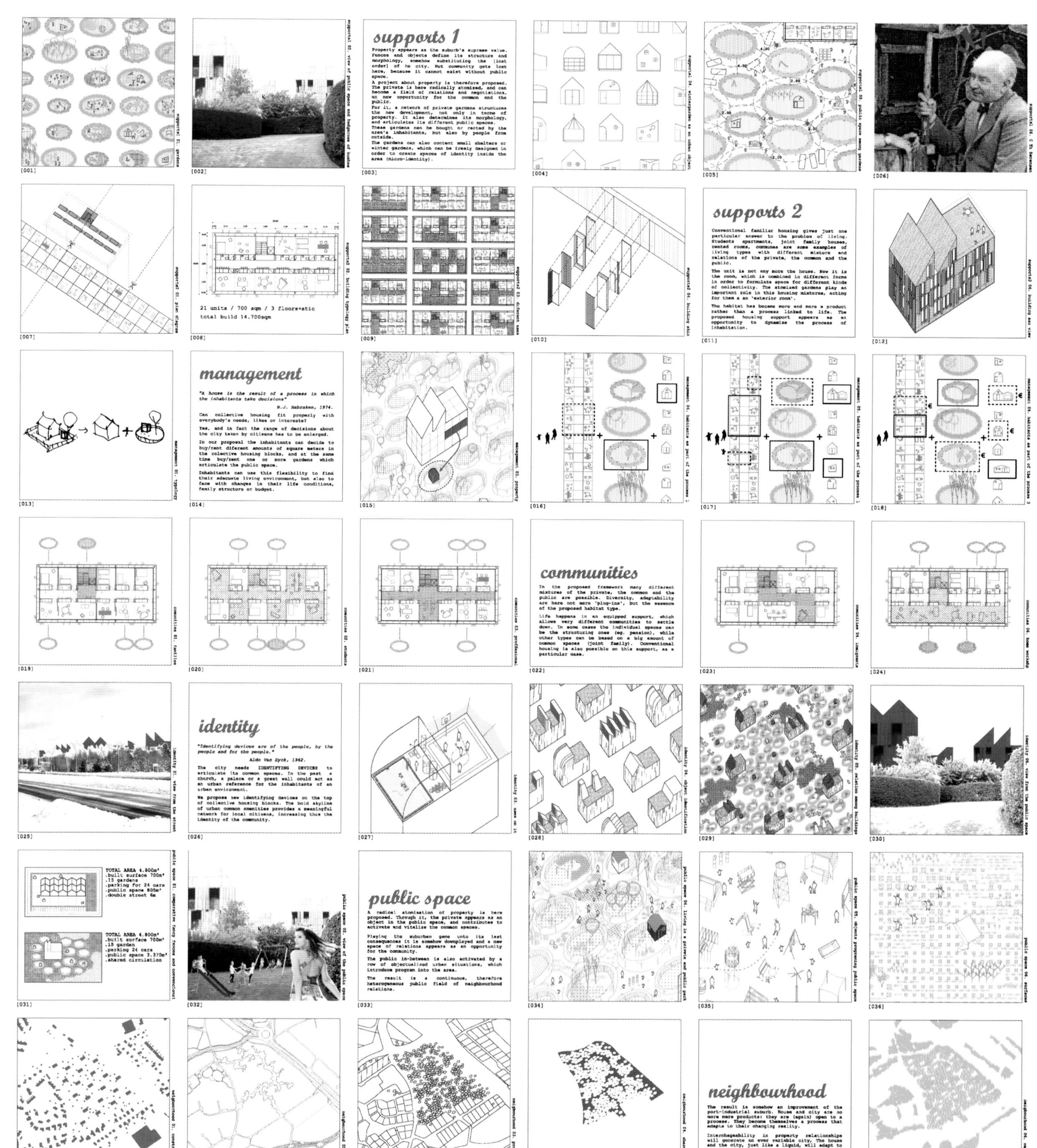

009 Fireproof Cider Box House | *Dai Nagasaka*

Team : Dai Nagasaka, Yoshihisa Ishibashi, Kayoko Nishida, Ikue Tanaka

Name of Competition : Competiton for Kishu-zai house

紀州材の家設計コンペ

延焼のおそれのない杉箱の家

防火のため多くの市街地で外壁を板で仕上げにくい時代です。
しかし、日本人にとって、美しい板を外壁に使えないことはとても残念です。
この案は敷地の寸法に着目し、「延焼のおそれのある部分」をかわした場所に「杉箱」を設けました。
防火規制区域であっても、敷地に一定の大きさがあれば木の表情を楽しめることを提案します。

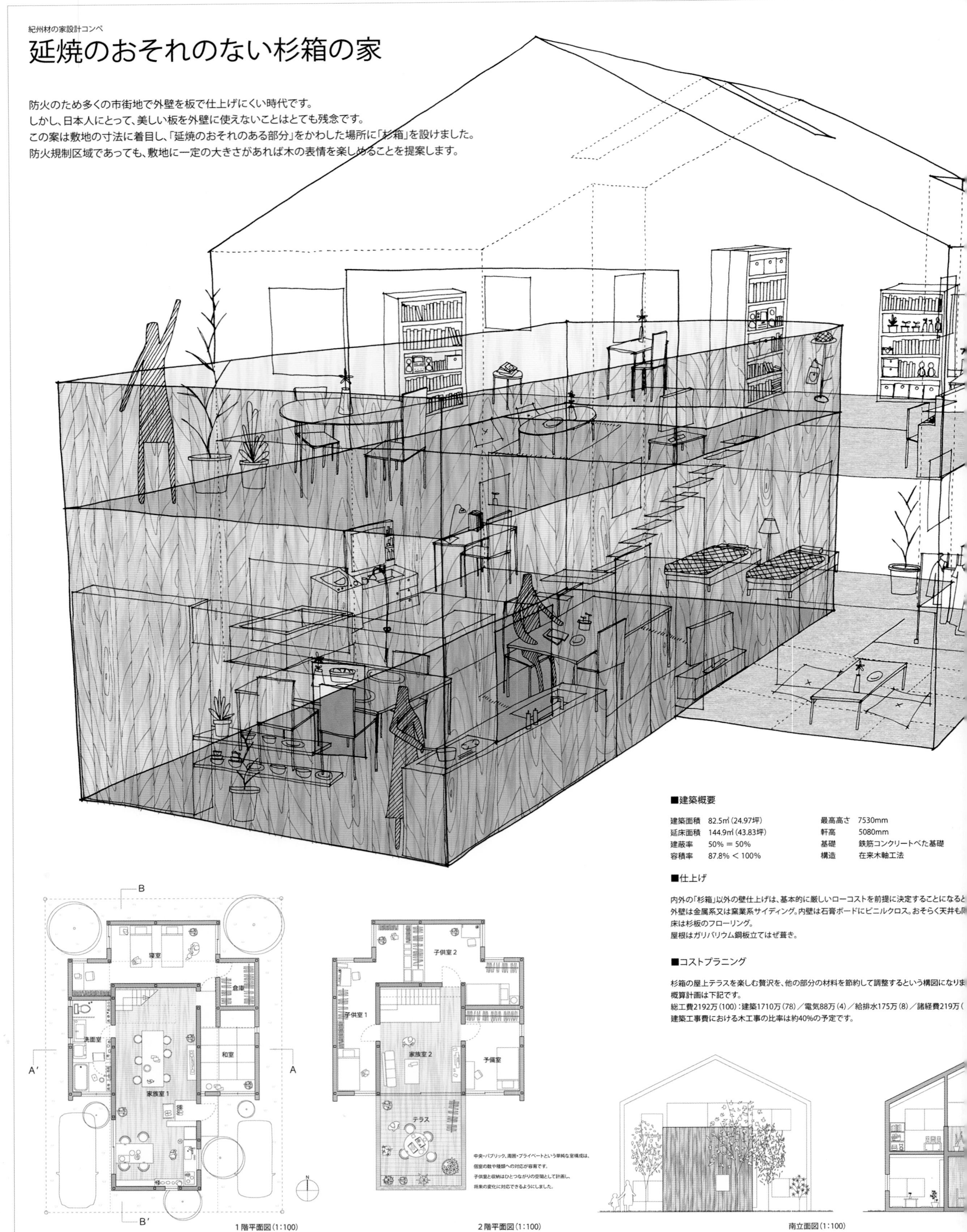

中央・パブリック、周囲・プライベートという単純な室構成は、
個室の数や種類への対応が容易です。
子供室と収納はひとつながりの空間として計画し、
将来の変化に対応できるようにしました。

1 階平面図（1:100）

2 階平面図（1:100）

南立面図（1:100）

■建築概要

建築面積	82.5㎡（24.97坪）	最高高さ	7530mm
延床面積	144.9㎡（43.83坪）	軒高	5080mm
建蔽率	50% ＝ 50%	基礎	鉄筋コンクリートべた基礎
容積率	87.8% ＜ 100%	構造	在来木軸工法

■仕上げ

内外の「杉箱」以外の壁仕上げは、基本的に厳しいローコストを前提に決定することになると
外壁は金属系又は窯業系サイディング。内壁は石膏ボードにビニルクロス。おそらく天井も
床は杉板のフローリング。
屋根はガリバリウム鋼板立てはぜ葺き。

■コストプラニング

杉箱の屋上テラスを楽しむ贅沢を、他の部分の材料を節約して調整するという構図になりま
概算計画は下記です。
総工費2192万（100）：建築1710万（78）／電気88万（4）／給排水175万（8）／諸経費219万（
建築工事費における木工事の比率は約40%の予定です。

■ダイアグラム

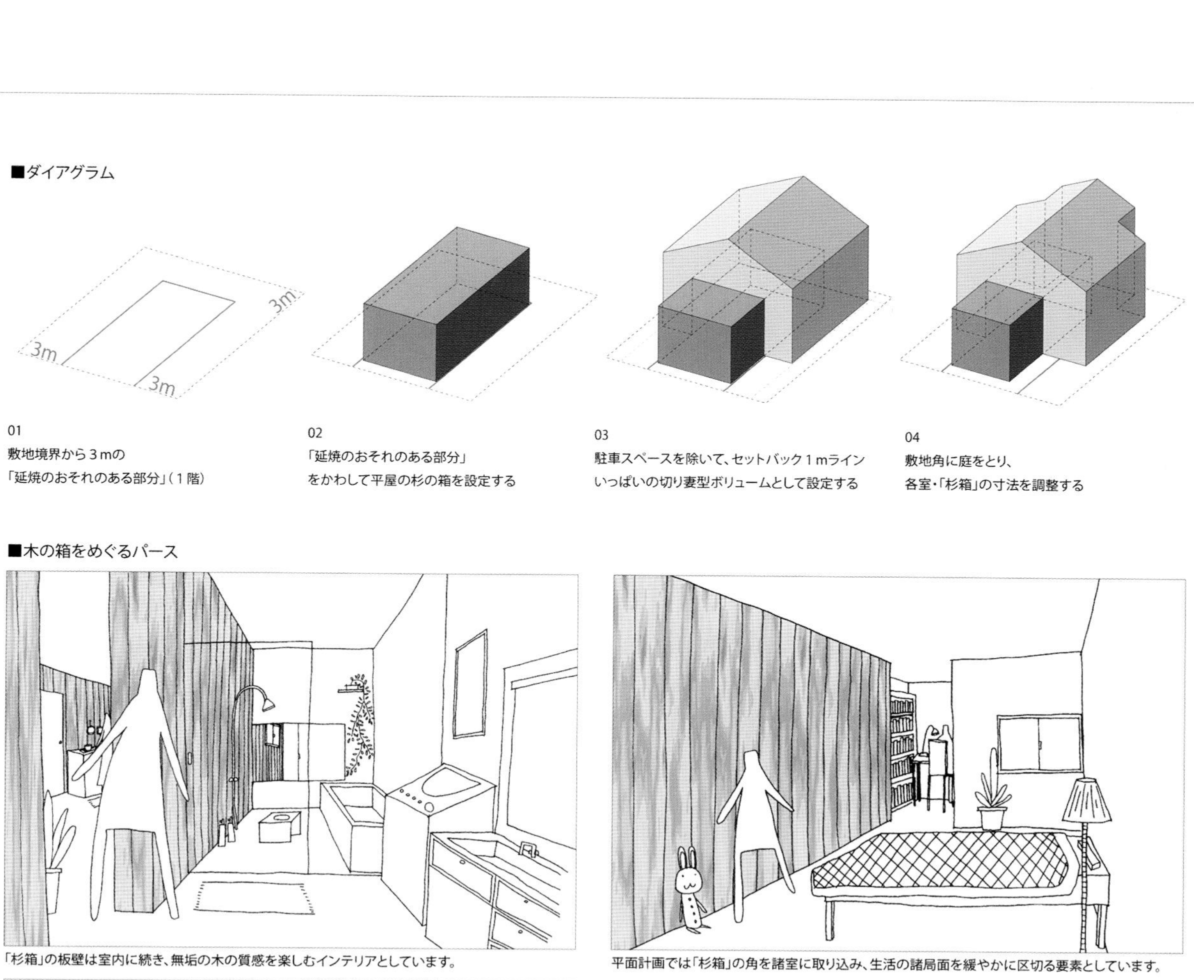

01
敷地境界から3mの
「延焼のおそれのある部分」（1階）

02
「延焼のおそれのある部分」
をかわして平屋の杉の箱を設定する

03
駐車スペースを除いて、セットバック1mライン
いっぱいの切り妻型ボリュームとして設定する

04
敷地角に庭をとり、
各室・「杉箱」の寸法を調整する

■木の箱をめぐるパース

「杉箱」の板壁は室内に続き、無垢の木の質感を楽しむインテリアとしています。

平面計画では「杉箱」の角を諸室に取り込み、生活の諸局面を緩やかに区切る要素としています。

1階　家族室1　正面の壁には、上部トップライトの光が落ちている

子供室1　「角」の向こうに本棚が見える

2階　家族室2　「杉箱」の手摺は屋内の腰壁となって連続する

テラス　夏には高木の枝が快い影を落とす

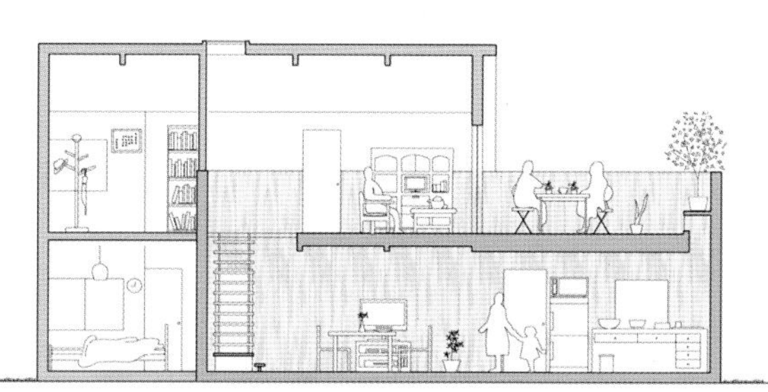

図(1:100)

B－B'断面図(1:100)

正面から見たパース

010 France_1 | *2:pm architectures*

Project : European Competition (W Prize)
Location : St Venant (France)
Design Team : 2:pm architectures + G. Benais (arch)

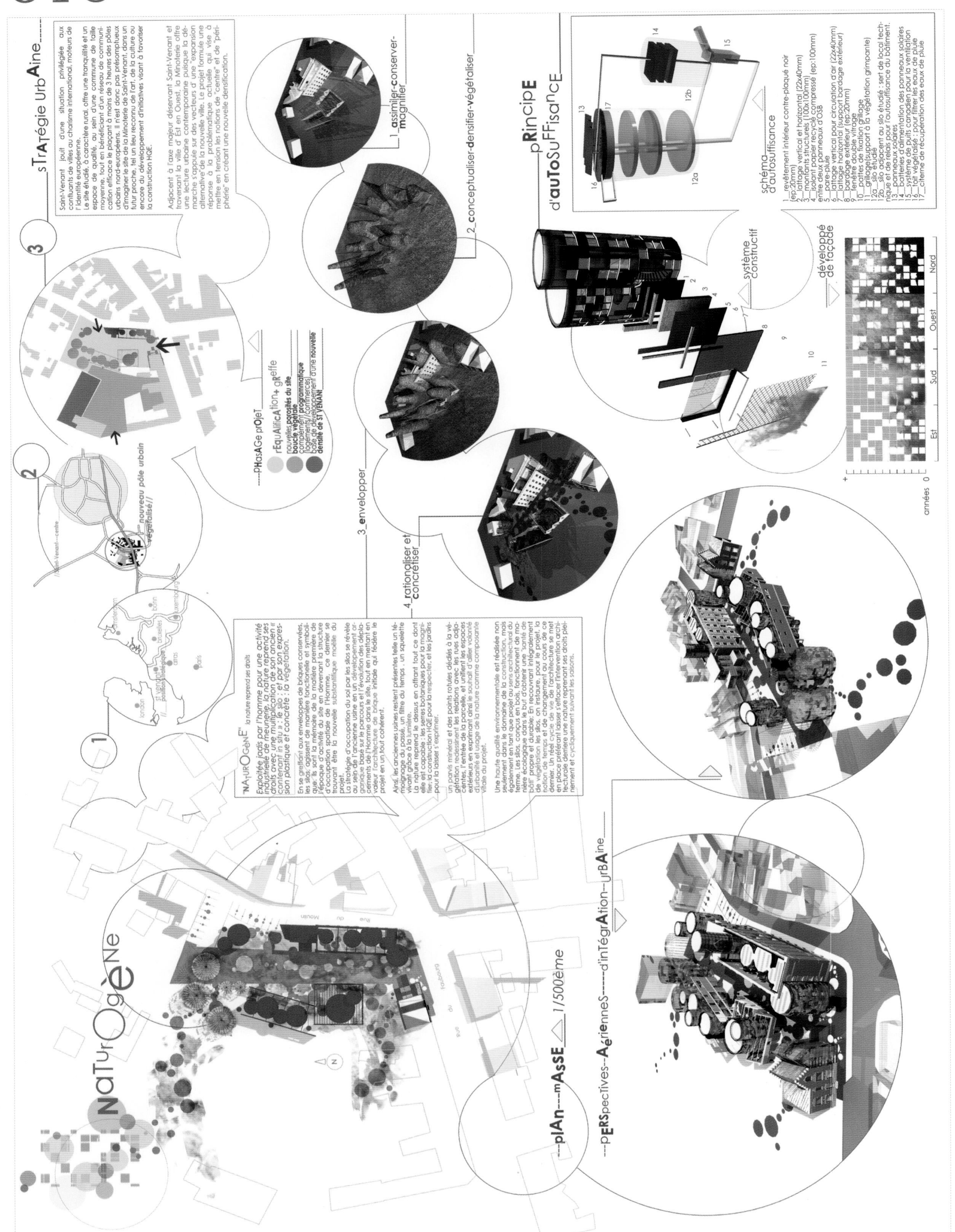

NaTurOgèNe

vUe intErieure dEpuis la galerie d'aRt contempOrain vers le parvis

vUe intErieure / extérieurE eSpaCe TaMpon dans la minOteriE dos à la galerie d'art contemporain

vUe intErieure SilO d'accueil grEffé à la miNoteRie

vue de la Rue du Faubourg : depuis l'ENtréE du site vers le parvis cENtral

vUe du parVis cENtral aMénagé en eSpace publIC paysagé

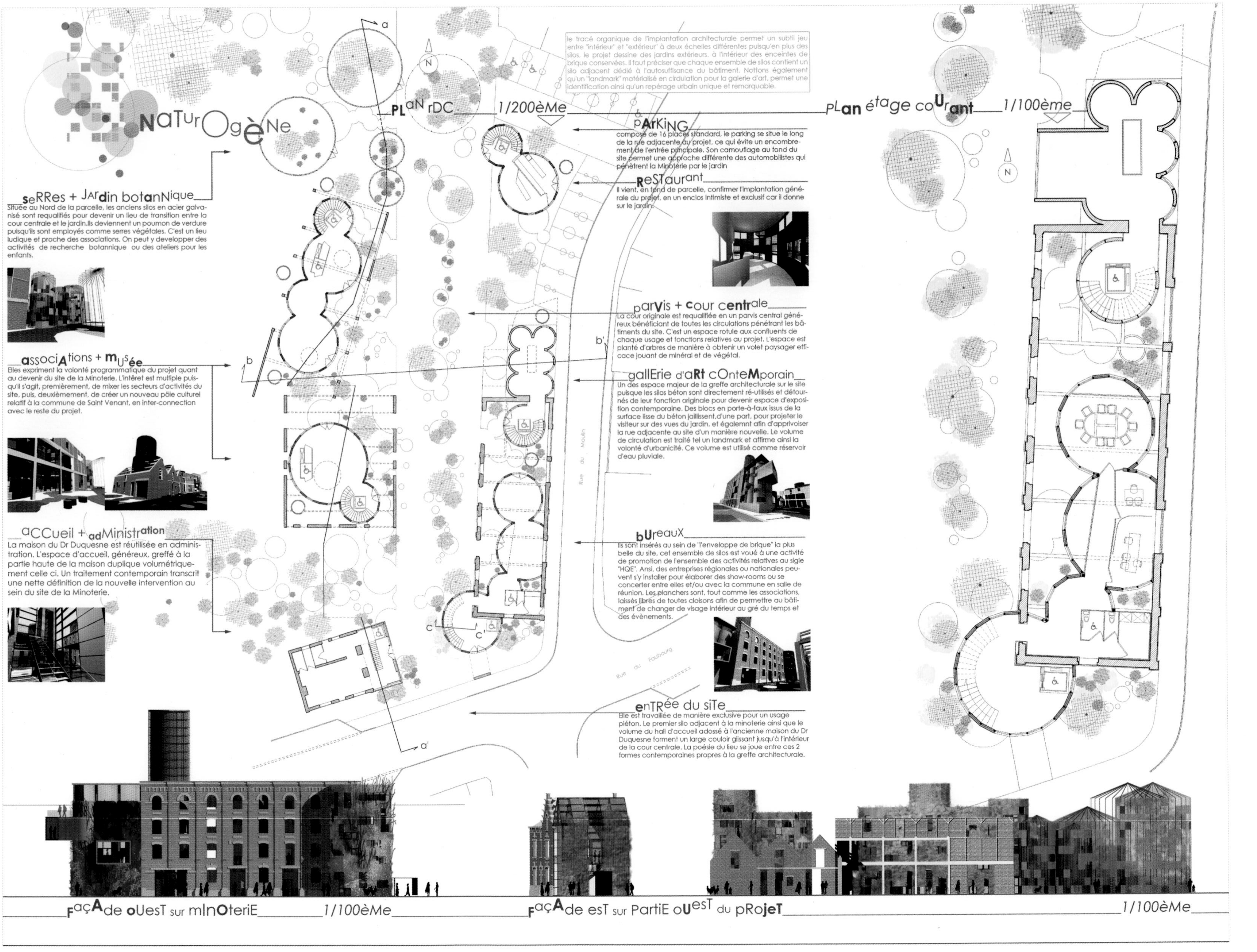
NaTurOgèNe
PLaN rDC 1/200èMe
PLan étage coUrant 1/100ème
le tracé organique de l'implantation architecturale permet un subtil jeu entre "intérieur" et "extérieur" à deux échelles différentes puisqu'en plus des silos, le projet dessine des jardins extérieurs, à l'intérieur des enceintes de brique conservées. Il faut préciser que chaque ensemble de silos contient un silo adjacent dédié à l'autosuffisance du bâtiment. Notions également qu'un "landmark" matérialisé en cirdulation pour la galerie d'art, permet une identification ainsi qu'un repérage urbain unique et remarquable.
seRRes + JArdin botanNique
Située au Nord de la parcelle, les anciens silos en acier galvanisé sont requalifiés pour devenir un lieu de transition entre la cour centrale et le jardin.Ils deviennent un poumon de verdure puisqu'ils sont employés comme serres végétales. C'est un lieu ludique et proche des associations. On peut y developper des activités de recherche botannique ou des ateliers pour les enfants.
associAtions + mUsée
Elles expriment la volonté programmatique du projet quant au devenir du site de la Minoterie. L'intêret est multiple puisqu'il s'agit, premièrement, de mixer les secteurs d'activités du site, puis, deuxièmement, de créer un nouveau pöle culturel relatif à la commune de Saint Venant, en inter-connection avec le reste du projet.
aCCueil + adMinistration
La maison du Dr Duquesne est réutilisée en administration. L'espace d'accueil, généreux, greffé à la partie haute de la maison duplique volumétriquement celle ci. Un traitement contemporain transcrit une nette définition de la nouvelle intervention au sein du site de la Minoterie.
pArKiNG
composé de 16 places standard, le parking se situe le long de la rue adjacente au projet, ce qui évite un encombrement de l'entrée principale. Son camouflage au fond du site permet une approche différente des automobilistes qui pénètrent la Minoterie par le jardin
ReSTaurant
Il vient, en fond de parcelle, confirmer l'implantation générale du projet, en un enclos intimiste et exclusif car il donne sur le jardin.
parVis + cour centrale
La cour originale est requalifiée en un parvis central généreux bénéficiant de toutes les circulations pénétrant les bâtiments du site. C'est un espace rotule aux confluents de chaque usage et fonctions relatives au projet. L'espace est planté d'arbres de manière à obtenir un volet paysager efficace jouant de minéral et de végétal.
gallErie d'aRt cOnteMporain
Un des espace majeur de la greffe architecturale sur le site puisque les silos béton sont directement ré-utilisés et détournés de leur fonction originale pour devenir espace d'exposition contemporaine. Des blocs en porte-à-faux issus de la surface lisse du béton jaillissent,d'une part, pour projeter le visiteur sur des vues du jardin, et égalemnt afin d'apprivoiser la rue adjacente au site d'un manière nouvelle. Le volume de circulation est traité tel un landmark et affirme ainsi la volonté d'urbanicité. Ce volume est utilisé comme réservoir d'eau pluviale.
bUreauX
Ils sont insérés au sein de "l'enveloppe de brique" la plus belle du site, cet ensemble de silos est voué à une activité de promotion de l'ensemble des activités relatives au sigle "HQE". Ansi, des entreprises régionales ou nationales peuvent s'y installer pour élaborer des show-rooms ou se concerter entre elles et/ou avec la commune en salle de réunion. Les planchers sont, tout comme les associations, laissés libres de toutes cloisons afin de permettre au bâtiment de changer de visage intérieur au gré du temps et des évènements.
enTRée du siTe
Elle est travaillée de manière exclusive pour un usage piéton. Le premier silo adjacent à la minoterie ainsi que le volume du hall d'accueil adossé à l'ancienne maison du Dr Duquesne forment un large couloir glissant jusqu'à l'intérieur de la cour centrale. La poésie du lieu se joue entre ces 2 formes contemporaines propres à la greffe architecturale.
Rue du Moulin
Rue du Faubourg
FaçAde oUesT sur mInOteriE 1/100èMe
FaçAde esT sur PartiE oUesT du pRojeT 1/100èMe

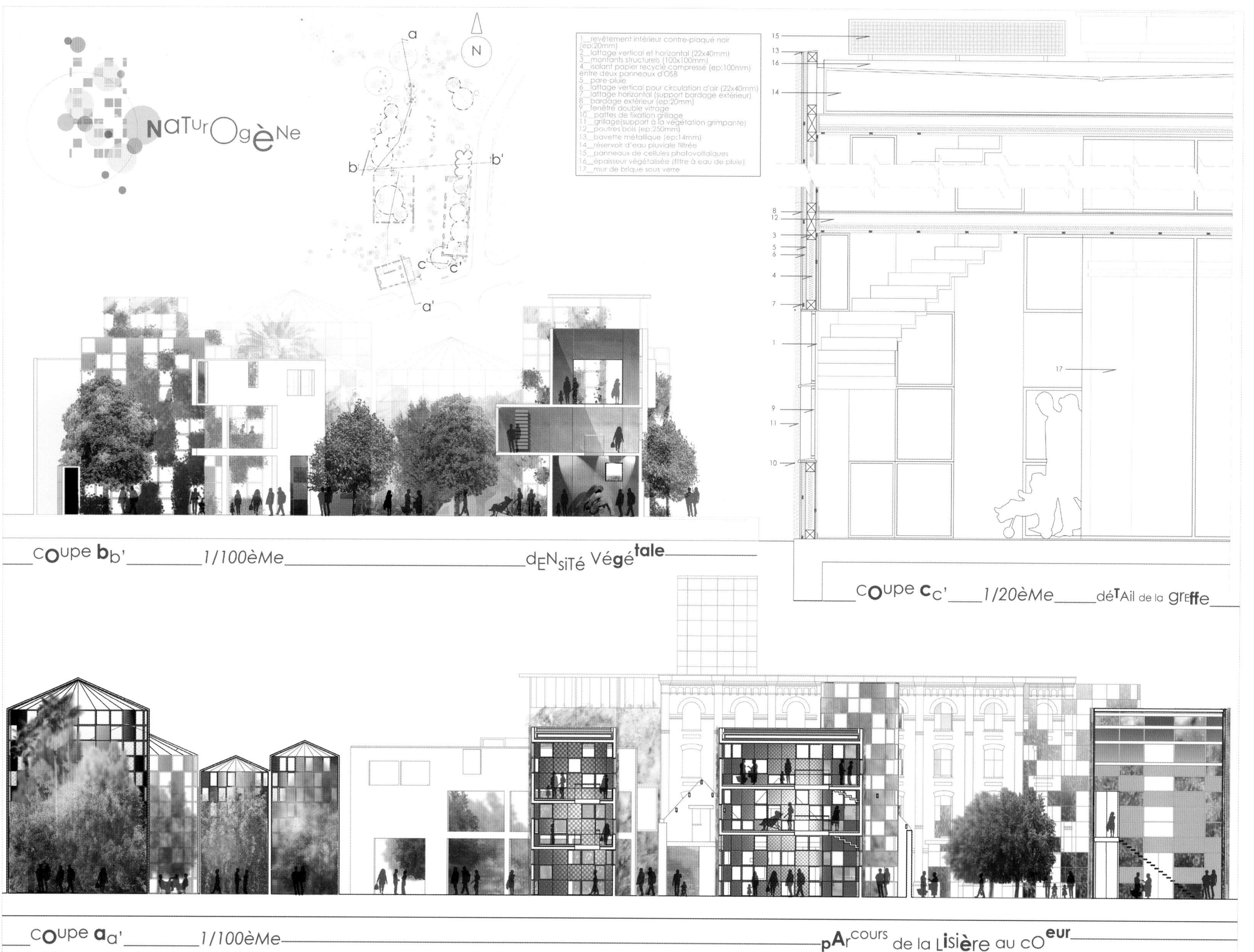
NaTurOgèNe
a
N
b
b'
c
c'
a'
1__revêtement intérieur contre-plaqué noir (ep:20mm)
2__lattage vertical et horizontal (22x40mm)
3__montants structurels (100x100mm)
4__isolant papier recyclé compressé (ep:100mm) entre deux panneaux d'OSB
5__pare-pluie
6__lattage vertical pour circulation d'air (22x40mm)
7__lattage horizontal (support bardage extérieur)
8__bardage extérieur (ep:20mm)
9__fenêtre double vitrage
10__pattes de fixation grillage
11__grillage(support à la végétation grimpante)
12__poutres bois (ep:250mm)
13__bavette métallique (ep:14mm)
14__réservoir d'eau pluviale filtrée
15__panneaux de cellules photovoltaïques
16__épaisseur végétalisée (filtre à eau de pluie)
17__mur de brique sous verre
coupe bb' 1/100èMe dENsiTé Végétale
coupe cc' 1/20èMe déTAil de la greffe
coupe aa' 1/100èMe pArcours de la Lisière au cOeur

011 France_2 | *2:pm architecture*

Project : French Competition for 11 passive Housings
Location : Savenay (France)
Design Team : 2:pm architectures

1 CONCOURS D'IDEES: MAISONS PASSIVES LIGERIENNES

11 LOGEMENTS BBC A TURQUANT

PERSPECTIVE INTERIEURE LOGEMENT EN «BANDE» OUVERT SUR LE PAYSAGE

L' acier comme système constructif innovant.

Le développement durable doit commencer par une réflexion globale de l'acte de construire, notamment concernant les materiaux. Il est important de prouver qu'aujourd'hui, construire de manière durable et peu énergivore, n'est plus forcément synonyme de construire en bois. En effet l'utilisation intensive d'un materiau peut devenir vite néfaste pour son marché économique.

L'acier est un matériau de construction permettant de prendre en compte les considérations de développement durable sur bien des aspects. L'acier est recyclable et régénérable à 100% c'est à dire qu'il est réutilisable indéfiniment et retrouve la totalité de ses propriétés d'origine après traitement en aciérie. De plus il est très souvent produit localement, l'acheminement du matériau de gros œuvre présente un bilan carbone faible. La mise en œuvre du système d'ossature acier en chantier se fait par assemblage. Les logements en acier sont faciles à démonter, on en récupère les éléments constitutifs et on les recycle.

Il est à ce jour peu utilisé en logement individuel ou collectif. Pourtant il permet une maîtrise des impacts du bâtiment sur son environnement par la légèreté de l'ossature, une logique d'économie des ressources et des chantiers dits « secs ». Il assure une gestion contrôlée des énergies et ressources à tous les moments de la vie du bâtiment. Il offre un environnement intérieur confortable autant dans la qualité de l'air que de la lumière ou de l'acoustique.

Les solutions proposées par l'acier et retenues pour le projet sont standardisées et performantes. La trame constructive de 60cm utilisée pour les panneaux de façades offre une multitude de possibilités répondant aux nécessités de l'accessibilité, du parking ou de l'agencement des chambres et pièces de vie. Les panneaux de remplissage seront agencés de manière à ne présenter aucun pont thermique au droit des structures (poteaux, poutres, nez de planchers) grâce à une isolation par l'extérieur. Les menuiseries en aluminium seront à rupture de ponts thermiques également. La taille des panneaux optimise également la rotation des camions les acheminant au moment du chantier du fait de leur faible taille et de leur légèreté.

Pour avoir une vue globale d'un bâtiment, il faut raisonner sur toutes les phases de sa vie car la construction d'un bâtiment ne correspond qu'à 10% de son coût total. Le développement durable est aujourd'hui à appréhender principalement selon les aspects environnementaux, économiques et sociaux mais aussi culturels, patrimoniaux ou bien touristiques…

L'aspect environnemental se caractérise par des chantiers à faible nuisance, car tout comme le bois, l'acier fait partie de la filière sèche qui permet un temps de chantier réduit (pas de séchage), un assemblage in situ d'éléments préfabriqués en atelier et un chantier propre (sans eau, sans boue, sans poussière et avec réduction des déplacements de véhicules. L'ossature légère et transparente permet une importante modularité des remplissages en fonction des nécessités thermiques ou lumineuses de l'endroit où l'on construit et un impact léger sur les sols.

L'aspect économique est mis en relief par une construction rapide dans le temps, un faible coût d'entretien, des solutions privilégiant les économies d'énergies, une optimisation des infrastructures et donc un impact faible sur les sols.

Et enfin l'apport de la construction en ossature métallique présente des avantages sociaux tels que l'aspect évolutif et modulaire des logements, la sécurité des chantiers du fait de la préfabrication, un acheminement des matériaux de construction léger, peu encombrant et facilement manipulables, de grandes ouvertures sur le paysage…

ETUDE VOLUMETRIQUE

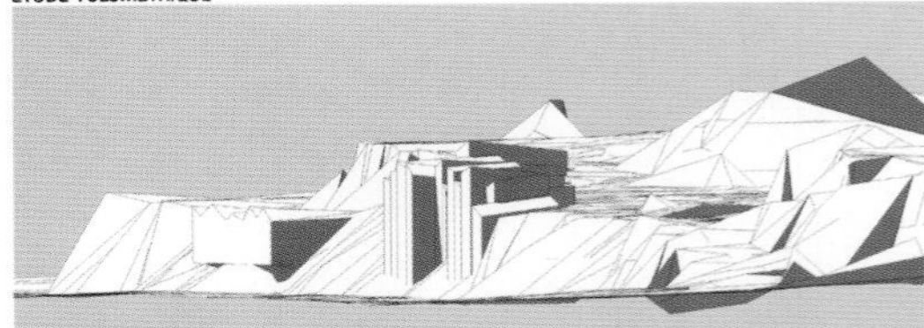

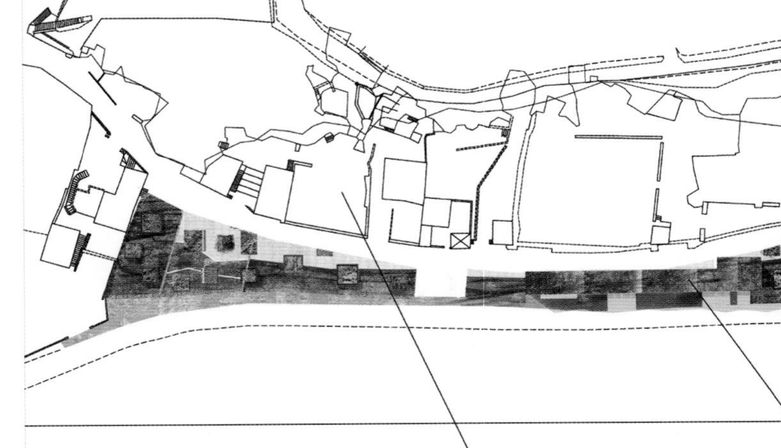

LA LOIRE

Le fleuve présent en contre bas présente ici une force importante pour le site. il apporte vent, fraicheur et bien être au site. Les dimensions en font un lieu d'immensité poussant à la contemplation, au désir de grand air.

HABITATS TROGLODYTES ET ARTISANAT D'ART.

Le Site d'étude est surplombé d'habitats creusés dans la roche ou se développe une activité caractéristique qui est celle de l'artisanant d'art. Forte identité locale, elle est la résonnance régionnale du pays ligérien. Le projet doit être un écho aux «métiers d'art en troglo». offrir un lien entre la route passante en contrebas et l'activité troglo.

LOGEMENTS «

Typologie de logem
3 appartements T3.
souligner la crête p
visibles de la rue du
sées, apportant au l
places de parkings
sée (inondable) tell
importantes au lieu.

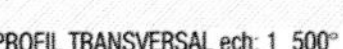

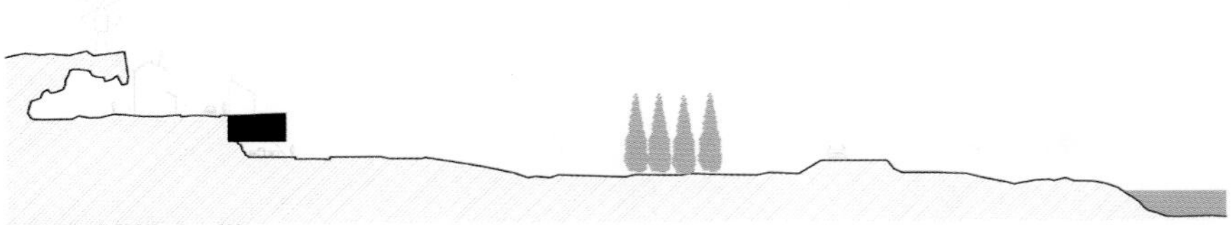

PROFIL TRANSVERSAL ech: 1_500°

ANALYSE DU SITE: LES POINTS POSITIFS

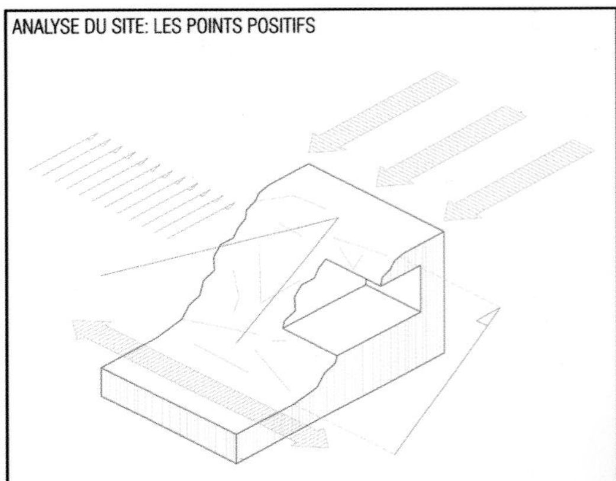

LES POINTS POSITIFS DU SITE DE TURQUANT:

>VENT PROFITABLE PROVENANT DU LIT DE LA LOIRE

>VUE OUVERTE SUR LA LOIRE

>FORTE PENTE SUR LE SITE OFFRANT DES POSSIBILITES TRES INTERESSANTES DE PROJET

>FORTE INFLUENCE DES METIERS D'ART PAR LE HAUT DU SITE. LES METIERS D'ART SONT ICI UNE VRAIE PLUS VALUE REGIONNALE ET CONTEXTUELLE; L'IDENTITE DE LA REGION EST CLAIREMENT AFFICHEE. NOTRE PROJET DOIT S'EN FAIRE L'ECHO AU NIVEAU DE LA ROUTE BASSE.

>LA POSITION DU SITE (ET DE TURQUANT) JOUIE D'UNE SITUATION IDEALE SUR UN CHEMIN TOURISTIQUE LONGEANT LA LOIRE. UN PARCOURS DE DECOUVERTE DE L'IDENTITE LIGERIENNE.

ANALYSE DU SITE: LES POINTS CONTRAIGNANTS

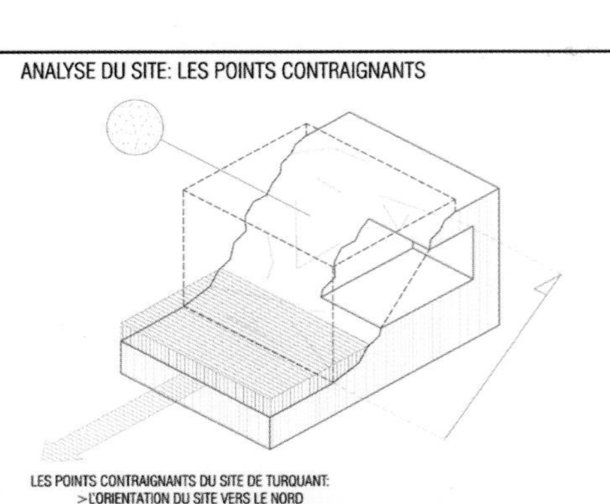

LES POINTS CONTRAIGNANTS DU SITE DE TURQUANT:

>L'ORIENTATION DU SITE VERS LE NORD

>LA LIMITE HAUTE DU PLU: NE PAS DEPASSER 1M DU NIVEAU HAUT.

CES DEUX CONTRAINTES LIMITENT ENORMEMENT LES APPORTS SOLAIRES POUR LES LOGEMENTS RENDANT LA CIBLE «BATIMENT PASSIF» IMPOSSIBLE A OBTENIR (CONTRAIREMENT A LA CIBLE «BBC».

>FORTE PENTE SUR LE SITE IMPOSANT DE TRAITER LES CIRCULATIONS HAUT-BAS DE MANIERE TRES PRECISES

>LA PRESENCE DE LA ZONE INONDABLE, LIMITANT L'USAGE DES REZ DE CHAUSSEES A DES PIECES D'APPOINTS (GARAGES, CELLIERS, ATELIERS DE BRICOLAGE ETC...)

>LA QUALITE DES SOLS POUSSANT A UNE VILIGENCE ACCRUE SUR LE TYPE DE FONDATIONS ET DE RETENUE DE TALUS. LE SOL EST COMPOSE DE CALCAIRE DUR A TRES FISSURE. LA ZONE EST CLASSE «ALEA TRES FORT CONCERNANT LES CARRIERES SOUTERRAINES. PRENDRE LES DISPOSITIONS REGLEMENTAIRES DU DTU 13.12

CONCEPT THERMIQUE ET ORGANISATIONNEL DU LOGEMENT

L'idée est de travailler sur une partition franche du module «logement» un noyau béton offrant forte inertie thermique et regroupant les pièces humides, passages de fluides, conduits des cheminées thermiques et locaux techniques). autour se développent les plateaux de vie, portés en façade, offrant une modularité optimum, ou les pièces sont hiérarchisées par des cloisons légères ou mobilier tout hauteur.

Ce concept est adapté au site de Turquant, très étiré, n'offrant parfois que 4 mètres pour développer le logement. Deux typologies de logements intermédiaires sont donc proposés ici: la typologie «longitudinnale» et la typologie dite «en plot».

Le diagramme suivant propose le principe d'adaptation du concept aux typologies permises par le site.
Ce principe de noyau offre une réelle flexibilité au logment et est surtout un important atout thermique. En effet, il permet de compenser de façon très notable le manque d'inertie de la construction acier. Il permet ainsi de profiter pleinement de tous les avantages de la construction acier et de contrecarrer ses carrences.

Les diagrammes ci contre proposent une illustration du rôle du noyau béton au sein du logement, en été et en hiver.

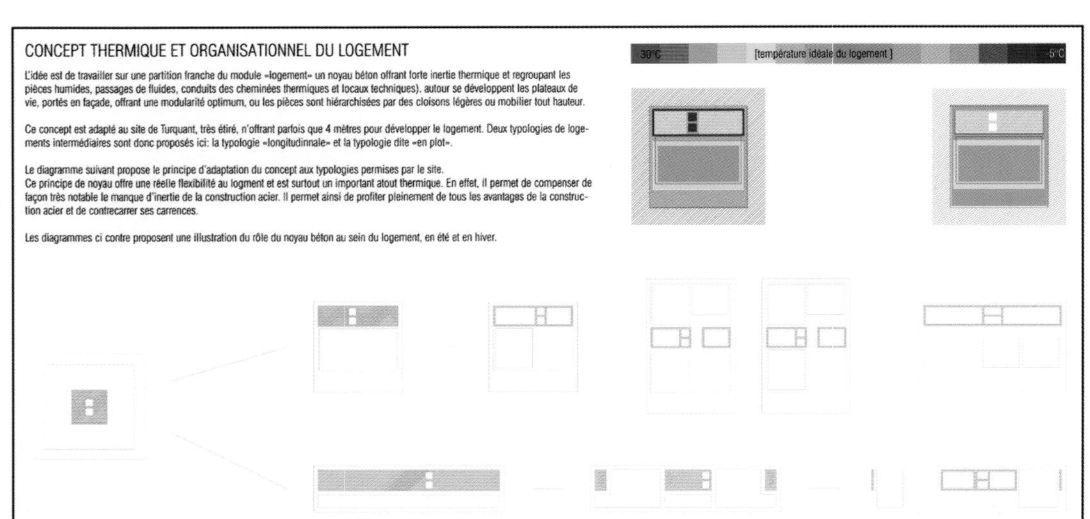

DEU
DEUX

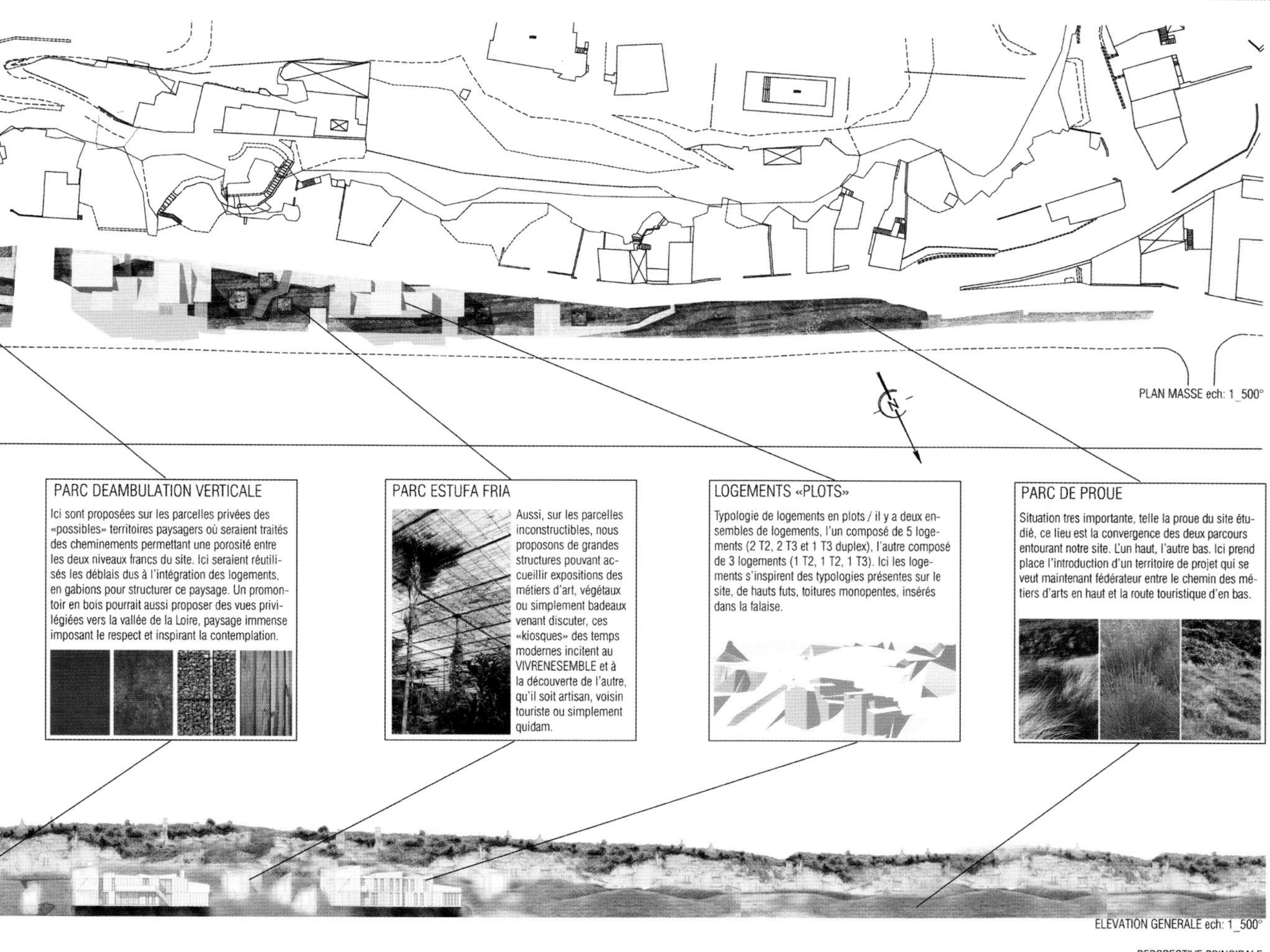

PLAN MASSE ech: 1_500°
N
PARC DEAMBULATION VERTICALE
Ici sont proposées sur les parcelles privées des «possibles» territoires paysagers où seraient traités des cheminements permettant une porosité entre les deux niveaux francs du site. Ici seraient réutilisés les déblais dus à l'intégration des logements, en gabions pour structurer ce paysage. Un promontoir en bois pourrait aussi proposer des vues privilégiées vers la vallée de la Loire, paysage immense imposant le respect et inspirant la contemplation.
PARC ESTUFA FRIA
Aussi, sur les parcelles inconstructibles, nous proposons de grandes structures pouvant accueillir expositions des métiers d'art, végétaux ou simplement badeaux venant discuter, ces «kiosques» des temps modernes incitent au VIVRENESEMBLE et à la découverte de l'autre, qu'il soit artisan, voisin touriste ou simplement quidam.
LOGEMENTS «PLOTS»
Typologie de logements en plots / il y a deux ensembles de logements, l'un composé de 5 logements (2 T2, 2 T3 et 1 T3 duplex), l'autre composé de 3 logements (1 T2, 1 T2, 1 T3). Ici les logements s'inspirent des typologies présentes sur le site, de hauts futs, toitures monopentes, insérés dans la falaise.
PARC DE PROUE
Situation tres importante, telle la proue du site étudié, ce lieu est la convergence des deux parcours entourant notre site. L'un haut, l'autre bas. Ici prend place l'introduction d'un territoire de projet qui se veut maintenant fédérateur entre le chemin des métiers d'arts en haut et la route touristique d'en bas.

ELEVATION GENERALE ech: 1_500°

PERSPECTIVE PRINCIPALE

PERSPECTIVE PARC ESTUFA FRIA

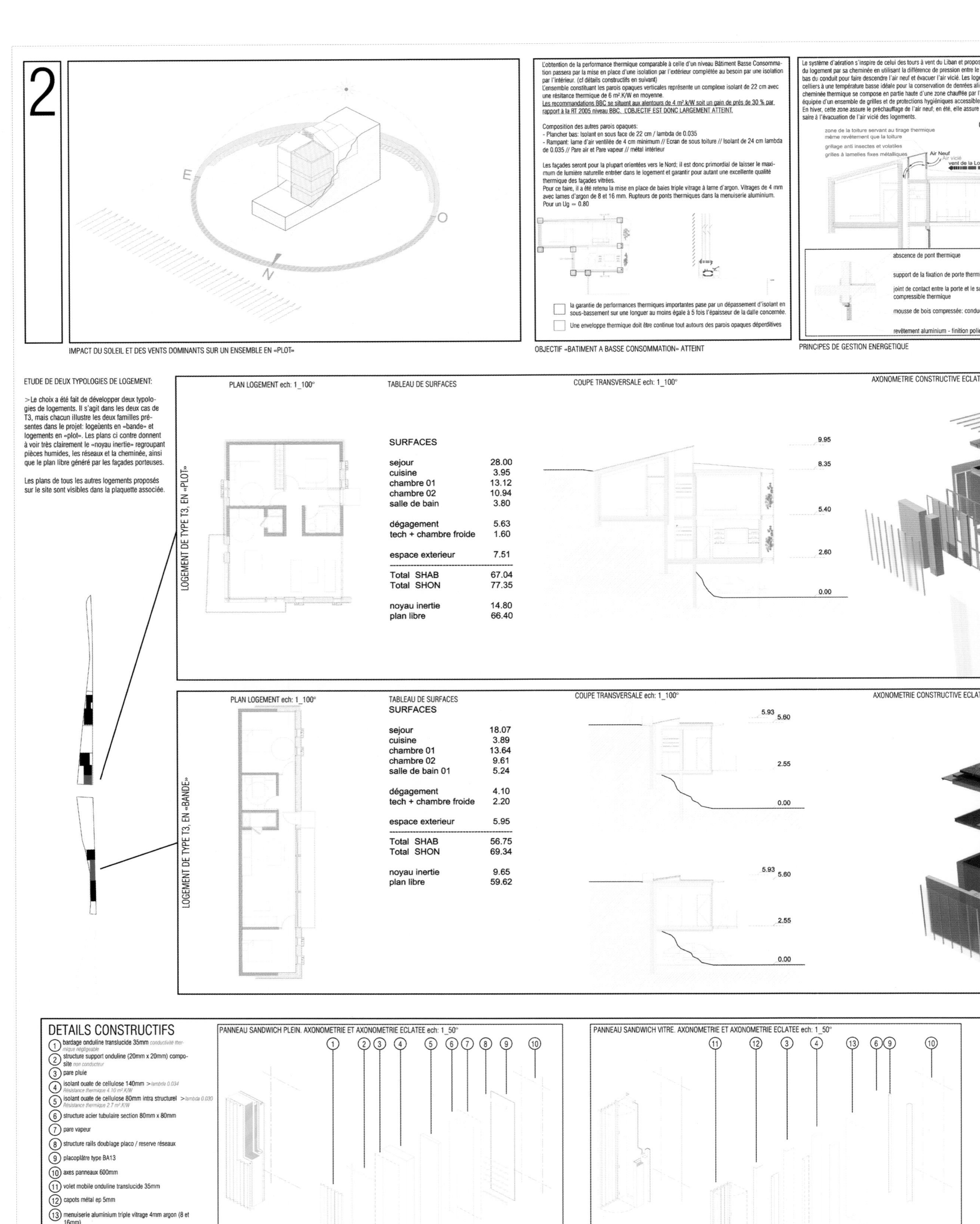

2
E
O
N
IMPACT DU SOLEIL ET DES VENTS DOMINANTS SUR UN ENSEMBLE EN «PLOT»
L'obtention de la performance thermique comparable à celle d'un niveau Bâtiment Basse Consommation passera par la mise en place d'une isolation par l'extérieur complétée au besoin par une isolation par l'intérieur. (cf détails constructifs en suivant)
L'ensemble constituant les parois opaques verticales représente un complexe isolant de 22 cm avec une résitance thermique de 6 m².K/W en moyenne.
Les recommandations BBC se situent aux alentours de 4 m².k/W soit un gain de prés de 30 % par rapport à la RT 2005 niveau BBC. L'OBJECTIF EST DONC LARGEMENT ATTEINT.
Composition des autres parois opaques:
- Plancher bas: Isolant en sous face de 22 cm / lambda de 0.035
- Rampant: lame d'air ventilée de 4 cm minimum // Ecran de sous toiture // Isolant de 24 cm lambda de 0.035 // Pare air et Pare vapeur // métal intérieur
Les façades seront pour la plupart orientées vers le Nord; il est donc primordial de laisser le maximum de lumière naturelle entréer dans le logement et garantir pour autant une excellente qualité thermique des façades vitrées.
Pour ce faire, il a été retenu la mise en place de baies triple vitrage à lame d'argon. Vitrages de 4 mm avec lames d'argon de 8 et 16 mm. Rupteurs de ponts thermiques dans la menuiserie aluminium. Pour un Ug = 0.80
la garantie de performances thermiques importantes pase par un dépassement d'isolant en sous-bassement sur une longuer au moins égale à 5 fois l'épaisseur de la dalle concernée.
Une enveloppe thermique doit être continue tout autours des parois opaques déperditives
OBJECTIF «BATIMENT A BASSE CONSOMMATION» ATTEINT
Le système d'aération s'inspire de celui des tours à vent du Liban et propose une
du logement par sa cheminée en utilisant la différence de pression entre le haut d
bas du conduit pour faire descendre l'air neuf et évacuer l'air vicié. Les logements
celliers à une température basse idéale pour la conservation de denrées alimenta
cheminée thermique se compose en partie haute d'une zone chauffée par l'énergi
équipée d'un ensemble de grilles et de protections hygiéniques accessibles à la
En hiver, cette zone assure le préchauffage de l'air neuf; en été, elle assure le tira
saire à l'évacuation de l'air vicié des logements.
CHEM
zone de la toiture servant au tirage thermique
même revêtement que la toiture
grillage anti insectes et volatiles
grilles à lamelles fixes métalliques
Air Neuf
Air vicié
vent de la Loire / v
abscence de pont thermique
support de la fixation de porte thermique
joint de contact entre la porte et le support: compressible thermique
mousse de bois compressée: conductivité
revêtement aluminium - finition polie
PRINCIPES DE GESTION ENERGETIQUE
ETUDE DE DEUX TYPOLOGIES DE LOGEMENT:
>Le choix a été fait de développer deux typologies de logements. Il s'agit dans les deux cas de T3, mais chacun illustre les deux familles présentes dans le projet: logeùents en «bande» et logements en «plot». Les plans ci contre donnent à voir très clairement le «noyau inertie» regroupant pièces humides, les réseaux et la cheminée, ainsi que le plan libre généré par les façades porteuses.
Les plans de tous les autres logements proposés sur le site sont visibles dans la plaquette associée.
LOGEMENT DE TYPE T3, EN «PLOT»
PLAN LOGEMENT ech: 1_100°
TABLEAU DE SURFACES
SURFACES
sejour 28.00
cuisine 3.95
chambre 01 13.12
chambre 02 10.94
salle de bain 3.80
dégagement 5.63
tech + chambre froide 1.60
espace exterieur 7.51
Total SHAB 67.04
Total SHON 77.35
noyau inertie 14.80
plan libre 66.40
COUPE TRANSVERSALE ech: 1_100°
9.95
8.35
5.40
2.60
0.00
AXONOMETRIE CONSTRUCTIVE ECLATEE
LOGEMENT DE TYPE T3, EN «BANDE»
PLAN LOGEMENT ech: 1_100°
TABLEAU DE SURFACES
SURFACES
sejour 18.07
cuisine 3.89
chambre 01 13.64
chambre 02 9.61
salle de bain 01 5.24
dégagement 4.10
tech + chambre froide 2.20
espace exterieur 5.95
Total SHAB 56.75
Total SHON 69.34
noyau inertie 9.65
plan libre 59.62
COUPE TRANSVERSALE ech: 1_100°
5.93
5.60
2.55
0.00
5.93
5.60
2.55
0.00
AXONOMETRIE CONSTRUCTIVE ECLATEE

DETAILS CONSTRUCTIFS

1. bardage onduline translucide 35mm *conductivité thermique négligeable*
2. structure support onduline (20mm x 20mm) composite *non conducteur*
3. pare pluie
4. isolant ouate de cellulose 140mm >*lambda 0.034 Résistance thermique 4.10 m².K/W*
5. isolant ouate de cellulose 80mm intra structurel >*lambda 0.030 Résistance thermique 2.7 m².K/W*
6. structure acier tubulaire section 80mm x 80mm
7. pare vapeur
8. structure rails doublage placo / reserve réseaux
9. placoplâtre type BA13
10. axes panneaux 600mm
11. volet mobile onduline translucide 35mm
12. capots métal ep 5mm
13. menuiserie aluminium triple vitrage 4mm argon (8 et 16mm)

ECHANTILLON DE MATERIALITE DE FACADE:

PANNEAU SANDWICH PLEIN. AXONOMETRIE ET AXONOMETRIE ECLATEE ech: 1_50°

1 2 3 4 5 6 7 8 9 10

PANNEAU SANDWICH VITRE. AXONOMETRIE ET AXONOMETRIE ECLATEE ech: 1_50°

11 12 3 4 13 6 9 10

ENERGETIQUE HIVER

, l'air extérieur est tout d'abord réchauffé par l'air extrait des pièces humides ment puis chauffé par l'ensemble thermodynamique. L'air chauffé est ensuite dans les pièces de vies et de sommeil. La production d'eau chaude sanitaire rée sur l'air extrait vers l'extérieur. La centrale présente également une fonction qui s'ouvre directement sur l'extérieur (sans passer par l'échangeur) et qui de récupérer la fraicheur en fin de nuit en été.

COUPE ENERGETIQUE ETE

En été, le sens de ventilation est inversé: l'air extérieur est pris sur une façade peu exposée avant d'être utilisé par la centrale double flux. Cette dernière assure la ventilation double flux by-pass, la production et le stockage de l'eau chaude sanitaire. En phase de production d'eau chaude sanitaire, l'ensemble thermodynamique rejette de l'air frais; ce dernier est insufflé dans le logement; ce système peut être assimilé à un rafraichissement passif.

Le local technique recevant l'ensemble thermodynamique associé à un local permettant le stockage de certains aliments doit être séparé du logement par une porte de type «chambre réfrigérée». Cette zone ne doit pas représenter une source trop importante de déperditions en hiver et ni d'apports de chaleur en été. De ce fait, la porte et son contact avec le mur de séparation sont traitées thermiquement et acoustiquement par la mise en place d'un système de joints en mousse compressible similaire à celle utilisée dans les ensembles frigorifiques.

RECUPERATION DES EAUX DE PLUIE

L'eau de pluie tout comme l'eau provenant de la connexion aux services urbains est filtrée et réutilisée pour l'usage de la maison ou l'arrosage des jardins communs. Cet ensemble de récupération sera installé en partie basse du rez de chaussée. Il permettra une autonomie de 15 jours pour un arrosage des plantes de la serre et l'éventuel lavage des surfaces et véhicules. Le trop plein sera raccordé au réseau des eaux pluviales. Les installations seront accessibles depuis l'extérieur pour la maintenance, notamment la vidange avant les périodes de gel.

La pompe de puisage sera mise en service par appel d'eau ce qui évite son fonctionnement continu.

Surface absorbante toiture
Air Extérieur 0°C / Vent de la Loire
3 °C
Air repris 20 °C
Zone tampon
Air chauffé 22 °C
Air rejeté 2 °C
Air chauffé 22 °C
Caisson double flux à récupération
Ballon Eau Chaude thermodynamique
Air chauffé 22 °C

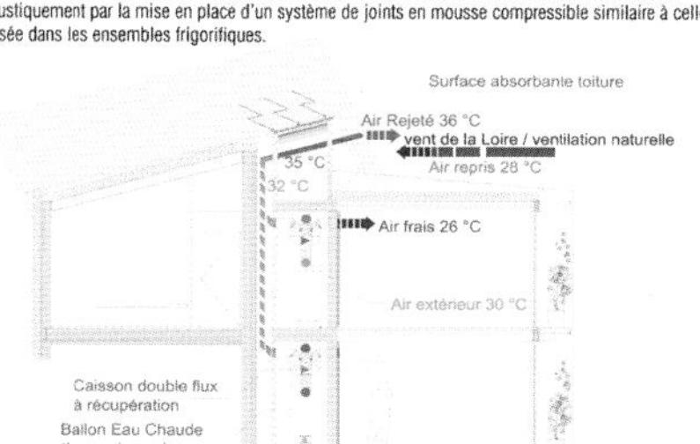

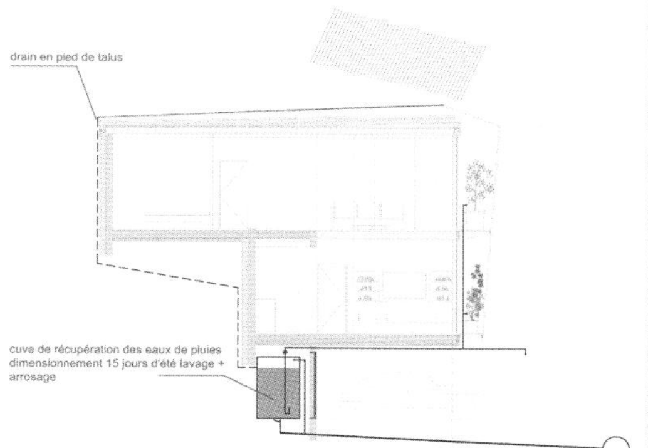

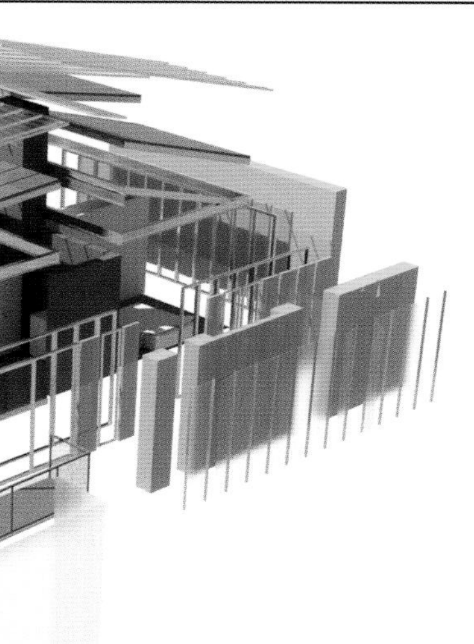

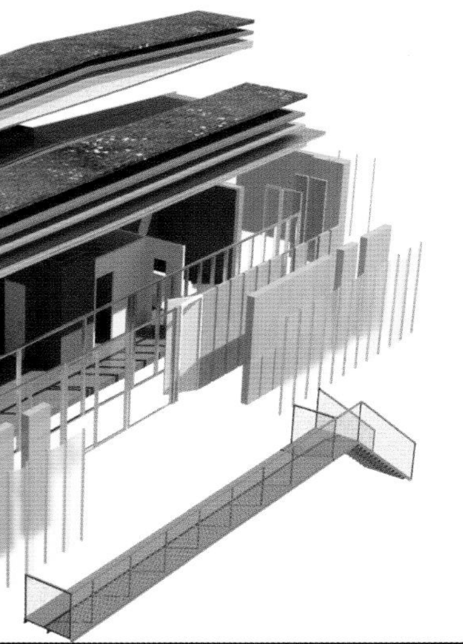

S PAROIS, PLANCHER INTERMEDIAIRE - PAROI ech: 1_20°

DETAIL JONCTIONS PLANCHER - BAS PAROIS - CONSOLE, PLANCHER INTERMEDIAIRE - PAROI - CONSOLE ech: 1_20°

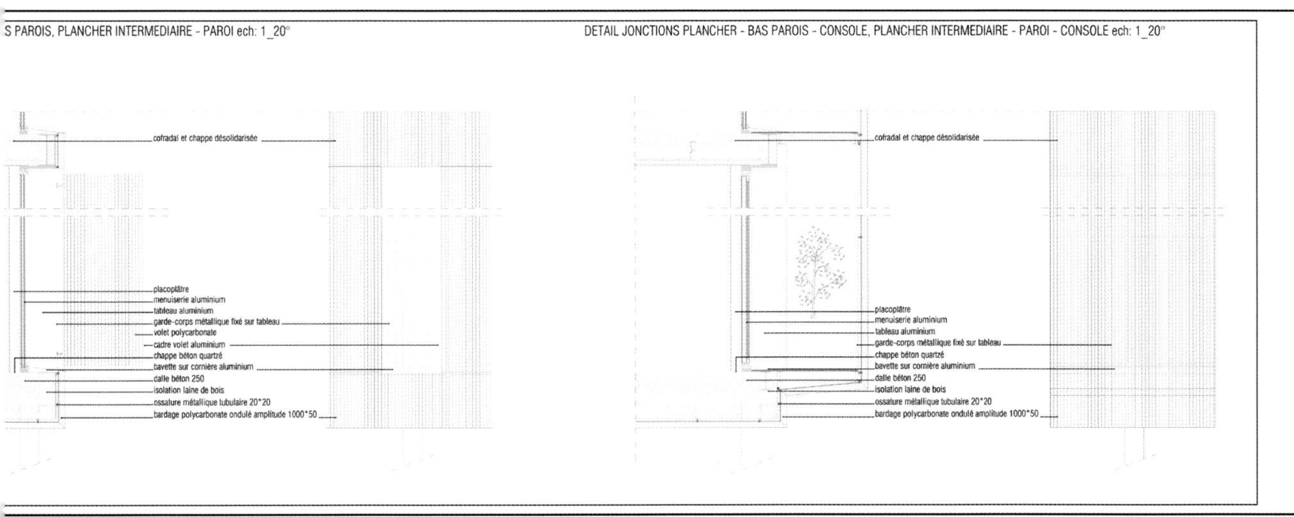

012 Garten> HOF | *arenas basabe palacios arquitectos*

Housing Development in Wien

Authors : Enrique Arenas Laorga, Luis Basabe Montalvo, Luis Palacios Labrador
Collaborators : Eva Miguel, Helena de Sebastian

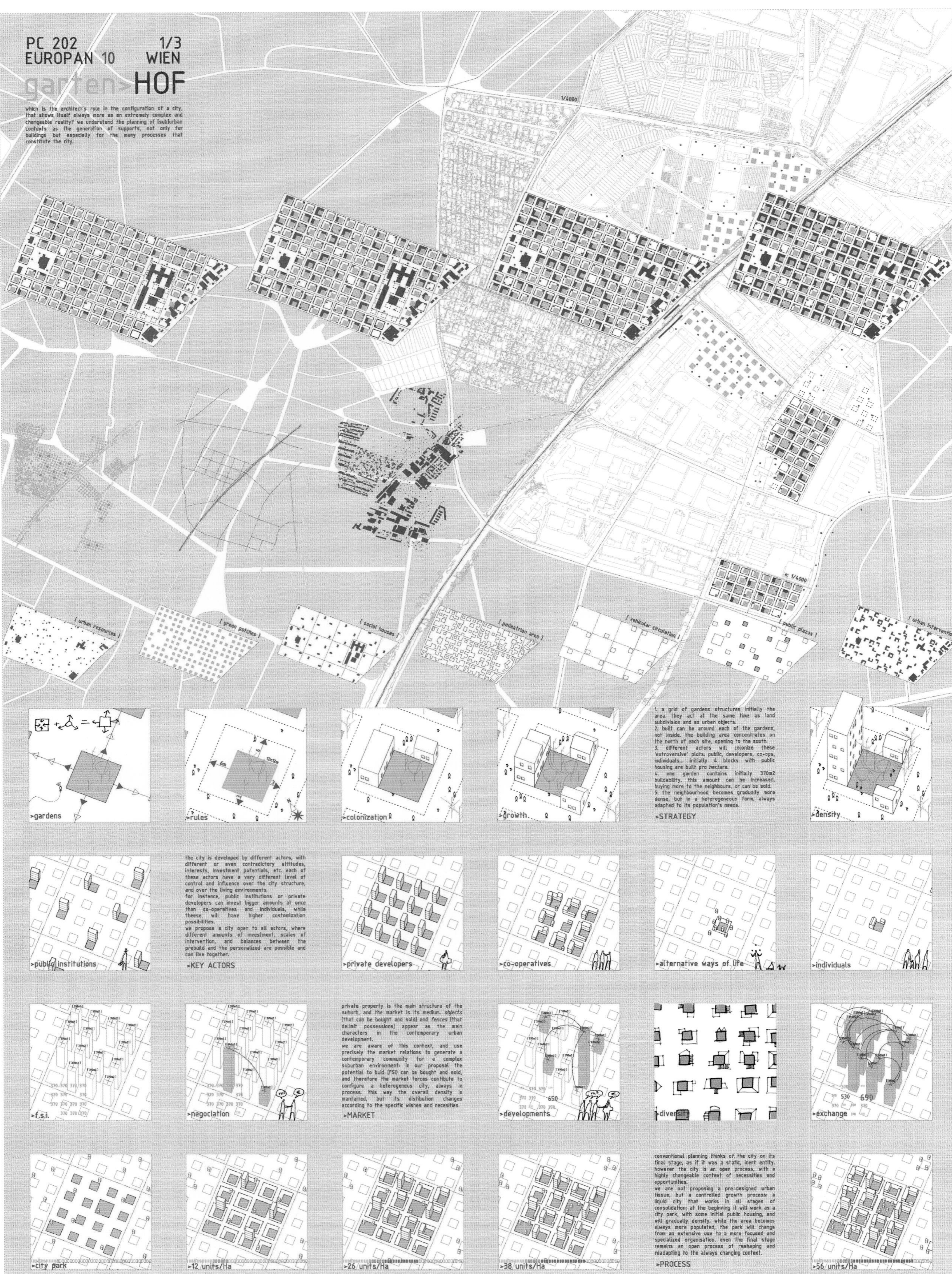

PC 202 2/3
EUROPAN 10 WIEN
garten>HOF
[urban situations]
[time builds section]
[plan 1 / 500]

PC 202 3/3
EUROPAN 10 WIEN
garten>HOF
2010. ENVIROMENTAL AREA
2010. SUMMER CINEMA
2010. MARKET
2010. LIFE SHOW
2010. CHILDREN SHOW
main actors
2010. PARKING
[?]
base grid 6+6
transformation mechanism
staircase
terrace roof
courtyard
dispositivos de transición
2010. OCUPATION
2035. DENSIFY
2060. RENT
2010. OCUPACION
[+]
[o]
[*]
2010. OCUPATION
70M2 working place
2025. DENSIFy
70M2 living
2040. DENSIFY
2015. OCUPATION
2020. OCUPATION
2020. RENT
35. DENSIFICACION Y TIPOS
70M2 working
100 m2 market
FOR SALE
>social housing
as an urban development's seed, each hectare contains initially 12 social housing units in four blocks
>hyperhouse
the economy of the hyperhouse lies in its ability to bring in family income through the renting of apartments, small bussines or workshops.
>open end houses
the house adapts itself to the always changing conditions, and has therefore a continuous personalization process. it is open to multinuclear families, group growth, etc.
>urban plazas
there is one every hectare. it is open to all kinds of urban activities, such as parking, sunday market, eislaufen, concerts, exhibitions, screenings, etc.
>playground
there is one every hectare. it serves the dwellers with common rest, celebrations and sport facilities.
>urban situations
the 3x3 standardized urban situation colorize the non built areas and structure the public urban space. they are easily transportable, interchangeable and removable.
>network
the whole area is divided in 1 Ha big squares, that can be considered urban units. the main traffic runs through their edges. inside these clusters only inhabitants slow traffic is permitted.

House of Memory | *2A+P/A*

Model : Marco Galofaro/Modelab
Photo : Sebastiano Costanzo

Type : Restricted Design Competition, Special Mention
Program : Cultural Center
Location : Milan, Italy
Year : 2011

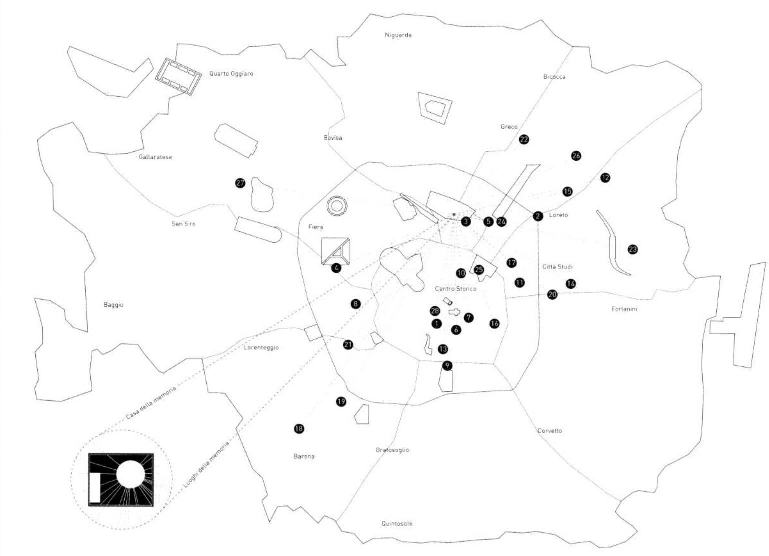

Mappa dei luoghi della memoria

Planivolumetrico 1:500

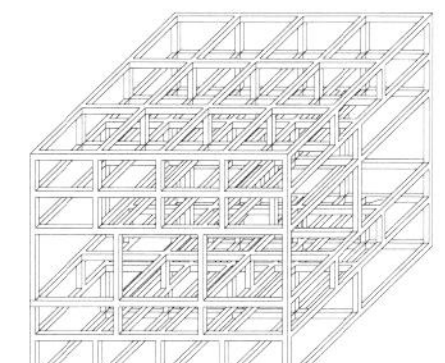

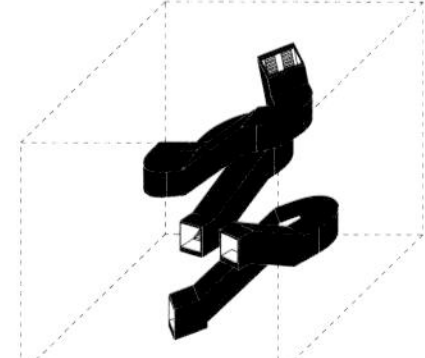

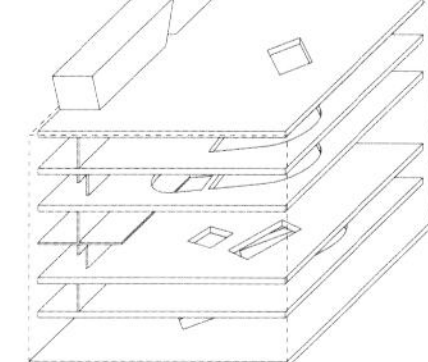

Schemi assonometrici 1:500

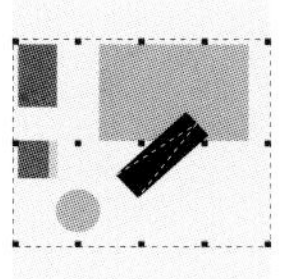

Piazza

Archivio

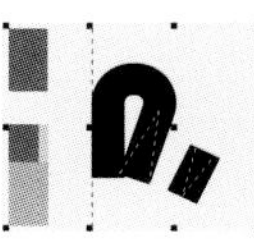

Spazio espositivo

Sala consultazione

Scala mobile
Connessioni verticali
Funzioni

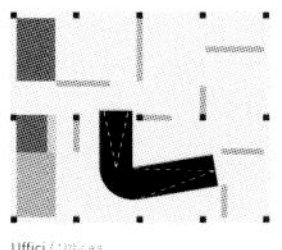

Uffici

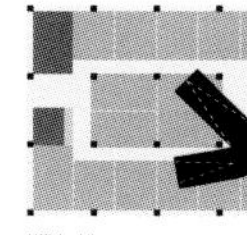

Uffici

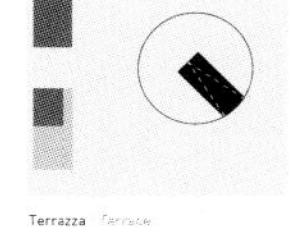

Terrazza

Coperture

Schemi funzionali 1:500

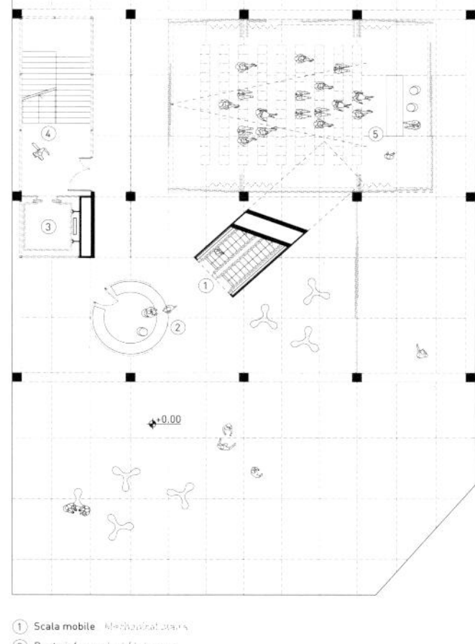

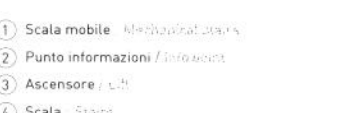

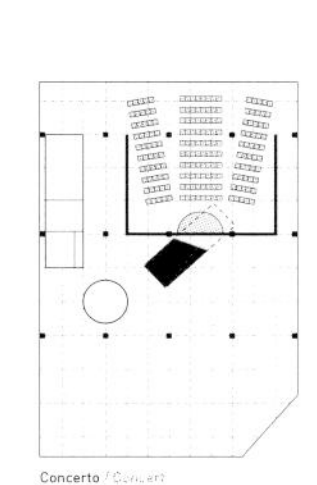

Sagra

Concerto

Schemi layout 1:500

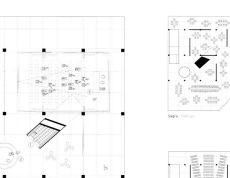

1. Scala mobile
2. Punto informazioni
3. Ascensore
4. Scala
5. Sala polifunzionale

Piano terra 1:200

Vista da / View from via F. Confalonieri

Vista dal parco / View from the park

2A+P/A studio associato
Casa della Memoria - Concorso di idee
Milano 21/4/2011
1

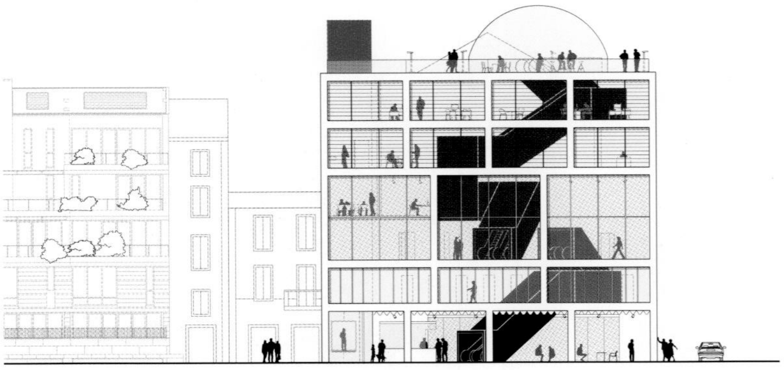

Prospetto Sud / South elevation 1:200

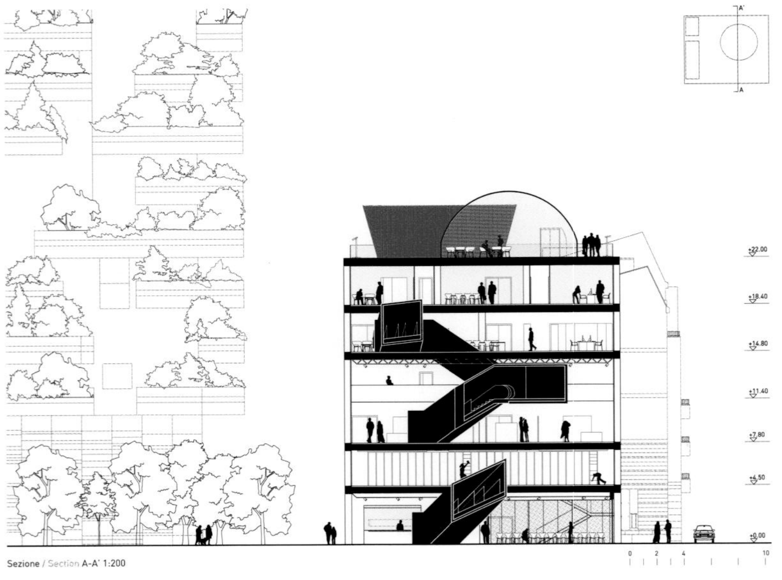

Sezione / Section A-A' 1:200

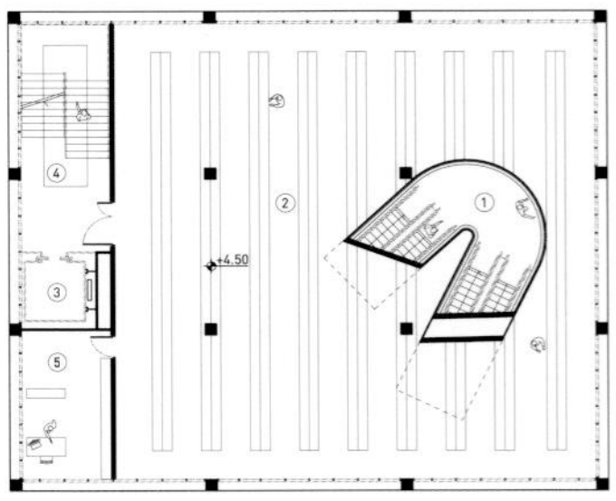

1. Scala mobile / Mechanical stairs
2. Archivio / Archive
3. Ascensore / Lift
4. Scala / Stairs
5. Addetto all'archivio / Archive assistant

Primo piano / First floor 1:200

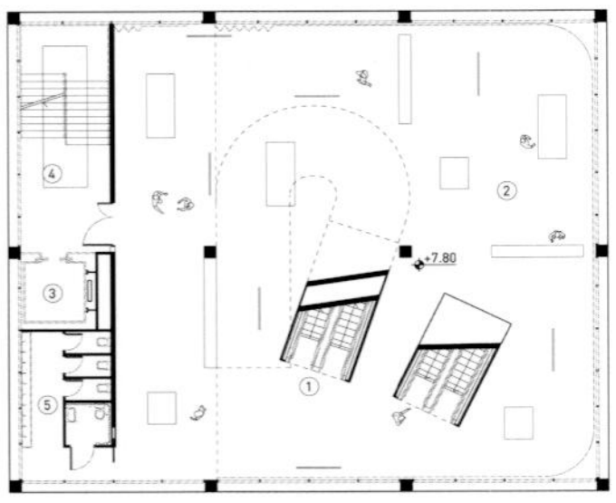

1. Scala mobile / Mechanical stairs
2. Sala espositiva / Exhibition
3. Ascensore / Lift
4. Scala / Stairs
5. Bagni / Toilets

Secondo piano / Second floor 1:200

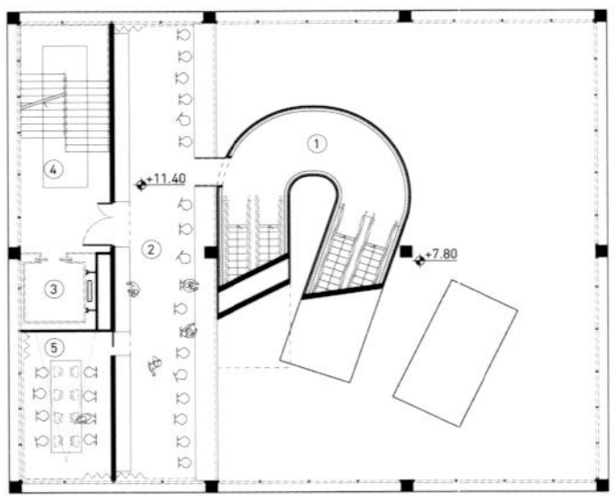

1. Scala mobile / Mechanical stairs
2. Sala consultazione / Consultation room
3. Ascensore / Lift
4. Scala / Stairs
5. Sala multimediale / Multimedia room

Terzo piano / Third floor 1:200

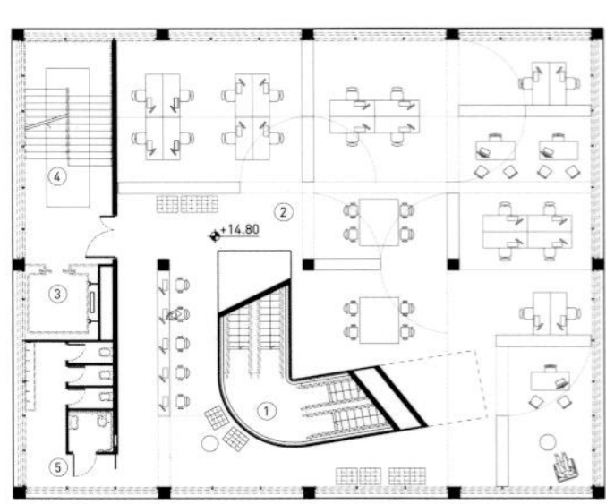

1. Scala mobile / Mechanical stairs
2. Uffici / Offices
3. Ascensore / Lift
4. Scala / Stairs
5. Bagni / Toilets

Quarto piano / Fourth floor 1:200

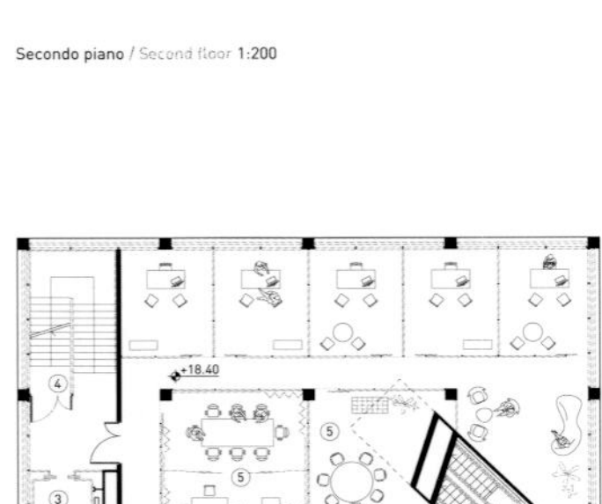

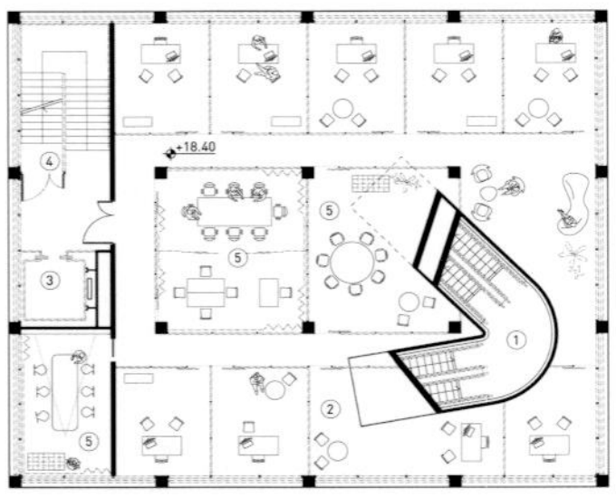

1. Scala mobile / Mechanical stairs
2. Uffici / Offices
3. Ascensore / Lift
4. Scala / Stairs
5. Sala riunione / Meeting room

Quinto piano / Fifth floor 1:200

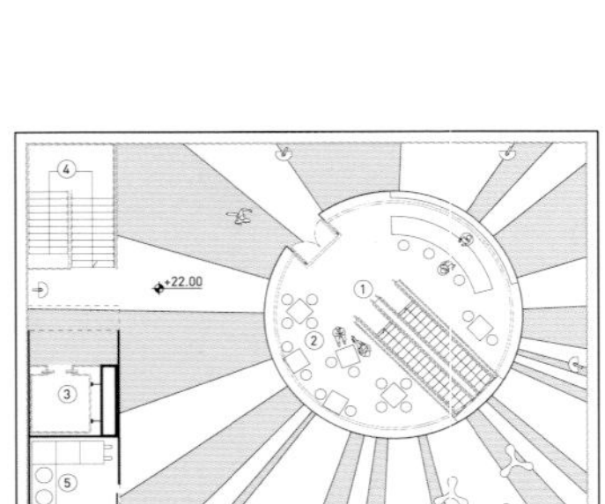

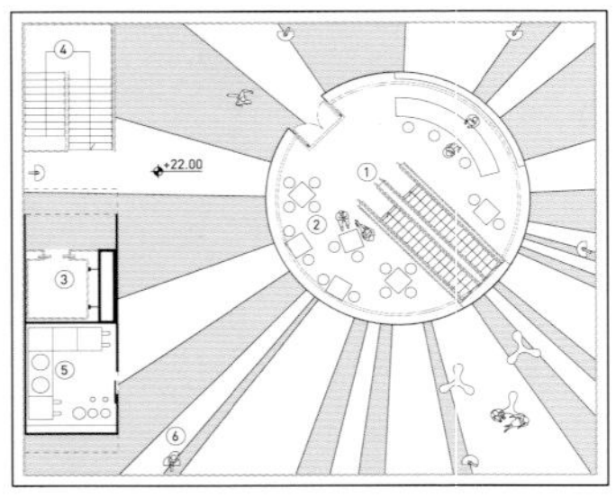

1. Scala mobile / Mechanical stairs
2. Bar / Caffe
3. Ascensore / Lift
4. Scala / Stairs
5. Locali tecnici / Technical spaces
6. Cannocchiale / Sightseeing Binocular

Terrazza / Terrace 1:200

Vista della scala mobile / View of the mechanical stairs

Sezione della scala mobile / Section of the mechanical stairs 1:50

2A+P/A studio associato
Casa della Memoria - Concorso di idee
Milano 21/4/2011
2

+22,00
+18,40
+14,80
+11,40
+7,80
+4,50
+0,00

Sezione / Section B-B' 1:200

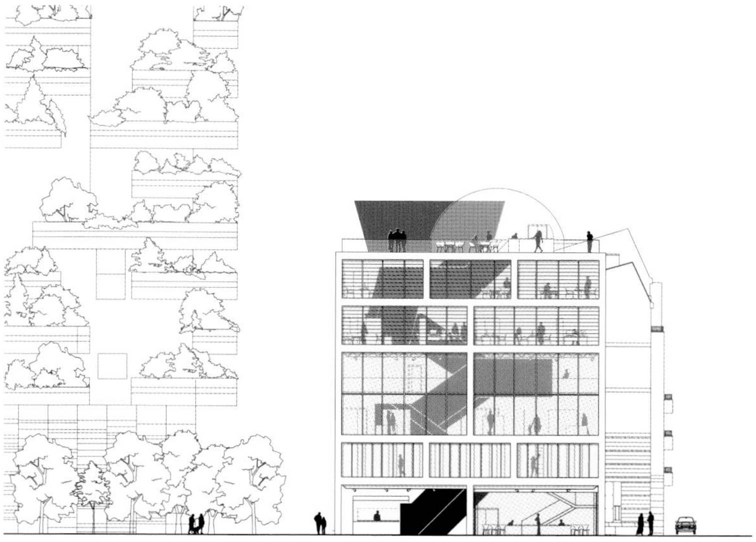

Prospetto est / East elevation 1:200

0 2 4 10

Sezione prospettica / Perspective section 1:100

0 1 2 5

Vista dello spazio espositivo / View of the exhibition

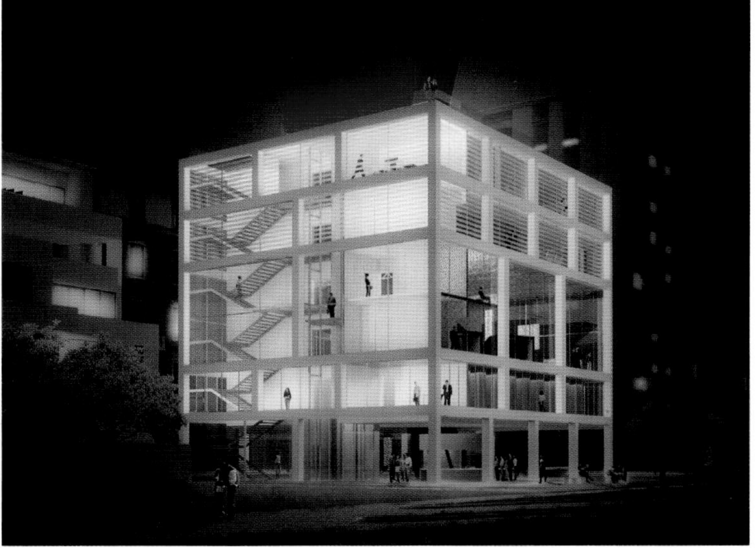

Vista dal parco / View from the park

2A+P/A studio associato
Casa della Memoria - Concorso di idee
Milano 21/4/2011

3

014 Granero House | *nodo17-architects*

Location : Húmera, Madrid, Spain
Design Team : Manuel Pérez Romero, Félix Toledo Lerín, Jaime Tarazona Lizarraga, Luis del Rey Cristobal
Model : Debora Mateo

Photographs : nodo17_architects
Project Type : Single Family House

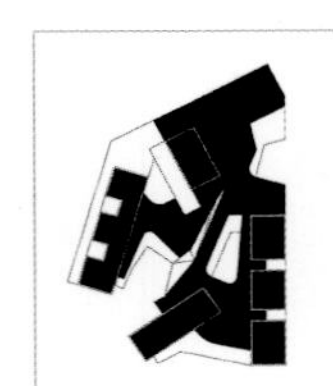

Company / Firm Name_ nodo17-architects/ Manuel Pérez Romero
Country_ Spain

Project Name_ GRANERO'S HOUSE
Location of Site_ Húmera_ Madrid. Spain.
Design Team_ Felix Toledo Lerín
Luis del Rey Cristóbal
Jaime Tarazona Lizarraga
Model_ Debora Mateo

Photographs_ nodo17_architects

Project Type_ Single Family House
Client_ Private

Site Area_ 3500 sm
Built-up Area_ 1700 sm

Date of completion_ (State- Executive projetct)

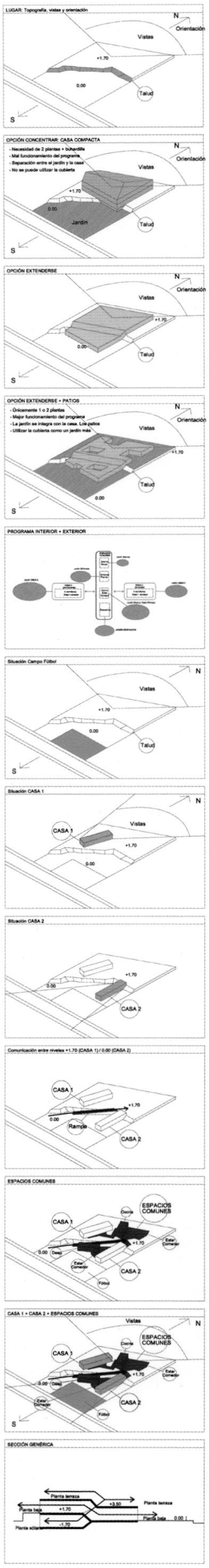

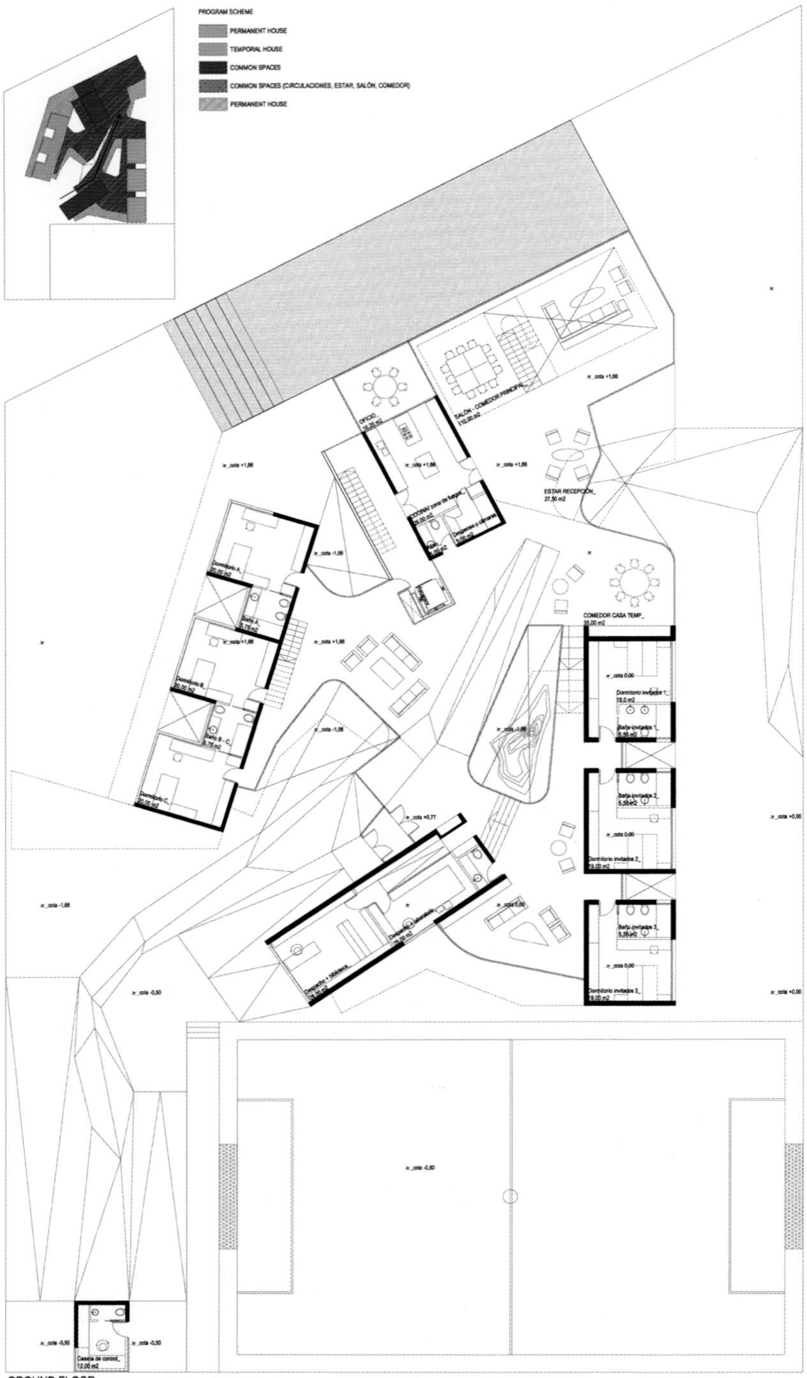

PROGRAM SCHEME
PERMANENT HOUSE
TEMPORAL HOUSE
COMMON SPACES
COMMON SPACES (CIRCULACIONES, ESTAR, SALÓN, COMEDOR)
PERMANENT HOUSE

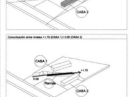

GROUND FLOOR_

0 1m 2m 5m 10m 20m

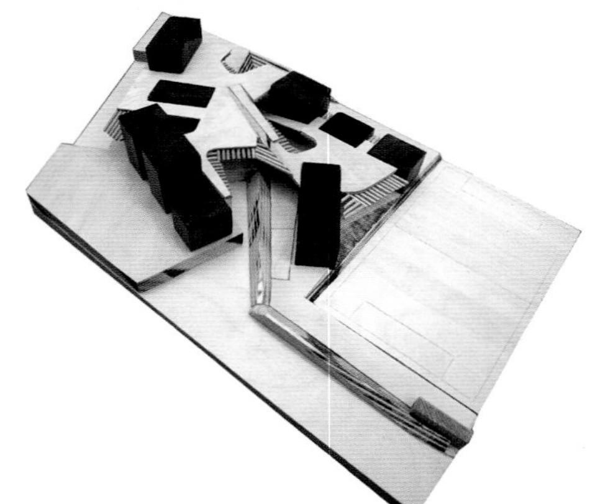

MODEL of the house_

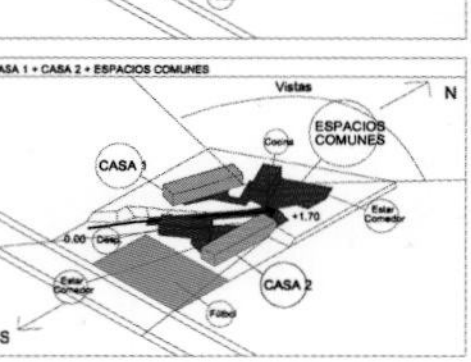

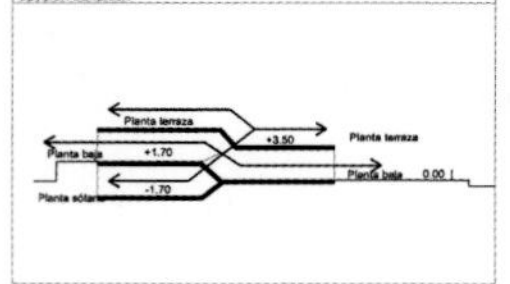

Interior views_

External views_

Living-Dike House | *nodo17-architects*

Photographs : nodo17_architects
Project Type : Single Family House

Location : Anaga, Tenerife, Canary Islands, Spain
Design Team : Manuel Pérez Romero, Félix Toledo Lerín, Jaime Tarazona Lizarraga, Luis del Rey Cristobal
Model : Debora Mateo

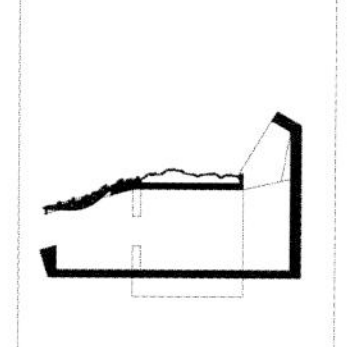

Company / Firm Name_ nodo17-architects/ Manuel Pérez Romero
Country_ Spain

Project Name_ LIVING-DIKE_ Anaga
Location of Site_ Anaga (LOS CATALANES)/ Tenerife/ Canary Island_ Spain

Design Team_ Félix Toledo Lerín
Jaime Tarazona Lizarraga
Luis del Rey Cristóbal.

Project Type_ Singular housing
Client_ private

Site Area_ 3.459,50 m2
Built-up Area_ 94,00 m2

Location area_

MODEL VIEWS_

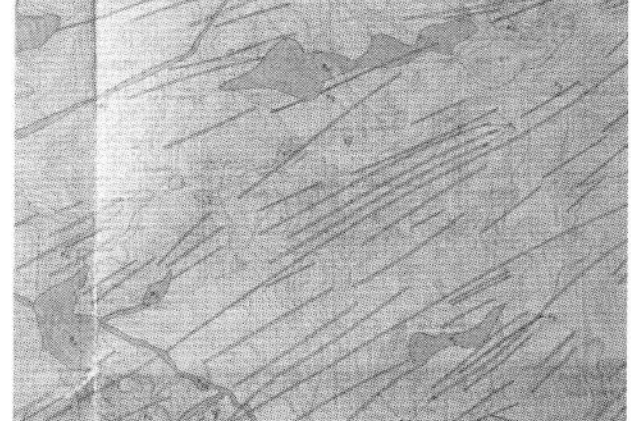

Geological dikes_

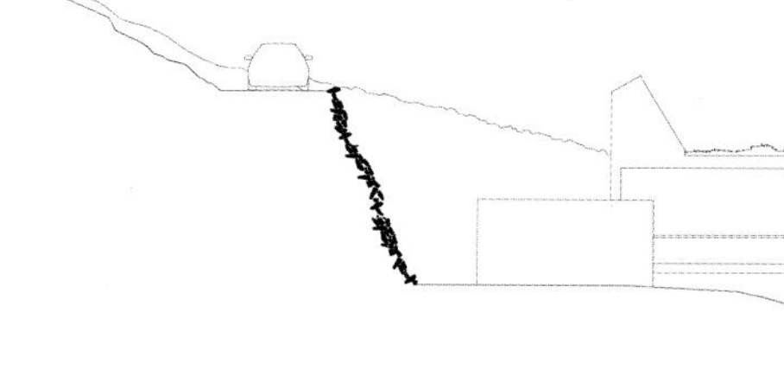

MAIN CUT_

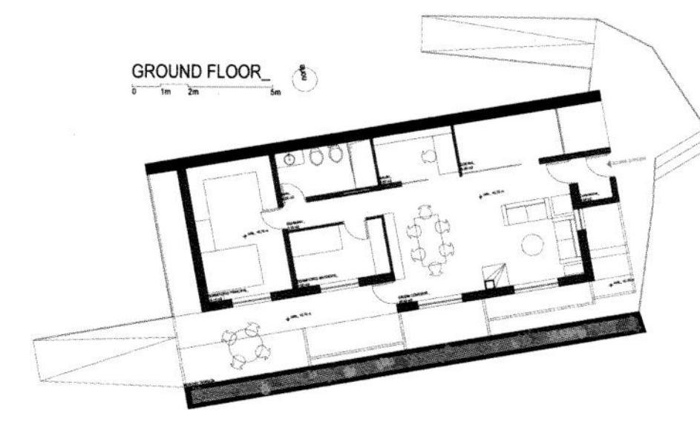

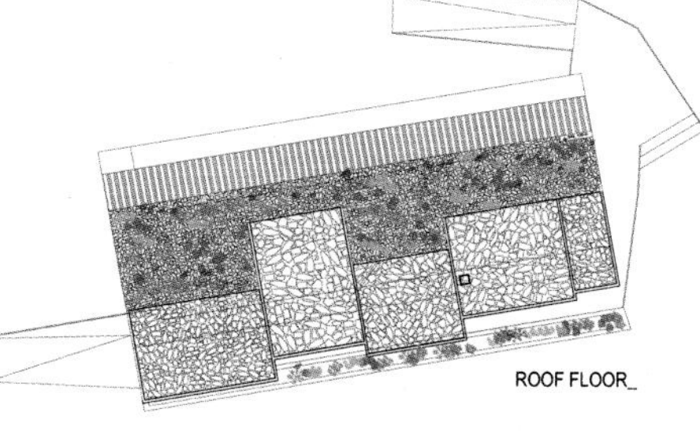

ROOF FLOOR_

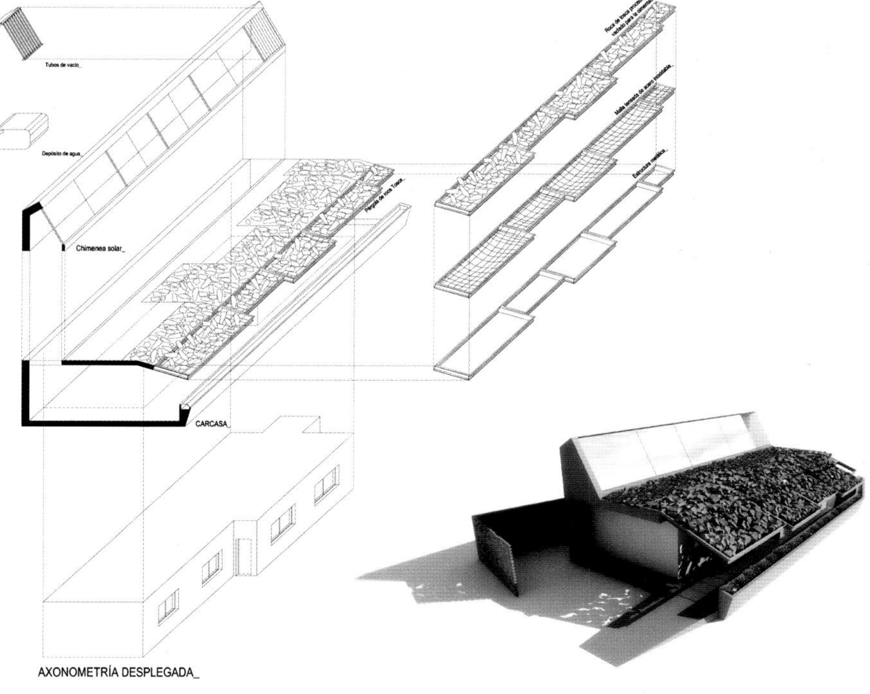

AXONOMETRÍA DESPLEGADA_

016 Intercultural Quarter | *BKK-3*

Location : Vienna, Austria
Team : Franz Sumnitsch, Jan Nieswand, Norman Jargstorff, Tina Krischmann, Renate Rodel, Friederike Welter

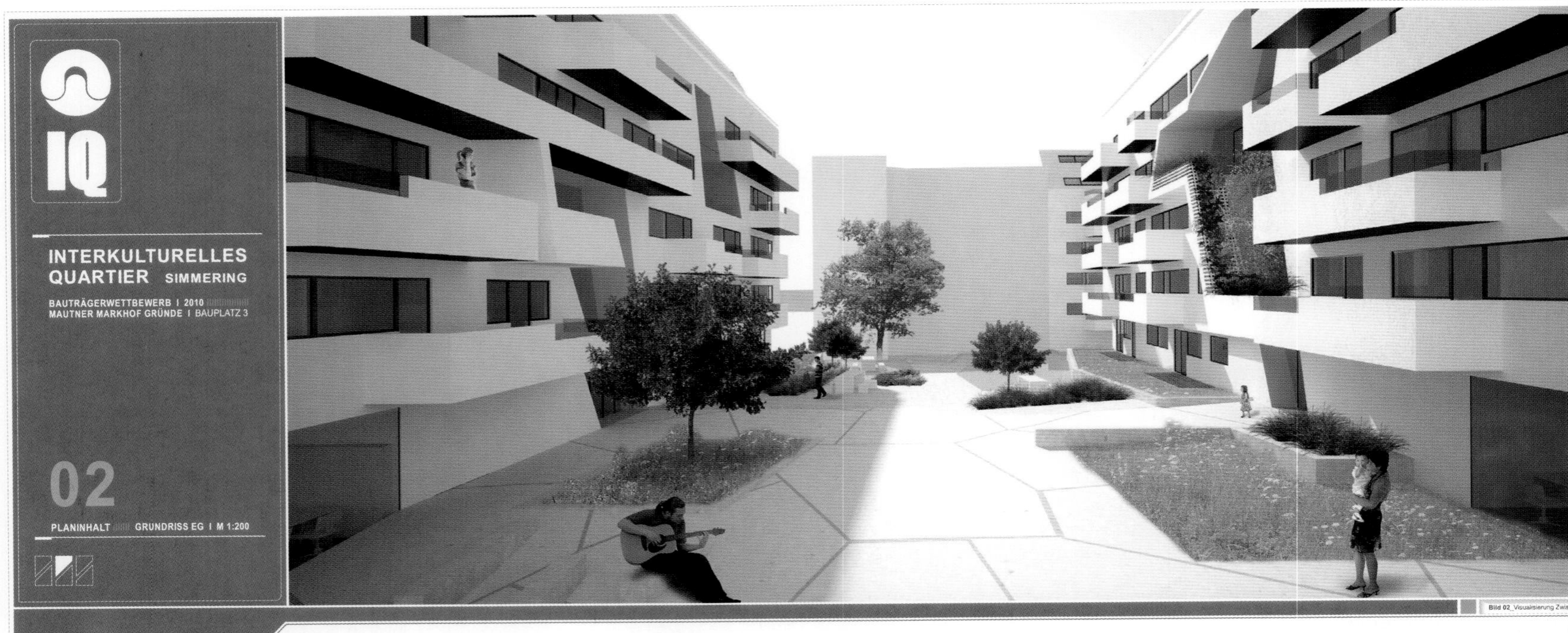

IQ- FREIRAUMKONZEPT

Die Anordnung der Freiräume mit unterschiedlichen Öffentlichkeitsgraden folgt einem Gradienten: *vom öffentlicheren zum privaten Nutzungsangebot* (von Norden nach Süden).
Zum übergeordneten Freiraumsystem knüpft dieser Freiraum mit einer offenen Platzgestaltung als Entrée, als Begegnung zu den Wohnbauten an. Dieser ist Begegnungsraum mit Bänken unter Zierkirschen, von denen der Blick über das gesamte Mautner Markhof Gelände ermöglicht wird und lädt auch zum Verweilen und Beobachten ein. Für BesucherInnen werden hier Radabstellanlagen angeboten.
Die Siedlung ist durchlässig und bietet Wegrelationen sowohl zum Straßenraum als auch zum Estragonplatz.

Der offenen Eingangssituation folgt der *wohnblockbezogene Freiraum*, der die Kommunikation fördert und gemeinschaftlich genutzt wird. Dieser ist mit Tisch- Bank Kombinationen ausgestattet und mit Blumenbeeten - bepflanzt mit Pfingstrosen, Wolfsmilch, Rosen, Anemonen und Gräsern - eingerahmt. Der Kleinkinderspielbereich mit Sandkiste und Kleinspielgeräten, wie Wippen, integriert sich mitten in der Anlage und ist bei den Hauseingängen situiert. Zierkirschen als kleinkronige Bäume sollen nur die Aufenthaltsbereiche aber nicht die Wohnungen beschatten.

Am Übergang zu den *privat nutzbaren Mietergärten ist ein Jugendrückzugsort* mit einer Liegepritsche angedacht. Wieder umfasst ein Pflanzbeet diesen Ort,der jedoch mit Hainbuchen auch ein wenig uneinsichtbar gestaltet sein soll.

136 Mieterbeete (flexible Teilung und Zusammenlegung der Mietergärten möglich) fördern das eigene Gärtnern und tragen zur gemeinsamen Kommuni-kation in der Siedlung bei. Die Beete mit einer Breite von 1,2 m² und 4,5 m Länge können bereits mit 5,5 m² einen Beitrag zur Selbstver-sorgung leisten. Eingefasst sind die Mietergärten mit einer kleinen Mauer, die Sitzhöhe hat, um sich beim Gärtnern auch ausruhen zu können. Ein Komposthaufen soll auch das ökologische Gärtnern för-dern. 19 Eigengärten mit durchschnittlich 55 m² ummanteln das Erdgeschoß. Eine Mauer mit einem integrierten Spalier aus Goldregen trennt die Eigengärten vom siedlungsöffentlichen Bereich, sodass der Privatsphäre mehr Raum gegeben werden kann. Die einheitliche Gestaltung der Gren-zen verleiht der gesamten Wohnhausanlage ein homogenes Gesicht.

Der BAuplatz ist an der östlichen und westlichen Grenze durch einen ÖKO-Wall eingefasst, der den Grünaspekt des Freiraums verstärkt.

Die Außenanlage umfaßt 4.448,99 m², davon sind 811,74 m² befestigt und 3.637,25 m² unbefestigt.

JUGENDTREFFPUNKT MIT LIEGEPRITSCHE
RASEN
WEISSE ZIERKIRSCHE
KLEINKINDERSPIELBEREICH MIT SANDKISTE UND SPIELGERÄTE IM FALLSCHUTZ
BEFESTIGTE FLÄCHE
WASSERDURCHLÄSSIGER BELAG - STABILIZER
SPALIER ZUR TRENNUNG DER EIGENGÄRTEN
MIETERBEETE FÜR GEMÜSE UND BLUMEN
WEG
SITZMAUER
EIGENGÄRTEN ZWISCHEN 30m² und 130m²
SITZINSEL
ROTE ZIERKIRSCHE
BLUMENBEETE
BETONGEMISCH GESTOCKT
FAHRRADABSTELLANLAGE
OUTDOOR SPIELBEREICH
NUSSBAUM
KOMPOSTHAUFEN
GRÜNER WALL MIT WEIDENGEBÜSCH ZUR ABGRENZUNG

EIGENGÄRTEN / FREIRAUM

DACHGARTEN

GRUNDRISS EG
FREIRAUMPLAN M 1:200

IQ

INTERKULTURELLES QUARTIER SIMMERING

BAUTRÄGERWETTBEWERB I 2010
MAUTNER MARKHOF GRÜNDE I BAUPLATZ 3

03

PLANINHALT GEMEINSCHAFTSZONEN

Bild 03_Visualisierung Hofbereich

Q- SOZIOLOGIE

ARCHITEKTUR GEMEINSCHAFTSRÄUME

Die Gemeinschaftsräume werden in den besten Wohnlagen errichtet. Damit ist die Zuordnung zu den Wohnungen auf kurzen Weg möglich und die soziale Kontrolle der Räume sehr ausgeprägt. Die Bewohnerschaft kümmert sich intensiver um diese Zonen, Vandalismus wird vorgebeugt und die Hausbewohner werden stärker an diese Kommunikationsorte gebunden. Die Lage ist ein wichtiger Faktor zur nachhaltigen Nutzung auch in Zukunft.
Die Architektur soll die verschiedenen Nutzungen so ineinander verweben, dass es einen Mehrwert für alle Räume gibt. Die Gemeinschaftsräume sollen als ein Fluss wahrgenommen werden obwohl sie durch Stockwerke und Glasscheiben getrennt sind.
Prinzipiell sind 2 Varianten der Gemeinschaftszonen geplant. In den äußeren Häusern A+B sind sie seitlich an das Atrium angeschlossenen und damit für alle Hausbewohner gleich erleb- und nutzbar.
Das mittlere Gebäude wird jedoch in 4 mehrgeschossige Mikronachbarschaften unterteilt. Das sind jeweils vom Stiegenhaus abgekoppelte 3 geschossige Gemeinschaftsbereiche mit viel Luftraum. An diese Mikronachbarschaft sind etwa 15 Wohnungen angeschlossen - die nächste Nachbarschaft erreicht man über das Stiegenhaus.
Mit dieser Struktur werden im Haus B die Gemeinschafts Nachbarschaftszonen um einiges individueller den Bewohnern zugeordnet. Gleichzeitig dient der Einschnitt auch der Belichtung der innen liegenden Erschließungszone, die in den beiden oberen Mikronachbarschaften noch zusätzlich durch große Oberlichtverglasungen belichtet werden. Die großzügige Vorzone zu den Wohnungen (etwa 10x5m) wird durch die Verglasung der Gemeinschaftsräume zu einer Einheit verschmolzen.

DACHGARTENKÜCHE

Der thematische Schwerpunkt auf interkulturelles Wohnen hat zu einem ganz besonderen Gemeinschaftsraum geführt. Beim Nachdenken über die Gemeinsamkeit der Kulturen hat sich die Esskultur als verbindendes Element herausgestellt. Hier wird die Verschiedenheit der Kulturen auch im Alltag als Bereicherung wahrgenommen.
Die Gemeinschaftsküche ist die Kommunikationsdrehscheibe und soll allen Bewohnern die Möglichkeit der Nutzung eröffnen. Hier finden sich beim Kochen und Essen die Menschen zusammen - noch immer der leichteste Einstieg in eine andere Kultur.
Kombiniert wird die Küche mit einem fast 300m² großen Dachgarten. Die Vielfalt der Elemente von Holzterrassen, Grasflächen, Kräuterbeeten und Pflanzen bietet für jede Nutzung einen speziellen Bereich an. Auch der Anbau von Küchenkräuter aus aller Welt ist ein Faktor zu emotionellen Anbindung der Bewohnerschaft.
Die Verbindung Küche mit dem Dachgarten eröffnet vielfältige Nutungen die auch die Schlechtwetternutzung umfassen. Ein großes Vordach erlaubt den Grillabend sogar bei einem Regenschauer weiterzuführen.
Neben der Küche wird durch die Atriumverglasung ein Ruheraum abgetrennt. Dieser Bereich des Dachgartens ist eher beschaulich angelegt, sodass eine komplentative Nutzung wie Yoga, Massage, Meditation auch ermöglicht wird. Das bis zu 2,5m hohe Atriumoberlicht trennt auch im Außenbereich die beiden gegensätzlichen Funktionen effektiv ab.

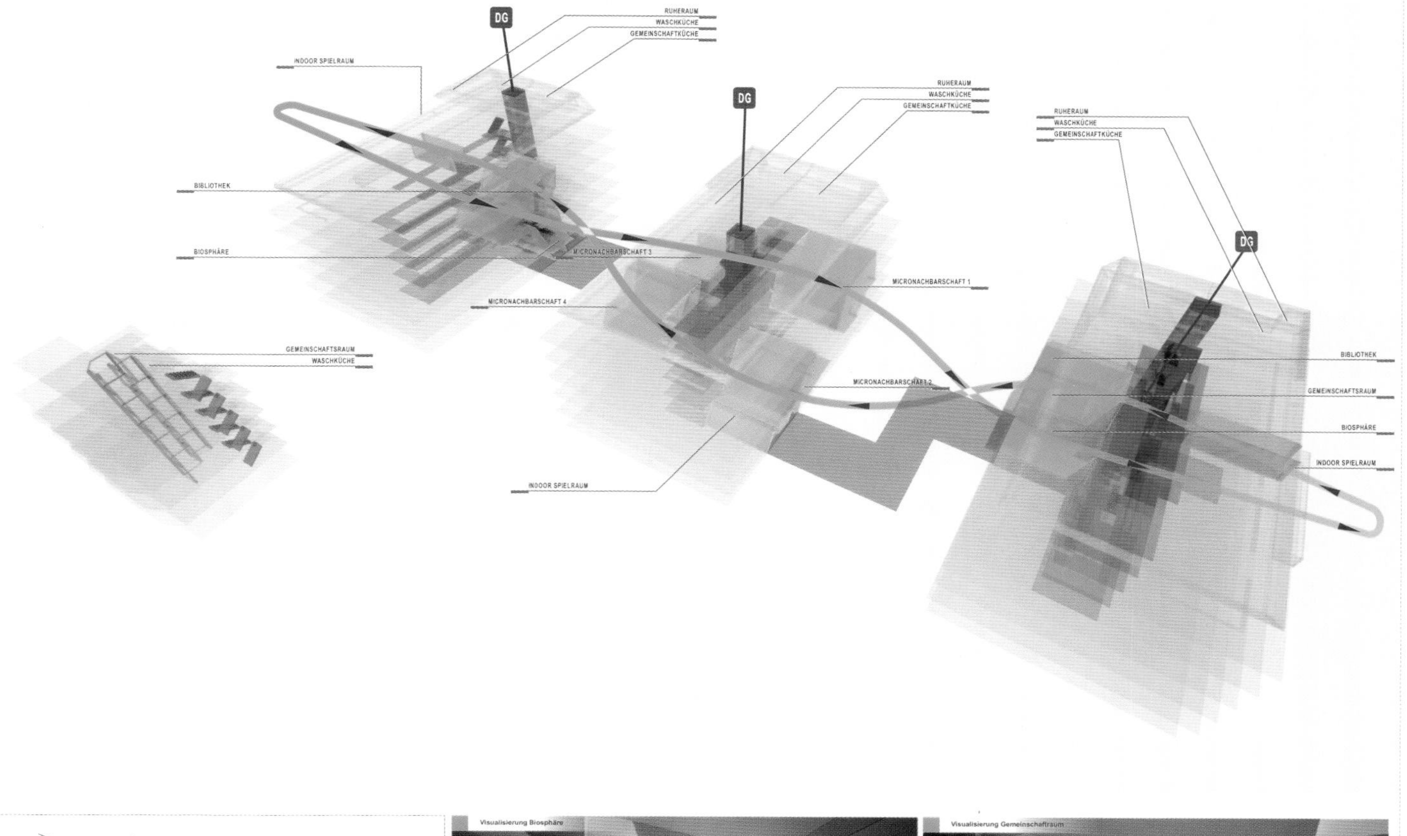

Q is looking for you!

usgrenzung entgegen gewirkt.
ie zukünftigen BewohnerInnen des IQ
Q for you! - Gemeinsame Interessen verbinden

as IQ - Interkulturelles Quartier Simmering stellt das Wohnen in ner vielfältigen, interkulturellen und toleranten Atmosphäre in den ittelpunkt: Das gemeinsame Interesse der zukünftigen Bewohnernen und Bewohner an einem Leben in einem weltoffenen Umfeld ringt diese zusammen, der „interkulturelle Mehrwert" der Anlage ist in Anreiz und ein Entscheidungsgrund für das Wohnen im IQ immering. Dieses gemeinsame Interesse und die damit verbunene Offenheit der Menschen bildet die Basis für die Herausbildung elfältiger (interethnischer) Nachbarschaftsbeziehungen und einer terkulturellen Atmosphäre.
as IQ Simmering legt den Fokus auf die Gemeinsamkeiten der ewohnerInnen und das Verbindende unter ihnen, nicht auf ihre ifferenzen und Unterschiede. „Kultur" wird - im Sinne eines „doing ulture" - als ein Prozess verstanden, der in einer Praxis des iteinander Tuns laufend hergestellt wird und auch ementsprechend wandelbar ist. Ethnizitäten und Kulturen stehen cht ein für alle Mal fest, sondern verändern sich ständig und sind „ ..) differenzierte Produkte einer bewegten und durch viele oziokulturelle Prozesse geprägten Geschichte." Mit diesem erständnis von „Kultur" wird der Festschreibung insbesondere von enschen mit Migrationshintergrund in einer ewigen Fremdeitsposition und damit ihrer gesellschaftlichen Simmering bringen it ihrer Lebensgeschichte und Erfahrung „Kultur" mit und entickeln sie beim Zusammenleben auch gemeinsam ein Stück weit eiter.

as IQ Simmering geht davon aus, dass unterschiedliche nsprüche und Wünsche von Menschen mit Migrationshintergrund nd von Menschen mit österreichischem Hintergrund ans Wohnen eniger „kulturell" als vor allem sozial bedingt sind: Die Höhe des ur Verfügung stehenden Einkommens oder die Größe des aushalts (Anzahl der Kinder, Mehr-Generationen-Haushalte etc.) nd für alle entscheidende Kriterien bei der Wohnungswahl - benso wie das Interesse am Wohnen in hellen, genügend großen, ut angebundenen Wohnungen in grüner Umgebung etc. Das IQ mmering stellt dieses gemeinsame Interesse in den Mittelpunkt, n breiter Mix aus Wohnungen mit verschiedenen Grundrissen und rößen kommt den unterschiedlichen Ansprüchen entgegen.

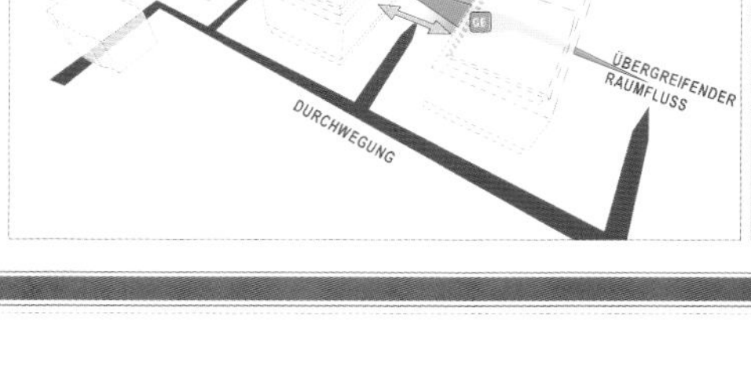

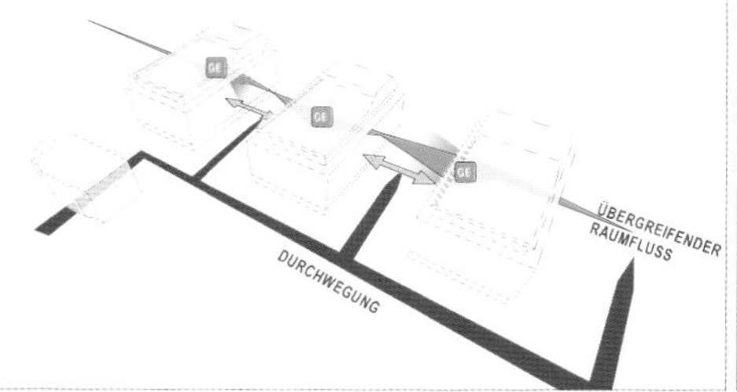

I Portici | *Alessandro Console Studio*

Promoter : Imprese Vellucci, Gruppo Zeppieri Costruzioni
Location : Frosinone, Italy
Typology : Housing
Project Team : Alessandro Console, Gina Oliva

01 Concorso Internazionale di idee "I Portici" per un complesso polifunzionale Residenza, Commercio, Spazi Pubblici a Frosinone

SWR2D2

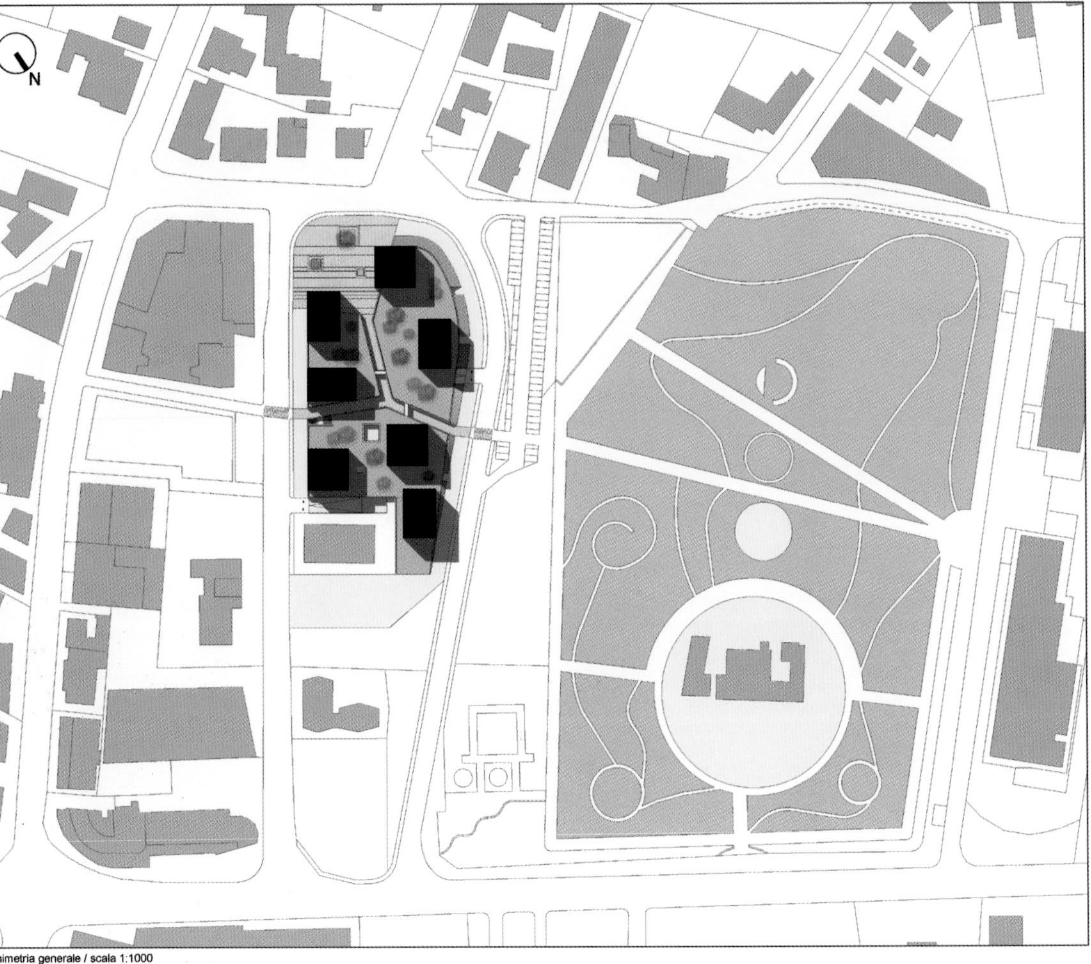

Planimetria generale / scala 1:1000

ACCESSIBILITA'
livello 0
- viabilità carrabile
- percorsi pedonali principali
- parcheggi pubblici
- accessi edifici residenziali
- accessi parcheggio interrato

SPAZI AD USO PUBBLICO
livello 0
- attività commerciali
- piazze:
  1. piazza pedonale
  2. piazza interna coperta

SPAZI PRIVATI E SEMIPUBBLICI
livello 1
- edifici residenziali
- accessi edifici residenziali
- spazi aperti semipubblici (aree verdi attrezzate e giardini condominiali)

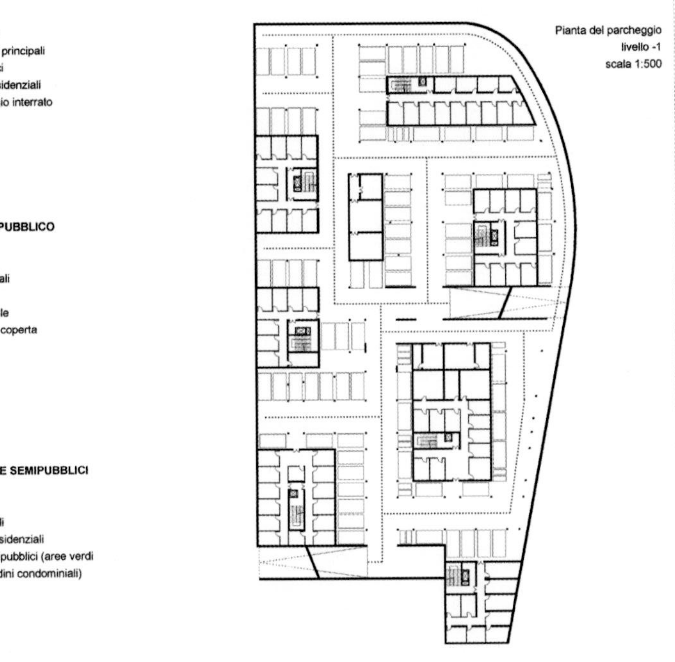

Pianta del parcheggio
livello -1
scala 1:500

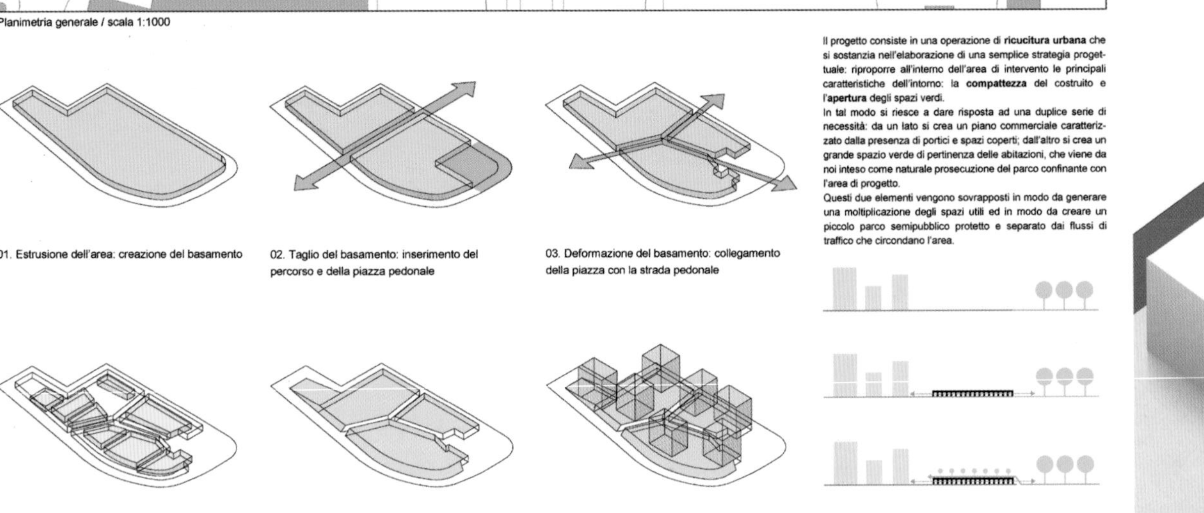

01. Estrusione dell'area: creazione del basamento

02. Taglio del basamento: inserimento del percorso e della piazza pedonale

03. Deformazione del basamento: collegamento della piazza con la strada pedonale

04. Erosione del basamento: differenziazione tra spazi commerciali e portici

05. Inclinazione del basamento: realizzazione del tetto verde

06. Sovrapposizione degli edifici residenziali

Il progetto consiste in una operazione di **ricucitura urbana** che si sostanzia nell'elaborazione di una semplice strategia progettuale: riproporre all'interno dell'area di intervento le principali caratteristiche dell'intorno: la **compattezza** del costruito e l'**apertura** degli spazi verdi.
In tal modo si riesce a dare risposta ad una duplice serie di necessità: da un lato si crea un piano commerciale caratterizzato dalla presenza di portici e spazi coperti; dall'altro si crea un grande spazio verde di pertinenza delle abitazioni, che viene da noi inteso come naturale prosecuzione del parco confinante con l'area di progetto.
Questi due elementi vengono sovrapposti in modo da generare una moltiplicazione degli spazi utili ed in modo da creare un piccolo parco semipubblico protetto e separato dai flussi di traffico che circondano l'area.

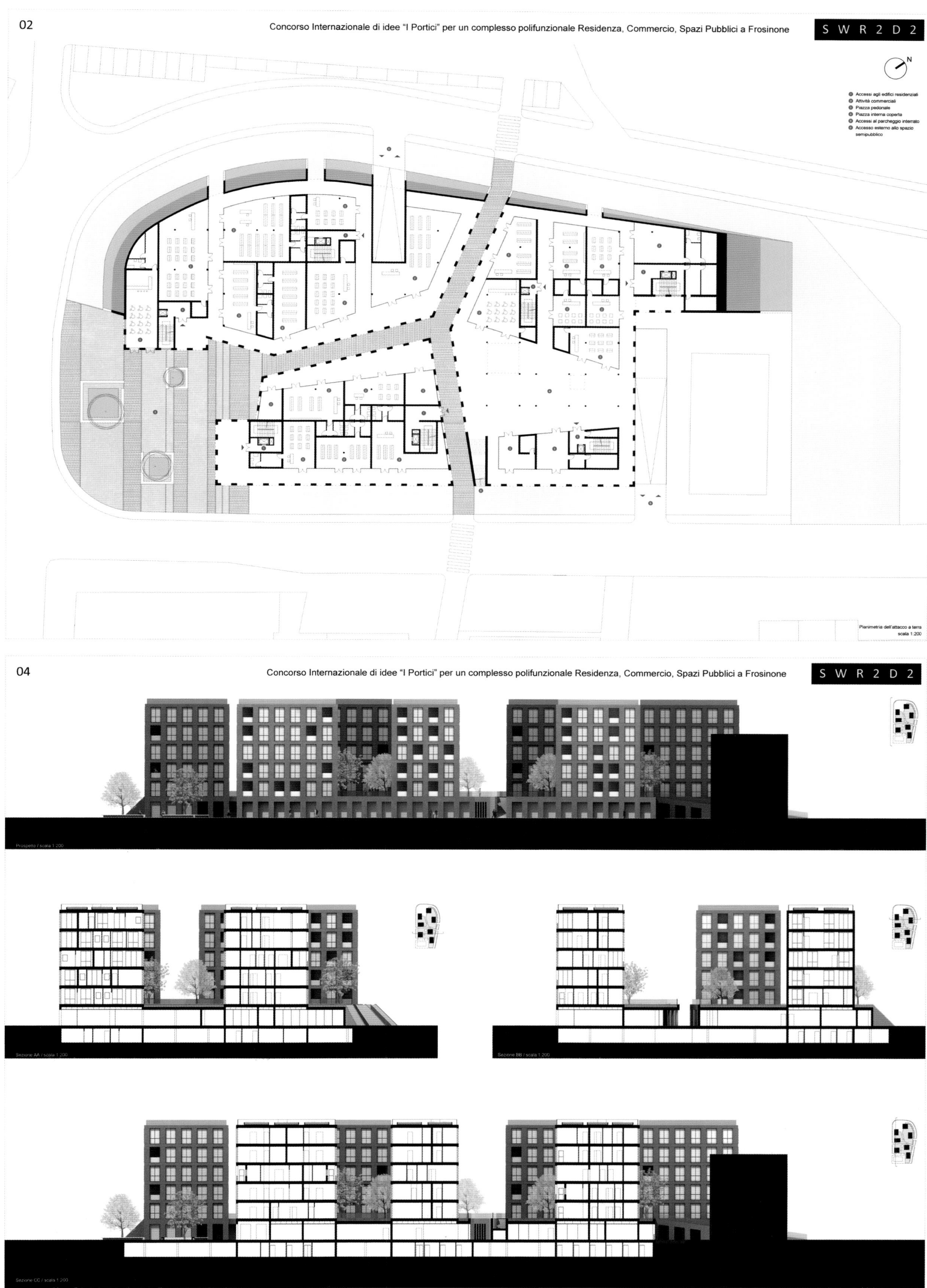
02
Concorso Internazionale di idee "I Portici" per un complesso polifunzionale Residenza, Commercio, Spazi Pubblici a Frosinone
S W R 2 D 2
N
Accessi agli edifici residenziali
Attivitá commerciali
Piazza pedonale
Piazza interna coperta
Accessi al parcheggio interrato
Accesso esterno allo spazio semipubblico
Planimetria dell'attacco a terra
scala 1:200
04
Concorso Internazionale di idee "I Portici" per un complesso polifunzionale Residenza, Commercio, Spazi Pubblici a Frosinone
S W R 2 D 2
Prospetto / scala 1:200
Sezione AA / scala 1:200
Sezione BB / scala 1:200
Sezione CC / scala 1:200

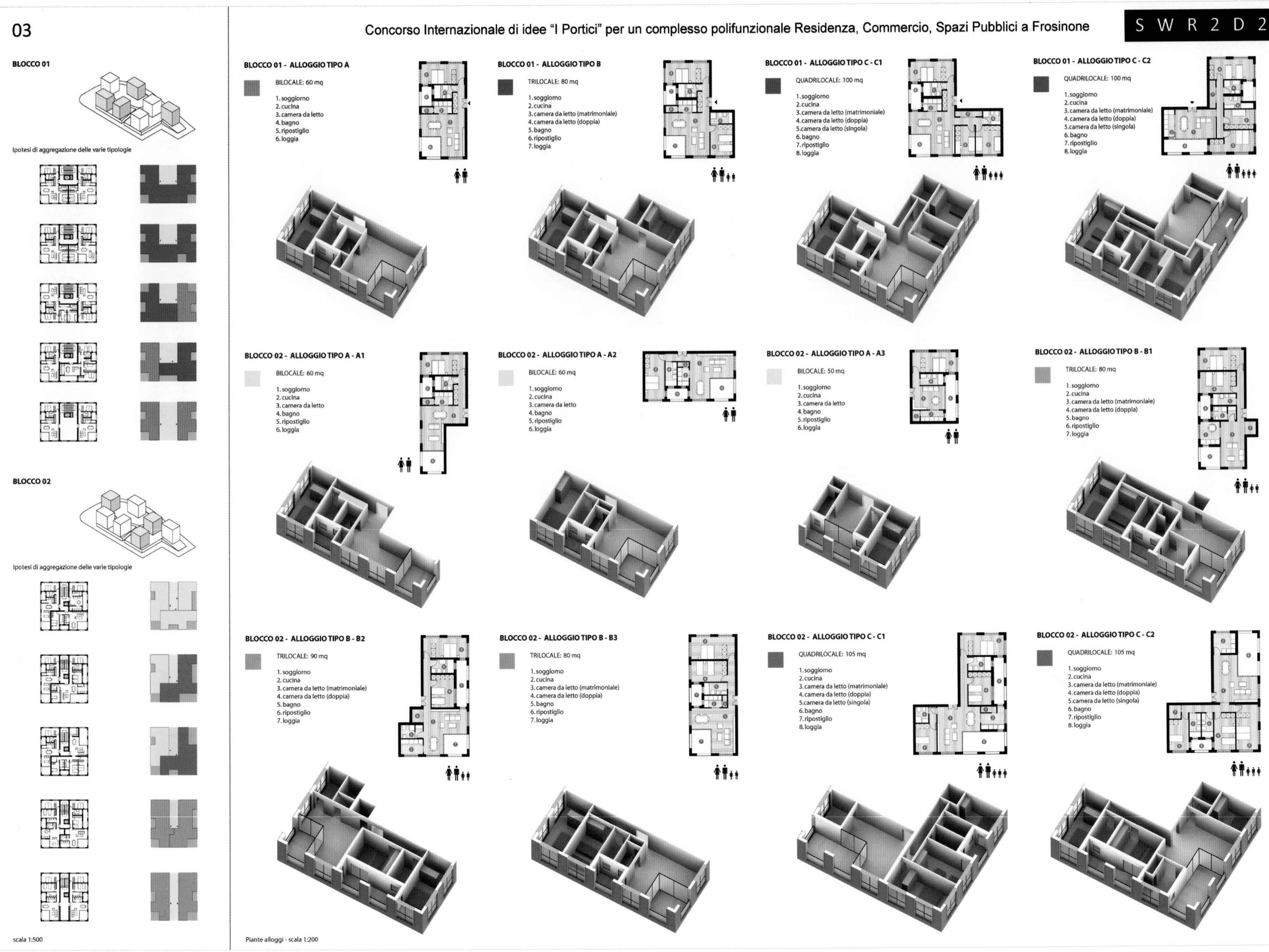
03
Concorso Internazionale di idee "I Portici" per un complesso polifunzionale Residenza, Commercio, Spazi Pubblici a Frosinone
S W R 2 D 2
BLOCCO 01
Ipotesi di aggregazione delle varie tipologie
BLOCCO 02
Ipotesi di aggregazione delle varie tipologie
scala 1:500
BLOCCO 01 - ALLOGGIO TIPO A
BILOCALE: 60 mq
1. soggiorno
2. cucina
3. camera da letto
4. bagno
5. ripostiglio
6. loggia
BLOCCO 01 - ALLOGGIO TIPO B
TRILOCALE: 80 mq
1. soggiorno
2. cucina
3. camera da letto (matrimoniale)
4. camera da letto (doppia)
5. bagno
6. ripostiglio
7. loggia
BLOCCO 01 - ALLOGGIO TIPO C - C1
QUADRILOCALE: 100 mq
1. soggiorno
2. cucina
3. camera da letto (matrimoniale)
4. camera da letto (doppia)
5. camera da letto (singola)
6. bagno
7. ripostiglio
8. loggia
BLOCCO 01 - ALLOGGIO TIPO C - C2
QUADRILOCALE: 100 mq
1. soggiorno
2. cucina
3. camera da letto (matrimoniale)
4. camera da letto (doppia)
5. camera da letto (singola)
6. bagno
7. ripostiglio
8. loggia
BLOCCO 02 - ALLOGGIO TIPO A - A1
BILOCALE: 60 mq
1. soggiorno
2. cucina
3. camera da letto
4. bagno
5. ripostiglio
6. loggia
BLOCCO 02 - ALLOGGIO TIPO A - A2
BILOCALE: 60 mq
1. soggiorno
2. cucina
3. camera da letto
4. bagno
5. ripostiglio
6. loggia
BLOCCO 02 - ALLOGGIO TIPO A - A3
BILOCALE: 50 mq
1. soggiorno
2. cucina
3. camera da letto
4. bagno
5. ripostiglio
6. loggia
BLOCCO 02 - ALLOGGIO TIPO B - B1
TRILOCALE: 80 mq
1. soggiorno
2. cucina
3. camera da letto (matrimoniale)
4. camera da letto (doppia)
5. bagno
6. ripostiglio
7. loggia
BLOCCO 02 - ALLOGGIO TIPO B - B2
TRILOCALE: 90 mq
1. soggiorno
2. cucina
3. camera da letto (matrimoniale)
4. camera da letto (doppia)
5. bagno
6. ripostiglio
7. loggia
BLOCCO 02 - ALLOGGIO TIPO B - B3
TRILOCALE: 80 mq
1. soggiorno
2. cucina
3. camera da letto (matrimoniale)
4. camera da letto (doppia)
5. bagno
6. ripostiglio
7. loggia
BLOCCO 02 - ALLOGGIO TIPO C - C1
QUADRILOCALE: 105 mq
1. soggiorno
2. cucina
3. camera da letto (matrimoniale)
4. camera da letto (doppia)
5. camera da letto (singola)
6. bagno
7. ripostiglio
8. loggia
BLOCCO 02 - ALLOGGIO TIPO C - C2
QUADRILOCALE: 105 mq
1. soggiorno
2. cucina
3. camera da letto (matrimoniale)
4. camera da letto (doppia)
5. camera da letto (singola)
6. bagno
7. ripostiglio
8. loggia
Piante alloggi - scala 1:200

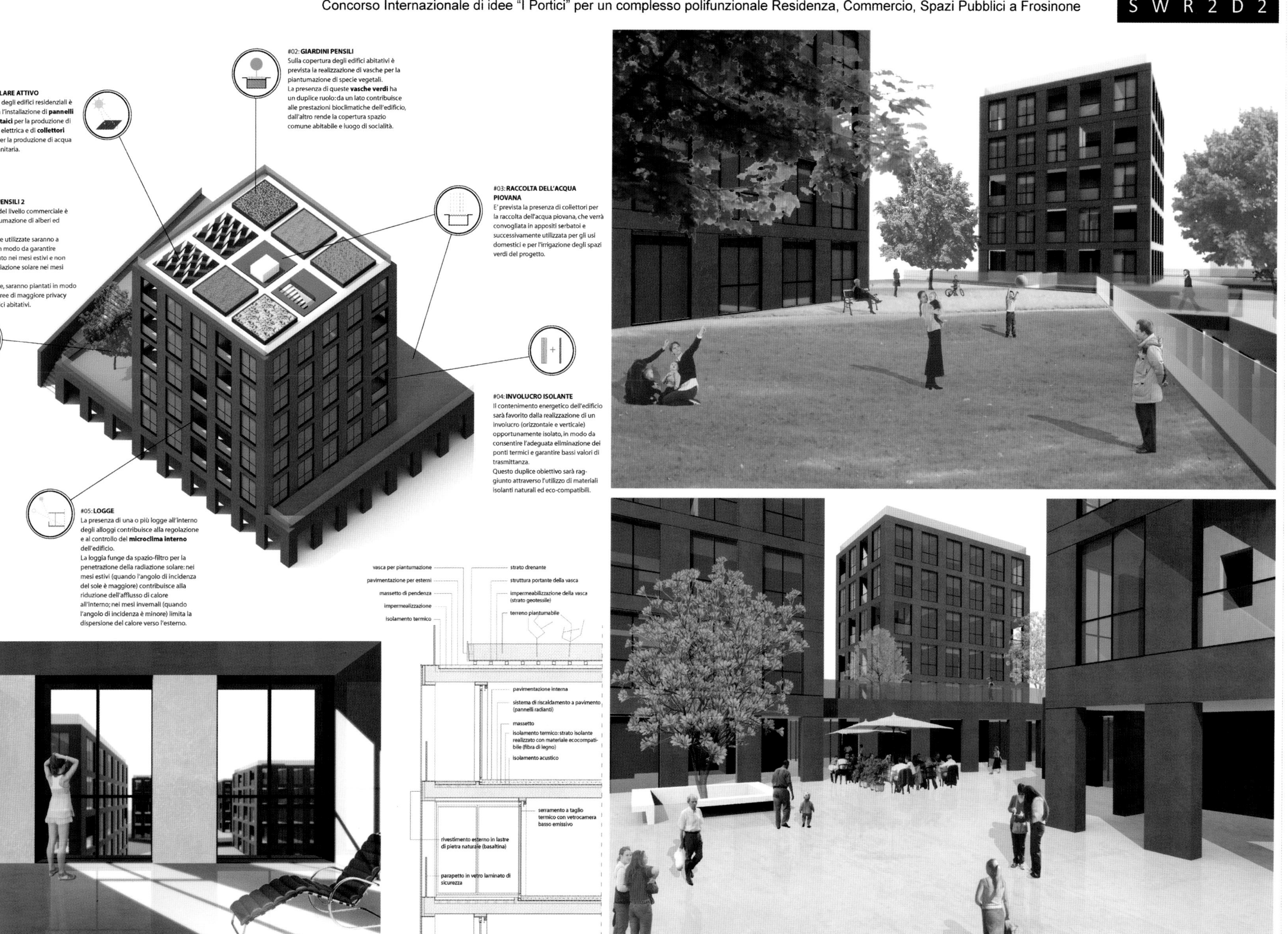
05
Concorso Internazionale di idee "I Portici" per un complesso polifunzionale Residenza, Commercio, Spazi Pubblici a Frosinone
S W R 2 D 2
#01: SOLARE ATTIVO
Sui tetti degli edifici residenziali è prevista l'installazione di pannelli fotovoltaici per la produzione di energia elettrica e di collettori solari per la produzione di acqua calda sanitaria.
#02: GIARDINI PENSILI
Sulla copertura degli edifici abitativi è prevista la realizzazione di vasche per la piantumazione di specie vegetali.
La presenza di queste vasche verdi ha un duplice ruolo: da un lato contribuisce alle prestazioni bioclimatiche dell'edificio, dall'altro rende la copertura spazio comune abitabile e luogo di socialità.
#06: GIARDINI PENSILI 2
Sulla copertura del livello commerciale è prevista la piantumazione di alberi ed arbusti.
Le specie arboree utilizzate saranno a foglia caduca, in modo da garantire l'ombreggiamento nei mesi estivi e non ostacolare la radiazione solare nei mesi invernali.
Gli arbusti, invece, saranno piantati in modo da creare delle aree di maggiore privacy intorno agli edifici abitativi.
#03: RACCOLTA DELL'ACQUA PIOVANA
E' prevista la presenza di collettori per la raccolta dell'acqua piovana, che verrà convogliata in appositi serbatoi e successivamente utilizzata per gli usi domestici e per l'irrigazione degli spazi verdi del progetto.
#04: INVOLUCRO ISOLANTE
Il contenimento energetico dell'edificio sarà favorito dalla realizzazione di un involucro (orizzontale e verticale) opportunamente isolato, in modo da consentire l'adeguata eliminazione dei ponti termici e garantire bassi valori di trasmittanza.
Questo duplice obiettivo sarà raggiunto attraverso l'utilizzo di materiali isolanti naturali ed eco-compatibili.
#05: LOGGE
La presenza di una o più logge all'interno degli alloggi contribuisce alla regolazione e al controllo del microclima interno dell'edificio.
La loggia funge da spazio-filtro per la penetrazione della radiazione solare: nei mesi estivi (quando l'angolo di incidenza del sole è maggiore) contribuisce alla riduzione dell'afflusso di calore all'interno; nei mesi invernali (quando l'angolo di incidenza è minore) limita la dispersione del calore verso l'esterno.
vasca per piantumazione
pavimentazione per esterni
massetto di pendenza
impermealizzazione
isolamento termico
strato drenante
struttura portante della vasca
impermeabilizzazione della vasca (strato geotessile)
terreno piantumabile
pavimentazione interna
sistema di riscaldamento a pavimento (pannelli radianti)
massetto
isolamento termico: strato isolante realizzato con materiale ecocompatibile (fibra di legno)
isolamento acustico
serramento a taglio termico con vetrocamera basso emissivo
rivestimento esterno in lastre di pietra naturale (basaltina)
parapetto in vetro laminato di sicurezza
Stralcio sezione edificio residenziale
scala 1:50

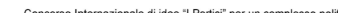

018 Nesting Thought | *b4architects*

Location : Winnipeg (Manitoba), Canada
Object : Warming Huts: An Art & Architecture Competition On Ice
Client : Inn at the Forks, ManitobaW Association of Architects, University of Manitoba, Faculty of Architects & Partners Program and KGS Group
Project Team : Agianluca Evels & Stefania Papitto

concept

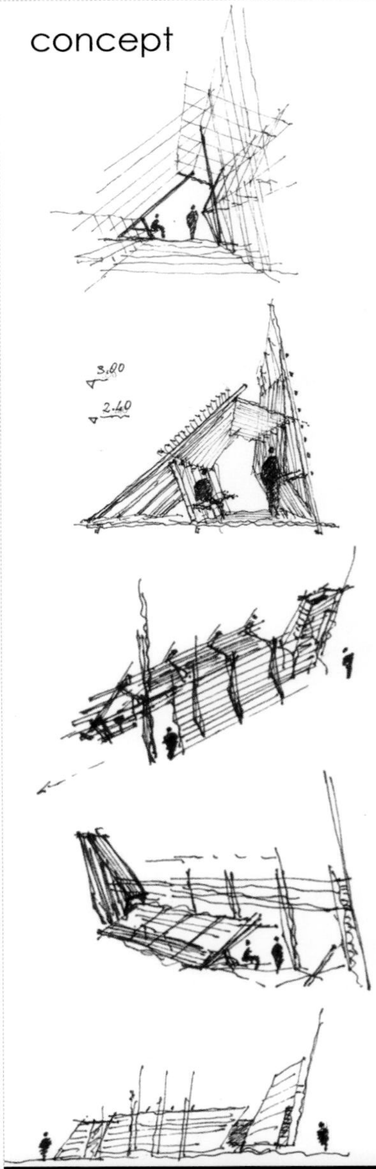

01

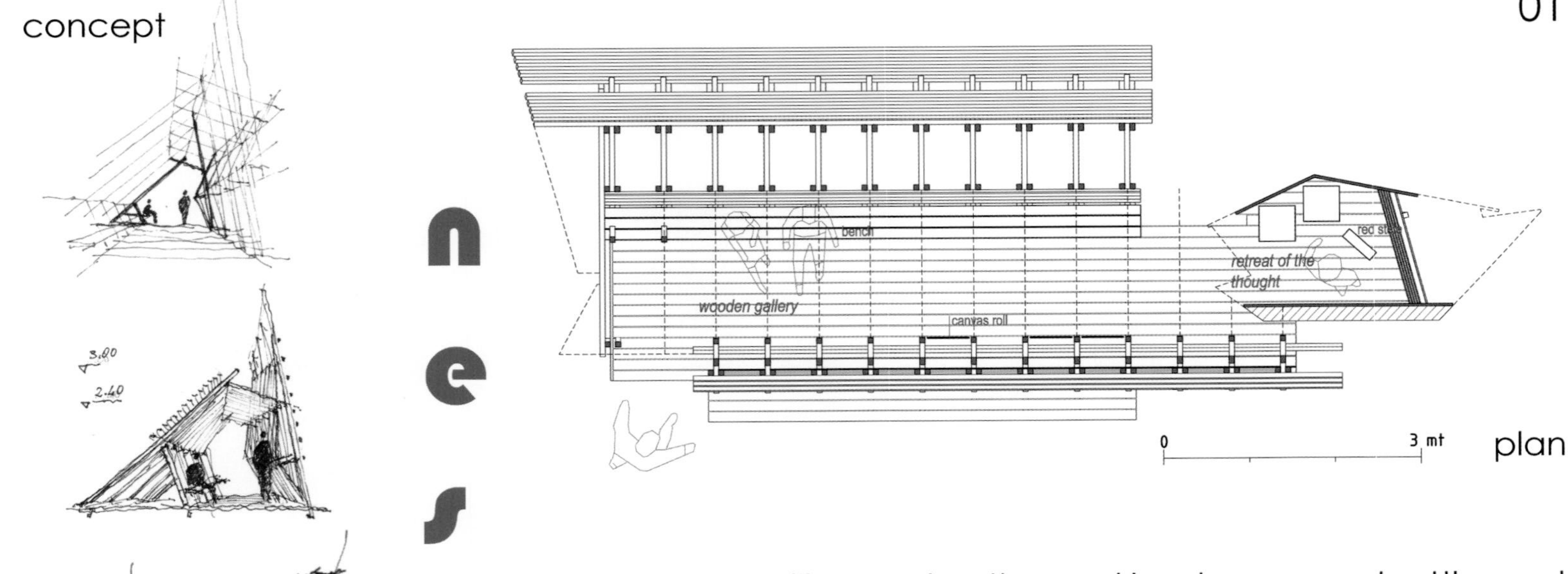

nesting thought

The wooden pavilion evokes the rural landscape and settlement structures of the ancient inhabitants of these latitudes. It offers to the visitors a sensory active experience. A short tunnel formed by light wooden stands is the first part of the pavilion which includes a seat for a short stop and three rolls of canvas attached to the posts where everyone can express thoughts and images. In this way, the pavilion becomes active atelier and the rollers after the event may be exposed to evoke the passage of visitors. The serial aspect of the gallery contrasts with the more intimate and confidential nature of the wooden tent, where can stay only two people. This 'retreat of thought' is illuminated by a red-colored stele that hides the radiant body. A grid of wooden slats together to polycarbonate surfaces ensure the necessary protection of the interior. At night, the pavilion becomes a lantern.

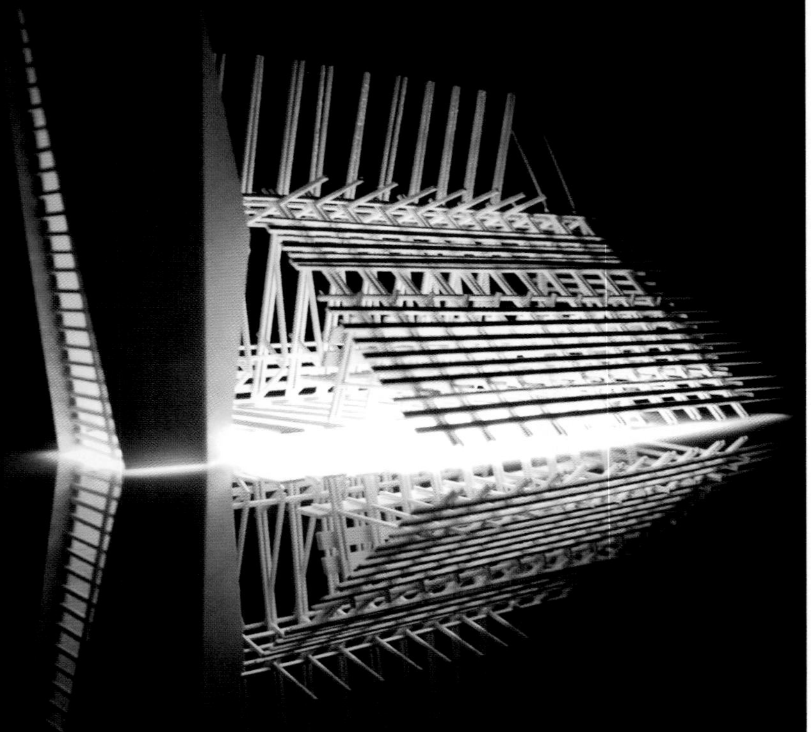

gianluca evels & stefania papitto

warming huts: an art & architecture competition on ice

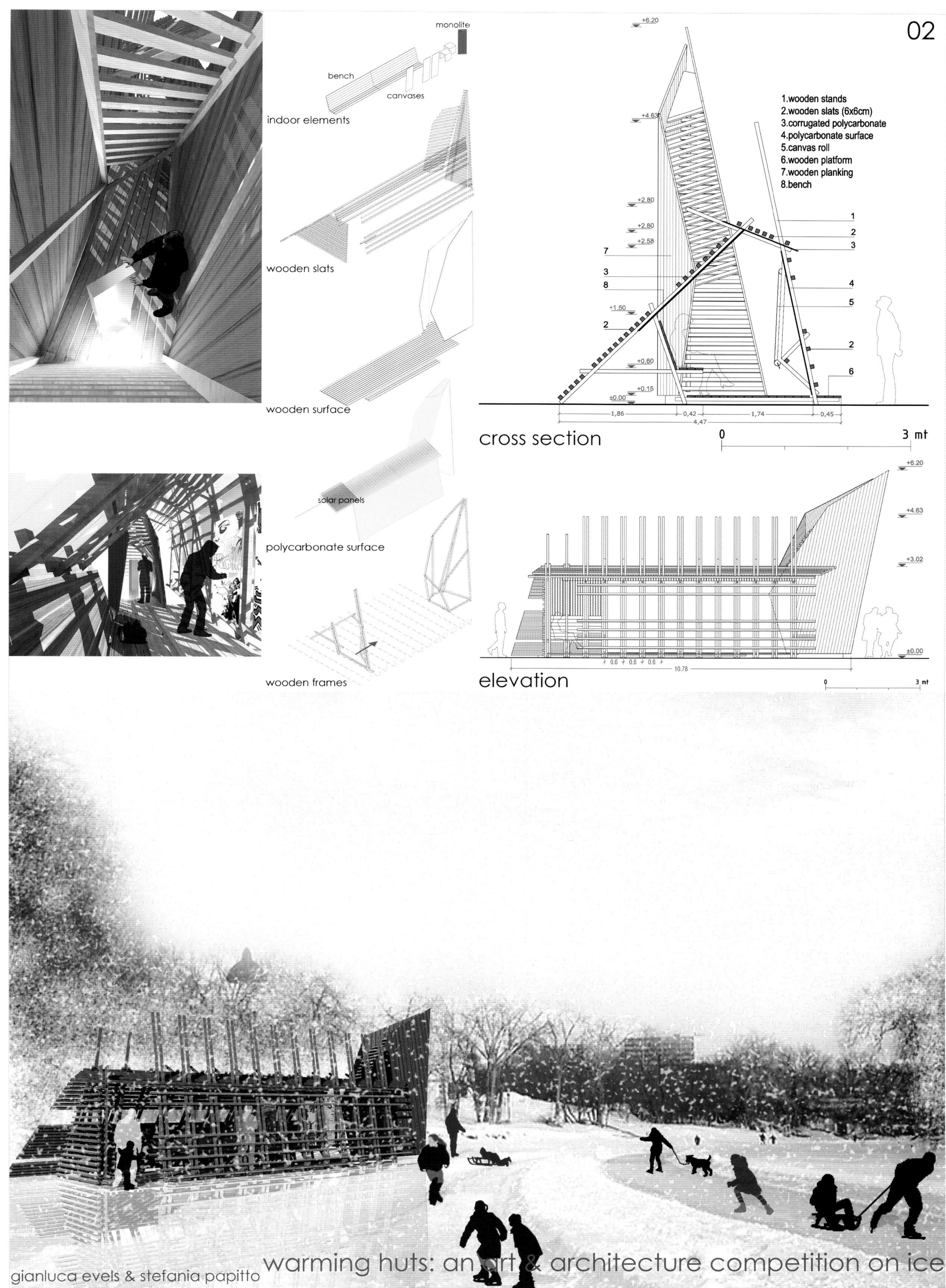
02
monolite
bench
canvases
indoor elements
wooden slats
wooden surface
solar panels
polycarbonate surface
wooden frames
1.wooden stands
2.wooden slats (6x6cm)
3.corrugated polycarbonate
4.polycarbonate surface
5.canvas roll
6.wooden platform
7.wooden planking
8.bench
cross section
0
3 mt
elevation
gianluca evels & stefania papitto
warming huts: an art & architecture competition on ice

019 North Face | *nodo17-architects*

Location : El Escorial, Madrid, Spain
Design Team : Manuel Pérez Romero, Félix Toledo Lerín, Noelia Somolinos, Luis del Rey Cristóbal

Project Type : Single Family House
Client : Garajes General Pardiñas S.A.

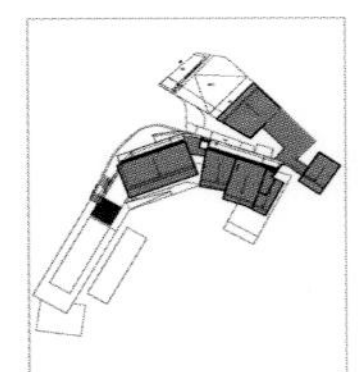

Company / Firm Name_ nodo17-architects/ Manuel Pérez Romero
Country_ spain

Project Name_ NORTH FACE
Location of Site_ El Escorial, Madrid. Spain
Design Team_ Félix Toledo Lerín
Noelia Somolinos
Luis del Rey Cristóbal

Project Type_ Single Family House_
Client_ Garajes General Pardiñas S.A.

Site Area_ 5100 sm
Built-up Area_ 1000 sm

Date of completion_ Under Construction

3D MODEL_ Víctor Quirós Quirós / Jaime López
Photographs_ nodo17_architects

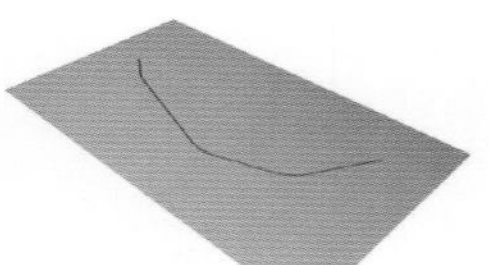
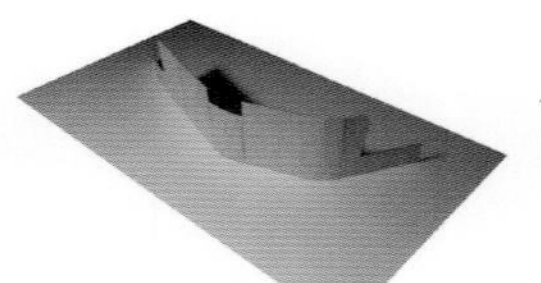
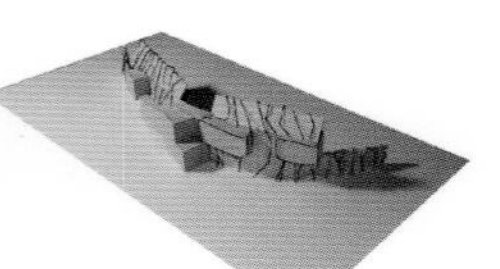
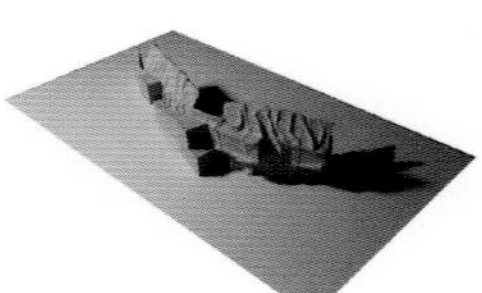

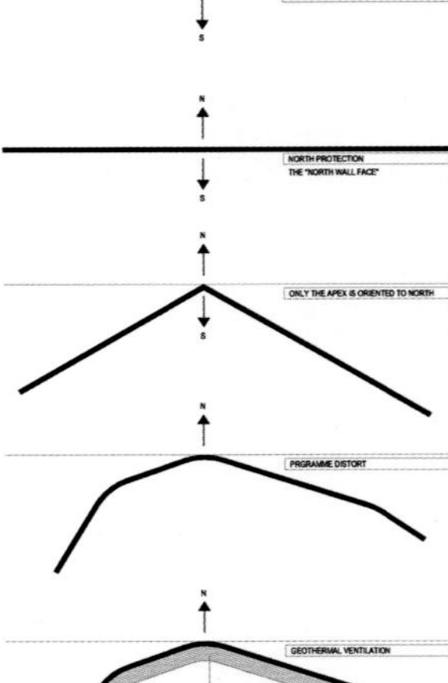

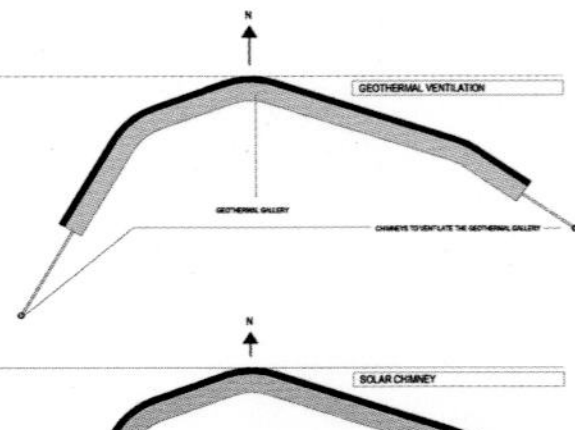

SKETCH PROCESS_

Working model_

north face

The "NORTH FACE" is a house protected by a climbing wall: wrapped and always wet, where the moss growth on the basatls stones. You will need a "good hand" for climbing it.
The house is devoloped along the "north face" wall, and it works like a thermal protector that receives air from a geothermal pipe and from a solar chimney.
The model shows only a part of the house: the North Face wall.
The main intention is to construct the most natural wall as posible. Almost like we cut a natural cliff and we carry it to the land. It is made of basalt stones and projected concrete.
The bullring is hence surrounded by smaller squares that house the different programs annexed to the main one. A single roof or marquee organizes the different activities and generates a public space sheltered from sun and rain. A new city square for Blanca.
The main elements that form this project are the following:

-The main square formed by the bullring and the stands, with the corresponding spaces for transit movement and entrances.

-The bubbles corresponding to the secondary squares that house the annex programs.

-The marquee which generates a new public space and classifies the different programs.

-The bullfighter's costume. The main square is 'dressed' with a skin of ceramic lattice that reproduces the intricate embroidery of bullfighters' costumes, and which at the same time is brightened by the different colors of the costumes.

GROUND FLOOR_

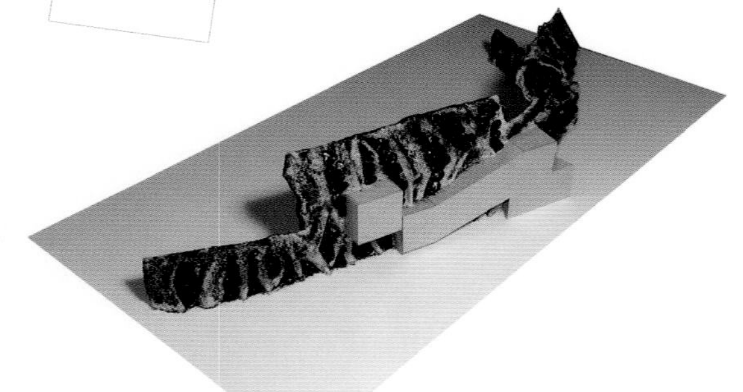

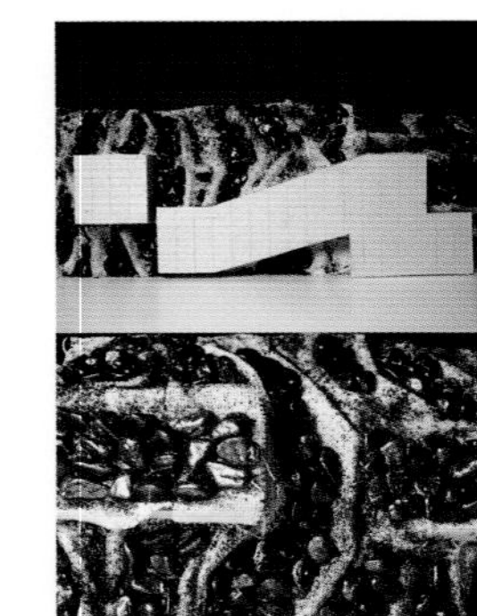

Model of the WALL_

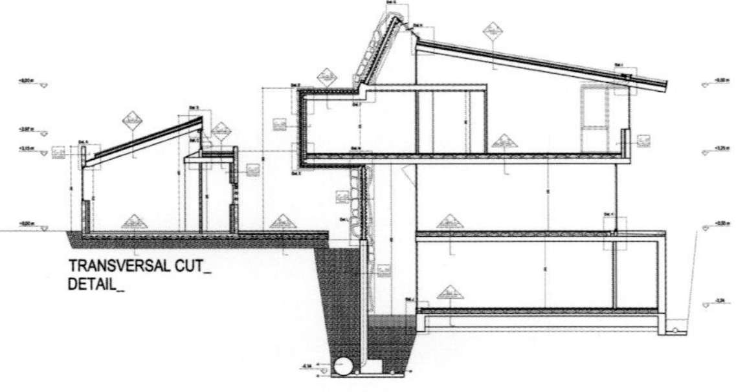

TRANSVERSAL CUT_
DETAIL_

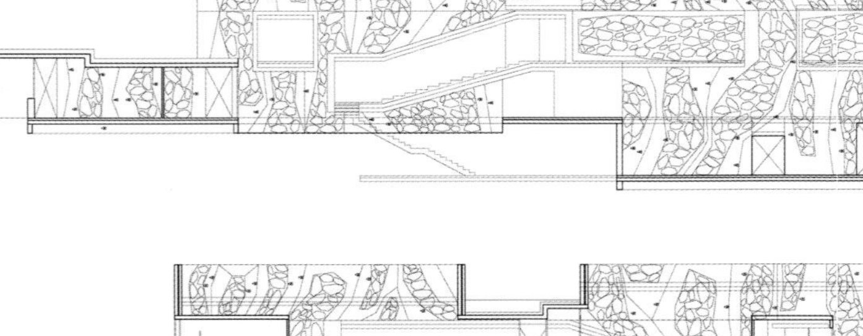

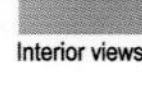

Interior views_

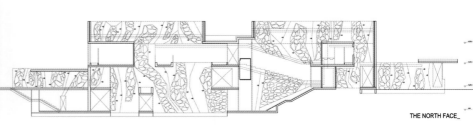

THE NORTH FACE_

Valley House | *nodo17-architects*

Model & Photographs : nodo17_architects
Project Type : Single Family House

Location : Hermigua, La Gomera, Canary Islands, Spain
Design Team : Manuel Pérez Romero, Félix Toledo Lerín, Jaime Tarazona Lizarraga, Luis del Rey Cristobal

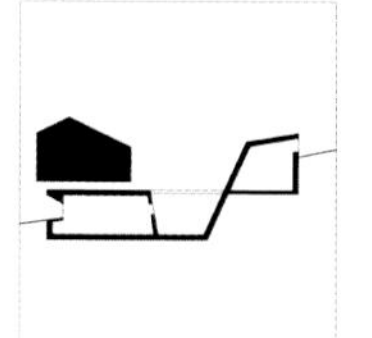

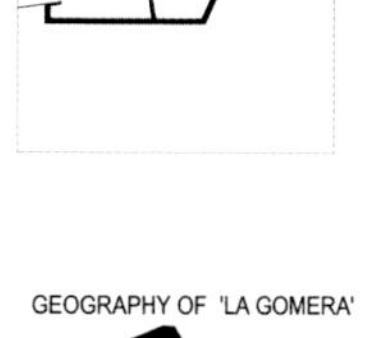

Company / Firm Name_ nodo17-architects/ Manuel Pérez Romero
Country_ Spain

Project Name_ VALLEY HOUSE
Location of Site_ Hermigua. La Gomera. Spain
Design Team_ Félix Toledo Lerín
Jaime Tarazona Lizarraga
Luis del Rey Cristóbal

Photographs_ nodo 17_ architects

Project Type_ Single Family House
Client_ Private

Site Area_ 670 sm
Built-up Area_ 264 sm

Date of completion_ (State- Executive projetct)

GEOGRAPHY OF 'LA GOMERA'

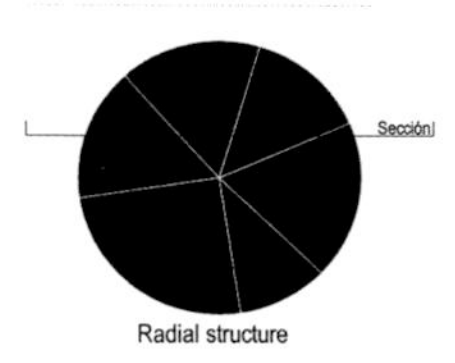

La Gomera, Ravines and Valleys

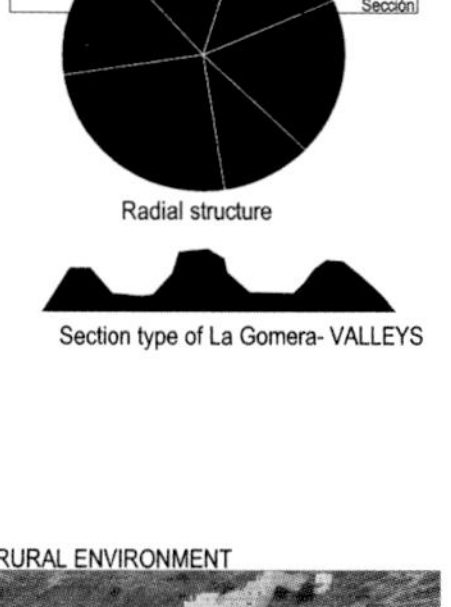

Radial structure

Section type of La Gomera- VALLEYS

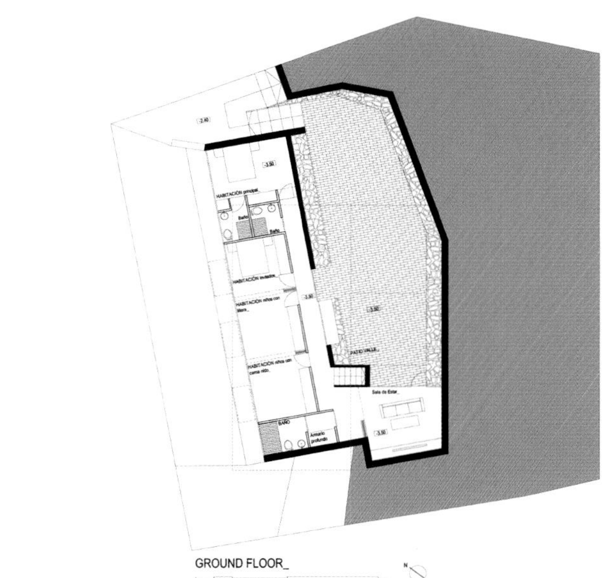

GROUND FLOOR_

IMÁGENES DE LA MAQUETA

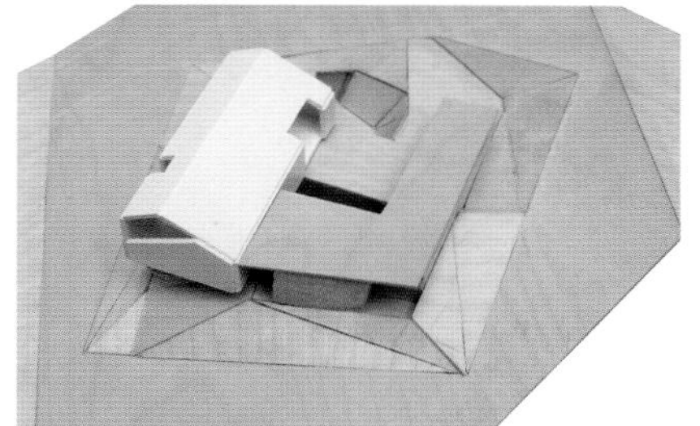

RURAL ENVIRONMENT

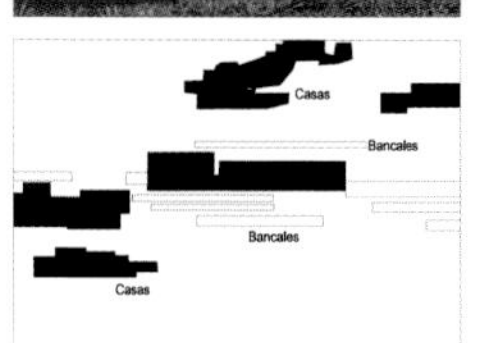

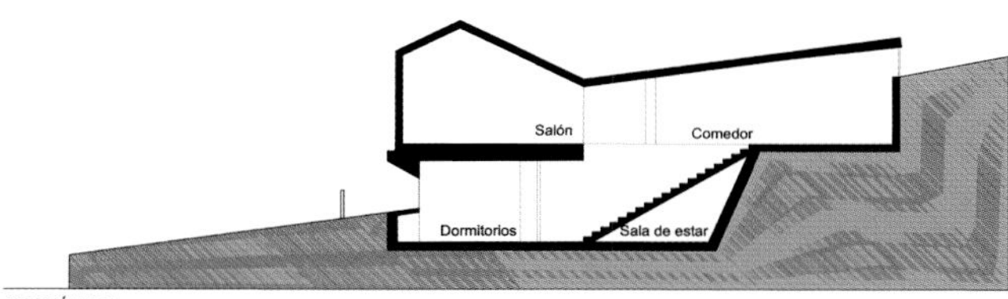

SECCIÓN BB'

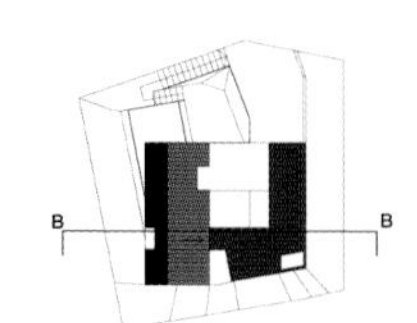

MODEL_

HOUSE AT THE EDGE OF THE VALLEY

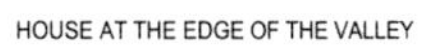

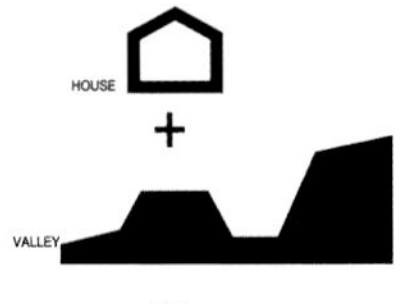

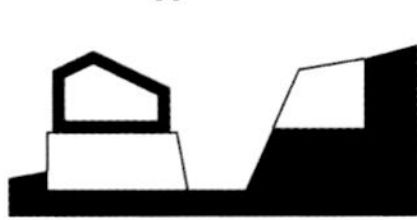

CASA AL BORDE DEL VALLE

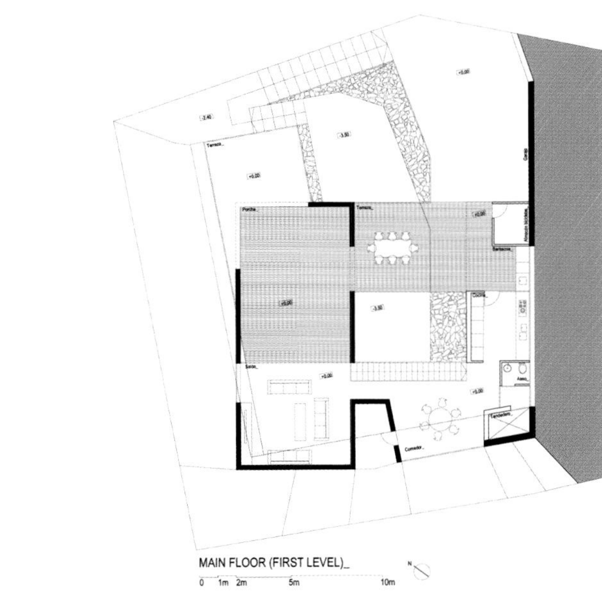

MAIN FLOOR (FIRST LEVEL)_

EXTERIOR VIEWS_

INTERIOR VIEWS_

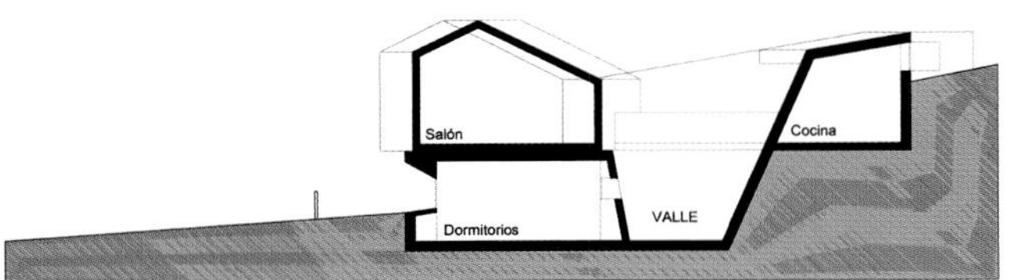

SECCIÓN AA'

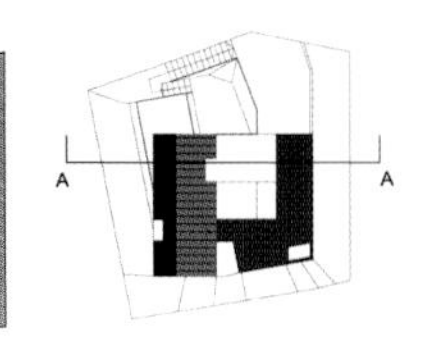

021 Y-Wing Housing | *Thurlow Small Architecture*

Project : The Plan-less House Competition Proposal
Design Team : Andrew Thurlow, Maia Small, Brandon Massey
Competition Sponsor : Shinkenchiku Residential Design Competition

Y-WING housing

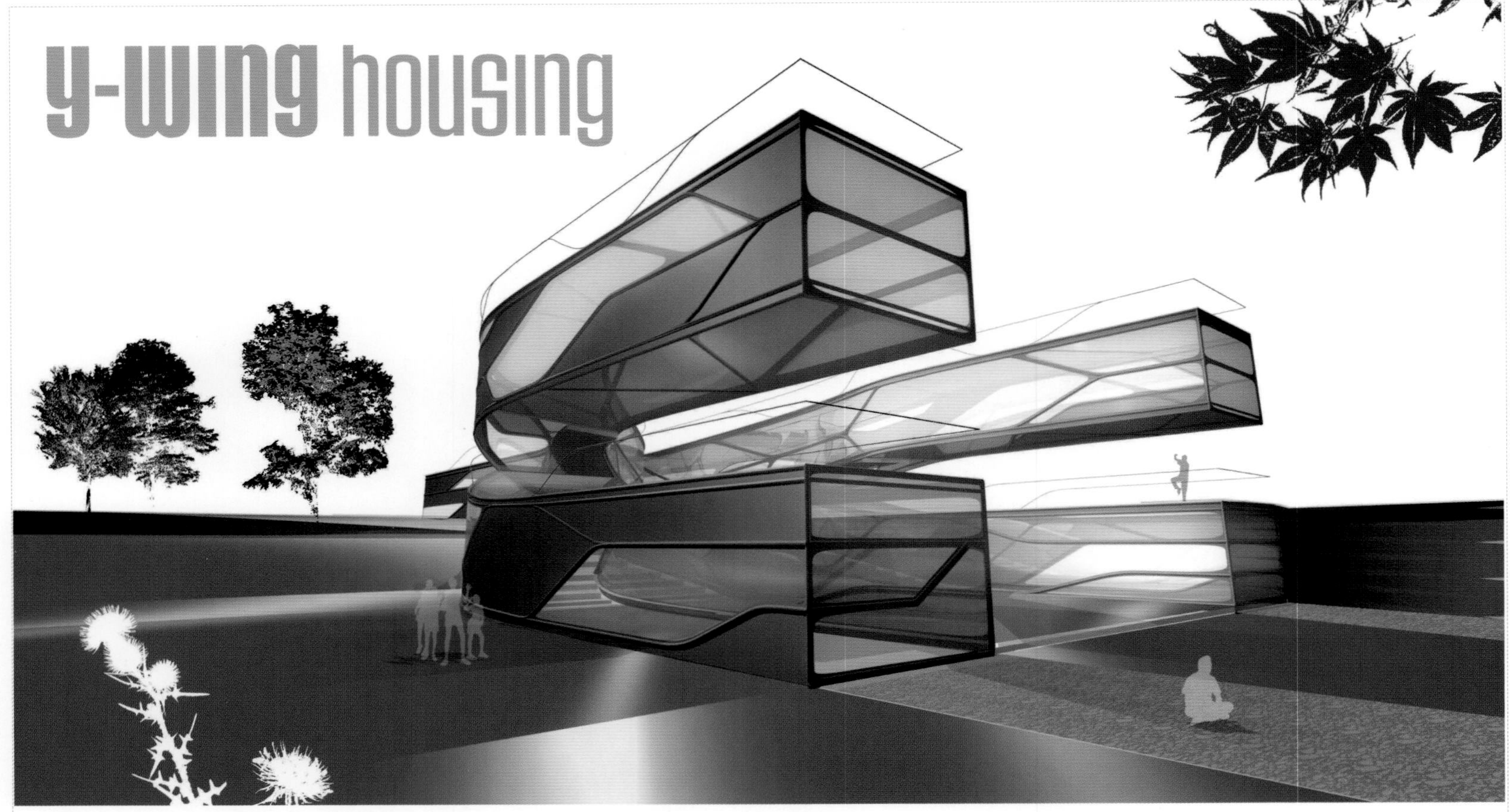

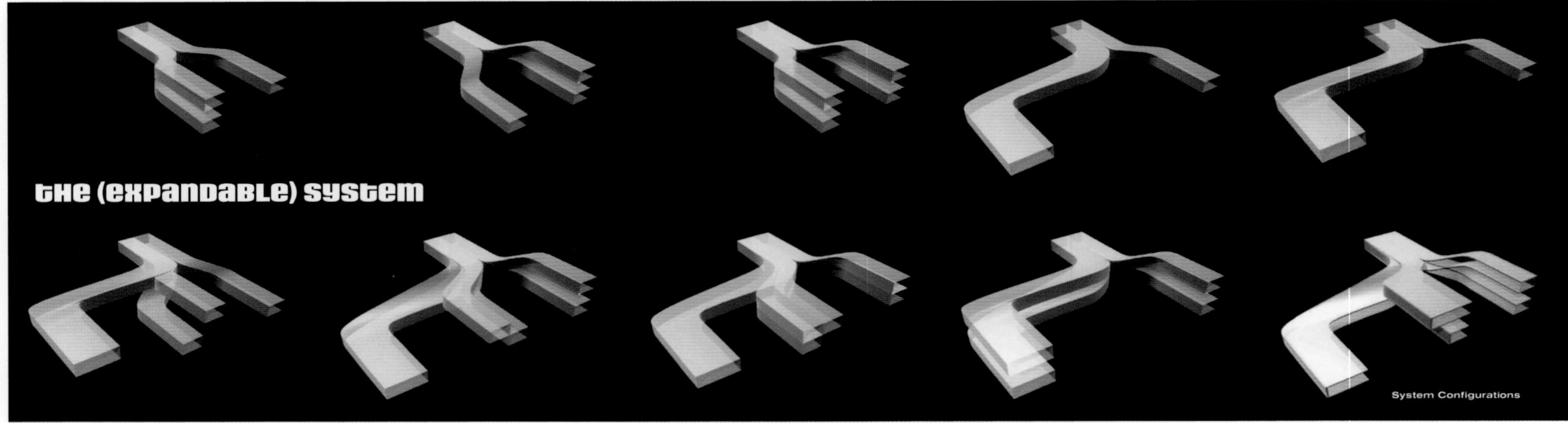

PLAN
a definition of boundary or order

"a diagram showing how something will be put in a neat, attractive, or required order"
Oxford English Dictionary

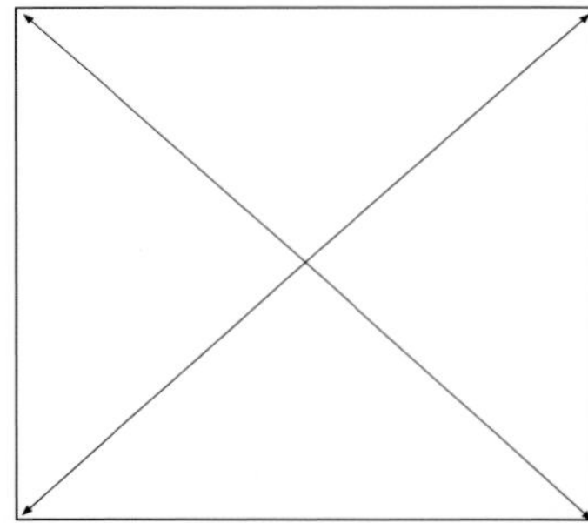

PLAN-LESS
a lack of definition of boundary or order

PLAN-NESS
the condition of defining boundaries or order

PLAN-LESS-NESS
the condition of defining no boundaries or order

PLAN-LESS-NESS

The Future is Open *(Linux ad copy)*
Despite an intention by many current political forces to promote construction of more and more definite boundaries and market globalization to steer us towards homogeneity through consolidation of land and commercial ownership, global landscapes are growing into increasingly complex layered systems, composites of cultural, economic and temporal modalities. Due to patterns of life that offer more global and less local pressures and the ease of international travel and temporary migration, contemporary culture fosters new "families" that are not longer defined only by strict racial, typological or economic categories, but cross and flex as subsequent generations increasingly embrace interracial marriage, non-married or non-reproductive couples, varieties of sexual orientation, divorce, secularism, single parent households, roommates, co-habitating multi-generational families, adoption, etc. To control these entropic environments we increasingly build gated communities, enclave business parks, privatized "public" space, viral quarantine and airport security checkpoints; we exert control over our edges, afraid of physical and psychic terrorism. We want free trade, as long as it isn't free. In reaction to this inherent contradiction, between the formation of loose social networks and the imposition of constricted spatial boundaries where existing political and economic powers quietly appropriate and coordinate public territory, our design proposes systems of variable boundary that reinforce both the natural organized blending and multiplicity of culture and natural environments. This multiplicity has the potential to create rich iterations and personal identity within common experience that requires a more variable relationship between time and space; thus, ownership, interior and exterior relationships, and living boundaries must become more flexible.

Y-Wing Housing The Y-Wing is less a specific architecture and more a system of spatial territories. The variability of the system works at two scales: the system components that allow for an infinitely expandable spatial envelop (it can infinitely extend by adding new wing that adapt to landscape: embed, rise, or fall; curl, hook or elongate) and the wall-less permeable skin system that allows for a gradation of interior and exterior: audial, visual, illumination, and air flow. The skin is not an enclosure system, it is a delineated spine of infrastructure from which water, energy, and materials flow.

Expandable System Housing must be variable: it must allow for changes within the family unit, additions of children or the elderly, subtractions of the empty nest or through death. The Y-wing does not preference a specific form, technology, or material, but instead suggests a variable individual unit that connects with other around it to create either larger units for expanding families or extended spaces for necessary use. Ownership models would need to follow this appropriation of neighboring and expanding territory-- for example, a Tenants in Common agreement or co-operative housing would allow for a series of structures to be owned together and distributed or redistributed among the various families or structures. The system itself extends arms into the landscape. These arms ride along side or conflate to create courtyard spaces and appropriate the landscape into the system of the house. Through stacking and conjoined configurations, it can figure into not only single-family housing, but multiples: apartments, row houses, and duplexes.

Permeable System The structural and programmatic lines, defined dimensionally by the modular, designate the elevation, the infrastructure, variable program, and the changing relationship between inside and outside. As planless, program is enhanced by specific spatial relationships and infrastructure availability, not defined by the architect. Openings allow for connection physically back into the landscape as well as views-- the elongated linearity drawing the inhabitant out into the landscape-- the new fenêtre longeur, if you will. Here the condition of plan-less-ness allows us to enter the exterior environment the interior environment and the exterior again at will, not as a transition, but as a seamless neutral passage in which interior and exterior are accepted simultaneously. The land forms around the house and forms it at the same time and the spaces within are shaped by the way in which one uses the outside. Space is also captured in between the volumes that is covered but not interior, cultivated but not controlled.

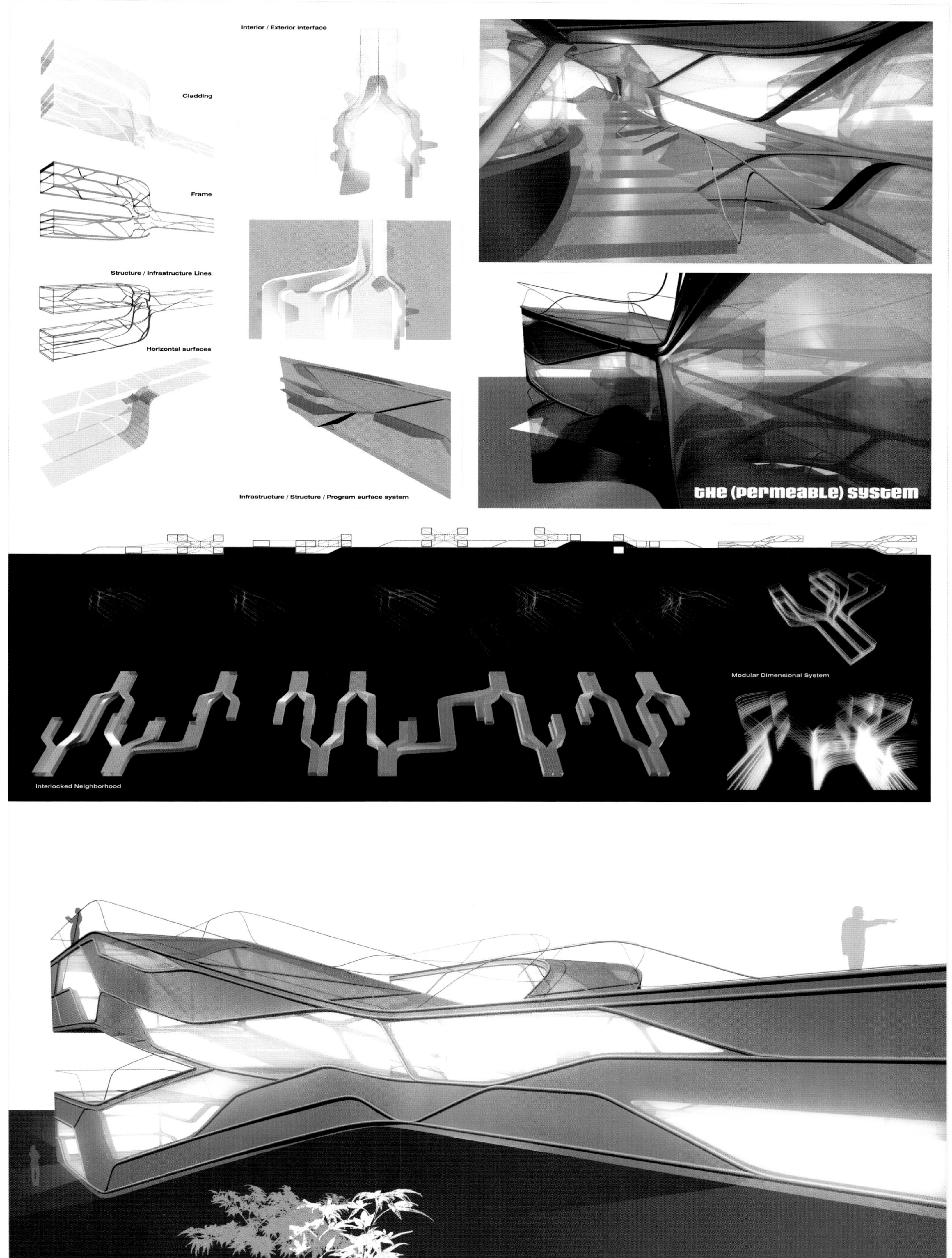
Interior / Exterior interface
Cladding
Frame
Structure / Infrastructure Lines
Horizontal surfaces
Infrastructure / Structure / Program surface system
the (permeable) system
Modular Dimensional System
Interlocked Neighborhood

022 Bubble House | *OCDC*

Project Team : Andy Ku, Kam Ku
Location : Los Angeles, USA
Typology : Single Family Housing
Size : 147m²

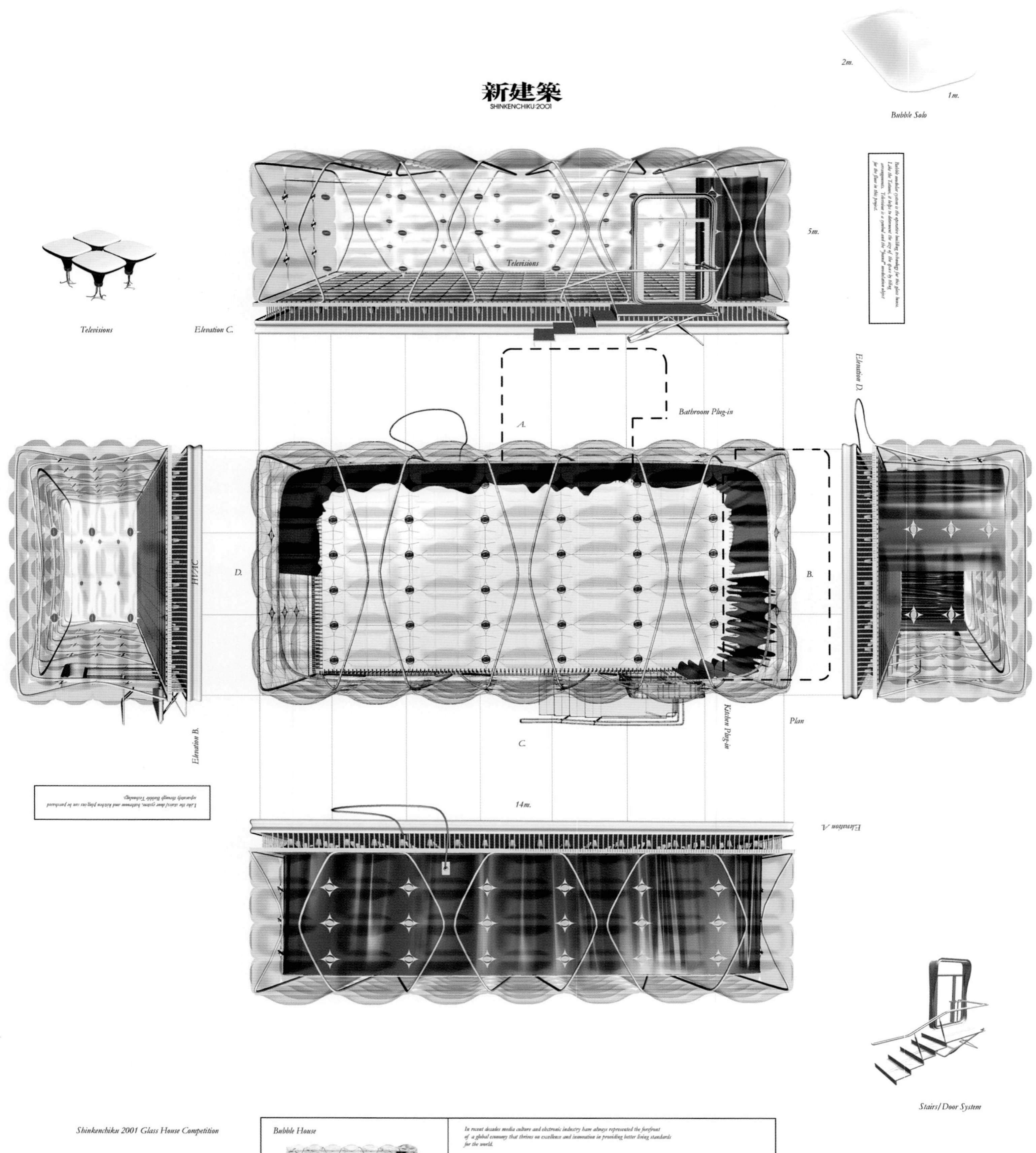

新建築
SHINKENCHIKU 2001
2m.
1m.
Bubble Solo
5m.
Televisions
Televisions
Elevation C.
Elevation D.
Bathroom Plug-in
A.
D.
HVAC
B.
C.
Kitchen Plug-in
Plan
Elevation B.
14m.
Elevation A.
Stairs/Door System
Shinkenchiku 2001 Glass House Competition
Bubble House
In recent decades media culture and electronic industry have always represented the forefront
of a global economy that thrives on excellence and innovation in providing better living standards
for the world.
The bubble house glorifies this economic phenomenon with a glass module configured space
that fills the entire floor with television monitors. This envelope formed by repetitive glass modules
contains a flexible space plan that is designed to anticipate different living arrangements.
The intent/experience of visual distortion/fragmentation through glass bubbles can be seen
as projections/reflections of multiple visions from within of the inviting sky above.

Car Park Housing | *OCDC*

Project Team : Andy Ku, Kam Ku, Olivia Ku
Location : Los Angeles, USA
Typology : Multi-family Housing
Size : Entire Site – 4,180 m² / Single Unit – 114 m²

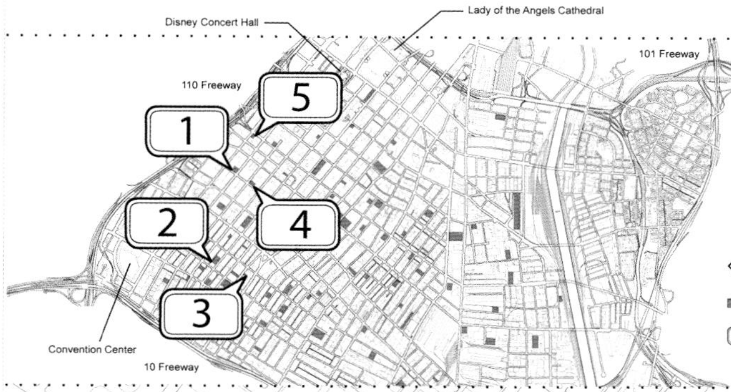

Disney Concert Hall
Lady of the Angels Cathedral
101 Freeway
110 Freeway
Convention Center
10 Freeway

Aerial map of dowtown Los Angeles:
A city surrounded by freeway systems

Indicates parking infrastructure locations
[parking garages and parking lots]

Indicates illustrated site examples [1-5]
see below from left to right

Shinkenchiku Central Glass Competition 2006

Car Park Housing

Decades of decentralization and lessened reliance on the downtown as a major hub for business and commerce has left behind a unique brand of modern infrastructure for Los Angeles that was widely constructed since and before the 1960s. This proposal seeks to transform the existing function of parking garages from car storage into a new solution for multi-housing facility.

The concept for Car Park housing does not eliminate the role of automobile as megalopolis connector. In fact, it relies on the power of spatial negotiation and car manufacturing technology to produce an emergent housing typology that remembers the past and performs all that is possible for the immediate future of Los Angeles.

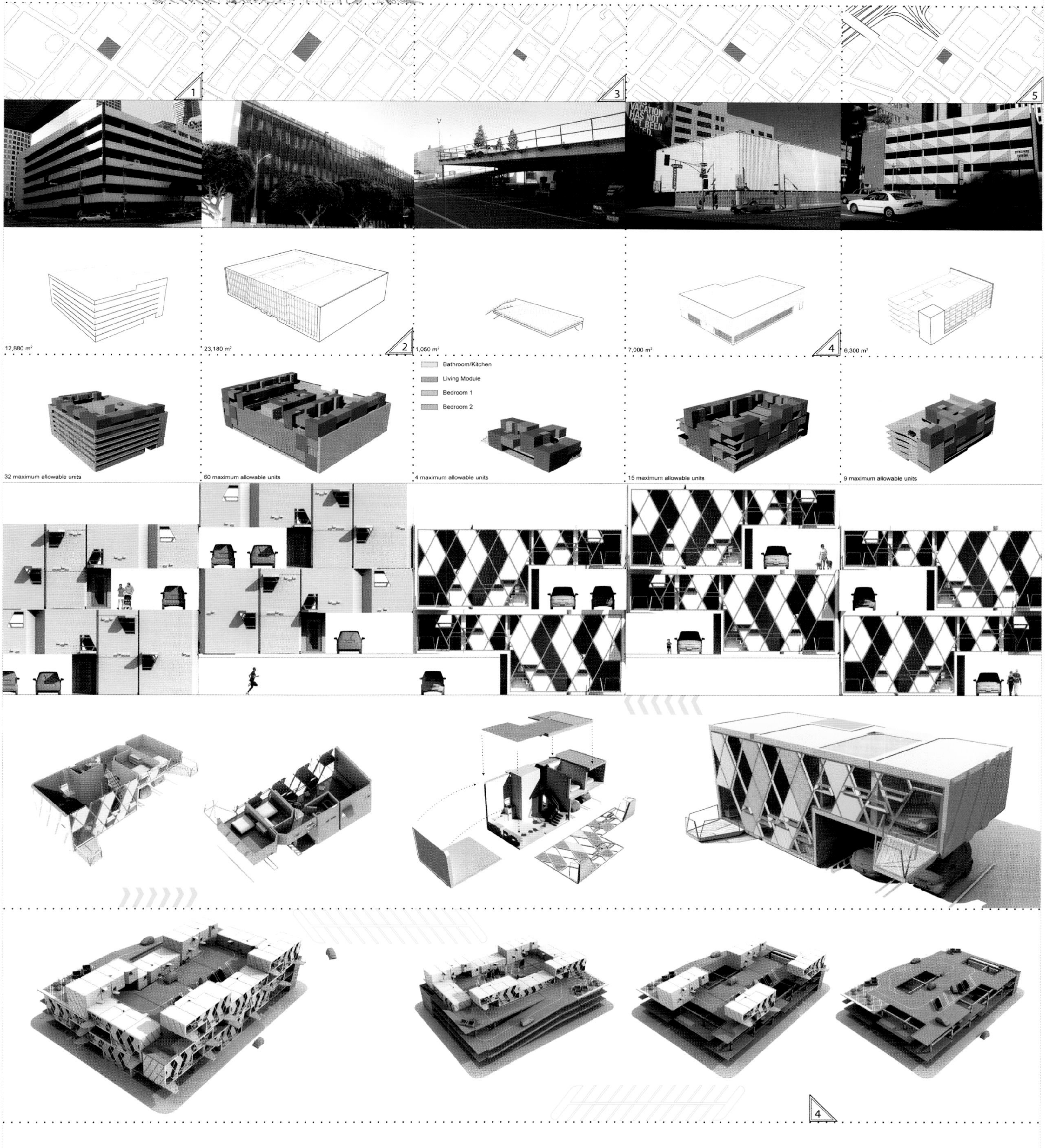

12,880 m²
23,180 m²
1,050 m²
7,000 m²
6,300 m²

Bathroom/Kitchen
Living Module
Bedroom 1
Bedroom 2

32 maximum allowable units
60 maximum allowable units
4 maximum allowable units
15 maximum allowable units
9 maximum allowable units

024 Butterfly House | *Donner Sorcinelli Architecture*

Location : Gapyeong, South Korea
Area : 866 sq.m / Built surface : 207 sq.m

Butterfly House
site_Gapyeong, South Korea year_2010 program_housing (no. 2 apartments) built surface_217 sq.m.

Donner Sorcinelli Architecture
Via Roma 51_31057 Silea (TV)_Italy
phone-fax_+390422363551
studio@donner-sorcinelli.it
www.doso.it

1

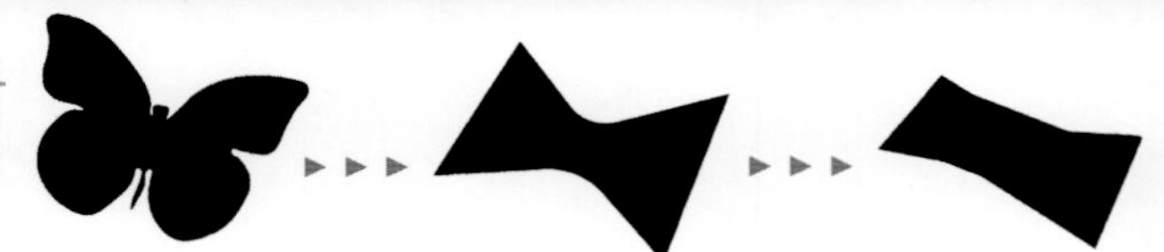

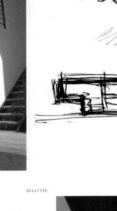

winter prevailing winds

closed barrier

summer prevailing breezes

wind collector system

winter

summer

natural ventilation

Butterfly House

site_Gapyeong, South Korea year_2010 program_housing (no. 2 apartments) built surface_217 sq.m.

Donner Sorcinelli Architecture
Via Roma 51_31057 Silea (TV)_Italy
phone-fax_+390422363551
studio@donner-sorcinelli.it
www.doso.it

2

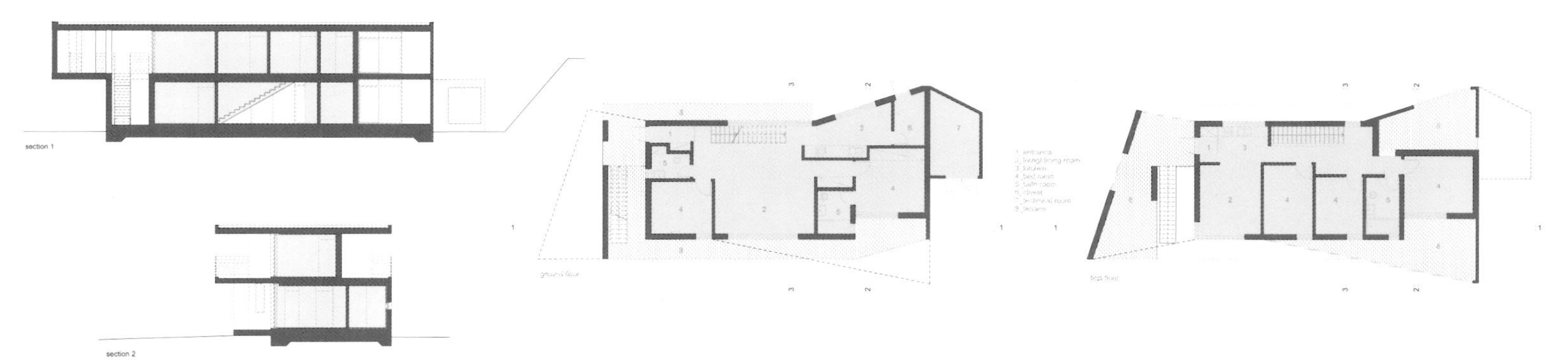

025 California Senior Housing | *Slot.*

Location : USA, California, Novato, Bahia Driveway / Topaz Driveway / Misty Road
Program : 26 Housing Units of approx. 90m² each, Retail Facilities, Public Areas
Client : Suburban Alternatives Land Trust & Northbay Family Homes
Construction Area : 6.3 ha

Design Concept
Center point of the design proposal is the concern for a unique and innovative design, which – despite its horizontal development – appears as a landmark.
The project is composed of numerous apparently homogenous boxes appearing as "shooting stars". They are formally contrasting to the most possible extend with the existing residential houses, while functionally intend to integrate into and complement the existing residential zone.
Social Integration
Basic principal for the new residential development is the concept of mixed uses (integration of small commercial units) as much as the prospected demand allows.
Each residential unit has an adjunct terraced garden for small-scale food production. Rather than a competitive business, this is to be understood as an occupational therapy for senior citizens. Products are sold in the "Senior Market" located at the most frequented corner between Topaz Drive and Bahia Drive. This market will provide the complete area with fresh fruits and vegetables and interlace the new residents with the existing local community.
Private Terrace
Aux
2B
S
Access Plaza
1B
Cross Section
Misty Road Extension
R
Community Plaza
Misty Road Parcel (B)
Community Plan 1"=50
Local Plaza
New Road Development
Local Plaza
Misty Road Parcel (B)

143 TOP

Bahia Driveway

Bahia Drive Parcel (A)

Topaz Driveway

Commercial Unit

Access Plaza

Private Terrace

Market Plaza

Senior Market

Cross Section

R

1B

2B

S

Aux

Modules

Module	Unit Number
Studio (S)	7
One Bedroom (1B)	9
Two Bedroom (2B)	3
Auxiliary (AUX)	10
Small Retail Store (R)	3
Medium Retail Store (R)	2
Small Office (R)	2
Green Terrace	19
Street	1
Plaza	11

RESIDENTIAL

COMMERCIAL

Area Chart

sq ft / unit	total sq ft
841	5,887
1,024	9,216
1,225	3,675
841	8,410
841	2,523
1,024	2,048
841	1,682
TOTAL CONSTRUCTED AREAS	33,441
1,075	20,425
24,725	24,725
3,917	43,087
TOTAL OUTDOOR AREAS	88,237
TOTAL ALL AREAS	121,678

Cost Chart (No prevailing Wages were used)

USD/ sq ft	USD/ unit	USD total
128.17 $	107,787.85 $	754,514.98 $
128.17 $	131,240.99 $	1,181,168.91 $
128.17 $	156,998.05 $	470,994.17 $
128.17 $	107,787.85 $	1,077,878.54 $
124.47 $	104,677.12 $	314,031.35 $
124.47 $	127,453.40 $	254,906.80 $
124.47 $	104,677.12 $	209,354.23 $
TOTAL CONSTRUCTED COSTS		4,262,848.96 $
4.18 $	4,498.15 $	85,388.85 $
68.00 $	1,681,318.72 $	1,681,318.72 $
68.00 $	266,358,97 $	2,929,948.68 $
TOTAL OUTDOOR COSTS		4,696,656.25 $
TOTAL ALL COSTS		8,959,505.21 $

Cross-Section in North-South Direction

Sustainability and Energy Concept

Apart from its social sustainability, the new development will have many ecological features, which classify it as sustainable such as the rainwater collection underneath every housing unit, which catches up with the unequal distribution of rain during the year, and an integrated household grey water system. This water will be used for irrigation of the terraced gardens attached to each housing unit.

In order to accomplish with the zero net energy goal, the building's façade is composed of a surface area that is almost totally covered with PV panels—single-crystal silicon on the roof, thin-film copper indium gallium diselenide on the sides. This façade can easily produce even more than a 100% of the prospected energy consumption.

A wood frame structure with phase-change material in the drywall creates highly insulating exterior walls, which maintain comfortable temperatures in the interior all year around. The new development will meet all necessary LEED energy certification standards.

4 to 5 Units around a Plaza

Private Terrace
Auxiliary Unit
2-Bedroom Unit
Private Terrace
Access from Street
Plaza on one Level
1-Bedroom Unit
2-Bedroom Unit
Auxiliary Unit
Private Terrace
Private Terrace
Private Terrace

Distribution by Program

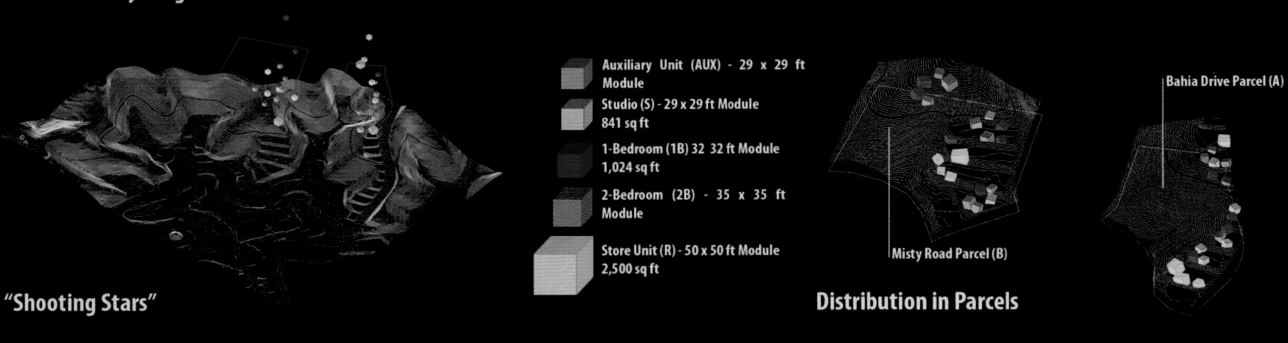

"Shooting Stars"

Distribution in Parcels

Misty Road Elevat

143

View from within Misty Road Parcel

Conceptual Diagrams

Site

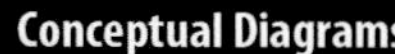

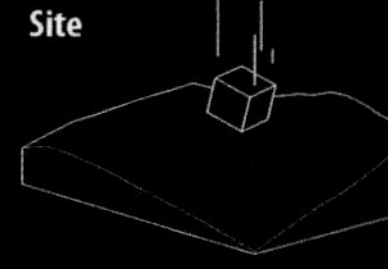

The housing program "falls" to any given site. Flexible to adapt the concept anywhere.

Slope Adjustment

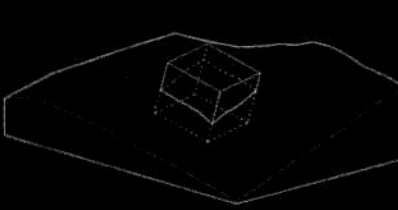

Just like a stone falling into sand, the houses adjust to the existing topography.

Excavation

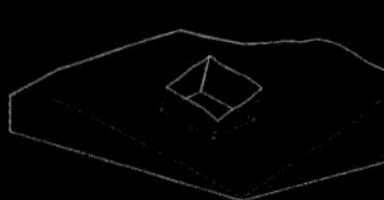

An excavation allows rainwater collection underneath each building.

Filling

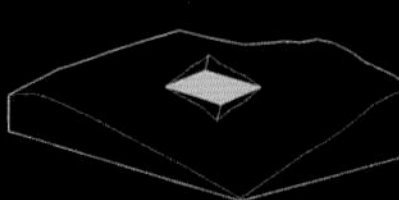

Consideration of plain floors in order to meet needs for seniors and ADA.

Transparency of Views

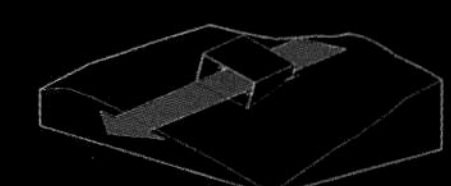

No interior walls reach the ceiling. This allows for an uninterrupted perception of the space.

Access Plaza

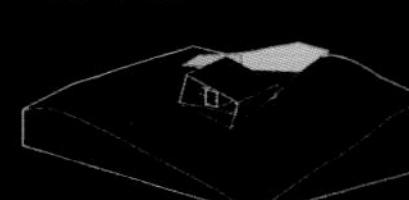

3 or more modules form an access plaza. This plaza connects the group of houses to the street.

Structure

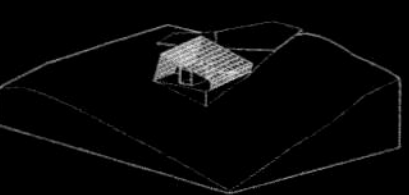

Wood frames structure the building.

Building Skin

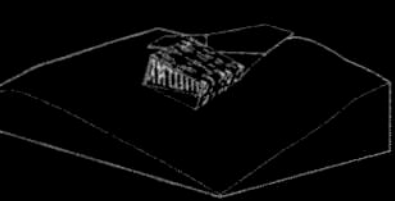

A modular solar panel skin is proposed to gain energy.

Projection

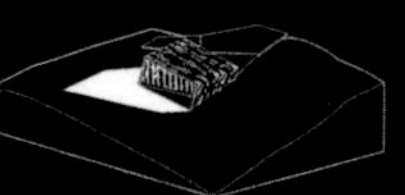

Projection of shadows mark the area for a private garden.

Terraces

Terraces for local food production result from the continuation of topographic lines.

Flexibility

The housing units have a simple and logical distribution of its program by respecting plain floors, which make stairs unnecessary.

This makes them highly flexible for their users. No interior walls reach the ceiling. This allows for an uninterrupted perception of the space.

Unit with 2 bedrooms

1,225 square feet

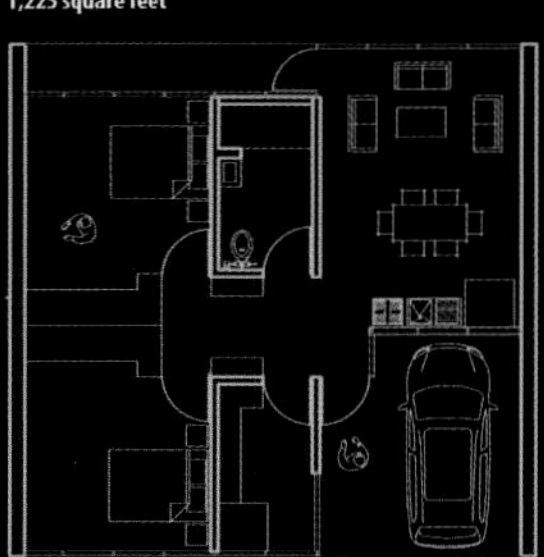

Unit with 1 Bedroom

1,024 square feet

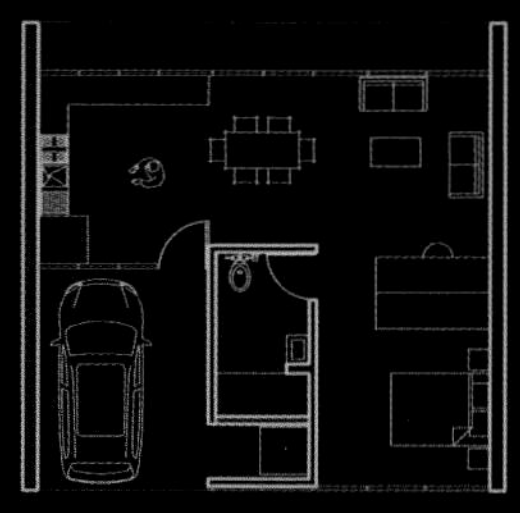

Unit Studio/ Auxiliary Unit

841 square feet

er Bahia Drive

Bahia Drive Elevation

026

Dingbat Trio | *OCDC*

Project Team : Juan Azcarate, Andy Ku, Kam Ku, Kin-Tak Yu
Location : Los Angeles, USA
Typology : Multi-family Housing
Size : Entire Site – 16,800 m²

Site /

Dingbats /

Slab Tectonics /

The Dingbat 2.0 is defined as character design and spatial typologies

Dingbat Field

This project approaches the Dingbat construction as a series of ever-expandable agencies yielding to spatial and economic logic. There are three main characters performing as housing typologies that generate the overall system: Stack Waffle, Vertical hut, and Drift Paradise. Each option and arrangement would facilitate multiple existing lifestyles and speculate on well-fitted forms for habitation. A horizontal slab emerges as the horizontal binding agent to connect the three characters into one ad hoc entity. The slab produces shared public zones that hybridize different usages and programs. This Dingbat field is designed to grow progressively and is calibrated to coexist with the current typology on site, furthermore, it is seeking to transform the Dingbat into a more urbanized identity.

The consideration for building each individual Dingbat probes the prefab culture and industrial design as a departure for research on possible material and assembly methods. Each unit and the sum of its parts are engineered to establish interchangeability and cross-characterized intelligence for the demand of various consumption desires and needs. The planning for parking and nature-scape are also priorities for establishing the character design and spatial logic for this Dingbat field. They are valued based upon degrees of physical proximity in relation to the actual living quarters and privacy. It is a spatial and material phenomenon generated by the constant demand for more open space and mobility in our world. This Dingbat field is a direct reflection on the current with a heightened supposition as our proposal.

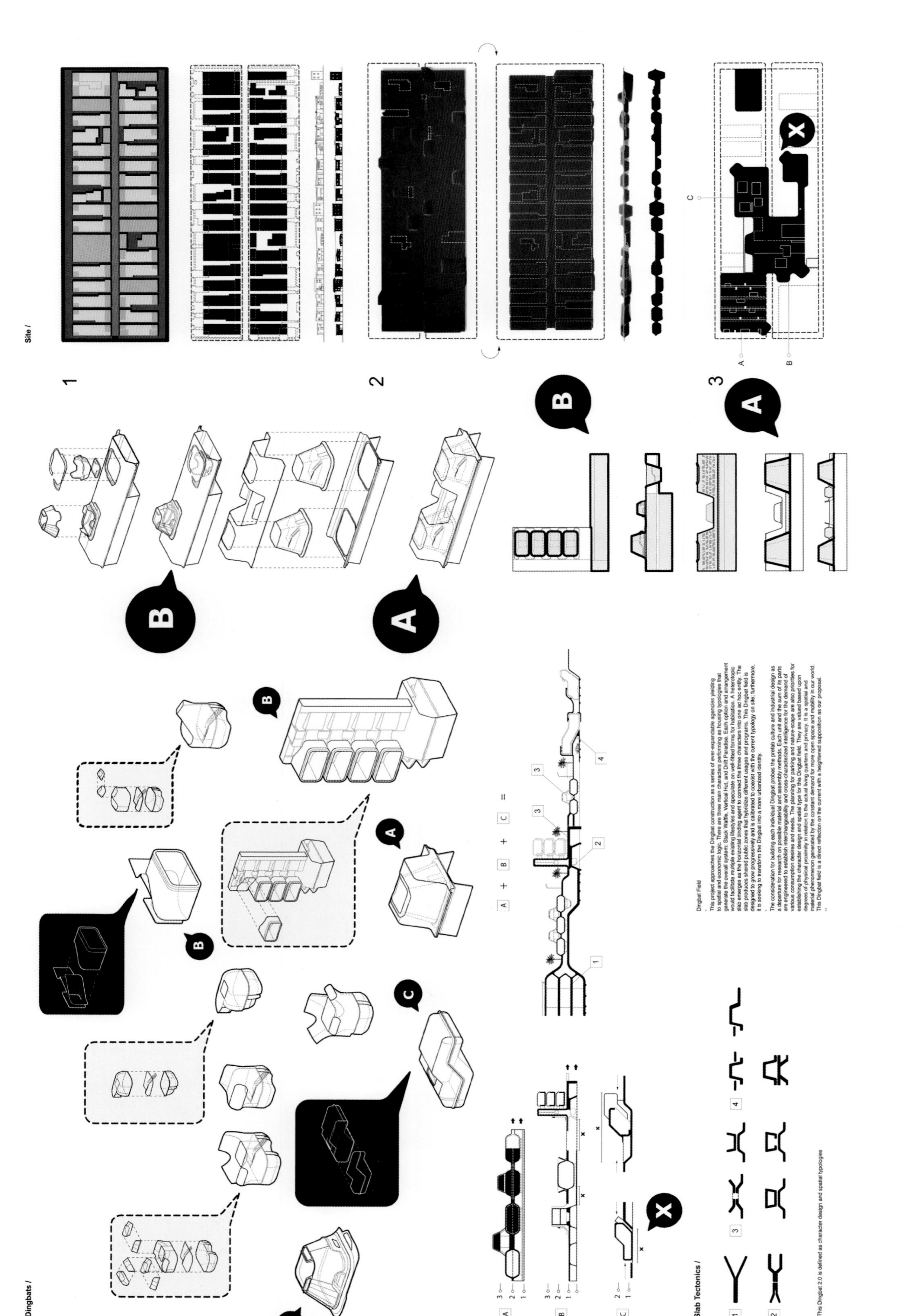

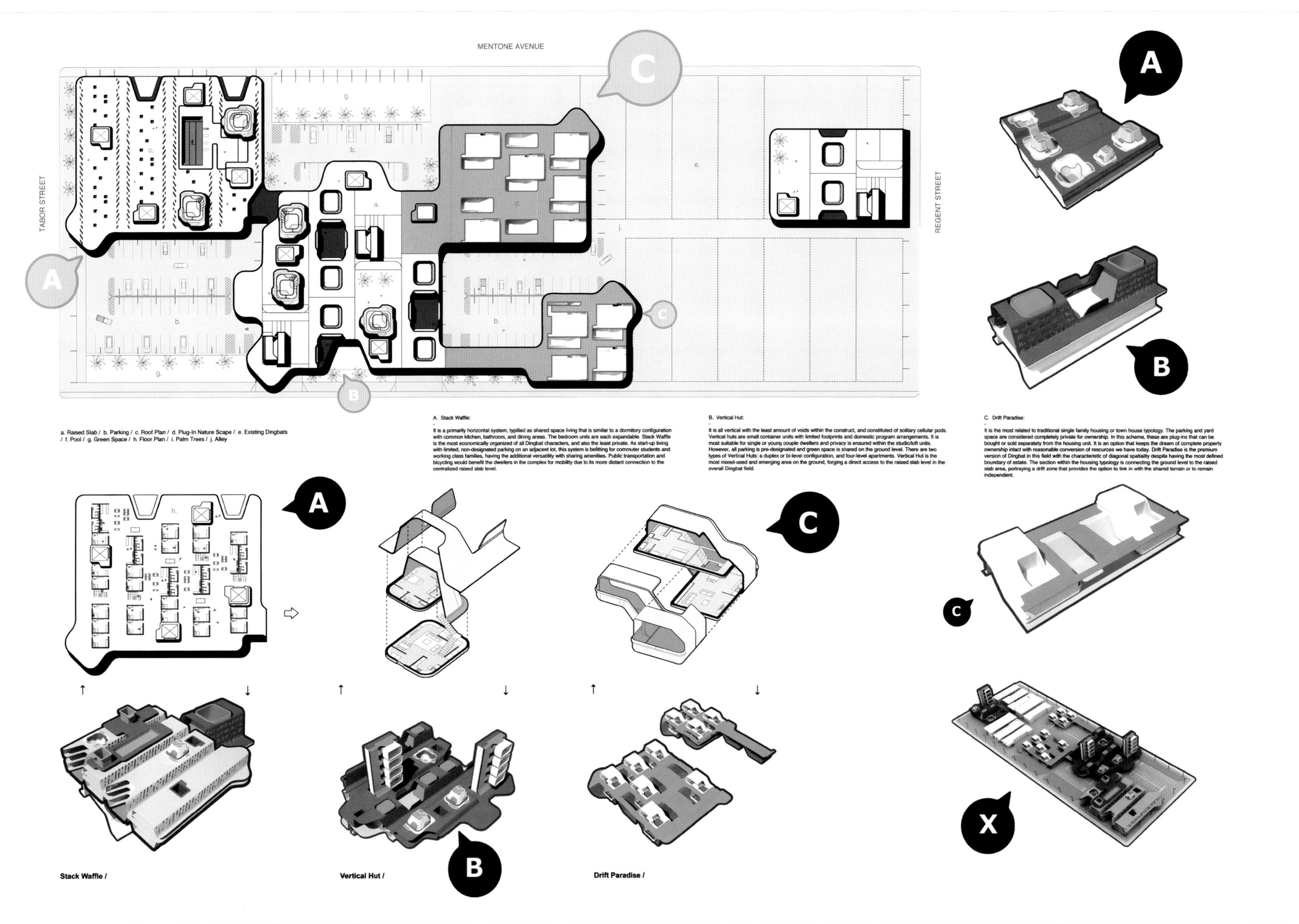

a. Raised Slab / b. Parking / c. Roof Plan / d. Plug-In Nature Scape / e. Existing Dingbats / f. Pool / g. Green Space / h. Floor Plan / i. Palm Trees / j. Alley

A. Stack Waffle:

-

It is a primarily horizontal system, typified as shared space living that is similar to a dormitory configuration with common kitchen, bathroom, and dining areas. The bedroom units are each expandable. Stack Waffle is the most economically organized of all Dingbat characters, and also the least private. As start-up living with limited, non-designated parking on an adjacent lot, this system is befitting for commuter students and working class families, having the additional versatility with sharing amenities. Public transportation and bicycling would benefit the dwellers in the complex for mobility due to its more distant connection to the centralized raised slab level.

B. Vertical Hut:

-

It is all vertical with the least amount of voids within the construct, and constituted of solitary cellular pods. Vertical huts are small container units with limited footprints and domestic program arrangements. It is most suitable for single or young couple dwellers and privacy is ensured within the studio/loft units. However, all parking is pre-designated and green space is shared on the ground level. There are two types of Vertical Huts: a duplex or bi-level configuration, and four-level apartments. Vertical Hut is the most mixed-used and emerging area on the ground, forging a direct access to the raised slab level in the overall Dingbat field.

C. Drift Paradise:

-

It is the most related to traditional single family housing or town house typology. The parking and yard space are considered completely private for ownership. In this scheme, these are plug-ins that can be bought or sold separately from the housing unit. It is an option that keeps the dream of complete property ownership intact with reasonable conversion of resources we have today. Drift Paradise is the premium version of Dingbat in this field with the characteristic of diagonal spatiality despite having the most defined boundary of estate. The section within the housing typology is connecting the ground level to the raised slab area, portraying a drift zone that provides the option to link in with the shared terrain or to remain independent.

027 Housing Estate in Zabrze | *ZALEWSKI ARCHITECTURE GROUP*

Participants : Krzysztof Zalewski, Adam Gil, Paweł Zalewski, Grzegorz Ziębik, Dorota Kniażewska
Typology : Residential buildings

Location : Zabrze, Poland
Construction Volume : 400,320 m²

PROJEKT KONCEPCYJNY
OSIEDLA MIESZKANIOWEGO
W ZABRZU

AUTORZY:
ZALEWSKI ARCHITECTURE GROUP
UL. KOŚCIUSZKI 30/9
44-100 GLIWICE

INWESTOR:
GPBP S.A.
UL. PLAC PIASTÓW 10
GLIWICE

ZALEWSKI
ARCHITECTURE GROUP

PROJEKT KONCEPCYJNY
OSIEDLA MIESZKANIOWEGO
W ZABRZU

AUTORZY:
ZALEWSKI ARCHITECTURE GROUP
UL. KOŚCIUSZKI 30/9
44-100 GLIWICE

INWESTOR:
GPBP S.A.
UL. PLAC PIASTÓW 10
GLIWICE

ZALEWSKI
ARCHITECTURE GROUP

BILANS TERENU

1.	POWIERZCHNIA DZIAŁKI	~14 017,00 m²
2.	POWIERZCHNIA ZABUDOWY BUDYNKU Z WEJŚCIEM OD POŁUDNIA (4 LOKALE MIESZKANIOWE)	215,18 m²
	POWIERZCHNIA ZABUDOWY BUDYNKU Z WEJŚCIEM OD PÓŁNOCY(4 LOKALE MIESZKANIOWE)	204,94 m²
3.	POWIERZCHNIA ZABUDOWY ŁĄCZNIE	2619,77 m²
4.	LICZBA MIESZKAŃ	50
5.	POWIERZCHNIA UŻYTKOWA MIESZKAŃ ŁĄCZNIE	4182,40 m²
6.	LICZBA MIEJSC PARKINGOWYCH	81
7.	POWIERZCHNIE POSZCZEGÓLNYCH MIESZKAŃ	

LP	TYP MIESZKANIA	POWIERZCHNIA UŻYTKOWA MIESZKAŃ	POWIERZCHNIA OGRÓDKA	ILOŚĆ POKOI W MIESZKANIU	ILOŚĆ MIESZKAŃ
a)	TYP 1	95,5 m²	~118,0	4	10
b)	TYP 2/ TYP 2B	80,3 m²	~60/60,0	3/3	5/5
c)	TYP 3/ TYP 3B/ TYP 3C	86,6 m²/79,4 m²/86,8 m²	~116,5/59,0/146,5	3/3/3	8/8/8
d)	TYP 4	67,0 m²	~61,0	2	6

SCHEMATY UKŁADU URBANISTYCZNEGO SKALA 1:2000

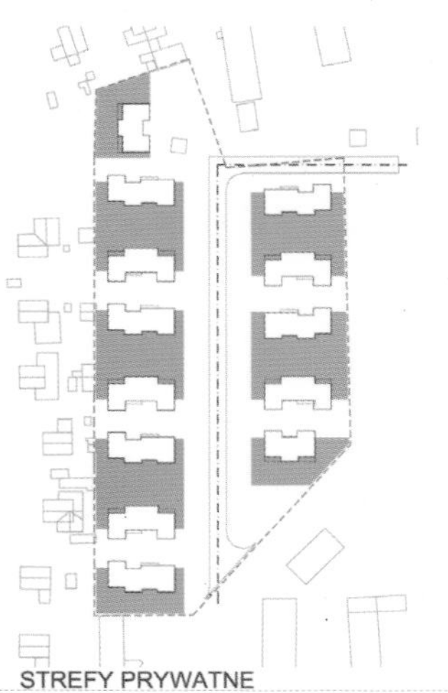

STREFY PRYWATNE

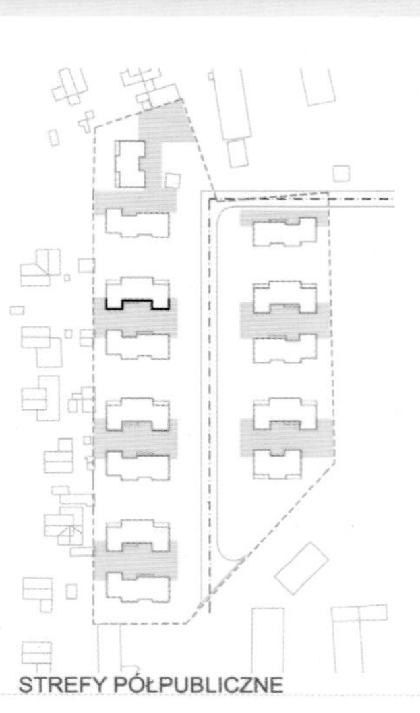

STREFY PÓŁPUBLICZNE

ZABUDOWA ORAZ WTÓRNY PODZIAŁ DZIAŁEK

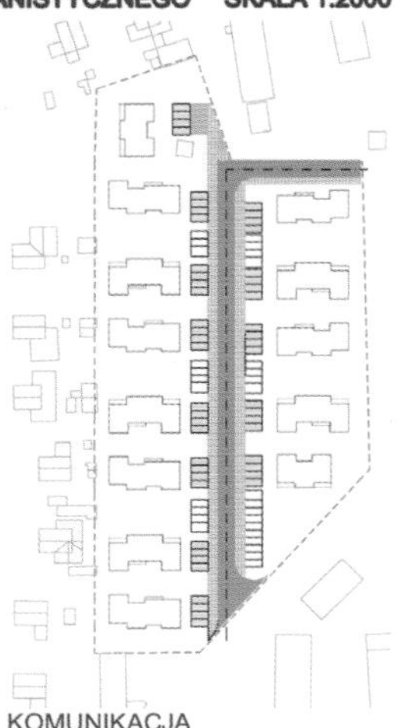

KOMUNIKACJA

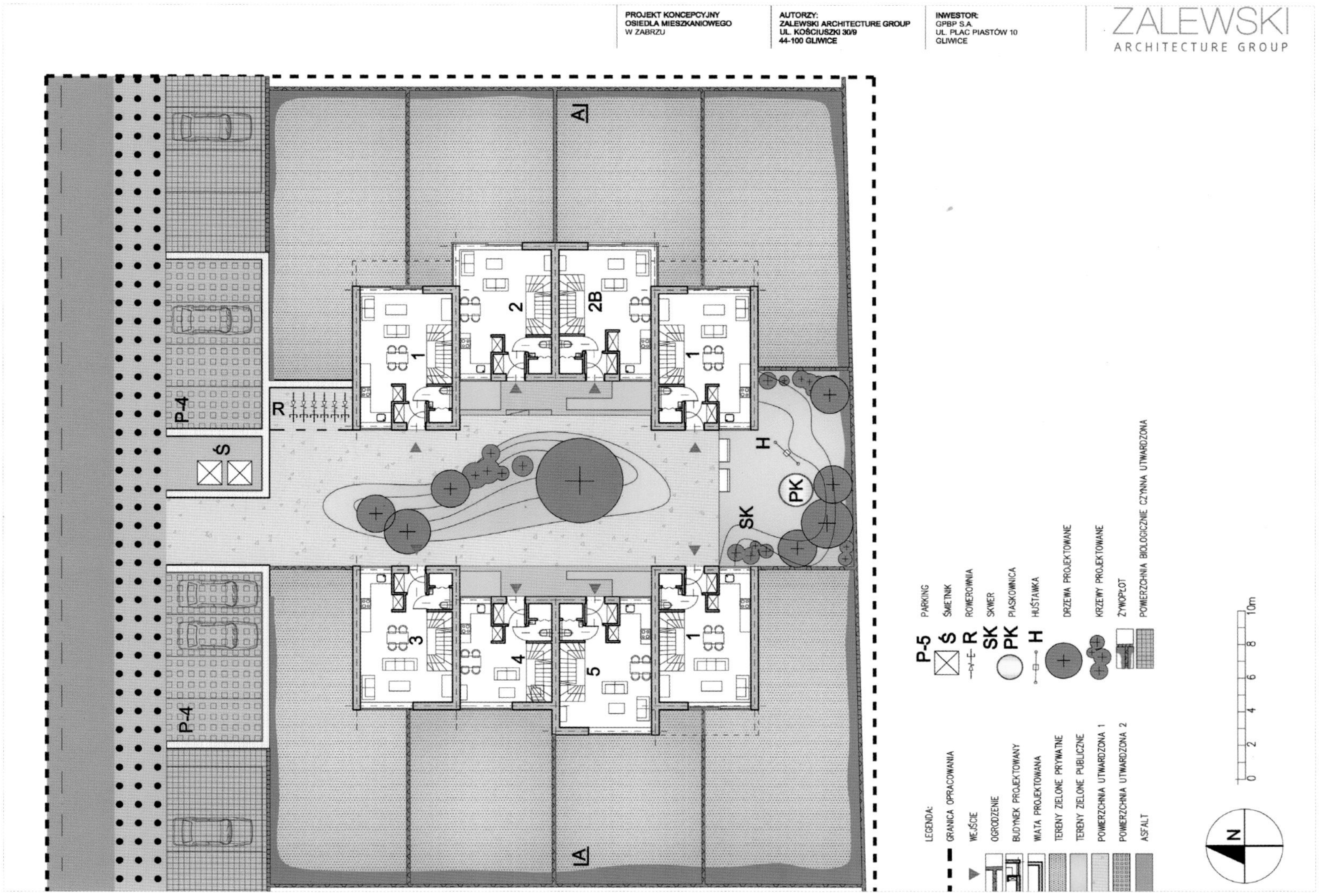

PROJEKT KONCEPCYJNY
OSIEDLA MIESZKANIOWEGO
W ZABRZU

AUTORZY:
ZALEWSKI ARCHITECTURE GROUP
UL. KOŚCIUSZKI 30/9
44-100 GLIWICE

INWESTOR:
GPBP S.A.
UL. PLAC PIASTÓW 10
GLIWICE

ZALEWSKI
ARCHITECTURE GROUP

LEGENDA:
GRANICA OPRACOWANIA
WEJŚCIE
OGRODZENIE
BUDYNEK PROJEKTOWANY
WIATA PROJEKTOWANA
TERENY ZIELONE PRYWATNE
TERENY ZIELONE PUBLICZNE
POWIERZCHNIA UTWARDZONA 1
POWIERZCHNIA UTWARDZONA 2
ASFALT

P-5 PARKING
Ś ŚMIETNIK
R ROWEROWNIA
SK SKWER
PK PIASKOWNICA
H HUŚTAWKA
DRZEWA PROJEKTOWANE
KRZEWY PROJEKTOWANE
ŻYWOPŁOT
POWIERZCHNIA BIOLOGICZNIE CZYNNA UTWARDZONA

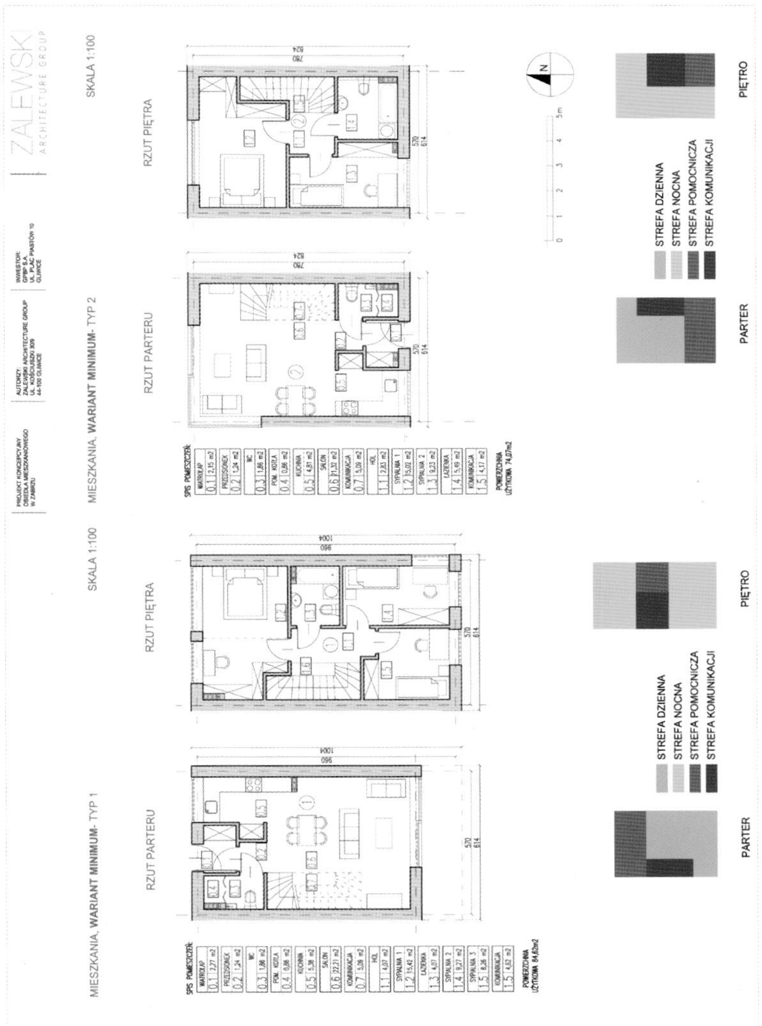

MIESZKANIA. WARIANT MINIMUM- TYP 1
SKALA 1:100
RZUT PARTERU
RZUT PIĘTRA

MIESZKANIA. WARIANT MINIMUM- TYP 2
SKALA 1:100
RZUT PARTERU
RZUT PIĘTRA

STREFA DZIENNA
STREFA NOCNA
STREFA POMOCNICZA
STREFA KOMUNIKACJI

PARTER
PIĘTRO

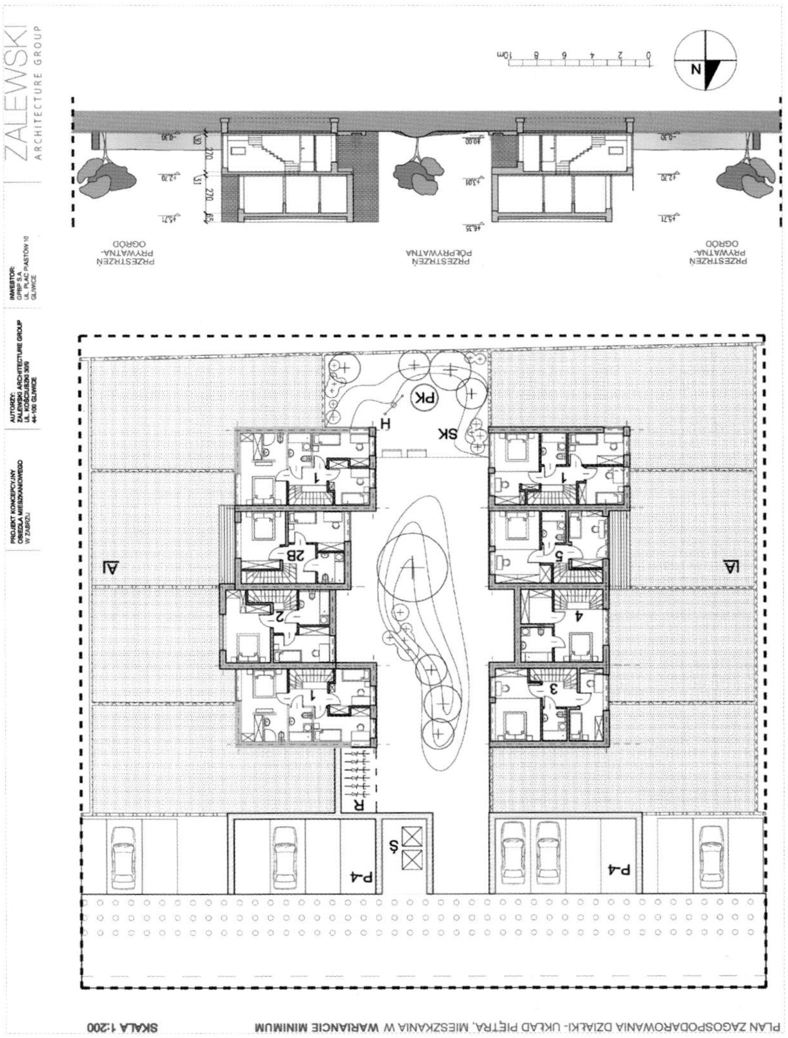

PRZESTRZEŃ PRYWATNA- OGRÓD
PRZESTRZEŃ PÓŁPRYWATNA
PRZESTRZEŃ PRYWATNA- OGRÓD

PLAN ZAGOSPODAROWANIA DZIAŁKI- UKŁAD PIĘTRA, MIESZKANIA W WARIANCIE MINIMUM
SKALA 1:200

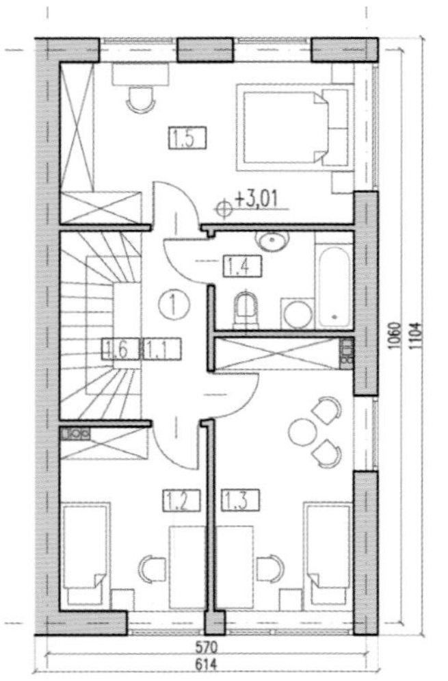

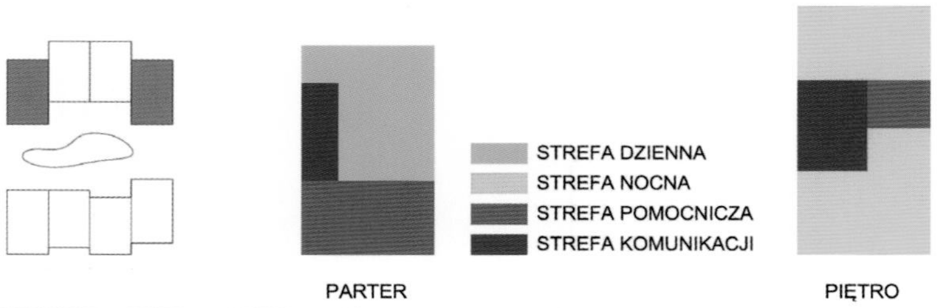

PROJEKT KONCEPCYJNY
OSIEDLA MIESZKANIOWEGO
W ZABRZU

AUTORZY:
ZALEWSKI ARCHITECTURE GROUP
UL. KOŚCIUSZKI 30/9
44-100 GLIWICE

INWESTOR:
GPBP S.A.
UL. PLAC PIASTÓW 10
GLIWICE

ZALEWSKI
ARCHITECTURE GROUP

SCHEMAT ALTERNATYWNYCH UKŁADÓW MIESZKAŃ

MOŻLIWE WARIANTY

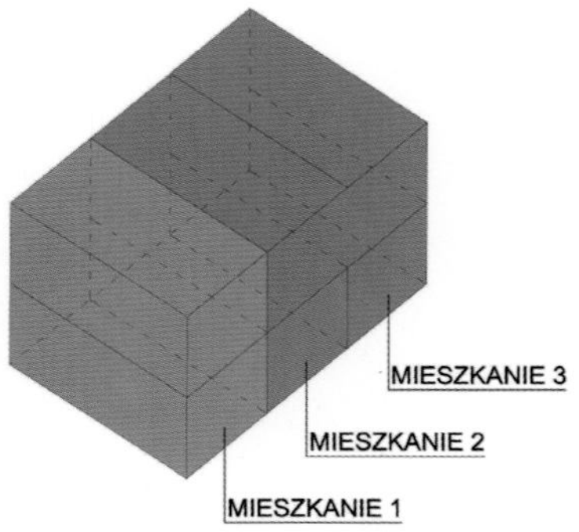

MIESZKANIE 3
MIESZKANIE 2
MIESZKANIE 1

MOŻLIWE POWIĘKSZANIE LUB ZMNIEJSZANIE POWIERZCHNI

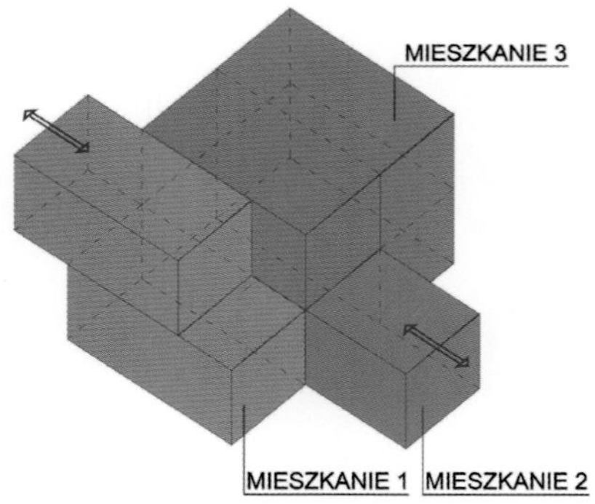

MIESZKANIE 3
MIESZKANIE 1
MIESZKANIE 2

ELASTYCZNA KONFIGURACJA POWIERZCHNI

MIESZKANIE- TYP 1

SKALA 1:100

RZUT PARTERU

RZUT PIĘTRA

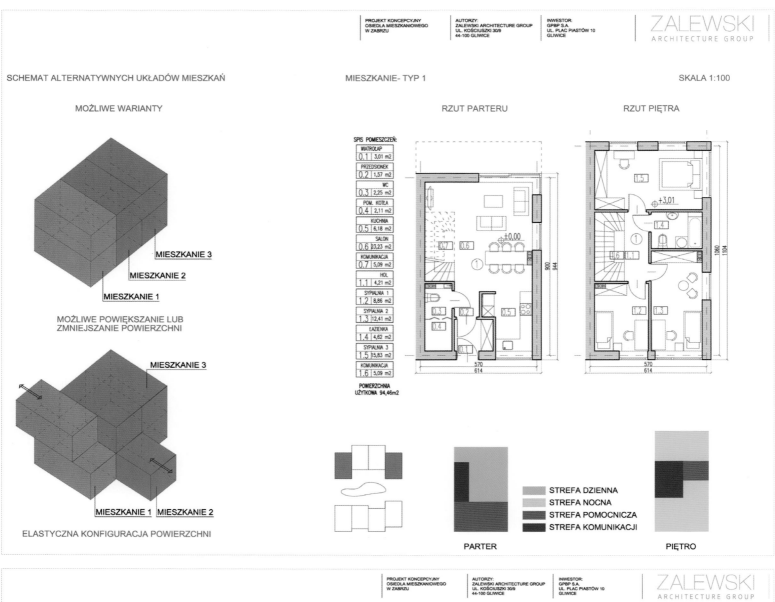

SPIS POMIESZCZEŃ:

0.1	WIATROŁAP	3,01 m2
0.2	PRZEDSIONEK	1,57 m2
0.3	WC	2,25 m2
0.4	POM. KOTŁA	2,11 m2
0.5	KUCHNIA	6,18 m2
0.6	SALON	23,23 m2
0.7	KOMUNIKACJA	5,09 m2
1.1	HOL	4,21 m2
1.2	SYPIALNIA 1	8,86 m2
1.3	SYPIALNIA 2	12,41 m2
1.4	ŁAZIENKA	4,62 m2
1.5	SYPIALNIA 3	15,83 m2
1.6	KOMUNIKACJA	5,09 m2

POWIERZCHNIA UŻYTKOWA 94,46m2

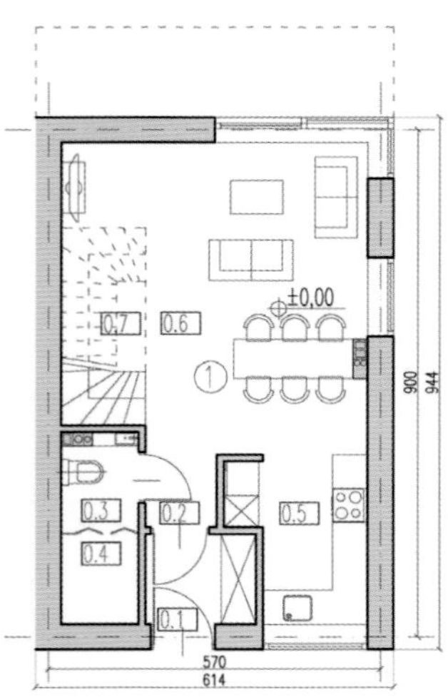

±0,00
900
944
570
614

+3,01
1060
1104
570
614

STREFA DZIENNA
STREFA NOCNA
STREFA POMOCNICZA
STREFA KOMUNIKACJI

PARTER

PIĘTRO

INWESTOR:
GPBP S.A.
UL. PLAC PIASTÓW 10
GLIWICE

KLIENT KTÓRY

- CHCE MIESZKAĆ W MIEŚCIE ALE NIE W BLOKU
- CHCE MIESZKAĆ W DOMU JEDNORODZINNYM
- NIE MA ŚRODKÓW NA BUDOWĘ DOMU

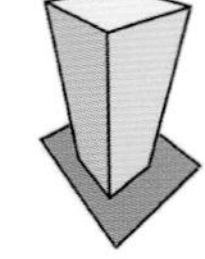

ZALETY BUDYNKU WIELORODZINNEGO

- NISKI METRAŻ = NIŻSZE KOSZTY
- BEZPIECZEŃSTWO = WIĘŹ SĄSIEDZKA
- WYKORZYSTANIE DZIAŁKI
- LOKALIZACJA W MIEŚCIE

+

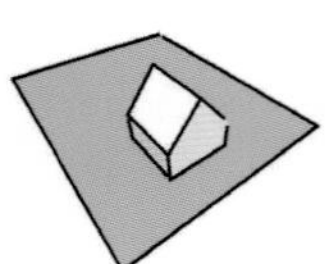

ZALETY BUDYNKU JEDNORODZINNEGO

- OGRÓD
- GARAŻ
- PRYWATNOŚĆ
- UKŁAD FUNKCJONALNY MIESZKANIA (STREFOWY)

=

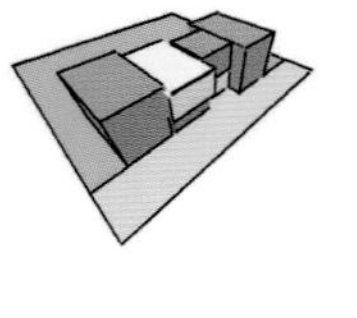

ZALETY PROPONOWANEJ KONCEPCJI

- MAŁY OGRÓD
- GARAŻ (PARKING)
- PRYWATNOŚĆ
- UKŁAD FUNKCJONALNY MIESZKANIA (STRUKTURA DOMU)
- OPTYMALNY METRAŻ = NISKIE KOSZTY UTRZYMANIA
- BEZPIECZEŃSTWO = WIĘŹ SĄSIEDZKA
- WYKORZYSTANIE DZIAŁKI
- LOKALIZACJA ŚRÓDMIEŚCIU
- ELASTYCZNOŚĆ UKŁADU FUNKCJONALNEGO
- MOŻLIWOŚĆ ETAPOWANIA ZABUDOWY
- MOŻLIWOŚĆ WYKSZTAŁCENIA (ZAMKNIĘCIA) MAŁYCH ZESPOŁÓW SĄSIEDZKICH

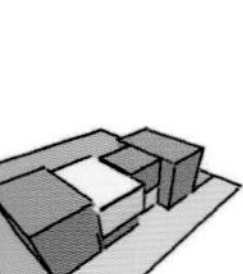

Upcycle House | *OCDC*

Project Team : Andy Ku, Kam Ku, Lionel Lambourn, Richard Yoo
Location : Los Angeles, USA
Typology : Single Family Housing

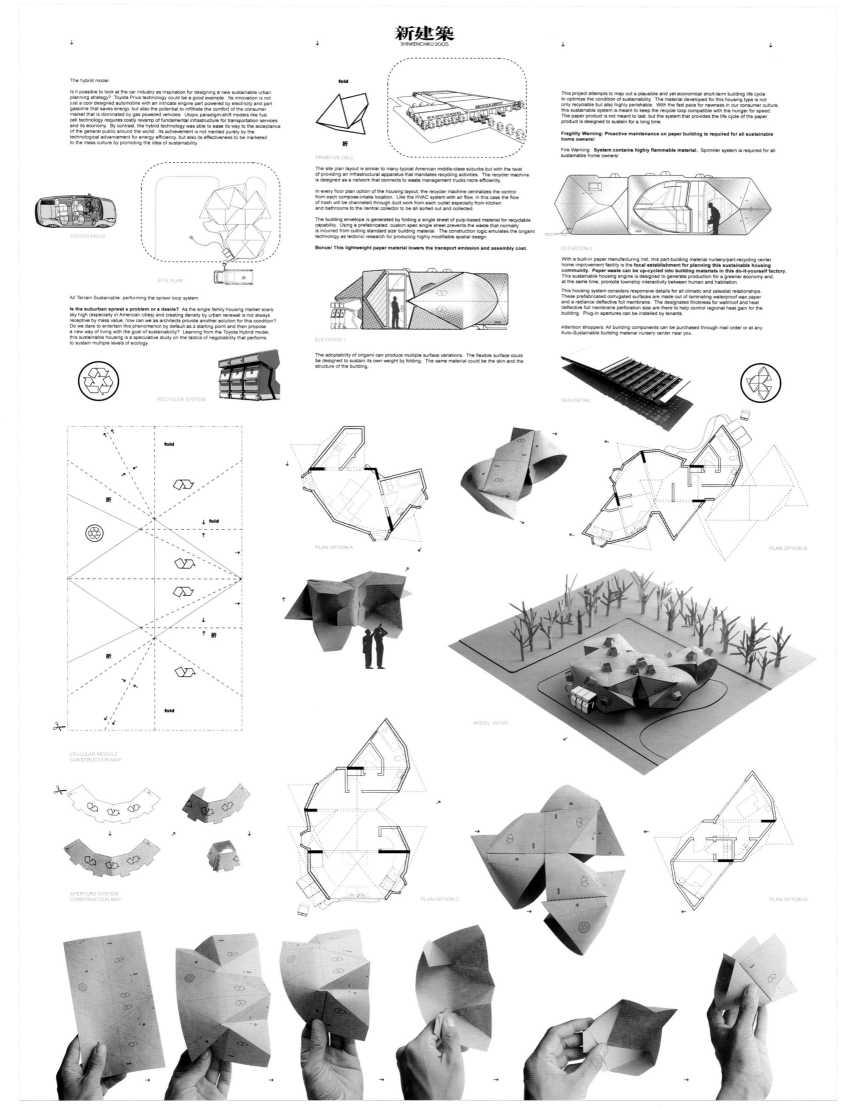

新建築
SHINKENCHIKU 2005

The hybrid model

Is it possible to look at the car industry as inspiration for designing a new sustainable urban planning strategy? Toyota Prius technology could be a good example. Its innovation is not just a cool designed automobile with an intricate engine part powered by electricity and part gasoline that saves energy, but also the potential to infiltrate the comfort of the consumer market that is dominated by gas powered vehicles. Utopic paradigm-shift models like fuel cell technology requires costly revamp of fundamental infrastructure for transportation services and its economy. By contrast, the hybrid technology was able to ease its way to the acceptance of the general public around the world. Its achievement is not merited purely by the technological advancement for energy efficiency, but also its effectiveness to be marketed to the mass culture by promoting the idea of sustainability.

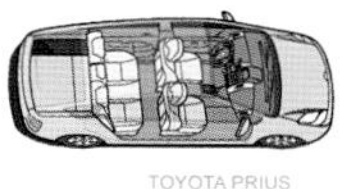

TOYOTA PRIUS

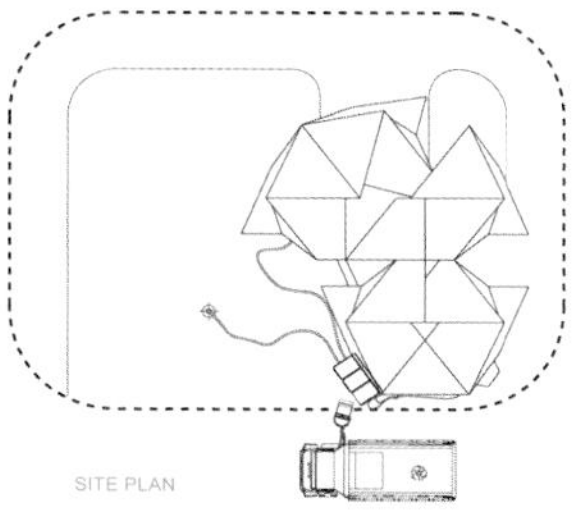

SITE PLAN

All Terrain Sustainable: performing the sprawl loop system

Is the suburban sprawl a problem or a desire? As the single family housing market soars sky high (especially in American cities) and creating density by urban renewal is not always receptive by mass value, how can we as architects provide another solution for this condition? Do we dare to entertain this phenomenon by default as a starting point and then propose a new way of living with the goal of sustainability? Learning from the Toyota Hybrid model, this sustainable housing is a speculative study on the tactics of negotiability that performs to sustain multiple levels of ecology.

RECYCLER SYSTEM

fold
折

PRIMITIVE CELL

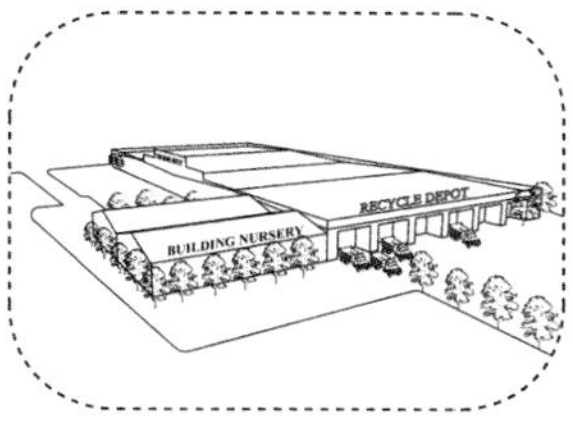

The site plan layout is similar to many typical American middle-class suburbs but with the twist of providing an infrastructural apparatus that mandates recycling activities. The recycler machine is designed as a network that connects to waste management trucks more efficiently.

In every floor plan option of the housing layout, the recycler machine centralizes the control from each compose-intake location. Like the HVAC system with air flow, in this case the flow of trash will be channeled through duct work from each outlet especially from kitchen and bathrooms to the central collector to be all sorted out and collected.

The building envelope is generated by folding a single sheet of pulp-based material for recyclable capability. Using a prefabricated, custom spec single sheet prevents the waste that normally is incurred from cutting standard size building material. The construction logic emulates the origami technology as tectonic research for producing highly modifiable spatial design.

Bonus! This lightweight paper material lowers the transport emission and assembly cost.

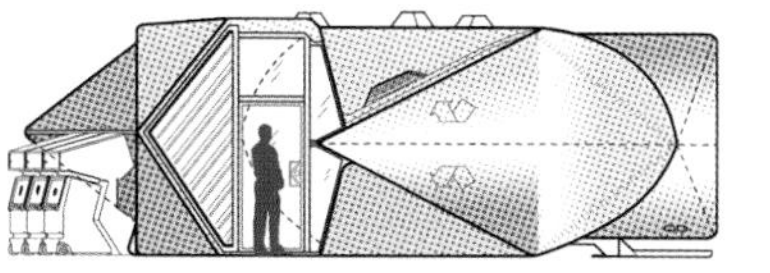

ELEVATION 1

The adoptability of origami can produce multiple surface variations. The flexible surface could be designed to sustain its own weight by folding. The same material could be the skin and the structure of the building.

This project attempts to map out a plausible and yet economical short-term building life cycle to optimize the condition of sustainability. The material developed for this housing type is not only recyclable but also highly perishable. With the fast pace for newness in our consumer culture, this sustainable system is meant to keep the recycle loop compatible with the hunger for speed. The paper product is not meant to last, but the system that provides the life cycle of the paper product is designed to sustain for a long time.

Fragility Warning: Proactive maintenance on paper building is required for all sustainable home owners!

Fire Warning: **System contains highly flammable material.** Sprinkler system is required for all sustainable home owners!

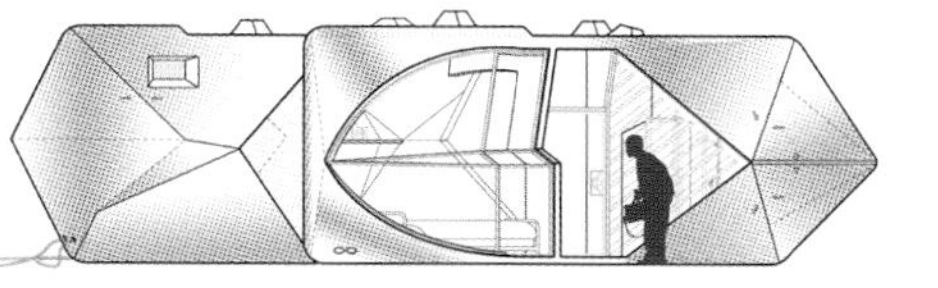

ELEVATION 2

With a built-in paper manufacturing mill, this part-building material nursery/part-recycling center home improvement facility is the **focal establishment for planning this sustainable housing community. Paper waste can be up-cycled into building materials in this do-it-yourself factory.** This sustainable housing engine is designed to generate production for a greener economy and, at the same time, promote township interactivity between human and habitation.

This housing system considers responsive details for all climatic and celestial relationships. These prefabricated corrugated surfaces are made out of laminating waterproof wax paper and a radiance deflective foil membrane. The designated thickness for wall/roof and heat deflective foil membrane perforation size are there to help control regional heat gain for the building. Plug-in apertures can be installed by tenants.

Attention shoppers: All building components can be purchased through mail order or at any Auto-Sustainable building material nursery center near you.

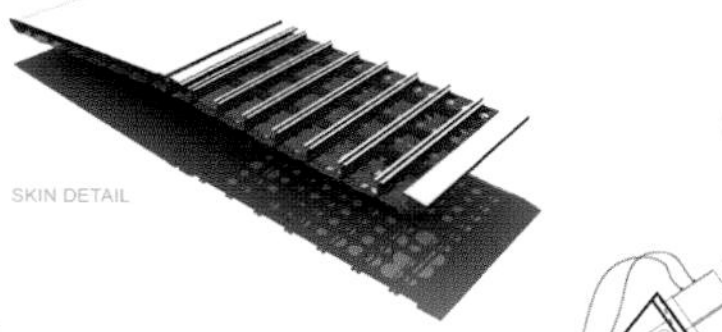

SKIN DETAIL

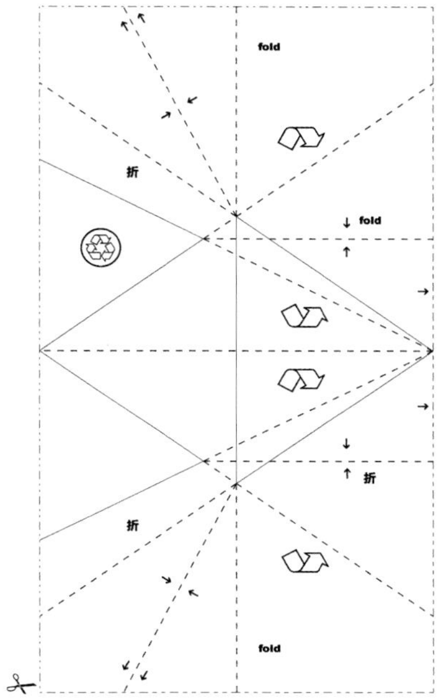

fold
折
fold
折
fold

CELLULAR MODULE CONSTRUCTION MAP

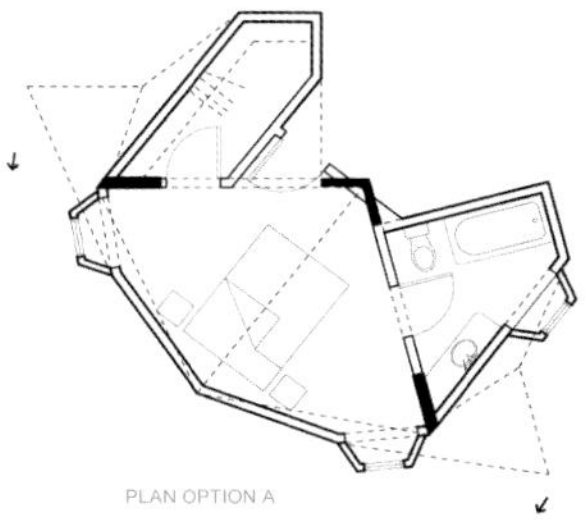

PLAN OPTION A

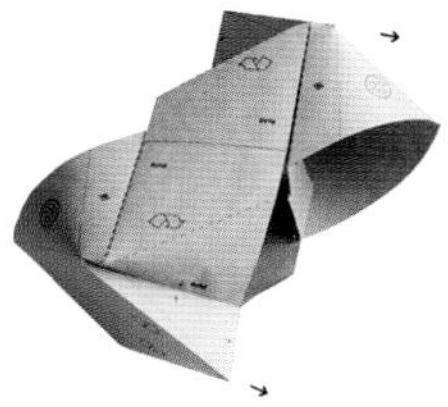

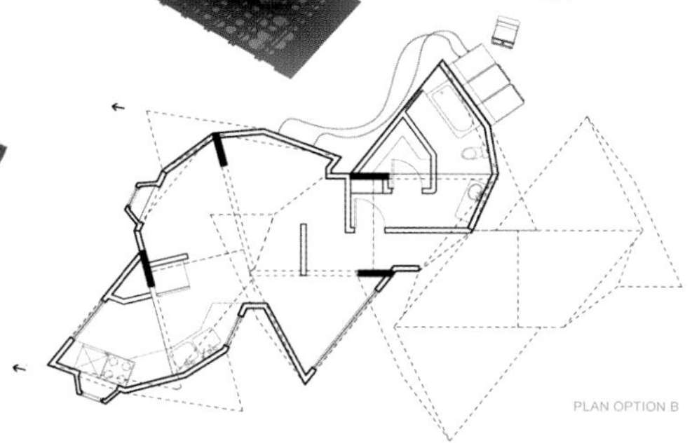

PLAN OPTION B

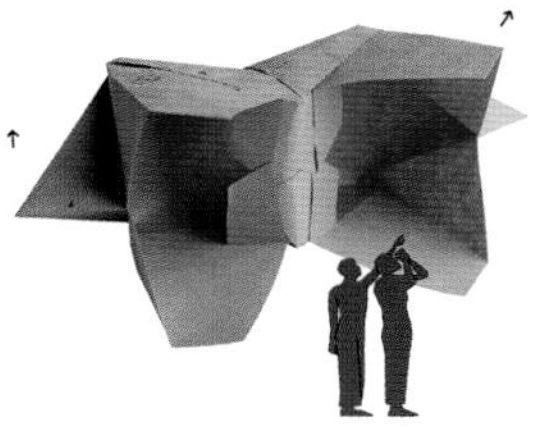

MODEL VIEWS

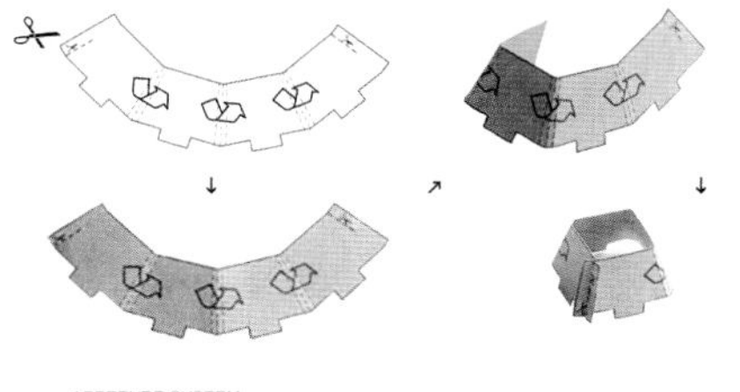

APERTURE SYSTEM CONSTRUCTION MAP

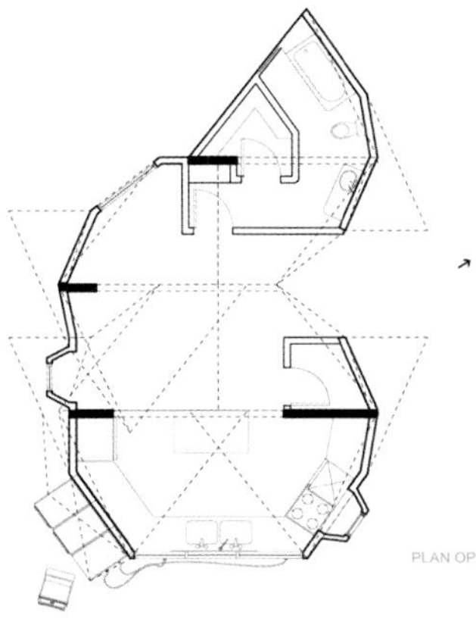

PLAN OPTION C

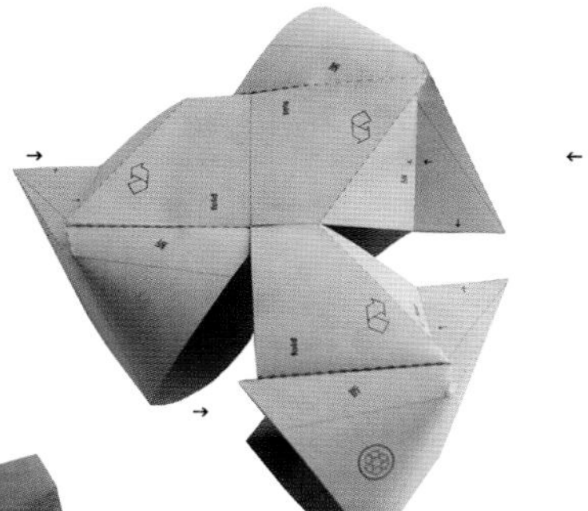

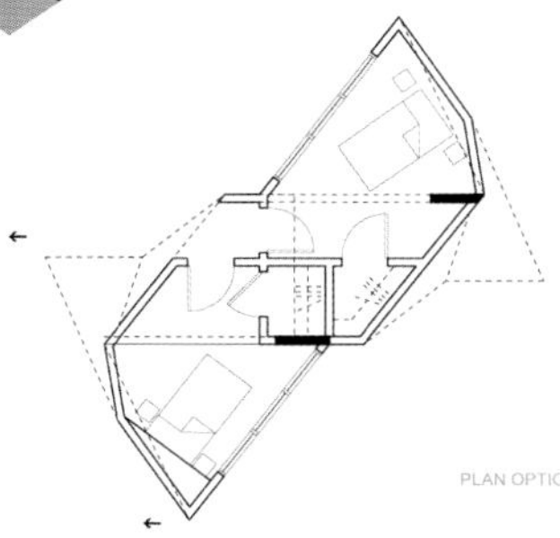

PLAN OPTION D

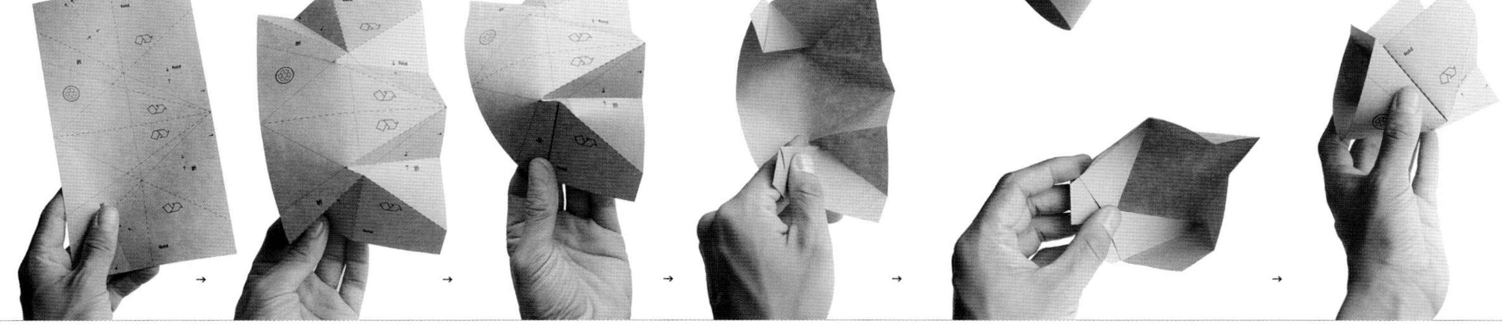

029

Europan Rioja | *REC ARQUITECTURA*

Location: Calahorra, Spain
Team: Oscar Daniel Ramirez, Jose Luis Jaspeado, Maria Jose Jimenez Muñoz, Gerardo Recoder

MJ 000

Y SIN EMBARGO... SE MUEVE

(GALILEO G. 1633)

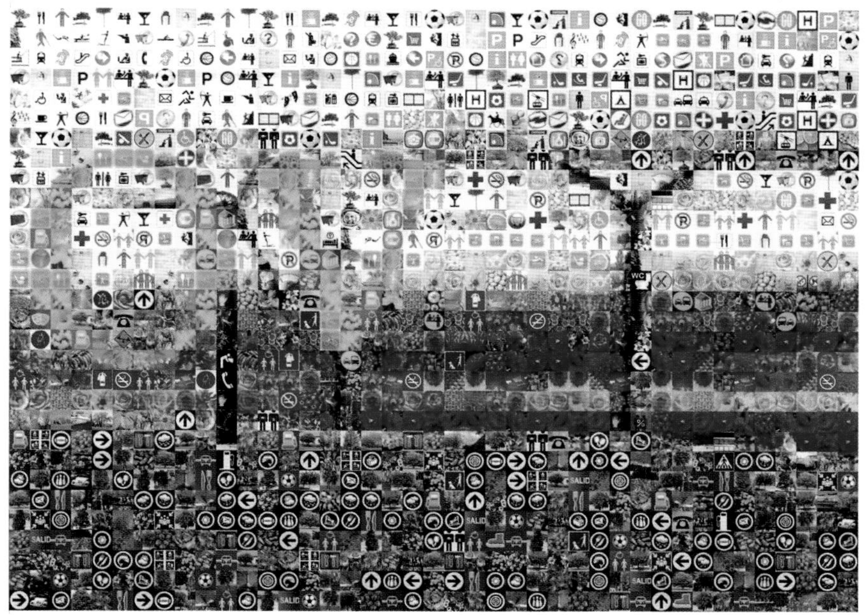

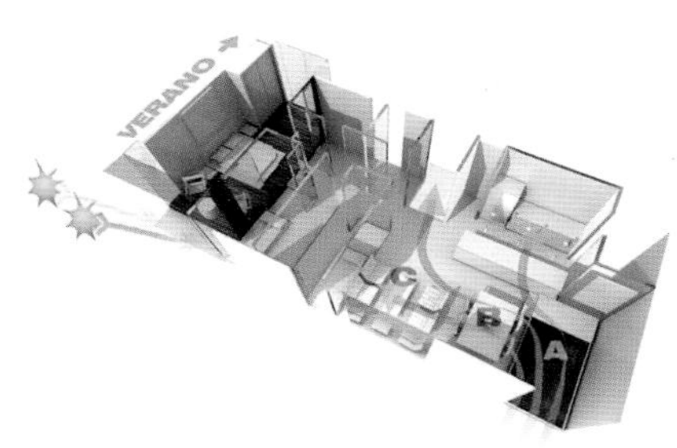

" La propuesta del movimiento no es la única, ni la integral, ni la mejor en cuestión de sostenibilidad, simplemente es una herramienta mas que se podrá sumar a las existentes "

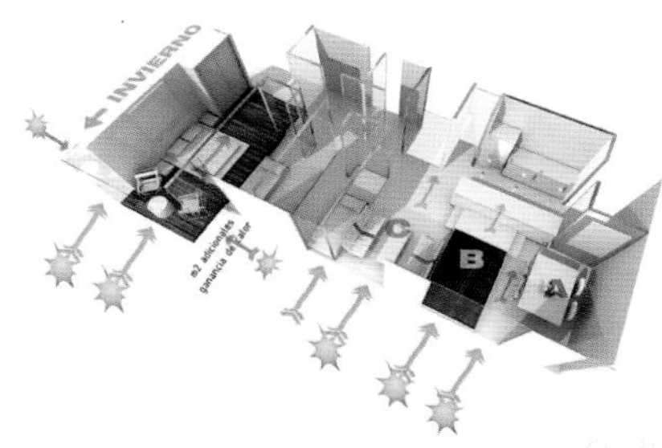

wi-fi libre , fomentando los grupos de tele trabajo, permitiendo al mismo tiempo la preocupación por el cuidado de los espacios públicos. (financiado por las mismas empresas de teletrabajo)

1 CUBIERTA NO TRANSITABLE SOBRE CARGA ANTIPUNZONANTE ACABADO DE GRAVA
2 AISLAMIENTO TÉRMICO e=4cm
3 LAMINA IMPERMEABILIZANTE
4 HORMIGON FORMACION PENDIENTE
5 CAPA DE COMPRESION e = 5cm
6 FORJADO DE VIGUETAS PREFABRICADAS Y BOVEDILLAS CERAMICAS
7 LOSA DE HORMIGON
8 CHAPA ALUMINIO DOBLE GOTERON, IGUAL COLOR CARPINTERIA EXTERIOR
9 FABRICA DE LADRILLO HUECO SENCILLO, CON ENFOSCADO Y PINTADO
10 ZUNCHO DE REMATE
11 CARPINTERIA DE ALUMINIO LACADO
12 VIDRIO TIPO CLIMATIC 3+3
13 SUELO DE MADERA
14 LAMINA PARA AISLAMIENTO ACUSTICO DE RUIDOS DE IMPACTO

VERANO INVIERNO

Comercios Verticales, en conexión con la ciudad existente.

Conexión de escaleras y rampas en zona de taludes para conectarse al proyecto nuevo, así como de pabellones flotados como miradores.

La tecnología empleada para el movimiento ha existido desde los primeros trenes y puertos, y sus costos de operación son mucho menores con respecto a los utilizados para climatizar, no proponemos el movimiento diario del los espacios, sino mas por temporadas.

Es bueno vivir donde uno a pensado o soñado, pero mejor aun en donde uno mismo puede manipular el espacio, haciendo sensible el movimiento de la vivienda a la estación del año, tipo y tiempo del habitante.

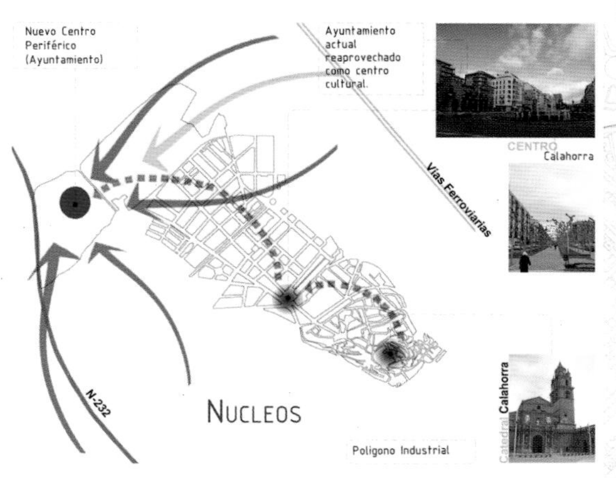

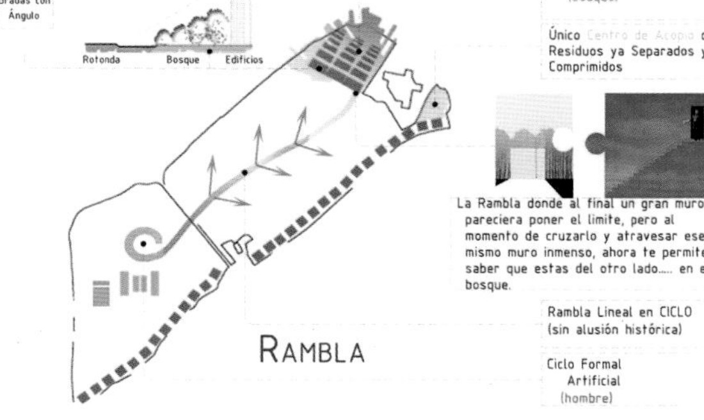

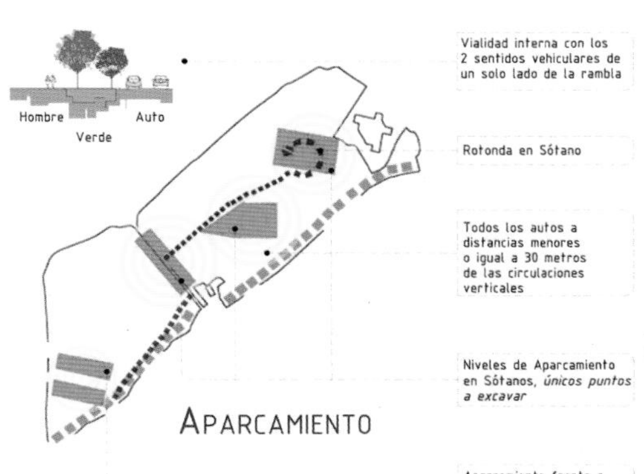

EUROPAN 9. CALAHORRA ESPAÑA

030 Baobab House | *Atelier do Cardoso*

Competition : Shortlisted, Select for the exhibition at Museu da Electricidade
Project : Patio and pavilion <A house in Luanda>, Lisbon Architecture Triennale 2010
<Let´s talk about houses>

Project Team : Mafalda Ribeiro Ambrósio + João Gomes Leitão
Colaborator : Manuela Cardial

Baobab House. 01

Memories of Africa.

Starting this exercise about an African house, come up to ours memory the circular straw matting that provided shelter on African landscape.

An investigation into the types of African and Angolan houses with circular plan and the way people live there, we found that most activities are conducted outside under the protection of a porch. It is in the outside of the house that people work, cook and socialize. The interior is just a shelter. The rooms are situated along the outer wall and common area serves as the central distribution area.
Our proposal involves the interpretation and inversion of this model, taking as its starting point the life of this family is passed on the outside protected by a porch. So, we propose a circular house with the outer space / patio in the center. With the rooms projected along the outer wall. And a porch that waves between the patio and the rooms.

The patio is the organizer of the program. Works as an extension of the interior spaces, since the wall of the porch are rotating panels that allow the full opening of the rooms to the patio. This flexibility allows each resident has a private space. The location of the courtyard in the center of the house allows the family to have an outdoor space with privacy and protected.

We propose a house using materials and construction techniques common in the architecture in Angola. Adobe walls, a structure of Mopane poles, a roof of compressed earth and panels of sisal.
The use of this material is not only due to its low cost, but aims to stimulate the local economy and employment creation. The construction of several houses or a neighborhood requires the establishment of the producing in factory of adobe bricks and sisal panels. The opening of carpentry workshops. And training technician builders.

The construction with adobe bricks it's the more common in Angola.
Adobe is a natural building material made from sand, clay and water with straw. This is shaped into bricks using frames. The mixture is roughly half sand (50%), one-third clay (35%), and one-sixth straw (15%). The straw is useful in binding the brick together and allowing the brick to dry evenly.
The blocks would be baked in the hot sun, thus, requiring no extra energy and limiting the environmental impact of the materials. The choice of using this technology represents the desire to introduce alternative and sustainable technologies within a context that is tied to standardise though not always optimal building practice.
Adobe bricks are laid by course. Each course is laid the whole length of the wall, overlapping at the corners on a layer of mud mortar. To place windows and door openings, a lintel is placed on top of the opening to support the bricks above.
Adobe structures are extremely durable and in hot climates, adobe buildings offer significant advantages due to their greater thermal mass. An adobe wall can serve as a significant heat reservoir due to the thermal properties inherent in the massive walls typical in adobe construction. In climates typified by hot days and cool nights, the high thermal mass of adobe levels out the heat transfer through the wall to the living space. The massive walls require a large and relatively long input of heat from the sun (radiation) and from the surrounding air (convection) before they warm through to the interior and begin to transfer heat to the living space. After the sun sets and the temperature drops, the warm wall will then continue to transfer heat to the interior for several hours due to the time lag effect.

The interior walls are constructed with adobe bricks using smaller frames.
Plaster is applied to the inside. The plaster is comprised of an appropriate mixture of sand, plaster and lime (Calcium hydroxide). Once it is applied it is floated and then, using a small rake-like implement, scratched. This must then dry before a second coat is applied. Once sufficiently dry the walls are painted.

The wood structure is made with Mopane. Mopane wood is one of southern Africa's heaviest timbers and is difficult to work because of its hardness. However, this also makes it termite resistant. For this reason it has long been used for building houses and fences.
The Mopane wood also is used for interior floor, because the termite-resistance and reddish coloring.

The uses of sisal want to encourage their production that has fallen since the 60s. Angola was one of the largest producers in the world.

Designed a circular house as well as urban strikes us as an asset to the project. We tried a geometry that might respond to a model city that do not far from the village of existing models. In these models prevailing social values of a community, values that have been losing with the times.

The house will be connected to networks of water supply and electricity. And also to the sewerage network.
In house systems are installed water-saving taps. Systems for the separation of the black water and the gray water. The gray water is purified and used to irrigate the orchard. There is also a system of recovery of the low rain water that is conducted to a deposit.

With these premises and the program application, we chose a distint lot, always in favor of a response to all factors implicit in a design competition, factors such as the development of thoughts and studies leading to limit their objectives.
Although the front and depth of the lot is not applied to the bases, do not go over the total area, is kept at an area of 250 m2 to 100 m2 of gross building area.

Through this model we have developed an urban design house resulting from the provision of these small bands and, through its curved geometry and organization of all the built elements, allows us to create spaces more or less compressed, providing an almost natural hierarchy of uses and speed of its transients, time to pause, fast or slow in passing, crossing, to be, to observe. This idea results in a sample of urban fabric with a range identical to a village, a small neighborhood with strong connections between its neighbors.

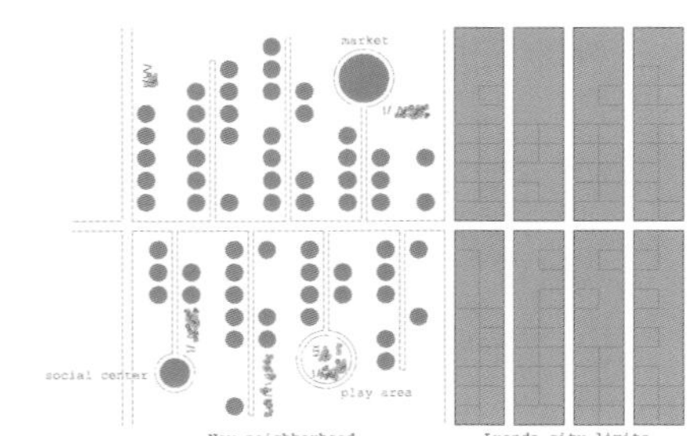

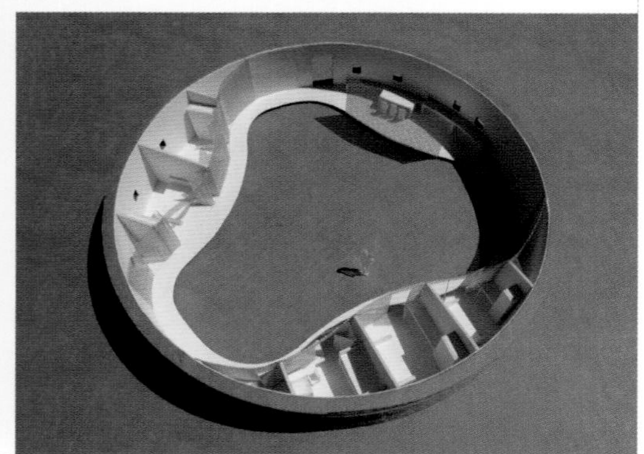

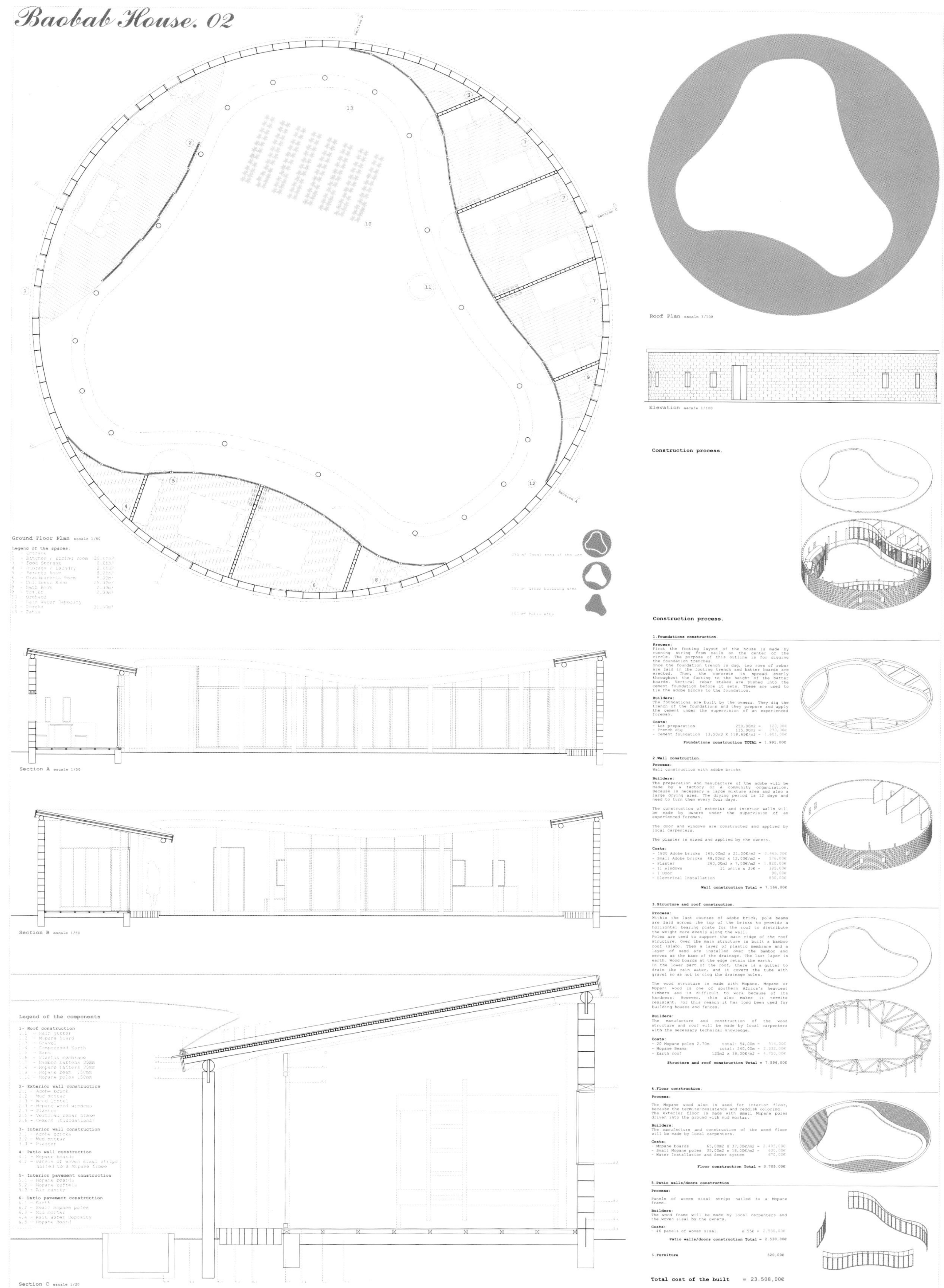
Baobab House. 02
Ground Floor Plan escale 1/50
Legend of the spaces:
Roof Plan escale 1/100
Elevation escale 1/100
Section A escale 1/50
Section B escale 1/50
Section C escale 1/20
Legend of the components
1- Roof construction
2- Exterior wall construction
3- Interior wall construction
4- Patio wall construction
5- Interior pavement construction
6- Patio pavement construction
Construction process.
Construction process.
1.Foundations construction.
Process:
First the footing layout of the house is made by running string from nails on the center of the circle. The purpose of this outline is for digging the foundation trenches.
Once the foundation trench is dug, two rows of rebar are laid in the footing trench and batter boards are erected. Then, the concrete is spread evenly throughout the footing to the height of the batter boards. Vertical rebar stakes are pushed into the cement foundation before it sets. These are used to tie the adobe blocks to the foundation.
Builders:
The foundations are built by the owners. They dig the trench of the foundations and they prepare and apply the cement under the supervision of an experienced foreman.
Costs:
- Lot preparation 250,00m2 = 120,00€
- Trench dig 135,00m2 = 270,00€
- Cement foundation 13,50m3 X 118.65€/m3 = 1.601,00€
Foundations construction TOTAL = 1.991,00€
2.Wall construction.
Process:
Wall construction with adobe bricks
Builders:
The preparation and manufacture of the adobe will be made by a factory or a community organization. Because is necessary a large mixture area and also a large drying area. The drying period is 12 days and need to turn them every four days.
The construction of exterior and interior walls will be made by owners under the supervision of an experienced foreman.
The door and windows are constructed and applied by local carpenters.
The plaster is mixed and applied by the owners.
Costs:
- 1800 Adobe bricks 165,00m2 x 21,00€/m2 = 3.465,00€
- Small Adobe bricks 48,00m2 x 12,00€/m2 = 576,00€
- Plaster 260,00m2 x 7,00€/m2 = 1.820,00€
- 11 windows 11 units x 35€ = 385,00€
- 1 Door 90,00€
- Electrical Installation 830,00€
Wall construction Total = 7.166,00€
3.Structure and roof construction.
Process:
Within the last courses of adobe brick, pole beams are laid across the top of the bricks to provide a horizontal bearing plate for the roof to distribute the weight more evenly along the wall.
Poles are used to support the main ridge of the roof structure. Over the main structure is built a bamboo roof (slab). Then a layer of plastic membrane and a layer of sand are installed over the bamboo and serves as the base of the drainage. The last layer is earth. Wood boards at the edge retain the earth.
In the lower part of the roof, there is a gutter to drain the rain water, and it covers the tube with gravel so as not to clog the drainage holes.
The wood structure is made with Mopane. Mopane or Mopani wood is one of southern Africa's heaviest timbers and is difficult to work because of its hardness. However, this also makes it termite resistant. For this reason it has long been used for building houses and fences.
Builders:
The manufacture and construction of the wood structure and roof will be made by local carpenters with the necessary technical knowledge.
Costs:
- 20 Mopane poles 2.70m total: 54,00m = 514,00€
- Mopane Beams total: 240,00m = 2.332,00€
- Earth roof 125m2 x 38,00€/m2 = 4.750,00€
Structure and roof construction Total = 7.596,00€
4.Floor construction.
Process:
The Mopane wood also is used for interior floor, because the termite-resistance and reddish coloring.
The exterior floor is made with small Mopane poles driven into the ground with mud mortar.
Builders:
The manufacture and construction of the wood floor will be made by local carpenters.
Costs:
- Mopane boards 65,00m2 x 37,00€/m2 = 2.405,00€
- Small Mopane poles 35,00m2 x 18,00€/m2 = 630,00€
- Water Installation and Sewer system 670,00€
Floor construction Total = 3.705,00€
5.Patio walls/doors construction
Process:
Panels of woven sisal strips nailed to a Mopane frame.
Builders:
The wood frame will be made by local carpenters and the woven sisal by the owners.
Costs:
- 46 panels of woven sisal x 55€ = 2.530,00€
Patio walls/doors construction Total = 2.530,00€
6.Furniture 520,00€
Total cost of the built = 23.508,00€

031 Plug-in Hanok | *MOTOElastico*

Project by : Simone Carena, Marco Bruno
Design Team : Minji Kim
Location : Seoul, South Korea

Plug-in Hanok

플러그인 한옥

Writing a New History
Hanok is a strong symbol of Korean Identity, but the culture that inhabited it has radically evolved. People living in Hanok had very few possessions, tidily arranged in the indoor cabinets. The Hanok was an empty house, and large part of the life of a family was happening outdoor:
preparing food,
playing,
meeting guests.
All this
has radically changed.
Our homes are now full of appliances and we need lots of space to store all our belongings:
clothes, books, toys, stuff.
To continue using the hanok as a home, and not only as a gallery, shop, teahouse or cafe, it is necessary to enhance its functionality in order to keep the identity of the original nucleus.

Plug-in
Taking advantage of the regular grid of the Hanok, we designed a modular extension system particularly suitable for those Hanok located in very dense urban conditions.
The units allow three different kind of extension:
_ along the perimeter
_ in the empty areas of the lot
_ above the original building
The units along the perimeter and above the building can be prefabricated and freely combined to obtain different formal configurations, while the one in the empty areas adapts to the dimensions of the site.

플러그인 한옥 - 파고다 타입 | PLUG-IN HANOK - PAGODA TYPE

한옥은 바로 밥과 국 같은 주식의 역할을 하고
반찬들은 입맛에 따라 달라진다
THE HANOK IS THE MAIN DISH WHILE
THE SIDE DISHES CHANGE ACCORDING TO TASTE

플러그인 한옥 - 타워 타입 | PLUG-IN HANOK - TOWER TYPE

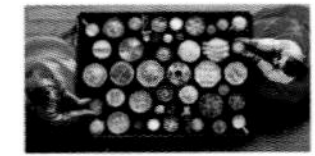

새로운 역사 쓰기
한옥은
한국의 정체성을 대표하는 상징이지만 한옥을 담고 있던 문화는 급진적인 발달과정을 거쳤다. 예전에 한옥에서 살던 우리 선조들은 소유물이 많지 않았기 때문에 방 내부에 있는 가구들만으로도 물건들을 깨끗이 정리하기에 충분하였다. 한옥은 비어있는 공간이었고 음식을 준비하거나 여흥을 즐기거나 손님을 맞이하는 등, 가정에서 이루어지는 생활의 많은 부분은 방의 내부보다는 마루나 마당 등의 외부공간에서 이루어졌다.
이 모든 것들은
급진적으로 변화하였다.
현재 우리들이 살고 있는 집은 가전제품으로 가득 차있고 옷, 책, 장난감 등 우리 소지품들을 수납할 수 있는 공간이 많이 필요하다. 한옥을 갤러리나 가게, 찻집 혹은 카페만이 아닌 주거용 한옥으로 이어가기 위해서는 한옥 본연의 정체성을 유지할 수 있도록 그에 맞는 기능성 향상이 필요하다.

플러그인
우리는 한옥 한 칸을 기본으로 하는 규칙적인 '그리드'를 활용하여 모듈 증축 시스템을 디자인하였다. 이는 특히 고밀도 도시 환경에 입지한 한옥들에 알맞은 시스템이다. 유닛들은 3개의 다른 증축방식을 가능하게 해준다.
_ 경계선을 따라서
_ 부지 내의 빈 공간 안에
_ 기존 건물 상부에
경계선을 따라서 만들어지는 유닛과 건물 위쪽에 올려지는 유닛의 경우 미리 조립식으로 제조하고 자유롭게 결합함으로써 다른 형태들을 얻을 수 있다. 반면에 빈 공간 안의 유닛은 대지의 크기에 순응하게 된다.

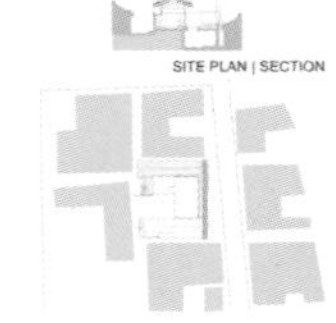

SITE PLAN | SECTION

플러그인 동선
PLUG-IN CIRCULATION

스파 + 화장실
SPA + BATHROOM

타워 투시도
TOWER VIEW

타워룸에서 한옥을 내려다보는 풍경
VIEW OVER THE HANOK ROOF FROM THE TOWER ROOM

3 Samples
The Hanok Plug-in system allows several variations. Here we present three of the most significant combinations with the purpose to define new typologies.

3가지 예시
한옥 플러그인 시스템은 몇몇의 변화를 가능하게 해준다. 새로운 유형들을 정의하기 위해 그 중에서도 가장 주요한 3개의 결합 형태를 여기서 선보이고 있다.

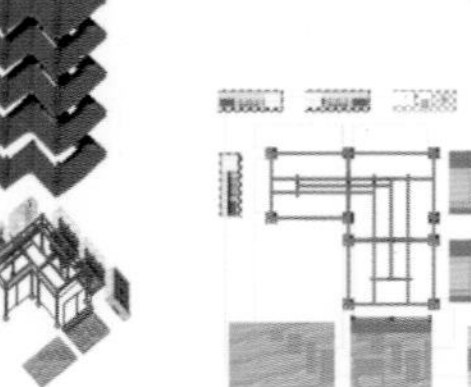

파고다 한옥 (Pagoda Hanok)은 기존 건물을 수직적으로 증축한 형태이다.
이는 건물의 표면을필요한 만큼 중복하여 얻게 된다. 이 새로운 강철 구조물은 단층주택을 도시의 소형 마천루로 탈바꿈시켜준다.

The Pagoda Hanok is the vertical extension of the original building, obtained duplicating the foot print surface as many times it is necessary.
The new structure, built using steel technology, turns a single storey villa into a urban mini skyscraper.

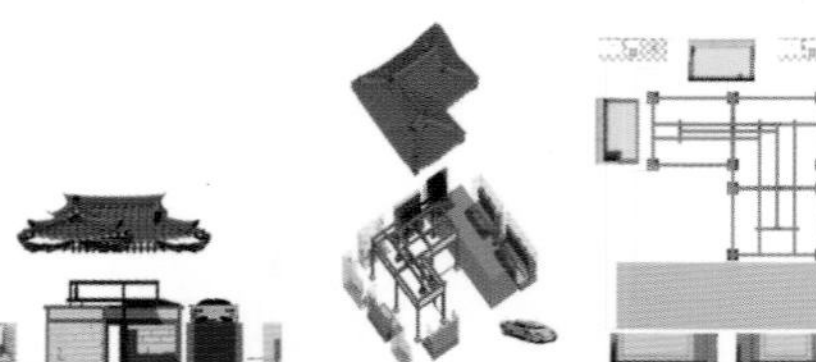

트랜스포트 한옥(Transport Hanok) 은 유닛들의 자유로운 결합을 가능하게 해준다. 새로운 건물의 지붕을 활용하여 한옥이 처음 지어졌을 당시에는 존재하지 않았던 자동차, 오토바이, 자전거, 쾌속정, 그리고 우주 로켓과 같은 갖가지 새로운 교통수단들을 위한 공간을 제공해준다. 지하철까지의 직행 통로로 건물을 공공교통시설과 바로 연결시켜준다.

The Transport Hanok offers a free combination of the units and takes advantage of the roof of the new building to provide space to all the transportation means that didn't exist at the time Hanok were invented: cars, motorcycles, bicycles, speed boats, helicopters and space rockets. A direct line to the subway system plugs the building in the public transportation system.

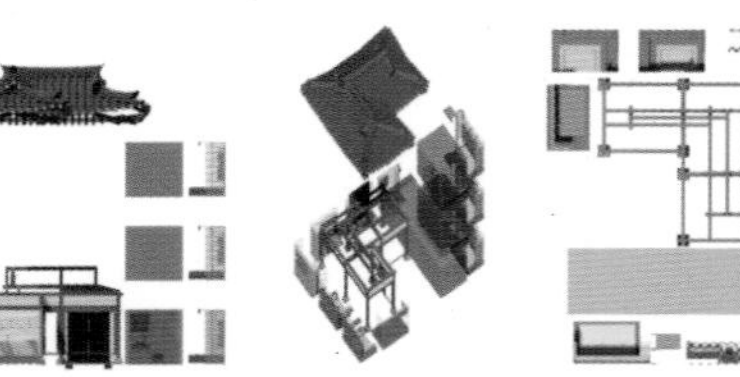

타워 한옥(Tower Hanok)은 대지의 빈 공간을 활용하여 한옥을 구성하는 '그리드'를 수직적으로 확장시켜준다. 계단으로 연결된 방들의 이웃들에게는 한정된 그림자만을 드리우며 도시의 새로운 아이콘에 생명을 불어넣는다.

The Tower Hanok
takes advantage of the empty area of in the site to extend vertically the grid.
A skinny pile of rooms connected by a stair, casting a very limited shadow over the neighbors, gives life to a new urban icon.

Treinuno | *studioNOWA*

032

Classification : Residential, Urban Regeneration
Client : BNL Real Estate
Designer : Marco Navarra_NOWA
Project Team : Maria Giacoma Marino_NOWA, Giuseppe Allegra, Salvatore Interlandi_NOWA, Adriano Marchisciana, Fortunato Dario Pappalardo_NOWA, Francesco Trovato (Officina22)
Collaborators : Giuseppe Libertino, Mario La Mattina
Consultant : D.L.C. s.r.l. Milano, METEC saggese Torino, Prof. Arch. Stefano Munarin

Nowa s.r.l.
coordinatore: Marco Navarra (capo progetto)
gruppo di progettazione: Maria Giacoma Marino, Giuseppe Allegra, Salvatore Interlandi, Adriano Marchisciana, Fortunato Pappalardo, Francesco Trovato (Officina22)
collaboratori: Giuseppe Libertino, Mario La Mattina
consulenti: D.L.C. s.r.l. Milano (strutture), METEC saggese Torino (impianti), Prof. Arch. Stefano Munarin Venezia (progetto urbano)

Le case, come occhi, proiettano a diverse quote la vita domestica sul paesaggio degli alberi in basso (tronchi, intrecci di rami, chiome) e della città antica in alto. Le difficoltà della topografia vengono trasformate in opportunità per differenziare e caratterizzare gli appartamenti attraverso la loro posizione.

Tre in uno.
I tre edifici tendono a formare un piccolo "pezzo di città":
L'EDIFICIO UNO reinterpreta le modalità insediative delle costruzioni presenti su via Bronacci Brunamonti caratterizzati da sostruzioni che sagomano a terrazze il suolo ricalcando il declivio della collina;
L'EDIFICIO DUE gioca il ruolo dell'edificio urbano per eccellenza definendo i fronti su piazza monteluce con aperture regolari e uno slittamento della facciata sul tetto e costruendo le soglie di accesso al lotto attraverso un equilibrio tra paramenti murari di sostegno del suolo e volumi sospesi;
L'EDIFICIO TRE sposta la quota più alta della strada verso la valle costruendo un piano speciale di residenze sospeso tra gli alberi con una visuale unica sul centro antico di Perugia.

Volti diversi.
In particolare, il progetto distingue quattro tipi di facciate: quelle che prospettano verso la città (per le quali si prevede un ritmo costante delle bucature), quelle verso la corte interna (caratterizzate da una distribuzione più aleatoria delle bucature), quelle verso la valle (caratterizzate dalla trasparenza delle superfici vetrate e dall'articolazione dei volumi attraverso logge, balconi, scavi e sbalzi) ed infine il tetto che, se in parte è trattato a giardino, verso monte si presenta però come una vera e propria facciata (e quindi come tale va trattato) rivolta verso piazza Monteluce. Il tetto facciata dell'edificio UNO rivolto a sud sarà rivestito di pannelli fotovoltaici.

Basamento giardini e recinto edificio 01
Intonaci con dettaglio cornici aperture
Tetti giardino edifici 1/2/3
Copertura fotovoltaica edificio 01 lato SUD
Brise soleil (facciata e copertura edifici 2/3)
Lastre copertura (edifici 2/3)

SUD Verso la valle
EST Verso l'hotel
NORD Verso la piazza
OVEST Verso la città
SUD Verso la valle

Nowa s.r.l.
coordinatore: Marco Navarra (capo progetto)
gruppo di progettazione: Maria Giacoma Marino, Giuseppe Allegra, Salvatore Interlandi, Adriano Marchisciana, Fortunato Pappalardo, Francesco Trovato (Officina22)
collaboratori: Giuseppe Libertino, Mario La Mattina
consulenti: D.L.C. s.r.l. Milano (strutture), METEC saggese Torino (impianti), Prof. Arch. Stefano Munarin Venezia (progetto urbano)

Monolocale 30mq
Bilocale 45mq
Trilocale 90mq
Quadrilocale duplex 110mq

Parcheggi e cantine
Percorsi d'accesso
Collegamenti verticali
Schema strutturale
Coperture (Pannelli fotovoltaici)
Tetti a giardino

Livello 05
Livello 04
Livello 03
Livello 02
Livello 01
Parcheggi e cantine 02
Parcheggi e cantine 01

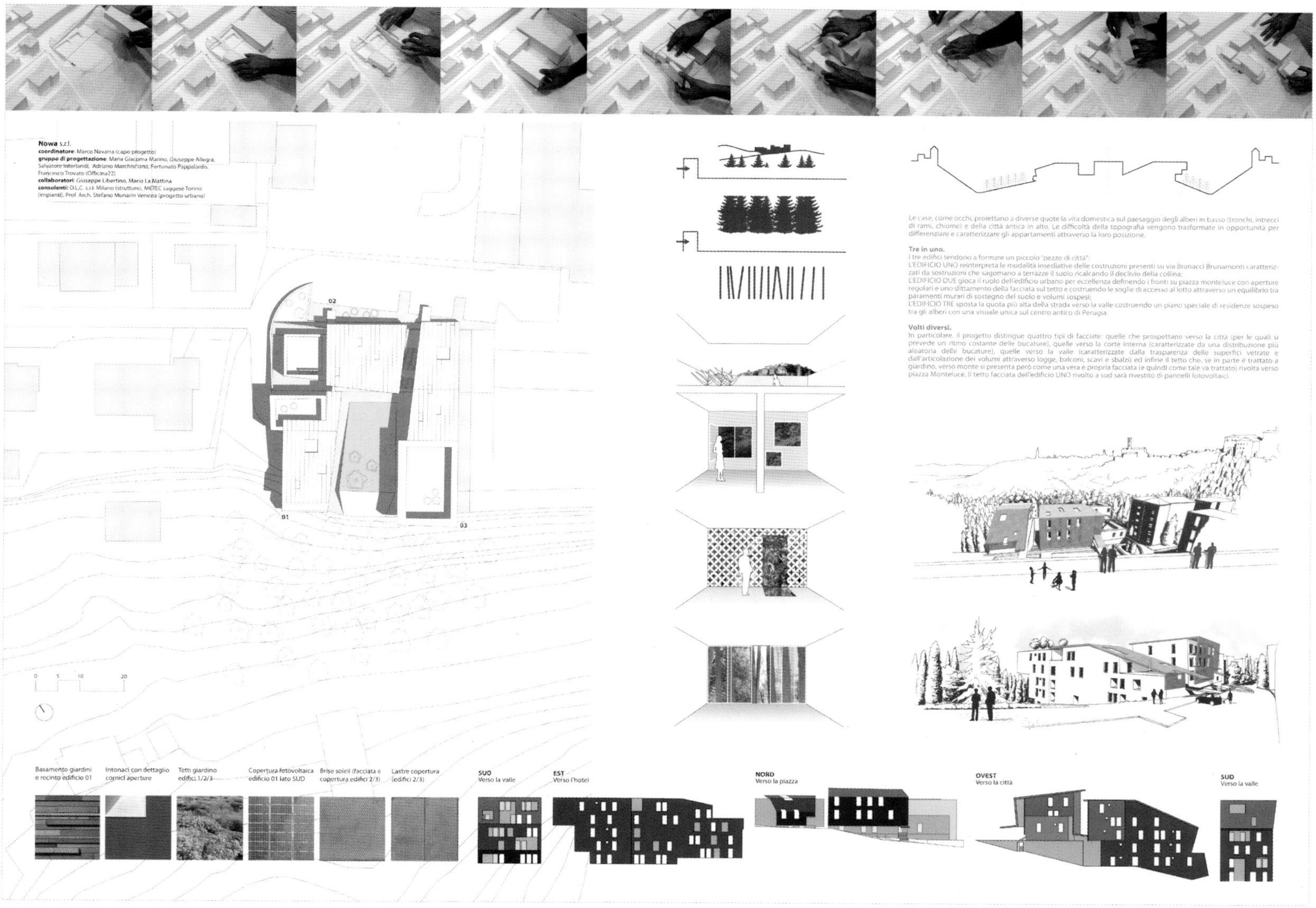

033 Northern Style Housing Complex | *Katsuhiro Miyamoto & Associates*

Result : Special Prize (unbuilt)
Location : Aomori-city, Aomori, Japan
Principal Use : Apartment house
Total Floor Area : 28,420m²

●ハイパールーフ
・マッシブな住棟のボリュームの表と裏から、それぞれ「夏の庭」と「冬の庭」と呼ぶヴォイドを欠き取ることで、住棟自体が最大で３層、平均約２層分の厚みを持つ大きな屋根（=「ハイパールーフ」）となる。
・ハイパールーフの下にできあがる多様なピロティ空間は、文化交流機能、店舗、保育所などを必要に応じて独立に配置する他、広域避難場所や、ねぶたの発進基地として利用することも可能である。

●夏の庭、冬の庭
・夏の庭‥‥大きく空が広がる。風通しがよい。緑陰がある。冬には積雪によってG.L.が変化する。すり鉢状の空間。
・冬の庭‥‥天井に開けられた孔から光がこぼれ落ちる。ピロティから光が回り込む。雪が積らない。暖かい空気の滞留。パンテオンのような断面構成。
・アンデュレーションのついた地表部では、夏の庭と冬の庭が交互に現れて、夏と冬で異なった風景が展開する。

●新しい雪国型パッサージュ
・ハイパールーフは地域に対して、雪を楽しむための、雁木に代わる「新しいパッサージュ」を提供する。
・国道４号線と平行して、中心市街地から本町公園～敷地～文化会館と東西方向に連続する、通り抜け可能な「裏道ネットワーク」の一部分を構成する。

●環境を調整する雪囲い
・敷地境界線に沿った住棟外壁やヴォイドの外側には「雪囲い」として、有孔折板を全周に巡らせる。
・温かい雰囲気のパッサージュ空間と対照的にシャープな印象を与える雪囲いは、冬の厳しい暴風雪に抗う盾であると同時に、有孔率を調整することで周辺オフィス街と集合住宅との関係の調停をはかる、環境調整機能をもった「ダブルスキン」となる。

●第５のファサード
・周辺のビルから俯瞰すると、フラットな屋根に開けられた様々ヴォイドやプライベート・コートの穴がつくる図像は、「第５のファサード」となる。
・特に、高層マンションを横に倒したマザーシップのような夜景は、外周の雪囲いを透過する光とともに、集合住宅の全体をねぶたのような「光る領域」として浮かび上がらせる。

●場所の記憶
・１２４年間そこにあり続けた小学校と、小学校を巡る地域住民の記憶を伝えるものとして、既存樹木は夏の庭に移植し、既存遊具は冬の庭に移設するなど、できるかぎり敷地内に残すように努める。

●Hyper roof
- We intend that the residential building itself will become a large roof (named 'hyper roof'), of which the maximum thickness is for three stories and the average one is for about two stories, by making the void named 'garden for summer' in the massive volume from above and 'garden for winter' from below.
- In the space of the pilotis with the diverse aspects under the 'hyper roof', each facility (community salon, shops, day nursery and so on) is placed properly without being loaded from the mass above, and this area may become a evacuation space and the starting point of 'Aomori NEBUTA festival' which is one of the Japanese representative festivals.

●Garden for summer and garden for winter
- In the garden for summer - The sky expands largely. A wind goes through. Trees make a shade. In winter, the ground level rises according to the deep snow cover. The space is like a bowl.
- In the garden for winter - The beam of sunlight streams through the opening at the top. The reflected light from the pilotis spreads out. The space is not snowed. A warm air keeps still. The section is like Parthenon.
- In the undulating ground, we can experience 'garden for summer' and 'garden for winter' alternately. So the different landscapes appear in summer and winter.

●New 'passage' for a snowy region
- The 'hyper roof' gives this area new 'passage' that replaces a traditional covered portico named 'Gangi', so that people take pleasure in heavy snow.
- This passage plays a part of a network of the back lane which runs from west to east (central urban area ~ 'Honmachi' park ~ this site ~ cultural hall), parallel to the National Highway 4.

●'Snowbreak' adjusting the relation with the surroundings
- The outside wall and the void along the boundry line are surrounded with the perforated and folded plates as 'snowbreak.'
- The snowbreak, which gives a sharp impression in contrast with the something warm in the 'passage' space, is a shield that protects the daily life of the residents from the snowstorm in winter ,and, at the same time, become a 'double skins' with a function adjusting the relation between the residential spaces and the office buildings around this site by altering the rate of the perforation.

●The fifth facade
- In looking downward this residential building from the buildings around it, the figure that the hole of various gardens and private courts are bored in the flat 'hyper roof' can be regarded as 'the fifth facade.'
- Especially in the night view of it like a mother ship or a highrise condominium building which lies down, the whole building appears as the volume of 'luminous field' like a NEBUTA with the light through the snowbreak.

●Memory of this place
- The existing trees will be transplanted to the garden for summer and the existing play equipments will be replaced to the garden for winter, so as to hand down the memory about the elementary school that had been in this site for about 120 years.

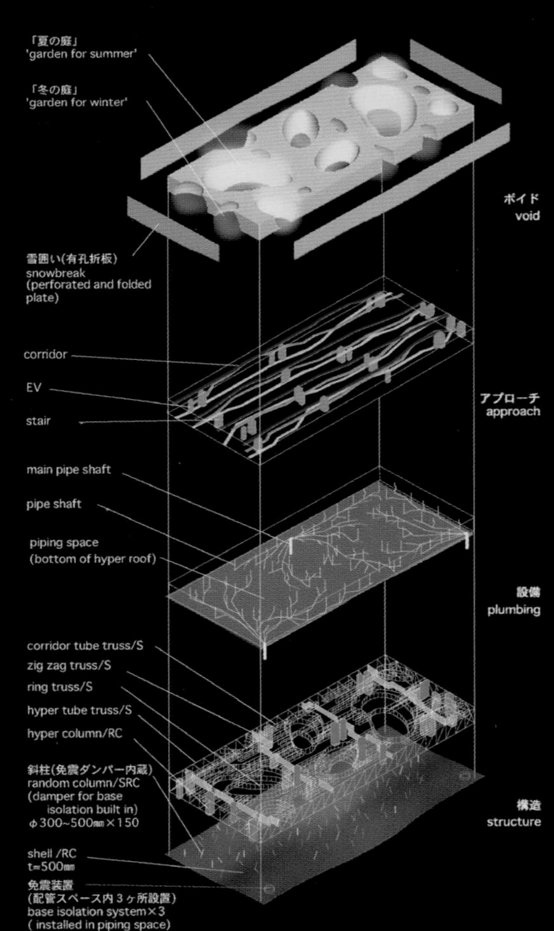

roof plan
S=1:1000

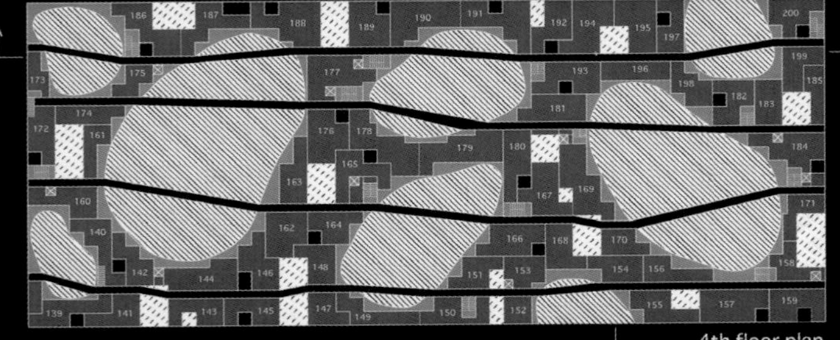

4th floor plan
S=1:1000

3rd floor plan
S=1:1000

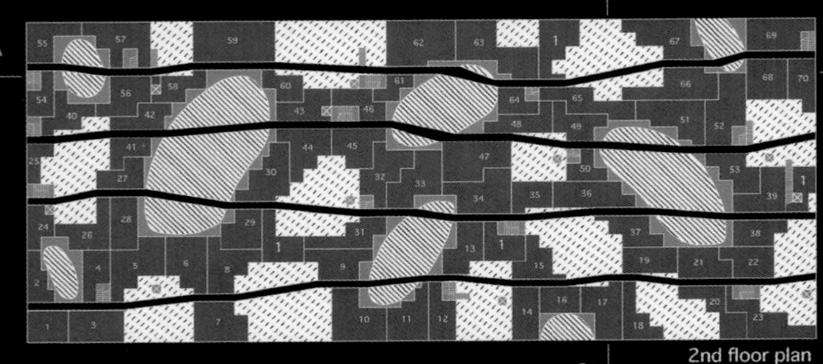

2nd floor plan
S=1:1000

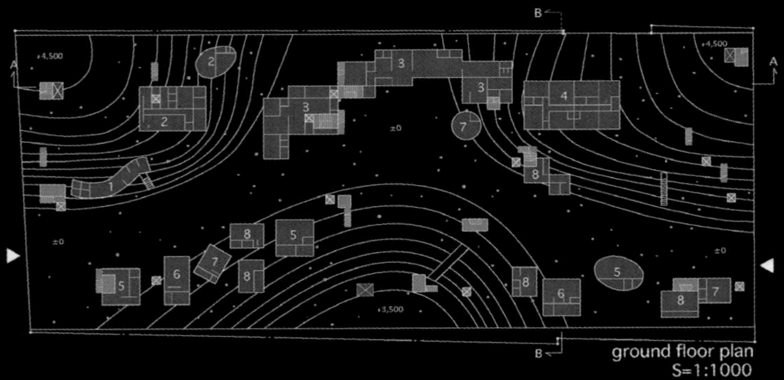

ground floor plan
S=1:1000

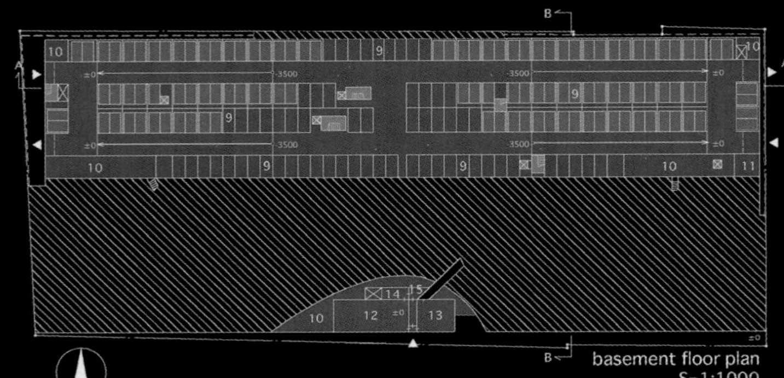

basement floor plan
S=1:1000

Northe

0209 22:00
wind speed 15.1m
wind direction WNW
air temperature −5.0℃
depth of snow fall 89㎝

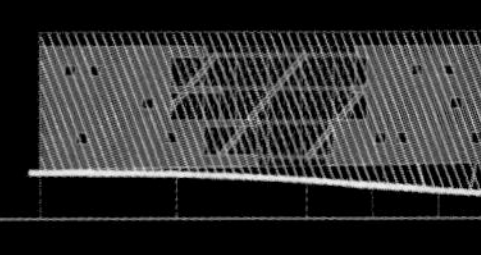

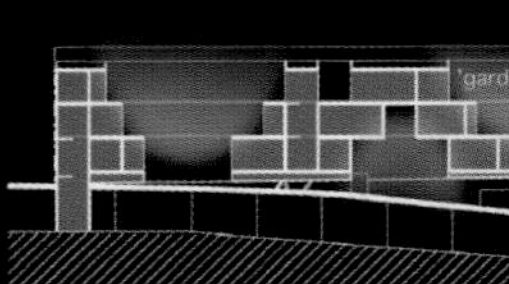

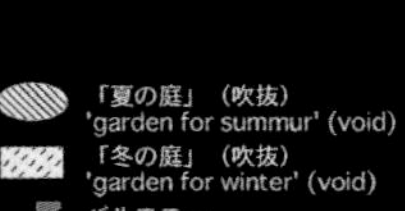

「夏の庭」（吹抜）
'garden for summur' (void)
「冬の庭」（吹抜）
'garden for winter' (void)
バルコニー
balcony
プライベートコート
private court
1 コミュニティサロン
community salon
2 児童室
children center
3 デイケアセンター
day care center

No.2916

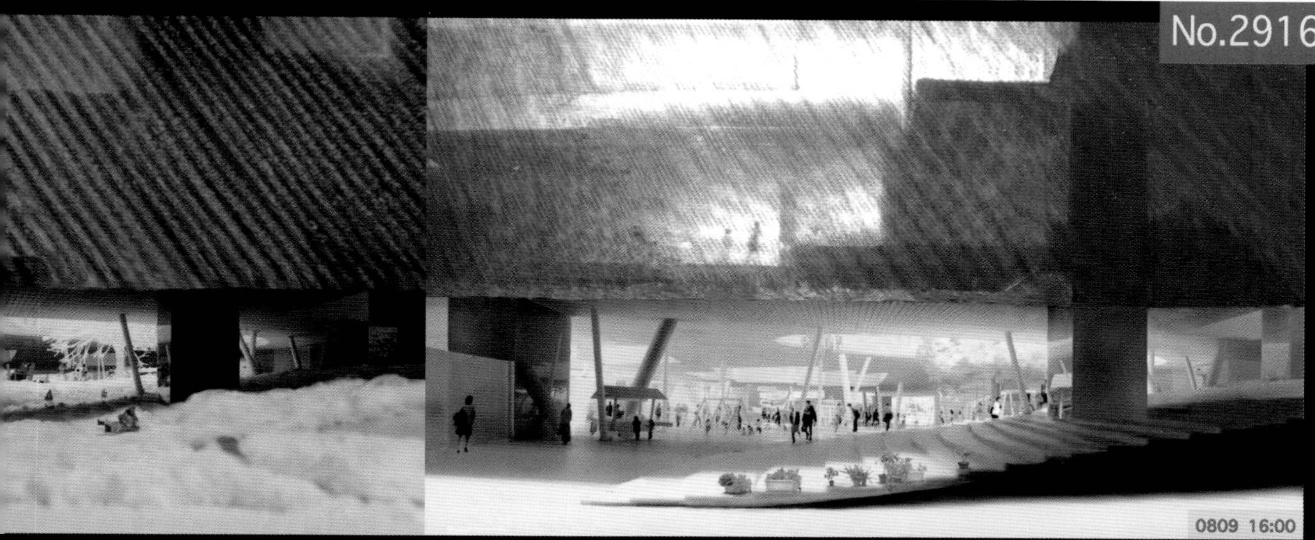

tyle Housing Complex In Aomori

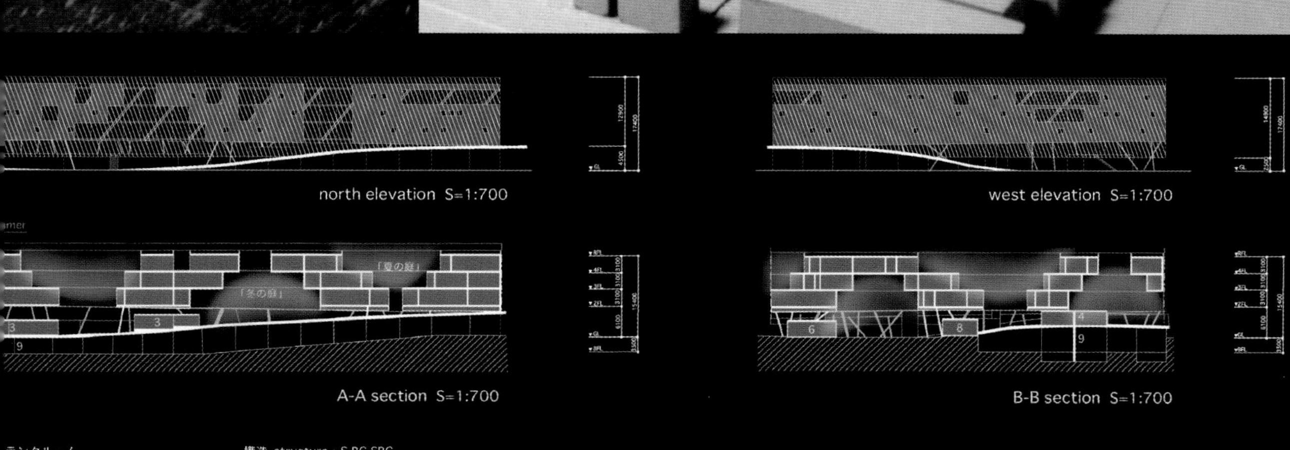

north elevation S=1:700

west elevation S=1:700

A-A section S=1:700

B-B section S=1:700

ランクルーム
unk room
火水槽
egestion tank
水槽
ater receiving tank
械室
echanical room
ンプ室
ater pump
気試験室
.D.F. room

構造 structure : S,RC,SRC
高さ height : 16.0m
住戸数 number of dwelling units : 200
建築面積 building area : 10,574㎡
建蔽率 building coverage ratio : 79.8%
延床面積 total floor area : 28,420㎡
容積率 floor area ratio : 171.6%
各施設床面積 floor area of each facility

・住宅 dwelling	20,848㎡
住戸部 dwelling unit	15,631㎡
共用部 common space	5,217㎡
・デイケアセンター day care center	536㎡
・児童館 children center	220㎡
・保育園 day nursery	276㎡
・コミュニティサロン community salon	470㎡
・店舗 shop	772㎡
・駐車場 parking	5,814㎡
駐車台数 number of parking units	291
住宅用 for dwelling	200
施設用 for facilities	91

back lane network

034 Chushinji Temple Priests' Quarters | *Katsuhiro Miyamoto & Associates*

Location : Minowa-machi, Kamiina-District, Nagano
Principal in Charge : Katsuhiro Miyamoto
Project Team : Isamu Tamaishi, Takenori Uotani

Structural Engineering : Hirokazu Toki (University of Shiga Prefecture), Takashi Manda (Takashi Manda structural design)
General Contractor : Shibusaki Kensetsu

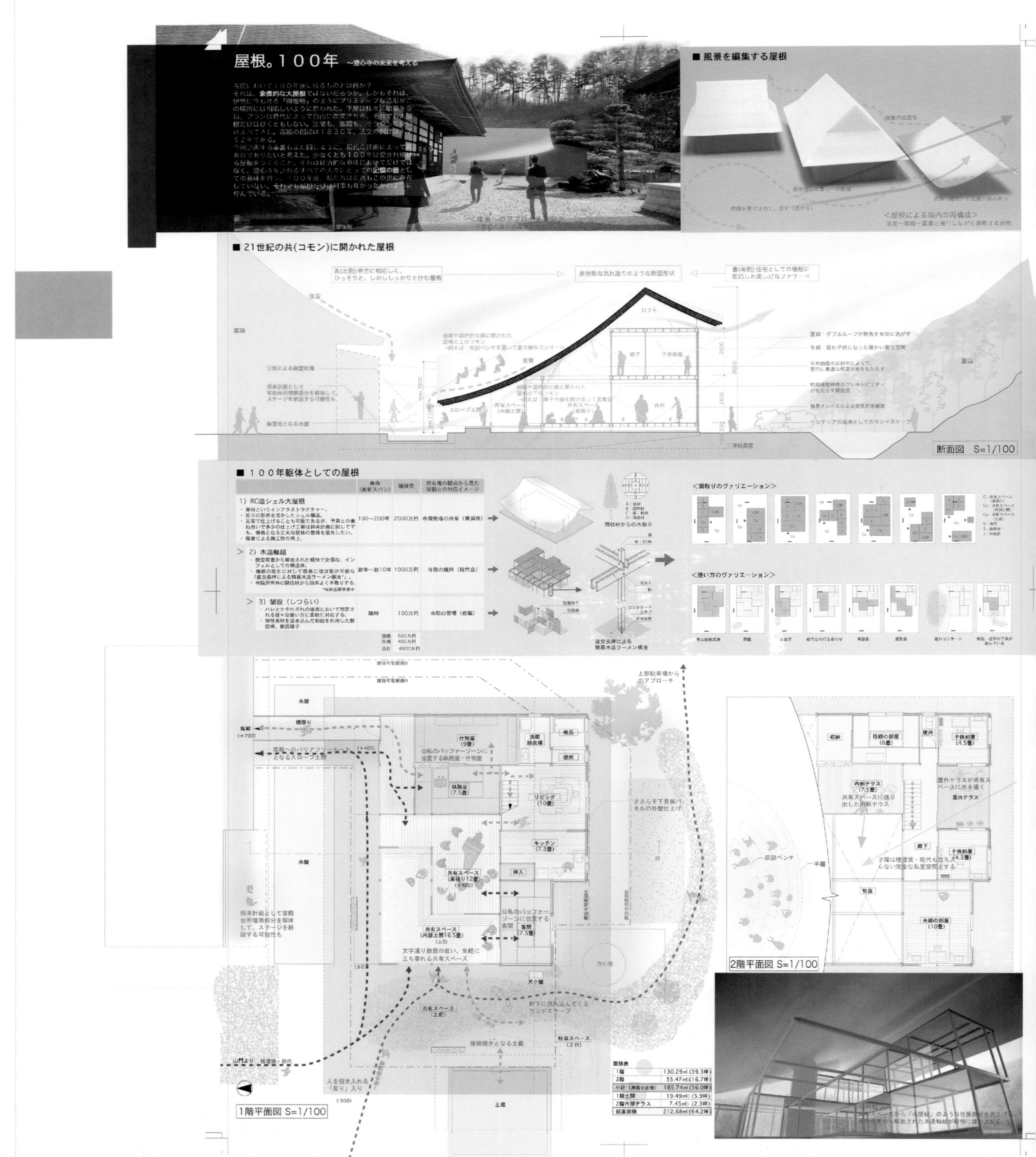

The Node | *NABITO ARCHITECTS & PARTNERS*

Date : 2011
Surface : 9.295 m²

Project phase : International Competition / 4th prize
Collaborators : Furio Sordini, Agita Putnina, Federica Bufano, Jorge Muñiz

Concorso Internazionale di idee "I PORTICI" per un complesso polifunzionale Residenze, Commercio e Spazi Pubblici a Frosinone

NABITO architects & partners s.l.p.

Tipologia dell'intervento:
Concorso internazionale "I Portici" per un complesso polifunzionale Residenza, Commercio e Spazi Pubblici a Frosinone

Cliente: Gruppo Zeppieri Costruzioni

Area di intervento complessiva: 11.618 mq

Superficie costruita: 9.295 mq

Superficie parcheggio interrato: 7.275 mq

Stima dei costi: xxx €

La soluzione progettuale sviluppata affronta e risolve complessivamente le richieste prospettate in sede di redazione del bando, interpretando lo schema progettuale fornito dalla committenza.
Si e' pensato di ampliare la visione delle soluzioni, non solo progettando adeguatamente il complesso polifunzionale da realizzare, ma anche tenendo in alta considerazione i suoi spazi aperti e coperti e le relazioni con l'intorno urbano di differenti caratteristiche.

FOTO AEREA - AREA INTERVENTO

SCHEMA SPAZI APERTI VERSO IL LATO URBANO ED IL CENTRO STORICO

SCHEMA SPAZI APERTI VERSO LA VILLA ED IL PARCO

SCHEMA VISTE E SOLEGGIAMENTO VERSO IL LATO URBANO ED IL CENTRO STORICO

SCHEMA VISTE E SOLEGGIAMENTO VERSO LA VILLA ED IL PARCO

ORIENTAMENTO EST-OVEST DI TUTTE LE TIPOLOGIE PER IL CORRETTO SOLEGGIAMENTO

ORIENTAMENTO NORD-SUD PER AVERE TUTTE LE TIPOLOGIE AFFACCIATE SULLA VILLA E SUL CENTRO STORICO DI FROSINONE

SLITTAMENTO DEI PIANI PER AMPLIFICARE IL VERDE DELLE LOGGE

PIANTA DELLE COPERTURE rapp. 1:1000

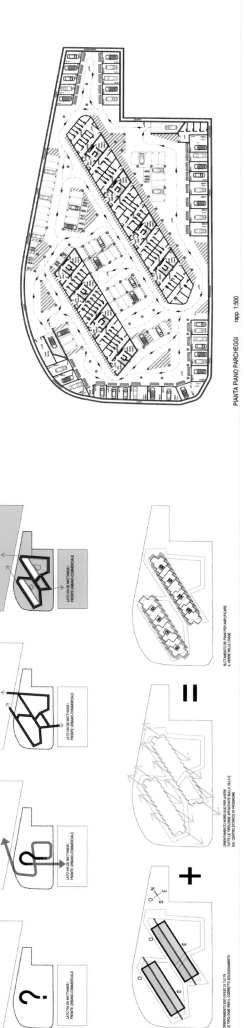

PIANTA PIANO PARCHEGGI rapp. 1:500

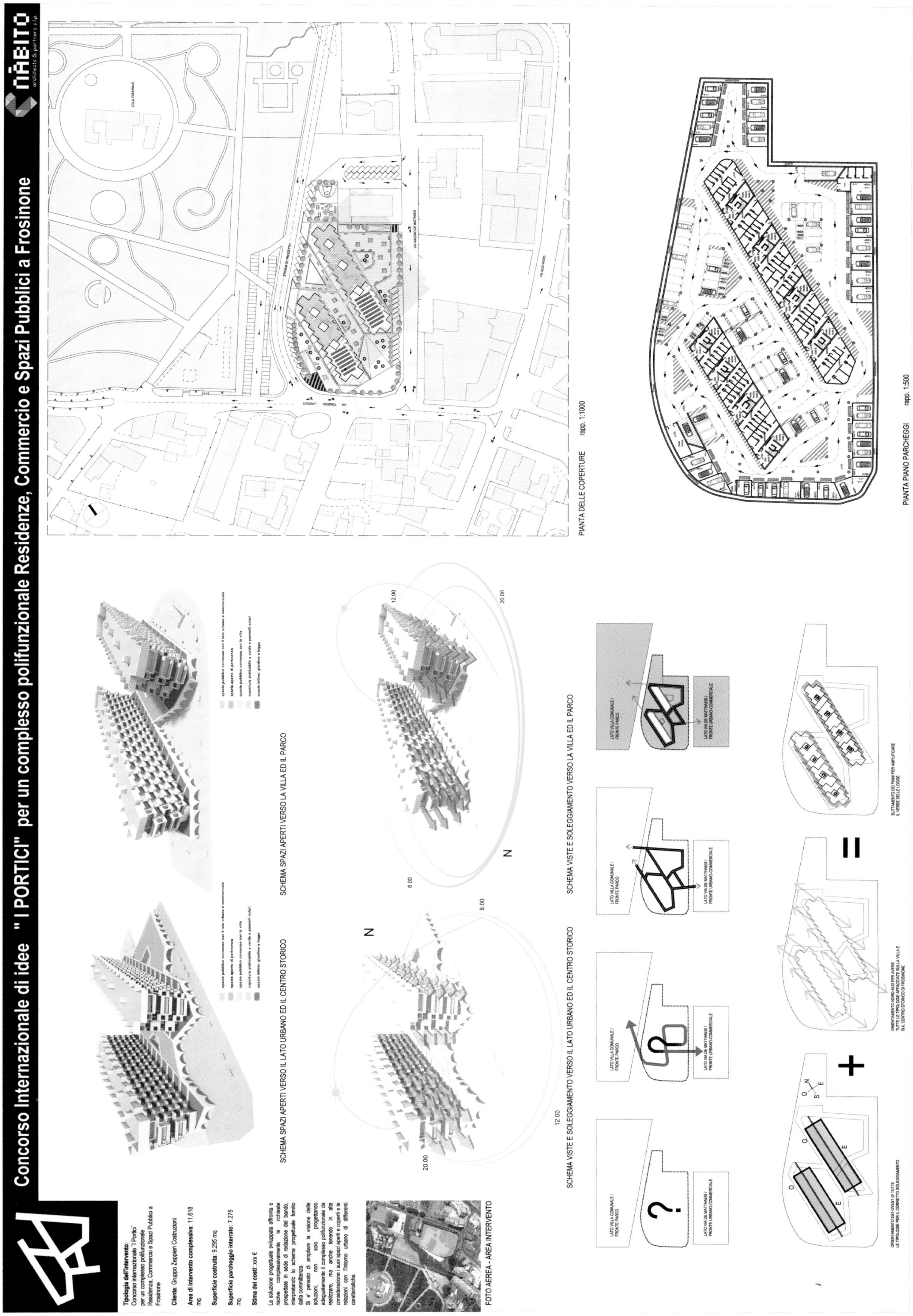

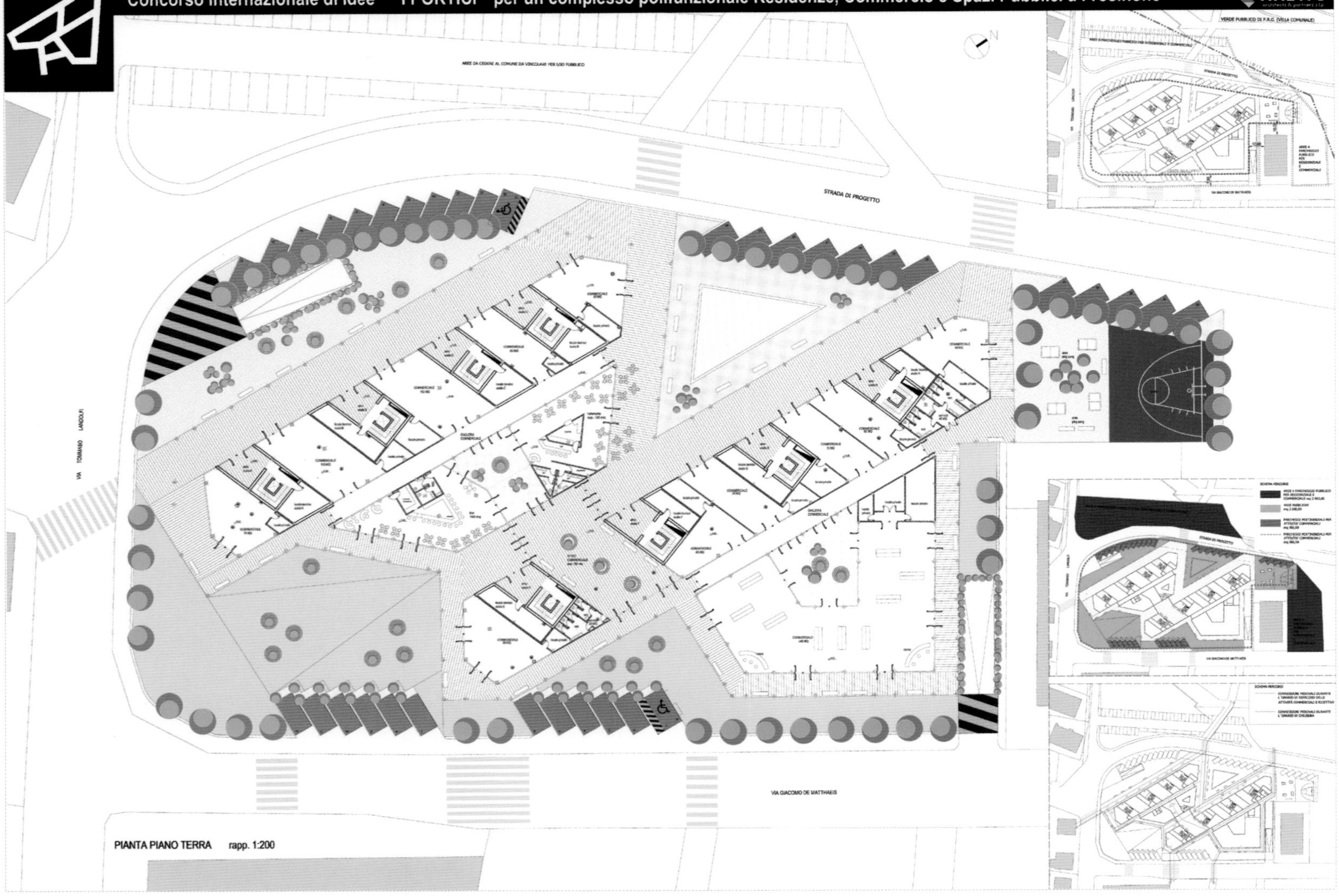

Concorso Internazionale di idee "I PORTICI" per un complesso polifunzionale Residenze, Commercio e Spazi Pubblici a Frosinone

nĀBITO

STRADA DI PROGETTO

VIA TOMMASO LANDOLFI

VIA GIACOMO DE MATTHAEIS

PIANTA PIANO TERRA rapp. 1:200

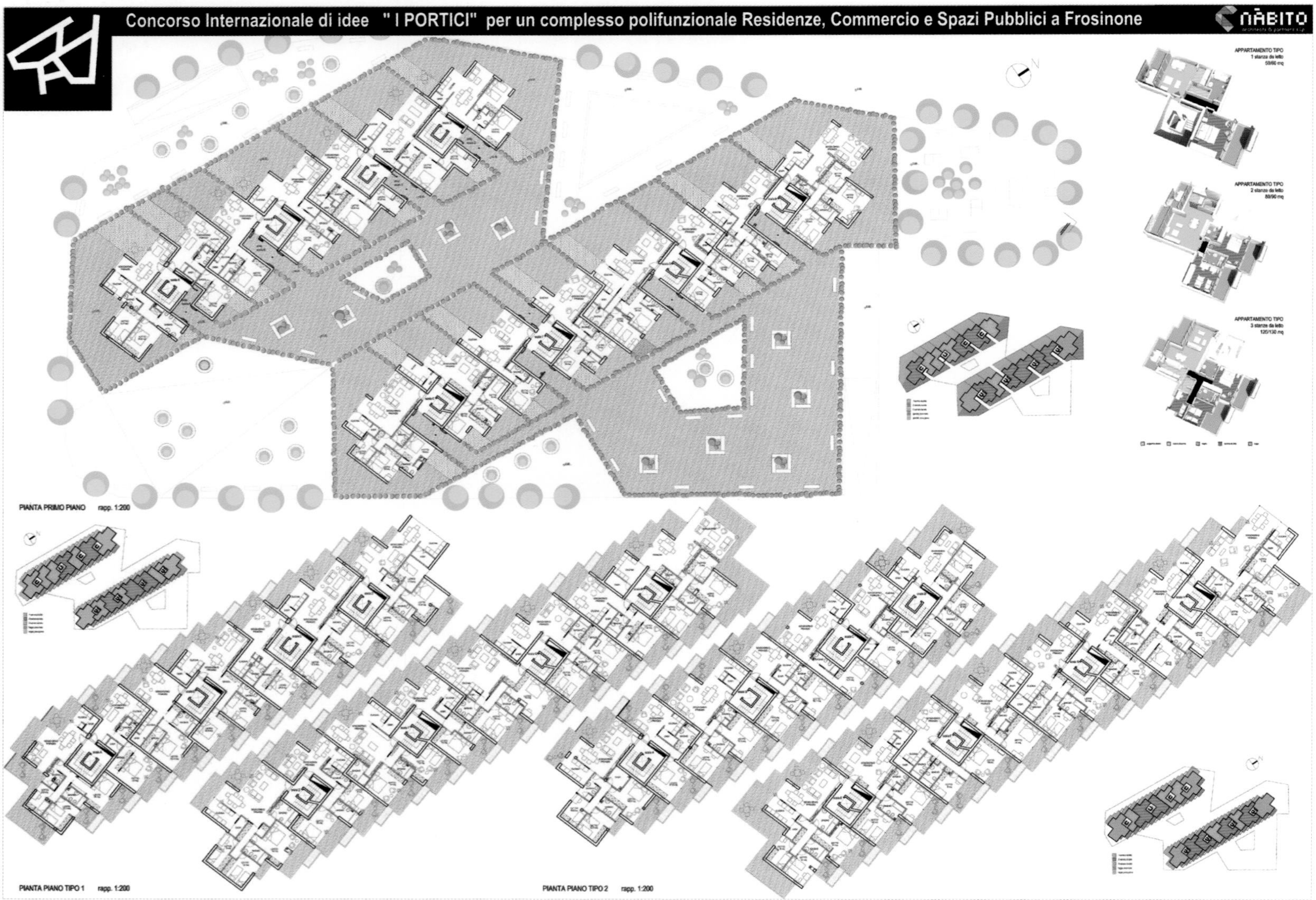

Concorso Internazionale di idee "I PORTICI" per un complesso polifunzionale Residenze, Commercio e Spazi Pubblici a Frosinone

nĀBITO

PIANTA PRIMO PIANO rapp. 1:200

PIANTA PIANO TIPO 1 rapp. 1:200

PIANTA PIANO TIPO 2 rapp. 1:200

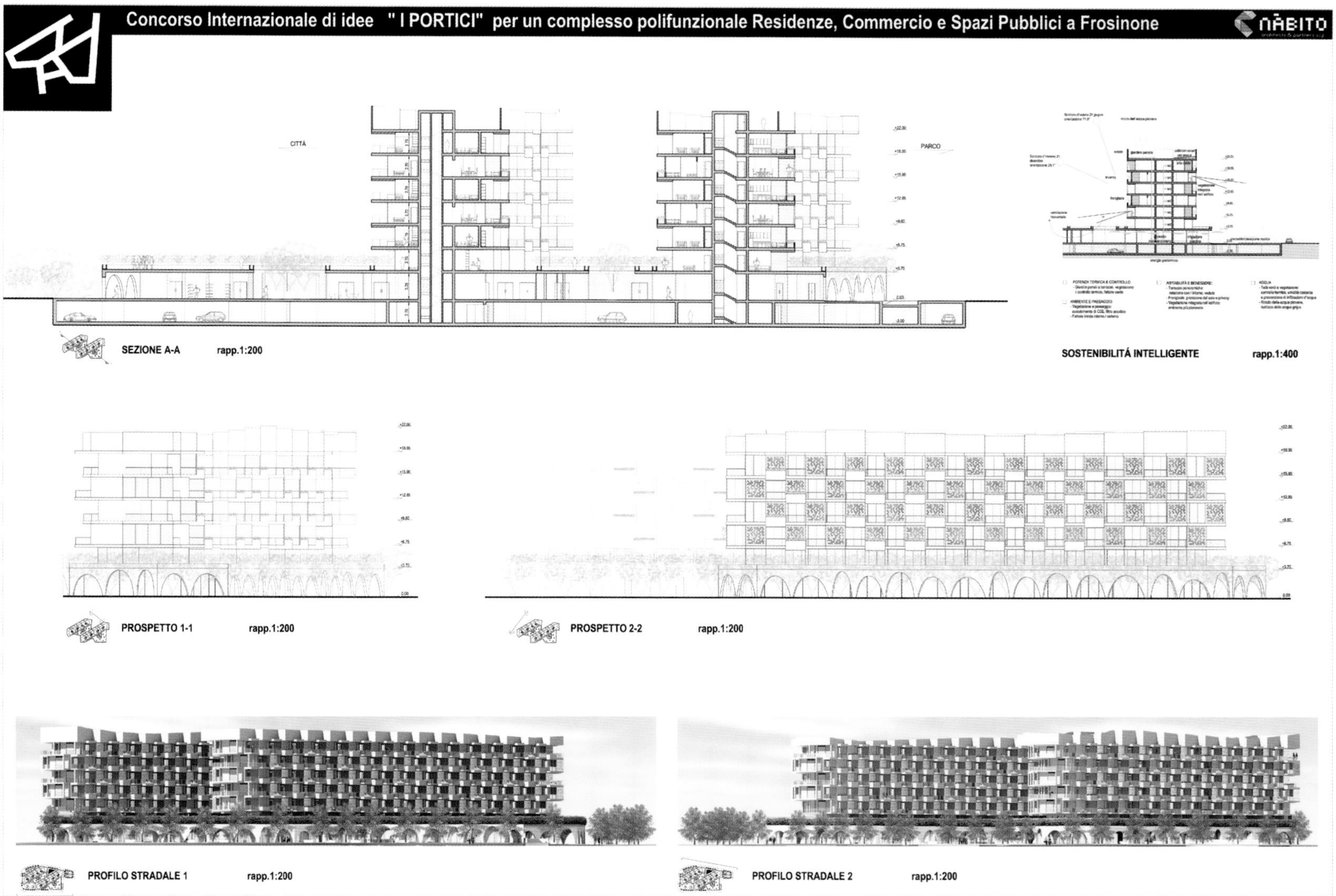
Concorso Internazionale di idee "I PORTICI" per un complesso polifunzionale Residenze, Commercio e Spazi Pubblici a Frosinone
nĀBITO
CITTÀ
PARCO
SEZIONE A-A rapp.1:200
SOSTENIBILITÁ INTELLIGENTE rapp.1:400
PROSPETTO 1-1 rapp.1:200
PROSPETTO 2-2 rapp.1:200
PROFILO STRADALE 1 rapp.1:200
PROFILO STRADALE 2 rapp.1:200

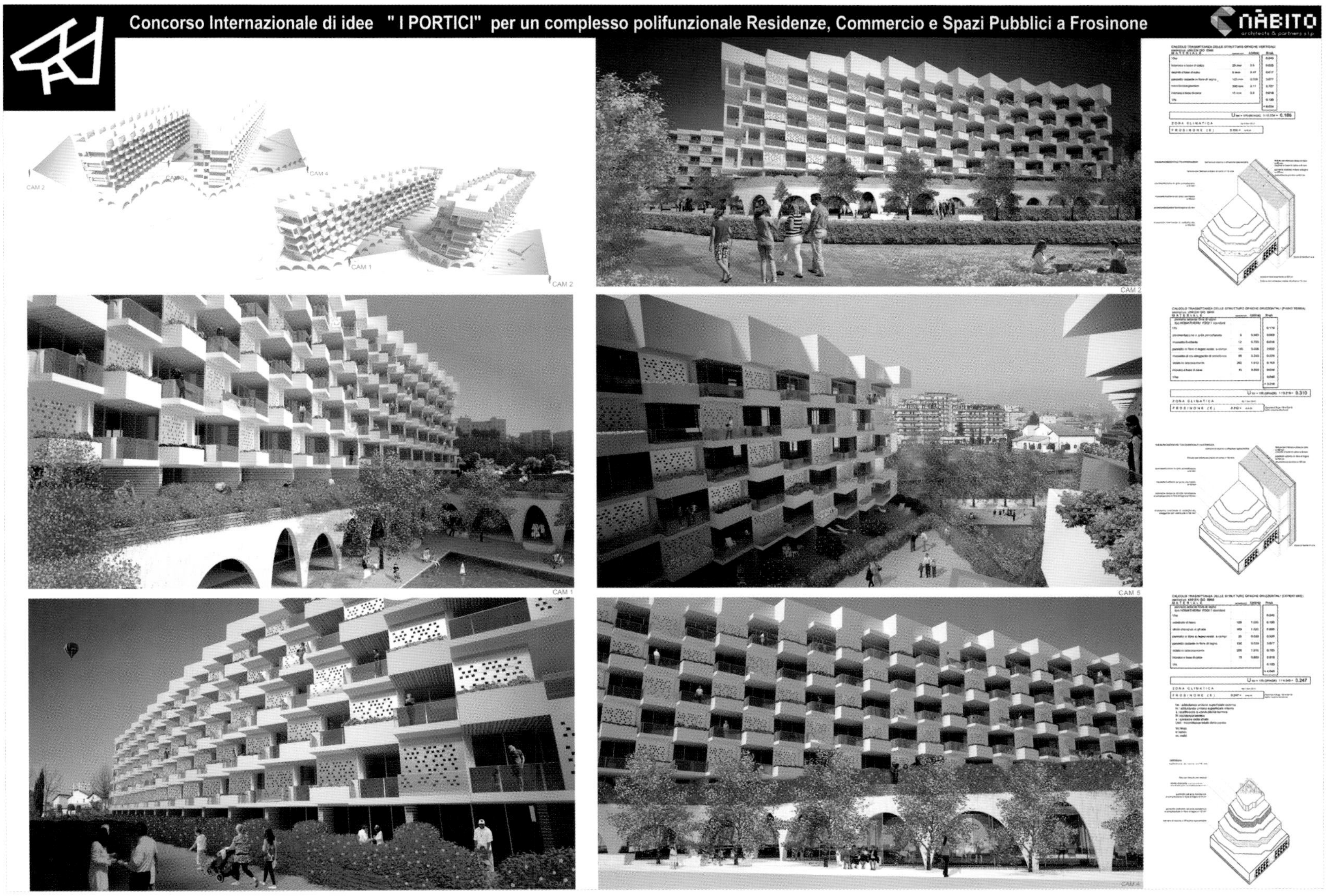
Concorso Internazionale di idee "I PORTICI" per un complesso polifunzionale Residenze, Commercio e Spazi Pubblici a Frosinone
nĀBITO
architects & partners
CAM 2
CAM 4
CAM 1
CAM 2
CAM 1
CAM 5
CAM 6

036 Stairscraper an Horizontal Skyscraper | *NABITO ARCHITECTS*

Assigned Task : Project design, site supervision, and security at design and execution
Project phase : International Idea Competition- First Prize / New York City
Team : Alessandra Faticanti, Roberto Ferlito, Sebastiano PalumboTeo Valli, Agita Putnina, Isidora Stecki, Sandra Stefanovic, Furio Sordini

THE STAIRSCRAPER

?

Typology: Residential - Apartment
Project:
Total Housing: Apartments.
New York, United States
Client: Actar publishers, Architizer.com, and Storefront for Art & Architecture

THE Stairscraper is a real provocation on the possibility of extending the housing to a Total Habitat sensitive to individual needs in a collective whole. So the passage from the private cottages (no spaces social bookmarking) to social cottages, maintaining individual and intimate space is evident.
THE STAIRScraper IS a superposition OF individual singular garden houses with the same characteristic of the horizontal sprawl but liberating the land and concentrating the uses and the energy. It is A social collective of individualities. The stair scraper is a complex 360 degree incorporate all kind of common facilities and public spaces at different levels maintaining the intimacy of the individual space with the same quality.

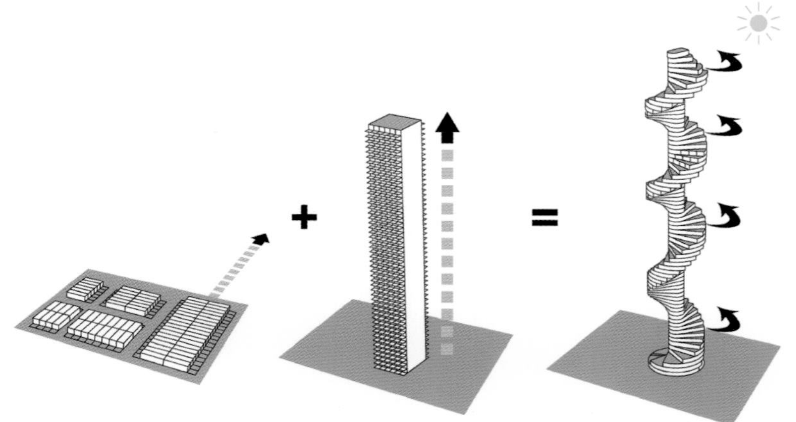

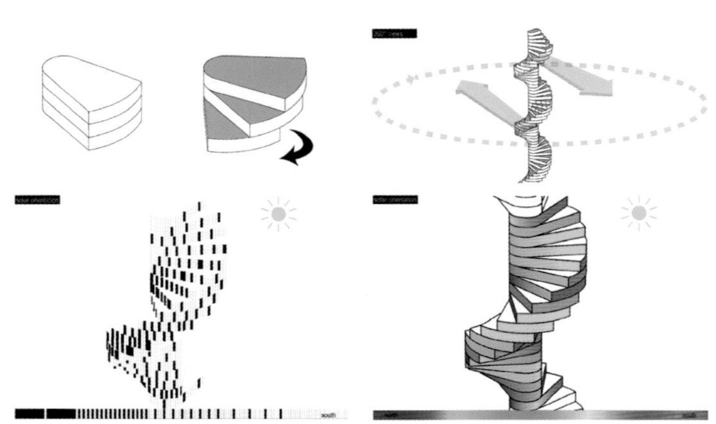

THE STAIRSCRAPER

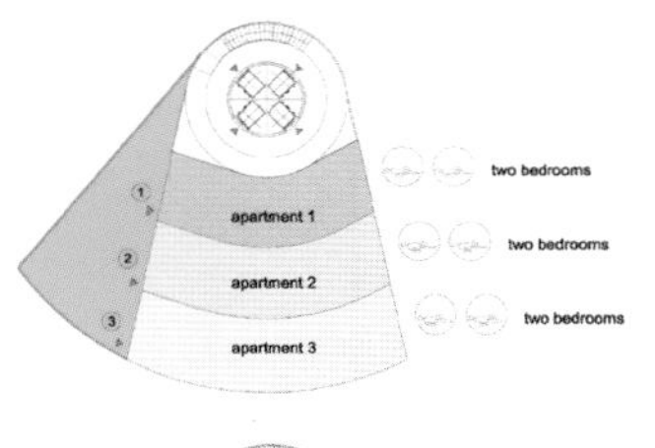

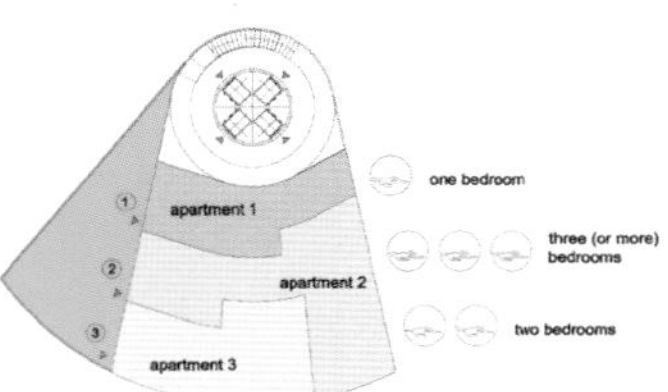

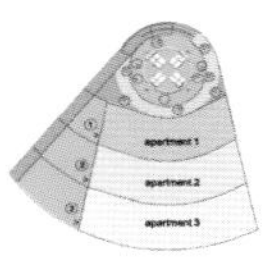

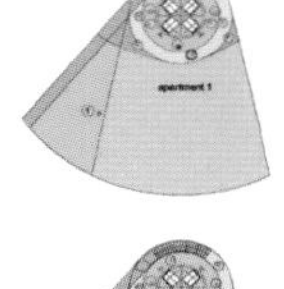

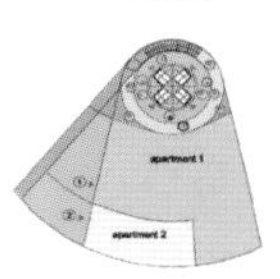

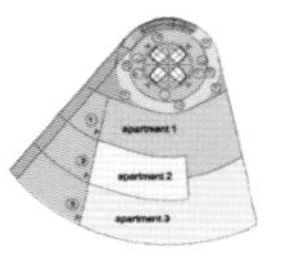

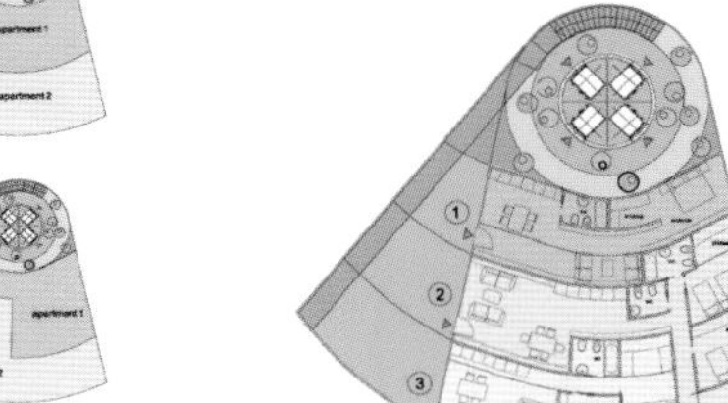

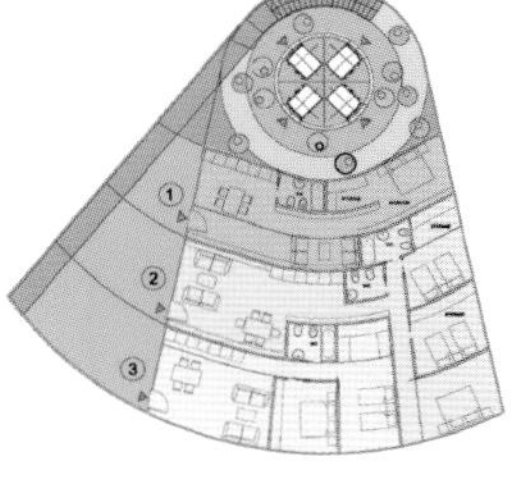

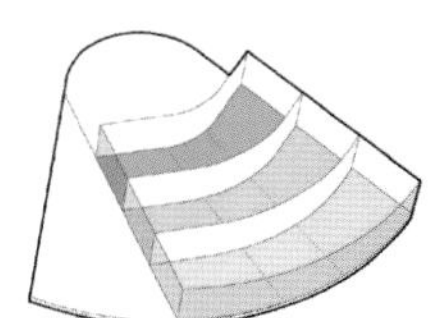

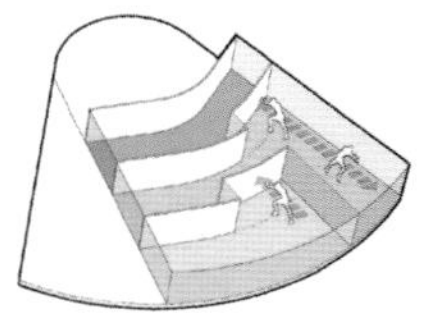

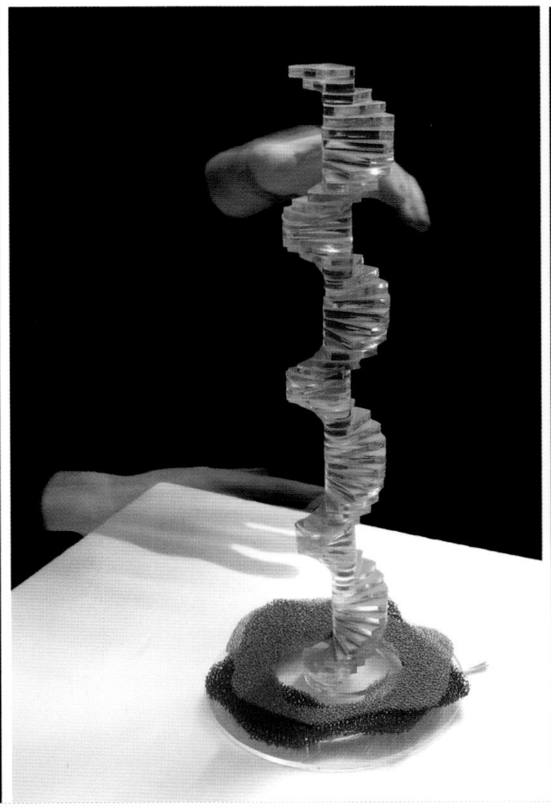

037 Torre Familia | *NABITO ARCHITECTS & PARTNERS*

Assigned Typology : Public
Client : Empresa Municipal de la Vivienda y Suelo de Madrid, S.A.
Project phase : Competition on going

Date : 2011 / Surface : 12,530m²
Collaborators : Madara Villere, Leonards Kalnins

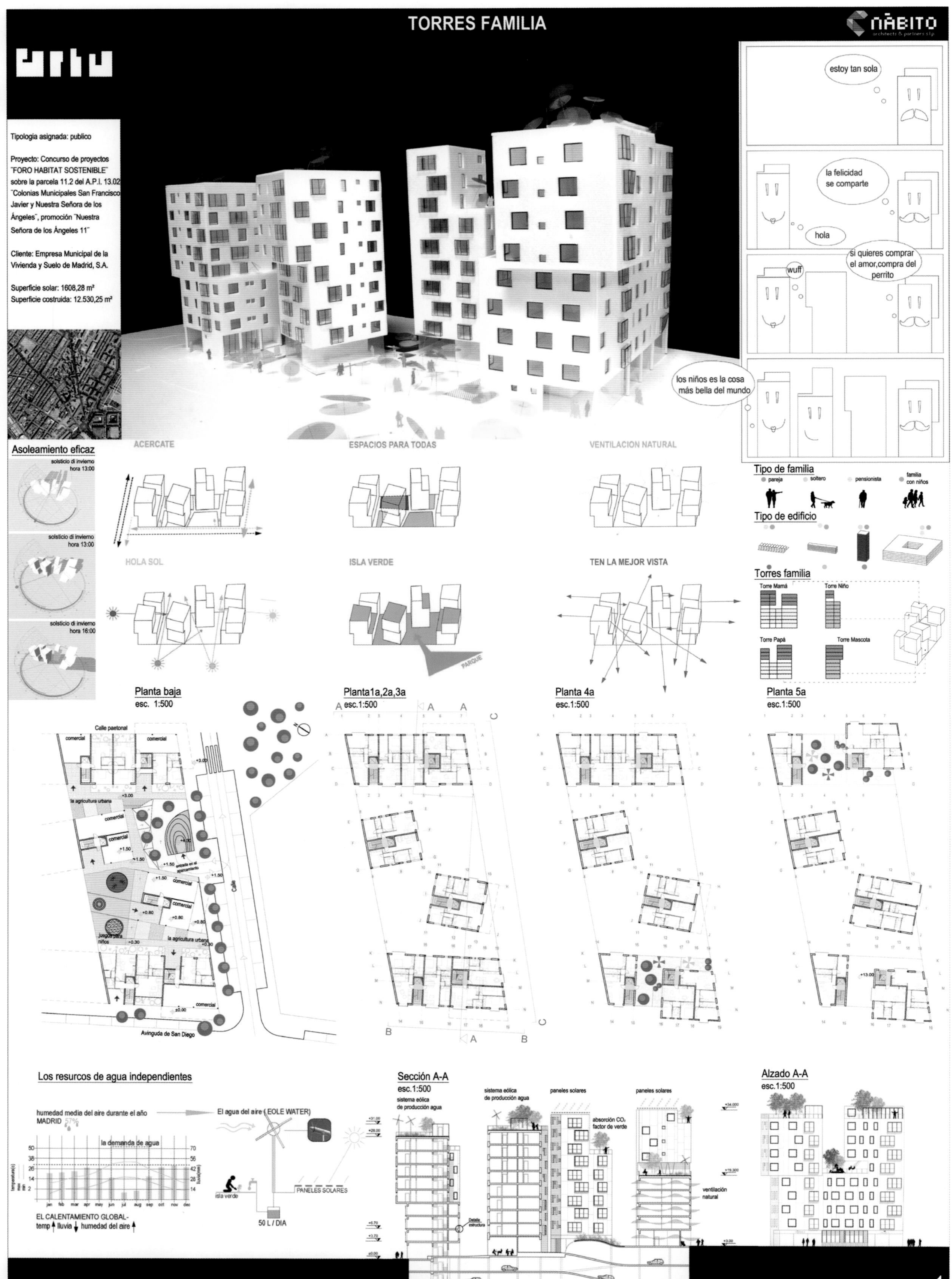

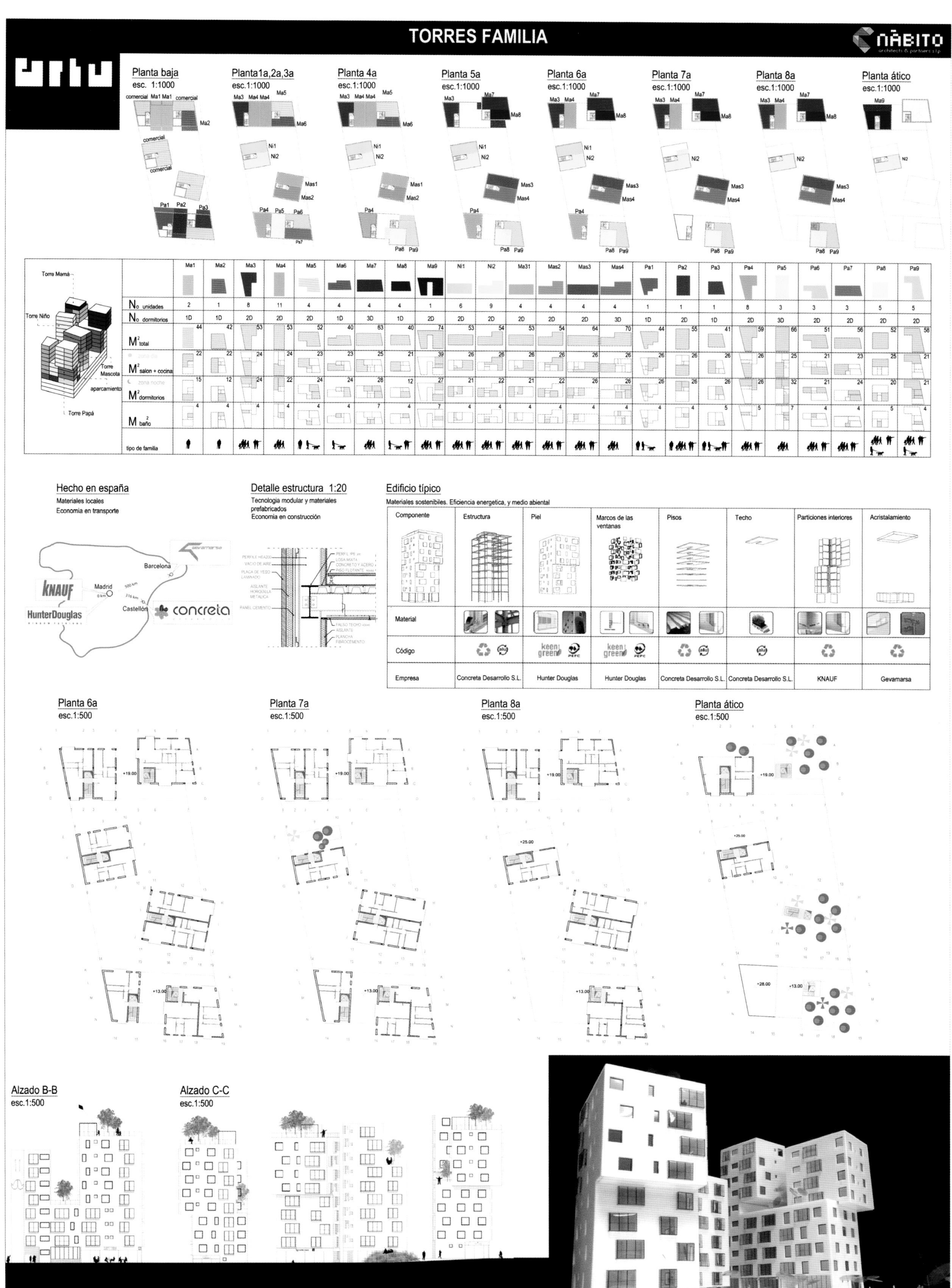
TORRES FAMILIA
NĀBITO
architects & partners s.l.p.
Planta baja
esc. 1:1000
Planta1a,2a,3a
esc.1:1000
Planta 4a
esc.1:1000
Planta 5a
esc.1:1000
Planta 6a
esc.1:1000
Planta 7a
esc.1:1000
Planta 8a
esc.1:1000
Planta ático
esc.1:1000
Torre Mamá
Torre Niño
Torre Mascota
aparcamiento
Torre Papá
No unidades
No dormitorios
M² total
M² salon + cocina
M² dormitorios
M² baño
tipo de familia
Hecho en españa
Materiales locales
Economia en transporte
Barcelona
Madrid
Castellón
KNAUF
HunterDouglas
concreta
Detalle estructura 1:20
Tecnologia modular y materiales prefabricados
Economia en construcción
Edificio típico
Materiales sostenibiles. Eficiencia energetica, y medio abiental
Componente
Estructura
Piel
Marcos de las ventanas
Pisos
Techo
Particiones interiores
Acristalamiento
Material
Código
Empresa
Concreta Desarrollo S.L.
Hunter Douglas
Hunter Douglas
Concreta Desarrollo S.L.
Concreta Desarrollo S.L.
KNAUF
Gevamarsa
Planta 6a
esc.1:500
Planta 7a
esc.1:500
Planta 8a
esc.1:500
Planta ático
esc.1:500
Alzado B-B
esc.1:500
Alzado C-C
esc.1:500
2

TORRES FAMILIA

n°	LEMA	VIVIENDAS n° total	1D	2D	3D	4D	% 1D	% 2D	% 3D	% 4D	superficies útil	const.	comp.	LOCALES n° total	superficies útil	const.	comp.	TRASTEROS n° total	superficies útil	const.	GARAJES n° plazas	superficies útil	const.	SUPERFICIES CONSTRUIDAS TOTAL	BR	SR	N° NUCLEOS COMUNIC.	RATIO CONST./ ÚTIL
DATOS EMVS		>= 100	5	75	20	0	5 %	75 %	20 %	0 %	5,494.46	7,966.96	=7516															>= 1,45
	AM 144	100	12	76	12	0	12 %	76 %	12 %	0 %	5,433.68	6,952.62	6,849.00	5	307.2	426.6	434.09	133	367.09	986	100	1038.75	3845.12	12,530.25	4,830.95	7,699.30	6	1.28

Urban House by Eternit | *Lima Urban Lab*

Location : Lima, Peru
Project Team : Pablo Diaz,Diego Rodriguez and Pamela Jara
Project Area : 400 sqm
Year : 2011

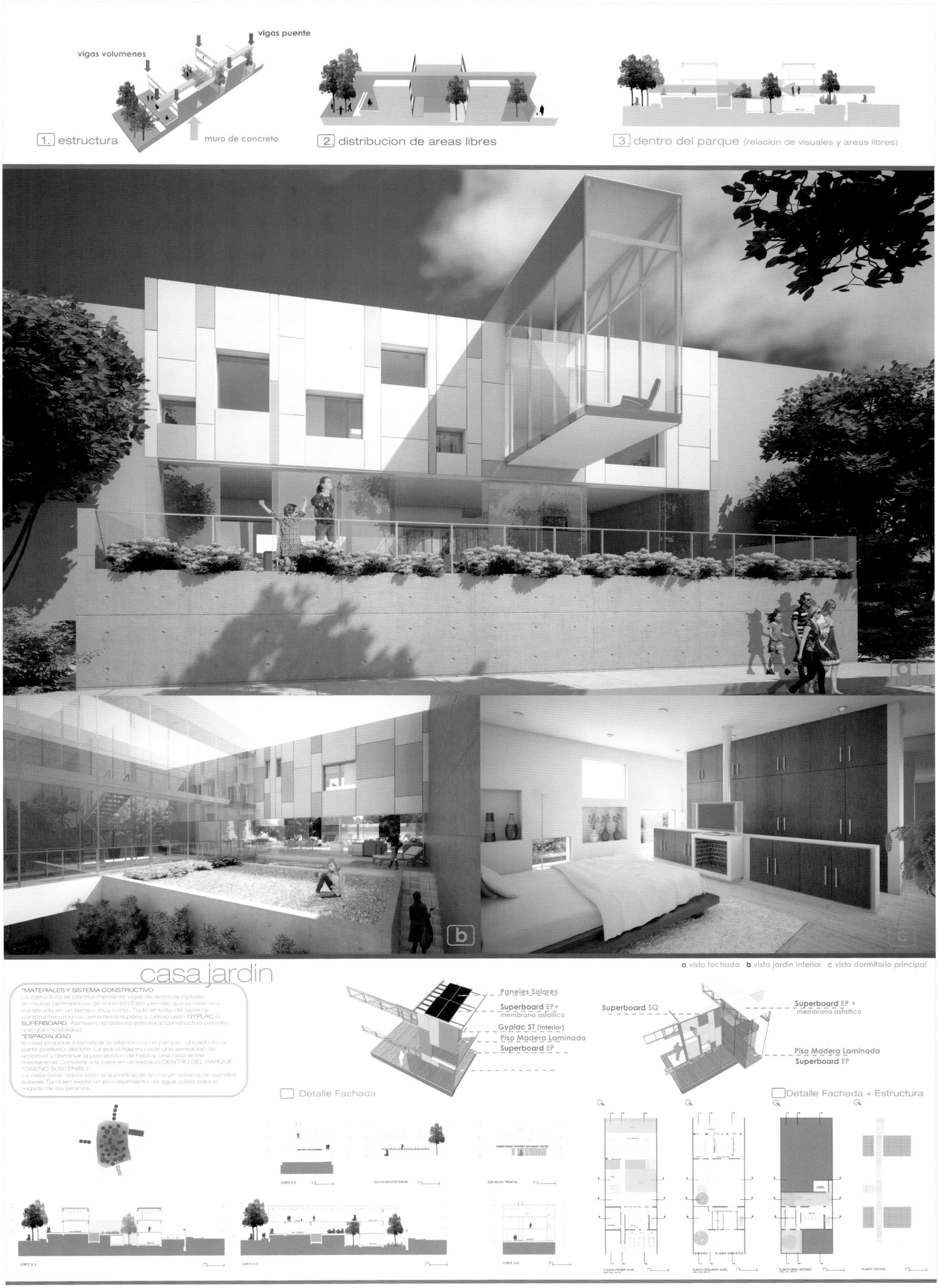

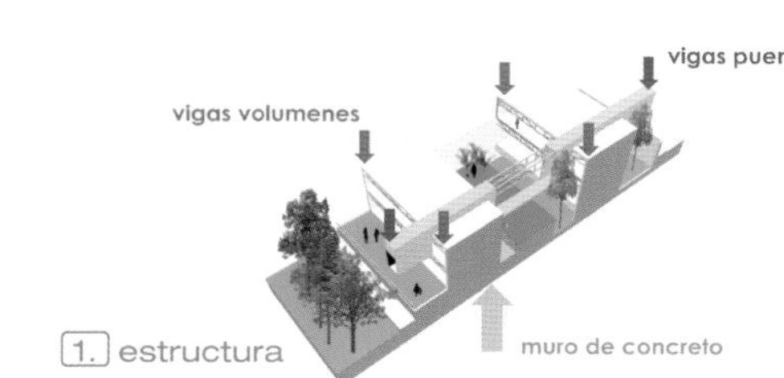

1. estructura

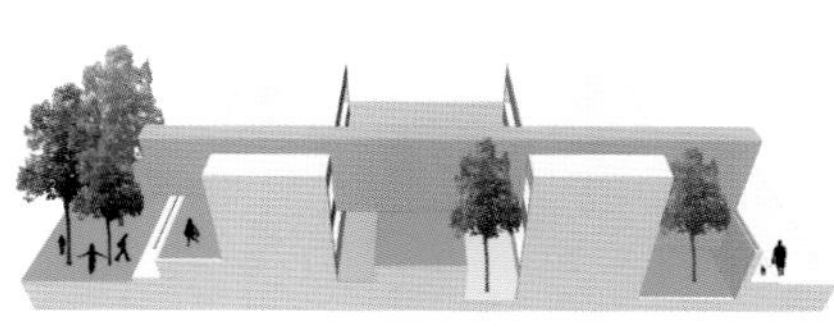

2. distribucion de areas libres

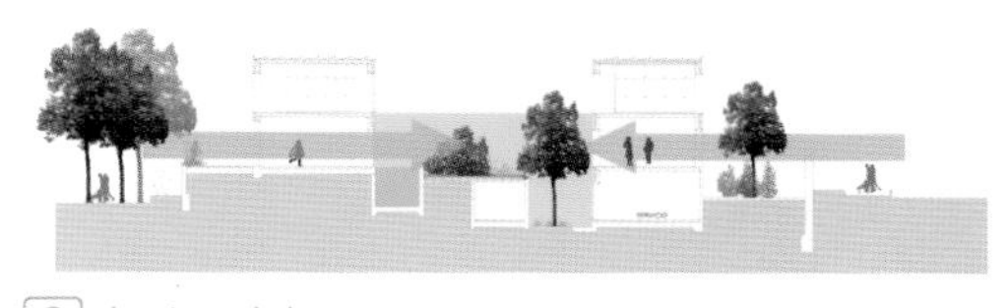

3. dentro del parque (relacion de visuales y areas libres)

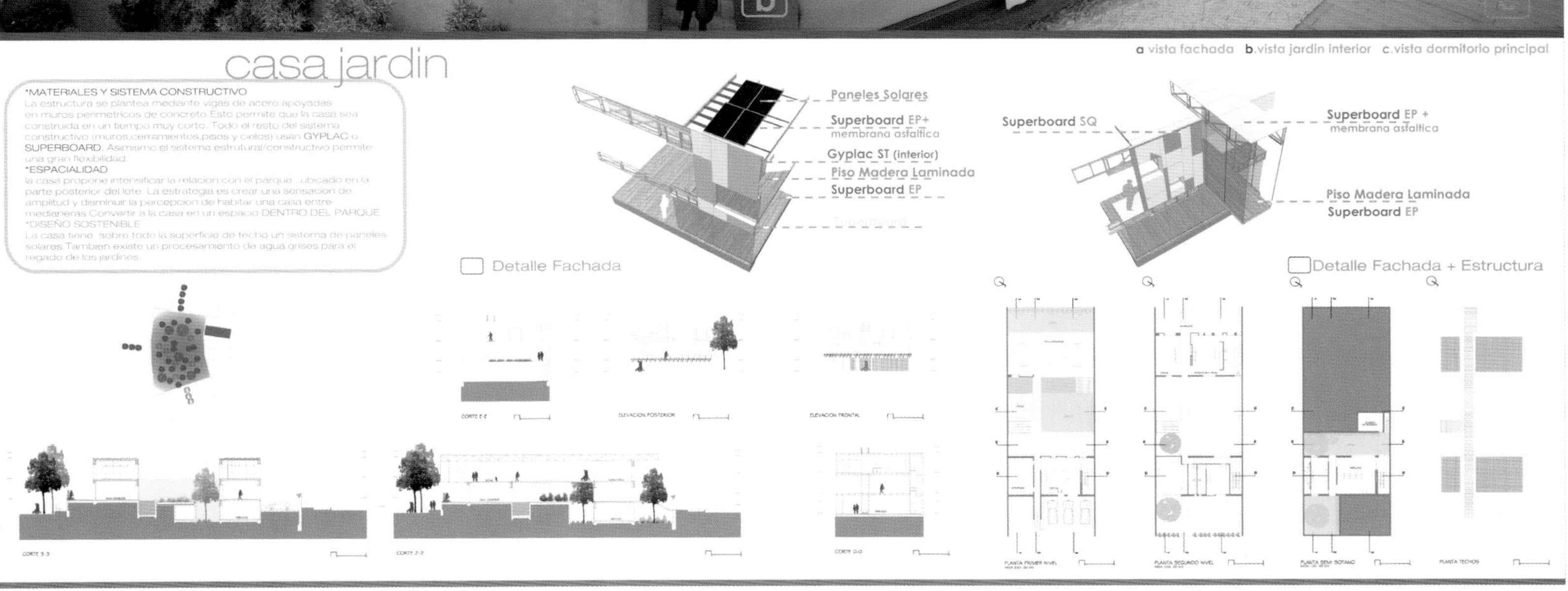

a vista fachada b.vista jardin interior c.vista dormitorio principal
casa jardin
*MATERIALES Y SISTEMA CONSTRUCTIVO
La estructura se plantea mediante vigas de acero apoyadas en muros perimetricos de concreto.Esto permite que la casa sea construida en un tiempo muy corto. Todo el resto del sistema constructivo (muros,cerramientos,pisos y cielos) usan GYPLAC o SUPERBOARD. Asimismo el sistema estrutural/constructivo permite una gran flexibilidad.
*ESPACIALIDAD
la casa propone intensificar la relacion con el parque , ubicado en la parte posterior del lote. La estrategia es crear una sensacion de amplitud y disminuir la percepcion de habitar una casa entre medianeras Convertir a la casa en un espacio DENTRO DEL PARQUE
*DISEÑO SOSTENIBLE
La casa tiene sobre todo la superficie de techo un sistema de paneles solares.Tambien existe un procesamiento de agua grises para el regado de los jardines.
Paneles Solares
Superboard EP+ membrana asfaltica
Gyplac ST (interior)
Piso Madera Laminada
Superboard EP
Detalle Fachada
Superboard SQ
Superboard EP + membrana asfaltica
Piso Madera Laminada
Superboard EP
Detalle Fachada + Estructura

039

HDW-01 | *remote-controlled*

House of the winds (One man highriser)
Location : Japan, Miyako Island
Typology : Leisure residence (40 sc meters of living space)
Design : Anton Markus Pasing

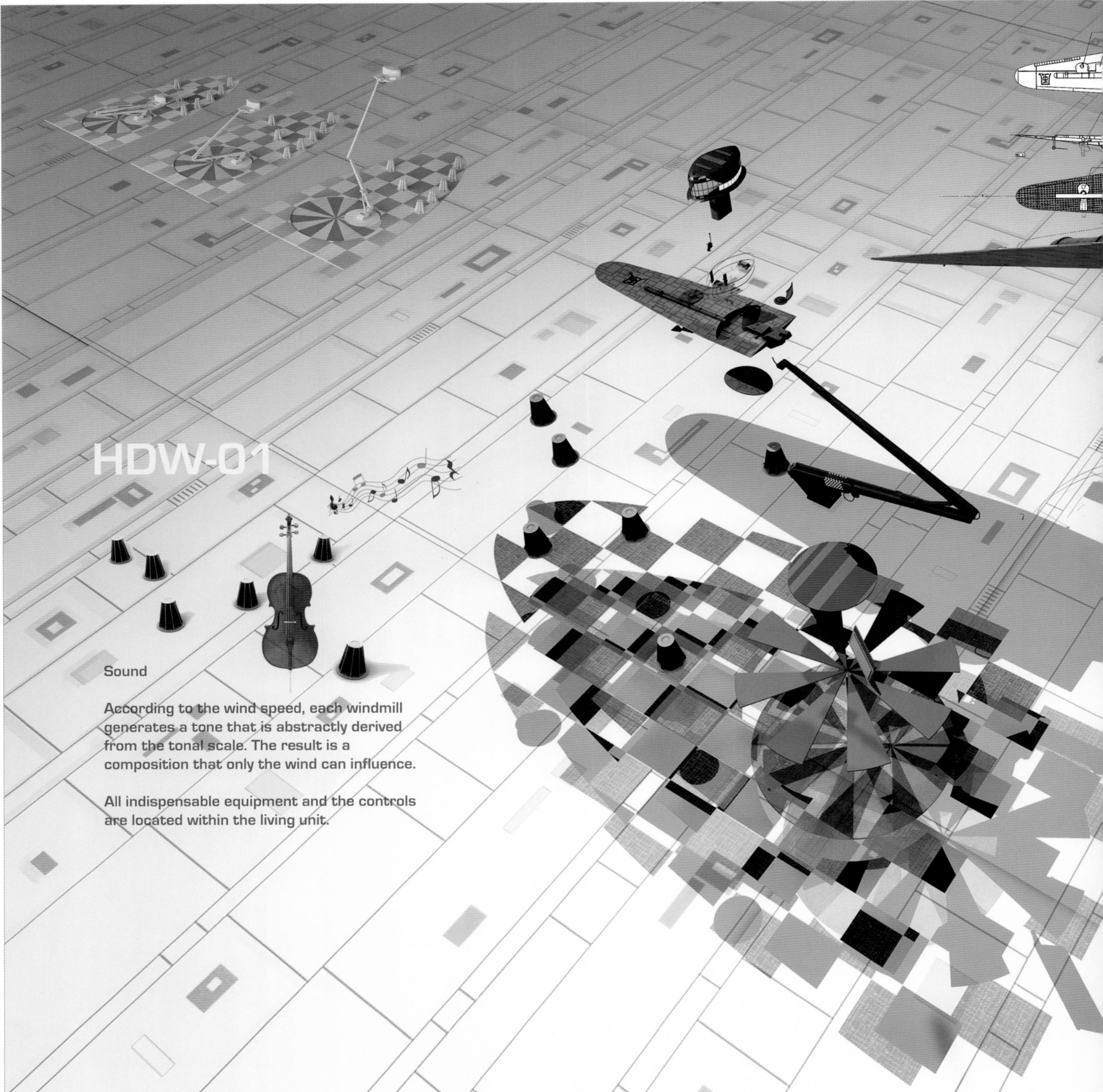

HDW-01

Sound

According to the wind speed, each windmill generates a tone that is abstractly derived from the tonal scale. The result is a composition that only the wind can influence.

All indispensable equipment and the controls are located within the living unit.

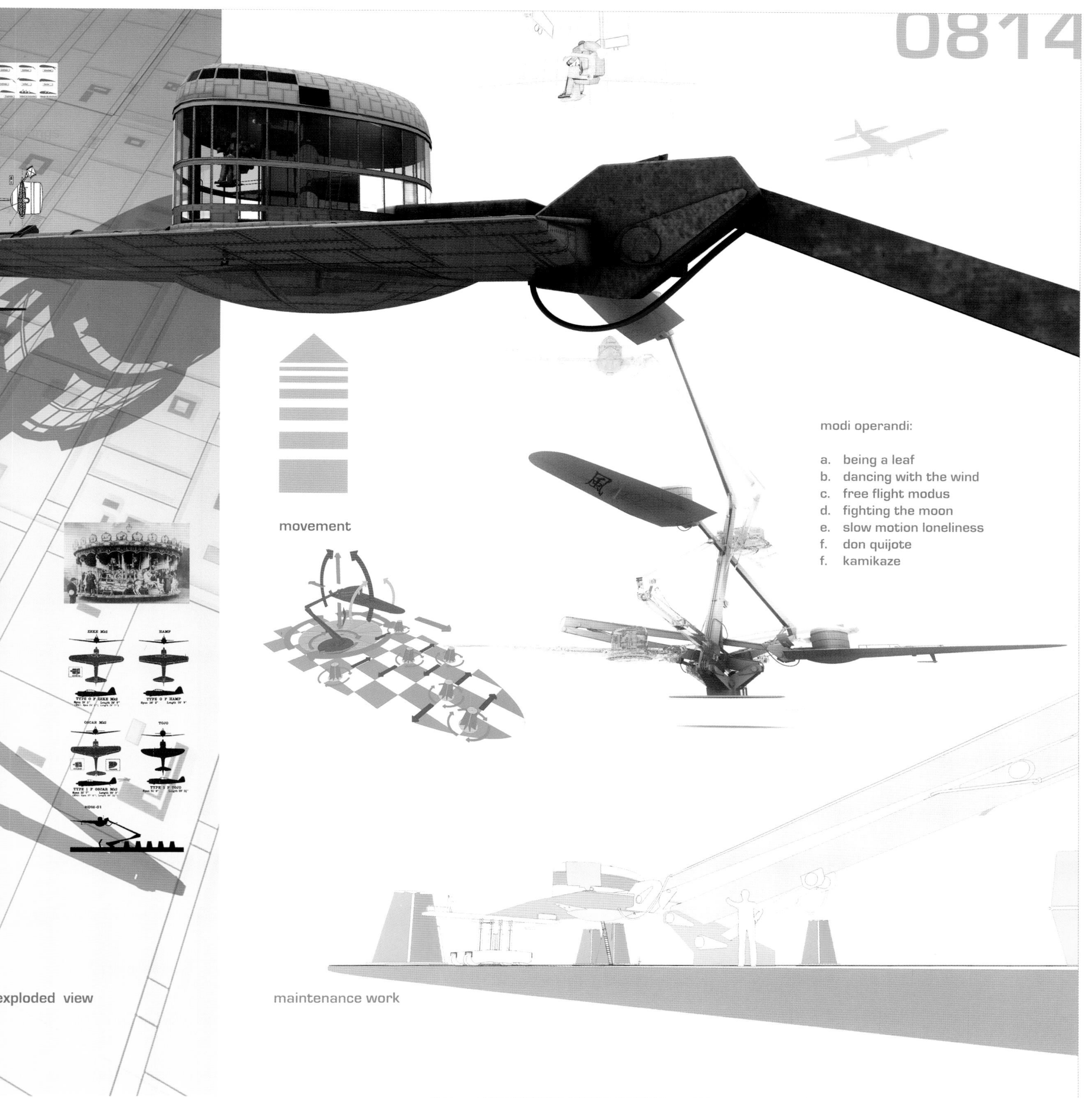
0814
modi operandi:
a. being a leaf
b. dancing with the wind
c. free flight modus
d. fighting the moon
e. slow motion loneliness
f. don quijote
f. kamikaze
movement
exploded view
maintenance work

HDW-01

House of the Winds

One man hirghriser

Introduction

Function as itself is senseless. There is no sense in function which goes beyond its nature. We have to make sure, that architecture will help us to fullfill our dreams and deep longing. One man, one life, one duty. Sustainability don´t just mean technoloty, Sustainability is a more a question of
Story

At a windy and lonely place, a former Japanese pilot brings his dream into being:

A house that is in almost constant motion, manually controlled and/or wind driven. Closer to a dancer or a leaf in the wind than to a house.

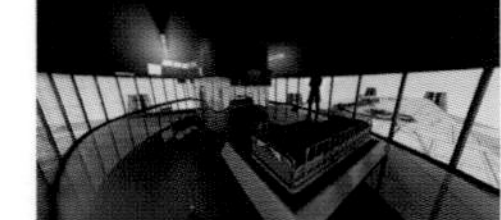
restroom

cockpit

elevation

Function

By means of changes to various parameters (wind, atmospheric conditions, light, etc.) the modes of movement
can be influenced.

Moreover, this routine can be temporarily transposed to manual control by switching the automatic pilot off.

The lifting arm is mounted on the ground on two discs that rotate independently of each other.

The vertical windmills are continually and automatically realigned according to the direction and speed of the wind so as to find the best possible position.

A wind sail on the ground acts as a passive wind catch and enhances the possibilities of movement.

view to the site

view from the wing

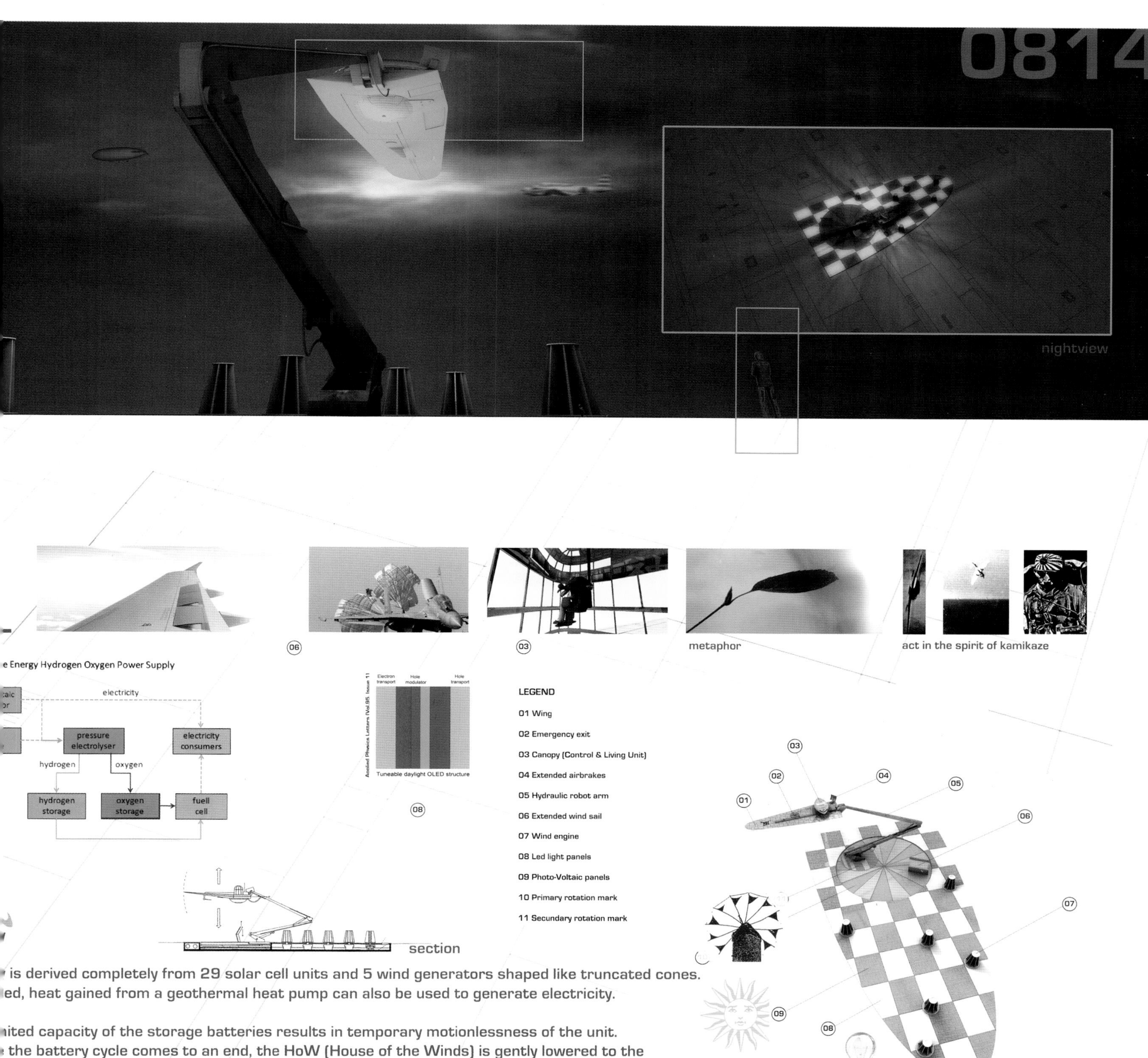

is derived completely from 29 solar cell units and 5 wind generators shaped like truncated cones. ed, heat gained from a geothermal heat pump can also be used to generate electricity.

ited capacity of the storage batteries results in temporary motionlessness of the unit. the battery cycle comes to an end, the HoW (House of the Winds) is gently lowered to the where it remains until the batteries are recharged.

er unit driven by airplane fuel serves as a reserve.

040 Minneapolis House | *Kevin Kennon Architects*

Location : Minneapolis, MN USA
Program : Single House
System : Reinforced Concrete
Area : 8,000 SQF
Floors : 2 Floors + Basement

MINNEAPOLIS HOUSE
MINNEAPOLIS, MN USA

Location : Minneapolis, MN USA
Program : Single House
System : Reinforced Concrete
Area : 8,000 SQF
Floors : 2 Floors + Basement

SITE PLAN

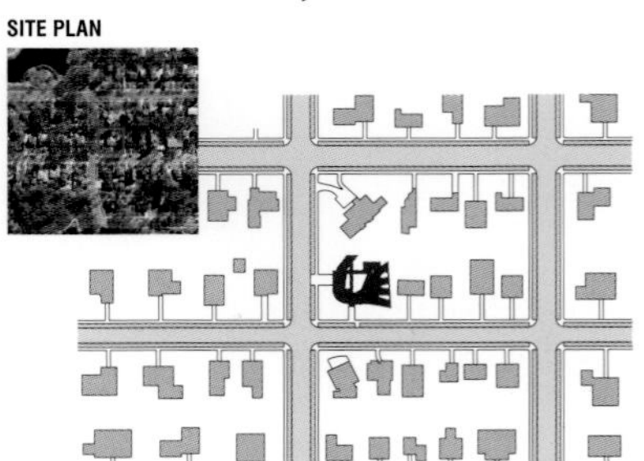

INTERIOR VIEWS

SPACE DIAGRAM

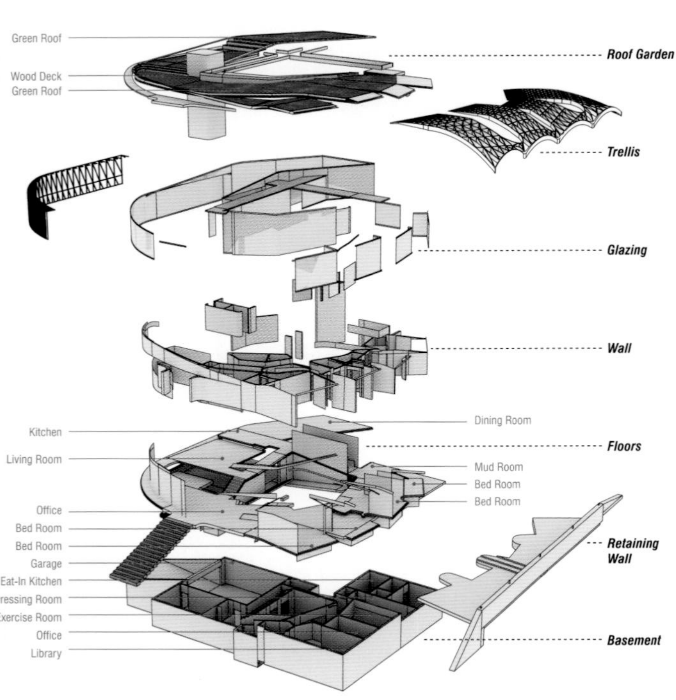

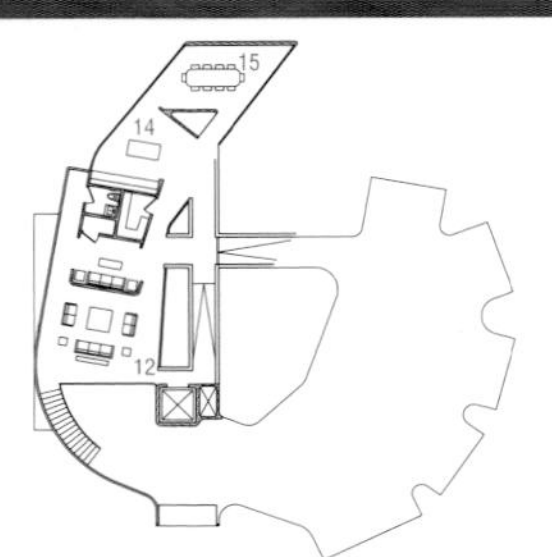

2ND FLOOR PLAN

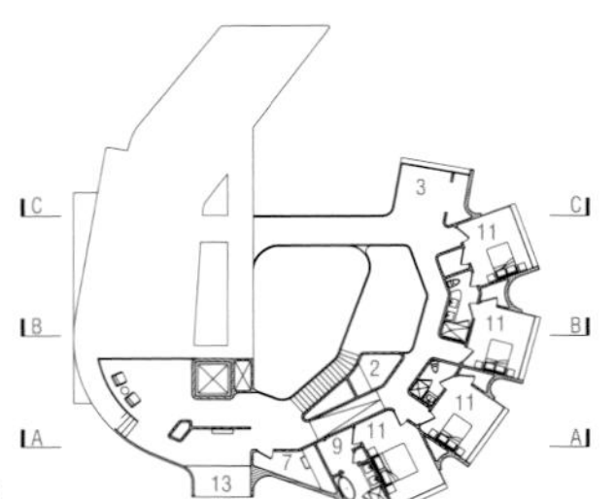

1ST FLOOR PLAN

1. Mech Room
2. Ele. Machine
3. Mud Room
4. Living Room
5. Storage
6. Library
7. Office
8. Exercise Room
9. Dressing Room
10. Eat-In Kitchen
11. Bed Room
12. Garage
13. Entrance
14. Kitchen
15. Dining Room
16. Storage
17. Corridor
18. Bath Room
19. Closet

BASEMENT FLOOR PLAN

AERIAL VIEW

SECTION C-C

SECTION B-B

SECTION A-A

Strawberry Fields Forever | *Horhizon consortium*

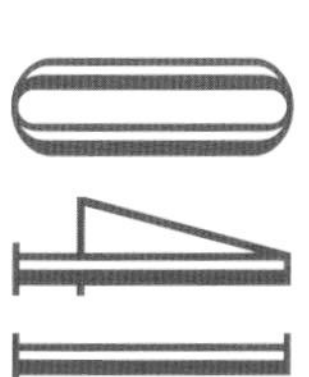

Team : Tobias Klein and Dietmar Koering with Kleopatra Chelmi, Eleanor Dodman and Graham K.Smith

STRAWBERRY FIELDS FOREVER

Proposal:

Cities can be very isolating; people live in high-density tower blocks but lead individual lives and do not commune with their neighbours. 'Growing your own' is something that can bring people together, however allotments are rapidly disappearing in cities, as land is reallocated for housing.

'Gathering' is initiated through social interaction and agricultural cultivation in a hybrid typology - a zero-carbon network of greenhouses and fields within high-density living; a space cultivated by the residents for the residents. Fruit and vegetable markets further extend the gathering space. Here produce is exchanged between residents; this establishes a community feel through shared activity.

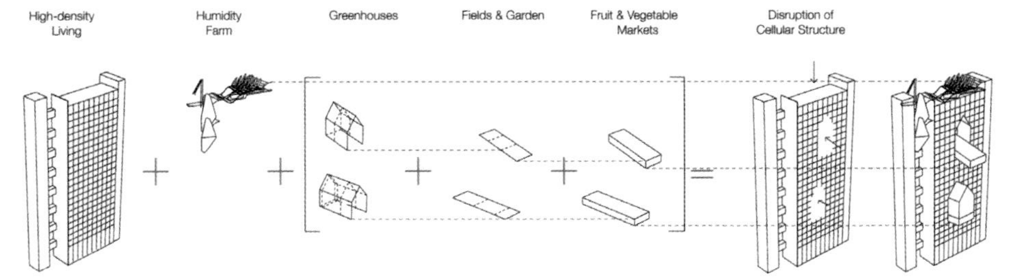

High-density Living + Humidity Farm + [Greenhouses + Fields & Garden + Fruit & Vegetable Markets] = Disruption of Cellular Structure

Insertion of greenhouse, market and connections to the humidity farm on the roof of the tower

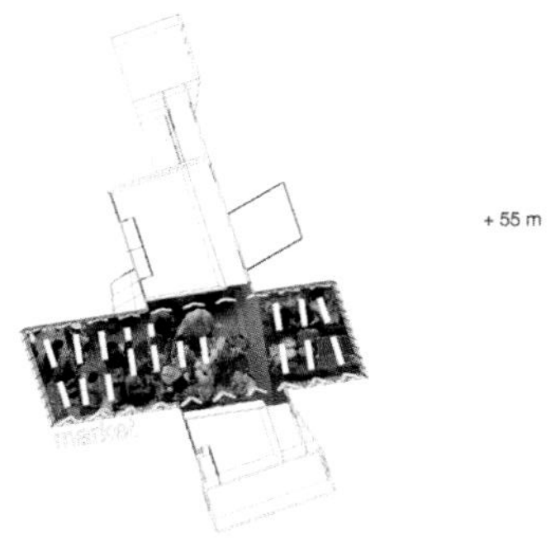

+ 55 m

Communal vegetable market

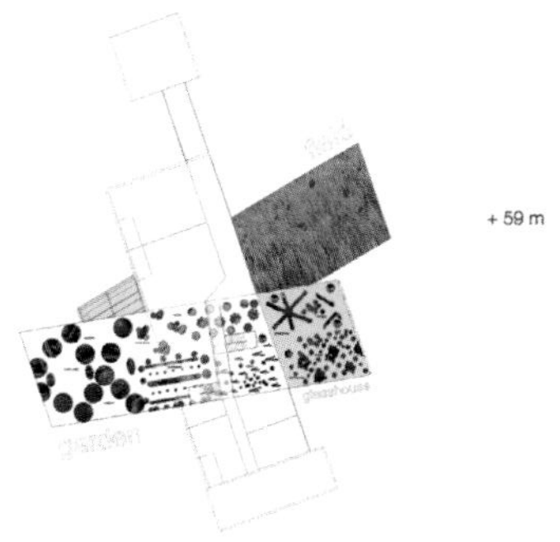

+ 59 m

Garden, Fields and Glasshouse - Plantation areas

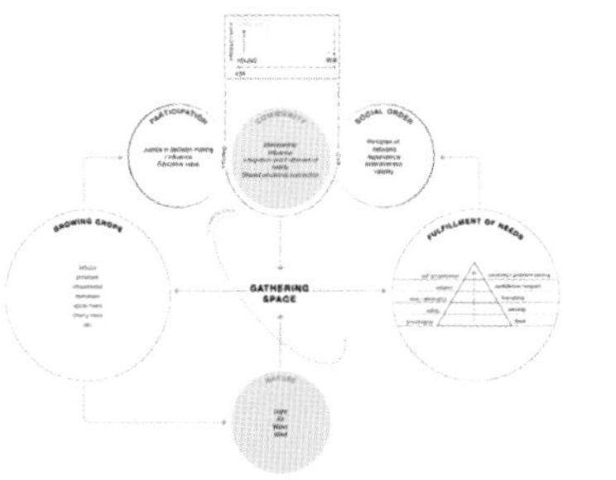

Gathering as a product of sustainable socio-agricultural activity

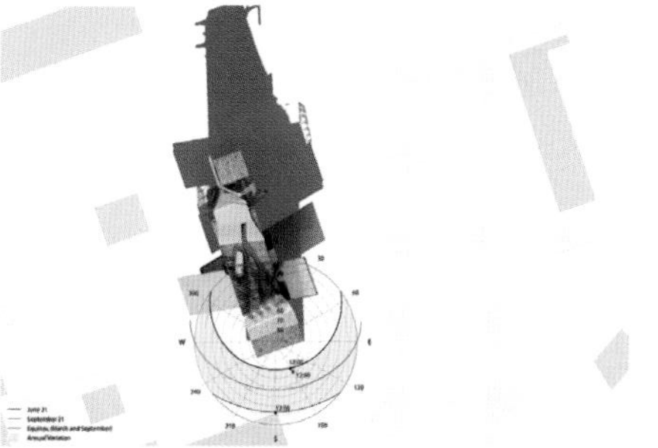

Siteplan showing solar patterns in relationship to Balfron Tower and cropcycle influences

Humidity farm; collecting water and renewable energies

Voided habitational field = Gathering space

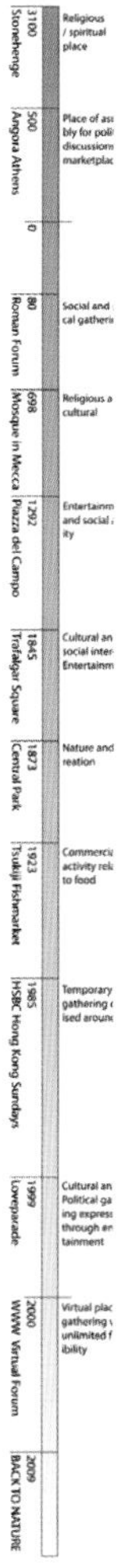

80% Of world population will live in towns and cities by 2050. It is 50% today.

23% Of each person's carbon footprint comes from the production of food and its transport

1.4m Number of allotments around the UK in 1943, which produced 1.3 million tonnes of food - half the nation's need of fruit and vegetables

80% Of London's food is imported

042 D3 Housing | *Horhizon consortium*

Type : Housing
Design : Johan Voordouw

Ref-URB. Ref-IND.

Forming a **refurb**ished **urb**an community by **re-f**inding the British **ind**ustrial landscape.

Like many mid-sized cities across western European and North America, **with the loss of manufacturing these cities have fallen into economic decline**. Leicester is but one of the many examples of cities in the United Kingdom that has increasingly suffered from the loss of industry and the inability to attract service industries due to its close proximity to larger centres such as London, Birmingham, Manchester and Liverpool.

This project seeks to re-establish a small-scale local industry, one around which a community can be built with a common purpose. The increased use of mixed-use development rarely deviates from a commercial / retail or leisure / high-end residential typology. This project seeks to establish a new more inclusive urban construct. **This community attempts to be more vertically integrated, connecting an industrial workplace, with housing and daily retail requirements**. This however does not intend to be an isolated commune but through its industry, connect to both the wider city and region beyond while it attempts to deliver its immediate requirements close to home.

View from observation point looking South

View from third floor apartment facing South

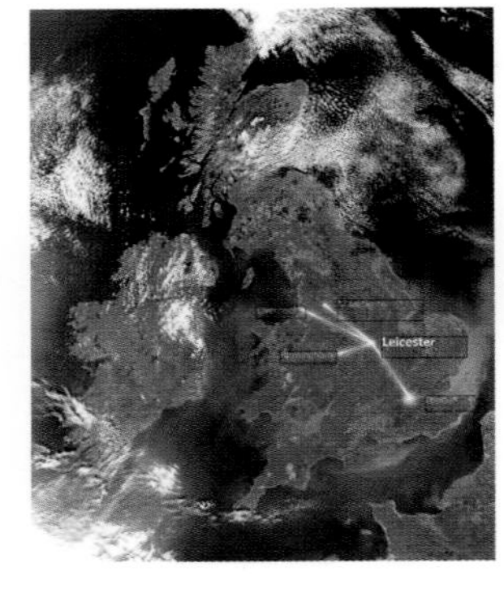

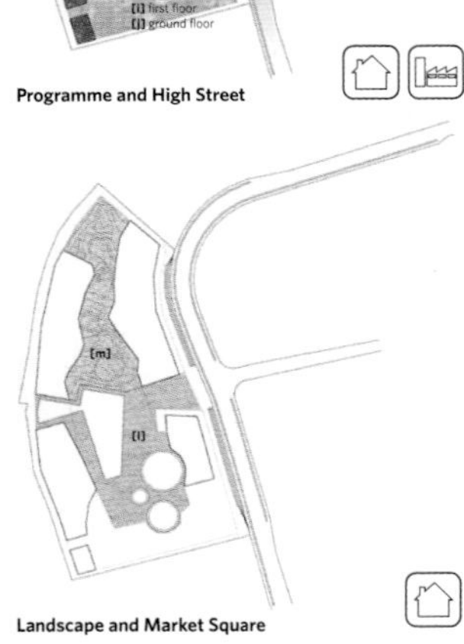

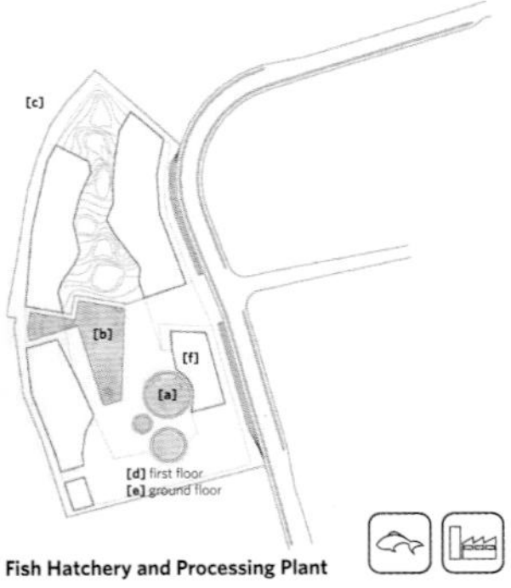

Fish Hatchery and Processing Plant

Programme and High Street

Landscape and Market Square

Leicester is located in the East Mid-lands in icestershire. It has a population of approx. 4 urban area of approx. 772 000 people.

The site is located on a derelict plot along the city centre. Adjacent to the site are a n mills from the 19th C. and an abandoned the east.

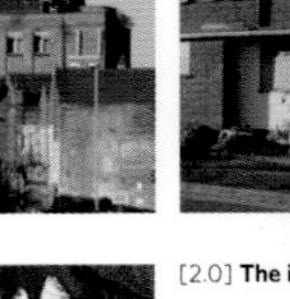

[2.0] **The in**

[a] The fish to entering After the fis the raised p located alor *def. high stre small scale b at mall) it is*

[4.0] **Re-in**

The commu toric scale **apartments** can occur in Furthermore over the car **[g]** Terrace

[5.0] **Re-in**

The market **munal spac** Currently, t dent housin create unsa **activity for sense of co**

1500-1

n

:entres in the UK, its industrial infrastructure **ect intends to re-appropriate such spaces for lopment and as a instigator or urban growth**. ks to define a new type of community, **one idustry back into the urban fabric** creating a le community which can build around a singu- ode.

ng plant.

lished **[b]** They are moved into the lock prior

fficient size they are caught and brought into either in the market **[e]** or the small cafe **[f]**

idential neighbourhood. The high street contains ores, restaurants, etc. rather than a retail hub (ie.

ation of historic types

illage was seen as a **small scale urban typol- ertically integrated community**. The fishing und one common purpose - the fishing itself ice of that industry in maintaining the boats, ent.
en extracted from the coast and re-inserted e British mid-lands.

use

ouses. The terraced house determine the his- atum for the community. **At six storeys the** which prevents the feeling of isolation which

e apartments are dual aspect looking both

et **[k]** High street

re

r individuals from the public of using a com- ting a vibrant, active community. ow-grade industrial sites and social and stu- t certain times of day and certainly at night **nd market square will create the necessary ty of the area as a whole and an increased** nentum for regeneration.

ing historic types
en and Market Square

rden - is a productive landscape, taking wa- Soar and filtering it to remove pollution so for the fish hatchery. It uses grasses within slowly cleaning the water. The landscape is en squares dotted throughout the cities of the S.

Industry Residential Commercial

Urban Centre Type
Places such as suburban communities with large retail hubs typical of North American and post-war European communities

High Street

High Street Type
Residential above a commercial vector, in this condition industry is completely removed from the city.

Market Sq. High Street

Ref-URB. Ref-IND.
Vertically Integrated Community
Integrates small-scale industry into a commercial and residential community creating a common focus and an employment node

[7.0] This community will be a re-interpretation of historic types with a High Street - **a commercial vector** with residential above, offering daily necessities such as shops, small cafés and restaurants, **an industrial centre** and **residences** which are constructed around a **communal garden and market square**.
This traditional typology will be re-worked to densify the city while retaining the necessity and scale of the typical English community.

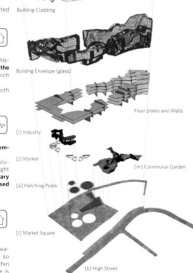

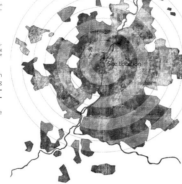

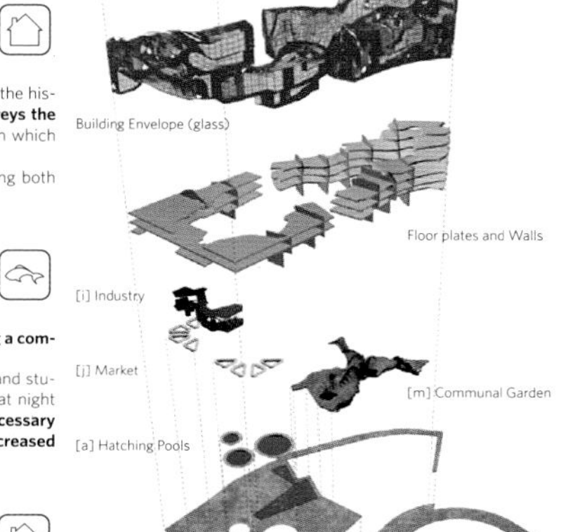

Site Location

[8.0] **Canal and River Network**
The site is adjacent to the River Soar, which meanders through the East-Midlands, within 16 km (10 miles) of the site the river has a length of 32 km (20miles) offering sufficient habitat for the fish to grow and mature.

[8.1] **Surrounding Ammenities**
Within the centre of Leicester are both numerous cafes and restaurants which offers a stable and continuous commercial outlet for the processed fish ranging from the local fish and chip shops to the more exclusive fine dining restaurants which are dotted throughout the city centre.
Currently the site is located on the fringe of a regenerated commercial hub. Located within walking distance is both the Highcross Shopping Centre, a mall which contains all necessary department and clothing stores and the Hayward, a 1960's development which will soon be refurbished. Furthermore, six existing grocery stores and the Central Market - a fruit and vegetable market with an indoor meat market are located within walking distance to further support the community. It is these neighbouring commercial and retail ventures that make this community more economically viable as a instigator or urban regeneration throughout Leicester's industrial warehouse district.
Additional facilities include two universities, two nearby parks and its general proximity to the main train station.

[8.2] **A Networked Community**
By creating a community with a common purpose it gives the project a consequential aspect, one that can be developed and in time expanded to re-establish an industrial / manufacturing hub to the economically depressed centres of the U.K.

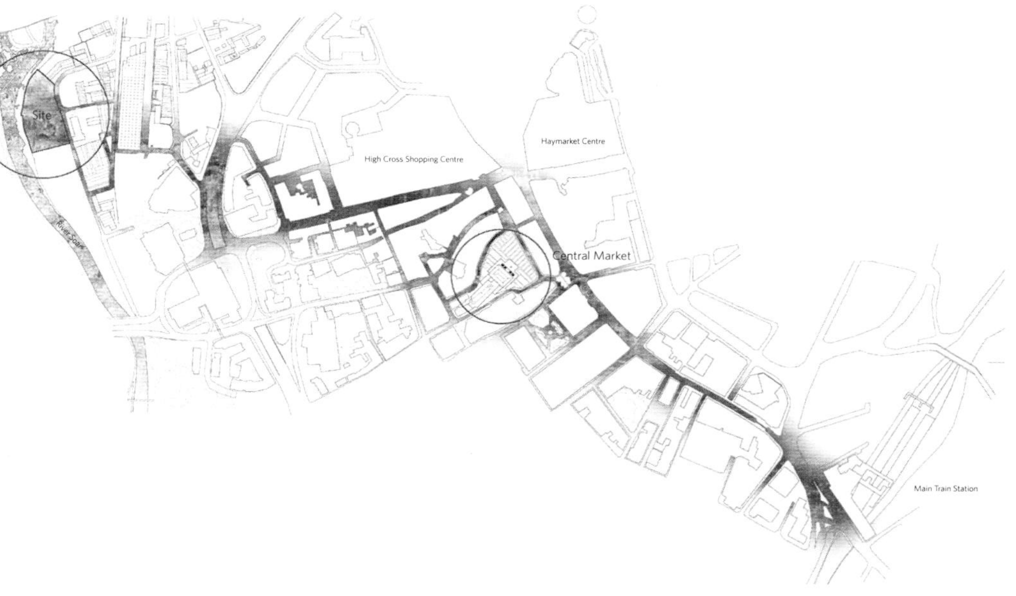

View North along the River Soar

View along the Market Square towards the residences

View up the High Street at the Market

[9.0] **Industrial Programme**

The industry is a medium scale fish farm. **Aqua-culture has increasingly become an economic driver in developing economies**. This concept has now been brought back to help re-establish industrial economies in decline. Using the extensive canal and river systems throughout the British 'mid-lands' the community revolves around a carp hatchery and processing plant, a fish indigenous to the United Kingdom. These **carp are harvested and sold both to local restaurants within Leicester and to the Fish Market** in the centre of the city.
As the industry expands it will use a larger extent of the existing canal & river network. The waste can be used in other agricultural processes further aiding to sustain the community. **By integrating industry and commerce within a residential neighbourhood it is intended that all three of these programmes can remain stable and sustainable**.

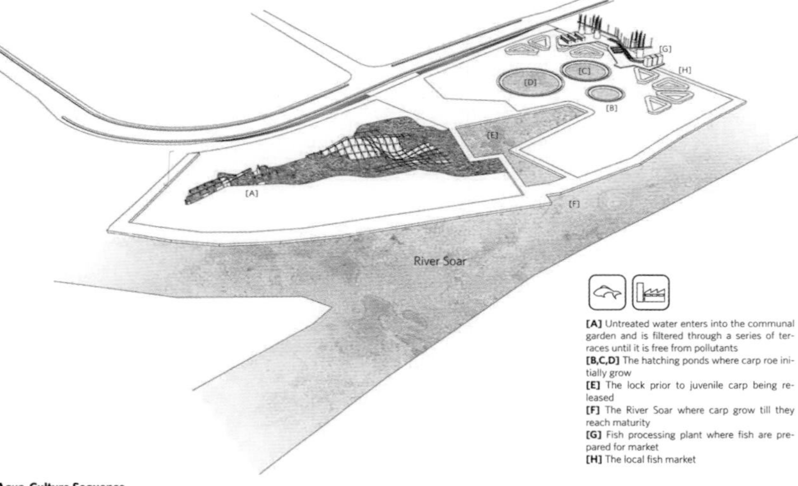

[A] Untreated water enters into the communal garden and is filtered through a series of terraces until it is free from pollutants
[B,C,D] The hatching ponds where carp roe initially grow
[E] The lock prior to juvenile carp being released
[F] The River Soar where carp grow till they reach maturity
[G] Fish processing plant where fish are prepared for market
[H] The local fish market

Aqua-Culture Sequence

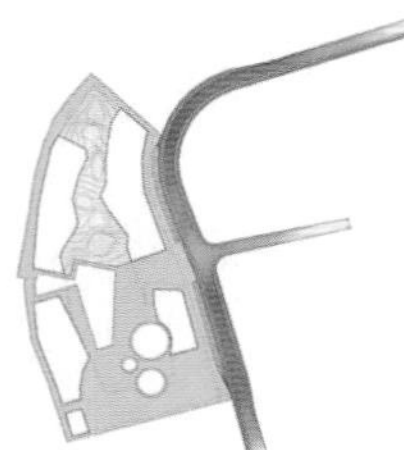

Access Diagram
Indicates the three modes of movement across and past the site. The streetscape has been divided into a vehicular road and a designated bike path, the pedestrian sidewalk is further separated from the traffic via a stair which acts as a threshold between the road and the High Street

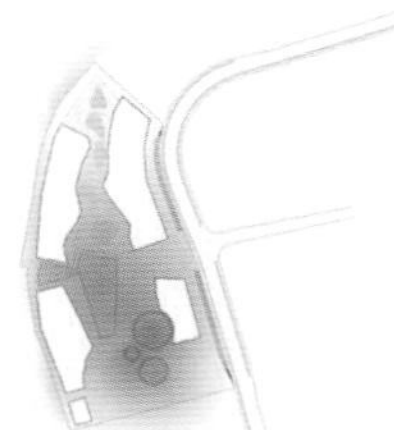

Drainage Diagram
The site has multiple drainage points to absorb water run-off from the extensive glass and cladding system. The rain either enters the hatching ponds, the lock or the communal garden.

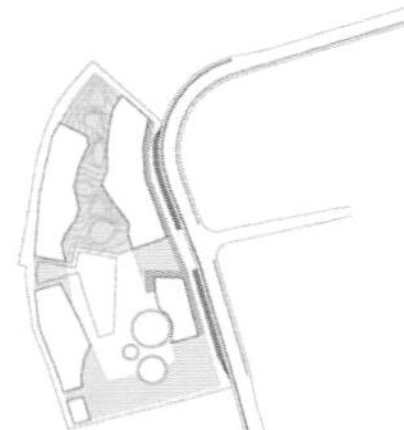

Threshold Diagram
A number of thresholds are used to spatially separate the building from the High Street. Moving from the streetscape one passes the bike lane, steps, the covered arcade for the shops and the stitching between the North and South building. These thresholds have been employed to develop the sequence into the more private square and communal garden that bound the residences, offering privacy to the occupants.

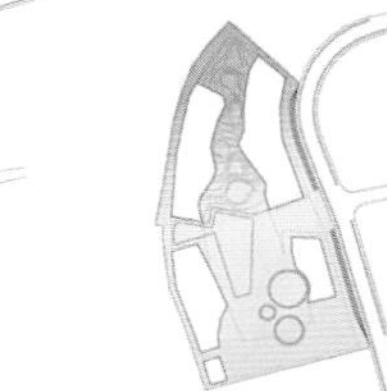

Solar Diagram
The orientation of the building square / garden creates a sou climate for the residents and den.
Locating the fish processing a south-end of the site keeps th and more within the shade buildings.

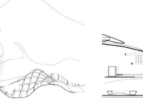

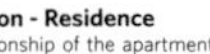

Schematic Section - Residence
Illustrates the relationship of the apartments to the canal and the communal garden and the general scale of the project.

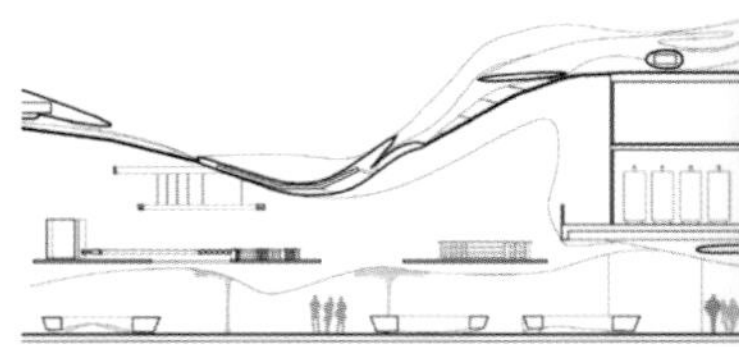

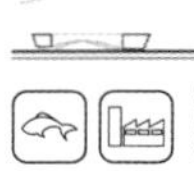

Schematic Section - Fish Processing and Market
Illustrates the relationship of the the fish processing factory to the fish market to the street.

1500-2

...anal gardens - the productive landscape that filters the water for the carp hatching ponds

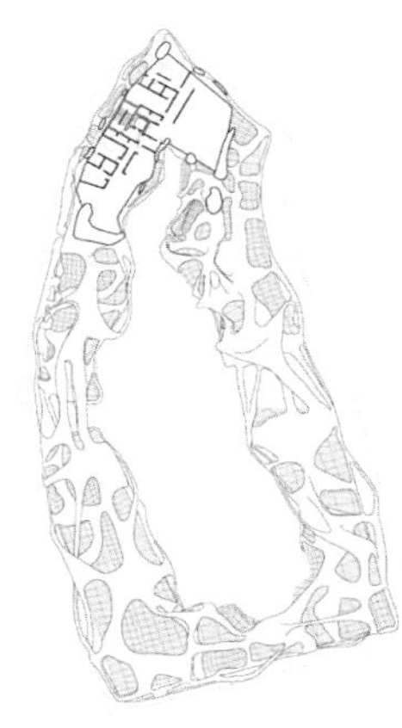

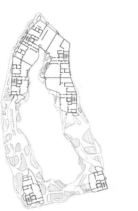

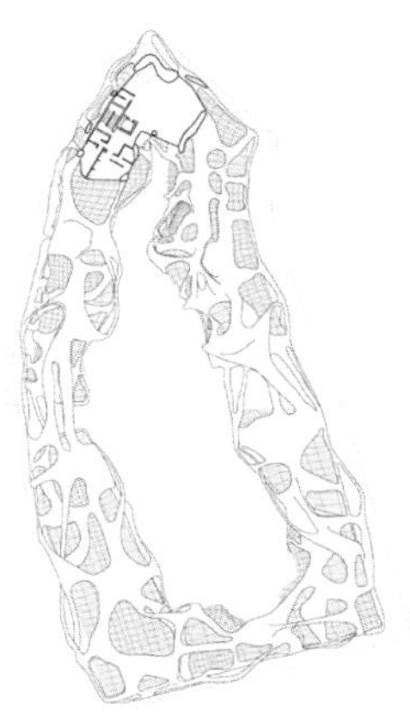

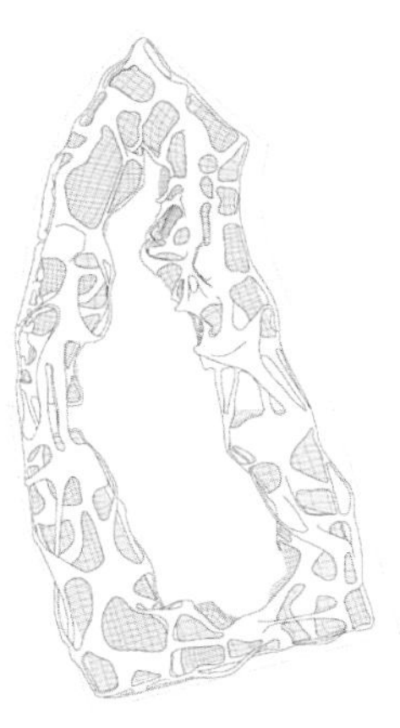

..., Square and Garden
...es access to the High Street and the ...d on the ground floor are the shops ...e, entrances into the residences and ...s along the canal

First Floor - Factory and Housing
The first floor contains the factory which connects to the market below. It also contains the first set of residences either as studio, one or two-bed apartments

Second to Fourth Floors
Contain only residential apartments, located between individual structural cores with lift and fire stairs.

Fifth Floor
The first penthouse floor with extensive views over both the River Soar and the market square

Sixth Floor
The uppermost residential floor, the space contains one two-bed apartment and extensive views across the city

Roof Plan
Shows the full extent of the cladding system and the formal complexity of the project.

043 Pol2 Housing Polgarstreet | *franz zt gmbh*

Location : Vienna, Austria
Function : Housing
Competition : 2011
Collaboration : Corinna Toell, Lucie Vencelidesova, Wolfgang Fischer, Michael Hasslacher

bauträgerwettbewerb „kostengünstiges wohnen“ polgarstrasse 30a

bauträger
GESIBA Gemeinnützige Siedlungs- und Bauaktiengesellschaft
GSG Gesellschaft für Stadtentwicklung und Stadterneuerung Gemeinnützige Ges.m.b.H.

architektur
Baumschlager Eberle
franz zt gmbh

statik + bauphysik
Dorr-Schober & Partner Ziviltechnikergesellschaft mbh

landschafsplanung
LAND IN SICHT Büro für Landschafsplanung

soziologe
Mag. Jochen Kugler, Strategische Kommunikation

soziale nachhaltigkeit - nutzungskonzept gemeinschaftsräume

viele raumkonzepte scheitern daran, dass sie zwar mit den besten absichten „erdacht“, von den menschen aber nicht angenommen und deshalb nicht genutzt werden. was expertinnen über den bedarf potentieller mieterinnen denken entspricht leider viel zu oft nicht dem, was diese tatsächlich wollen. es folgt eine zweistufige strategie:

1) entsprechend des gestellten themas „ kostengünstiges wohnen“ sind die wohnungen bewusst klein und einfach gehalten, um den mietpreis so gering wie möglich zu machen. andererseits soll und darf dabei nicht auf die sozialen bedürfnisse vergessen werden: die möglichkeit, freunde zu einem essen zu sich nach hause einzuladen, nimmt dabei einen wichtigen platz ein. wer niemanden zu sich einladen kann – weil er/sie keinen platz hat, oder die wohnung nicht „präsentabel“ ist – verliert soziale kontakte. basierend auf dieser überlegung werden als „initialzündung“ 2 der insgesamt 5 gemeinschaftsräume für gemeinsame treffen mit freunden und/oder nachbarn konzipiert: ein grösserer raum fungiert dabei als mehrzweck- und partyraum mit terrasse (zu leerzeiten „mehrfachgenutzt“ als indoorspielfläche); ein intimerer raum dient als „ open kitchen“ mit offener küche und essbereich zum gemeinschaftlichem kochen und essen.

2) für die nutzungsfixierung der 3 weiteren gemeinschaftsräume verfolgt das vorliegende projekt ein partizipatives raumkonzept, wie es etwa in den projekten der lokalen agenda 21 zur anwendung kommt:: um zu wissen, was die menschen brauchen, fragen wir sie selbst und geben ihnen die möglichkeit, ihren raum selbst zu gestalten und zu entwickeln. weil sich bedürfnisse über die jahre ändern können (etwa weil sich die mieterstruktur ändert), wird dieser partizipative prozess über die jahre kontinuierlich weitergeführt.

konkret bedeutet dies:
drei gemeinschaftsräumen werden so gebaut (notwendige anschlüsse, modulares system,...), dass ein möglichst breite nutzung möglich ist. die nutzungskonzepte für diese räume werden in einem moderierten partizipativen prozess von allen interessierten mieterinnen gleichberechtigt entwickelt

für die moderation dieser prozesse, sowie für mögliche raumausgestaltungen wird ein eigenes budget zur verfügung gestellt die bestehenden nutzungen werden in regelmäßigen abständen (z.b.: 1x jährlich) gemeinsam reflektiert. änderungen sind – so von den mieterinnen gewünscht – jederzeit möglich. auch für diese nutzungsänderungen stehen budgetposten zur verfügung

damit sind die gemeinschaftsräume nicht nur „bedürfnisadäquat“. die aktive beteiligung am gestaltungsprozess führt gleichzeitig zu einer viel stärkeren identifikation der mieterinnen mit ihren räumen. das wirkt sich nicht nur positiv auf die nutzung der räume aus, sondern auch auf die sorgfalt, mit der mit ihnen umgegangen wird. die nutzung aller gemeinschaftsräume wird mit einer reservierungsliste (web oder aushang) unter den mietern selbst geregelt. eine „moderationsperson“ wird lediglich bei konfliktsituationen hinzugezogen.

gründerzeit reloaded

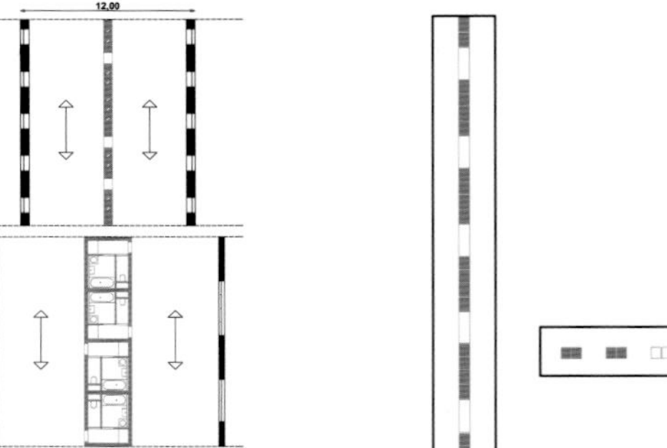

gründerzeit + struktur

als leitbild für die räumliche aufteilung der wohnungen dient die gründerzeitliche struktur von aussenwand-mittelmauer-aussenwand inkl. der freihaltung des eigentlichen wohnraums von ent-/versorgungsleitungen. diese struktur besticht durch ihre grosse flexibilität und nutzungsneutralität in querrichtung.

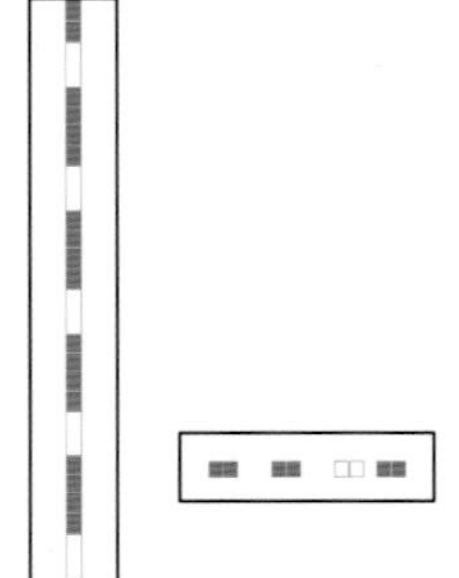

sanitärzone + stiegenhauskerne

sämtliche sanitärräume sind gemeinsam mit den stiegenhauskernen konzentriert in einer mittelzone angeordnet. dadurch ist eine einfache installationsführung gewährleistet. der schallschutz zwischen den wohnungen wir aufgrund der zonierung erhöht. an den aussenwände entstehen flexibel ausformulierbare wohnräume.

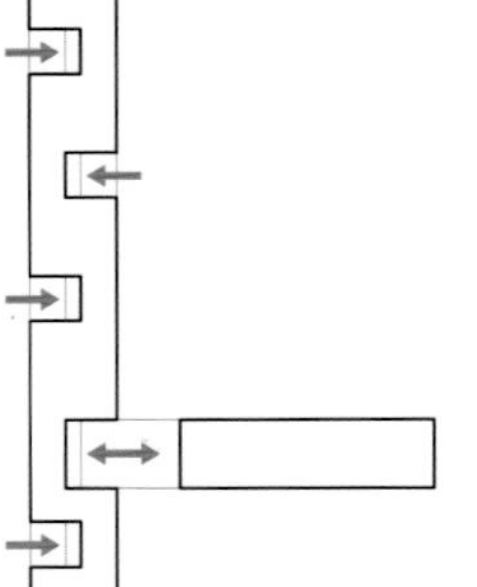

erschließung + gemeinschaftsräume

die erschließzung der wohnungen erfolgt über effiziente stiegenhauskerne in der mittelzone in der form von 4-spännern. zur belichtung wird der liftschacht verglast und als lichtschacht aufgewertet. je stiegenhaus ist ein ein- oder zweigeschoßiger gemeinschaftsraum angeordnet. er bringt zusätzlich tageslicht in die vertikalerschließung und gewährleistet einen außenbezug.

dachterrasse + mieterbeete

hochwertige dachflächen werden den mietern zur gemeinschaftlichen nutzung zur verfügung gestellt: jedem stiegenhaus ist ein freibereich mit anmietbaren mieterbeeten zugeordnet. dadurch entstehen überschaubare und geschütze einheiten, die distanz zwischen küche und gemüsefeld wir minimiert. am dach des querriegels wird im geschützten innenhof eine große gemeinschaftsdachterrasse angeboten.

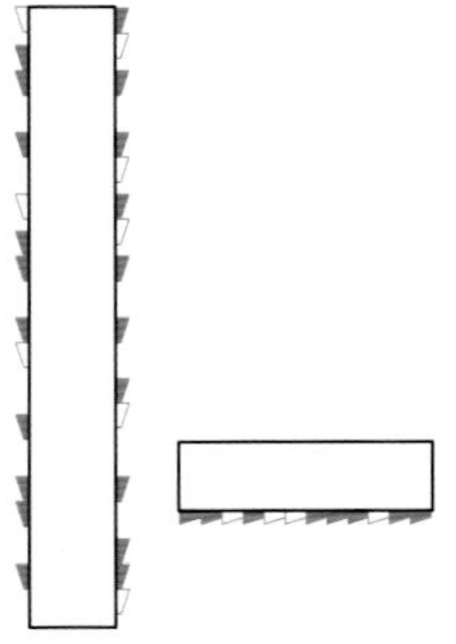

loggien + balkone

jeder wohnung ist ein privater freiraum “vorgehängt“, der aus einer kombination von loggia und balkon entsteht (=ballogia). So ergibt sich bei angemessener grösse eine gut nutzbare tiefe von im mittel. 175cm. der schräge zuschnitt dient der „ abgrenzung“ vom nachbarn und der „ zuwendung“ zur „besseren“ himmelsrichtung: an der polgarstrasse nach westen, hofseitig nach süden. die oberfläche der ballogien bestehen aus neutralen betonfertigteilen, die von jedem mieter auf der innenseite farblich individuell gestaltet werden können.

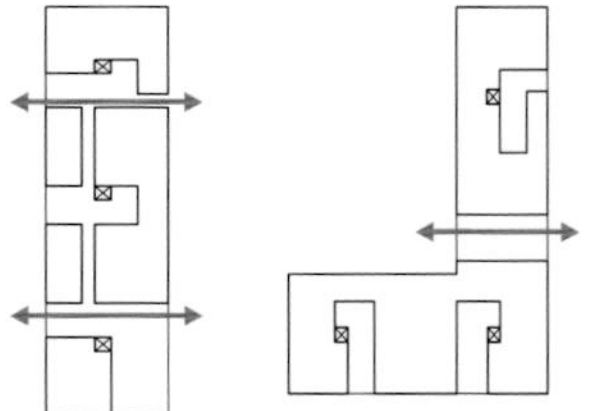

durchwegung

differenzierte wegeführung mit durchgängen im erdgeschoss
-> räumliche vernetzung mit wohnquartier
wegeführung/ erschließung als kommunikative zonen
-> belebte und attraktive begegnungsräume
-> hohe akzeptanz und sicherheitsgefühl

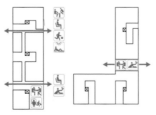

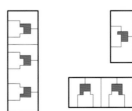

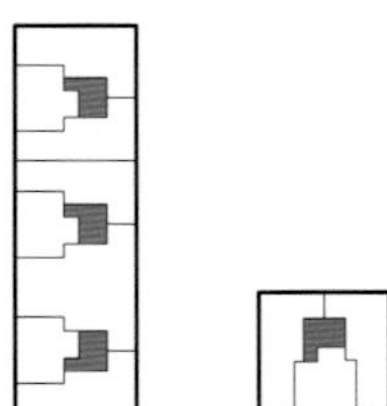

gemeinschaft

großzügige, kommunikative eingangshallen mit sitzgelegenheiten
gemeinschaftsflächen an den durchgängen (indoorspielbereich, tisch-tennis, „freundeecke“ mit küchenzeile, „waschplatz“, „runder tisch“)
gemeinschaftlicher innenhof („kleine rasenfreiheit“, sitzbänke, kleinkinderspielen)
-> hoher freizeitwert, steigerung der lebensqualität
-> hohe identifikation

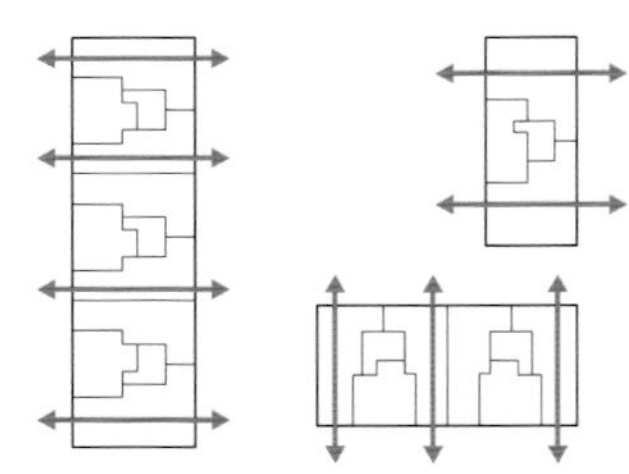

erschliessung

flächengeringe treppenhäuser mit natürlicher Belichtung/ Be- und Entlüftung
3-spänner mit überschaubaren hausgemeinschaften
-> identifikation und wir- gefühl

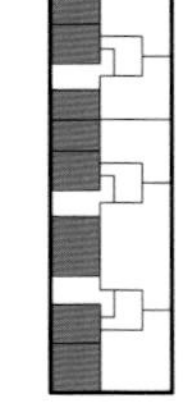

wohnungsstruktur

ab 2-zimmer-wohnungen durchgesteckte wohneinheiten mit querlüftung
70% durchgesteckte wohnungen, 30% monoorientierte Wohnungen nach westen/ süden
differenziertes angebot von 2- bis 5-zimmerwohnungen
-> hohe soziale durchmischung

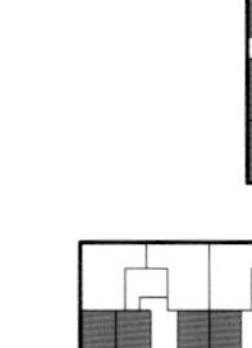

orientierung

- gut belichtetes, offenes wohnen nach süden/ westen
- ruhige, private schlafzimmer nach osten/ norden
- nebenräume, sanitärräume in mittelzone
- einfachen installationsführung und hohen wirtschaftlichkeit
- durch bündelung küchen- und sanitärbereiche

franz

perspektive polgarstrasse

die leichtigkeit der masse
der kompakte baukörper sitzt leichtfüßig am boden und erweitert sich höckerartig im dachgeschoß. die robuste grundstruktur bietet ein solides gerüst zum andocken zusätzlicher elemente.

die vielfalt in der gemeinschaft
im erdgeschoß bilden fahrradräume ein einladendes foyer. die gemeinschaftsräume zeichnen sich durch großzügige verglasungen an der fassade ab. das dachgeschoß bildet windgeschütze nischen für mieterbeete.

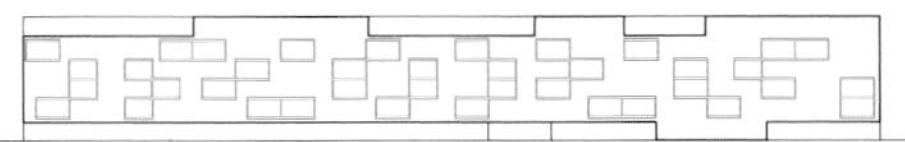

die summe der einzelnen teile
die loggien bilden einerseits geschützte individuelle freiräume und schließen sich ande-rerseits zu gemeinschaftlichen clustern zusammen. mit einfachen seriellen elementen entsteht ein differenziertes fassadenbild. die gestaltung des innenenlebens erfolgt im laufe der nutzung durch die bewohner als setzkasten des lebens.

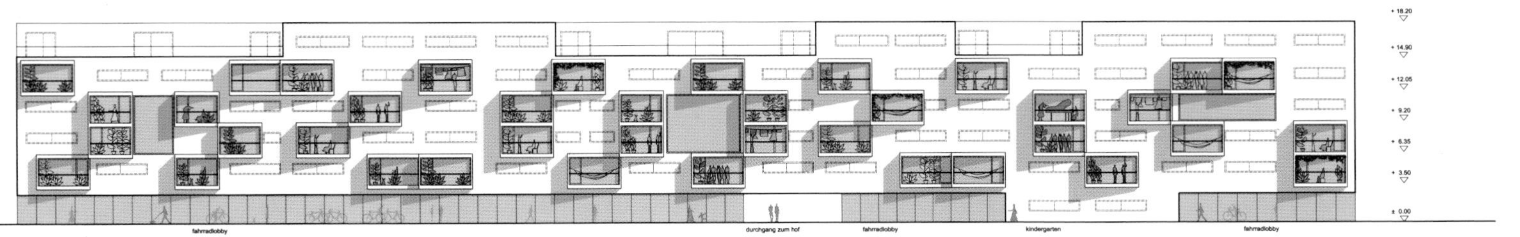

ansicht polgarstrasse 1:200

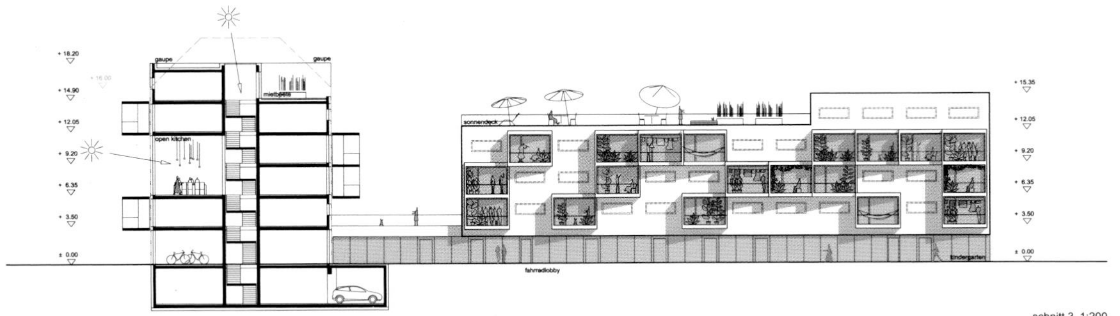

schnitt 3 1:200

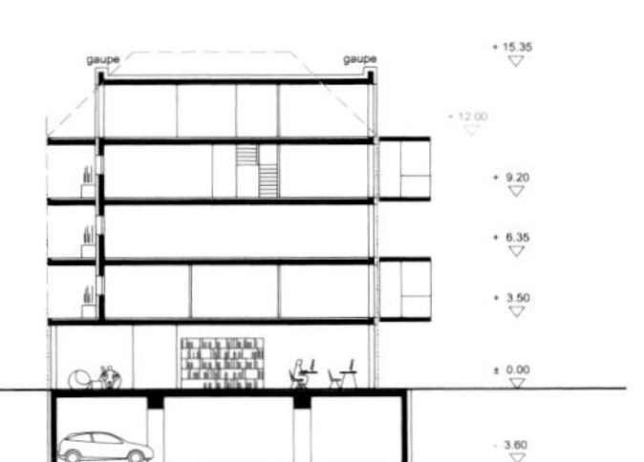

schnitt 4 1:200

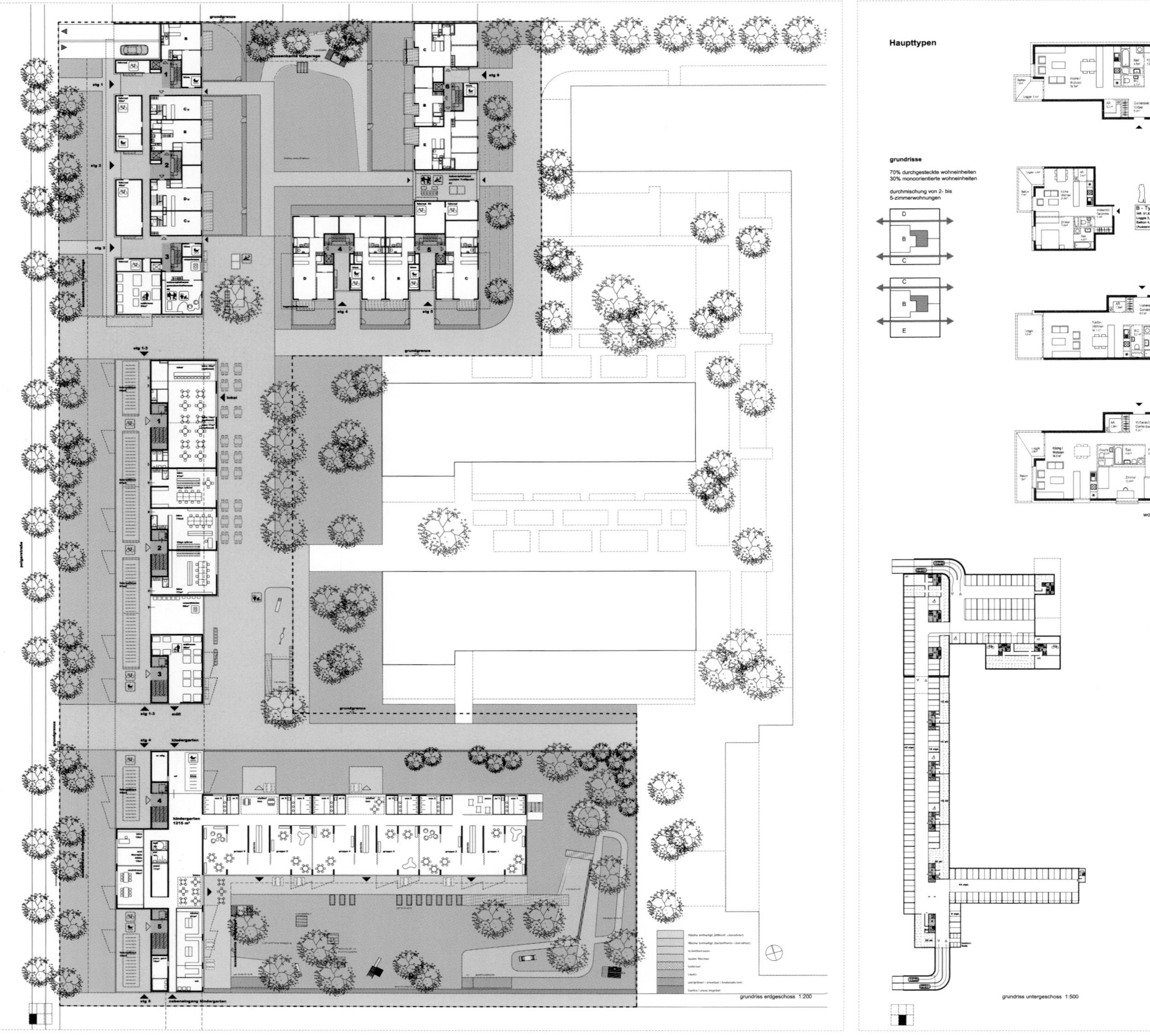
Haupttypen
grundrisse
70% durchgesteckte wohneinheiten
30% monoorientierte wohneinheiten
durchmischung von 2- bis
5-zimmerwohnungen
D
B
C
C
B
E
B - Typ
"single"
wohnungsgrundrisse 1:100
grundriss untergeschoss 1:500
grundriss erdgeschoss 1:200

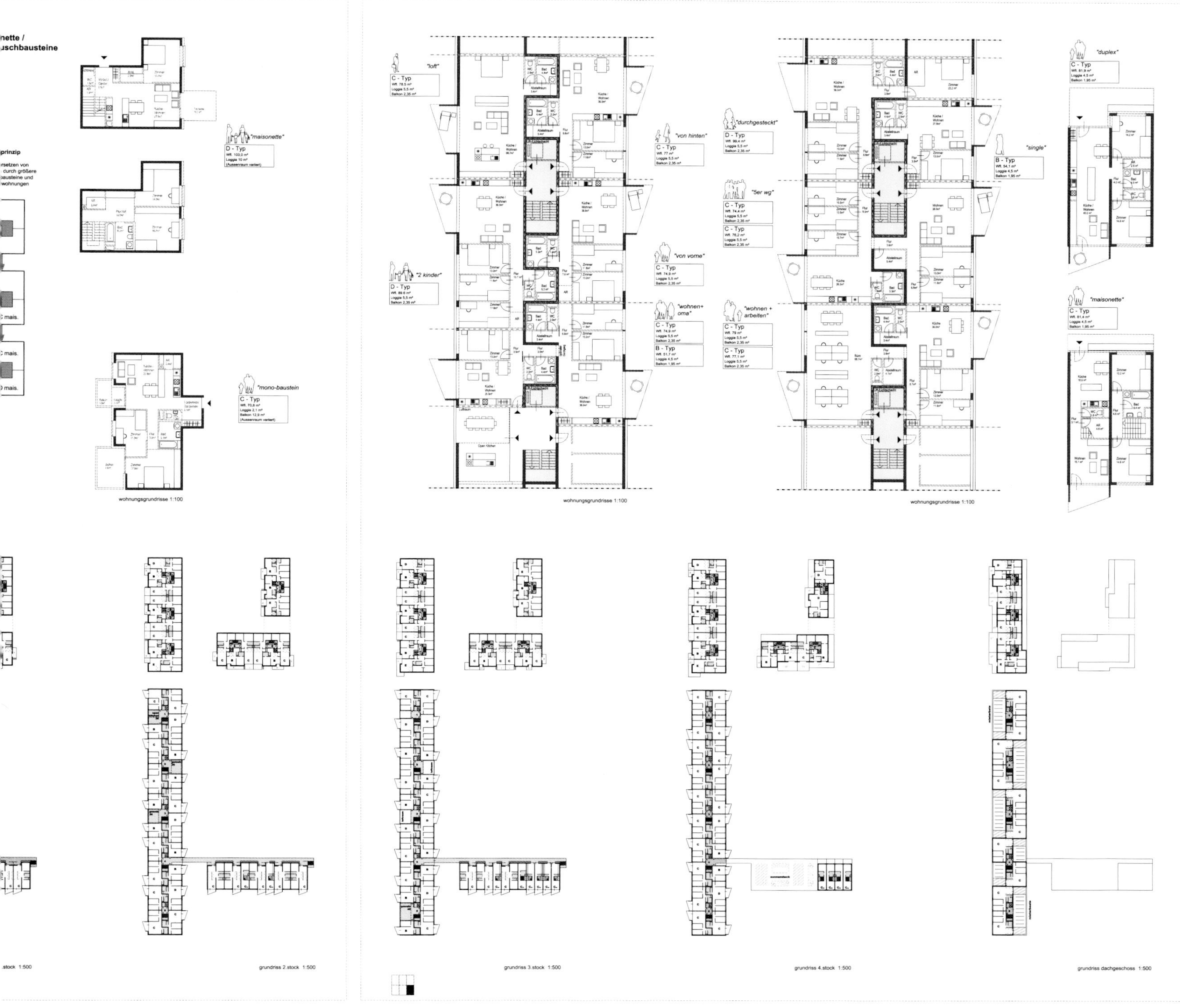

044 Modular City | *KLAIR Architecture*

Project Description : Urban Housing Block
Designer/Architect : KLAIR + Nenad Basic + Benjamin Vigot
Competition Entry December 2011

BDS605

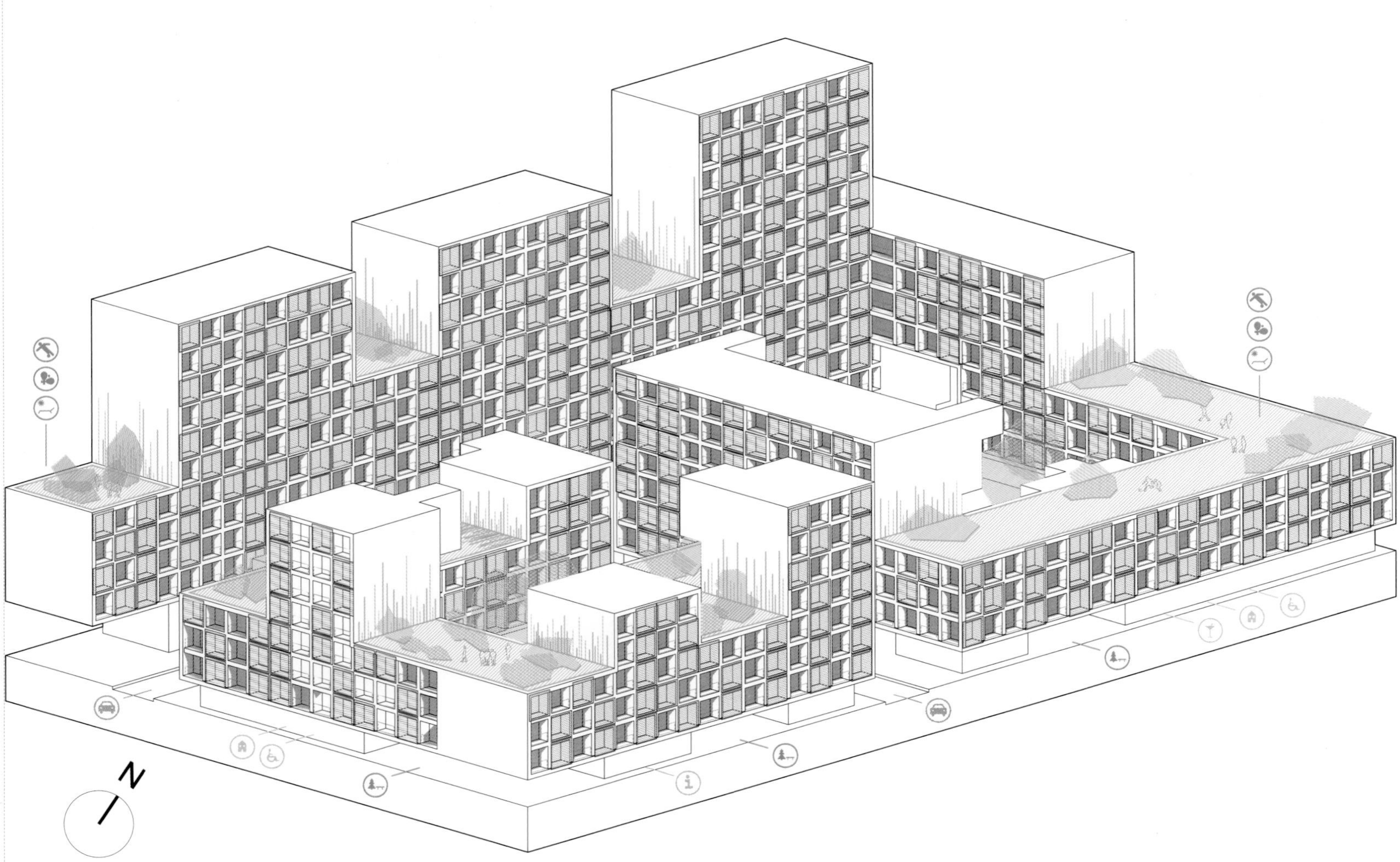

MODULAR CITY

B2

GROSS FLOOR AREA : 28.000 m2
NET/GROSS FLOOR AREA RATIO : 0,81
FACADE/FLOOR AREA RATIO : 0,65
ENTRY CODE : BDS605

The proposed scheme develops not a predefined urban shape but a system that allows the colonization of a site with changing characteristics.

The preliminary study shows how through a series of "basic block typologies" – the closed block, the open block and the mixed block – the final scheme is achieved. It sums up the interesting sides of urban living - protection, community living and free space. In order not to be monofunctional, the proposed scheme is developed as a cut-out of urban fabric, with different scales, atmospheres and building types, while still keeping a high level of standardization.

A catalogue of apartments is developed upon the same geometrical base. It is based on a subdivisible grid of 25x25 (12.5 x 12.5) meters as a carrier of the basic module which enables the development of different scenarios. All apartments (except the one room apt - studio type) have a double orientation and they get exposed to the sun two times a day. This enables a very flexible orientation of the block.

The open spaces are organized on three scales - as a landscape park on the ground floor, smaller gardens on building rooftops accessible only to inhabitants of that very building and pri-

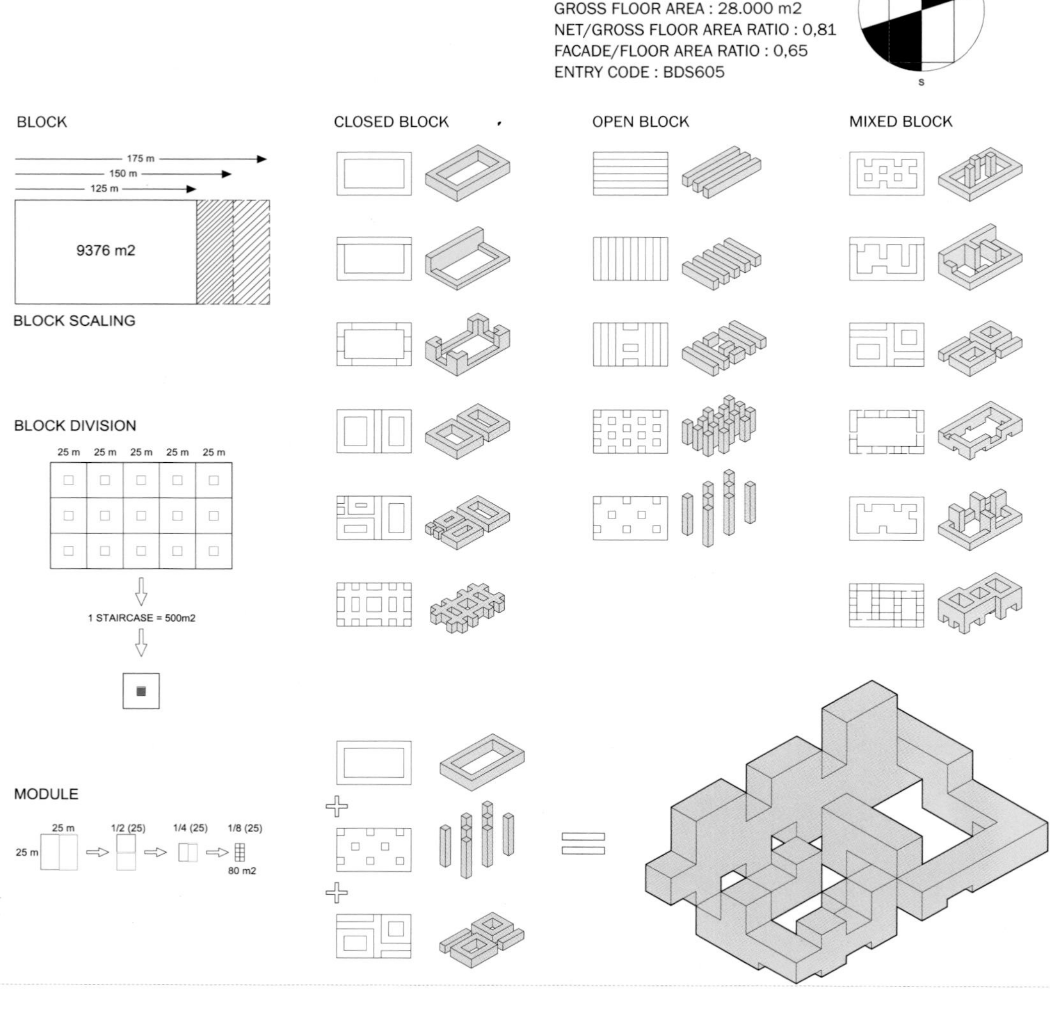

BDS605

AERIAL VIEW

VIEW OF THE INSIDE OF THE BLOCK

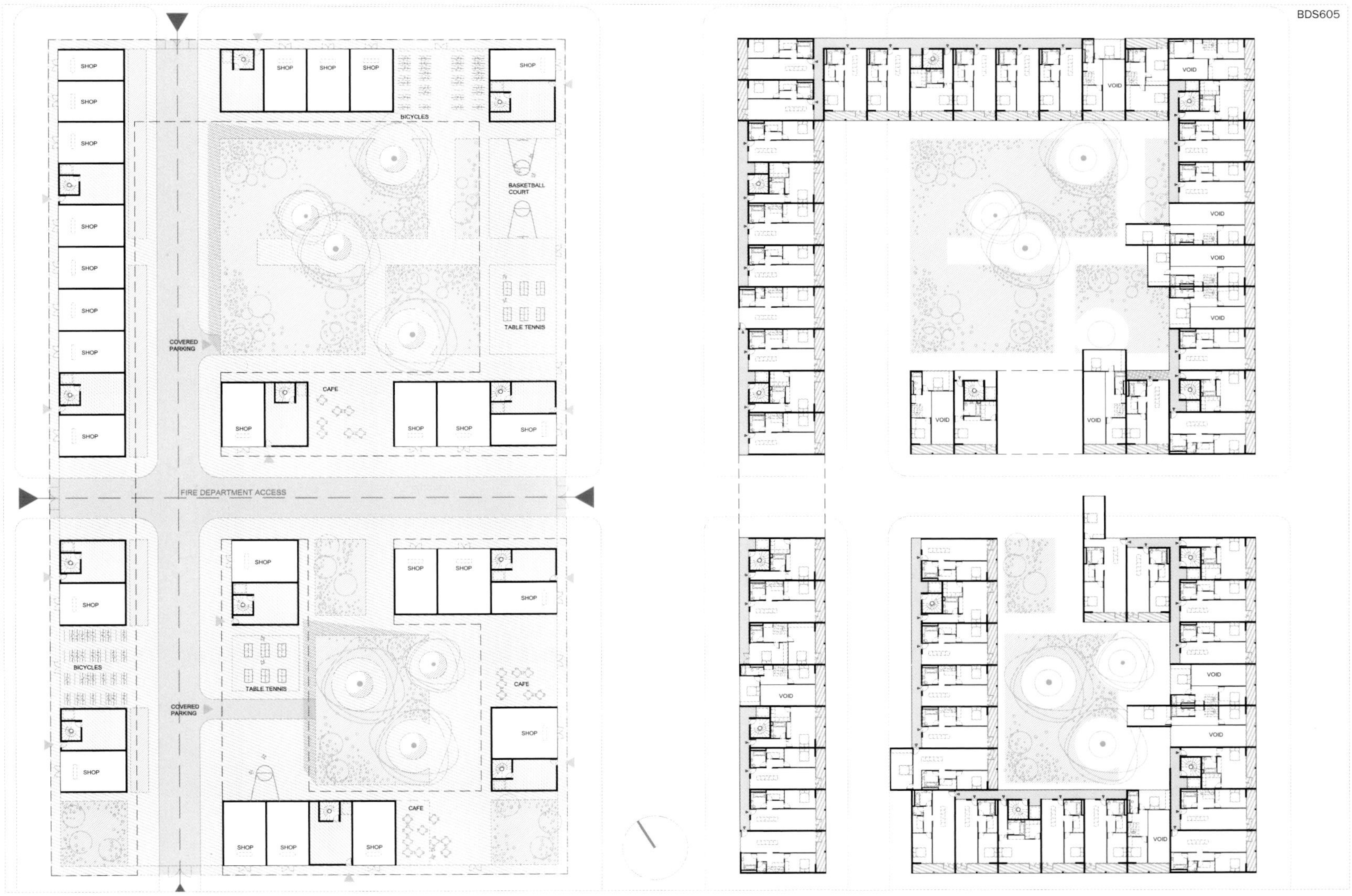

BDS605

SHOP SHOP SHOP SHOP SHOP SHOP SHOP SHOP SHOP SHOP SHOP

BICYCLES

BASKETBALL COURT

TABLE TENNIS

COVERED PARKING

CAFE

SHOP SHOP SHOP SHOP

FIRE DEPARTMENT ACCESS

SHOP SHOP SHOP SHOP SHOP

BICYCLES

TABLE TENNIS

COVERED PARKING

CAFE

SHOP SHOP

CAFE

SHOP SHOP SHOP

VOID VOID VOID VOID VOID VOID VOID VOID VOID VOID VOID

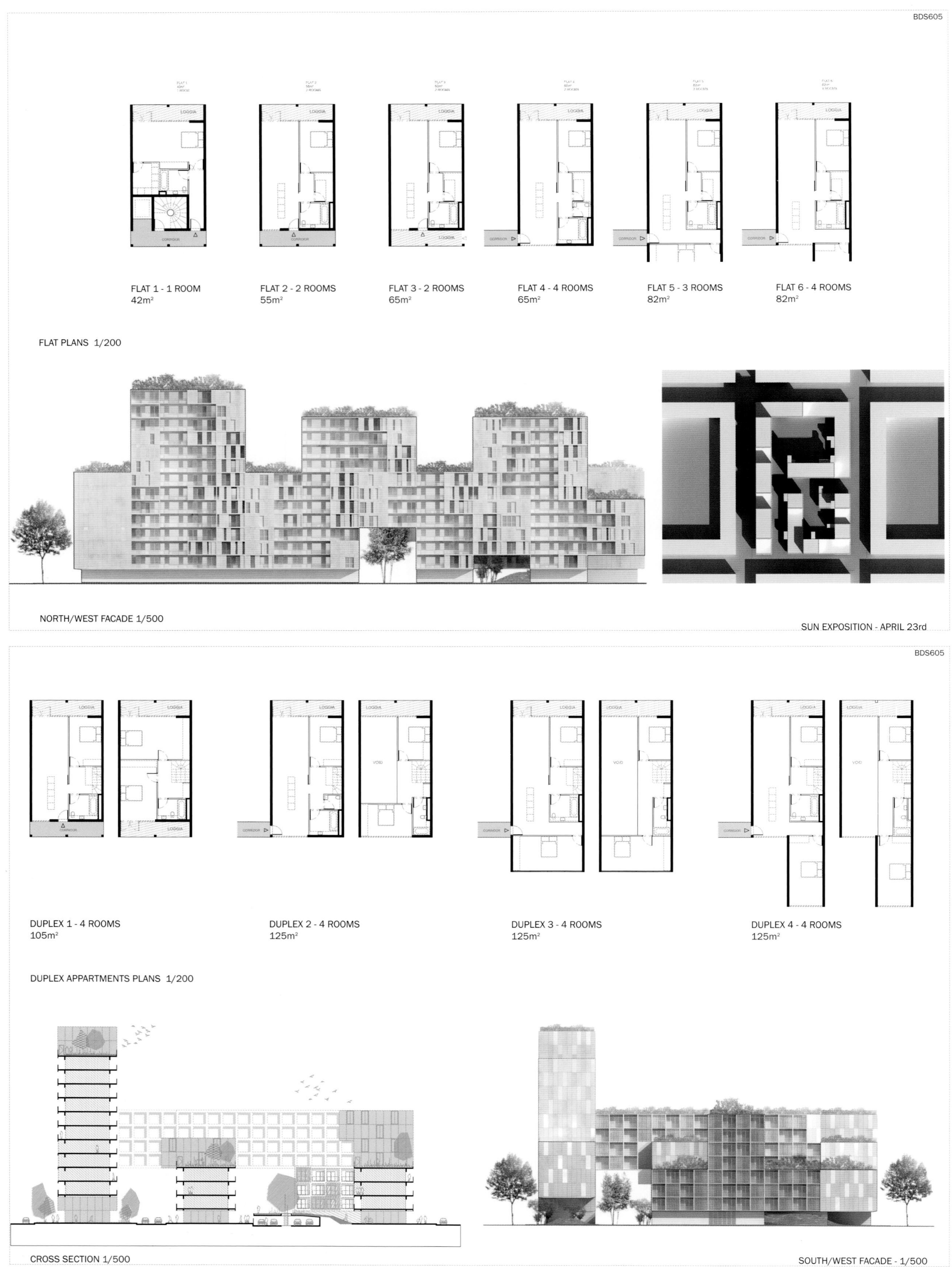
BDS605
FLAT 1 - 1 ROOM
42m²
FLAT 2 - 2 ROOMS
55m²
FLAT 3 - 2 ROOMS
65m²
FLAT 4 - 4 ROOMS
65m²
FLAT 5 - 3 ROOMS
82m²
FLAT 6 - 4 ROOMS
82m²
FLAT PLANS 1/200
NORTH/WEST FACADE 1/500
SUN EXPOSITION - APRIL 23rd
BDS605
DUPLEX 1 - 4 ROOMS
105m²
DUPLEX 2 - 4 ROOMS
125m²
DUPLEX 3 - 4 ROOMS
125m²
DUPLEX 4 - 4 ROOMS
125m²
DUPLEX APPARTMENTS PLANS 1/200
CROSS SECTION 1/500
SOUTH/WEST FACADE - 1/500

COM | *KLAIR Architecture*

Project Description : Social Housing (32 apartment units)
Location : Colombes, France
Designer/Architect : KLAIR + ECDM + Nenad Basic
Competition Entry May 2011

LOT3 / 18 LOGEMENTS _vue perspective depuis l'Allée de l'Ile Marante

LOT7 / 14 LOGEMENTS _vue perspective depuis l'Allée jardinée de l'Ile Marante

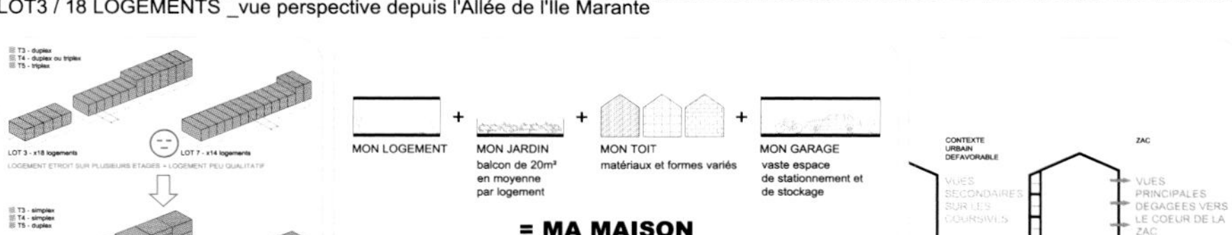

AVOIR UNE MAISON, C'EST AVOIR AUTANT D'ESPACES ET D'ELEMENTS INDIVIDUALISES

ORIENTATION

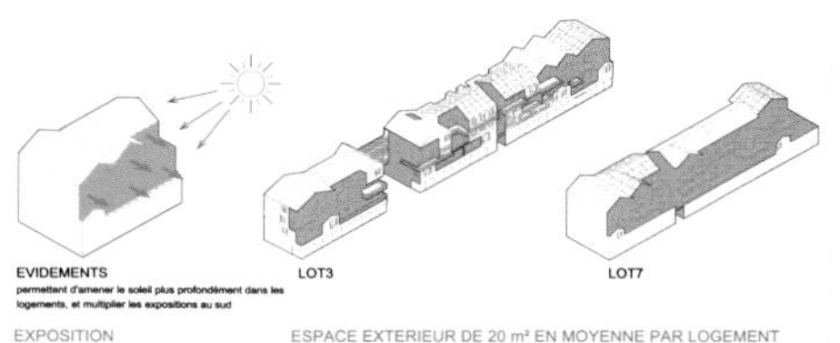

EXPOSITION

ESPACE EXTERIEUR DE 20 m² EN MOYENNE PAR LOGEMENT

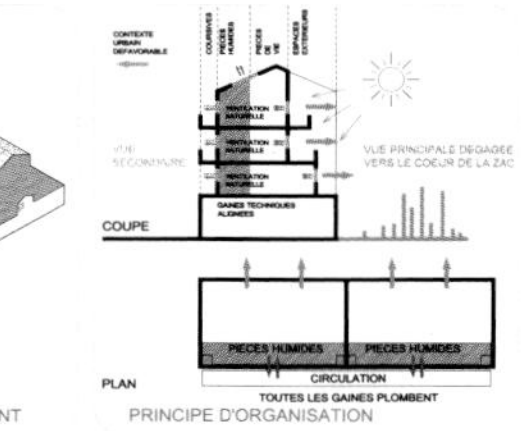

PRINCIPE D'ORGANISATION

_schémas de principe

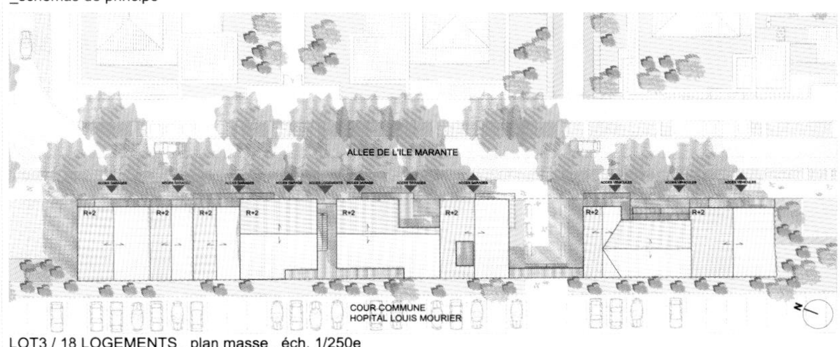

LOT3 / 18 LOGEMENTS _plan masse _éch. 1/250e

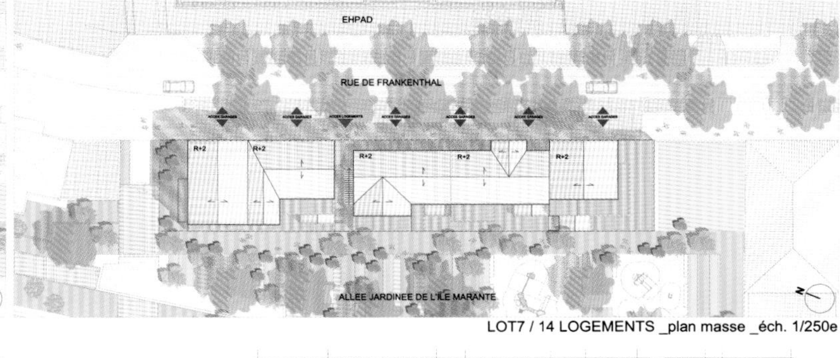

LOT7 / 14 LOGEMENTS _plan masse _éch. 1/250e

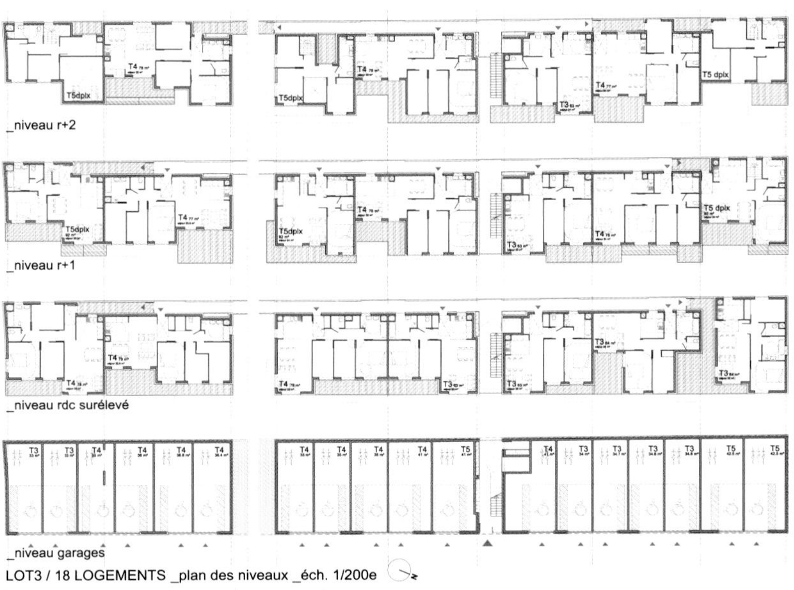

LOT3 / 18 LOGEMENTS _plan des niveaux _éch. 1/200e

LOT3 _coupe _éch. 1/200e

LOT7 _coupe _éch. 1/200e

LOT3 & 7 _coupes de principe

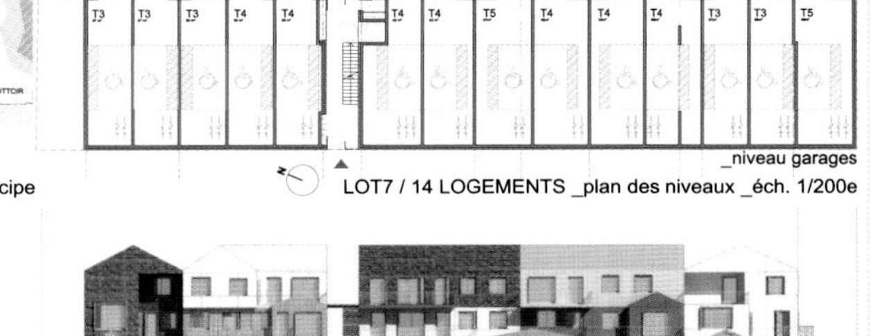

LOT7 / 14 LOGEMENTS _plan des niveaux _éch. 1/200e

LOT3 / 18 LOGEMENTS _façade est sur l'Allée de l'Ile Marante _éch. 1/200e

LOT7 / 14 LOGEMENTS _façade ouest sur l'Allée jardinée de l'Ile Marante _éch. 1/200e

Expansiel Codévam COLOMBES / ZAC DE L'ILE MARANTE - LOT 3 et 7 _32 LOGEMENTS INDIVIDUELS EN ACCESSION SOCIALE ecdm KLNB LE 31 MAI 2010

046 Amel101 | LUIS ARREDONDO_ARCHITECT

Project : Social Housing Competition
Participants : Luis Arredondo
Location : Madrid, Spain
Client : EMVS / Year : 2011

CONCURSO DE PROYECTOS SOBRE LA PARCELA 9.1 EN "NUESTRA SEÑORA DE LOS ÁNGELES 6"_LEMA_AMEL101_1/3

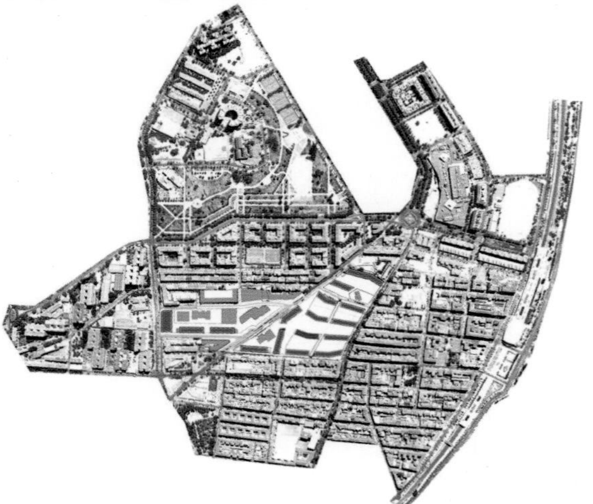

SITUACIÓN 1/10.000

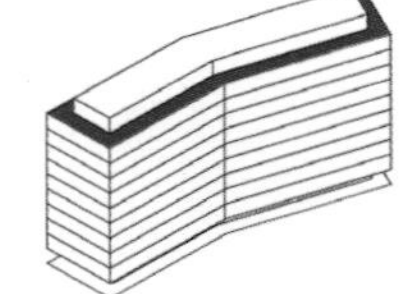

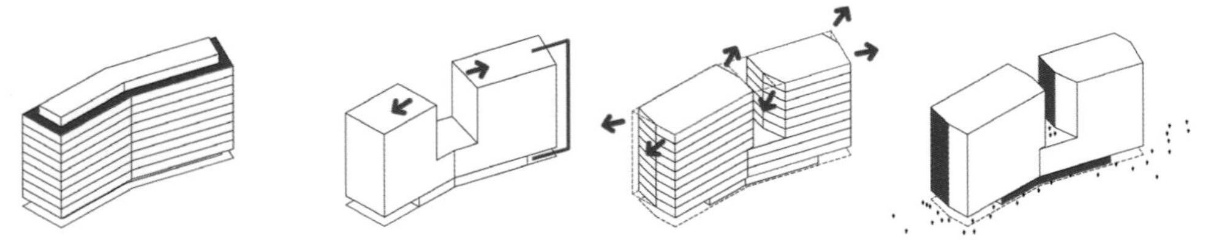

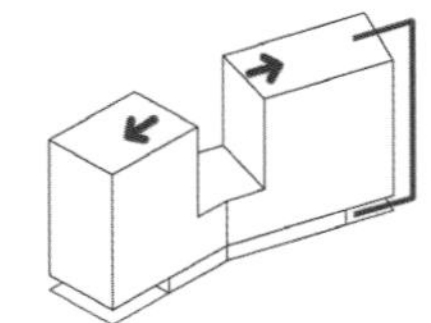

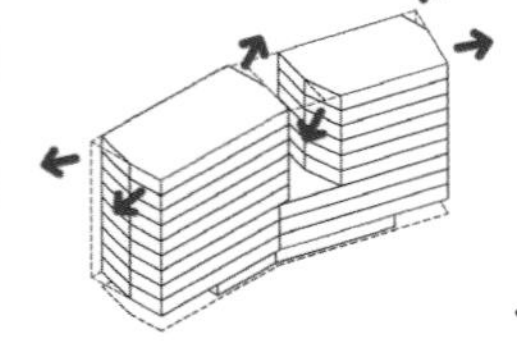

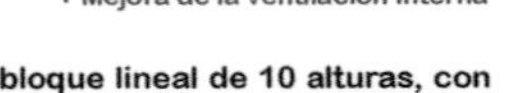

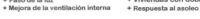

PARCELA DE ACTUACIÓN
+ Profundidad edificio 12m
+ Edificabilidad: 7.500 m2
+ Alturas permitidas: PBP+IX+A
+ Volumen pantalla

REAJUSTE DE LA VOLUMETRÍA
+ Permeabilidad del edificio
+ Los áticos los pasamos a la PB
+ Paso de la luz
+ Mejora de la ventilación interna

INTERPRETACIÓN DEL LUGAR
+ Economía de núcleos
+ Visuales abiertas
+ Viviendas con doble orientación
+ Respuesta al asoleo

VOLUMETRÍA FINAL
+ Ventilación y vistas transversales
+ Nuevos pasos en planta baja
+ Contacto espacios libres
+ Edificio contundente

El planeamiento propone un bloque lineal de 10 alturas, con posibilidad de ático, permitiendo una profundidad de edificación de 12 m.
Proponemos un edificio con con dos núcleos verticales y viviendas a ambos lados. Para lograr el doble objetivo de permitir la permeabilidad del edificio, eliminando el efecto pantalla, y mejorar la calidad de las viviendas, trabajamos la volumetría separando el volumen en dos cuerpos independientes en altura.

El edificio interpreta el entorno, abriéndose a la orientación sur, y buscando visuales lejanas, a la vez que permite el paso de la luz, aportando un espacio libre entre edificios de mayor calidad.
El sistema de organización está basado en dos barras de servicios paralelas que acompañan a los espacios servidos, y dos barras de almacenamiento en fachada que permiten una flexibilidad total del espacio interior, que está distribuido por medio de habitaciones-mueble.

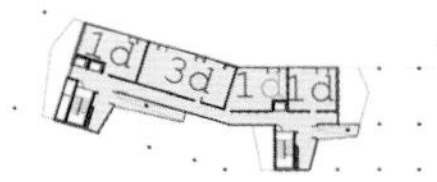

_tipologías

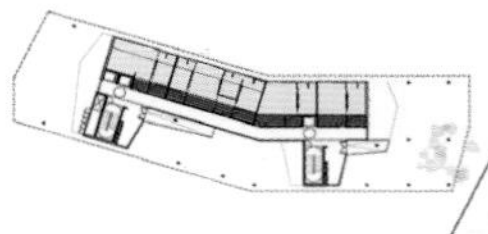

_barras de servicios

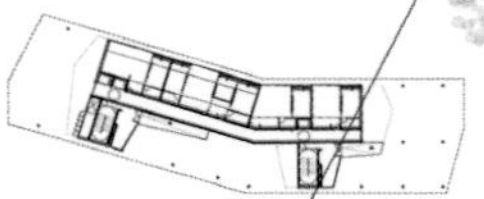

_almacenamiento y estructura

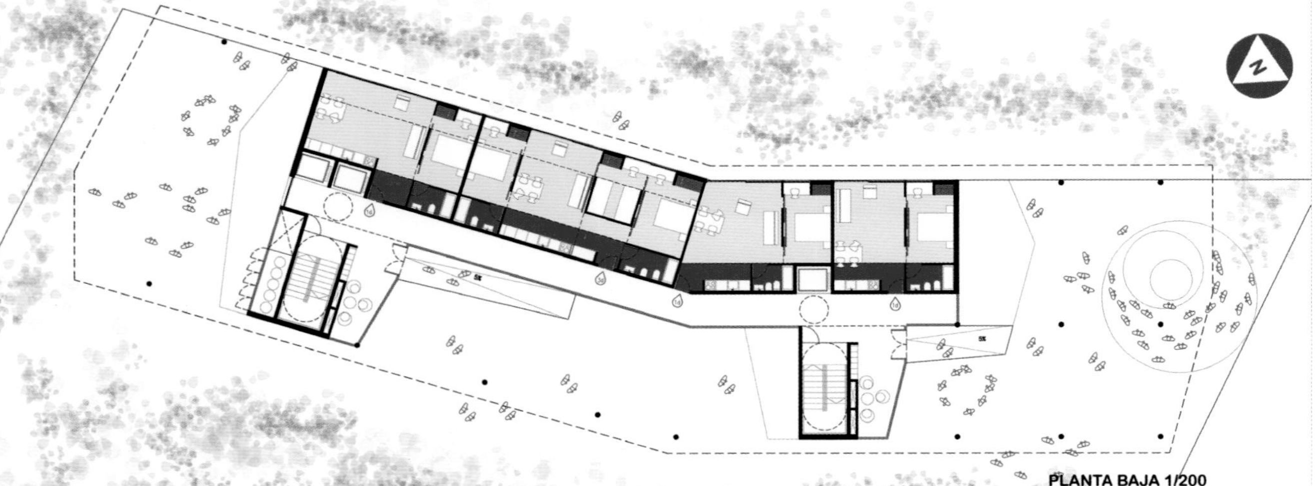

PLANTA BAJA 1/200

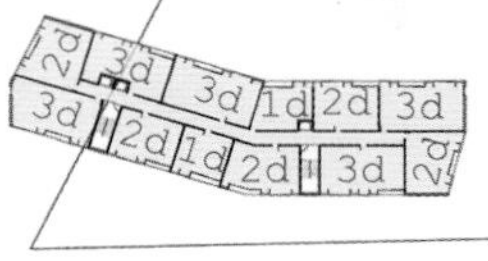

_tipologías

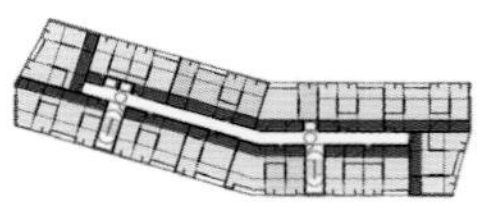

_barras de servicios

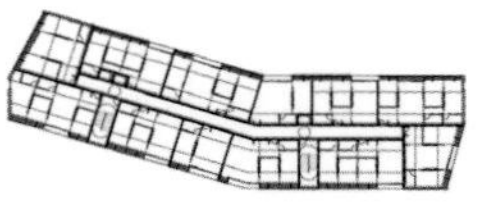

_almacenamiento y estructura

PLANTA PRIMERA 1/200

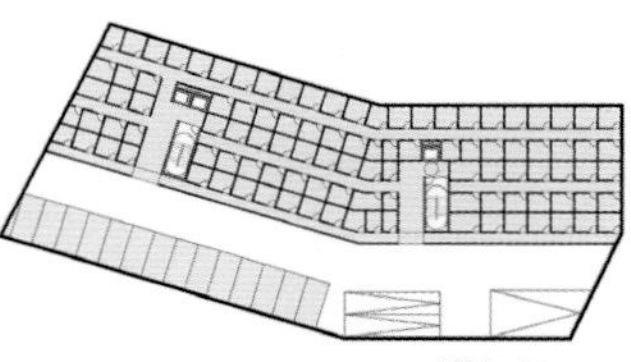

PLANTA -1 1/400 — 100 trasteros, 14 plazas aparcamiento

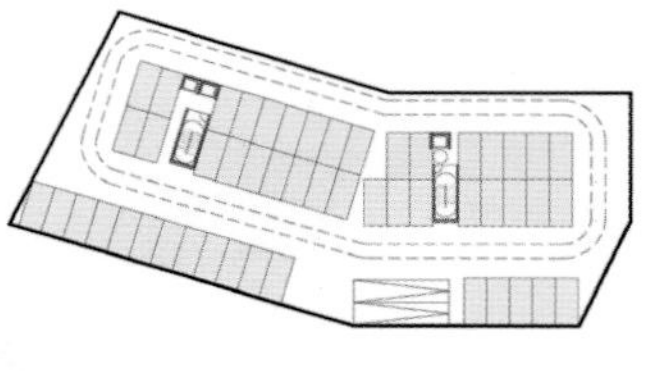

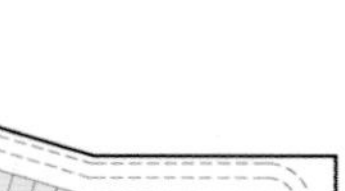

PLANTA -2 y -3 1/400 — 52 plazas aparcamiento por planta

CONCURSO DE PROYECTOS SOBRE LA PARCELA 9.1 EN "NUESTRA SEÑORA DE LOS ÁNGELES 6"_LEMA_AMEL101_2/3

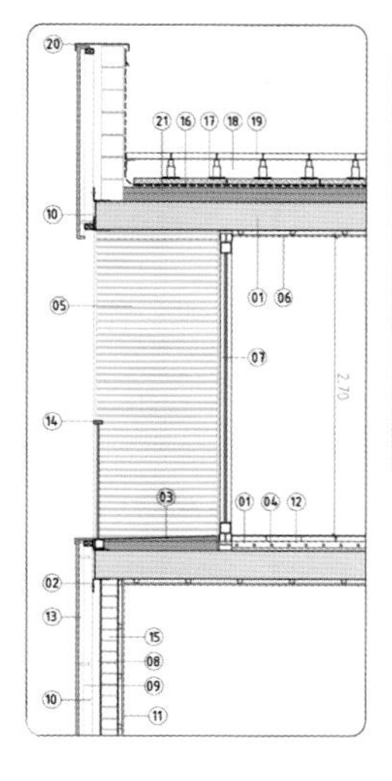

LEYENDA CONSTRUCTIVA

01 Forjado hormigón
02 Conectores
03 Pavimento exterior
04 Suelo radiante
05 Plafón exterior ligero
06 Falso techo cartón-yeso
07 Carpintería doble vidrio
08 Aislamiento térmico
09 Panel GRC
10 Subestructura aluminio
11 Carton-yeso semi directo
12 Terrazo
13 Poliuretano preyectado
14 Barandilla
15 Ladrillo cerámico
16 Lámina impermeabilizante
17 Aislamento poliestireno extrusionado
18 Pie regulable
19 Pavimento de hormigón prefabricado
20 Chapa de aluminio lacado
21 Hormigón de pendientes

PRESUPUESTO

Derribos	532.625,00 €
Movimiento de tierras	266.312,50 €
Cimentación	319.575,00 €
Estructura	585.887,50 €
Coberta	213.050,00 €
Fachada carpinterias	319.575,00 €
Fachada aislamiento	106.525,00 €
Fachada_obra	159.787,50 €
Fachada revestimiento	372.837,50 €
Fachada_vidrio	319.575,00 €
Divisiones_puertas	53.262,50 €
Divisiones tabiqueria	106.525,00 €
Instalaciones audio	53.262,50 €
Climatización	106.525,00 €
Electricidad	159.787,50 €
Fontanería	266.312,50 €
Instalación gas	106.525,00 €
Saneamiento	106.525,00 €
Instalción ventilación	53.262,50 €
Revestimiento pavimentación	319.575,00 €
Revestimiento alicatados	106.525,00 €
Revestimiento escaleras	159.787,50 €
Revestimiento yeso	159.787,50 €
Revestimiento pintura	106.525,00 €
Revestimiento techo	106.525,00 €
Decoración	53.262,50 €
Urbanización	106.525,00 €
	5.326.250,00 €

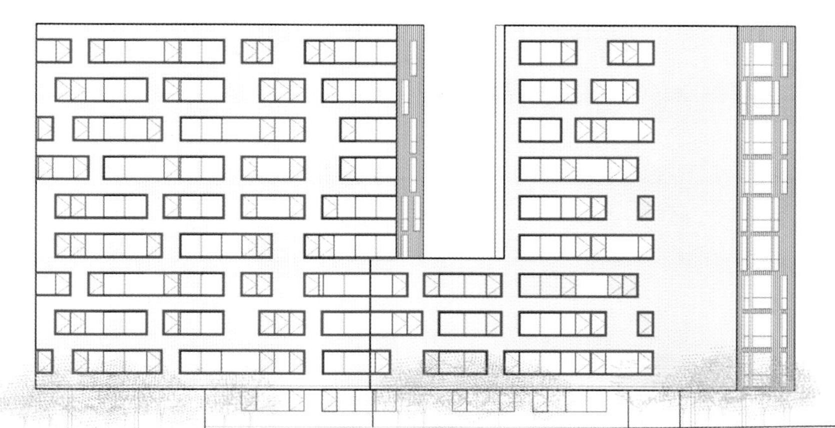

ALZADO SUR 1/300

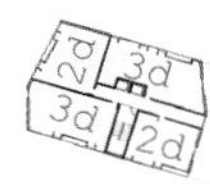

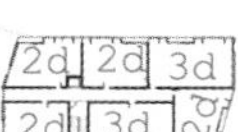

_tipologías

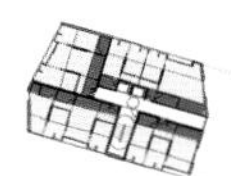

_barras de servicios

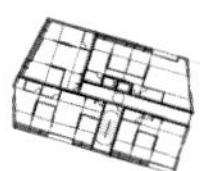

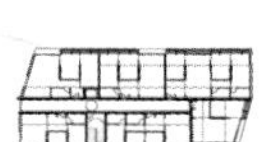

_almacenamiento y estructura

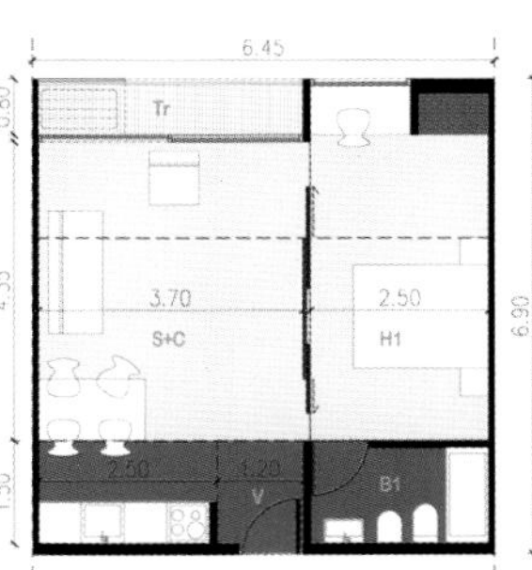

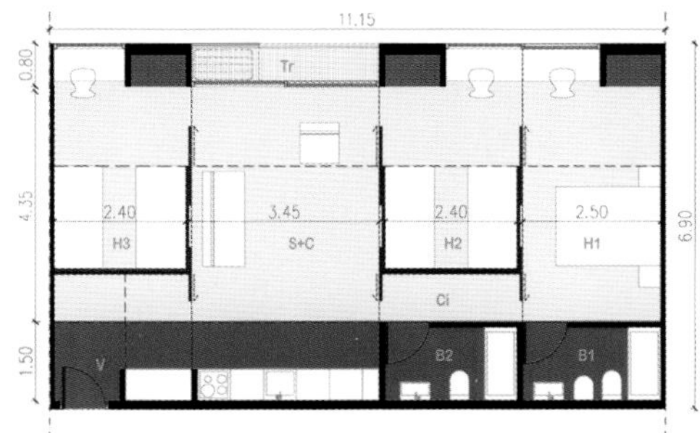

PLANTAS 4-9_ 1/200

HABITACIÓN-MUEBLE

Las tipologías se organizan por medio de dos barras paralelas, una de almacenamiento y otra de servicios, que generan un espacio diáfano ordenado por medio de las habitaciones-mueble.

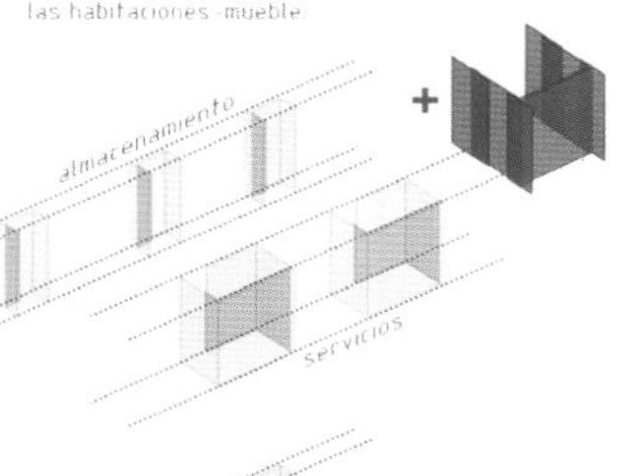

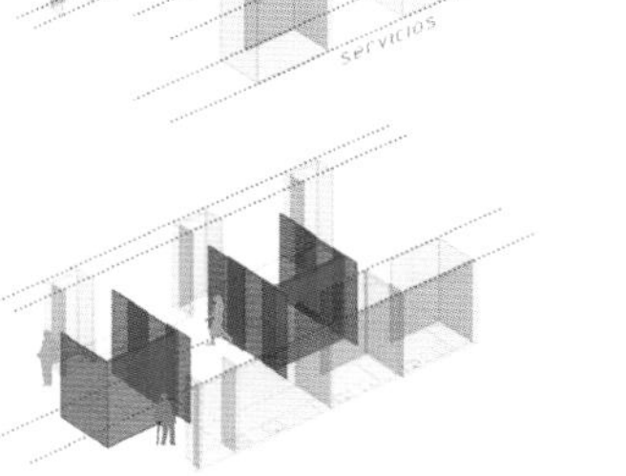

TIPO 1D

SUP. INTERIORES		sup. útil
S+C	sala estar+cocina	20.01
H1	dormitorio 1	12.83
H2	dormitorio 2	-
B1	baño principal	3.58
B2	baño secundario	-
C	cocina	-
V	vestíbulo	1.90
Ci	circulaciones	-
TOTAL ÚTIL INTERIOR		38.32m2
SUP. EXTERIORES		
Tr	TERRAZAS	2.96

TIPO 2D

SUP. INTERIORES		sup. útil
S+C	sala estar+cocina	23.78
H1	dormitorio 1	12.83
H2	dormitorio 2	10.08
B1	baño principal	3.58
B2	baño secundario	-
C	cocina	-
V	vestíbulo	2.05
Ci	circulaciones	-
TOTAL ÚTIL INTERIOR		52.32m2
SUP. EXTERIORES		
Tr	TERRAZAS	2.96

TIPO 3D

SUP. INTERIORES		sup. útil
S+C	sala estar+cocina	23.78
H1	dormitorio 1	12.83
H2	dormitorio 2	10.08
H3	dormitorio 3	10.08
B1	baño principal	3.58
B2	baño secundario	3.58
V	vestíbulo	2.05
Ci	circulaciones	2.34
TOTAL ÚTIL INTERIOR		68.32m2
SUP. EXTERIORES		
Tr	TERRAZAS	2.96

TIPOLOGÍAS 1/100

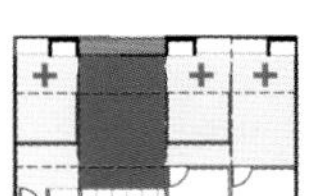

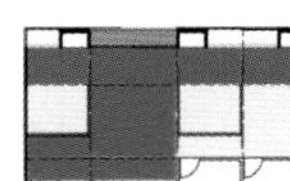

ESPACIO COMODÍN
SALA DE ESTAR LOGITUDINAL

Se genera una doble circulación alrededor de las habitaciones-mueble, permitiendo extender la sala de estar a todo el ancho de la vivienda, transformando el espacio y aportando una nueva forma de entender el espacio común dentro de la vivienda.

ESTUDIO TIPOLOGÍA

Bandact | *LUIS ARREDONDO_ARCHITECT*

Project : Social Housing Competition
Participants : Luis Arredondo
Collaborators : Amaia Artaetxebarria

Location : Madrid, Spain
Client : EMVS / Year : 2011

CONCURSO DE PROYECTOS SOBRE LA PARCELA 12.1 EN "NUESTRA SEÑORA DE LOS ÁNGELES 12"_LEMA_BANDACT_1/3

SITUACIÓN 1/10.000

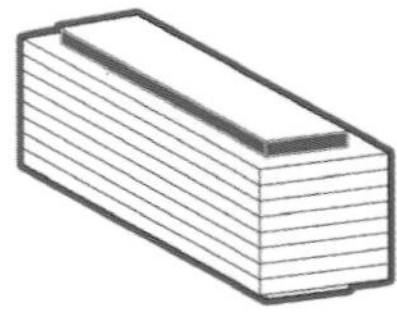

PARCELA DE ACTUACIÓN
+ Profundidad edificio 15m
+ Edificabilidad: 5.800 m2
+ Alturas permitidas: PBP+VIII+A
+ Volumen pantalla

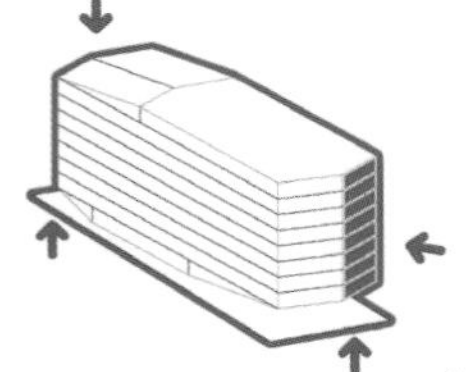

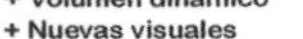

REAJUSTE DE LA VOLUMETRÍA
+ Relación con el parque
+ Los áticos los pasamos a la PB
+ Volumen dinámico
+ Nuevas visuales

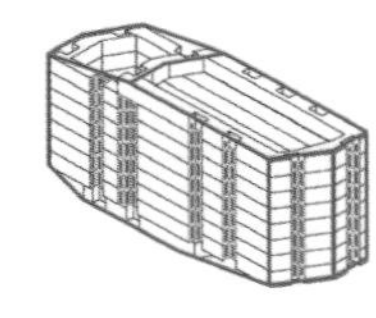

BANDA ACTIVA
+ Economía de núcleos
+ Patios-terrazas-gran ventana
+ Banda de servicios en fachada
+ Nuevo espacio comodín

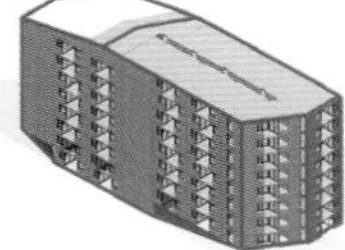

VOLUMETRÍA FINAL
+ Volumentría contundente
+ Nuevos pasos en planta baja
+ Contacto espacios libres
+ Edificio contundente

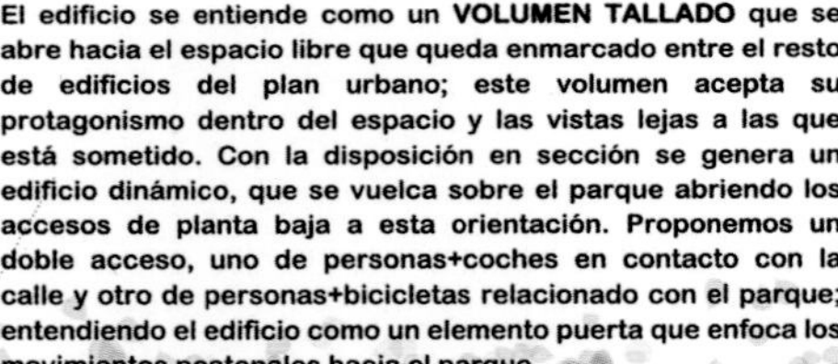

El edificio se entiende como un **VOLUMEN TALLADO** que se abre hacia el espacio libre que queda enmarcado entre el resto de edificios del plan urbano; este volumen acepta su protagonismo dentro del espacio y las vistas lejas a las que está sometido. Con la disposición en sección se genera un edificio dinámico, que se vuelca sobre el parque abriendo los accesos de planta baja a esta orientación. Proponemos un doble acceso, uno de personas+coches en contacto con la calle y otro de personas+bicicletas relacionado con el parque; entendiendo el edificio como un elemento puerta que enfoca los movimientos peatonales hacia el parque.

A nivel funcional proponemos una **BANDA ACTIVA** en fachada, compuesta por los espacios servidores y por una terraza-patio entendida como habitación exterior. Conseguimos con este sistema una perfecta ventilación e iluminación de todos los espacios de la vivienda, por medio de una gran ventana que se pliega a lo largo de esta terraza-patio proporcionando nuevas visuales y aumentando la flexibilidad interior.

La **HABITACIÓN EXTERIOR** es el comodín de la vivienda, un espacio con dimensión suficiente para ser útil, permitiendo combinaciones con los diferentes espacios interiores, pasando de esta forma a ser el protagonista de la distribución de la vivienda.

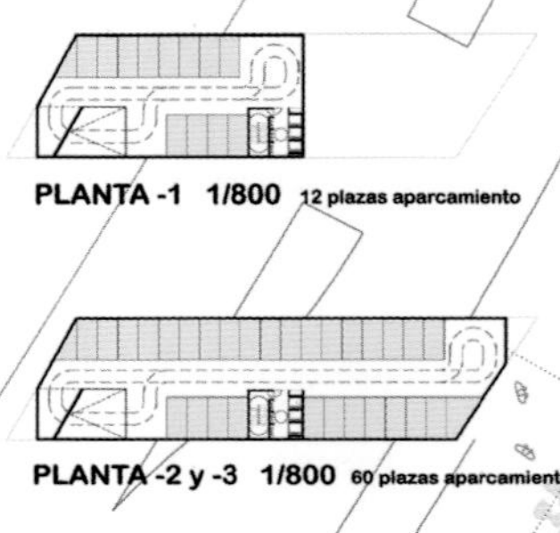

PLANTA -1 1/800 12 plazas aparcamiento

PLANTA -2 y -3 1/800 60 plazas aparcamiento

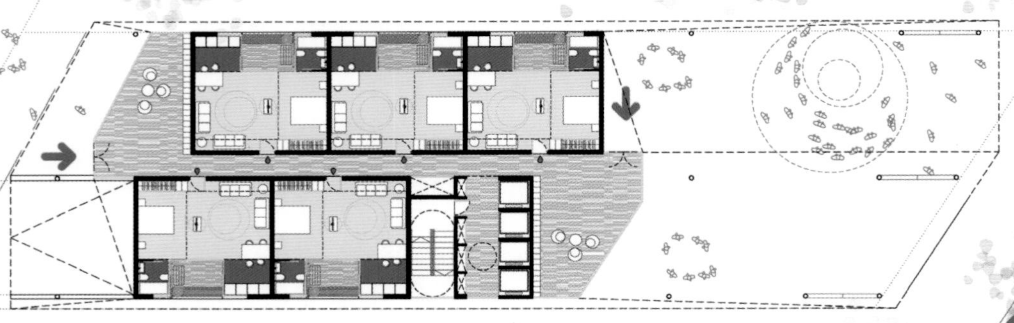

PLANTA BAJA 1/200

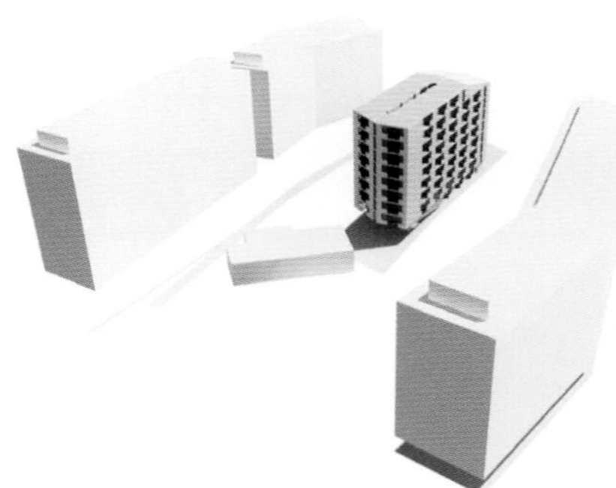

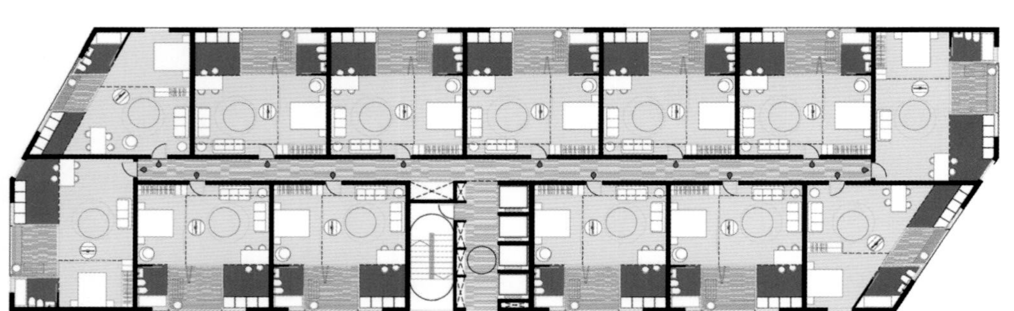

PLANTAS 1-7 1/200

CONCURSO DE PROYECTOS SOBRE LA PARCELA 12.1 EN "NUESTRA SEÑORA DE LOS ÁNGELES 12"_LEMA_BANDACT_2/3

LEYENDA CONSTRUCTIVA

01 Forjado hormigón
02 Conectores
03 Pavimento exterior
04 Suelo radiante
05 Plafón exterior ligero
06 Falso techo cartón-yeso
07 Carpintería doble vidrio
08 Aislamiento térmico
09 Panel GRC
10 Subestructura aluminio
11 Carton-yeso semi directo
12 Terrazo
13 Poliuretano preyectado
14 Barandilla
15 Ladrillo cerámico
16 Lámina impermeabilizante
17 Aislamento poliestireno extrusionado
18 Pie regulable
19 Pavimento de hormigón prefabricado
20 Chapa de aluminio lacado
21 Hormigón de pendientes

PRESUPUESTO

Movimiento de tierras	69.126,00 €
Cimentación	345.630,00 €
Estructura	345.630,00 €
Coberta	138.252,00 €
Fachada carpinterias	241.941,00 €
Fachada aislamiento	172.815,00 €
Fachada_obra	241.941,00 €
Fachada revestimiento	414.756,00 €
Fachada_vidrio	138.252,00 €
Divisiones_puertas	276.504,00 €
Divisiones tabiquería	69.126,00 €
Electricidad	138.252,00 €
Fontaneria	207.378,00 €
Instalación gas	34.563,00 €
saneamiento	172.815,00 €
Instalción ventilación	103.689,00 €
Revestimiento pavimentación	138.252,00 €
Urbanización	207.378,00 €
	3.456.300,00 €

ALZADO NORTE 1/400

PLANTA 8_ 1/200

AXONOMETRÍA VIVIENDA

TIPOLOGÍA 1/100

TERRAZA-PATIO

El espacio de terraza pasa a ser una zona comdín que multipilca la flexibilidad de la vivienda, ya que su dimensión le concede el grado de espacio útil. Puede ser una zona de estudio, un dormitorio de verano, un comedor exterior, una ampliación del salón...

VIVIENDA TIPO

SUP. INTERIORES		sup. útil
S+C	sala estar+cocina	25.00
H1	dormitorio 1	11.22
H2	dormitorio 2	-
B1	baño principal	3.68
B2	baño secundario	-
C	cocina	-
V	vestíbulo	-
Ci	circulaciones	-
TOTAL ÚTIL		40.04m2
+ Tr	terraza	6.58m2

ESPACIO COMODÍN

LA GRAN VENTANA

La decisión de centralizar la ventilación e iluminación de la vivienda, aporta una obertura de cara al exterior mucho mayor que en un caso tradicional pasando a ser el centro de visuales de la unidad.

ESTUDIO TIPOLOGÍA

048 Zigzag | *LUIS ARREDONDO_ARCHITECT*

Project : Social Housing Competition
Participants : Luis Arredondo
Collaborators : Amaia Artaetxebarria

Location : Madrid, Spain
Client : EMVS / Year : 2011

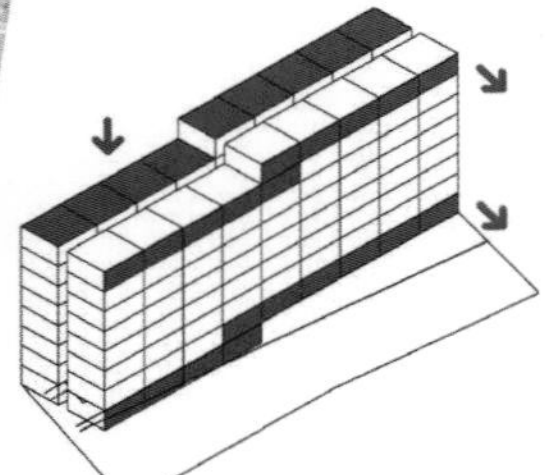

PARCELA DE ACTUACIÓN
+ Edificabilidad: 8.000 m2
+ Alturas permitidas: PBP+VII+A
+ Adaptación al terreno
- 50% viviendas mal orientadas

REAJUSTE DE LA VOLUMETRÍA
+ Adaptación a la parcela
+ Doble barra+1 vivienda extra
+ Variación altura
- Patio interior mínimo

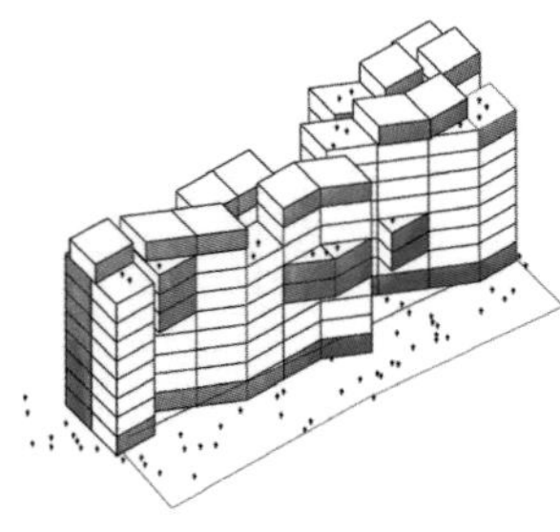

INTERPRETACIÓN DEL LUGAR
+ Malla anisótropa adaptada a los límites
+ Visuales abiertas
+ Accesos abiertos
+ Respuesta al asoleo

SITUACIÓN

La disposición y dimensión del solar de actuación parece obligar a un sistema de viviendas con orientación N-S con pasillo central, lo que condena a la mitad de las viviendas de la promoción a una mala orientación. Proponemos romper la barra con una nueva malla anisótropa, sistemática y estructural, que permite alinearse a dos de las caras del solar y trazar diagonales con orientación sur, las dos barras iniciales se deslizan y se enrollan sobre sí mismas, sacando el máximo partido del edificio y de su entorno. El edificio interpreta el entorno, abriéndose a la orientación sur, y buscando visuales lejanas, a la vez que permite el paso de la luz, aportando un espacio libre entre edificios de mayor calidad.

Este sistema genera una edificación que elimina la sensación de edificio pantalla, con una fachada de profundidad variable. A la vez que abre los pasillos centrales a la calle y entre las diferentes plantas, evitando la sensación túnel.

La tipología de vivienda está basada una barra de servicios y acceso y otra de espacios servidos, con una corredera que permite la unificación del espacio. Se hace una propuesta de mobiliario organizada en un paquete que aglutina cama abatible, armario y mesa de estudio, aumentando la flexibilidad interior. Su envolvente sesgada permite un aumento de las visuales y genera una nueva sensación espacial abierta al exterior, apoyada en un único hueco tridimensional que agrupa la terraza y las dos ventanas del dormitorio.

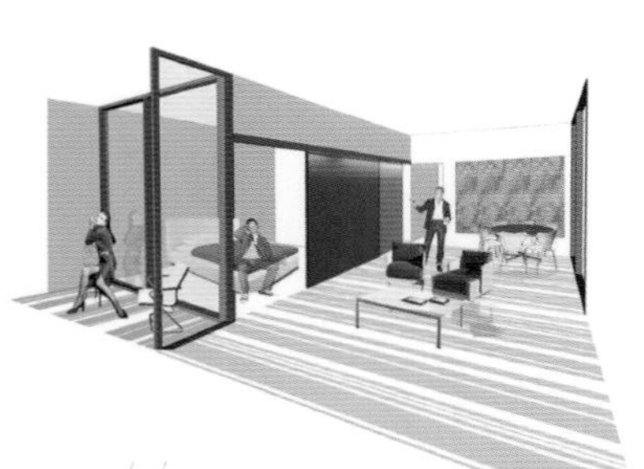

LEYENDA CONSTRUCTIVA

01 Forjado hormigón
02 Conectores
03 Pavimento exterior
04 Suelo radiante
05 Plafón exterior ligero
06 Falso techo cartón-yeso
07 Carpintería doble vidrio
08 Aislamiento térmico
09 Panel GRC
10 Subestructura aluminio
11 Carton-yeso semi directo
12 Terrazo
13 Poliuretano preyectado
14 Barandilla
15 Ladrillo cerámico
16 Lámina impermeabilizante
17 Aislamiento poliestireno extrusionado
18 Pie regulable
19 Pavimento de hormigón prefabricado
20 Chapa de aluminio lacado
21 Hormigón de pendientes

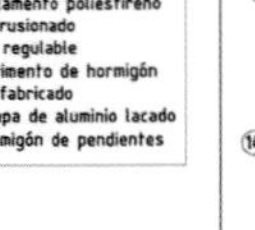

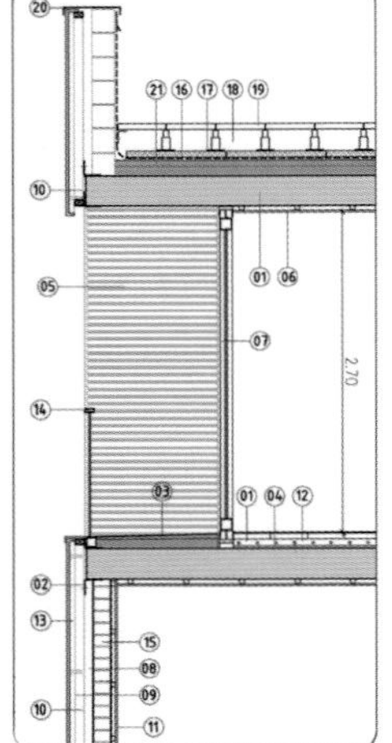

DETALLE 1/50

PRESUPUESTO

Derribos	0,00 €
Movimiento de tierras	690.270,00 €
Cimentación	739.575,00 €
Estructura	493.050,00 €
Coberta	197.220,00 €
Fachada carpinterías	295.830,00 €
Fachada aislamiento	98.610,00 €
Fachada_obra	147.915,00 €
Fachada revestimiento	197.220,00 €
Fachada_vidrio	295.830,00 €
Divisiones_puertas	49.305,00 €
Divisiones tabiquería	98.610,00 €
Instalaciones audio	49.305,00 €
Climatización	49.305,00 €
Electricidad	147.915,00 €
Fontanería	147.915,00 €
Instalación gas	98.610,00 €
Saneamiento	98.610,00 €
Instalción ventilación	49.305,00 €
Revestimiento pavimentación	197.220,00 €
Revestimiento alicatados	98.610,00 €
Revestimiento escaleras	147.915,00 €
Revestimiento yeso	147.915,00 €
Revestimiento pintura	98.610,00 €
Revestimiento techo	98.610,00 €
Decoración	98.610,00 €
Urbanización	98.610,00 €
	4.935.500,00 €

VOLUMETRÍA FINAL
+ Ventilación y vistas transversales
+ Nuevos pasos en planta baja
+ Contacto espacios libres
+ Edificio permeable

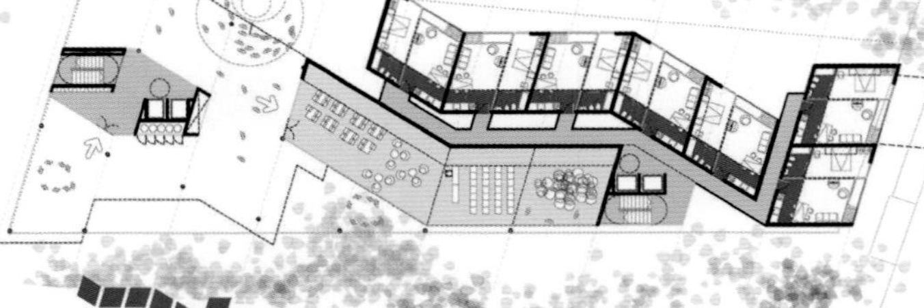

PLANTA 0 _COTA 622.45
1/400

AXONOMETRÍA

PLANTA 0 _COTA 618.75
1/1000

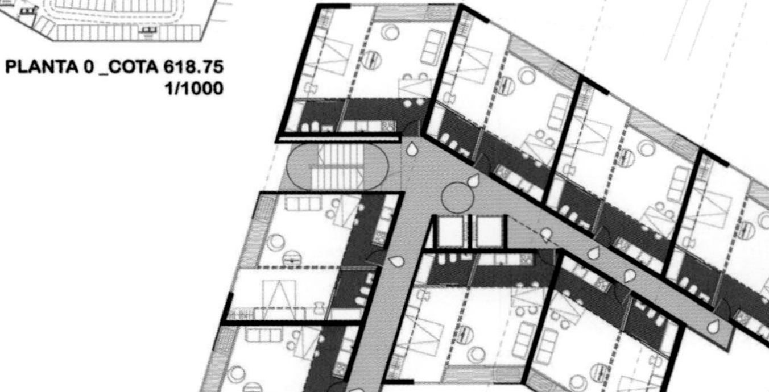

PLANTA PRIMERA y SEGUNDA
1/200

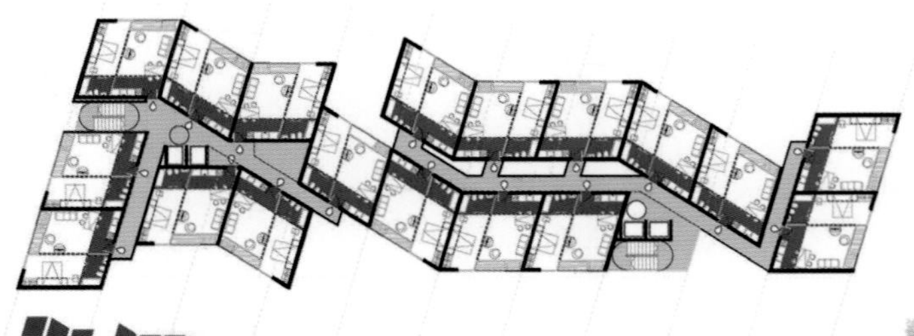

PLANTA TERCERA y CUARTA
1/400

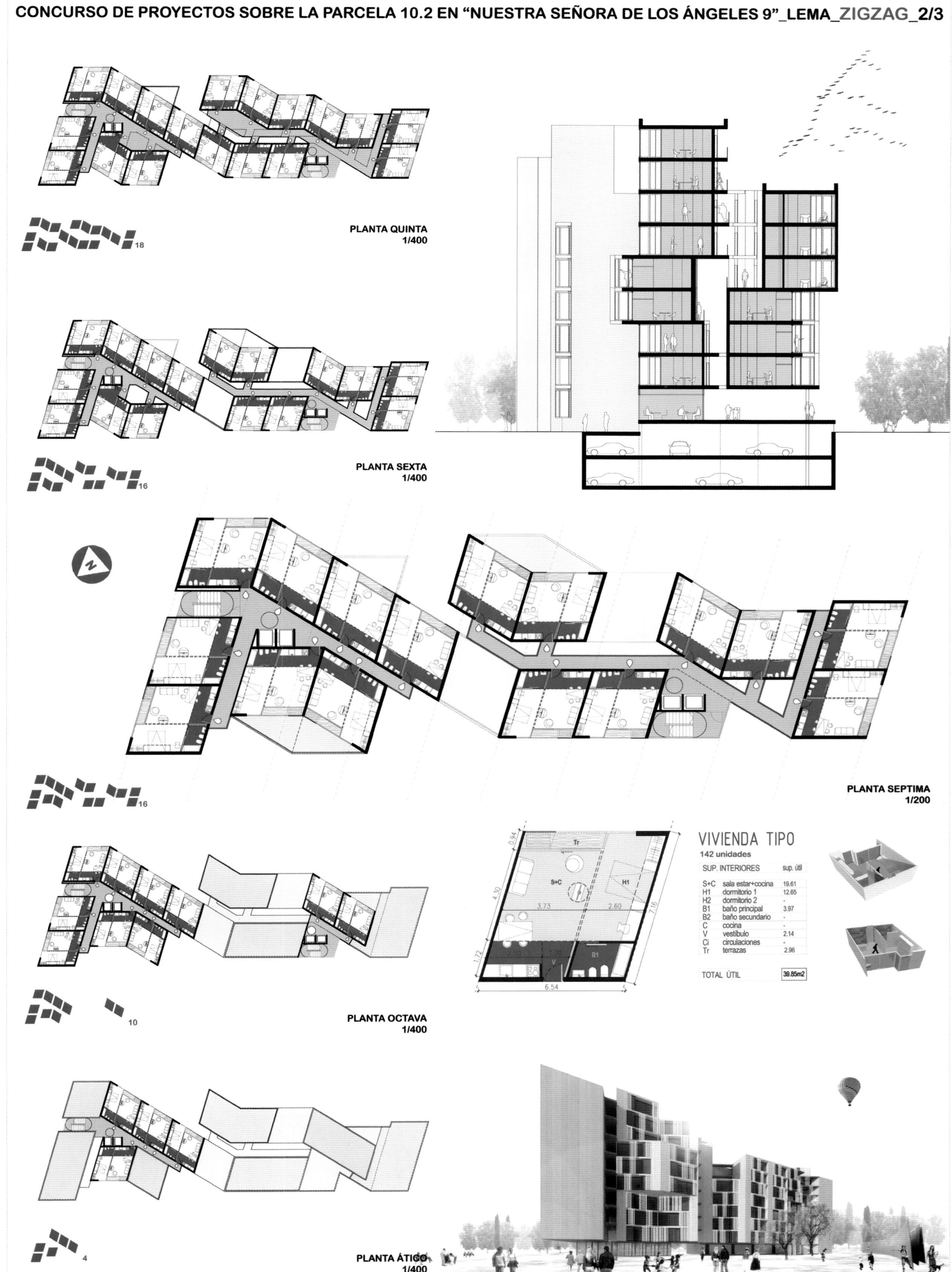
CONCURSO DE PROYECTOS SOBRE LA PARCELA 10.2 EN "NUESTRA SEÑORA DE LOS ÁNGELES 9"_LEMA_ZIGZAG_2/3
18
PLANTA QUINTA
1/400
16
PLANTA SEXTA
1/400
16
PLANTA SEPTIMA
1/200
Tr
S+C
H1
0.94
4.30
3.73
2.60
7.16
1.72
1.81
1.20
V
B1
6.54
VIVIENDA TIPO
142 unidades
SUP. INTERIORES sup. útil
S+C sala estar+cocina 19.61
H1 dormitorio 1 12.65
H2 dormitorio 2 -
B1 baño principal 3.97
B2 baño secundario -
C cocina -
V vestíbulo 2.14
Ci circulaciones -
Tr terrazas 2.96
TOTAL ÚTIL 39.85m2
10
PLANTA OCTAVA
1/400
4
PLANTA ÁTICO
1/400

049 Replica | *LUIS ARREDONDO_ARCHITECT*

Project : Social Housing Competition
Participants : Luis Arredondo
Collaborators : Amaia Artaetxebarria

Location : Madrid, Spain
Client : EMVS / Year : 2011

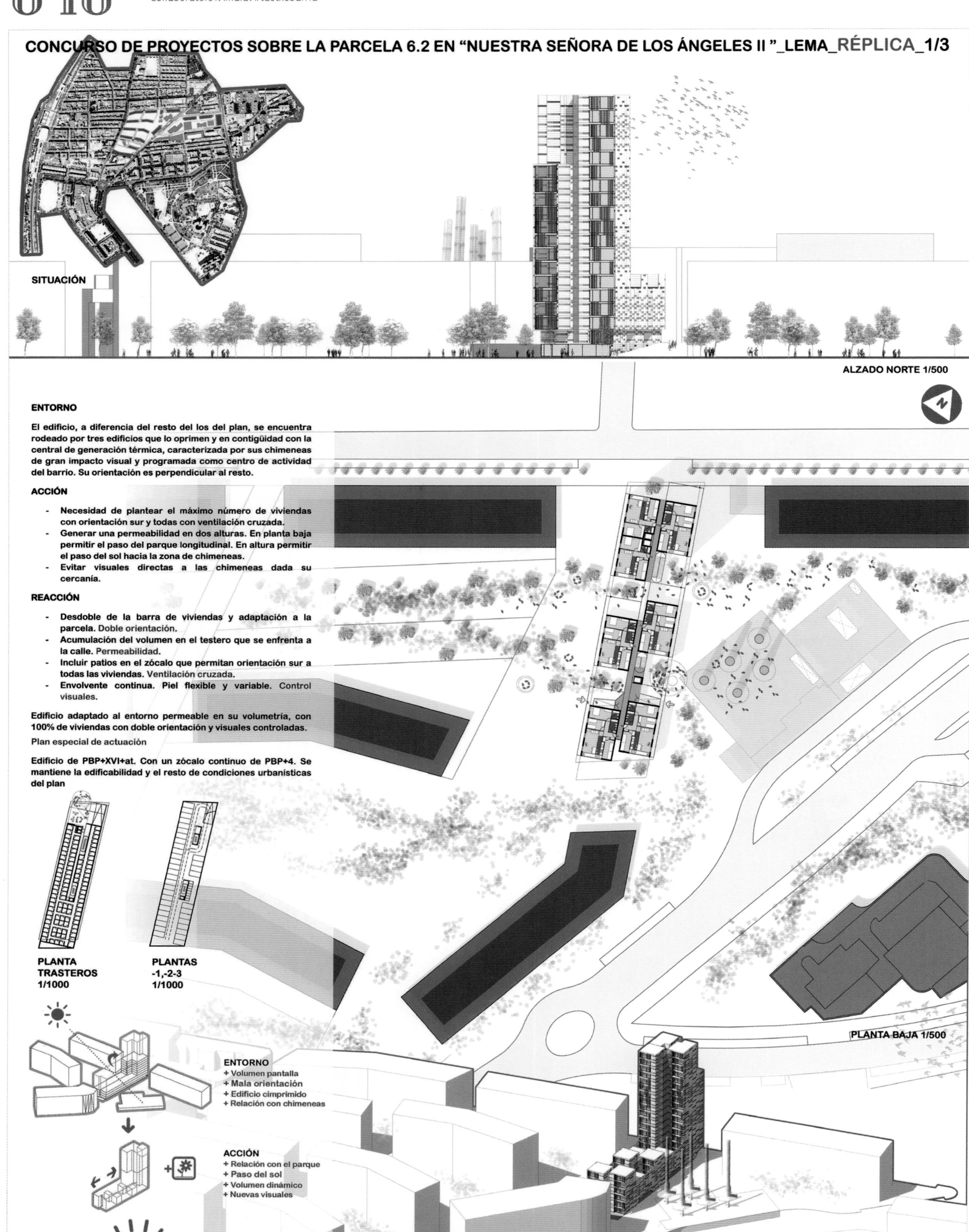

CONCURSO DE PROYECTOS SOBRE LA PARCELA 6.2 EN "NUESTRA SEÑORA DE LOS ÁNGELES II "_LEMA_RÉPLICA_1/3
SITUACIÓN
ALZADO NORTE 1/500
ENTORNO
El edificio, a diferencia del resto del los del plan, se encuentra rodeado por tres edificios que lo oprimen y en contigüidad con la central de generación térmica, caracterizada por sus chimeneas de gran impacto visual y programada como centro de actividad del barrio. Su orientación es perpendicular al resto.
ACCIÓN
- Necesidad de plantear el máximo número de viviendas con orientación sur y todas con ventilación cruzada.
- Generar una permeabilidad en dos alturas. En planta baja permitir el paso del parque longitudinal. En altura permitir el paso del sol hacia la zona de chimeneas.
- Evitar visuales directas a las chimeneas dada su cercanía.
REACCIÓN
- Desdoble de la barra de viviendas y adaptación a la parcela. Doble orientación.
- Acumulación del volumen en el testero que se enfrenta a la calle. Permeabilidad.
- Incluir patios en el zócalo que permitan orientación sur a todas las viviendas. Ventilación cruzada.
- Envolvente continua. Piel flexible y variable. Control visuales.
Edificio adaptado al entorno permeable en su volumetría, con 100% de viviendas con doble orientación y visuales controladas.
Plan especial de actuación
Edificio de PBP+XVI+at. Con un zócalo continuo de PBP+4. Se mantiene la edificabilidad y el resto de condiciones urbanísticas del plan
PLANTA TRASTEROS 1/1000
PLANTAS -1,-2-3 1/1000
PLANTA BAJA 1/500
ENTORNO
+ Volumen pantalla
+ Mala orientación
+ Edificio cimprimido
+ Relación con chimeneas
ACCIÓN
+ Relación con el parque
+ Paso del sol
+ Volumen dinámico
+ Nuevas visuales
REACCIÓN
+ Nueva volmuen adaptado
+ Permeabilidad
+ 100% ventilación cruzada
+ Piel dinámica

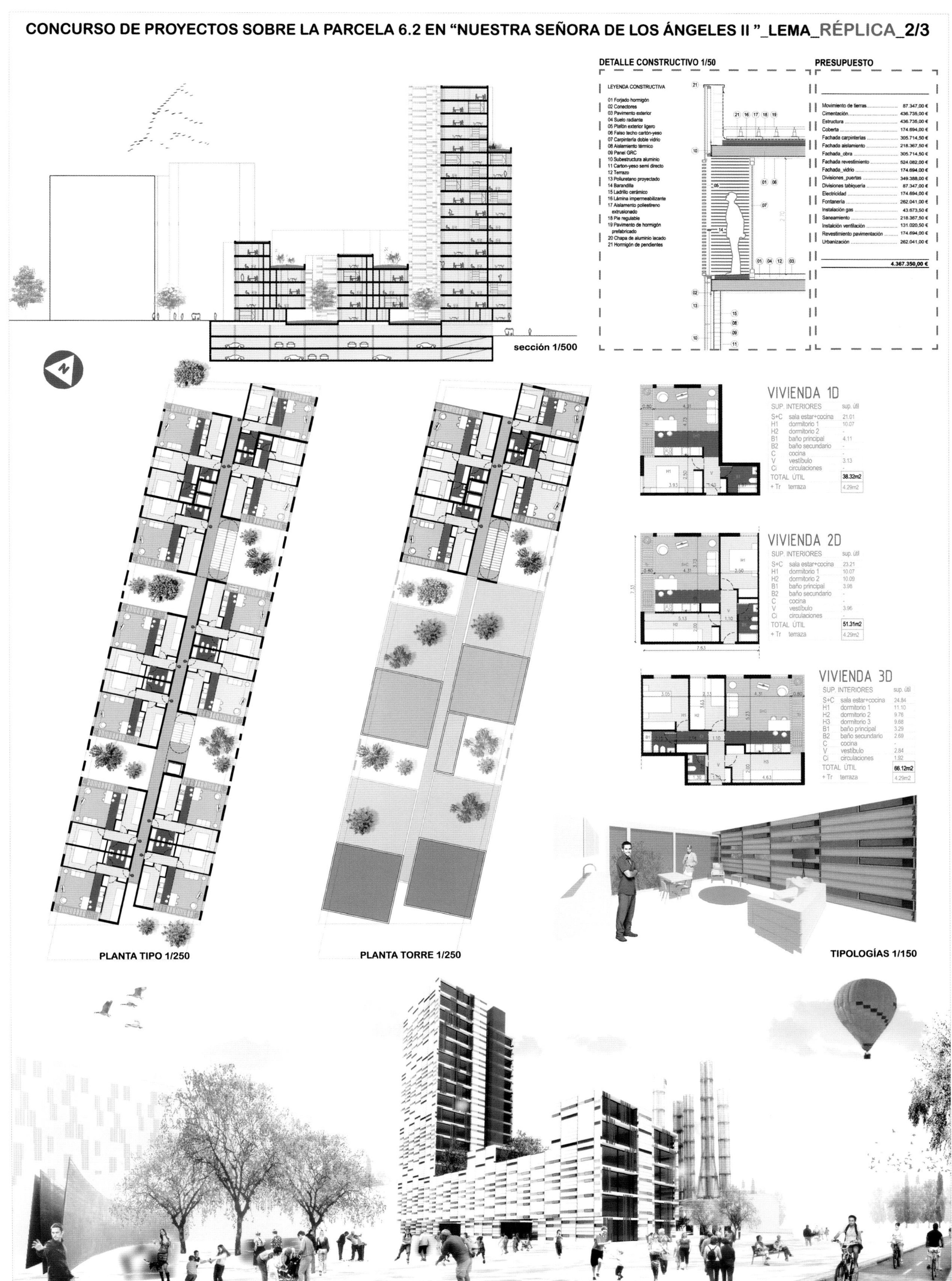
CONCURSO DE PROYECTOS SOBRE LA PARCELA 6.2 EN "NUESTRA SEÑORA DE LOS ÁNGELES II "_LEMA_RÉPLICA_2/3
DETALLE CONSTRUCTIVO 1/50
LEYENDA CONSTRUCTIVA
01 Forjado hormigón
02 Conectores
03 Pavimento exterior
04 Suelo radiante
05 Plafón exterior ligero
06 Falso techo cartón-yeso
07 Carpintería doble vidrio
08 Aislamiento térmico
09 Panel GRC
10 Subestructura aluminio
11 Carton-yeso semi directo
12 Terrazo
13 Poliuretano proyectado
14 Barandilla
15 Ladrillo cerámico
16 Lámina impermeabilizante
17 Aislamiento poliestireno extrusionado
18 Pie regulable
19 Pavimento de hormigón prefabricado
20 Chapa de aluminio lacado
21 Hormigón de pendientes
PRESUPUESTO
Movimiento de tierras 87.347,00 €
Cimentación 436.735,00 €
Estructura 436.735,00 €
Coberta 174.694,00 €
Fachada carpinterías 305.714,50 €
Fachada aislamiento 218.367,50 €
Fachada_obra 305.714,50 €
Fachada revestimiento 524.082,00 €
Fachada_vidrio 174.694,00 €
Divisiones_puertas 349.388,00 €
Divisiones tabiquería 87.347,00 €
Electricidad 174.694,00 €
Fontanería 262.041,00 €
Instalación gas 43.673,50 €
Saneamiento 218.367,50 €
Instalción ventilación 131.020,50 €
Revestimiento pavimentación 174.694,00 €
Urbanización 262.041,00 €
4.367.350,00 €
sección 1/500
VIVIENDA 1D
SUP. INTERIORES sup. útil
S+C sala estar+cocina 21.01
H1 dormitorio 1 10.07
H2 dormitorio 2 -
B1 baño principal 4.11
B2 baño secundario -
C cocina -
V vestíbulo 3.13
Ci circulaciones -
TOTAL ÚTIL 38.32m2
+ Tr terraza 4.29m2
VIVIENDA 2D
SUP. INTERIORES sup. útil
S+C sala estar+cocina 23.21
H1 dormitorio 1 10.07
H2 dormitorio 2 10.09
B1 baño principal 3.98
B2 baño secundario -
C cocina -
V vestíbulo 3.96
Ci circulaciones -
TOTAL ÚTIL 51.31m2
+ Tr terraza 4.29m2
VIVIENDA 3D
SUP. INTERIORES sup. útil
S+C sala estar+cocina 24.84
H1 dormitorio 1 11.10
H2 dormitorio 2 9.76
H3 dormitorio 3 9.68
B1 baño principal 3.29
B2 baño secundario 2.69
C cocina -
V vestíbulo 2.84
Ci circulaciones 1.92
TOTAL ÚTIL 66.12m2
+ Tr terraza 4.29m2
PLANTA TIPO 1/250
PLANTA TORRE 1/250
TIPOLOGÍAS 1/150

050 Concavo_Convexo | *LUIS ARREDONDO_ARCHITECT*

Project : Social Housing Competition
Participants : Luis Arredondo
Location : Melilla, Spain

Client : Melilla
Year : 2011

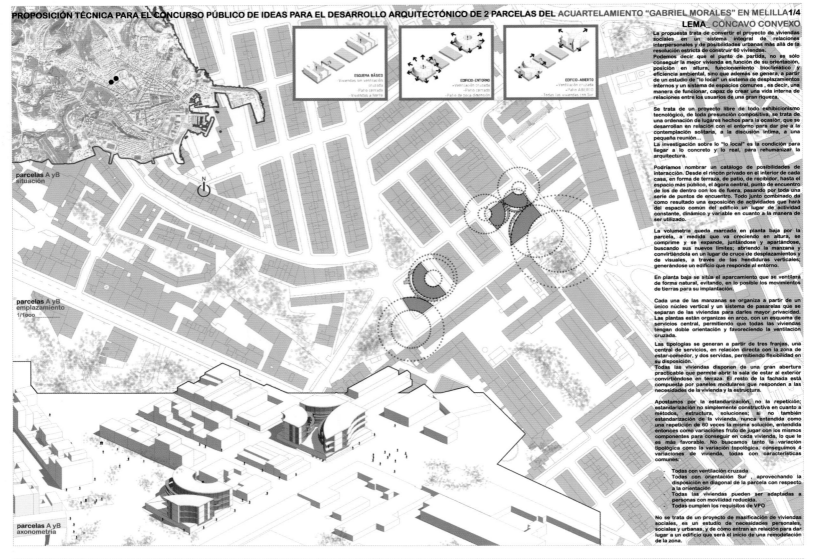

PROPOSICIÓN TÉCNICA PARA EL CONCURSO PÚBLICO DE IDEAS PARA EL DESARROLLO ARQUITECTÓNICO DE 2 PARCELAS DEL ACUARTELAMIENTO "GABRIEL MORALES" EN MELILLA1/4

LEMA_ CÓNCAVO CONVEXO

ESQUEMA BÁSICO
- Viviendas sin ventilación cruzada
- Patio cerrado
- Viviendas a Norte

EDIFICIO-ENTORNO
+ Ventilación cruzada
- Patio cerrado
- Patio de poca dimensión

EDIFICIO-ABIERTO
+ Ventilación cruzada
+ Patio ABIERTO
- Todas las viviendas con Sur

La propuesta trata de convertir el proyecto de viviendas sociales en un sistema integral de relaciones interpersonales y de posibilidades urbanas más allá de la resolución estricta de construir 60 viviendas.
Podemos decir que el punto de partida, no es sólo conseguir la mejor vivienda en función de su orientación, posición en altura, funcionamiento bioclimático y eficiencia ambiental, sino que además se genera, a partir de un estudio de "lo local" un sistema de desplazamientos internos y un sistema de espacios comunes , es decir, una manera de funcionar, capaz de crear una vida interna de relaciones entre los usuarios de una gran riqueza.

Se trata de un proyecto libre de todo exhibicionismo tecnológico, de toda presunción compositiva, se trata de una ordenación de lugares hechos para la ocasión, que se desarrollan en relación con el entorno para dar pie a la contemplación solitaria, a la discusión íntima, a una pequeña reunión...
La investigación sobre lo "lo local" es la condición para llegar a lo concreto y lo real, para rehumanizar la arquitectura.

Podríamos nombrar un catálogo de posibilidades de interacción. Desde el rincón privado en el interior de cada casa, en forma de terraza, de patio, de recibidor, hasta el espacio más público, el ágora central, punto de encuentro de los de dentro con los de fuera, pasando por toda una serie de puntos de encuentro. Todo junto combinado da como resultado una exposición de actividades que hará del espacio común del edificio un lugar de actividad constante, dinámico y variable en cuanto a la manera de ser utilizado.

La volumetría queda marcada en planta baja por la parcela, a medida que va creciendo en altura, se comprime y se expande, juntándose y apartándose, buscando sus nuevos límites; abriendo la manzana y convirtiéndola en un lugar de cruce de desplazamientos y de visuales, a través de las hendiduras verticales; generándose un edificio que responde al entorno.

En planta baja se sitúa el aparcamiento que se ventilará de forma natural, evitando, en lo posible los movimientos de tierras para su implantación.

Cada una de las manzanas se organiza a partir de un único núcleo vertical y un sistema de pasarelas que se separan de las viviendas para darles mayor privacidad. Las plantas están organizas en arco, con un esquema de servicios central, permitiendo que todas las viviendas tengan doble orientación y favoreciendo la ventilación cruzada.

Las tipologías se generan a partir de tres franjas, una central de servicios, en relación directa con la zona de estar-comedor, y dos servidas, permitiendo flexibilidad en su disposición.
Todas las viviendas disponen de una gran abertura practicable que permite abrir la sala de estar al exterior convirtiéndose en terraza. El resto de la fachada está compuesta por paneles modulares que responden a las necesidades de la vivienda y la estructura.

Apostamos por la estandarización, no la repetición; estandarización no simplemente constructiva en cuanto a métodos, estructura, soluciones; si no también estandarización de la vivienda, nunca entendida como una repetición de 60 veces la misma solución, entendida entonces como variaciones fruto de jugar con los mismos componentes para conseguir en cada vivienda, lo que le es más favorable. No buscamos tanto la variación tipológica como la variación topológica, conseguimos 4 variaciones de vivienda, todas con características comunes:

- Todas con ventilación cruzada
- Todas con orientación Sur , aprovechando la disposición en diagonal de la parcela con respecto a la orientación
- Todas las viviendas pueden ser adaptadas a personas con movilidad reducida.
- Todas cumplen los requisitos de VPO

No se trata de un proyecto de masificación de viviendas sociales, es un estudio de necesidades personales, sociales y urbanas, y de cómo entran en relación para dar lugar a un edificio que será el inicio de una remodelación de la zona.

parcelas A yB
situación

parcelas A yB
emplazamiento
1/1ooo

parcelas A yB
axonometría

PROPOSICIÓN TÉCNICA PARA EL CONCURSO PÚBLICO DE IDEAS PARA EL DESARROLLO ARQUITECTÓNICO DE 2 PARCELAS DEL ACUARTELAMIENTO "GABRIEL MORALES" EN MELILLA2/4

LEMA_ CÓNCAVO CONVEXO

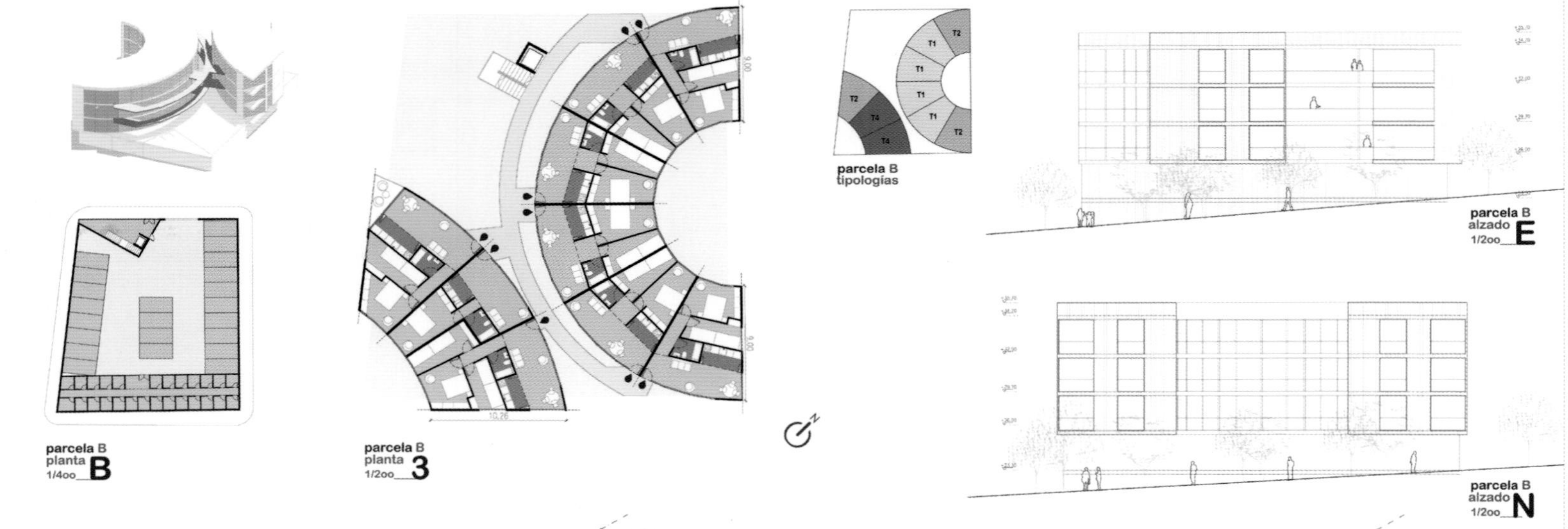

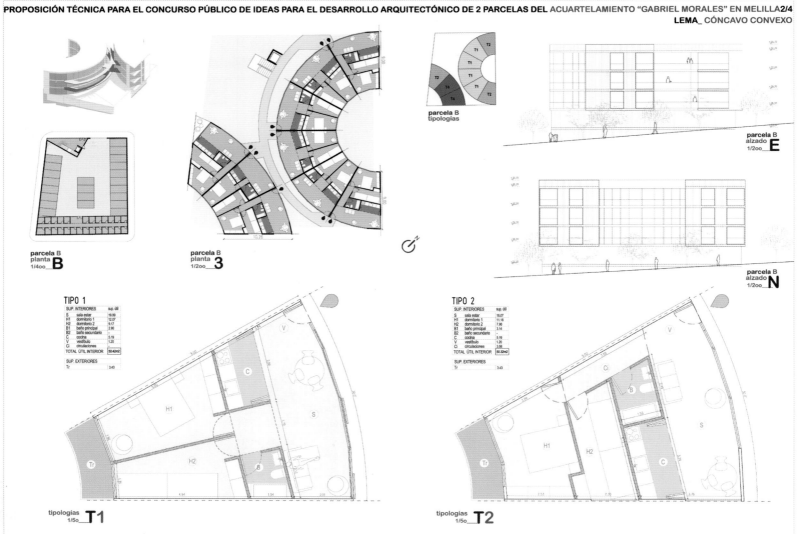

parcela B
tipologías

parcela B
planta
1/4oo **B**

parcela B
planta
1/2oo **3**

parcela B
alzado
1/2oo **E**

parcela B
alzado
1/2oo **N**

TIPO 1

SUP. INTERIORES		sup. útil
S	sala estar	19.99
H1	dormitorio 1	12.07
H2	dormitorio 2	9.17
B1	baño principal	2.80
B2	baño secundario	-
C	cocina	5.19
V	vestíbulo	1.20
Ci	circulaciones	-
TOTAL ÚTIL INTERIOR		50.42m2
SUP. EXTERIORES		
Tr		3.43

TIPO 2

SUP. INTERIORES		sup. útil
S	sala estar	18.07
H1	dormitorio 1	11.16
H2	dormitorio 2	7.96
B1	baño principal	3.14
B2	baño secundario	-
C	cocina	5.19
V	vestíbulo	1.20
Ci	circulaciones	3.58
TOTAL ÚTIL INTERIOR		50.32m2
SUP. EXTERIORES		
Tr		3.43

tipologías
1/5o **T1**

tipologías
1/5o **T2**

PROPOSICIÓN TÉCNICA PARA EL CONCURSO PÚBLICO DE IDEAS PARA EL DESARROLLO ARQUITECTÓNICO DE 2 PARCELAS DEL ACUARTELAMIENTO "GABRIEL MORALES" EN MELILLA3/4

LEMA_ CÓNCAVO CONVEXO

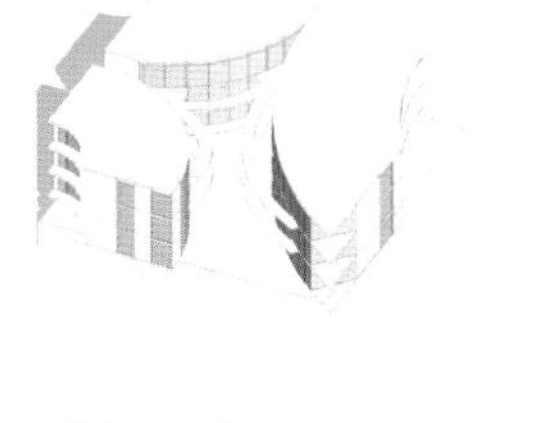

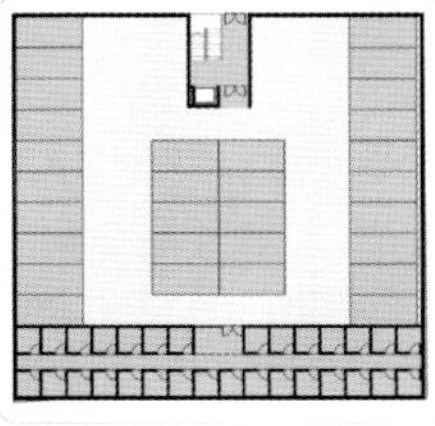

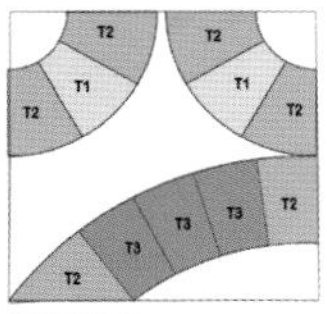

parcela A
tipologías

parcela A
alzado E
1/2oo

parcela A
planta B
1/4oo

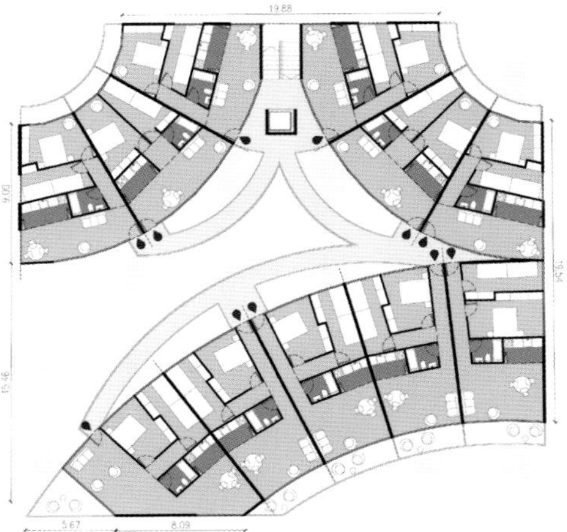

parcela A
planta 3
1/2oo

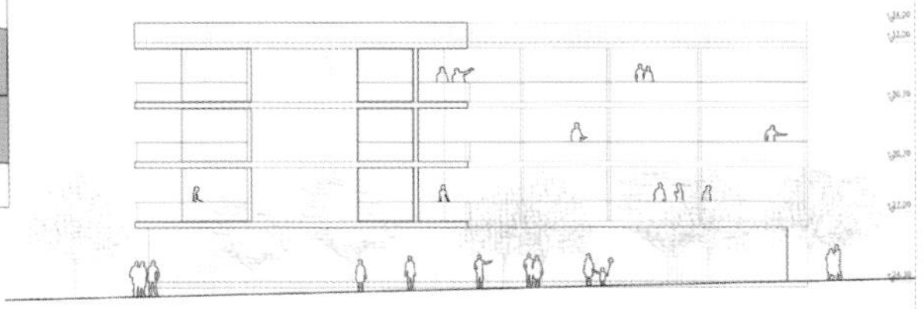

TIPO 4a

SUP. INTERIORES		sup. útil
S	sala estar	17.21
H1	dormitorio 1	13.57
H2	dormitorio 2	-
B1	baño principal	3.50
B2	baño secundario	-
C	cocina	4.50
V	vestíbulo	1.20
Ci	circulaciones	1.28
TOTAL ÚTIL INTERIOR		41.18m2
SUP. EXTERIORES		
Tr		-

TIPO 4b

SUP. INTERIORES		sup. útil
S	sala estar	17.21
H1	dormitorio 1	11.86
H2	dormitorio 2	7.97
B1	dormitorio 3	9.98
B2	baño principal	4.16
C	cocina	5.19
V	vestíbulo	1.20
Ci	circulaciones	3.45
TOTAL ÚTIL INTERIOR		61.02m2
SUP. EXTERIORES		
Tr		-

TIPO 3

SUP. INTERIORES		sup. útil
S	sala estar	17.68
H1	dormitorio 1	10.82
H2	dormitorio 2	9.21
B1	baño principal	2.95
B2	baño secundario	-
C	cocina	5.19
V	vestíbulo	1.20
Ci	circulaciones	7.60
TOTAL ÚTIL INTERIOR		54.65m2
SUP. EXTERIORES		
Tr		6.13

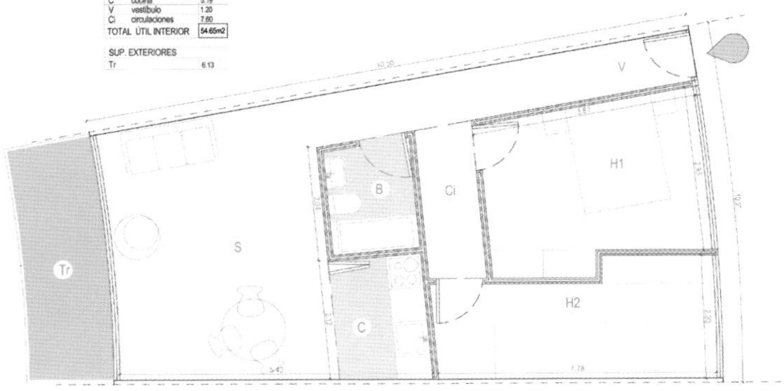

tipologías T3
1/5o

tipologías T4
1/5o

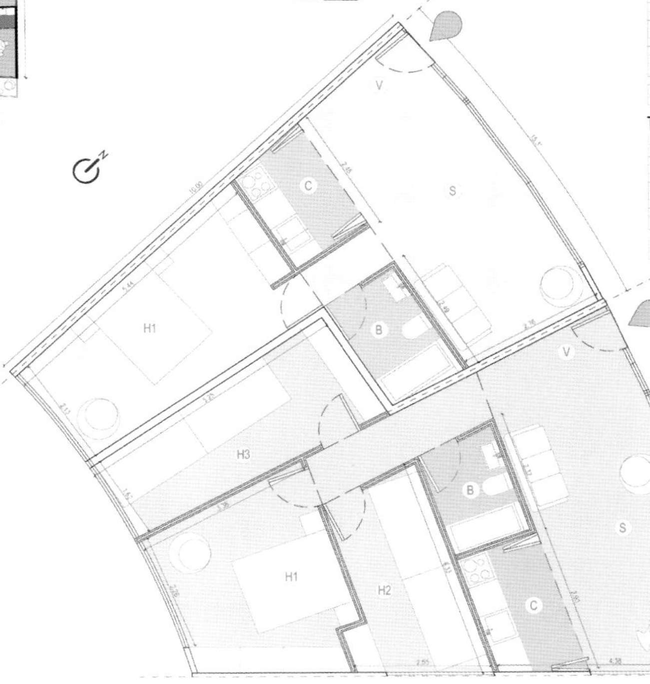

PROPOSICIÓN TÉCNICA PARA EL CONCURSO PÚBLICO DE IDEAS PARA EL DESARROLLO ARQUITECTÓNICO DE 2 PARCELAS DEL ACUARTELAMIENTO "GABRIEL MORALES" EN MELILLA4/4

LEMA_ CÓNCAVO CONVEXO

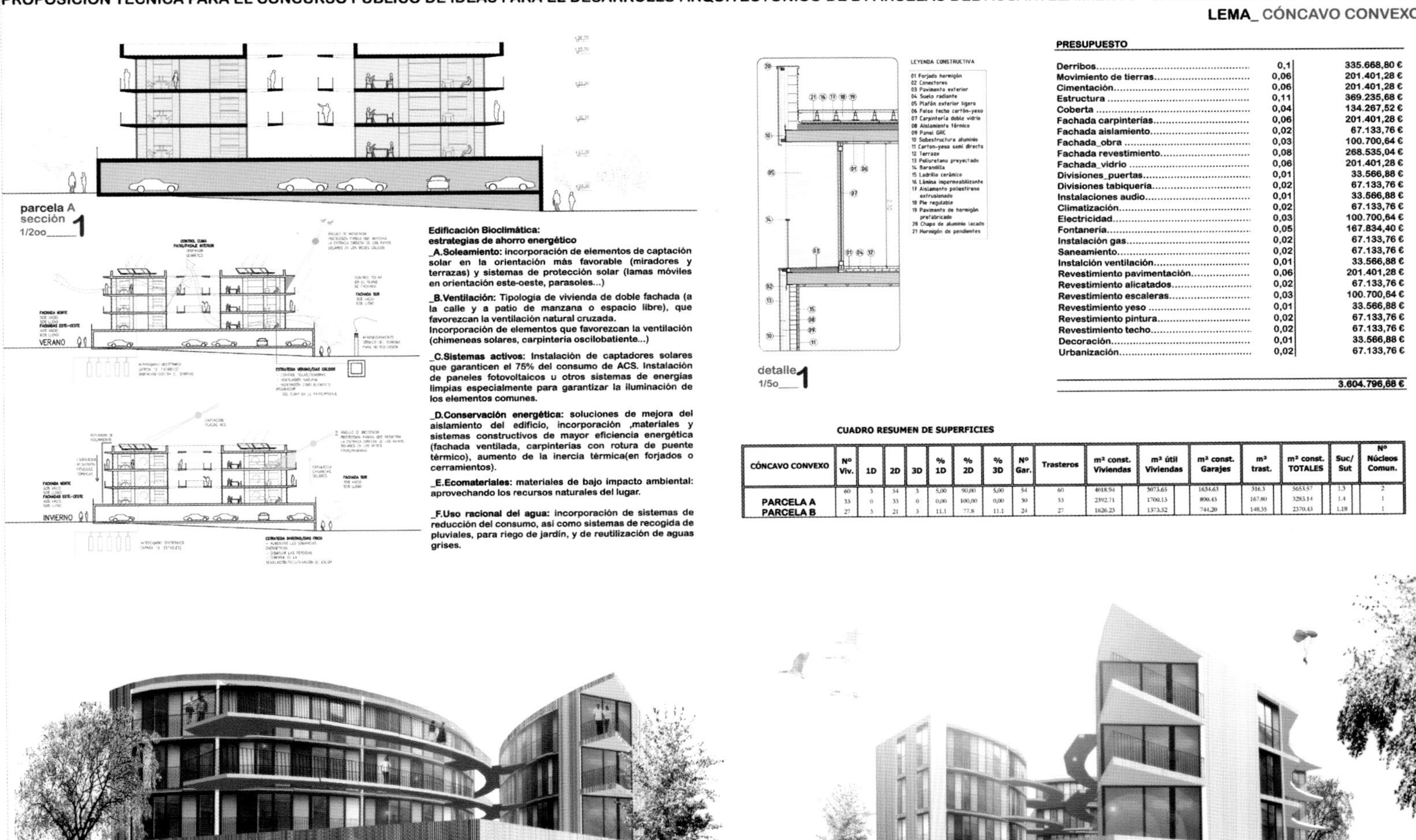

parcela A
sección 1
1/2oo

VERANO

INVIERNO

Edificación Bioclimática:
estrategias de ahorro energético

_A.Soleamiento: incorporación de elementos de captación solar en la orientación más favorable (miradores y terrazas) y sistemas de protección solar (lamas móviles en orientación este-oeste, parasoles...)

_B.Ventilación: Tipología de vivienda de doble fachada (a la calle y a patio de manzana o espacio libre), que favorezcan la ventilación natural cruzada.
Incorporación de elementos que favorezcan la ventilación (chimeneas solares, carpintería oscilobatiente...)

_C.Sistemas activos: Instalación de captadores solares que garanticen el 75% del consumo de ACS. Instalación de paneles fotovoltaicos u otros sistemas de energías limpias especialmente para garantizar la iluminación de los elementos comunes.

_D.Conservación energética: soluciones de mejora del aislamiento del edificio, incorporación ,materiales y sistemas constructivos de mayor eficiencia energética (fachada ventilada, carpinterías con rotura de puente térmico), aumento de la inercia térmica(en forjados o cerramientos).

_E.Ecomateriales: materiales de bajo impacto ambiental: aprovechando los recursos naturales del lugar.

_F.Uso racional del agua: incorporación de sistemas de reducción del consumo, así como sistemas de recogida de pluviales, para riego de jardín, y de reutilización de aguas grises.

LEYENDA CONSTRUCTIVA

01 Forjado hormigón
02 Conectores
03 Pavimento exterior
04 Suelo radiante
05 Plafón exterior ligero
06 Falso techo cartón-yeso
07 Carpintería doble vidrio
08 Aislamiento térmico
09 Panel GRC
10 Subestructura aluminio
11 Carton-yeso semi directo
12 Terrazo
13 Poliuretano preyectado
14 Barandilla
15 Ladrillo cerámico
16 Lámina impermeabilizante
17 Aislamento poliestireno extrusionado
18 Pie regulable
19 Pavimento de hormigón prefabricado
20 Chapa de aluminio lacado
21 Hormigón de pendientes

detalle 1
1/5o

PRESUPUESTO

Derribos	0,1	335.668,80 €
Movimiento de tierras	0,06	201.401,28 €
Cimentación	0,06	201.401,28 €
Estructura	0,11	369.235,68 €
Coberta	0,04	134.267,52 €
Fachada carpinterías	0,06	201.401,28 €
Fachada aislamiento	0,02	67.133,76 €
Fachada_obra	0,03	100.700,64 €
Fachada revestimiento	0,08	268.535,04 €
Fachada_vidrio	0,06	201.401,28 €
Divisiones_puertas	0,01	33.566,88 €
Divisiones tabiquería	0,02	67.133,76 €
Instalaciones audio	0,01	33.566,88 €
Climatización	0,02	67.133,76 €
Electricidad	0,03	100.700,64 €
Fontanería	0,05	167.834,40 €
Instalación gas	0,02	67.133,76 €
Saneamiento	0,02	67.133,76 €
Instalción ventilación	0,01	33.566,88 €
Revestimiento pavimentación	0,06	201.401,28 €
Revestimiento alicatados	0,02	67.133,76 €
Revestimiento escaleras	0,03	100.700,64 €
Revestimiento yeso	0,01	33.566,88 €
Revestimiento pintura	0,02	67.133,76 €
Revestimiento techo	0,02	67.133,76 €
Decoración	0,01	33.566,88 €
Urbanización	0,02	67.133,76 €
		3.604.796,68 €

CUADRO RESUMEN DE SUPERFICIES

CÓNCAVO CONVEXO	Nº Viv.	1D	2D	3D	% 1D	% 2D	% 3D	Nº Gar.	Trasteros	m² const. Viviendas	m² útil Viviendas	m² const. Garajes	m² trast.	m² const. TOTALES	Suc/ Sut	Nº Núcleos Comun.
	60	3	54	3	5,00	90,00	5,00	54	60	4018.94	3073.65	1634.63	316.3	5653.57	1.3	2
PARCELA A	33	0	33	0	0,00	100,00	0,00	30	33	2392.71	1700.13	890.43	167.80	3283.14	1.4	1
PARCELA B	27	3	21	3	11.1	77.8	11.1	24	27	1626.23	1373.32	744.20	148.35	2370.43	1.18	1

Design : Dimitris Gourdoukis & Katerina Tryfonidou

Project : Design for a self-sufficient settlement
Typology : Emergency housing

inflateit

Inflateit is a **modular**, **self-learning** experiment, that relies upon an **interactive**, **self informative** process.

The process begins with the generation of random elevation patterns. Those patterns are getting tested in a lighting simulation software (ecotect) for different locations, seasons and times so an initial database of solutions is created. Each time that units have to be produced, random patterns are tested until a satisfactory solution is found. The tests are added to the database.

The feedback of the users is used in order to re-evaluate the data collected. The production of new units is becoming a self-learning process for the program. At the same time the users with their feedback are altering the initial standards in a never-ending, multiple exchange and altering of information.

The growth of the database is strictly related to the growth of the inflateit settlements and follows similar self-referencial patterns. The data stored in the database gets transformed from data regarding lighting strategies to data regarding relationships

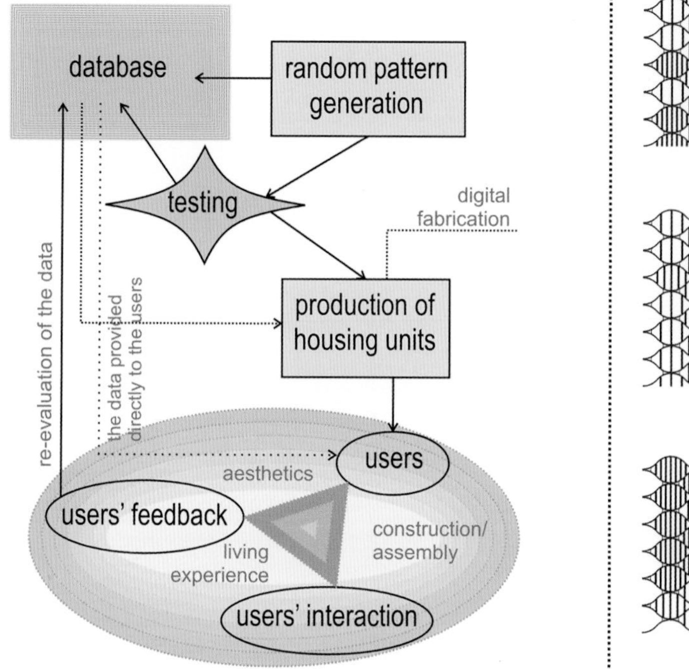

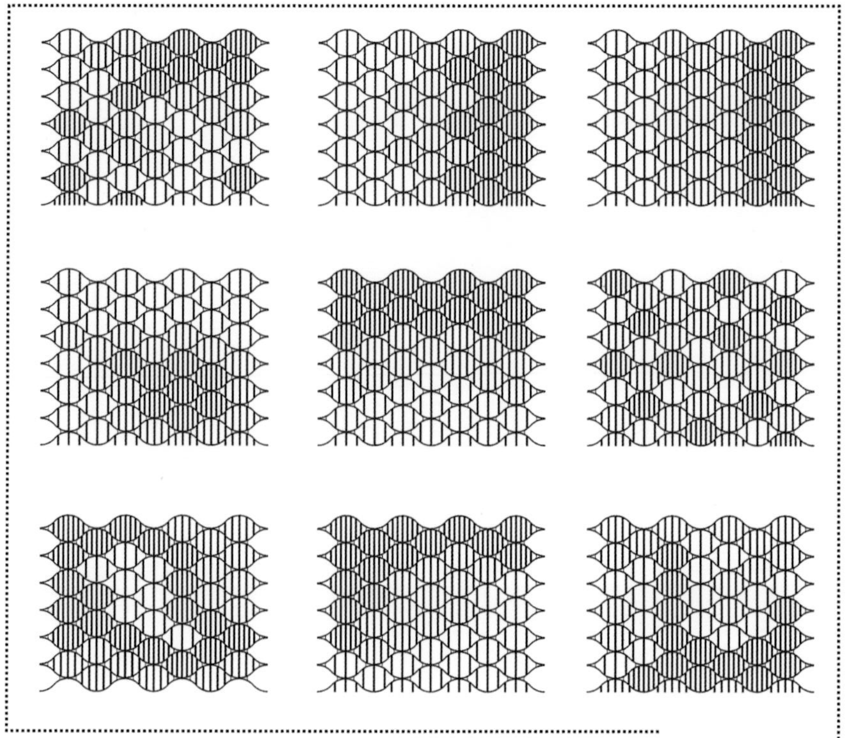

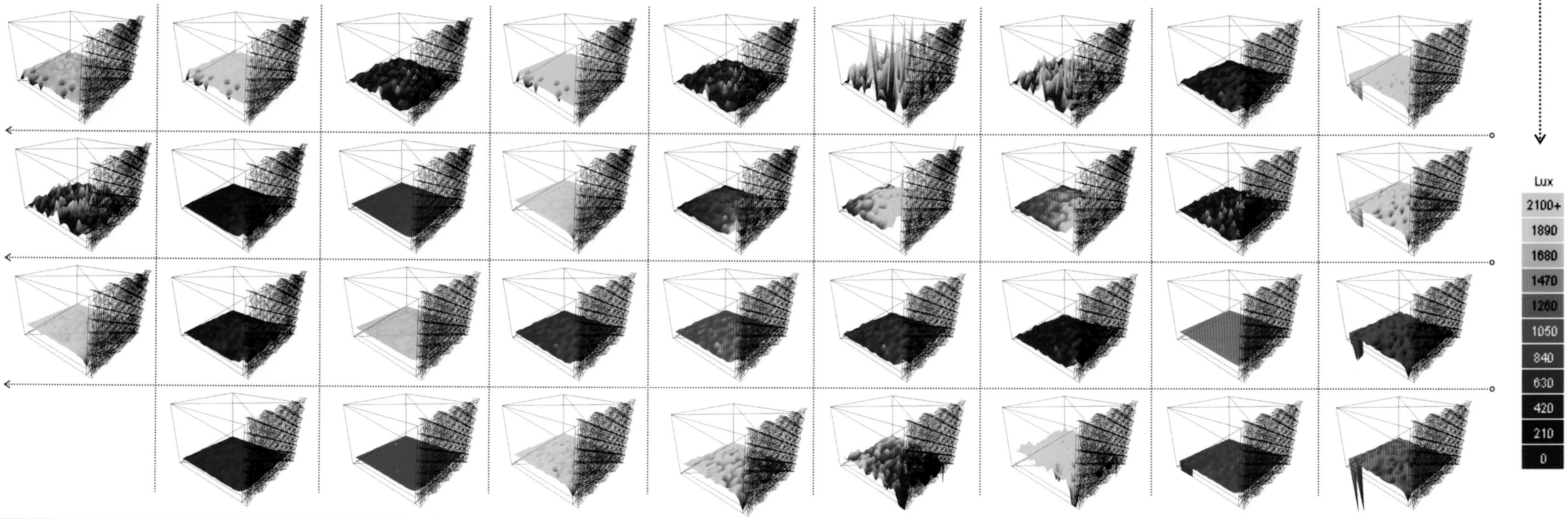

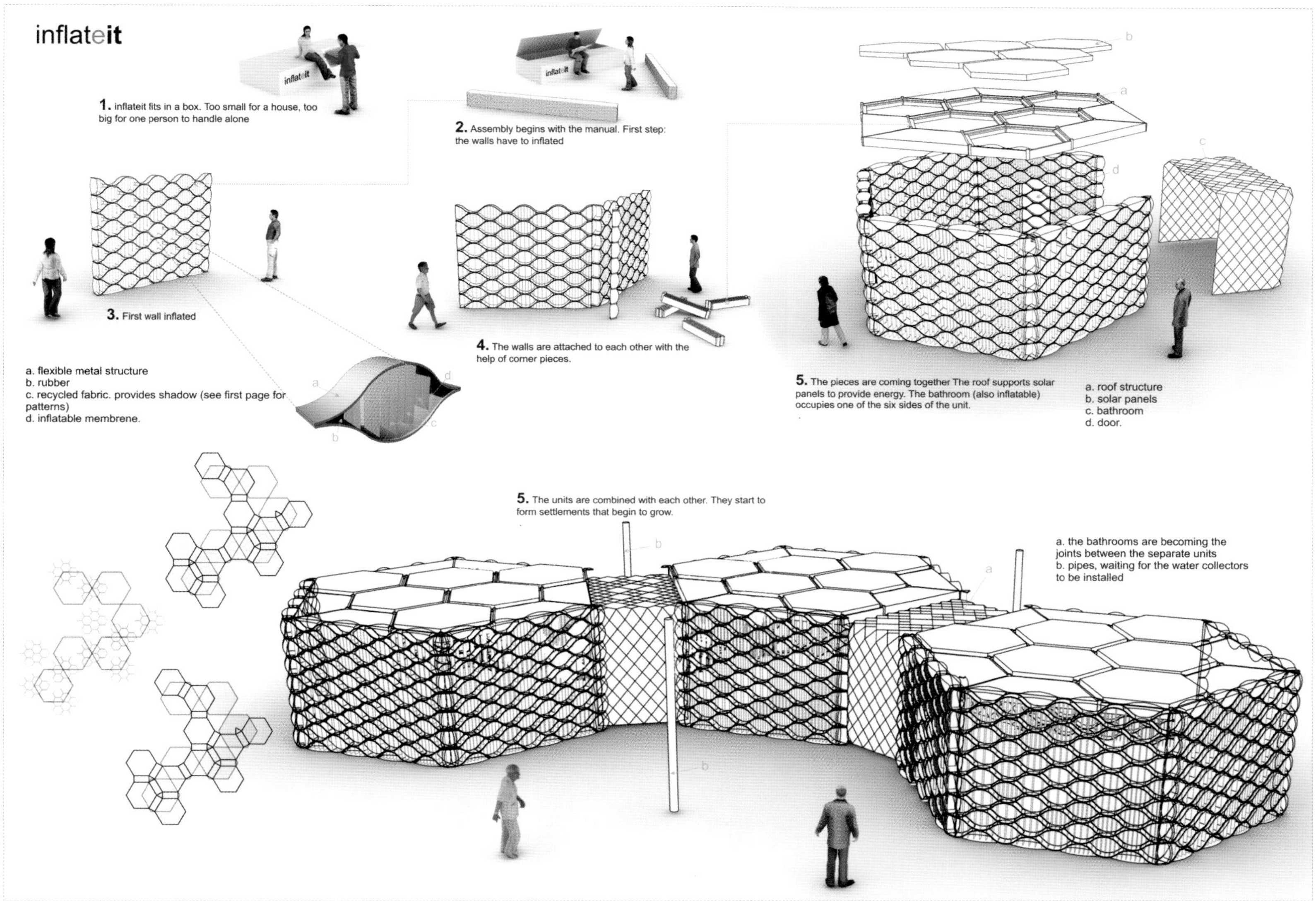

inflateit

1. inflateit fits in a box. Too small for a house, too big for one person to handle alone

2. Assembly begins with the manual. First step: the walls have to inflated

3. First wall inflated

4. The walls are attached to each other with the help of corner pieces.

a. flexible metal structure
b. rubber
c. recycled fabric. provides shadow (see first page for patterns)
d. inflatable membrene.

5. The pieces are coming together The roof supports solar panels to provide energy. The bathroom (also inflatable) occupies one of the six sides of the unit.

a. roof structure
b. solar panels
c. bathroom
d. door.

5. The units are combined with each other. They start to form settlements that begin to grow.

a. the bathrooms are becoming the joints between the separate units
b. pipes, waiting for the water collectors to be installed

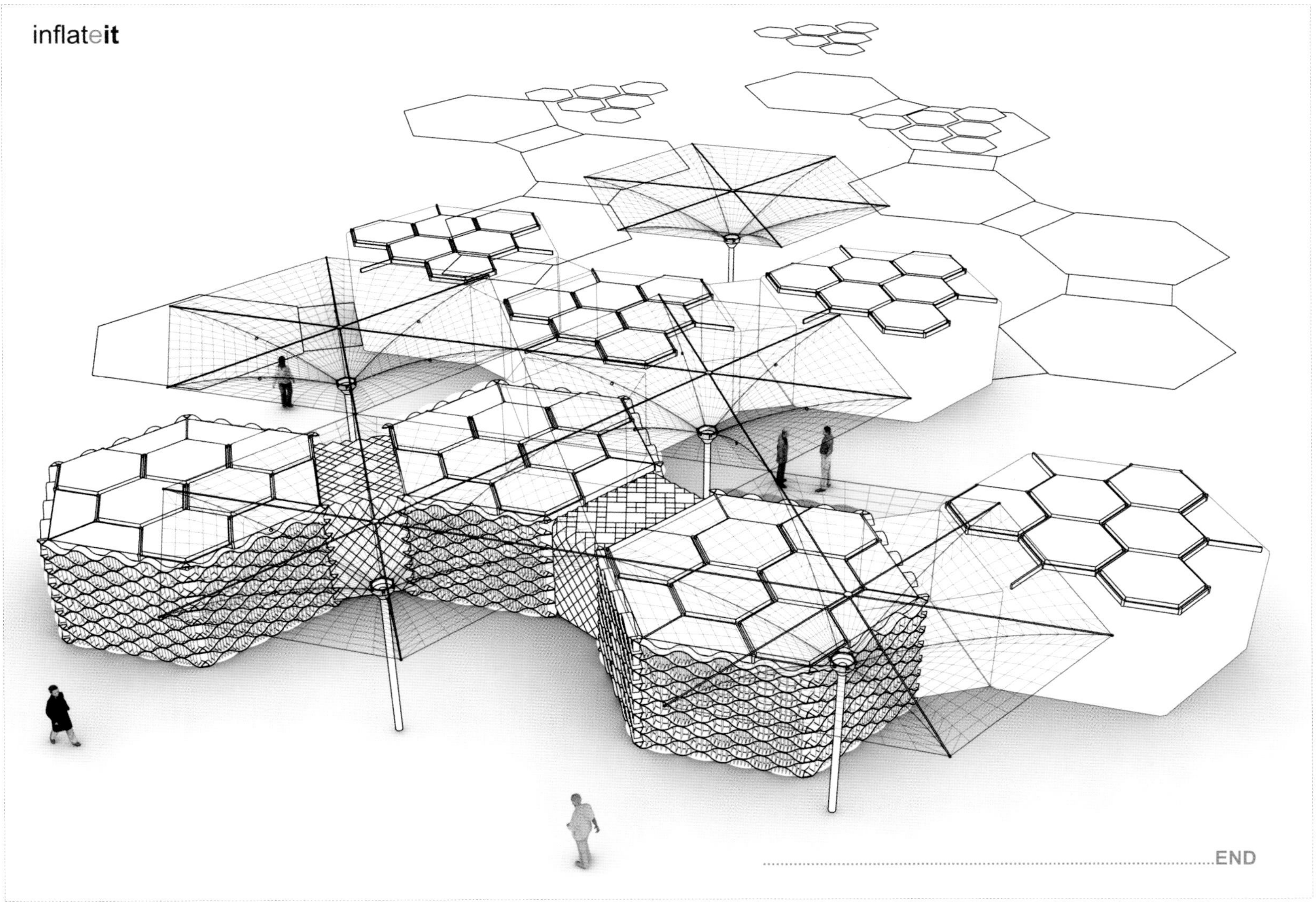

inflateit

..........END

052 Kuelap | *Marchi_Architectes*

Title : The Endless Structure

Team : Architecture (Adelaïde et Nicola Marchi[Marchi_Architectes]), Art Director(Timoteo Niccolo), Project Manager(Pia Lê), 3D images(Ryuta Amae [Japan])

Location : Cauca Valley (Colombia)
Built area (GFA) : 60 sqm / Client : IaaC (Spain)

Participants : Luis Aguirre Manso
Collaborators : Maite García Aznar, Elena Morales Virgili
Project : Self-sufficient house in Cauca Valley
Typology : Residential building

053

harvest home

the handmade vegetable steel house

01

The self-sufficient housing concept especially makes sense where along with a strong demand, qualified labour and technical resources are scarce. In the last 40 years, about 3 million people have been forced to leave their homes in Colombia, making it the country with the highest number of displaced people in the world. The demand of dwellings in the country is more than 1,4 million and the Cauca Valley is the place where the most humanitarian help is needed. However the development potential in is significant, and it is in this south-occidental region, placed between the Occidental and Central mountain chain, where a superb construction material is already present and grows in a natural way: bamboo.

Bamboo houses are easy to build, qualified labour is not required and they are particularly suited to the climate and conditions of the valley. Bamboo -gramineae from the rice family- is a versatile, light-weight, biodegradable and sustainable raw material, and besides that it differs from other woods in the fact that it grows up again after being cut. An eighteen meter high tree cut takes 60 years to replace; an eighteen meter high bamboo -also called guadua- takes only 59 days.
The harvest of one hectare of bamboo is equivalent to 3.5 houses. The valley watered by the River Cauca has more than 8300 hectares and about 5000 families a year are moving in, so using bamboo is the most convenient choice.
The self-sufficient house brings an activity to the newly established community, and its self-sufficient design guarantees families' resources. Environmental conditions are excellent in this intertropical climate, where the temperature is constant year round. Furthermore, earth-quake resistant qualities of this vegetable steel ensure the stability in this risk area.

Houses in the Cauca valley are ready for harvest. Their occupants will have a hand made and sustainable place to live in, while the bamboo will grow up again in this fertile Colombian region.

'the harvest process'

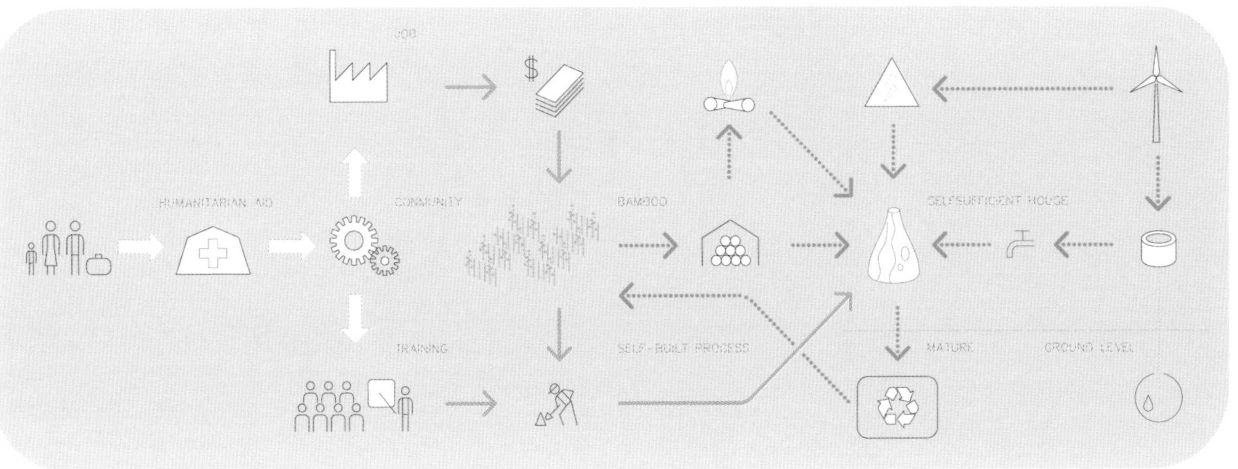

harvest home

the handmade vegetable steel house

02

The bamboo house is an organic element that rises over the landscape's valley. Its 'non-site specific' quality allows it to be versatile in different sites. The base, wide and stable, contains the day-activities program, whereas the first floor accommodates the bedrooms around the central chimney. Its slender figure becomes a milestone; a little tower placed on the site marking the final destination and the place of a new home for the displaced people. The random opes made between the nerves of its sewed skin allows to choose views in all directions.

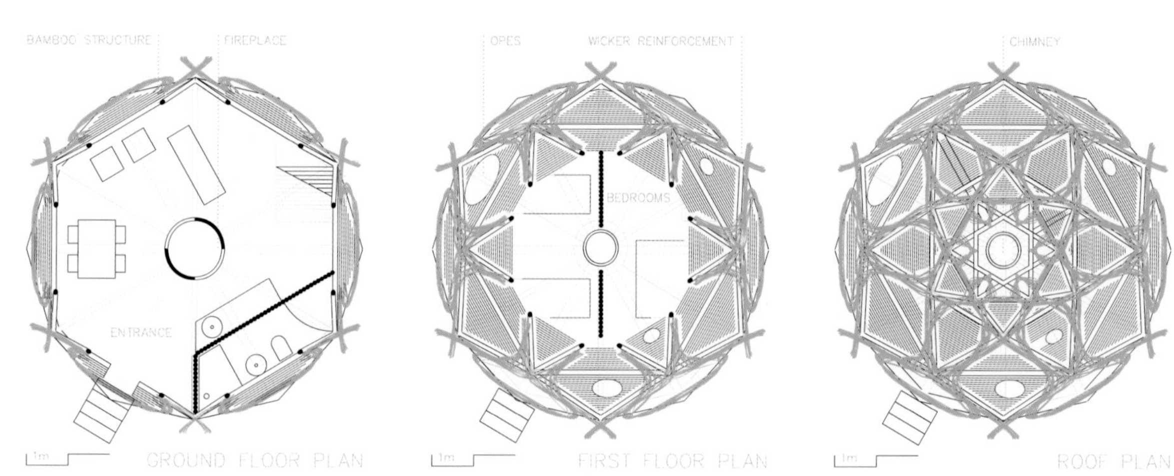

harvest home

the handmade vegetable steel house

03

The building is above ground level to protect the structure against dampness. The bamboo shell, inspired by the icosahedron geometry, has four bar nodes to reduce the number of legs of the foundation. These nodes are built cutting the ends of the bamboo rods in a particular way, and fixing them by means of screws. A wicker mesh is used to reinforce the structure. This flexible fiber, abundant in the valley, sews the whole shell together.
The external walls are made using rods of bamboo as well. The windows openings are made by cutting into the finished surface. This skin with its small gaps provides the level of ventilation required for the climate of the area, keeping the interior cool and dry. The amount of bamboo necessary to build a single house costs approximately 95 euro.
The central fireplace is used both for the kitchen as well as for the living area and is built in stone and settled on the ground. The steel chimney provides heating for the bedrooms above. Installations are simple and located underneath the house, were a space for the wood storage is also provided.

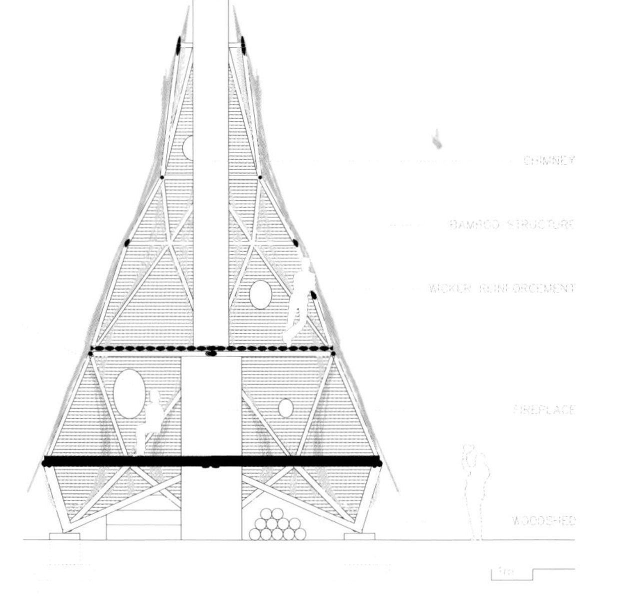

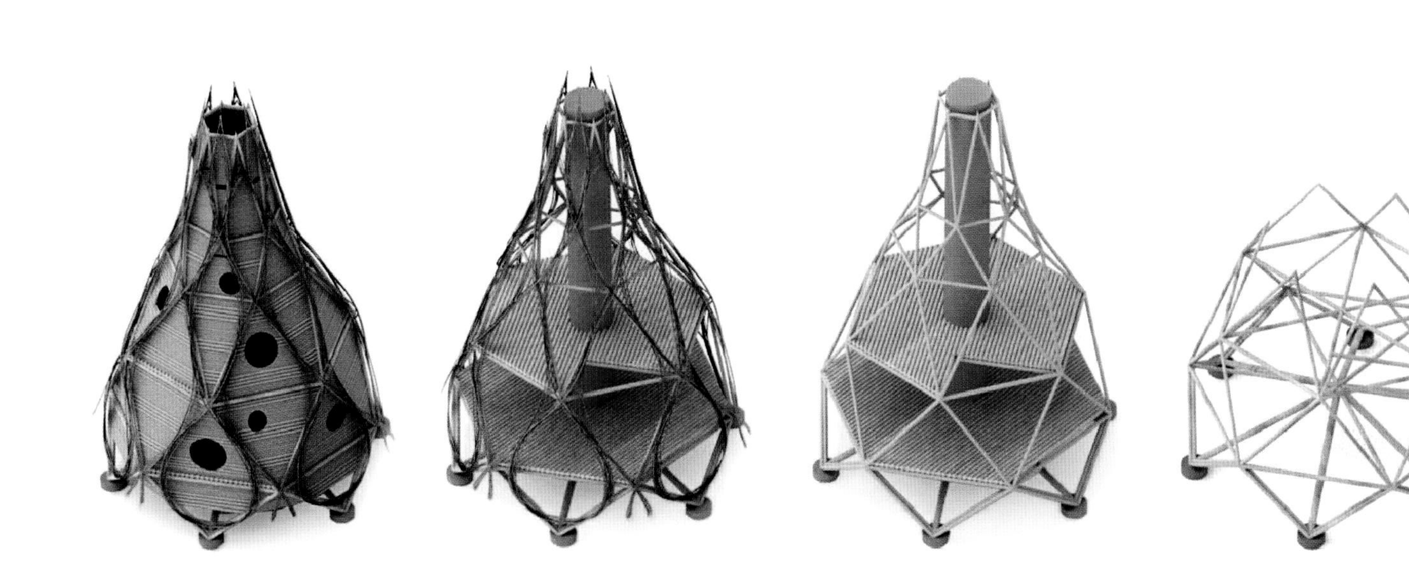

Architect : Keiichi Hayashi
Project : Renovation of Apartment for 'LIVING & DESIGN' Exhibition in Japan

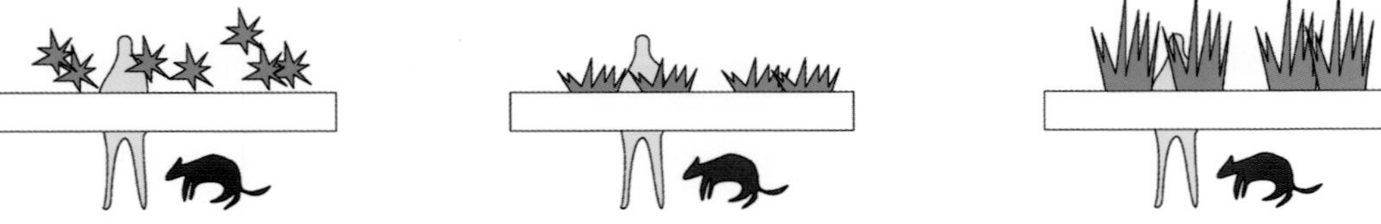

changes of phase and the strength of partition by plant type and growth

Living with Dog

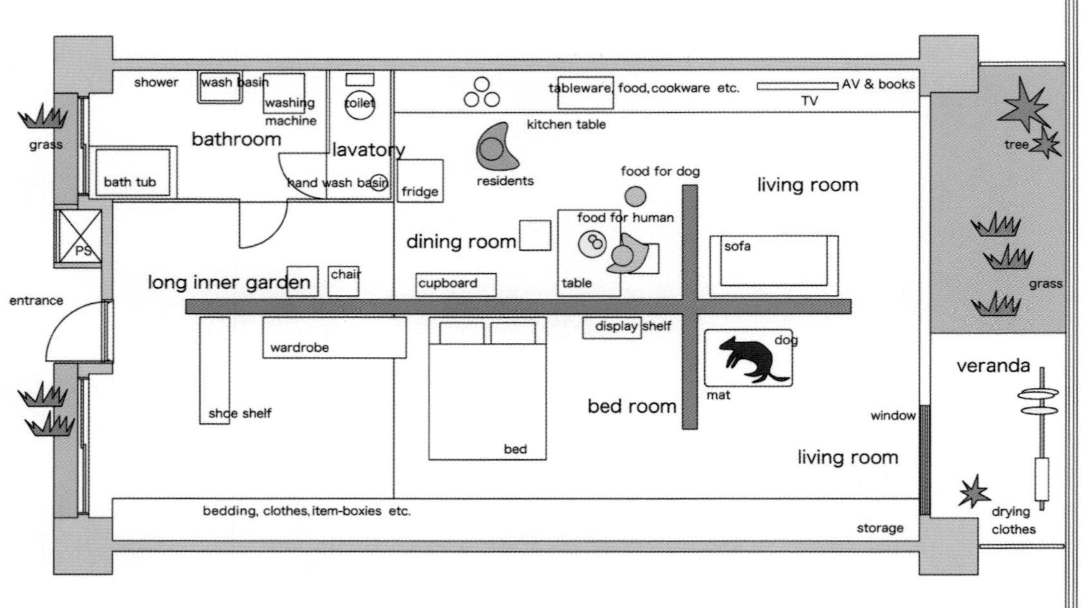

plan S=1:30

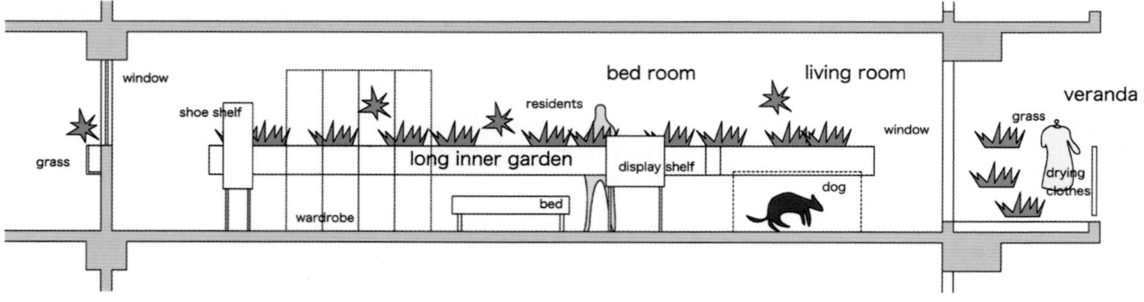

section S=1:30

I planned a long cross-shaped innner garden to partition an empty apartment into four spaces. The residents can control the strength of the partition depending on which plants they use- each kind of plants is different in its height and shape of leaves. And the phase of the partition will change with the growth of the plants gradually.

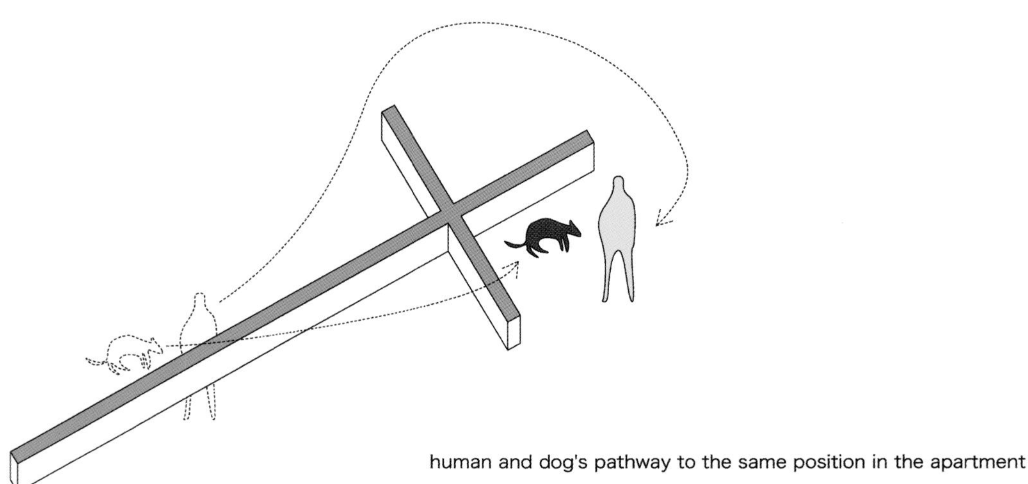

human and dog's pathway to the same position in the apartment

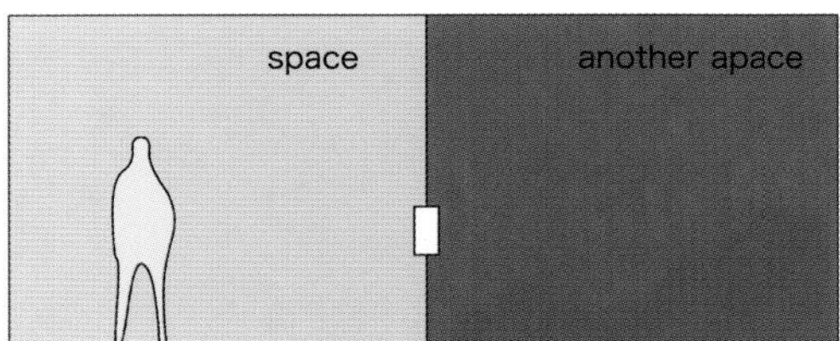

human's perception of the space

dog's perception of the space

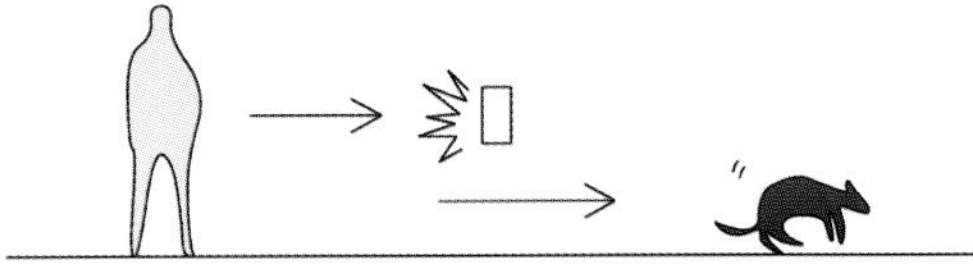

difference of the affects between human and dog

occurrence caused by the different affects

The partition is lifted from the floor so that the dog can pass under it freely. In fact, the space for the residents is partitioned but for the dog is not partitioned. Naturally, the human's behavior and dog's one are different. I planned the adequate partition for each of them so that it gave richness to the space. And I wish that occurrences which are caused by the partition would give the residents and dog a joy of life.

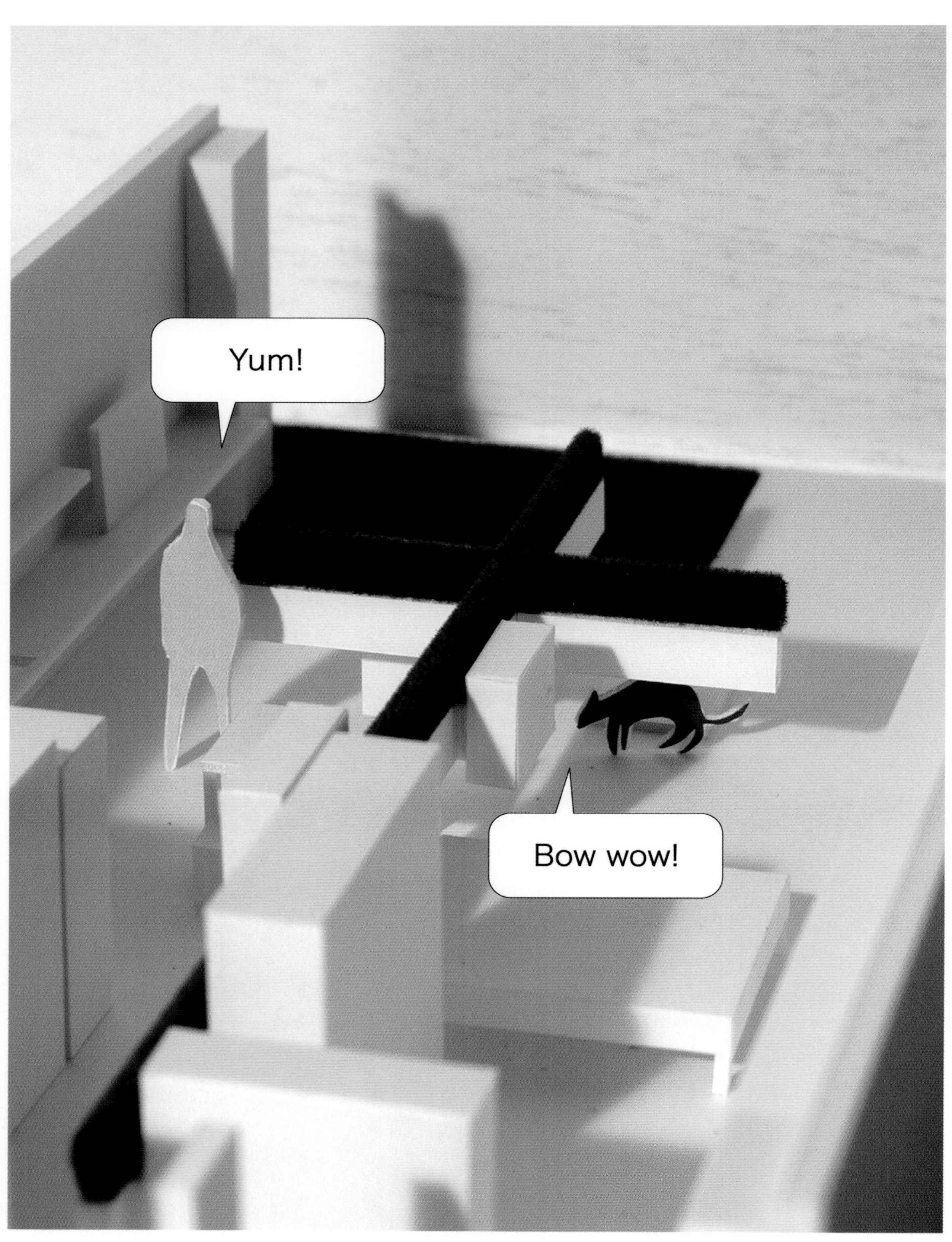

one scene in this room

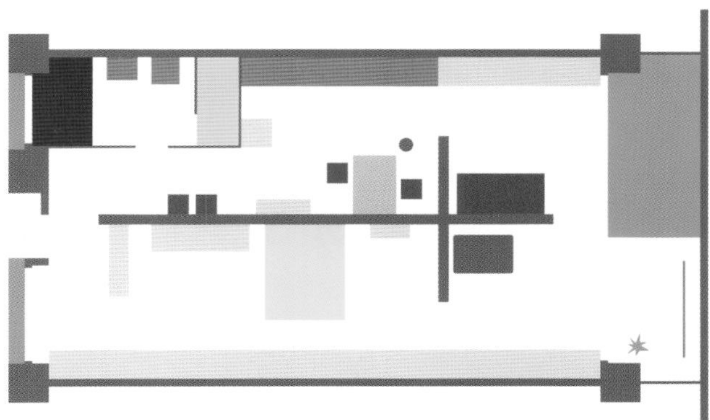

room for human

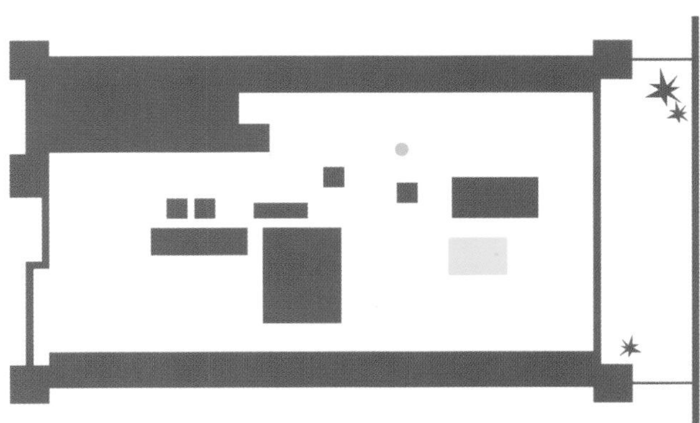

room for dog

tone variation of the affects

tone of obstacle
tone of walking
tone of eating
tone of sleeping
tone of sitting
tone of storing
tone of working
tone of bathing
tone of excreting
tone of gardening

Notes of the classification tones
One object can have multiple tones in some cases. For example, the partition for a human in this room can have 'tone of obstacle' or 'tone of gardening' depending on the feeling of the subject. I simplfied the classification tones boldly, in order to clarify the maps.

I referred to the following book for drawing the maps and writing the text.

Jacob von Uexküll, STREIFZÜGE DURCH DIE UMWELTEN VON TIEREN UND MENSCHEN. (translated by Toshitaka Hidaka and Setsuko Haneda. 2005. Iwnami Shoten.)

The maps are colored according to the usage of the residents and dog in this room by the tone of affects on an object such a partition, furniture and floor. It is obvious that the partitio n, which appears in the resident's umwelt, disappears in the dog's umwelt. In addition, even practical objects for the residents can be obstacles for the dog.

'T' House
Phoenix, Arizona USA

The site for the 'T' House is located at the edge of a residential neighborhood that abuts the North Mountain Preserve in Phoenix, Arizona. It possesses an expansive view of the Phoenix city skyline to the south. Northwest of the project location a rocky hilltop protrudes from the desert preserve.

The house is organized into a slender bar acting as an edge bracket that ends the residential fabric to the east and frames a rectilinear front yard area. This bracketed yard harbors a dense mesquite tree grove that mitigates the boundary between street and residence and shades the eastern façade of the residence. The house occupies the hill and site by this bracketing and by mimicking the steep pitch. The monopitch roof of the house is visible from the neighboring areas and is therefore covered with a rock bed to match the surroundings and to imply that the building was pushed upward from the desert floor.

Approach promenade follows to the highest point of the site. Visitors ascend the site towards the hilltop protrusion where parking, pool, and entry access occur. Visitors descend the incline of the slope into the residence where they occupy a series of platforms of public spaces. Private sleeping spaces can be accessed from behind the dining level platform.

An expression of extrusion encompasses the project. 'T' profile steel members at 1' o.c. that structure the levels and the roof surround the house externally. The steel members provide external sun shading for the glass behind. The steel bars (plus steel sheet composed opaque façade areas) are allowed to oxidize naturally and are removed occasionally to strategically allow for uninterrupted views of the landscape from within the residence spaces. Internally the house offers a reduced, refined palette of ebonized wood and polished white or integrally colored plaster.

View from south

Site plan

Living / sitting space

'T' House
blank studio architecture | PHOENIX, ARIZONA, USA

Littles Road Residence | *blank studio architecture*

056

View from courtyard

Littles Road Residence
Queenstown, New Zealand

The Littles Road Residence is located on the South Island of New Zealand, minutes north of Queenstown. The house is situated within a grassy plateau on the property that will remain an active grazing area for sheep. The residence has views across the Shotover River to the south and west and is surrounded by expansive mountain views that include Coronet Peak, Cecil Peak, and The Remarkables.

The residence is organized into three primary components. The house is arranged beneath three linear vaults and it split into two parts with the primary living spaces in the northern portion and the guest suite in the southern zone. These two components bracket a gracious outdoor courtyard area. The entry sequence passes beneath a long vault and into the courtyard zone. This courtyard is lushly planted and stands in contrast to the neatly goat-trimmed grasses surrounding the residence.

Conceptually, the residence is a glazed pavilion set within the grazing field. Separating the house and courtyard from the grassland enclosing it is a unifying wood screen made up of a series of hinged, operable panels each measuring 2.7 meters high by 1.2 meters wide. In a gesture to anchor the project to its place, the panels are composed of a native Blackwood species that has had been water-jet cut in a pattern that abstracts the windswept, delicate grasses blanketing the surrounding hillsides.

The roof vaults also connect the building to place. The gently folded forms recall the mountainous surroundings or even the tectonic plates that have collided to create this island nation and continue to generate earthquakes experienced throughout the South Pacific. Perhaps one can interpret the vaults as a reflection of the commonly used corrugated iron that clads many utilitarian farm buildings. Regardless, upon approach the building presents an elegant silhouette reminiscent of a noble shed.

Internally the residence's spaces are organized neatly beneath the vaults and offer a reduced palette of light wood floors and polished white plaster walls and ceilings. Illumination evenly up lights the vaults and emphasizes the unadorned, uninterrupted flow of space beneath the sheltering forms.

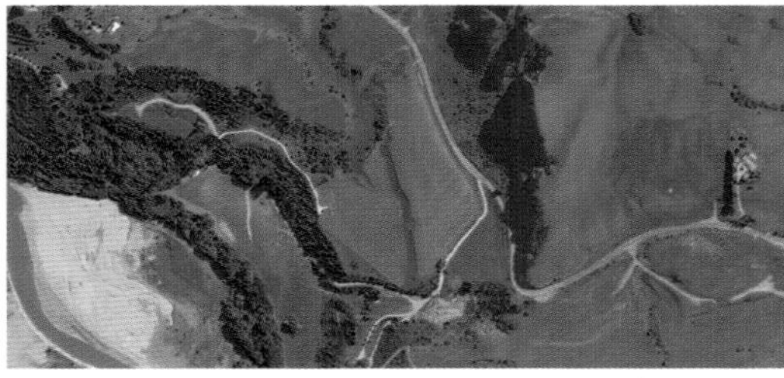
Site plan

Dining area

Living area

Master bedroom area

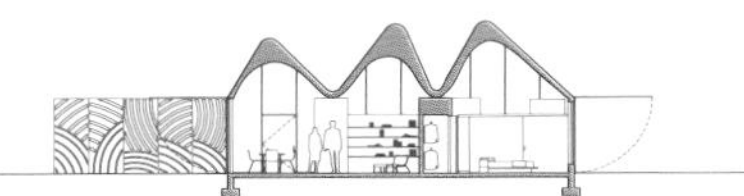

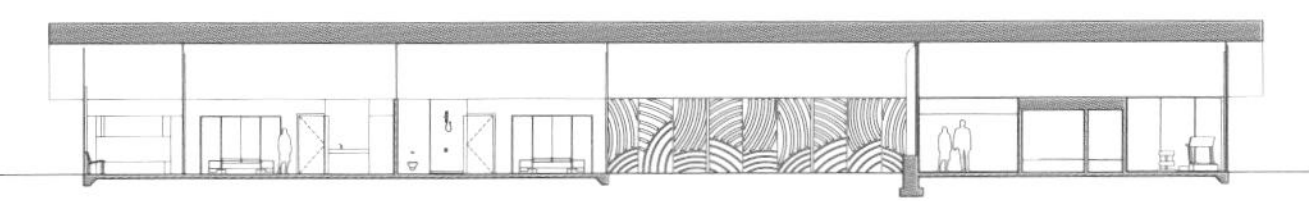

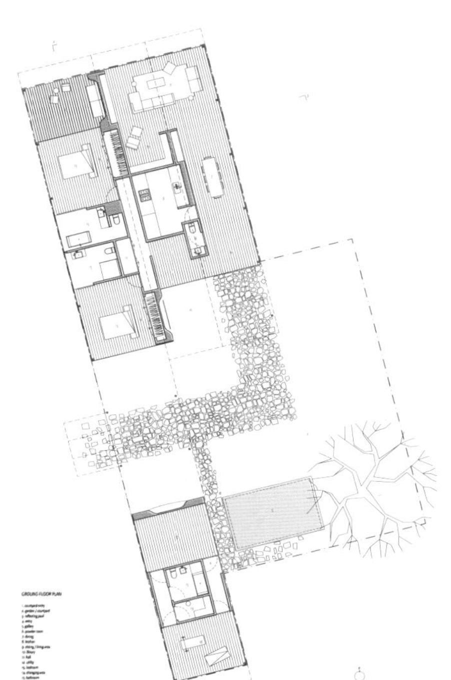

Exterior view with screens closed and open

Littles Road Residence

blank studio architecture | PHOENIX, ARIZONA, USA

057 Ecobitat | *Figura Arquitetos office*

Architect : Felipe Campolina
Use : Residential
Dimension : 32m²

ECOBITAT 1/4

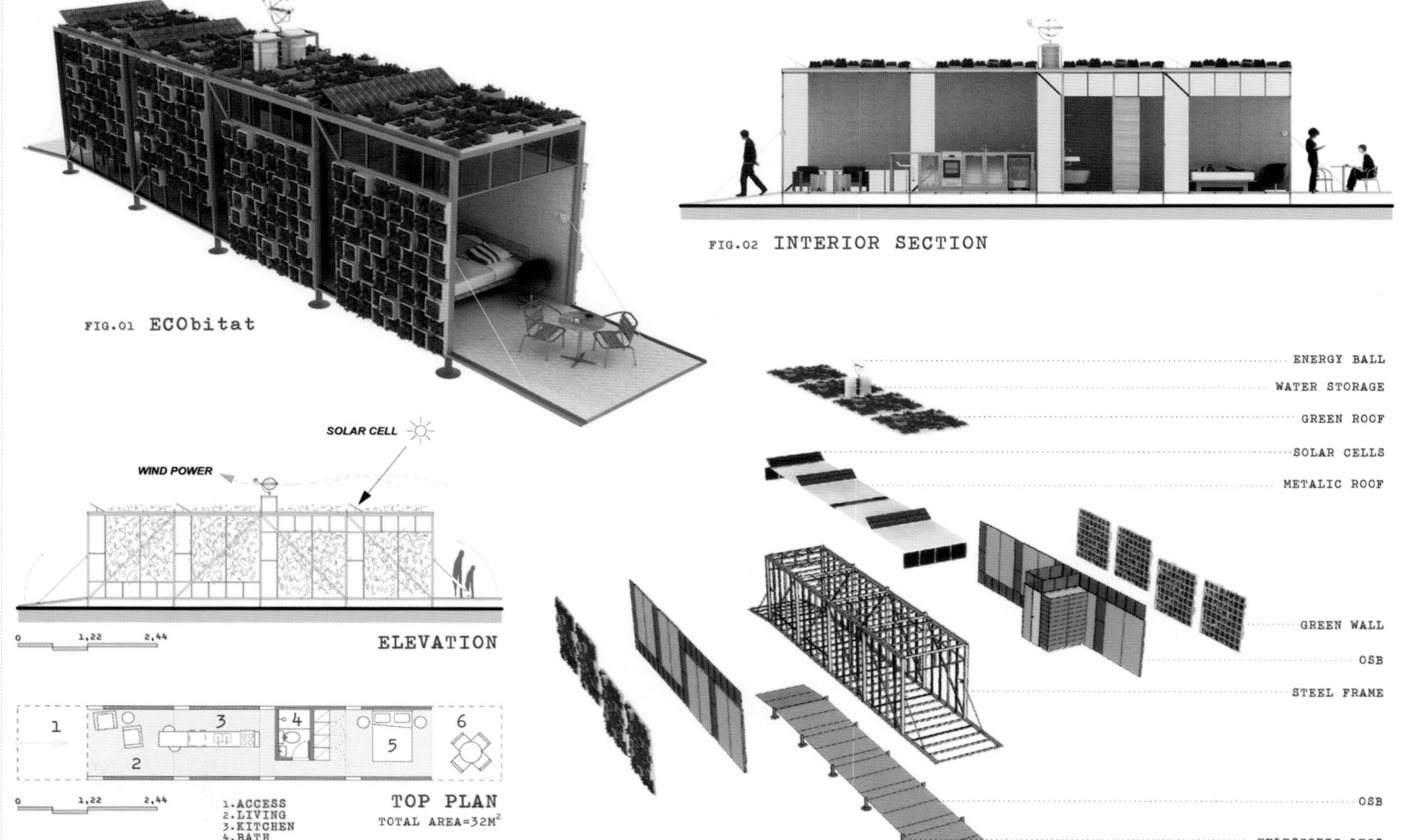

ECOBITAT 2/4

ECOBITAT 3/4

ECOBITAT 4/4

A New Way to Inhabit | *Figura Arquitetos office*

Architect : Felipe Campolina
Use : Residential
Dimension : 252 units (32m² each)

HOUSING. A NEW WAY TO INHABIT.

ably becomes
lew concepts for
are emerging
serve special
e of manufacture,

onstruction
ocial issues. This
standard **OSB**
defining flexible
d adequate for
industrial
of manufactured

a huge tower
ates an empty
ve those units,
come and go.

units that can
ith others. A
de rails built-in
ntal trasfering.
ouse lift located
there is a
d fire escape).
jection area on
implementation
reduced.

ge cities, either
he demand. It
vertically,

: ANYWHERE

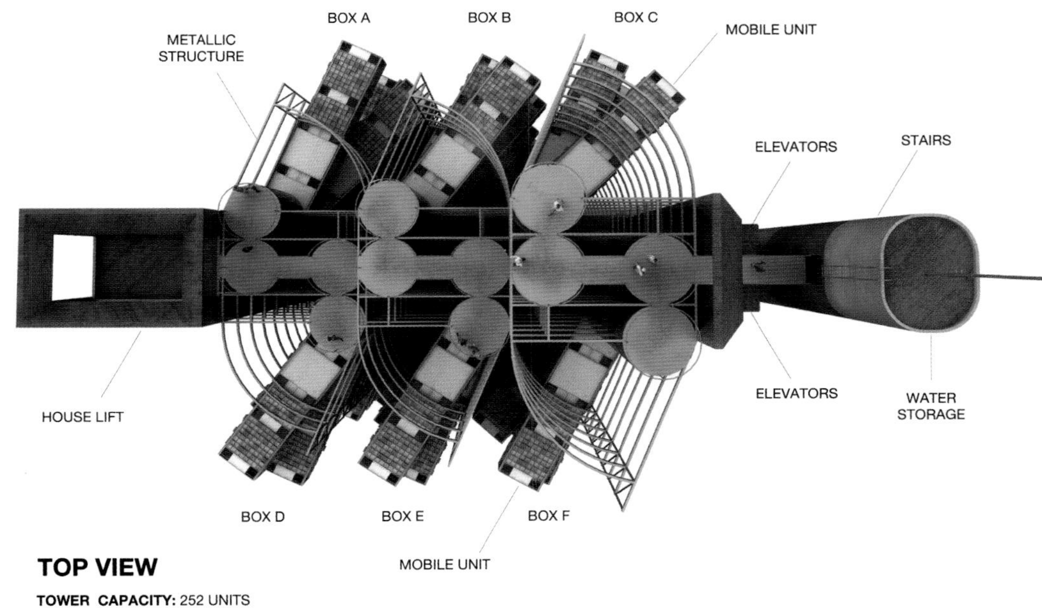

TOP VIEW

TOWER CAPACITY: 252 UNITS

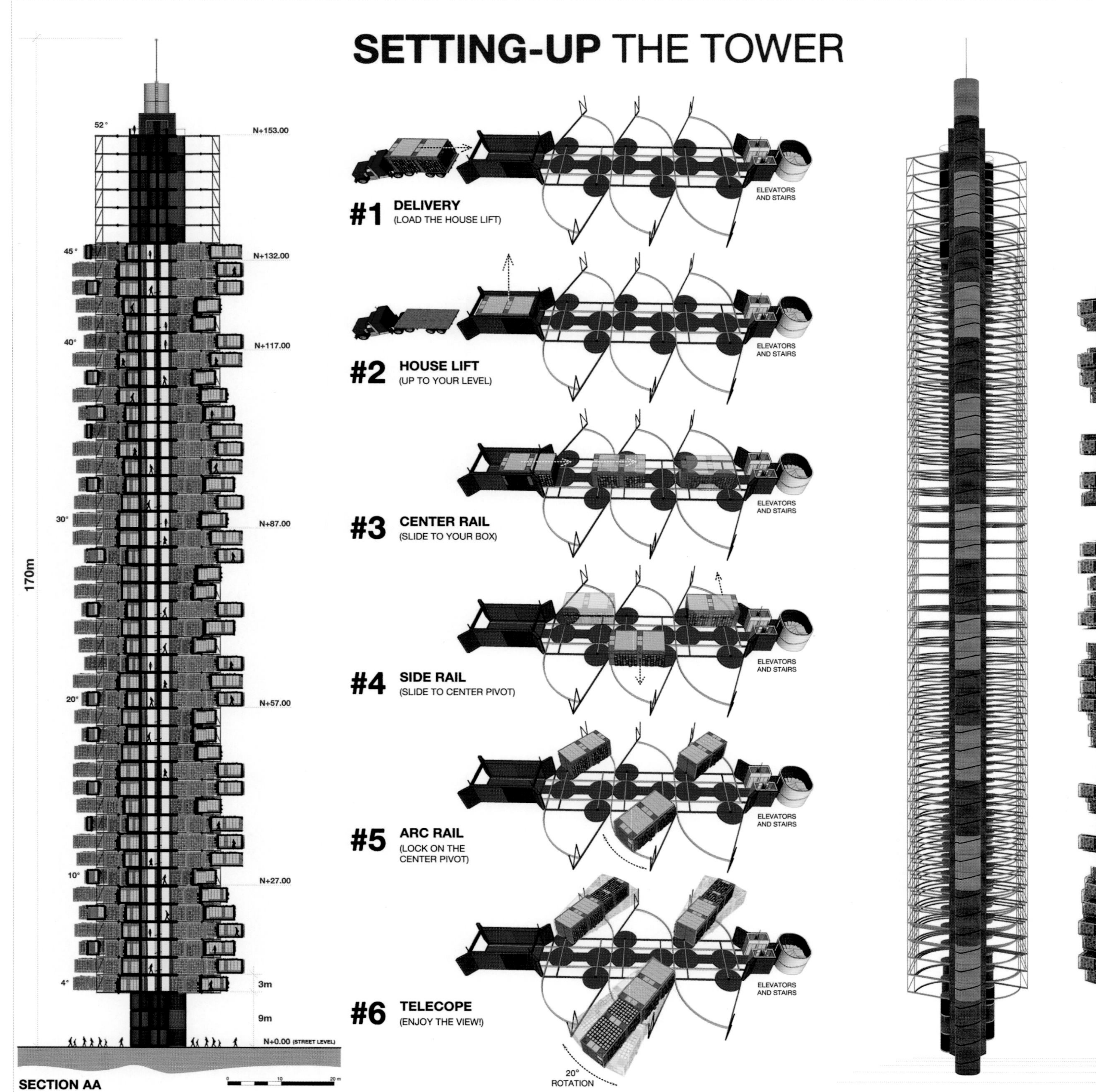
SETTING-UP THE TOWER
#1 DELIVERY
(LOAD THE HOUSE LIFT)
#2 HOUSE LIFT
(UP TO YOUR LEVEL)
#3 CENTER RAIL
(SLIDE TO YOUR BOX)
#4 SIDE RAIL
(SLIDE TO CENTER PIVOT)
#5 ARC RAIL
(LOCK ON THE CENTER PIVOT)
#6 TELECOPE
(ENJOY THE VIEW!)
ELEVATORS AND STAIRS
20° ROTATION
52°
N+153.00
45°
N+132.00
40°
N+117.00
30°
N+87.00
20°
N+57.00
10°
N+27.00
4°
3m
9m
N+0.00 (STREET LEVEL)
170m
SECTION AA

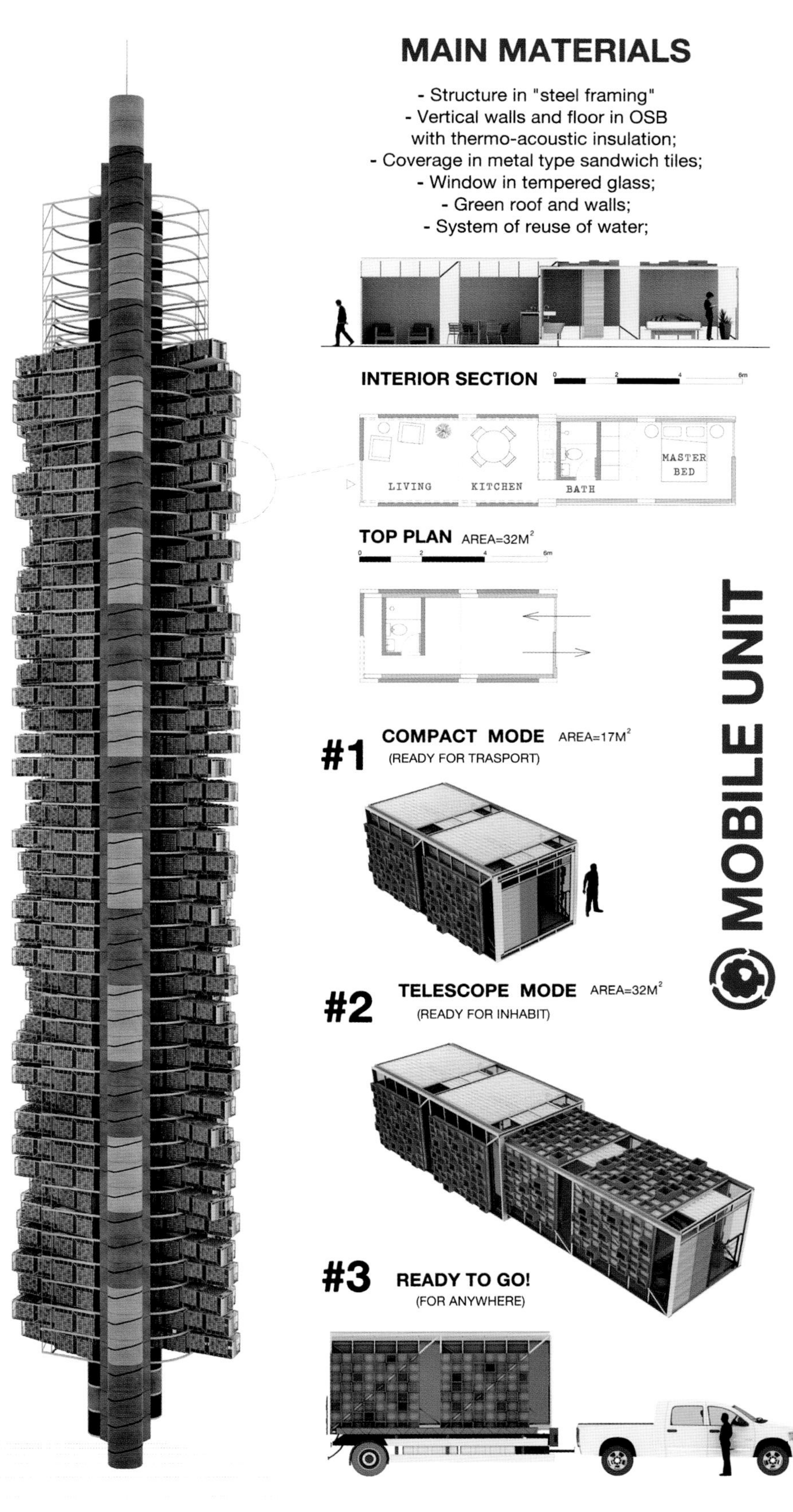
MAIN MATERIALS
- Structure in "steel framing"
- Vertical walls and floor in OSB with thermo-acoustic insulation;
- Coverage in metal type sandwich tiles;
- Window in tempered glass;
- Green roof and walls;
- System of reuse of water;
INTERIOR SECTION
LIVING
KITCHEN
BATH
MASTER BED
TOP PLAN AREA=32M²
MOBILE UNIT
#1 COMPACT MODE AREA=17M²
(READY FOR TRASPORT)
#2 TELESCOPE MODE AREA=32M²
(READY FOR INHABIT)
#3 READY TO GO!
(FOR ANYWHERE)

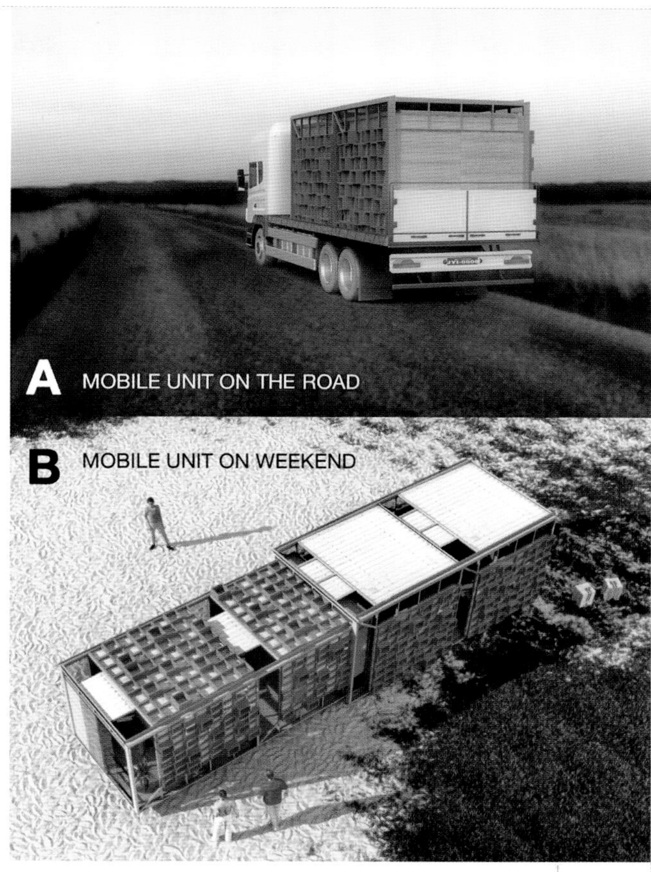
A MOBILE UNIT ON THE ROAD
B MOBILE UNIT ON WEEKEND

C MOBILE UNIT IN THE CITY

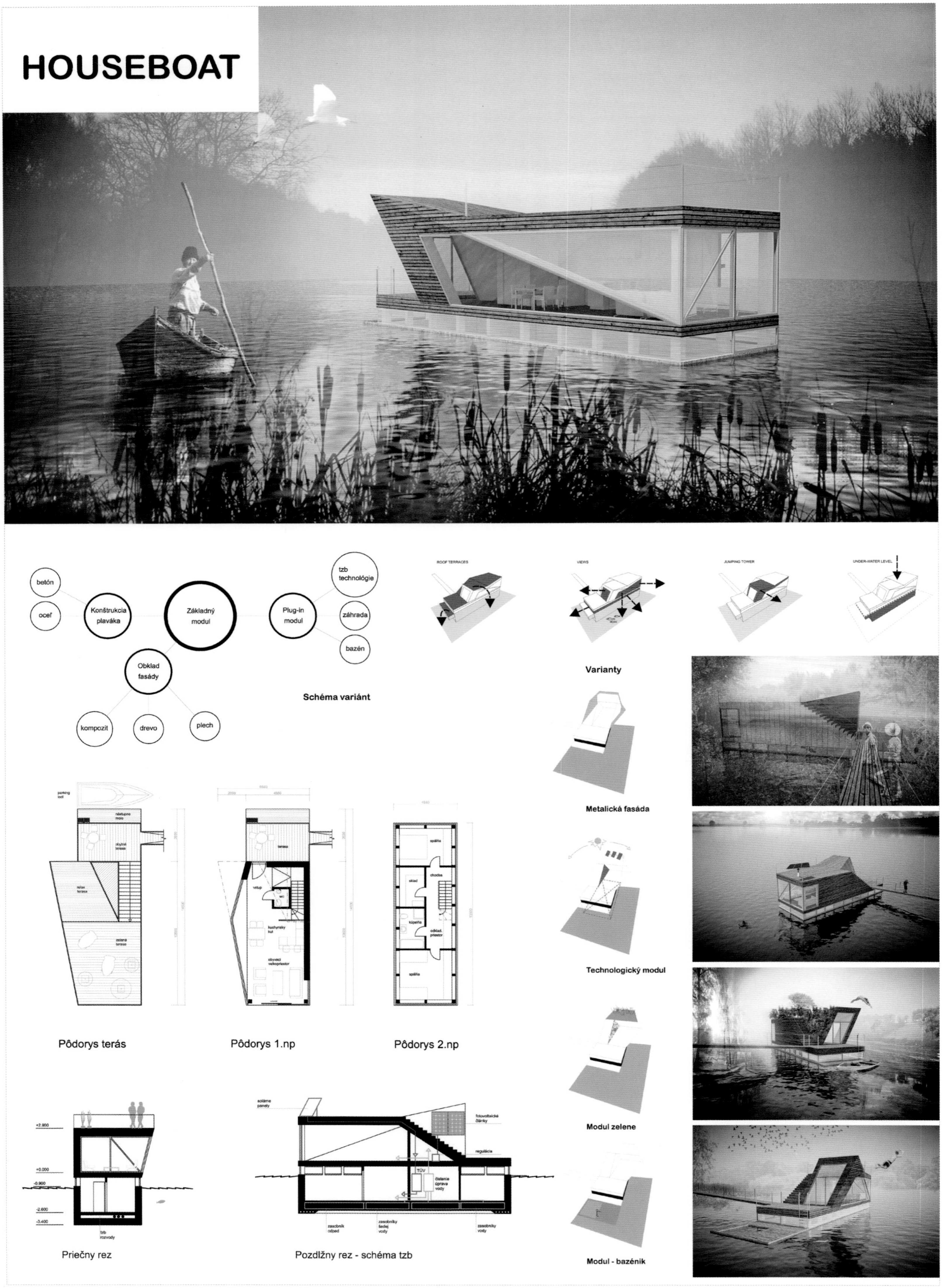

betón
oceľ
Konštrukcia plaváka
Základný modul
Plug-in modul
tzb technológie
záhrada
bazén
Obklad fasády
kompozit
drevo
plech

Schéma variánt

ROOF TERRACES
VIEWS
JUMPING TOWER
UNDER-WATER LEVEL

Varianty

Metalická fasáda

Technologický modul

Modul zelene

Modul - bazénik

Pôdorys terás

Pôdorys 1.np

Pôdorys 2.np

Priečny rez

Pozdĺžny rez - schéma tzb

Chalés LN | *Figura Arquitetos office*

Architects : Felipe Campolina, Tiago Viegas
Location : Brazil
Use : Residential
Dimension : 12 units (20m² each)

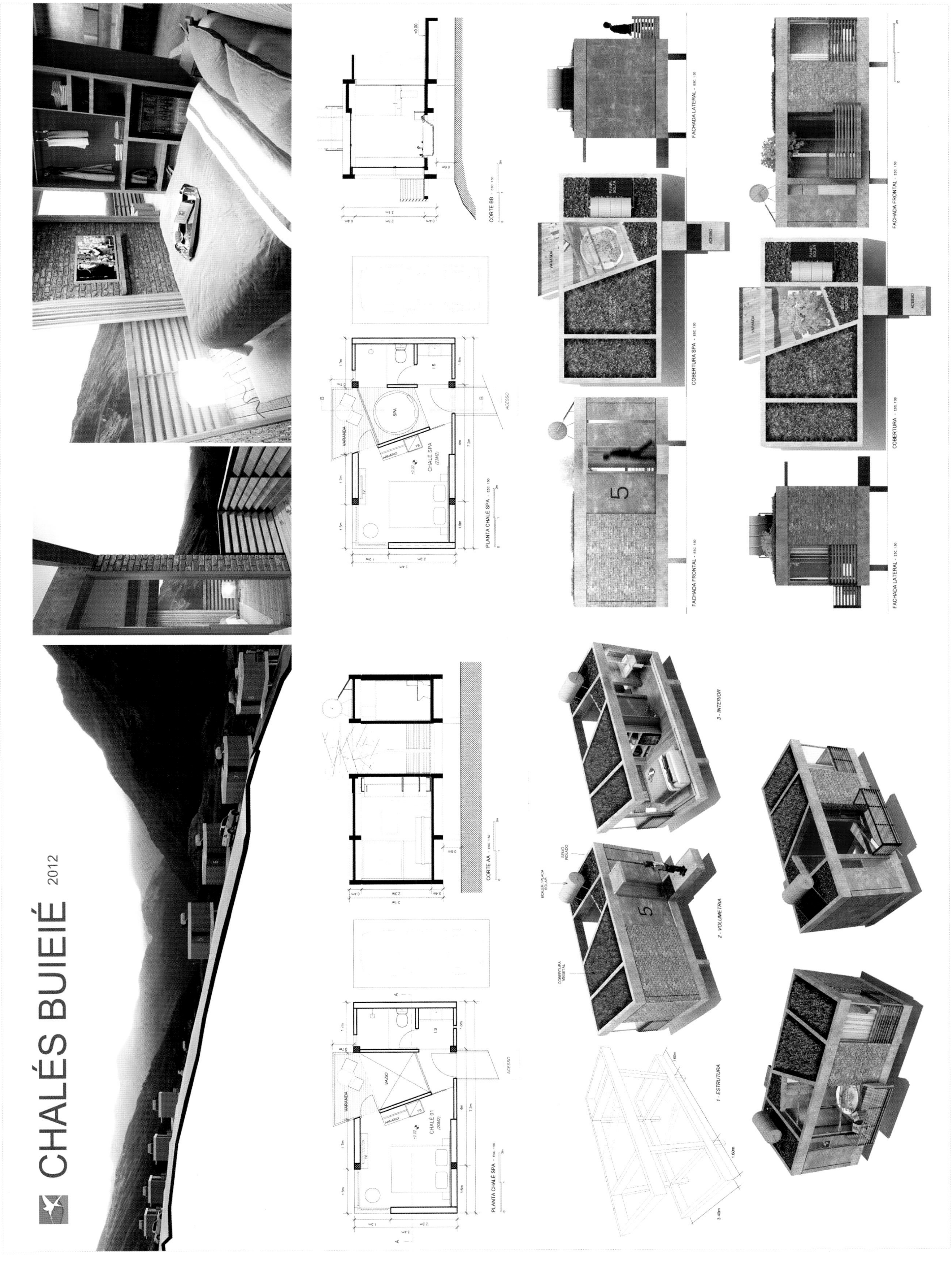

CHALÉS BUIEIÉ 2012

PLANTA CHALÉ SPA

CORTE AA

CORTE BB

FACHADA LATERAL

COBERTURA SPA

FACHADA FRONTAL

COBERTURA

1 - ESTRUTURA

2 - VOLUMETRIA

3 - INTERIOR

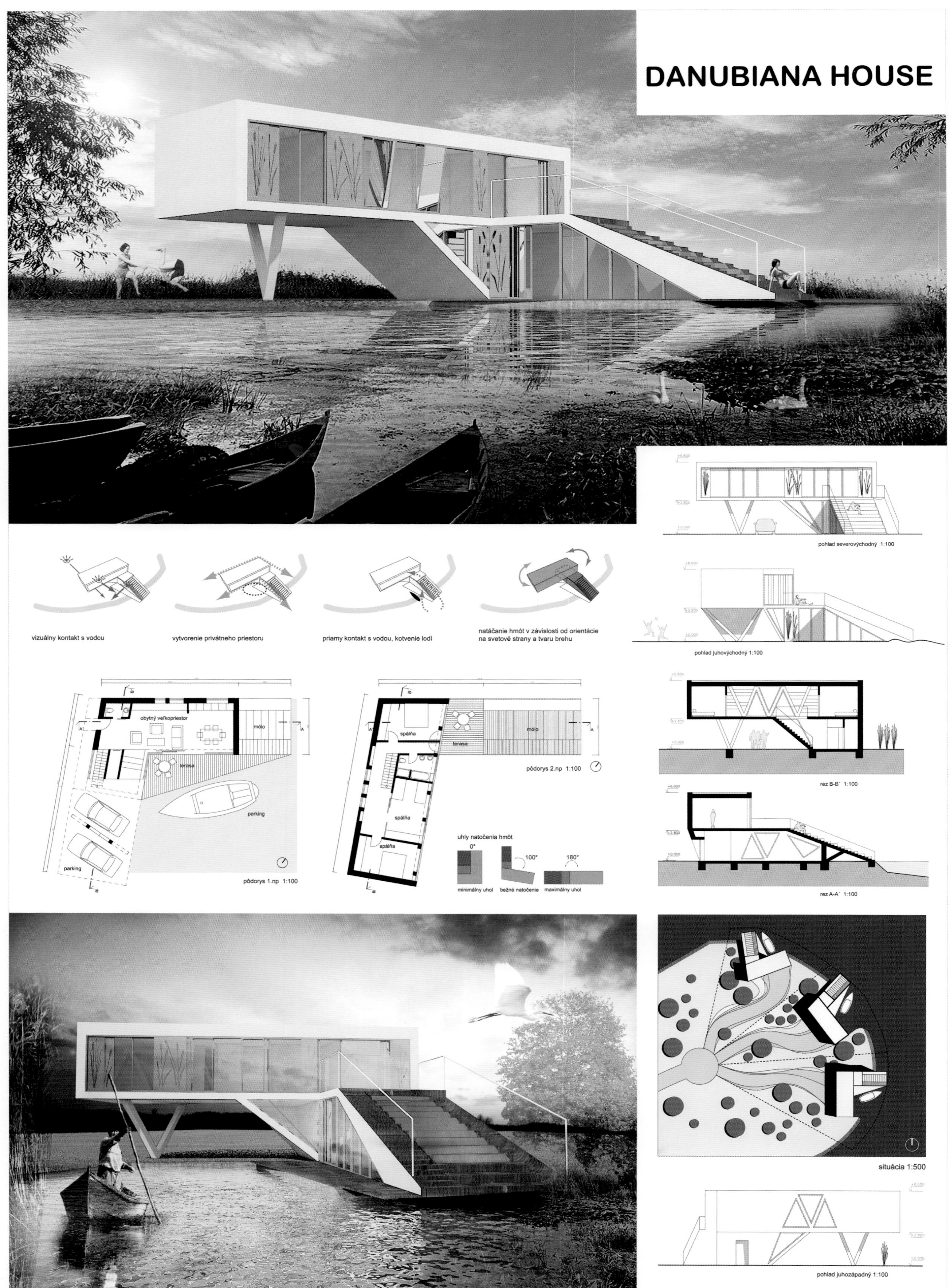
DANUBIANA HOUSE
pohlad severovýchodný 1:100
vizuálny kontakt s vodou
vytvorenie privátneho priestoru
priamy kontakt s vodou, kotvenie lodí
natáčanie hmôt v závislosti od orientácie na svetové strany a tvaru brehu
pohlad juhovýchodný 1:100
obytný veľkopriestor
mólo
terasa
parking
pôdorys 1.np 1:100
spálňa
pôdorys 2.np 1:100
uhly natočenia hmôt
0°
100°
180°
minimálny uhol
bežné natočenie
maximálny uhol
rez B-B´ 1:100
rez A-A´ 1:100
situácia 1:500
pohlad juhozápadný 1:100

ECO CAPSULA

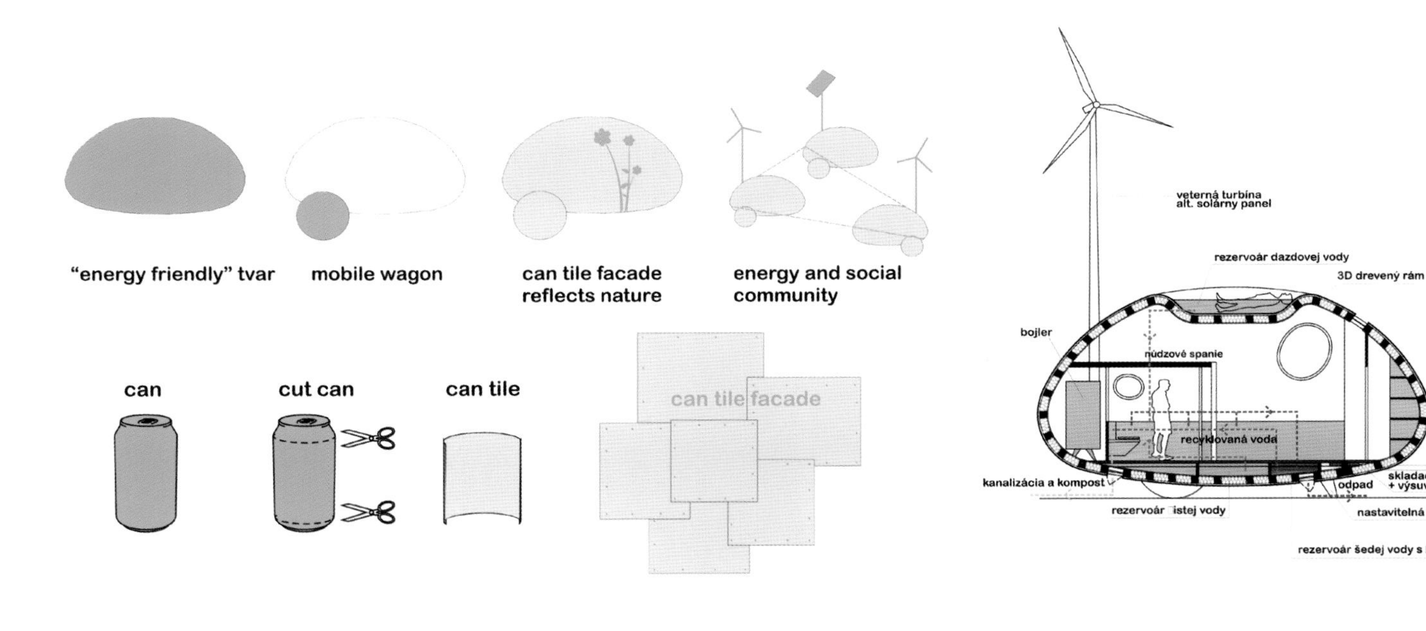
"energy friendly" tvar
mobile wagon
can tile facade reflects nature
energy and social community
can
cut can
can tile
can tile facade
veterná turbína
alt. solárny panel
rezervoár dazdovej vody
3D drevený rám
bojler
núdzové spanie
recyklovaná voda
4200 mm
kanalizácia a kompost
odpad
skladacie schody + výsuvne kolesá
rezervoár istej vody
nastavitelná "noha"
rezervoár šedej vody s istiacim mechanizmom

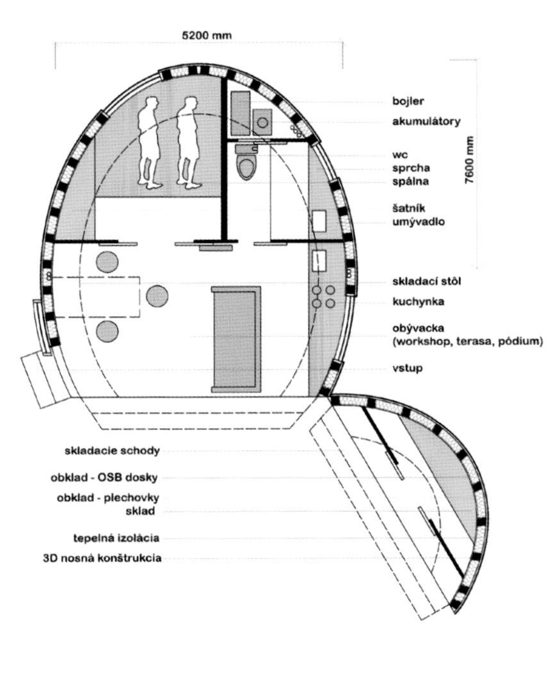
5200 mm
bojler
akumulátory
wc
sprcha
spálna
7600 mm
šatník
umývadlo
skladací stôl
kuchynka
obývacka
(workshop, terasa, pódium)
vstup
skladacie schody
obklad - OSB dosky
obklad - plechovky
sklad
tepelná izolácia
3D nosná konštrukcia

063 Open Block | *2A+P/A*

Type : Design Competition "AAA Architetti cercasi", Honourable Mention
Program : Housing
Project : 2A+P/A, Tommaso Arcangioli, Angelo Grasso, T Spoon

Location : Milan, Italy
Year : 2010

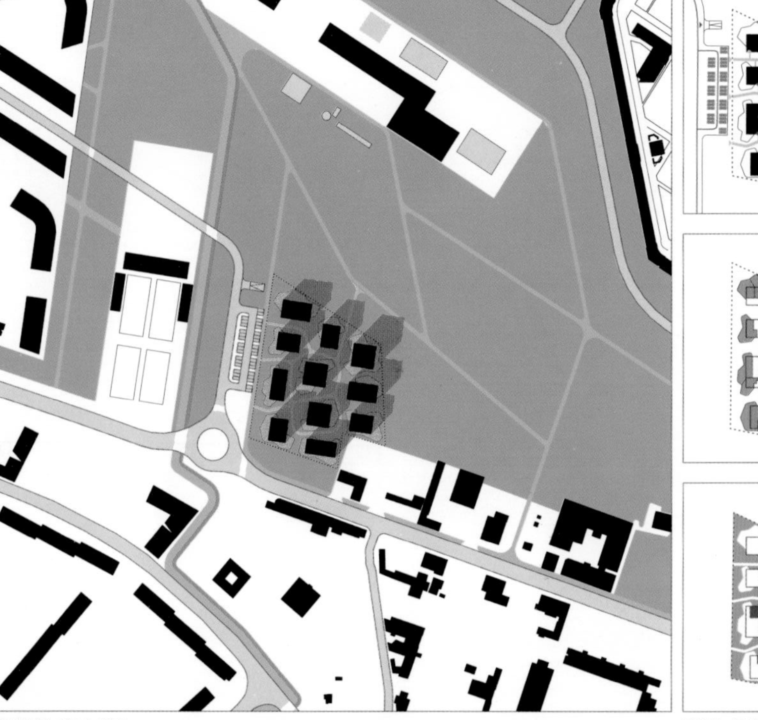

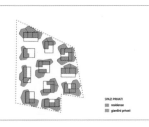

INQUADRAMENTO - SCALA 1:2000

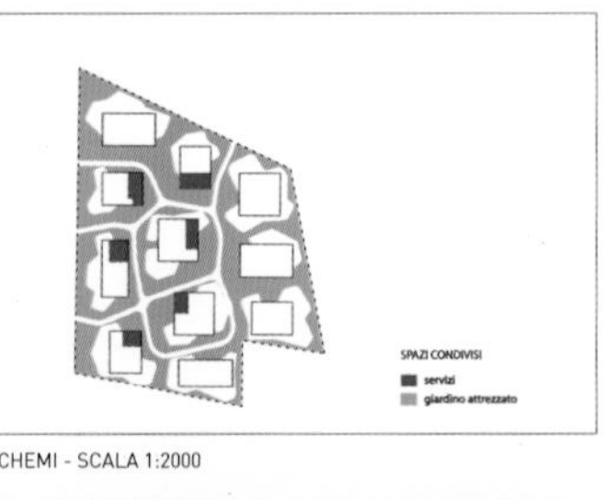

SCHEMI - SCALA 1:2000

Il progetto propone un cambio di scala rispetto al piano d'intervento nel quale si inserisce, nel tentativo di connettersi e dialogare con l'area della Cascina Merlata e allo stesso tempo proporre un'alternativa possibile rispetto agli insediamenti di edilizia residenziale previsti.
La proposta è quella di strutturare l'intervento come un isolato urbano immerso nel verde e costituito da vari edifici, con l'obiettivo di definire un sistema articolato di vuoti al suo interno. Il progetto rappresenta sostanzialmente una porzione di città in cui i diversi elementi, posti uno accanto all'altro, generano di volta in volta, scorci, vicoli, slarghi e piazze in continuità con gli spazi naturali che circondano l'area.
Il progetto sviluppa un insediamento residenziale costituito da undici edifici di diversa tipologia edilizia, differenti in altezza e per trattamento delle facciate. Il masterplan è composto da tre edifici a torre, due corpi a ballatoio e sei edifici in linea, ulteriormente differenziati tra loro a seconda dell'orientamento in cui sono posizionati.
Ogni tipo edilizio ha caratteristiche differenti. La torre è caratterizzata dall'uso di logge e grandi aperture vetrate. Il ballatoio presenta una pelle esterna che riveste da un lato gli elementi di distribuzione semi-pubblici e dall'altro delle grandi terrazze private. La linea A è arricchita da terrazzini e finestre modulari. La linea B da grandi vetrate con tende regolabili.
L'uso delle coperture si differenzia grazie a dispositivi come pergole e tetti a shed con sistemi integrati solari e fotovoltaici, serre e attici con patii e terrazze verdi.
Le altezze degli edifici, che vanno da un minimo di sei livelli ad un massimo di otto, sono state studiate per avere, da una parte, uno profilo differenziato e, dall'altra, garantire, nel rispetto delle distanze minime consentite, l'adeguata illuminazione naturale degli alloggi e degli spazi aperti.
I diversi tipi edilizi sono stati pensati per ospitare il maggior numero possibile di tipologie abitative differenti, al fine di andare incontro alle diverse necessità e desideri della comunità.
L'obiettivo di questo progetto è quello di creare un preciso rapporto tra pieno e vuoto, tra tipologia edilizia e caratteristiche dello spazio aperto: pubblico, semi-pubblico e privato.
Il progetto propone un intervento dove gli edifici, occupando solo il 25% della superficie dell'area, lasciano libero il suolo a percorsi, giardini e spazi comuni, orti, playground e giardini privati delle residenze ai piani terra.
Queste strategie garantiscono che l'intero progetto appaia come una parte di città, dove la varietà e l'alternanza di spazi, di materiali e di colori, restituiscano nell'immediato un'idea di complessità urbana.

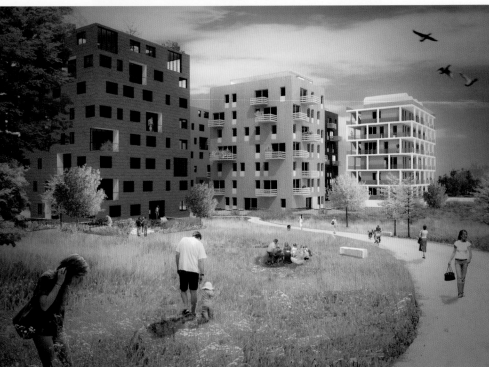

PROFILO SEZIONE - SCALA 1:500

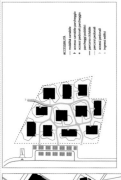

MASTERPLAN (+1.2M) - SCALA 1:500

VISTA DAL PARCO

M1LAN0 2

PIANO -2

PIANO -1

PIANO TERRA

PIANO 1

PIANO 2

PIANO 3

PIANO 4

PIANO 5

PIANO 6

PIANO 7

SCHEMI FUNZIONALI E AGGREGATIVI - SCALA 1:2000

LINEA A

LINEA B

TORRE

BALLATOIO

TIPI EDILIZI / PIANO TIPO - SCALA 1:500

TIPOLOGIE - SCALA 1:300

PROFILO SEZIONE - SCALA 1:500

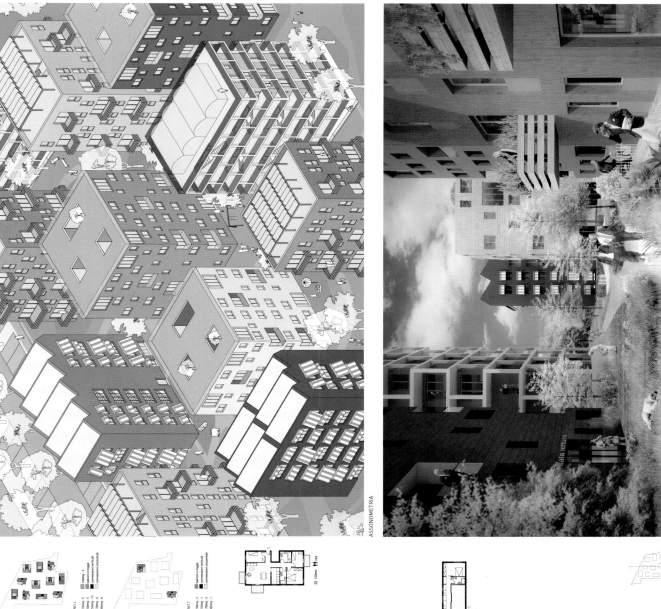

ASSONOMETRIA

VISTA INTERNA

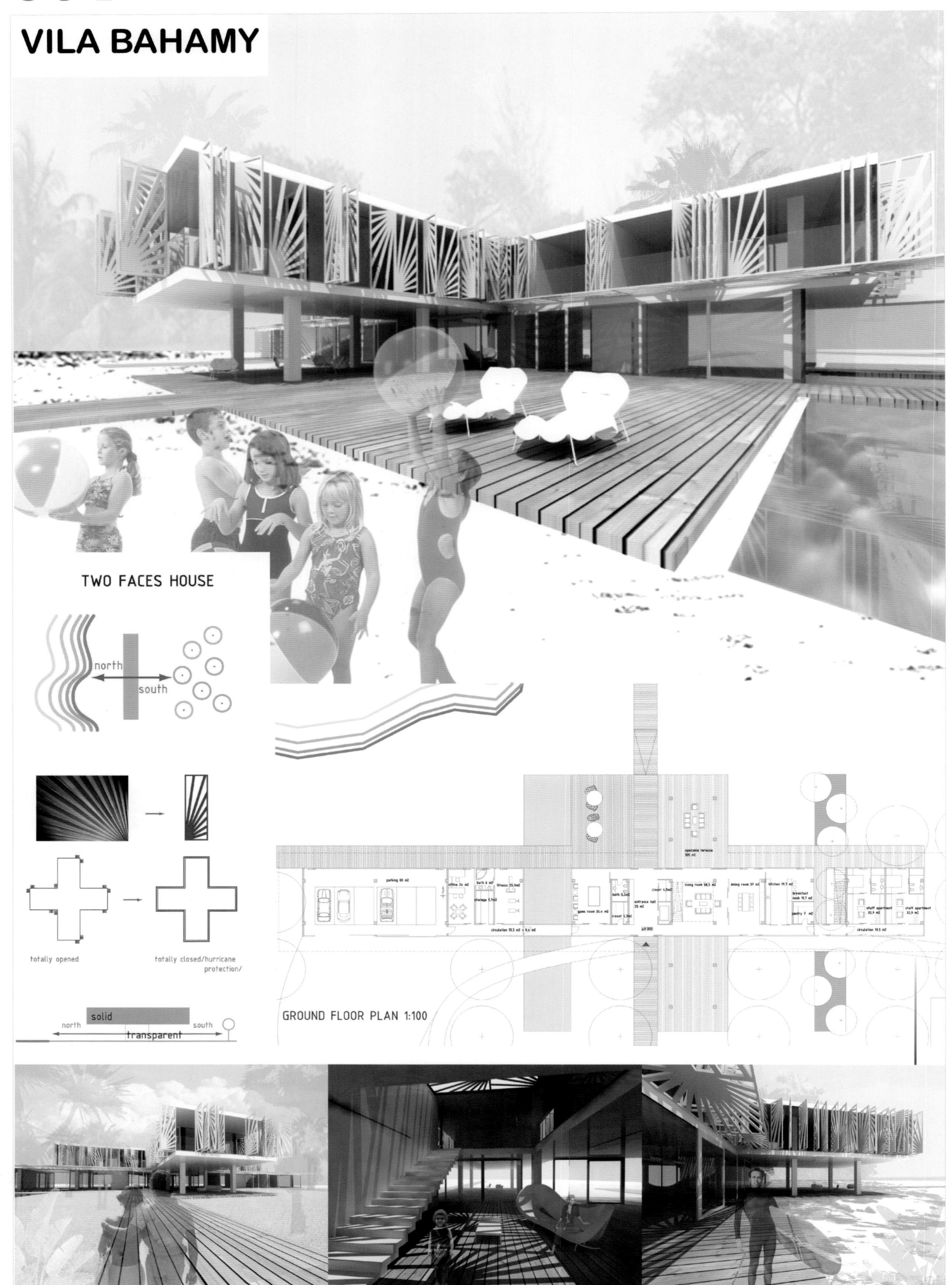
VILA BAHAMY
TWO FACES HOUSE
north
south
totally opened
totally closed/hurricane protection/
solid
north
south
transparent
GROUND FLOOR PLAN 1:100

Urban Block | *2A+P/A*

Model : Marco Galofaro / Modelab
Photo: Sebastiano Costanzo

Type : International design competition "A101 Urban Block"
Program : Housing
Location : Moscow, Russia / Year : 2011

OP3N8L

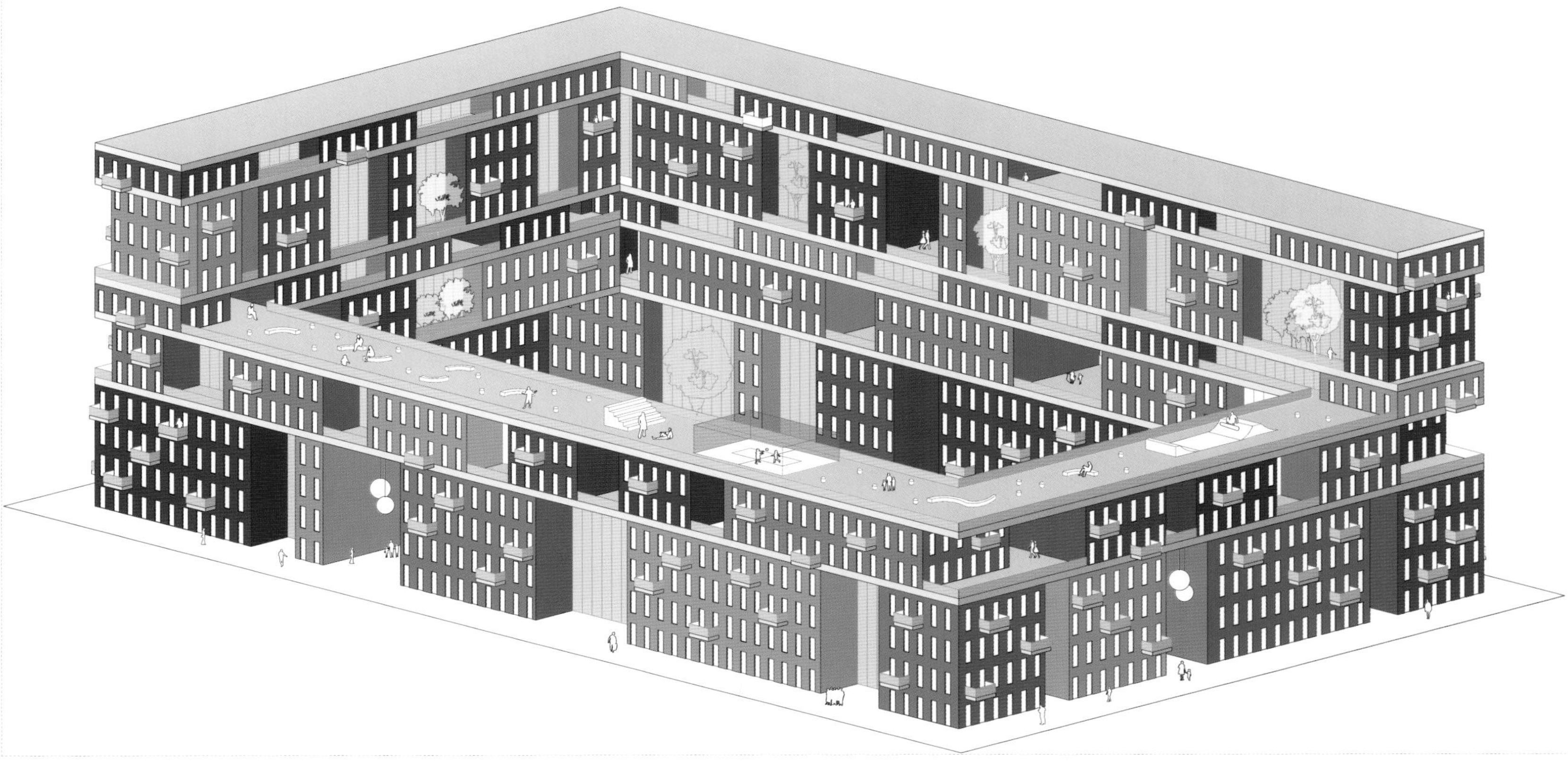

OPEN BLOCK

A1

GROSS FLOOR AREA: 27.982 sqm
NET/GROSS FLOOR AREA RATIO: 0,83
FACADE/FLOOR AREA RATIO: 0,51
ENTRY CODE: OP3N8L

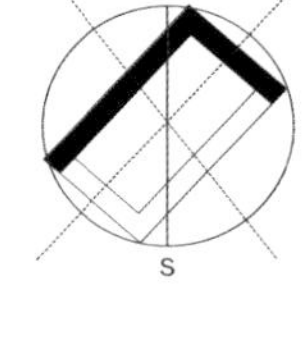

The project develops a complex and articulate habitat where simple forms are able to set the block as an open and flexible system. The chosen typology is the courtyard. It has been modeled to let the solar radiation get inside the court and, at the same time, to provide sheltering from the northern winds. It is composed by two L shaped buildings, with different heights, put together to make a block characterized by different voids as connective and shared spaces. The building is developed through a series of main floors, sustained by simple boxes with different heights and colors. The spaces between the volumes are the places where private and shared confront themselves: common terraces and winter gardens are the spaces where inhabitants can meet and be engaged in social relations, while private terraces are open and protected spaces, natural extensions of the apartments. The inhabitants of the block exclusively use the court which is the most public space of the project. Huge artificial hills, benches and playgrounds create a space that is public and private at the same time. In the actual configuration of the project, the ground floor is commercial, with shops and offices. In this sense it has been conceived to be positioned inside an urban quarter. Nevertheless, the flexibility of the project makes it easy to modify it, according to other environmental and social contexts.

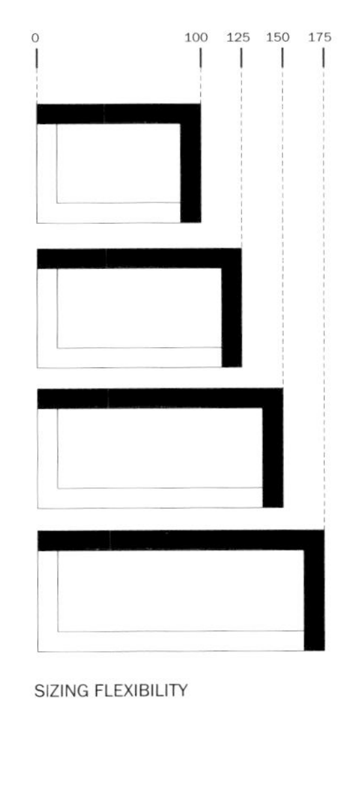

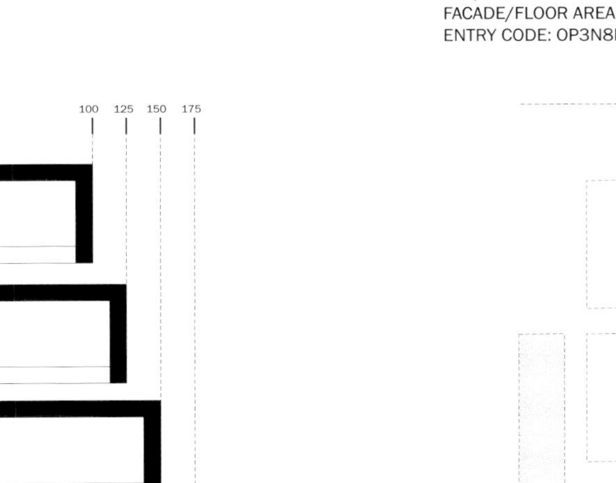

SIZING FLEXIBILITY

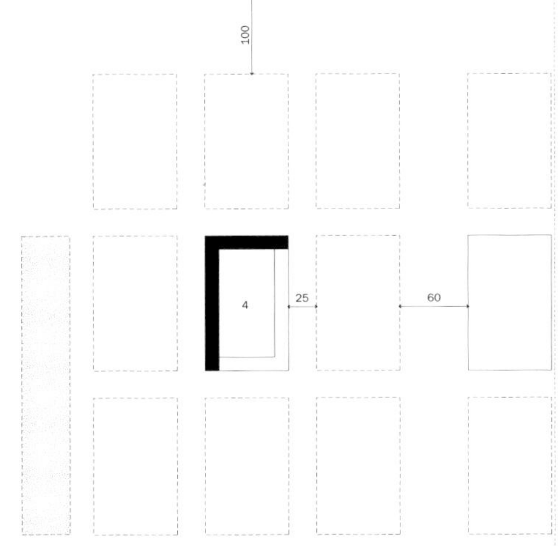

URBAN QUARTER POSITIONING

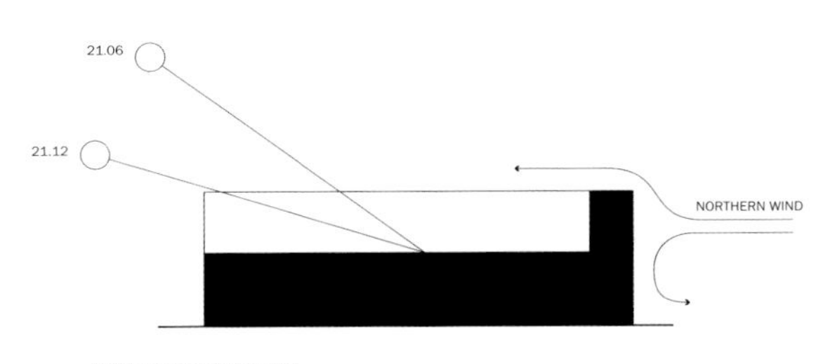

BIOCLIMATIC STRATEGY

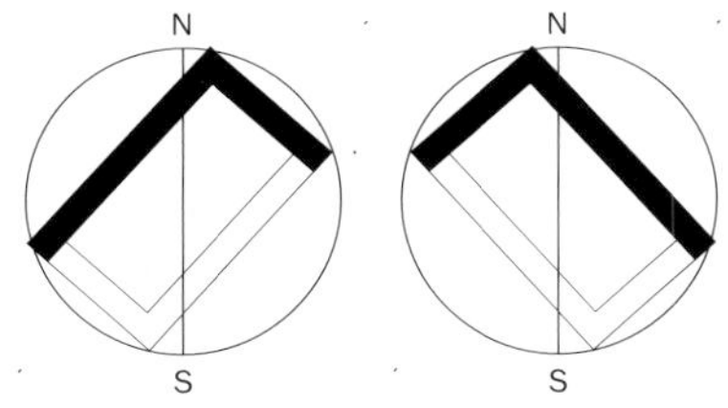

MIRRORING AND ORIENTATION

OP3N8L

OP3N

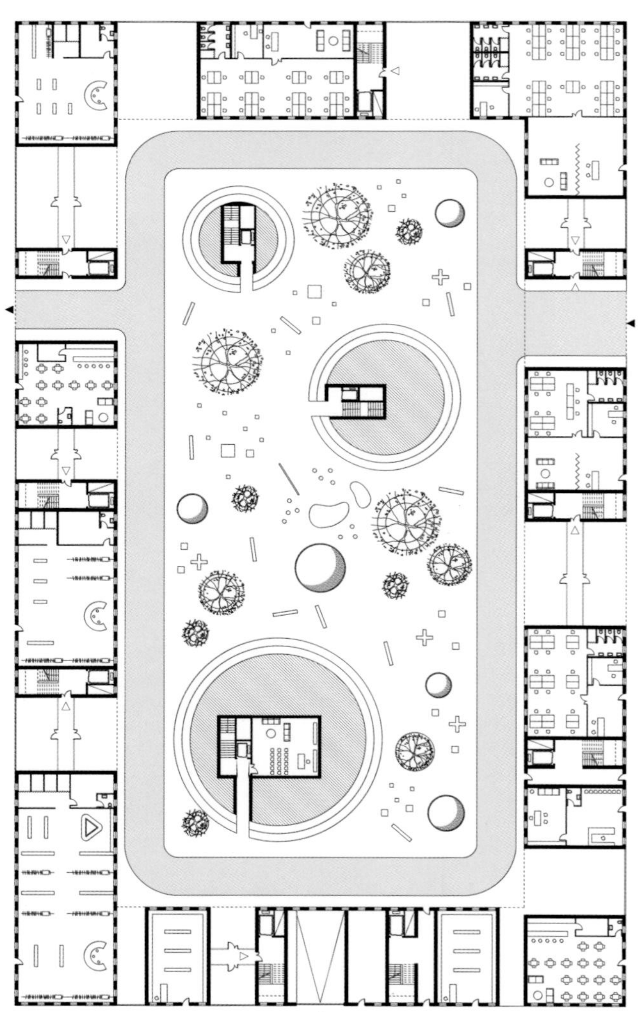

GROUND FLOOR 1:500

UPPER FLOOR 1:500

OP3N8L

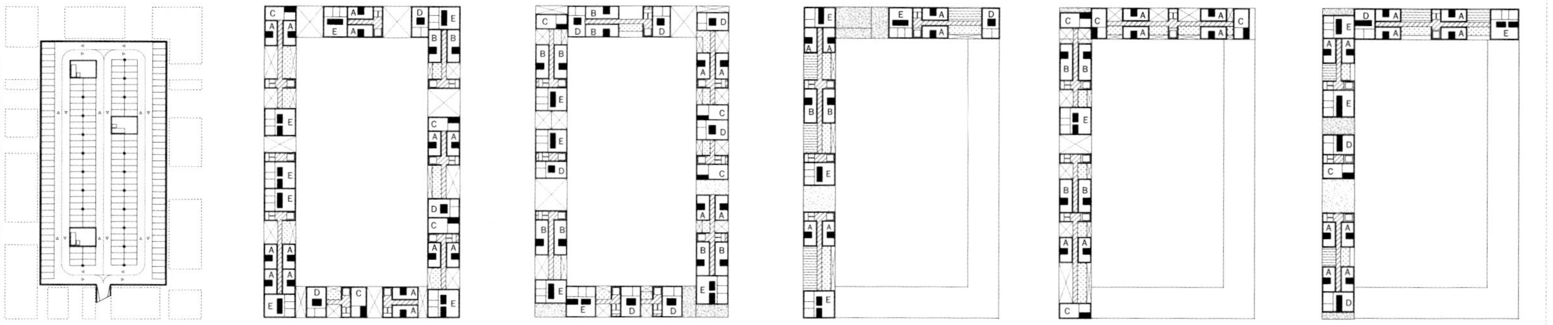

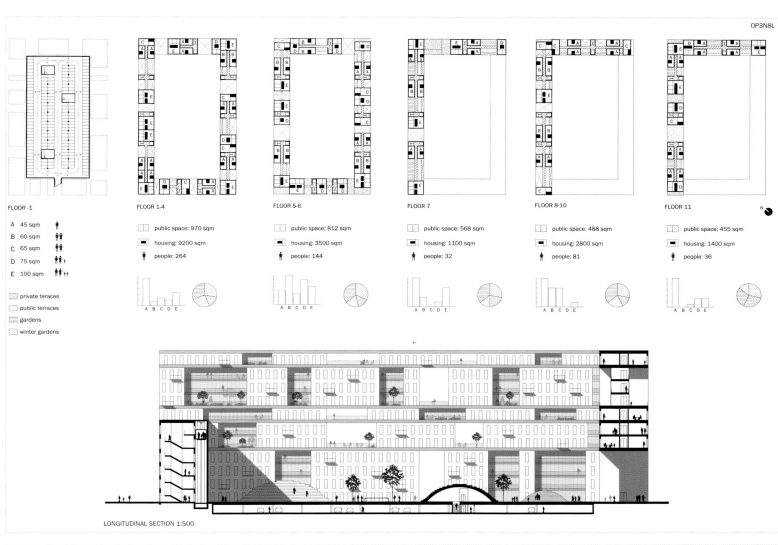

FLOOR -1

A 45 sqm
B 60 sqm
C 65 sqm
D 75 sqm
E 100 sqm

private teraces
public terraces
gardens
winter gardens

FLOOR 1-4

public space: 970 sqm
housing: 9200 sqm
people: 264

FLOOR 5-6

public space: 812 sqm
housing: 3500 sqm
people: 144

FLOOR 7

public space: 568 sqm
housing: 1100 sqm
people: 32

FLOOR 8-10

public space: 488 sqm
housing: 2800 sqm
people: 81

FLOOR 11

public space: 455 sqm
housing: 1400 sqm
people: 36

LONGITUDINAL SECTION 1:500

OP3N8L

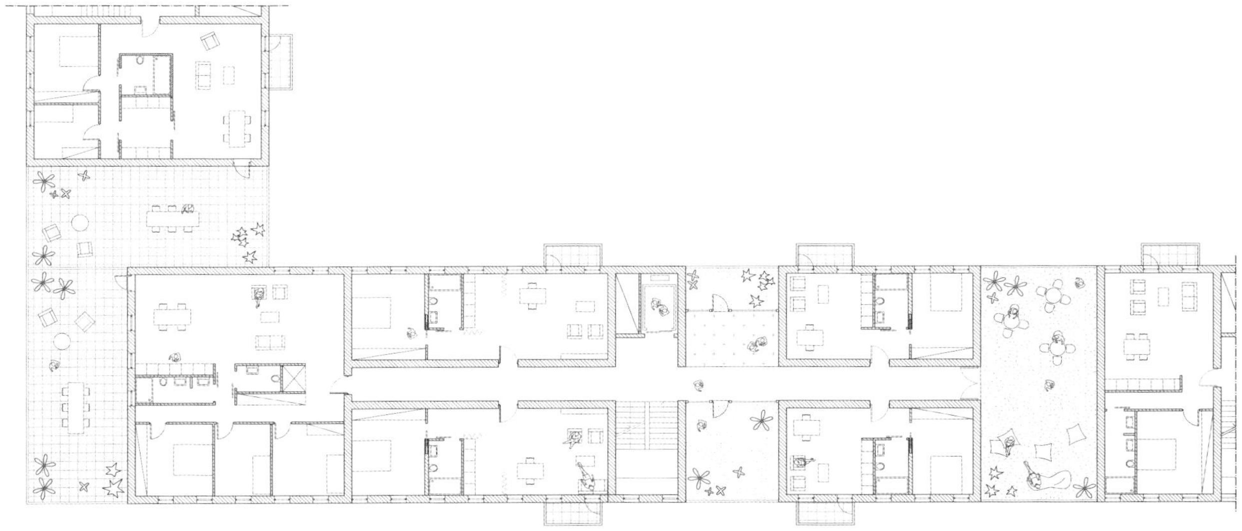

FLOOR PLAN SAMPLE 1:200

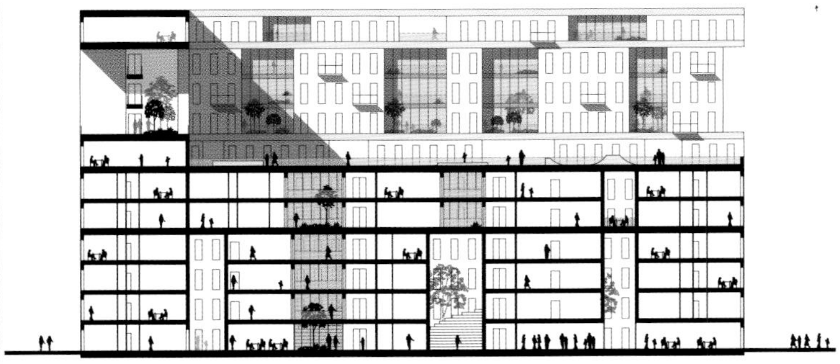

TRANSVERSAL SECTION 1:500

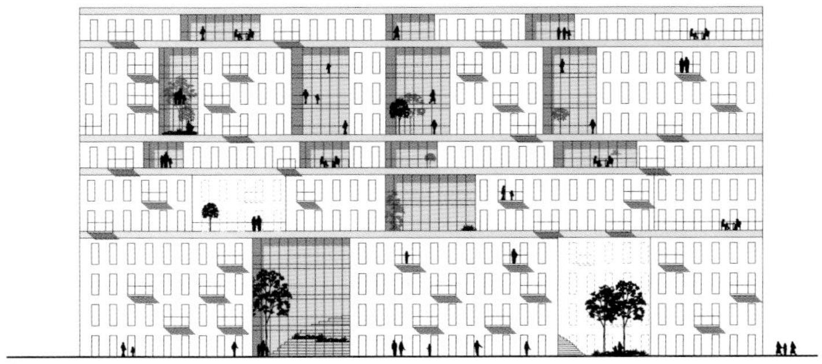

NORTH ELEVATION 1:500

066 Alesund Fjord New Waterfront | *Carloslampreia[x]arquitectos*

Location : Alesund, Norway
Project : Carlos Lampreia
Project team : [x architects]- Rui Rocha, Leonor Contreiras, Jorge Guerra
Consultants : Alvaro Cidrais(urbanscape), Antonio Maccara(digital image)

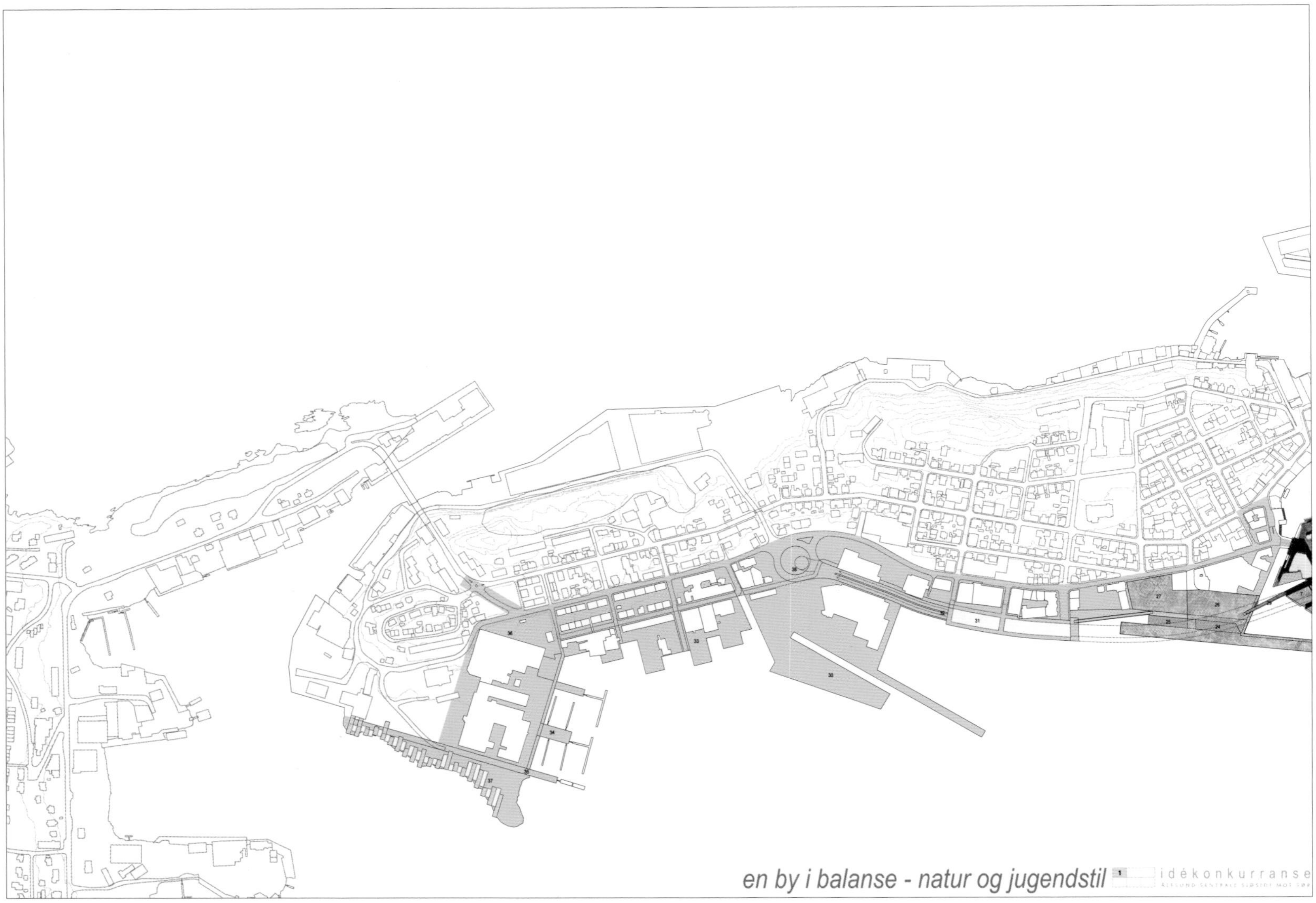

en by i balanse - natur og jugendstil 1 idékonkurranse

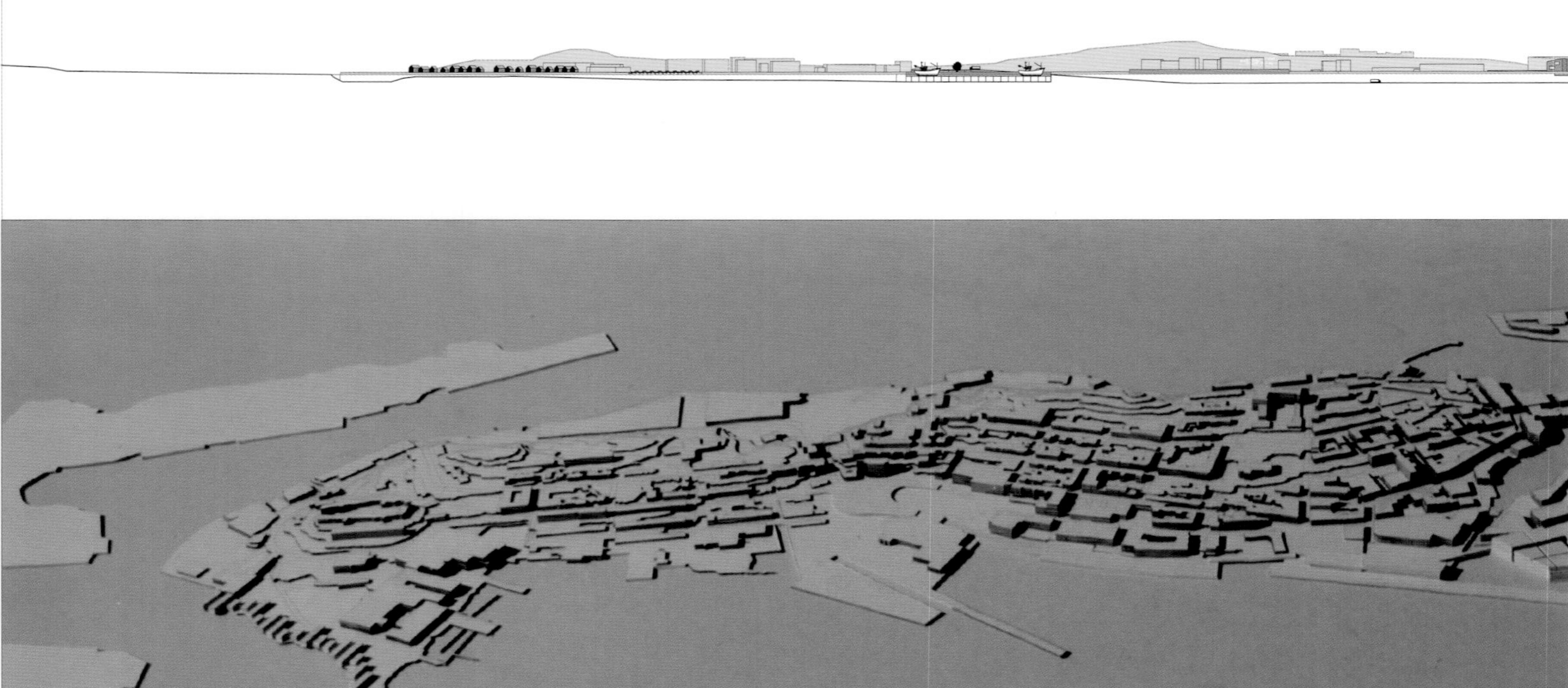

Jugendstil - ingen annen stilretning enn Jugendstil har i så stor grad, og med større fascinasjon, iaktatt og latt seg inspirere av naturen. Bruken av former fra plantelivet utgjør et hovedkjennetegn ved stilen, både som dekorelement og som modell for selve gjenstandenes struktur. [in norsk ordbok]

00-introduksjon
Vi bruker dette som inspirasjon til å bringe mer natur inn i byrommet, bevare og understreke jugendbyen og planlegge større bygningsmasse, men samtidig gi rom for innbyggernes behov for vegetasjon og frisk luft, trygg ferdsel og tilgjengelighet.

0-KONSEPTER
a.Formasjon av Borgundfjorden ved Ålesund, vann og stein
b.Fisken, trebebyggelsen, husene og bryggene
c.Bybrannen, Jugendstil og murbyen
d.Ødeleggelsen av fjellet med Rønnebergvillaen og den økende befolkningstettheten i byen

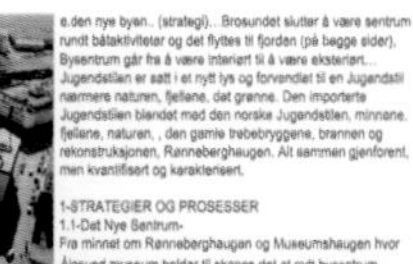

e.den nye byen.. (strategi)...Brosundet slutter å være sentrum rundt båtaktiviteter og det flyttes til fjorden (på begge sider). Bysentrum går fra å være interiørt til å være eksteriørt... Jugendstilen er satt i et nytt lys og forvandlet til en Jugendstil nærmere naturen, fjellene, det grønne. Den importerte Jugendstilen blandet med den norske Jugendstilen, minnene, fjellene, naturen, , den gamle trebebryggene, brannen og rekonstruksjonen, Rønneberghaugen. Alt sammen gjenforent, men kvantifisert og karakterisert.

1-STRATEGIER OG PROSESSER
1.1-Det Nye Sentrum-
Fra minnet om Rønneberghaugen og Museumshaugen hvor Ålesund museum holder til skapes det et nytt bysentrum.
En ny, åpen handlegate binder sammen en tenkt ny inngang til Ålesund museum med Hellebroa, og denne bryter samtidig ned rådhusklossen i retning øst vest. Et nytt handelssenter skapes og fylles med en ny lesesal, mediarom og Rønneberg salong med utsikt til Brosundet og fjorden.

en by i balanse - natur og jugendstil 4 idékonkurranse

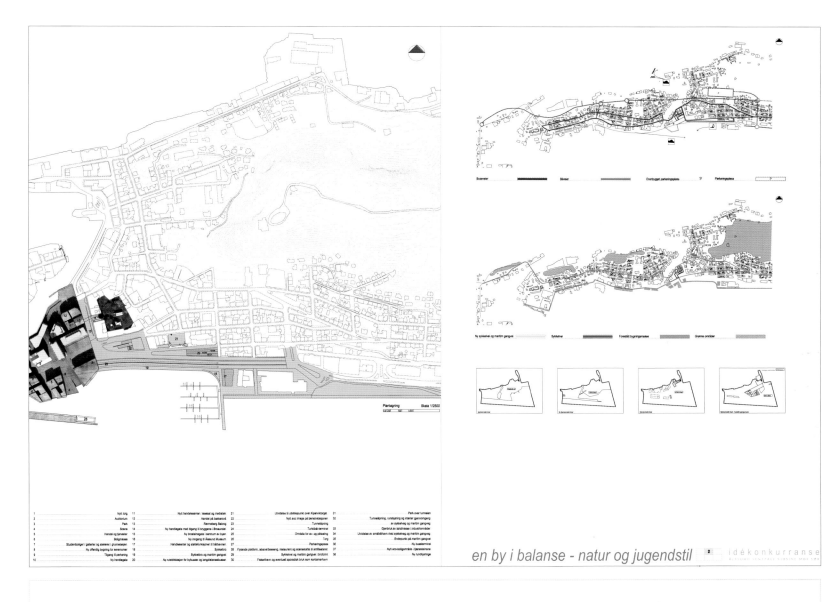

Bussveier Bilveier Overbygget parkeringsplass Parkeringsplass

Ny sykkelvei og maritim gangvei Sykkelvei Foreslått bygningsmasse Grønne områder

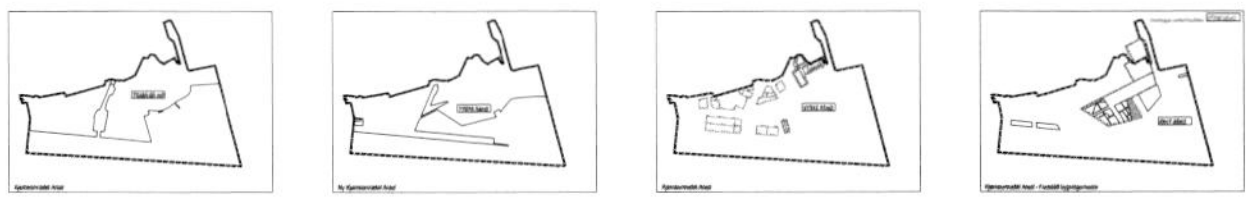

Plantegning Skala 1/2500

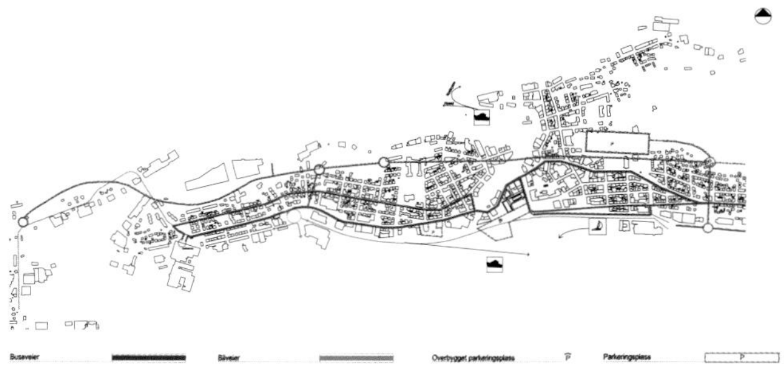

1	Nytt torg	11	Nytt handelssenter / lesesal og mediatek	21	Utvidelse til utsiktspunkt over Kiperviktorget	31	Park over tunnelen
2	Auditorium	12	Handel på bakkenivå	22	Nytt eco image på bensinstasjonen	32	Tunnelåpning, rundkjøring og interiør gjennomgang av sykkelveg og maritim gangveg
3	Park	13	Rønneberg Salong	23	Tunnelåpning	33	Gjenbruk av landmasse i industriområder
4	Scene	14	Ny handlegate med tilgang til bryggene i Brosundet	24	Turistbåt-terminal	34	Utvidelse av småbåthavn med sykkelveg og maritim gangveg
5	Handel og tjenester	15	Ny brosteinsgate i sentrum av byen	25	Område for av- og påstigning	35	Endepunkt på maritim gangvei
6	Boligmasse	16	Ny inngang til Ålesund Museum	26	Torg	36	Ny bussterminal
7	Studentboliger / gallerier og atelierer i grunnetasjen	17	Handlesenter og støttefunksjoner til båthavnen	27	Parkeringsplass	37	Nytt eco-boligområde i fjæresteinene
8	Ny offentlig bygning for seremonier	18	Sykkelbro	28	Flytende platform, isbane/basseng, restaurant og scenestøtte til amfiteateret	38	Ny rundkjøringe
9	Tilgang til parkering	19	Sykkelbro og maritim gangvei	29	Sykkelvei og maritim gangvei i broform		
10	Ny handlegate	20	Ny rutebilstasjon for bybusser og langdistansebusser	30	Fiskerihavn og eventuell sporadisk bruk som kontainerhavn		

en by i balanse - natur og jugendstil 2 idékonkurranse

Snitt

Høsten - kl.12:00

En annen gate går gjennom bygget i retning nord syd og forbinder bryggene ved Brosundet med gatene i det nye sentrum. Veien går gjennom de nye bygningene og skaper på den måten en handlegate som er beskyttet mot vær og vind mellom Rønnebergata og det nye auditoriet ved fjorden.
Disse gatene strekker seg mot syd i retning mot det nye sentrum, dominert av et langstrakt torg som er beskyttet mot været, men åpen mot fjorden og hvor de nye funksjonene er integrert.
Det nye auditoriet og sammenstillingen av de nye bygningene gjør inntrykk der de beveger seg ut mot den nye viken som skapes ved byggingen av ny kai mot syd, og et nytt kommunalt bygg, dekorert med trykte jugendstil motiver, som avslutter torget.
De nye bygningene gir mulighet for beskyttelse, adgang til sol og grønne lunger i de store åpne og tildekte parkene og tar opp konseptet med det kontemporere språk som omhandler fusjon mellom de naturlige elementer av stein, av vegetasjon og det historiske jugendstil sentrum.

1.2 - DEN NYE VIKEN OG KANALER

Brosundet blir omdirigert til den nye viken, hvor den gir vann til det nye sentrum, og den nye turistbåt-terminalen blir på den måten gitt mer avstand og forbundet til Aspøya med tilgang ved hjelp av en ny gang og sykkelbro som blir ført internt i de nye bygningene som omslutter torget.
Turistbåt-terminalen er del av et nytt system av platformer som har egen identitet (conceptual iceberg) slik at den ikke blander seg med den urbane og geologiske identiteten til øya.
Der er tre slike platformer; **Kvennaneset** med småbåthavn integrert i det nye boligområdet, konseptuelt basert på tradisjonell trehusbebyggelse og trebrygger som hviler over fjæresteinene, **Skutvika** med fiskebåthavn og tilhørende industri og **Prestebrygga** med turistbåt-terminalen. Alle er visuelt basert på drivende isfjell, store hvite flater som hjelper til å reflektere naturlig lys.
Meierikaia vil bli fornyet med fergeterminal for langevågsbåten etc., småbåthavn og på den måten bli den nye byhavnen, sammen med oppgradering av Sunnmøre Meieri til å omfatte museum og kommersielt område for meieriprodukter.
Nært dette området finner vi også den nye rutebilstasjonen, ved Kiperviktorget, som blir utvidet med en platform ut mot Borgundfjorden.
Dette er også hvor vi finner inngangen til ny tunnel.

1.3-NYE TRAFIKKLØSNINGER

Den nye tunnelen som er tenkt, med inngang under det nye auditorium og utgang i Skutvika vil ta av for all trafikk som skal direkte til Aspøy, Skarbøvik og Hessa, slik at denne unngår sentrum av byen. Denne løsningen regnes som en Low-Cost, som ikke involverer så mye boring/fjellsprenging, men vi vurderer også løsningen med tunnel gjennom Aksla og kun parkering ved foten av Fjellstua nær byparken.
Den reduserte trafikken gjennom sentrum skjer via eksisterende vei mellom Meierikaia, via Posthuskrysset til Skansekaia. Det nye sentrum på Sydsiden har ikke adgang for biler, kun en utvidet parkering under det nye sentrum, siden trafikken nå blir ledet perifert forbi Hellebroa til Aspøy.
Toppen av den nye tunnelen blir dekt av en eco-struktur av grønne lunger, maritim gangvei og sykkelsti som fletter seg inn i det urbane nettverk, som foreslått i planene, mellom Meierikaia og småbåthavna på Kvennaneset. Offentlig transport i sentrum vil bli utført av busser med mindre dimensjon og hyppigere avganger og tar utgangspunkt i den nye rutebilstasjonen på Kiperviktorget, og langdistansebusser vil også ta utgangspunkt her. Stasjon for bussene, parkering, foreslås imidlertid på Kvennaneset, ved eller i de store eksisterende industribygninger.
Systemet komplementeres med bysykler med utgangspunkt i det nye sentrum, og nye sykkelveier både mot øst og mot vest, uten store høydeforskjeller.

1.3-NYE TRAFIKKLØSNINGER

Den nye tunnelen som er tenkt, med inngang under det nye auditorium og utgang i Skutvika vil ta av for all trafikk som skal direkte til Aspøy, Skarbøvik og Hessa, slik at denne unngår sentrum av byen. Denne løsningen regnes som en Low-Cost, som ikke involverer så mye boring/fjellsprenging, men vi vurderer også løsningen med tunnel gjennom Aksla og kun parkering ved foten av Fjellstua nær byparken.
Den reduserte trafikken gjennom sentrum skjer via eksisterende vei mellom Meierikaia, via Posthuskrysset til

en by i balanse - natur og jugendstil 5 idékonkurranse

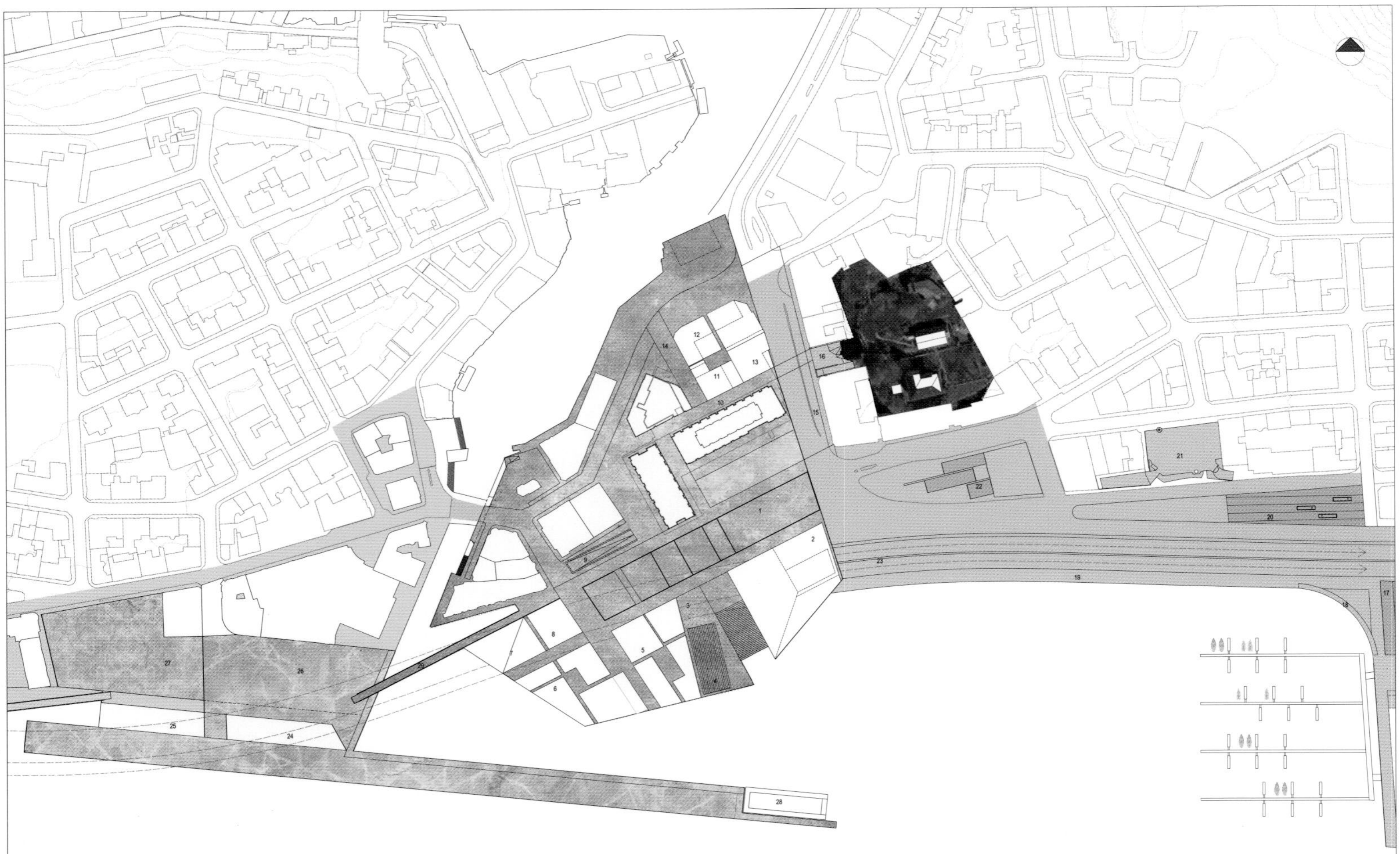

Plantegning Skala 1/1000

1	Nytt torg	11	Nytt handelssenter / lesesal og mediatek	21	Utvidelse til utkikkspunkt over Kiperviktorget
2	Auditorium	12	Handel på bakkenivå	22	Nytt eco image på bensinstasjonen
3	Park	13	Ranneberg Salong	23	Tunneløpning
4	Scene	14	Ny handlegate med tilgang til bryggene i Brosundet	24	Turistbåt-terminal
5	Handel og tjenester	15	Ny brosteinsgate i sentrum av byen	25	Område for av- og pålasting
6	Boligmasse	16	Ny inngang til Ålesund Museum	26	Torg
7	Studentboliger / gallerier og atelierer i grunnetasjen	17	Handlesenter og støttefunksjoner til båthavnen	27	Parkeringsplass
8	Ny offentlig bygning for seremonier	18	Sykkelbro	28	Flytende platform, isbane/basseng, restaurant og scenestøtte til amfiteateret
9	Tilgang til parkering	19	Sykkelbro og maritim gangvei	29	Sykkelvei og maritim gangvei i broformt
10	Ny handlegate	20	Ny rutebilstasjon for bybusser og langdistansebusser		

en by i balanse - natur og jugendstil 3 idékonkurranse

vår - kl.12:00

Høsten - kl.16:00

vår - kl.16:00

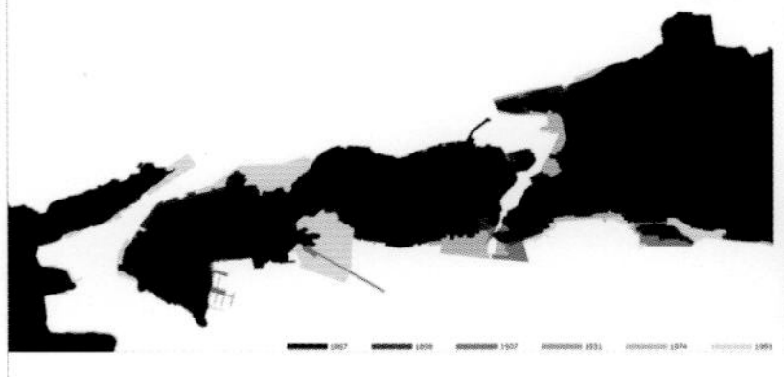

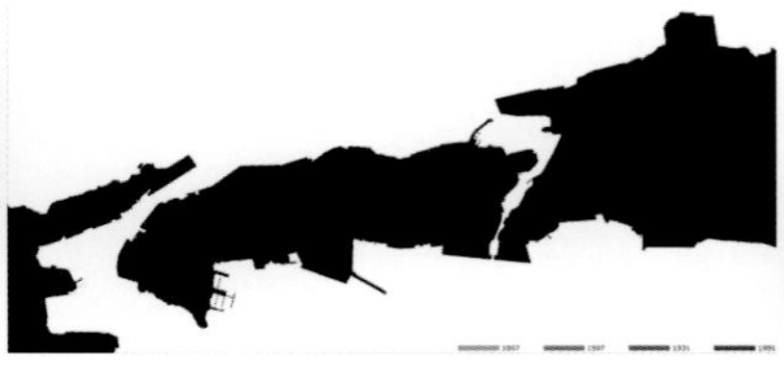

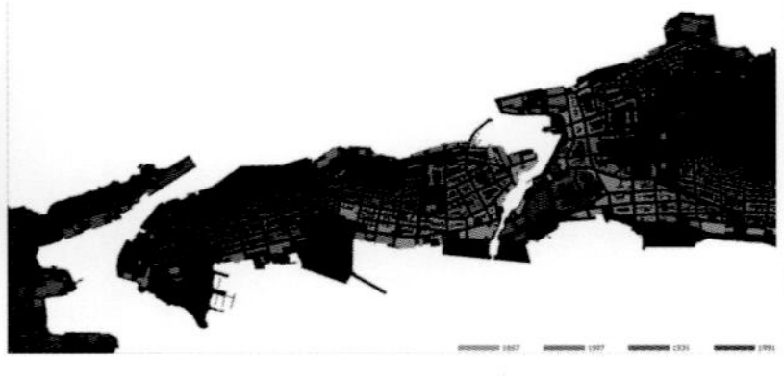

Skansekaia. Det nye sentrum på Sydsiden har ikke adgang for biler, kun en utvidet parkering under det nye sentrum, siden trafikken nå blir ledet perifert forbi Hellebroa til Aspøy. Toppen av den nye tunnelen blir dekt av en eco-struktur av grønne lunger, maritim gangvei og sykkelsti som fletter seg inn i det urbane nettverk, som foreslått i planene, mellom Meierikaia og småbåthavna på Kvennaneset. Offentlig transport i sentrum vil bli utført av busser med mindre dimensjon og hyppigere avganger og tar utgangspunkt i den nye rutebilstasjonen på Kiperviktorget, og langdistansebusser vil også ta utgangspunkt her. Stasjon for bussene, parkering, foreslås imidlertid på Kvennaneset, ved eller i de store eksisterende industribygninger. Systemet komplementeres med bysykler med utgangspunkt i det nye sentrum, og nye sykkelveier både mot øst og mot vest, uten store høydeforskjeller.

1.4 KAMPEN MOT KLIMAET LYS

De spesielle klimatiske forhold i byen gjør at det er fokusert på to forhold, å skape beskyttelse på den ene siden og åpne opp på den andre siden for å kunne utnytte best mulig timene med sol.

VIND

Det nye naboiaget i sentrum, beveger seg med, i og mellom eksisterende bygninger for å kunne beskytte best mulig mot de dominerende vindretninger Sørvest og Nord-Nordvest, og utvider det disponible gatesystemet mellom bygningsmassen.

REGN OG SNØ

Det nye gatesystemet og de åpne områdene inkluderer også en del overbygde torg og nye gater, som vil være rettere og med mulighet for å tildekkes med et system av glidende glasspaneler på toppen av bygningene. På den måten introduseres et kunstig komlimentært system som beskytter mot nedbør, og det tenkes også at dette systemet kan inneholde belysning for å kunne reprodusere lysintensitet til dagslys.

en by i balanse - natur og jugendstil 6 idékonkurranse

Atlanticcity | *2:pm architectures*

Project : International Competition an holocaust memorial
Location : Atlantic City(US)
Design Team : 2:pm architectures + G. Benais(arch)

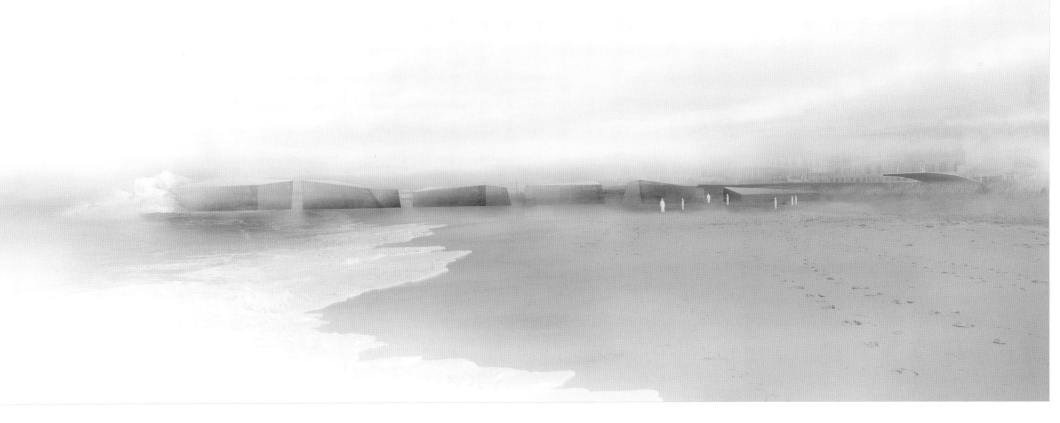

KADZIDLO02

STEPS to MEMORY

'Free man, you will always cherish the sea! The sea is your mirror; you contemplate your soul' C. Baudelaire.

***Freedom**, Man's eternal quest, the quest of all Humankind, all Peoples. Freedom, an absolute right for which Man must constantly strive. Evoking man as a free man, thinking like a free man, imagining man as free man, freed by the **ocean's infinite power**. 'Steps To Memory' is the cement, the solid bond between man and the horizon. It unbinds infinity for our **meditative contemplation**. And in so doing frees the mind from the shackles of the material world and offers us an **escape** into the boundless realm of imagination and memory as the soul soars high above the ocean waves.*

*The boardwalk lifts us above sea level, and from this elevated position the eye surveys the **serenely simple blocks** of concrete slicing majestically across the beach, as the sunlight plays across their surface, mirroring infinitesimal changes in weather, reflecting back the changing tides, season after season, century after century, leisurely progressing through **time immemorial**. The blocks turn their **inaccessible faces to the sky**, probing the skyline, engaging in mutual contemplation and debate with the horizon, inviting us all to partake in its meditation.*

*From the beach, the blocks appear to be 'walls', **linking** sky and earth, ocean and boardwalk. The space between each stone is redolent with architectural **sensations** - each space brings change or expectation, questions or future possibles. Some grip us like a vice, others open up passageways bathed in shade; some offer shelter from the wind, while others invite us to feel its full force. They protect us from the rain or retain the water brought by changing tides.*

*Grains of sand blow in on the wind and huddle in the concave hollows of the stone's surface, bearing eloquent witness to the **changing faces** of the site.*

*'Steps To Memory' is inspired by formal and conceptual **minimalism** and awakens heartfelt **emotions in the soul** of each man.*

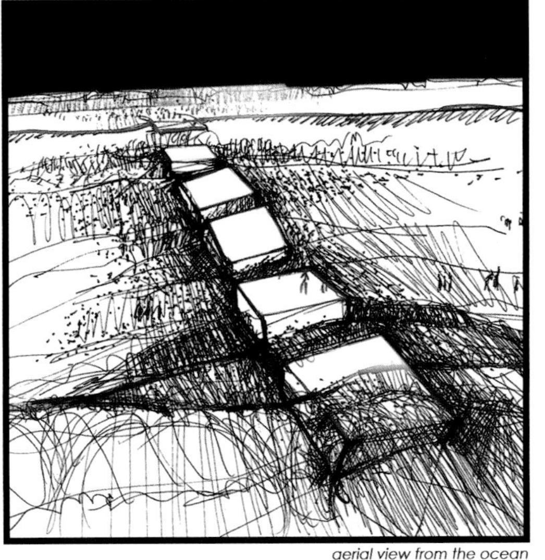

aerial view from the ocean

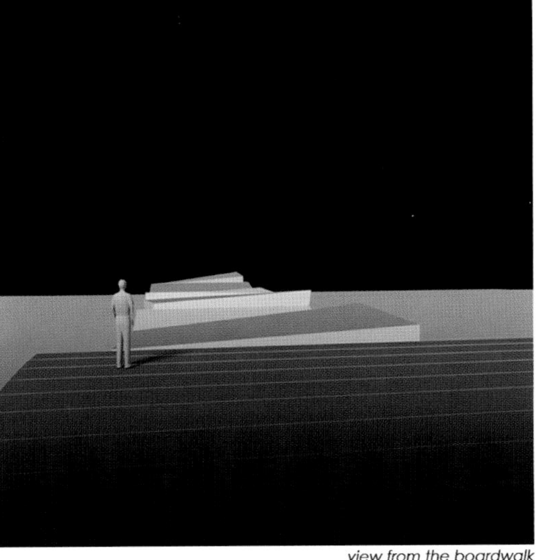

view from the boardwalk

068 Calamari Union | *Lapo Ruffi Architetto*

Promotional Organization : Europan Finland
Client : Municipality of Turku (FI)
Architect : Lapo Ruffi (capogruppo_teamleader), Lorenzo Santini
Collaborators : Anna Biagioni, Giancarlo Bucciero, Nicholas Diddi

Result : Shortlisted Project
Site area : 95.549mq_sqm

turku

1

CALAMARI UNION

LAND PLOT

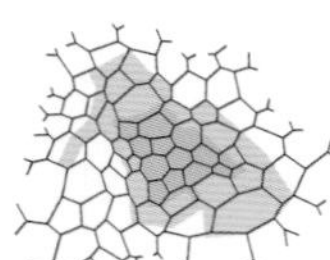

NEW TOPOGRAPHY

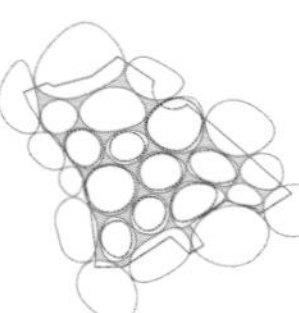

CELLULAR STRUCTURE

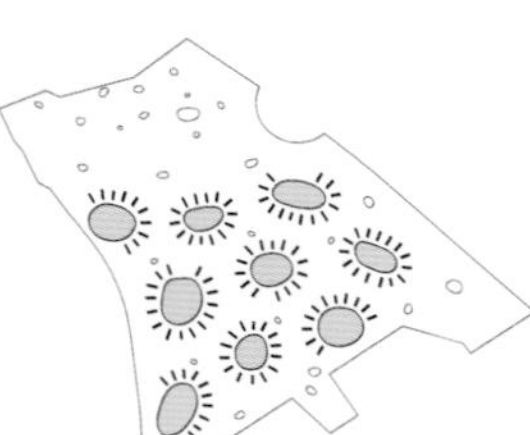

CURVILINEAR SETTLEMENTS

PRIMITIVE FUTURE

The new settlement comes out of an interpretation of the site, where by uniting roads, signs of the territory and property borders emerges a cellular design like a new topography, a polygonal network that reminds the alveolar structures. The definition of the new architectures places its basis on the extension of this urban structure. It is similar to a *tessellation* by *Voronoi*, in which the aggregation of the dwellings that form open courtyards becomes the first layer against noise; they are raised one floor near the main roads and at the heads of the *Tupas*, opening up to nature and sunlight on the other side. Sinuous forms, initially ended, open up toward the landscape and pre-existing structures, visually tying themselves into the place and letting nature enter inside the courtyards; the new complex comes out of a cognitive re-reading of archetypal forms and like a modern *Goseck circle*, takes the observer back to images of ancient settlements, moving the project toward pure, primordial architectures and toward a primitive future.

LIMEN

Limen in Latin means *limit*, but also *threshold*, *entrance*. The project designs constructed borders, which are not created to separate, but to create a series of settings, or variable scenes, that change according to one's position, generating spaces for connections and opportunities. The houses, joined by a continuous glass strip that reflects the natural surroundings, make up open and fluid courtyards, designing a place able to multiply human passions; the line of dwellings describes an appropriate space that accompanies the flow of nature, creating social stages for the life of man. The new architectures look for dialog between nature, the pre-existing structures and new signs, that willingly interrupt themselves giving an unfinished, or infinite, sensation, entering therefore in a strong relationship with Nature. That which is born as limit becomes the crux between private and collective spaces, defining two different but continuous external places; the border is indistinct.

LIVING IDENTITY

The first reaction that the new settlement aims to promote is to link collectivity with the place it populated, facilitating a sense of belonging for the inhabitants in the existing neighborhoods and then for who will live in the new settlement. This is the first objective that the neighborhood poses, using places like Port Arthur, Mantymaki and Marrti as inspiration, where spaces aided socialization between people, increasing a sense of public spirit and the pleasure of living.

Semi-aerial view

500 m
100
50
0

Site plan

N

blurred *borders*

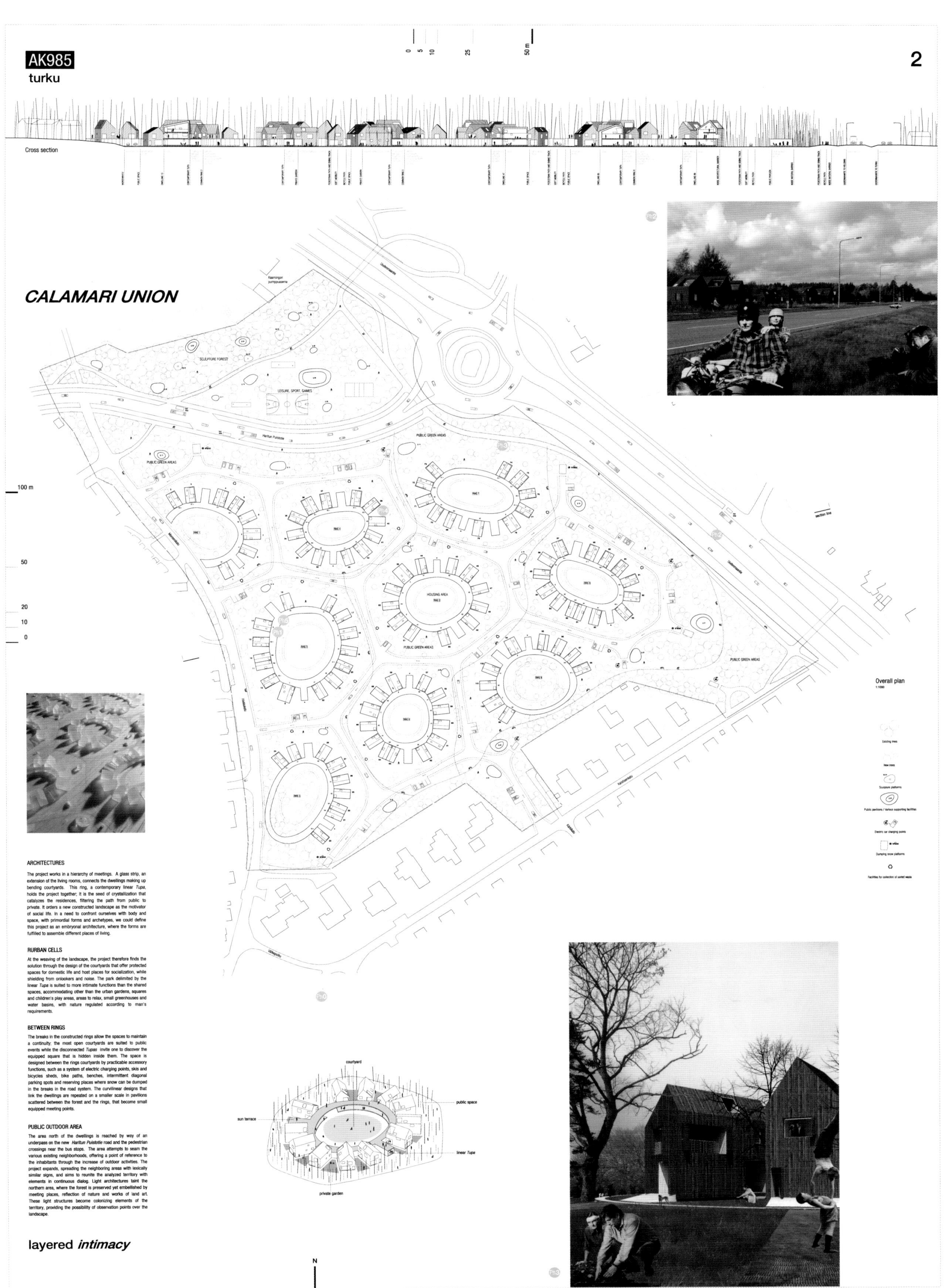
AK985
turku
2
0
5
10
25
50 m
Cross section
CALAMARI UNION
SCULPTURE FOREST
LEISURE, SPORT, GAMES
PUBLIC GREEN AREAS
HOUSING AREA
section line
100 m
50
20
10
0
Overall plan
1:1000
Existing trees
New trees
Sculpture platforms
Public pavilions / Various supporting facilities
Electric car charging points
Dumping snow platforms
Facilities for collection of sorted waste
ARCHITECTURES
The project works in a hierarchy of meetings. A glass strip, an extension of the living rooms, connects the dwellings making up bending courtyards. This ring, a contemporary linear *Tupa*, holds the project together; it is the seed of crystallization that catalyzes the residences, filtering the path from public to private. It orders a new constructed landscape as the motivator of social life. In a need to confront ourselves with body and space, with primordial forms and archetypes, we could define this project as an embryonal architecture, where the forms are fulfilled to assemble different places of living.
RURBAN CELLS
At the weaving of the landscape, the project therefore finds the solution through the design of the courtyards that offer protected spaces for domestic life and host places for socialization, while shielding from onlookers and noise. The park delimited by the linear *Tupa* is suited to more intimate functions than the shared spaces, accommodating other than the urban gardens, squares and children's play areas, areas to relax, small greenhouses and water basins, with nature regulated according to man's requirements.
BETWEEN RINGS
The breaks in the constructed rings allow the spaces to maintain a continuity; the most open courtyards are suited to public events while the disconnected *Tupas* invite one to discover the equipped square that is hidden inside them. The space is designed between the rings courtyards by practicable accessory functions, such as a system of electric charging points, skis and bicycles sheds, bike paths, benches, intermittent diagonal parking spots and reserving places where snow can be dumped in the breaks in the road system. The curvilinear designs that link the dwellings are repeated on a smaller scale in pavilions scattered between the forest and the rings, that become small equipped meeting points.
PUBLIC OUTDOOR AREA
The area north of the dwellings is reached by way of an underpass on the new *Haritun Puistotie* road and the pedestrian crossings near the bus stops. The area attempts to seam the various existing neighborhoods, offering a point of reference to the inhabitants through the increase of outdoor activities. The project expands, spreading the neighboring areas with lexically similar signs, and aims to reunite the analyzed territory with elements in continuous dialog. Light architectures taint the northern area, where the forest is preserved yet embellished by meeting places, reflection of nature and works of land art. These light structures become colonizing elements of the territory, providing the possibility of observation points over the landscape.
layered *intimacy*
courtyard
public space
sun terrace
linear *Tupa*
private garden
N

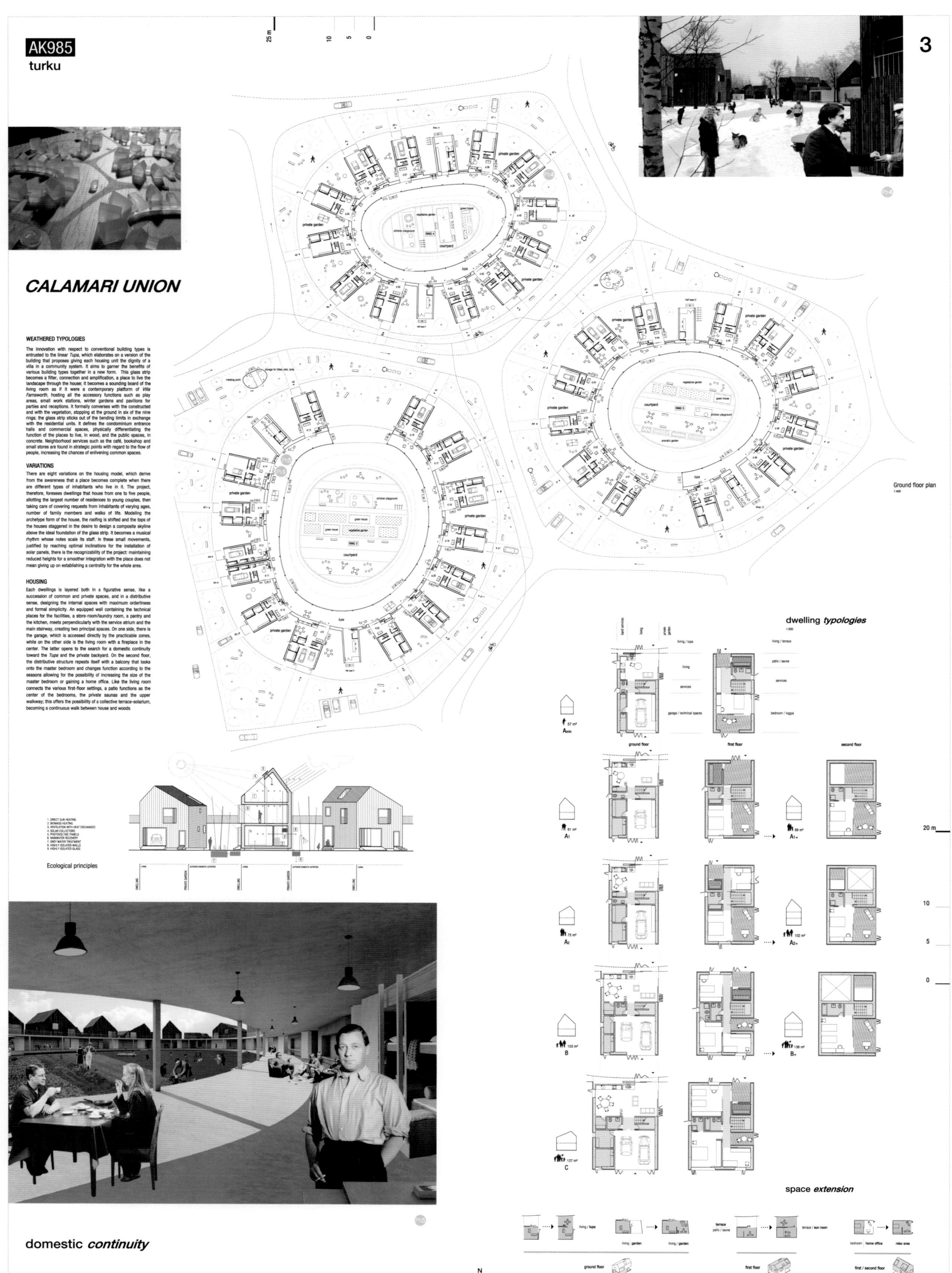
AK985
turku
3
CALAMARI UNION
WEATHERED TYPOLOGIES
The innovation with respect to conventional building types is entrusted to the linear *Tupa*, which elaborates on a version of the building that proposes giving each housing unit the dignity of a villa in a community system. It aims to garner the benefits of various building types together in a new form. This glass strip becomes a filter, connection and amplification, a place to live the landscape through the house; it becomes a sounding board of the living room as if it were a contemporary platform of *Villa Farnsworth*, hosting all the accessory functions such as play areas, small work stations, winter gardens and pavilions for parties and receptions. It formally converses with the constructed and with the vegetation, stopping at the ground in six of the nine rings; the glass strip sticks out of the bending limits in exchange with the residential units. It defines the condominium entrance halls and commercial spaces, physically differentiating the function of the places to live, in wood, and the public spaces, in concrete. Neighborhood services such as the café, bookshop and small stores are found in strategic points with regard to the flow of people, increasing the chances of enlivening common spaces.
VARIATIONS
There are eight variations on the housing model, which derive from the awareness that a place becomes complete when there are different types of inhabitants who live in it. The project, therefore, foresees dwellings that house from one to five people, allotting the largest number of residences to young couples, then taking care of covering requests from inhabitants of varying ages, number of family members and walks of life. Modeling the archetype form of the house, the roofing is shifted and the tops of the houses staggered in the desire to design a composite skyline above the ideal foundation of the glass strip. It becomes a musical rhythm whose notes scale its staff. In these small movements, justified by reaching optimal inclinations for the installation of solar panels, there is the recognizability of the project: maintaining reduced heights for a smoother integration with the place does not mean giving up on establishing a centrality for the whole area.
HOUSING
Each dwellings is layered both in a figurative sense, like a succession of common and private spaces, and in a distributive sense, designing the internal spaces with maximum orderliness and formal simplicity. An equipped wall containing the technical places for the facilities, a store-room/laundry room, a pantry and the kitchen, meets perpendicularly with the service atrium and the main stairway, creating two principal spaces. On one side, there is the garage, which is accessed directly by the practicable zones, while on the other side is the living room with a fireplace in the center. The latter opens to the search for a domestic continuity toward the *Tupa* and the private backyard. On the second floor, the distributive structure repeats itself with a balcony that looks onto the master bedroom and changes function according to the seasons allowing for the possibility of increasing the size of the master bedroom or gaining a home office. Like the living room connects the various first-floor settings, a patio functions as the center of the bedrooms, the private saunas and the upper walkway; this offers the possibility of a collective terrace-solarium, becoming a continuous walk between house and woods
25 m
10
5
0
private garden
courtyard
Ground floor plan
Ecological principles
dwelling *typologies*
ground floor
first floor
second floor
A1
A1+
A2
A2+
B
B+
C
20 m
10
5
0
space *extension*
domestic *continuity*
N

Floating Clouds | *2A+P/A*

Type : International Ideas Competition "Europan10"
Program : Urban planning
Project : 2A+P/A, Angelo Grasso
Location : Dunkerque, Francia

PP219
Dunkerque

FLOATING CLOUDS I 01

DUNKERQUE'S ATTRACTIONS

Port area
Industrial area
Museum boat
Cathedral
Storage
University
Light tower
Boat basin
Central square
Waterfront
Stadium
Rail station
Shopping mall
Historic tower
Beach
River station
Ferry boat
Museum
Theatre
Leisure pier

DUNKERQUE TOURIST MAP

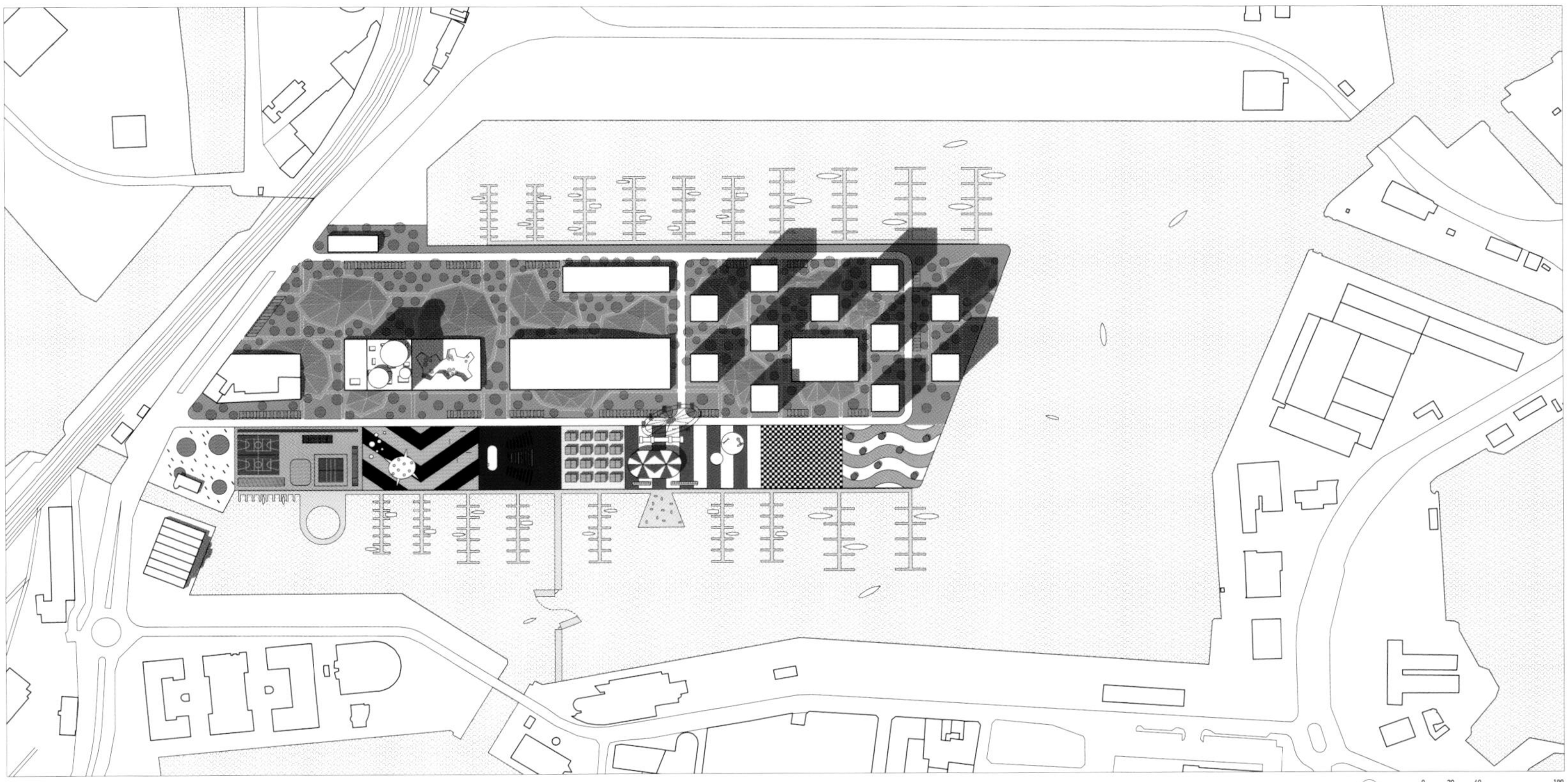

1.10000 0 100 200 500

MASTERPLAN

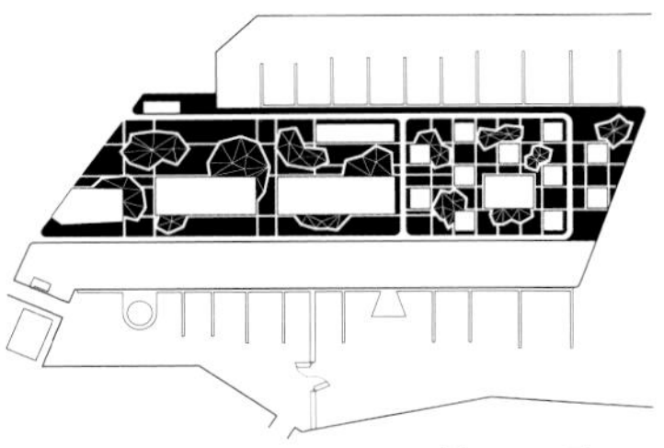

1.2000 0 20 40 100

GROUNDS
Natural
Artificial

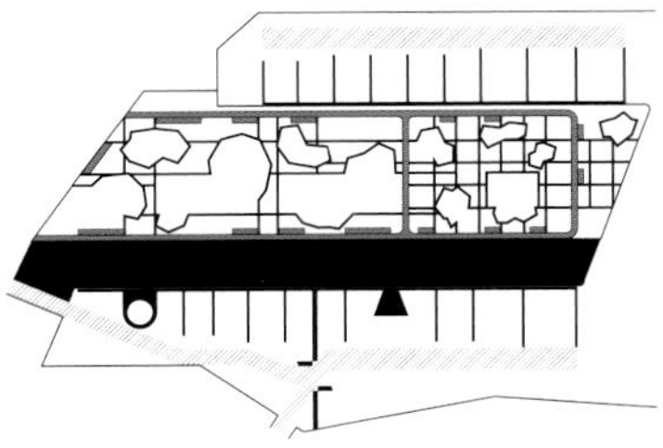

MOBILITY
Pedestrian
Driveway
Waterway

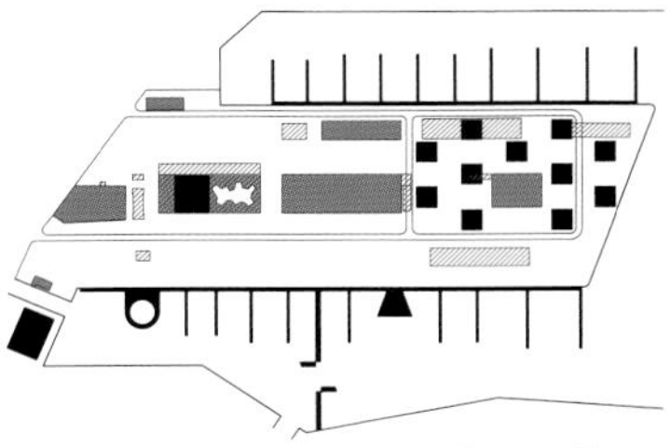

BUILDINGS
Exist
New
Demolish

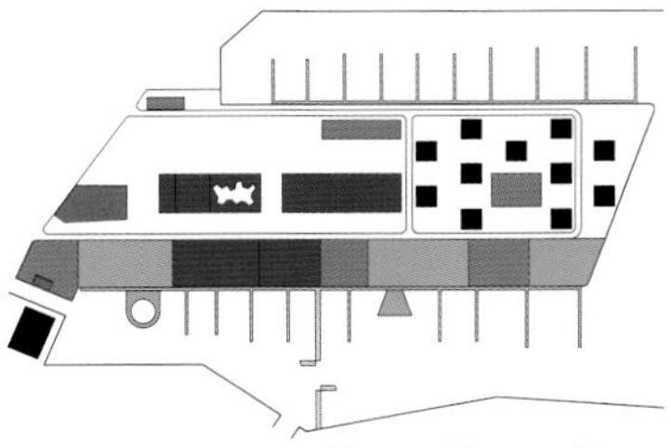

FUNCTIONS
Residential
Recreational
Cultural
Facilities
Receptive

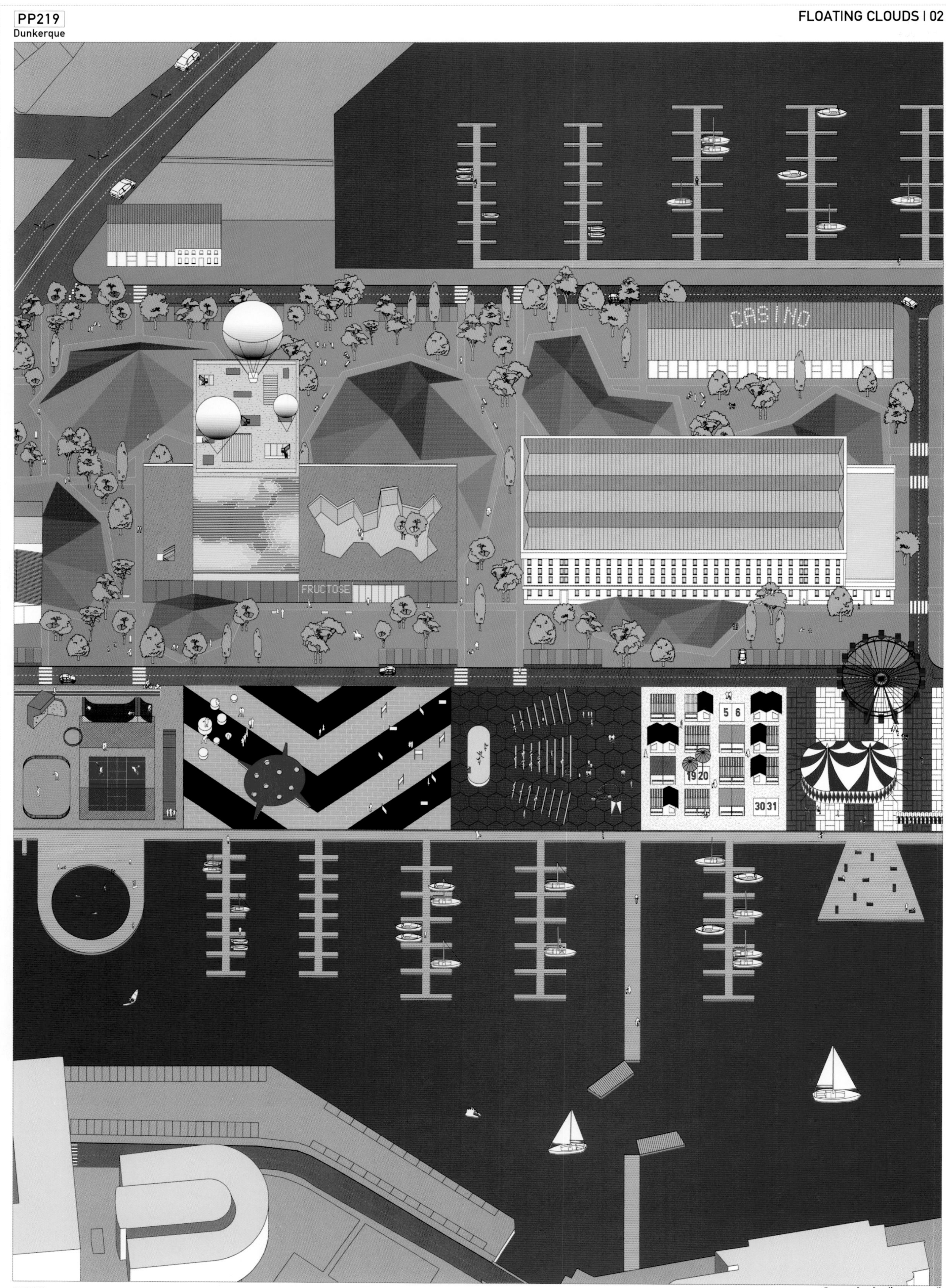
PP219
Dunkerque
FLOATING CLOUDS | 02
CASINO
FRUCTOSE
5 6
19 20
30 31
AXONOMETRI
1:500

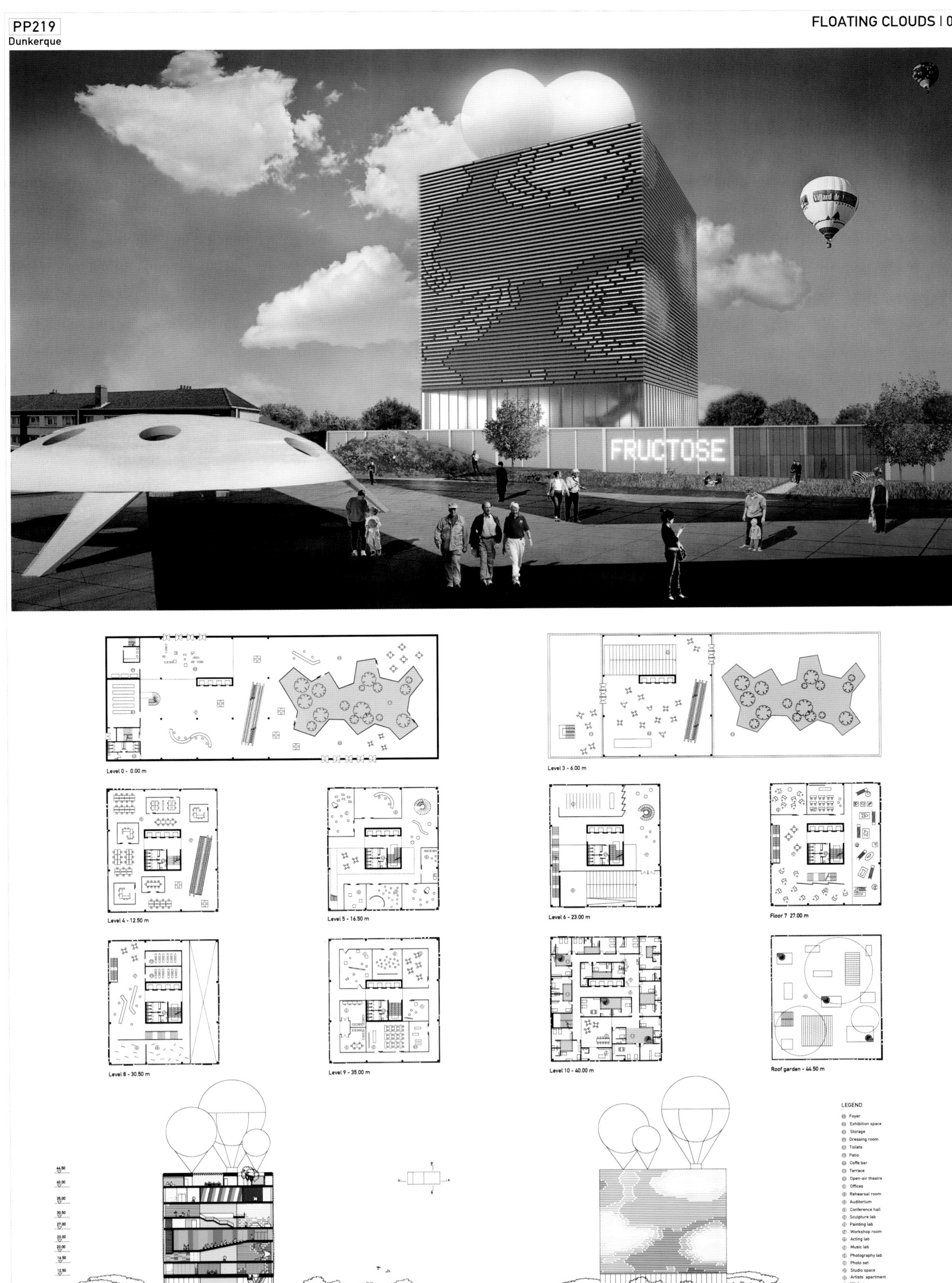
PP219
Dunkerque
FLOATING CLOUDS | 03
FRUCTOSE
Level 0 - 0.00 m
Level 3 - 6.00 m
Level 4 - 12.50 m
Level 5 - 16.50 m
Level 6 - 23.00 m
Floor 7 27.00 m
Level 8 - 30.50 m
Level 9 - 35.00 m
Level 10 - 40.00 m
Roof garden - 44.50 m
Section AA'
Section BB'
LEGEND
Foyer
Exhibition space
Storage
Dressing room
Toilets
Patio
Coffe bar
Terrace
Open-air theatre
Offices
Rehearsal room
Auditorium
Conference hall
Sculpture lab
Painting lab
Workshop room
Acting lab
Music lab
Photography lab
Photo set
Studio space
Artists' apartment
Kitchen
Sharing space
Roof garden
1:500
0 5 10 25

070

Austria | *2:pm architectures*

Project : European Urbanism Competition
Location : Graz, Austria
Design Team : 2:pm architectures + L. Brenterc'h(arch) + N. Van Bever(Landscape designer)
Competition Results : Jury Phase 2

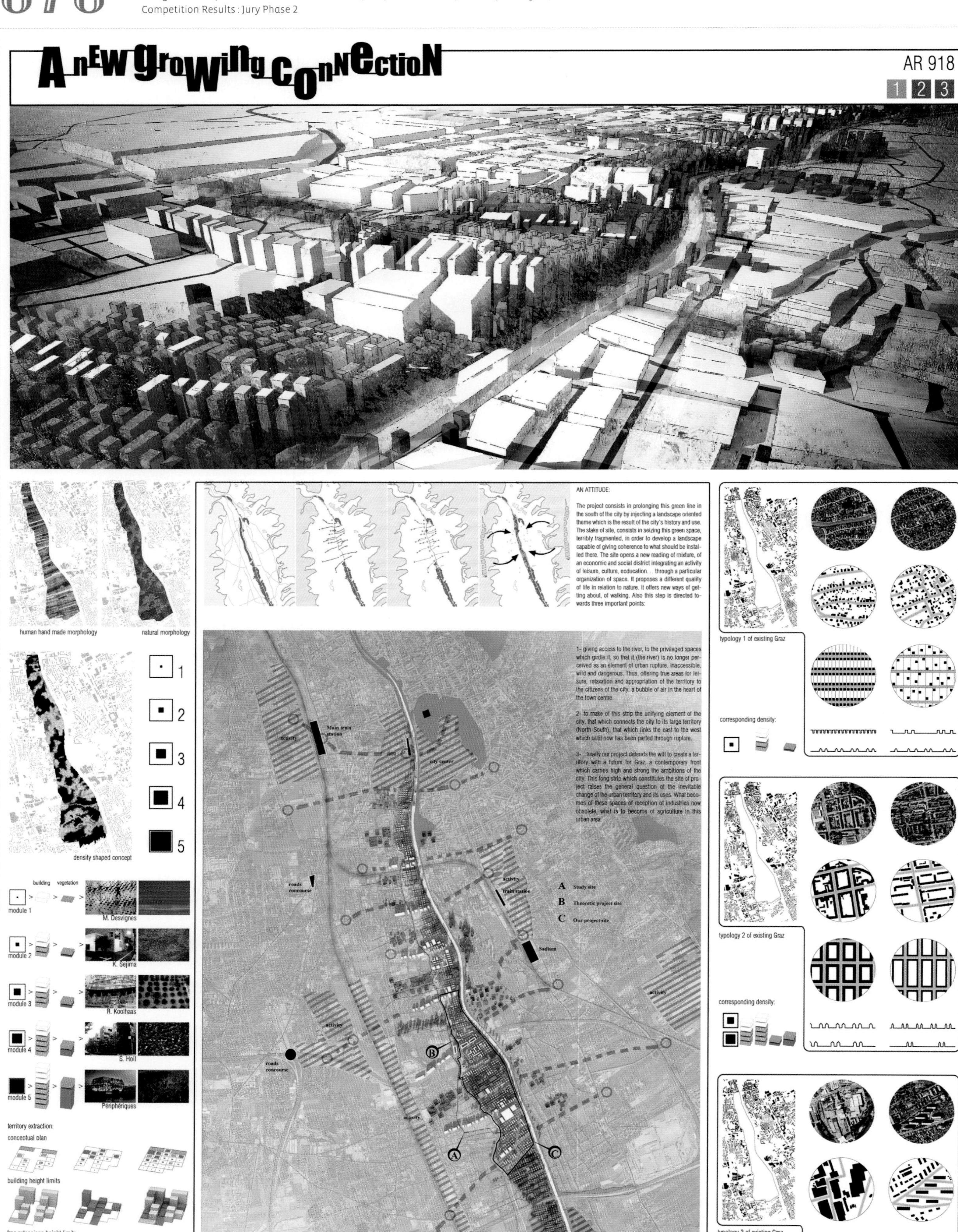

A new growing connection

AR 918

A - Take care of the landscape by creating new sports areas and walking ways
B - Densify the actual housing areas with new environementals housing
C - Little compagny and group housing
D - Kept the actual activity of the building on 1/3 of the building
Transform one part of the actuel building to a new office building
E - Head center of office buildings connect to the airport and the city center by the tramway
F - Densify the actual housing areas with new environementals housing
G - Sport and leisure areas
H - new housing and group housing
I - Office and activity center
J - Main park with public building
K - new housing and group housing
L - new housing and group housing
M - Office and activity center
N - little center and cultural building near the river
O - Little center
P - new housing and group housing area

bati_entrerpises
85 060 M² SHOB
85 060 M² X 0.9 X 1 = 78 500 SHON

bati_connerces
11 740 M² SHOB
11 740 M² X 0.9 X 3 = 31 690 SHON

scale 1.300e

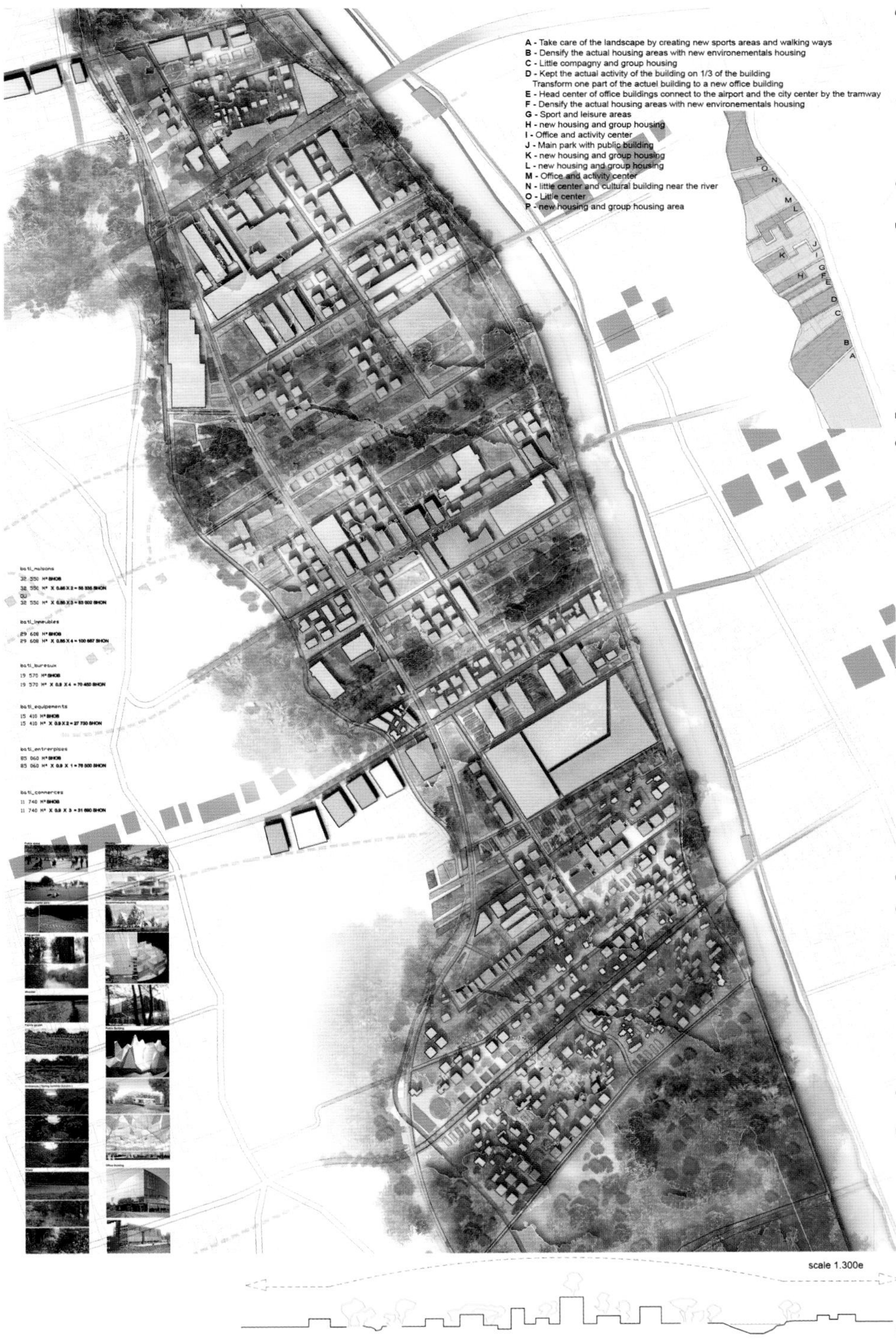

CONSERVATION - CONSTRUCTION

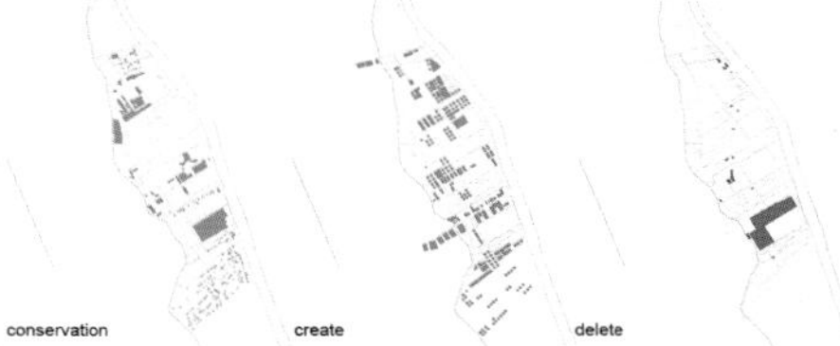

conservation — create — delete

Area DEVELOPMENT
The opposition city/nature is on its way to being resolved. Solidarity between urban and rural, between intensity and diffuse town planning, is henceforth essential when thinking of the shape of the future cities. The play of transposition of natural elements creates another reality, of a mass and of important shapes, reassuring, which gives scene to void. By constructing small dense islands, induced by the natural configuration of the site, it is possible to give the territory an image that everyone can understand and a coherent physical presence, also taking into account the infrastructures, for eminently urban uses. The development of a new urban ensemble of intermediate scale seeks new proximities between both the habitat and the workplace, between city and nature, between production and consumption... The reinforcement of the existing poles such as certain historical centres, poles of activities, heavy infrastructures, forests or parks calls for the adapted development of the intermediate zones in their specific qualities: flexibility, mixture of the functions between residential habitat, schools, small businesses and local services.

URBAN PLANNING - PROGRAM

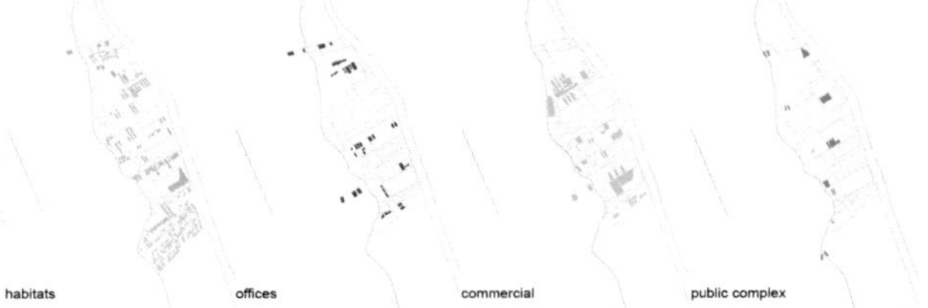

habitats — offices — commercial — public complex

CADASTRAL - CONNEXION

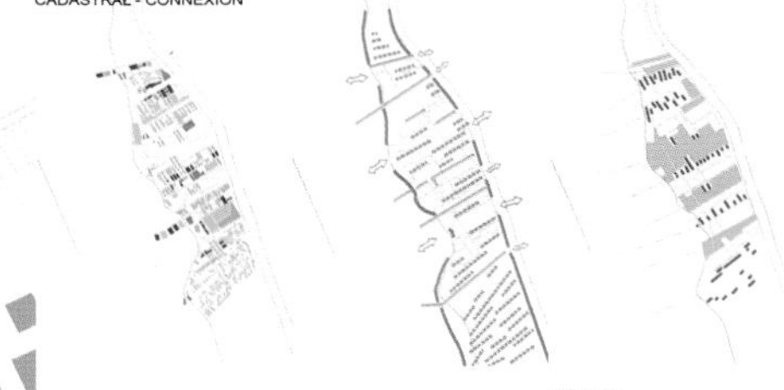

Through a process which borrows an urban form belonging to Graz. It reveals two identity fragments of territory of the mountain and the plain being able to support a new installation. Besides these organic qualities this extract develops a form which allows strong urban polarities (full) and permeabilities (empty) in order to recreate the physical bonds of landscape in the East-West direction, to connect the various districts of the city. Translated into pixel plan, this fragment creates the city. In black; strong urban densities structured by the more important, higher buildings, in white; the voids which are the lungs of the city, the weak densities. The entire unit is irrigated and related to its environment by the screen viaire. The pixel itself is a measuring unit, a scale of territory equivalent to a house or a tree of great size.

TRAFFIC

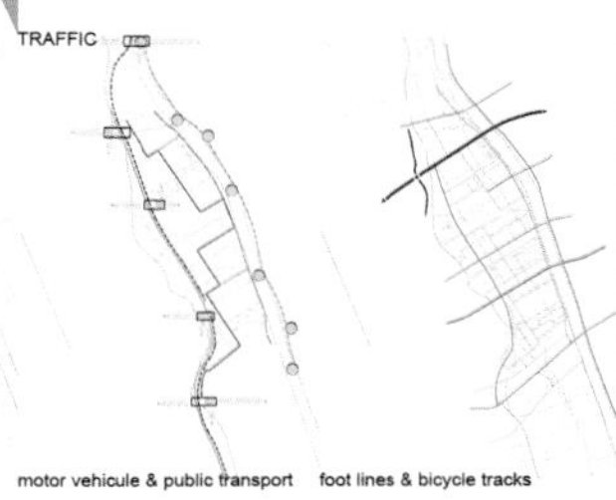

motor vehicule & public transport — foot lines & bicycle tracks

CIRCULATIONS
This neighborhood opens a new mixture of live and uses. This coexistence also brings several urban systems; some controlled by public transport, others governed by the car, others still structured by the softer modes. It must also take into account the speed at which the urbanization phenomenon operates as well as the existing characteristics of urban infrastructure and the existing appropriateness of the ecological area. As much as the intense poles must be connected to each other by a fast, effective and reliable, primarily public, transport network, as much as it is also important that the light city implies more personalized means.

The project seeks a hierarchy of the uses compared to the different sectors. Therefore, the poles of activities generate knots, where the various systems meet; points of articulation of the various modes of transport, the passing of one speed with another, and thus from one time space to another. Places of centrality and intensity connecting itself to the city. On its entirety, the site accommodates several car park silos, distributed according to the needs of the different sectors. The concept of sustainable development is considered here by the anticipation of future different uses. These buildings are thus dimensioned so as to be reusable as future dwellings or offices without requiring any considerable work. In addition, the current railroad is rehabilitated in the form of tramway connecting the town centre to the airport. It therefore offers public transport making it possible to distribute the site, and to open up to the city.
Effects of proximity created by strong densities and the mixture of uses, enhance the possible improvement concerning the efficiency of energy of the buildings and the movement towards an urban mobility based on walking, the use of bicycles and public transport and the high consumption of natural resources are essential components of any strategy aiming at dissociating a high standard of living. The site brings a strategy of transition for individual transport by allowing a restoration of the public domain; more greenery, widener pavements, paths ways, cycle tracks... Also, bicycles could be at disposal of the walkers and of the inhabitants, though a system of hiring, with the possibility of returning them to another station and of connecting them to other transport networks, interfaces allowing one to continue their journey be train, bus, way river shuttle... Therefore the site supports short, local travel not exceeding 10 minutes either in public transport, by bicycle, or on foot.

GREEN AREA

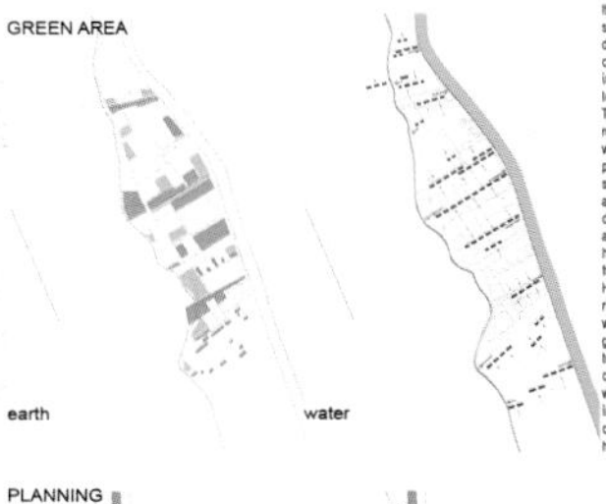

earth — water

LANDSCAPE
It is a city park. The landscape quality of the place is made after an identification of the territory in all its dimensions, in order to benefit from its riches, and to stimulate them in the project. To extend the forest, to exploit and direct the city towards it; the continuity of natural space in south Graz becomes a major asset ensuring the green continuity of the linen. The project seeks thus, the means of preserving the heritage of this site, making it durable in the long run. This site therefore becomes more than a new neighborhood but becomes a new destination of leisure for its population.
This part taken from the vegetation intervention of the site it is not only an aesthetic measure, but is used to reduce for example, the degree of impermeability of the grounds, thus allowing direct evacuation of surface water, in particular for the strong polarities. In addition, it filters, the particles of suspended dust in the air, and prevents the formation of thermal small islands above dense spaces. It initially acts to understand that it, on the scale of a vast territory, the coexistence of these many essences present different textures, very different colors and matters, possesses coherence, and their concentration in a more reduced place becomes relatively more delicate. The work consists of a selection operated in a list proposed by our landscape designer, the selection allowing the consideration of transitions in order for the entity to be readable. Trees of various sizes, shrubs, the herbaceous, tree ferns etc follow a composition in order to carve out the vegetable mass layer by layer, starting from the cartography of the general site.
However, the Wall also generates a break between the Western bank and the Eastern bank. These visual, sensory ruptures and symbolic systems in relation to the river were underlined by the intervention of Vito Vicconci wishing regain a new reading through an "architectural island ". Observing this territory under the glance of the geography and its history shows how this strong landscape unit connects the local scale with that of the large territory. Graz is grafted on the "Mur , river artery offering a true natural band which penetrates the middle of the city. It allows to link external activities in a feeling of proximity with the landscape. Access to the river edge, rich with varied wild flora and fauna, makes it possible to discover the nature of the Wall. The project refits the banks in a long public space. This promenade along the river opens in rhythm on the park, and various attractions, cultural, leisure and relaxing points and playgrounds, organized around small shops, such as restaurants, refreshment bar...

PLANNING

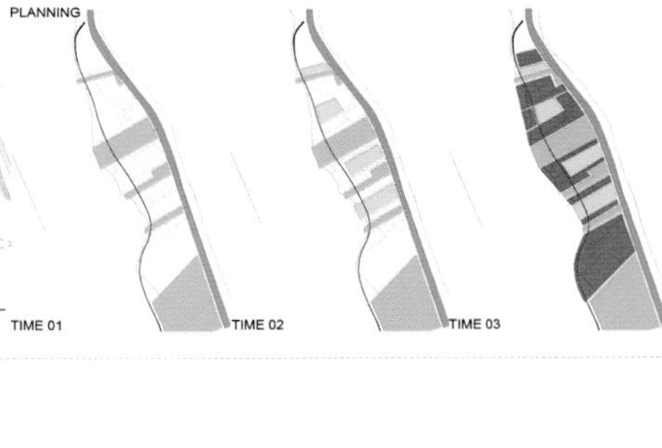

TIME 01 — TIME 02 — TIME 03

Our work on this typically industrial object is done in 4 phases:

01. Connect the forest and the city center with new walking way and cycle track

02. Create new public park to open the view between the montain and the lowland

03. Create en Tram line to connect the airport and the new small center to the city center

04. Transformation of lands to new urban areas

05. Complete the local buildings by new environmental's buildings

A new growing connection

AR 918

1 2 3

landscape study

volume section _ 1/1000

plan _ 1/1000

section _ 1/1000

dwellings study

volume section _ 1/1000

plans _ 1/1000

offices study

volume sections _ 1/1000

plans _ 1/1000

existing greenhouse re-use study > market place

volume section _ 1/1000

plans _ 1/1000

France_3 | *2:pm architectures*

Project : European Urbanism Competition
Location : Savenay, France
Design Team : 2:pm architectures + S. Baudry, C. Chauvet, E. Chaparro, F. Chagny, E. Perret(arch)
Competition Results : waiting for results(January 2012)

AE983
SAVENAY

PERMACITY

1

Espaces verts et agriculture : La commune de Savenay est située dans un vaste écrin agricole et forestier. Si la ville tend à se développer au sud des rails, pourquoi le paysage ne tendrait pas à se développer vers le nord ? N'imperméabilisons aucun nouveaux sols et implantons-nous uniquement sur la zone d'activité existante. Le grand paysage entre alors en résistance. Il s'étendra dans le futur quartier.

Hydrographie : Zone inondable. Il est nécessaire d'étirer les systèmes de gestion des eaux qui entourent les champs bordant l'estuaire de la Loire dans le nouveau quartier. Ces noues feront par ailleurs partie intégrante du cadre de vie offert aux habitants, produisant leurs propres faune et flore.

Pôles attractifs et circulations douces : L'estuaire de la Loire est à seulement quelques km de Savenay et n'est pourtant pas accessible facilement. Il est possible d'ouvrir la ville vers ce paysage singulier par le biais de circulations douces, de promenades (20 min en vélo, 1 h à pied). Un franchissement au dessus des voies ferrées assurera la liaison entre le vieux centre, le nouveau quartier et l'estuaire.

Réseau ferré et réseau routier : Véritable balafre territoriale, les voies ferrée ne sont franchissables qu'aux extrémités de la zone d'étude. Il est aujourd'hui primordiale de les franchir au cœur de la ville. Les boulevards Branly et Pasteur deviendront un boulevard urbain à la fois capable de drainer les flux d'une départementale fréquentée, et de révéler une véritable place pour les piétons et les cyclistes.

Vues et perspectives dominantes : La cohésion entre vieille ville et nouveau quartier passera en partie par la topographie du site. Elle permet une relation visuelle étroite entre le grand paysage au sud et le clocher de l'église au nord, véritable icône géographique. Nous conserverons les perspectives vers l'estuaire, et en offrirons de nouvelles vers la ville haute.

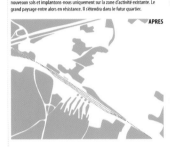

IGN 2019

Plan masse - 1/2000

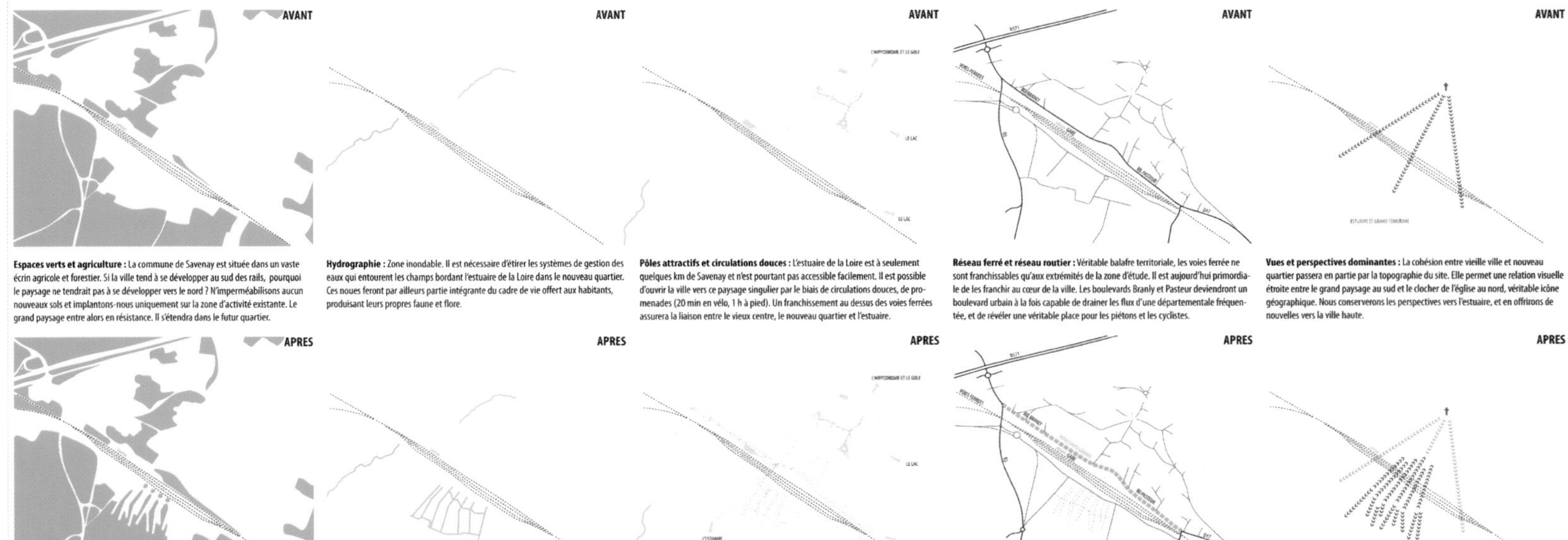

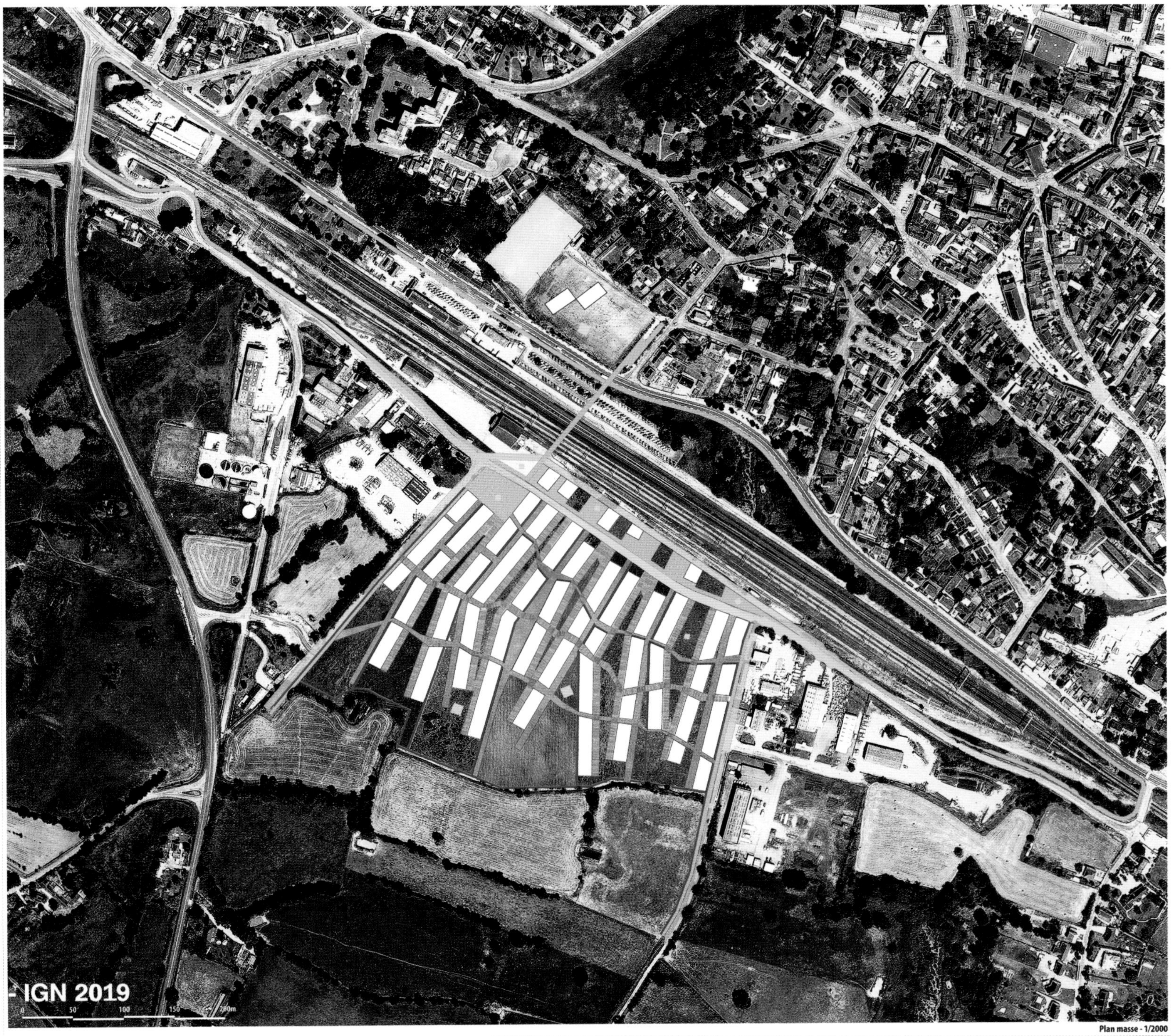

AE983
SAVENAY

PERMACITY

2

Une des deux venelles piétonnes transversales et sa noue

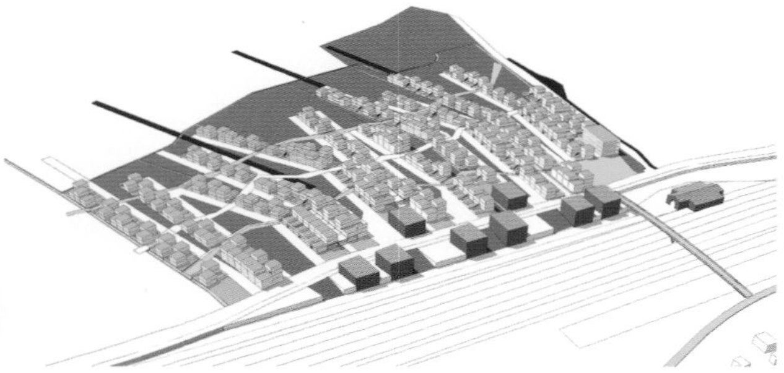

Le front bâti du nouveau quartier dialogue avec les voies ferrées et la vieille ville.

7

Coupe sur une rue paysagère

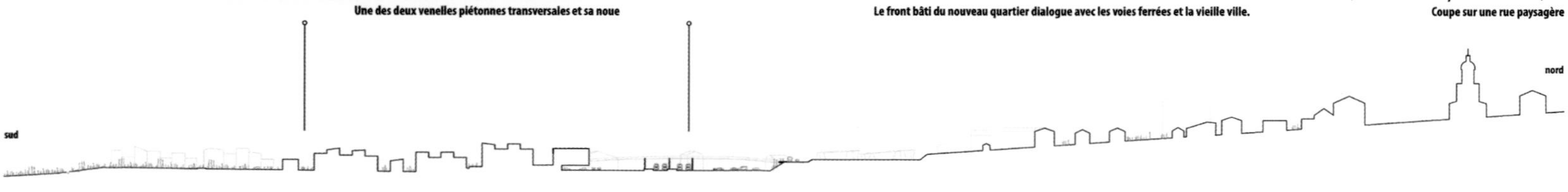

sud

nord

Coupe longitudinale - 1/1500

Le grand paysage s'insère entre les lanières.

5 2

Coupe sur une venelle piétonne et sa noue

Une venelle piétonne et sa noue

est

ouest

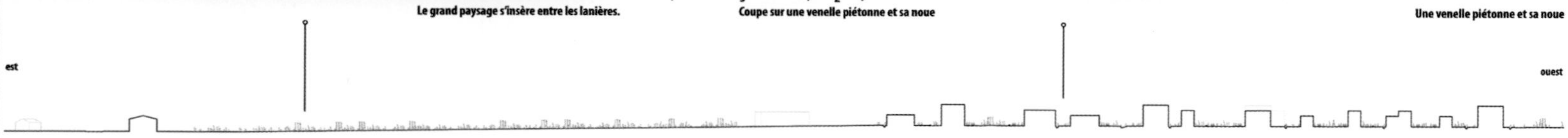

Coupe transversale - 1/1500

Vue générale du nouveau quartier - dialogue avec la ville existante

AE983 SAVENAY

PERMACITY

3

Maison individuelle standard

Maison individuelle périphérie centre ville Savenay

Maison individuelle centre ville Savenay

Maison individuelle groupée Savenay + son espace public partagé

De l'habitat consommateur d'espace à l'habitat *permanent*

	centre ville savenay logement/habitant projet 100 personnes 54 logements 100 personnes	perma-city savenay logement/habitant 40 logements 100 personnes	repartitions première phase (2014) 200 logements 500 personnes	
	16.5 T3, 26 T2, 1.6 T6, 4 T5, 5.6 T4	12 T3, 8 T2, 4 T6, 8 T5, 8 T4	60 T3, 40 T2, 20 T6, 40T5, 40 T4	
T2	26 personnes vivent seules dans 26 T2	8 personnes vivent seules dans 8 T2	total : 40 collectif : 40	50 m² + 12.5m²
T3	33 personnes vivent à 2 dans 16.5 T3	24 personnes vivent à 2 dans 12 T3	total : 60 collectif : 30 individuel : 30	62.5m² + 12.5m²
T4	17 personnes vivent à 3 dans 5.6 T4	24 personnes vivent à 3 dans 8 T4	total : 40 collectif : 20 individuel : 20	75m² + 12.5m²
T5	16 personnes vivent à 4 dans 4 T5	32 personnes vivent à 4 dans 8 T5	total : 40 collectif : 20 individuel : 20	87.5m² + 12.5m²
T6	8 personnes vivent à 5 ou + 1.6 T5 ou +	20 personnes vivent à 5 ou + 4 T5 ou +	total : 20 collectif : 10 individuel : 10	100m² + 12.5m²

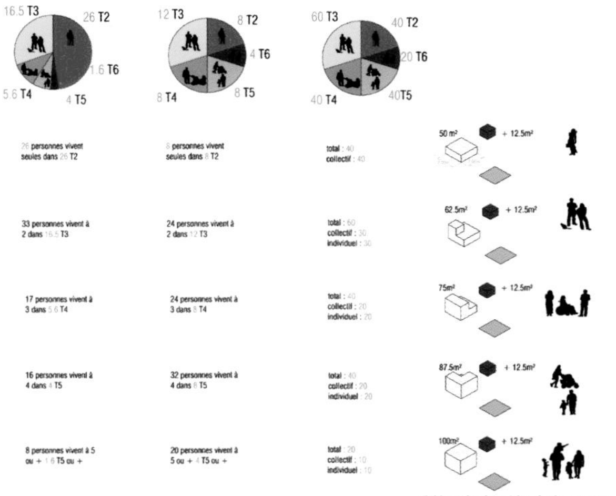

Tableau de répartition des logements

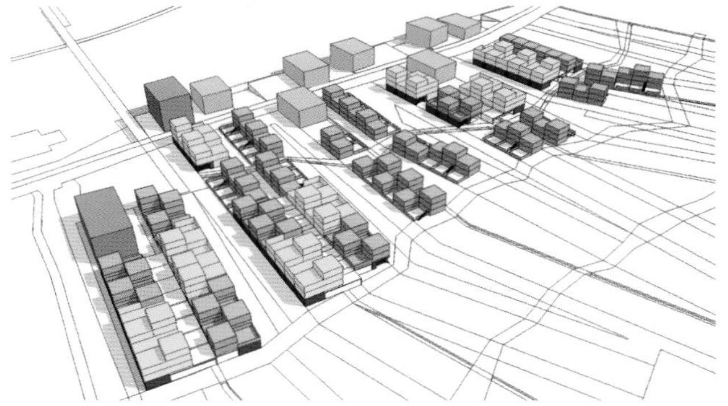

Bureaux - 5000m²

Siège de la Communauté des communes Loire et Sillon - 1200m²

Multi-accueils de la petite enfance - 1000m²

Logements individuels et individuels groupés - 6125m²

Logements collectifs - 8125m²

Commerces et « pièces en plus » - 2500m²

Répartition programmatique

Parcelle à urbaniser en première phase

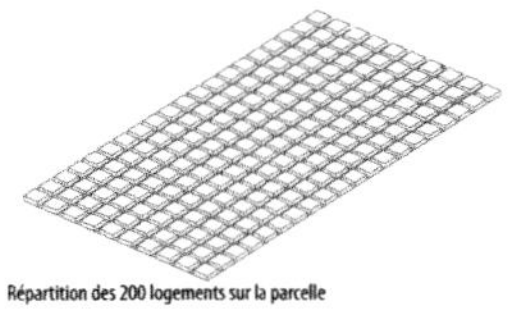

Répartition des 200 logements sur la parcelle

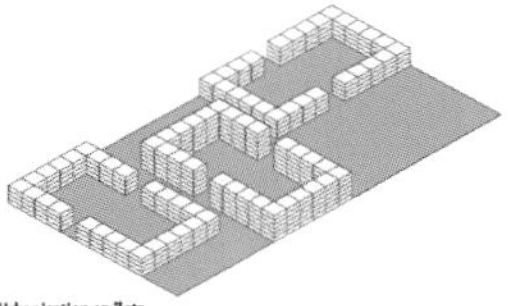

Urbanisation en îlots

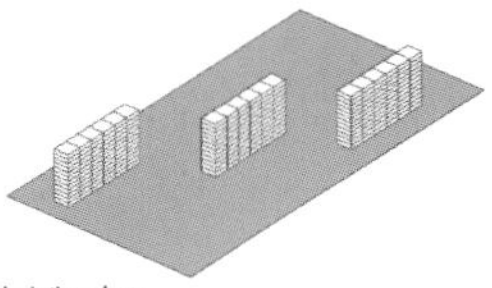

Urbanisation en barre

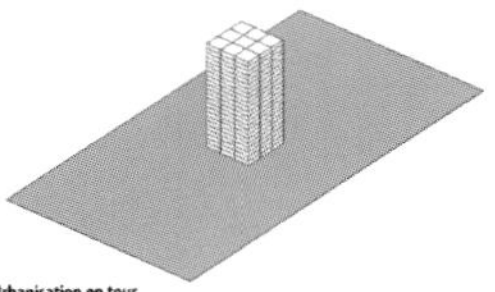

Urbanisation en tour

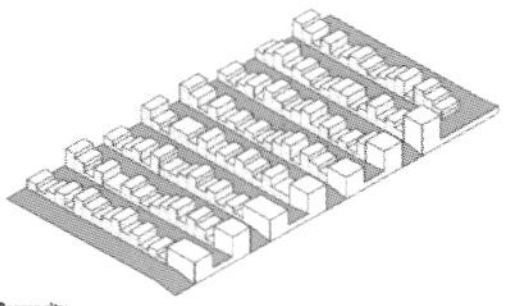

Permacity

sur rue

sur venelle

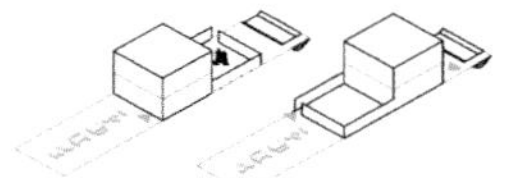

Logements individuels accollés

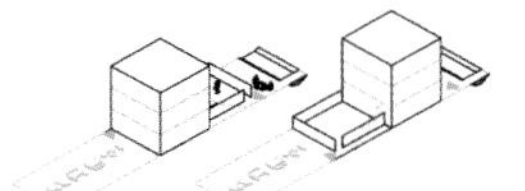

Logements individuels superposés

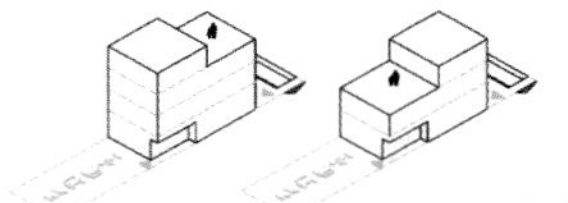

Logements collectifs intermédiaires

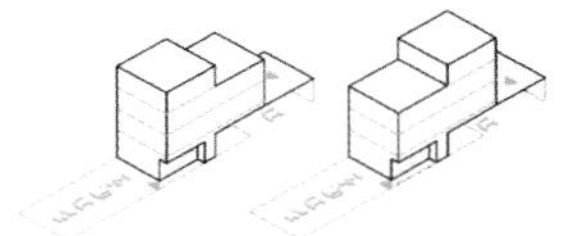

Logements individuels accollés ou superposés sur parking

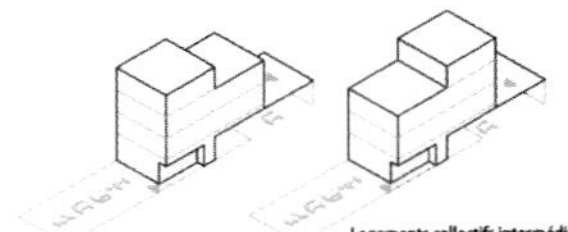

Logements collectifs intermédiaires sur parking

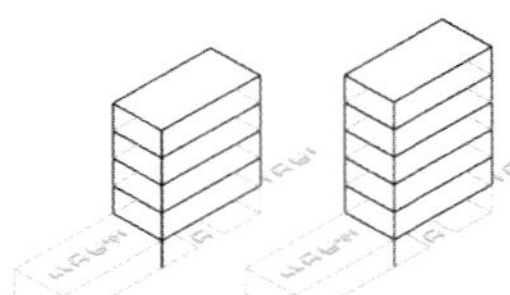

Tertiaire - équipement sur parking

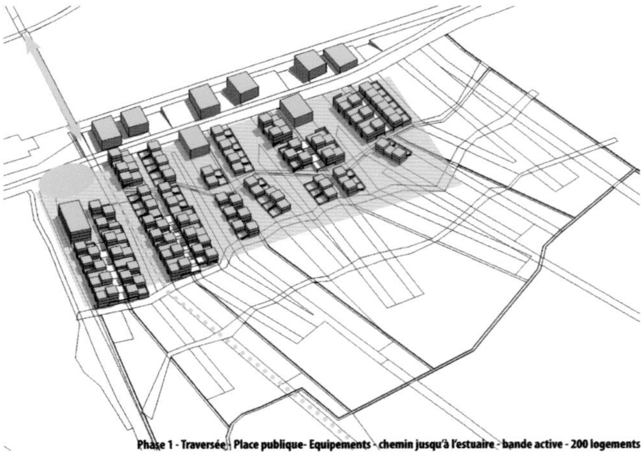

Phase 1 - Traversée - Place publique - Equipements - chemin jusqu'à l'estuaire - bande active - 200 logements

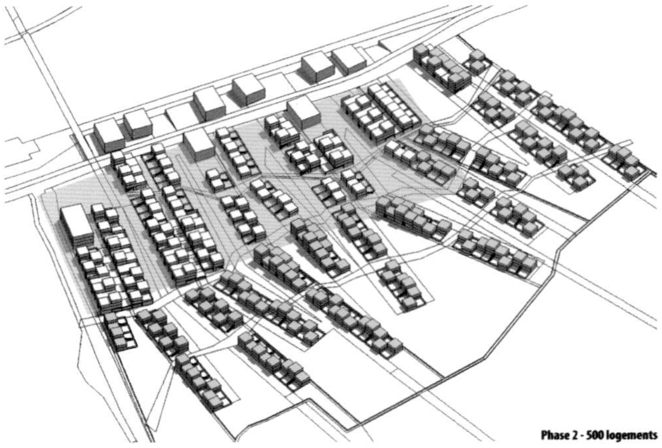

Phase 2 - 500 logements

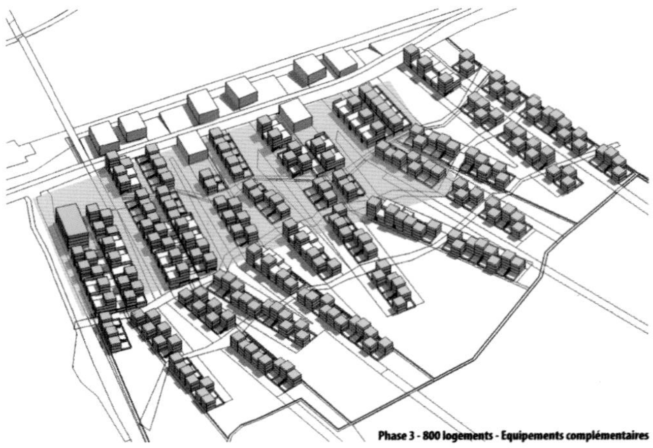

Phase 3 - 800 logements - Equipements complémentaires

072 Green City Graz | *BKK-3*

Location : Graz, Austria
Architecture competition for a landscape garden / housing development 2011
Team : Franz Sumnitsch, Ondrej Chybik, Michal Kristof, Matej Strba, Frank Schilder

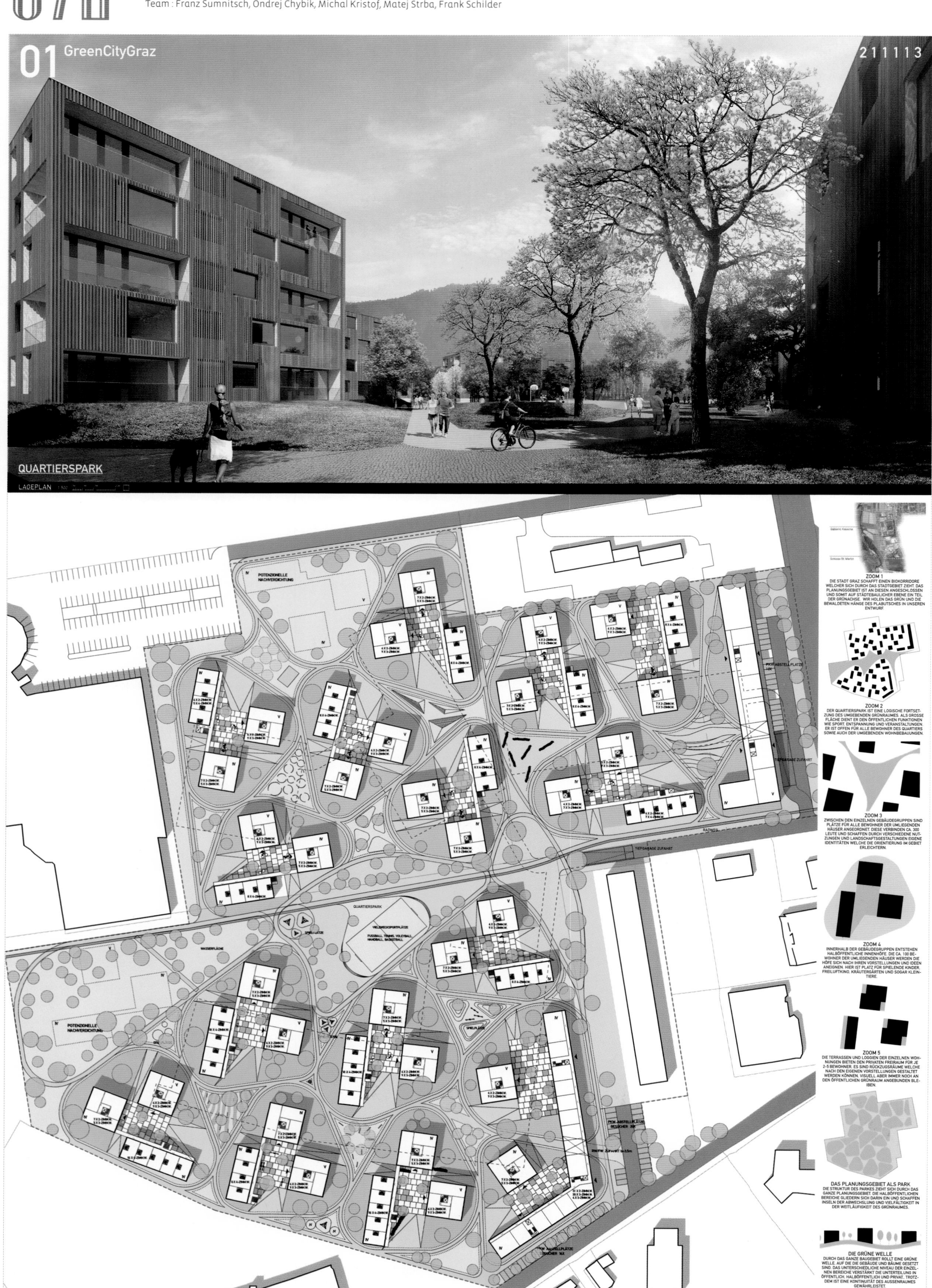

04 GreenCityGraz

211113

WOHNZIMMER

UMWELT

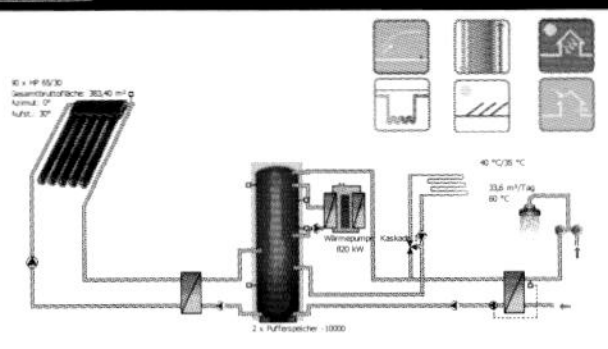

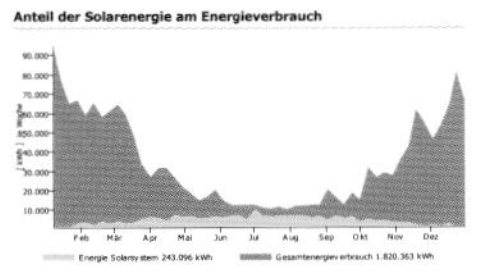

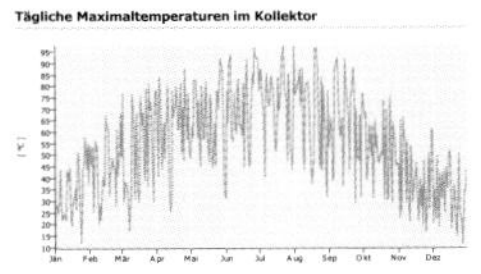

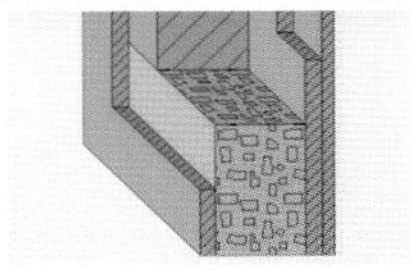

Masse	133,9 kg/m²
$OI3_{KON}$	-31 Pkt/m²
PEI n. e.	166,91 MJ/m²
GWP100	-77,0806 kg CO_2/m²
AP	0,093986 kg SO_2/m²

MATERIALIEN

DIE VERWENDETEN BAUSTOFFE WERDEN NACH RÜCKBAUBARKEIT UND WIEDERVERWERTBARKEIT AUSGESUCHT. DAS FÜR PRODUKTION, TRANSPORT UND RÜCKBAU VERBRAUCHTE CO2 SOLLTE SO GERING WIE MÖGLICH GEHALTEN WERDEN. GEACHTET WIRD AUCH AUF DIE TRENNUNG VON SYSTEMEN MIT UNTERSCHIEDLICHER LEBENSDAUER.

Ergebnisse der Jahressimulation

Installierte Kollektorleistung:	268,38 kW	
Installierte Kollektorfläche (Brutto):	383,4 m²	
Einstrahlung Kollektorfläche (Bezugsfläche):	368,91 MWh	1.276,96 kWh/m²
Abgegebene Energie Kollektoren:	251,12 MWh	869,22 kWh/m²
Abgegebene Energie Kollektorkreis:	243,10 MWh	841,45 kWh/m²
Energielieferung Trinkwarmwassererwärmung:	710,45 MWh	
Energielieferung Heizwärme:	1101,07 MWh	
Energie Solarsystem:	243,1 MWh	
Zugeführte Energie Zusatzheizung:	1577,27 MWh	
Einsparung Strom:		**78.622,4 kWh**
Vermiedene CO2-Emissionen:		**52.362,52 kg**
Deckungsanteil gesamt:		**13,4 %**
Anteilige Energieeinsparung (EN 12976):		**13,3 %**
Systemnutzungsgrad:		**65,9 %**

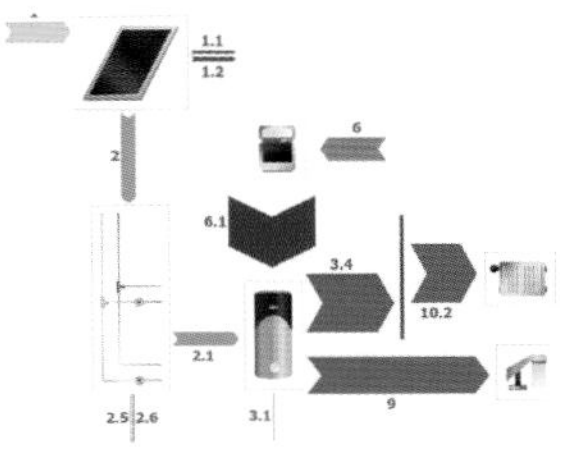

Legende

1	Einstrahlung Kollektorfläche (Bezugsfläche)	369 MWh	
1.1	Optische Kollektorverluste	40 MWh	40 MWh
1.2	Thermische Kollektorverluste	78 MWh	
2	Energie vom Kollektorfeld	251 MWh	251 MWh
2.1	Solarenergie an Speicher	243 MWh	
2.5	Rohrverluste innen	2.820 kWh	2.820 kWh
2.6	Rohrverluste außen	5.201 kWh	
3.1	Speicherverluste	8.678 kWh	8.678
3.4	Speicher an Heizung	1.101 MWh	
6	Endenergie	437 MWh	437 MWh
6.1	Zusatzenergie an Speicher	1.577 MWh	
9	WW-Energie aus dem Speicher	710 MWh	710 MWh
10.2	Wärme an NT-Heizung	1.101 MWh	

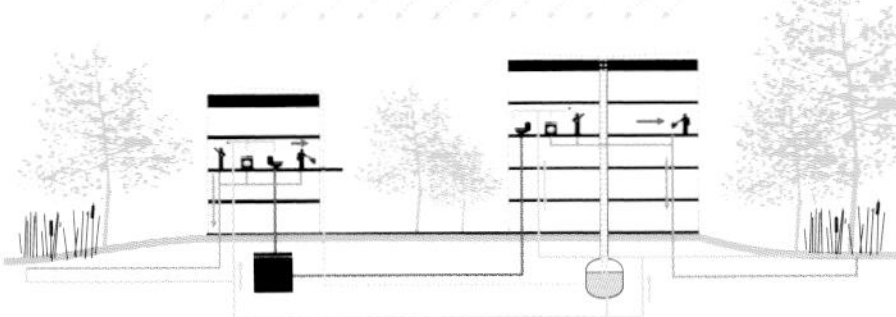

WASSERNUTZUNG

DER WASSERBEDARF WIRD SO WEIT WIE MÖGLICH REDUZIERT. REGENWASSER UND BRUNNENWASSER WERDEN Z.B. FÜR TOILETTENSPÜLUNG GENUTZT. DAS GERING VERSCHMUTZTE GRAUWASSER KANN ÜBER BIOLOGISCHE KLÄRANALGEN GEFILTERT UND DEM WASSERKREISLAUF SCHNELL WIEDER ZUGEFÜHRT WERDEN.

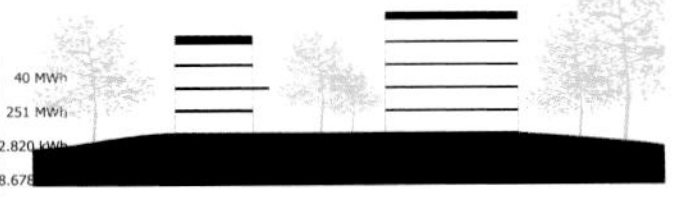

MIKROKLIMA

DER INNENHOF MIT SEINEN UMLIEGENDEN GEBÄUDEN IST VOR DER WITTERUNG TEILWEISE GESCHÜTZT. HIER KANN SICH EIN EIGENES MIKROKLIMA AUSBILDEN. IM SOMMER SORGEN DIE BÄUME FÜR VERSCHATTUNG UND KÜHLUNG. DIE FRISCHE LUFT VON DEN UMLIEGENDEN GRÜNBEREICHEN WIRD WIE IN EINEM LUFTKANAL ZU DEN WOHNUNGEN GELEITET.

SOZIALE

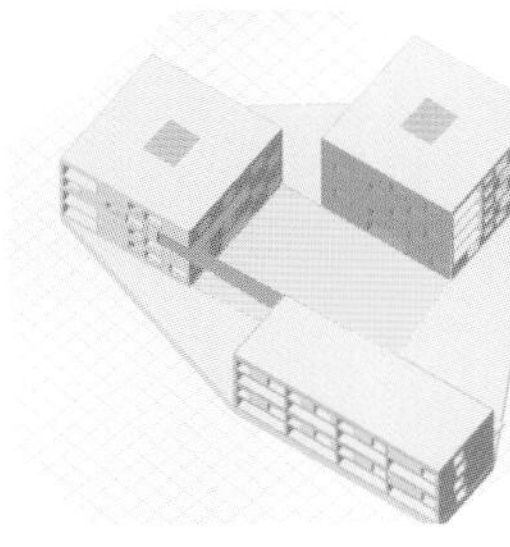

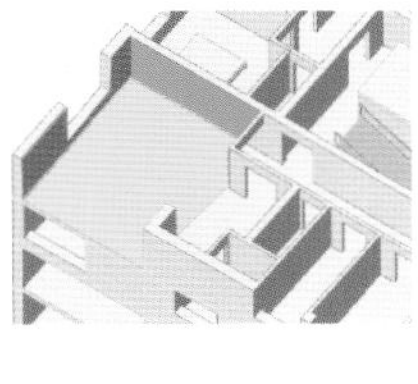

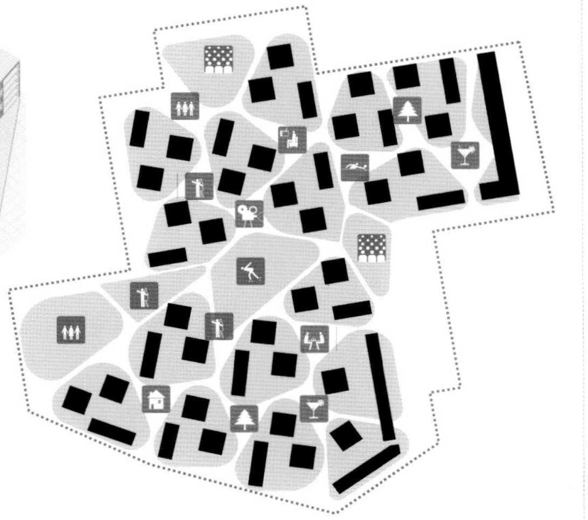

DAS WOHNZIMMER DRAUSSEN

DER INNENHOF IST GLEICHZEITIG DAS ÖFFENTLICHE WOHNZIMMER FÜR ALLE BEWOHNER. DAS MATERIALKONZEPT ZIEHT SICH VON DEN WOHNUNGEN IN DEN HOF DURCH. SOMIT WIRD DER SPRUNG IM MASSTAB VON KLEIN ZU GROSS GESCHAFFT UND DEN BEWOHNERN GEHOLFEN, SICH MIT DEM HAUS ZU IDENTIFIZIEREN. SIE SOLLEN SICH IN DER HALBÖFFENTLICHEN FREIFLÄCHE GENAUSO WOHL FÜHLEN WIE IN IHRER EIGENEN WOHNUNG.

SOZIALE NACHHALTIGKEIT

JEDER BEREICH DES PLANUNGSGEBIETES BIETET RAUM FÜR UNTERSCHIEDLICHE AKTIVITÄTEN. DIE DIFFERENZIERTEN WOHNUNGSTYPOLOGIEN GEWÄHRLEISTEN EINE GUTE SOZIALE DURCHMISCHUNG. DIE HALBÖFFENTLICHEN FREIFLÄCHEN UND DIE INNENHÖFE MIT IHREN VERSCHIEDENEN NUTZUNGEN SORGEN DAFÜR, DASS DAS GEBIET VON DEN BEWOHNERN GUT ANGENOMMEN WIRD UND MIT LEBEN GEFÜLLT IST.

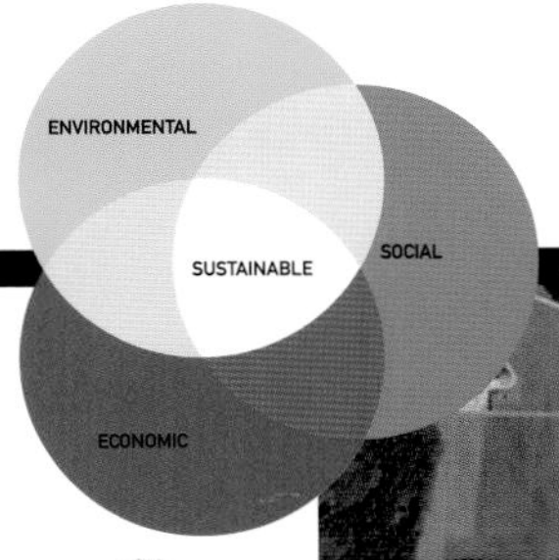

WIRTSCHAFT

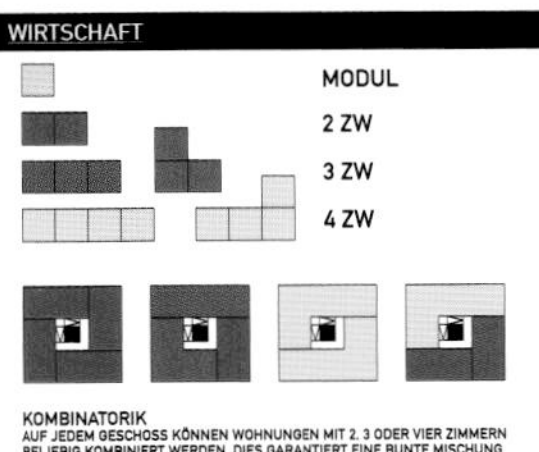

KOMBINATORIK

AUF JEDEM GESCHOSS KÖNNEN WOHNUNGEN MIT 2, 3 ODER VIER ZIMMERN BELIEBIG KOMBINIERT WERDEN. DIES GARANTIERT EINE BUNTE MISCHUNG DER BEWOHNER UND TRÄGT ZUR SOZIALEN NACHHALTIGKEIT DER EINHEITEN BEI. ALTE, JUNGE UND FAMILIEN SCHAFFEN GEMEINSAM EINEN LEBENDIGEN MIKROKOSMOS.

FERTIGTEILE

GEBAUT WIRD MIT HOLZFERTIGTEILELEMENTEN. DURCH DEN HOHEN VORFERTIGUNGSGRAD ERREICHT MAN EINE WEIT SCHNELLERE BAUZEIT UND DAMIT ÖKONOMISCHERE ERRICHTUNG ALS BEI HERKÖMMLICHER MASSIVBAUWEISE. DIE HOHE PRODUKTIONSGENAUIGKEIT BEDINGT EINE MÜHLOSE MONTAGE UND GERINGE ABWEICHUNGEN VON DER PLANUNG.

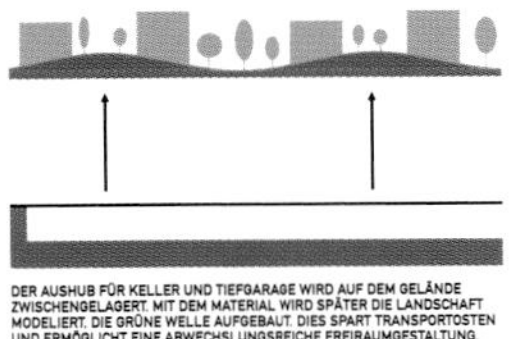

DER AUSHUB FÜR KELLER UND TIEFGARAGE WIRD AUF DEM GELÄNDE ZWISCHENGELAGERT. MIT DEM MATERIAL WIRD SPÄTER DIE LANDSCHAFT MODELIERT, DIE GRÜNE WELLE AUFGEBAUT. DIES SPART TRANSPORTOSTEN UND ERMÖGLICHT EINE ABWECHSLUNGSREICHE FREIRAUMGESTALTUNG.

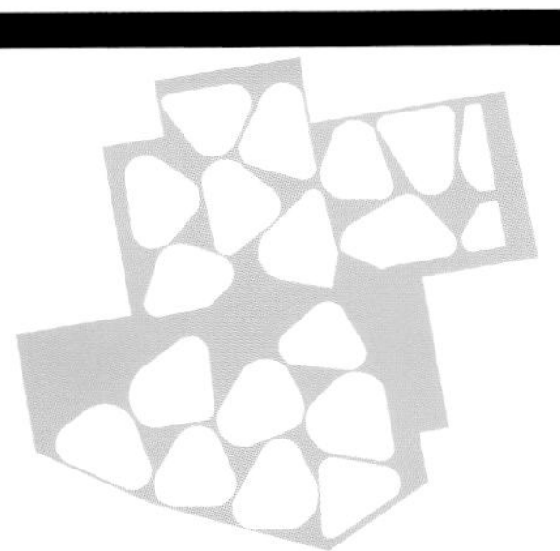

NUR DER ÖFFENTLICHE BEREICH DER GRÜNFLÄCHEN WIRD VON DER STADT GRAZ BEWIRTSCHAFTET. DIE FLÄCHEN ZWISCHEN DEN GEBÄUDEGRUPPEN WERDEN – OBWOHL EBENFALLS GEMEINGUT – VON DEN BEWOHNERN IN STAND GEHALTEN. DIES SPART DER STADT KOSTEN UND VERMITTELT DEN BEWOHNERN EINE FESTERE BINDUNG ZU IHREM LEBENSRAUM.

DIE BÄUME IM QUARTIERSPARK WERDEN IN DER ERSTEN BAUPHASE GEPFLANZT. GEWÄHLT WERDEN KLEINE BÄUME. DIESE SIND BILLIGER ALS BEREITS GROSS GEWACHSENE UND SOMIT KANN EINE QUALITÄTSVOLLERE BEPFLANZUNG UMGESETZT WERDEN. WENN DIE LETZTEN BEWOHNER IN IHRE WOHNUNGEN EINZIEHEN, SIND DIE BÄUME BEREITS GROSS GEWORDEN.

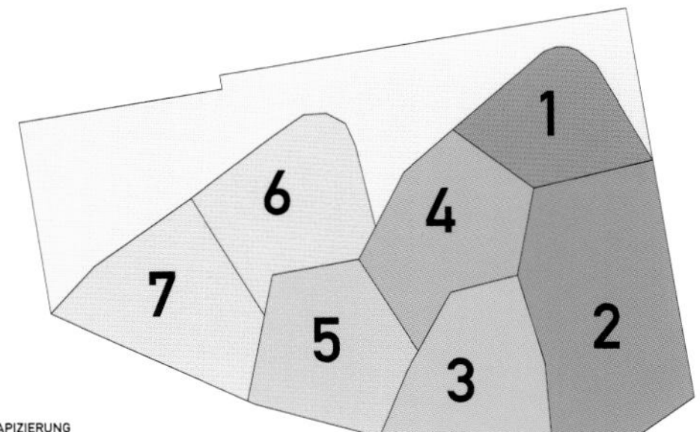

ETAPIZIERUNG

LUFTBILD

073 Ciudad Del Medio Ambiente | *modostudio*

Location : Santomera, Spagna
Client : Dirección General de Medio Natural de la Región de Murcia (Consejería de Industria y Medio Ambiente)
Phase : International Competition – Winning Project

Surface : 130 ha
Cost : € 16,000,000,00
Design team : Adhocmsl(Juan Antonio Sánchez, Miguel Mesa del Castillo, Riccardo Crespi), Barbarela studio(Juan Carlos Castro), Best Before(Enrique Nieto), Modostudio(Fabio

21Z09V

panel // 01

CIUDAD DEL MEDIO AMBIENTE. ESTRATEGIA MEDIOAMBIENTAL

REFLEXION PREVIA
Las características del conjunto de canteras abandonadas sobre las que pretende instalarse la CIUDAD DEL MEDIO AMBIENTE exigen un posicionamiento medioambiental previo al establecimiento de una estrategia de intervención. La discusión principal se centrará en el alcance de la rehabilitación en relación a unas condiciones anteriores al inicio de la actividad extractiva. La magnitud de las extracciones y el grado de alteración geomorfológico es de tal envergadura que creemos que conduce directamente a la aceptación en algún grado de lo que hoy hay, eliminando cualquier posibilidad de recuperación de lo que en su día fue por una ausencia manifiesta de viabilidad.

La situación actual presenta un claro impacto paisajístico negativo en el entorno, que llamaremos impacto externo, pero, por el contrario, ofrece un atractivo paisajístico si se recorre interiormente, que llamaremos valor interno. El criterio general de intervención resultará de un doble objetivo:
- la reducción del impacto externo en el mayor grado posible
- la potenciación de los valores internos con los recursos disponibles.

La metodología de trabajo desarrollada se estructura de acuerdo al siguiente proceso que desarrollaremos a continuación:
a) caracterización selectiva del medio físico
b) análisis de riesgos geológicos
c) establecimiento de medidas de rehabilitación ecológica y paisajística

ANALISIS DEL MEDIO FISICO
Inicialmente se ha realizado un estudio del medio para conocer aquellas características que consideramos necesarias para determinar los sistemas y procedimientos más aconsejables para la rehabilitación ecológica y la recuperación ambiental del espacio. Diferenciando dos niveles, se han analizado los siguientes aspectos:
Encuadre geográfico:
- Uso del suelo.
- Edafología.
- Espacios protegidos.
Area de actuación:
- Relieve / inclinación y orientación de pendientes
- Hidrología / cauces, escorrentía y espacios endorreicos
- Soleamiento / en diferentes días y horarios.

EVALUACION DE RIESGOS
La condición de espacio público que pretende rescatarse en las canteras exige un estudio profundo y detallado de la situación geológica actual, dirigido a la evaluación y valoración de riesgos existentes.

Esta identificación de riesgos permitirá:
- El establecimiento de medidas de eliminación y/o reducción.
- La selección de los espacios interiores más adecuados para la programación de actividades en función de la ausencia de riesgo.
Pendientes de un estudio con mayor profundidad, mediante prospecciones mecánicas y análisis geofísicos avanzados, se han identificado las situaciones siguientes:
- Desprendimientos de grandes bloques de roca por inestabilidad.
- Desprendimientos de roca meteorizada por inestabilidad y erosión.
- Rellenos incontrolados con riesgo de deslizamientos.
- Zonas de escorrentía y de riesgo de inundación.
- Posible aparición de karstificaciones.
- Localización de fallas y diaclasas con peligro de rotura de taludes por acciones sísmicas.
- Riesgos de rotura por raíces de arbolado.

MEDIDAS DE REHABILITACION ECOLOGICA Y PAISAJISTICA
De acuerdo al criterio de intervención establecido las medidas de intervención que se proponen son:
- Para la reducción del impacto visual de la cantera:
- adaptación morfológica, por remodelado, mediante voladuras en cabecera de los bancos para mejorar las condiciones de talud y microvoladuras puntuales para generación de huecos, repisas, salientes, etc.
- apantallamiento visual de las zonas de frente, mediante utilización de geotextiles y mulches
- aplicación de técnicas de envejecimiento del banco de explotación para reducir los contrastes cromáticos.

- Para la integración de las actuaciones:
- implantación de una cubierta vegetal, en función de la microclimatología, topografía y las propiedades físico-químicas del suelo, impulsando procesos sucesionales hacia comunidades vegetales maduras, en equilibrio con el medio y con gran capacidad de automantenimiento.
- Modificación de las condiciones del suelo, por escarificado, aportación de tierra vegetal, incremento de la disponibilidad hídrica de escorrentía, sistemas de riego y mulches.
- Selección de especies vegetales autóctonas.

- Para la selección de especies se proponen aplicar dos vectores:
- En reflejo de las distintas comunidades vegetales presentes en el entorno según las diversas estructuras fisonómicas y que caracterizan los hábitats naturales de interés prioritario: 1520, 6220, 5330 y 8210.
- Por gradiente de mantenimiento e intervención, desde áreas centrales intensivas hasta bordes de intervención mínima como nexo de conexión con el entorno restaurado de la cantera.

- Complementariamente se propone
- el control de los flujos de escorrentía y de erosión del suelo producidos por eventos lluviosos de carácter torrencial.
- Impulsar el refugio y hábitat de fauna de medios semiáridos.

MEMORIA TÉCNICA DE REHABILITACIÓN
Como se ha explicado anteriormente, la especial singularidad de estas canteras aconseja el enfocar su rehabilitación hacia la generación de un producto de alto valor turístico y educacional. En este sentido, la cuestión de la seguridad de uso jugará un papel determinante en todo el proceso de toma de decisiones.
Otra consideración fundamental será corregir el impacto visual que los frentes de cantera tienen sobre la autovía A-7, para generar un frente atractivo que más allá de camuflar la intervención humana sobre el paisaje explique la intervención en clave de regeneración de un espacio y su conversión en un espacio de uso público.

PROPUESTA DE PROCESO DE REHABILITACIÓN
1.- Eliminación de los riesgos de accidentes y de impactos exteriores. El estado general de la cantera es crítico en lo concerniente a la seguridad. Como se ha visto en el estudio geotécnico, se trata de bancos muy fragmentados y meteorizados que hacen muy difícil su trabajo en condiciones de seguridad. Se realizará un estudio del estado de los frentes en profundidad, lo que implicará señalización, corrección de áreas peligrosas (cortes, limpieza de taludes, microvoladuras de taludes inestables, ...), construcción de canales perimetrales que desvíen las aguas de escorrentía superficial...
2.- Control de formas o geometrías. Conocido el anteproyecto de utilización de la cantera, se procederá a reducir y/o eliminar los riesgos de erosión, diseño de taludes y pendientes estables, adaptación al proyecto previsto, etc. En nuestro caso sólo se ha detectado una zona especialmente complicada, se trata de la primera cuenca por donde se accede a la cantera, donde aparece una rampa que conecta la meseta de acceso con con la meseta superior. La altura del frente de cantera cercano, y el mal estado del mismo hacen casi inviable la utilización de dicha rampa de manera natural. Estudios posteriores deben determinar la conveniencia de corregir el talud principal de dicho frente para garantizar el uso de dicha rampa. En caso de no poderse, sería el edificio el que cumpliría exclusivamente tal función de conexión entre ambas mesetas.
3.- Control y tratamiento de aguas. Contamos con dos lugares principales de almacenamiento natural del agua de escorrentía, que se convertirán en estanques para su utilización posterior en el riego de las especies revegetadas. Se debe realizar a través de canales construidos que evacuen el agua rápidamente, disminuyendo su tiempo de residencia en los materiales de la mina y llevándola a los lugares de almacenamiento.
Esta recogida y almacenamiento superficial del agua es interesantes puesto que favorece la aparición de plantas tales como typhas, musgos, juncos... que realizan un importante papel depurador o fijador de sustancias tóxicas. Estos pantanales fomentan la creación de ambientes reductores donde muchos de los problemas derivados de las explotaciones mineras, como la acidez de las aguas y la presencia de concentraciones anómalas de metales, pueden ser controladas por los cambios que se provocan por los procesos redox.
En principio, el uso exclusivo de esta aguas recogidas para riego de vegetación favorable, y la composición de los minerales de la cantera, no exije el tratamiento de dichas aguas.
4.-Restauración de los suelos y la cubierta vegetal. Evidentemente, los suelos de la cantera, prácticamente materiales originales deteriorados, presentan unas características físicas y fisicoquímicas muy limitantes para el desarrollo de la vegetación, estas se deben corregir mediante técnicas de mejora y fertilización:
a) Incorporación de residuos orgánicos de todo tipo (estiércoles, composts, biodepósitos marinos bajo bateas de mejillón, despojos de mataderos, etc), debido a que incorporan carbono y otros elementos biogénicos, suministran productos metabolizables para la fauna que comienza a colonizarlos al tiempo que se evita el daño que podrían causar al acumularlos en otros lugares.
b) Introducción de plantas que tengan posibilidad de fijar nitrógeno atmosférico.
5.- Recuperación de las comunidades faunísticas. La fauna representa uno de los principales valores naturales de un espacio y un importante mecanismo de reciclaje de nutrientes. En nuestro caso además, la presencia de una escuela de caza en la intervención nos permite pensar en la introducción en estado de cautiverio de especies amenazadas.
Otra cuestión importante sería la apertura de corredores transversales, utilizando los bordes no alterados, para permitir el paso e inserción de especies animales autóctonas.
6.- Recuperación paisajística. Todas las fases anteriores deben de estar orientadas de modo que se vaya avanzando en el logro de una integración paisajística. Sin embargo, dada la escasez de vegetación del entorno de las canteras, se hace improcedente su integración en el sentido de camuflaje y pérdida de reconocimiento visual.
Nuestra propuesta trabaja desde un plantemaniento más cercano a la rehabilitación en el sentido de reconversión en un espacio de alto interés social y medioambiental, pero de características claramente diferenciadas respecto del ecosistema del que procede.
El valor especialmente didáctico que este tipo de espacios transformados por la actividad industrial del hombre puede tener, junto con la introducción de los usos previstos por las bases del concurso, permiten pensar en el éxito de una operación encaminada a la generación de un nuevo paisaje.

TRATAMIENTO DE TALUDES CON ALTO RIESGO DE DESPRENDIMIENTOS

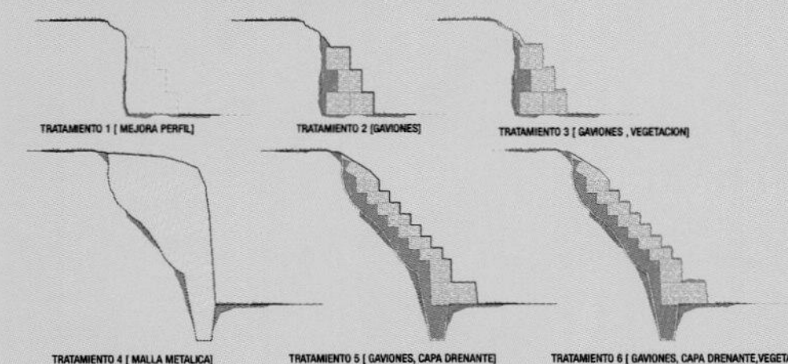

PRESUPUESTO ESTIMADO

ACTUACIONES PREVIAS			
DESMONTES			900.000,00 €
CONSOLIDACIONES			600.000,00 €
VOLADURAS			400.000,00 €
RESTO			1.200.000,00 €
		TOTAL ACTUACIONES PREVIAS	3.100.000,00 €
ESTUDIOS, ENSAYOS Y PROYECTOS			
ESTUDIOS Y ENSAYOS			450.000,00 €
PROYECTOS			580.000,00 €
		TOTAL ESTUDIOS Y ENSAYOS	1.030.000,00 €
URBANIZACION			
ALTA	60,00 €	3.000,00 m2	180.000,00 €
MEDIA	30,00 €	10.000,00 m2	300.000,00 €
BAJA	20,00 €	120.000,00 m2	2.400.000,00 €
		TOTAL URBANIZACIÓN	2.880.000,00 €
ARQUITECTURA			
EDIFICIO 1	1.500,00 €	600,00 m2	900.000,00 €
EDIFICIO 2	1.500,00 €	800,00 m2	1.200.000,00 €
MOBILIARIO			12.000,00 €
		TOTAL ARQUITECTURA	2.112.000,00 €
DISPOSITIVOS DE CAPTACIÓN DE ENERGÍA			
SOL			500.000,00 €
VIENTO			200.000,00 €
AGUA			400.000,00 €
		TOTAL DISPOSITIVOS DE CAPTACIÓN	1.100.000,00 €
MOBILIARIO EXTERIOR			
PROTECCIONES	150,00 €	14.876,80 m2	2.231.520,00 €
MOBILIARIO Y SEÑALECTICA		m2	180.000,00 €
		TOTAL PROGRAMAS DE AGUA	2.411.520,00 €
		TOTAL PRESUPUESTO ESTIMADO	**12.633.520,00 €**
		TOTAL PRESUPUESTO ESTIMADO CON IVA	**14.654.883,20 €**

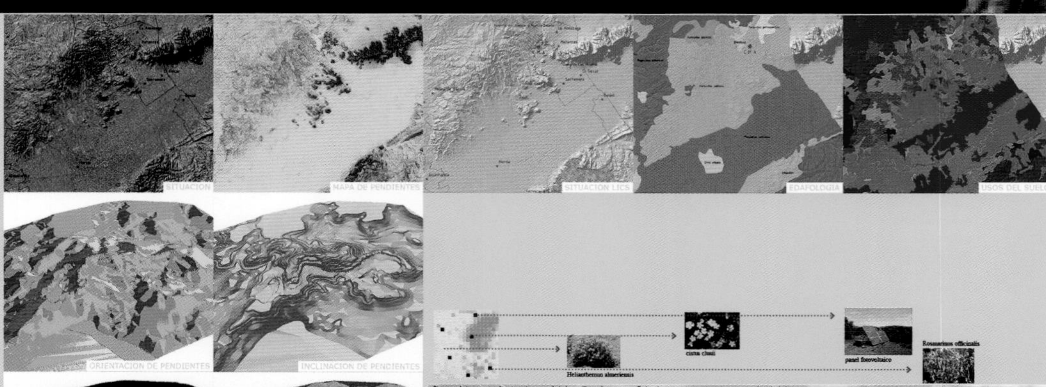

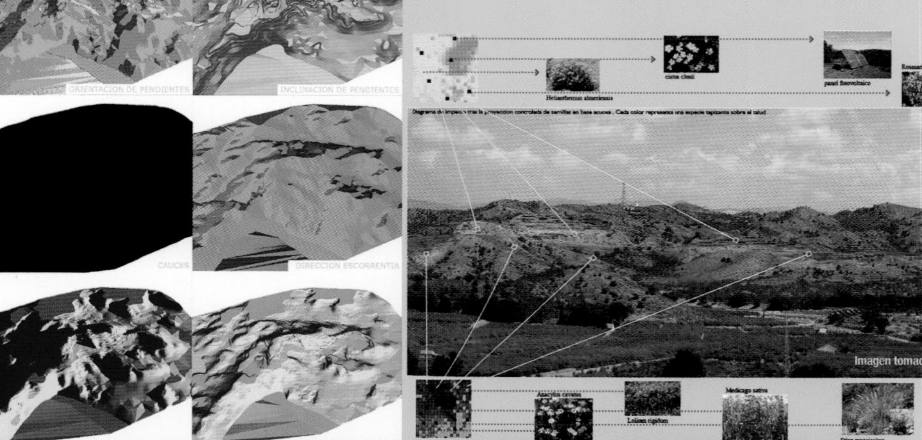

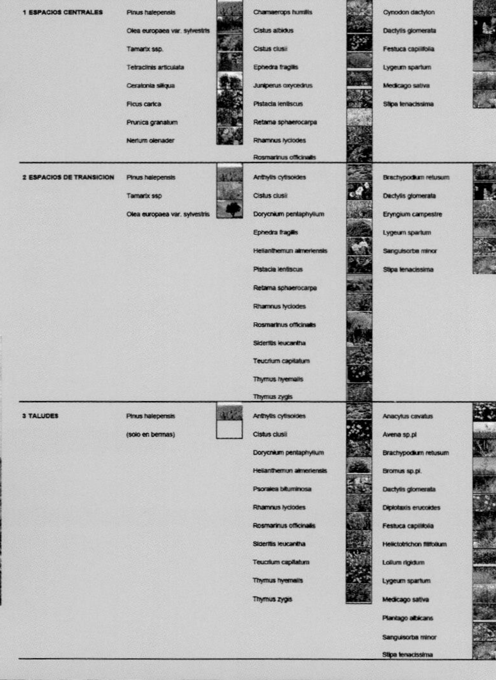

Unidad de actuacion	Especies: Arbóreas	Arbustivas y semiarbustivas	Herbáceas
1 ESPACIOS CENTRALES	Pinus halepensis	Chamaerops humilis	Cynodon dactylon
	Olea europaea var. sylvestris	Cistus albidus	Dactylis glomerata
	Tamarix ssp.	Cistus clusii	Festuca capillifolia
	Tetraclinis articulata	Ephedra fragilis	Lygeum spartum
	Ceratonia siliqua	Juniperus oxycedrus	Medicago sativa
	Ficus carica	Pistacia lentiscus	Stipa tenacissima
	Prunica granatum	Retama sphaerocarpa	
	Nerium olenader	Rhamnus lyciodes	
		Rosmarinus officinalis	
2 ESPACIOS DE TRANSICION	Pinus halepensis	Anthyllis cytisoides	Brachypodium retusum
	Tamarix ssp	Cistus clusii	Dactylis glomerata
	Olea europaea var. sylvestris	Dorycnium pentaphyllum	Eryngium campestre
		Ephedra fragilis	Lygeum spartum
		Helianthemun almeriensis	Sanguisorba minor
		Pistacia lentiscus	Stipa tenacissima
		Retama sphaerocarpa	
		Rhamnus lyciodes	
		Rosmarinus officinalis	
		Sideritis leucantha	
		Teucrium capitatum	
		Thymus hyemalis	
		Thymus zygis	
3 TALUDES	Pinus halepensis	Anthyllis cytisoides	Anacyclus cavatus
	(solo en bermas)	Cistus clusii	Avena sp.pl
		Dorycnium pentaphyllum	Brachypodium retusum
		Helianthemun almeriensis	Bromus sp.pl.
		Psoralea bituminosa	Dactylis glomerata
		Rhamnus lyciodes	Diplotaxis erucoides
		Rosmarinus officinalis	Festuca capillifolia
		Sideritis leucantha	Helictotrichon filifolium
		Teucrium capitatum	Lolium rigidum
		Thymus hyemalis	Lygeum spartum
		Thymus zygis	Medicago sativa
			Plantago albicans
			Sanguisorba minor
			Stipa tenacissima

ESTRATEGÍAS GENERALES/

Ciudad del Medio Ambiente
En un contexto regional de aparición constante de ofertas de ocupación del tiempo libre, la clave de su supervivencia es la fuerte especialización del producto generado y la capacidad de presentarse al público como una oferta intensa, necesaria y unitaria. La Ciudad del Medio Ambiente de Murcia, por su ambición, tamaño y ubicación, debe pensarse además desde su centralidad en el mapa metropolitano de Murcia, pero también en el mapa de ofertas de ocupación del tiempo libre de los ciudadanos, con la intención además de convertirse en una referencia obligada por su innovación en este tipo de intervenciones.

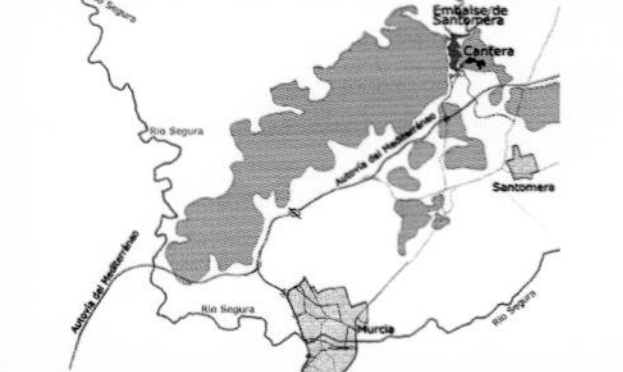

identidad y producto
Esta propuesta intenta dotar de unidad e identidad a un conjunto de requerimientos heterogéneos a partir de unas aproximaciones estratégicas que se perfeccionarán en el transcurso de los sucesivos proyectos y estudios específicos.

Dicha heterogeneidad aparece concretada en las bases del concurso en dos grandes grupos: los aspectos medioambientales, encaminados a rehabilitar la cantera entendida como espacio natural degradado, y los programáticos, entendidos como implantes funcionales a partir de las necesidades concretas de la Administración convocante del concurso.

Sin embargo, el objetivo fundamental de la propuesta debe ser identificar un producto que genere interés en el mayor número posible de grupos sociales y de suficiente identidad como para ser reconocido y valorado como la ciudad del Medio Ambiente de Murcia.

calidad paisajística y didáctica
Los procesos de extración de mineral, además de considerarse desastres ecológicos, producen un fuerte impacto visual al exterior, pero sobre todo tienen generan paisajes internos extremadamente caracterizados, de baja fragilidad visual y de enorme calidad paisajística. Proponemos utilizar estos paisajes como la primera oportunidad de proyecto.

Desde un punto de vista de la sostenibilidad social, la supervivencia de la memoria histórica y de la cultura técnica que estos paisajes artificiales contienen, nos permiten pensar también nuestra intervención como un paisaje didáctico donde los valores ambientales, técnicos, antropológicos, económicos, culturales y geofísicos componen un continuo que la propuesta tratará de descifrar y poner en valor.

máxima seguridad y sostenibilidad
La antigua cantera de Los Ásperos nos ha dejado unos 1.800 metros lineales de frente de cantera, y unos 1.200 metros lineales de frente abierto. El estado de ambos bordes es altamente peligroso para su conversión en un lugar de uso público. Como estrategia inicial de intervención se propone trabajar desde la máxima seguridad, transformando lo menos posible las zonas peligrosas y desplegando la ocupación humana desde los puntos de mayor seguridad de las 13 Ha donde se desarrolla la intervención.

Desplegar nuestra propuesta desde estos puntos de máxima seguridad nos permite además concentrar recursos y avanzar progresivamente en la definición de objetivos finales. Entendemos que la sostenibilidad de los propios procesos de génesis de la institución es un argumento fundamental para controlar el resultado final.

Cibinel, Roberto Laurenti, Giorgio Martocchia)
Consultants : Victor Manuel Castillo Sánchez(Forestal engineering), Maria Dolores Martínez-Mena García(Biology), Julián Pérez Castillo(Structural engineering)

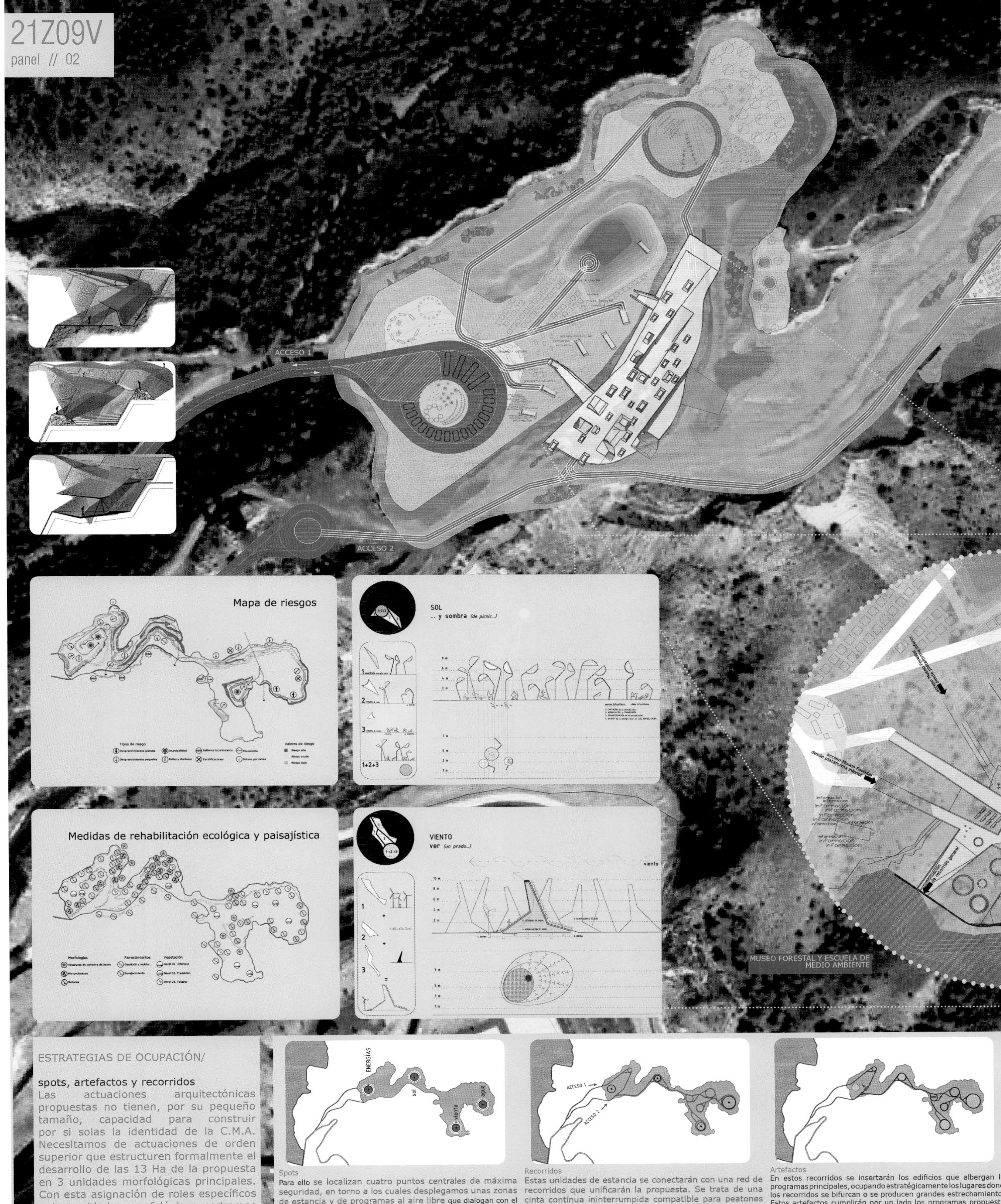

ESTRATEGIAS DE OCUPACIÓN/

spots, artefactos y recorridos

Las actuaciones arquitectónicas propuestas no tienen, por su pequeño tamaño, capacidad para construir por si solas la identidad de la C.M.A. Necesitamos de actuaciones de orden superior que estructuren formalmente el desarrollo de las 13 Ha de la propuesta en 3 unidades morfológicas principales. Con esta asignación de roles específicos a las unidades morfológicas podremos pensar la C.M.A. como un dispositivo docente y educativo unificado y a escala del paisaje.

Spots

Para ello se localizan cuatro puntos centrales de máxima seguridad, en torno a los cuales desplegamos unas zonas de estancia y de programas al aire libre que dialogan con el tamaño de la cantera. Permiten utilizar y entender la C.M.A.como un parque al margen de las edificaciones arquitectónicas, en horarios más amplios y con un público más amplio.
Con estas manchas se intenta activar y especializar cada espacio dotándolos de artefactos que gestionan y representan los distintos tipos de energía: Así, aparecen espacios donde el sol, el viento, el agua y sus respectivas posibilidades de captación tecnológicas aparecen representados en unidades morfológicas claramente diferenciadas.

El primer spot, el de llegada, representa la síntesis de los otros tres en su manifestación más destructiva, la catástrofe natural. Con esta intervención, queremos equiparar las catástrofes naturales y las producidas por la industria humana en lo que de común tienen, la liberación de cantidades enormes de energía en procesos que la ciencia está llegando a desvelar.

Recorridos

Estas unidades de estancia se conectarán con una red de recorridos que unificarán la propuesta. Se trata de una cinta contínua ininterrumpida compatible para peatones y vehículos que irá acompañada de actuaciones de revegetación y de protección y clausura en ambos lados. Se diseñarán desde el entendimiento de la cantera como museo al aire libre y desde el reconocimiento de su alto interés formal y espacial.

Se proponen dos accesos a las canteras, que se corresponden con los dos accesos originales. Por un lado un acceso de público general previsto o espontáneo, que deja su vehículo en la primera cuenca visual y desarrolla su recorrido peatonalmente. Hablamos de un visitante lúdico y ocasional, y un visitante organizado que llega por razones formativas.

Por otro lado un acceso rodado que conduce directamente a los edificios y recorre toda la intervención. Hablamos de un usuario profesional

Artefactos

En estos recorridos se insertarán los edificios que albergan los programas principales, ocupando estratégicamente los lugares donde los recorridos se bifurcan o se producen grandes estrechamientos. Estos artefactos cumplirán por un lado los programas propuestos por las bases, y además actuarán a modo de prótesis para salvar peatonalmente discontinuidades en el terreno.

Formalmente, nuestros artefactos actúan respetando al máximo el lugar donde se implantan y proponen una imagen fuerte y tecnológica. Entendemos que es esta la mejor opción para incorporarlos a un discurso formal unitario, puesto que su tamaño es muy reducido en comparación con el lugar donde se insertan.

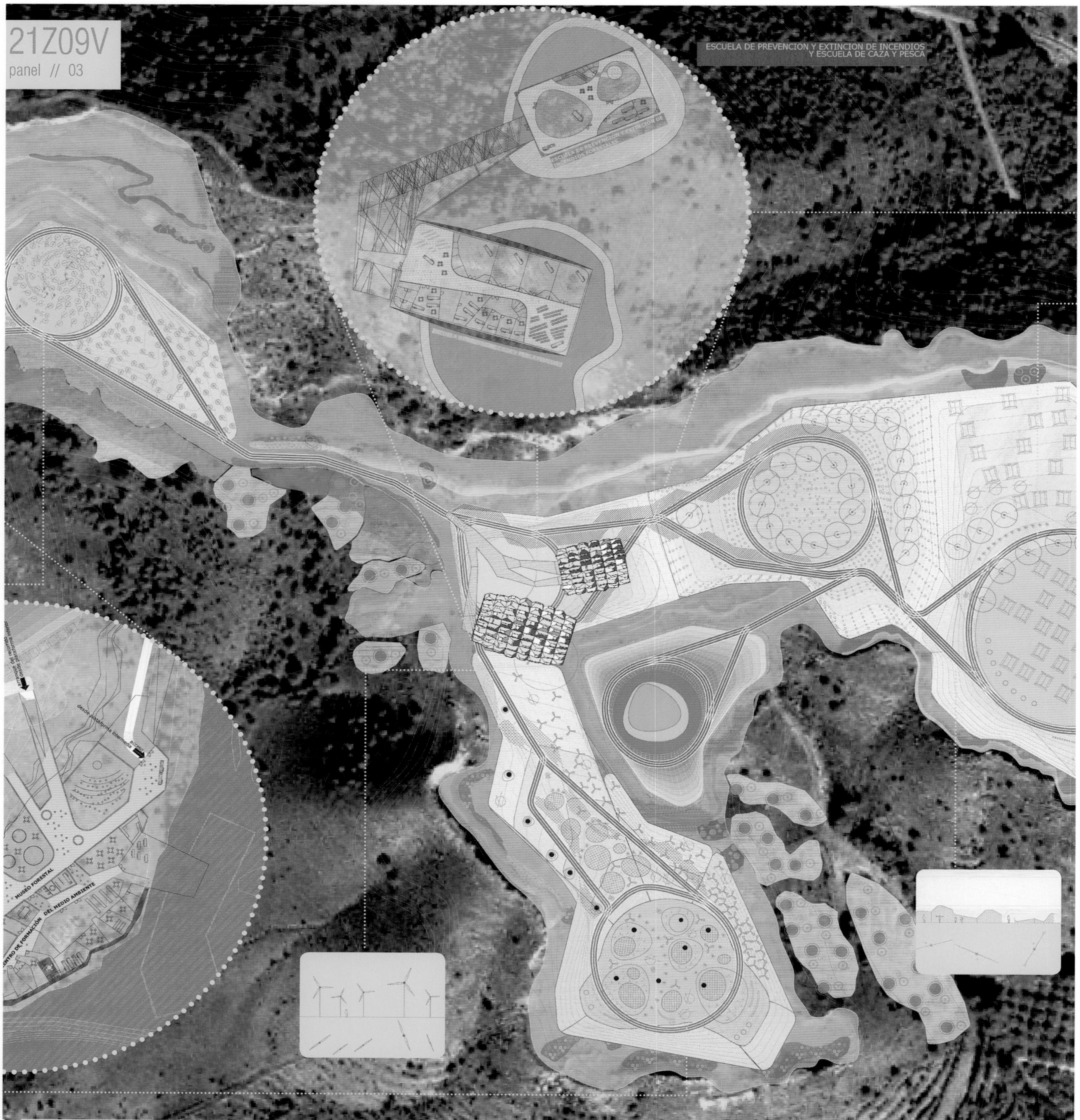

ESTRATEGIAS DE OCUPACIÓN/

Escorrentías y programas complementarios

De manera complementaria a las 3 grandes unidades estructurantes, aparecen otras de orden menor y de distinto origen que completan la intervención y sirven de estaciones intermedias a las anteriores.

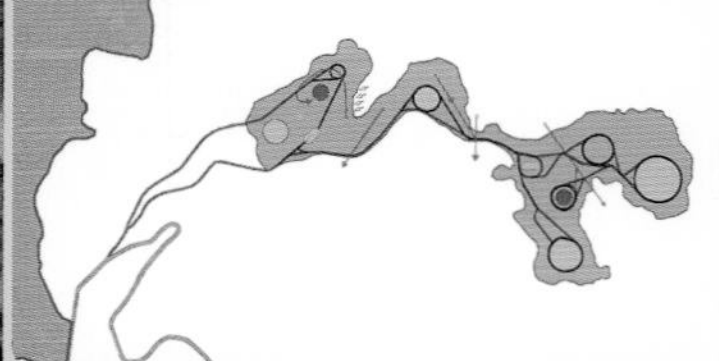

Escorrentias/Acumulación de H2O

En el estudio inicial de escorrentías existentes, aparecen dos lugares naturales de acumulación de agua. Proponemos que pasen a formar parte de la red secundaria de elementos estructurantes, convirtiendo estos lugares en depósitos de agua en superficie que se utilizará posteriormente para el riego de las especies vegetales utilizadas.

Los recorridos del agua hasta llegar a sus puntos de acumulación se harán en superficie, en canales que favorecerán la aparición de especies vegetales en su entorno propio y evitarán la erosión que observamos en la actualidad.

Paralelamente se "grafiarán" y reconocerán en el terreno a partir de su construcción física los caudales de escorrentía que atraviesan la cantera sin depositar su agua en ella. Entendemos que estos aportes son también necesarios para las zonas bajas de los montes donde se desarrolló la cantera

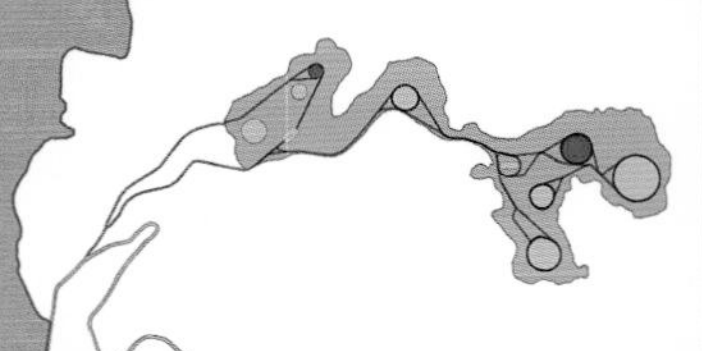

Programas complementarios

Aparecen finalmente unos spots más pequeños, situados en lugares de paso y conexión entre las unidades mayores, que utilizamos para alojar los áreas complementarias a los programas principales y a otros introducidos por nosotros que pretenden intensificar y completar las unidades originales.

Uno de ellos constituirá el campo de prácticas de la Escuela de Prevención y Extinción de Incendios Forestales, convenientemente aislado y protegido de los recorridos, pero con una presencia visual que consideramos relevante.

El otro, más cerca del ingreso, se propone como aulario al aire libre, una infraestructura polivalente y de bajo coste que permitirá completar la oferta formativa en periodos de bonanza climática.

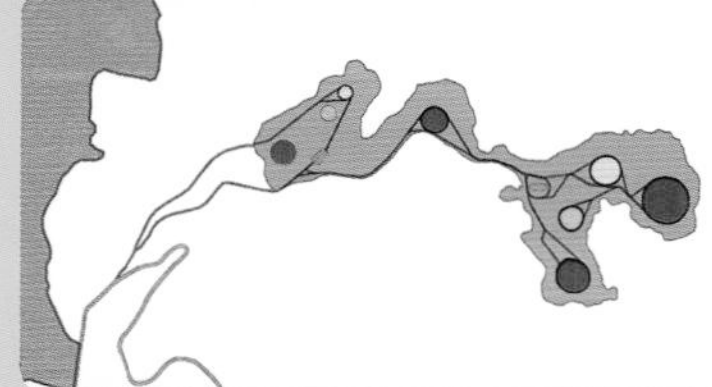

diagrama de elementos estructurantes

Nuestra intervención se propone así como un modelo teórico de intervención paisajística de rehabilitación de espacios naturales degradados aplicado a un ejemplo concreto, donde se produce un implante programático que se estructura a partir del reconocimiento morfológico del lugar donde se implanta.

El resultado es un catálogo de elementos estructurantes de la intervención donde todas las estrategias quedan formalmente definidas y pendientes de desarrollos específicos. Entendemos que de esta manera se consigue el objetivo inicial de dotar de identidad y unidad morfológica al conjunto.

21Z09V
panel // 04
CONCURSO DE IDEAS PARA LA REDACCIÓN DEL PROYECTO LA CIUDAD DEL MEDIO AMBIENTE

ESTRATEGIAS ARQUITECTÓNICAS/

Agrupación y especialización
Siguiendo el razonamiento de mínimo impacto y de reconocimiento de las cualidades del lugar, la arquitectura propuesta se implanta en su lugar a modo de objeto ajeno que se relaciona con su contexto por oposición y por su valor de utilidad.

agrupación de edificios
Desde el principio nos pareció conveniente agrupar los cuatro programas expuestos en las bases en dos grandes piezas arquitectónicas. Cuatro fueron las razones:
1.-La pequeñísima escala de los programas entendidos como piezas independientes, incapaces de negociar con la escala del paisaje.
2.- La cantera se configura como dos grandes cuencas visuales unidas por un cordón estrecho de comunicación donde se ubica una tercera cuenca. La agrupación de los programas en dos edificios nos permite especializar el paisaje de las dos primeras y articular el paso entre ambas.
3.- Intentar minimizar la dispersión de recursos económicos y de mantenimiento.
4.- Pero la decisión definitiva tiene que ver con el tipo y cantidad de público previsto: adultos y niños. Con esta agrupación intentamos concentrar la afluencia de público infantil en torno al acceso a la cantera, dejando para la zona interior los programas destinados a adultos.

Centro de Formación del Medio Ambiente + Museo Forestal
Interpretamos ambos programas como orientados a un público predominantemente infantil. Por esta razón unificamos ambos y los situamos en las proximidades del acceso natural a las canteras. Se trata del acceso más escenográfico pues constituye una cuenca visual cerrada y desde donde se divisa el Pantano de Santomera y gran parte de la finca de Los Cuadros.

De esta manera, y en la búsqueda de la seguridad máxima, limitamos el movimiento del público infantil a zonas muy controladas.

Este edificio se complementa con una zona de recogida de aguas y una zona de aulario al aire libre que lo completa.
Este cráter inicial es además el más interesante desde el punto de vista de transparentización de todos los procesos y agentes intervinientes en el proceso de formación de la cantera, ya que aparecen restos de implantes tecnológicos, tiene vistas al pantano, y presenta los mayores bancos de cantera de toda la intervención.

Escuela Regional de Caza y Pesca Fluvial + Escuela de Prevención y Extinción de Incendios Forestales
En principio, se trata de dos programas dirigidos a un público adulto y sujeto a horarios muy concretos. Los situamos en el segundo punto elegido, vinculados a sus espacios de apoyo, campos de práctica.

Esta edificación se dota de un acceso rodado restringido para usuarios especializados y programados, así como para vehículos de mantenimiento.

Como se ha adelantado anteriormente, el campo de prácticas de la Escuela de Prevención constituye un laboratorio visual del impacto del fuego sobre los ecosistemas que merece ser expuesto y explicado con gran rigor.

Le Cret-Du-Locle | *modostudio*

Location : Le Crêt-du-Locle, Switzerland
Client : Ville de La Chaux-de-Fonds, Ville du Locle
Type : Urban planning international competition - sixth prize

Design team : Fabio Cibinel, Roberto Laurenti, Giorgio Martocchia, Chor-Tung Chan
Consultants : Stephan Tischer(Landscape)

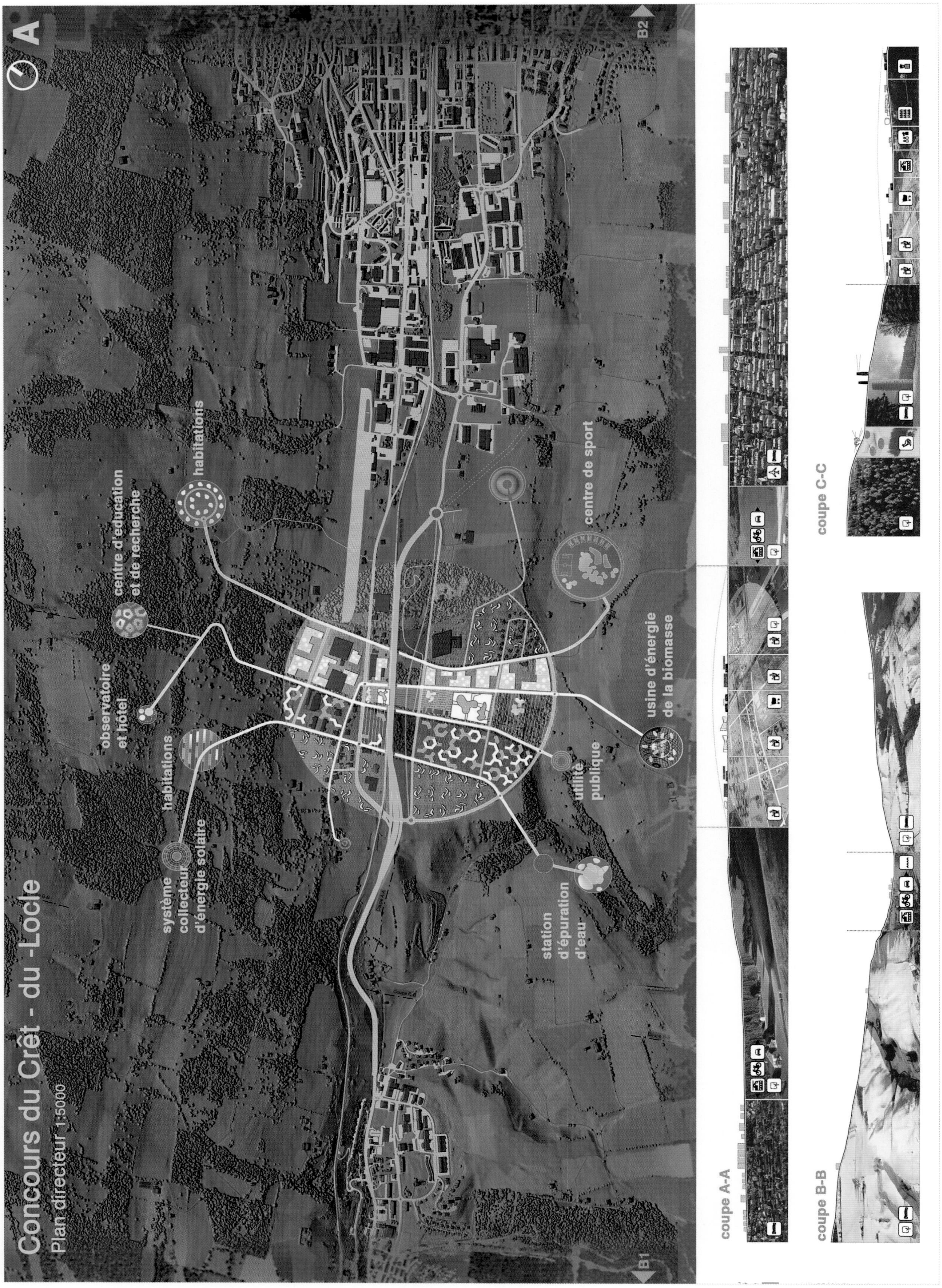

Concours du Crêt - du -Locle
Plan directeur 1:5000

A
B1
B2

centre d'education et de recherche
habitations
observatoire et hôtel
habitations
système collecteur d'énergie solaire
centre de sport
usine d'énergie de la biomasse
utilité publique
station d'épuration d'eau

coupe A-A
coupe B-B
coupe C-C

B1
Concours du Crêt - du -Locle
La Crêt-du-Locle est un nœud à l'intérieur du réseau macro-urbain dans le paysage du Jura, l'ensemble étant lié par son développement économique inter-dépendant. La Crêt-du-Locle est une charnière qui apporte une connexion flexible et un mode de communication entre Le Locle et La Chaux-de-Fonds. La Crêt-du-Locle est un seuil qui marque l'entrée de Le Locle et de la Chaux-de-Fonds. Elle empêche leur aglomération et leur homogénéisation et préserve leurs spécificités. La Crêt-du-Locle est une enceinte définie et autonome. Elle est capable d'assurer son existance sans pour autant mettre en danger les ressources des générations futures. La Crêt-du-Locle est un micro-réseau en elle-même qui fonctionne comme une entité. Elle opère avec la même précision qu'un appareil de mesure de temps.
La Crêt-du-Locle est respectueuse vis-à-vis de son paysage, mais n'a jamais peur d'assumer son existence.
Bâle
Berne
Lausanne
400 milliers habitants
200 milliers habitants
5 milliers habitants
La route des microtechniques
Lcl CdL CdF
1850 1890 1950 2005 2005 1950 1890 1850
Comme deux aimants aux pôles opposés, les deux villes s'étendent l'une vers l'autre au fil des années. La Crêt-du-Locle peut être considérée comme le centre de cette attraction
Lcl
CdL
CdF
Le district bien distinct au centre crée une barrière à l'éventuelle homogénéisation des deux villes. Au lieu de cela, la Crêt-du-Locle organisera et renforçera le développement des deux villes
Lcl
CdL
CdF
Le développement central est assuré par des parcs, des structures de loisirs, une gestion des déchets raisonnée et une structure de gestion de l'énergie en périphérie.
paysage
CdL
Tout autour, les fontions d'appui périphériques protègent et permettent le développement du paysage.

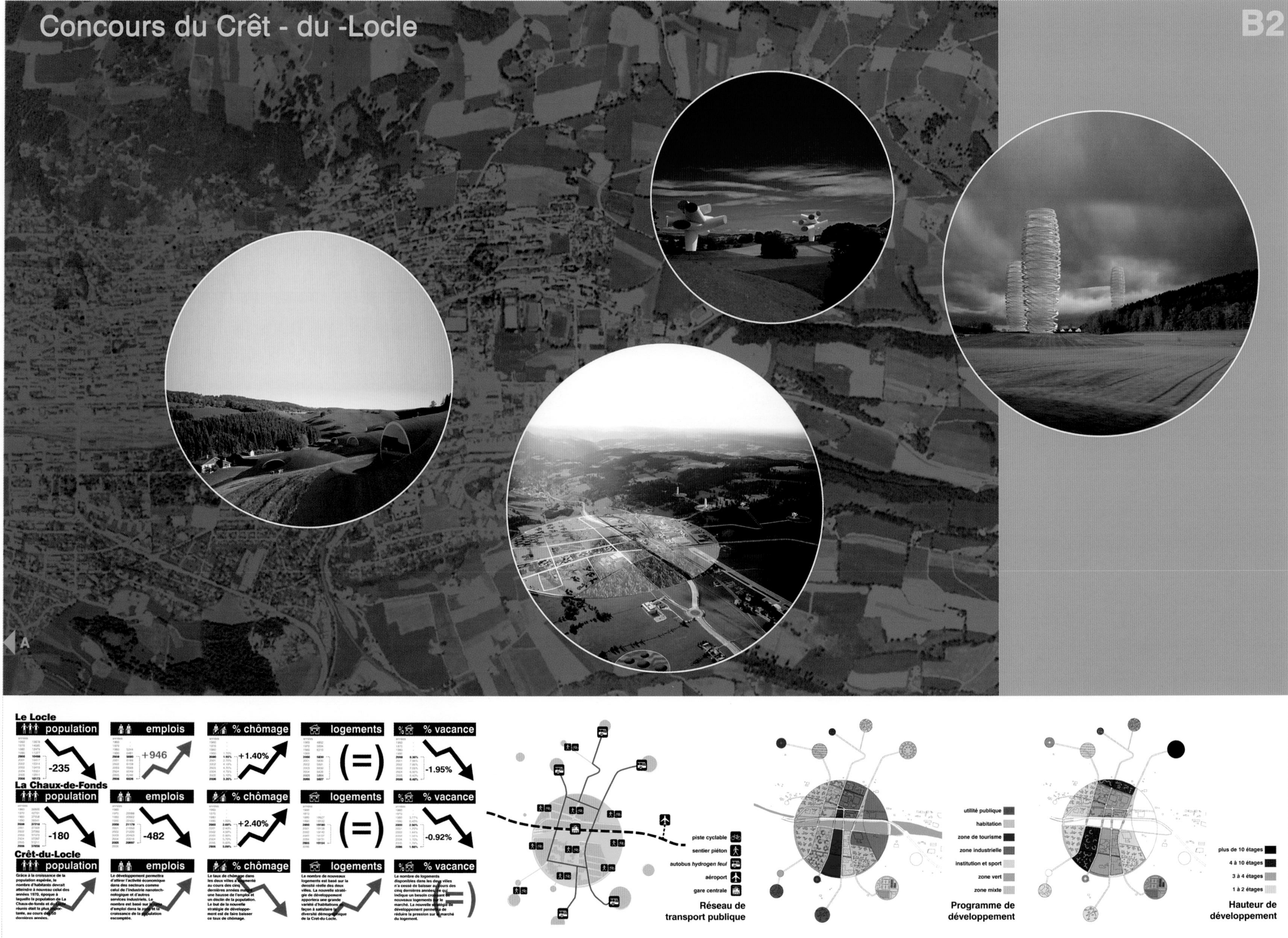
Concours du Crêt - du -Locle
B2
A
Le Locle
population
-235
emplois
+946
% chômage
+1.40%
logements
(=)
% vacance
-1.95%
La Chaux-de-Fonds
population
-180
emplois
-482
% chômage
+2.40%
logements
(=)
% vacance
-0.92%
Crêt-du-Locle
population
Grâce à la croissance de la population espérée, le nombre d'habitants devrait atteindre à nouveau celui des années 1970, époque à laquelle la population de La Chaux-de-fonds et du Locle réunis était la plus importante, au cours des 50 dernières années.
emplois
Le développement permettra d'attirer l'activité économique dans des secteurs comme celui de l'industrie nanotechnologique et d'autres services industriels. Le nombre est basé sur le ratio d'emploi dans la zone et la croissance de la population escomptée.
% chômage
Le taux de chômage dans les deux villes a augmenté au cours des cinq dernières années malgré une hausse de l'emploi et un déclin de la population. Le but de la nouvelle stratégie de développement est de faire baisser ce taux de chômage.
logements
Le nombre de nouveaux logements est basé sur la densité réelle des deux villes. La nouvelle stratégie de développement apportera une grande variété d'habitations de façon à satisfaire la diversité démographique de la Cret-du-Locle.
% vacance
Le nombre de logements disponibles dans les deux villes n'a cessé de baisser au cours des cinq dernières années, ce qui indique un besoin croissant de nouveaux logements sur le marché. La nouvelle stratégie de développement permettra de réduire la pression sur le marché du logement.
(=)
piste cyclable
sentier piéton
autobus hydrogen feul
aéroport
gare centrale
Réseau de transport publique
utilité publique
habitation
zone de tourisme
zone industrielle
institution et sport
zone vert
zone mixte
Programme de développement
plus de 10 étages
4 à 10 étages
3 à 4 étages
1 à 2 étages
Hauteur de développement

Switzerland | *2:pm architectures*

Project : European Urbanism Competition
Location : Aigle(Switzerland)
Design Team : 2:pm architectures + Dauphins(arch)
Competition Results : Waiting for Results(January 2012)

FP123
AIGLE

SCÈNE ET PLACES

PROPOS 1

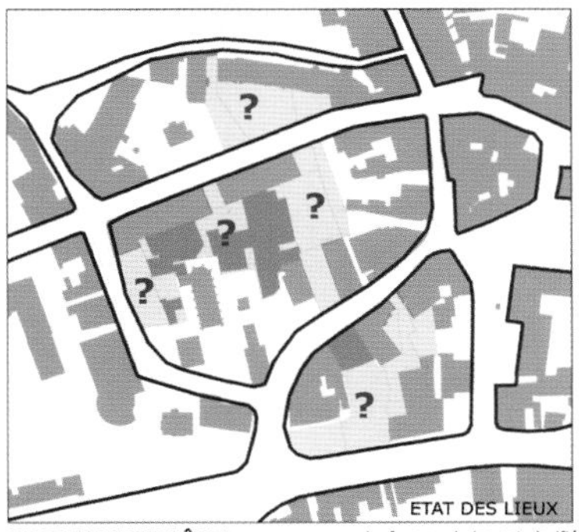

ETAT DES LIEUX

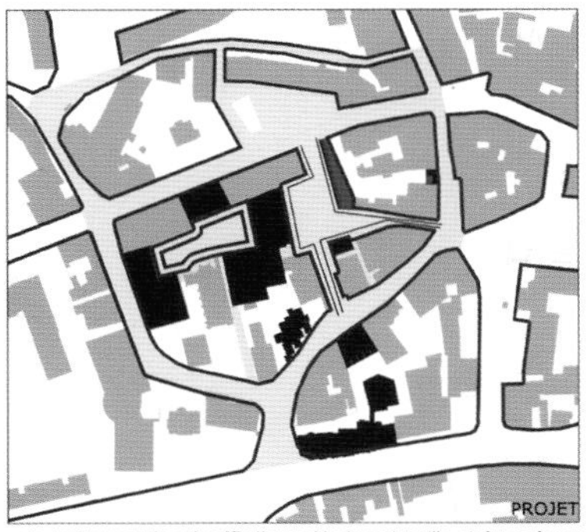

PROJET

MORPHOLOGIE BÂTIE

La forme urbaine est clarifiée. **Un vaste traitement de sol unifie** l'ensemble du centre ville et **deux places complémentaires** , l'une ouverte et l'autre contenue, harmonisent les espaces. De nouveaux lieux à découvrir s'offrent aux flanneurs, et enrichissent le dessin urbain.

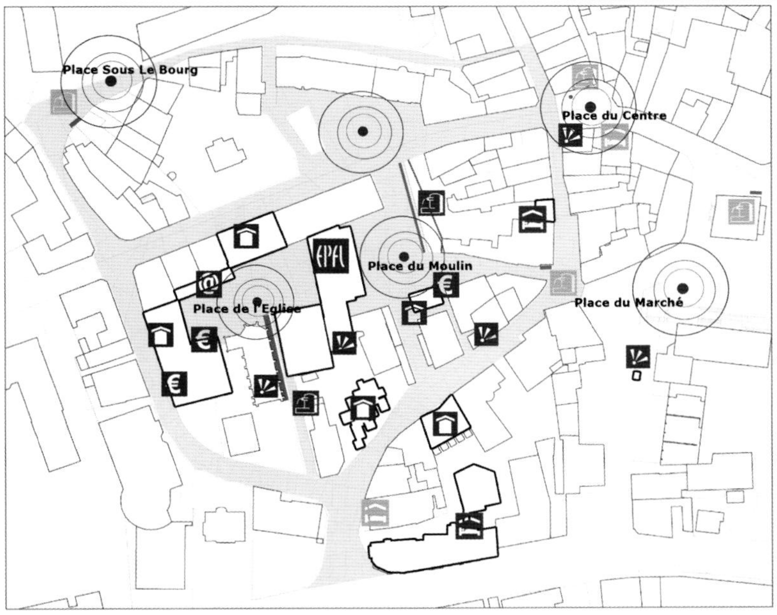

Place Sous Le Bourg
Place du Centre
Place du Moulin
Place de l'Eglise
Place du Marché

Emprise de l'aménagement urbain traduisant l'**unité du centre historique** et son exploitation pour des **usages partagés**

Zones piétonnes attenantes (Place du Marché, Place Sous Le Bourg)

Réseau des places :
Deux nouvelles places requalifient le centre historique, la Place du Moulin Neuf (place ouverte) et la Place de l'Eglise (place contenue).

Centre de Recherche et de Formation de la Vigne et du Vin :
Un équipement d'enseignement dédié à la préservation, la mise en valeur et l'exploitation du patrimoine viticole local et régional. Ce programme peut être mis en relation avec l'EPFL.

Signaux urbains :
Belvédère des pompiers
Eglise catholique
Temple
Moulin Neuf
Tour de l'Horloge

Festival des Fontaines :
Deux fontaines contemporaines, Fontaine de l'Eglise et Fontaine du Moulin Neuf, amorcent l'organisation d'un festival annuel des arts de la rue.

Hébergements saisonniers :
Ce type d'activité permet de faire d'Aigle une étape de choix dans la découverte de la région du Chablais.

Nouveaux logements :
Afin d'accueillir une croissance démographique dans le centre il est nécessaire de fournir des logements en accession ou en location, ou encore des logements étudiants à proximité du centre du vin.

Des espaces de **connectivité**

Des **commerces** de proximité

ESPACES DE SOCIABILITÉ

L'ensemble du centre historique, redevenu piéton, accueille de **nouveaux programmes par petites touches** afin de dynamiser Aigle. Deux programmes majeurs accentuent l'**attractivité** : Le centre de Recherche de la Vigne et du Vin et le Festival des Fontaines. Le patrimoine culturel comme un tuteur fiable à l'épanouissement d'une ville.

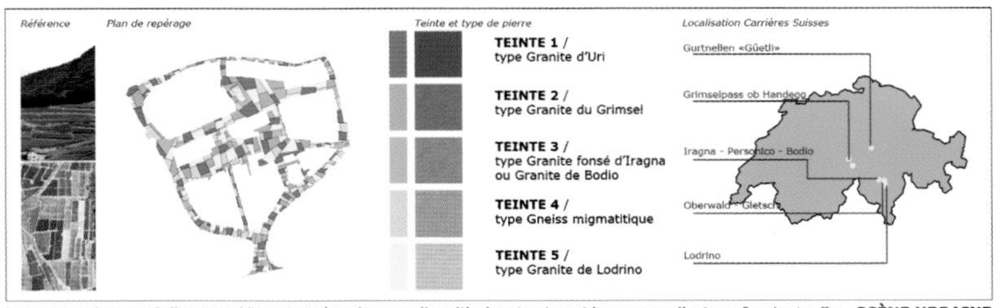

Référence — Plan de repérage — Teinte et type de pierre — Localisation Carrières Suisses

TEINTE 1 /
type Granite d'Uri

TEINTE 2 /
type Granite du Grimsel

TEINTE 3 /
type Granite fonsé d'Iragna ou Granite de Bodio

TEINTE 4 /
type Gneiss migmatitique

TEINTE 5 /
type Granite de Lodrino

Iragna - Personico - Bodio
Lodrino

SCÈNE URBAINE

Le nouveau calepinage de l'espace public est inspiré par **les parcelles viticoles structurant le paysage allentour**. Son dessin offre un panel de cinq revêtements en pierres issues des carrières suisses. Le sol devient alors **support de nouveaux usages**, un espace d'expression identitaire.

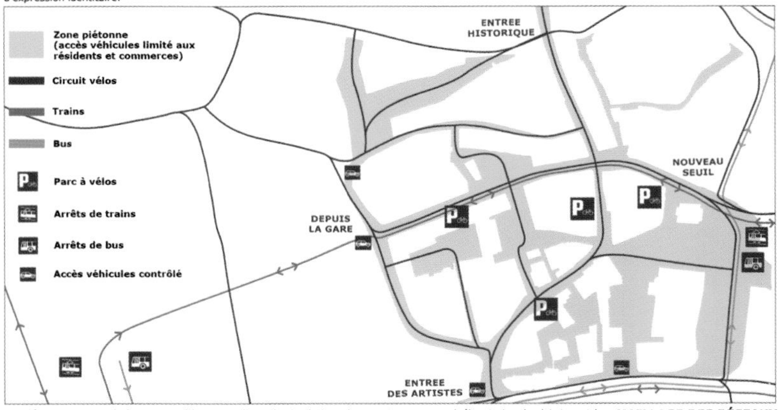

Zone piétonne (accès véhicules limité aux résidents et commerces)
Circuit vélos
Trains
Bus
Parc à vélos
Arrêts de trains
Arrêts de bus
Accès véhicules contrôlé

ENTREE HISTORIQUE
NOUVEAU SEUIL
DEPUIS LA GARE
ENTREE DES ARTISTES

MAILLAGE DES RÉSEAUX

Le piéton a reconquis le centre ville. Un maillage de circulations douces et communes (vélos, trains, bus) irriguent les **espaces urbains retrouvés**. Des circuits cyclistes balisés, ponctués de parcs à vélos, sont aménagés en lieu et place des voies voitures. L'accès au centre historique est alors interdit à ces dernières sauf pour les riverains et les commerçants.

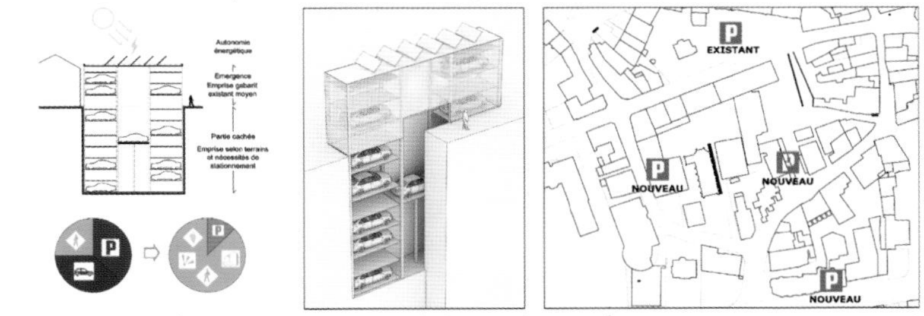

EXISTANT
NOUVEAU
NOUVEAU
NOUVEAU

RÉDUCTION DE L'EMPRISE DES VOITURES

Il est important de **reconsidérer la place de la voiture** en centre ville. De vastes surfaces sont retrouvées en mutualisant les espaces de stationnement. Des parkings silos, empilant les voitures, permettent de **dégager le sol** et son exploitation n'est plus entravée.

Aigle Verre en Main — Festival des Fontaines — Dimanche

OCCUPATION SPATIALE

En aménageant un traitement urbain unificateur et en donnant la priorité aux piétons, **le centre historique peut devenir une véritable scène** où s'expriment tous les évènements culturels. L'espace et l'identité d'Aigle sont restitués aux promeneurs.

INTERVENTIONS

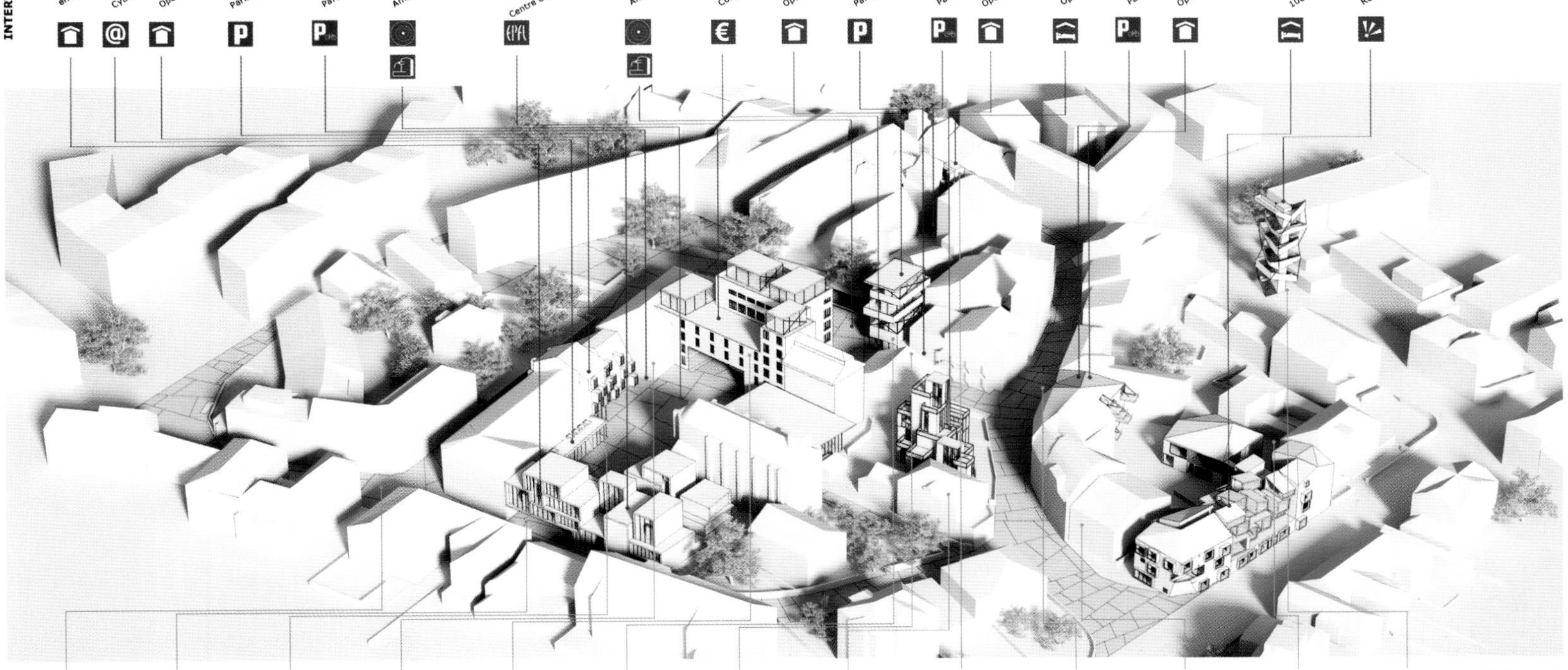

Opération de 15 logements en pont sur la Place de l'Eglise
Cyber café
Opération de 25 logements étudiants en pont sur la Place de l'Eglise
Parking silo intégré aux logements
Parc à vélos intégré aux logements étudiants
Aménagement de la Place de l'Eglise et de sa fontaine
Restructuration du Moulin Neuf en Centre de Recherche et de Formation de la Vigne et du Vin (EPFL)
Aménagement de la Place du Moulin et de sa fontaine
Commerce de proximité
Opération de 3 logements en accession
Parking silo sur pignon aveugle existant
Parc à vélos intégré
Opération de 7 logements en accession
Opération de 4 chambres d'hôtes
Parc à vélos intégré
Opération de 10 logements mettant en relation coeur d'îlot et rue
Auberge de jeunesse 106 lits et 7 appartements
Restructuration de la tour des pompiers en belvédère sur le paysage

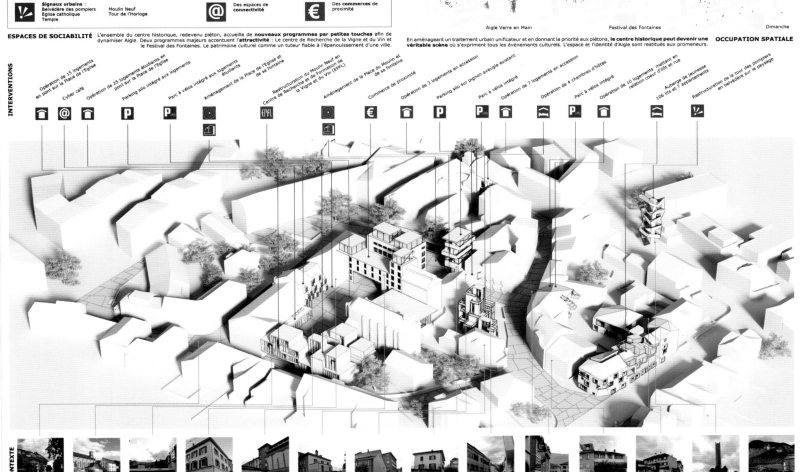

CONTEXTE

FP123
AIGLE

SCÈNE ET PLACES

ENTRE DEUX : 5 LOGEMENTS IMBRIQUÉS

Pour éviter l'exode du centre historique il est crucial de repenser l'occupation des parcelles afin de **dégager de l'espace habitable**. La densification du tissu urbain semble être une nécessité.

Cette opération de cinq logements adopte une géométrie d'imbrication limitant l'emprise au sol et préservant l'intimité des voisins en s'en éloignant à mesure que le bâtiment s'élève.

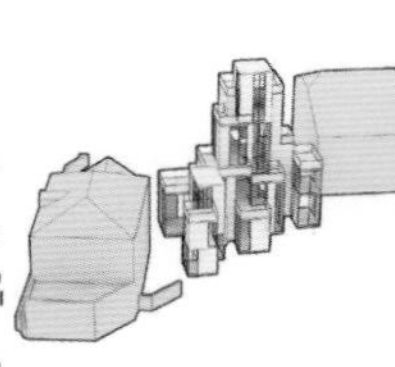

ACCUEILLIR : AUBERGE DE JEUNESSE

Plusieurs coutures urbaines clarifient la lecture et les limites des ilôts. Des espaces aujourd'hui «non définis» deviennent un **potentiel de densification**.

Cette opération d'auberge de jeunesse s'inscrit sur une des entrées de ville : l'entrée des artistes. Sa position d'angle agit comme un repère marquant le seuil de la ville historique. D'une capacité de cent six lits et de sept appartements, elle fournit un nouveau type d'hébergement, vecteur d'attractivité.

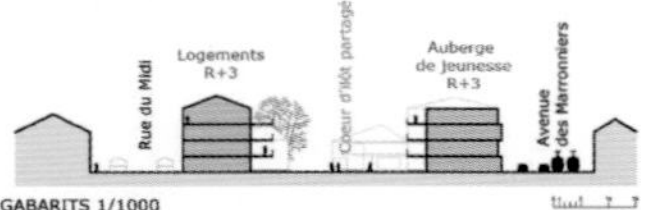

GABARITS 1/1000

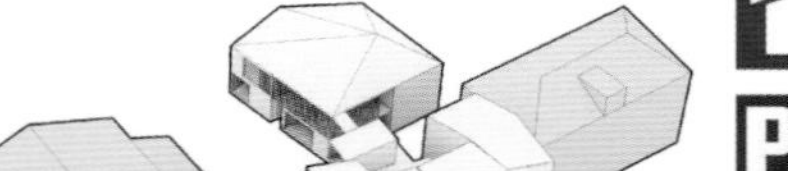

LIEN : 10 LOGEMENTS ENTRE RUE ET COEUR D'ILÔT

Démolir et reconstruire font partie de la requalification d'un tissu urbain à condition de préserver une **harmonie avec les gabarits existants**.

Cette opération de dix logements tire parti du réaménagement de l'ilôt entier. Elle entretient deux rapports distincts: un premier sur la rue où une inflection du bâtiment ponctue la linéarité de la façade urbaine. Un seccond sur le coeur d'ilôt où de larges balcons ouvrent la vue sur la montagne.

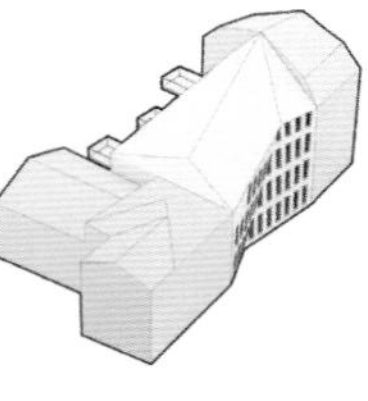

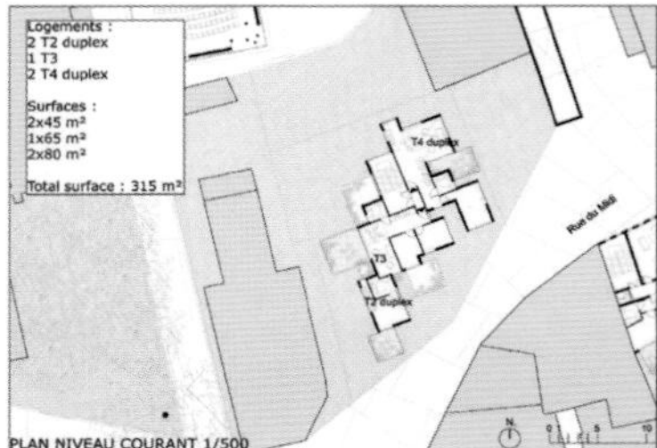

PLAN NIVEAU COURANT 1/500

PLAN REZ DE CHAUSSÉE 1/1000

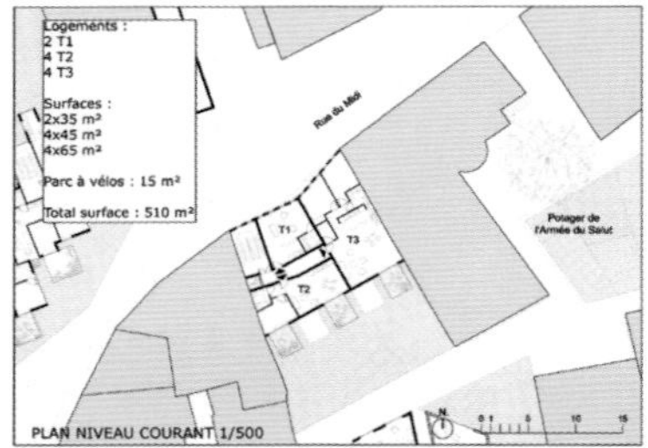

PLAN NIVEAU COURANT 1/500

FP123
AIGLE

SCÈNE ET PLACES

SUR LA PLACE : 3 LOGEMENTS SUR UN COMMERCE

La nouvelle place du Moulin s'inscrit dans un **réseau de placettes** ponctuant le centre d'évènements urbains singuliers.

Cette opération allie deux usages tout en travaillant sur la densité de la parcelle utilisée. Chaque logement est ceinturé d'une allège de 1,60 m obturant la vue depuis le sol. Les vitrages hauts apportent la lumière du ciel, seule la cime des montagnes reste visible.

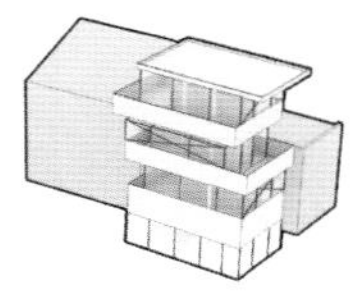

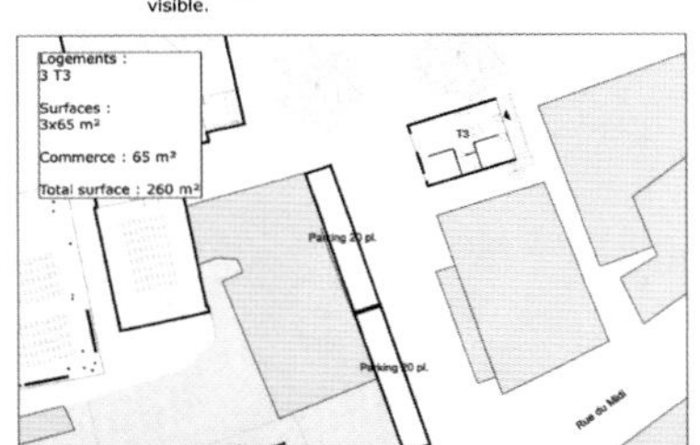

PATRIMOINE : RECONVERTION DU MOULIN NEUF EN CENTRE DE RECHERCHE DE LA VIGNE ET DU VIN

Au delà de la vielle pierre, la **préservation du patrimoine** doit aussi s'attacher à la conservation d'une **mémoire collective** qui peut parfois s'inscrire dans des bâtiments semblant anodins.

S'adapter pour durer:
Cette opération de reconvertion du Moulin Neuf a deux conséquences sur le patrimoine d'Aigle. Le bâtiment, un repère sur le site, est conservé dans les mémoires, et son usage met en valeur un autre aspect de l'identité de la ville, les vignes. Le domaine de l'enseignement et de la recherche reliera Aigle à Lausanne au travers d'une caractéristique locale: le vin. Salles de cours et amphithéâtre animent les deux places nouvellement aménagées.

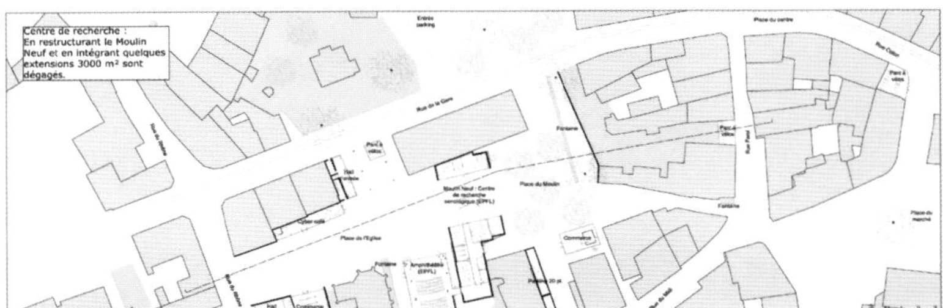

EN PONT : 15 LOGEMENTS ENTRE RUE ET PLACE

Agencer une place contenue engendre ici des morphologies de bâtiments ponts. Cette singularité trouve **un écho à la mémoire urbaine** du centre historique.

Cette opération de quinze logements traversants est distribuée par une coursive à ciel ouvert. Sa morphologie recadre la rue du Rhône d'un côté, et contient la place de l'autre.

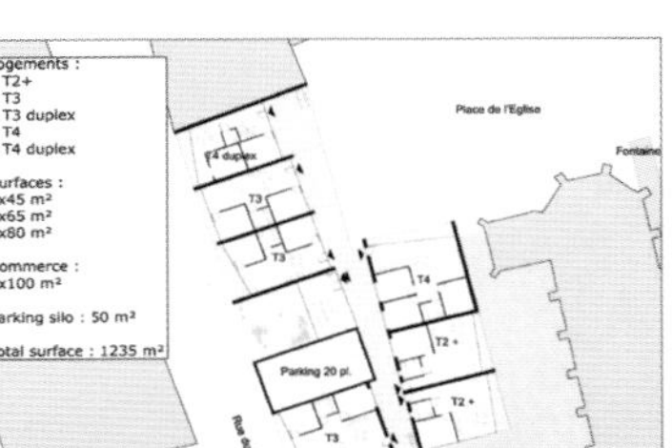

076 Mexico 2030 | *Slot.*

Location : Azcapotzalco, Mexico City
Program : Urban Conversion of former industrial Areas to a Mixed Use Development
Project Type : Competition

Client : Colegio de Arquitectos, Mexico
Year of Design : 2011
Construction Area : 600 ha / Credits : Slot.

Última Edición

MEXICO 2030

VIERNES
2 DE DICIEMBRE DE 2030

UNA CIUDAD CON PROYECTO.

$ 10

AÑO: 113 I NÚMERO 34.267

MÉXICO, DF 4 PÁGINAS

A veinte años después de su aprobación, Ciudad Fortuna sobrepasa las expectativas de un Subcentro Urbano

Primer proyecto de una exitosa conversión urbana

CIUDAD FORTUNA 2030

Desde la capital, Rodrigo Rodríguez, 2 de Noviembre, 2030

El jefe del gobierno del Distrito Federal Carlos Ángel Torres y el gobernador del Estado de México Leonardo Ayala destacaron los enormes logros de mejoramiento urbano que se realizaron en Ciudad Fortuna.

"Ciudad Fortuna ha sido el más ambicioso proyecto de revitalización urbana en Latinoamérica. Ubicado a tan sólo seis kilómetros del Centro Histórico de la Ciudad de México y con facilidad conectiva a la infraestructura de la ciudad continuando la Avenida de los Insurgentes, la Ciudad de México se ha vuelto pionera en Latinoamérica ante el enfrentamiento del colapso de las megaciudades", explicó el jefe del gobierno capitalino ayer y agregó: "En apenas veinte años pudimos concentrar el crecimiento de la Zona Metropolitana del Valle de México en un subcentro de alto rendimiento."

"Todos los criterios importantes para una ciudad sostenible se hacen evidentes con este proyecto ejemplar" agregó el gobernador del Estado de México Leonardo Ayala y lo particularizó en una lista de características que incluyen: energía sustentable, el buen manejo de recursos y la reducción de gases invernaderos que revierten el cambio climático sin limitar la calidad de vida de sus ciudadanos.

Con un total de 600 hectáreas, Ciudad Fortuna se desarrolló en los últimos veinte años dando lugar a alrededor de 300,000 habitantes y ofreciendo el mismo número de puestos de trabajo. El concepto de "Una Ciudad Adentro de una Ciudad" ganó varios premios a nivel mundial por su carácter autosustentable que reduce significativamente los problemas de tránsito. Una fina mezcla entre diferentes usos y una amplia variedad de tipologías para vivienda y oficinas que favorecen su buen funcionamiento.

Así mismo, Ciudad Fortuna es una mezcla de diferentes sectores sociales lo cual resulta en una ciudad más democrática donde todos tienen acceso libre a los servicios y dónde existe un diálogo entre sus ciudadanos. El alto porcentaje de áreas verdes se logró a partir de la alta densidad aplicada y que aumenta conforme se acerca a su centro. Un parque lineal de tres kilómetros de largo forma la columna vertebral y da una clara orientación.

"El uso del coche dentro del subcentro es casi innecesario ya que todo es accesible peatonalmente, por medio de ciclovías o en transportes públicos de última generación", explica Ángel Torres y agregó: "La Ciudad de México encontró la fórmula para crecer sin agobiar el medio ambiente. Nuestras emisiones de dióxido de carbono se han reducido en un 20% en comparación con las que teníamos en el año 2011. La Ciudad de México encontró la cura para el colapso que muchas megaciudades del mundo están viviendo hoy en día."

Trampolín

La Ciudad de México funge como embudo para toda Latinoamérica

La competencia por la mejor posición económica a nivel mundial se decide cada vez menos entre los países dando prioridad a sus ciudades. Así, podemos observar que las ciudades tienen que ser creativas para no perder la gracia de sus ciudadanos, empresas y turistas.

A lo largo de los últimos años, muchas ciudades del planeta han desarrollado una identidad simple, clara y fácil de entender y transmitir, que movilice a las mejores iniciativas y personas. Para desarrollar esta visión es muy importante el aspecto de la elección de la imagen que se proyecta; se requiere un modelo ideológico.

En la competencia mundial entre ciudades, la Ciudad de México ha encontrado su identidad específica en un aspecto geopolítico, y gracias a su ubicación cercana a los Estados Unidos que todavía representa la economía más fuerte del mundo; un portal para el tráfico entre Latinoamérica y los Estados Unidos o más general, entre Latinoamérica y el mundo desarrollado. De igual manera este umbral funciona inversamente para el primer mundo que hace negocios con Latinoamérica. La "Ciudad Trampolín".

El desarrollo de nuevos subcentros urbanos muestra buenos avances

El Plan de Desarrollo Urbano 2050 está en rápido crecimiento

Esteban Rendón, director del Superministerio de Desarrollo Urbano de la ZMVM está satisfecho con los avances de los tres nuevos Subcentros Urbanos. "Tomando como ejemplo su hermano mayor "Ciudad Fortuna", los tres nuevos subcentros en los municipios de Naucalpan, Ecatepec y Tlalnepantla están tomando forma y se desarrollan más rápido que lo previsto", destacó Esteban Rendón ayer en la presentación del reporte anual de su ministerio.

La columna vertebral del Plan de Desarrollo 2050 consiste en el desarrollo de tres nuevos subcentros en áreas industriales subutilizadas en la ZMVM. Cada uno de los nuevos subcentros tiene un área de aproximadamente 500 hectáreas y esta muy bien conectado con el resto de la ciudad através de las líneas del tren suburbano ya existentes de las líneas 2 y 3.

"Las exigencias de crecimiento y densificación de nuestra ciudad son enormes en los años a venir", explica Esteban Rendón, indicando que la Ciudad de México es reconocida en el mundo por la implementación de Subcentros Urbanos de gran tamaño. "Nuestra estrategia de densificación urbana a través de Subcentros Urbanos nos ha dado mucho crédito al nivel mundial y nos ha convertido en líderes de la rehabilitación urbana en toda Latinoamérica."

El Superministerio de Desarrollo Urbano para la ZMVM es una dependencia gubernamental formado por el SEDUVI del Distrito Federal y la Secretaría de Comunicaciones y Transportes del Estado de México comenzó sus labores hace ya una década con el fin de reducir los procesos burocráticos entre las dos entidades políticas y así dar solución a una problemática regional. A lo largo de la planeación del Subcentro Ciudad Fortuna tener un solo ministerio coordinando la planeación y el desarrollo fue de vital importancia.

Red de trenes suburbanos en crecimiento continuo

Grupos ciudadanos y políticos de todos los partidos exigen la construcción de la cuarta línea del tren suburbano de Buenavista a San Ángel

Ya son tres las líneas del tren suburbano en la ZMVM y con esto no basta. Varias voces exigen la siguiente pieza en la red del tren suburbano. Se trata de una cuarta línea que extendería la estación Buenavista con San Ángel en el sur de la ciudad y conectará los nuevos subcentros con los ya establecidos como son Reforma e Insurgentes.

"Con esta nueva línea todos los subcentros de la ciudad estarían conectados con trenes suburbanos y el tiempo máximo entre un subcentro y otro sería de no más de 10 minutos", explica Margarita García, diputado del PRI.

El financiamiento de la nueva línea da respuesta al obstáculo más grande, a diferencia de la situación con las tres líneas en operación, que se construyeron en corredores libres en territorio federal sin necesidad de un mayor número de puentes o túneles. "La situación con esta nueva línea es diferente", afirma Ricardo Navarrete, líder del grupo ciudadano, "porque un túnel debajo de la Avenida de los Insurgentes cuesta mucho dinero."

Red de trenes suburbanos

Sin embargo, los beneficios de la nueva línea son tan grandes y obvios que nadie duda de su pronta realización. "Pensar de comunicarse de San Ángel a uno de los nuevos subcentros en el norte de la ciudad en tan sólo 10 minutos estaría acompañado de un ahorro de tiempo de más de una hora", dice Ricardo Navarrete.

El nuevo Tenochtitlán - Conoce su renacimiento

El área de la ZMVM no ha crecido en los últimos quince años

Confirma directora del INEGI que la Ciudad no se expandió en áreas desde el año 2015

La Zona Metropolitana del Valle de México continúa en crecimiento con una tasa anual de 3.5%. Sin embargo, la mancha urbana se ha mantenido del mismo tamaño por décimo año consecutivo, gracias a las políticas ambientales establecidas hace ya diecisiete años. Mientras que los metros cuadrados construidos en la ZMVM subieron por 36 % en los últimos 18 años, tan sólo se invadieron 2.6% de áreas vírgenes nuevos en el mismo tiempo. Paralelamente, se pudo lograr la generación de más parques y áreas verdes adentro de la ZMVM.

La ciudad de México ha tenido enormes logros en la reducción de la expansión urbana que desde mitad del siglo XX empezó a invadir zonas no aptas para su construcción como son áreas en peligro de inundación o zonas montañosas. Así mismo logró la protección de la Reserva Ecológica del Parque Nacional Ajusco, cuyos bosques se encontraban amenazados por el crecimiento de la mancha urbana que se había expandido sin control sobre las partes bajas cercanas a la zona del parque.

"Gracias a las políticas de hace casi veinte años, la Ciudad de México ha logrado mantener su entorno boscoso y ha aprovechado de manera óptima su infraestructura existente", explica Juana Herrera, directora del INEGI en su reporte anual.

La tecnología a favor del medio ambiente

La venta de coches con tecnología sustentable en marcha adelante

Cada día son más los coches híbridos que usan tecnologías sustentables en la Ciudad de México. Según los números de ventas por la compañía X presentados ayer, la venta en la ZMVM de este año suma 302,189 coches que no emiten dióxido de carbón.

Esta tendencia es resultados del programa "Cambia tu coche ya" que está subsidiado por los gobiernos del Estado de México y del Distrito Federal. "Estamos muy contentos con este movimiento y esperamos que aún más ciudadanos se decidan a participar en este programa", dijo el vicepresidente de X ayer en una conferencia de prensa.

Coche híbrido

El programa "Cambia tu coche ya" subsidia la compra de un coche sustentable con el 30 % de su precio si el coche con tecnología convencional se achatara al mismo tiempo. Con este programa, los gobiernos de los Estados participantes esperan lograr un mejoramiento significativo del medio ambiente.

Crecimiento de la Ciudad de México

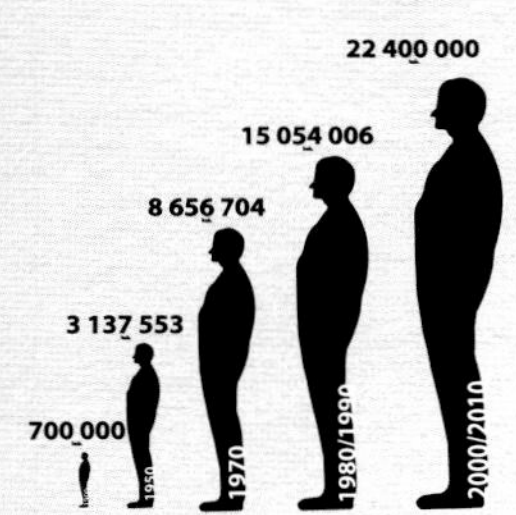

Crecimiento de población entre 1900 y 2010

La Ciudad de México siempre perteneció al circulo de las ciudades más grandes en el planeta. Aún antes de la conquista española en 1521, el antiguo Tenochtitlán contaba ya con cuatro veces de la población de Londres.

Desde los años 1950, la ciudad se encuentra en un crecimiento acelerado continuo. Mientras que su crecimiento hasta los años ochenta se caracterizaba por el binomio, área - población, el crecimiento hoy en día se define básicamente por las áreas ya que el crecimiento de la población se ha desacelerado constantemente.

A pesar de esta tendencia y a pesar de ser una de las ciudades más grandes del mundo, el perímetro de la mancha urbana en relación a su población tiene aún dimensiones aceptables al compararlo con ciudades como Los Ángeles o Shangai. Esta condición favorece muchos aspectos que son importantes para la visión de una ciudad sustentable.

Para mantener esta situación y respetando las necesidades previstas de crecimiento en áreas del futuro, la Ciudad de México necesita un concepto de crecimiento vertical, que al mismo tiempo restrinja la expansión horizontal.

La importancia del Estado de México

Crecimineto en áreas

La Zona Metropolitana de la Ciudad de México engloba tres entidades administrativas. Una parte se extiende en el Distrito Federal, la parte más antigua y céntrica, otra parte en el Estado de México y una tercera pequeña parte en el Estado de Hidalgo. La planeación de la ciudad se hizo por separado sin encontrar un concepto abarcando todas las entidades administrativas por demasiados años.

La Ciudad de México tuvo su crecimiento más acelerado entre 1930 y 1950, período en el cual inicia su expansión hacia el Estado de México. De 1950 a 1980, iniciando la conurbación con el Estado de México. En la actualidad la población se divide casi por igual entre el D.F. y el Estado de México. Sin embar¬go, el crecimiento urbano actual domina en el Estado de México, mientras que el D.F. tiende a estabilizarse.

Desde 1980 se inició una migración centro-periferia y una estrecha vinculación con las ciudades de Pachuca, Puebla, Tlaxcala, Cuernavaca y Toluca, conformando una corona regional.

Para controlar el futuro crecimiento de la ciudad, existe una gran necesidad de ver la Ciudad de México como un gran organismo que requiere un concepto de planeación coordinado y unido.

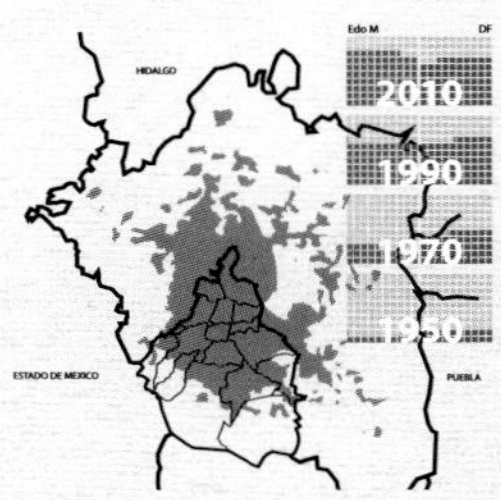

Crecimiento de áreas en el Estado de México (rojo) y el Distrito Federal (azul) entre 1950 y 2010

Limitaciones

Condiciones geográficas y naturales

Desde sus inicios, la Ciudad de México ha enfrentado limitaciones en su construcción. Cuando el conquistador español Hernán Cortés tomó la decisión de construir la nueva capital encima del antiguo Tenochtitlán, la batalla contra el agua comenzaba sin haber iniciado la construcción. La desecación del lago Texcoco llevó a muchos problemas que hasta hoy causan dificultades, lo cual se manifiesta en las numerosas inundaciones que la Ciudad de México sufre cada año. Otra consecuencia de construir en un subsuelo no firme son los riesgos causados por sismos. Gracias a la ingeniería moderna hemos encontrado maneras de enfrentar este reto.

Otra limitación que enfrenta la Ciudad de México la constituyen las montañas boscosas que contornean casi toda la ciudad. En muchas ocasiones la mancha urbana ya sobrepasó el límite e invadió zonas que no se prestan para su urbanización. Según la SEMARNAP, "el rápido crecimiento de los últimos 50 años ocurrió a costa de la expansión no planificada de áreas urbanas residenciales, así como por asentamientos ilegales no planificados en las áreas periféricas, no siempre aptas para el desarrollo ur¬bano. Esto ha acarreado grandes presiones sobre los espacios y recursos natura¬les, y dificultades en el aprovisionamiento de diferentes insumos y servicios a los habitantes; y ha originado un mosaico diverso de espacios intraurbanos, según su grado de consolidación urbana y las condiciones socioeconómicas de la po¬blación que los habita, así como la vulnerabilidad y riesgo al que se exponen."

Invasión de áreas no aptas para su construcción

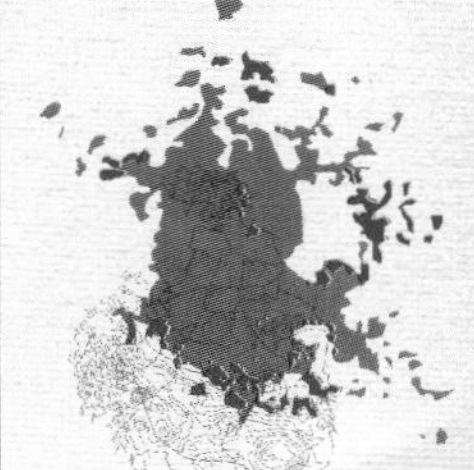

Las inundaciones y los terremotos debido al subsuelo y la zona sísmica en la cual se ubica la Ciudad de México son condiciones irreversibles dadas las decisiones se tomaron en tiempos pasados, sin embargo son controlables.

A diferencia de estos dos aspectos, la invasión de zonas naturales para el futuro crecimiento de la ciudad se puede frenar eficazmente. Estamos todavía a buen tiempo. La necesidad de un freno a la expansión horizontal es incuestionable. La respuesta se encuentra en la densificación de zonas subutilizadas dentro de la mancha urbana de forma vertical.

Movilidad

Transporte individual y transporte público

La planeación del transporte individual y público de la Ciudad de México no está uno si no varios pasos atrás de sus necesidades, hecho que se manifiesta en muchas horas perdidas en el tráfico.

Mientras que la necesidad de viajes en la Ciudad de México aumenta cada día, hay que encontrar un concepto de trafico robusto y eficiente para las siguientes décadas. Sólo así se asegura que no sufra la actividad económica de la ciudad debido a limitaciones del movimiento.

Red del metro en relación con la mancha urbana de la ZMVM

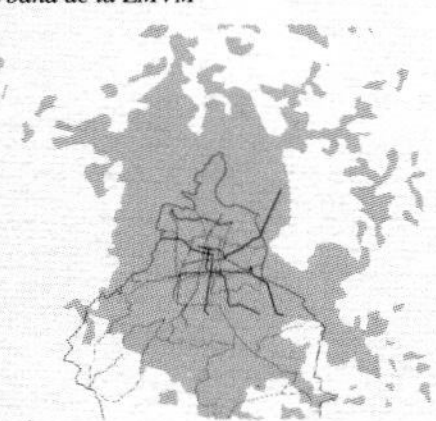

El transporte público de la ciudad está subsidiado para los sectores más pobres y por esto la decisión por el uso de transporte individual o colectivo en la Ciudad de México depende básicamente a la clase socio-económico a la cual pertenezcan sus habitantes. Mientras que la clase trabajadora y los pobres tienden al uso del transporte público, las clases más altas usan casi exclusivamente el transporte individual motorizado, independientemente si un viaje pudiera realizarse más rápido y cómodamente con el transporte público. Este fenómeno conlleva el descuido del transporte público y al poco desarrolló del sistema en las últimas décadas.

Aunque el sistema de metro de la Ciudad de México se está en continuo desarrollo, sus líneas no llegan más allá del centro de la ciudad y deja la periferia subdesarrollada. Además, todas las líneas existentes ya llegaron a su límite de capacidad, ya que ni el tamaño ni la frecuencia de tacto se pueden aumentar.

Línea 1 del tren suburbano en áreas de baja densidad urbana

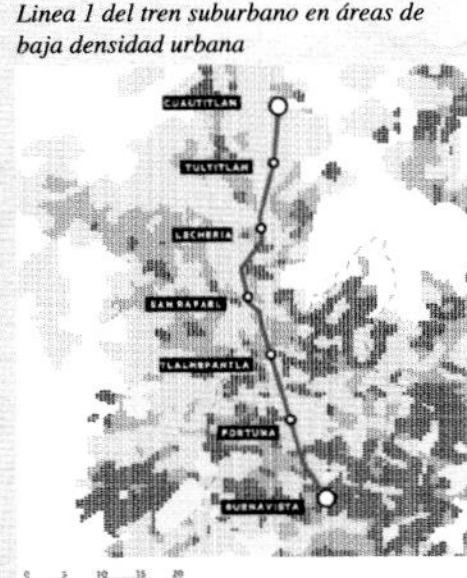

Uno de los intentos de cambiar esta condición resultó en la planeación del tren suburbano que recorre de manera muy rápida grandes distancias conectando el norte de la ciudad con el centro. Debido a que el tren usa vías ferroviales existentes que antes conectaban áreas industriales, la densidad a lo largo de la línea y alrededor de sus estaciones es muy baja. Allí existe un gran potencial de densificación, tomando en cuenta que ya poseen una infraestructura excelente que todavía no llegó a sus límites de capacidad en cuanto a la frecuencia de tacto.

Calidad de vida de los ciudadanos

Pirámide de edades

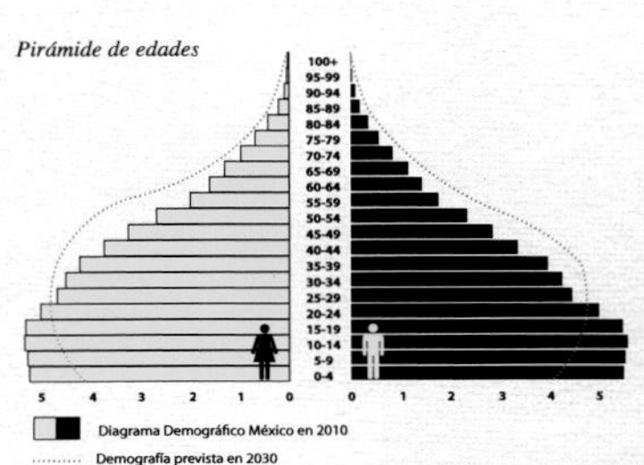

La calidad de vida en la Ciudad de México tiene muchos déficits. Según la Encuesta Mundial sobre Calidad de Vida 2007 hecho por Mercer Human Resource Consulting, la Ciudad de México se posiciona en el lugar 211 de 215 ciudades examinadas. El ranking considera factores como la calidad y disponibilidad de suministros médicos, niveles de contaminación ambiental, enfermedades infecciosas así como la eficiencia de la remoción de deshechos y los sistemas de tratamiento de aguas negras, potabilidad del agua y la presencia de animales e insectos dañinos.

De acuerdo con la UNESCO, es recomendable tener un mínimo de 12 metros cuadrados de áreas verdes por habitante en las ciudades para poseer un ambiente aceptablemente sano. En la Ciudad de México se calcula actualmente una superficie de solo 3 metros cuadrados, lo cual hace el déficit evidente.

De la misma manera habrá que tomar en cuenta los cambios afectados por una composición de la sociedad diferente en el año 2030; mientras que la imagen actual de la población esta marcada por jóvenes, las calles de la Ciudad de México del año 2030 se van a caracterizar por una población vieja. Este cambio hace aún más necesario un cambio en los factores que determinen la calidad de vida.

Estos factores podrían ser un sistema de transporte público eficiente y seguro, un aumento en actividades culturales abiertos a todo público en un ambiente libre de contaminantes.

La economía de la Ciudad de México

El crecimiento del sector de servicios a costo del sector de producción

La separación de la economía en tres sectores de actividad ayuda a clasificarla y nos explica su composición. La extracción de materias primas se reconoce como el sector primario, la manufactura como el sector secundario y los servicios como el terciario. La composición de los porcentajes explica el progreso del desarrollo de un país o una aglomeración urbana. Un país con un alto sector primario es menos desarrollado que un país con un alto sector terciario.

En la Ciudad de México, el sector terciario (los servicios) tiene el porcentaje mas alto con tendencia creciente, mientras que el sector secundario(la industria)se ha reducido año por año. Este fenómeno es conocido en todas las aglomeraciones urbanas grandes de países en vías de desarrollo o ya desarrollados. Las razones por esto son obvias, porque las ciudades que representan el corazón económico, cultural y social del país se han convertido en lugares con un alto porcentaje de servicios modernos y debido a esta transformación, tienen cada vez menos industria.

Estos cambios en la economía de la Ciudad de México se reflejan en cambios gradualesen todas partes de la ciudad, la industria se retira y se reemplaza por otros usos. Se puede observar que este proceso empezó en las delegaciones del Distrito Federal más céntricos, como son la delegación Cuauhtémoc, Miguel Hidalgo y Benito Juárez, y se está extendiendo hasta los municipios del Estado de México.

Y la ciudad de México no está sola con este fenómeno; los cambios en la actividad económica que vemos aquí son parte de un proceso mundial. Muchas ciudades del mundo desarrollado ya lo enfrentaron hace dos o tres décadas. Y la globalización acelera el fenómeno aun más en los países en vías de desarrollo.

Desarrollo de los tres sectores de la economía entre 1930 y 2030

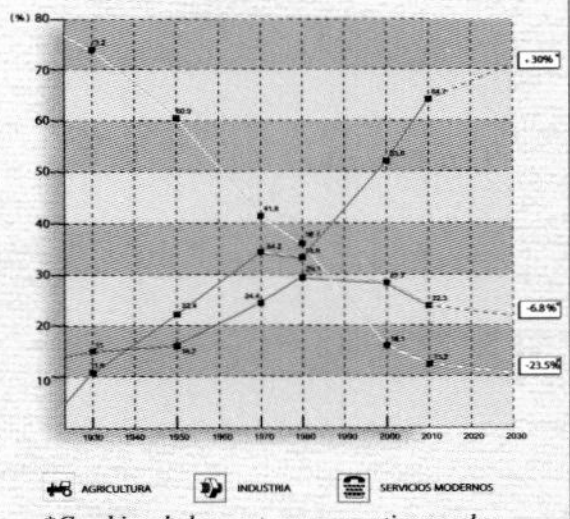

**Cambios de los sectores respectivos en los últimos 30 años*

Casos análogos de conversiones urbanas alrededor del globo

¿Cómo se manifiestan los cambios en la estructura y la imagen de nuestras ciudades?

Para contestar esta pregunta, vale la pena echar un vistazo a ciudades que han vivido este cambio décadas atrás. El proceso está conocido bajo el termino de "conversión urbana", quiere decir el cambio de un uso a otro. En su mayoría se trata de áreas industriales que se convirtieron en áreas de usos mixtos, porque la industria abandonó estas zonas debido a la falta de espacio o el nivel de contaminación que producían.

Baltimore en los Estados Unidos fue la primera ciudad donde se realizó una conversión urbana en el año 1958. La zona del puerto interior que poseía muchas bodegas vacías se convirtió en un atractivo destino turístico con una multitud de comercios pequeños y restaurantes. No fue sino hasta los años ochenta, cuando el movimiento de la revitalización urbana llegó a Europa. Londres como primer ciudad en el viejo continente revitalizó su puerto en 1981. El proyecto conocido como "Docklands" respondió a la necesidad de vivienda accesible e infraestructura social. El ambiente por el agua junto con el río Támesis brindó un sitio único que se convirtió en el lugar con mayor construcción de vivienda en Londres.

Proyectos de Conversiones urbanas en el mundo

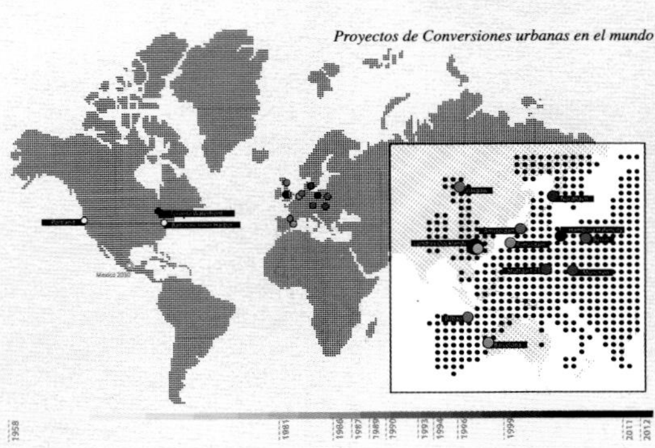

El ejemplo de Barcelona, que utilizó los juegos olímpicos para una conversión fundamental abriéndose al mar, o Bilbao en los años 1985 y 1989. En los Países Bajos, Roterdam y Ámsterdam convirtieron sus puertos abandonados en atractivas zonas de usos mixtos y las conectaban con ambiciosos proyectos de infraestructura con el centro de la ciudad.

El movimiento de la conversión urbana ganó mucha popularidad en Alemania en los años noventa. Ciudades como Munich, Stuttgart y Frankfurt propusieron construir estaciones de tren y infraestructura ferrovial de manera subterránea para así liberar centenares de hectáreas con la mejor ubicación junto a los centros históricos. Los llamados "Proyectos 21" enfrentaron dificultades en su realización costosa y solo Stuttgart 21 logró ser realizado.

En los primeros años del siglo XXI el movimiento se concentró nuevamente a ciudades cerca al agua como por ejemplo Hamburgo que actualmente está transformando su puerto antiguo en 150 hectáreas de usos mixtos, o el proyecto más ambicioso en la actualidad, reconocido como Nordhavnen, el antiguo puerto de Copenhagen resolverá 300 hectáreas de usos mixtos en 2020.

¿Cómo se podrían reflejar los cambios efectuados por el cambió de la economía en el ambiente construido de la Ciudad de México?

La Ciudad de México no tiene puertos abandonados, sin embargo tiene por lo menos cuatro zonas industriales en desuso. Todas se encuentran en el norte de la Zona Metropolitana del Valle de México. Sus tamaños varían entre 300 y 600 hectáreas.

Estas zonas industriales podrían cambiar su uso y convertirse en zonas de usos mixtos, con vivienda, oficinas, comercios y programas complementarios, ya que su infraestructura inicial ya se encuentra ahí, además muchas de dichas áreas se encuentran en puntos estratégicos.

Subcentros

Un freno al crecimiento horizontal

Cuando una ciudad ha vivido un crecimiento considerable y su tamaño supera varios millones de habitantes, un sólo centro ya no da abasto para soportar a todos los movimientos que genera el tránsito, el comercio y los servicios. Si además esta ciudad funge como el corazón económico, social y cultural del país, un solo centro deja de ser suficiente para garantizar su bien funcionamiento.

Esto ya ha pasado en la Ciudad de México y desde hace muchos años y se generaron subcentros adentro de la mancha urbana o en su periferia. En el mejor de los casos, estos subcentros poseen la mayoría de los servicios que una ciudad normalmente tiene para funcionar de manera independiente.

Otro aspecto importante en cuanto a los subcentros es su ubicación referente a la ubicación del centro, su conectividad con el mismo y la conectividad y distancias referente a otros subcentros de la misma ciudad.

Analizando la situación en la Ciudad de México, encontramos que el primer subcentro se formó hace muchos años a lo largo de la Avenida Reforma como subcentro lineal en competencia al centro histórico. Con el boom económico de los años setena, se desarrolló un segundo subcentro a lo largo de la Avenida de los Insurgentes, igualmente de manera lineal y formó dos polos económicos y sociales alrededor del World TradeCenter y otro por San Ángel.

Ambos subcentros, el de Reforma y el de Insurgentes se formaron cuando la ciudad alrededor aún no se desarrollaba completamente lo cual permitió que los subcentros crecieran lo necesario. En cuanto a sus ubicaciones y las distancias entre sí y el centro histórico, los dos subcentros se integraban muy bien en la estructura existente de la ciudad y permitían una conectividad muy buena.

Sin embargo la ciudad siguió creciendo y se empezó a desarrollar otro subcentro en los años noventa en la periferia, lo que conocemos como Santa Fe. Uno de los puntos críticos es su relativa distancia del centro histórico de la ciudad, esto se hubiera podido compensar con una conectividad adecuada tanto del transporte individual como del transporte público. Este aspecto importante no se consideró suficientemente y hoy en día sufrimos las consecuencias que se expresan en tiempos de traslado inaceptables.

El último subcentro que se desarrolló en la ciudad al principio del siglo 21 conocido como Interlomas, ésta tiene los mismos problemas que Santa Fe – lejanía del centro y escases de infraestructura necesaria.

Esto nos lleva a otro aspecto importante de los subcentros y al mismo tiempo nos remite a su definición. Un subcentro – como se deduce de su nombre - debería funcionar de manera independiente, lo que haría traslados de gran escala innecesarios. Pero Santa Fe o Interlomas están lejos de ser un subcentro independiente ya que no son inclusivas. Existen ejércitos de trabajadores en posiciones de cuello azul que no pueden permitirse el lujo de vivir en Santa Fe debido al concepto de vivienda de lujo que se aplicado ahí. Esto trajo como consecuencia problemáticas de orden urbano.

Mapa con los subcentros existentes (negro) y posibles nuevos subcentros (blanco)

Las metas para un buen subcentro urbano

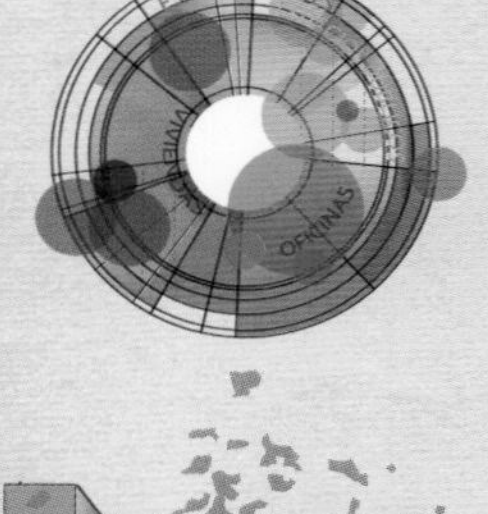

El subcentro ideal mezcla sus usos tanto horizontalmente como verticalmente

Pensando en el futuro de la Ciudad de México, una ciudad que todavía no llegó a su culminación de crecimiento, ¿cuáles serían los subcentros a desarrollar en el siglo 21?

Para contestar esta pregunta, habrá que definir primero las metas para el subcentro ideal y muchas de las respuestas se encuentran en la historia de la ciudad, tanto por lo positivo como por lo negativo. Así mismo la situación actual ha traído nuevos retos como por ejemplo el enfrentamiento al cambio climático y a escases de recursos naturale. ¿Cuántos subcentros y de qué tamaño se requieren? ¿Dónde los construimos considerando que la ciudad parece agotada? Preguntas sobre preguntas.

Usos y estructura social - Un buen subcentro necesita una buena y sana estructura en cuanto a sus usos, esto quiere decir que las ofertas de trabajo, vivienda, servicios complementarios y actividades de esparcimiento, se encuentran equilibradas. Y no solo esto, para no repetir los errores del urbanismo moderno, la mezcla de los usos mencionados tiene que planearse de una manera muy fina para evitar zonas muertas. Y con respecto a los errores que se hicieron en Santa Fe, el subcentro necesitara un equilibrio sano entre las diferentes clases sociales que tenemos en el país. Ninguna clase social debería estar excluida.

Densidad y fuerza – Para que el subcentro funcione como tal, su imagen cuenta. Tendrá que tener la fuerza formal para generar presencia en la silueta de la ciudad através de su verticalidad con uno o varios edificios que tengan carácter de hito. Todos los subcentros que tenemos hoy en día en la Ciudad de México cuentan con esta característica. La densidad traerá otros beneficios como son los caminos cortos que vuelven innecesario el uso de un medio de transporte porque muchos caminos se hacen a pie. El ahorro de tiempo representa otro aspecto positivo.

Ubicación – La ubicación de los subcentros debería medirse con respecto a su interrelación entre sí y el centro geográfico de la ciudad. La posibilidad de ubicarlos en la periferia no parece opción para la Ciudad de México porque geográficamente se observan grandes limitaciones para más construcción. Así que hay que buscar el espacio adentro de la mancha urbana en áreas que sufrieron cambios de su uso y permiten una conversión urbana. Su distancia con respecto al resto de la ciudad es importante y no debería ser demasiado lejos.

Conectividad – Para evitar los errores de Santa Fe, una buena conectividad tanto del transporte individual como del transporte colectivo será premisa para su buen funcionamiento. El subcentro debería encontrarse en ejes naturales de la ciudad que permite su conectividad. Sistemas de transporte subutilizados como vías del tren o corredores urbanos funcionarían como conectores.

Transporte interno – Un buen sistema de transporte público dentro del subcentro deberá ser la columna vertebral del mismo. Todo debería basarse en él y las distancias máximas para llegar a una parada de transporte público no podrá ser mayor a los 600 metros de distancia o 10 minutos caminando.

Análisis del Industrial Vallejo

La zona conocida como Industrial Vallejo se ubica en el norte del Distrito Federal en la delegación Azcapotzalco. Cuenta con un total de 600 hectáreas y tiene un uso industrial no contaminante. Se compone en su mayoría de bodegas y centros logísticos.

La estructura urbana se compone de varios elementos urbanos; en la esquina surponiente del industrial existe la estación Pantaco, una estación de trenes de carga, en la esquina norponiente hay varias instalaciones educativas. La zona consiste en su mayoría de bodegas industriales y está definida por lotes con una profundidad estandarizada de 150 metros. Se organiza mediante una malla general de manzanas de aproximadamente 300 por 600 metros, además existe una red de vías ferroviarias que se extiende por toda la zona y da abasto a los diferentes lotes industriales.

Densidad

Clave para una ciudad sustentable

Una alta densidad es clave para el desarrollo del subcentro, de esta manera los caminos son relativamente cortos y las distancias y necesidades de movilidad se resuelven sin mayor problema. Según Brent Toderian, director de planeación urbana de Vancouver, "el siglo 21 va ser el siglo de la densificación y ciudades que entienden esto, no solamente tienen éxito con los objetivos sustentables, pero van a ser competitivos, resistentes y formidables lugares para vivir".

La densificación estratégica ofrece además beneficios positivos más allá de un subcentro urbano: considerando el crecimiento continuo de la población mundial y la migración continua de personas a las ciudades alrededor del mundo, la densificación de todos los asentamientos urbanos puede tomar un papel crítico si queremos mejorar la salud del planeta.

Ciudad Fortuna tiene cinco anillos con diferentes densidades que se valen de diferentes tipologías. La zona de mayor densidad se ubica alrededor del parque central y se manifiesta en torres de entre quince y veinte niveles. Moviéndose desde el centro hacia la orilla, la densidad disminuye progresivamente. La segunda más densa zona se encuentra en el siguiente anillo, con 12 niveles como máximo. El tercer anillo disminuye drásticamente su densidad debido a un cambio de tipologías; pabellones de usos complementarios se ubican dentro de un parque. Los últimos dos anillos aumentan su densidad nuevamente usando tipologías de usos mixtos con un máximo de 6 niveles.

DENSIDADES

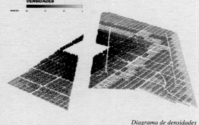

Diagrama de densidades

La transformación gradual

La transformación de Zona Industrial al Subcentro Urbano de usos mixtos se realizará gradualmente a lo largo de los siguientes años a por medio de la reutilización de la infraestructura, la lotificación, la determinación del uso de suelo y de densidades y la definición de áreas libres, entre otros.

Uno de los aspectos más fuertes del nuevo subcentro es el uso de la infraestructura existente. Las calles con sus sistemas de drenaje, y suministro de agua y electricidad ya existen y por lo tanto no representarán un gasto. La red de vías ferroviarias se convierte en un lazo de transporte público interno del subcentro.

Los nuevos predios del subcentro harán uso de la lotificación existente de la zona industrial. Según las necesidades del mercado, éstas se transformarán gradualmente y cambiarán sus densidades y usos.

El plan maestro define la ubicación de áreas verdes, las densidades y el porcentaje correspondiente de cada uso, ya sea residencial, comercial o de oficinas. La velocidad con la cual se transformará la zona en un subcentro depende de la situación económica y política.

Uso de suelo

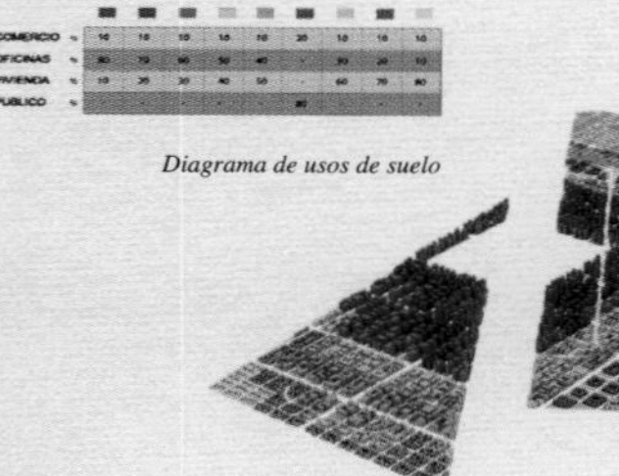

COMERCIO %	10	10	10	10	10	20	10	10	10
OFICINAS %	80	70	60	50	40	-	30	20	10
VIVIENDA %	10	20	30	40	50	-	60	70	80
PUBLICO %	-	-	-	-	-	80	-	-	-

Diagrama de usos de suelo

El uso de suelo define el coeficiente entre áreas con construcción y áreas libres, además define los porcentajes correspondientes a su uso, ya sea habitacional, comercial o de oficinas. Junto con la densidad resulta ser un fiable factor de planeación.

Ciudad Fortuna tiene varias zonas de diferentes usos. Con excepción de la zona de usos complementarios que se representa en un anillo rodeando la parte más céntrica, todas las zonas tienen una mezcla de usos. Se diferencian sólo por los porcentajes correspondientes.

La zona más céntrica se define por un alto porcentaje de oficinas, seguido por viviendas y comercios en los niveles más bajos y se basa en la idea de tener un centro de comercio nacional e internacional con grandes corporativos y un alto número de oficinas.

Un aspecto importante consiste en siempre tener comercios en la planta baja con el fin de actividades durante todo el día y no crear zonas muertas en las noches que sólo funcionen durante ciertas horas del día.

LOS COMPONENTES DEL SUBCENTRO

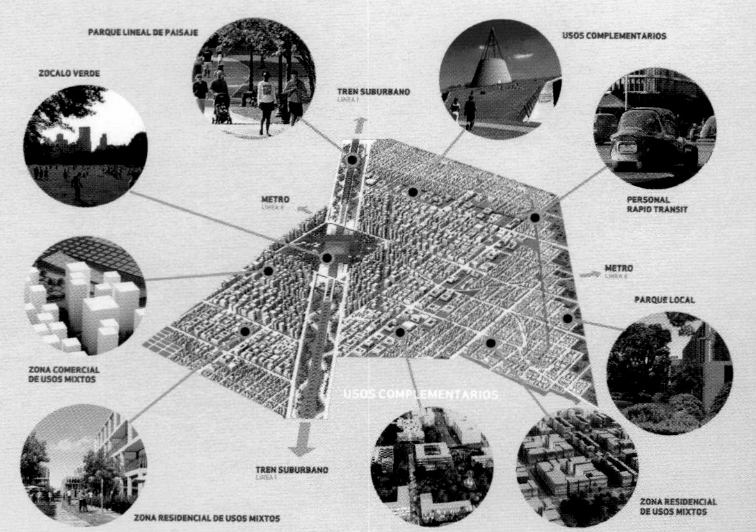

Calidad de vida

El peatón se contempla como participante principal y más importante en el nuevo subcentro. Ciudad Fortuna se construye alrededor de él y no del coche. Todas las decisiones están hechas en función de la prioridad por el peatón, un principio que no se ha visto en la Ciudad de México hasta el momento.

Las plantas bajas de los edificios se funden con el espacio público de tal forma que se remeten. Así se refuerza el diálogo entre la calle y los edificios. Los niveles de calles y banquetas se eliminan convirtiendo todo en espacio público agradable. Lo mismo pasa con el transporte público del sistema Personal Rapid Transit que se integra al espacio urbano sin formar una barrera.

La franja de usos complementarios

Ciudad Fortuna tiene un centro altamente denso y compacto, cuya densidad baja continuamente hacia sus orillas. Como consecuencia de la densidad, la tipología predominante en el centro son bloques de usos mixtos bastante compactos, que no permiten tipologías más abiertas con menos densidad en su tejido.

Para ubicar las tipologías de menor densidad y mayor apertura de carácter público, se definió una zona de usos complementarios entre las franjas más densas del centro y las menos densas en su orilla. Esta franja verde se percibe como un parque urbano, que se complementa con edificios de diferentes tamaños. Estos edificios, que se perciben como pabellones o solitarios, se mezclan entre lo verde rompiendo con la estructura rígida de su contexto.

Los usos complementarios constan de todo tipo de edificios públicos como pueden ser escuelas, hospitales, instituciones culturales y museos. Edificios gubernamentales podrían ubicarse allí de igual manera. Lo mismo aplicaría para elementos urbanos como los tianguis que pueden tener un alto valor cultural.

La construcción de esta franja comenzará con un parque que gradualmente se densificará, según las necesidades de crecimiento del subcentro, manteniendo siempre carácter de parque.

Tipologías de áreas verdes

No sólo el espacio público es verde; la vegetación en las calles prosigue en los interiores verdes de los bloques, los espacios semipúblicos. Todos los edificios en esta cuarta franja de tipologías que forman un bloque urbano comparten un patio interno con amenidades para todos su habitantes ofreciendo un máximo de vegetación.

La plaza y el eje lineal verde

Los dos elementos más importantes que definen la estructura del subcentro son la plaza central, un enorme parque de 650 por 650 metros y el eje lineal verde con unos 250 metros de ancho que marca el corredor urbano acompañado por el tren suburbano.

La plaza central, centro geográfico y logístico de Ciudad Fortuna es un enorme parque urbano con una estación intermodal en su centro que conecta los diferentes medios de transporte como el tren suburbano que circula en dirección norte-sur, la línea 6 del metro circulando en dirección oriente-poniente y el nuevo sistema de Personal Rapid Transit.

El gran vacío del parque central se equilibra con una alta densidad alrededor. Por tal motivo las construcciones más altas con unos quince a veinte niveles se alinean alrededor. Su uso es mixto con un alto porcentaje de oficinas. La vivienda más atractiva de Ciudad Fortuna se encuentra en los niveles más elevados de las torres con vista al parque central. La mezcla de usos ayuda que el centro tenga actividades las 24 horas, lo cual evita problemas de seguridad.

Si fuera un zócalo verde, el parque central de Ciudad Fortuna es el punto que da orientación y funciona como centro en un tejido urbano denso y complejo. Concentra los flujos peatonales y del transporte público desempeñándose como corazón del subcentro.

A diferencia, el parque lineal ordena las generalidades del subcentro y funciona como columna vertebral. Es parte de un eje aún más largo que conecta Ciudad Fortuna con las zonas industriales en el norte a lo largo de más de quince kilómetros. El parque lineal conecta el subcentro con su contexto urbano y garantiza su funcionamiento en una escala más grande.

Sus características son diferentes a las del parque central, no sólo por sus dimensiones sino también por su uso; es un parque de paisaje en el cual grandes partes se dirigen a la naturaleza. Ofrece muchas oportunidades para pasar el tiempo y practicar deportes. Tiene el potencial de convertirse en un espacio verde para toda la ciudad.

Ciudad Fortuna genera diálogo entre ciudadano y comercio

Convencionalmente las ciudades suelen generar fronteras muy rígidas entre el espacio público y el privado, las áreas del público por lo general se ven confinadas por los paramentos de los edificios y las calles. En el caso de Ciudad Fortuna la "barrera" es altamente permeable, los edificios en sus primeros niveles se abren eliminando la división entre el espacio público y privado y como consecuencia, el espacio público se ve beneficiado por una extensión virtual que invita al ciudadano a hacer uso de espacios que convencionalmente habían sido restringidos. De tal manera, la transición entre espacio público al privado se vuelve una experiencia más sutil. Esta apertura además ayuda al comercio ya que la exploración a las áreas comerciales es incentivada.

El sistema de transporte híbrido

El *Personal Rapid Transit* es un sistema de transporte urbano desarrollado en Corea y actualmente probado en el aeropuerto de Londres, que consiste de vehículos eléctricos que circulan sin conductor por vías especiales con capacidad de cuatro a seis personas. Van directamente entre dos puntos específicos y sin hacer escalas innecesarias.

El sistema trae muchas comodidades para el usuario, es un 50 % más eficiente energéticamente que los autobuses o los trenes y hasta un 70% más que los coches privados. Ofrecen también ventajas económicas con respecto a otros transportes públicos; mientras que la milla lineal de metro subterránea cuesta 200 millones de dólares en promedio, el sistema Personal Rapid Transit cuesta tan sólo 40 millones de dólares por milla – incluyendo vías, vehículos y estaciones.

Conclusión

Ciudad Fortuna es un proyecto de conversión urbana que reemplazará la zona industrial Vallejo ubicado en el norte del Distrito Federal con oficinas, hoteles, comercios, edificios públicos y áreas residenciales. Será el proyecto de revitalización y conversión urbana más importante del país y de todo Latinoamérica. Su construcción está previsto para el año 2030 y el concepto de una conversión gradual permite cambios y adaptaciones a la situación económica y política de la ciudad y del país. Con sus 600 hectáreas es sin duda uno de los proyectos urbanos más ambiciosos al nivel mundial.

El nuevo subcentro toma en cuenta los efectos causados por la terciarización de la economía en la Ciudad de México y propone una fina mezcla de los diferentes usos. Al mismo tiempo aumenta su densidad limitando el crecimiento horizontal y convirtiéndolo en un crecimiento vertical, ayudando a salvar a la Ciudad de México del colapso causado por su extensión en la periferia.

Ciudad Fortuna es un proyecto totalmente sustentable gracias a su transporte híbrido que integrará los diferentes modos de transporte individual y público. El tren suburbano y la línea 6 del metro garantizarán la conexión del subcentro con la ciudad y sus demás subcentros, mientras que el Personal Rapid Transit circulará por vías especiales en el interior del subcentro. Sin embargo la mayoría de los viajes se realizarán caminando o en bicicleta para hacer el uso del coche innecesario. El tránsito vehicular estará en sintonía con la ciudad y no causará ningún conflicto.

Esto mejorará la calidad de vida de sus habitantes. Además, con 30% de áreas verdes el subcentro recuperará los espacios públicos, haciéndolos accesibles creando zonas agradables para todos los grupos sociales, independiente de su edad o sexo.

Una vez desarrollada, Ciudad Fortuna dará lugar a 300,000 nuevos habitantes y el mismo número de puestos de trabajo, ya sea en las torres de oficinas o en uno de los muchos nuevos comercios que se instalan en las plantas bajas del subcentro.

Con estos principios y las medidas tomadas desde su planeación, se prevea que Ciudad Fortuna reduce sus emisiones de dióxido de carbón drásticamente en comparación con los que hoy en día emite la Ciudad de México en promedio. Los mayores mejoramientos se notaran en los ahorros de dióxido de carbón emitido por las necesidades de transporte.Ciudad Fortuna tiene una huella ecológica menor a la del promedio de la ZMVM.

Huella ecológica menor = Caldiad de Vida mayor

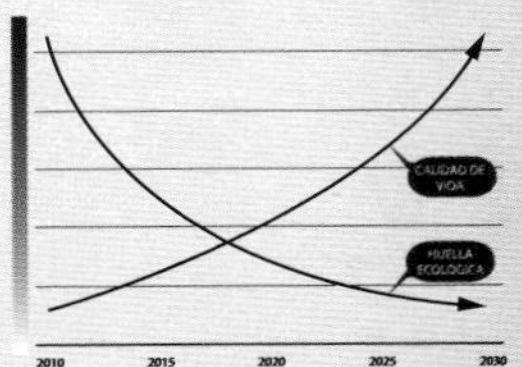

077

Gabion Field | *Thurlow Small Architecture*

National AIDS Memorial Finalist Proposal
Location : Golden Gate Park, San Francisco, CA
Competition Sponsor : National AIDS Memorial Grove

Design Team : Phase 1 Andrew Thurlow, Maia Small; Phase 2 Jose Goncalves, Eric Scott, Theodore Duboc; Mark Kelley, MACK5(Cost Estimating), Mark Cavagnero Associates(Local Architect); Snehal Intwala, 3D Systems, Inc.(Fabrication Support)
Award : Selected as one of Five Finalists, Completed Phase 2

The past itself, as historical change continues to accelerate, has become the most surreal of subjects - making it possible... to see a new beauty in what is vanishing. susan sontag

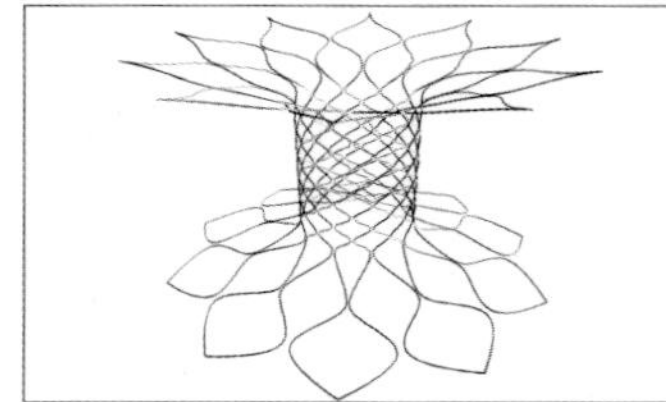
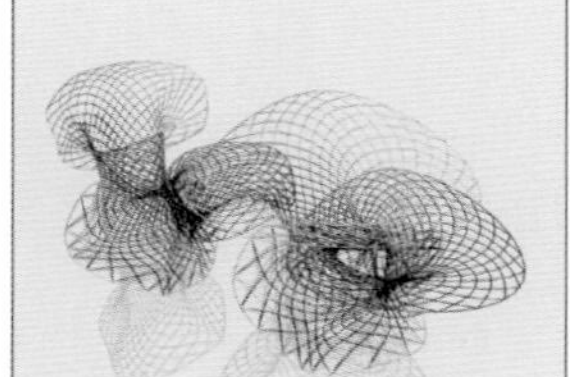
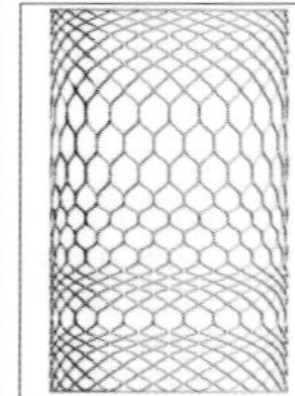
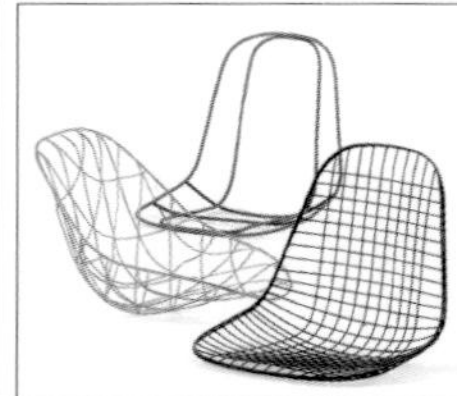

national **AIDS** memorial

golden gate park, san francisco

Existence is no more than the precarious attainment of relevance in an intensely mobile **flux of past, present, and future.** susan sontag

Context

Unlike the instantaneous and overwhelming disasters that the world has seen recently through political and natural destruction, the pandemic of AIDS has crept and spread towards societal erosion over decades. But while the destruction is vast, there is no singular marker in time of remembrance, anniversary of an event that becomes a collective acknowledgement. Instead, linkages of individual stories have become a global network; sadness and loss has become not only a personal and local process, but a global emotional experience. We experience grief through a new sense of scale.

In an environment of a disease that captures and changes lives throughout the world, over time, incrementally, in hidden and overt ways, in all economic and social environments, through political passages:

Our design proposal is **more a memorial landscape than monument**.

It is a loose and interactive system of distributed components, an open network of landscape organized by choreographed figures; it is not a fixed, pristine, idealized object intend to charm or abstract a complex experience. The project deploys wire-mesh-architecture in the existing landscape of the Memorial Grove in Golden Gate Park. These objects, as a landscape of spirit, elevate a series of layers of screening and overlapping to express light weight organizations of air and space, containers of program, eddies and swirls of density. They also house remembrance by becoming a framework for memento, such as for red ribbons-- or the improptu self-organized memorials, such as in New York City after 9/11. (Imagine the impossibility of a red ribbon appended on a wire for every person who contracted HIV...) The wire frameworks offer a structure for layers of memory so that remembrance is not abstract, but instead has texture, individuality-- so that it remains conscious and alive.

Material / System

The wire components are distributed into the surrounding forest and out into the meadow where they densify and help to form organized spaces. The wire is deformed to create benches, walls and portals. The wire lattice also creates an atmosphere of framework, without interfering with the lush surroundings nor treading heavily upon the ground. The figures become more angelic, more spirits in the material world that guide the space of the memorial garden. The figures, as trunks, operate like columns of collected space, similar in scale and nature like surrounding trees. They would be both visual clues of an(other) type of garden space and space defining objects.

The wire-mesh-components shape space, they are meshes which consist of braids and linkages, a form of architectural drapery, like webs floating in the air, "strong yet delicate in appearance." The individual wires are joined together, creating an airy and light structure that can be extended in multiple directions. The spatial gabions are coated with bonded rilsan, specified with either a shiny, highly reflective white nylon coating, for maximum reflection as an enhancement of the picturesque pointalism throughout the site, or with an ultra-matt grey-white nylon, to absorb more light, for greying effects to coincide with the fog and for enhanced atmospherics. The ribbons would seem to almost hang suspended in space.

space goes through them...looking at them we can notice that they are made by air. like a sculpture.

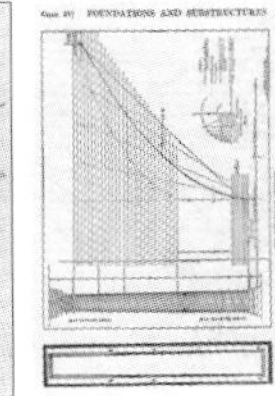

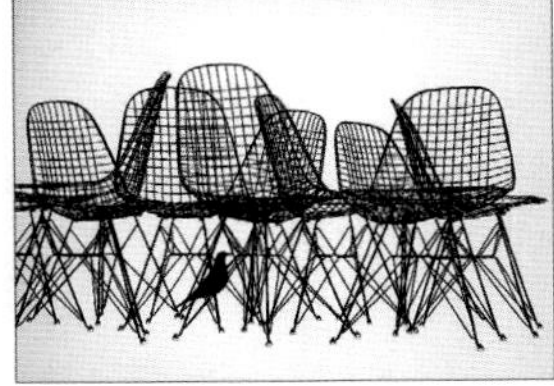
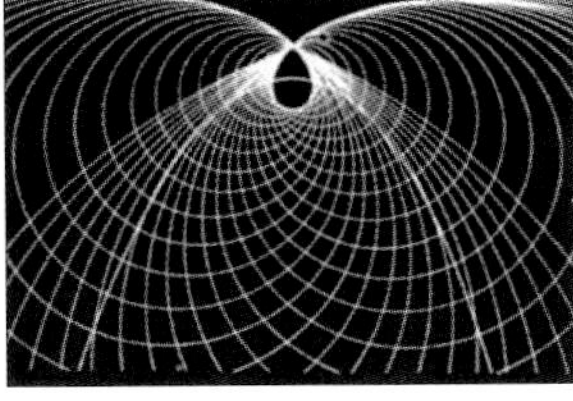
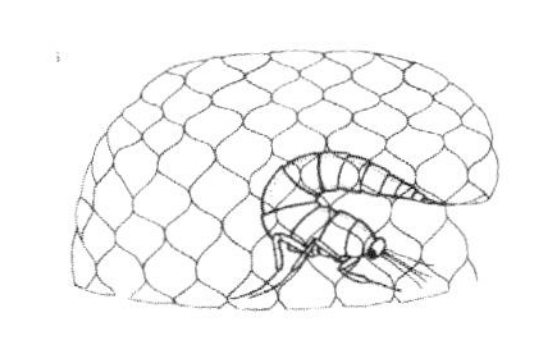
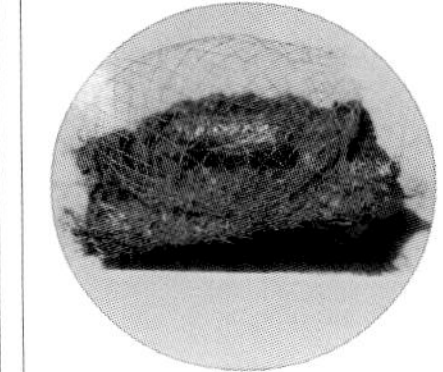

Recycled Urban Space | *Dai Nagasaka*

Project member : Kohei Okada, Aiko Goto
Model Production Member : Yusuke Kondo, Minoru Inaoka, Yasufumi Onishi, Naomi Kinoshita, Aiko Matsuda, Shogo Kawata, Yutaka Kikuchi
Name of Competition : UIA International Competition

"Recycled Urban Space"

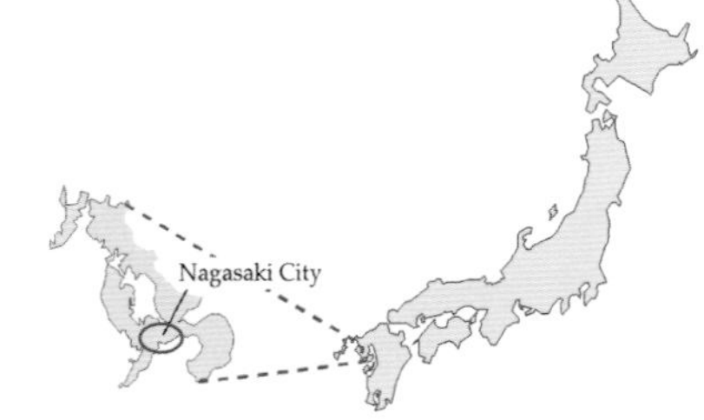

Renewal Plan for a Steep Slope Topography in Nagasaki.

The site is a steeply sloped topography residential area of Nagasaki. In view of the qualities of the topography, access to the area is by means of narrowly terraced alleys and intermittent stairways. So, cars are not able to pass through. Despite being near the city center, the topography makes it seem so far away. This topographical condition is not uncommon for many port and fishing towns in an island country like Japan. In the Building Regulations of Japan, there are two positions taken for these type of areas: one is to just demolish, or another is to leave it as it is until it disintegrates. There are no plans and regulations that make use of the specific qualities of the area. In a site like this, the relation of the roadway and the lots is very important. It is necessary to take them as one entity instead of separate elements. This proposal attempts to do that. In this plan, we propose, a low rise housing scheme with the road ways thatcan also allow passage of cars. It is not a proposal to solve the issue of accessibility, rather, it is a scheme that aims to make use of the existing order of things and the environment. It will be possible with gradual construction, a part by part and a step by step process. In other words, it is an "Recycled Urban Space". The objects of the recycle arethe "site condition or topography" and the "Residence Rights or Landrights". These can be expressed physically as embankment and stairway.
Likewise, by taking the people and the place as a set it is possible to encourage the continuity of a community. The proposal is, for the city administration to establish the apportioning of the lots and the layout of the roadways. The forms and timing of the renewal and rebuilding of the structures would depend on the residents. It is also possible to make choices on how to manage the area: as a publicly managed housing area, or as a collectively managed effort.
The steeply sloped topography is reflected in the collective form of the housing which consequently creates a distinct form of the floor plan. As a whole, the planned area and the unplanned area are mixed, thus resulting in a energetic "Recycled Urban Space".

The Present State of the Site
The site indicated in the plan ends at the bus street which is behind the apartment building in the upper left corner of the picture. The difference of a land height of the site if apporoximately 100m.

Overlooking the Nagasaki Port

A retaining wall covered with green

A slope with stone pavements

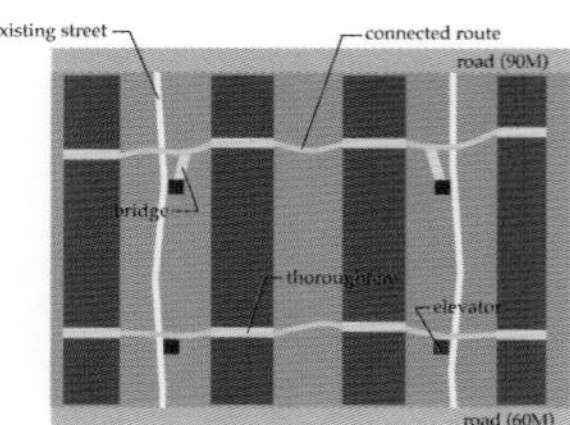

The Basic Structure of Roadways and Housing Buildings
A green belt and a building are arranged alternately between the roads. The green belt is planned to include the existing stairs. Paths are a little less than 1m wide and arranged along the contour.

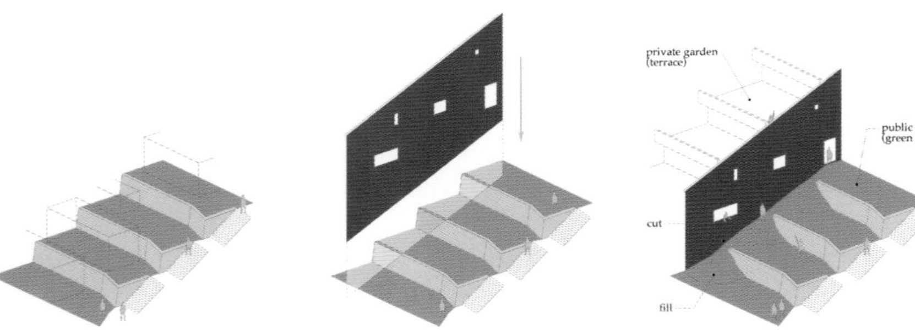

The Relationship of the Existing Environment and the New Housing Complex

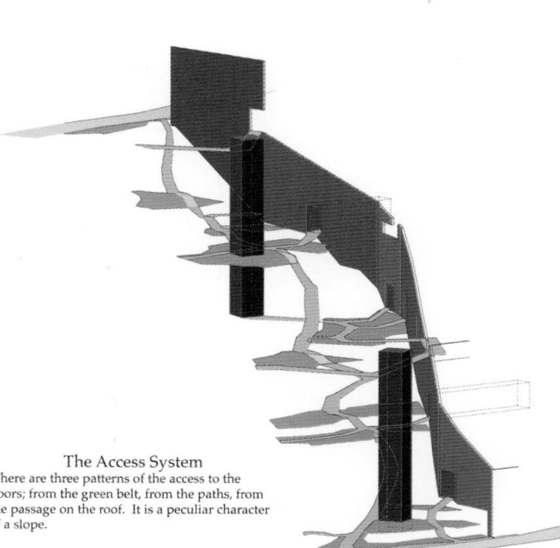

The Access System
There are three patterns of the access to the doors; from the green belt, from the paths, from the passage on the roof. It is a peculiar character of a slope.

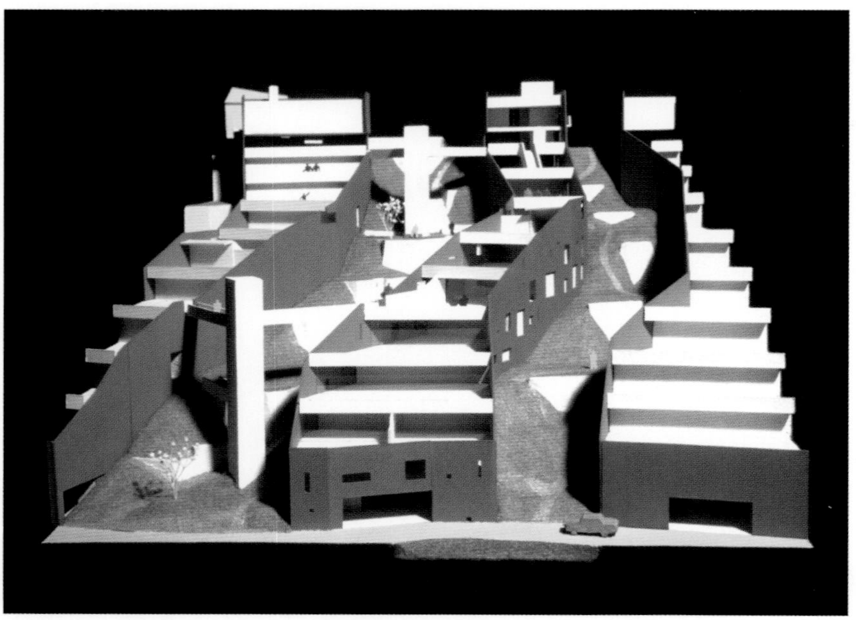

The Housing Complex
The brown walls take account of the color of brick-built buildings that remain in Nagasaki.

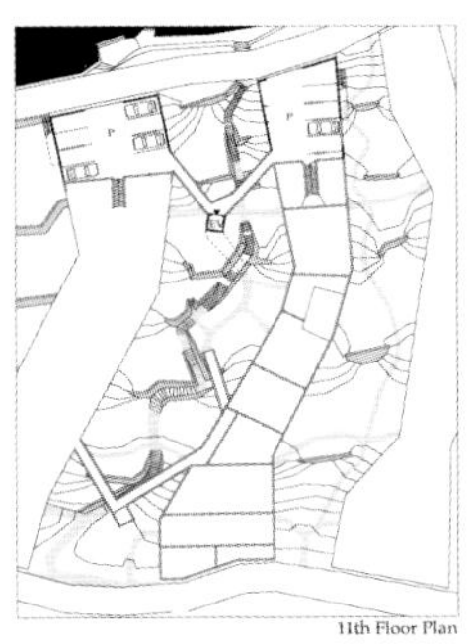
11th Floor Plan

8th Floor Plan

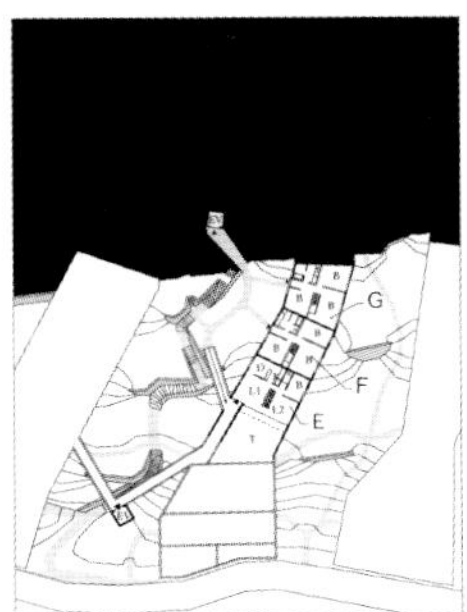

6th Floor Plan

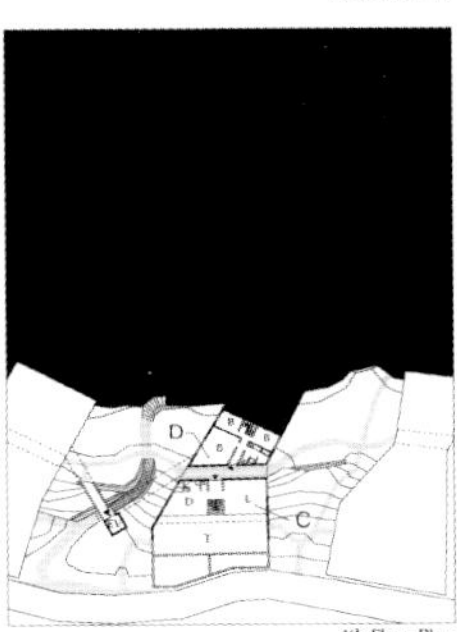

4th Floor Plan

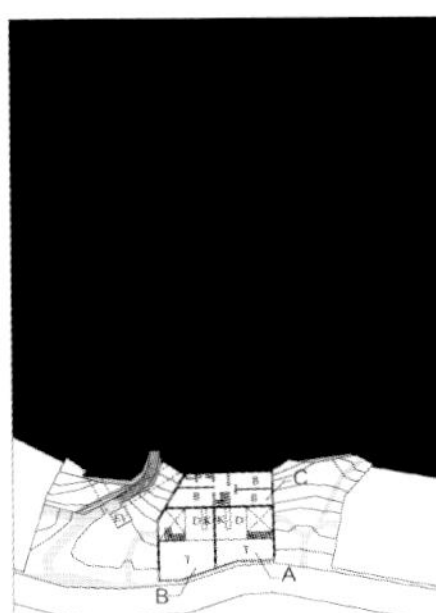

3rd Floor Plan

1st Floor Plan

The Site Plan of the Existing Buildings
The buildings line up parallel to the contour in a form of a mortar.

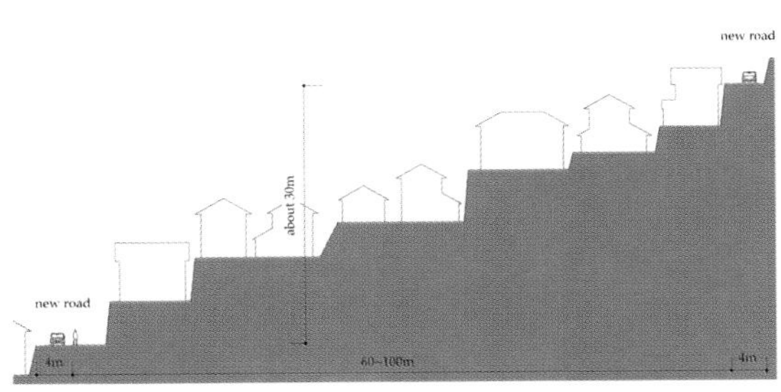

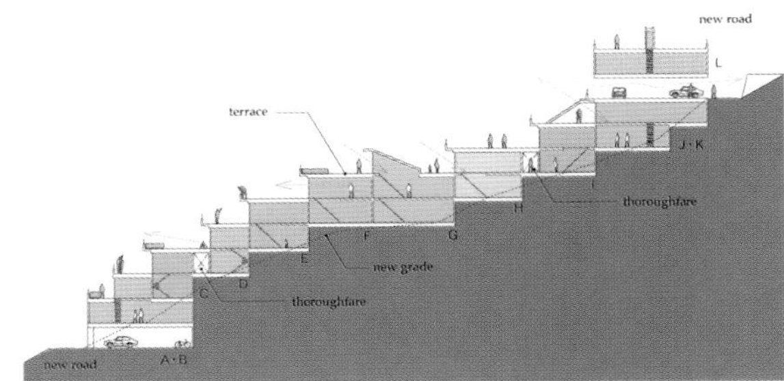

The Section of the City Block / The section of the existing building + The section of the newly built road → The section of the housing complex
Each dwelling unit is a maisonette and has contact with the ground and also a large roof terrace from which a panorama is obtained. Except the units on the level one higher and also one lower than two front roads, all the units are accessible from the elevators. Two paths are connected with the elevators and contribute to the circulation network of the whole site.

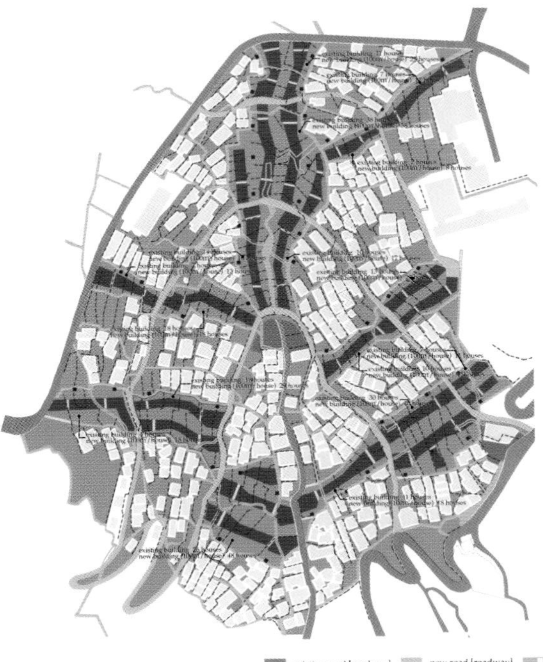

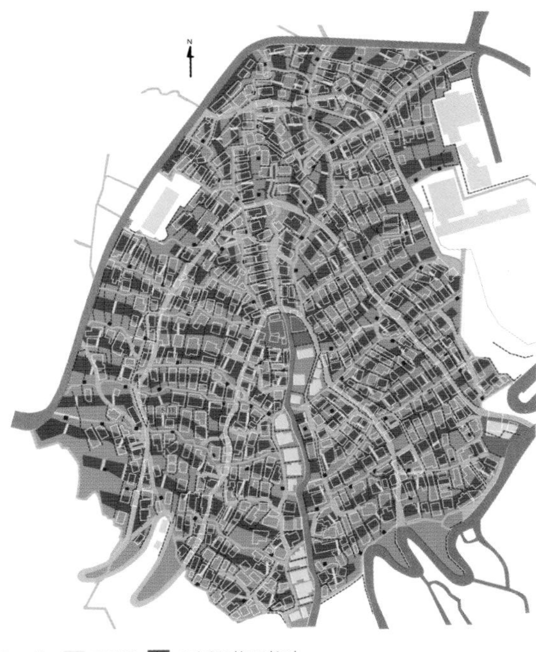

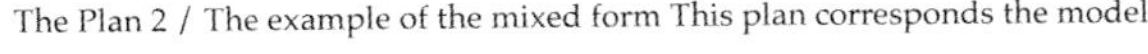

The Plan of the Housing Complex
They are 12-story, and each dwelling unit is a maisonette. They have contact with the ground providing the living environment of low-rise townhouse. The connection of two elevators is made through the green belt. The possession rate of a parking lot is 100 percent. The size of each dwelling unit is 94 to 120· u. In this example, the number of the units is increased from 18 to 26, and it is 44 percent increase.

The Plan 2 / The example of the mixed form This plan corresponds the model.

It shows the state in which a part of the city blocks is replaced by new housing complex. On the assumption that elevators are used publicly, the blocks with a good vertical connection are chosen.

The Plan 1 / The case of all the existing buildings replaced by the same form of new housing complex

The planned roadways are almost flat with the basic width of 4m (Note1). The height difference between two roadways is apporoximately 30m, and this distance is decided from the condition in which people can make a connection of two elevators provided in each building without using stairs and access all the doors (Note2). The number of the dwelling units is planned to be 15 to 20 percent more than the number of the units which presently exist with the thought of profit.

Note 1: According to the Japanese Building Standards Act, the minimum width of a front road on which a building can be constructed is 4m.

Note 2: The possession of elevators, new housing complex, and existing buildings is examined and compared in the public case, the private case, and the case in between. Adjacent buildings own the elevators jointly, and if the existing buildings remain, their residents are accessible to them.

Symbiosis
Or how to become self sufficient

A town is a dissipative system that needs to exchange with the outside natural world to get to a level of dynamic balance. To become a self sufficient entity, where the waste is absorbed and the energy and materials are constantly produced and renewed, a continuous exchange with the system of nature must be included in the planning.

From these premises, the starting point for the project is to consider the future town as an environment which does not oppose itself to the natural context. **The challenge is to get a dense and vibrant urban space, without interrupting the existing natural conditions, but including them in a continuous exchange with the built environment**. To get to this goal, nature and town have to grow together in a strong relationship as two interconnected ecosystems.

Landscape is not considered as a static entity, - suitable for leisure and preserved only for its esthetic values -, but as a **living complex merged with the dynamic urban structure** and its «flux exchanges» of energy, waste, information and so on. At the same time the built context is thought as flexible, evolutive and complex, as an organic being from its beginning.

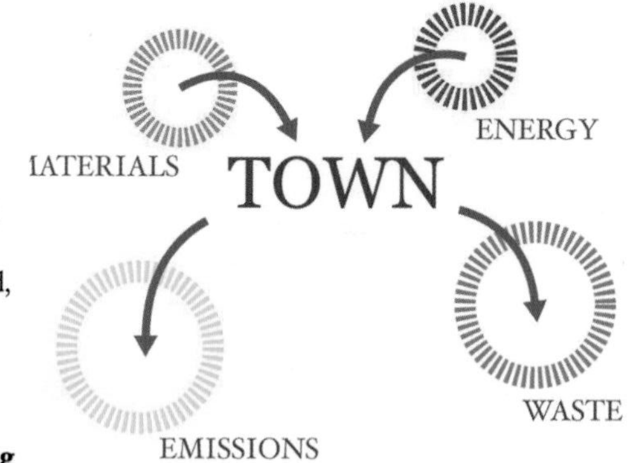

Dissipative system
In thermodynamics is a system which is far from equilibrium. This term can be used to describe a contemporary town: it takes energy and materials from far away, produces huge emissions and wastes that are not absorbed.

System in dynamic equilibrium
In thermodynamics is a system where the rate of every internal forward reaction is equal to the rate of its backward reaction: for a town it means a system where inputs and outputs are balanced, waste is recycled, energy and materials are produced, emissions are absorbed.

Symbiosis
In order for the town to become a system in dynamic equilibrium, - a self-sufficient entity -, town must reach a symbiosis with nature, a relationships from which both benefits.

The old model
A single city centre concentrates urban intensity while the other districts are mono-functional and sub-urban. Landscape is relegated to the exterior margins of the town and doesn't interact with it.

An innovative town
More nodes (districts) act each one as a city centre with intensity, social and functional mixity and spacial variety. Landscape flows uninterrupted through the town and participate to its life.

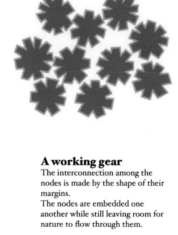

Nodes and network
While made up of different districts, the town is a continuous organism where each node is closely related to the others.

A working gear
The interconnection among the nodes is made by the shape of their margins.
The nodes are embedded one another while still leaving room for nature to flow through them.

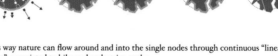

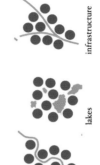

A town as a network

Instead of thinking on a town of 20000 inhabitants made up of a centre that slowly flows until the margins and superposes itself to the existing areas, we considered more nodes closely interconnected among them.

This first step allows to avoid a situation where we have only one intense city centre and the rest of the town works as an orbit, turning around in a relationship city/ suburban areas.

Here, each node is part of a network that constitutes the whole town and the way the single nodes are connected one another lets nature flow throw the system, making a balanced void/full system at this scale. The flexibility of the network allows to include in the system the ever-changing conditions of landscape and infrastructures, easily adapting to an enormous amount of possibly pre-existing situations.

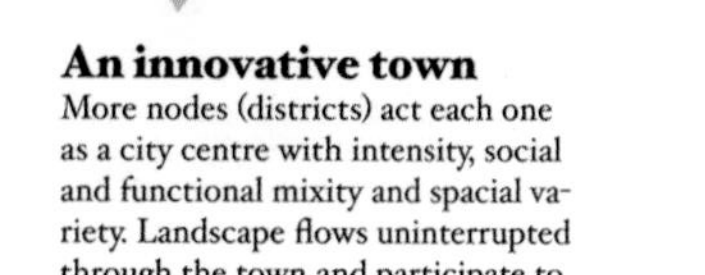

Margins
How to make all of the neighborhoods open to the natural environments?
If the perimeter of each node is a line where built and natural environment touch, modifying this line we obtain a longer perimeter, without augmenting the total surface.

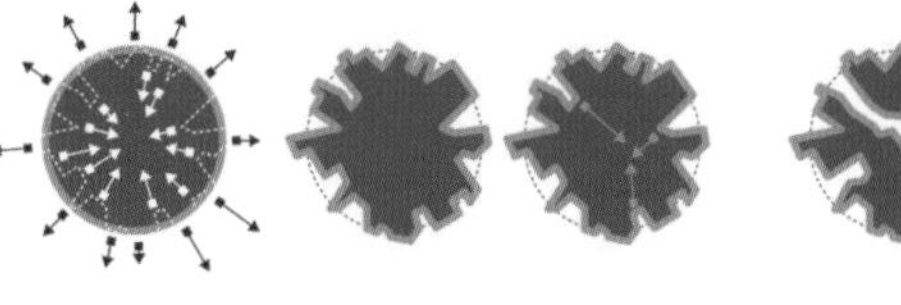
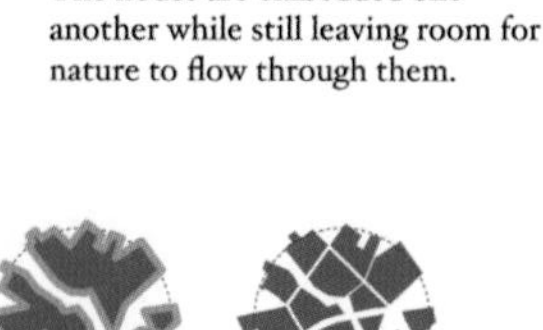

This way nature can flow around and into the single nodes through continuous "linear parks", associated to bike and pedestrian paths.
Higher buildings usually face these strips of land in the districts..

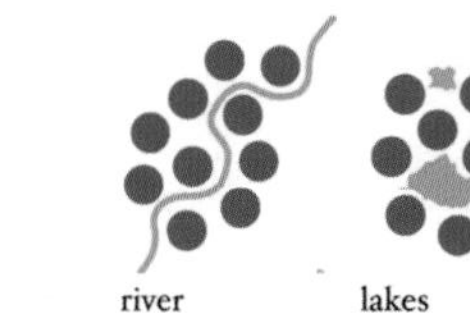

Some possible pre-existing situations and how the nodes relate to them

symbiosis - 01

Shape of the nodes

Form follows energy and needs

Each node can host up to 2000 people, this reduced scale allowing to deal with the need for a **self-sufficient urban unit** on different scales.
The basic shape and the nature of a single node is given by taking into account several parameters: the radius of each node measures about 250 m, which makes the **maximal distance inside a pole of 500 m, 5 minutes on foot**. This distance determines the diffuse presence of the basic services (day-care, retail, kindergartens, meeting points, small sport structures, local banks, entertainment ...), letting **each node work as a city centre in the city** and allowing each inhabitant to easily take advantage by this situation. The public transportation stops are located so that their distance from each point of the town is maximum 500 m.

The needs for heating can be satisfied, at the scale of a node, by a small CHP plant (combined heating and power) of 2 MW, and fueled by recycled waste, biomass or pelt, (all renewable products which can be obtained in the district proximity). This small plant provides, at the same time, 10% of electricity (the remaining 90% is obtained by more renewable sources on a town scale). The energy provided by the CHP, (heating and electricity) is then distributed in the buildings included in a radius of 250 m, **this short distance allowing a very small dispersion**. (CHP is most efficient when the heat can be used on site or very close to it).

Like in the old towns, where the "shape" of the districts depended on the need for water and on the access to the market, in this project the dimensions of the nodes are similarly determined by the needs, in terms of energy, of "urban life" and easy pedestrian access to services .

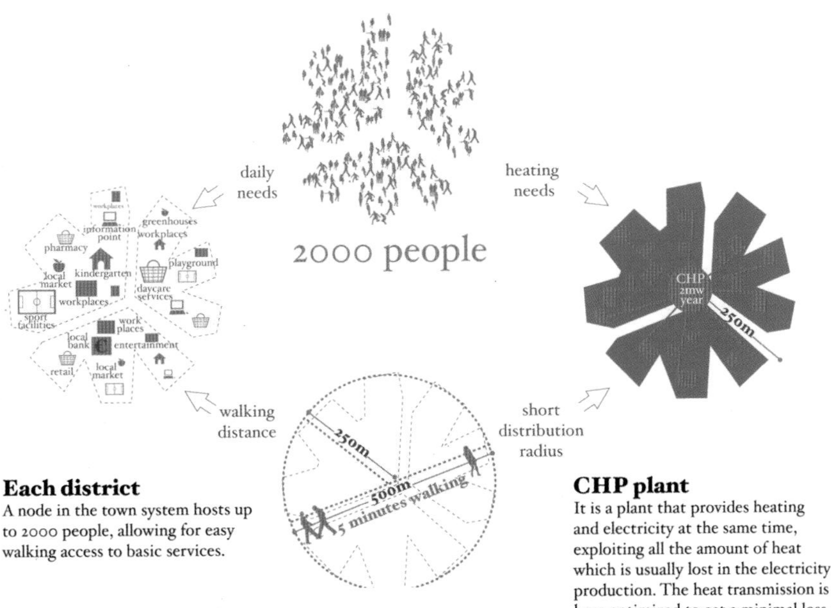

Each district
A node in the town system hosts up to 2000 people, allowing for easy walking access to basic services.

CHP plant
It is a plant that provides heating and electricity at the same time, exploiting all the amount of heat which is usually lost in the electricity production. The heat transmission is here optimized to get a minimal loss.

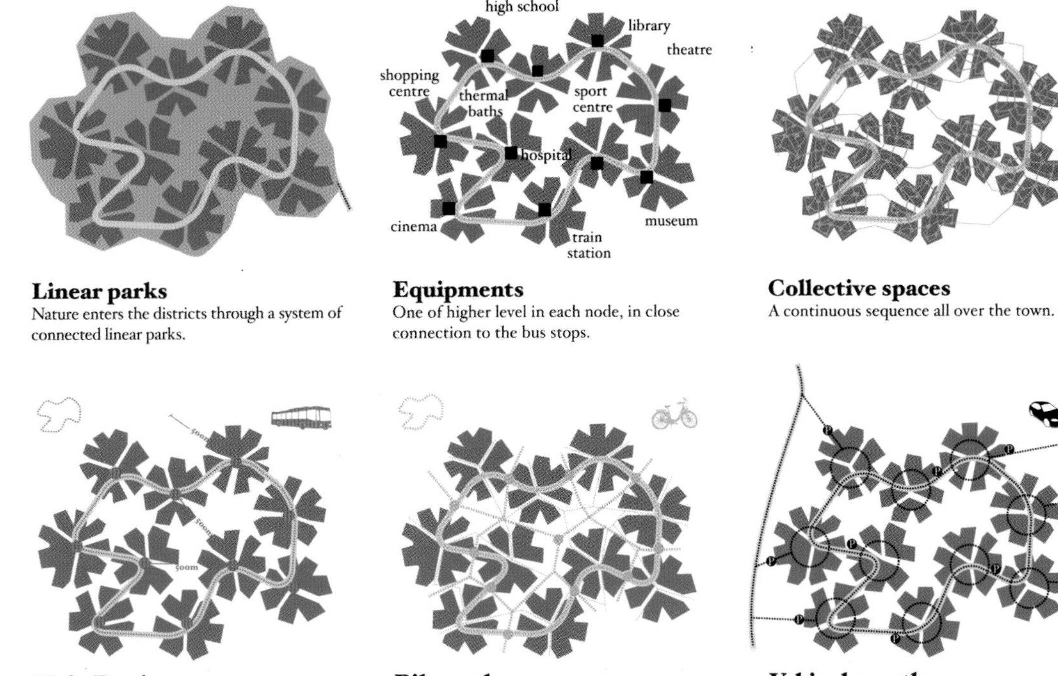

Linear parks
Nature enters the districts through a system of connected linear parks.

Equipments
One of higher level in each node, in close connection to the bus stops.

Collective spaces
A continuous sequence all over the town.

Main Bus lane
Each bus stop is located at max 500 m or 5 minutes walking- from each point of the town

Bike paths
Tot. distance 3,5 km - 10 minutes by bike.
Express paths
Leisure paths

Vehicular paths
Connecting local to regional. Main parking facilities are located just outside each node.

The backbone as a continuous centre

The single nodes are crossed by a **large boulevard** which is the **backbone of the transportation system**, works as the main path for the public transport (electric bus), and is associated to cars and bike lanes. This path, crossing all the nodes, becomes a commercial street and the main visual and physical connection among the districts. The silhouettes and volumes of the buildings opening on this street will result in a diverse though coherent unity at first glance, while at a more close look will reveal the identities of the crossed districts, making the **travelling on this line a sequence of visual experiences**. More than a connecting line, the backbone constitutes the "continuous centre" of the whole town that leads to the main squares and public buildings in each district. Starting from these, a continuous system of paths and collective spaces reaches all the single wards and building units.
Car traffic is directed from the main boulevard through each district and reconnects itself to the exterior car lines (motorways etc) linking the town with the regional and national system. Parking facilities are located just outside the single nodes, while in the sub-districts car access is restricted.

Cycle routes and footpaths

A meshed grid of bike paths and footpaths links city districts, urban spaces and passes through the natural areas connecting the different nodes through multiple accesses. There are two kinds of bike paths express ways and leisure ways, the first are intended to be a real alternative to car, they cross the districts in a fast way and are served by a system of bike sharing points: the whole systems allows to get from one point to another by bike in a maximum of 10 minutes (3,5 km is the longest possible distance in the town).

Linking backbone
Main transportation boulevard and commercial area.

Energy cycle

From waste to production

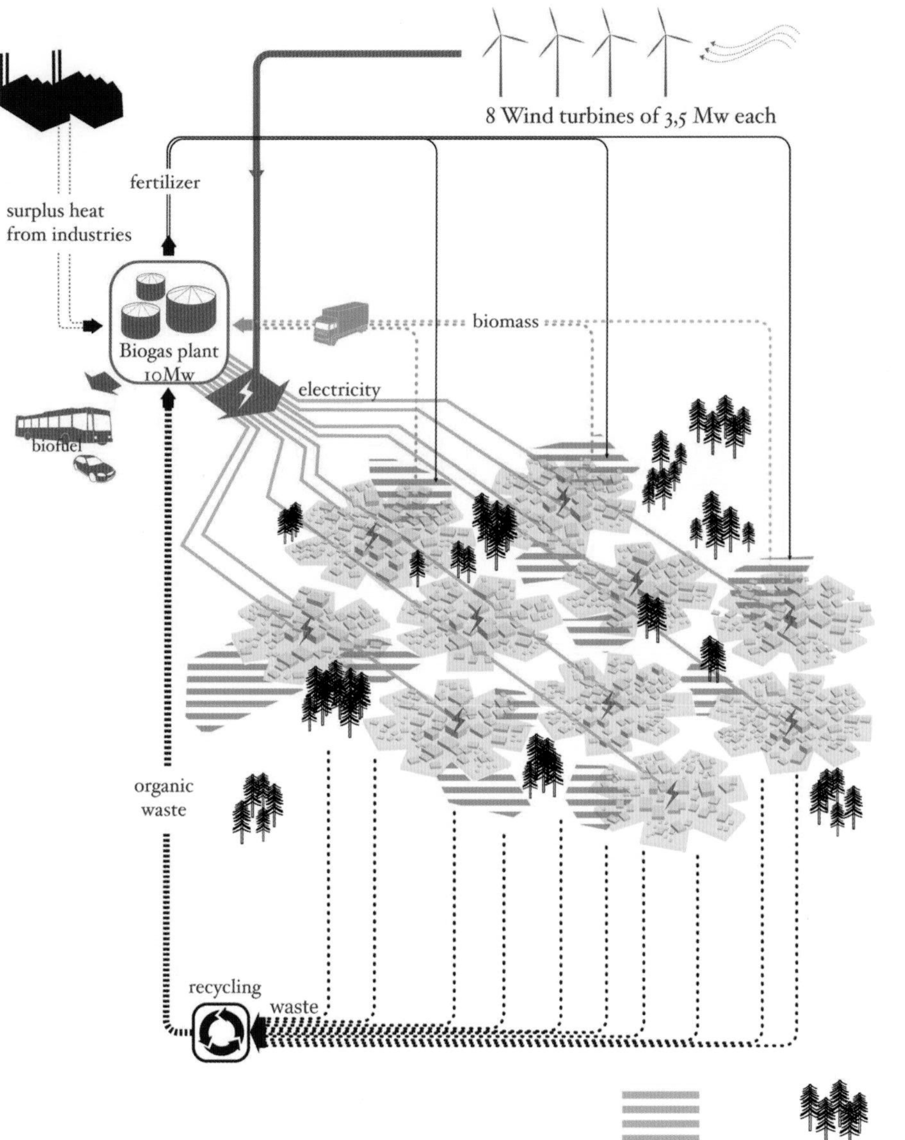

Town
Electricity is provided by 8 wind turbines and through the biogas produced in a biogas plant (10 MW). Biogas is obtained by: organic waste produced in the town and in the agriculture plots nearby; by biomass from forest and agriculture. The surplus heat from industries is also used. The biogas plant generates biofuel to power public and private vehicles. The digester liquor is a fertilizer that can be used in agriculture and forest areas.

The issue of ecological efficiency is taken as a key point for the process of designing the town and it influences the orientations at each level. A **holistic approach** helps conceiving a strategy that takes into account a whole range of multiple processes, parameters and actors influencing one another.

The efficiency is always considered as a design tool, taken as a basic parameter and never as a slogan added in the end of the conception. Neither is it a mechanical calculation that doesn't take into account the economical, social and spacial impact of each choice.

Each issue is treated on multiple scales or at the more suitable level while the different stages are then connected one another.

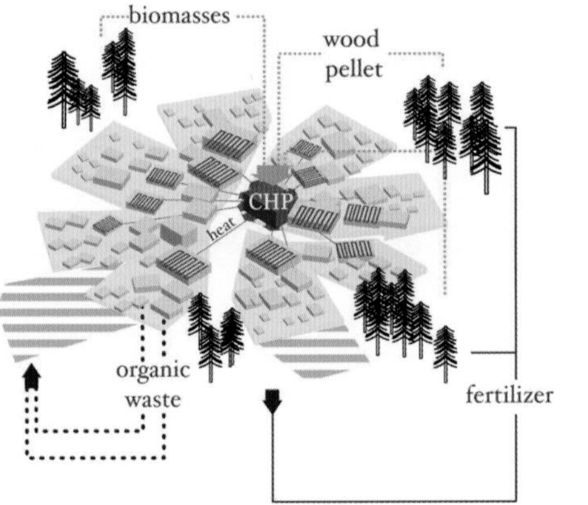

Node
A CHP (combined heat and power) of 3MW provides heat for bigger buildings in each node. The short transmission radius (250 m max) allows a minimal thermal dispersion. The plant is powered by wood pellet and chips from the local forests, a carbon neutral source.

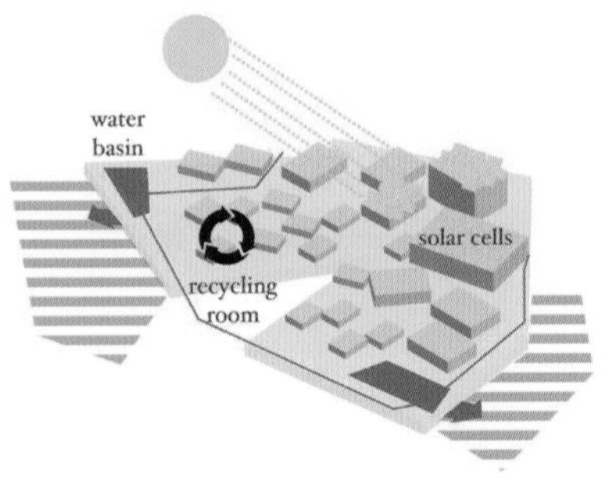

Buildings
Passive strategies are applied in design: double skin, extra insulation, smart orientation. Heat in smaller units is provided through a geothermal power pump.

The scales considered are: **The whole town as a urban network** (20000 people) - the **nodes/distict** (2000 people) – **sub districts** (250-400 people) – **single buildings**.

The choice of approaching each environmental issue on the appropriate scale is accompanied to a **campaign of information** connected to the specific tasks, enforcing the sense of responsibility of each individual and community involved. Incentives can promote the best practices and community can act as a network for sharing knowledge on each scale.

This will help people to consider themselves as active actors in the process, as up to 50% of the carbon footprint depends on people choices and lifestyles.

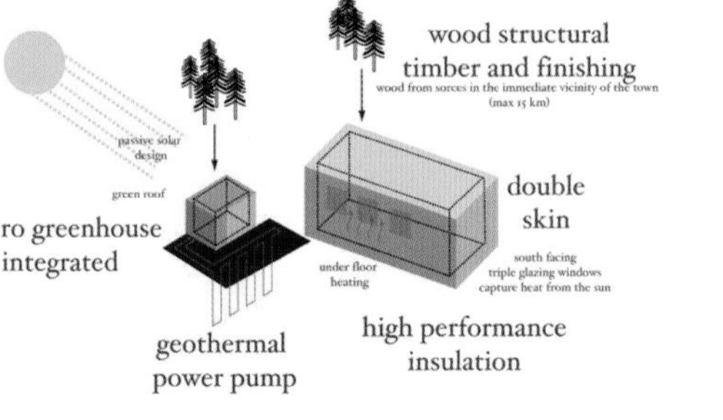

Sub-district
Solar cells on higher buildings and parking buildings provide 2MW in the whole town. Water is collected in basins and used for agriculture plots nearby and for watering.

Carbon neutral energy production

The resource of biogas plant is organic matter, the production of plant's photosynthesis.
Plants produce oxygen and carbohydrates from carbon dioxides by photosynthesis. So, there is a balance between the exhaustion of carbon dioxides into the atmosphere and absorption of carbon dioxides from the atmosphere, making the system carbon neutral

Solar cells, wind turbines, geothermic pumps and wood pellets generate electricity without releasing CO_2.

symbiosis - 03

Layers of eco efficiency

LEVEL / LAYERS OF ECO EFFICIENCY	**Energy production** Efficiency obtained by combination of more renewable sources	**Energy efficiency strategies** Reducing needs	**Waste management** Reintroducing in a cycle	**Water management** Save and reuse	**Mobility** Improving colocation (live+work) walk + bike + public transportation	**Construction** Using of low carbon and recyclable materials	**Green/Ecosystems** O_2 production and preservation of biodiversity	**Food** Direct production to consumption
Urban network **Town level**	Electricity: - 1 Biogas Power Plant producing 10 MW (Biogas obtained from : organic and animal waste, biomass, surplus heat from industries). - 8 wind turbines producing 3,5 MW/each (exploiting the wind tunnel phenomenon in the area close to the railway).	- Avoiding sprawling, the shape of the town allows the optimization of the resources	- Waste is separated at source and either directly recycled or used to produce biogas. BIOGAS	- Rainwater and snowmelt from the streets to be collected and treated in a variety of differentways. - The water collected in basins and then drained out into canals through the whole network.	- Main boulevard as backbone : electric or biofuel bus system, with dedicated bus lanes. - Bike sharing services - Express - fast - bike paths (max existing distance within the town is 3,5 km / 10 min) - Leisure - slow - bike paths (through nature, green spaces) - Limitation of private vehicular traffic. Incentives for non-oil vehicles (electric, biofueled, ethanol)	- Wood for construction available from sources in the immediate vicinity of the town (less than 15 km).	- Deforestation is reduced by densification of the built areas - Ecosystems stay connected through the organization of the nodes. - Underpasses for animals are planned under infrastructures.	- Continuity between agricultural plots and built areas.
District level	Heating+electricity: - 1 Small scale CHP producing 3 MW in each district - Combined heat and power production, powered by biomass, wood pellets, waste. Suitable for large buildings.	- Public lighting with leds + solar cells.	- Compost used for local agriculture production.	- Basins collecting surface water to reuse in agriculture.	- Max existing distance in the district level to be 500m (5 minutes on foot). First need and daily services are within this radius. - Parking located closely to bikesharing centres and bus stops. Small distance residence-work cuts the need for cars.	- Urban furniture made with recycled materials	- Green continuity through the districts by linear parks.	- Local agricultural production sold in the markets.
Sub-District level	Electricity: - Solar cells integrated in higher buildings + parking producing 2 MW in total (whole town) Cooling: - Narrow floor-plates enable natural ventilation	Reduction of electric energy needs, by: - orientation of the blocks, - relationship of the blocks to the street, - the choice of limiting the number of floors improves the access of light inside each building.	- Automated Vacuum Collection (Pneumatic waste trasport system directed to recycling plants). - Local and block-based recycling rooms and places for the exchange (or selling) of used goods in the community.	- Basins collecting surface water to reuse for watering.	- Bike-sharing points - Cars: limited access to residential areas. - Fuel station and car sharing for cars running on electricity, biogas or ethanol. BIOGAS	- Permeable paving. - Use of available local materials in sub-district main buildings.	- Constant balance between green and built areas.	- Shared greenhouses providing food for the local communities.
Building	Heating : - Small units : geothermal capture system (heat pumps), under-floor diffusion. Cooling: - Double ventilation.	- Reduction of heating demand by: passive technology integrated, (smart distribution of functions, double skin, ext. isolation). Reduction of electric energy needs, by: - more access to light - tight buildings - orientation	- Waste sorting.	- Greywater recycling for wc. - Eco-friendly installations (energy class A: washing machines and dishwashers, low flush toilets and air mixer taps). BIOGAS	- Public covered foot and bike paths as an alternative to open air streets (during cold seasons).	- Wood structural timber and finishing. - Narrow floor plates , modular structures can be used for retail, office, residential. - Dry construction methods, totally reversible and recyclable	- Greenroofs and terraces.	- Integrated micro greenhouses in buildings. - Vegetable self production.
RESULTS	- 100% of electric energy is produced by combining renewable sources: - wind turbines, biogas, solar power - biofuels, geothermal power - 100% of heating is produced by combining renewable sources: wood pellets, biomasses	- 40% reduction of energy needs. **Average consumption (buildings): 65 kWh / m2**	- All waste is recycled - 80% of organic waste is converted into biosolids and used as fertilizer or to product biogas.	- 50% less of water consumption + - 50% recuperation of storm water: treated and reused for agriculture fields. - Grey water is reused	- 80% of residents and workers journeys shall be by public transport, on foot and by bicycle.	- Embodied carbon in buildings is reduced by 55%	- Preservation of biodiversity through the town. - Production of O_2.	- 50% of vegetables come from the sub district greenhouses of from close agricoltural plot
CO_2 EMISSIONS	Biogas production: carbon neutral Renewable sources: carbon neutral **CO_2 : 0**	Normal CO_2 emission in operational phase: 2600 Kg/m2 **Reduced tot CO_2 emission in operational phase: 500 Kg/m2** Total reduction of CO_2 emission in operational phase: 2100 Kg/m2			CO_2 emissions reduced over time thanks to co-location (living close to workplace), incentives for biofuel and electric cars and an efficient public transportation system.	Using wood instead of concrete Concrete CO_2: 550 Kg/m2 to **Wood CO_2 : 300 Kg/m2** (for houses and workplaces)	Planting : O_2 as carbon offsetting.	Reduced carbon emissions for food by 10%.

Two ecosystems

A multiplicity of lifestyles

The shape of the urban nodes guarantees the continuity of the existing ecosystems, adapts itself progressively to the specific features of the territory and absorbs the impact of infrastructures.

The two systems (**urban/landscape**) are in a continuous interdependency:
- Agriculture areas produce biomass which generates energy for heating. The agricultural production of the areas nearby can be partially sold in the urban markets and consumed by the town population, obtaining **direct connection between production and consume** without wasting energy in the transportation (30 m2 of agricultural land feeds the vegetable needs for one person in a year).
- Forests are **O2 producers**. Regenerative forests closed to the town provide building materials, cutting the costs of transportation, while wood waste is used as fuel (pellet) to get energy through the CHPs.
- **Landscape is seen as an infrastructure**, hosting bike paths and footpaths and connecting the different districts.
- **Citizen** can be employed in the management and cultivation of the territories.
- Playful activities, sport, learning can take place in those areas of the city/ecosystem allowing people to **live at the same time in a dense and intense urban context while being in a close contact with nature**: this double perception of the overall urban context helps improving the variety of the urban tissue and the diversity of lifestyles.

1. bus stop
2. bike path
3. bike sharing point
4. main square
5. public building
6. commercial arcades
7. local square
8. chp
9. covered path
10. local market
11. shared greenhouse
12. shared sauna
13. playground
14. sport field
15. shared working place
16. basin
17. greenhouse
18. agricultural field
19. common laundry

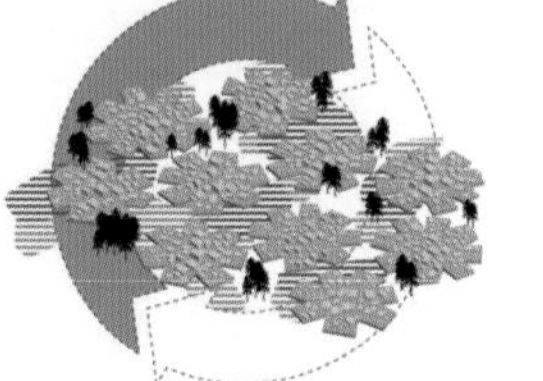

This new model of town is seen as a **synthesis** between the needs of contemporary citizen to be in contact to a lively environment close to work and leisure opportunities, which is usually intended to be in a city, and a more relaxed and independent way of living, closed to nature and "related" to open spaces.
Those last needs led worldwide to the constant presence of urban sprawl: large territory-consuming units, car dependent and anti-urban conditions. While not endorsing this kind of attitude more and more present nowadays, we must understand the basic will behind it and try to **imagine urban conditions which can be attractive for larger segments of population**.

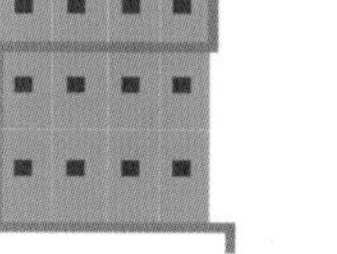

or

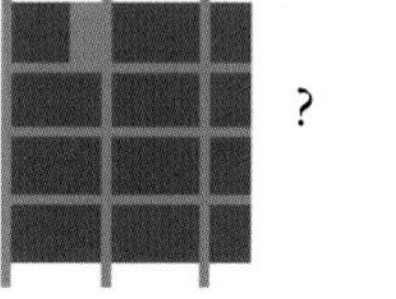

?

Best of them!

Instead of choosing between independent units close to nature or a compact urban tissue, we propose a model that assumes the advantages of the two situations.

An ever-changing urban tissue

A wide range of housing units types and types of commercial premises allows for **social mixité and urban variety**. Most of the housing units are low rising with medium density. This solution avoids sprawl while letting - at the same time - individual access to each unit. Plots of small dimensions can be more easily sold on the market.

Common spaces flow through the districts, opening in local gathering spaces and outdoor activities through footpaths, arcades, courtyards and green spaces. The strong relationship between built units and the continuous collective space shapes each district as a town unit, with intensity and urban life, it guarantees a town identity and a complexity of spaces, while providing meeting places in each district.

This collective space develops into multiple scenarios where sequences of paths and squares get interior and exterior, opened and covered, and by overlapping give birth to different uses of the city through the seasons. The town itself provides ever-changing sequences of spaces, showing different faces through the time.

There's always the possibility to get to each point through interior or at least covered passages, while higher and larger buildings can be crossed in the ground floor as public gateways. This allows to walk on every weather condition and avoids the need for private cars.

Residential areas are always equipped with shared facilities that help improving the sense of community and make life in the wards more attractive for workers and residents.

Flexible, evolutive

Choices in space and time

The density mixity (co-presence and distribution of multiple functions) is an important indicator taken into account: it is usually a characteristic of city centres and it disappears in mono-functional suburban areas. Here it informs each sector of the city and it is usually obtained as an hybridization of the residential types. This is made possible by choosing structures that can be used for residential, as well as for offices and retail, opened to possible changes of destinations through time. This flexibility helps to absorb future changing of uses and needs in the town.

Quality of the environment for working, close to residence, flexible and different. New forms of working (such as remote working) have been taken into account leading to a **multiplicity of spaces**. These range from small units directly connected to the residential unit to "open studio" in the block, **big spaces that can be shared and rented for different periods**, even time of the day or the week, allowing to optimize resources in common, to bigger spaces, in direct connection to public transport stops. A great amount of natural light is always present in the buildings, and the way the places are scattered in the districts, merged with other functions on each scale and location, makes **working in the town a way to participate to its rhythm and production**.

gym
multiple floors work space
business open space
block sauna
+housing
open air wi-fi working
+housing
+housing
block atelier
retail
house and office associated
business open space
shared working place

years
CONSTRUCTION PERIOD OF THE TOWN
+5 +10 +15 +20 +30 +40 +50

population
10000
20000
20000 ±5000

energy
forest regeneration
first wind turbine
completion of 8 wind turbines
wind turbines maintenance
construction chp plant
completion of the Biogas plant
completion of 10 CHP plants
biofuel production from Biogas plant
TOWN BECOMES CARBON NEUTRAL (ENERGY-TRANSPORTATION)
Biogas plant maintenance
electric stations

mobility
private and public transport becomes oil-free
mixity of functions and proximity work-living makes walking and cycling a real alternative to any transportation
incentives for biofuel cars
incentives for electric cars

program

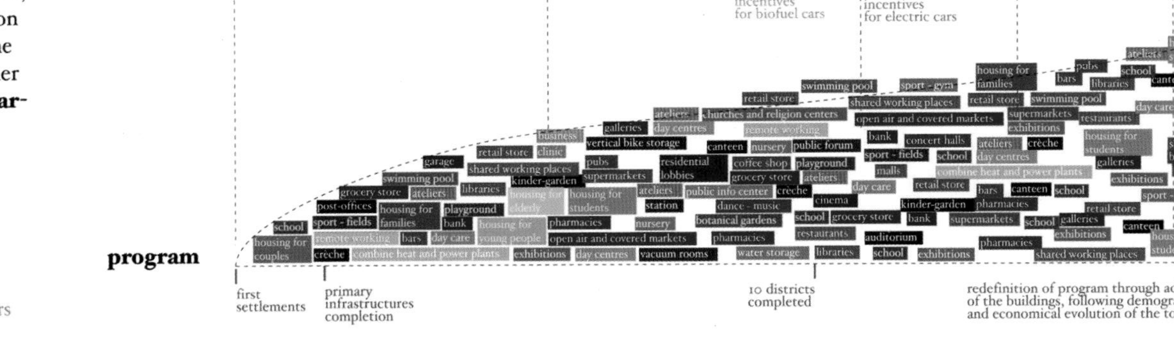

first settlements
primary infrastructures completion
10 districts completed
redefinition of program through adaptation of the buildings, following demographic, social and economical evolution of the town.

Time span of 50 years

The town develops and consolidates during its first 15 to 20 years, (providing the resources for 20000 people, becoming energetically self sufficient and carbon neutral). Its conception allows for the continual adaptation of the program and of the mobility's efficiency through time, following the ever-changing needs from its birth stage to the far future.

Construction materials

- Upper floors: Mainly timber frame - shorter span residential structures.
- Lower floors: Concrete prefab, suitable for flexible retail and office destinations.
- Provisions of wood from within a radius of 15 km around the town.
- Other local materials when available (gravel, etc.).
- Reinforced isolation within frame or external.
- Double windows, double skins and buffer zones on the south.
- Modular structures, narrow floor plates for natural ventilation and greater access to natural light.

Density mixity and diffusion of program in every part of the town

symbiosis - 06

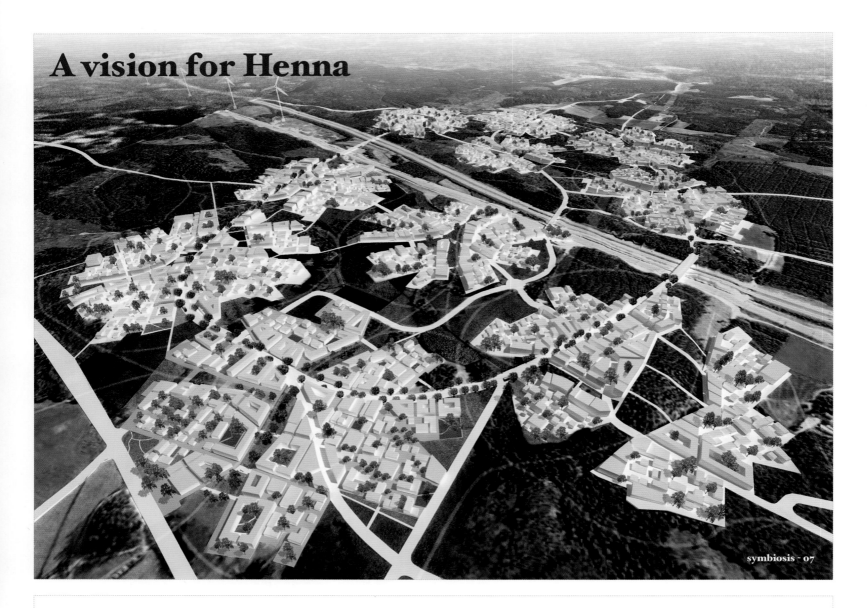

A vision for Henna

symbiosis - 07

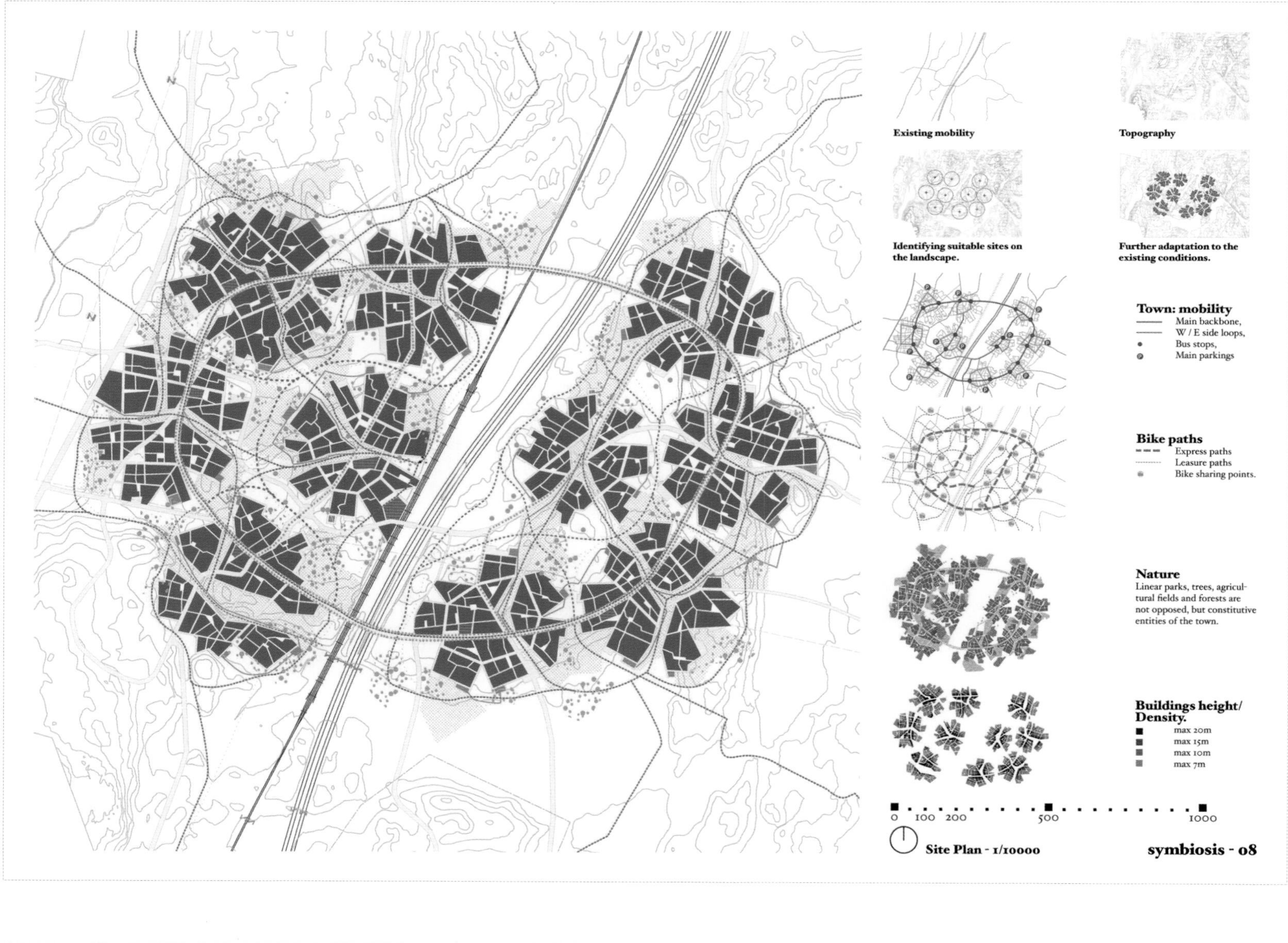

Existing mobility

Topography

Identifying suitable sites on the landscape.

Further adaptation to the existing conditions.

Town: mobility
Main backbone,
W / E side loops,
Bus stops,
Main parkings

Bike paths
Express paths
Leasure paths
Bike sharing points.

Nature
Linear parks, trees, agricultural fields and forests are not opposed, but constitutive entities of the town.

Buildings height/ Density.
max 20m
max 15m
max 10m
max 7m

0 100 200 500 1000

Site Plan - 1/10000

symbiosis - 08

LANDSCAPE
INTEGRATED
NOISE BARRIERS

RAILWAY
STATION

Double perception.
Each neighborhood opens on the natural environment, while hosting inside a dense urban character.

The residential area close to the railway station.
Medium density dwellings with individual access, mixed with retail stores and working spaces.

0 100 200 500

Site Plan - 1/5000

symbiosis - 09

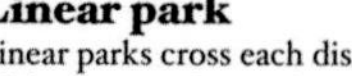

Linear park
Linear parks cross each district of the town and provide space for leasure, sport and meeting, while working as light infrastructures.

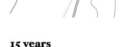

The boulevards
Rich and vibrant urban spaces develop along and around these paths. Squares, main buildings and commercial areas open on them.

2 years
Construction of the first 3 nodes on the west side of the railway.
Small train station, (first phase).

5 years
Expansion of the five nodes on the west side.
Connection of the west nodes by the west loop.
Construction of the first node on the east side, along the road crossing the railway.

5 years
Most of the west nodes and their mobility is completed.
Construction of the second loop is started with two new bridges crossing the railway (south and north).

15 years
Completion of the west side with the expansion of the train station. (second phase).
Main backbone connecting the two sides is completed.
Five years to the completion of the entire town.

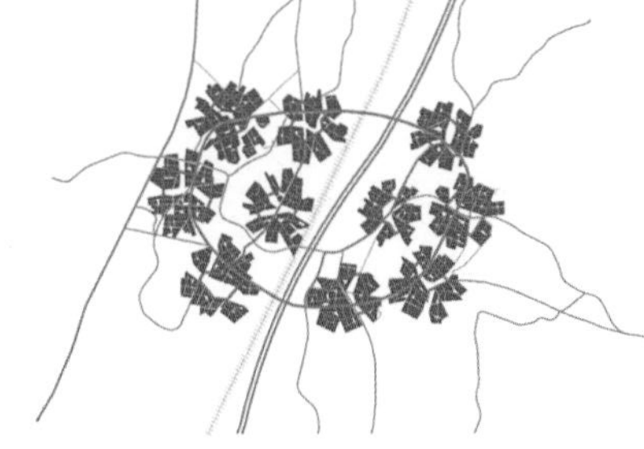

20 years
The town is completed. Primary and secondary infrastructures balance the relationship between the two sides of the town.

symbiosis - 10

Henna

Our vision for a town

Relationship with town model

Our proposal for an innovative town is extremely adaptable to a large variety of possible existing conditions, so that the landscape has to be shaped only in minimal part, in order to fit the new implantation. We took the special existing features of the Henna site: infrastructure, topography, presence of forests and agriculture etc. and included them in the planning from the beginning. We then found the locations for the single nodes/districts and adapted the shape of the new infrastructures, to connect them with the existing network.

The theoretical approach appears perfectly suitable for Henna since its territory is characterized nowadays by very strong ecosystems and a complexity of different productive environments. These last can be integrated in the planning; used as a contributors for the production of energy; be preserved by the town implantation and even be fed by the fertilizer the town itself will produce. **The site specific features and identity will not be erased but will be enlighten by their new relationship**.

The new Henna and its territory

Shape and infrastructures
The town develops on the two sides of the railway; the central station is located in a district which is easily reachable from the other by all kinds of transportation. Instead of providing a single transportation backbone, as explained in the model town, we shaped this line in order to make two loops, one on the west side and one on the east and then connecting them by a larger one crossing both side. This choice was made to **strengthen the local transportation system on both sides of the railway** and to follow the demand to build the town on the west side, first. The west side loop will be the first one to be completed and will allow to get an efficient public transportation system since the early stages of the town construction.

The impact of noise from the motorway is avoided through **sound barriers** which are integrated with the existing landscape.

The margins of the single nodes follow the agricultural limits, the existing topographic features and, **like platforms overlooking the sea**, they become territories from where one can be confronted to the landscape's beauty and complexity. The linear parks run through the districts like canals, but they are also infrastructures: going across them, one can reach different points of town, while always staying in an natural though urban ambience.

The bike paths will cross the natural areas. They will follow some existing, informal country routes, while the mere crossing of the fields will be avoided as much as possible. The materials constituting them are permeable and natural and merge with the existing soil conditions.

Energy production
The wind tunnel, created by the railway line, will be exploited locating the wind turbines in correspondence with it, far enough from the inhabited centre to avoid noise and visual annoyance.
The biogas plant will be situated close to the future industrial plants, to easily recycle their heat losses and be served by the same infrastructures.

Sun and weather
Through the districts, the single buildings are placed to **reach maximal access to light**; their heights, shape and orientations enable to get two sides which are south - oriented, while squares are always placed to be enlightened.
The presence of covered footpaths and the use of part of the ground floor of many buildings as covered gateways appears appropriate to the rigid winter climate of Henna, **allowing to walk in every condition**.

Construction materials
Wood from regenerative forest is employed for the construction of the buildings, both for structure and finishing, while the gravel extracted from the pit will be used for the structures of main buildings following availability.
All of the local resources are therefore used.

Henna identity

The special conditions of Henna in relationship with the region, made us wonder what would be the type of life citizens and workers would look for, while choosing this particular location to live. What would make it different, compared to the other areas easily reachable through the regional network? What would give Henna a special identity, making it a ***unicum*** in the whole country? How to give - from the beginning - an identity to a town where there are not historical phases shaping it through the decades, but everything comes almost at the same time?

Ecology is not a label
The idea is to promote a town which is self sufficient, ecological and energetically efficient, while not associating it to the cliché of the "eco-city" and its nowadays ubiquitous "aesthetics".
Here, a small ecological footprint is obtained by restoring a close contact and exchange with the surrounding territory, optimizing the town shape to the mobility issues, the energy production and saving and using up to date technologies to reinterpret the archetypical relationship town/nature. We have chosen not to expose

the contemporary high tech tools as a flag that would only help to get a easy, (and easily obsolescent), "ecological image", for a fast acknowledgement.
While still encouraging inhabitants' consciousness of their role in keeping a small footprint, we still think their role as citizens cannot only be limited to their awareness toward the town efficiency. Their will of belonging to this town cannot only be related to its ecological features or image.

20000 inhabitants
Doesn't make it a metropolis but it is a critical threshold to get a urban feeling and intensity. People who choose to live in a town of this scale could do this for a multiplicity of reasons, from the need to avoid congested centres to that of belonging to a community with a human dimension, from the will of getting more space and open space to the feel of living closer to nature.

How dense?
The question of density is nowadays a basic topic for each urban project and discussion. We approached the subject not too mechanistically, at first, to avoid the consequences of a strictly quantitative way to relate to the issue. Density by itself is not a correct indicator of the quality of a space/urban plan: there are not so dense cities which are perceived as obsessive and claustrophobic, while some really dense places are enjoyable to live, giving the feeling of a more open and lively centre (the commonly known example of Barcelona). We avoided really low densities to get a compact urban unity, saving natural spaces and excluding a suburban atmosphere. At the same time we did not choose buildings and blocks too high, in order to preserve a maximum access to light and a nice connection to the streets. Lastly we avoided a too concentrated urban impact in term of resources and access compared to this small/medium sized town. In the choice of volumes and urban scenarios we aimed for a **comfortable relationship between open spaces and constructions**, for a rhythm of the built environment which feels coherent to the human scale, for residential units which are individualized while still underlining the sense of belonging to a community.

Through the districts the built density varies, like it would be in a town that has been constructed through time, to guarantee a urban-scape that is constantly changing and to offer a wide range of opportunities for the future householders.

Diversity
The proposed urban types and their combination makes the town a complex organism composed by subdistricts differing a lot one another. The mixed structures range from closed to opened courtyards, open compositions of mini blocks of different sizes, terraced houses, superposed semi-detached houses and offices, small apartment blocks facing a town square, porous blocks with public accessible ground floor and so on. The way these different urban types compose themselves with the network of public spaces and interact with the variety of landscape typologies, gives birth to a very rich urban plot where there are always new sides to discover even if it's a medium sized town.

Overcoming of the old town/landscape dichotomy

The domestic ambiances, the everyday space that connote a town, here meets a territory that has become no longer familiar for contemporary urban inhabitants.
The ambiguous geographies of a land to discover are merged with the urban fabric, creating stripes of lands through the buildings.
These spaces, where the built environment is therefore suspended, are constitutive parts of the town: this territory becomes a strong part of the urban unit, not its opposition.
While the town gets a territorial dimension, the territory assumes an urban character. The two subjects establish different layers of relationships through a strategic presence of mixed uses in both of them and the definition of new, lighter infrastructures.

Levels of flexibility and evolution
A town generates its own complex dynamics, it is a system evolving through time. There are different ways the multiple elements constituting the town interact with the time scale. The open territory works as a tableau for more ephemeral uses, ever-changing in short time, following the seasons, the light, night and day, the times of the year, even following the rhythm of agriculture. **The activities which take place in the linear parks are more connected to the uses of the town: the sequence of collective space, (open and covered, public and semi-public), allows the prosecution of activities taking place in the building**. Small units scattered through all the district host the local shared spaces, saunas, gym, laundries on different urban scales and their destination can change in time, following needs. Buildings in themselves are adaptable to different functions in time; retail, offices, housing allowing margins for auto-organization trough time, as well as new forms of urban life.

In the eventuality that the town will have more than 20000 inhabitants in the future, its expansion is possible, following the principle of nodes of 2000 people connected with the existing ones. This strategy will guarantee a balanced growth to the town.

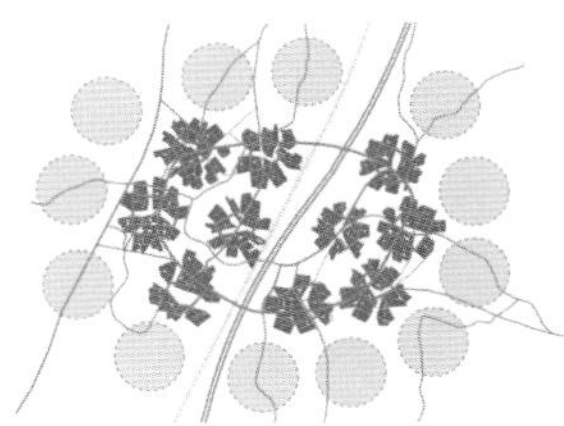

A new way of living in a town

Henna will get **the richness of a big city**, where there are always new areas to explore and events to be surprised from, **with the advantages of a smaller scale town**, where work and opportunities are close and a sense of community characterizes the urban life.
At the same time its special relationship with its territory will give birth to a completely new concept of town where the limit between the built and natural environment is faded. The feeling of inhabiting an urban unit will be completely reinvented. Everyday people can choose their way to go to work and live the town, the transportation they use, the landscape they cross. There are plenty of ways to experience the town itself, through the built urban connections, the backbone line, the dense urban wards, travelling through the linear parks or crossing the fields or even the forests.

080

Synapsiedlung | *Lapo Ruffi Architetto*

Client : Municipality of Montreux
Design Team : Lapo Ruffi, Vanessa Giandonati, Antonio Monaci, Lorenzo Santini
Collaborators : Benedetta Agostini, Francesca Nesi, Ilaria Rauty

Result : First Prize
Site area : 25.566mq_sqm

The objective of a new attractive density inside the residential area of Montreux and the possibility of building an urban centrality represent the guidelines of this project while determining its key points: the origin of a system of structures able to dialog amongst themselves while spilling over into the surrounding landscape. They are a network of connections, like a transposition, with fibers denser than those of historic paths. They become a web of fluxes, impulses of connection between the buildings and the neighborhood. They are the creation of a diffused system of public shared spaces among the residences; the system of connections and the territory able to generate *centrality*.

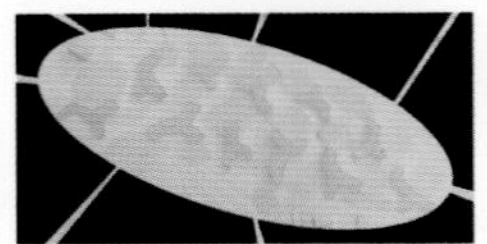

In connection with debates on the opportunity of a reasoned urban density, in opposition to the "twentieth century" planning system, the new buildings of this inhabited landscape design an urban layout along weaving lines. They are like *synapses of living*, or a continuous connection, uninterrupted, among the parts of the same system.The search for a new city layout is interrelated to the neighboring realities of village (Chailly, Clarens and Baugy) where historicized architecture presents itself in a continuous dialog with the landscape, becoming *centrality on the territory*.

And it is here, becoming centrality, that the project finds its first affirmation. The placement of the area Aux Grands Prés at the north of the city makes it a possible "*access point*" to the urban territory of Montreux, in the point where the countryside seems to give itself over to the city. Centrality means this as well; interweaving an inhabited space able to come to life with an architectural and functional character serving the territory, between them and the landscape. It is also inserting the architecture inside the existing urban fabrics understood as a junction able to generate successive levels of interaction with the place: a virological architecture as Wiel Arets defined in his travel toward the contemporaneity with which he treated the conviction: "unlike medicine, architecture does not have any intention to take the city back to its original state. Medical or surgical intervention is verified while architectural intervention in the city is not."

The new architectures of the "triplicity" of form, figure with three faces on the landscape, are arranged along an axial *system of synapses*, making up an *urban network* between the project area and the adjacent zones: the neighborhood. The spaces that this interweaving generates, therefore, become the vacancies where the citizen can regain possession of the territory through their multi-functionality, that which we can call a self-management of the inhabited space, the self-management of its times: *social stages*.

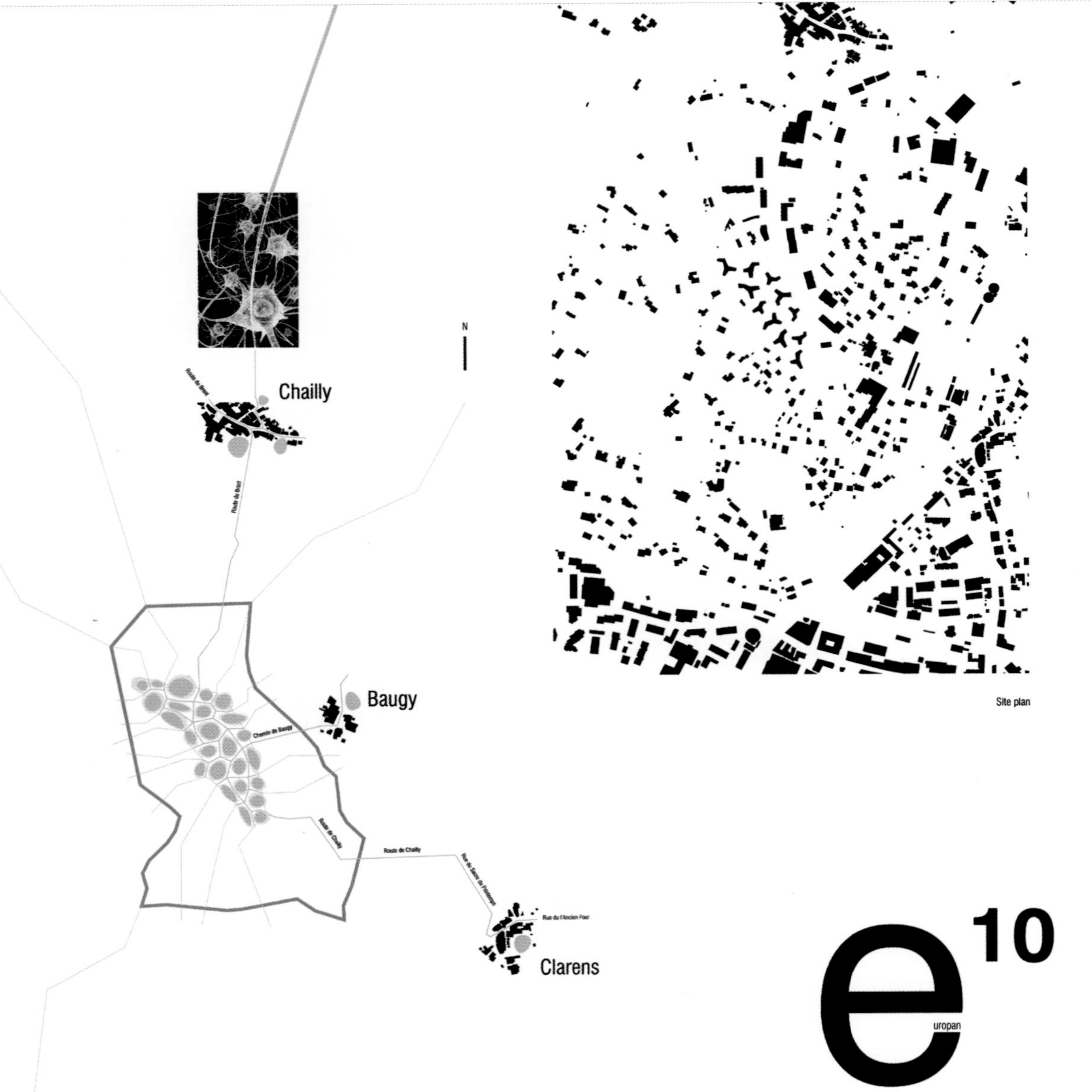

Ordering the structures along the line of movement of the synapses means generating a complete structure. It is *ordered fragmentation* of the inhabited space where fragment does not constitute discord when the origin resides in the order of the completed sentence. Homogeneity of the intervention avoids estrangement of singular structures.

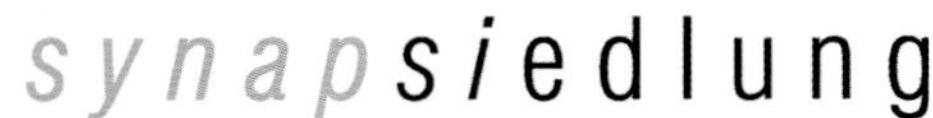

To talk about social stage signifies the definition of a space of the city as a comparison between the inhabitant and the place. The relationship of contact between landscape and new structures is composed of volumetries at the ground floor that moving along the fabric generator of the project, show themselves as an *extrusion of the landscape* at various levels, as if it was to open in a series of circumstances to welcome them in its organicity.

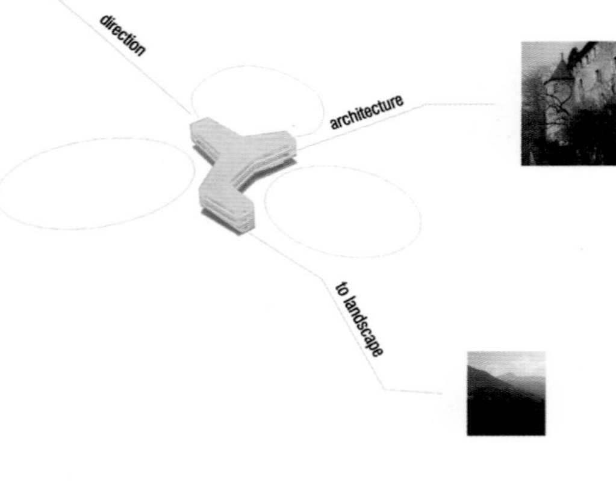

The liberated space between the multi-functional structures on the ground floor creates the area where *twenty-five equipped cells* define the spaces allocated to free time, in addition to the traditional apartment, house and garden. In these cells, social vegetable gardens contribute to the origin of a naturbanization, or the production of a portion of *green city* controlled by the citizens, as they are the first to recognize their own needs. There will be spaces of the residential area intended as a market, spaces as "a place to meet, chat, play, fight, envy, court and feel proud", then playgrounds for children, pétanque grounds, landscaped green areas and shady areas like city forests. Facing onto these shared spaces, there are structures on the ground floor of the buildings offering services to the neighborhood like café, a bistrot, small commercial spaces, places for vegetable garden maintenance, market activity, artisan shops and atelier.
The covered area is equal to 17% of the total project area, demonstrating how much intervention is aimed at maintaining a *balance with the landscape* in this part of the city.

The residential structures, as if balanced above these volumes of public functionality, generate a second zone of built-up space that sees its development on three levels. The multiplicity of the typologies (individual collective living, grouped individual living, protected housing and economic housing) allows the attainment of that *flexibility* and *social mixité* necessary for a new vision of living where the risk of a mute aggregate is avoided.
In the total of eleven architectural synapses, the buildings S1 and S3 are planned to house the Nursery school and Kindergarten in a part of the lot where the remodeled hilly area allows the creation of patios as protected spaces for the schools.
In the north area of the lot, building S11, Neighborhood *cultural center*, represents the willingness to connote the urban intervention of a space serving the whole community as a connecting point between both the project area and the neighborhood, the neighborhood and the city. Entering into the ground, it allows the exploitation of the covering as a projection of the landscape on what is built.

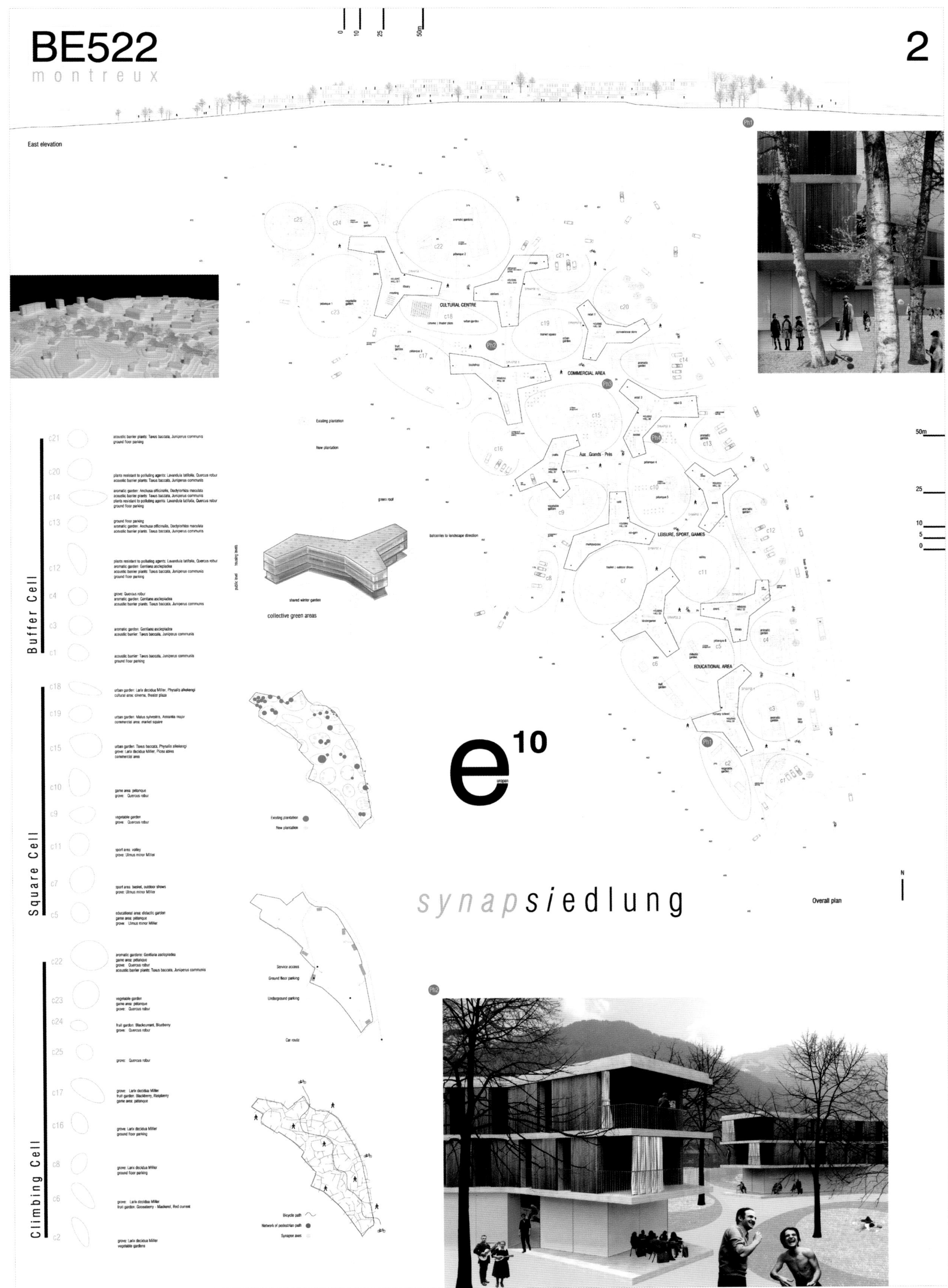

BE522
montreux
2
0
10
25
50m
East elevation

c21 — acoustic barrier plants: Taxus baccata, Juniperus communis / ground floor parking

c20 — plants resistant to polluting agents: Lavandula latifolia, Quercus robur / acoustic barrier plants: Taxus baccata, Juniperus communis

c14 — aromatic garden: Anchusa officinalis, Dactylorhiza maculata / acoustic barrier plants: Taxus baccata, Juniperus communis / plants resistant to polluting agents: Lavandula latifolia, Quercus robur / ground floor parking

c13 — ground floor parking / aromatic garden: Anchusa officinalis, Dactylorhiza maculata / acoustic barrier plants: Taxus baccata, Juniperus communis

c12 — plants resistant to polluting agents: Lavandula latifolia, Quercus robur / aromatic garden: Gentiana asclepiadea / acoustic barrier plants: Taxus baccata, Juniperus communis / ground floor parking

c4 — grove: Quercus robur / aromatic garden: Gentiana asclepiadea / acoustic barrier plants: Taxus baccata, Juniperus communis

c3 — aromatic garden: Gentiana asclepiadea / acoustic barrier: Taxus baccata, Juniperus communis

c1 — acoustic barrier: Taxus baccata, Juniperus communis / ground floor parking

c18 — urban garden: Larix decidua Miller, Physalis alkekengi / cultural area: cinema, theater plaza

c19 — urban garden: Malus sylvestris, Anisantha major / commercial area: market square

c15 — urban garden: Taxus baccata, Physalis alkekengi / grove: Larix decidua Miller, Picea abies / commercial area

c10 — game area: pétanque / grove: Quercus robur

c9 — vegetable garden / grove: Quercus robur

c11 — sport area: volley / grove: Ulmus minor Miller

c7 — sport area: basket, outdoor shows / grove: Ulmus minor Miller

c5 — educational area: didactic garden / game area: pétanque / grove: Ulmus minor Miller

c22 — aromatic garden: Gentiana asclepiadea / game area: pétanque / grove: Quercus robur / acoustic barrier plants: Taxus baccata, Juniperus communis

c23 — vegetable garden / game area: pétanque / grove: Quercus robur

c24 — fruit garden: Blackberry, Blueberry / grove: Quercus robur

c25 — grove: Quercus robur

c17 — grove: Larix decidua Miller / fruit garden: Blackberry, Raspberry / game area: pétanque

c16 — grove: Larix decidua Miller / ground floor parking

c8 — grove: Larix decidua Miller / ground floor parking

c6 — grove: Larix decidua Miller / fruit garden: Gooseberry - Mackerel, Red currant

c2 — grove: Larix decidua Miller / vegetable gardens

Existing plantation
New plantation

green roof

shared winter garden

balconies to landscape direction

public field / housing fields

Existing plantation
New plantation

Service access
Ground floor parking
Underground parking
Car route

Bicycle path
Network of pedestrian paths
Synapse axes

CULTURAL CENTRE
c18
cinema | theater plaza
urban garden

COMMERCIAL AREA
LEISURE, SPORT, GAMES
EDUCATIONAL AREA
Aux Grands - Prés
collective green areas
Buffer Cell
Square Cell
Climbing Cell
e
10
synapsiedlung
Overall plan
N

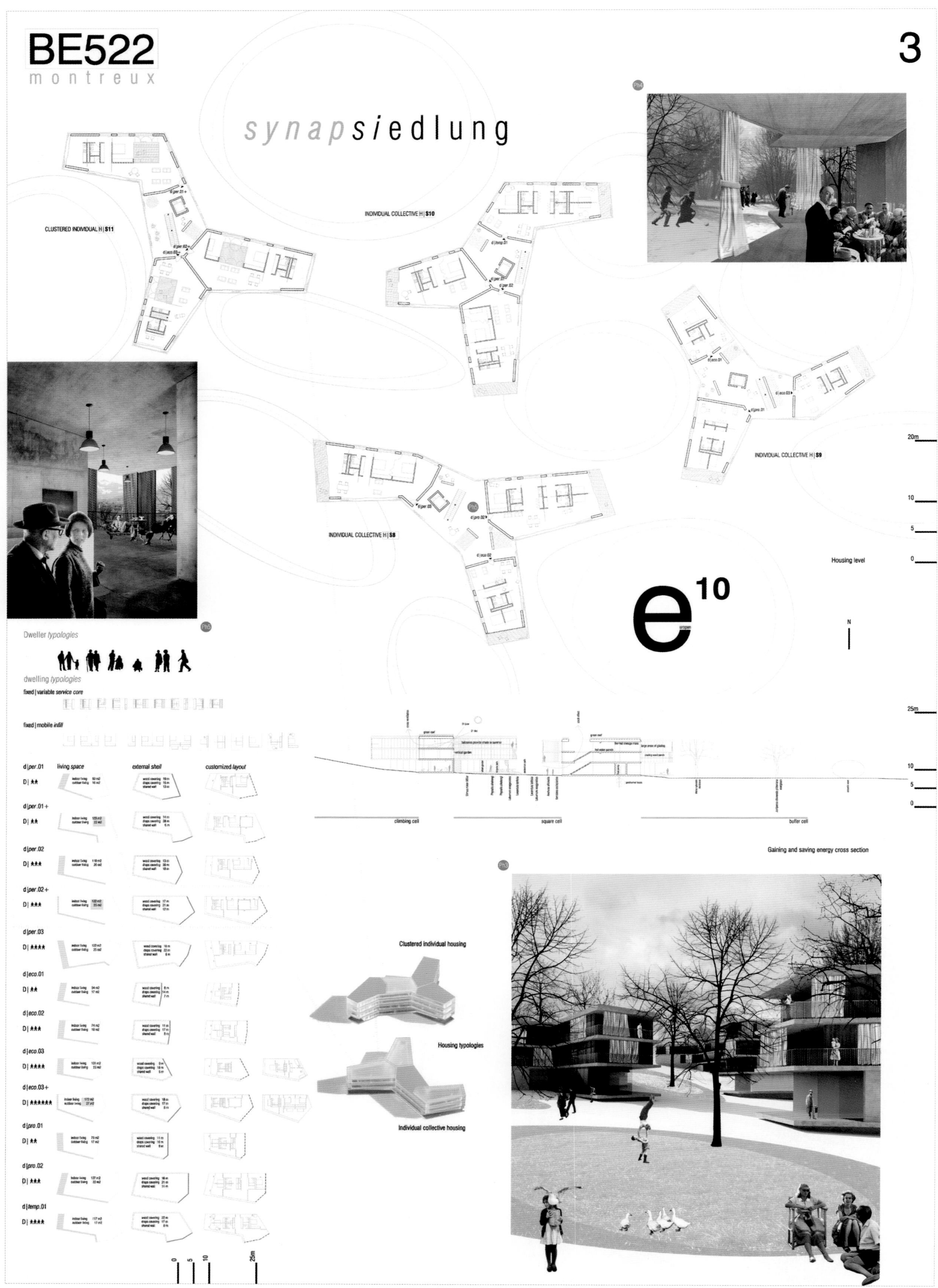
BE522
montreux
3
synapsiedlung
CLUSTERED INDIVIDUAL H | S11
INDIVIDUAL COLLECTIVE H | S10
INDIVIDUAL COLLECTIVE H | S9
INDIVIDUAL COLLECTIVE H | S8
Housing level
e10
Dweller typologies
dwelling typologies
fixed | variable service core
fixed | mobile infill
living space
external shell
customized layout
Gaining and saving energy cross section
climbing cell
square cell
buffer cell
Clustered individual housing
Housing typologies
Individual collective housing

Tranversal Processes | *arenas basabe palacios arquitectos*

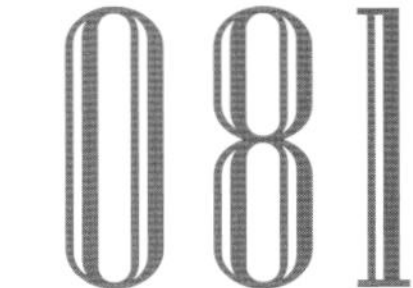

Urban Rehabilitation in Elda(Spain)
Authors : Enrique Arenas Laorga, Luis Basabe Montalvo, Luis Palacios Labrador
Collaborators : Eva Miguel, Helena de Sebastian

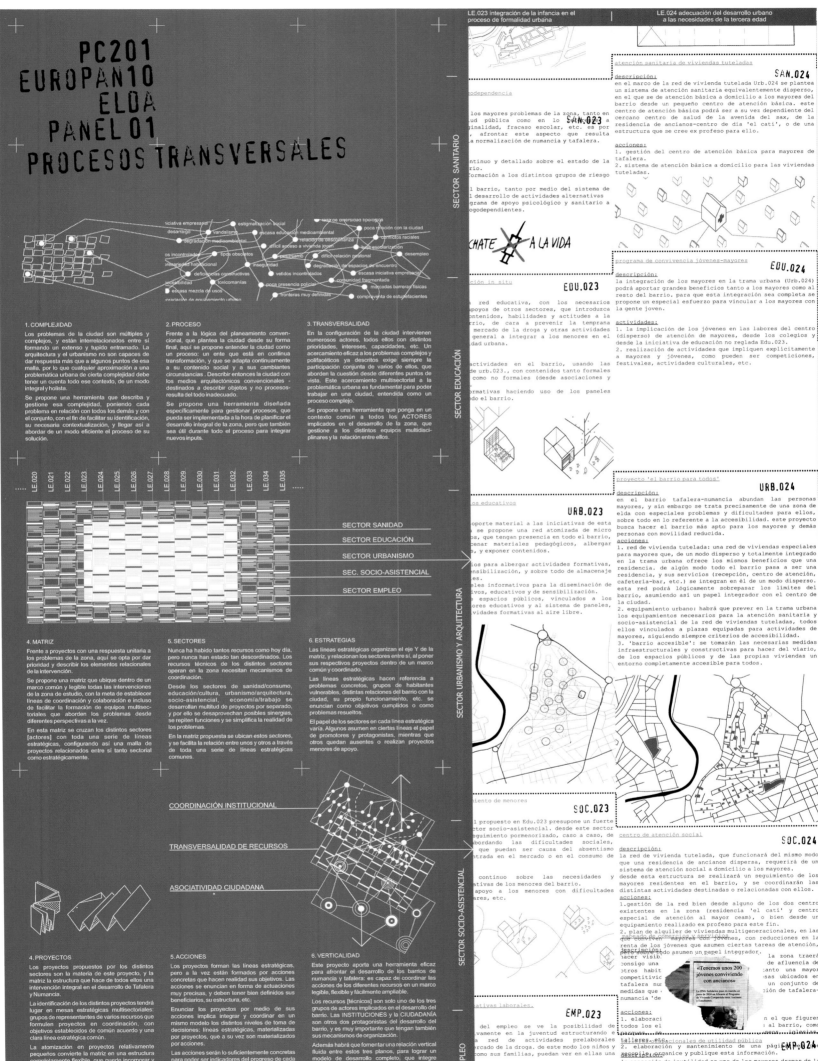

PC201 EUROPAN10 ELDA PANEL 01 PROCESOS TRANSVERSALES

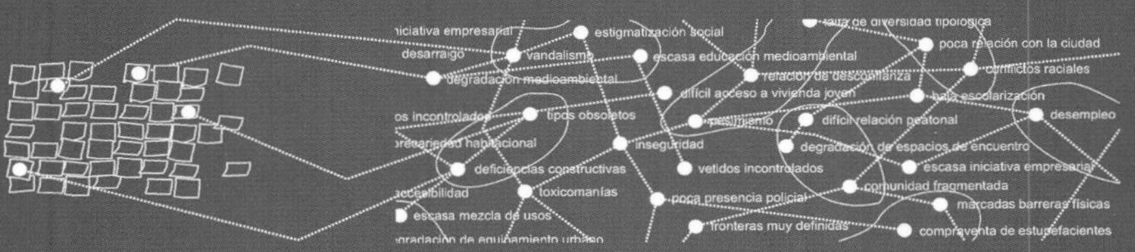

1. COMPLEJIDAD

Los problemas de la ciudad son múltiples y complejos, y están interrelacionados entre sí formando un extenso y tupido entramado. La arquitectura y el urbanismo no son capaces de dar respuesta más que a algunos puntos de esa malla, por lo que cualquier aproximación a una problemática urbana de cierta complejidad debe tener un cuenta todo ese contexto, de un modo integral y holista.

Se propone una herramienta que describa y gestione esa complejidad, poniendo cada problema en relación con todos los demás y con el conjunto, con el fin de facilitar su identificación, su necesaria contextualización, y llegar así a abordar de un modo eficiente el proceso de su solución.

2. PROCESO

Frente a la lógica del planeamiento convencional, que plantea la ciudad desde su forma final, aquí se propone entender la ciudad como un proceso: un ente que está en continua transformación, y que se adapta continuamente a su contenido social y a sus cambiantes circunstancias. Describir entonces la ciudad con los medios arquitectónicos convencionales - destinados a describir objetos y no procesos- resulta del todo inadecuado.

Se propone una herramienta diseñada específicamente para gestionar procesos, que pueda ser implementada a la hora de planificar el desarrollo integral de la zona, pero que también sea útil durante todo el proceso para integrar nuevos inputs.

3. TRANSVERSALIDAD

En la configuración de la ciudad intervienen numerosos actores, todos ellos con distintos prioridades, intereses, capacidades, etc. Un acercamiento eficaz a los problemas complejos y polifacéticos ya descritos exige siempre la participación conjunta de varios de ellos, que aborden la cuestión desde diferentes puntos de vista. Este acercamiento multisectorial a la problemática urbana es fundamental para poder trabajar en una ciudad, entendida como un proceso complejo.

Se propone una herramienta que ponga en un contexto común a todos los ACTORES implicados en el desarrollo de la zona, que gestione a los distintos equipos multidisciplinares y la relación entre ellos.

LE.020 LE.021 LE.022 LE.023 LE.024 LE.025 LE.026 LE.027 LE.028 LE.029 LE.030 LE.031 LE.032 LE.033 LE.034 LE.035

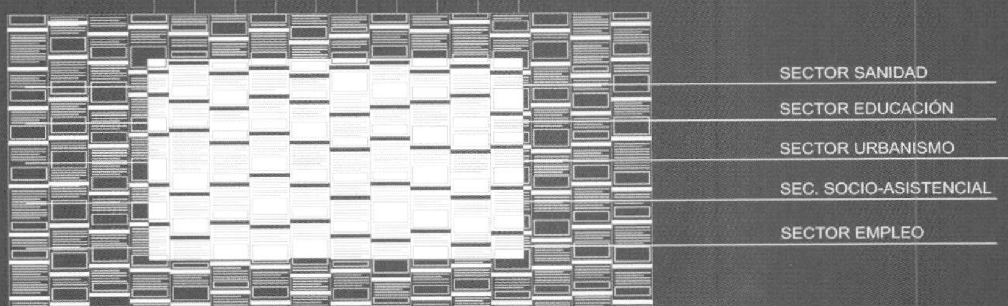

SECTOR SANIDAD
SECTOR EDUCACIÓN
SECTOR URBANISMO
SEC. SOCIO-ASISTENCIAL
SECTOR EMPLEO

4. MATRIZ

Frente a proyectos con una respuesta unitaria a los problemas de la zona, aquí se opta por dar prioridad y describir los elementos relacionales de la intervención.

Se propone una matriz que ubique dentro de un marco común y legible todas las intervenciones de la zona de estudio, con la meta de establecer líneas de coordinación y colaboración e incluso de facilitar la formación de equipos multisectoriales que aborden los problemas desde diferentes perspectivas a la vez.

En esta matriz se cruzan los distintos sectores [actores] con toda una serie de líneas estratégicas, configurando así una malla de proyectos relacionados entre sí tanto sectorial como estratégicamente.

5. SECTORES

Nunca ha habido tantos recursos como hoy día, pero nunca han estado tan descordinados. Los recursos técnicos de los distintos sectores operan en la zona necesitan mecanismos de coordinación.

Desde los sectores de sanidad/consumo, educación/cultura, urbanismo/arquitectura, socio-asistencial, economía/trabajo se desarrollan multitud de proyectos por separado, y por ello se desaprovechan posibles sinergias, se repiten funciones y se simplifica la realidad de los problemas.

En la matriz propuesta se ubican estos sectores, y se facilita la relación entre unos y otros a través de toda una serie de líneas estratégicas comunes.

6. ESTRATEGIAS

Las líneas estratégicas organizan el eje Y de la matriz, y relacionan los sectores entre sí, al poner sus respectivos proyectos dentro de un marco común y coordinado.

Las líneas estratégicas hacen referencia a problemas concretos, grupos de habitantes vulnerables, distintas relaciones del barrio con la ciudad, su propio funcionamiento, etc. como problemas resueltos.

El papel de los sectores en cada línea estratégica varía. Algunos asumen en ciertas líneas el papel de promotores y protagonistas, mientras que otros quedan ausentes o realizan proyectos menores de apoyo.

COORDINACIÓN INSTITUCIONAL
TRANSVERSALIDAD DE RECURSOS
ASOCIATIVIDAD CIUDADANA

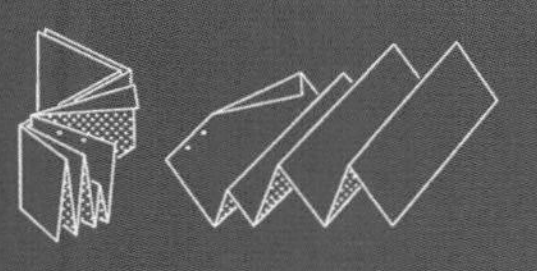

4. PROYECTOS

Los proyectos propuestos por los distintos sectores son la materia de este proyecto, y la matriz la estructura que hace de todos ellos una intervención integral en el desarrollo de Tafalera y Numancia.

La identificación de los distintos proyectos tendrá lugar en mesas estratégicas multisectoriales: grupos de representantes de varios recursos que formulen proyectos en coordinación, con objetivos establecidos de común acuerdo y una clara línea estratégica común.

La atomización en proyectos relativamente pequeños convierte la matriz en una estructura completamente flexible, que puede incorporar y eliminar piezas, y reconfigurarse ante cualquier cambio circunstancial.

5. ACCIONES

Los proyectos forman las líneas estratégicas, pero a la vez están formados por acciones concretas que hacen realidad sus objetivos. Las acciones se enuncian en forma de actuaciones muy precisas, y deben tener bien definidos sus beneficiarios, su estructura, etc.

Enunciar los proyectos por medio de sus acciones implica integrar y coordinar en un mismo modelo los distintos niveles de toma de decisiones: líneas estratégicas, materializadas por proyectos, que a su vez son materializados por acciones.

Las acciones serán lo suficientemente concretas para poder ser indicadores del progreso de cada proyecto.

6. VERTICALIDAD

Este proyecto aporta una herramienta eficaz para afrontar el desarrollo de los barrios de numancia y tafalera: es capaz de coordinar las acciones de los diferentes recursos en un marco legible, flexible y fácilmente ampliable.

Los recursos [técnicos] son solo uno de los tres grupos de actores implicados en el desarrollo del barrio. Las INSTITUCIONES y la CIUDADANÍA son otros dos protagonistas del desarrollo del barrio, y es muy importante que tengan también sus mecanismos de organización.

Además habrá que fomentar una relación vertical fluida entre estos tres planos, para lograr un modelo de desarrollo completo, que integre todas las fuerzas implicadas en la configuración de la zona.

SECTOR SANITARIO
SECTOR EDUCACIÓN
SECTOR URBANISMO Y ARQUITECTURA
SECTOR SOCIO-ASISTENCIAL
SECTOR EMPLEO

LE.023 integración de la infancia en el proceso de formalidad urbana

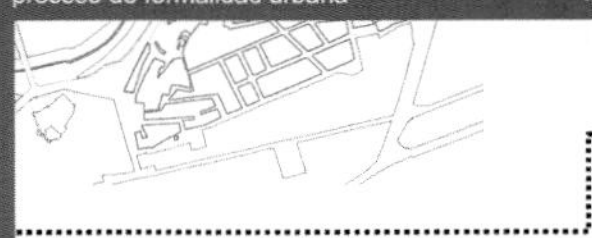

LE.024 adecuación del desarrollo urbano a las necesidades de la tercera edad

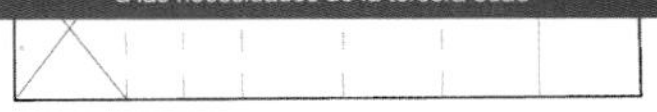

odependencia

SAN.023

los mayores problemas de la zona, tanto en
ud pública como en lo [...] a
ginalidad, fracaso escolar, etc. es por
, afrontar este aspecto que resulta
a normalización de numancia y tafalera.

ntinuo y detallado sobre el estado de la
rio.
formación a los distintos grupos de riesgo

l barrio, tanto por medio del sistema de
l desarrollo de actividades alternativas
grama de apoyo psicológico y sanitario a
ogodependientes.

CHATE A LA VIDA

atención sanitaria de viviendas tuteladas

SAN.024

descripción:
en el marco de la red de vivienda tutelada Urb.024 se plantea un sistema de atención sanitaria equivalentemente disperso, en el que se de atención básica a domicilio a los mayores del barrio desde un pequeño centro de atención básica. este centro de atención básica podrá ser a su vez dependiente del cercano centro de salud de la avenida del sax, de la residencia de ancianos-centro de día 'el cati', o de una estructura que se cree ex profeso para ello.

acciones:
1. gestión del centro de atención básica para mayores de tafalera.
2. sistema de atención básica a domicilio para las viviendas tuteladas.

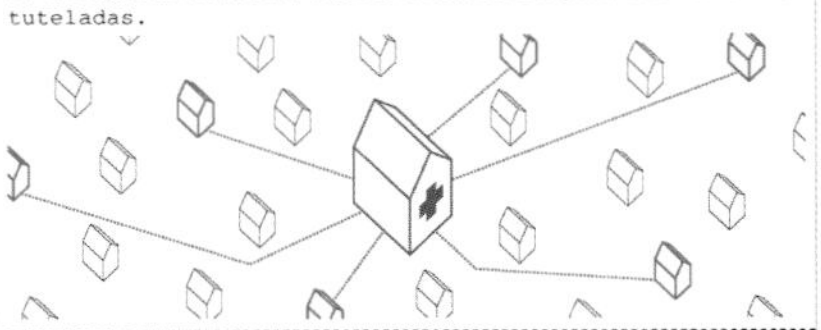

ción in situ

EDU.023

red educativa, con los necesarios
apoyos de otros sectores, que introduzca
ontenidos, habilidades y actitudes a la
rrio, de cara a prevenir la temprana
mercado de la droga y otras actividades
general a integrar a los menores en el
dad urbana.

actividades en el barrio, usando las
de urb.023., con contenidos tanto formales
como no formales (desde asociaciones y

ormativas haciendo uso de los paneles
do el barrio.

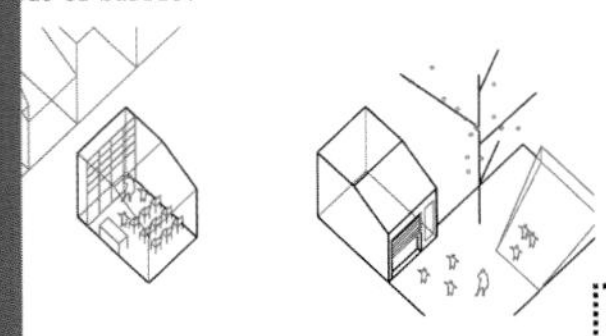

programa de convivencia jóvenes-mayores

EDU.024

descripción:
la integración de los mayores en la trama urbana (Urb.024) podrá aportar grandes beneficios tanto a los mayores como al resto del barrio. para que esta integración sea completa se propone un especial esfuerzo para vincular a los mayores con la gente joven.

actividades:
1. la implicación de los jóvenes en las labores del centro (disperso) de atención de mayores, desde los colegios y desde la iniciativa de educación no reglada Edu.023.
2. realización de actividades que impliquen explícitamente a mayores y jóvenes, como pueden ser competiciones, festivales, actividades culturales, etc.

os educativos

URB.023

oporte material a las iniciativas de esta
se propone una red atomizada de micro
os, que tengan presencia en todo el barrio,
cenar materiales pedagógicos, albergar
s, y exponer contenidos.

ios para albergar actividades formativas,
nsibilización, y sobre todo de almacenaje
es.
eles informativos para la diseminación de
ivos, educativos y de sensibilización.
espacios públicos, vinculados a los
ores educativos y al sistema de paneles,
vidades formativas al aire libre.

proyecto 'el barrio para todos'

URB.024

descripción:
en el barrio tafalera-numancia abundan las personas mayores, y sin embargo se trata precisamente de una zona de elda con especiales problemas y dificultades para ellos, sobre todo en lo referente a la accesibilidad. este proyecto busca hacer el barrio más apto para los mayores y demás personas con movilidad reducida.

acciones:
1. red de vivienda tutelada: una red de viviendas especiales para mayores que, de un modo disperso y totalmente integrado en la trama urbana ofrece los mismos beneficios que una residencia. de algún modo todo el barrio pasa a ser una residencia, y sus servicios (recepción, centro de atención, cafetería-bar, etc.) se integran en él de un modo disperso. esta red podrá lógicamente sobrepasar los límites del barrio, asumiendo así un papel integrador con el centro de la ciudad.
2. equipamiento urbano: habrá que prever en la trama urbana los equipamientos necesarios para la atención sanitaria y socio-asistencial de la red de viviendas tuteladas, todos ellos vinculados a plazas equipadas para actividades de mayores, siguiendo siempre criterios de accesibilidad.
3. 'barrio accesible': se tomarán las necesarias medidas infraestructurales y constructivas para hacer del viario, de los espacios públicos y de las propias viviendas un entorno completamente accesible para todos.

iento de menores

SOC.023

l propuesto en Edu.023 presupone un fuerte
ctor socio-asistencial. desde este sector
eguimiento pormenorizado, caso a caso, de
bordando las dificultades sociales,
que puedan ser causa del absentismo
ntrada en el mercado o en el consumo de

continuo sobre las necesidades y
ativas de los menores del barrio.
apoyo a los menores con dificultades
ares, etc.

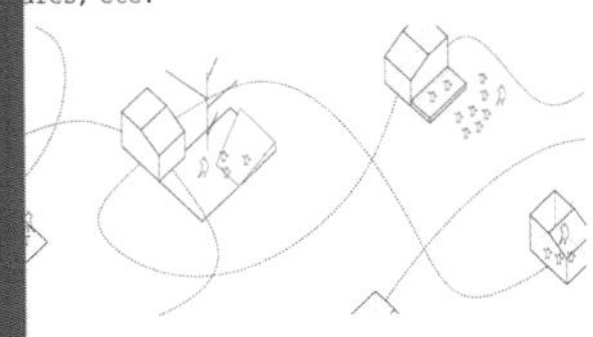

centro de atención social

SOC.024

descripción:
la red de vivienda tutelada, que funcionará del mismo modo que una residencia de ancianos dispersa, requerirá de un sistema de atención social a domicilio a los mayores.
desde esta estructura se realizará un seguimiento de los mayores residentes en el barrio, y se coordinarán las distintas actividades destinadas o relacionadas con ellos.

acciones:
1. gestión de la red bien desde alguno de los dos centro existentes en la zona (residencia 'el cati' y centro especial de atención al mayor ceam), o bien desde un equipamiento realizado ex profeso para este fin.
2. plan de alquiler de viviendas multigeneracionales, en las que conviven mayores con jóvenes, con reducciones en la renta de los jóvenes que asumen ciertas tareas de atención, pero sobre todo asumen un papel integrador.

mapeado de comercios y servicios

descripción:
hacer visib[...] la zona traerá
consigo una [...] de afluencia de
otros habit[...] tanto una mayor
competitivic[...] sas ubicados en
tafalera nu[...] un conjunto de
medidas que [...] ción de tafalera-
numancia 'de

«Tenemos unos 200 jóvenes conviviendo con ancianos»

La ONG Solidarios puso en marcha en junio de 2010 en Alicante el Programa de Vivienda Compartida entre Ancianos y Estudiantes.

acciones:
1. elaboraci[...] n el que figuren
todos los el[...] al barrio, como
parques, se[...] seos, iglesias,
talleres, etc.
2. elaboración y mantenimiento de una página web que recopile, organice y publique esta información.

ativas laborales.

EMP.023

del empleo se ve la posibilidad de
vamente en la juventud estructurando e
a red de actividades prelaborales
ercado de la droga. de este modo los niños y
como sus familias, puedan ver en ellas una

ector empleo se podrá gestionar un sistema
ra las familias que apoyen la correcta
sus hijos, así como la red de educación no

talleres ocupacionales de utilidad pública

EMP.024

descripción:
la sensación de inutilidad es uno de los mayores dramas de la gente mayor, que ven desplazado su papel en la comunidad. por ello es necesario, desde el sector de empleo, tener en

LE.025 gestión responsable y eficiente de los residuos

el interior de los patios particulares.

no solo se propone eliminar la presencia de residuos, sino que se plantea transformar tafalera-numancia en xxxxxxxxun enclave ejemplar en lo que se refiere a la salubridad y limpieza.

PC201
EUROPAN10
ELDA
PANEL 02

proyecto 'tafalera limpia-tafalera sana' — SAN.025

descripción:
la insalubridad que conlleva la presencia generalizada e ilegal de residuos implica toda una serie de problemas y riesgos:
-presencia de roedores, culebras y perros salvajes.
-fuente de infecciones y enfermedades, sobre todo para la infancia que juega en la zona.
-objetos y materiales peligrosos.
-contaminación del ambiente, del suelo y del agua.
-malos olores y degradación del paisaje urbano.
-contribuye a la condición de marginalidad e inseguridad de la zona.

acciones:
1. un diagnóstico detallado de focos de insalubridad, de sus riesgos para la salud, así como una evaluación de sus causas de cara a establecer una matriz de soluciones.
2. un proyecto de concienciación y educación sanitaria que incluya el tema de los residuos, informando sobre los riesgos de una mala gestión de los residuos, y sobre las maneras correctas de prevenirlos.

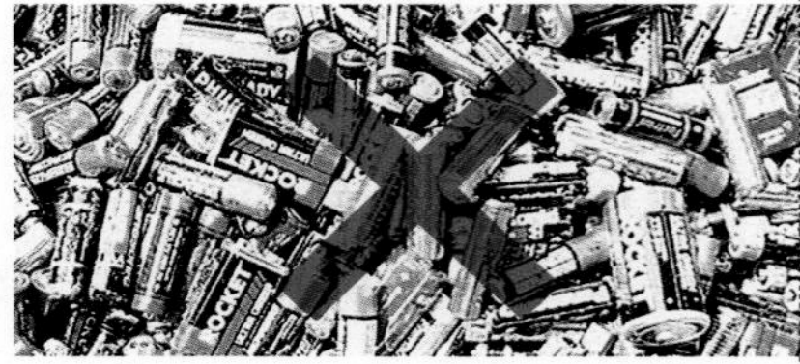

talleres de sensibilización — EDU.025

descripción:
la gestión responsable de los residuos se fundamenta sobre un conjunto de hábitos adquiridos a menudo durante la infancia. por ello parece importante abordar este tema tan crucial desde el sector educativo.

acciones:
1. desarrollo de talleres de formación sobre la basura, sus riesgos y sus potenciales, así como sobre su separación, su procesamiento, reutilización, reciclaje, y uso como fuente de energía. estos talleres podrán tener lugar en los colegios de la zona, así como en la red de espacios educativos Edu.024.
2. introducir horizontalmente la temática de la gestión de residuos en las distintas instituciones e iniciativas educativas de la zona. de este modo se abordará el tema en los distintos proyectos educativos de guarderías, colegios, institutos, centros de capacitación laboral, iniciativas de educación no formal, etc.

sistema de gestión eficiente de residuos — URB.025

descripción:
para hacer de tafalera-numancia no solo un lugar limpio, sino un paradigma reconocido en gestión de residuos, será necesaria la implantación de una red infraestructural puntera, que permita la separación, reciclaje y reutilización de la basura, así como su uso para producción energética, que pueda abastecer y enriquecer el barrio.

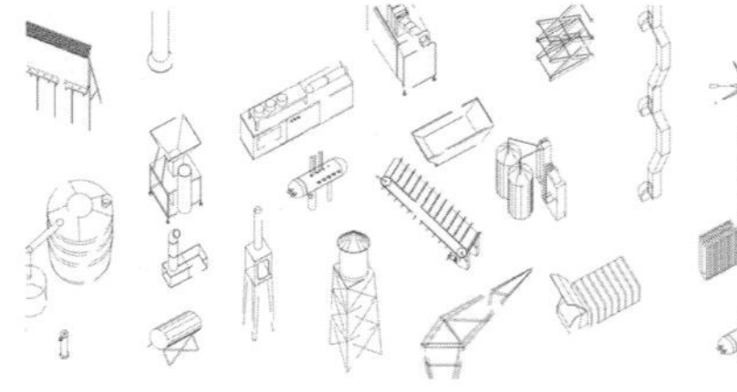

acciones:
1. se propone un sistema descentralizado que esté apoyado por el resto de programas de sensibilización, capacitación y seguimiento de la LE.025: una red de infraestructuras integrada en el propio tejido urbano, que va desde la escala doméstica (separación, calderas de biomasa) hasta otras de barrio o incluso para todo el municipio (centro de separación de basura).
el resultado es que todo el barrio se convierte en un eficiente procesador de gran parte de los residuos.
los principales elementos de esta red son:
1. separación a escala doméstica.
2. dispositivos de compostaje a escala doméstica.
3. biodigestores (gas) / calderas de biomasa (calor) cada cinco domicilios.
4. puntos de recogida selectiva.
5. dispositivos de prensado de cartón, papel, plástico, lata para su posterior venta.

influencia en los hábitos de salubridad — SOC.025

descripción:
el descuido del entorno tiene a menudo sus raíces en problemas de índole social, cultural, etc. por ello abordar el problema de la presencia generalizada de basuras sin entrar a solucionar sus causas promete ser una tarea poco fructífera.
en este sentido el apoyo desde el ámbito socio-asistencial se ve como algo absolutamente necesario para introducir hábitos responsables en las familias y demás colectivos del barrio.
acciones:
1. Se trabajará sobre todo en la gestión de residuos a escala doméstica: correcta separación, uso de las calderas de biomasa, así como en el mantenimiento del entorno inmediato de cada domicilio.

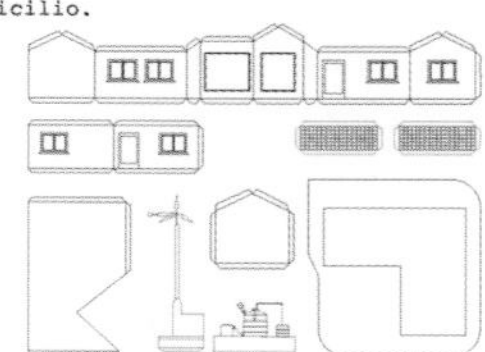

programa 'negocio-basura' — EMP.025

descripción
la basura es una fuente económica y de empleo de primer orden. es fuente de materiales y energía, y su gestión es fuente de actividad económica y de empleo. entender la basura no solo como algo que debe ser retirado, sino precisamente como fuente de recursos, es necesario de cara a gestionarla de un modo auténticamente sostenible.

LE.026 adecuación del barrio para optimizar los recursos energéticos

control sanitario de los espacios públicos y de la edificación — SAN.026

descripción:
para su correcta inserción en la ciudad, el barrio debe adecuarse a los estándares de salubridad, tanto en sus espacios públicos como en la edificación. por ello será esencial el diagnóstico, asesoramiento y posterior control sanitario de la intervención.

acciones:
1. diagnóstico sobre el estado sanitario de la edificación de los barrios tafalera y numancia, de cara a enfocar y priorizar su rehabilitación integral.
2. asesoramiento sanitario en el proceso de rehabilitación del barrio.
3. control sanitario continuado de los edificios, comercios, zonas residenciales y espacios públicos, durante y después del proceso de rehabilitación.

proyecto educativo 'la casa verde' — EDU.026

descripción:
proyecto educativo en torno a la vivienda piloto sostenible (cfr. emp.026), de formación y sensibilización en materia de ahorro de energía, de gestión ecológica de residuos y de consumo responsable del agua.
la 'casa verde' piloto se usará como centro de (in)formación, documentación y capacitación en materia de sostenibilidad a escala doméstica.
acciones:
1. Recopilar, archivar y poner a disposición del público documentación y tecnologías referidas a la gestión responsable de la energía, el agua y los residuos.
2. Difundir actitudes que lleven a una mayor eficiencia y respeto al medioambiente, por medio de visitas de grupos, colectivos, colegios, e individuales particulares. Además podrán realizarse desde la 'casa verde' campañas informativas, cursos y actividades con ese fin.
3. Desarrollar talleres de capacitación laboral destinados a mejorar las tecnologías de construcción y de instalaciones en la edificación (cfr. emp.26).

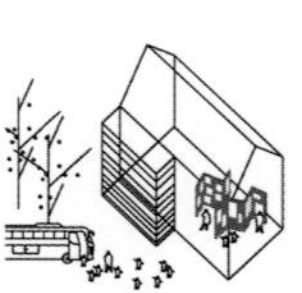
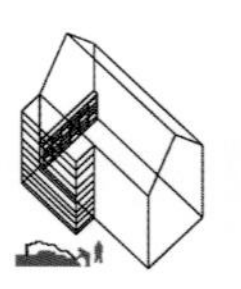
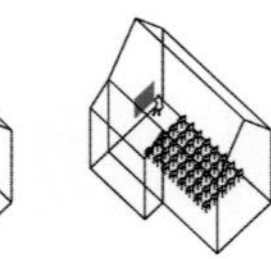

prog. de rehabilitación de viviendas — URB.026

descripción:
"rehabilitar un edificio puede suponer un ahorro energético del 60% respecto a derribarlo y volver a construirlo, y evita numerosos impactos ambientales. (...) además, la rehabilitación minimiza los problemas de desarraigo e insostenibilidad social de poblaciones con carencias económicas." (margarita luxán, conama 2009).

acciones:
1. programa integral de rehabilitación del barrio de numancia-tafalera, tomando como referencia las exigencias del cte, en el cual se desarrolle la rehabilitación sostenible de los espacios públicos del barrio, y también se informe, incentive, co-financie y coordine la rehabilitación de las viviendas.
2. implantación de medidas punteras en gestión de residuos, ahorro energético y gestión del agua, de modo que el barrio pueda llegar a ser modélico, y su proceso de rehabilitación sea un proyecto piloto exportable al resto de elda, de la región, o incluso a escalas mayores.
3. proceso de implantación de nuevo tejido, en la parte norte del área de estudio, que se regirá igualmente por criterios de sostenibilidad energética y medioambiental, tanto en lo referente a su definición como a sus procesos constructivos.

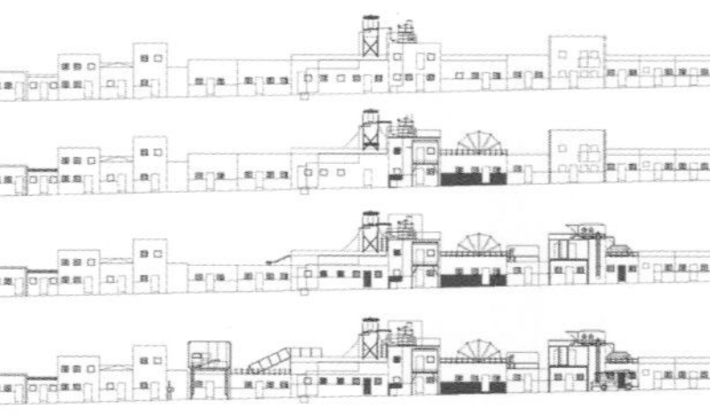

gestión social del proceso de rehabilitación — SOC.026

descripción:
el éxito de los procesos de rehabilitación de barrios socialmente complejos proviene en gran medida del acompañamiento de una buena gestión social. realojos, necesidades específicas, dificultades económicas, familiares o físicas, etc. hacen que un proceso de rehabilitación no sea solo algo físico, sino que sobre todo un proceso de adaptación y reubicación social

acciones:
1. analice las condiciones sociales del hábitat, los lugares de necesidades especiales y de precariedad urgente.
2. gestione los realojos y adaptaciones temporales que pueda llegar a haber en el proceso de rehabilitación.
3. informe y asesore a los particulares sobre las necesidades de la rehabilitación de sus viviendas, así como sobre las posibilidades de financiación y sobre los trámites administrativos a seguir.

proyecto de capacitación 'la casa verde' — EMP.026

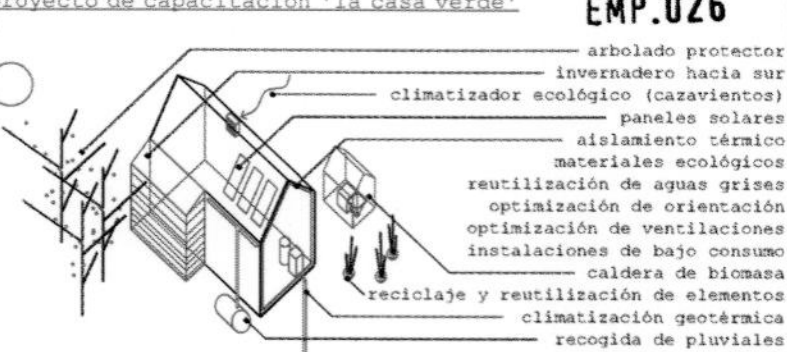

descripción:
se propone la construcción de una vivienda sostenible piloto, que sea ejemplar en materia de sostenibilidad tanto medioambiental como económica.
la propia construcción del prototipo tendrá la forma de un taller de capacitación laboral, en el que se transmitirán técnicas constructivas y de instalaciones que mejoren la

LE.027 fortalecimiento de la identidad del barrio

diagnóstico sanitario — SAN.027

descripción:
uno de los mayores problemas sanitarios consiste en no tener cláramente definidos cuáles son las necesidades reales. para ello es necesario generar los mecanismos necesarios de diagnóstico que operen de forma continuada, para conocer en cada momento el estado real de la salud comunitaria.
acciones:
1. preparaciones previas: delimitar y definir la comunidad objeto de análisis, conocer las principales fuentes de información, (cuantitativa y cualitativa). contacto con ciudadanía, instituciones y recursos de la comunidad.
2. recogida de información en función de la importancia otorgada, su disponibilidad y el coste de su obtención.
3. elaboración de la información, descartando la que no sea útil, y resumiéndola en indicadores.
4. interpretar los resultados
5. describir las limitaciones y dificultades encontradas.
6. elaborar un documento que sirva de base para la priorización de problemas.

programa 'configura tu barrio' — EDU.027

descripción:
se proponen que desde centros educativos del barrio se desarrollen intervenciones de personalización de la edificación, , siempre con asesoramiento y supervisión de expertos. la meta es por un lado fomentar la labor configuradora de los jóvenes en la comunidad, y por otro generar una imagen única y cambiante, con la que se identifique el barrio.
acciones:
1. actividades de pintura de fachadas de distintas casas y equipamientos de toda la zona.
2. intervenciones e instalaciones efímeras en el espacio público, haciendo uso de la red de plazas, o en los parques de la zona.
3. jardinería productiva: establecimiento de pequeños huertos en el espacio público, vinculados al programa educativo de los centros escolares.

creación de nuevas centralidades — URB.027

descripción:
de cara a fortalecer la identidad del barrio se propone una red de nuevas centralidades, que sirvan de referencia, que establezcan una jerarquía de espacios y que marquen unas coordenadas para todo el barrio.

acciones:
1. creación de una red jerarquizada de espacios públicos que estructuren la zona y orienten el tránsito. estas plazas forman un sistema disperso, vinculado a los pequeños espacios educativos, que está presente en toda la zona.
2. acondicionamiento del cerro de tafalera, que tiene las mejores vistas de la ciudad, como espacio verde central para la zona, y referencia para el resto de la ciudad.
3. fortalecimiento de la identidad por medio de 'dotaciones dispersas', como las viviendas tuteladas, que funcionan como una residencia pero integrada en todo el área, o las instalaciones educativas.

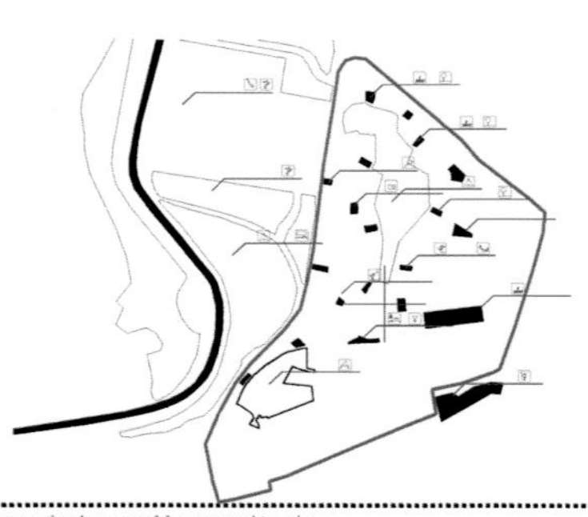

proceso de desarrollo comunitario — SOC.027

descripción:
parece necesario impulsar un proceso integral de desarrollo comunitario: un espacio de encuentro, intercambio, colaboración y coordinación de los distintos recursos técnicos, instituciones y ciudadanos, que permita avanzar en una programación coherente de la intervención social (en sentido amplio), y para propiciar y facilitar una progresiva y creíble participación comunitaria.
acciones:
1. diagnóstico comunitario: que integre y supere los conocimientos existentes, dispersos y sectorializados, y que implique a la propia comunidad en su elaboración.
2. programación: establecer líneas de acción que coordinen a la ciudadanía, los recursos técnicos y las instituciones, siguiendo criterios de transversalidad.
3. evaluación continua del proceso.

Fomento del asociacionismo empresarial — EMP.027

descripción:
parece necesario canalizar esfuerzos comunes, hallar sinergias y establecer vínculos en la actividad económica de la zona, que mejoren la producción, el comercio y la iniciativa, y así mejoren su presencia y competitividad en el resto de la ciudad.
acciones:
1. fomentar e incentivar la creación de cooperativas y asociaciones empresariales, a partir de actividades ya existentes, de cara a aumentar la competitividad.
2. crear marcos de coordinación para las distintas áreas de actividad económica, que establezcan estrategias comunes, e incentivar la participación en estos marcos.

LE.028 inserción del barrio en el tejido urbano

no es posible el acceso rodado a varios puntos tanto en numancia como en tafalera.

promoción de actuaciones de salud en colectivos vulnerables — SAN.028

descripción:
existen en el barrio colectivos especialmente vulnerables en materia de salud, por sus hábitos de vida y alimentación, por la precariedad del entorno, por desinformación y sobre todo por problemas de drogodependencia. se realizarán actuaciones de salud destinadas específicamente a estos grupos, de cara a darles un acceso a la sanidad adecuado a sus necesidades.

acciones:
1. análisis e identificación de los distintos grupos de riesgo, de cara a formular programas y acciones concretos para cada uno.
2. acciones de información y sensibilización, sobre hábitos de vida sanos, acceso a la sanidad pública, problemas específicos, etc.
3. acciones sanitarias específicas para problemas concretos, como la drogodependencia, algunas enfermedades infecciosas, parásitos, enfermedades bucales, etc.
3. mejora del acceso al sistema sanitario público de las personas excluidas, por su informalidad, su falta de información, etc.

aumentar la visibilidad de tafalera — EDU.028

descripción:
la meta de este proyecto es lograr introducir tafalera en el 'campo de visión' del resto de la ciudad, y lograr que sea conocida introduciendo su conocimiento y estudio en programas escolares, culturales, etc.

acciones:
1. difusión del presente y de la historia de tafalera, muy importante para conocer elda, en programas educativos de toda la ciudad.
2. desarrollo de una publicación que de a conocer el contexto y la historia del barrio.
3. integrar una serie de puntos relevantes de tafalera en otra red mayor de puntos de interés histórico-cultural de todo elda

estructura conectora — URB.028

descripción:
conectar el tejido existente y ampliado de tafalera, con el resto de la ciudad, especialmente con el barrio de numancia y con la avenida de santa bárbara. se tendrán en cuenta las prioridades de conexión y la marcada topografía del lugar.

acciones:
1. generación de nuevos tejidos viarios en el cerro de tafalera y a lo largo de la avenida de la mora, siguiendo la huella histórica, los fuertes condicionantes topográficos y las posibilidades de conexión con los tejidos y los espacios públicos adyacentes.
2. transporte público: potenciar el paso de autobuses y la proliferación de las paradas. incluir parada de autobuses regionales que aumente la visibilidad de la zona.
3. red peatonal: aprovechando la peculiar topografía del barrio y la prominente ubicación del cerro de tafalera se cruza una red de recorridos peatonales a la propuesta de viario, conectando los diferentes parques existentes en la zona.

incorporación plena e igualitaria de la población gitana — SOC.028

descripción:
la mayor parte de la población de elda y una parte importante de la de numancia es de etnia gitana. parece fundamental incorporar a la comunidad gitana en el proceso de desarrollo urbano, fomentando su participación activa y garantizando su situación de igualdad.

acciones:
1. fomento de la representación de la comunidad gitana en asociaciones, actividades, instituciones, etc. del barrio, y de todo elda.
2. dar a conocer las especificidades culturales de la comunidad gitana al resto de la ciudad, por medio de festivales, exposiciones, publicaciones, etc.

mapeado de comercios y servicios — EMP.028

descripción:
hacer visible la actividad económica de la zona traerá consigo una mayor visibilidad, un aumento de afluencia de otros habitantes de elda, y por lo tanto una mayor competitividad de los comercios y empresas ubicados en tafalera numancia. se proponen por ello un conjunto de medidas que contibuyan a esta mayor percepción de tafalera-numancia 'desde fuera'.

acciones:
1. elaboración y publicación de un mapa en el que figuren todos los elementos que pueden atraer usos al barrio, como parques, servicios, tiendas, bares, paseos, iglesias, etc.
2. elaboración y mantenimiento de una página web que recopile, organice y publique esta información.

PROCESOS TRANSVERSALES

PC201 EUROPAN10 ELDA PANEL03

LE.029 regeneración y ampliación del tejido comunitario

plan de salud comunitaria

SAN.029

descripción:
la estructura sanitaria [...] papel muy fundamental en la estructuración del tejido social de una comunidad. para ello las políticas sanitarias no pueden limitarse a su función de curación (modelo asistencial), sino que deben dedicarse a la promoción de la salud (modelo salubrista). no bastará con ir satisfaciendo al paso de las necesidades, sino que será necesario elaborar un plan de salud para el barrio. un plan semejante, que quiera intervenir sobre la salud comunitaria, presentará las siguientes etapas:
acciones:
1. diagnóstico: identificar los problemas y necesidades de salud de la población y establecer un orden de prioridades.
2. programación: concebir y poner en marcha programas para responder a los problemas prioritarios.
3. evaluación: valorar el impacto de estos programas sobre la salud de la población.

fomento del asociacionismo juvenil

EDU.029

descripción:
el dinamismo social y la participación activa de los ciudadanos en el funcionamiento y en el proceso de desarrollo de su barrio es un medidor básico de la fuerza de esa comunidad. la medida en la que una comunidad está estructurada, por medio de asociaciones, clubes, peñas, cofradías, etc. da idea de su cohesión, y de su fuerza para reaccionar a problemas tanto internos como externos. por ello parece importante impulsar desde el sector educativo actitudes cívicas y participativas, así como la creación estructuras comunitarias.
acciones:
1. fomentar desde colegios la creación de asociaciones, equipos, peñas etc., facilitando materiales, espacios, etc.
2. poner a disposición de asociaciones juveniles el uso de los espacios educativos Edu.023, e incluirlas en su programación.
3. introducción de dinamizadores sociales que, tanto en colegios como en el propio barrio, informen, asesoren y fomenten el asociacionismo juvenil.

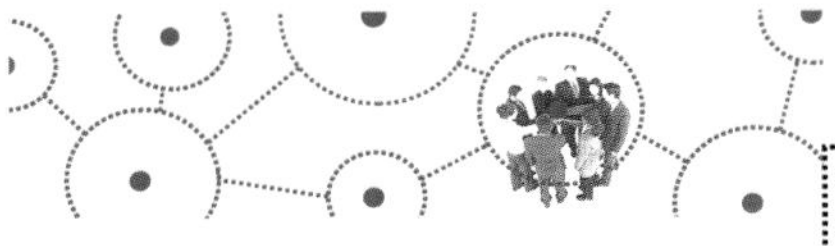

tejido urbano en el cerro de tafalera

URB.029

descripción:
la intervención en el barrio es compleja. no se trata de sustituir lo que ya hay, sino de reactivar el desarrollo urbano para que tafalera-numancia pase de una dinámica autodestructiva a un desarrollo normalizado como un tejido más de la ciudad. no debe entenderse como una intervención arquitectónica unitaria, sino más bien como el soporte de un proceso de desarrollo urbano y de adaptación a las cambiantes necesidades que no debe parar nunca. habrá que tener en cuenta los siguientes principios:
1. escála mínima de intervención, evitando proyectos arquitectónicos grandes y unitarios, de cara a alcanzar una ciudad más 'líquida', capaz de reaccionar al contexto cambiante de necesidades.
2. diversidad tipológica y programática, que apoye el pluralismo en el barrio. integración del equipamiento y de la actividad en el propio tejido, de un modo disperso.
3. 'el barrio para todos': la formulación del nuevo tejido deberá tener en cuenta a los ciudadanos con una situación menos favorable, por ejemplo en temas de accesibilidad.
4. participación, ya que solo la propia comunidad es capaz de dirigir un proceso de crecimiento orgánico.
5. primacía del espacio público, que debe ser el estructurante del tejido urbano.
acciones:
1. proyecto de rehabilitación del barrio de numancia, poniéndolo al día en las actuales exigencias de accesibilidad, sostenibilidad y habitabilidad (cfr. Urb.026).
2. creación de nuevos tejidos sustitutivos en las zonas ya vacías y en las zonas más degradadas de tafalera. este nuevo tejido se forma a partir de las huellas de viario y edificación ya existentes, y está principalmente condicionado por la marcada topografía del lugar.

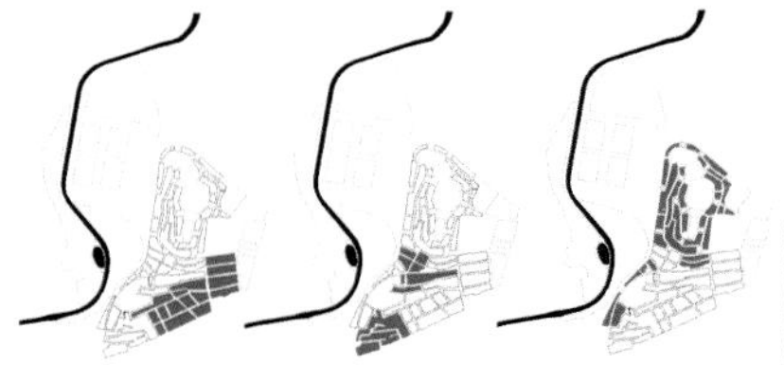

dinamización social

SOC.029

descripción:
el proceso de desarrollo de un barrio debe suceder sobre todo a nivel social. el desarrollo urbanístico, o el económico, deben estar al servicio del desarrollo integral de la comunidad, y la formación de un tejido urbanístico debe subordinarse a la creación o consolidación de un tejido social.

acciones:
1. de este modo desde el sector socioasistencial se propone por un lado, pero no solo, dar apoyo y respuesta a los problemas sociales derivados de un desarrollo urbanístico, como pueden ser los realojos, las desigualdades, etc.
2. por otro lado se asume el papel de impulsar la autoorganización de la propia comunidad para hacer posible un proceso de participación ciudadana que realmente guíe el desarrollo del barrio en todas sus dimensiones.

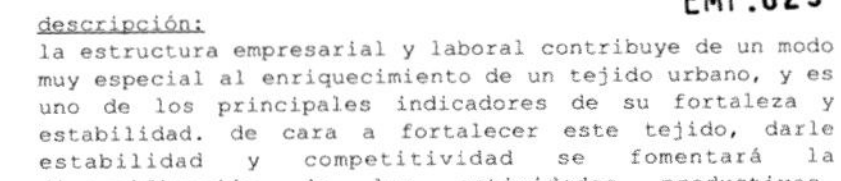

diversificación de las actividades económicas en la zona

EMP.029

descripción:
la estructura empresarial y laboral contribuye de un modo muy especial al enriquecimiento de un tejido urbano, y es uno de los principales indicadores de su fortaleza y estabilidad. de cara a fortalecer este tejido, darle estabilidad y competitividad se fomentará la diversificación de las actividades productivas, empresariales y comerciales de la zona.

acciones:
1. introducción de nuevas actividades económicas, por medio de incentivos, información, asesoramiento y formación
2. fomento del trabajo en casa, viviendas taller, etc.

LE.030 mejora de la imagen del barrio

cercano centro de salud de la avenida del sax, de la residencia de ancianos-centro de día 'el catí', o de una estructura que se cree ex profeso para ello.

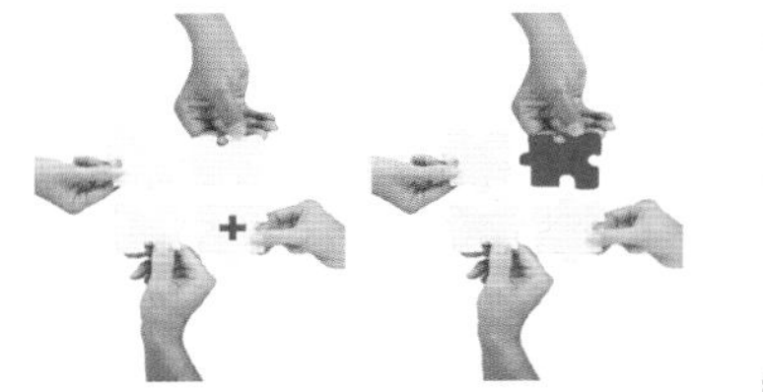

fortalecer la identidad histórica de tafalera

EDU.030

descripción:
ubicada junto al centro de la ciudad de elda, tafalera tiene una rica historia, que se remonta a los orígenes industriales de la ciudad, y constituye una parte importante de su patrimonio histórico. redescubrir y difundir el valor cultural del barrio tendrá grandes beneficios para su integración con el resto de la ciudad, y será una valiosa aportación para la conurbación elda-petrer.

acciones:
1. fomentar la investigación en la historia del barrio y en su patrimonio, con el fin de estructurarla y hacerla fácil de difundir.
2. fomentar el estudio de la historia del barrio en los colegios e institutos de elda, como parte esencial de la propia identidad.
2. elaboraR materiales de difusión, como libros y folletos, que presenten el barrio como el contexto rico en historia y cultura que es.

dotar a tafalera de una fachada

URB.030

descripción:
el barrio tafalera presenta un aspecto deteriorado y en decadencia y su presencia en elda es percibida como algo negativo. desde la avenida de la mora se presenta como un frente en ruinas, y desde los tejidos adyacentes aparece como 'trasera'. se propone aquí mejorar la presencia del conjunto tafalera en la ciudad, de modo que se convierta en un tejido esencial para la trama urbana.

acciones:
1. rehabilitación y construcción de los frentes a la avenida de la mora y a la avenida de la libertad, que son la fachada principal del barrio a dos vías importantes, y que en la actualidad presentan un aspecto degradado y ruinoso.
2. permeabilizar el parque del cerro hacia la ciudad, ofreciendo a sus habitantes un espacio público verde de gran calidad, de enorme potencial paisajístico por su prominente situación sobre elda.
3. recuperación del patrimonio histórico de tafalera y numancia, testigo del origen de la conurbación, que va desde el respeto a la trama hasta la conservación de algunas viviendas prototípicas de su época.

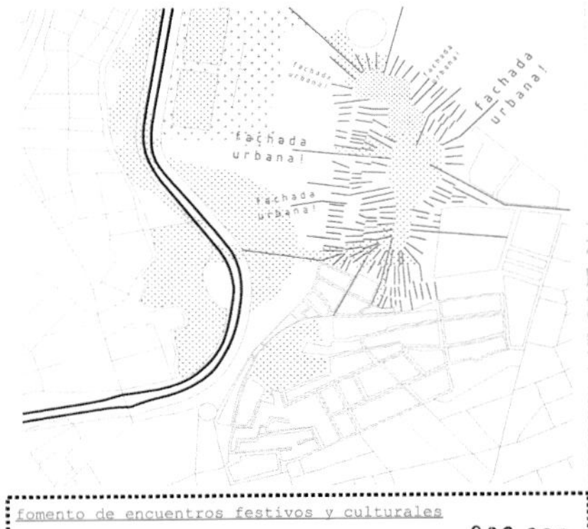

fomento de encuentros festivos y culturales

SOC.030

descripción:
los festivales, los eventos populares y los actos culturales son importantes elementos de relación, capaces de vincular a habitantes de distintos barrios, o incluso de distintas poblaciones. por ello se propone fomentar actos de este tipo, que por un lado contribuyen a la cohesión del barrio, y por otro lado lo muestran hacia fuera y presentan su cara más positiva.
acciones:
1. programación de festividades y eventos en la que se implique el mayor número de comunidades, asociaciones, colectivos y grupos.
2. difusión de dicha programación, por medio de carteles, folletos y una página web.

gestión social del proceso de rehabilitación

descripción:
el éxito de los procesos de rehabilitación de barrios socialmente complejos proviene en gran medida del acompañamiento de una buena gestión social. realojos, necesidades específicas, dificultades económicas, familiares o físicas, etc. hacen que un proceso de rehabilitación no sea solo algo físico, sino sobre todo un proceso de adaptación y reubicación social

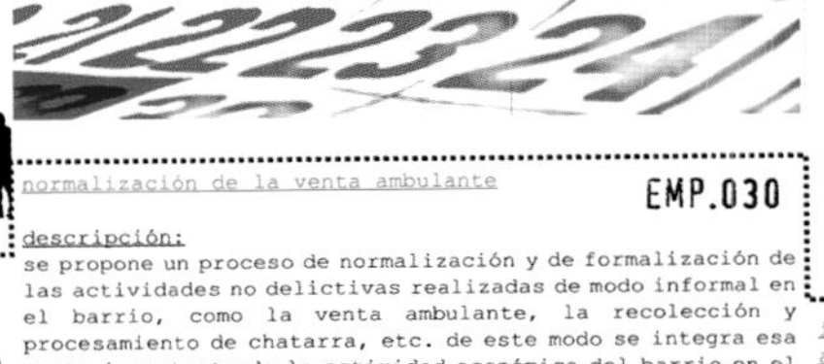

normalización de la venta ambulante

EMP.030

descripción:
se propone un proceso de normalización y de formalización de las actividades no delictivas realizadas de modo informal en el barrio, como la venta ambulante, la recolección y procesamiento de chatarra, etc. de este modo se integra esa parte importante de la actividad económica del barrio en el proceso formal de desarrollo urbano.

acciones:
1. informar, asesorar e incentivar la formalización de las distintas actividades económicas
2. implantar una red de consultoría microempresarial para mejorar la competitividad de actividades económicas tradicionales y específicas del barrio.
3. facilitar el acceso a financiación, por medio de créditos, microcréditos, préstamos de bajo interés, etc.

LE.031. inserción del barrio en el paisaje

1. estudio diagnóstico sobre los principales riesgos de salud en los espacios públicos
2. controles periódicos sobre el estado de salubridad de los parques: residuos, animales, parásitos, etc.

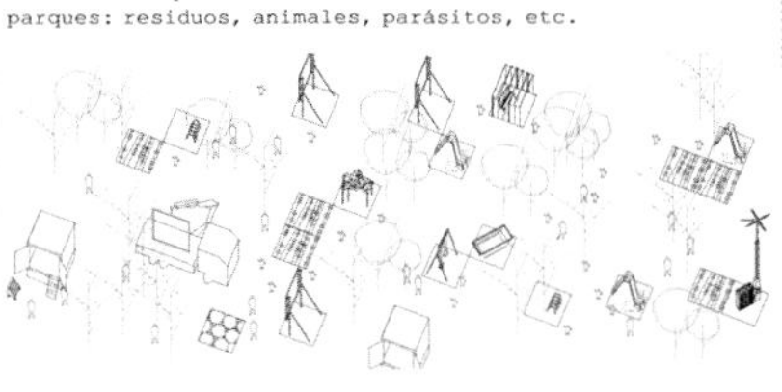

fomento del uso del entorno natural para actividades escolares

EDU.031

descripción:
una de las condiciones más decisivas para el buen mantenimiento de los espacios verdes es que estos tengan un uso continuado. los parques en desuso pasan a ser entornos inseguros, degradados y víctimas del vandalismo. por ello se propone fomentar el desarrollo de actividades educativas, tanto formales como no formales, que por un lado se beneficien de estos espacios, pero por otro los llenen de actividad y colaboren a configurarlos.
acciones:
1. informar a educadores e instituciones educativas sobre este programa, e incentivar su participación con contenidos, materiales, etc.
2. facilitar la adecuación del propuesto parque del cerro y de los demás espacios los espacios verdes para la realización de actividades concretas.
3. preparación de un programa de eventos de distinta regularidad que doten de actividad el parque del cerro de tafalera.

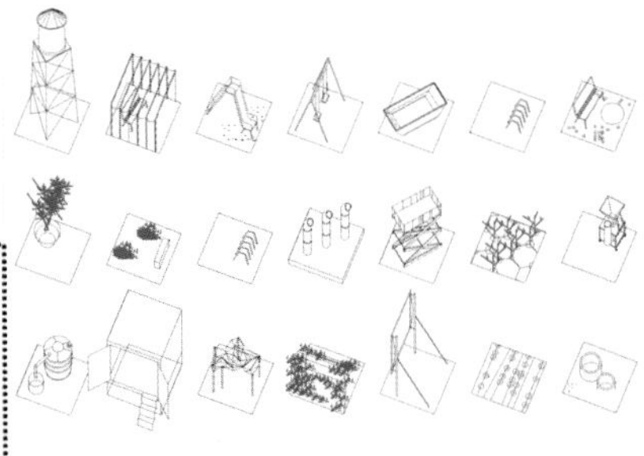

creación del parque del cerro tafalera y de una red de espacios públicos

URB.031

descripción:
el poderoso paisaje del cerro de tafalera, desde el que se domina visualmente toda la conurbación elda-petrer, se presenta como uno de los principales valores de la zona, y por tanto como un importante potencial para su desarrollo. se propone estructurar el barrio en torno a un parque, que comprende la cima del cerro, y que se relaciona con el resto de la ciudad a través de una malla de plazas espacios verdes. el barrio entero pasa a quedar integrado en el paisaje.

acciones:
1. acondicionamiento del cerro de tafalera como parque central del nuevo desarrollo urbano. se destacará su valor como mirador, y estará habilitado para albergar actividades y eventos (teatro, conciertos, festivales, etc.)
2. creación de una red de espacios públicos, compuesta por plazas y espacios verdes, que en continuidad con el nuevo parque y con los espacios verdes ya existentes vertebra paisajísticamente la zona.

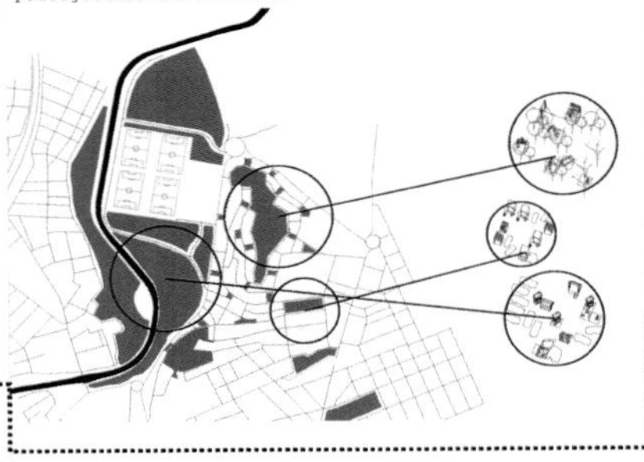

diseño participativo y multisectorial del entorno

SOC.031

descripción:
de cara a una mayor eficacia en los trabajos de diseño y rehabilitación de barrios, un aspecto fundamental es que estos proyectos no queden como intervenciones exógenas, sino que han de tener en cuenta a los habitantes del barrio. que la propia comunidad participe en el proceso de diseño de su entorno es crucial para su posterior uso, respeto y mantenimiento, ya que de esta manera el barrio es considerado como algo propio.
acciones:
1. talleres de participación ciudadana para la toma de decisiones respecto a las dotaciones de situaciones urbanas que incorporará el barrio.2. impulsar el uso de espacio público por parte de los ciudadanos, como medio de activación del tejido de parques y paseos: como sedes asociaciones de moros, de ajedrez, de mus, de dominó, etc.

implicación laboral de los habitantes en el acondicionamiento paisajístico de su barrio.

EMP.031

descripción:
para evitar abandono, vandalismo y demás actitudes que suponen un deterioro del entorno, una estrategia de gran efectividad es el empleo de los habitantes del barrio en la adecuación paisajística, especialmente de los jóvenes.

acciones:
1. jornadas de trabajo para jóvenes en el cuidado del entorno.
2. plan de empleo para los ciudadanos del barrio en las

LE.032 fortalecimiento de las estructuras familiares de la zona

programa de salud familiar

SAN.0

descripción:
una parte importante de los problemas de salud tien origen en hábitos nocivos adquiridos en el entorno fami una alimentación desequilibrada, el tabaquismo y el co abusivo de alcohol, deficiencias en la higiene, etc. l a problemas de salud que podían haber sido evitado previsión. se propone por ello un programa dest específicamente a mejorar la salud en el contexto famil

acciones:
1. realizar una campaña de mejora de los há alimenticios, higiénicos y sanitarios en las familias zona.
2. mejorar el acceso a la salud pública por parte d familias, por medio de regularizaciones, informac asesoramiento.
3. apoyo a las familias de drogodependientes.

implicación de las familias en los programas educativos

EDU.032

descripción:
el fracaso escolar, el absentismo o la pasividad colegio son problemas que tienen a menudo una est relación con la indiferencia hacia la educación por del entorno familiar. para lograr una mayor integració contexto escolar y el familiar se propone un esfuerz implicar a los adultos en actividades escolares, asuman la educación de sus hijos como algo propio.

acciones:
1. implicar a padres y parientes de los estudiant programas y actividades educativas destinadas a sus h tanto en el ámbito formal como en el no formal.
2. seguimiento riguroso de los casos de absentismo esc y a través del sector socioasistencial intervenir en entornos familiares.

fomentar la incorporación de nueva población joven al b

URB.032

descripción:
posibilitar el relevo generacional de los ba envejecidos o en decadencia es uno de los grandes ret urbanismo actual. en el barrio de numancia, y sobre t el de tafalera, parece necesario un intenso proce revitalización del tejido social, que introduzca pobl nueva y sana en el barrio. desde los sectores del urbani la arquitectura se ve posible impulsar este proceso y el soporte físico necesario.

acciones:
1. garantizar las condiciones de seguridad, salubri calidad ambiental del barrio, para posibilitar la lleg nuevos habitantes.
2. enriquecer el equipamiento de la zona para fami niños, etc, como comercio de proximidad, juegos infant etc.
3. diversificar la tipologías del barrio, de mod contenga una mezcla de familias, jóvenes, may viviendas-taller, etc.
4. ampliación del barrio, destinado específicamen contener y organizar esta diversidad.

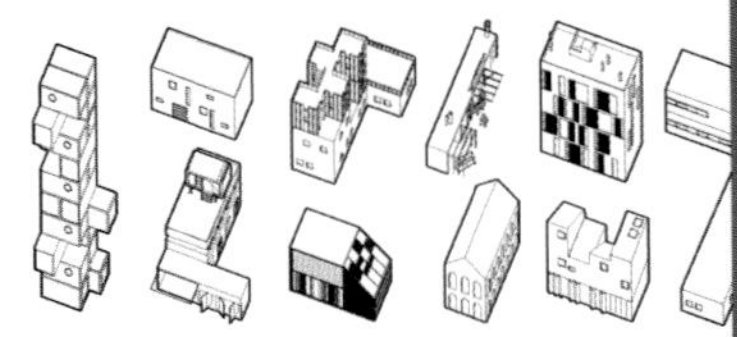

seguimiento y apoyo a las familias desestructuradas

SOC.032

descripción:
el problema de la desestructuración familiar es uno d principales en contextos de exclusión y marginalid requiere una respuesta integral y transversal. aun desde el sector socio-asistencial se abordará el directo a los miembros vulnerables de las fam desestructuradas.

acciones:
1. estudiar la situación social de las familias del ba de cara a identificar los principales problem necesidades.
2. red de apoyo a las familias desestructurada especialmente a sus miembros más vulnerables (n ancianos, mujeres, etc.)

mapeado de comercios y servicios

descripción:
hacer visible la actividad económica de la zona consigo una mayor visibilidad, un aumento de afluenc otros habitantes de elda, y por lo tanto una competitividad de los comercios y empresas ubicad tafalera numancia. se proponen por ello un conjun medidas que contibuyan a esta mayor percepción de tafa numancia 'desde fuera'.
acciones:
1. elaboración y publicación de un mapa en el que fi todos los elementos que pueden atraer usos al barrio, parques, servicios, tiendas, bares, paseos, fie talleres, etc.
2. elaboración y mantenimiento de una página web recopile, organice y publique esta información.

fomento de la igualdad de oportunidades para la mujer

EMP.03

descripción:
en contextos socialmente complejos, con problema exclusión social, la situación de la mujer se prese menudo como especialmente vulnerable. también en el á laboral sufren las mujeres por lo general una situ discriminatoria, en lo referente a responsabilid sueldos, inestabilidad, etc.
se propone un programa de medidas que fomenten la igu de la mujer en el campo laboral, y en consecuenci fortalezcan su situación dentro de la estructura famil en general su presencia en la comunidad.
acciones:
1. desarrollar una campaña de información y sensibiliz sobre igualdad de género, dirigida a las mujeres general a toda la población de la zona.
2. fomentar la integración de la mujer en el ámbito lab informando e incentivando el empleo de mujere

PROCESOS TRANSVERSALES

082

Inhabiting the Sky | *Leon11*

Coordination and Leadership : Ana Peñalba Estebanez and Maria Mallo
Team : Ana Peñalba, Maria Mallo, Jaime López, Ignacio A.Monteserín, Beatriz Crespo, Alicia Domingo, Javier Gutierrez, Jorge López

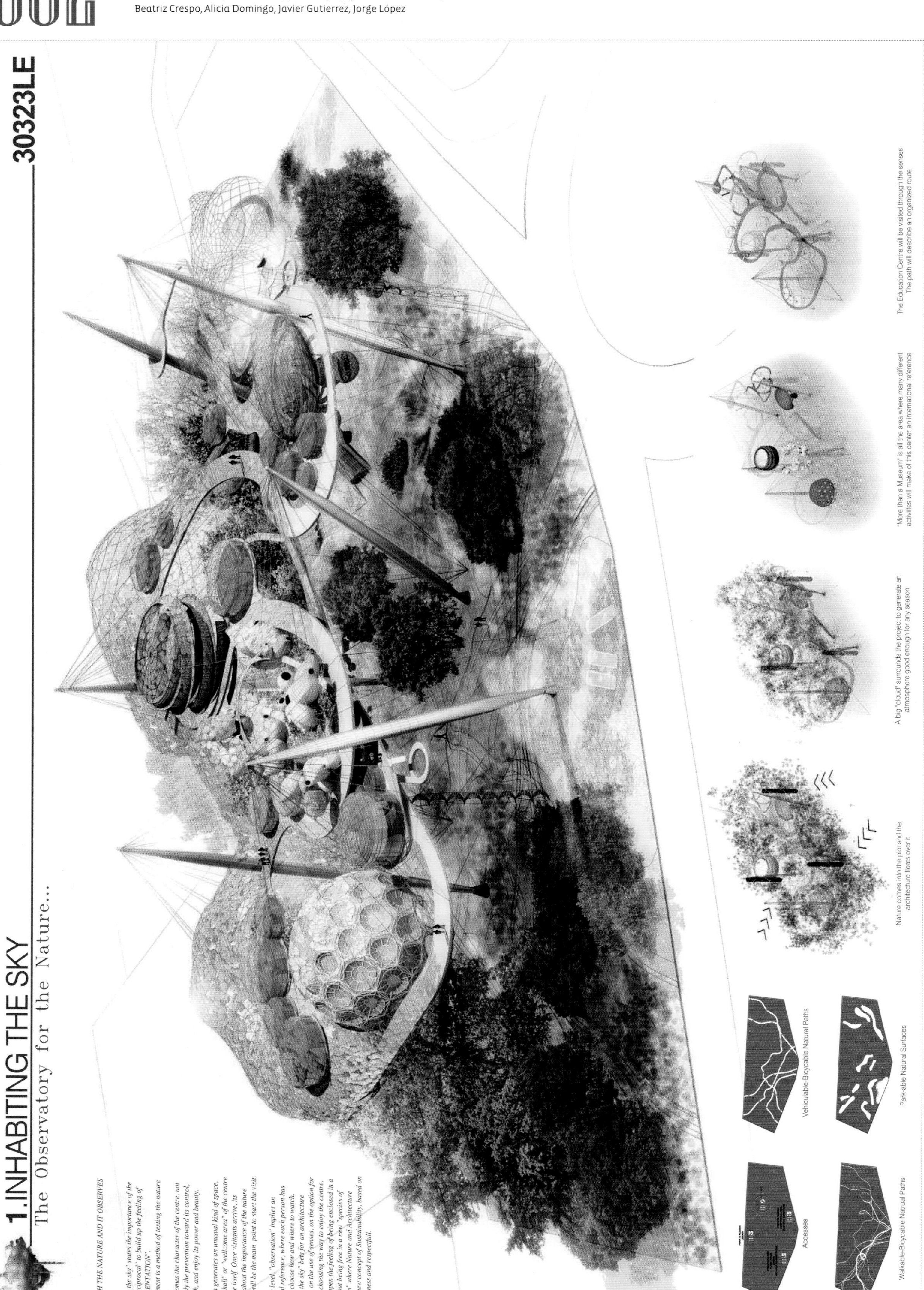
1.INHABITING THE SKY
The Observatory for the Nature...
30323LE
WE WATCH THE NATURE AND IT OBSERVES US...
"Inhabiting the sky" states the importance of the concept "reciprocal" to build up the feeling of "EXPERIMENTATION".
"An Experiment is a method of testing the nature of reality".
Nature becomes the character of the centre, not just for study the prevention toward its control, but to watch, and enjoy its power and beauty.
Its situation generates an unusual kind of space, where the "hall" or "wellcome area" of the centre is the nature itself. Once visitants arrive, its awareness about the importance of the nature among us, will be the main point to start the visit.
At the same level, "observation" implies an uni-personal reference, where each person has the right to choose how and where to watch. "Inhabiting the sky" bets for an architecture based on it, on the use of senses, on the option for the visitant choosing the way to enjoy the centre. It never happen the feeling of being enclosed in a "building" but being free in a new "species of construction" where Nature and Architecture build up a new concept of Sustainability, based on love, awareness and respectfull.
Accesses
Vehiculable-Bicycable Natural Paths
Walkable-Bicycable Natrual Paths
Park-able Natural Surfaces
Nature comes into the plot and the architecture floats over it
A big "cloud" surrounds the project to generate an atmosphere good enough for any season
"More than a Museum" is all the area where many different activiites will make of this center an international reference
The Education Centre will be visited through the senses
The path will describe an organized route

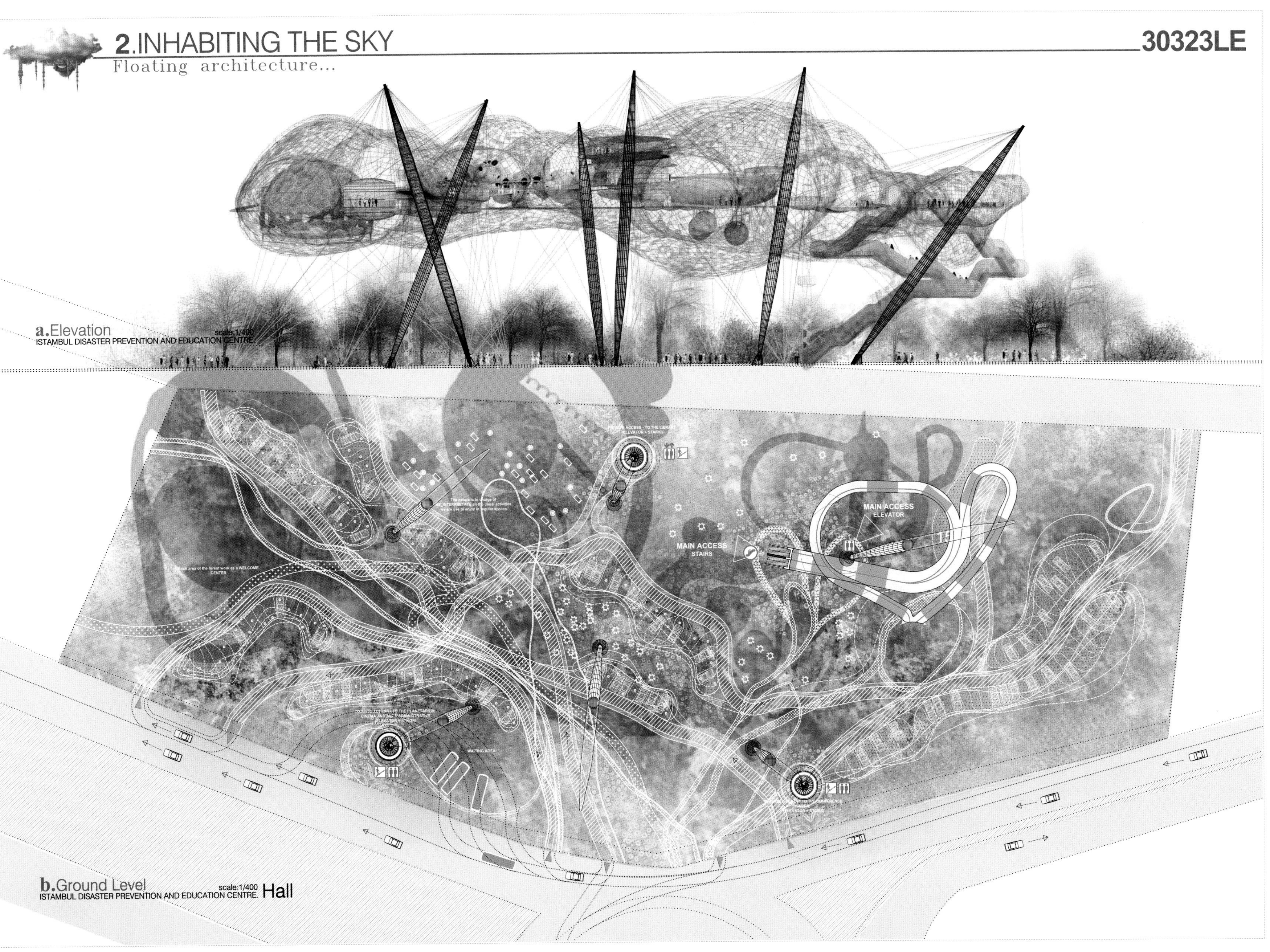
2.INHABITING THE SKY
Floating architecture...
30323LE
a.Elevation
scale:1/400
ISTAMBUL DISASTER PREVENTION AND EDUCATION CENTRE
MAIN ACCESS
ELEVATOR
MAIN ACCESS
STAIRS
b.Ground Level
scale:1/400
ISTAMBUL DISASTER PREVENTION AND EDUCATION CENTRE.
Hall

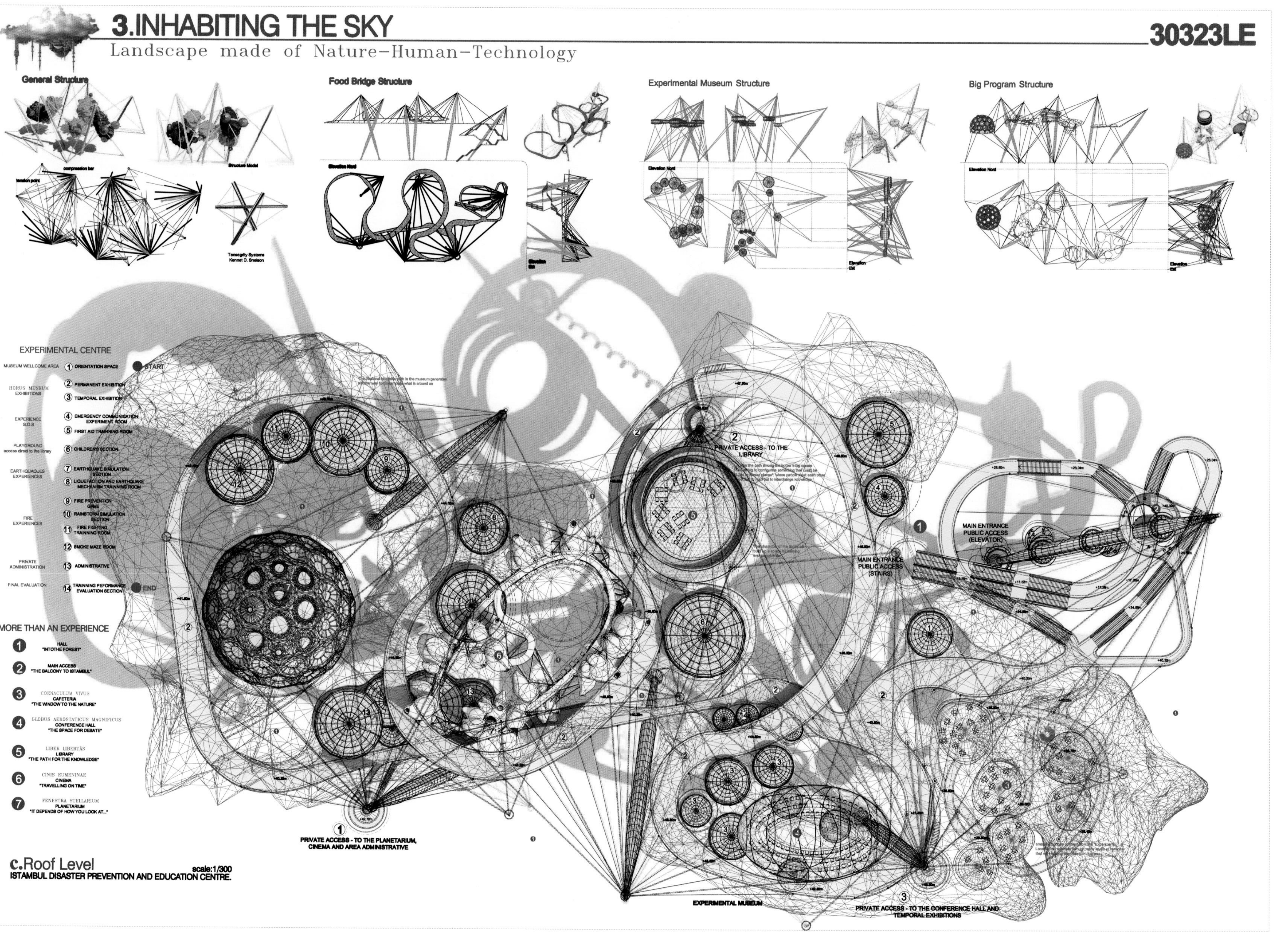

3.INHABITING THE SKY
Landscape made of Nature–Human–Technology
30323LE
General Structure
compression bar
tension point
Structure Model
Tensegrity Systems Kennet D. Snelson
Food Bridge Structure
Elevation Nord
Experimental Museum Structure
Elevation Nord
Big Program Structure
Elevation Nord
EXPERIMENTAL CENTRE
MUSEUM WELLCOME AREA
1 ORIENTATION SPACE
START
HORUS MUSEUM EXHIBITIONS
2 PERMANENT EXHIBITION
3 TEMPORAL EXHIBITION
EXPERIENCE S.O.S
4 EMERGENCY COMMUNICATION EXPERIMENT ROOM
5 FIRST AID TRAINING ROOM
PLAYGROUND access direct to the library
6 CHILDREN'S SECTION
EARTHQUAQUES EXPERIENCES
7 EARTHQUAKE SIMULATION SECTION
8 LIQUEFACTION AND EARTHQUAKE MECHANISM TRAINING ROOM
FIRE EXPERIENCES
9 FIRE PREVENTION GAME
10 RAINSTORM SIMULATION SECTION
11 FIRE FIGHTING TRAINING ROOM
12 SMOKE MAZE ROOM
PRIVATE ADMINISTRATION
13 ADMINISTRATIVE
FINAL EVALUATION
14 TRAINING PEFORMANCE EVALUATION SECTION
END
MORE THAN AN EXPERIENCE
1 HALL "INTO THE FOREST"
2 MAIN ACCESS "THE BALCONY TO ISTAMBUL"
3 COENACULUM VIVUS CAFETERIA "THE WINDOW TO THE NATURE"
4 GLOBUS AEROSTATICUS MAGNIFICUS CONFERENCE HALL "THE SPACE FOR DEBATE"
5 LIBER LIBERTAS LIBRARY "THE PATH FOR THE KNOWLEDGE"
6 CINIS EUMENINAE CINEMA "TRAVELLING ON TIME"
7 FENESTRA STELLARIUM PLANETARIUM "IT DEPENDS OF HOW YOU LOOK AT..."
c.Roof Level
scale:1/300
ISTAMBUL DISASTER PREVENTION AND EDUCATION CENTRE.
1 PRIVATE ACCESS - TO THE PLANETARIUM, CINEMA AND AREA ADMINISTRATIVE
2 PRIVATE ACCESS - TO THE LIBRARY
MAIN ENTRANCE PUBLIC ACCESS (ELEVATOR)
MAIN ENTRANCE PUBLIC ACCESS (STAIRS)
EXPERIMENTAL MUSEUM
3 PRIVATE ACCESS - TO THE CONFERENCE HALL AND TEMPORAL EXHIBITIONS

4.INHABITING THE SKY
The main hall of the centre is a forest...
Karl Popper, the great philosopher of science, divided the world into two categories: clocks and clouds. The clocks are clean ordered systems that can be used through reductionism and the clouds are a mess epistemic "highly irregular, disordered, more or less unpredictable." The mistake of modern science is to pretend that everything is a clock, which is why we let ourselves be seduced again and again and again by false promises of brain scans and genetic sequences. We believe that we will get to understand nature the moment we find the accurate tool which gets to cut up its joints with. But this approach is doomed to failure.
We do not live in an universe of cloks. We live in an universe of clouds.
"Inhabiting the sky" shows the strong conection among Nature-Technology-Human..

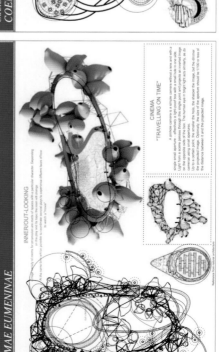

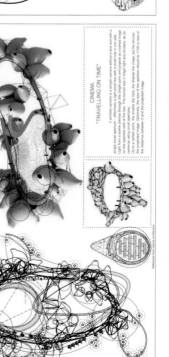

5.INHABITING THE SKY

Archi–nature typologies

30323LE

Static Typologies

CONFERENCE ROOM — GLOBUS AEROSTATICUS MAGNIFICUS

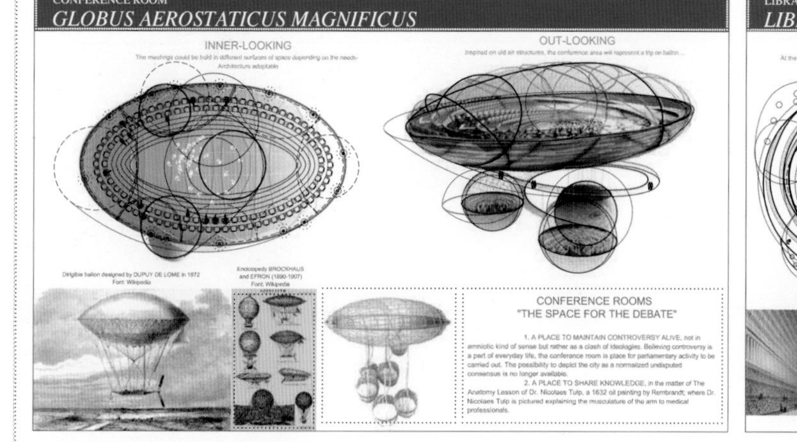

CONFERENCE ROOMS
"THE SPACE FOR THE DEBATE"

1. A PLACE TO MAINTAIN CONTROVERSY ALIVE, not in amniotic kind of sense but rather as a clash of ideologies. Believing controversy is a part of everyday life, the conference room is place for parliamentary activity to be carried out. The possibility to depict the city as a normalized undisputed consensus is no longer available.

2. A PLACE TO SHARE KNOWLEDGE, in the matter of The Anatomy Lesson of Dr. Nicolaes Tulp, a 1632 oil painting by Rembrandt; where Dr. Nicolaes Tulp is pictured explaining the musculature of the arm to medical professionals.

LIBRARY — LIBER LIBERTAS

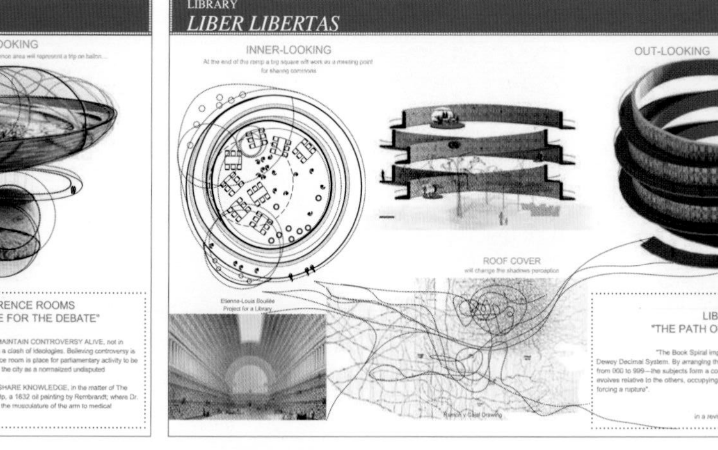

LIBRARY
"THE PATH OF KNOWLEDGE"

"The Book Spiral implies a reclamation of the much-compromised Dewey Decimal System. By arranging the collection in a continuous ribbon—running from 000 to 999—the subjects form a coexistence that approaches the organic: each evolves relative to the others, occupying more or less space on the ribbon, but never forcing a rupture".

Nico Saieh from ArchDaily
in a review of The Seattle Public Library by O.M.A.

CINEMAS — CINEMAE EUMENINAE

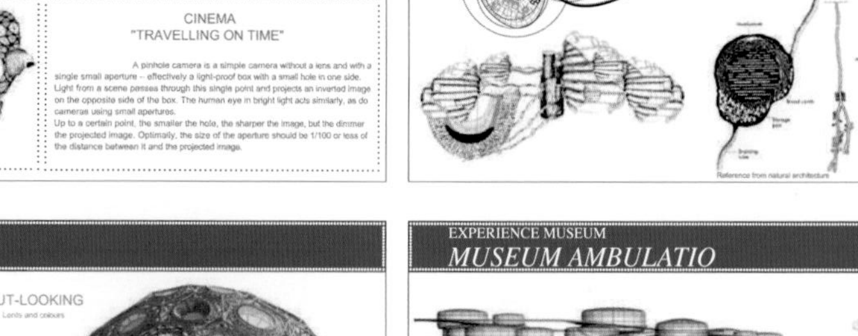

CINEMA
"TRAVELLING ON TIME"

A pinhole camera is a simple camera without a lens and with a single small aperture -- effectively a light-proof box with a small hole in one side. Light from a scene passes through this single point and projects an inverted image on the opposite side of the box. The human eye in bright light acts similarly, as do cameras using small apertures.

Up to a certain point, the smaller the hole, the sharper the image, but the dimmer the projected image. Optimally, the size of the aperture should be 1/100 or less of the distance between it and the projected image.

CAFETERIA — COENACULUM VIVUS

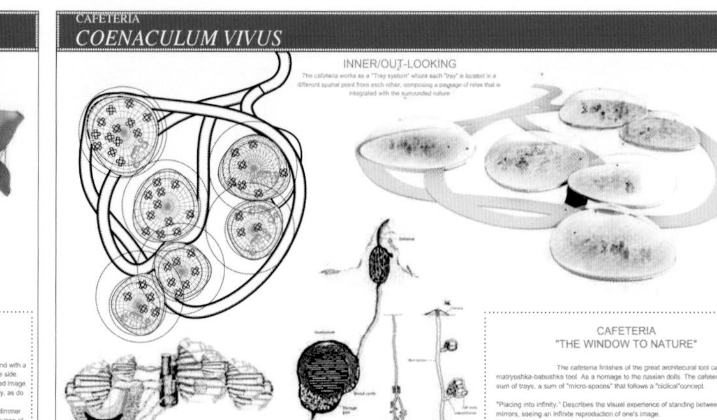

CAFETERIA
"THE WINDOW TO NATURE"

The cafeteria finishes of the great architecural tool called the matryoshka-babushka tool. As a homage to the russian dolls. The cafeteria is a sum of trays, a sum of "micro-spaces" that follows a "ciclical"concept.

"Placing into infinity." Describes the visual experience of standing between two mirrors, seeing an infinite reproduction of one's image.

This area represents a formal technique in which a space contains a smaller copy of itself and the sequence appearing to recur infinitely.

PLANETARIUM — FENESTRA STELLARIUM

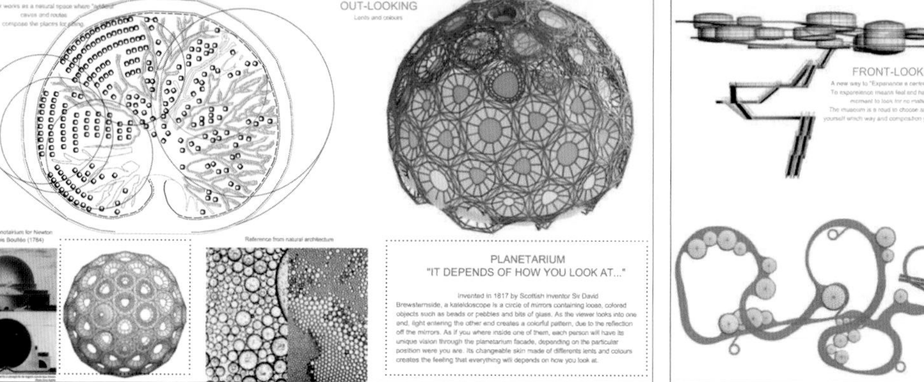

PLANETARIUM
"IT DEPENDS OF HOW YOU LOOK AT..."

Invented in 1817 by Scottish inventor Sir David Brewsternside, a kaleidoscope is a circle of mirrors containing loose, colored objects such as beads or pebbles and bits of glass. As the viewer looks into one end, light entering the other end creates a colorful pattern, due to the reflection off the mirrors. As if you where inside one of them, each person will have its unique vision through the planetarium facade, depending on the particular position were you are. Its changeable skin made of differents lents and colours creates the feeling that everything will depends on how you look at.

EXPERIENCE MUSEUM — MUSEUM AMBULATIO

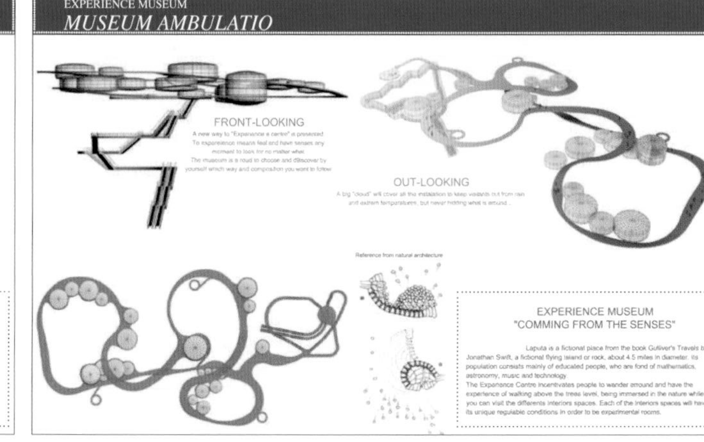

EXPERIENCE MUSEUM
"COMMING FROM THE SENSES"

Laputa is a fictional place from the book Gulliver's Travels by Jonathan Swift, a fictional flying island or rock, about 4.5 miles in diameter. its population consists mainly of educated people, who are fond of mathematics, astronomy, music and technology.

The Experience Centre incentivates people to wander arround and have the experience of walking above the trees level, being immersed in the nature while you can visit the differents interiors spaces. Each of the interiors spaces will have its unique reguiable conditions in order to be experimental rooms.

Dinamic Typologies

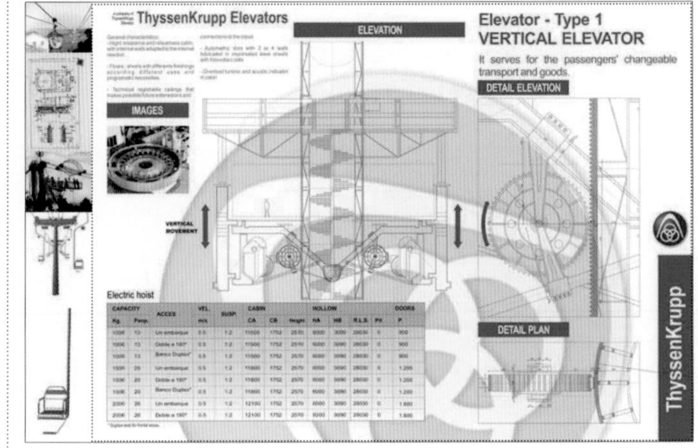

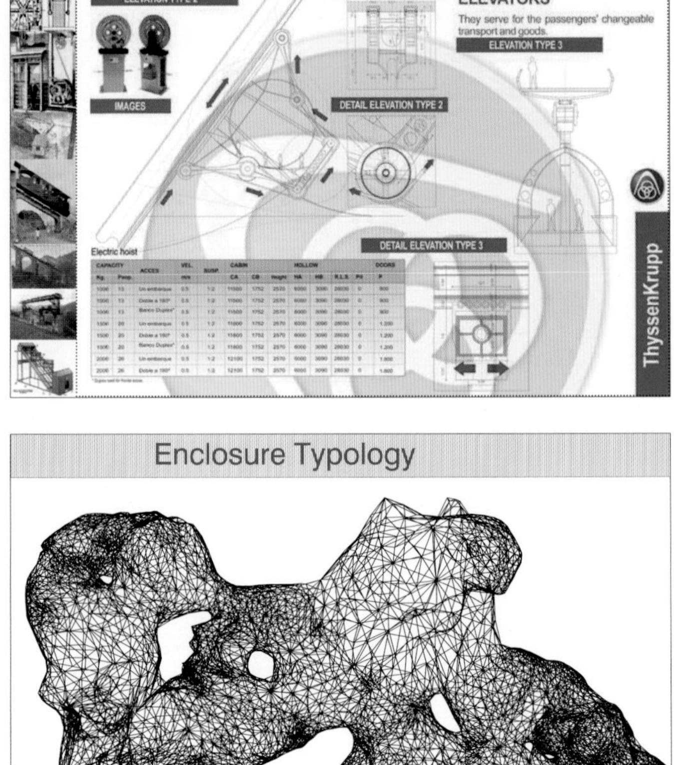

Enclosure Typology

Ujpest City Centre | *3LHD*

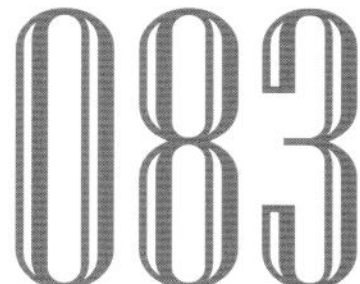

Project number : 159
City : Budapest
Country : Hungary
Type : retail, public, culture, business, leisure, sport, residential, urban
3D : Freya
Project team : Sasa Begovic, Marko Dabrovic, Tatjana Grozdanic Begovic, Silvije Novak, Paula Kukuljica, Nives Krsnik Rister, Leon Lazaneo, Eugen Popovic
Project team collaborators : Vibor Granic, Zeljko Mohorovic
Project : 17.03.2008. - 28.04.2008.

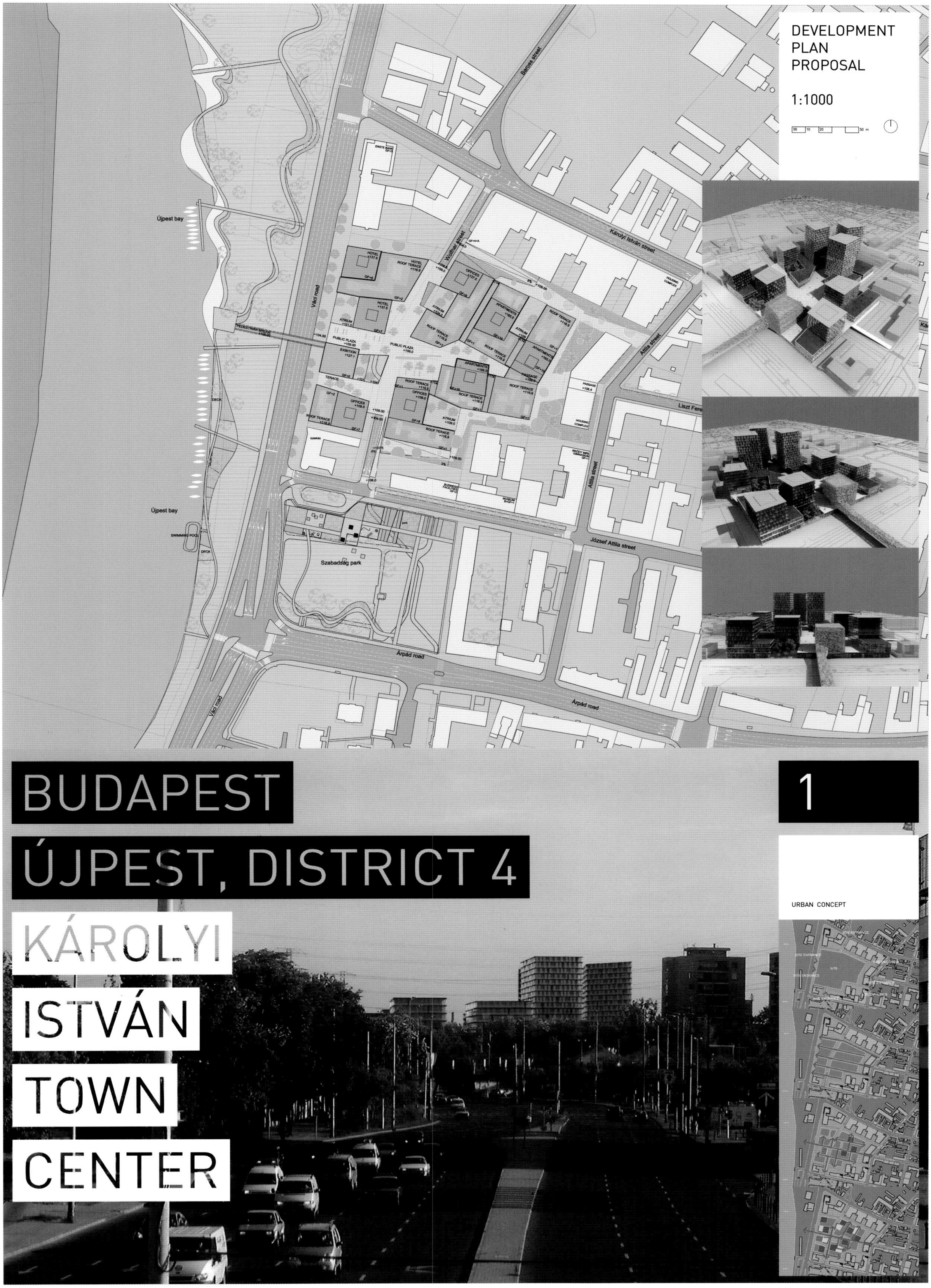

DEVELOPMENT PLAN PROPOSAL

1:1000

Újpest bay

Váci road

Károlyi István street

Wolfner street

Attila street

Liszt Ferenc

József Attila street

Szabadság park

Árpád road

Váci road

BUDAPEST

ÚJPEST, DISTRICT 4

KÁROLYI ISTVÁN TOWN CENTER

1

URBAN CONCEPT

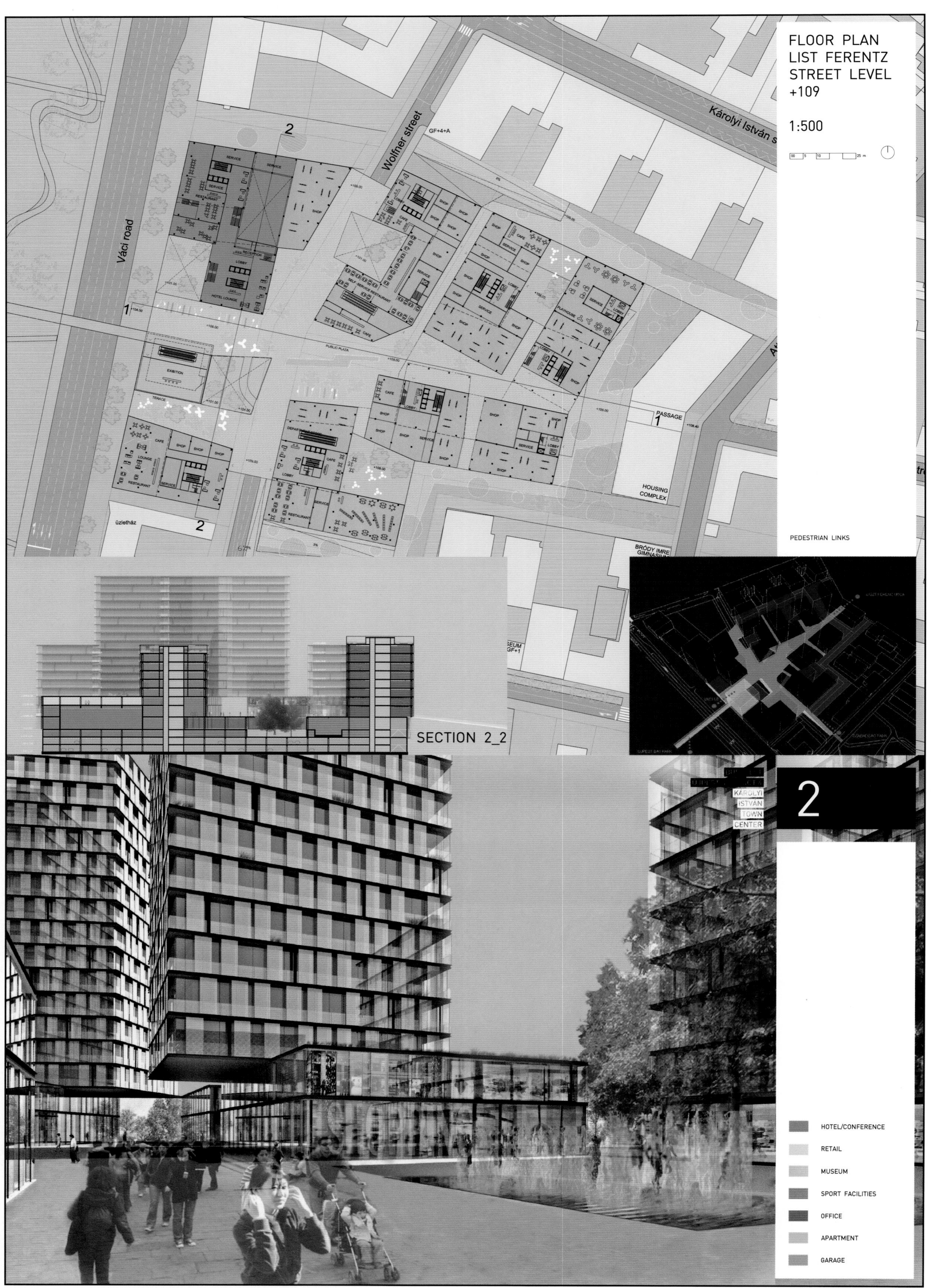
FLOOR PLAN
LIST FERENTZ
STREET LEVEL
+109
1:500
Károlyi István s
Wolfner street
Váci road
PUBLIC PLAZA
PASSAGE
HOUSING COMPLEX
üzletház
PEDESTRIAN LINKS
SECTION 2_2
KÁROLYI
ISTVÁN
TOWN
CENTER
2
HOTEL/CONFERENCE
RETAIL
MUSEUM
SPORT FACILITIES
OFFICE
APARTMENT
GARAGE

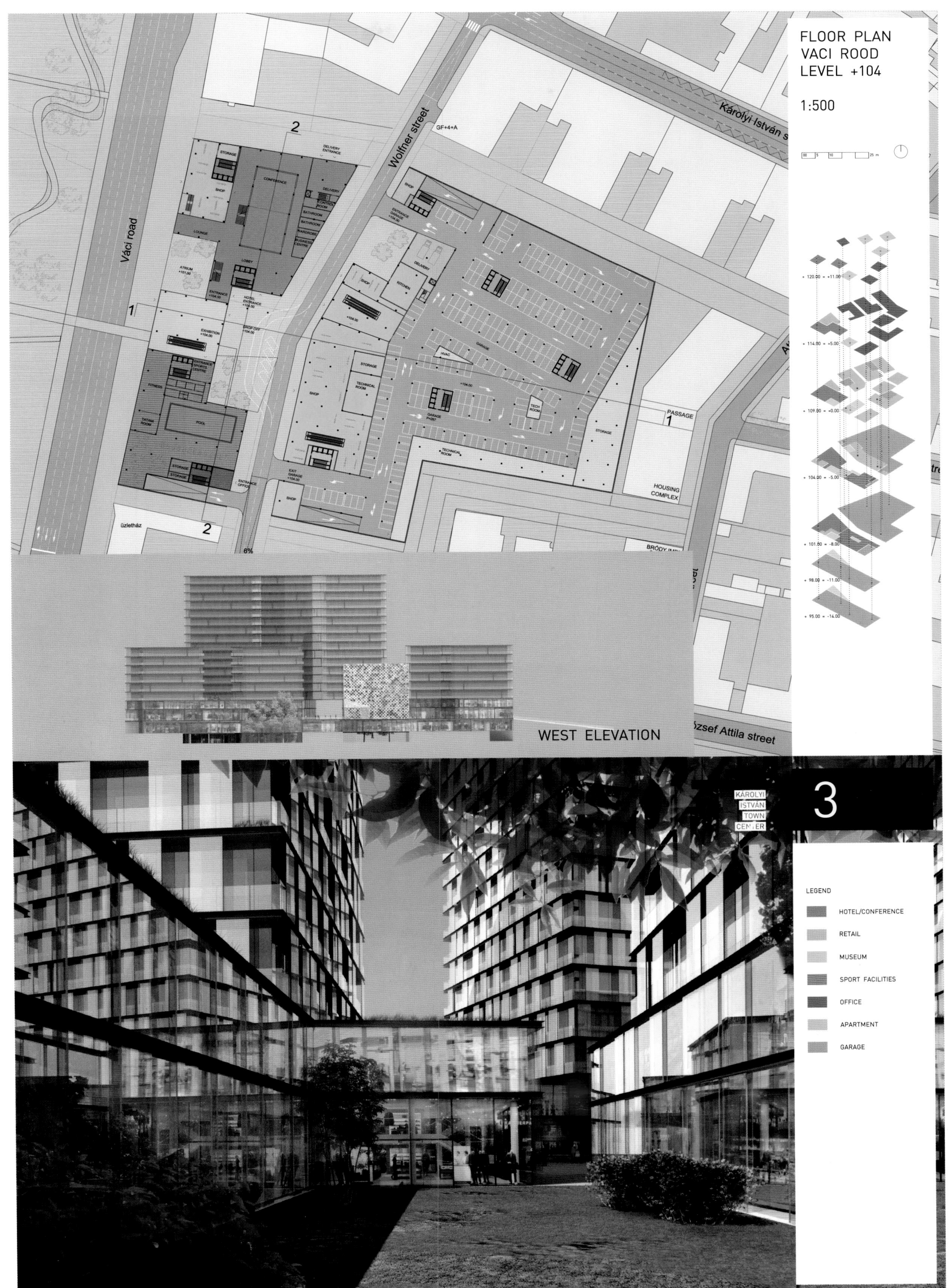

FLOOR PLAN
VACI ROOD
LEVEL +104
1:500
Váci road
Wolfner street
Károlyi István s
HOUSING COMPLEX
PASSAGE
WEST ELEVATION
József Attila street
KÁROLYI
ISTVÁN
TOWN
CENTER
3
LEGEND
HOTEL/CONFERENCE
RETAIL
MUSEUM
SPORT FACILITIES
OFFICE
APARTMENT
GARAGE

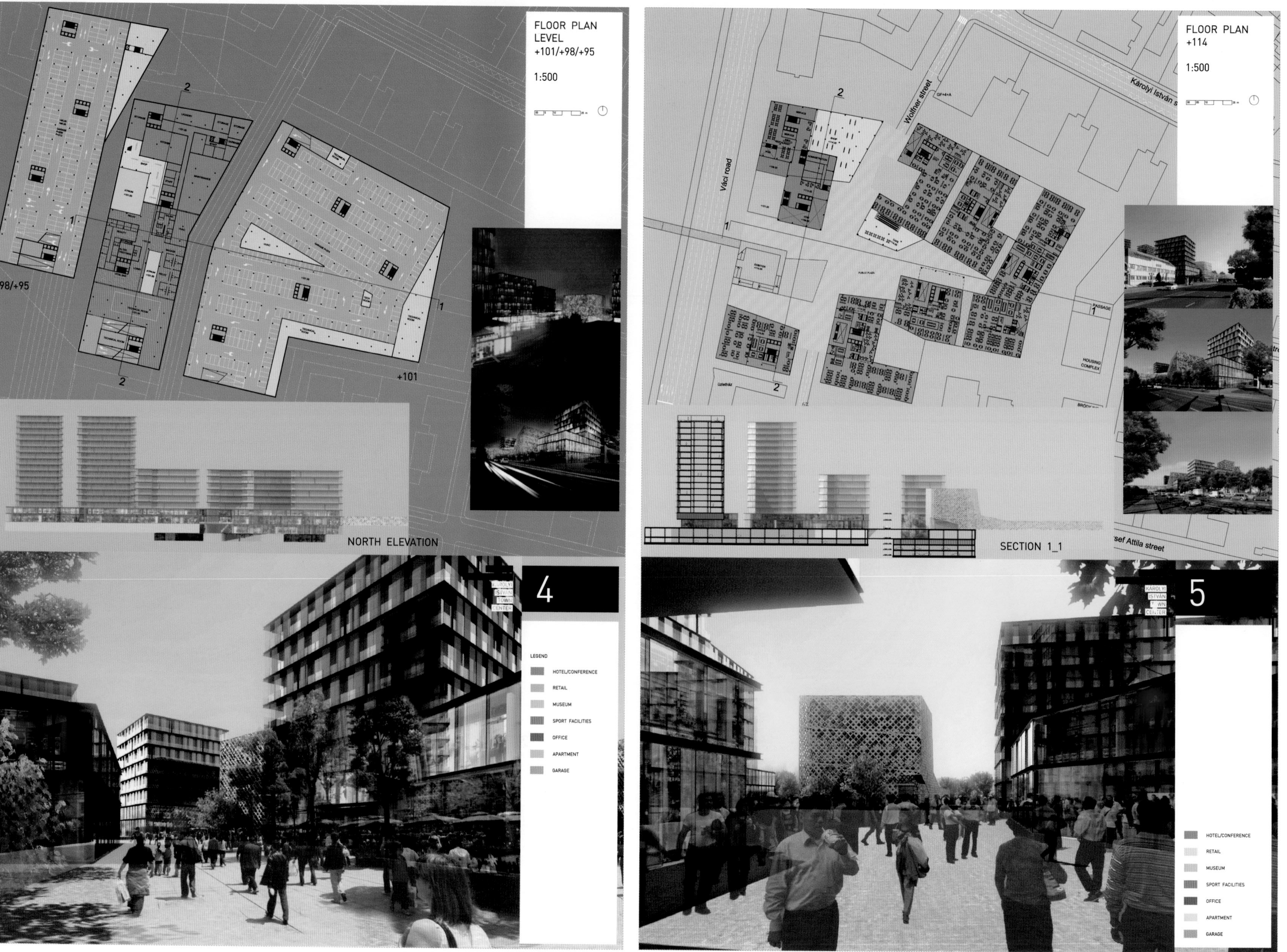
FLOOR PLAN
LEVEL
+101/+98/+95
1:500
+98/+95
+101
NORTH ELEVATION
FLOOR PLAN
+114
1:500
Károlyi István s
Wolfner street
Váci road
PASSAGE
HOUSING COMPLEX
sef Attila street
SECTION 1_1
4
KÁROLYI ISTVÁN TOWN CENTER
LEGEND
HOTEL/CONFERENCE
RETAIL
MUSEUM
SPORT FACILITIES
OFFICE
APARTMENT
GARAGE
5
KÁROLYI ISTVÁN TOWN CENTER
HOTEL/CONFERENCE
RETAIL
MUSEUM
SPORT FACILITIES
OFFICE
APARTMENT
GARAGE

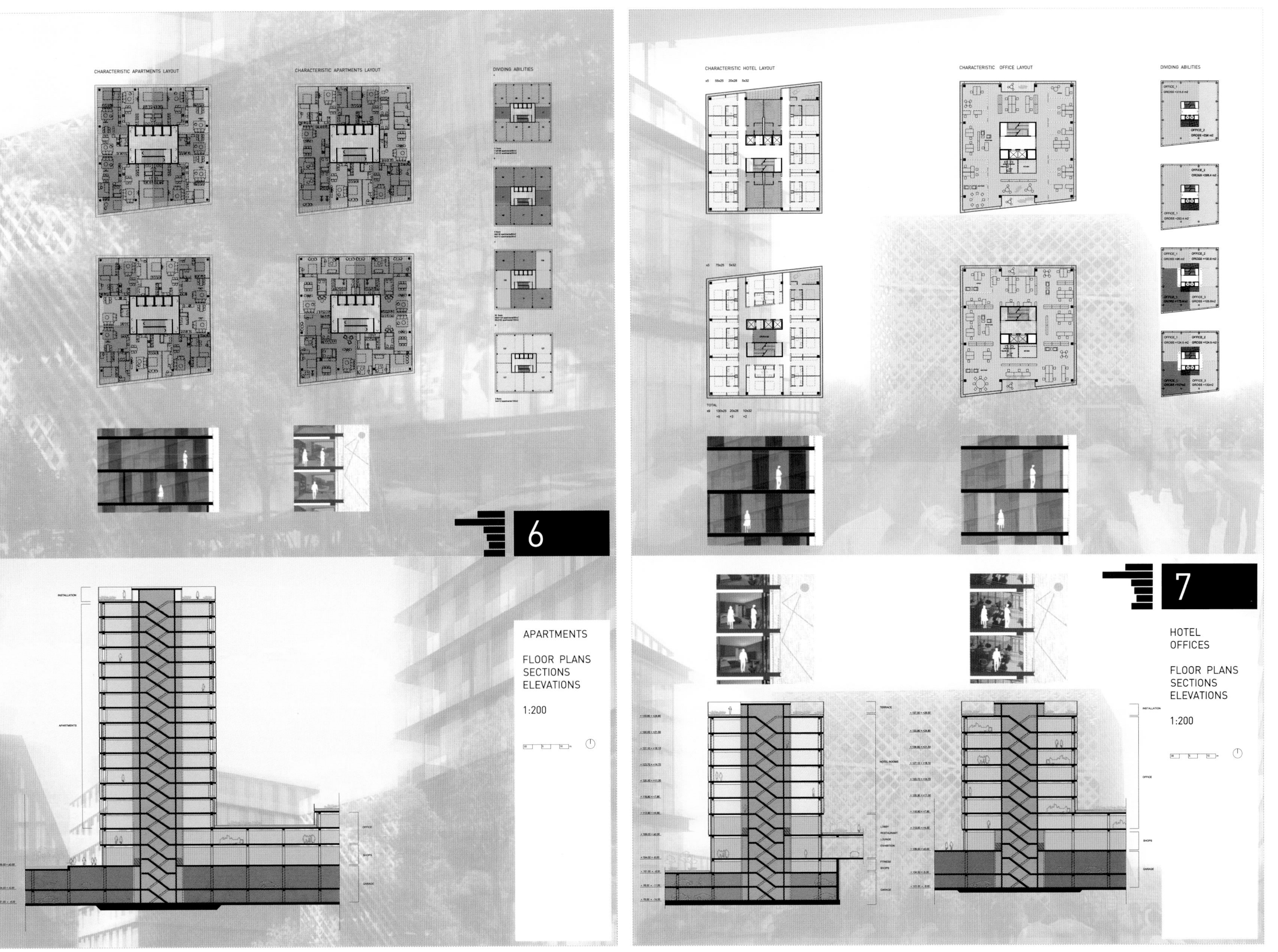
CHARACTERISTIC APARTMENTS LAYOUT
CHARACTERISTIC APARTMENTS LAYOUT
DIVIDING ABILITIES
6
APARTMENTS
FLOOR PLANS
SECTIONS
ELEVATIONS
1:200
CHARACTERISTIC HOTEL LAYOUT
CHARACTERISTIC OFFICE LAYOUT
DIVIDING ABILITIES
7
HOTEL
OFFICES
FLOOR PLANS
SECTIONS
ELEVATIONS
1:200

084 Duilovo Waterfront Masterplan | *3LHD*

Location : Split, Croatia
Type : Public, Urban Planning
Client : City of Split
Project Team : Sasa Begovic, Marko Dabrovic, Tatjana Grozdanic Begovic, Silvije Novak, Danira Matosic, Martina Ruzic, Filip Dubrovski, Gorana Barbaric, Drazen Pejkovic
3D : Drazen Pejkovic, Lemonade, 3LHD

pješak

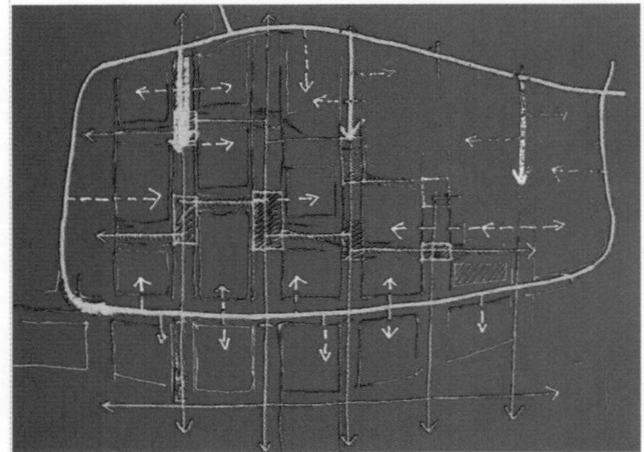

promet

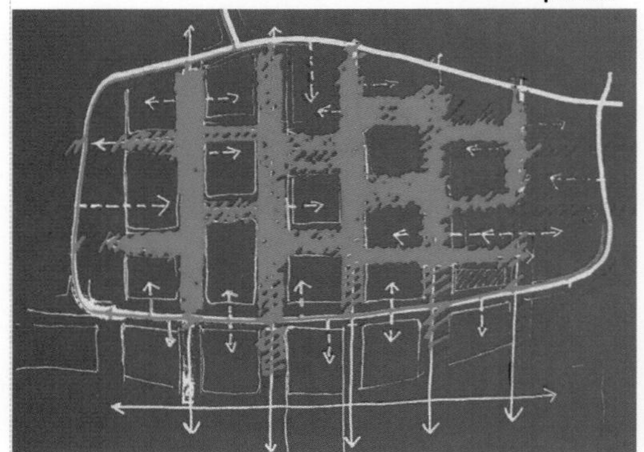

zelenilo

matrica

1:5000 - postojeći urbani kontekst

1:5000 - urbanističko rješenje s postojećim planovima u primjeni

SWS 2015
South Waterfront Split

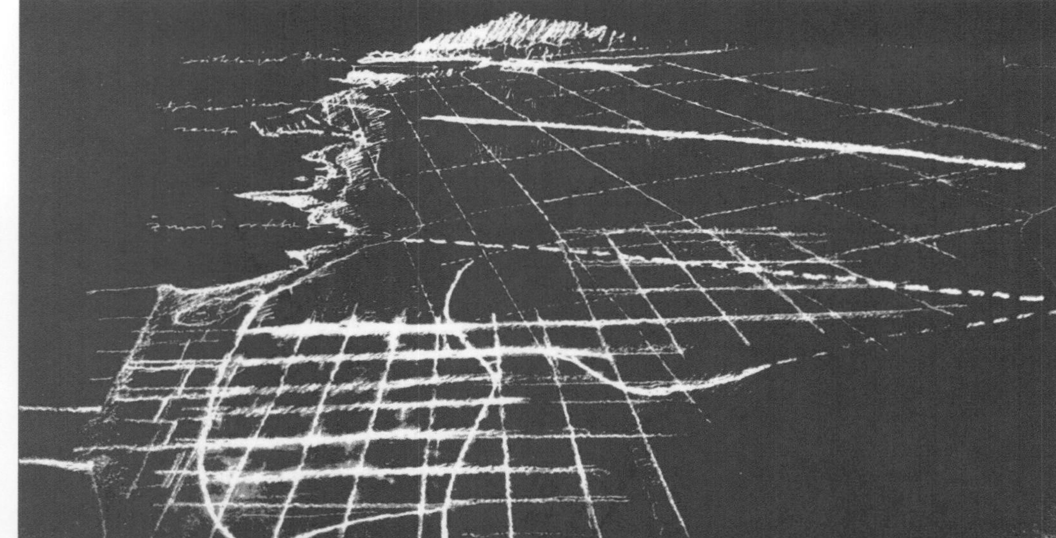

koncept

reference

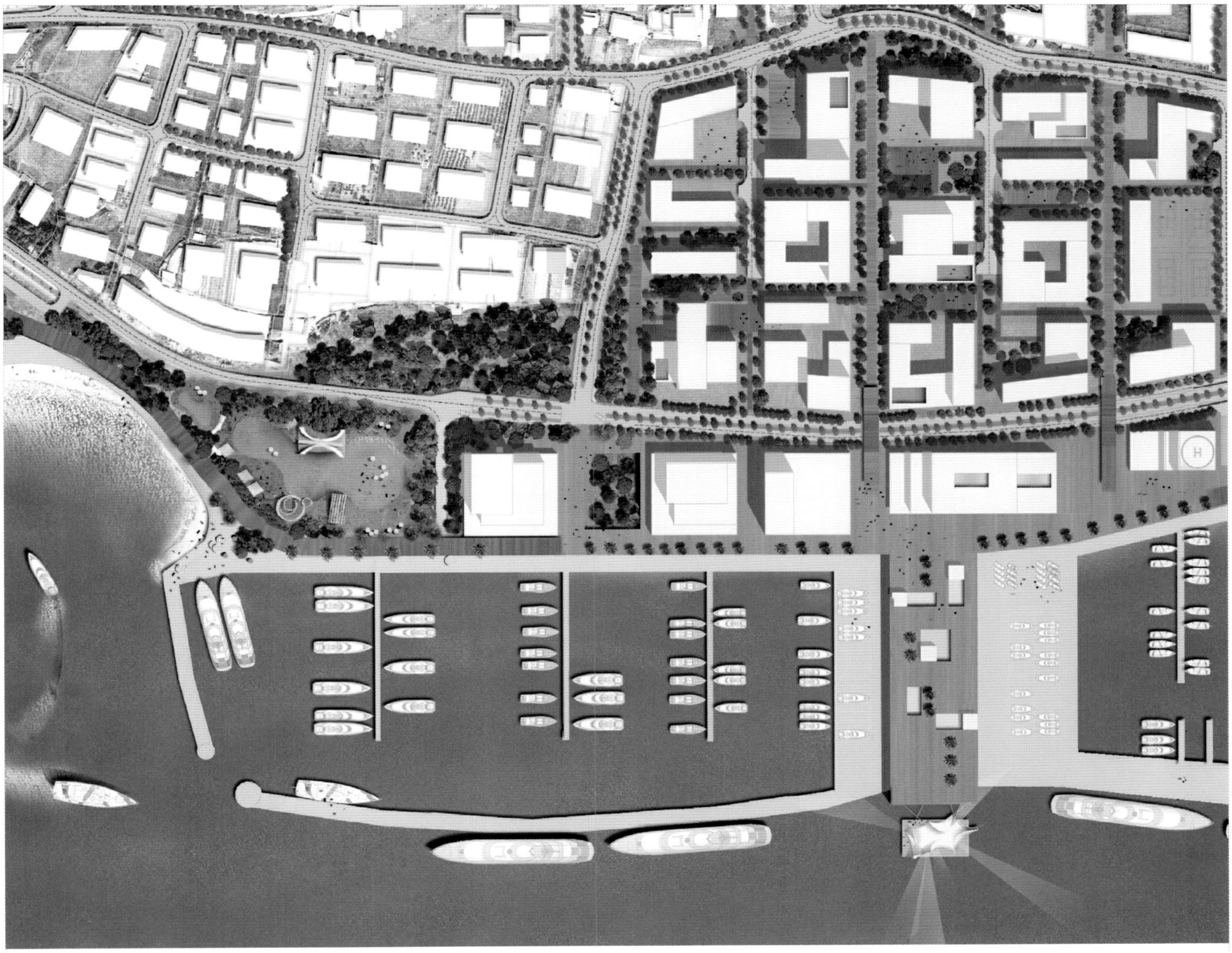

SWS 2015

South Waterfront Split

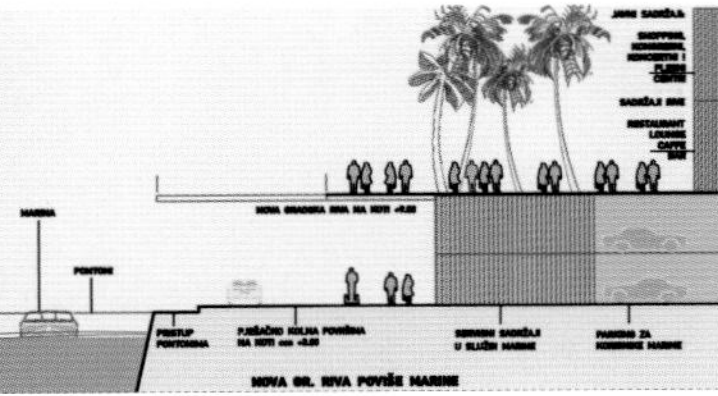

urbanističko rješenje 1:1000

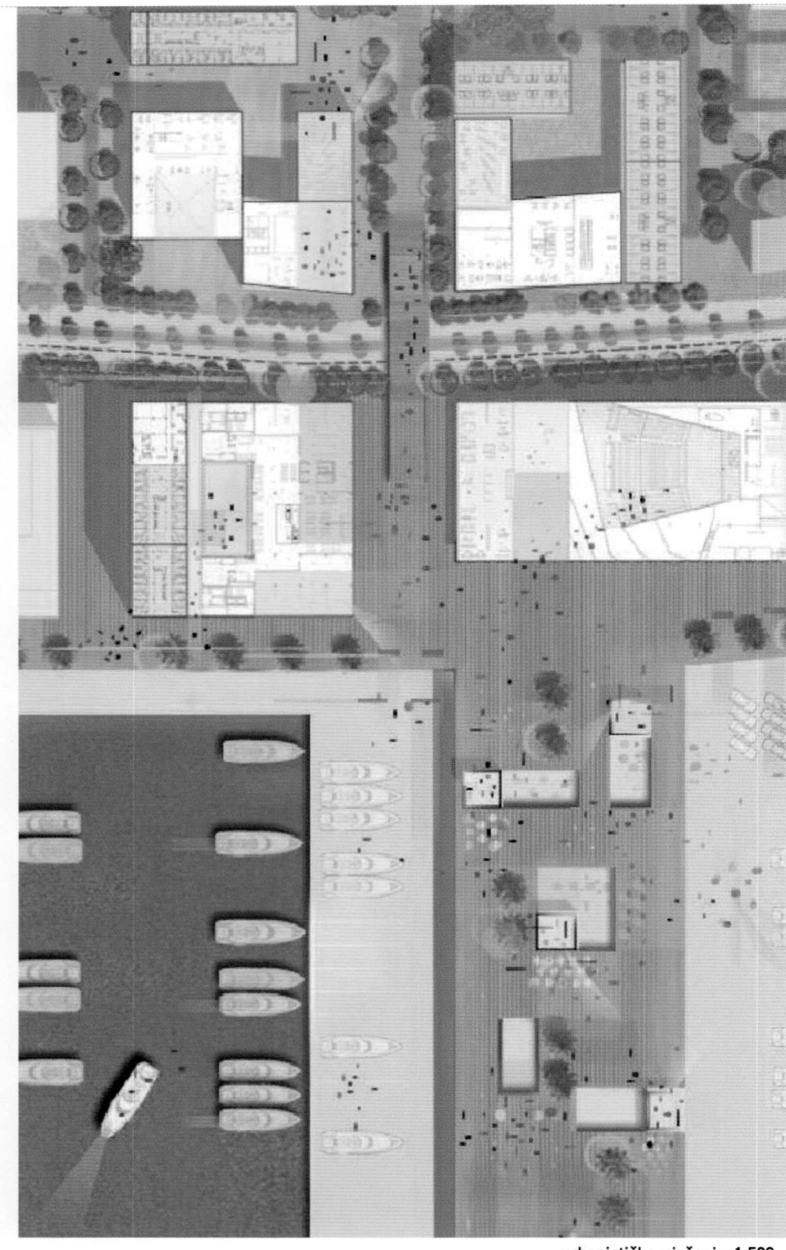

urbanističko rješenje 1:500

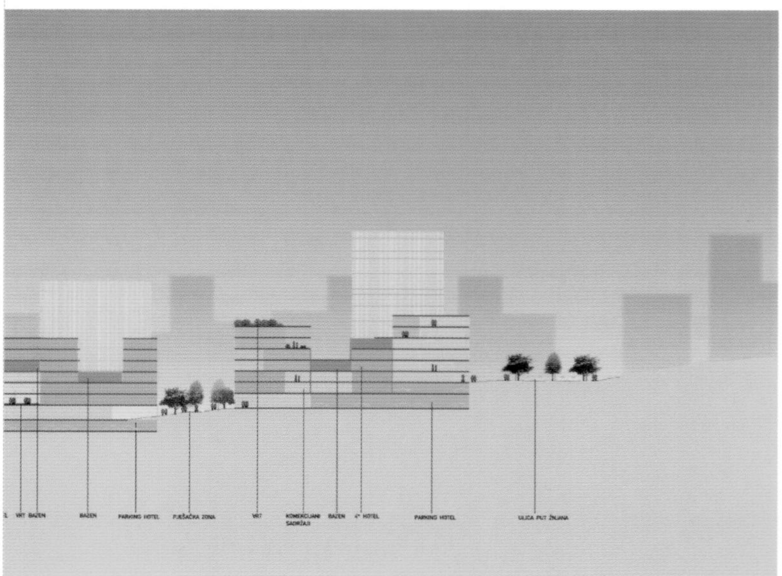

presjek 1:500

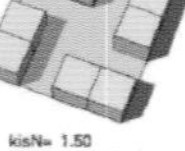

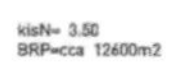
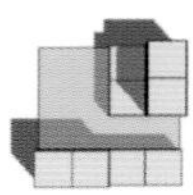

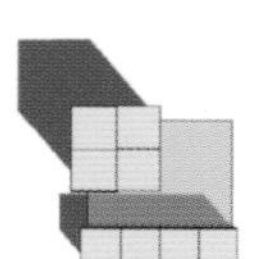

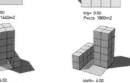

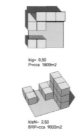

varijantne tipologije/kis/kig/BRP

reference

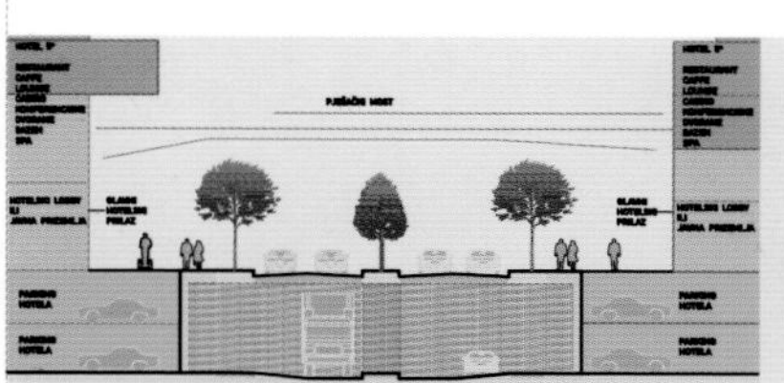
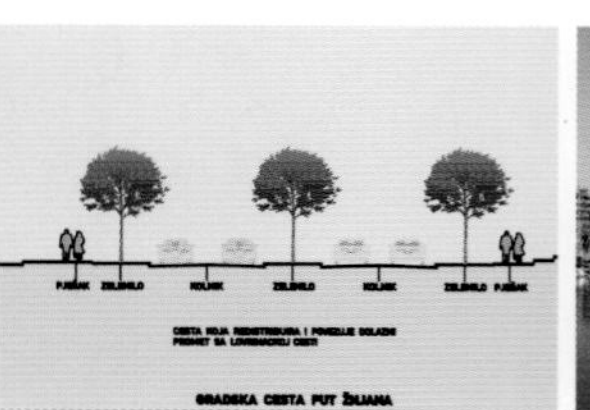

pogled iz zraka noću

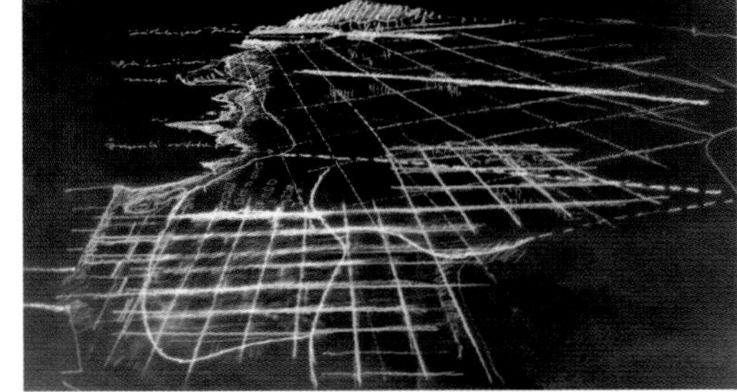

konceptualna skica

potezi pogled sjever-jug

marina

SWS 2015

South Waterfront Split

nova riva

aquapark

reference

085 Mali Maj | *3LHD*

Location : Pore, Croatia
Type : Public, Sport, Residential, Urbanism
Client : Grad Porec
Project team : Sasa Begovic, Marko Dabrovic, Tatjana Grozdanic Begovic, Silvije Novak, Irena Mazer, Tomislav Soldo, Vibor Granic, Ida Ister
3D : Boris Goreta

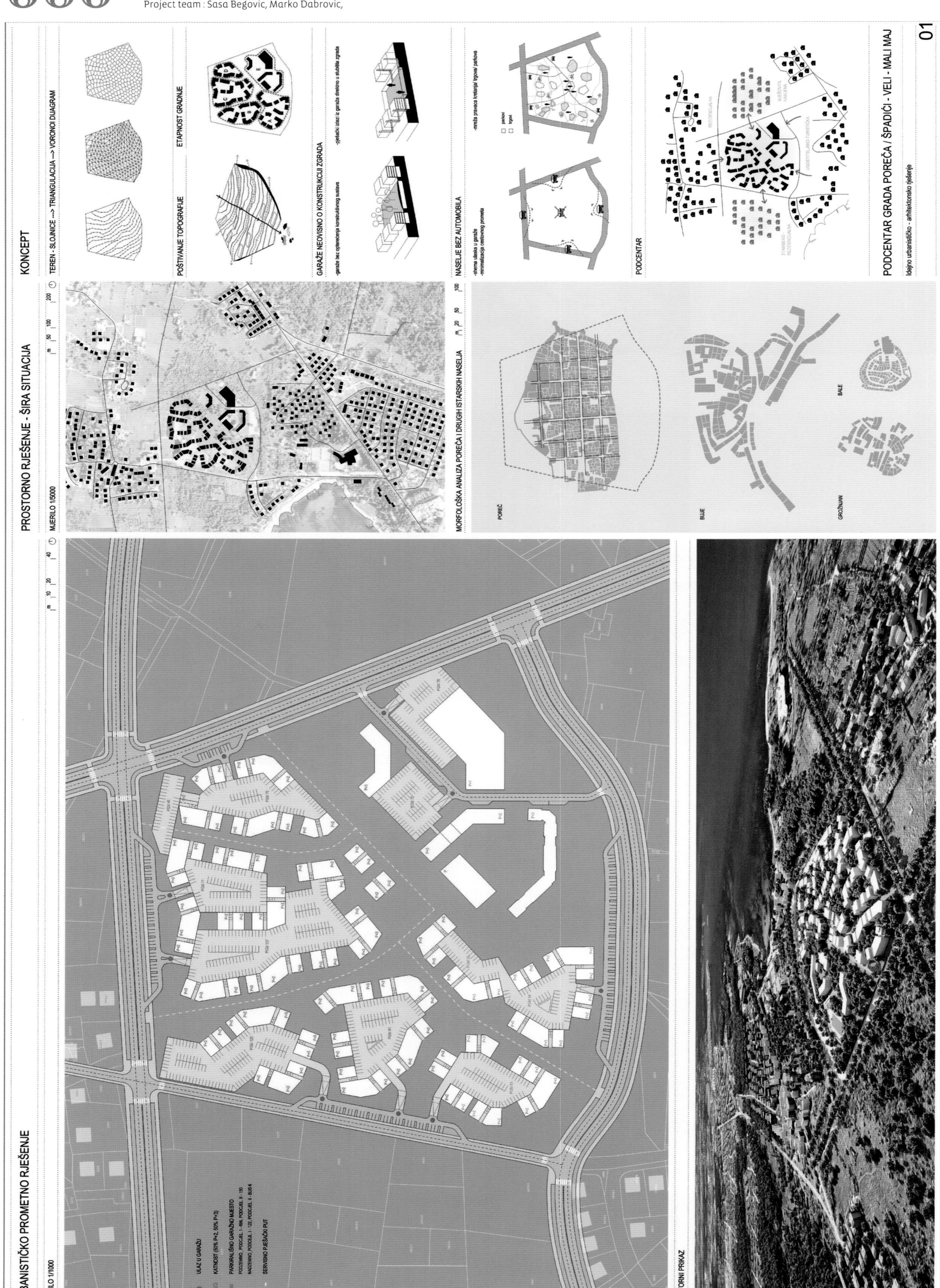

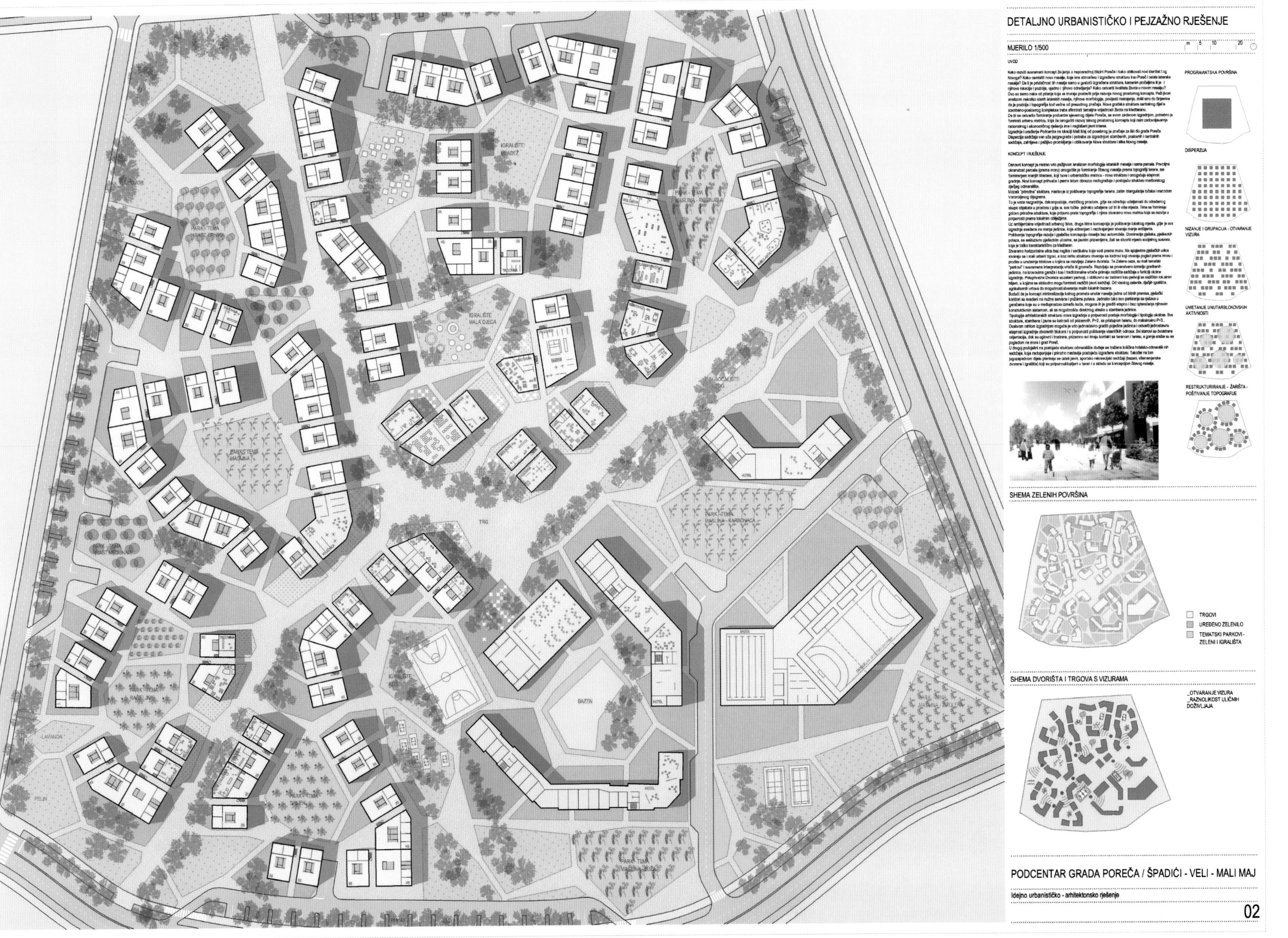
DETALJNO URBANISTIČKO I PEJZAŽNO RJEŠENJE
MJERILO 1/500
UVOD
KONCEPT I RJEŠENJE
PROGRAMATSKA POVRŠINA
DISPERZIJA
NIZANJE I GRUPACIJA - OTVARANJE VIZURA
UMETANJE UNUTARBLOKOVSKIH AKTIVNOSTI
RESTRUKTURIRANJE - ŽARIŠTA - POŠTIVANJE TOPOGRAFIJE
SHEMA ZELENIH POVRŠINA
TRGOVI
UREĐENO ZELENILO
TEMATSKI PARKOVI - ZELENI I IGRALIŠTA
SHEMA DVORIŠTA I TRGOVA S VIZURAMA
_OTVARANJE VIZURA
_RAZNOLIKOST ULIČNIH DOŽIVLJAJA
TRG
BAZEN
HOTEL
IGRALIŠTE MALA DJECA
PODCENTAR GRADA POREČA / ŠPADIĆI - VELI - MALI MAJ
Idejno urbanističko - arhitektonsko rješenje
02

PROGRAMSKO RJEŠENJE GRAĐEVINA
MJERILO 1/500
m 5 10 20
ORIJENTACIJA STANOVA
PROLAZNO PRIZEMLJE
PROLAZNO PRIZEMLJE
FORMIRANJE JAVNE ZONE I MJESTA GRADSKOG KARAKTERA I SOCIOLOŠKOG SUSRETA
SHEMA PRIZEMLJA - NAMJENA
TRGOVINE
UGOSTITELJSTVO
STAMBENO
KULTURA
HOTELI
ZDRAVSTVO
SPORT
PODCENTAR GRADA POREČA / ŠPADIĆI - VELI - MALI MAJ
Idejno urbanističko - arhitektonsko rješenje
03

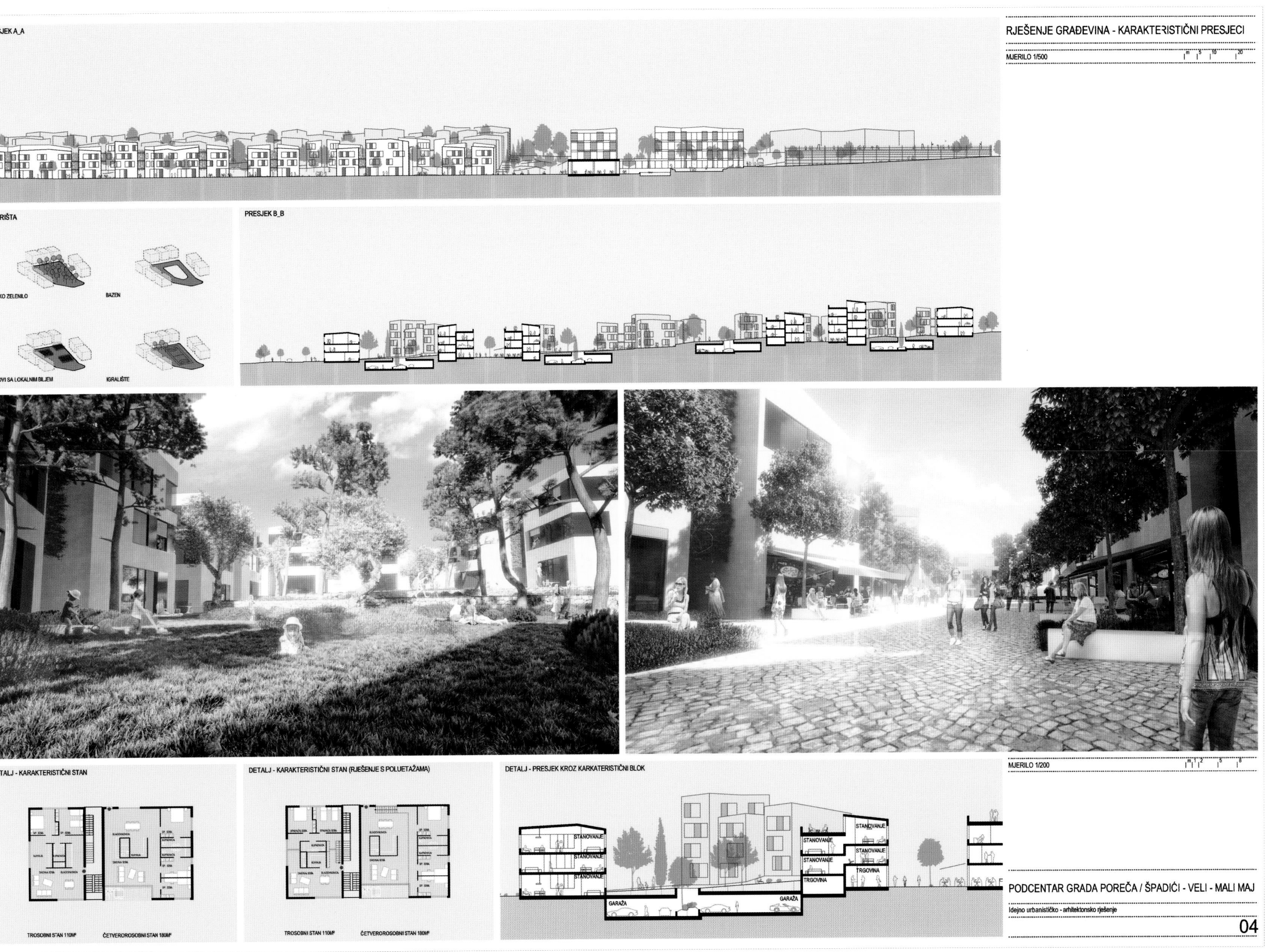
RJEŠENJE GRAĐEVINA - KARAKTERISTIČNI PRESJECI
MJERILO 1/500
PRESJEK A_A
DVORIŠTA
VISOKO ZELENILO
BAZEN
VRTOVI SA LOKALNIM BILJEM
IGRALIŠTE
PRESJEK B_B
DETALJ - KARAKTERISTIČNI STAN
TROSOBNI STAN 110M²
ČETVEROSOBNI STAN 180M²
DETALJ - KARAKTERISTIČNI STAN (RJEŠENJE S POLUETAŽAMA)
TROSOBNI STAN 110M²
ČETVEROSOBNI STAN 180M²
DETALJ - PRESJEK KROZ KARAKTERISTIČNI BLOK
STANOVANJE
TRGOVINA
GARAŽA
MJERILO 1/200
PODCENTAR GRADA POREČA / ŠPADIĆI - VELI - MALI MAJ
Idejno urbanističko - arhitektonsko rješenje
04

Tallinn - Green Cement | *XML Architecture Research Urbanism*

Project : Urban Strategy and Two Markethalls
Program : Fishmarket, Designmarket, Foodmarket, Creative workshopspace
Area : Masterplan 1km² / Buildings 800m²

Client : Chief Government Architect Estonia / Europan Estonia
Location : Tallinn, Estonia
Status : Competition, First Prize

TH115 - TALLINN - GREEN CEMENT 001

GREEN CEMENT

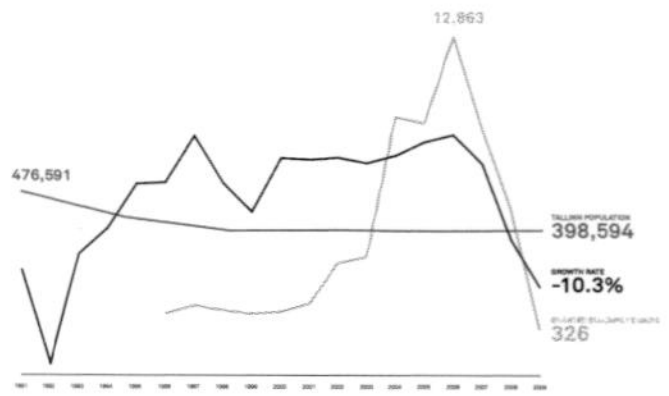

TALLINN POPULATION VS. ESTONIA GROWTH RATE VS. BUILDING PERMITS 1991-2009 (SOURCE: WWW.STAT.EE)

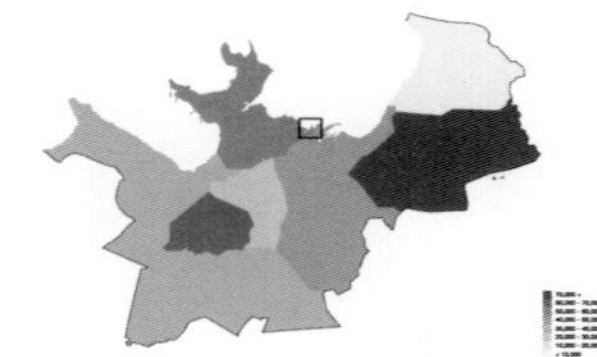

POPULATION PER DISTRICT (SOURCE: COMPETITION BRIEF)

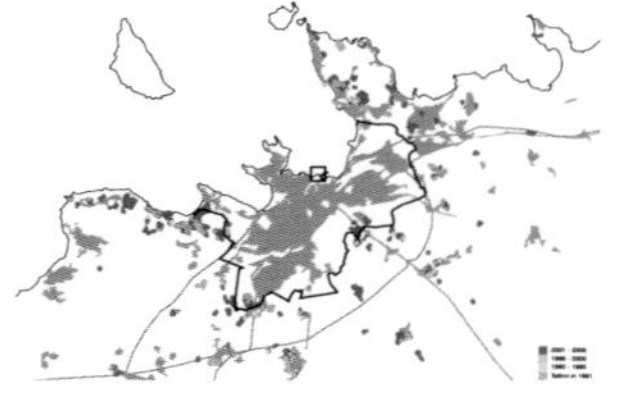

URBAN GROWTH (1990-2008)

PROPERTY VALUE MAP (SOURCE: WWW.KV.EE , MAY 2009)

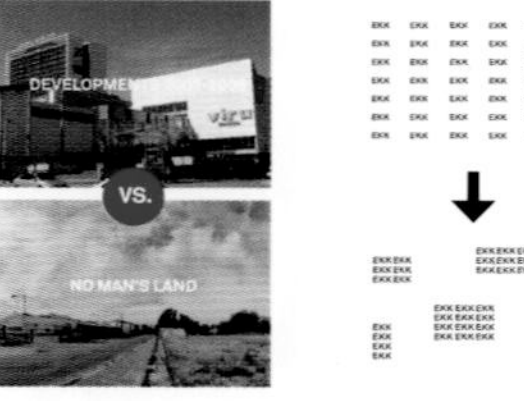

URBAN CONDITION: AUTOMATICALLY ALLOCATING PROGRAMS TO ALL UNDEFINED AREAS WITHIN A SPRAWLING CITY MEANS THAT SCANT AVAILABLE RESOURCES MUST BE DISTRIBUTED OVER A MULTITUDE OF NEEDS. INSTEAD, THIS PROPOSAL FOCUSES ON A STRATEGY OF CREATING CONTRASTS.

LAND COVER ESTONIA FOREST. OVER 50% OF ESTONIA IS COVERED BY FOREST.

Since the fall of the Berlin Wall, which was a prelude to Estonia's independence, the country has experienced a period of turbulent growth. With a capital that has been characterized by the New York Times as 'Silicon Valley on the Baltic Sea,' Estonia's G.D.P. has boomed and the number of new construction projects has multiplied since the beginning of the 21st century. Paradoxically, this period of strong economic growth and intense building activity has seen a parallel decrease in the population of Talinn. Now that the global recession is strongly impacting on Estonia's economy and construction activities have slowed down significantly, this may be a decisive moment for Talinn to evaluate its situation and utilize this breathing space to formulate new urban scenarios for the future.

A quick analysis shows that, for Talinn, the economic boom and the explosive increase in building activity of the past 15 years has materialized in the form of urban sprawl. Construction has been particularly strong at the periphery, and the majority of the city's population now lives at a considerable distance from the city center. A notable aspect of Talinn's urban sprawl is that there is little variation in the value of its real estate and few locations are considered distinctly more attractive than others. Another important feature is the steady decline in residential density over a period of 50 years, a decline that has accelerated since the country's independence.

Hence, after 40 years of communist social engineering and urban development followed by the post-independence construction outburst, Talinn's sprawling urban plan is characterized by two extremes: areas with new, primarily self-referential conditions alternated with vast expanses of no-man's land. The city has recently formulated the ambition to strengthen its relationship to the surrounding water. However, in view of current economic and demographic conditions, it may be argued that this is not the most sustainable and realistic scenario. An attempt to fill the city's voids with any kind of program is highly dubious, and it is the zones between urban area and water in particular that consist of meaningless stretches of unused space, former military terrain, and dockland areas.

Automatically allocating programs to all undefined areas within a sprawling city means that scant available resources must be distributed over a multitude of needs. Instead, this proposal focuses on a strategy of creating contrasts. Here, differences between various parts of the city are reinforced by filling undefined areas with woodlands. These woodlands will have a major impact on Talinn, in various ways. Naturally changing with the seasons, the woods transform stretches of no-mans's land into meaningful spaces. By filling no-man's land with woodlands, locations that are to be developed in the future will have added value and buildings realized on these locations will be special, regardless of their architecture; each fragment in the landscape becomes unique instead of disappearing into urban oblivion. Depending on future trends, certain urban areas may be allocated to the woodlands, or vice versa. Thus, the city will have room for expansion and reduction, all within the same organic system. The woodlands provide the 'Green Cement' needed to bind Talinn's fragmented structure, giving consistency to the city's urban fabric. A clear contrast between the city and the woodlands is an affirmation of the true identity of Tallin as capital of Estonia, where over 50% of the land is covered by forests. The Green Cement scenario allows Talinn to grow -- literally -- into a modern metropolis characterized by clearly delineated public spaces rather than an endless sprawl of indistinctness.

One of the fragments in this new urban landscape is the cluster that contains the Cultural Factory, the Linnahall, the new City Administration Building and the new Market Twins. The Market Twins are two rectangular generic halls, which house the fish market, and the food and design markets respectively. The modest architecture of the halls is complemented by interiors in which market activities are organized through the placement of stalls and daylighting. In the fish market hall, the long lines of the fish stalls follow the shoreline and the hall's daylighting runs in the same direction, providing a clear overview in an essentially chaotic marketplace. The public space created by the area between the fish market hall and the Linnahall becomes part of the new route along the shoreline, which can be seen from this viewpoint through the filter of lanes between the lined fish stalls. The second hall houses the design market and the food market. Here, daylighting is organized in a gradient that consists of a variety of apertures. Like open spaces in the woods where sunlight shines through, the concentration of programmatic activities at various spots in this hall is accentuated by daylighting. The placement of market stalls and furniture helps to highlight various areas within this space. Besides the food market and the design market, this hall houses a restaurant, a small conference center and a creative workshop area. These programs will allow the hall to develop into an informal civic hall that complements the formal City Administration Building located across the street.

Clearly delineated by Green Cement, the project creates a public space in which the Linnahall, the City Administration Building and the Market Twins become genuine actors, each with their own roles. The clear demarcation of the boundaries through the adjacent woodlands allows the site to develop into a meaningful public space, with a program that will be truly rooted in Talinn's urban fabric.

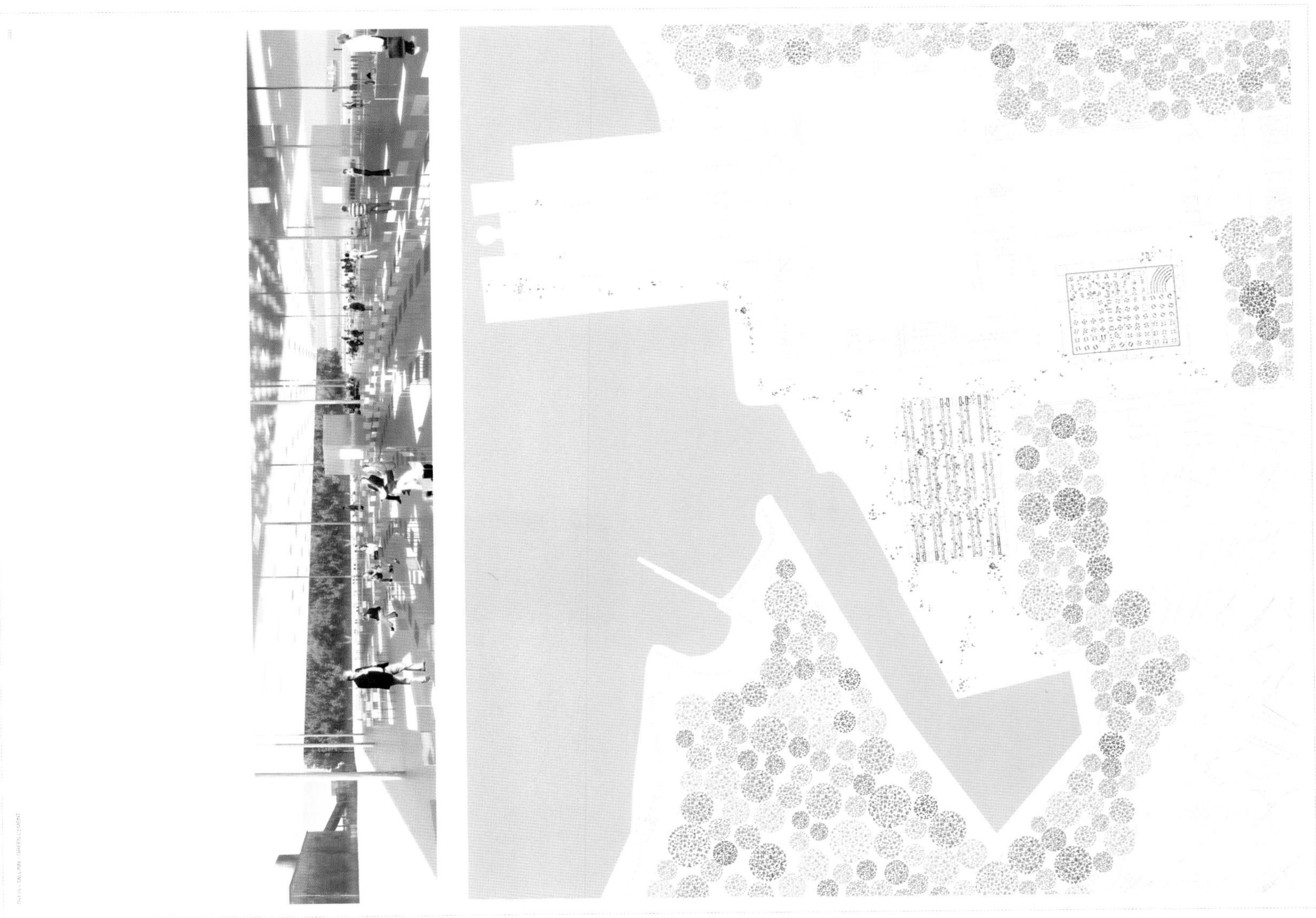

Alnus glutinosa
Alnus incana
Betula pendula
Fraxinus excelsior
Picea abies
Pinus sylvestris
Populus tremula
Quercus robur

AUTUMN
WINTER
SPRING
SUMMER

087 D3 Natural Systems | *Horhizon consortium*

Biosynthetic Ecology : Hybridized Farm Bridge as a City Garden
1st Place Winner Sustainable Worldwide Category D3 Natural Systems Design Competition
Type : Agriculture and Urbanism
Design : Kenny Kinugasa Tsui, Lorene Faure

Urban Agriculture Biosynthetic Ecology: Hybridized Farm Bridge as a City Garden

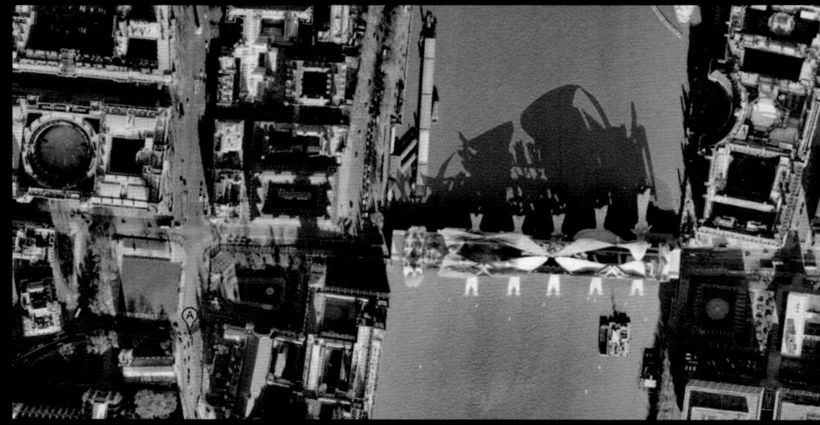

Introduction - An architectural vision of a sustainable future
Most cities in the world rely on a vulnerable system of food supply; hence they are most likely to feel the effects of any food shortages. In UK, it is estimated that Londoners consumed 6.9 million tones of food per year, of which 81% came from outside the UK. The country's food supply is almost totally dependent on oil (95% of the food we eat is oil-dependent) and if the oil supply to Britain were suddenly cut off, figures show that it would take just three full days before law and order broke down. *(Sources from London Yields: Urban Agriculture. An exhibition held at the Building Centre, London during 9 April - 30 May 2009)*
The transformation of cities from consumers of food to generators of agricultural products not only increases food security but also contributes to sustainability, improved health and poverty alleviation.
This has driven an in-depth research based investigation into the proposition of an urban agricultural building hybridized with biological matter, as a semi-living system that informs a biosynthetic ecology that would provide food for Londoners.
The architectural proposal is a technological food production farm built on top of the existing Westminster Bridge in central London. The design of an archifoliage 'veils' system allows a variable input from the surrounding natural habitat and human influence into a public garden spectacle, while preserving its original function as a road bridge. The veils morphologically adapts to the existing stone bridge and forms a number of floating docks on the Thames River that accommodates the function of food delivery through water vehicles, as well as leisure activities such as canoeing and kayaking.

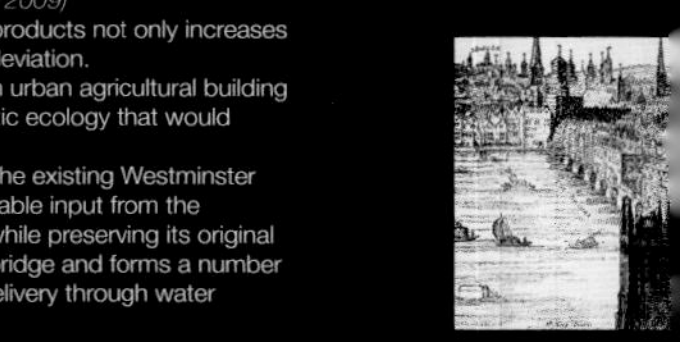

Depth of Research - An innovative technological approach
The rapid development of innovative technological approaches in the realm of biology, biomechanics, biotechnology, aerodynamics, and hydrodynamics are becoming of immense significance to architecture, demanding our attention due to their inevitable cultural, aesthetic and technical implications. This results in the 'biologicalisation' phenomenon in architecture. The line between natural and the artificial is progressively blurred.

Below: A synthetic living flesh - Archifoliage 'Veils'
Based on the research into plant flowers fertilization and fermentation mechanisms, the proposed artificial synthetic structures creates a family of responsive and interrelated typological growth structures to nurture specific crop plants living systems.

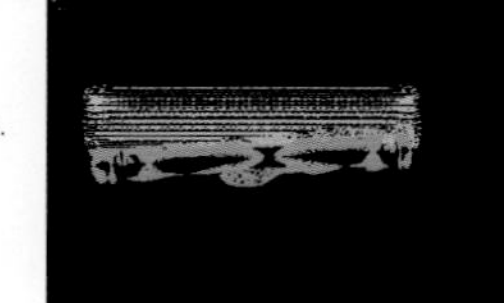
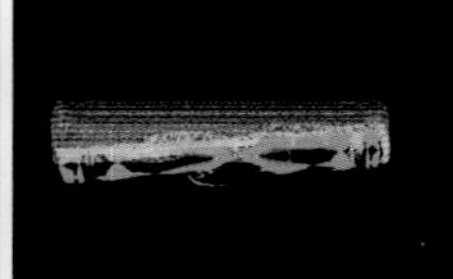
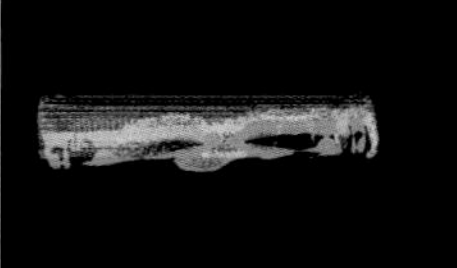
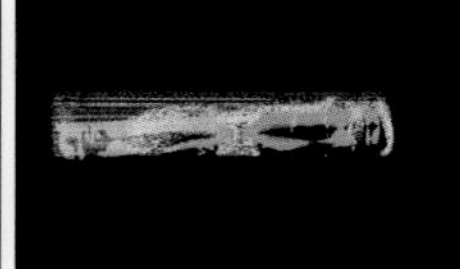

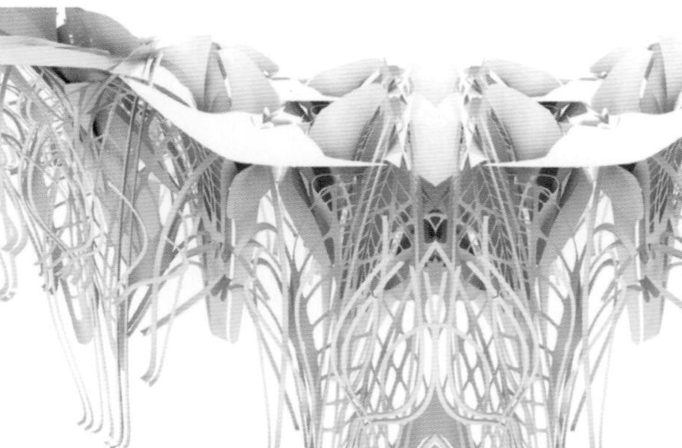

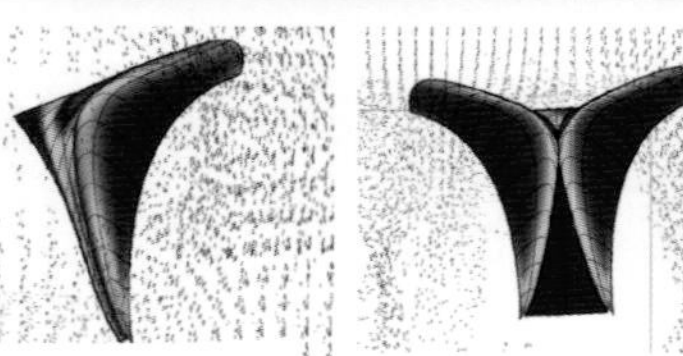

Archi-zantedeschia elliottiana - beans

Archi-zantedeschia aethiopica - guord

Archi-zantedeschia rehmannii - cucumbers

Archi-zantedeschia albomaculata - yam

Arch[illegible] jucu[illegible] toma[illegible] herb[illegible]

Archifoliage typologies - Araceae
A catalogue of variations was generated to manage a degree of transpiration, solar and water flow along the veil surfaces to enable a multiplicity of conditions and responses for optimized c[illegible] plant growths. They modulate the micro weather environment for each plant growth species.

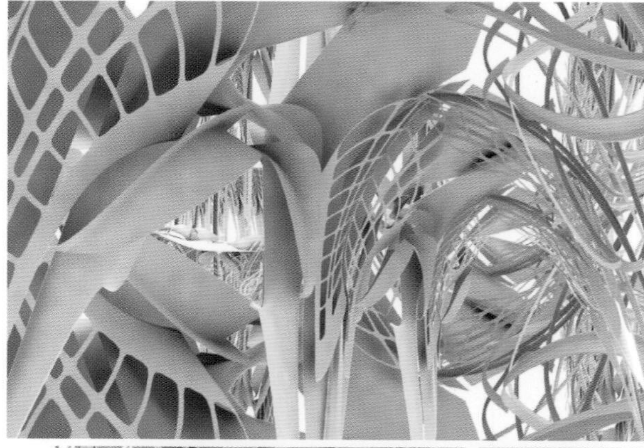

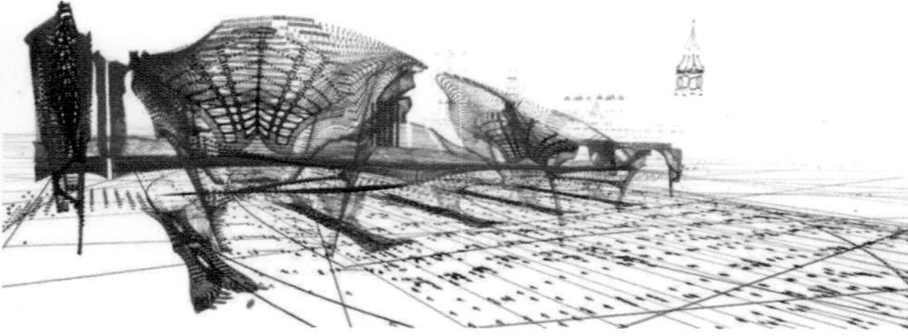

Below: Vector fields - ecological synthetic flesh
Fluid dynamic design processes. The infrastructural flows of the road bridge, pedestrian, and water vehicles¬ are analyzed in a time-based urban dynamics. The environmental criteria and conditions of have been studied.

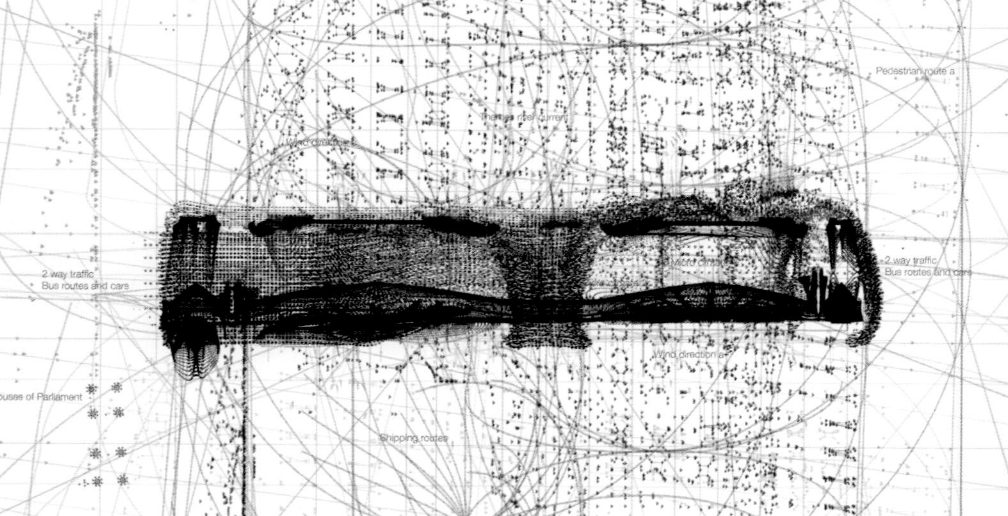

1154

Hydromorphic membrane structures - water collection retractable roof membrane
The transparent foldable PVC roof canopy acts as a condenser for reclaiming water for storage which is then used for watering the crops. The technique for this lightweight system is simple and its cost of maintenance is low.
The folding geometry of the roof canopy takes inspiration from the plant family of Araceae and maximizes its surface area for heat exchange. It dissipates its heat at night and allows for the condensation of water vapor from the air, as well as directing rain water to the white funnels.

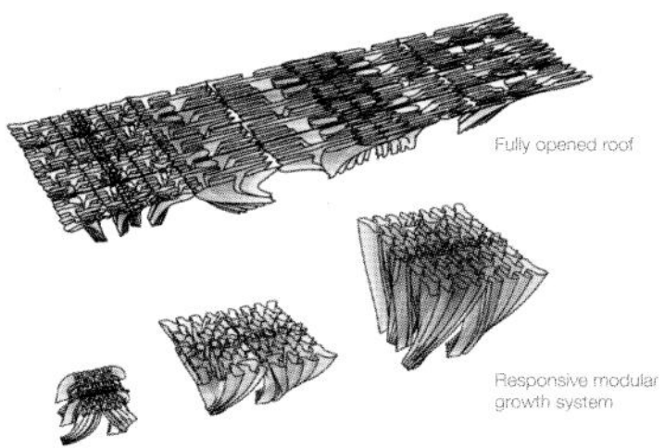

Right: Identity in the city - Retractable roof glows during year round events
The roof canopy is electronically controlled using a simple cable pulley system to 'open' and expand to cover a bigger area during rain and night dew time for condensation. The transparent material can be beautifully lit during community events which could be seen clearly from the surrounding neighborhood.

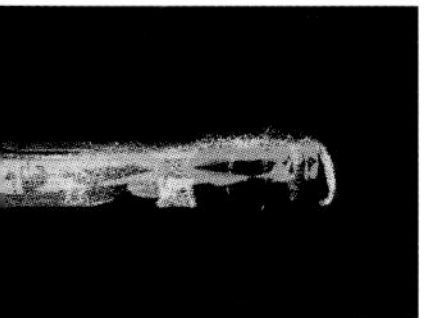

Left: Fluid dynamic studies for biosynthetic responsive structures
Process of time based documentation and analysis

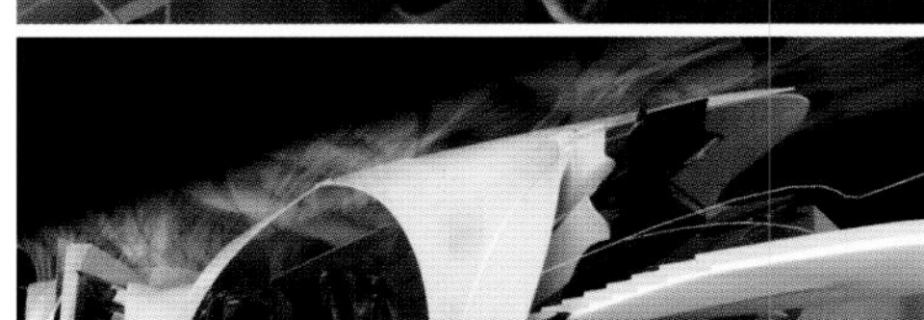

Below: Transgenic organisms hybrid
The biological phenomena in morphological terms have been studied and applied principles as a means to develop new structural and formal systems. The designed synthetic archifoliage veil structures are each tailored to nurture different species of living crop to grow symbiotically in an optimized condition.

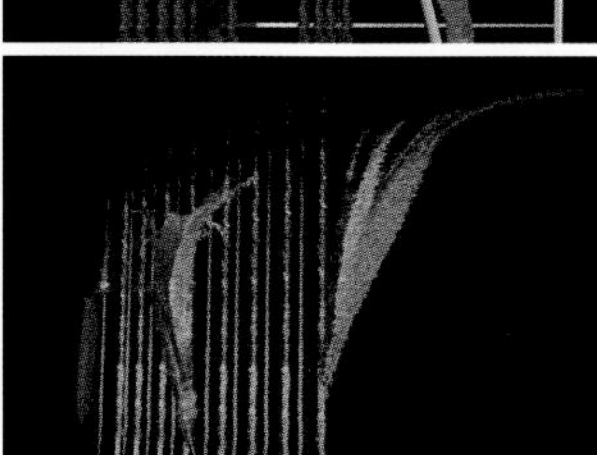

The geometries of the crops as a seasonal vegetation skin
The above images records growth pattern for a climbing plant (hop plant) on the archifoliage system. The resultant geometry of the vegetation is generated from the differentiated nurturing forms of the archifoliage veil structures.
The vegetation forms a soft outer skin for the building, which changes seasonally according to the annual growth and cultivation of the farm.

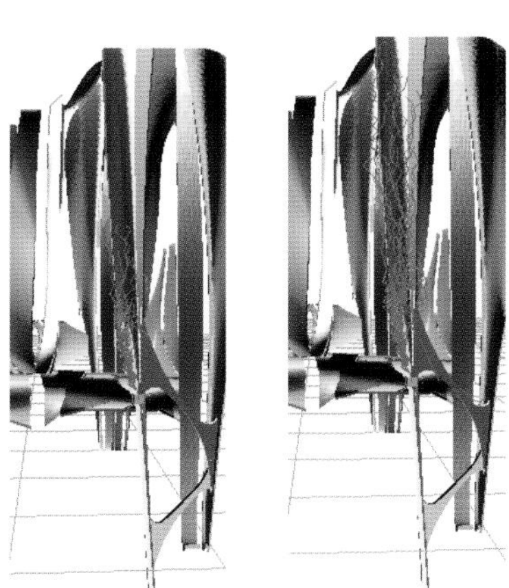

Hydromorphic structures - Time based study for plant growth
Seeds are simulated to grow on the synthetic veil; it is dependent on the micro climate created by the veil.

Circle01 PAR:21892 Px:-20.09 Py:12.23 Pz:-3.73
r1 Y:2658 F:5022 Px:25.07 Py:0.0 Pz:0.45
Gravity01 Px:0.0 Py:0.0 Pz:0.0

chifoliage Veils - Innovation in the use of nceptual process generators
design of the archifoliage Veils system researched dynamics as the conceptual and technical basis for eographing complex interactions of crop growth from putationally generated vector fields. The ecological ronmental data such as sunlight, temperature and rain is rporated into the iterative design progression of the veils ly typologies.

hifoliage typologies - Araceae
eae is a family of monocotyledonous flowering plants in h flowers are borne on a type of inflorescence called a dix. The spadix is usually accompanied by, and sometimes ially enclosed in a leaf-like hood.
tedeschia and Anthurium are two well known members of family.

variation of archifoliage are studied:
i-zantedeschia elliottiana - beans
i-zantedeschia aethiopica - guord
i-zantedeschia rehmannii - cucumbers
i-zantedeschia albomaculata - yam
i-zantedeschia jucunda - squashes, tomatoes, salads and s

ectiveness of the design relative to its rounding context
cultural and political impact of the site requires a poetic synthesis in llel to the technologically driven research. The Westminster Bridge is in e proximity to the iconic building of the 'Big Ben' clock tower and the ament building, the heart of a tourist destination in London.
existing road bridge does not respond to the change of flux of the city, her does it sustain much of its iconic value when compared to other e famous bridges in London such as London Bridge and Tower bridge. infrastructural flows of the road bridge, pedestrian, and water cles- are analyzed in a time-based urban dynamics. The environmental ria and conditions of have been studied. Five modular typologies that ulate crop growths has been designed as 'Performative structures' that litate organizations and actions in the ecosystem and interconnected ables that make up the 'active context'.

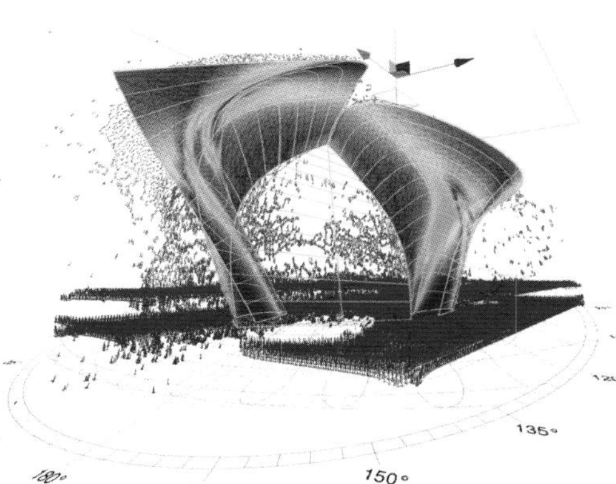

Archi-zantedeschia rehmannii
Study for the Archifoliage veil. An invention for a material property capable of response and changes of the external and internal changes to modulate micro and macro bio environments.

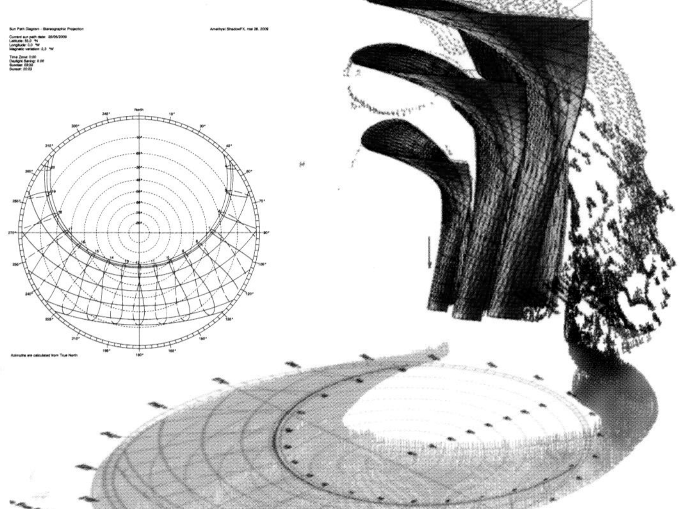

Archi-zantedeschia jucunda
Study for the Archifoliage veil. Wind flow, rain and air temperature is simulated. The foliage blend variable input from the surrounding environmental influences into providing a microclimate for squashes, tomatoes, and salad crop growths.

nal section
roof canopy

docks

n
ridge
of main crop farm for climbing plants
a flexible space flexible vending 'Bin-pods'
ue and sky walk for pedestrians
es existing road access
of a series of delivery docks

Urban Agriculture Biosynthetic Ecology: Hybridized Farm Bridge as a City Garden

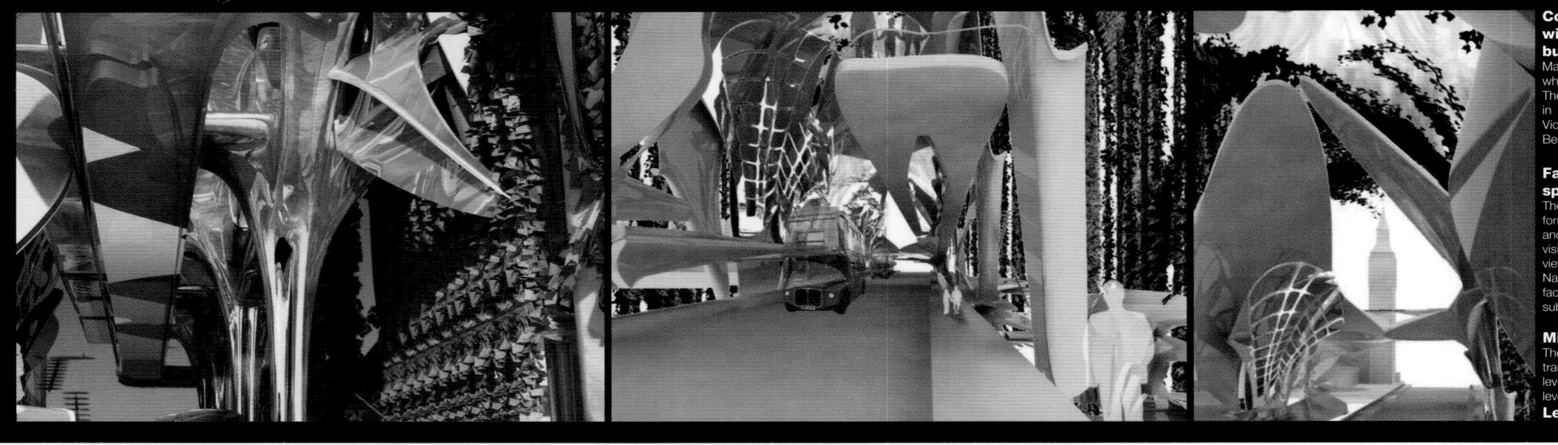

Colours a with the buildings
Market stalls where cust These pods in coherence Victorian orn Ben and the

Far left spaces
The elegant forms create and surprise visitors to go viewing balc Natural dayl facade to t sublime cath

Middle: F
The new tranportantic level, while levels of the

Left: A ne

1154

Left: Floating system of docks for water delivery transport and leisure canoes and kayaks
The new hybridized bridge creates a new way of transport through a series of floating water docking systems for water transport vehicles such as small delivery boats for food delivery, as well as canoes and kayaks for public leisure activities.

The biosynthetic garden - A biomimetic landscape of botanic lushness and exuberance
The living flesh creates a zone of CO2 absorbers from the local atmosphere in a process skin to natural photosynthesis, this acts as a catalyst for the living plants and synthetic plant structures to grow and release oxygen back into the atmosphere. The impact of human interference, such as light and air pollution from the road bridge and river Thames, is processed ecologically so that it is beneficial in developing and strengthening the food production process.

Key

Cross section / Longitudinal section

a. Retractable PVC water collection roof canopy
b. Archifoliage Veils structure
c. Flexible 'Bin-pods'
d.Tomato farm
e. Viewing balcony 1F
f. Beans farm
g. Staircase ramp down to floating docks
h. Green skin enclosure
i. Cumcumber farm
j. Storage
k. Loading area
l. Bus stop
m. Community space
n. Houses of Parliament

Farmer's Market | *Horhizon consortium*

Beer Hops Farm – Brewerymarket
3rd Place Winner Farmer's Market International Design Competition
Type : Agriculture and Urbanism
Design : Kenny Kinugasa Tsui, Lorene Faure

Urban Agriculture Beer Hops Farm - Brewerymarket

Introduction

This urban agricultural proposal is a 'Beer Hops Farm Brewerymarket' that aims to create a new place for the exchange of goods and service in the historic Highland Square district of West Highlands neighborhood. The Brewerymarket's main entrance is on West 32 Avenue, enroute to Downtown Denver where the annual American Beer Festival at the Colorado Convention Center is held. The building acts as a 'reception' to the global events of Denver and strengthens West Highland neighborhood's local identity through an innovative year round programming including hop plant farming, beer making, and providing flexible vending market spaces with a community events venue for arts and music performances.

Architectural interpretations

Hop plant (Humulus Lupulus) is a vigorous climbing vegetation and hops are used primarily as an important flavoring and stability agent in the beer making process. The proposal creates the sensual experience of a vibrant 'garden' where the hops are farmed on hop poles to create the building's green main facade. The adjustable assembly systems of the modular vending bins are inspired from the natural material properties of hop pods.

Artistic inspiration from nature - Water collection retractable roof membrane

The transparent foldable PVC roof canopy acts as a condenser for reclaiming water for storage which is then used in the brewery and watering for the beer hops farm facade. The technique for this lightweight system is simple and its cost of maintenance is low.

The folding geometry of the roof canopy takes inspiration from a plant and maximizes its surface area for heat exchange. It dissipates its heat at night and allows for the condensation of water vapor from the air, as well as directing rain water to the white funnels.

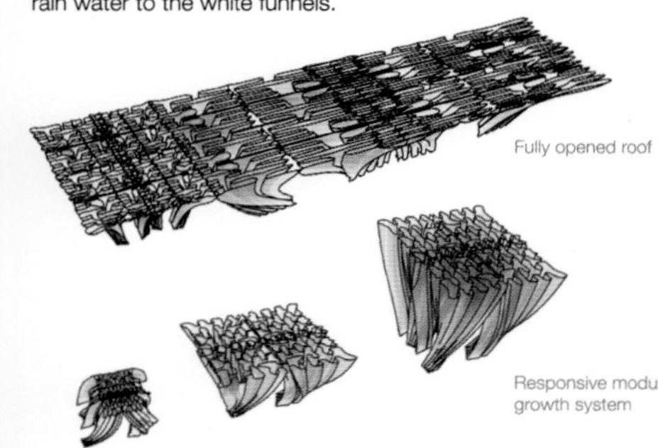

Left: Identity in the neighborhood - Retractable roof glows during year round events

The roof canopy is electronically controlled using a simple cable pulley system to 'open' and expand to cover a bigger area during rain and night dew time for condensation. The transparent material can be beautifully lit during community events which could be seen clearly from the surrounding neighborhood.

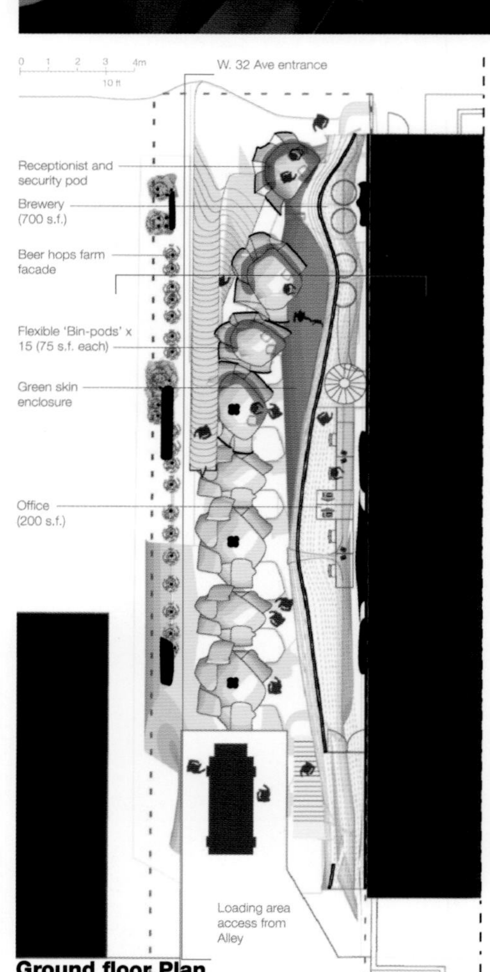

Ground floor Plan

- The flexible open and enclosed public spaces on all levels provide year round opportunities for events.

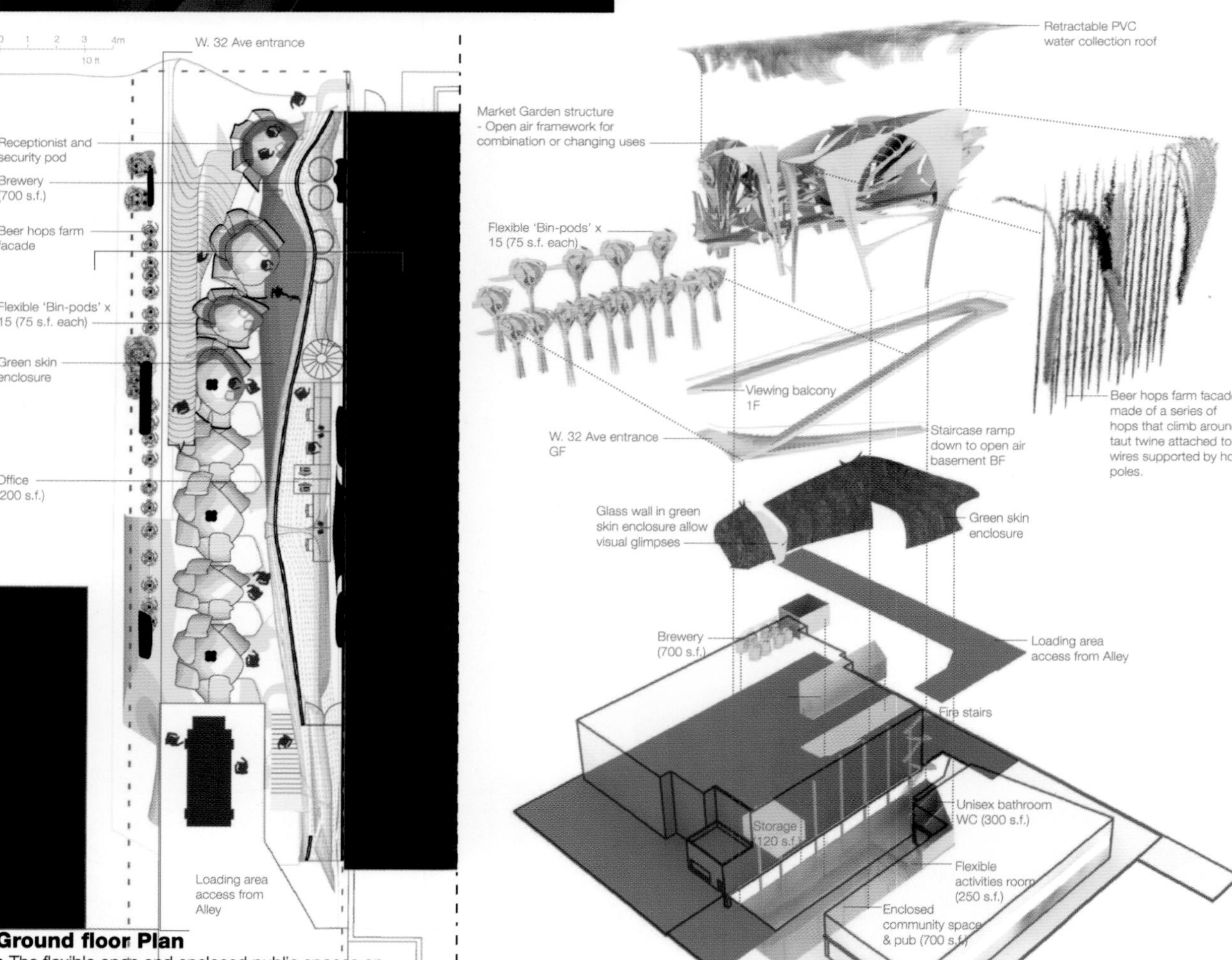

Key

Cross section / Longitudinal sectic

a. Retractable PVC water collection roof canopy
b. Market Garden structure
c. Flexible 'Bin-pods' x 15 (75 s.f. each)
d. Beer hops farm facade
e. Viewing balcony 1F
f. W. 32 Ave entrance GF
g. Staircase ramp down to open air basement B
h. Green skin enclosure
i. Glimpses through the glass wall
j. Brewery (700 s.f.)
k. Loading area access from Alley
l. Office (200 s.f.)
m. Fire stairs
n. Storage (120 s.f.)
o. Unisex bathroom WC (300 s.f.)
p. Flexible activities room (250 s.f.)
q. Enclosed community space (700 s.f.)

A vertical garden of earthly deligh

The Brewerymarket is a living 'garden' that inha
is filled with wonderful opportunities for urban cu
through the pavilion-like copper vending 'Bin-po
spaces, creating opportunities for a sensual and
pleasant plant smells and rays of natural daylight

Multiple cross programming of pub

The local community can use the flexible spaces
including art exhibitions, educational workshops,
'Bin-pods' during the day and weekends. At nig
events while the glowing roof canopy is expande

A viable identity for community out

The Brewerymarket would be identified as a loca
provides opportunities for the community to be i
participate in farming, harvesting, and brewing be
to the attractions created by the annual America

Far left: Sublime & eventful spaces
The elegant geometries of the architectural forms create intimate spaces for exploration and surprises. The staircase ramp entices public visitors to go up to the upper vendor's level and viewing balcony.

Natural daylight filters through the beer hops farm facade to the interior lower levels, creating a sublime cathedral-like experience.

Left: Enticing public & community
The main entrance is positioned on 32nd Avenue. Upon arrival, an enticing circulation ramp directs one's curiosity to finding the copper vending 'Bin-pods' on the upper level and the lower level brewery.

The green skin on the ground area provides enclosure for the lower level spaces such as the brewery and the office, with openings to provide visual transparency and natural daylight.

West longitudinal section
A contemporary public place

- The lower level consists of a flexible space for art and music performances, a community venue and a pub in the brewery area.
- The upper level consists of flexible vending 'Bin-pods' for arts and crafts.

der
that links all
poetic appreciation of

n array of flexible events
use the adjustable vending
vith festive art and music

and local produce. The brewery
the hop farm, where they could
as a global and touristic connection
own Denver.

089

Unesco | *Horhizon consortium*

Cultural Alignments – Architecture Coexisting with World Heritage Sites
Type : Masterplan
Design : Johan Voordouw

CULTURAL ALIGNMENTS - Architecture Coexisting with World Heritage Sites
43rd Annual Central Glass International Design Competition, 2008

Each UNESCO World Heritage Site is a moment and a monument rich in cultural history. This project seeks to strengthen these connections to our communal past by linking places to other related World Heritage Sites.

The term 'cultural alignments' describes both the architecture's physical and programmatic intensions. The project sought to use architecture as a conduit for preservation and education of both a specific site and of a growing network.

Every site would develop a pavilion that would physically shift to reveal differing spatial alignments creating continually varied spaces of informed connection in which visitors can experience the breadth of UNESCO's programs. Simultaneously each new alignment expresses how World Heritage ties to other sites revealing the diverse characteristics that make each site unique but relevant in a broader historical and geo-typological context.

The constructed and perceived axis illustrates a specific alignment of connectedness, linking specific locations and associating sites in terms of chronology, typology and geography forming a multi-layered map of our local, regional and international heritage.

Vivaigle | *gutiérrez-delafuente arquitectos*

Location : Aigle, Switzerland
Client : City of Aigle, Europan

Program : At the heart of the city - activation of the inner city of Aigle with 6acupuncture actions and a public space healing therapy
Architects : Natalia Gutiérrez & Julio de la Fuente
Collaborators : Paul-Rouven Denz

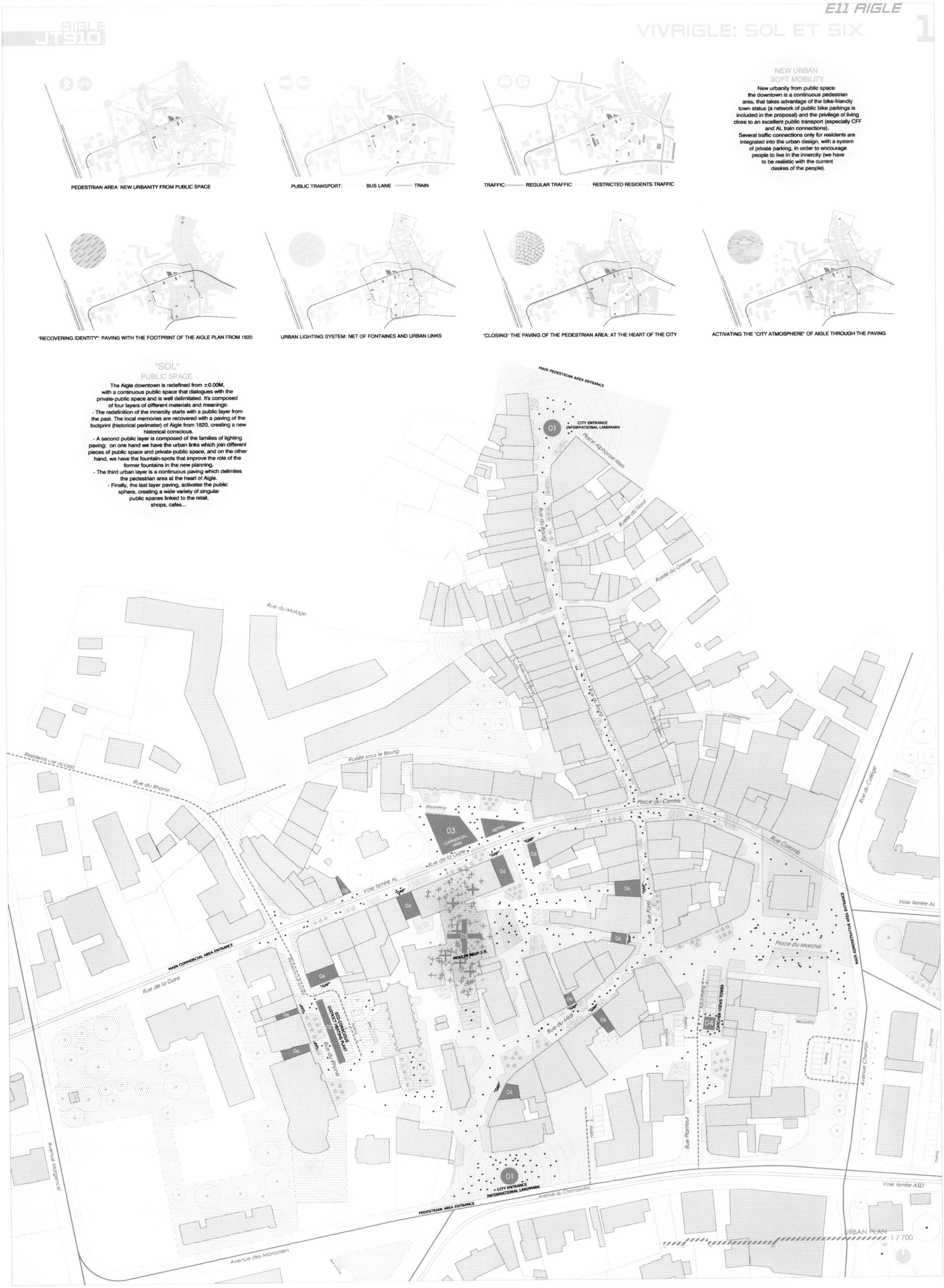

E11 AIGLE

AIGLE JT910

VIVAIGLE: SOL ET SIX

1

PEDESTRIAN AREA: NEW URBANITY FROM PUBLIC SPACE

PUBLIC TRANSPORT: BUS LANE TRAIN

TRAFFIC: REGULAR TRAFFIC RESTRICTED RESIDENTS TRAFFIC

NEW URBAN SOFT MOBILITY

New urbanity from public space: the downtown is a continuous pedestrian area, that takes advantage of the bike-friendly town status (a network of public bike parkings is included in the proposal) and the privilege of living close to an excellent public transport (especially CFF and AL train connections).
Several traffic connections only for residents are integrated into the urban design, with a system of private parking, in order to encourage people to live in the innercity (we have to be realistic with the current desires of the people).

"RECOVERING IDENTITY": PAVING WITH THE FOOTPRINT OF THE AIGLE PLAN FROM 1820

URBAN LIGHTING SYSTEM: NET OF FONTAINES AND URBAN LINKS

"CLOSING" THE PAVING OF THE PEDESTRIAN AREA: AT THE HEART OF THE CITY

ACTIVATING THE "CITY ATMOSPHERE" OF AIGLE THROUGH THE PAVING

"SOL" PUBLIC SPACE

The Aigle downtown is redefined from ±0.00M, with a continuous public space that dialogues with the private-public space and is well delimitated. It's composed of four layers of different materials and meanings:
- The redefinition of the innercity starts with a public layer from the past. The local memories are recovered with a paving of the footprint (historical perimeter) of Aigle from 1820, creating a new historical conscious.
- A second public layer is composed of the families of lighting paving: on one hand we have the urban links which join different pieces of public space and private-public space, and on the other hand, we have the fountain-spots that improve the role of the former fountains in the new planning.
- The third urban layer is a continuous paving which delimites the pedestrian area at the heart of Aigle.
- Finally, the last layer paving, activates the public sphere, creating a wide variety of singular public spaces linked to the retail, shops, cafes...

MAIN PEDESTRIAN AREA ENTRANCE

CITY ENTRANCE INFORMATIONAL LANDMARK

MAIN COMMERCIAL AREA ENTRANCE

PEDESTRIAN AREA ENTRANCE

URBAN PLAN 1/700

AIGLE JT910

E11 AIGLE

VIVAIGLE: SOL ET SIX 2

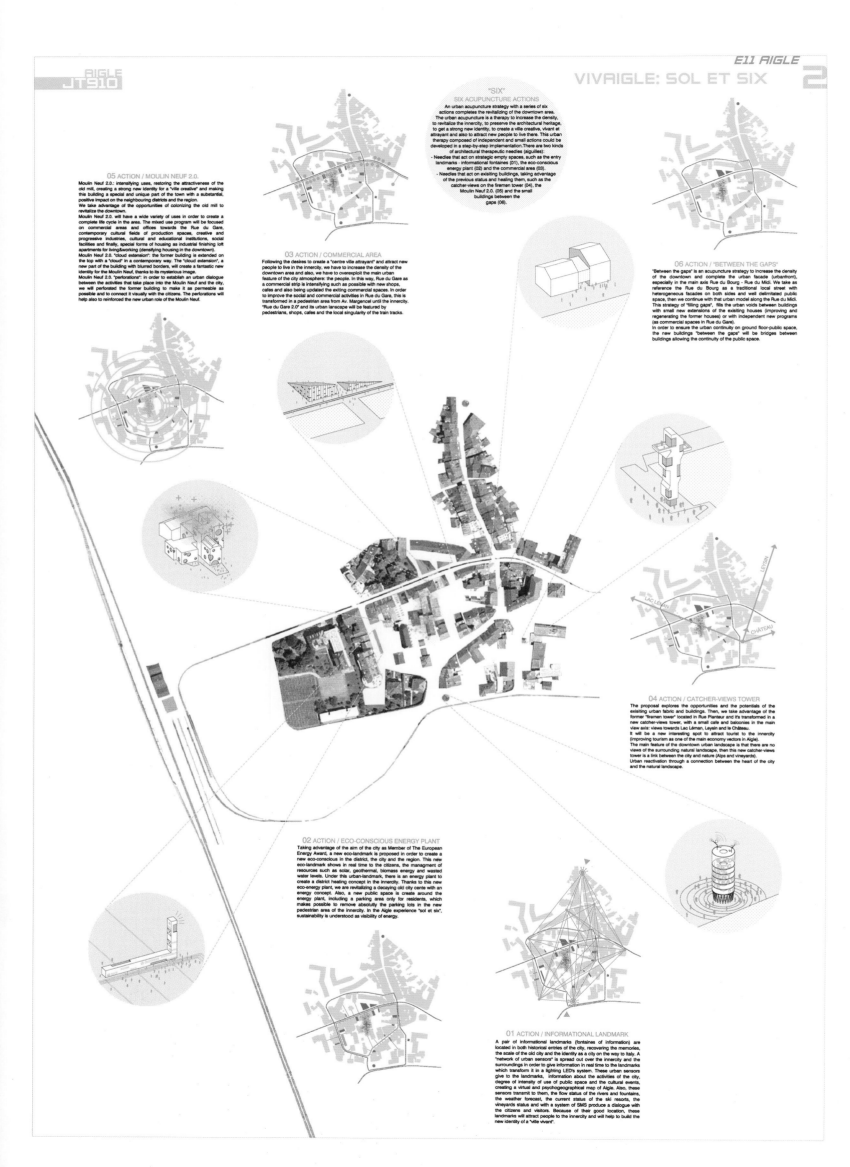

"SIX"

SIX ACUPUNCTURE ACTIONS

An urban acupuncture strategy with a series of six actions completes the revitalizing of the downtown area. The urban acupuncture is a therapy to increase the density, to revitalize the innercity, to preserve the architectural heritage, to get a strong new identity, to create a ville creative, vivant et attrayant and also to attract new people to live there. This urban therapy composed of independent and small actions could be developed in a step-by-step implementation.There are two kinds of architectural therapeutic needles (aiguilles):

- Needles that act on strategic empty spaces, such as the entry landmarks - informational fontaines (01), the eco-conscious energy plant (02) and the commercial area (03).
- Needles that act on exisiting buildings, taking advantage of the previous status and healing them, such as the catcher-views on the firemen tower (04), the Moulin Neuf 2.0. (05) and the small buildings between the gaps (06).

05 ACTION / MOULIN NEUF 2.0.

Moulin Neuf 2.0.: intensifying uses, restoring the attractiveness of the old mill, creating a strong new identity for a "ville creative" and making this building a special and unique part of the town with a substantial, positive impact on the neighbouring districts and the region.

We take advantage of the opportunities of colonizing the old mill to revitalize the downtown.

Moulin Neuf 2.0. will have a wide variety of uses in order to create a complete life cycle in the area. The mixed use program will be focused on commercial areas and offices towards the Rue du Gare, contemporary cultural fields of production spaces, creative and progressive industries, cultural and educational institutions, social facilities and finally, special forms of housing as industrial finishing loft apartments for living&working (densifying housing in the downtown).

Moulin Neuf 2.0. "cloud extension": the former building is extended on the top with a "cloud" in a contemporary way. The "cloud extension", a new part of the building with blurred borders, will create a fantastic new identity for the Moulin Neuf, thanks to its mysterious image.

Moulin Neuf 2.0. "perforations": in order to establish an urban dialogue between the activities that take place into the Moulin Neuf and the city, we will perforated the former building to make it as permeable as possible and to connect it visually with the citizens. The perforations will help also to reinforced the new urban role of the Moulin Neuf.

03 ACTION / COMMERCIAL AREA

Following the desires to create a "centre ville attrayant" and attract new people to live in the innercity, we have to increase the density of the downtown area and also, we have to overexploit the main urban feature of the city atmosphere: the people. In this way, Rue du Gare as a commercial strip is intensifying such as possible with new shops, cafes and also being updated the exiting commercial spaces. In order to improve the social and commercial activities in Rue du Gare, this is transformed in a pedestrian area from Av. Margencel until the innercity. "Rue du Gare 2.0" and its urban lanscape will be featured by pedestrians, shops, cafes and the local singularity of the train tracks.

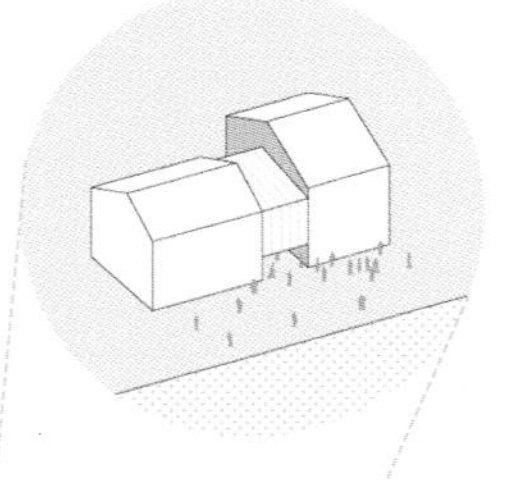

06 ACTION / "BETWEEN THE GAPS"

"Between the gaps" is an acupuncture strategy to increase the density of the downtown and complete the urban facade (urbanfront), especially in the main axis Rue du Bourg - Rue du Midi. We take as reference the Rue du Bourg as a traditional local street with heterogeneous facades on both sides and well delimitated public space, then we continue with that urban model along the Rue du Midi. This strategy of "filling gaps", fills the urban voids between buildings with small new extensions of the exisiting houses (improving and regenerating the former houses) or with independent new programs (as commercial spaces in Rue du Gare).

In order to ensure the urban continuity on ground floor-public space, the new buildings "between the gaps" will be bridges between buildings allowing the continuity of the public space.

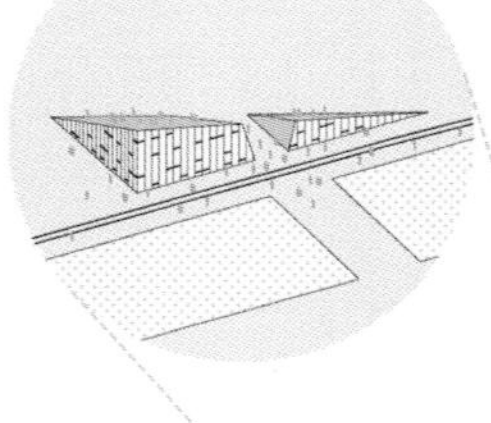

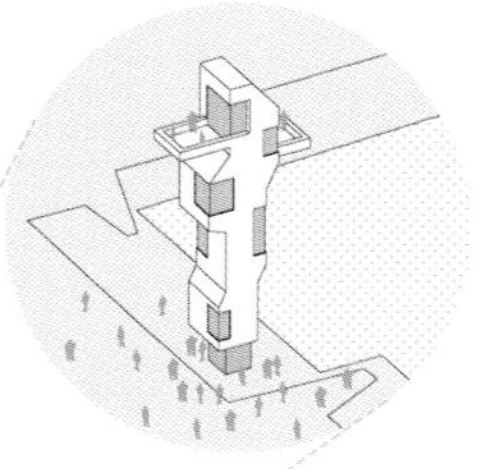

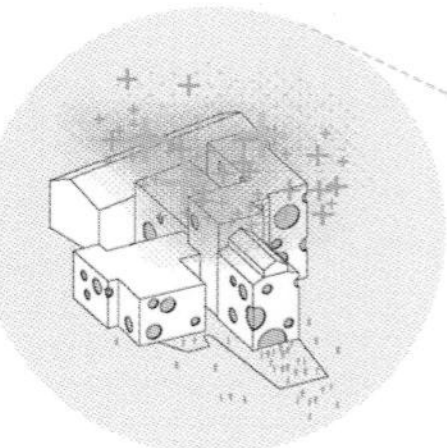

04 ACTION / CATCHER-VIEWS TOWER

The proposal explores the opportunities and the potentials of the exisiting urban fabric and buildings. Then, we take advantage of the former "firemen tower" located in Rue Planteur and it's transformed in a new catcher-views tower, with a small cafe and balconies in the main view axis: views towards Lac Léman, Leysin and le Château.

It will be a new interesting spot to attract tourist to the innercity (improving tourism as one of the main economy vectors in Aigle).

The main feature of the downtown urban landscape is that there are no views of the surrounding natural landscape, then this new catcher-views tower is a link between the city and nature (Alps and vineyards).

Urban reactivation through a connection between the heart of the city and the natural landscape.

02 ACTION / ECO-CONSCIOUS ENERGY PLANT

Taking advantage of the aim of the city as Member of The European Energy Award, a new eco-landmark is proposed in order to create a new eco-conscious in the district, the city and the region. This new eco-landmark shows in real time to the citizens, the managment of resources such as solar, geothermal, biomass energy and wasted water levels. Under this urban-landmark, there is an energy plant to create a district heating concept in the innercity. Thanks to this new eco-energy plant, we are revitalizing a decaying old city cente with an energy concept. Also, a new public space is create around the energy plant, including a parking area only for residents, which makes possible to remove absolutly the parking lots in the new pedestrian area of the innercity. In the Aigle experience "sol et six", sustainability is understood as visibility of energy.

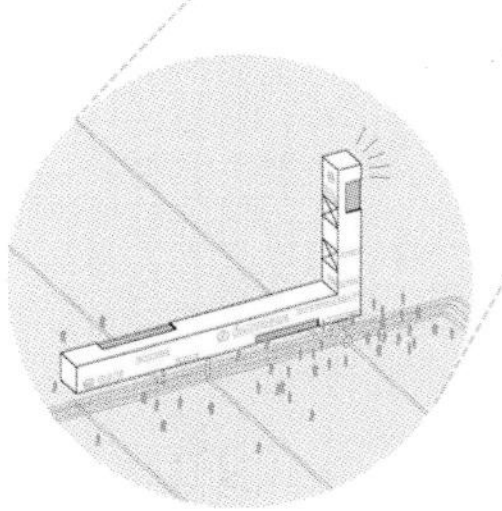

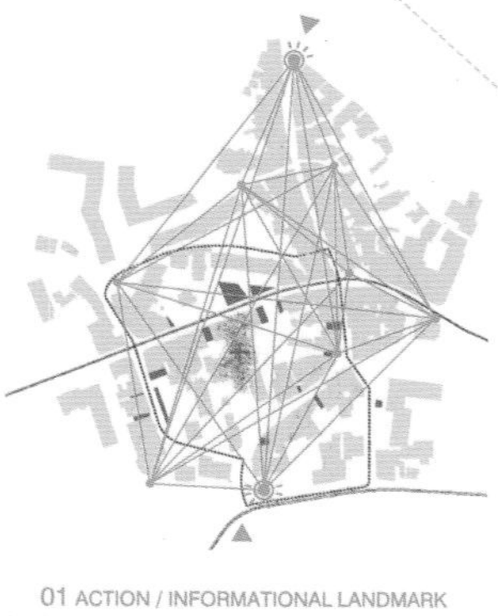

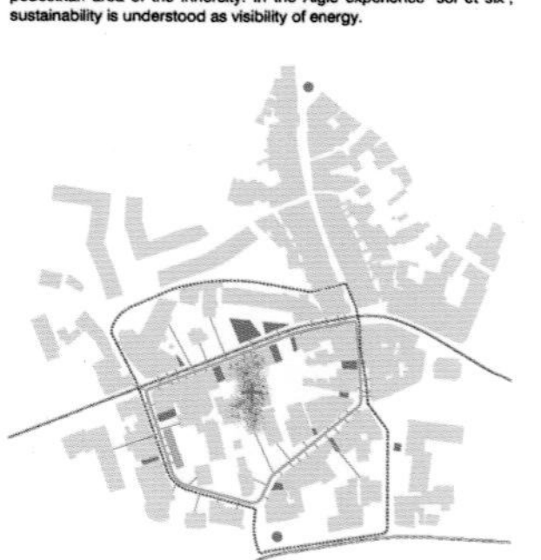

01 ACTION / INFORMATIONAL LANDMARK

A pair of informational landmarks (fontaines of information) are located in both historical entries of the city, recovering the memories, the scale of the old city and the identity as a city on the way to Italy. A "network of urban sensors" is spread out over the innercity and the surroundings in order to give information in real time to the landmarks which transform it in a lighting LED's system. These urban sensors give to the landmarks, information about the activities of the city, degree of intensity of use of public space and the cultural events, creating a virtual and psychogeographical map of Aigle. Also, these sensors transmit to them, the flow status of the rivers and fountains, the weather forecast, the current status of the ski resorts, the vineyards status and with a system of SMS produce a dialogue with the citizens and visitors. Because of their good location, these landmarks will attract people to the innercity and will help to build the new identity of a "ville vivant".

E11 AIGLE

VIVAIGLE: SOL ET SIX

3

AU CROISEMENT RUE DU MIDI, CHEMIN DES MARRONNIERS ET AV CHAMOSSAIRE
ENTRANCE-LANDMARK LIGHTING STATUS= LOW INTENSITY OF USE OF PUBLIC SPACE

HOTEL-DE-VILLE ET PLACE DU MARCHE

SUR RUE DE LA GARE, A L'ANGLE DE LA RUE DU RHONE

EN PLEIN COEUR DE AIGLE, RUE DU MIDI

AU CROISEMENT RUE DU MIDI, CHEMIN DES MARRONNIERS ET AV.CHAMOSSAIRE
ENTRANCE-LANDMARK LIGHTING STATUS= HIGH INTENSITY OF USE OF PUBLIC SPACE

RUE DU MIDI

RUE DE LA GARE

ANGLE RUE DE LA GARE, RUE DU RHONE

RUE DU RHONE

ANGLE RUE PLANTOUR, AVENUE DU CHAMOSSAIRE

RUE FAREL

ANGLE RUE DE LA GARE, RUE FAREL, RUE DU BOURG

Leo Major | *gutiérrez-delafuente arquitectos*

Project : 1st Prize National Competition Transite 06 for the World Architecture Day
Program : World Architecture Day Art Work Ligthing art installation
Location : Almería, Spain

Architects : Natalia Gutiérrez & Julio de la Fuente
Client : City of Almería, Junta de Andalucía, COA Almería

almería / leo major / 1/2

una galaxia artificial de LED y fibra óptica , representa en todo momento con distintos grados de intensidad luminosa , la actividad pública del barrio, gracias a unos medidores de actividad colocados en los bares del entorno que mandan la señal en tiempo real a la medianera-galaxia.

foto/cúmulo estelar de las pléyades

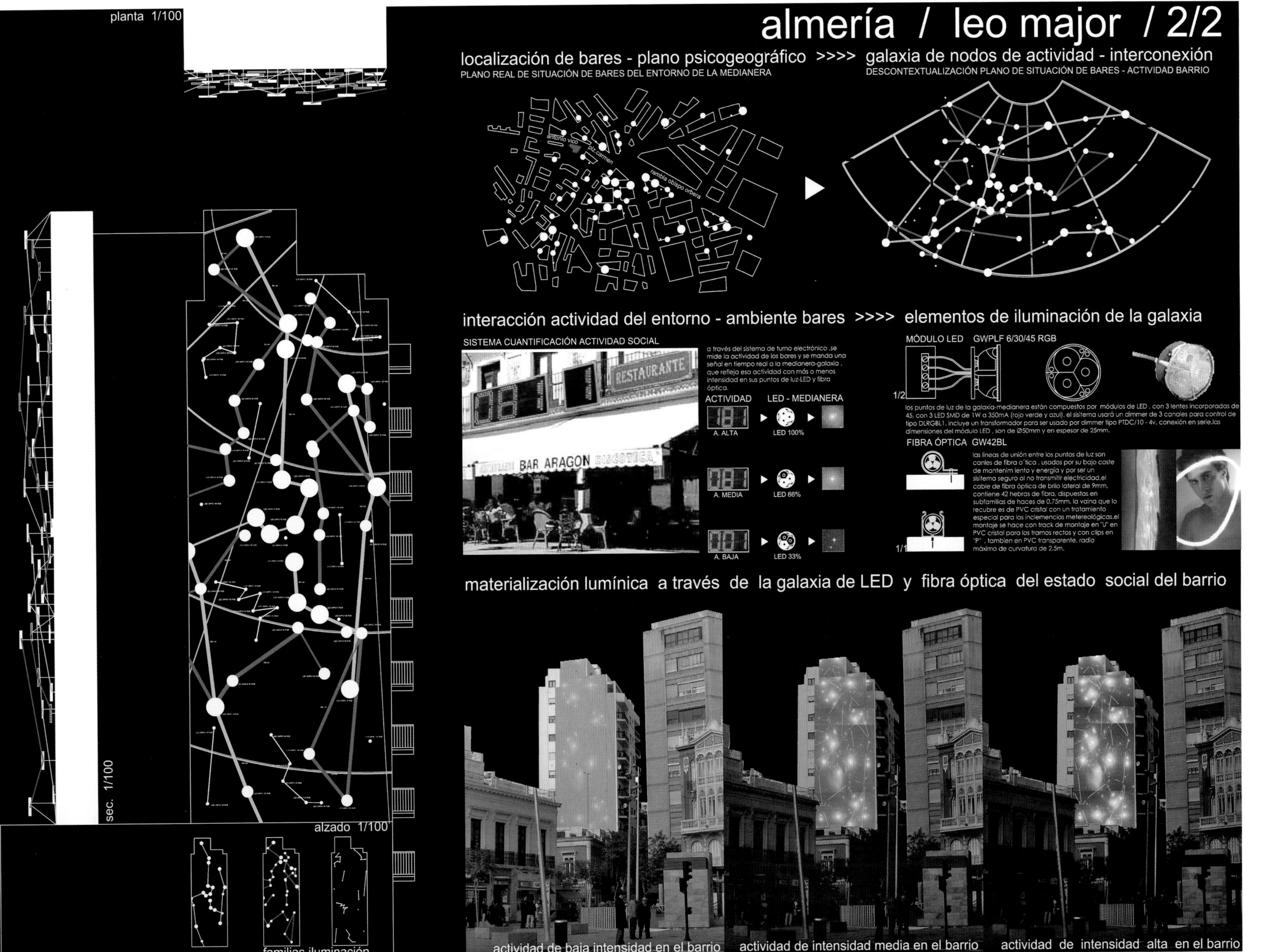
almería / leo major / 2/2
planta 1/100
localización de bares - plano psicogeográfico >>>> galaxia de nodos de actividad - interconexión
PLANO REAL DE SITUACIÓN DE BARES DEL ENTORNO DE LA MEDIANERA
DESCONTEXTUALIZACIÓN PLANO DE SITUACIÓN DE BARES - ACTIVIDAD BARRIO
antonio vico
plz.carmen
rambla obispo orbera
interacción actividad del entorno - ambiente bares >>>> elementos de iluminación de la galaxia
SISTEMA CUANTIFICACIÓN ACTIVIDAD SOCIAL
RESTAURANTE
BAR ARAGON
a través del sistema de turno electrónico ,se mide la actividad de los bares y se manda una señal en tiempo real a la medianera-galaxia , que refleja esa actividad con más o menos intensidad en sus puntos de luz-LED y fibra óptica.
ACTIVIDAD
LED - MEDIANERA
A. ALTA
LED 100%
A. MEDIA
LED 66%
A. BAJA
LED 33%
MÓDULO LED GWPLF 6/30/45 RGB
1/2
los puntos de luz de la galaxia-medianera están compuestos por módulos de LED , con 3 lentes incorporadas de 45, con 3 LED SMD de 1W a 350mA (rojo verde y azul). el sisitema usará un dimmer de 3 canales para control de tipo DLRGBL1. incluye un transformador para ser usado por dimmer tipo PTDC/10 - 4v. conexión en serie.las dimensiones del módulo LED , son de Ø50mm y en espesor de 25mm.
FIBRA ÓPTICA GW42BL
las lineas de unión entre los puntos de luz son canles de fibra o´tica , usados por su bajo coste de mantenim iento y energía y por ser un sisitema seguro al no transmitir electricidad.el cable de fibra óptica de brilo lateral de 9mm, contiene 42 hebras de fibra, dispuestas en subfamilias de haces de 0.75mm, la vaina que lo recubre es de PVC cristal con un tratamiento especial para las inclemencias metereológicas.el montaje se hace con track de montaje en "U" en PVC cristal para los tramos rectos y con clips en "P" , tambien en PVC transparente. radio máximo de curvatura de 2.5m.
1/1
materialización lumínica a través de la galaxia de LED y fibra óptica del estado social del barrio
sec. 1/100
alzado 1/100
familias iluminación
actividad de baja intensidad en el barrio
actividad de intensidad media en el barrio
actividad de intensidad alta en el barrio

092 Desmaterialitations | *gutiérrez-delafuente arquitectos*

Project : 2nd Prize International Competition Europan 09 AMA "Local mutations"
Programme : Urban regeneration of an old industrial mining area in the core of the Asturias Metropolitan Area
Location : AMA, Asturias Metropolitan Area, Spain

Architects : Natalia Gutiérrez & Julio de la Fuente
Client : Hunosa, Principado de Asturias, Europan

NJ373

DESMATERIALIZACIONES >> ENTRE EL ORBAYU Y LA HULLA AMA

SISTEMA PARA LA CREACIÓN DE UNA RED DE 30 POZOS

ESTE TRABAJO RESUELVE EL EMPLAZAMIENTO AMA PROPONIENDO UN SISTEMA PARA CREAR UNA RED CON LOS 30 POZOS , EXTRAPOLANDO PRIMERO LOS CONDICIONANTES Y SOLUCIONES COMUNES A LOS TODOS LOS EMPLAZAMIENTOS Y ENSAYANDO EL SISTEMA SOBRE EL POZO CONCRETO DE SAN ANTONIO.
EL SISTEMA ARRANCA EN LA ESCALA TERRITORIAL , DEFINIENDO LA RED VIRTUAL, DOTANDO A ESTA DE PROGRAMA , CONFIRIÉNDOLA UNA MORFOLOGÍA Y UNA MANERA DE ADAPTARSE A LOS LÍMITES. DESPUÉS SE PLANTEA EL DOTAR AL SISTEMA DE UNA IDENTIDAD A TRAVÉS DE UNA OPERACIÓN DE LAND-ART Y UNA MATERIALIDAD SENSIBLE CON LA CUENCA MINERA, SU HISTORIA, CLIMA...
LAS FICHAS QUE SE ADJUNTAN FIJAN EL SISTEMA. LA CREACIÓN DE ESTA RED DE 30 POZOS ESTARÍA APOYADA EN EL TIEMPO Y SERÍA VIABLE ECONÓMICAMENTE GRACIAS A QUE PRIMERO SE ASENTARÍAN LOS PROGRAMAS TERCIARIOS VINCULADOS A LA INDUSTRIA DEL TURISMO, QUE SERÍAN UN MOTOR (YA CONOCIDO Y ÓPTIMO)PARA EL POSTERIOR DESARROLLO DE LA RED.

AUTO-TEST DE LA PROPUESTA AL GUANTE LANZADO POR EUROPAN 9 PARA ESTE EMPLAZAMIENTO:
- LA SITUACIÓN DE AISLAMIENTO SE RESUELVE COMO UN SISTEMA DE BOLSAS NODALES DE ACTIVIDAD APOYADAS EN UN SISTEMA DE INFRAESTRUCTURAS LINEALES. LA CONECTIVIDAD E INTERRELACIÓN ENTRE LOS DISTINTOS PUNTOS DEL TERRITORIO SE APOYA EN UNA OPERACIÓN DE LAND-ART Y EN LA CREACIÓN DE UNA IDENTIDAD PROPIA DE LOS EMPLAZAMIENTOS, QUE LOS INTEGRA DENTRO DE UN CONJUNTO. ADEMÁS, EN LA RED SE DA UN RELACIÓN PROGRAMÁTICA , AL CONFIGURAR UN POTENTE PROGRAMA ENTRE TODAS LAS ÁREAS DE ACTUACIÓN JUNTAS, ESTABLECIÉNDOSE ASÍ UNA CONEXIÓN EN EL TERRITORIO MÁS FUERTE QUE LA MERAMENTE FÍSICA.
- A ESCALA LOCAL, LAS BARRERAS FÍSICAS SE RESUELVEN MEDIANTE PARQUES LINEALES DE BORDE QUE ARTICULAN DIVERSOS PROGRAMAS NODALES QUE ACTIVAN EL BORDE.
- LAS RUINAS SE INTEGRAN EN LA ACTUACIÓN, SIENDO LOS FOCOS ATRACTORES DE ACTIVIDAD (TURISMO). SE INTEGRAN AL CEDERLE A LO "NUEVO" SU IDENTIDAD: ENTRE EL ORBAYU Y LA HULLA.
- LAS TRAMAS URBANAS PROPUESTAS RECORREN DE FORMA LINEAL GRAN PARTE DEL TERRITORIO Y A SU PASO VAN ARTICULANDO FRAGMENTOS OLVIDADOS Y DESCONECTADOS.

EL TERRITORIO >> RED 30 POZOS

UNA RED VIRTUAL QUE UNE LOS 30 POZOS SE TRAZA SOBRE EL TERRITORIO INDEPENDIENTEMENTE DEL SOPORTE FÍSICO.
- SE PRODUCE UN CAMBIO EN LA ECONOMÍA DE LA REGIÓN MINERA , SE PASA DE UNA ACTIVIDAD INDUSTRIAL A UNA TERCIARIA . LOS POZOS DE EXTRACCIÓN SE CONSERVAN COMO RUINAS ARQUEOLÓGICO-INDUSTRIALES QUE FUNCIONAN COMO ATRACTORES DE ACTIVIDAD, PREDOMINANDO LA ACTIVIDAD TURÍSTICA COMO GENERADORA DE EMPLEO Y RIQUEZA.
-SE CREA UN PROGRAMA TURÍSTICO Y DE SERVICIOS PARA LOS HABITANTES QUE ES GLOBAL PARA TODA LA REGIÓN , ESTE COMPLETO PROGRAMA A ESCALA COMARCAL SE DISEMINA POR LOS DISTINTOS POZOS , DOTANDO DE PROGRAMA A LA RED Y CREANDO ASÍ LOS FLUJOS ENTRE LOS POZOS, DE MANERA QUE LA RED VIRTUAL FUNCIONE.

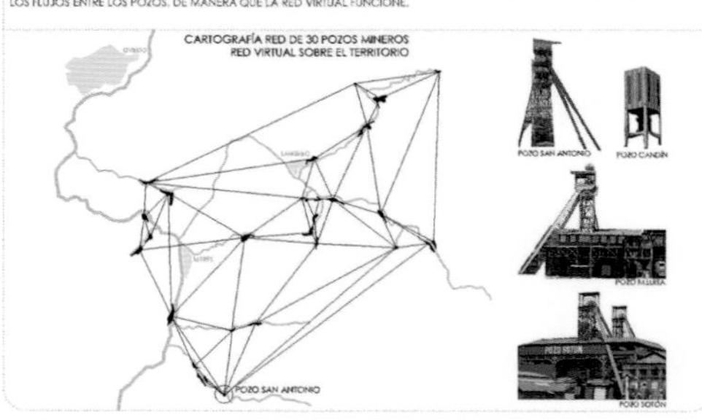

EL TERRITORIO >> "DOMINER LE SITE"

"DOMINER LE SITE, DEVENIR L'EQUIVALENCE DES RELIEFS NATURELS, CHANGER LA DIMENSION , DEVENIR RELIEF ARTIFICIEL, PAYSAGE..." CLAUDE PARENT 1966, MANIFIESTO "DOMINER LE SITE"
SE PROPONE CREAR UN MOTOR A PARTE DEL PROGRAMÁTICO, PARA QUE LOS POZOS FUNCIONEN COMO ATRACTORES DE FLUJOS. LOS SINUOSOS VALLES IMPIDEN TENER UN CONTROL TOTAL DEL TERRITORIO DESDE LO ALTO DE UN SOLO PUNTO , ASÍ QUE PARA SACIAR LA NATURAL CURIOSIDAD DEL HOMBRE POR DOMINAR EL ENTORNO, SE PROPONE SITUAR EN LOS POZOS TORRES MIRADOR DESDE LAS QUE CONTEMPLAR LA REGIÓN , DANDO UN MOTIVO PARA ACERCARSE A LOS PUNTOS DE LA RED.
LA SUMA DE LAS PEQUEÑAS CONQUISTAS VISUALES DESDE CADA NODO DAN UNA VISIÓN GLOBAL DEL ENTORNO. LA RED FUNCIONA.

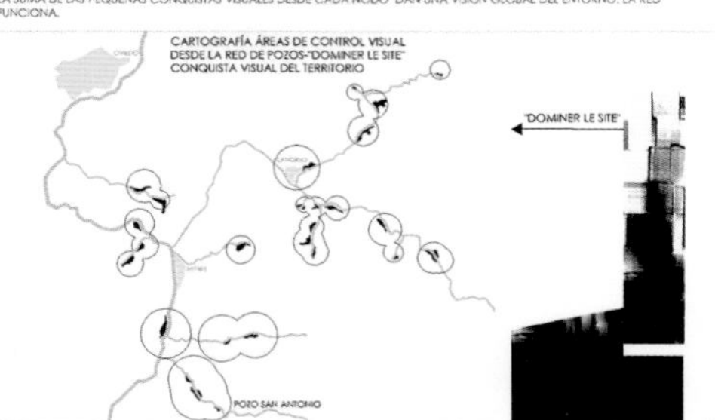

EL TERRITORIO >> HABITATS LINEALES

SE MANTIENE Y SE POTENCIA EL CONCEPTO DE HABITAT LINEAL, ASÍ QUE COMO PRIMERA MEDIDA SE ANALIZAN LA CARACTERÍSTICAS DE LAS MORFOLOGÍAS LINEALES EXISTENTES, CON ESPECIAL ATENCIÓN AL TRATAMIENTO DE LOS BORDES. LA CARRETERA DEJARÍA DE SER EFECTIVA SI HUBIESE MUCHOS NUDOS E INCORPORACIONES, POR ESO PLANTEAMOS UN SISTEMA DE ASENTAMIENTOS LINEALES CON BOLSAS O NODOS DE ACTIVIDAD APOYADOS EN PARQUES LINEALES DE BORDE.

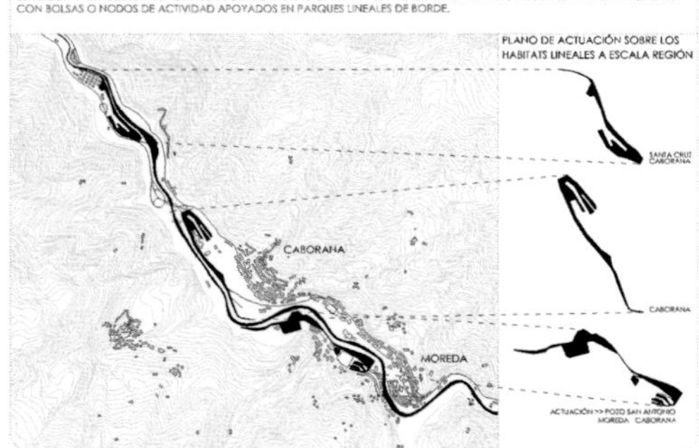

RECUPERACIÓN PAISAJÍSTICA

"RUNNING FENCE", SONOMA ET MARIN COUNTIES CALIFORNIE. 1972-76 - CHRISTO & JEANNE-CLAUDE

IMAGEN ACTUACIÓN BORDE - PAISAJE

EL FENÓMENO >> DOBLE PROGRAMA

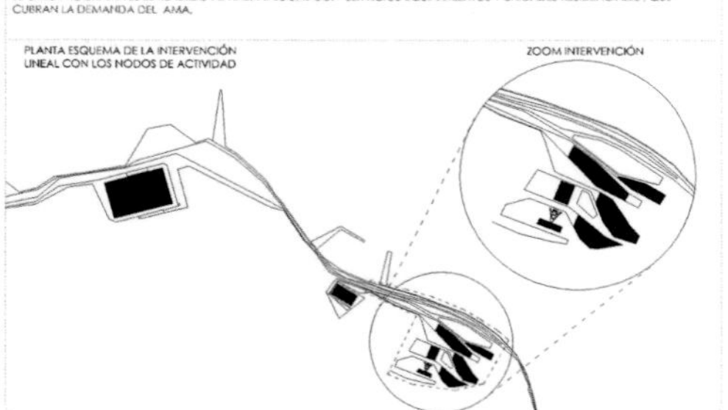

DESMATERIALIZACIONES

FOTO DE ARCHIVO - POZO SAN ANTONIO - ENTRE LA HULLA Y EL ORBAYU

FOTO ACTUAL - TARDE DE ORBAYU

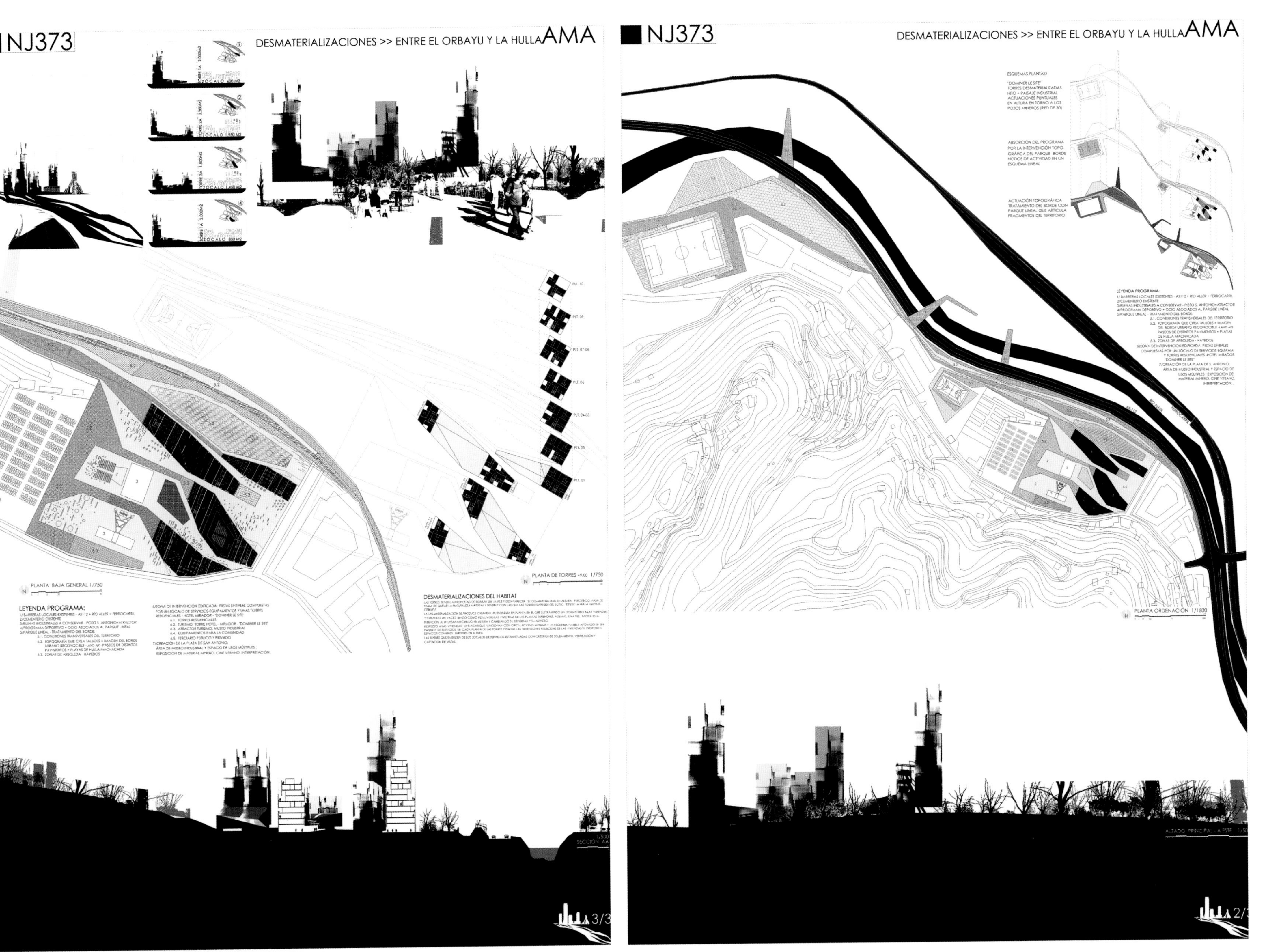
NJ373
DESMATERIALIZACIONES >> ENTRE EL ORBAYU Y LA HULLA AMA
PLANTA BAJA GENERAL 1/750
LEYENDA PROGRAMA:
PLANTA DE TORRES +9.00 1/750
DESMATERIALIZACIONES DEL HABITAT
3/3
NJ373
DESMATERIALIZACIONES >> ENTRE EL ORBAYU Y LA HULLA AMA
ESQUEMAS PLANTAS/
"DOMINER LE SITE"
TORRES DESMATERIALIZADAS
HITO + PAISAJE INDUSTRIAL
ACTUACIONES PUNTUALES
EN ALTURA EN TORNO A LOS
POZOS MINEROS (RED DE 30)
ABSORCIÓN DEL PROGRAMA
POR LA INTERVENCIÓN TOPO-
GRÁFICA DEL PARQUE BORDE
NODOS DE ACTIVIDAD EN UN
ESQUEMA LINEAL
ACTUACIÓN TOPOGRÁFICA
TRATAMIENTO DEL BORDE CON
PARQUE LINEAL QUE ARTICULA
FRAGMENTOS DEL TERRITORIO
LEYENDA PROGRAMA:
PLANTA ORDENACIÓN 1/1500
2/3

093 Local Land Art Identity | *gutiérrez-delafuente arquitectos*

Project : 2nd Prize International Competition Europan 10 Forchheim "Thinking an Urban Interface"
Program : Urban Conversion of The Old Wassner Industrial Area and Urban Regeneration of the Forchheim North District

Location : Forchheim, Germany
Architects : Natalia Gutiérrez & Julio de la Fuente
Client : Stadt Forchheim, Europan

HOW TO RESOLVE SOCIAL & URBAN PROBLEMS THROUGH A NEW STRONG IDENTITY....

THE INDUSTRIAL WAASNER AREA MEMORY IS MAINTAINED, BUT THERE IS NOTHING NOSTALGIC ABOUT THIS....WE PRESERVE THIS AIM IN ORDER TO SUBVERT IT.

BEFORE, PEOPLE SPENT THEIR TIME AND HEALTH IN THE INDUSTRIAL BUILDINGS, NOW WE SUBVERT IT AND THE INDUSTRIAL BUILDINGS ARE TRANSFORMED TO BE OF SERVICE TO THE PEOPLE'S HEALTH AND THEIR LEISURE. A GREAT ECONOMICAL AND SOCIAL CHANGE IN THE AREA IS TAKING PLACE THROUGH A NEW IDENTITY.

THE TRADEMARK DESIGNED FOR THE NEW COMPLEX IS THE PERFECT EXPRESSION OF THIS IDEA. IT WILL BE A SYMBOL. THE TRADEMARK TRANSFORMS THE OLD DIE-CAST ROTORS MANUFACTURED IN WAASNER COMPANY IN NEW ELEMENTS WHERE LIFE AND FLOWERS CAN GROW. THIS IS AN EXPRESSION OF THE NEW "USEFUL LIFE CYCLE" OF THE WAASNER AREA.

URBAN CONCEPTION

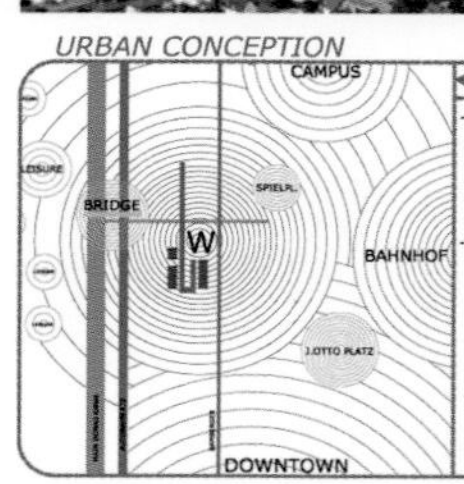

NODES NEW CENTRALITY VECTORS

-NODES: A NEW CENTRALITY IS CREATED. WAASNER AREA IS A SELF-SUFFICIENT PEDESTRIAN SCALE AREA THANKS TO THE REAL MIXED USE PROGRAM. THIS NEW CENTRALITY STARTS TO DIALOGUE WITH THE OTHERS CENTRALITIES SUCH AS DOWNTOWN, "SOCIAL CITY " MAIN PUBLIC SPACE, BAHNHOF, NORTH SCHOOLS CAMPUS AND THE OTHER SIDE OF THE KANAL

-VECTORS:
-LONGITUDINAL (SOUTH-NORTH): WE TAKE THE LINEAR MORPHOLOGY AS ANSWER TO THE BOUNDARY CONDITIONS AND THE EXISTING BARRIERS (KANAL, A73, BAMBERGER ST.). MOREOVER, WE INTEGRATE IN THE SAME AREA THE EXISTING NORTH COMMERCIAL BUILDINGS (LIDL) AND THE PETROL STATION, ALSO WE INTEGRATE IN THE INTERVENTION THE EXISTING SOCIAL AND MULTI-STOREY HOUSES.
-CROSS (EAST-WEST): WE COHESION THE DIFFERENT URBAN PIECES THROUGH THE CONTINUITY OF PUBLIC SPACE IN THIS AXIS. WE "SEW" NORTH FORCHHEIM IN THE CROSS WAY, FROM THE BAHNHOF TO THE OTHER SIDE OF THE MAIN DONAU KANAL.

LEISURE | MAIN DONAU KANAL | AUTOBAHN A73 | BAMBERGER STRASSE

URBAN CROSS INTERFACE

WE HAVE SEVERAL KINDS OF FABRICs IN CROSS WAY. WE FIND A HARD TRANSITION FROM SINGLE HOUSES TO MULTI STOREY HOUSES, WITH SOME BARRIERS AND "LONGITUDINAL WOUNDS" AS THE KANAL, A73 AND AN INDUSTRIAL AREA.
THE MAIN GOAL IS TO CONNECT IN THE CROSS DIRECTION EACH PIECE OF CITY THANKS TO THE PUBLIC SPACE AND A SOCIAL LAYER ON LEVEL ±0.00M. A STRONG CROSS CONNECTION IS REQUIRED.

FIRSTLY, WE CREATE A URBAN VOID IN WAASNER AREA, WE REUSE TWO BUILDINGS TO MAINTAIN THE HISTORICAL VIEWS AND THE CURRENT SOUND BARRIERS. WE TRANSFORM THE BUILDINGS WITH SPORT AND SOCIAL FACILITIES. THEN WE DENSIFY THE AREA WITH A LONGITUDINAL MIXED USE BUILDING. FINALLY, THIS BUILDING AND THE EXISTING TOO, ARE MODIFIED TO CREATE CROSS CONNECTIONS AND 100% OF PERMEABILITY ON GROUND FLOOR. THE NORTH AREA IS COHESIONED THANKS TO THE CONTINUOUS PUBLIC SPACE.

CURRENTLY WAASNER AREA SITUATION
URBAN VOID & REUSED BUILDINGS
MIXED USE DENSITY & FACILITIES
CONTINUITY OF CROSS PUBLIC SPACE

ABOUT PUBLIC SPACE

FIRSTLY, WE PROPOSED A DOUBLE SCALE PUBLIC SPACE:
-SPACE WHICH IS ENJOYED BY NEIGHBOURS AND PEOPLE FROM "SOCIAL CITY".
-SPACE WHICH IS AN ATTRACTOR FOR PEOPLE FROM THE WHOLE CITY. AN INTERESTING MIX WILL TAKE PLACE THEN.

SECONDLY, WE PROPOSED TWO KINDS OF PUBLIC SPACE:
-OPENED PUBLIC SPACE.
-COVERED PUBLIC SPACE (REF:SONY CENTER, BERLIN). THIS SPACE COULD BE SPONSORED BY WAASNER COMPANY TO RESPECT THE LOCAL COLLECTIVE MEMORY. (MARKET, PERFORMANCES, BIER-COVERED-GARTEN....)

FINALLY, WE PROPOSED THREE KINDS OF PUBLIC SPACE MANAGEMENT:
-PUBLIC-PUBLIC SPACE: MANAGED BY STADT FORCHHEIM.
-HYBRID SPACE: MANAGED BY NEIGHBORHOOD ASSOCIATIONS (IN CONNECTION WITH "SOCIAL CITY")
-PRIVATE-PUBLIC SPACE: MANAGED BY PRIVATE OWNERS.

NEW URBAN DIALOGUE

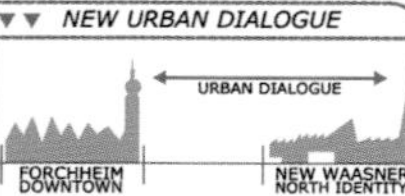

PEOPLE FROM NORTH FORCHHEIM ARE PROUD OF THEIR DISTRICT BECAUSE OF THE NEW IDENTITY. NOW, THIS AREA CAN DIALOGUE WITH THE OLD FORCHHEIM:

MIDDLE AGE CITY	NEW WAASNER AREA
ST. MARTIN'S CHURCH	ECO-URBAN LANDMARK
TRADITIONAL ARCHITECTURE	MODERN ARCHITECTURE
KULTURPFALZ / PFALZMUSEUM	ART PUBLIC SPACES
14th CENTURY WALL PAINTINGS	CONTEMPORARY ART
SMALL SHOPS / RETAIL	SMALL SHOPS / RETAIL
COMPLETE LIFE CYCLE	COMPLETE LIFE CYCLE
PEDESTRIAN SCALE	PEDESTRIAN SCALE

SOCIOLOGICAL PROGRAM

MIXED USED = LIFE CYCLE

A COMPLETE MIXED USE PROGRAM IS CREATED TO ATTRACT PEOPLE TO A PERFECT LIFE CYCLE.THIS PROGRAM CHANGES THE INDUSTRIAL WAASNER AREA IN A PIECE OF REAL CITY WHICH IS ABLE TO DIALOGUE WITH THE DOWNTOWN AND TRANSFORM NORTH FORCHHEIM.

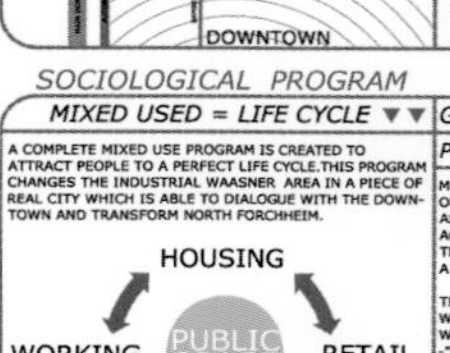

GENERATIONAL USES CROSSING

PREVENTIVE & HEALING ACUPUNCTURE

MOST OF THE NORTH FORCHHEIM PROBLEMES ARE FOCUSED ON ELDERLY AND YOUNG PEOPLE.
AS RESULT OF THIS PROBLEM, WE PROPOSE TWO KINDS OF ACUPUNCTURE IN OLD WAASNER AREA WHICH IS ABLE TO TRANSFORM THE WHOLE NORTH NEIGHBORHOOD THROUGH A PRECISE AND INTENSIVE ACTION IN WAASNER AREA.

THE GOAL IS TO REACH A COMPLETE SOCIAL COHESION WITH THE STRATEGY OF GENERATIONAL USES CROSSING. WE GET THAT IDEA WITH A DOUBLE KIND OF ACUPUNCTURE
-"PREVENTIVE ACUPUNCTURE" WORKS TO AVOID YOUNG PEOPLE LEAVE THE CITY AND TO IMPROVE THEIR SOCIAL FACILITIES, TRAINING AND SUITABLE JOBS.
-"HEALING ACUPUNCTURE" WORKS TO IMPROVE THE ELDERLY PEOPLE'S LIFE. THEY ARE STILL USEFUL, AND THEY HAVE TO BUILD A NEW SOCIETY WITH THE OTHER GENERATIONS.

IF BOTH KINDS OF ACUPUNCTURE WORK , WE WILL BE ABLE TO REACH A NEW SOCIAL COHESION IN NORTH AREA.

ECONOMIC SYSTEM

HOW TO DEVELOPE THE WAASNER AREA WITH A VIABLE MANAGEMENT? HOW TO OBTAIN YIELD AND AT THE SAME TIME TO CREATE SOCIAL AND CULTURAL FACILITIES AND A HIGH QUALITY PUBLIC SPACE?

WE PROPOSE A HIGH DENSITY BUILDING THAT CONCENTRATES THE MIXED USE PROGRAM AND WHICH IS SOLD IN THE PRIVATE SECTOR. THE PUBLIC SPACE AND THE SOCIAL AND SPORTS FACILITIES IN THE OLD INDUSTRIAL BUILDINGS WILL BE AFFORDED THROUGH THAT PRIVATE INVESTMENT. THE CYCLE WORKS!!!

SPORT & SOCIAL FACILITIES ← €€ ← PRIVATE €€ SALE WAASNER → €€ → PUBLIC SPACE

INDUSTRIAL RUINS MANAGEMENT

THE AREA IS GOING TO SUFFER A GREAT ECONOMIC AND SOCIAL CHANGE. WE SUBVERT THE OLD INDUSTRIAL BUILDINGS WITH A CHANGE OF USES. BEFORE PEOPLE USED TO GO THERE TO WORK AND NOW PEOPLE ARE GOING THERE TO ENJOY THEMSELVES, TO DO SPORTS, TO TAKE LESSONS, TO SOCIALIZE... IT'S A SYMBOL OF THE CHANGE. "SOCIAL CITY" PEOPLE WILL BE PROUD OF THEIR NEIGHBORHOOD. THE "AIM" OF THE AREA IS GOING TO CHANGE.
WE REUSED THE INDUSTRIAL BUILDINGS TO MAINTAIN THE COLLECTIVE MEMORIES OF THE PLACE AND THE ACOUSTIC EAST BARRIER TO BAMBERGER STRASSE. WE INTEND TO MAKE THE BUILDINGS MORE PERMEABLE ON THE GROUND FLOOR TO IMPROVE THE PUBLIC SPACE CONTINUITY.
ALSO WE PROPOSE BRIDGES TO CONNECT THESE BUILDINGS WITH THE MAIN MIXED USE BUILDING TO CREATE A REAL MIXED USE IN SEVERAL LEVELS. MATTA-CLARK ART-WORKS ARE TAKEN AS REFERENCE TO TRANSFORM THE OLD BUILDINGS IN CONTEMPORARY AND QUALIFIED SPACES.

01

02

MATERIAL & LOCAL IDENTITY

03

LOCAL IDENTITY

IN THE WAY OF CREATING A STRONG IDENTITY THROUGH A LOCAL LAND ART ACTION, WE ARE VERY CLOSE TO THE REGIONAL ITEMS AND REFERENCES. OVER THESE, WE ARE ABLE TO CREATE A NEW LANGUAGE WITH THESE TOOLS. LOCAL REFERENCES ARE COMPOSED BY OUR MEMORIES.

IN ADDITION TO THESE LOCAL REFERENCES, WE USE SOME WORKS OF FELICE VARINI, CHRISTO&JEANE-CLAUDE, AND GORDON MATTA-CLARK, ABOUT HOW TO TRANSFORM A PLACE WITH A MINIMAL ACTION ALONG THE TERRITORY.

THAT "LAND ART IDENTITY" WILL HAVE TWO SCALES:
-LOCAL SCALE, WHERE NORTH FORCHHEIM PEOPLE WILL RECOGNIZE & WILL BE PROUD OF THEIR NEIGHBORHOOD.
-REGIONAL SCALE, THE STRONG IDENTITY WILL BE KNOWN OUTSIDE THE CITY AND IT WILL BE A REFERENT RECYCLED INDUSTRIAL AREA.

04

MEMORIES AND ART-WORKS

01 "CUTTING EDGE", NEW YORK 1969, BY GORDON MATTA-CLARK
02 PHOTO TAKEN IN RECLYCED INDUSTRIAL AREA, LONDON, SUMMER 2008, BY US.
03 PHOTO TAKEN IN KAISERBURG, NÜRNBERG SPRING 2009, BY US.
04 REGIONAL FLAG.
05 "QUART DE DISQUE ET ARCS DE CERCLES", VILLE DE FONTENAY-LE-COMTE 2003, BY FELICE VARINI.
06 "RUNNING FENCE", SONOMA ET MARIN COUNTIES, CALIFORNIE 1972-76, BY CHRISTO & JEANNE-CLAUDE
07 DOWNTOWN FORCHHEIM VIEW. 2009. WEBSITE.
08 PHOTO OF HALF-TIMBERED WALLS TAKEN IN FORCHHEIM, SPRING 2009, BY US.
09 PHOTO OF TRADITIONAL SLOPE ROOF TAKEN IN FORCHHEIM, SPRING 2009, BY US.

05

NEW COLLECTIVE IDENTITY

THROUGH ECO-SOCIAL CONSCIENCE

IN THE SAME WAY THAT THIS NEW LOCAL IDENTITY IS CREATED THROUGH A SIMPLE ACTION, WE PROPOSE TO CREATE A NEW ECO-IDENTITY THROUGH A NEW COLLECTIVE CONSCIENCE ABOUT ENERGY MANAGEMENT AND NATURAL RESOURCES, SPECIALLY THE WATER. WE PROPOSE TWO MAIN ACTIONS FOR IT:

-THE NEW LANDMARK CONTAINS THE INSTALLATIONS OF THE COMPLEX. IT SHOWS BY ITSELF IN REAL TIME THE STATE OF MANAGEMENT OF RESOURCES (SOLAR ENERGY, GEOTHERMAL, BIOMASS, WASTED WATER ...), SO PEOPLE WILL HAVE A CONSCIENCE ABOUT IT. THAT INFO-ENERGY LANDMARK WILL BE A NEW URBAN AND SOCIAL REFERENCE IN FORCHHEIM AND THE REGION.

-ABOUT WATER, WE PROPOSED SOME GREEN-PLATFORMS AREA IN THE MAIN DONAU KANAL WITH PLANTS TO RECYCLE GREY AND STORM WATER. THIS WATER WILL BE REUSED AND WILL BE PART OF THE NEW PUBLIC SPACE AS "WATER CIRCLES" AND PLAYGROUND AREAS.

06

HYBRID SCALE

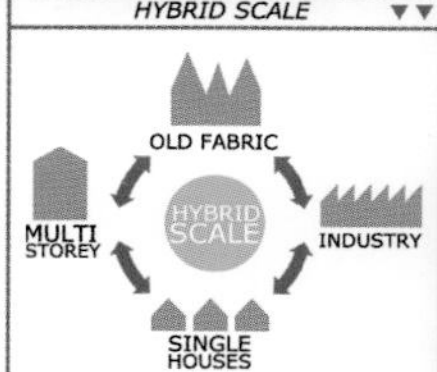

07

HYBRID TYPOLOGY

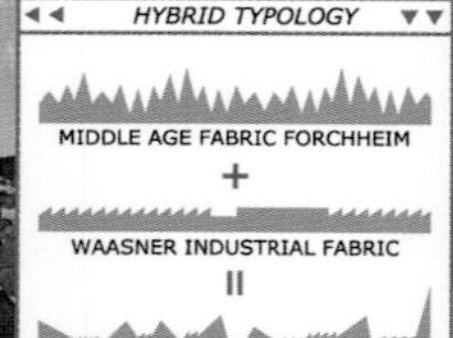

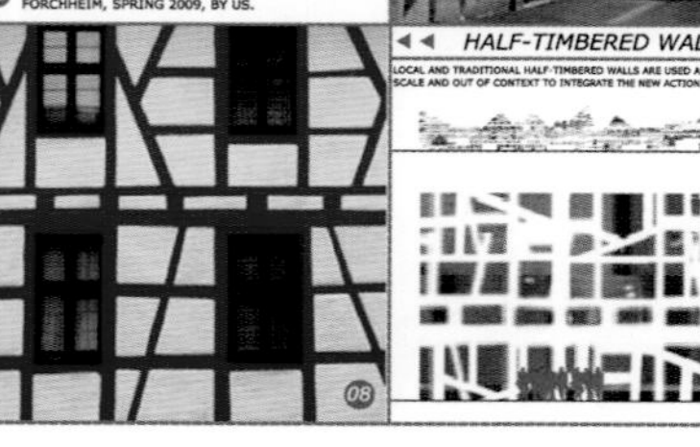
08

HALF-TIMBERED WALLS

LOCAL AND TRADITIONAL HALF-TIMBERED WALLS ARE USED AS REFERENCE OUT OF SCALE AND OUT OF CONTEXT TO INTEGRATE THE NEW ACTION.

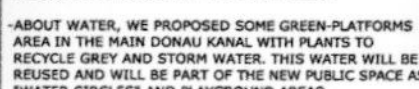

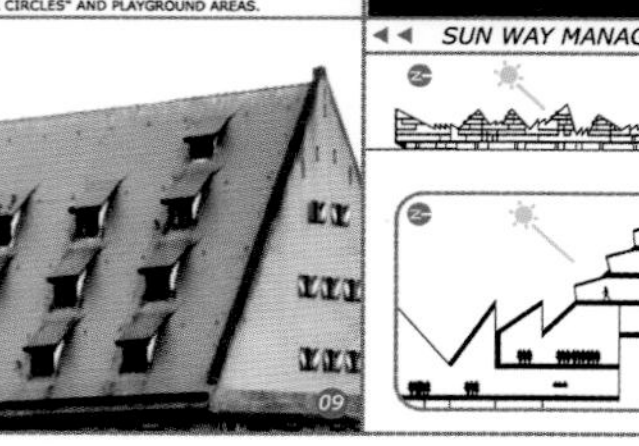
09

SUN WAY MANAGEMENT

MODEL / URBAN CONTEXT & DETAILS

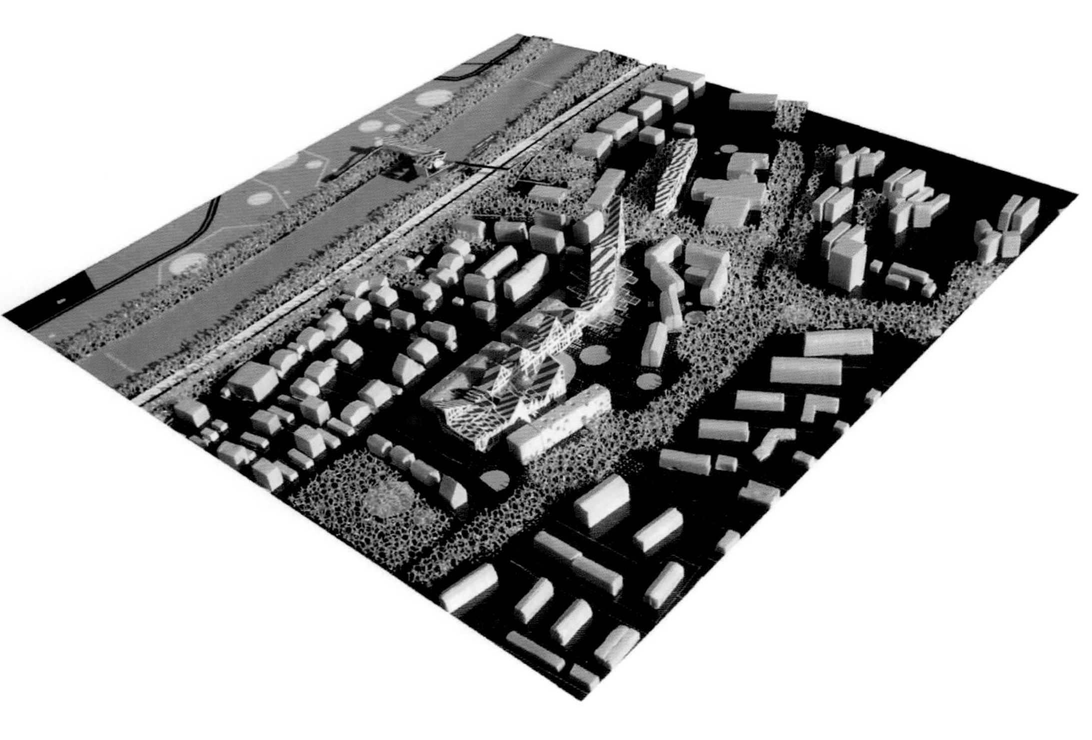

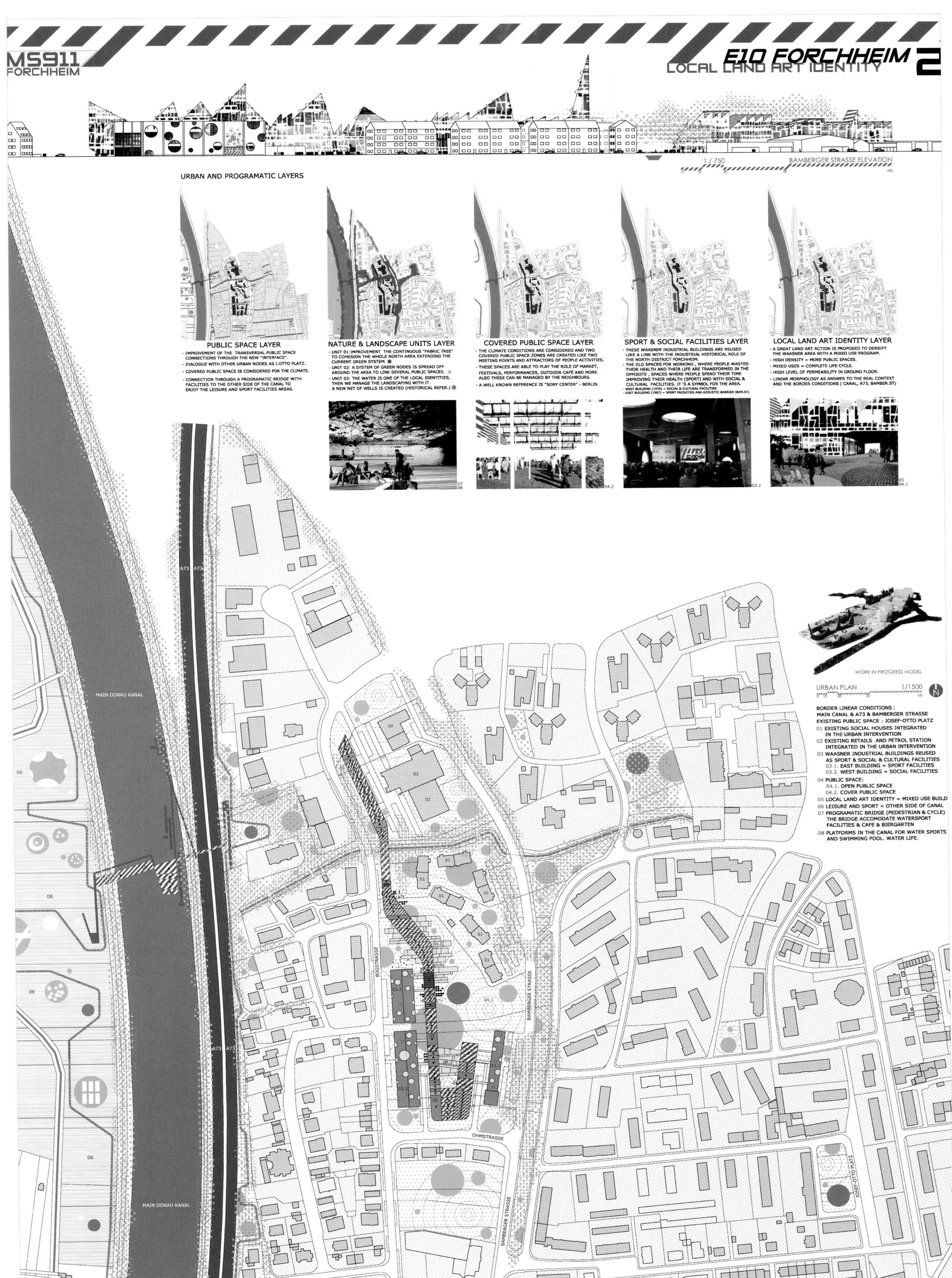
MS911
FORCHHEIM
E10 FORCHHEIM 2
LOCAL LAND ART IDENTITY
1/750
BAMBERGER STRASSE ELEVATION
URBAN AND PROGRAMATIC LAYERS
PUBLIC SPACE LAYER
- IMPROVEMENT OF THE TRANSVERSAL PUBLIC SPACE CONNECTIONS THROUGH THE NEW "INTERFACE".
- DIALOGUE WITH OTHER URBAN NODES AS J.OTTO PLATZ.
- COVERED PUBLIC SPACE IS CONSIDERED FOR THE CLIMATE.
- CONNECTION THROUGH A PROGRAMATIC BRIDGE WITH FACILITIES TO THE OTHER SIDE OF THE CANAL TO ENJOY THE LEISURE AND SPORT FACILITIES AREAS.
NATURE & LANDSCAPE UNITS LAYER
- UNIT 01:IMPROVEMENT THE CONTINUOUS "FABRIC TREE" TO COHESION THE WHOLE NORTH AREA EXTENDING THE CURRENT GREEN SYSTEM.
- UNIT 02: A SYSTEM OF GREEN NODES IS SPREAD OFF AROUND THE AREA TO LINK SEVERAL PUBLIC SPACES.
- UNIT 03: THE WATER IS ONE OF THE LOCAL IDENTITIES, THEN WE MANAGE THE LANDSCAPING WITH IT. A NEW NET OF WELLS IS CREATED (HISTORICAL REFER.)
COVERED PUBLIC SPACE LAYER
- THE CLIMATE CONDITIONS ARE CONSIDERED AND TWO COVERED PUBLIC SPACE ZONES ARE CREATED LIKE TWO MEETING POINTS AND ATTRACTORS OF PEOPLE ACTIVITIES.
- THESE SPACES ARE ABLE TO PLAY THE ROLE OF MARKET, FESTIVALS, PERFORMANCES, OUTDOOR CAFÉ AND MORE. ALSO THESE CAN BE MANAGED BY THE NEIGHBOURS.
- A WELL KNOWN REFERENCE IS "SONY CENTER" - BERLIN.
SPORT & SOCIAL FACILITIES LAYER
- THESE WAASNER INDUSTRIAL BUILDINGS ARE REUSED LIKE A LINK WITH THE INDUSTRIAL HISTORICAL ROLE OF THE NORTH DISTRICT FORCHHEIM.
- THE OLD SPACES FOR WORKING , WHERE PEOPLE WASTED THEIR HEALTH AND THEIR LIFE ARE TRANSFORMED IN THE OPPOSITE , SPACES WHERE PEOPLE SPEND THEIR TIME IMPROVING THEIR HEALTH (SPORT) AND WITH SOCIAL & CULTURAL FACILITIES. IT 'S A SYMBOL FOR THE AREA.
- WEST BUILDING (1970) = SOCIAL & CULTURAL FACILITIES
- EAST BUILDING (1987) = SPORT FACILITIES AND ACOUSTIC BARRIER (BAM.ST)
LOCAL LAND ART IDENTITY LAYER
- A GREAT LAND ART ACTION IS PROPOSED TO DENSIFY THE WAASNER AREA WITH A MIXED USE PROGRAM.
- HIGH DENSITY = MORE PUBLIC SPACES.
- MIXED USES = COMPLETE LIFE CYCLE.
- HIGH LEVEL OF PERMEABILITY IN GROUND FLOOR.
- LINEAR MORPHOLOGY AS ANSWER TO THE REAL CONTEXT AND THE BORDER CONDITIONS (CANAL, A73, BAMBER.ST)
WORK IN PROGRESS MODEL
URBAN PLAN 1/1500
BORDER LINEAR CONDITIONS :
MAIN CANAL & A73 & BAMBERGER STRASSE
EXISTING PUBLIC SPACE : JOSEF-OTTO PLATZ
01 EXISTING SOCIAL HOUSES INTEGRATED IN THE URBAN INTERVENTION
02 EXISTING RETAILS AND PETROL STATION INTEGRATED IN THE URBAN INTERVENTION
03 WAASNER INDUSTRIAL BUILDINGS REUSED AS SPORT & SOCIAL & CULTURAL FACILITIES
03.1. EAST BUILDING = SPORT FACILITIES
03.2. WEST BUILDING = SOCIAL FACILITIES
04 PUBLIC SPACE:
04.1. OPEN PUBLIC SPACE
04.2. COVER PUBLIC SPACE
05 LOCAL LAND ART IDENTITY = MIXED USE BUILD
06 LEISURE AND SPORT = OTHER SIDE OF CANAL
07 PROGRAMATIC BRIDGE (PEDESTRIAN & CYCLE) THE BRIDGE ACCOMODATE WATERSPORT FACILITIES & CAFE & BIERGARTEN
08 PLATFORMS IN THE CANAL FOR WATER SPORTS AND SWIMMING POOL. WATER LIFE.
MAIN DONAU KANAL
A73
BUGSTRASSE
BAMBERGER STRASSE
OHMSTRASSE
JOSEF-OTTO PLATZ

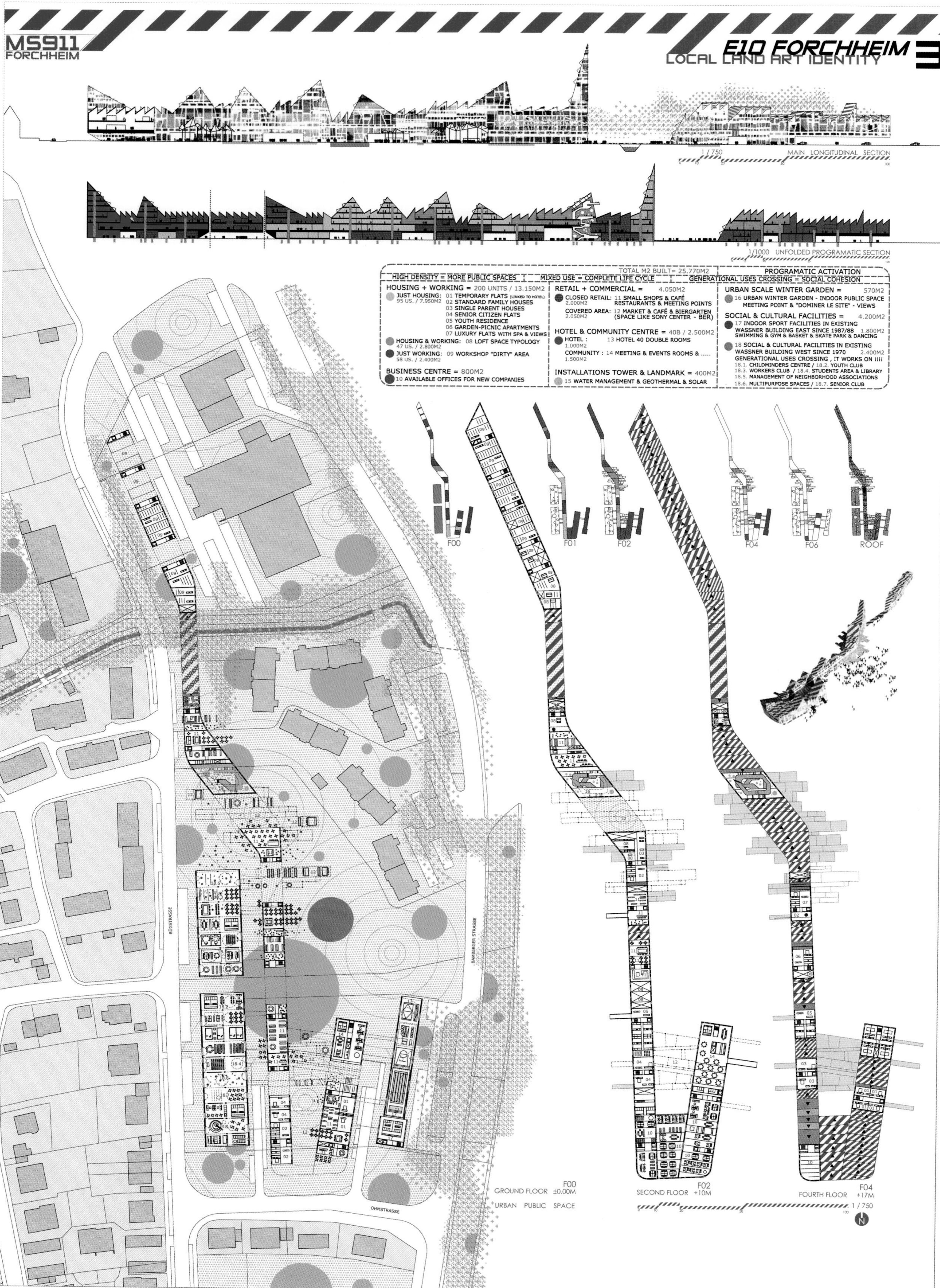

MS911
FORCHHEIM
E10 FORCHHEIM 3
LOCAL LAND ART IDENTITY
1 / 750 MAIN LONGITUDINAL SECTION
1/1000 UNFOLDED PROGRAMATIC SECTION
TOTAL M2 BUILT= 25.770M2
HIGH DENSITY = MORE PUBLIC SPACES
MIXED USE = COMPLETE LIFE CYCLE
PROGRAMATIC ACTIVATION
GENERATIONAL USES CROSSING = SOCIAL COHESION
HOUSING + WORKING = 200 UNITS / 13.150M2
JUST HOUSING: 95 US. / 7.950M2
01 TEMPORARY FLATS (LINKED TO HOTEL)
02 STANDARD FAMILY HOUSES
03 SINGLE PARENT HOUSES
04 SENIOR CITIZEN FLATS
05 YOUTH RESIDENCE
06 GARDEN-PICNIC APARTMENTS
07 LUXURY FLATS WITH SPA & VIEWS
HOUSING & WORKING: 47 US. / 2.800M2 08 LOFT SPACE TYPOLOGY
JUST WORKING: 58 US. / 2.400M2 09 WORKSHOP "DIRTY" AREA
BUSINESS CENTRE = 800M2
10 AVAILABLE OFFICES FOR NEW COMPANIES
RETAIL + COMMERCIAL = 4.050M2
CLOSED RETAIL: 2.000M2 11 SMALL SHOPS & CAFÉ RESTAURANTS & MEETING POINTS
COVERED AREA: 2.050M2 12 MARKET & CAFÉ & BIERGARTEN (SPACE LIKE SONY CENTER - BER)
HOTEL & COMMUNITY CENTRE = 40B / 2.500M2
HOTEL : 1.000M2 13 HOTEL 40 DOUBLE ROOMS
COMMUNITY : 1.500M2 14 MEETING & EVENTS ROOMS & .....
INSTALLATIONS TOWER & LANDMARK = 400M2
15 WATER MANAGEMENT & GEOTHERMAL & SOLAR
URBAN SCALE WINTER GARDEN = 570M2
16 URBAN WINTER GARDEN - INDOOR PUBLIC SPACE MEETING POINT & "DOMINER LE SITE" - VIEWS
SOCIAL & CULTURAL FACILITIES = 4.200M2
17 INDOOR SPORT FACILITIES IN EXISTING WASSNER BUILDING EAST SINCE 1987/88 1.800M2
SWIMMING & GYM & BASKET & SKATE PARK & DANCING
18 SOCIAL & CULTURAL FACILITIES IN EXISTING WASSNER BUILDING WEST SINCE 1970 2.400M2
GENERATIONAL USES CROSSING , IT WORKS ON ¡¡¡¡
18.1. CHILDMINDERS CENTRE / 18.2. YOUTH CLUB
18.3. WORKERS CLUB / 18.4. STUDENTS AREA & LIBRARY
18.5. MANAGEMENT OF NEIGHBORHOOD ASSOCIATIONS
18.6. MULTIPURPOSE SPACES / 18.7. SENIOR CLUB
F00
F01
F02
F04
F06
ROOF
BÜGSTRASSE
BAMBERGER STRASSE
OHMSTRASSE
F00
GROUND FLOOR ±0.00M
URBAN PUBLIC SPACE
F02
SECOND FLOOR +10M
F04
FOURTH FLOOR +17M
1 / 750

Flow | *object-e architecture*

Location : St. Louis, USA
Year : 2010 - Honorable mention

Design : Dimitris Gourdoukis
Project : entry for the Steedman Competition 2010
Typology : Urban Design

FLOW

2010ST539
Panel 1/3

A. Subtle Master Planning

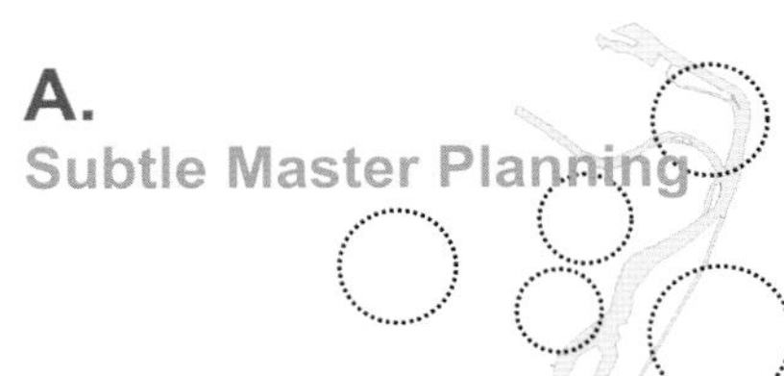

Master planning is not attempting to impose any centrally decided, strict direction. It is supporting already existing elements and is providing the necessary infrastructure for possibilities to arise.

B. Field of Possibilities

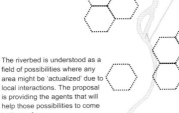

The riverbed is understood as a field of possibilities where any area might be 'actualized' due to local interactions. The proposal is providing the agents that will help those possibilities to come to the surface.

C. Data Flow

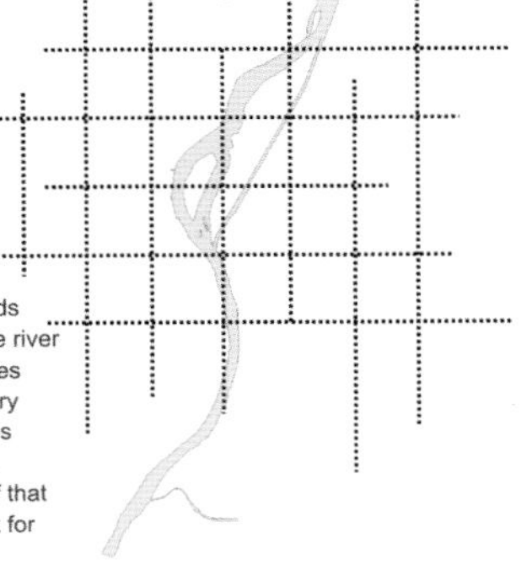

The flow of water and goods from north to south that the river accommodated for centuries becomes in the 21st century flow of information, which is controller and transmitted, transforming the display of that data flow into a monument for contemporary societies

Recreation

The old Chain of Rocks Bridge is a beautiful example of metal structure and one of the few pedestrian bridges of the Missisipi. The views that it offers to the river and to the surroundings are special, and it is also an ideal spot for bird watching in late winter-beginning of spring, when the eagles fly across the area. The areas around the two banks at the Old Chain of Rocks Bridge will be designed as public spaces for hosting activities such as biking, hiking, canoeing, and daily excursions. On the Illinois side, on the Chouteau island, there will be interventions on the landscape in the direction of restoring the 'wildlife' character it used to have, rather than the agricultural one it gradually obtained over the decades. This will be achieved with a landscape approach of recreating prairies and marshes, including of course the infrastructure for the **recreational** activities.

Biotope / Ecotourism

The Confluence is a Natural monument of great significance at a local and State level, and by cultivating ecotourism this important site will become more available and accessible. The existing Confluence Point State Park will be restored and expanded and the activities will be enriched. Specific areas for camping, bird watching and canoeing will be created, and a new network of safe and exciting hiking and biking trails will be traced. Along the Mississippi banks there will be two sea taxi stations from where visitors will be able to move along the river and visit other natural sites via a **water means of transportation**. The direction of the development is that of ecotourism, aiming at very light human intervention at the environmental site, which is **low impact** and **small scale**. The goal is to educate the traveler through the direct interaction with nature, as well as to foster respect for the natural heritage. Furthermore, via the **sea taxi route** the Confluence site will be part of a network of recreational areas of natural beauty along the Mississippi.

Access to the River

The riverbanks differentiate greatly along the St. Louis Mississippi area; in some parts the riverbank is a soft edge with wild flora growing without any human intervention. In these areas the riverbanks are not accessible due to the lack of designated trails, paths and road formations. In other places the riverbanks have an urban character, as for example around the Arch, where there is a hard edge with a sense of urban public space. Both extends of hardness and softness - along with all the conditions in between - are valuable for the **differentiation** and variation of the environment along the river. What is necessary is that the strategic planning makes it clear where one condition is desirable and where the other is more appropriate. The project's approach on this issue is to locate certain areas of access to the river, where living public spaces will be created at the riverbanks. At these areas of access to the river there will be located piers, seating, observations points and sea taxi stations. Also at these points the Floating Market, a farmer's market located on platforms moving in the Mississippi, will be hosted. The project aims at the creation of spaces close to nature, more urban or less urban according to the surroundings, but with a focus of creating spaces were people can **interact** publicly at the proximity of water.

Monumentality

The Arch consists the iconic image of the city of St. Louis. It is monumental because of its being out of scale of its surroundings. In this project the monumentality is a key aspect of the proposal but it is expressed in a different way. The monumental character of the gesture lays on the tribute it pays to the Mississippi river. It is a discrete, quiet, human scale homage to the forces of nature and to the nurturing **flow** of the water. The interventions are all aligned with sustainable, non-invasive, ecological ideology. There is a landmark, however, which represents in a monumental way the quintessence of our times: It is a tower where information collected from the river will be displayed on its facades, thus creating a **constantly changing** data wall. The Tower is in no way competing neither with its size nor with its function with the Arch. But as the Arch, the Tower is also a **metaphor** : in past times the flow of water was linking places, people and ideas, north and south - nowadays the flow of information attempts to do the same.

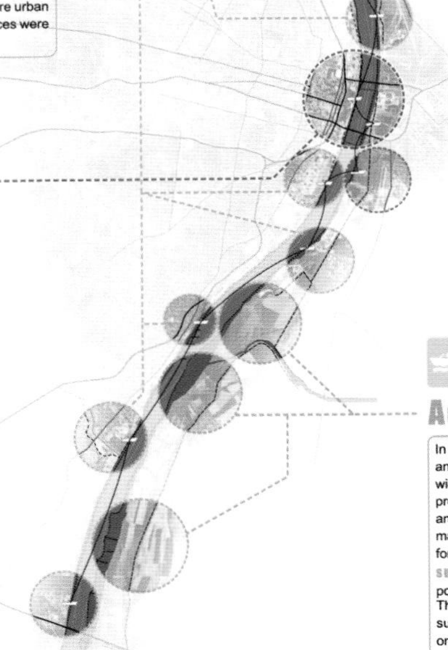

Agriculture / Agrotourism

At the Southern part of the Chouteau island the landscape will smoothly change from the more "wildlife" prairie character of the Northern part, to a more agricultural setting. Here agriculture will (continue to) be the main activity, thus being reinforced with interaction with visitors. All crops will be organically cultivated in a sustainable, biodynamic manner. **Agrotourism** will be develop, with the form of organized farms where visitors will find accommodation and will be able to get involved with agricultural activities, consume and buy local handmade foods and artisanal products. Visitors will have the opportunity to take part at harvesting, picking seeds, gardening, horse riding, preparing meals and doing arts and crafts activities.

Agriculture

In this area agriculture will be the main activity and restoration and preservation of farmland will take place. After the necessary soil preparation, all crops will be grown organically and biodynamically. The goal is for this area to maintain its original character and landscape formation, but at the same time to obtain a **sustainable way of producing** without polluting the ecosystem and the river.
The vegetables and grains produced will be supplying the Floating Market, where only organic products will be traded.

FLOW

2010ST539
PANEL 2/3

infrastructure networks

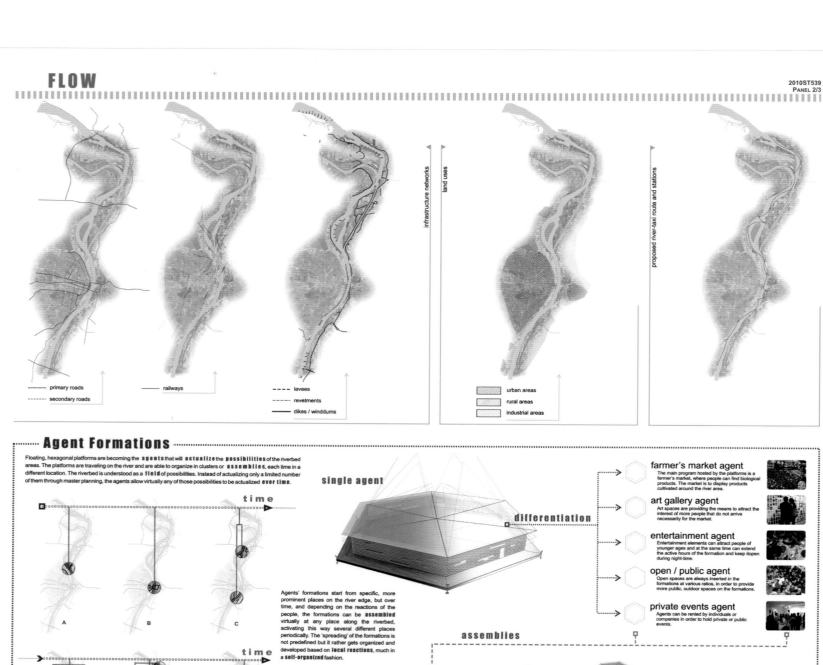

- primary roads
- secondary roads
- railways
- levees
- revetments
- dikes / winddums

land uses

- urban areas
- rural areas
- industrial areas

proposed river-taxi route and stations

Agent Formations

Floating, hexagonal platforms are becoming the **agents** that will **actualize** the **possibilities** of the riverbed areas. The platforms are traveling on the river and are able to organize in clusters or **assemblies**, each time in a different location. The riverbed is understood as a **field** of possibilities. Instead of actualizing only a limited number of them through master planning, the agents allow virtually any of those possibilities to be actualized **over time**.

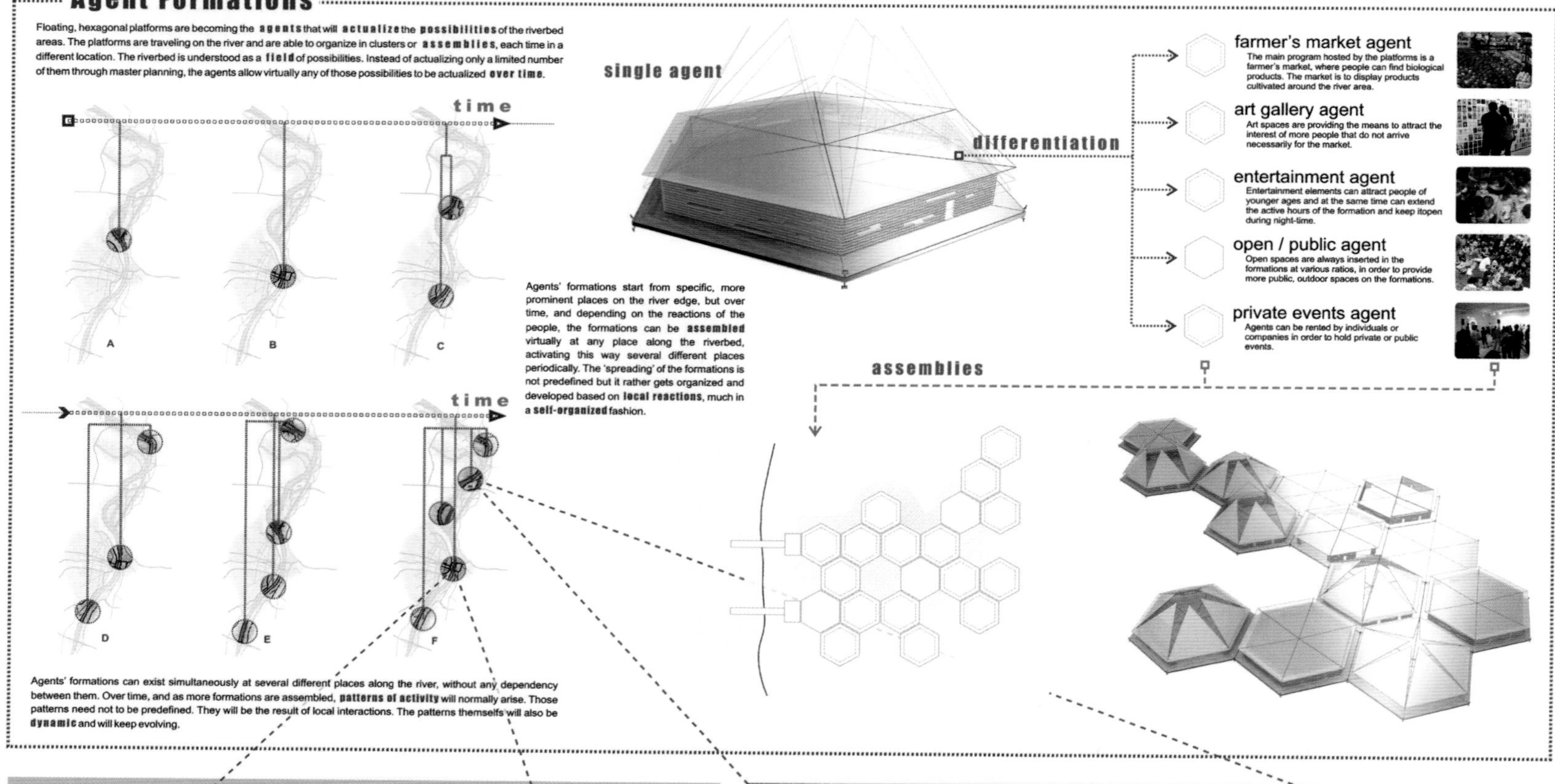

time
A
B
C
time
D
E
F
single agent
differentiation
farmer's market agent
The main program hosted by the platforms is a farmer's market, where people can find biological products. The market is to display products cultivated around the river area.
art gallery agent
Art spaces are providing the means to attract the interest of more people that do not arrive necessarily for the market.
entertainment agent
Entertainment elements can attract people of younger ages and at the same time can extend the active hours of the formation and keep itopen during night-time.
open / public agent
Open spaces are always inserted in the formations at various ratios, in order to provide more public, outdoor spaces on the formations.
private events agent
Agents can be rented by individuals or companies in order to hold private or public events.
assemblies

Agents' formations start from specific, more prominent places on the river edge, but over time, and depending on the reactions of the people, the formations can be **assembled** virtually at any place along the riverbed, activating this way several different places periodically. The 'spreading' of the formations is not predefined but it rather gets organized and developed based on **local reactions**, much in a **self-organized** fashion.

Agents' formations can exist simultaneously at several different places along the river, without any dependency between them. Over time, and as more formations are assembled, **patterns of activity** will normally arise. Those patterns need not to be predefined. They will be the result of local interactions. The patterns themselfs will also be **dynamic** and will keep evolving.

the edge of the river across the Arch, flooded, with a platform assembly and the data tower

the Chouteau island and the Chain of Rock bridge

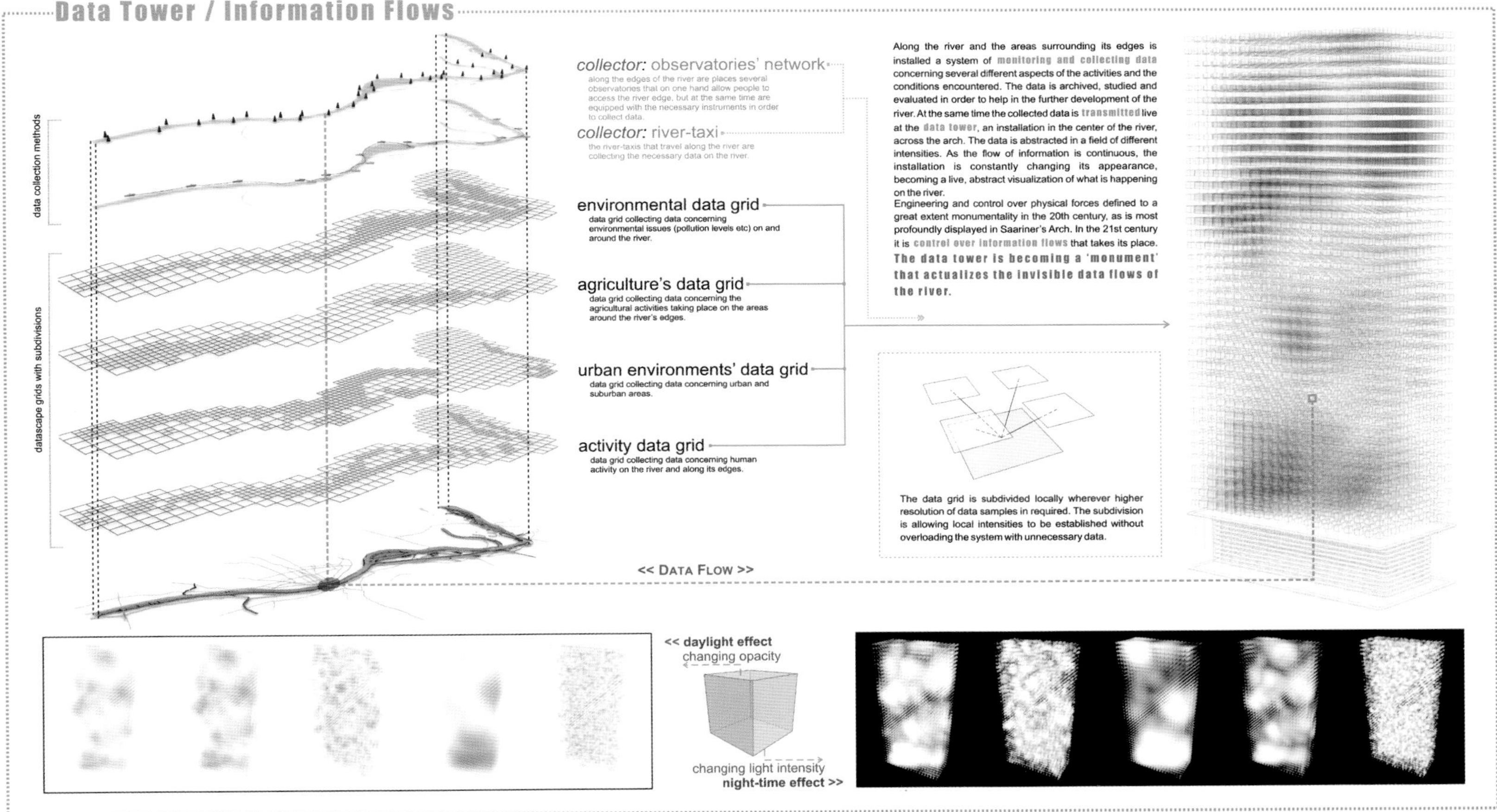

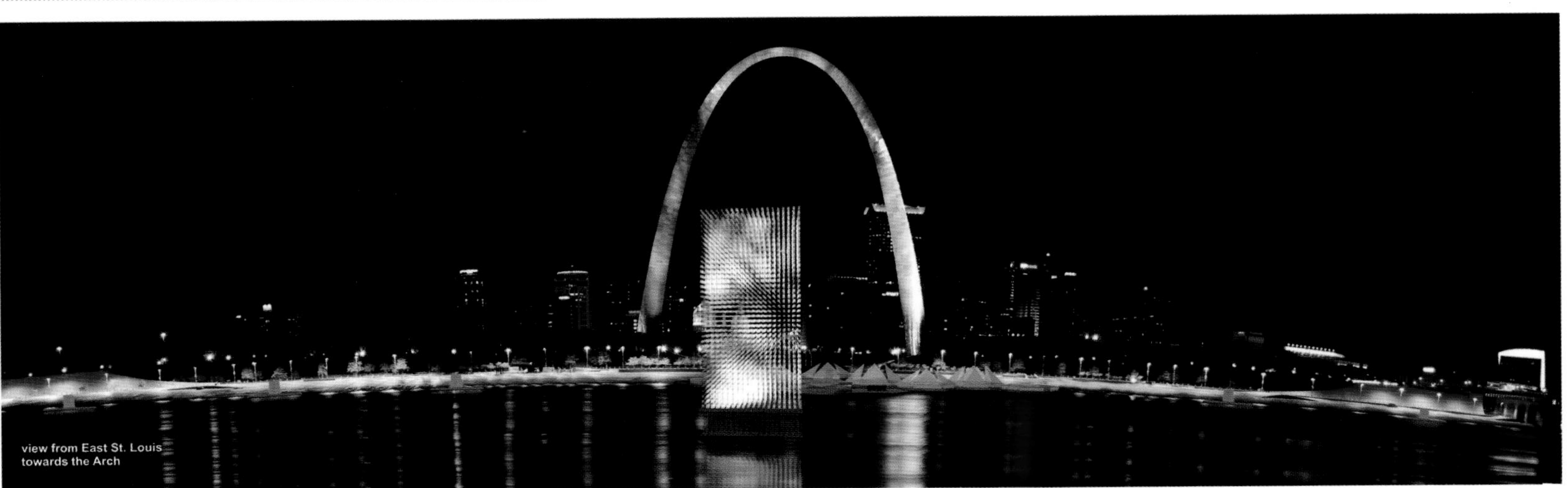
view from East St. Louis towards the Arch

Roundabout Prophylaxis | *Fake Industries Architectural Agonism*

Participants : Cristina Goberna, Urtzi Grau
Project : Europan 11 - Recycling a Connection Space in Alcorcón - Runner up
Typology : Urban planning + Housing proposal
Location : Alcorcon, Spain

Construction Volume : Housing 60,000m², Cubatur 356.000m³
Client : Ayuntamiento de Alcorcón / Year : 2011

FKOO4 - Alcorcon
Roundabout Prophylactics
Rotula Profilactica

Or how a transparent ring and an invisible structure of plastic domesticity could protect the outskirts' landscape, stop a brick tsunami and seduce industries for unexpected superficial activities.
Como un anillo transparente y una estructura invisible de domesticidad de plástico puede proteger el paisaje del extrarradio, parar un tsunami de ladrillo y seducir a la industria para superficiales e inesperadas actividades.

1

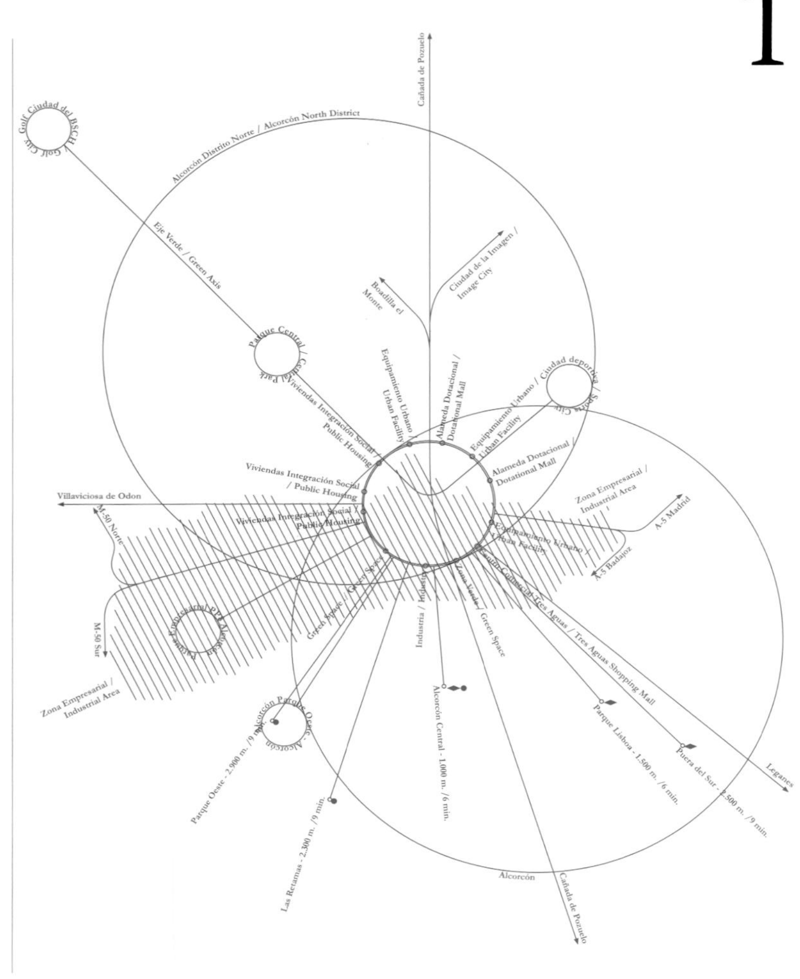

The mix of industrial areas, agricultural terrains and empty lots that surrounds la Cañada de Pozuelo is a fantastic example of the *Descampado* Landscape. There is no need to re-integrate the site into the city. It is already part of it. Its excellent location and unique urban conditions call for preservation – or even intensification – of its existing qualities. Instead of attempting to unify or homogenize the area, we prefer to start with what is existing and to capitalize on it (this also forms the basis of our approach to sustainability).

Current Conditions
Located in the north border of the Indisutrial Area Cañada de Pozuelo, part of the commercial industrial corridor associated to the highway A-5 that connects Madrid and Lisbon, the area of study enjoys direct connections to the A-5 and the M-50 completed with the proximity to public mass transportation. The site is in walking distance from two public transit systems Cercanias (Parque Oeste, Las Retamas, Alcorcon Central) and Metro (Alcorcon Central, Parque de Lisboa, Puerta del Sur)

Such intense connectivity contrasts with its character of *descampado*. It consist of fragments – mainly empty – that differ in function and size, with a common denominator, low intensity of informal use in transition between the city and an agricultural landscape. These open spaces are potentially more important than the impulse to add new buildings. The preservation of the periphery landscape and informal leisure associated form connections within the area and to the surrounding city.

The possibility of Alcorcón Distrito Norte:
The plan for the extension of Alcorcón in the North side of the A-5 is in fact a complete new city. Structured around a system of linear green public spaces – *Alamedas Dotacionales* – and massive parks – Central Park and the future Sport City of Atletico de Madrid – its urban structure is independent from the existing Alcorcón. The Industrial-Commercial corridor surrounding the A-5 intensifies the autonomy of the operation. Our goal is therefore to articulate the connections between the two cities, as a superposition of the existing industrial areas and the new system of green public spaces of the Distrito Norte.

Yet, it would be naive not to mention the Spanish economic meltdown in the context of the proposed brief. As we all know, the inability of families to pay their mortgages has resulted in a landscape of foreclosures. Closely connected, the banks refusal to grant new credits translates in unaffordability of new property, which generates a panorama of empty housing blocks. And we cannot forget that the housing bubble that started it all was pumped up by operations identical to Alcorcón Distrito Norte. The difference, however, is painfully obvious. Previous operations developed during the economic bonanza succeed even is some remain incomplete. But how a plan that doubles the size of the municipality exhausting its land is going to be developed in the current economy? Not only there has been a decrease on the overall building rate, but also, the governmental tendency seems to shift towards policies that emphasize rehabilitation and preservation over new construction.

In this context, it is more than justifiable to consider the Alcorcón Distrito Norte Alcorcon might – or should – not take place. At least it would be proper to admit the possibility for it not to being developed immediately. In sight of this evidence, this proposal admits both scenarios and it is structured in two complementary stages that preserve the existing conditions, form connections with the city and propose news forms of domesticity. Hence, the ultimate agenda for this proposal could be summarized in the following points:

La mezcla de areas industrials, terrenos agricolas y solares vacios que rodean la Cañada de Pozuelo es un ejemplo fantástico de paisaje de Descampado. No hay necesidad de reintegrarlo en la ciudad, ya es parte de la misma. Su excelente localización y condiciones urbanas únicas son perfectas para ser conservadas o incluso intensificadase de sus cualidades existentes. En vez de intentar unificar u homogeneizar el área, preferimos comenzar con las existencias , sacándoles provecho como parte de nuestra estrategia de sostenibilidad, y asi convertir el área en una excelente rotonda de conexiones adyacentes.

Condiciones Actuales
Situada en el límite norte del área industrial Cañada de Pozuelo, un sector del corredor industrial asociado a la autopista A-5que conecta Madrid y Lisboa, el área de estudio disfruta de conexión directa con las vias A-5 y M-50, completadas con la proximidad de transporte público Cercanías (Parque Oeste, Las Retamas, Alcorcón Central) y el metro (Alcorcón Central, Parque de Lisboa, Puerta del Sur), de los que se encuentra a una distancia susceptible de ser recorrida a pie.
Esta intensa conectividad contrasta con su carácter de descampado consistente en fragmentos-mayoritariamente vacíos-que difieren en tamaño y función teniendo un denominador común: baja intensidad de uso informal en la transición entre la ciudad y el paisaje agrícola. Estos espacios abiertos son potencialmente más importantes que el impulso a añadir nuevos edificios. La conservación del paisaje de periferia y el ocio informal asociado al mismo, forma conexiones entre el área y la ciudad que la rodea.

El Distrito Norte de Alcorcon:
El plan para la extensión de Alcorcón hacia el lado norte de la vía A-5 es de hecho una nueva ciudad, cuya configuración urbana se estructura alrededor de un sistema linear de espacios verdes públicos -Alamedas Dotacionales- y parques masivos -Central Park y la futura Ciudad Deportiva del Atlético de Madrid-y es independiente del Alcorcón existente. El corredor Industrial-Comercial situado alrededor de la via A-5 intensifica la autonomía de la operación. Nuestro objetivo es por tanto, articular las conexiones entre las dos ciudades como una superposición de las áreas industriales y el nuevo sistema de espacios verdes públicos del Distrito Norte.

Sin embargo seria naïve no mencionar la crisis económica actual que sufre España en el contexto del brief de este concurso. Como todos sabemos, la incapacidad de las familias de pagar sus hipotecas ha resultado en un amplio panorama de desahucios. Íntimamente conectado con este hecho, la negación de los bancos a ofrecer nuevos créditos, se traduce en la imposibilidad de comprar nuevas propiedades por parte del público, lo que genera un extenso panorama de bloques vacíos. No podemos olvidar que la burbuja inmobiliaria que comenzó todo fue inflada por operaciones idénticas a la del Distrito Norte de Alcorcon. En cualquier caso, la diferencia es desafortunadamente obvia. Operaciones previas desarrolladas durante la bonnza económica tuvieron éxito incluso quedando algunas incompletas. Pero como un plan que dobla en tamaño de la municipalidad, agotando el terreno puede ser desarrollado en las actuales condiciones económicas? No solo ha habido un descenso en el ratio general de la construcción, también la tendencia gubernamental parece girar hacia políticas que enfatizan la rehabilitación y preservación sobre la construcción.

En este contexto, es más que justificable considerar el Distrito Norte de Alcorcon no puede ni debe realizarse inmediatamente. En vistas de esta evidencia, esta propuesta admite ambas posibilidades, y se estructura en dos pases complementarios que conservan las condiciones existentes, forman conexiones con la ciudad, y proponen nuevas formas de domesticidad. Por tanto, los objetivos de esta propuesta se pueden resumir en los siguientes tres puntos:

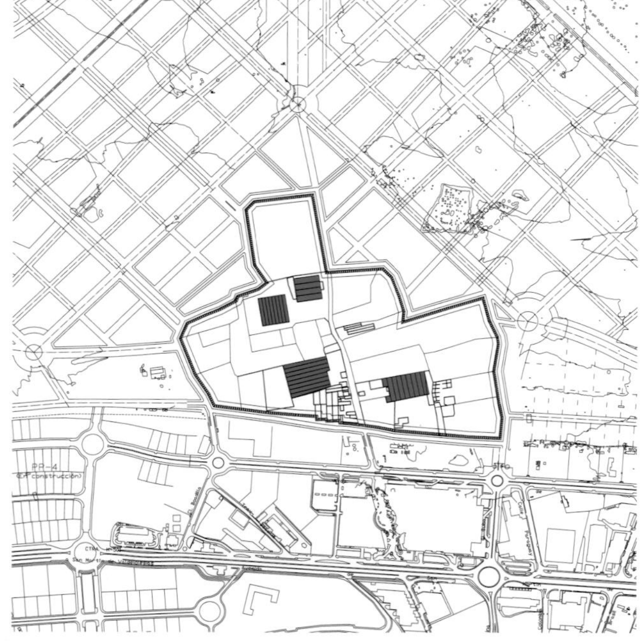

1. The protection of the descampado :

Instead of hiding or destroying the amalgam of agricultural and industrial landscape found in the outskirts of any city, this proposal highlights its potential, leaving the fragmented nature as protected wild areas of public use. In phase one, the landscape is left untouched by concentrating all new building on the factory's roofs, mixing industrial and domestic uses. Phase two concentrates the construction in a ring along the site's perimeter that preserves the existing landscape blocking the urban sprawl.

2. Two new types of affordable domesticity:
Phase one adds to the current regulations loft-like housing as compatible use in the industrial areas. Encouraging greenhouse constructions on the factory's roofs, the plan intends to provide cheap housing organized in vast and raw units, design to be acclimatized by natural techniques. The linear ring-like building of the second phase contains only identical rooms of 30m2 connected directly avoiding the use of hallways. Both designs facilitate the incorporation of commercial uses as ateliers or small business in the housing fabric, resulting in a

3. The site as an urban roundabout:
It phase one intensifies the conditions of *descampado* by leaving the landscape untouched, phase two transforms the site in a massive roundabout, icon of centrality and communication, that connects the existing Alarcón and the future Distrito Norte. The roundabout articulates the public spaces and facilities of the new plan with the industrial and commercial existing fabric, providing a new type of public space in the center of the city.

1. La proteccion del Descampado
En vez de esconder o destruir el paisaje agrario e industrial del extrarradio de cualquier ciudad, esta propuesta subraya su potencial, dejando su fragmentada naturaleza como áreas salvajes y protegidas para uso público. En la fase uno, es decir, si no se construye el Distrito Norte de Alcorcón o si su construcción se retrasa ostensiblemente, el paisaje se mantiene intacto al concentrar todas las nuevas edificaciones encima de las industrias, mezclando así, usos industriales y domésticos. En la fase dos, es decir, si se construye el Distrito Norte de Alcorcón, la construcción se concentra en un anillo alrededor del perímetro del solar, preservando así el paisaje existente y bloqueando la expansión urbana.

2. Dos nuevas formas de domesticidad:
La fase uno añade a las actuales regulaciones, viviendas loft, como usos compatibles en áreas industriales. Potenciando el uso de construcciones tipo invernadero encima de los edificios industriales, el plan pretende proporcionar viviendas económicas organizadas en vastas y desnudas unidades, aclimatadas con técnicas naturales. El edificio anillo de la fase dos solamente contiene solo habitaciones idénticas de 30m2 conectadas directamente de manera que eviten el uso del pasillo. Ambos diseños facilitan la incorporación de usos comerciales como talleres o pequeños negocios en su tejido urbano.

3. El solar como rotunda urbana:
Si la fase uno intensifica la condición de Descampado al dejar el paisaje intacto, la fase dos transforma el solar en una gran rotonda, icono de centralidad y comunicación, que conecta el Alcorcón existente y el futuro Distrito Norte. La rotonda articula los espacios públicos y facilita el nuevo plan con un tejido existente industrial y comercial, suministrando un nuevo tipo de espacio en el centro de la ciudad.

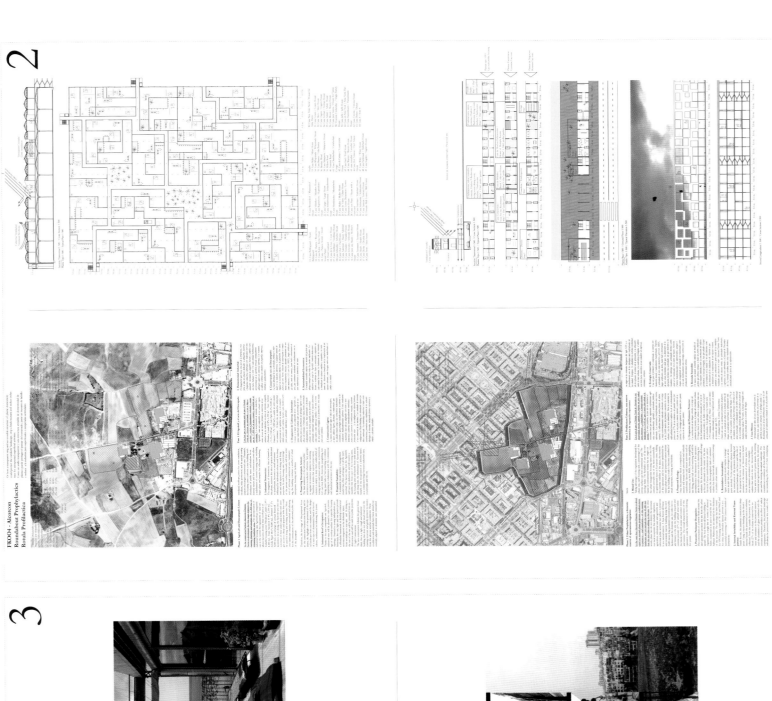

FKOO4 - Alcorcon
Roundabout Prophylactics
Rotula Profilactica

Or how a transparent ring and an invisible structure of plastic domesticity could protect the outskirts' landscape, stop a brick tsunami and seduce industries for unexpected superficial activities.

Como un anillo transparente y una estructura invisible de domesticidad de plastico puede proteger el paisaje del extrarradio, parar un tsunami de ladrillo y seducir a la industria para superficiales e inesperadas actividades.

3

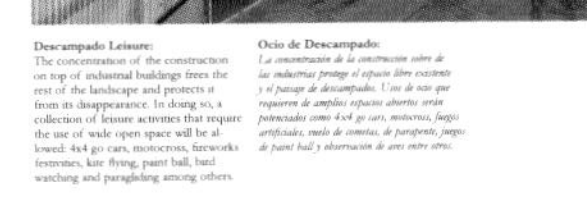

Descampado Leisure:
The concentration of the construction on top of industrial buildings frees the rest of the landscape and protects it from its disappearance. In doing so, a collection of leisure activities that require the use of wide open space will be allowed: 4x4 go cars, motocross, fireworks festivities, kite flying, paint ball, bird watching and paragliding among others.

Ocio de Descampado:
La concentración de la construcción sobre de las industrias protege el espacio libre existente y el paisaje de descampados. Usos de ocio que requieren de amplios espacios abiertos serán potenciados como 4x4 go cars, motocross, fuegos artificiales, vuelo de cometas, de parapente, juegos de paint ball y observación de aves entre otros.

The Agro-Loft:
Wide and affordable units built on the top on industries in matt building configuration. Their incoming inhabitants are able to choose their constructed surface depending on their financial possibilities. Their structure is based in the green-house ideal in which natural acclimatization is potentiated. A new compatible use category allows a mix of domestic and industrial use and the use of the units for working and living purposes.

El Agroloft:
Amplias y baratas unidades de vivienda serán construidas encima de las industrias, a modo de matt-buildings. Su estructura se basará en el concepto del invernadero en las que se potenciarán métodos de climatización natural. Sus habitantes podrán elegir la superficie de las unidades dependiendo de sus posibilidades económicas. Una doble categoría urbana, mezcla usos domésticos e industriales, permite el uso de las unidades de vivienda para actividades laborales y usos terciarios. Los habitantes pueden dedicar un porcentaje de sus superficie a oficina, taller, teatro, restaurante, bar etc.

Architectural Prophylaxis:
The constructed ring that protects the site's landscape from the urban sprawl, forces a reflection regarding housing typology. Based in a line of single rooms 6x 5m connected in their axis avoiding the use of hallways, it rethinks flexibility bringing back 19th Century notions of domesticity. The effect is one of an extreme sense of lightness and transparency. The interior façade is cladded with a mirror finishing to infinitely reflect the protected landscape. The exterior façade will foster transparency towards the interior of the block so that the landscape is always visible from the outside.

Profilaxis Arquitectónica:
El anillo de construcción que protege el área del crecimiento urbano obliga a una reflexión sobre la vivienda. Dado que el edificio se organiza en apartamentos de habitaciones de 6m de ancho y 5 de largo conectadas en su eje y sin pasillo entre ellas, recupera una versión de domesticidad del siglo XIX. Además se consigue un aumentado efecto de transparencia y ligereza radical. La fachada interior está acabada en espejo de manera que el paisaje interior se refleja hasta el infinito. La fachada exterior es transparente para que desde la ciudad el paisaje protegido sea visible.

Canned Nature:
The concentration of the construction in a perimeter ring has a double agenda: On one side it radically protects the existing landscape. On the other, it liberates the area for leisure uses that require wide open spaces as 4x4 go cars, motocross, fireworks festivities, kite flying, paint ball, bird watching and paragliding among others.

Naturaleza en Conserva:
La concentración de construcción de viviendas propuestas en un anillo perimetral al área de actuación tiene doble intención: Por una parte protege de manera radical el paisaje existente, por otra libera el espacio para usos de ocio que requieren de amplios espacios libres como 4x4 go cars, motocross, fuegos artificiales, vuelo de cometas, de parapente, juegos de paint ball y observación de aves entre otros.

FKOO4 - Alcorcon
Roundabout Prophylactics
Rotula Profilactica

2

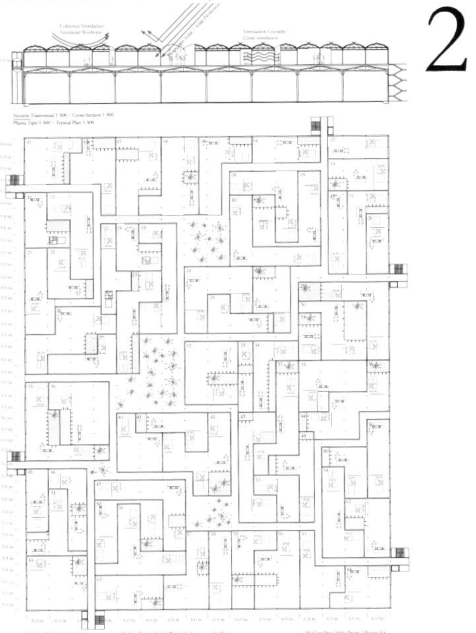

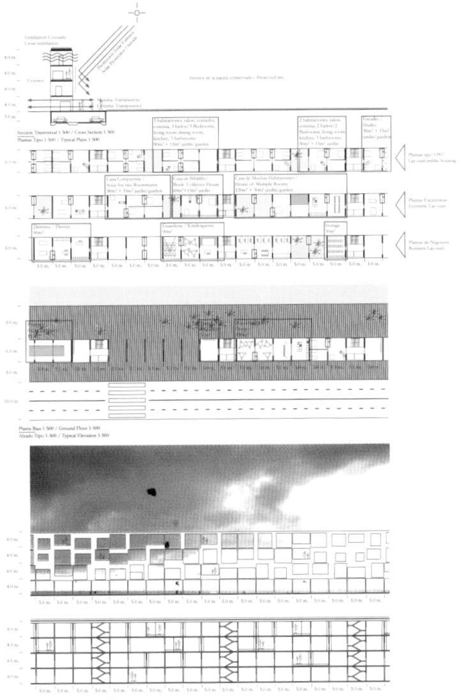

096 Inje(un)ction | *object-e architecture*

Design : Dimitris Gourdoukis & Christos Gourdoukis
Project : Entry for the Competition AthensX4
Typology : Urban Intervention
Location : Athens, Greece
Year : 2011 - shortlisted

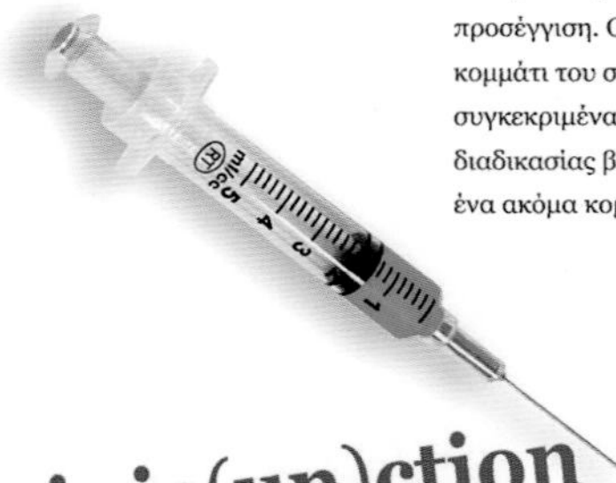

inje(un)ction

Η προτεινόμενη επέμβαση έχει ως στόχο να διερευνήσει τη σχέση **φυσικού** και **ανθρωπογενούς** στοιχείου μέσα στο χώρο της πόλης και να δοκιμάσει μία διαφορετική προσέγγιση. Οι μέχρι τώρα προσεγγίσεις αντιμετωπίζουν το 'φυσικό' στοιχείο ως ένα ακόμα κομμάτι του σχεδιασμού. Δηλαδή ως κάτι που σχεδιάζεται με σαφήνεια, χωροθετείται συγκεκριμένα, και αναπτύσσεται ελεγχόμενα και προκαθορισμένα. Το αποτέλεσμα μία τέτοιας διαδικασίας βέβαια, μόνο κατ' όνομα θα μπορούσε να θεωρηθεί φυσικό. Στην ουσία αποτελεί ένα ακόμα κομμάτι του ανθρωπογενούς περιβάλλοντος της πόλης.

Ταυτόχρονα, η συνειδητοποίηση της επιτακτικής ανάγκης αναθεώρησης των τρόπων διαχείρισης της ενέργειας και του περιβάλλοντος έχει οδηγήσει σε μία τάση όλα και μεγαλύτερης χρήσης - σχεδιασμένων - φυσικών στοιχείων με πρόφαση την περιβαλλοντολογική ευαισθησία. Όλα αυτά όμως χωρίς να υπάρχει πραγματική **επαναδιαπραγμάτευση** της σχέσης του ανθρώπου με το φυσικό περιβάλλον. Η λογική που υπερισχύει είναι: 'όσο το δυνατόν περισσότερο πράσινο, αρκεί αυτό να μην απειλεί τις συνήθειες και τους τρόπους με τους οποίους έχουμε συνηθίσει να ζούμε.

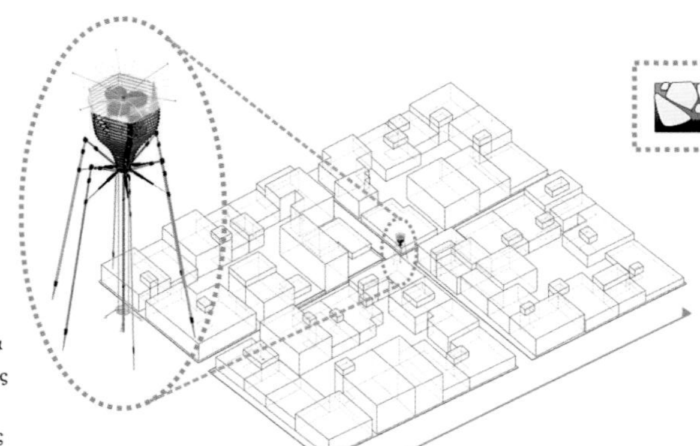

A. Το σύστημα εγκαθίσταται στο κέντρο του σταυρού. Συνδέεται κατακόρυφα με το δίκτυο αποχέτευσης απορροφώντας από εκεί απόβλητα. Τα απόβλητα μετατρέπονται σε υγρό λίπασμα.

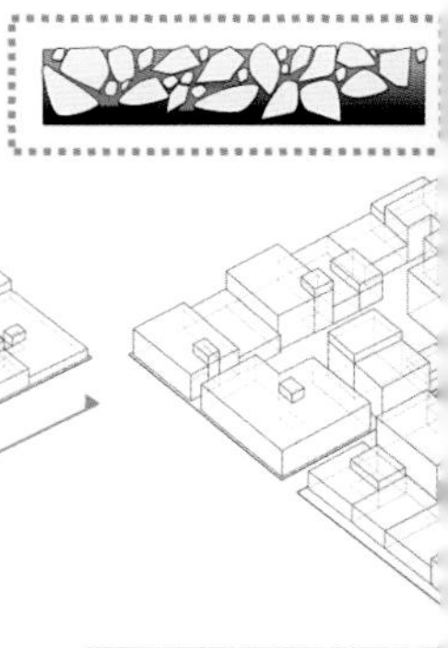

B. Υγρό λίπασμα, μικρο
από τους βιο-αντιδρο
άσφαλτο. Δημιουργο
δημιουργία πολύ απλ
κάτω από την άσφαλ

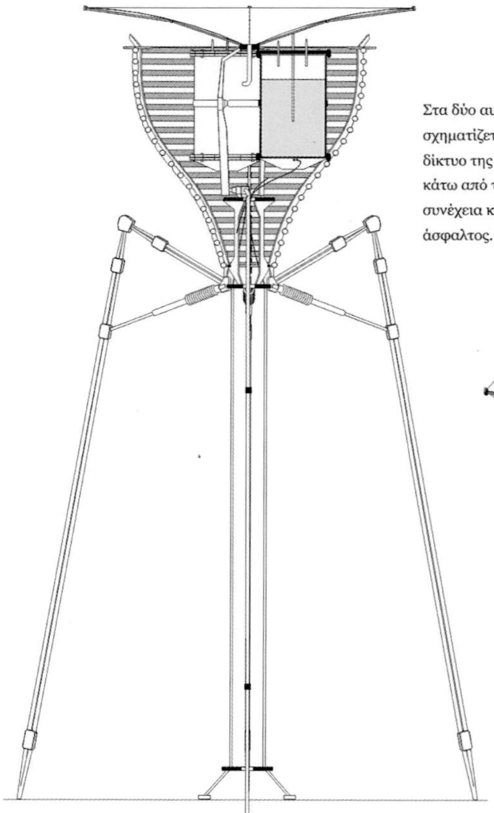

Στα δύο αυτά θέματα η πρόταση προσπαθεί να διερευνήσει πιθανές **εναλλακτικές**. Προτείνεται η εγκατάσταση στο κέντρο του σταυρού που σχηματίζεται μεταξύ των τεσσάρων τετραγώνων ενός μηχανισμού, που περιέχει τρεις βιο-αντιδραστήρες, και απορροφάει απόβλητα από το δίκτυο της αποχέτευσης. Τα απόβλητα αυτά επεξεργάζονται και διοχετεύονται - εν είδει λιπάσματος - μαζί με μικρο-οργανισμούς στο έδαφος κάτω από την άσφαλτο. Έτσι δημιουργούνται σταδιακά οι απαραίτητες συνθήκες για την ανάπτυξη στην αρχή μικρο-οργανισμών και στη συνέχεια και πιο σύνθετων ενδογενών φυτών, που βρίσκοντας πρόσφορο έδαφος αναπτύσσονται διεκδικώντας το χώρο που καταλαμβάνει η άσφαλτος. Όσο η ανάπτυξη συνεχίζεται, η άσφαλτος υποχωρεί και δίνει τη θέση της στο εν μέρη ανεξέλεγκτο φυσικό στοιχείο.

inje(un)ction:

Απώτερος στόχος της πρότασης είναι να υπογραμμίσει την ανάγκη **αναθεώρησης** της στάσης μας απέναντι στο φυσικό στοιχείο, απέναντι στο τι θεωρούμε "όμορφο" και "αποδεκτό" και τι "αντιαισθητικό" και "ενοχλητικό". Τα ανθρώπινα απόβλητα για παράδειγμα είναι ένα στοιχείο που θα μπορούσε να χρησιμοποιηθεί και αξιοποιηθεί για την παρασκευή λιπάσματος ή ενέργειας. Μία όχι τόσο ελεγχόμενη εκδοχή του φυσικού στοιχείου θα μπορούσε ίσως να δώσει νέες διαστάσεις στους χώρους της πόλης και να δημιουργήσει καινούργιες συνθήκες ζωής. Αλλά για να γίνουν αυτά είναι απαραίτητη η αναθεώρηση των **"ανέσεων"** και **συνηθειών** μας.

αξονική τομή της κατασκευής

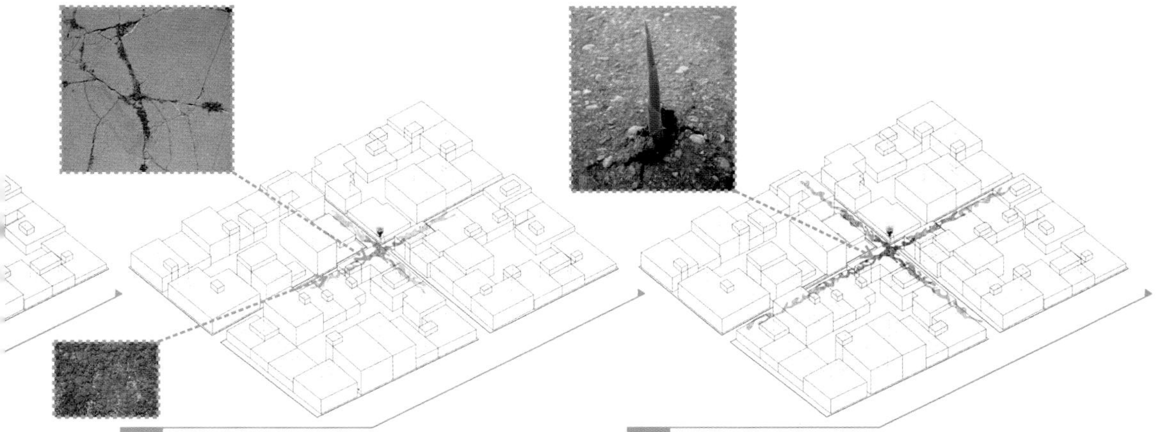

ύονται
ην
τη
ονται

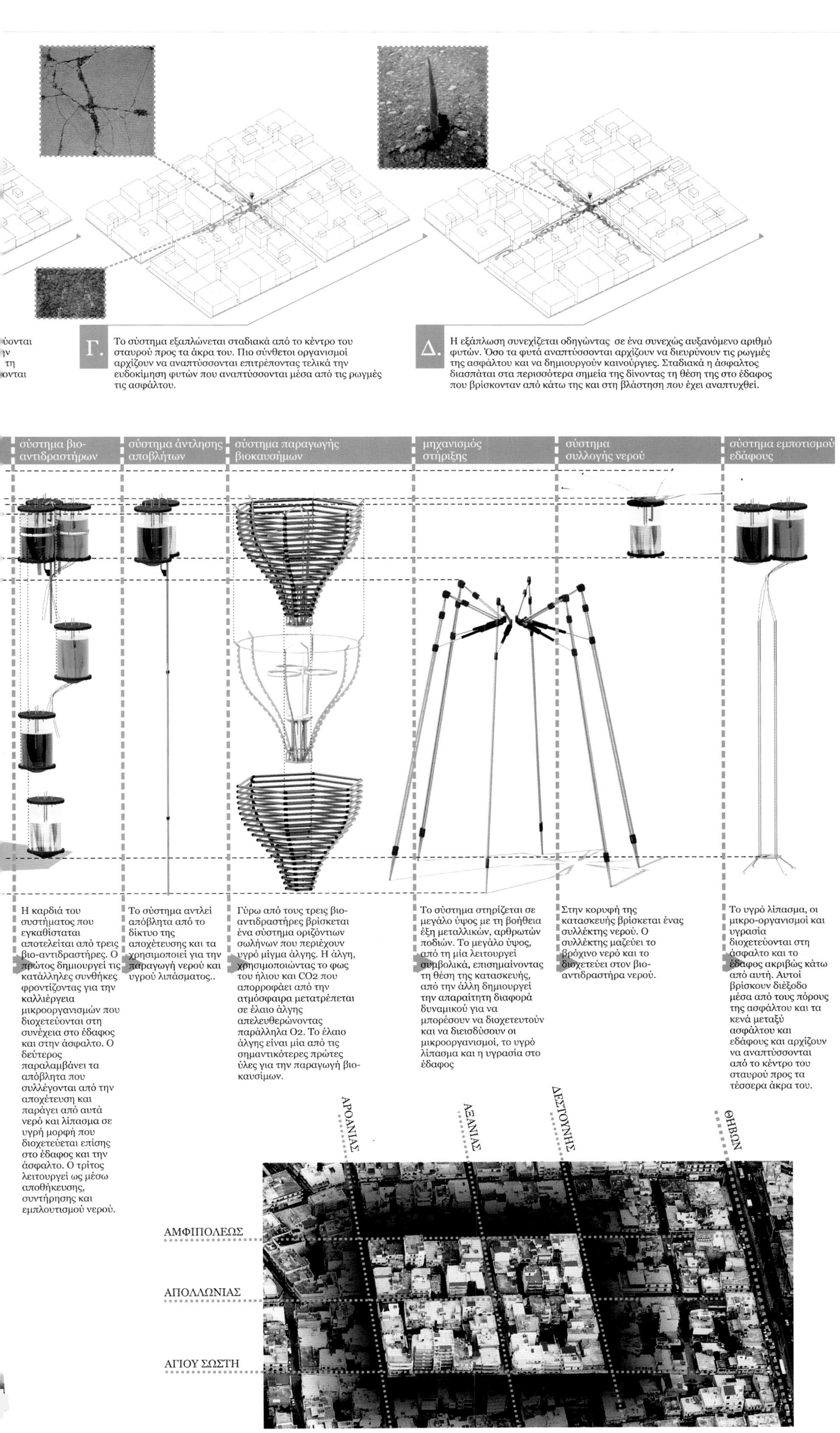

Γ. Το σύστημα εξαπλώνεται σταδιακά από το κέντρο του σταυρού προς τα άκρα του. Πιο σύνθετοι οργανισμοί αρχίζουν να αναπτύσσονται επιτρέποντας τελικά την ευδοκίμηση φυτών που αναπτύσσονται μέσα από τις ρωγμές τις ασφάλτου.

Δ. Η εξάπλωση συνεχίζεται οδηγώντας σε ένα συνεχώς αυξανόμενο αριθμό φυτών. Όσο τα φυτά αναπτύσσονται αρχίζουν να διευρύνουν τις ρωγμές της ασφάλτου και να δημιουργούν καινούργιες. Σταδιακά η άσφαλτος διασπάται στα περισσότερα σημεία της δίνοντας τη θέση της στο έδαφος που βρίσκονταν από κάτω της και στη βλάστηση που έχει αναπτυχθεί.

σύστημα βιο-αντιδραστήρων	σύστημα άντλησης αποβλήτων	σύστημα παραγωγής βιοκαυσίμων	μηχανισμός στήριξης	σύστημα συλλογής νερού	σύστημα εμποτισμού εδάφους

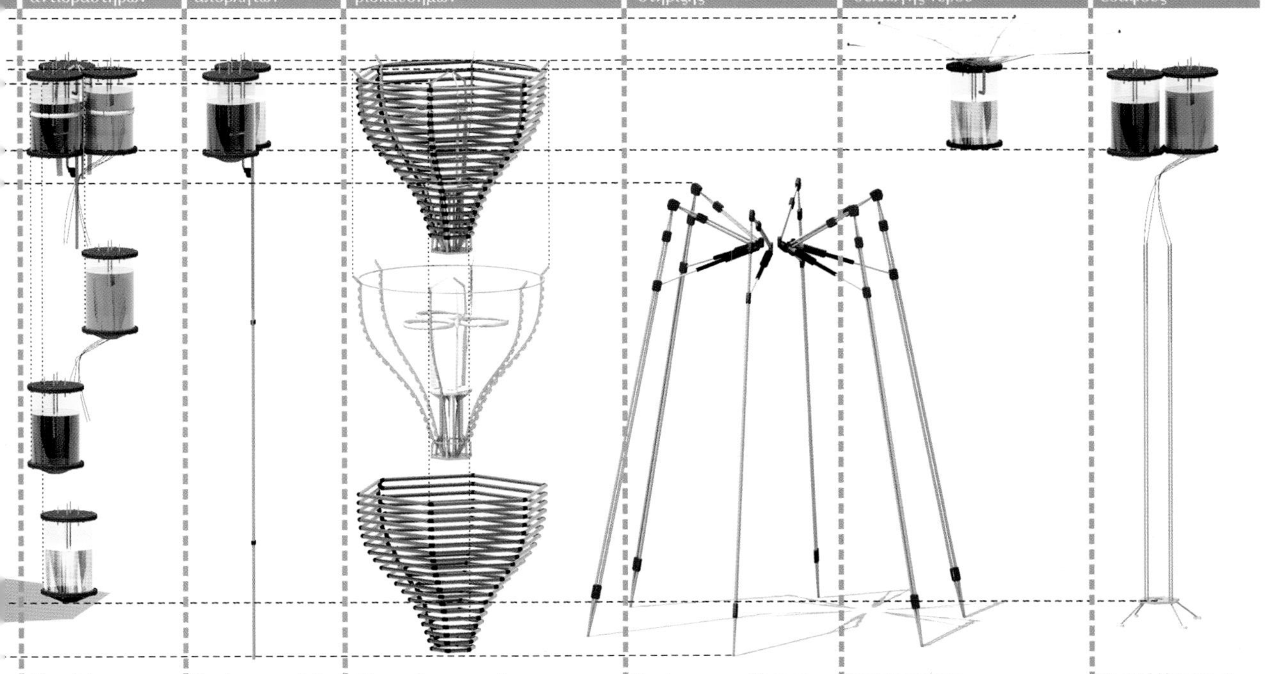

σύστημα βιο-αντιδραστήρων: Η καρδιά του συστήματος που εγκαθίσταται αποτελείται από τρεις βιο-αντιδραστήρες. Ο πρώτος δημιουργεί τις κατάλληλες συνθήκες φροντίζοντας για την καλλιέργεια μικροοργανισμών που διοχετεύονται στη συνέχεια στο έδαφος και στην άσφαλτο. Ο δεύτερος παραλαμβάνει τα απόβλητα που συλλέγονται από την αποχέτευση και παράγει από αυτά νερό και λίπασμα σε υγρή μορφή που διοχετεύεται επίσης στο έδαφος και την άσφαλτο. Ο τρίτος λειτουργεί ως μέσω αποθήκευσης, συντήρησης και εμπλουτισμού νερού.

σύστημα άντλησης αποβλήτων: Το σύστημα αντλεί απόβλητα από το δίκτυο της αποχέτευσης και τα χρησιμοποιεί για την παραγωγή νερού και υγρού λιπάσματος..

σύστημα παραγωγής βιοκαυσίμων: Γύρω από τους τρεις βιο-αντιδραστήρες βρίσκεται ένα σύστημα οριζόντιων σωλήνων που περιέχουν υγρό μίγμα άλγης. Η άλγη, χρησιμοποιώντας το φως του ήλιου και CO_2 που απορροφάει από την ατμόσφαιρα μετατρέπεται σε έλαιο άλγης απελευθερώνοντας παράλληλα O_2. Το έλαιο άλγης είναι μία από τις σημαντικότερες πρώτες ύλες για την παραγωγή βιο-καυσίμων.

μηχανισμός στήριξης: Το σύστημα στηρίζεται σε μεγάλο ύψος με τη βοήθεια έξη μεταλλικών, αρθρωτών ποδιών. Το μεγάλο ύψος, από τη μία λειτουργεί συμβολικά, επισημαίνοντας τη θέση της κατασκευής, από την άλλη δημιουργεί την απαραίτητη διαφορά δυναμικού για να μπορέσουν να διοχετευτούν και να διεισδύσουν οι μικροοργανισμοί, το υγρό λίπασμα και η υγρασία στο έδαφος

σύστημα συλλογής νερού: Στην κορυφή της κατασκευής βρίσκεται ένας συλλέκτης νερού. Ο συλλέκτης μαζεύει το βρόχινο νερό και το διοχετεύει στον βιο-αντιδραστήρα νερού.

σύστημα εμποτισμού εδάφους: Το υγρό λίπασμα, οι μικρο-οργανισμοί και υγρασία διοχετεύονται στη άσφαλτο και το έδαφος ακριβώς κάτω από αυτή. Αυτοί βρίσκουν διέξοδο μέσα από τους πόρους της ασφάλτου και τα κενά μεταξύ ασφάλτου και εδάφους και αρχίζουν να αναπτύσσονται από το κέντρο του σταυρού προς τα τέσσερα άκρα του.

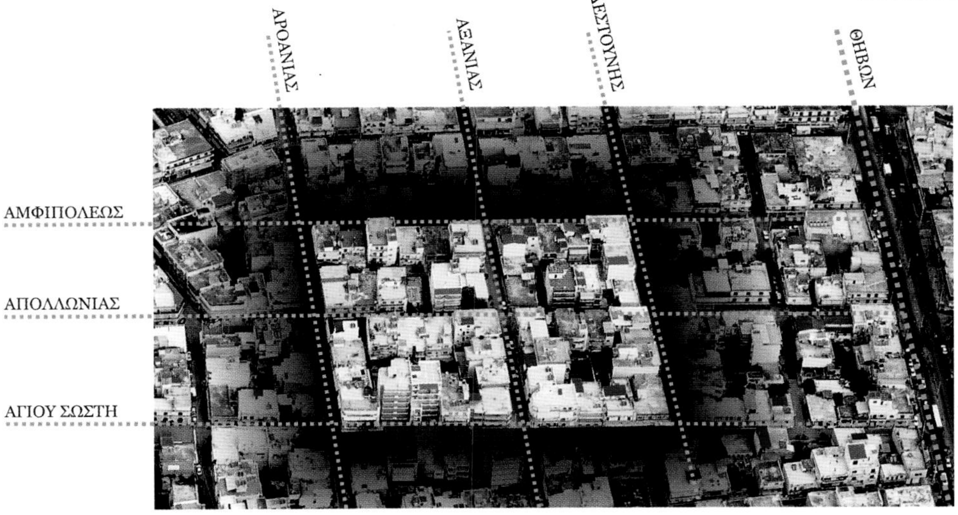
ΑΡΟΑΝΙΑΣ
ΑΞΑΝΙΑΣ
ΔΕΣΤΟΥΝΗΣ
ΘΗΒΩΝ
ΑΜΦΙΠΟΛΕΩΣ
ΑΠΟΛΛΩΝΙΑΣ
ΑΓΙΟΥ ΣΩΣΤΗ

097 Para*site | *object-e architecture*

Design : Dimitris Gourdoukis & Katerina Tryfonidou
Project : entry for the St. Louis Follies Competition
Typology : Urban Intervention
Location : St. Louis, USA

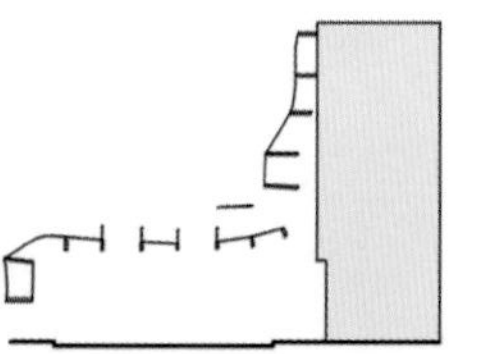
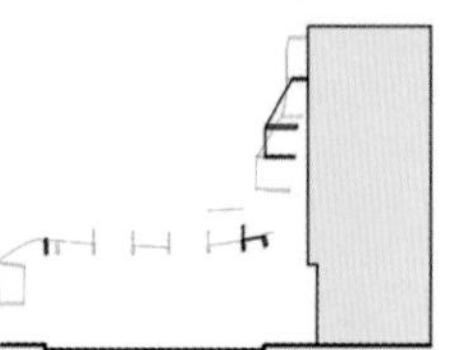
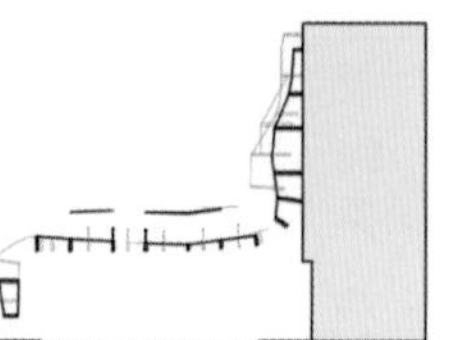
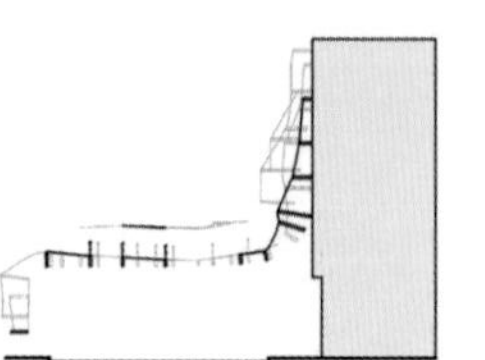
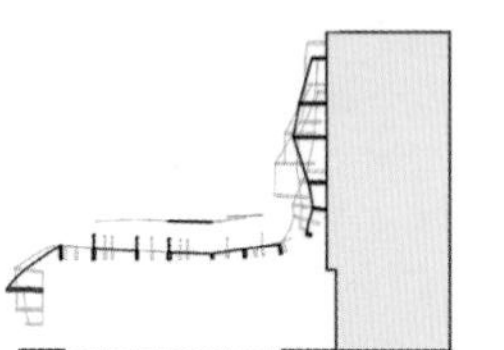
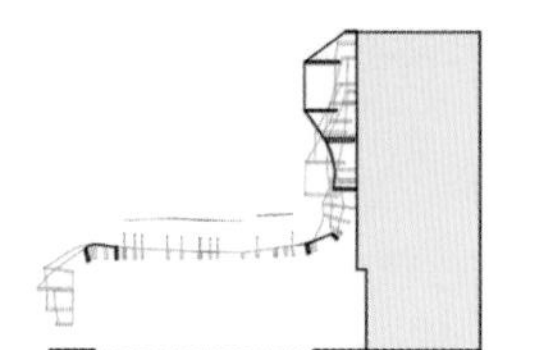
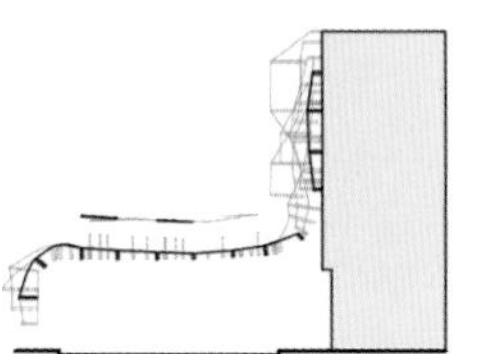

para*site

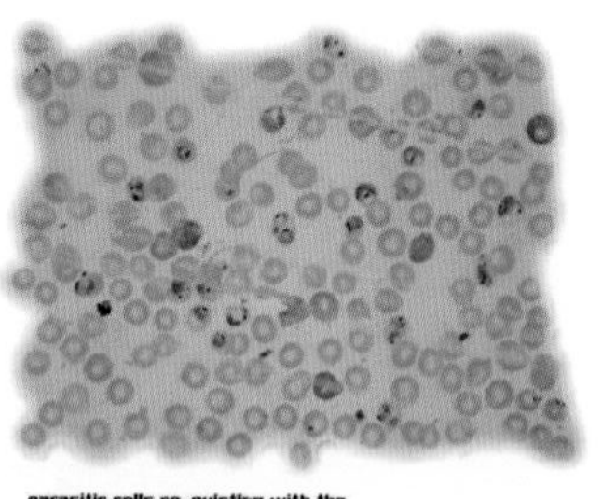
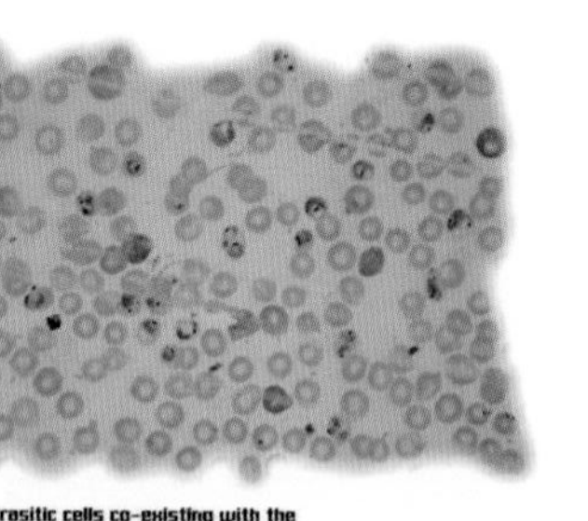
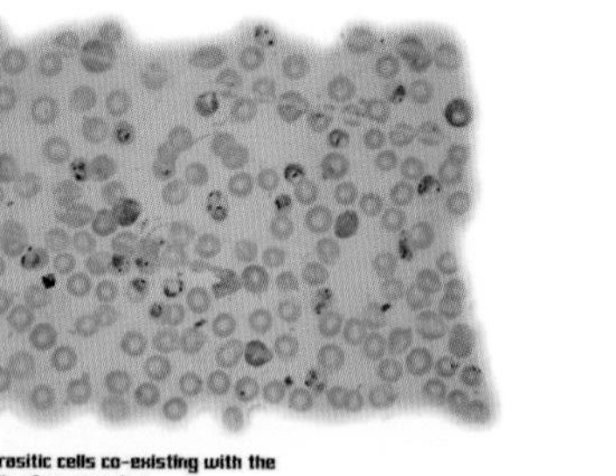
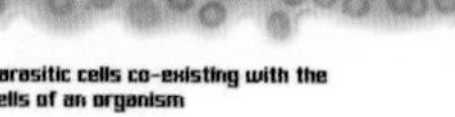
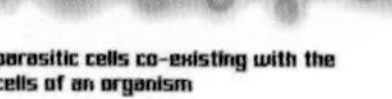

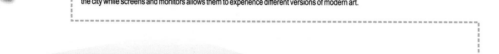

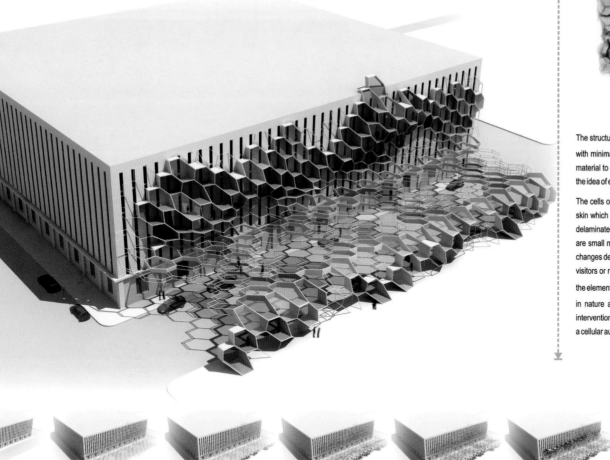

parasitic cells co-existing with the cells of an organism

Parasitism is one version of symbiosis, a phenomenon in which two organisms which are phylogenetically unrelated co-exist over a prolonged period of time, and where the one of the two profits of the symbiosis while the other does not. In the city, many spaces are created using existing buildings as their structural systems. Spaces made spontaneously, in left over areas "infect" the urban tissue in a condition similar to parasitism. These spaces are using the existing urban structure as the territory and an unusual sense of symbiosis appears: the city is enriched by these spaces although it does not control them, and the parasites take advantage of leftover spaces of the city to use as their territory of invasion. The project attempts to look at the intervention as a parasite to the rigid, static yet monumental axis of market str in downtown St. Louis. The space is an information- multimedia knot, on one of the most important axis in St. Louis. The users will have the opportunity to walk inside the mesh, experience different views of the city while screens and monitors allows them to experience different versions of modern art.

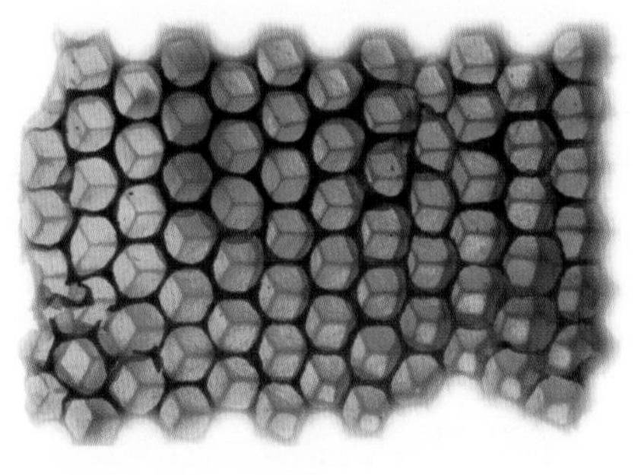

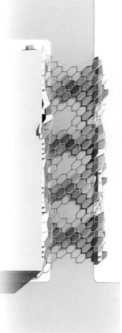

The structure proposed is that of a **honeycomb**: the hexagon tiles the plane with minimal perimeter per piece area. Thus a hexagonal structure uses the least material to create a lattice of cells with a given volume. The honeycomb introduces the idea of economy, apparent in nature as well as in the expansion of the city.

The cells of the honeycomb change colors every one minute; it is a transformable skin which at some points is adjacent to the garage facades and at other points it delaminates to create bridges, sheds and passages. Inside some of the cells there are small multimedia stations that people can visit. The way the color of each cell changes depend on the state of the cells next to it, as well as whether it is occupied by visitors or not. The system where one element transforms according to the state of the elements around it is called a **cellular automaton** and it is found both in nature and in algorithmic man-made and computer generated patterns. The intervention on the garage façade creates a transformable parasite that performs as a cellular automaton.

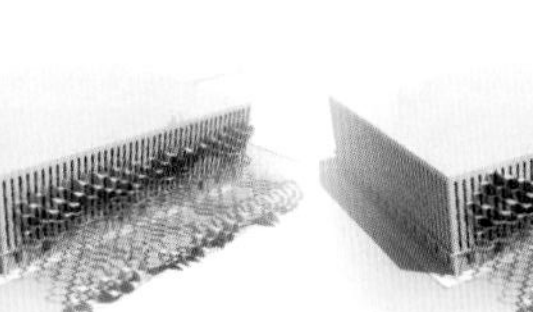
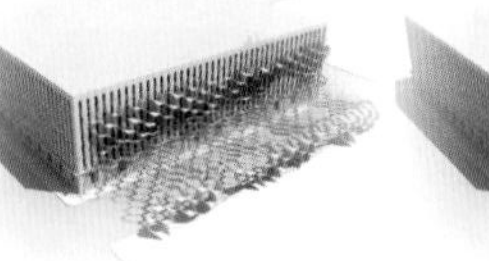
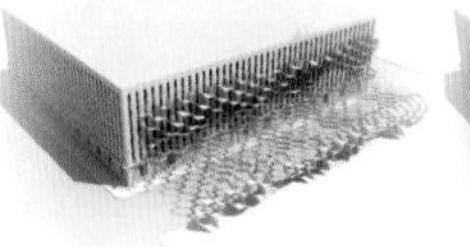

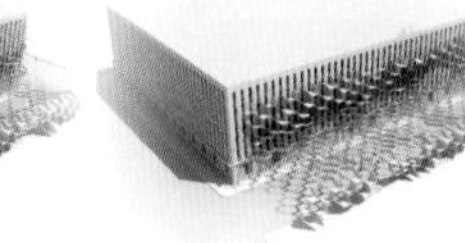
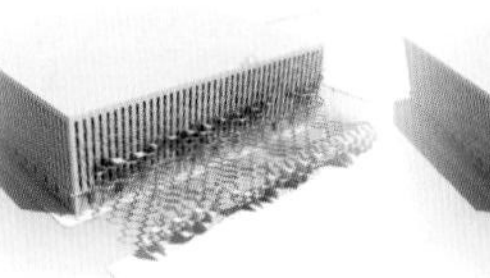

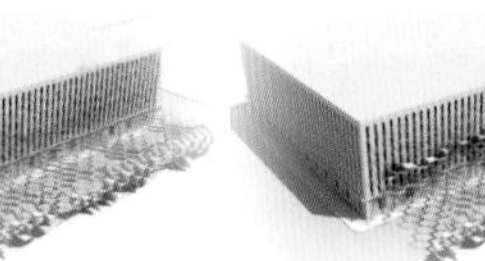
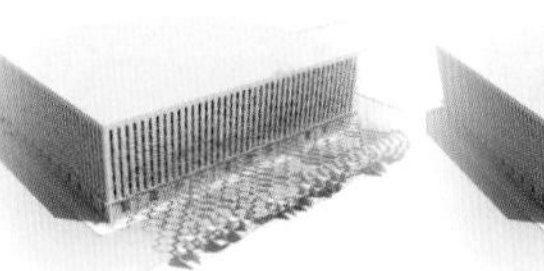

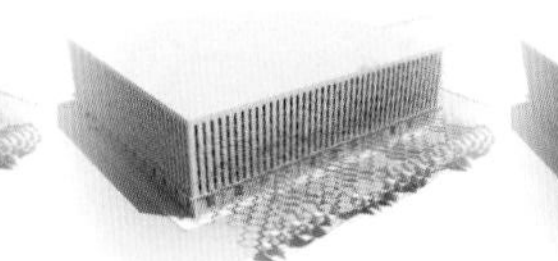

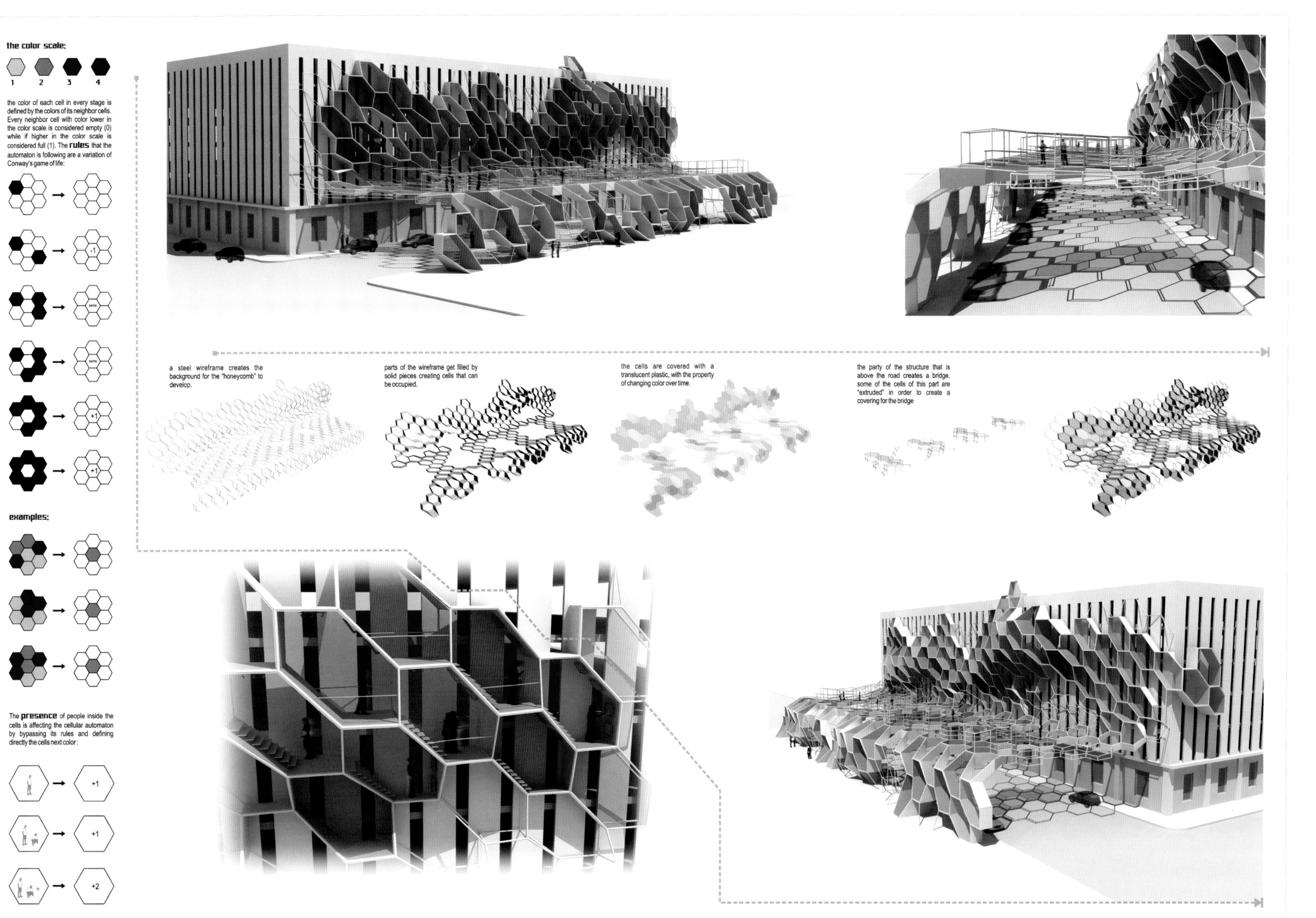

the color scale:
1
2
3
4
the color of each cell in every stage is defined by the colors of its neighbor cells. Every neighbor cell with color lower in the color scale is considered empty (0) while if higher in the color scale is considered full (1). The rules that the automaton is following are a variation of Conway's game of life:
-1
same
same
+1
+1
examples:
The presence of people inside the cells is affecting the cellular automaton by bypassing its rules and defining directly the cells next color:
+1
+1
+2
a steel wireframe creates the background for the "honeycomb" to develop.
parts of the wireframe get filled by solid pieces creating cells that can be occupied.
the cells are covered with a translucent plastic, with the property of changing color over time.
the party of the structure that is above the road creates a bridge. some of the cells of this part are "extruded" in order to create a covering for the bridge

098 Arbatax Waterfront | *ZO_loft*

Architect : Filomena Acquaviva, Andrea Cingoli, Francesca Fontana, Michele Manigrasso, Roberto Potenza
Client : Comune di Toroli (OG)
Location : Arbatax (OG) Italy

Design : 2011
Award : shortlisted

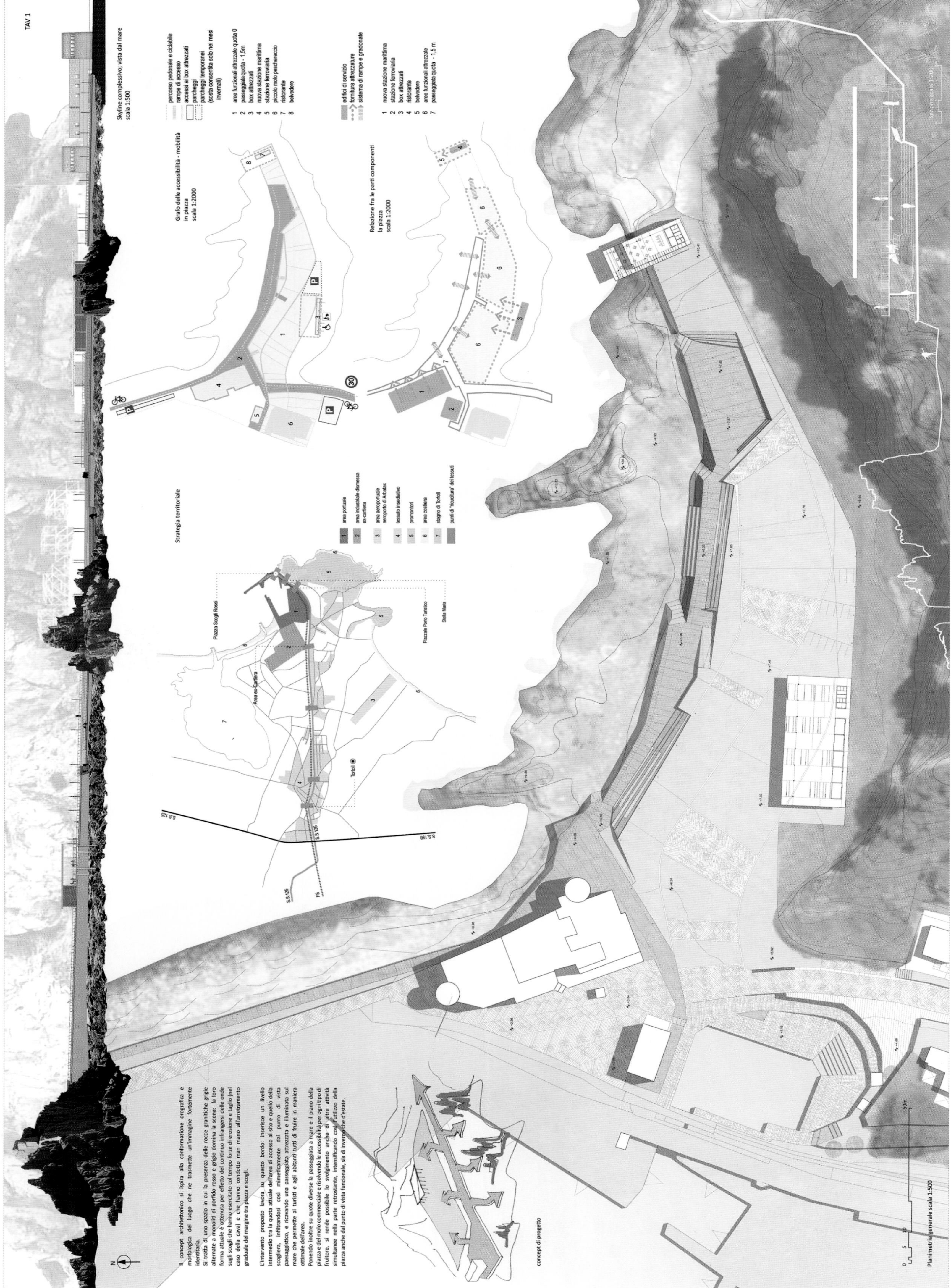

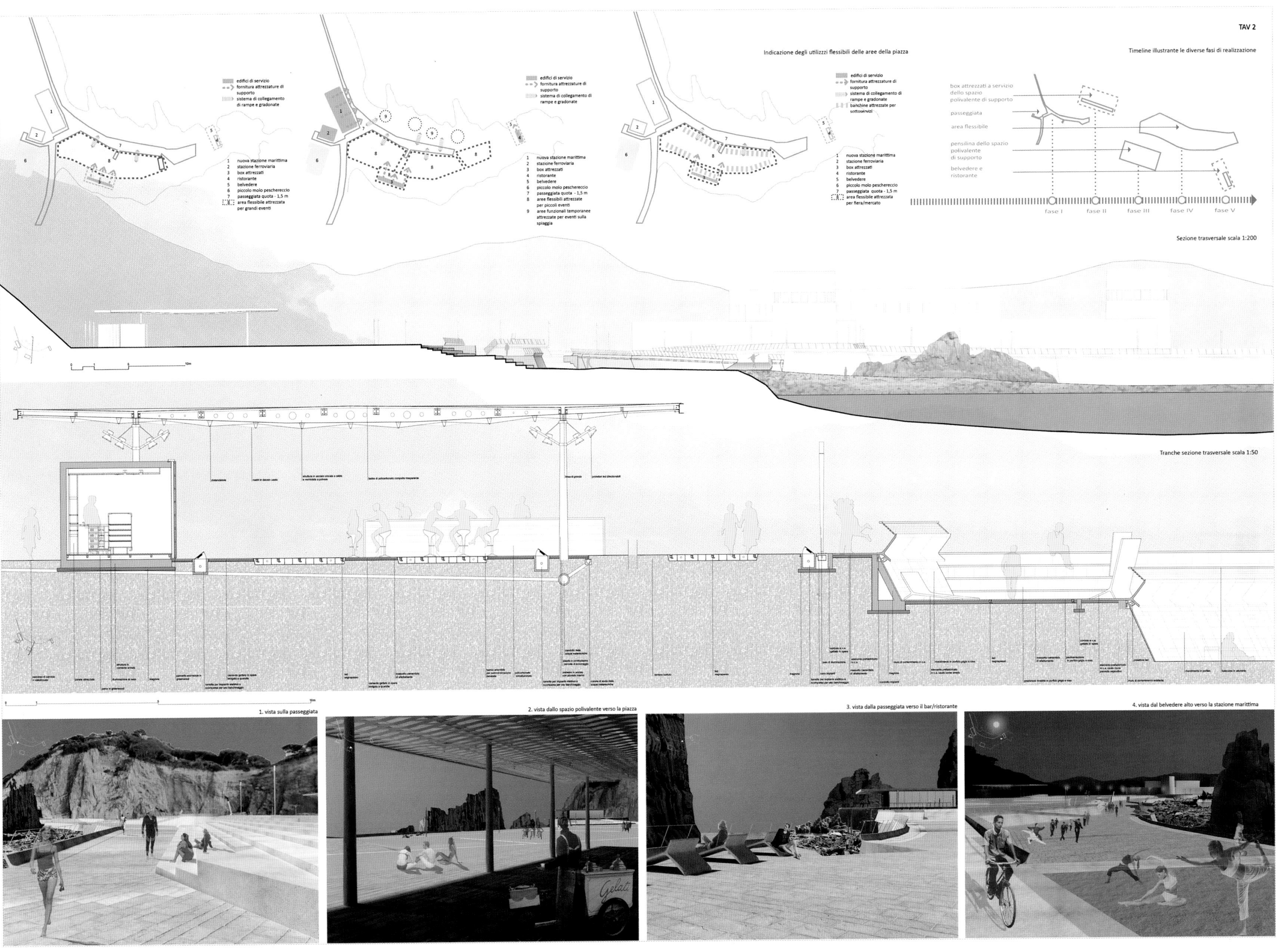
TAV 2
Indicazione degli utilizzi flessibili delle aree della piazza
Timeline illustrante le diverse fasi di realizzazione
edifici di servizio
fornitura attrezzature di supporto
sistema di collegamento di rampe e gradonate
1 nuova stazione marittima
2 stazione ferroviaria
3 box attrezzati
4 ristorante
5 belvedere
6 piccolo molo peschereccio
7 passeggiata quota - 1,5 m
area flessibile attrezzata per grandi eventi
edifici di servizio
fornitura attrezzature di supporto
sistema di collegamento di rampe e gradonate
1 nuova stazione marittima
2 stazione ferroviaria
3 box attrezzati
4 ristorante
5 belvedere
6 piccolo molo peschereccio
7 passeggiata quota - 1,5 m
8 aree flessibili attrezzate per piccoli eventi
9 aree funzionali temporanee attrezzate per eventi sulla spiaggia
edifici di servizio
fornitura attrezzature di supporto
sistema di collegamento di rampe e gradonate
banchine attrezzate per sottoservizi
1 nuova stazione marittima
2 stazione ferroviaria
3 box attrezzati
4 ristorante
5 belvedere
6 piccolo molo peschereccio
7 passeggiata quota - 1,5 m
area flessibile attrezzata per fiera/mercato
box attrezzati a servizio dello spazio polivalente di supporto
passeggiata
area flessibile
pensilina dello spazio polivalente di supporto
belvedere e ristorante
fase I
fase II
fase III
fase IV
fase V
Sezione trasversale scala 1:200
Tranche sezione trasversale scala 1:50
1. vista sulla passeggiata
2. vista dallo spazio polivalente verso la piazza
3. vista dalla passeggiata verso il bar/ristorante
4. vista dal belvedere alto verso la stazione marittima
Gelati

099 Viale Vittoria | *ZO_loft*

Architect : Paolo Emilio Bellisario, Valerio Bracci, Ilias Fragkakis
Client : Comune di Jesi (AN)
Location : Jesi (AN) Italy
Award : 1° prize

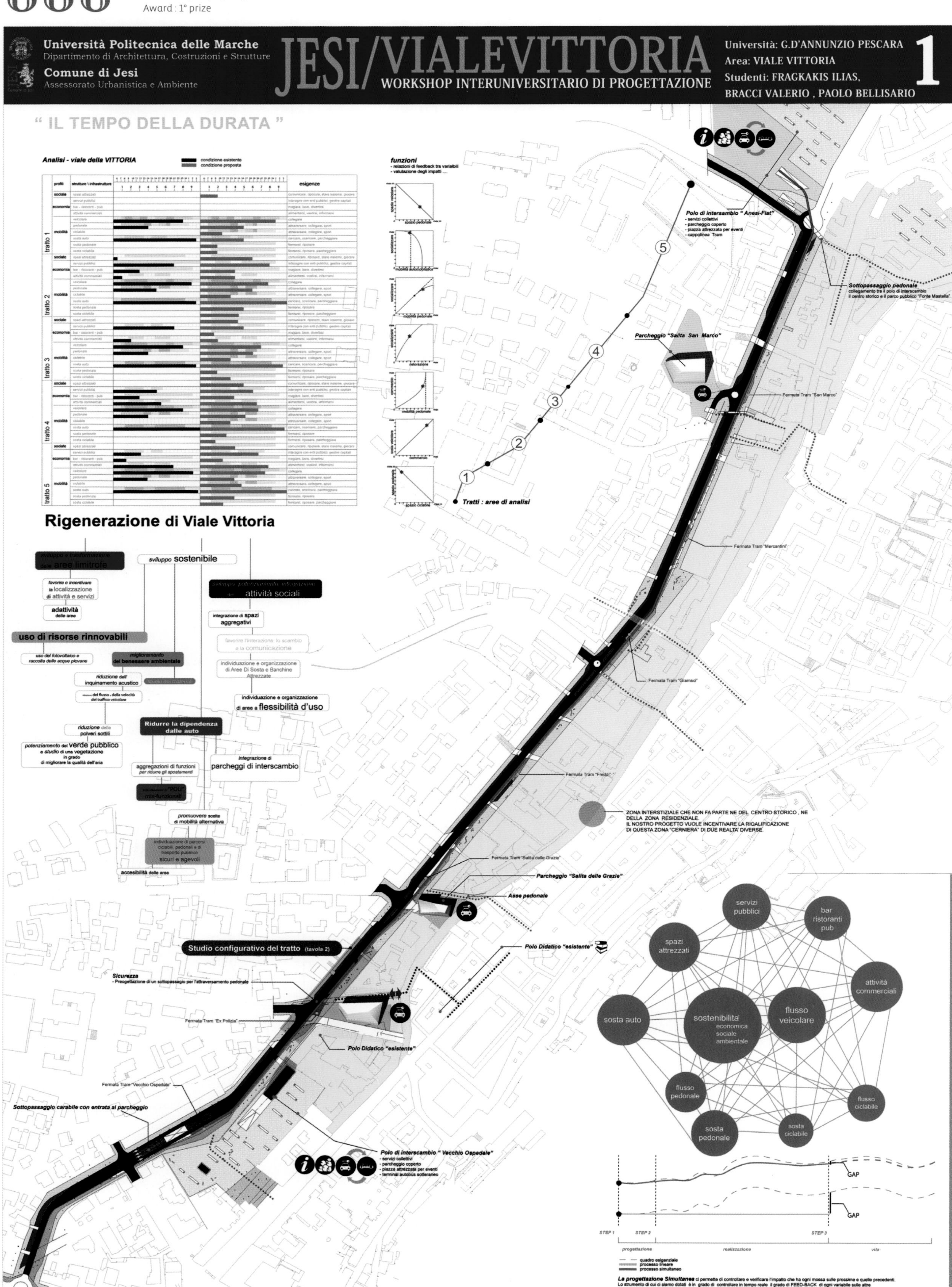

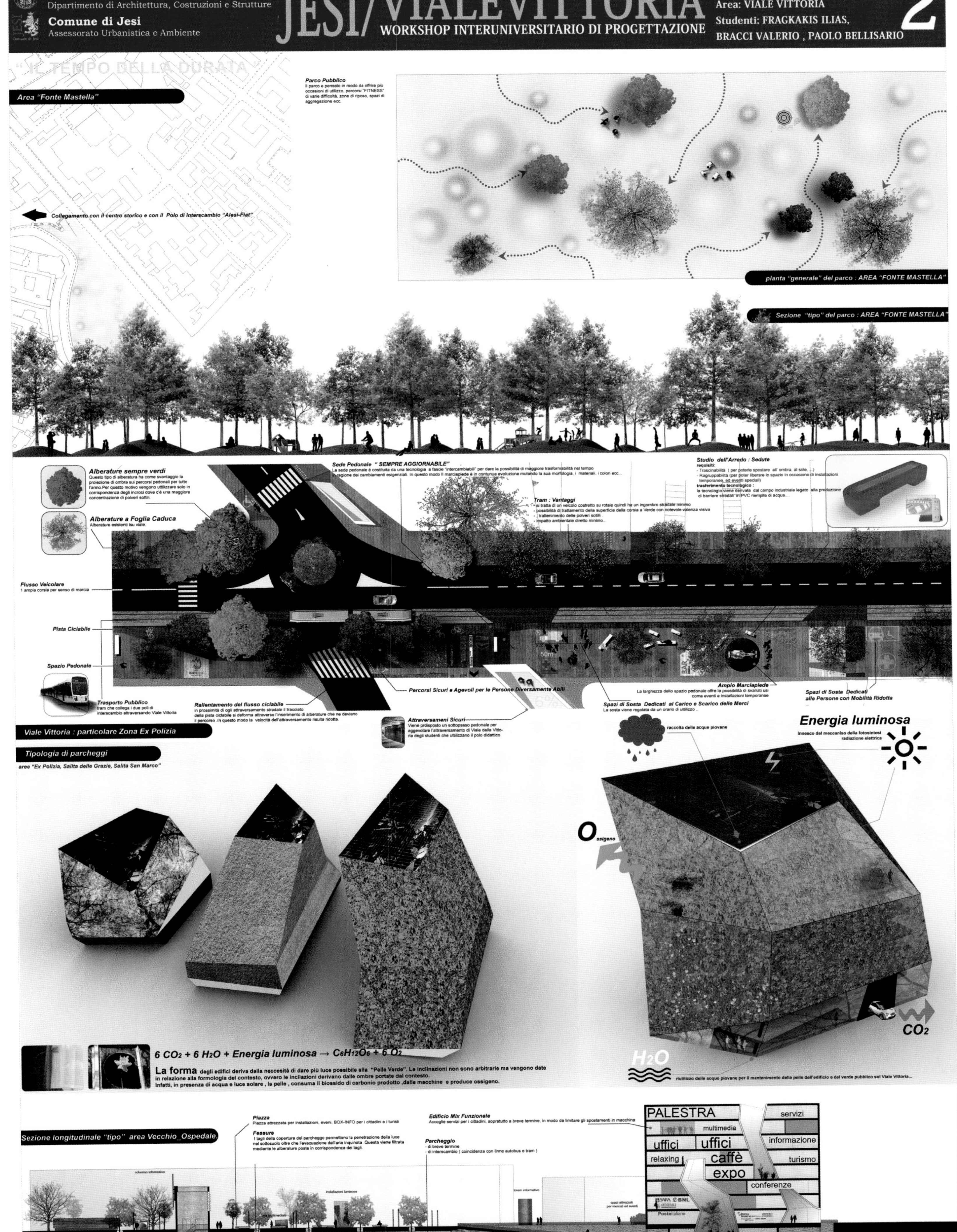
Università Politecnica delle Marche
Dipartimento di Architettura, Costruzioni e Strutture
Comune di Jesi
Assessorato Urbanistica e Ambiente
JESI/VIALEVITTORIA
WORKSHOP INTERUNIVERSITARIO DI PROGETTAZIONE
Università: G.D'ANNUNZIO PESCARA
Area: VIALE VITTORIA
Studenti: FRAGKAKIS ILIAS, BRACCI VALERIO , PAOLO BELLISARIO
2
"IL TEMPO DELLA DURATA"
Area "Fonte Mastella"
Parco Pubblico
Il parco e pensato in modo da offrire più occasioni di utilizzo, percorsi "FITNESS" di varie difficoltà, zone di riposo, spazi di aggregazione ecc.
Collegamento con il centro storico e con il Polo di Interscambio "Alesi-Fiat"
pianta "generale" del parco : AREA "FONTE MASTELLA"
Sezione "tipo" del parco : AREA "FONTE MASTELLA"
Alberature sempre verdi
Questo tipo di alberatura ha come svantaggio la proiezione di ombra sui percorsi pedonali per tutto l'anno.Per questo motivo vengono utilizzare solo in corrispondenza degli incroci dove c'è una maggiore concentrazione di polveri sottili.
Alberature a Foglia Caduca
Alberature esistenti isu viale.
Sede Pedonale " SEMPRE AGGIORNABILE"
La sede pedonale è costituita da una tecnologia a fascie "intercambiabili" per dare la possibilità di maggiore trasformabilità nel tempo in ragione dei cambiamenti esigenziali. In questo modo Il marciapiede è in continua evoluzione mutando la sua morfologia, i materiali, i colori ecc...
Tram : Vantaggi
- si tratta di un veicolo costretto su rotaie quindi ha un ingombro stradale minimo
- possibilità di trattamento della superficie della corsia a Verde con notevole valenza visiva
- trattenimento delle polveri sottili
- impatto ambientale diretto minimo...
Studio dell'Arredo : Sedute
requisiti:
- Trascinabilità (per poterle spostare all' ombra, al sole, ...)
- Ragruppabilità (per poter liberare lo spazio in occasione di installazioni temporanee, ed eventi speciali)
trasferimento tecnologico :
la tecnologia viene derivata dal campo industriale legato alla produzione di barriere stradali in PVC riempite di acqua....
Flusso Veicolare
1 ampia corsia per senso di marcia
Pista Ciclabile
Spazio Pedonale
Trasporto Pubblico
tram che collega i due poli di interscambio attraversando Viale Vittoria
Rallentamento del flusso ciclabile
in prossimità di ogli attraversamento stradale il tracciato della pista ciclabile si deforma attraverso l'inserimento di alberature che ne deviano il percorso .In questo modo la velocità dell'attraversamento risulta ridotta.
Percorsi Sicuri e Agevoli per le Persone Diversamente Abili
Attraversameni Sicuri
Viene prdisposto un sottopasso pedonale per aggevolare l'attraversamento di Viale della Vittoria degli studenti che utilizzano il polo didattico.
Ampio Marciapiede
La larghezza dello spazio pedonale offre la possibilità di svariati usi come eventi e installazioni temporanee
Spazi di Sosta Dedicati al Carico e Scarico delle Merci
La sosta viene regolata da un orario di utilizzo ..
Spazi di Sosta Dedicati alle Persone con Mobilità Ridotta
50m
BAR
Viale Vittoria : particolare Zona Ex Polizia
Tipologia di parcheggi
aree "Ex Polizia, Salita delle Grazie, Salita San Marco"
raccolta delle acque piovane
Energia luminosa
innesco del meccaniso della fotosintesi radiazione elettrica
Ossigeno
CO_2
H_2O
$6 CO_2 + 6 H_2O$ + Energia luminosa $\rightarrow C_6H_{12}O_6 + 6 O_2$
La forma degli edifici deriva dalla neccesità di dare più luce possibile alla "Pelle Verde". Le inclinazioni non sono arbitrarie ma vengono date in relazione alla formologia del contesto, ovvero le incilazioni derivano dalle ombre portate dal contesto.
Infatti, in presenza di acqua e luce solare , la pelle , consuma il biossido di carbonio prodotto ,dalle macchine e produce ossigeno.
riutilizzo delle acque piovane per il mantenimento della pelle dell'edificio e del verde pubblico sul Viale Vittoria...
Sezione longitudinale "tipo" area Vecchio_Ospedale.
Piazza
Piazza attrezzata per installazioni, eveni, BOX-INFO per i cittadini e i turisti
Fessure
I tagli della copertura del parcheggio permettono la penetrazione della luce nel sottosuolo oltre che l'evacuazione dell'aria inquinata .Questa viene filtrata mediante le alberature poste in corrispondenza dei tagli.
Edificio Mix Funzionale
Accoglie servizi per i cittadini, sopratutto a breve termine, in modo da limitare gli spostamenti in macchina
Parcheggio
- di breve termine
- di interscambio (coincidenza con linne autobus e tram)
PALESTRA
servizi
multimedia
uffici
uffici
informazione
relaxing
caffè
turismo
expo
conferenze

Town&Country | *Arquipelago Studio*

Noted as a Finalist to the London Farm Tower Competition

Project Team : Gregory Marinic(Principal), Karen Mendoza, Alejandra Rios, Andrea Barrero, Stephanie Garcia

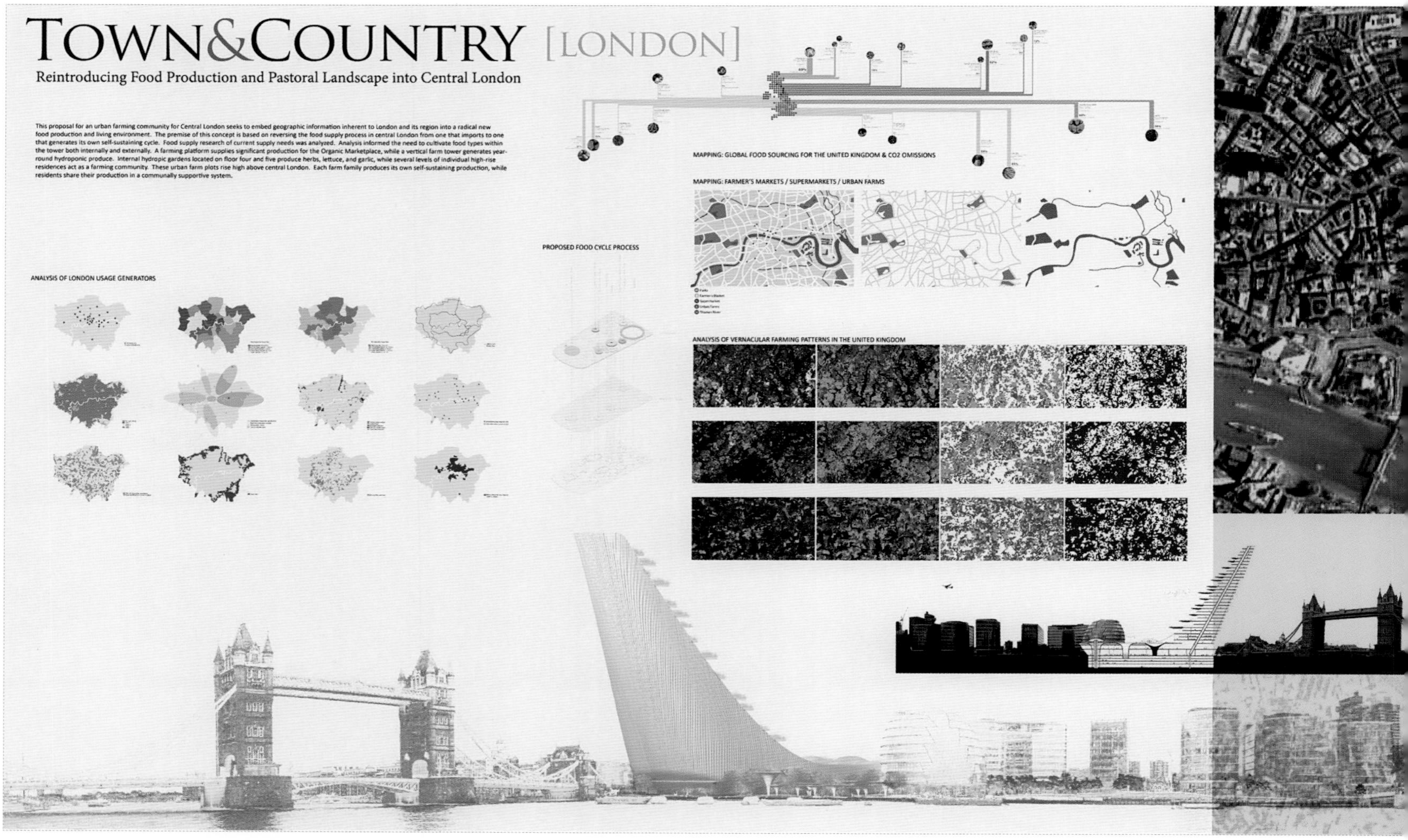

TOWN&COUNTRY [LONDON]

Reintroducing Food Production and Pastoral Landscape into Central London

This proposal for an urban farming community for Central London seeks to embed geographic information inherent to London and its region into a radical new food production and living environment. The premise of this concept is based on reversing the food supply process in central London from one that imports to one that generates its own self-sustaining cycle. Food supply research of current supply needs was analyzed. Analysis informed the need to cultivate food types within the tower both internally and externally. A farming platform supplies significant production for the Organic Marketplace, while a vertical farm tower generates year-round hydroponic produce. Internal hydropic gardens located on floor four and five produce herbs, lettuce, and garlic, while several levels of individual high-rise residences act as a farming community. These urban farm plots rise high above central London. Each farm family produces its own self-sustaining production, while residents share their production in a communally supportive system.

ANALYSIS OF LONDON USAGE GENERATORS

PROPOSED FOOD CYCLE PROCESS

MAPPING: GLOBAL FOOD SOURCING FOR THE UNITED KINGDOM & CO2 OMISSIONS

MAPPING: FARMER'S MARKETS / SUPERMARKETS / URBAN FARMS

ANALYSIS OF VERNACULAR FARMING PATTERNS IN THE UNITED KINGDOM

VERTICAL HYDROPONIC GARDENS

The 21st Century Right of Way | *Ian Caine + Derek Hoeferlin*

101

Location : Long Island, New York, USA
Client : Build a Better Burb Competition – Sponsored by the Long Island Index, a Project of the Rauch Foundation
Year : 2010, Finalist

Participants : Ian Caine and Derek Hoeferlin – co-lead Designers; Jing Chen, Xi Chen, Akshita Sivakumar, Jonathan Stitelman – team
Project : Design Solution for Suburban Downtowns
Typology : Infrastructure, Private and Public Space, Mixed-Use

21c R.O.W.

The 21st Century Right-of-Way

Principles

The 21st Century Right of Way...

IS RADICAL BUT REAL

21c R.O.W. is a new suburban concept that will fundamentally alter the physical and legal structure of the strip. 21c R.O.W. is also cost effective and ready for immediate implementation on Long Island.

DOES NOT REQUIRE ANY NEW TECHNOLOGY

21c R.O.W. begins with the assumption that we cannot 'invent' a solution for our suburban predicament. 21c R.O.W. accepts the prevalence of the automobile for the next 25 years while critiquing our reliance on uncoordinated, redundant parking infrastructure.

REQUIRES COLLECTIVE THOUGHT AND ACTION

21c R.O.W. is implemented locally through the introduction of a new, coordinated municipal zoning structure.

BALANCES PUBLIC AND PRIVATE INTERESTS

21c R.O.W. repositions the public sector as the long term guardian of infrastructure and public space, while freeing up the private sector to do what it does best: innovate and money-make.

Long Island Index Targeted Downtowns for Development

96 low
31 medium
29 high potential
LIRR expansion
LIE expansion

Mall Type
Grid Type
Strip Type

17 of the 29 high potential downtowns are Strips

EXISTING
SINGULAR R.O.W.

INTERVENTION
21c R.O.W.

The 21st CENTURY RIGHT OF WAY
21c R.O.W. expands existing singular public right-of-ways through private lots to create efficent parking, multiple access and comprehensive water management. In order to minimize the impact on developers, this right-of-way will track along existing demising lot lines--essentially acting as a thickened easement. Developers, in return for giving up this underutilized land, will receive full access to this new public infrastructure.

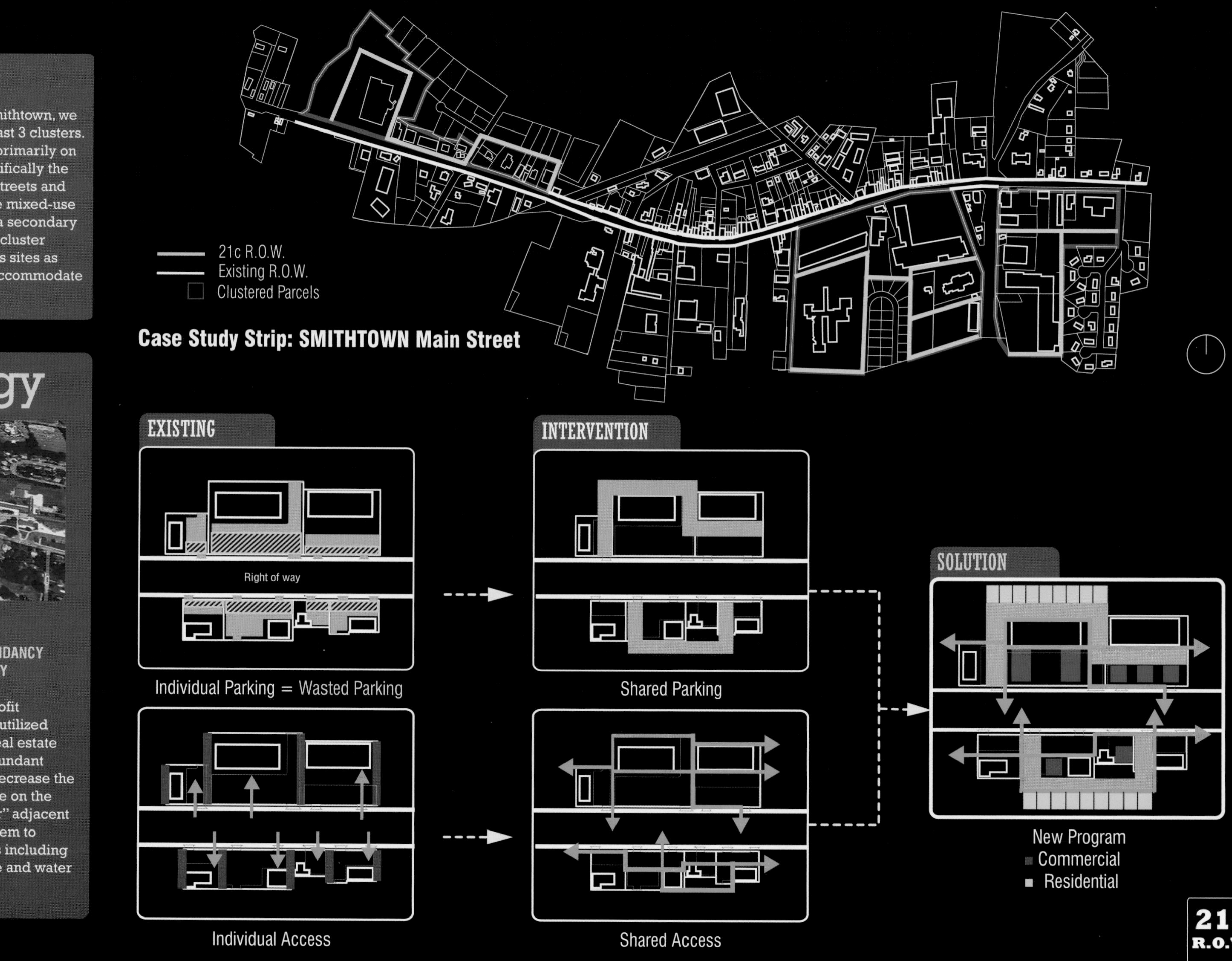
CLUSTERED PARCELS
In the case of downtown Smithtown, we see the possibility for at least 3 clusters. We base cluster selection primarily on physical morphology; specifically the physical proximity of lots, streets and blocks. The desire to create mixed-use program within clusters is a secondary consideration. Criteria for cluster selection will change across sites as planning officials seek to accommodate local conditions.
Strategy
INDIVIDUAL PARKING = REDUNDANCY
CLUSTERED LOTS = EFFICIENCY
One of the best ways to retrofit thousands of acres of underutilized asphalt is to decrease the real estate devoted to parking and redundant infrastructure. In order to decrease the total amount of infrastructure on the strip, we propose to "cluster" adjacent parcels, thereby allowing them to share critical infrastructures including parking, pedestrian, bicycle and water management.
21c R.O.W.
Existing R.O.W.
Clustered Parcels
Case Study Strip: SMITHTOWN Main Street
EXISTING
Right of way
Individual Parking = Wasted Parking
Individual Access
INTERVENTION
Shared Parking
Shared Access
SOLUTION
New Program
Commercial
Residential
21c
R.O.W.

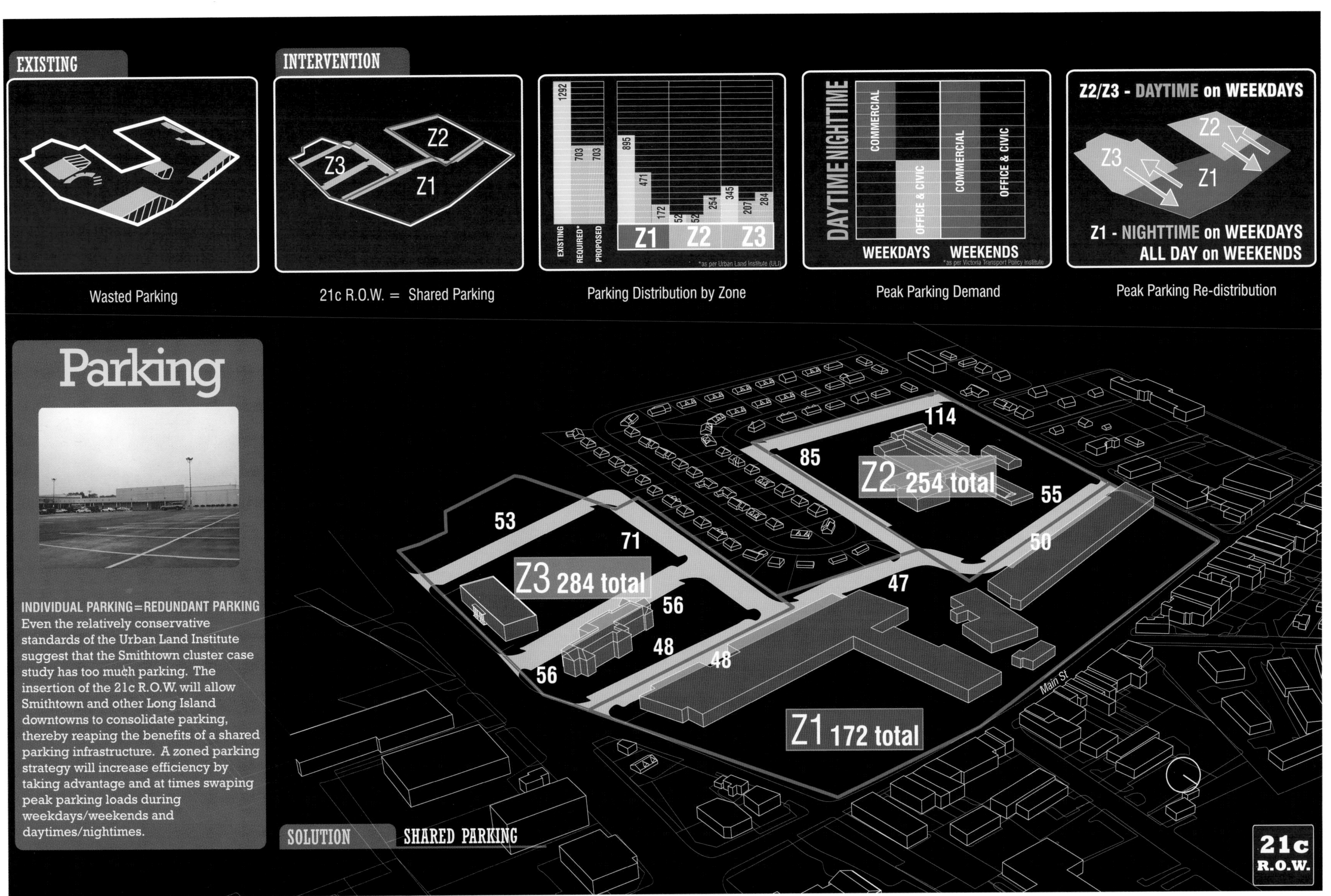

INDIVIDUAL PARKING=REDUNDANT PARKING

Even the relatively conservative standards of the Urban Land Institute suggest that the Smithtown cluster case study has too much parking. The insertion of the 21c R.O.W. will allow Smithtown and other Long Island downtowns to consolidate parking, thereby reaping the benefits of a shared parking infrastructure. A zoned parking strategy will increase efficiency by taking advantage and at times swaping peak parking loads during weekdays/weekends and daytimes/nightimes.

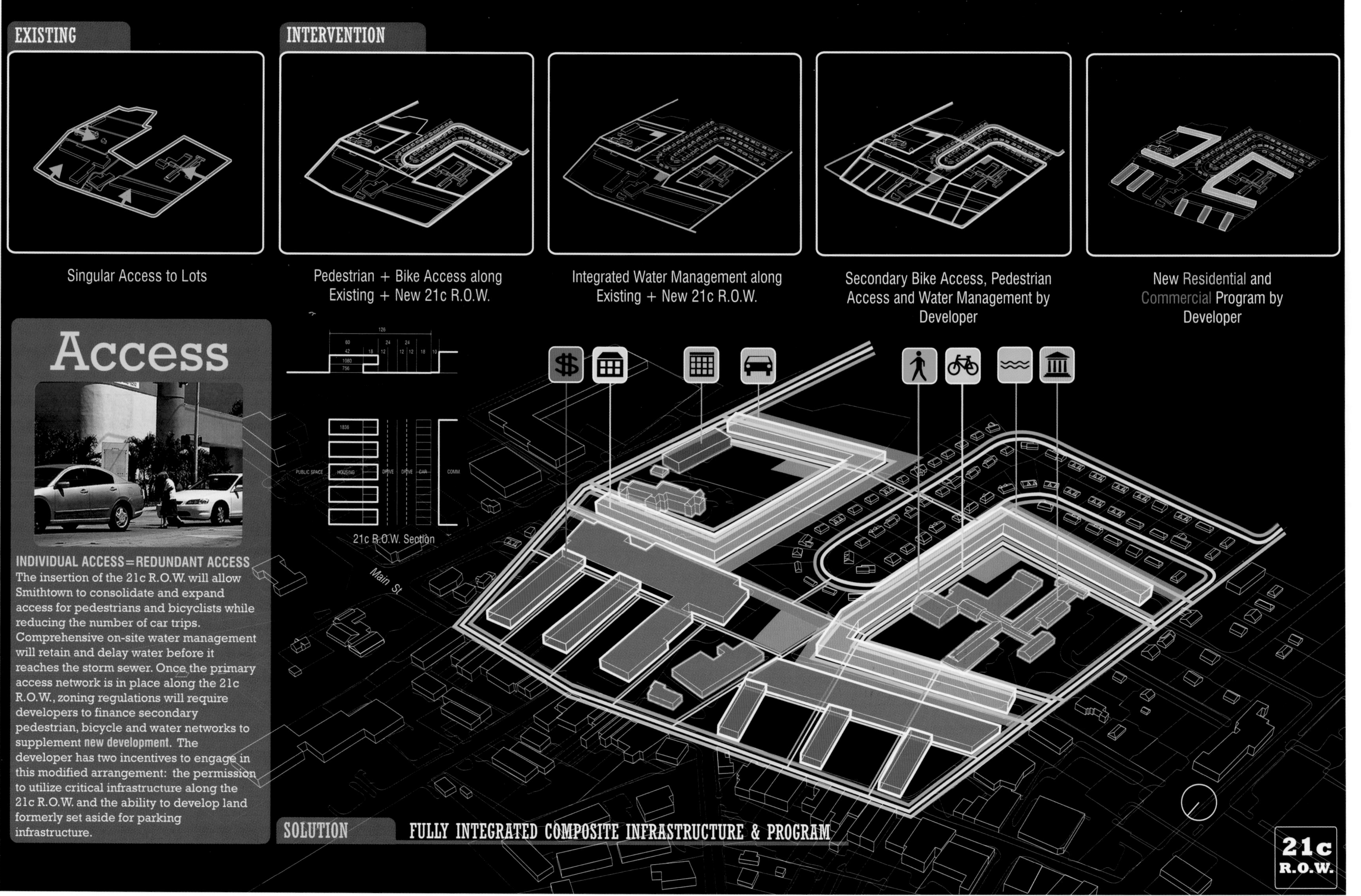
EXISTING
INTERVENTION
Singular Access to Lots
Pedestrian + Bike Access along Existing + New 21c R.O.W.
Integrated Water Management along Existing + New 21c R.O.W.
Secondary Bike Access, Pedestrian Access and Water Management by Developer
New Residential and Commercial Program by Developer
Access
INDIVIDUAL ACCESS=REDUNDANT ACCESS
The insertion of the 21c R.O.W. will allow Smithtown to consolidate and expand access for pedestrians and bicyclists while reducing the number of car trips. Comprehensive on-site water management will retain and delay water before it reaches the storm sewer. Once the primary access network is in place along the 21c R.O.W., zoning regulations will require developers to finance secondary pedestrian, bicycle and water networks to supplement new development. The developer has two incentives to engage in this modified arrangement: the permission to utilize critical infrastructure along the 21c R.O.W. and the ability to develop land formerly set aside for parking infrastructure.
21c R.O.W. Section
Main St
SOLUTION
FULLY INTEGRATED COMPOSITE INFRASTRUCTURE & PROGRAM
21c
R.O.W.

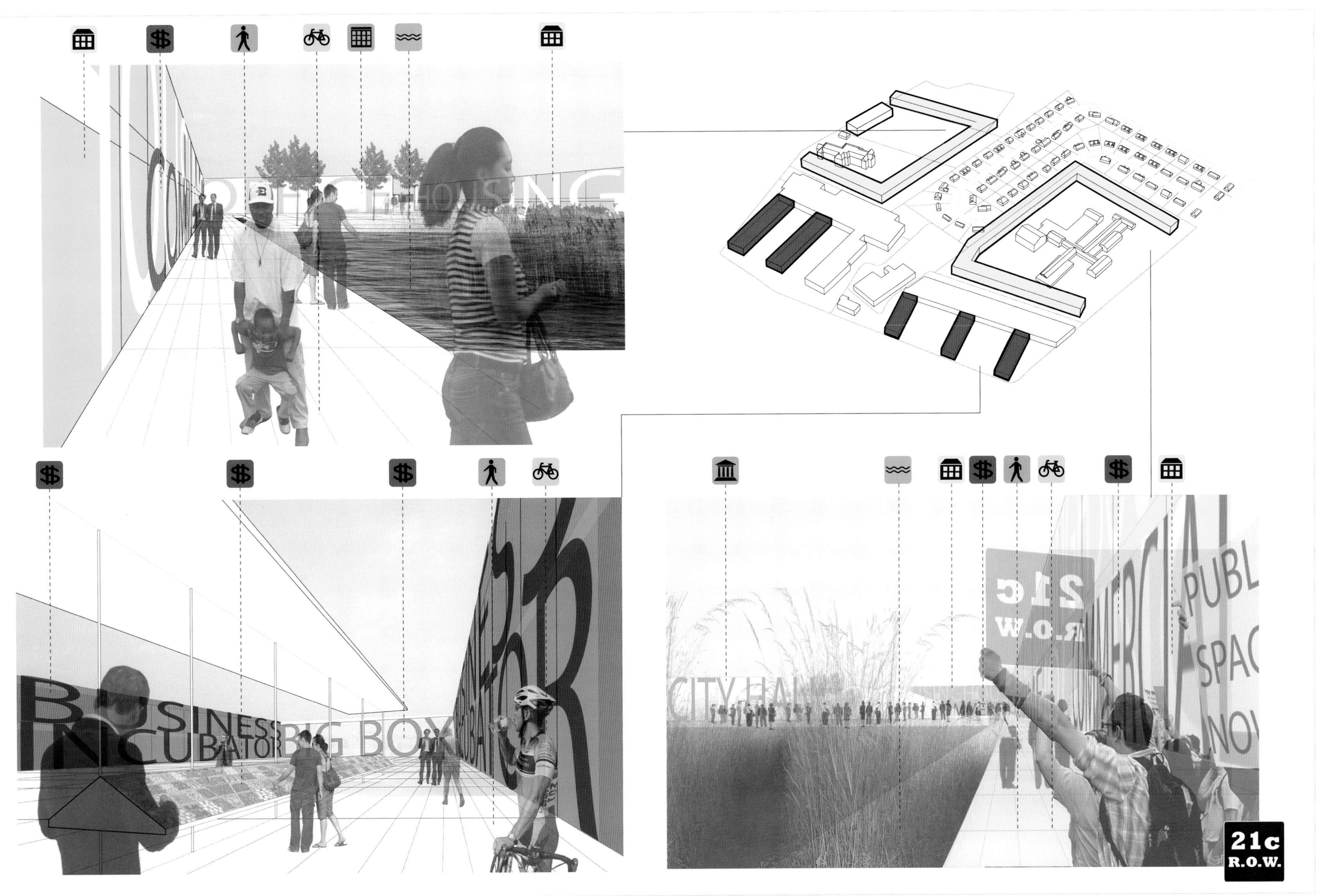
HOUSING
BUSINESS
INCUBATOR
BIG BOX
CITY HALL
21c
R.O.W.

102

The 100 Year Plan | *Ian Caine + Derek Hoeferlin*

Participants : Ian Caine and Derek Hoeferlin, co-lead Designers; Michael Heller, Research Assistant
Project : Design Solution for Sea Level Rise
Typology : Adaptive Infrastructure and Comprehensive Water Management Design
Location : San Francisco Bay, California, USA

Client : Rising Tides Competition – sponsored by San Francisco Bay Conservation and Development Commission

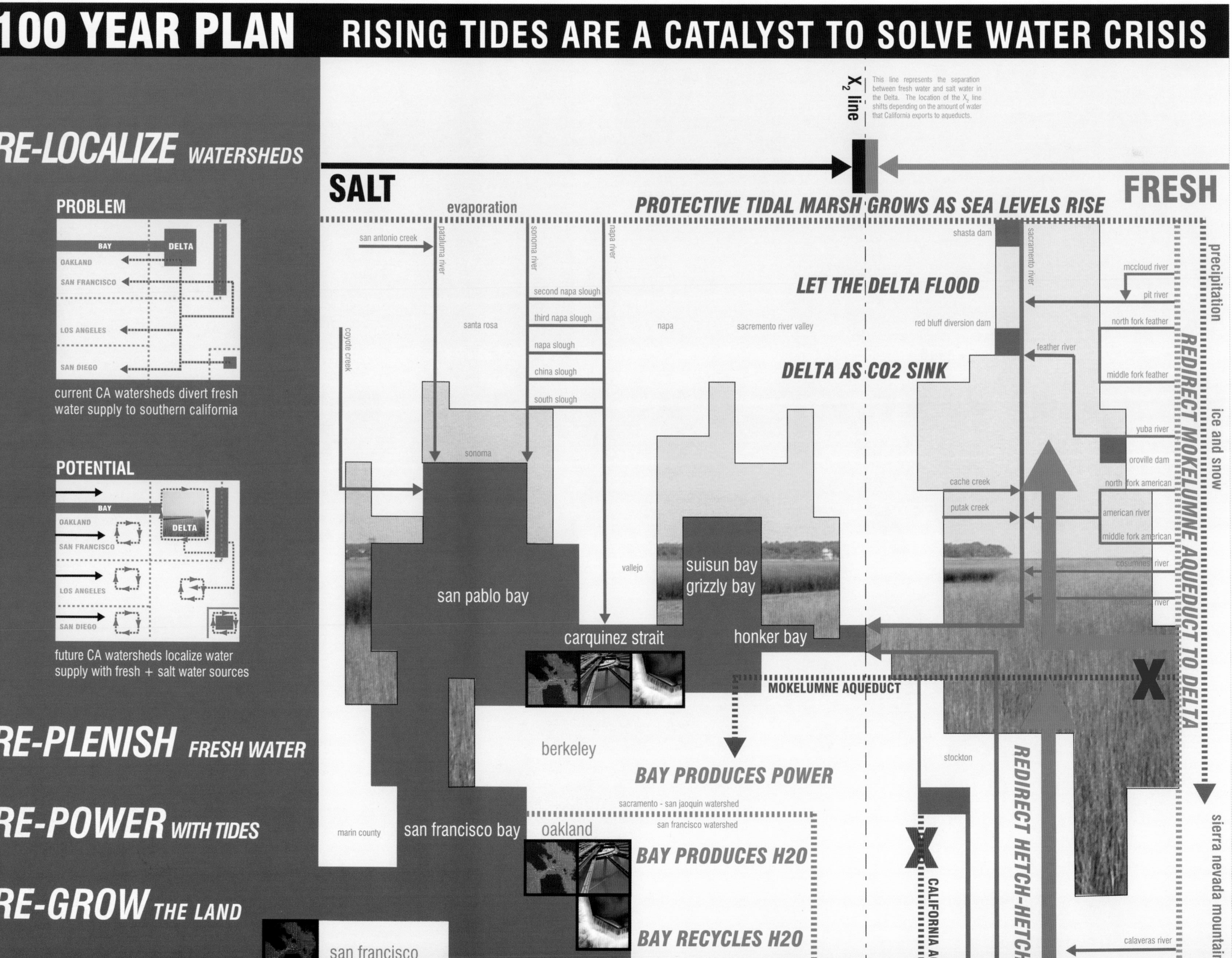

of rising tides can provide a catalyst which leads us to comprehensively **RE-BALANCE** the water system in **CALIFORNIA AND BEYOND**.
Our **100 YEAR PLAN** is political first and foremost. It advocates for an ambitious policy-based **TOOLKIT** that trades the "watershed hopping" method of massive water transport (which is energy intensive and environmentally destructive) for a more localized approach. We propose fresh water via sustainable desalination and water recycling programs along with tidal marsh regeneration, powered and protected by **RISING TIDES** over the course of the next 100 years.
HETCH-HETCHY AQUEDUCT
san francisco watershed
hetch-hetchy dam reservoir
tuolumne river
merced river
san joaquin river
central valley
friant dam
friant-kern canal
cross valley canal
LA AQUEDUCT
san luis reservoir
san luis canal
RE-LOCALIZE WATERSHEDS
PROTECTIVE TIDAL MARSH GROWS AS SEA LEVELS RISE
san jose
san francisco watershed
pajaro watershed
to southern california
TOOLKIT
BAY:
DELTA:
DESALINATION
Growing coastal populations and the subsequent demand for freshwater have transformed the economics of desalination, making it a viable method for providing freshwater. The environmental impact of desalination, particularly from brine, can be greatly reduced through planning and combination with other water infrastructures.
marine life screening
reverse osmosis
ph adjustment
TIDAL MARSH
potable water
SALT
mitigated brine output
TIDAL POWER
Tidal action provides a clean, renewable and predictable source of energy. Both tidal stream at bay inlets and tidal lagoons at points of maximum tidal differential are environmentally viable.These methods harvest an infinite power source to address the large demands of desalination and water recycling. Excess power is available for export to off-set reliance on fossil fuels.
export power
chemical treatment
biosolid harvesting
solid screening
WATER RECYCLING
Water recycling is an essential tool in responsible water management. It is increasingly relevant as water usage continues to grow. The process collects and cleans waste water including raw sewage and run-off from residential, commercial and agricultural uses.
X_2 line
This line represents the separation between fresh water and salt water in the Delta. The location of the X_2 line shifts depending on the amount of water that California exports to aqueducts.
TIDAL MARSH
Tidal marshes have three productive outcomes: they are environmentally friendly storm surge barriers (the sponge effect); they grow as sea levels rise by depositing sediment (the growth effect); they remove carbon from the air (the carbon sink effect).
CO_2 sink
grow earth
protection
grow earth
water + sediment
FRESH
9461OP

103 The Tsunami + Coral Reef Research Network | *Ian Caine + Derek Hoeferlin*

Participants : Ian Caine and Derek Hoeferlin – co-lead designers; Jing Chen, Xi Chen, Akshita Sivakumar, Jonathan Stitelman – team
Project : Design Solution for Climate Change and Tsunamis
Typology : Water-Based Research-Visitor Center/ Armature for Environmental Regeneration

Location : Kuta Beach, Bali, Indonesia
Client : Bali 2010 Marine Research Center in Indonesia Competition – sponsored by Arquitectum and Pelita Harapan University

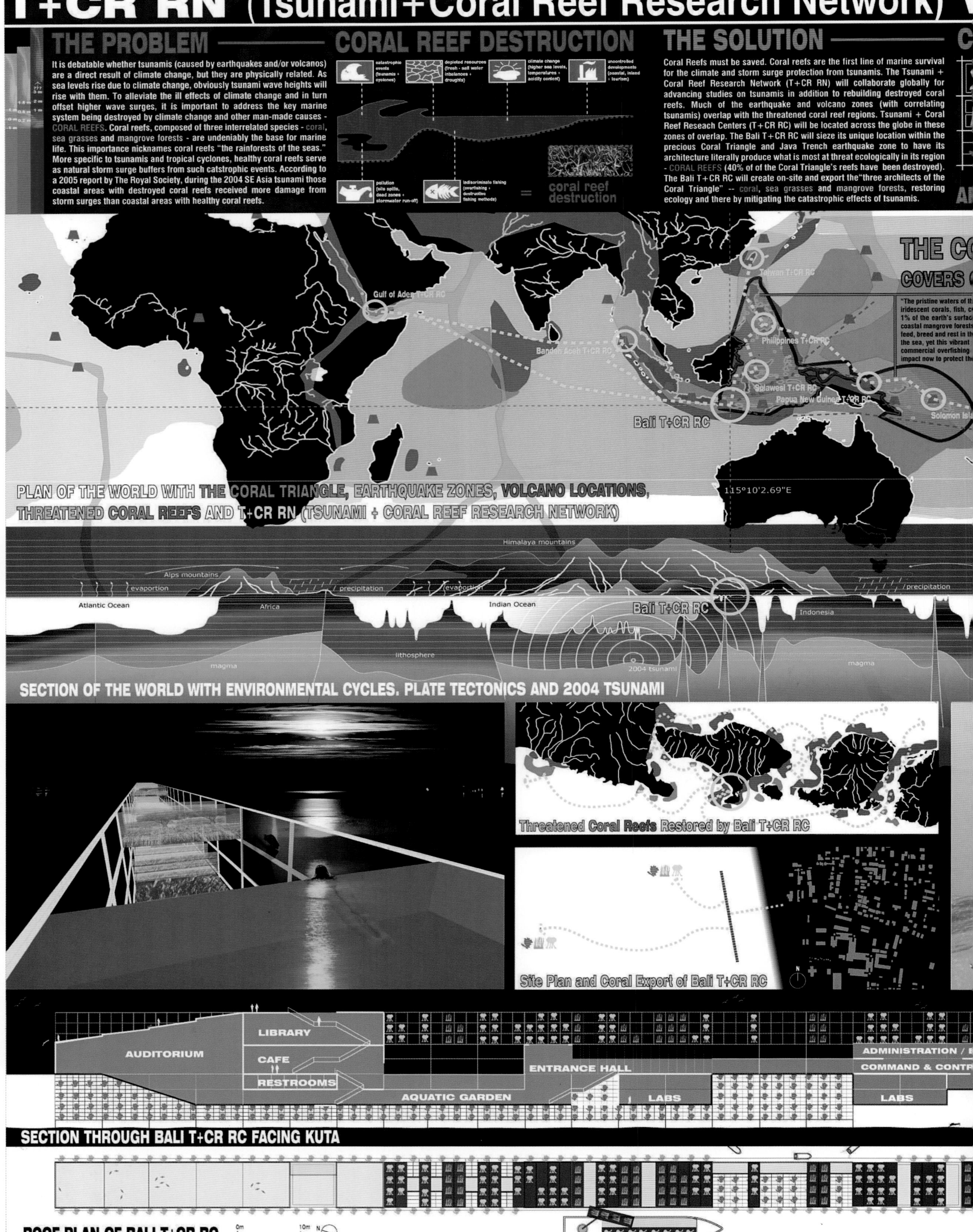

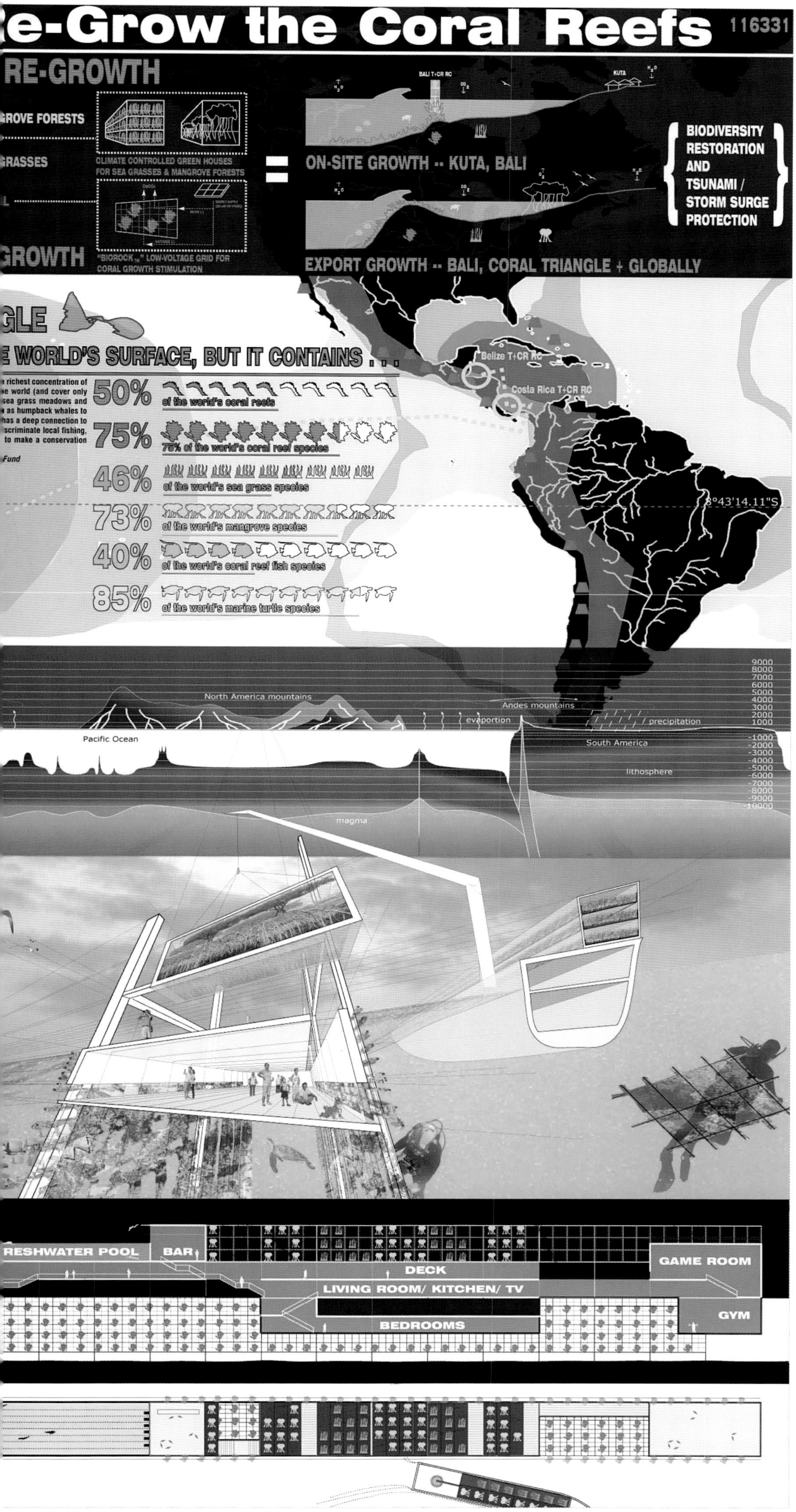
e-Grow the Coral Reefs
116331
RE-GROWTH
ROVE FORESTS
RASSES
CLIMATE CONTROLLED GREEN HOUSES
FOR SEA GRASSES & MANGROVE FORESTS
ROWTH
"BIOROCK™" LOW-VOLTAGE GRID FOR
CORAL GROWTH STIMULATION
BALI T+CR RC
KUTA
ON-SITE GROWTH -- KUTA, BALI
EXPORT GROWTH -- BALI, CORAL TRIANGLE + GLOBALLY
BIODIVERSITY
RESTORATION
AND
TSUNAMI /
STORM SURGE
PROTECTION
GLE
E WORLD'S SURFACE, BUT IT CONTAINS . . .
richest concentration of
e world (and cover only
sea grass meadows and
as humpback whales to
has a deep connection to
scriminate local fishing,
to make a conservation
Fund
50%
of the world's coral reefs
75%
75% of the world's coral reef species
46%
of the world's sea grass species
73%
of the world's mangrove species
40%
of the world's coral reef fish species
85%
of the world's marine turtle species
Belize T+CR RC
Costa Rica T+CR RC
8°43'14.11"S
North America mountains
Andes mountains
evaporation
precipitation
9000
8000
7000
6000
5000
4000
3000
2000
1000
Pacific Ocean
South America
lithosphere
magma
-1000
-2000
-3000
-4000
-5000
-6000
-7000
-8000
-9000
-10000
RESHWATER POOL
BAR
DECK
GAME ROOM
LIVING ROOM/ KITCHEN/ TV
BEDROOMS
GYM

A Dynamic Multi-level Gateway the Crossroads of Cultures and Nature for 21st century Pittsburgh

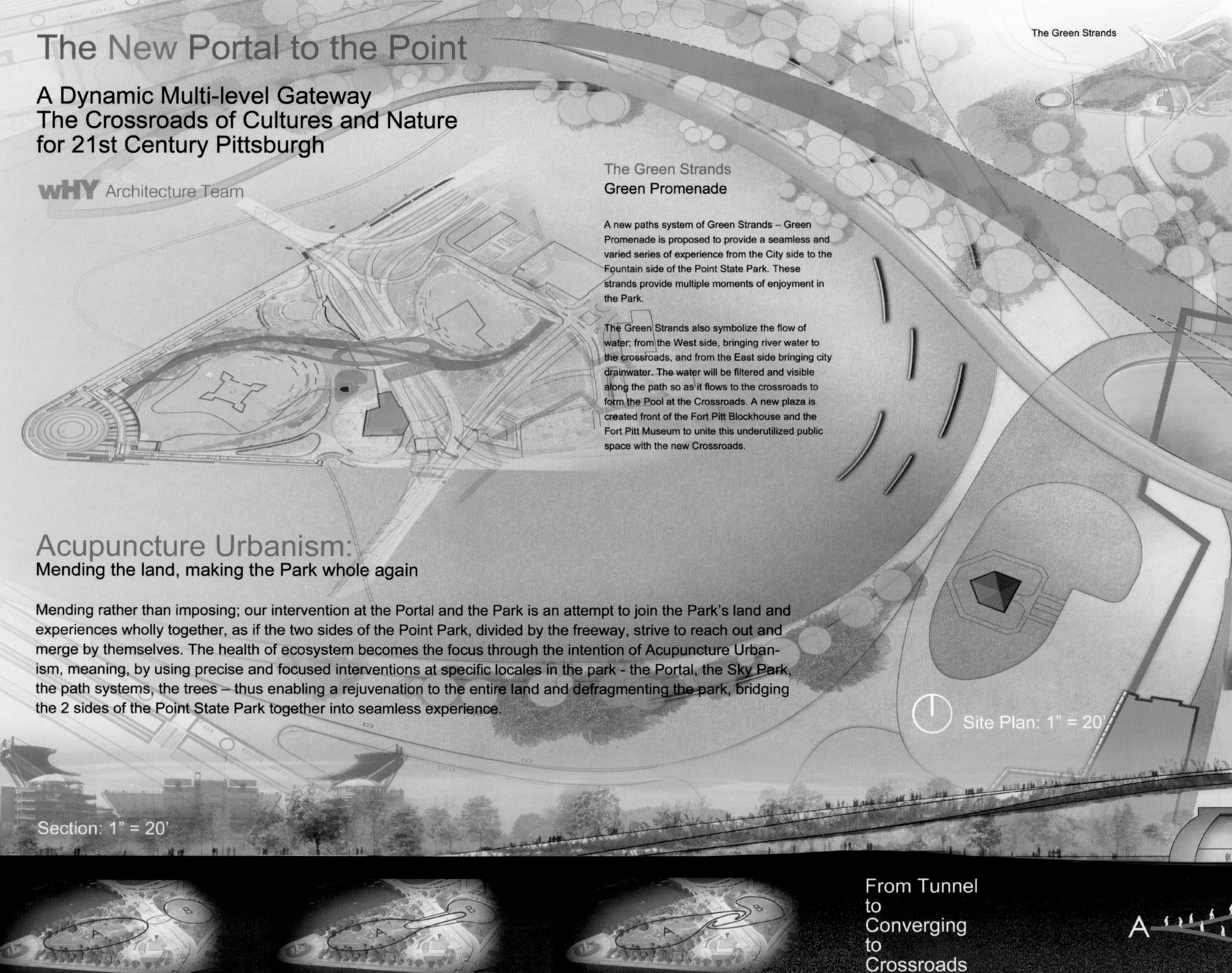
The New Portal to the Point
A Dynamic Multi-level Gateway
The Crossroads of Cultures and Nature
for 21st Century Pittsburgh
wHY Architecture Team
The Green Strands
The Green Strands
Green Promenade
A new paths system of Green Strands – Green Promenade is proposed to provide a seamless and varied series of experience from the City side to the Fountain side of the Point State Park. These strands provide multiple moments of enjoyment in the Park.
The Green Strands also symbolize the flow of water; from the West side, bringing river water to the crossroads, and from the East side bringing city drainwater. The water will be filtered and visible along the path so as it flows to the crossroads to form the Pool at the Crossroads. A new plaza is created front of the Fort Pitt Blockhouse and the Fort Pitt Museum to unite this underutilized public space with the new Crossroads.
Acupuncture Urbanism:
Mending the land, making the Park whole again
Mending rather than imposing; our intervention at the Portal and the Park is an attempt to join the Park's land and experiences wholly together, as if the two sides of the Point Park, divided by the freeway, strive to reach out and merge by themselves. The health of ecosystem becomes the focus through the intention of Acupuncture Urbanism, meaning, by using precise and focused interventions at specific locales in the park - the Portal, the Sky Park, the path systems, the trees – thus enabling a rejuvenation to the entire land and defragmenting the park, bridging the 2 sides of the Point State Park together into seamless experience.
Site Plan: 1" = 20'
Section: 1" = 20'
From Tunnel
to
Converging
to
Crossroads

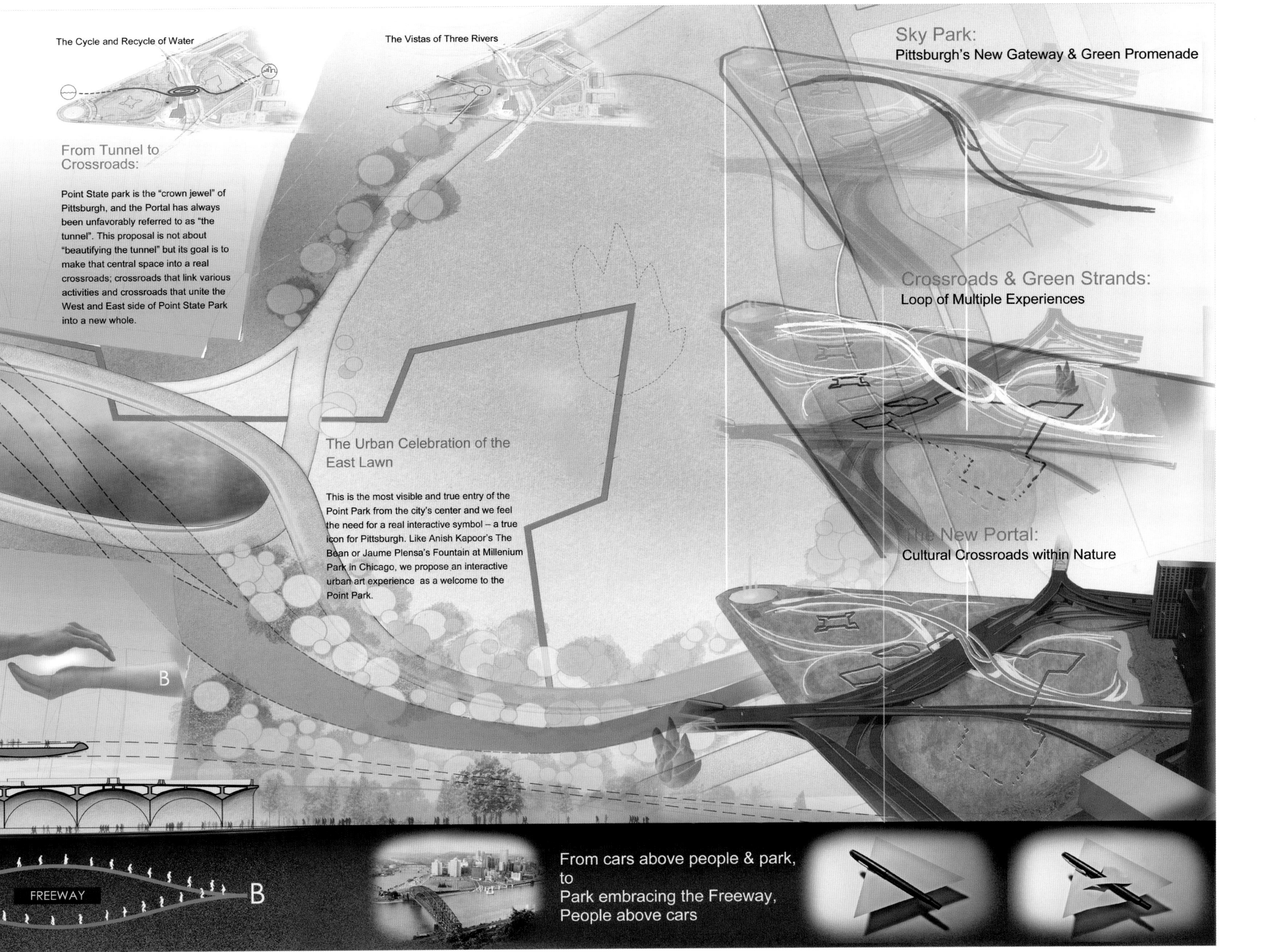

The Cycle and Recycle of Water
The Vistas of Three Rivers
From Tunnel to Crossroads:
Point State park is the "crown jewel" of Pittsburgh, and the Portal has always been unfavorably referred to as "the tunnel". This proposal is not about "beautifying the tunnel" but its goal is to make that central space into a real crossroads; crossroads that link various activities and crossroads that unite the West and East side of Point State Park into a new whole.
The Urban Celebration of the East Lawn
This is the most visible and true entry of the Point Park from the city's center and we feel the need for a real interactive symbol – a true icon for Pittsburgh. Like Anish Kapoor's The Bean or Jaume Plensa's Fountain at Millenium Park in Chicago, we propose an interactive urban art experience as a welcome to the Point Park.
Sky Park:
Pittsburgh's New Gateway & Green Promenade
Crossroads & Green Strands:
Loop of Multiple Experiences
The New Portal:
Cultural Crossroads within Nature
B
B
FREEWAY
From cars above people & park,
to
Park embracing the Freeway,
People above cars

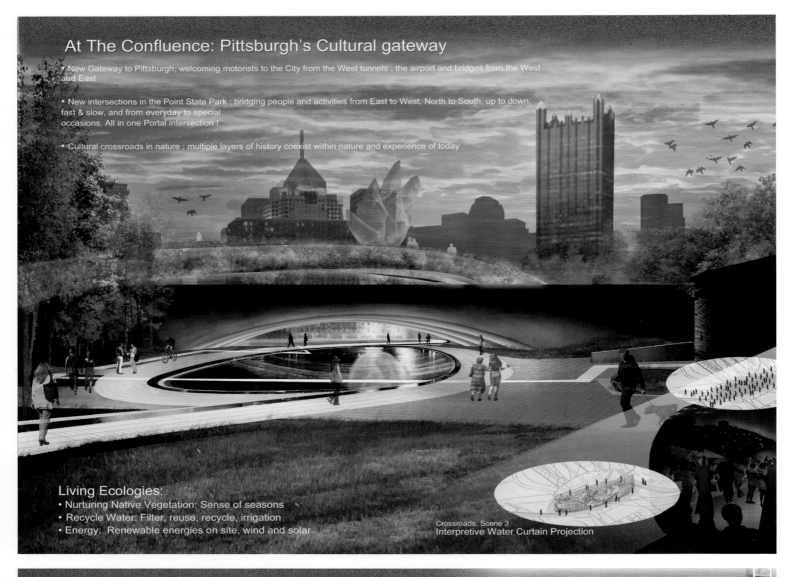

At The Confluence: Pittsburgh's Cultural gateway

• New Gateway to Pittsburgh; welcoming motorists to the City from the West tunnels , the airport and bridges from the West and East

• New intersections in the Point State Park ; bridging people and activities from East to West, North to South, up to down, fast & slow, and from everyday to special occasions. All in one Portal intersection !

• Cultural crossroads in nature ; multiple layers of history coexist within nature and experience of today

Living Ecologies:

• Nurturing Native Vegetation: Sense of seasons
• Recycle Water: Filter, reuse, recycle, irrigation
• Energy: Renewable energies on site, wind and solar

Crossroads: Scene 3
Interpretive Water Curtain Projection

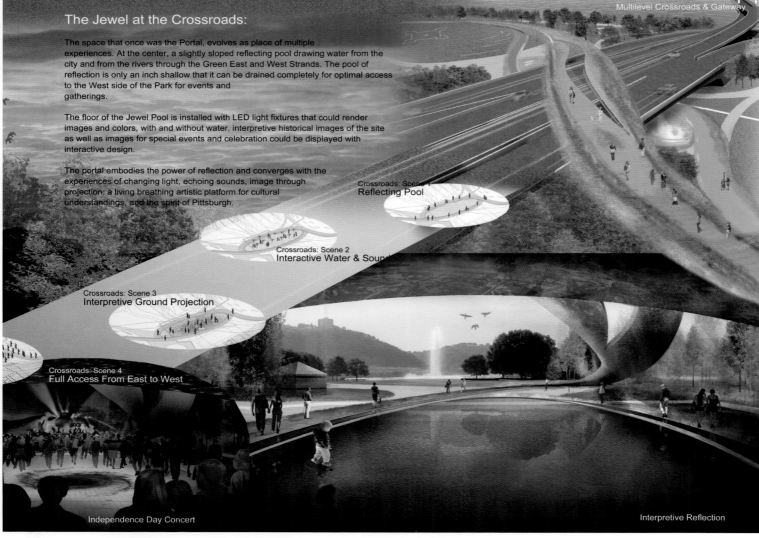

The Jewel at the Crossroads:

The space that once was the Portal, evolves as place of multiple experiences. At the center, a slightly sloped reflecting pool drawing water from the city and from the rivers through the Green East and West Strands. The pool of reflection is only an inch shallow that it can be drained completely for optimal access to the West side of the Park for events and gatherings.

The floor of the Jewel Pool is installed with LED light fixtures that could render images and colors, with and without water, interpretive historical images of the site as well as images for special events and celebration could be displayed with interactive design.

The portal embodies the power of reflection and converges with the experiences of changing light, echoing sounds, image through projection: a living breathing artistic platform for cultural understandings, and the spirit of Pittsburgh.

Multilevel Crossroads & Gateway

Crossroads: Scene 1
Reflecting Pool

Crossroads: Scene 2
Interactive Water & Sound

Crossroads: Scene 3
Interpretive Ground Projection

Crossroads: Scene 4
Full Access From East to West

Independence Day Concert

Interpretive Reflection

The New Portal to the Point
A Dynamic Multi-level Gateway
The Crossroads of Cultures and Nature
for 21st Century Pittsburgh
wHY Architecture Team
The Green Strands
The Cycle and Recycle of Water
The Vistas of Three Rivers
Sky Park:
Pittsburgh's New Gateway & Green Promenade
The Green Strands
Green Promenade
A new paths system of Green Strands -- Green Promenade is proposed to provide a seamless and varied series of experience from the City side to the Fountain side of the Point State Park. These strands provide multiple moments of enjoyment in the Park.
The Green Strands also symbolize the flow of water; from the West side, bringing river water to the crossroads, and from the East side bringing city drainwater. The water will be filtered and visible along the path so as it flows to the crossroads to form the Pool at the Crossroads. A new plaza is created front of the Fort Pitt Blockhouse and the Fort Pitt Museum to unite this underutilized public space with the new Crossroads.
From Tunnel to Crossroads:
Point State park is the "crown jewel" of Pittsburgh, and the Portal has always been unfavorably referred to as "the tunnel". This proposal is not about "beautifying the tunnel" but its goal is to make that central space into a real crossroads; crossroads that link various activities and crossroads that unite the West and East side of Point State Park into a new whole.
Crossroads & Green Strands:
Loop of Multiple Experiences
The Urban Celebration of the East Lawn
This is the most visible and true entry of the Point Park from the city's center and we feel the need for a real interactive symbol – a true icon for Pittsburgh. Like Anish Kapoor's The Bean or Jaume Plensa's Fountain at Millenium Park in Chicago, we propose an interactive urban art experience as a welcome to the Point Park.
New Portal:
Cultural Crossroads within Nature
Acupuncture Urbanism:
Mending the land, making the Park whole again
Mending rather than imposing; our intervention at the Portal and the Park is an attempt to join the Park's land and experiences wholly together, as if the two sides of the Point Park, divided by the freeway, strive to reach out and merge by themselves. The health of ecosystem becomes the focus through the intention of Acupuncture Urbanism, meaning, by using precise and focused interventions at specific locales in the park - the Portal, the Sky Park, the path systems, the trees – thus enabling a rejuvenation to the entire land and defragmenting the park, bridging the 2 sides of the Point State Park together into seamless experience.
A
B
Section: 1" = 20'
Section: 1" = 20'
Site Plan: 1" = 20'
From Tunnel
to
Converging
to
Crossroads
A
FREEWAY
B
From cars above people & park,
to
Park embracing the Freeway,
People above cars
At The Confluence: Pittsburgh's Cultural gateway
• New Gateway to Pittsburgh; welcoming motorists to the City from the West tunnels , the airport and bridges from the West and East
• New intersections in the Point State Park : bridging people and activities from East to West, North to South, up to down, fast & slow, and from everyday to special occasions. All in one Portal intersection !
• Cultural crossroads in nature ; multiple layers of history coexist within nature and experience of today
The Jewel at the Crossroads:
The space that once was the Portal, evolves as place of multiple experiences. At the center, a slightly sloped reflecting pool drawing water from the city and from the rivers through the Green East and West Strands. The pool of reflection is only an inch shallow that it can be drained completely for optimal access to the West side of the Park for events and gatherings.
The floor of the Jewel Pool is installed with LED light fixtures that could render images and colors, with and without water, interpretive historical images of the site as well as images for special events and celebration could be displayed with interactive design.
The portal embodies the power of reflection and converges with the experiences of changing light, echoing sounds, image through projection: a living breathing artistic platform for cultural understandings, and the spirit of Pittsburgh.
Multilevel Crossroads & Gateway
Reflecting Pool
Crossroads: Scene 2
Interactive Water & Sound
Crossroads: Scene 3
Interpretive Ground Projection
Crossroads: Scene 4
Full Access From East to West

Between the Lines | *Posad*

Participants : Posad-spatial Strategies
Project : Nodal And Regional Development
Typology : Urban Design
Location : Skien-Porsgrunn, Norway

Size of projectsite : +11km in length
Client : Europan 11 / Year : 2011 – honorable mention

PS 404
Skien-Porsgrunn, Norway

I

Between The Lines

Nodal development on the shores of the Telemarksvassdraget

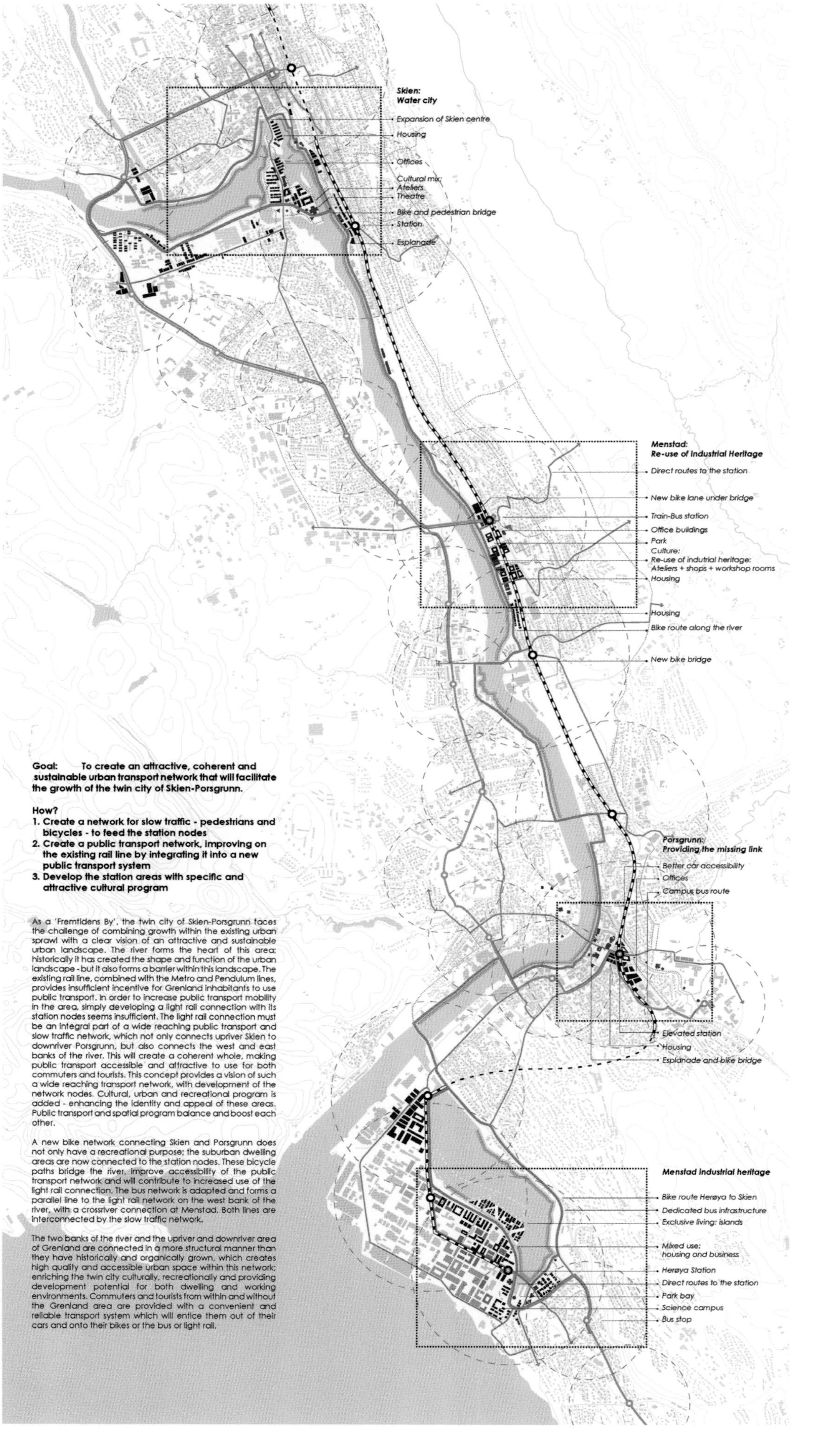

Skien: Water city
- *Expansion of Skien centre*
- *Housing*
- *Offices*
- *Cultural mix: Ateliers, Theatre*
- *Bike and pedestrian bridge*
- *Station*
- *Esplanade*

Menstad: Re-use of Industrial Heritage
- *Direct routes to the station*
- *New bike lane under bridge*
- *Train-Bus station*
- *Office buildings*
- *Park*
- *Culture: Re-use of indutrial heritage: Ateliers + shops + workshop rooms*
- *Housing*
- *Housing*
- *Bike route along the river*
- *New bike bridge*

Porsgrunn: Providing the missing link
- *Better car accessibility*
- *Offices*
- *Campus bus route*
- *Elevated station*
- *Housing*
- *Esplnade and bike bridge*

Menstad industrial heritage
- *Bike route Herøya to Skien*
- *Dedicated bus infrastructure*
- *Exclusive living: islands*
- *Mixed use: housing and business*
- *Herøya Station*
- *Direct routes to the station*
- *Park bay*
- *Science campus*
- *Bus stop*

Goal: **To create an attractive, coherent and sustainable urban transport network that will facilitate the growth of the twin city of Skien-Porsgrunn.**

How?

1. **Create a network for slow traffic - pedestrians and bicycles - to feed the station nodes**
2. **Create a public transport network, improving on the existing rail line by integrating it into a new public transport system**
3. **Develop the station areas with specific and attractive cultural program**

As a 'Fremtidens By', the twin city of Skien-Porsgrunn faces the challenge of combining growth within the existing urban sprawl with a clear vision of an attractive and sustainable urban landscape. The river forms the heart of this area; historically it has created the shape and function of the urban landscape - but it also forms a barrier within this landscape. The existing rail line, combined with the Metro and Pendulum lines, provides insufficient incentive for Grenland inhabitants to use public transport. In order to increase public transport mobility in the area, simply developing a light rail connection with its station nodes seems insufficient. The light rail connection must be an integral part of a wide reaching public transport and slow traffic network, which not only connects upriver Skien to downriver Porsgrunn, but also connects the west and east banks of the river. This will create a coherent whole, making public transport accessible and attractive to use for both commuters and tourists. This concept provides a vision of such a wide reaching transport network, with development of the network nodes. Cultural, urban and recreational program is added - enhancing the identity and appeal of these areas. Public transport and spatial program balance and boost each other.

A new bike network connecting Skien and Porsgrunn does not only have a recreational purpose; the suburban dwelling areas are now connected to the station nodes. These bicycle paths bridge the river, improve accessibility of the public transport network and will contribute to increased use of the light rail connection. The bus network is adapted and forms a parallel line to the light rail network on the west bank of the river, with a crossriver connection at Menstad. Both lines are interconnected by the slow traffic network.

The two banks of the river and the upriver and downriver area of Grenland are connected in a more structural manner than they have historically and organically grown, which creates high quality and accessible urban space within this network; enriching the twin city culturally, recreationally and providing development potential for both dwelling and working environments. Commuters and tourists from within and without the Grenland area are provided with a convenient and reliable transport system which will entice them out of their cars and onto their bikes or the bus or light rail.

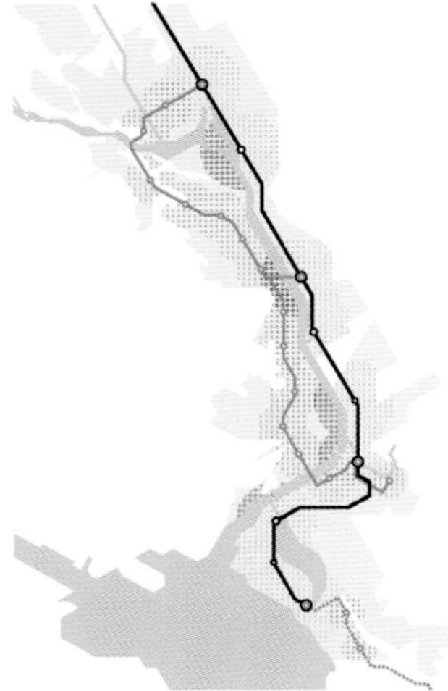

The public transport network of the twin city consists of a twin system which is interconnected. One half of the system consists of a light rail connection based on the existing rail connection, the other half is a fast bus network on a dedicated bus lane replacing one of the Metrolines. This system - in conjunction with the existing Metro and Pendulum network - covers a far wider area than the current network does and provides more opportunity and incentive for Grenlanders to use public transport. Four new slow traffic bridges make the catchement areas of bus and lightrail strech out to both sides of the river.

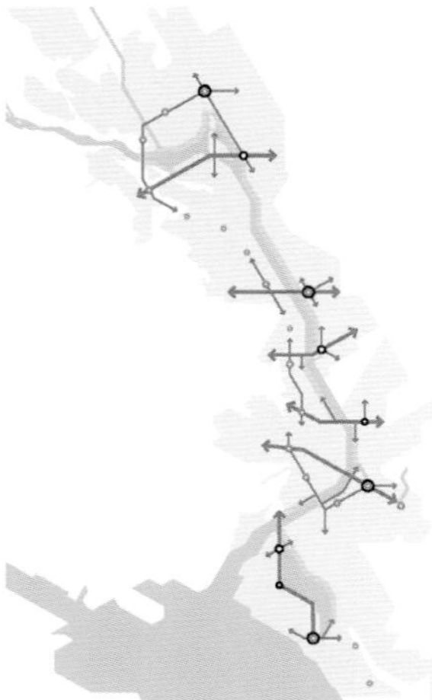

Bicycle lanes are the driving force of the public transport system. By creating new riverbank connections, public transport becomes accessible for a larger group of inhabitants. The networks also form the basis for new urban and cultural development.

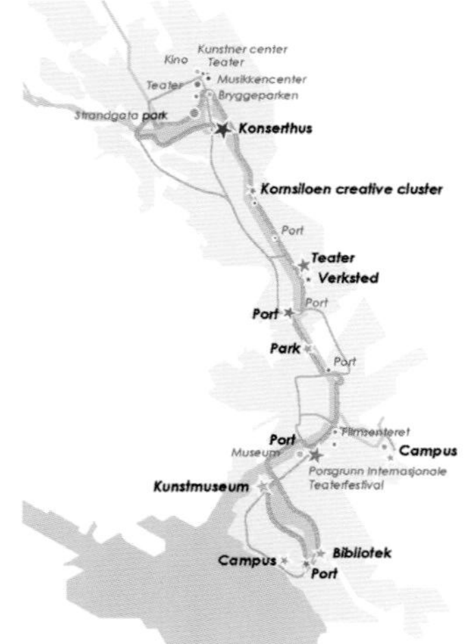

Cultural development is a focal point for the twin city of Skien-Porsgrunn. The existing urban environment already incorporates many cultural functions. By strengthening and increasing this cultural program and tying it to bus and light rail stops, a unique selling point is created for the twin city; it will become the sustainable cultural capital of the region.

- Light rail stop
- Bus stop
- Bus line
- Slow traffic routes
- New program
- Special program
- Waterfront

N

0 250 500 1250m

View along the river esplanade to Skien and the new concert hall

Skien - Water City

The development of a new public transport network provides a boost in development potential for Skien, which is an interesting and appealing city already. By tying the slow traffic network, car and bus connections and the light rail connection together in this urban node, there is a huge opportunity for qualitative development.

The concept comprises a lengthened city centre and a new vista across the Skiensleva; the face Skien displays to the south will be modern and will provide rich cultural program. The cycle path which starts in the historic centre of Skien extends via the east bank to the south. A new bridge will connect the island with the new light rail station.

The island has two distinct identities. The first is epitomized in the view of the city from the south; a new urban silhouette which contains cultural and office program. The developments on the west side of the island are on a smaller scale; dwelling on the 'rural' side of the island means a living environment which is green and peaceful, on the edge of the bay leading into the Telemark Canal. These two environments form a coherent but distinctive whole which strengthens the identity of Skien in itself and as a constituent of the twin city. Skien forms the northern tip of the twin city.

The stations at this point present the motivation for a slow traffic connection to the island – providing the island with access to nye Forestad station. This new bicycle bridge intersects the new bicycle route which travels from Skien to Herøya. This bike path flows its way along the river, forming a new quayside esplanade which is alluring to daily traffic, day trippers and tourists alike.

Porsgrunn - Providing The Missing Link

The historic centre of Porsgrunn, the west bank of the river and the university campus are currently divided from each other by the parallel lines of river and rail. At present, the rail track cleaves the centre in two. Raising the rail line and its station will enable a direct route from the centre to the university campus. Not only that, but the traditional street grid pattern which is present on the western side of the tracks can be extended to the east – for example the Rådhusgata, creating a new coherent whole. The station site is developed as an extension of the city centre – a pedestrian area with smallscale shopping facilities and other local functions. Raising the tracks also allows for an improved crossing of the Hovenggata and the Sverresgate. Both thoroughfares are no longer impacted by the rail line.

The route from campus to centre is extended across the Porsgrunn river. A bridge across the water to the west will make the station accessible for people living on the other side of the river. Existing west bank dwellers will be able to use the station, but the west bank will also become more attractive as living space for students and university staff, which in turn creates a wider basis for potential development of the station area.

Bridging the gap between east and west banks and between centre and campus will make the station node a logical place for office and urban development, in view of its increased accessibility circle. The station node now lies at the heart of a new urban space which extends from the university campus in the east all the way across the water to the west bank of Porsgrunn river. The new city of Porsgrunn comprises the entirety of the area, including the previously solitary western shore, which now has huge potential for qualitative housing development.

Creative cluster near Menstad station

Menstad - Re-use of Industrial Heritage

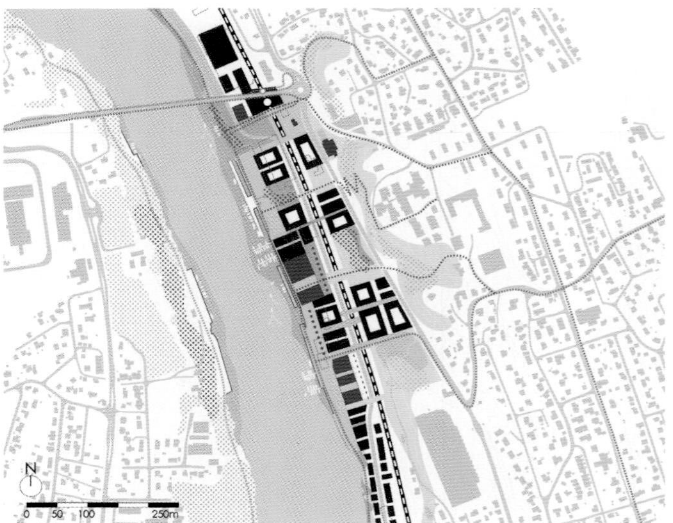

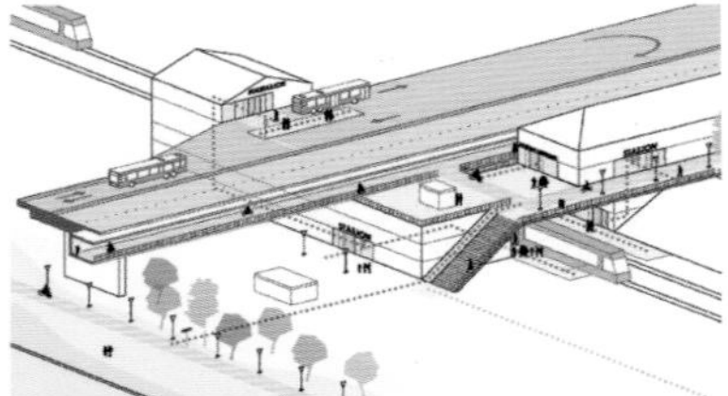

Menstad public transport node
By transforming the exsisting bike path into a dedicated busline a optimal interchnage can be made at Menstad station. The bike path is no attached underneath the Menstad bridge. The station forms a hub for train, light rail, bus, car, bike and pedestrians, connecting all modalities.

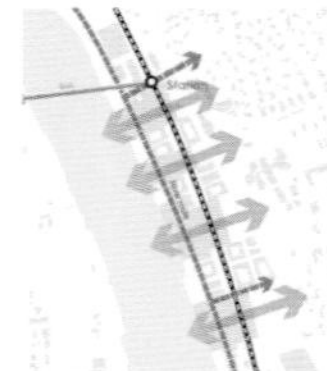

Slow traffic
Connections through the green corridors connect to the station and the Porsgrunn-Skien route.

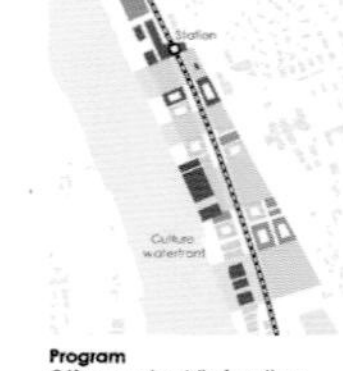

Program
Offices and public functions around the station. Housing and cultural program in the South.

The Menstad bridge is an icon within the twin city; it is one of the only existing river crossings in the area. At this spot, the station forms the motive for crosslinking the bus and train networks. Beside the station, on the industrial heritage site, there is room for new cultural program: workshop spaces, exhibition areas and theatre. Surrounding the station and cultural site, there is a development opportunity for new living spaces on the riverfront. Closer to the road and the rail track, smallscale industrial and office program will form a recognisable spatial identity. Along the road and within the site itself, new architecture will speak the same visual language as the existing industrial edifices and archetypes.

Within the gaps in the architectural fabric there is room for the pylons; these areas will form green connections to the dwelling area on the eastern hillsides. Along the waterfront, we will find the new bicycle paths which connect the various town centres within the twin city with each other and with the stations and stops.

Solely developing the station node without the supporting networks which travel in all directions – not just following the existing rail infrastructure – would neither provide a large enough basis for new program at the station site nor for the exploitation of the light rail itself. In order to develop this area and transform it to an attractive district, it is imperative that the station area is disclosed in all directions, to all potential public transport travellers – using the combination of slow traffic, bus networks and light rail. This new transport network will provide the inhabitants of the wider area with the means to enjoy this new light rail and spatial program; it will form a system that is not just dependent on commuters, but which will become the daily urban system for Grenland's population.

Herøya - Transformation Livable Industrial Site

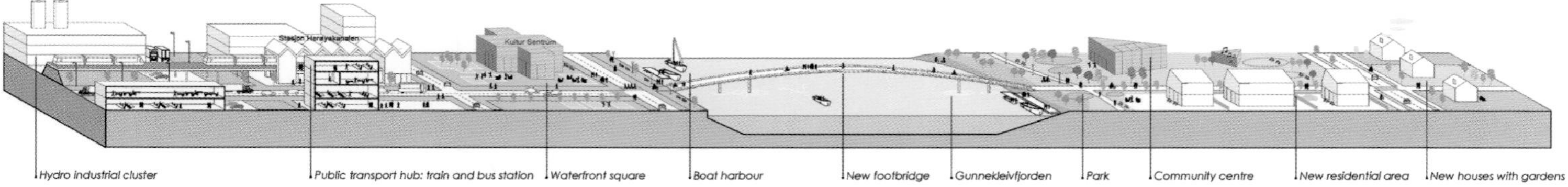

Slow traffic routes

- Bike and pedestrian routes run along the small bay
- The route connects Herøya with Porsgrunn and Skien

Program

- Industries
- Housing
- Station and office program
- Public functions and culture
- Research campus - University

Green public space
Views and spaces

1. Green bay
2. public parks and open views
3. Vista's to the North shore and hills (4)

All within range of public transport

Herøya forms one of the engines of the local economy, but also provides potentially beautiful living spaces. By transforming the area gradually, industry will remain active and new working and dwelling environments will increasingly come into existence. The light rail cuts its way through the Herøya site and creates a spatial division; to the north-eastern side of the tracks a working and living environment on the water's edge comes to life. This area may be extended at some later point with small dwelling islands. The islands will provide an entirely new quality of living within the twin city; living space on the waterfront, protected and sheltered, with a view of the lake and surrounding hills.

To the south of the tracks, the industrial landscape will progressively transform to a service-related knowledge economy. The university will have the opportunity to establish research laboratories, there is room for student housing and office program.

The entire area is perfectly accessible; the light rail will have three stops – close to the industrial sites and in the heart of the new living and working district. This last station will also have transfer facilities onto the bus network.

The extensive pedestrian area forms the beating heart of this neighbourhood. The plaza with surrounding housing and offices in connected to the east bank of the water by footbridge. On the shore of the bay this new urban program will gradually metamorphose into a dwelling area with detached housing, large gardens and an atmosphere of peace and tranquility.

This concept will recreate Herøya as a new and dynamic urban district with its own city centre, unique spatial qualities and perfect accessibility.

IV751

france- REIMS

VELOVILLE-ROULE À REIMS

1

Velo-ville

Establishing a mix use Velo-centric neighborhood for Reims. The need for economic stimulation, local connectivity and healthier living can be addressed by this new light industry. The existing aviation industry offers a skill set that could easily be transferred to supply the 75,000 bicycles needed for the city's proposed bike share network. A fully connected network of safe bike lanes will connect the neighborhood. Once connectivity is established a bike share system can be introduced that provides an affordable and accessible transit method for potential users such as school students, commuters, the local community and leisure activities. This new infrastructure would create a comfortable and effective environment for bikers that would be unique to the Reims identity. This identity shift from agriculture and vineyards, could be a catalyst for the bike repair and fabrication of the existing aviation service industry while promoting a healthy (both for the individual and the environment) form of transit in the neighborhood. This Reims neighborhood becomes a prototype for other outlying neighborhoods within the city and A COUNTRY.

why Reims needs an intervention???

The absorption of the new into the old to secure the cohesion with the city of Reims and the vineyards is the ambition of the project. Alternating landscape of built and inbuilt, urban and green we want to create a flexible vision reacting to different urban conditions. We create:

1. Clear identity,
2. Looser fit of functions,
3. Better connectivity,
4. Ecological regeneration,
5. Public domain as an experience.

radicalize local products (wine, champagne)
promote economic self suffiency
blurring boundaries between architecture and nature

New identity is proposed by looking at existing city of Reims blocs to integrate through a network of 5 existing building typologies of Reims:

From the ZONE close to:

1. bd. henri vasnier , we focused on individual expressions, personal interpretation of living,
2. bd. henri henrot- we look at life and building typologies,
3. Av de l' Europe- we look at the street curvature
4. Av. jean Jaures -we look at people, how they spend free time,
5. boulevard de la paix- we observe public, semi public and private spaces

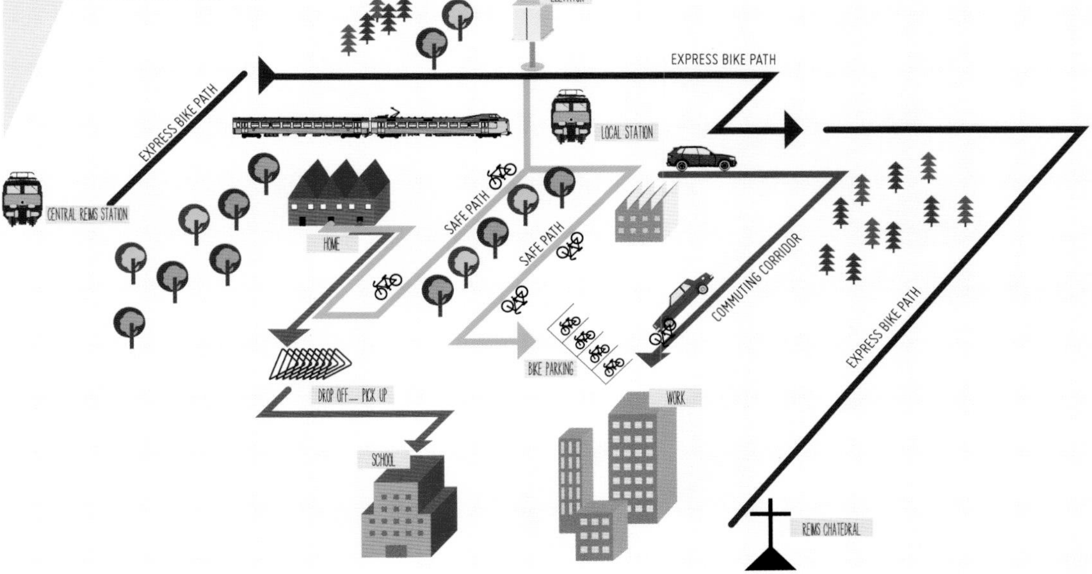

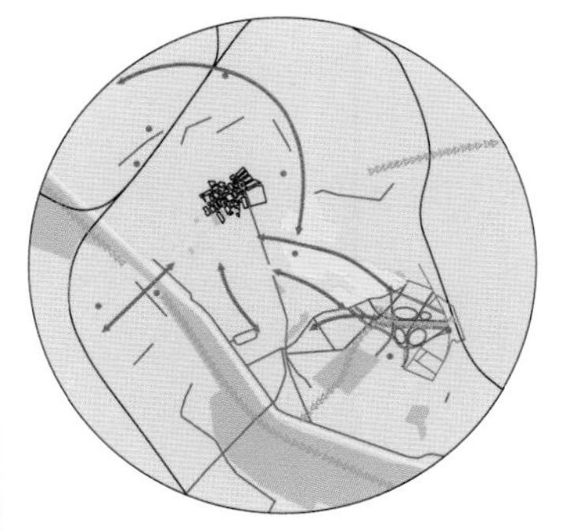

promote the use of bicycles:

multimodal concept:

- Moulin de campus Reims
- city center
- green zone
- new streets
- existing bypass
- existing cycling zone
- interchanges
- railways
- existing tram lines
- tram line to establish
- existing bus lines
- bus lines to establish

maps R 1: 10 000

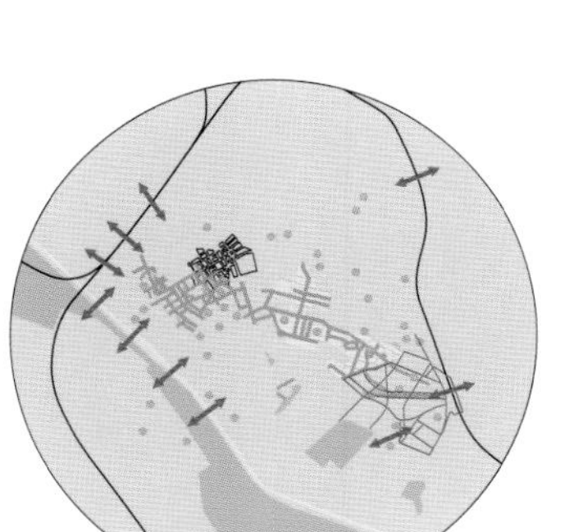

pedestrian places:

maps R 1: 10 000

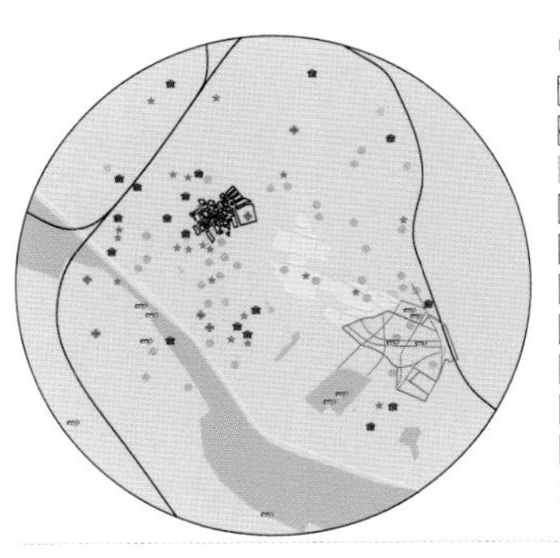

multimodal concept:

- Moulin de campus Reims
- city center
- green zone
- town hall, prefectures, train station, administrative building
- health facilities
- sport equipment (swimming pool, stadium icerink, sports building)
- kindergarden, elementary school, collages and universities
- railways
- cultural facilities, libraries, theaters
- commercial areas

maps R 1: 10 000

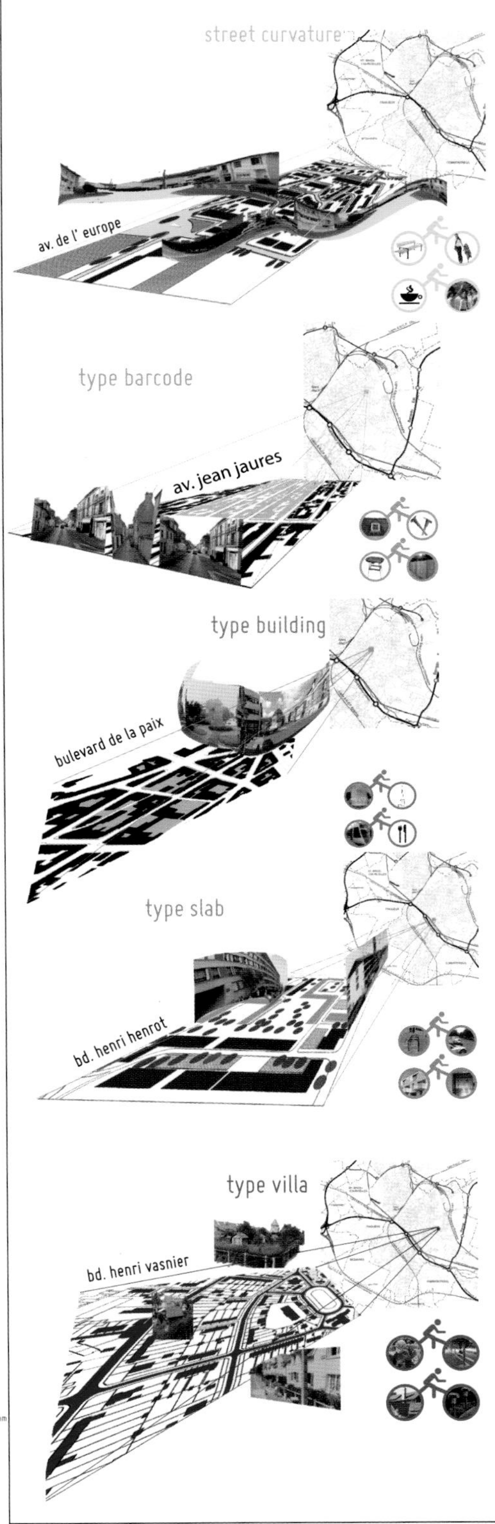

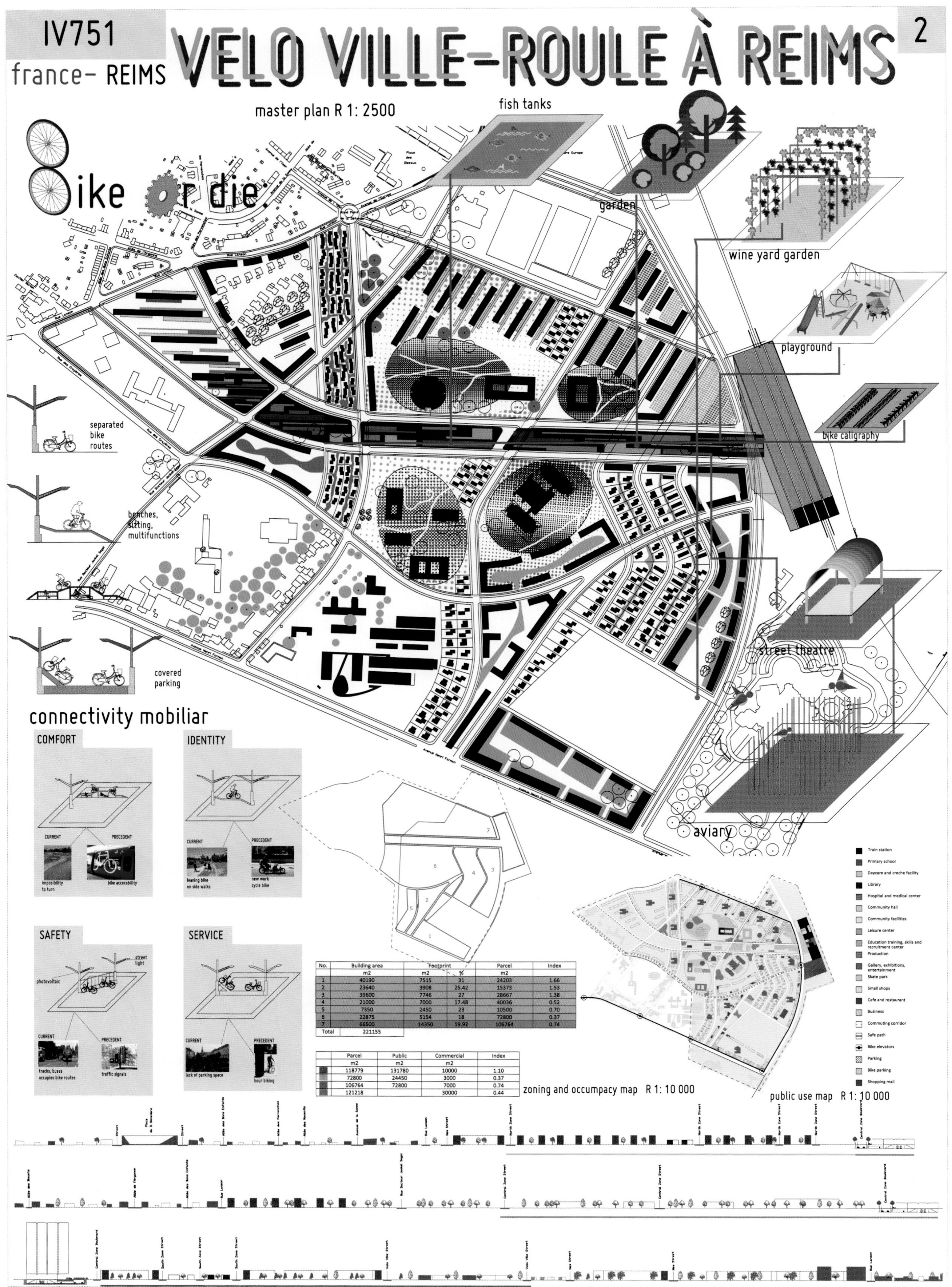

No.	Building area	Footprint		Parcel	Index
	m2	m2	%	m2	
1	40190	7515	31	24203	1.66
2	23640	3908	25.42	15373	1.53
3	39600	7746	27	28667	1.38
4	21000	7000	17.48	40036	0.52
5	7350	2450	23	10500	0.70
6	22875	5154	18	72800	0.37
7	66500	14350	19.92	106764	0.74
Total	221155				

	Parcel	Public	Commercial	Index
	m2	m2	m2	
	118779	131780	10000	1.10
	72800	24450	3000	0.37
	106764	72800	7000	0.74
	121218		30000	0.44

IV571 france- REIMS VELOVILLE-ROULE À REIMS 3

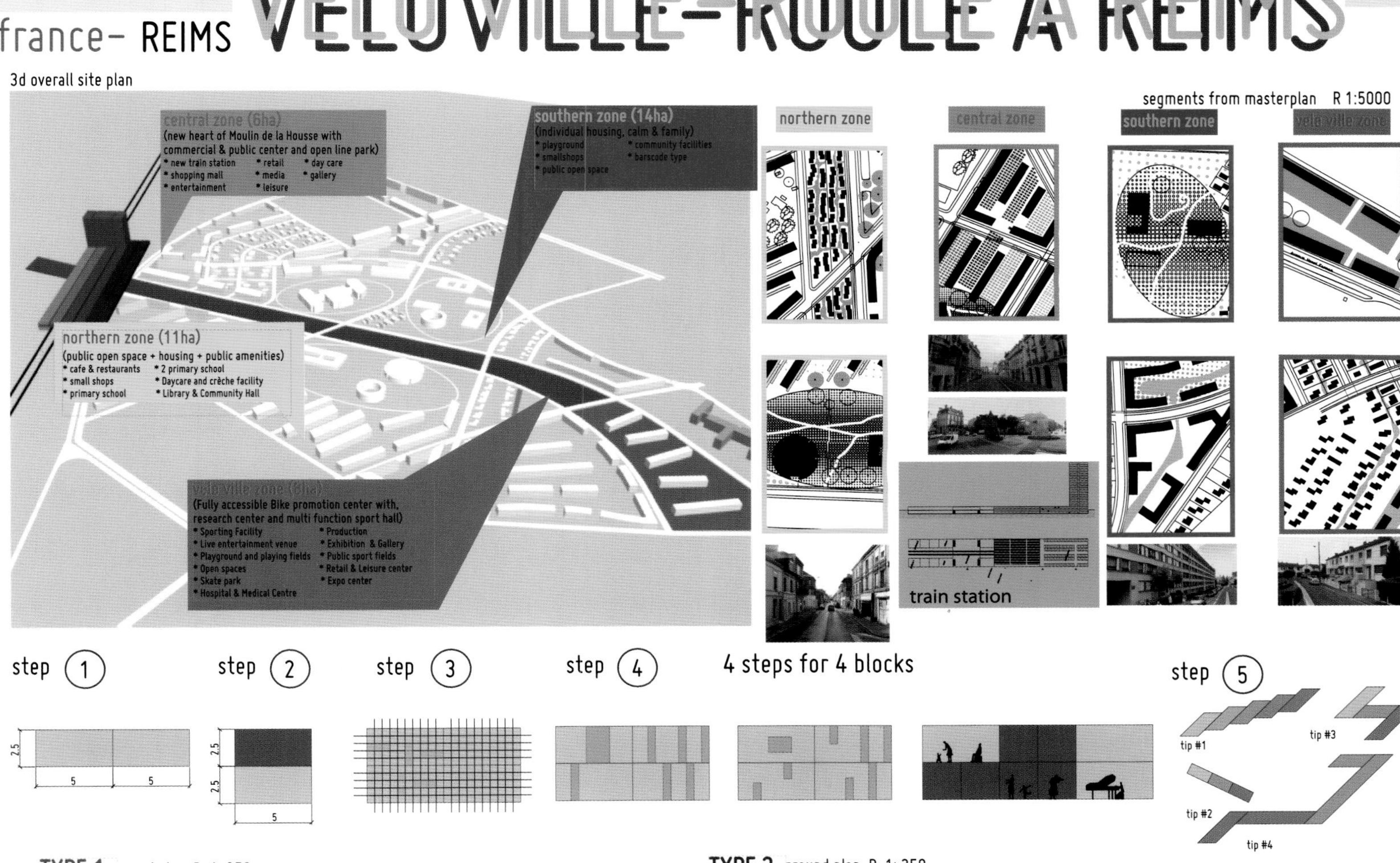

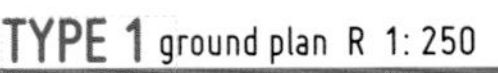

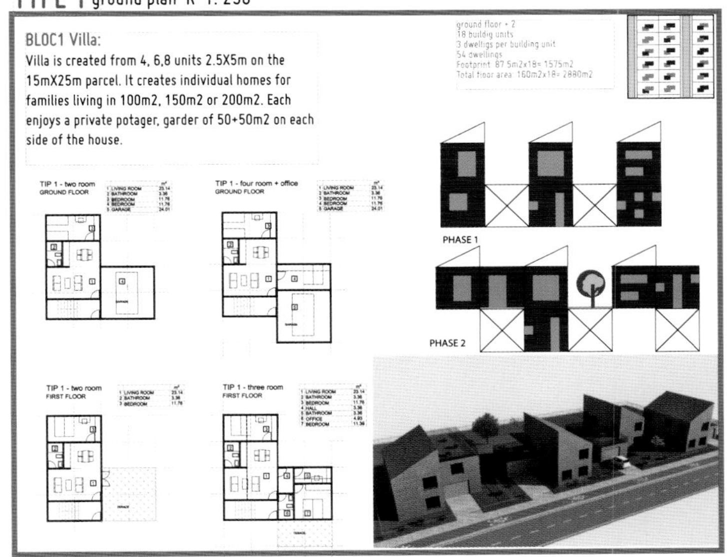

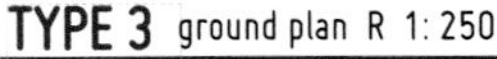

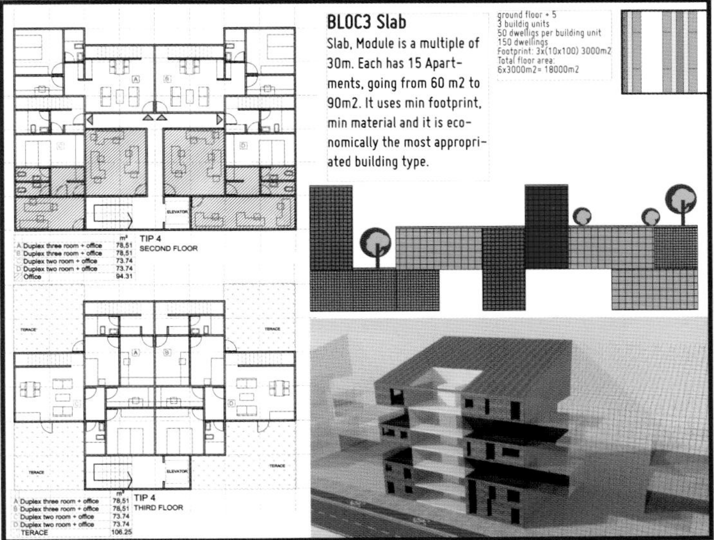

BLOC3 Slab
Slab, Module is a multiple of 30m. Each has 15 Apartments, going from 60 m2 to 90m2. It uses min footprint, min material and it is economically the most appropriated building type.
TIP 4 SECOND FLOOR
TIP 4 THIRD FLOOR

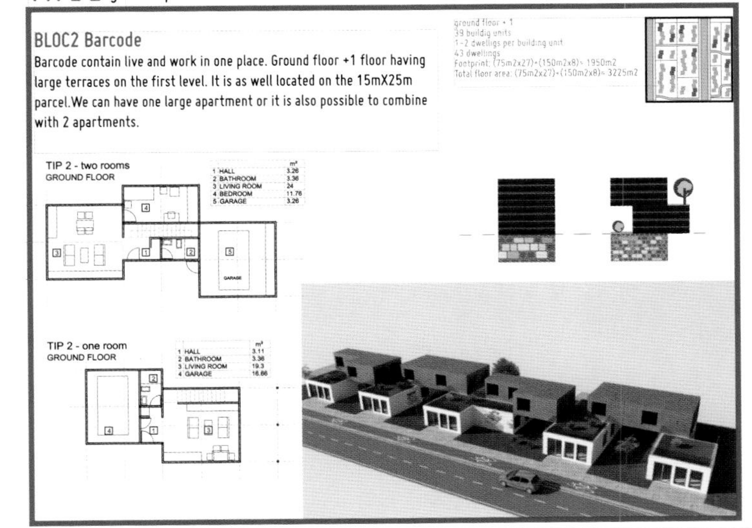

TYPE 2 ground plan R 1: 250
BLOC2 Barcode
Barcode contain live and work in one place. Ground floor +1 floor having large terraces on the first level. It is as well located on the 15mX25m parcel. We can have one large apartment or it is also possible to combine with 2 apartments.
TIP 2 - two rooms GROUND FLOOR
TIP 2 - one room GROUND FLOOR

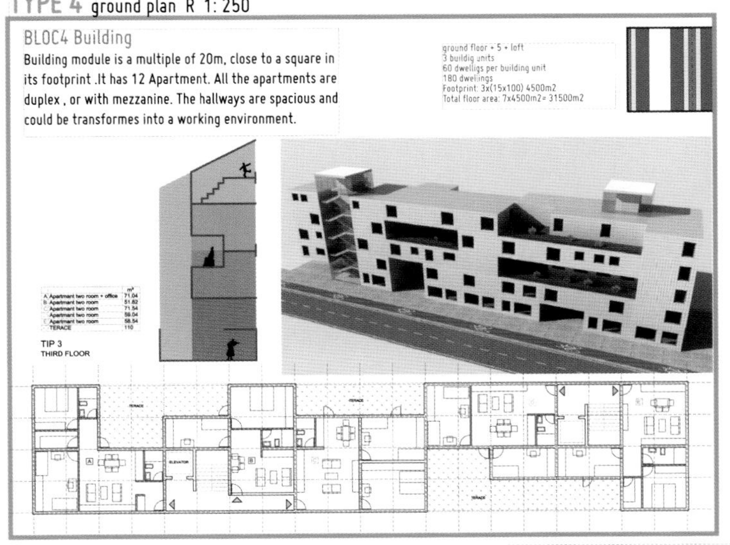

TYPE 4 ground plan R 1: 250
BLOC4 Building
Building module is a multiple of 20m, close to a square in its footprint. It has 12 Apartment. All the apartments are duplex, or with mezzanine. The hallways are spacious and could be transformes into a working environment.
TIP 3 THIRD FLOOR

107

Brik | *Posad*

Participants : Posad-spatial Strategies
Project : Bike-Friendly Neighborhood
Typology : Urban Design/Redevelopment
Location : Rotterdam, the Netherlands

Size of projectsite : $1.25 km^2$
Client : Dutch Cyclist Association (Fietsersbond)

BRIK MEER DAN EEN FIETSNETWERK

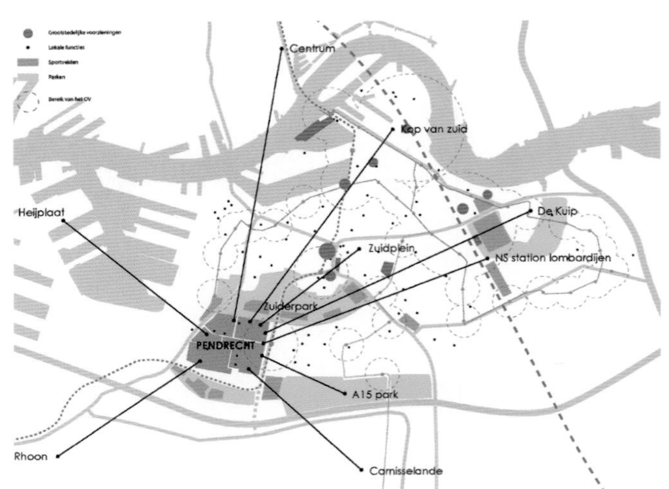

Pendrecht maakt onderdeel uit van de zuidelijke tuinsteden van Rotterdam (samen met Zuidwijk, Lombardijen en Groot IJsselmonde) en heeft een zeer ideologische inslag. De wijk was bedoeld om bij te dragen aan een verbeterd leefmilieu voor de massa. Typerend voor de wijk zijn de zogenoemde 'stempels'; verschillende bouwblokken om een gemeenschappelijke tuin. In de jaren net na de oorlog leefden gezinnen van vijf personen in één-kamer appartementen, in de tuinsteden konden zij een vierkamerwoning van 60m2 betrekken. De babyboomers maakten volop gebruik van het ruim aanwezige gemeenschappelijke tuinen in de wijken en het Zuiderpark.

Twintig jaar na de oplevering van de wijk in 1970, wordt de Erasmuslijn aangelegd met eindstation Slinge. Deze gebeurtenis lijkt de omslag voor de tuinsteden in te zetten. De nieuwe bereikbaarheid - die de wijk maar beperkt bedient - zorgt ervoor dat veel voorzieningen zich naar het stadscentrum verplaatsen. De jongeren trekken langzaam weg en de leegstaande huizen worden gevuld met immigranten die aangetrokken worden door de groei van de havens. De gemeenschappelijke tuinen worden slecht onderhouden en niemand gebruikt ze. De wijk is een betekenisloze plek tussen periferie en stad worden. Pendrecht stond onlangs op de tweede plaats van slechtste buurten van Nederland.
Kenmerkend aan een probleemwijk zoals Pendrecht zijn het lage inkomen, de beperkte arbeidsparticipatie en een groot aantal (niet westerse) allochtonen maar ook een beperkte aanwezigheid van openbaar vervoer. Het auto- en fietsbezit in deze wijken is ook veel lager zijn dan in de rest van Nederland. Het aantal zelfstandigen is in deze wijk juist hoger.

Het verbeteren van de fietsbereikbaarheid en het fietsgebruik biedt gelijktijdig een bijdrage in de oplossing van de hierboven beschreven problemen. De ondernemingszin binnen Pendrecht wordt daarin opgepakt als onderdeel binnen het fietsnetwerk.

Het voorgestelde netwerk is toegespitst op het ontwerp van de wijk door Lotte Stam-Beese. Het assenkruis waar alle voorzieningen en scholen aan liggen wordt versterkt. De groene kwaliteit van de singels wordt uitgebreid tot langgerekte arboretums waar ruimte is voor een echte fietsweg. De vervoers-as langs het wijkcentrum krijgt een duidelijk profiel met ruimte voor openbaar vervoer, fiets en auto. Samen binden ze de wijk en verbinden ze het met de regio. De route wordt gedragen, aangeduid, versterkt en aangevuld door Brikken.

Een Brik biedt naast parkeerruimte ook plek aan een kleine economische functie. De bewaker zou een kleine krantenkiosk bij het station kunnen runnen, een fietsenmaker of een groenteboer met groente uit de tuinstad.
's Ochtend opent de stalling, de stalen buitenkant van de Brik wordt opgetild en heeft openingen naar alle zijden. 's Avonds sluit de Brik en is het een robuust, vandalismebestendig lichtobject ter oriëntatie in de wijk.

AUTOBEZIT PER HUISHOUDEN

	1,0
	0,65
	-
	0,5

- Weinig autobezit

FIETSBEZIT (% VAN AANTAL INWONERS)

	84%
	67%
	-
	61%

- Weinig fietsen

AFKOMST

	AUTOCHTONEN	WESTERSE ALLOCHTONEN	NIET WESTERSE ALLOCHTONEN
	84%	8%	8%
	55%	10%	35%
	52%	8%	40%
	40%	9%	51%

- Veel nationaliteiten, onbekend met fiets-cultuur

NIET WERKENDE WERKZOEKENDEN

	% BEROEPSBEVOLKING	BEROEPSBEVOLKING	NIET WERKENDE WERKZOEKENDEN
	6%	10.939.921	692.210
	13%	406.203	51.728
	15%	157.068	23.306
	20%	7.705	1.509

- Hoge werkloosheid

ZELFSTANDIGEN (% BEROEPSBEVOLKING)

	7%
	4%
	5%
	11%

- Veel zelfstandig ondernemers

BESTEEDBAAR INKOMEN (€ PER INKOMENSONTVANGER)

	17.700
	17.000
	15.800
	15.400

- Laag inkomen

BRON: CBS 2007

Een netwerk van fietsenstallingen
Brikken- in Pendrecht:

- Oriëntatie en de basis voor een route door de wijk
- Ruimte voor economische impulsen in en rond de stalling
- Een nieuwe vorm van verlichting, een bijdrage aan de sociale veiligheid in de wijk

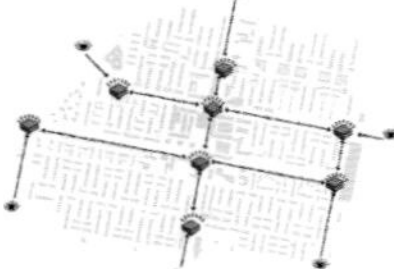

Sterke assen door de wijk
groene ruimte en ruimte voor verkeer:

- Brede groene 'shared space' zone waar de auto welkom is in het domein van de fietser en voetganger. De 'fietsweg' door de wijk bepaalt de lijn, de auto volgt
- De groene zone en de hoofd autostructuur verbinden de wijk aan de regio: Pendrecht bereikbaar voor auto, fiets en voetganger

Haarvaten van het weefsel
De introductie van kleinschalige verbindingen - olifanten-' of 'kerkpaden':

- De groene binnengebieden van de gestempelde bouwblokken worden onderdeel van de straat; het activeren van de openbare ruimte.
- Directe verbindingen met de grote assen in de wijk brengen de wijk dichter bij de winkels, scholen, de Brikken en de regio.

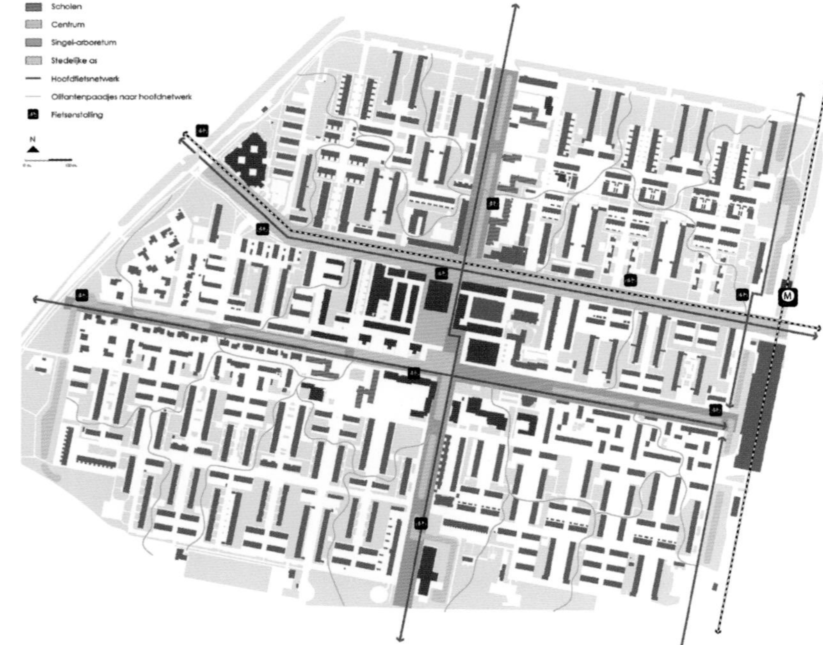

Van huis via school naar het werk:

1. Over de kleine paden, door de binnentuinen, naar de 'fietsweg'

2. Oude kranten en lege flessen kunnen bij school worden ingeleverd, gelijktijdig met het wegbrengen van de kinderen

3. De fiets stallen, een krant en appel kopen in de Brik en dan met de metro of tram naar je werk ergens in Rotterdam Zuid, of gewoon doorfietsen naar het Zuiderpark...

Bij de school is de Brik een fietsenstalling-met-groentewinkel, de groenten uit de schooltuin kan naast groenten uit directe omgeving worden verkocht. Een Brik is altijd meer dan stalling alleen: een wegwijzer, een verlichtingselement, kiosk, recyclepunt, fietsenshop of een informatiepunt om kennis te maken met de Nederlandse fietscultuur. Met deze functies worden concrete problemen in de wijk aangepakt: werkloosheid, sociale onveiligheid en bereikbaarheid.

De paden zorgen voor een directe verbinding naar de fietsweg, een veilige en snelle route door Pendrecht. De scholen die aan deze route zijn goed bereikbaar, hebben een degelijke stalling maar worden ook onderdeel van een sociaal-ruimtelijk netwerk. De Brikken koppelen schooltuinen aan ondernemers, kinderen aan het groene (speel)gebied en veiligheid aan gebruik.

Het alleen neerzetten van een fietsenstalling in een wijk als Pendrecht voegt weinig toe; inkomsten zijn laag net als het fietsbezit. De Brikken, de verbindende assen, de sociale functies maken een compleet systeem waarbij het hebben van een fiets meer nut heeft dan nu. De eerste voorwaarde naar gebruik is zo gelegd: een degelijke basis, een Brik.

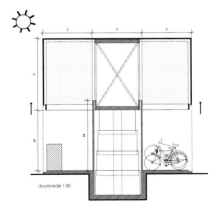

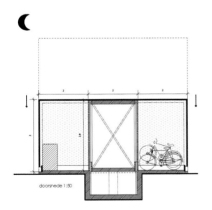

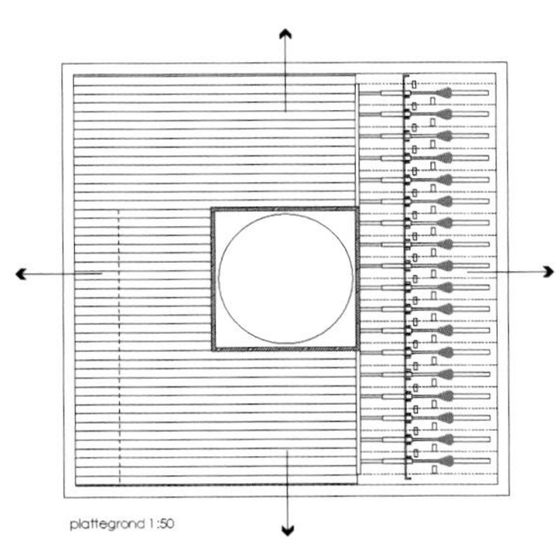

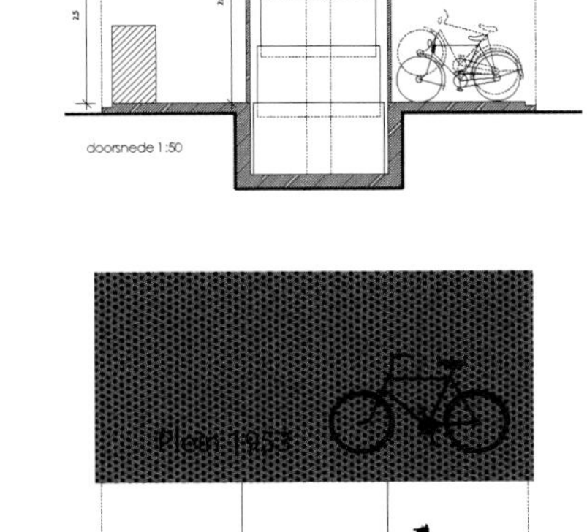

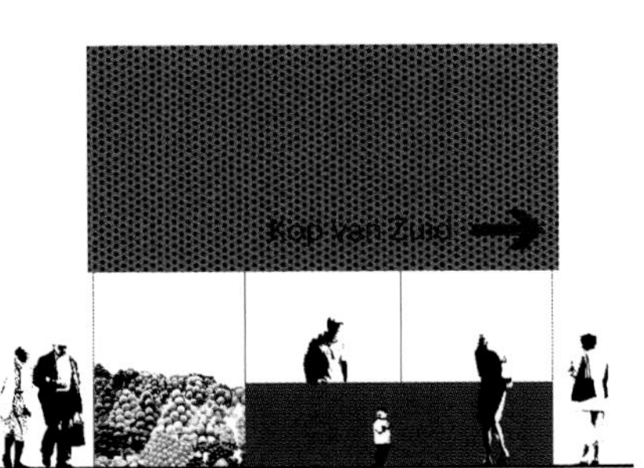

De Brik heeft een vrij indeelbare plattegrond waarbij 3/8 deel altijd in gebruik als fietsenstalling. Door de bouw heeft de Brik een alzijdige en open uitstraling.

De Brik opent zich in de ochtend door middel van een hydraulisch liftsysteem. Het mechanisme is vergelijkbaar met de liften in autogarages en de personenliften op kleine treinstations. De liften zijn makkelijk inpasbaar en behoeven weinig onderhoud. De vierkante kern zorgt in geopende toestand voor stabiliteit.

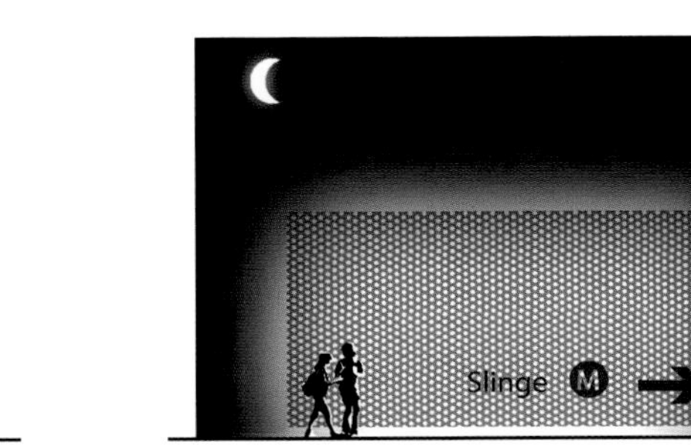

De kap is gemaakt van geperforeerd corten-staal en transformeert 's avonds naar een vandalisme bestendig lichtobject.

108 Own Harvest | *Posad*

Participants : Posad-spatial Strategies
Project : Spatial Strategy To Improve Quality Of Living Environment
Typology : Research Design/Regional Planning
Location : Province of South-Holland, the Netherlands

Size of Projectsite : 800km²
Client : Province of South-Holland

Eigen oogst

N
5 km

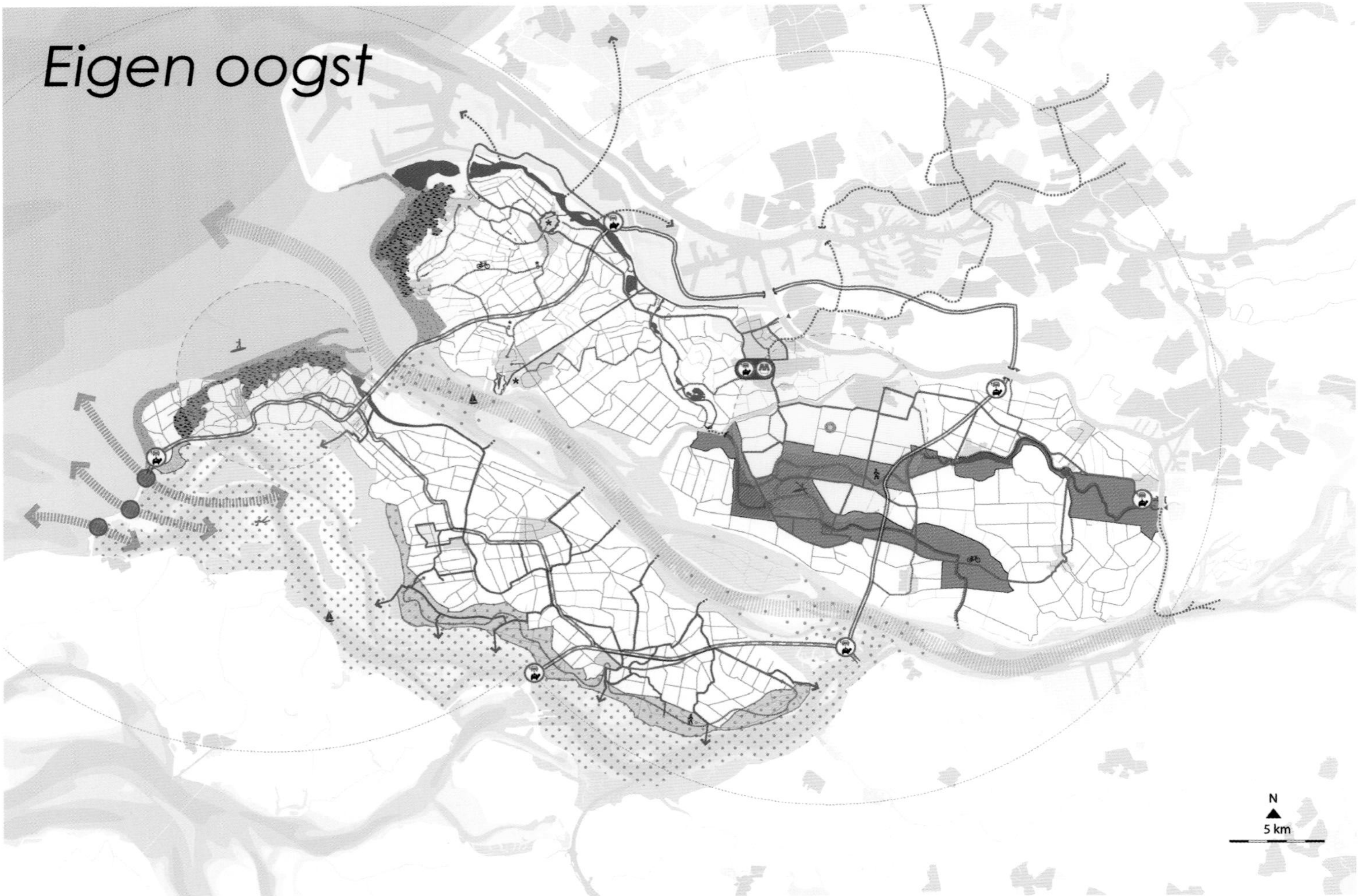

Toekomststrategie Zuid-Hollandse eilanden

Zuid Holland bestaat – naast de grootstedelijke gebieden van de Randstad – uit een aantal kenmerkende grote landschappen. De strandzone met de binnenduinrand, de veenweide gebieden van het Groene Hart en de Zuid Hollandse eilanden. Er is er een genuanceerdere beschrijving te maken van de diversiteit van de landschappen, maar het schept een beeld van de tweedeling van deze provincie: grote landschappen en (dicht)stedelijk gebied.

Deze grote landschappen of landschappelijke gebieden zijn in grote mate afhankelijk van dit stedelijk gebied, ze worden erdoor bedreigd maar een deel van de welvaart en voorzieningen liggen juist daar. Het gevolg is dat de landschappen snel gezien worden als een last of een restgebied waar invulling altijd leidt tot conflicten of waar de investeringen nooit opwegen tegen de baten.
De strategie die hier beschreven en geïllustreerd is, biedt mogelijkheden tot verandering binnen deze status quo: het landschap kan ook een lust zijn, baten hebben die iets toevoegen aan het stedelijk gebied, die zelfs de provincie als geheel kunnen versterken; landschappelijk, ecologisch en economisch. Het noodzakelijk transport van zoet water wordt één met recreatie en ruimte voor natuur, verzilting en de noodzaak tot doorspoelen met het creëren van nieuwe landschappen en andere vormen van landbouw.

Concept
Met het gebruik van de gebiedskenmerken is tevens getracht de regio minder afhankelijk te maken van de stad. Niet door programma toe te voegen wat al te vinden is in het stedelijk gebied maar door functies, landschappen en kansen te scheppen waar in de stad geen ruimte voor is en die voor de stad ook een waardevolle aanvulling kunnen zijn.

Noodzaak
Een aantal veranderingen in het gebied komen voort uit noodzaak; naast demografische ontwikkeling ook de wateropgave. Er verandert veel aan de bevolkingsverdeling en -opbouw in het gebied. Jongeren trekken weg en de babyboomgeneratie gaat langzaam naar de 65; het gebied vergrijst sterk en snel. De vergrijzing en leegloop van het gebied creëren een vraag naar zorg, naar een economische motor, iemand die het dorp en het land onderhoud. Het keren van de leegloop of het terugbrengen van zowel ouderen als jongeren is noodzakelijk om dat te bereiken.

De eilanden hebben al eeuwen onder invloed gestaan van de krachten van water, het heeft het gebied letterlijk gevormd. De grote wateren tussen de eilanden zijn in de afgelopen decennia gevormd, aangepast en getemd. Deze ingrepen hebben tot nu toe al grote gevolgen gehad; positief: veiligheid en zoetwaterkwaliteit en negatief: terugloop van soortenrijkdom en de achteruitgang van de waterkwaliteit. Ook nu zijn ingrepen noodzakelijk deels om problemen uit het verleden op te lossen, deels om nieuwe problemen tegen te gaan. Het ' Kierbesluit' , de verzilting van het Volkerak-Zoommeer en de ontwikkeling van een 'afsluitbaar-open' Rijnmond zijn noodzakelijke ingrepen om de ecologie van het gebied te verbeteren, de waterkwaliteit te verbeteren en de veiligheid te vergroten.

Oplossingen
De strategie heeft als uitgangspunt *de noodzaak*: krimp, klimaatverandering, waterkwaliteit en ecologie stellen ons voor enorme opgaven. Deze noodzaak geeft ook nieuwe mogelijkheden:
De noodzakelijke ingrepen gebruiken als basis voor de ontwikkeling van recreatie, een nieuwe lokale economische impuls en een nieuw duurzaamheidsperspectief voor het hele gebied.

Bebouwing
Bedrijventerrein / kassen
Water
Bestaand water onderdeel van krekennetwerk
Zoutwater
Nieuw landschap
Binnenduinrand
Strand
Zilte landbouw
Max. hoogwaardige gebruiksgebied geothermiek (5 km)
Max. laagwaardige gebruiksgebied geothermiek (20 km)
Snelweg
Provinciale weg
Lokale weg
Metro
Fietspad
Inname voor waterberging
Stroomrichting
Doorspoelen Goerree Overflakkee
Getijdencentrale
Electrischnetwerk transferpunt
Geothermische bron
Fietsrecreatief knooppunt
Wandelroute
Kanoroute
Waterrecreatie
Duikrecreatie
Vestingwerk / historisch stadscentrum

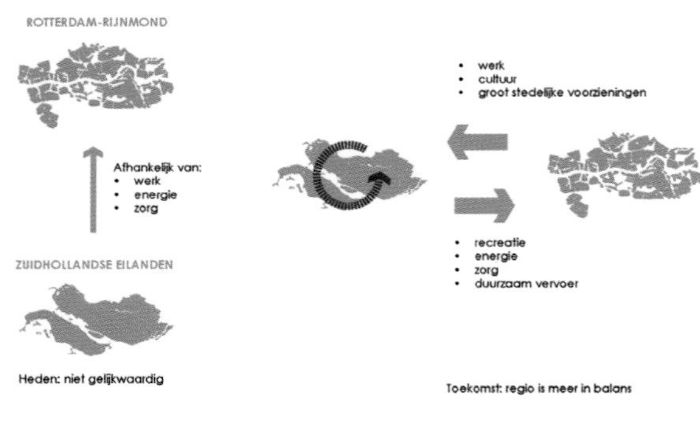

Heden: niet gelijkwaardig

Toekomst: regio is meer in balans

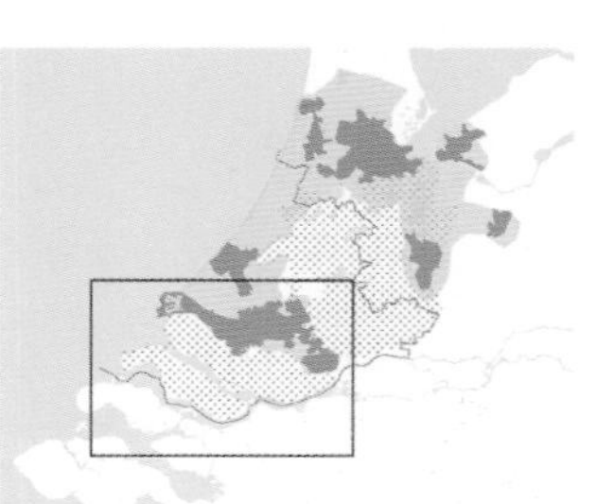
Twee grote niet stedelijke gebieden buiten de Randstad: het Groene hart en de Zuid-Hollandse eilanden

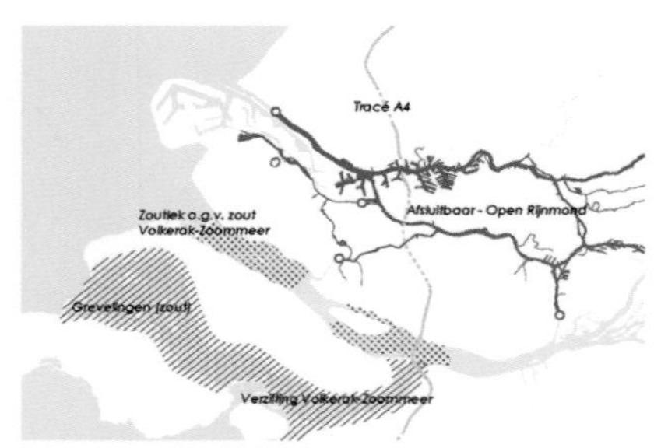

Wateropgave voor zuid-west Nederland

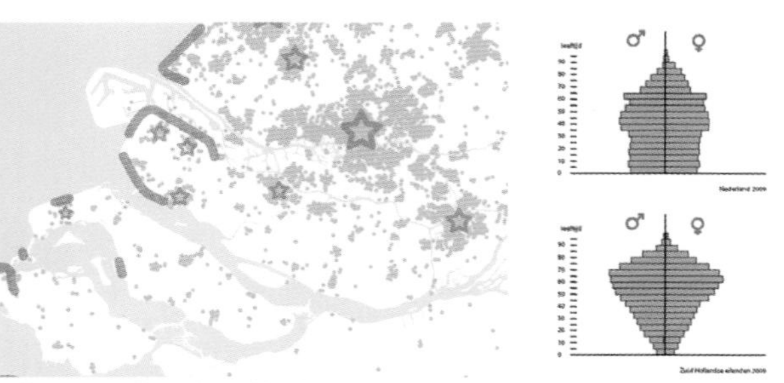

Nauwelijks water- en verblijfsrecreatie op de Zuid-Hollandse eilanden

Bevolkingssamenstelling

Water

Zilte teelt aan de zuidkant van Goeree Overflakkee

De stijgende zeespiegel, een toch al zilte bodem en de verzilting van Goeree-Overflakkee geeft problemen voor zoet oppervlaktewater. Het slootwater is brak of wordt het als gevolg van deze veranderingen. Door water over Goeree-Overflakkee heen te pompen – vanuit het Haringvliet – is een deel van deze verzilting te bestrijden. Hierdoor ontstaat een gradiënt op het eiland: het noordelijk deel van het eiland is zoet en het zuidelijk deel is in toenemende mate brak. Nieuwe teelten kunnen een oplossing zijn voor dit zuidelijk deel, deze teelten kunnen ook nieuwe (productie)landschappen vormen. Landschappen die we nu nog niet kennen. Na eeuwen van inpolderen - de creatie van het veenweidelandschap - is het mogelijk een nieuw (polder) landschap te creëren; een vervolg op een rijke traditie van het 'maken' van land.

Doorsnede Goederede

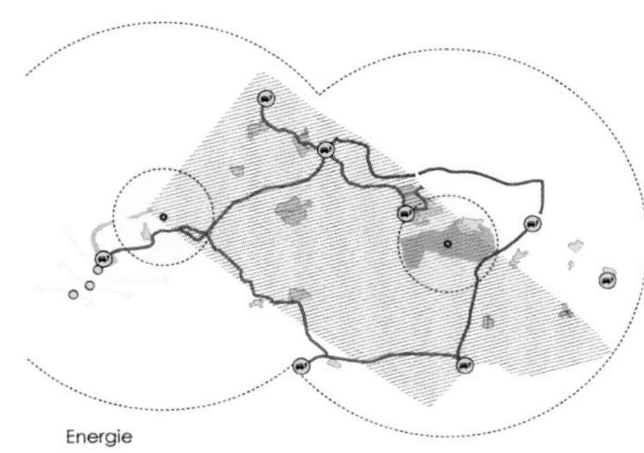

Energie

Recreatie op de kop van Goeree Overflakkee met warmwaterbaden uit geothermiek

De Zuid Hollandse eilanden hebben in de bodem een aantal goed exploitabele aardlagen liggen, lagen die geschikt zijn voor warmtewinning. Met deze geothermische energie kunnen kassen, huizen en bedrijven verwarmd worden maar er kan ook stroom mee opgewekt worden, in een straal van ca. 5 km stroom opgewekt worden en worden gebruikt voor stadsverwarming, industriële processen en de grote kassencomplexen. In een straal van maximaal 20 kilometer van de put kunnen recreatieve voorzieningen - de recreatieve kustontwikkeling op Goeree voorzien worden van warmte. Ondiepe geothermie, in dezelfde put, biedt daarnaast de mogelijkheid om kantoren, huizen en bedrijven te koelen. Deze warmte en koude uit de eigen ondergrond, uit de eigen regio, maakt ruimtelijke ontwikkelingen in het gebied duurzamer, laagdrempeliger en uniek. De kenmerken van het gebied, de bevolking en het landschap maken een andere vorm van recreatie mogelijk. Een luxe, rustige en goed in het landschap gepaste recreatie. Een recreatieontwikkeling als deze biedt gelijk kansen voor zorgontwikkeling voor de grijze generatie: een generatie die op zoek is naar rust en luxe en daar voor bereid is te betalen.

Recreatie

Oude kreek in de Hoekse Waard gebruiken als zoetwater buffer, transport en gebruiken als motor voor recreatie

Waterrecreatie nabij Mijnsheerenland

Natuurlijke oevers ter vergroting van soortenrijkdom

Sterk recreatief netwerk gekoppeld aan water

Nationaal Landschap de Hoekse Waard kan een doorvoer en bergingsgebied zijn als alternatief voor het verzilte Haringvliet. Hiermee is de watertoevoer aan het Rotterdamse Haven en Delfland te waarborgen. Door het water bovengronds – in de vorm van sloten, kanalen en kreken – te transporteren kan gelijktijdig het probleem van bodemdaling deels worden tegengegaan. Het nieuwe watersysteem in de Hoekse Waard bied ruimte aan recreanten maar er ontstaat ook een nieuw biotoop; een langgerekte zoetwater 'kreek' gelegen in polderlandschap. Recreatief maar ook ecologische een verrijking voor het gebied.

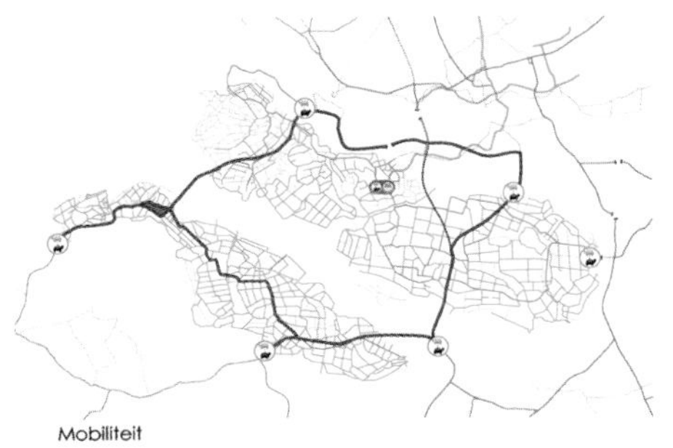

Mobiliteit

Er is geen alternatief voor de auto in dunbevolkte gebieden; er is geen volledig dekkend openbaar systeem. Het gebruik van de auto is hier dus een gegeven, juist hier biedt een stap naar duurzaam vervoer winst. De winst is te behalen door een scheiding aan te brengen in het doorgaande verkeer – over de snelwegen – en het lokale verkeer.
Een bewoner/gebruiker van het gebied kan in een transferium zijn elektrische auto inruilen voor een 'normale' auto om zijn weg buiten de eilanden te vervolgen. Snelwegen die door de regio lopen zijn ononderbroken, wil men echter van de snelweg af dan blijft de auto op fossiele brandstof staan en wordt overgestapt in een elektrische auto. De stroom voor deze auto's komt van de geothermische warmte uit de regio zelf: eigen oogst.

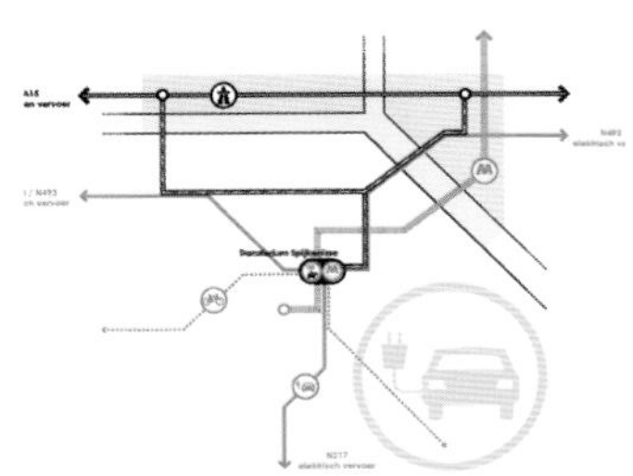

Schematische weergave van transferpunt voor elektrisch netwerk

109 Golden Grip | *Posad*

Participants : Posad-Spatial Strategies
Project : Development Strategy of Business Park
Typology : Urban Design
Location : Gouda, the Netherlands
Size of projectsite : 62,5 ha
Client : grAp, Architecture Centre of Gouda

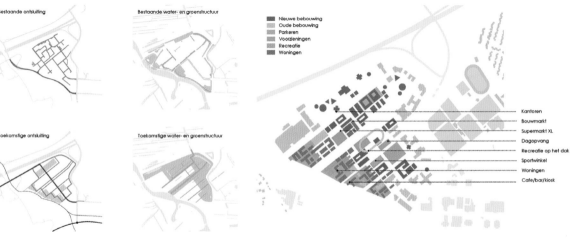

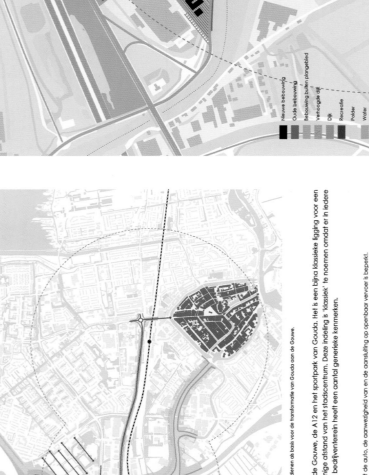

GOUWE GREEP

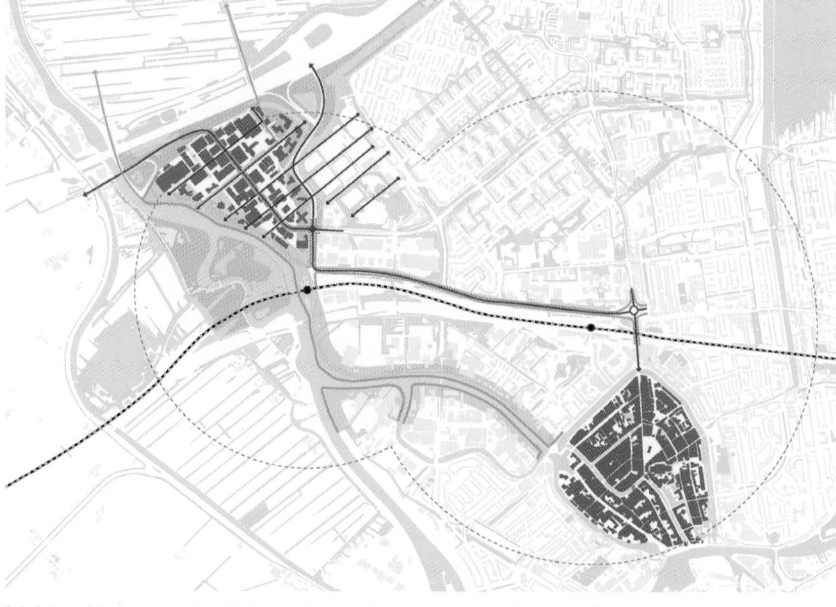
De ligging tussen stad en land en de goede ontsluitingsmogelijkheden dienen als basis voor de transformatie van Gouda aan de Gouwe.

Bedrijventerrein Goudse Poort is ingeklemd tussen de Gouwe, de A12 en het sportpark van Gouda. Het is een bijna klassieke ligging voor een bedrijventerrein: dicht tegen de infrastructuur op enige afstand van het stadscentrum. Deze indeling is 'klassiek' te noemen omdat er in iedere stad in Nederland op dezelfde wijze gewerkt is: het bedrijventerrein heeft een aantal generieke kenmerken.

Generieke kenmerken en problemen
- Het gebied is bijna alleen bereikbaar met de auto, de aanwezigheid van en de aansluiting op openbaar vervoer is beperkt.
- Bedrijventerreinen kennen een sterke mono functionaliteit
- Er is beperkt toezicht of sociale controle (met name in de avonduren)
- Bedrijventerreinen hebben niets met de stad te maken: er is geen echte relatie met het centrum
- Het is vaak het eerste wat iemand ziet bij binnenkomst van de stad: het bedrijventerrein is de poort naar de stad geworden.

Unieke eigenschappen van Gouda en Goudse Poort?
- Gouda is een stad dichtbij het water: de Gouwe en de Hollandse IJssel
- Om de stad ligt een rijk en open polderlandschap
- Goudse poort heeft een goede bereikbaarheid: trein, auto en in de toekomst zelfs lightrail

De eigenschappen zijn echter niet altijd even goed benut; de relatie tussen de stad als geheel en het water wordt ontkend. De stad lijkt na de afdichting van de binnenstad in 1953 vergeten te zijn een stad aan het water te zijn. Het open polderlandschap is alleen nog op afstand te ervaren, de structuur van de polder die zo belangrijk is geweest voor de ontwikkeling van de stad is niet meer terug te vinden in de structuur van de stad.

Doel
Door functies naast elkaar te positioneren en elkaars functie te gebruiken en werking te versterken kan een monofunctioneel bedrijventerrein veranderen in een levendig, stedelijk, gebied met bedrijven en woningen, maatschappelijke functies en landschap. Het doel is geenszins om alle bedrijven weg te vegen van het terrein; een stad heeft bedrijvigheid hard nodig. Een monofunctioneel, parasitair aan de stad en het landschap ontkennend element in de stad – het bedrijventerrein – is iets van de vorige eeuw. Een modern en toekomstbestendig gebied gaat uit van (gedeeltelijke) functiemenging, gebruik van landschappelijke kwaliteiten en de ambitie om een onderdeel te worden van de stad.

Greep
Naast bedrijventerreinen zijn er in de stad meerdere functies die langzaam richting periferie geschoven worden. Door deze - voor de stad essentiële functies - te mengen kan het bedrijventerrein een uiterst dynamisch gebied worden met ruimte voor sport en recreatie, winkels en bedrijven, parken en fietsroutes.
Door structuur van de wegen in het gebied aan te passen is het mogelijk een voetgangersgebied – de auto is te gast op de kade, er is ruimte voor laden en lossen - te maken. De hoofdontsluiting loopt niet langer langs het water maar door het hart van het gebied, dit maakt het gebied overzichtelijker en beter bereikbaar
De dijkzone is bij uitstek geschikt voor wonen en werken, hier zou de ligging van Gouda aan het water weer vorm krijgen. Door de dijk langs de Gouwe nieuw vorm te geven, te verbreden de polder in, ontstaat ruimte voor wonen en werken met zicht op en over het water. Op dit moment wordt door het Hoogheemraadschap gekeken naar mogelijkheden voor dijkversterking en de aanleg van keringen in de Gouwe. Dit momentum zou gegrepen moeten worden om de stad aan het water te leggen op basis van de versterking van de dijken.

Plankaart

Bestaande ontsluiting

Bestaande water- en groenstructuur

Toekomstige ontsluiting

Toekomstige water- en groenstructuur

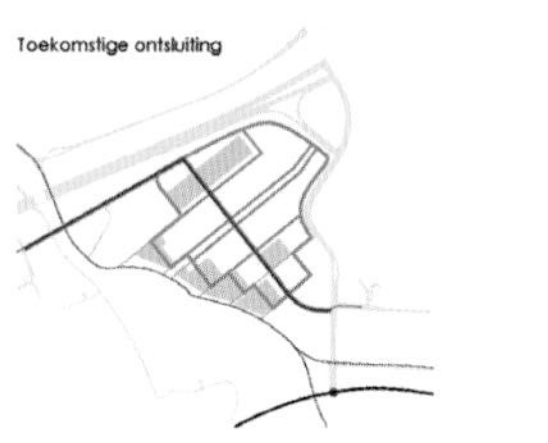

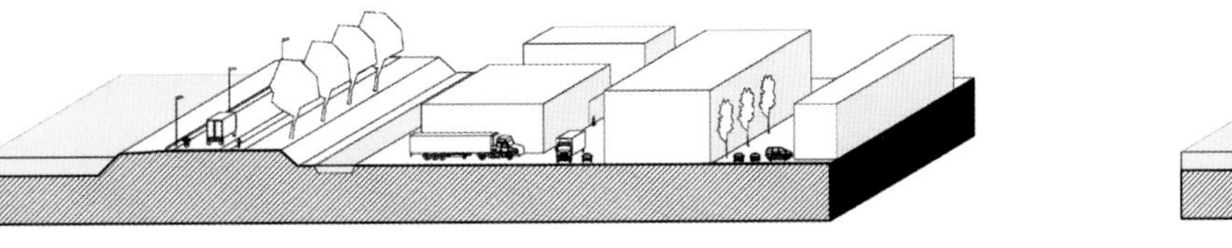

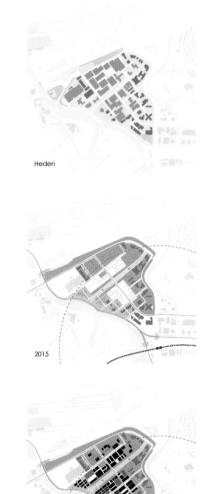

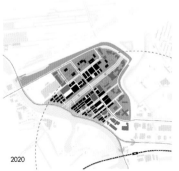

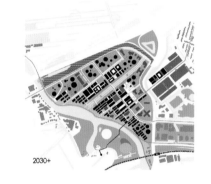

Dijk langs de Gouwe in de bestaande situatie

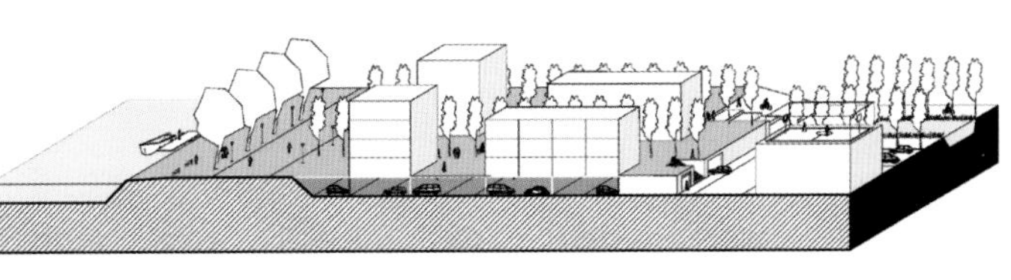

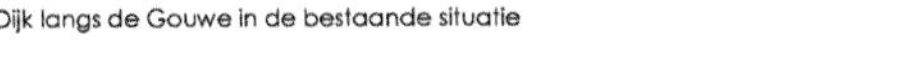

Situatie met verbrede en bebouwde dijk langs de Gouwe

De verbrede dijk geeft zicht over het water maar maakt ook mogelijk dat de structuur van het bedrijventerrein verandert: de lijnen van de polder zoals die tot in de jaren 50 van de vorige eeuw nog te zien waren worden gebruikt als basis voor de verkaveling. Binnen deze structuur kan de herkenbaarheid van het polderlandschap – sloten, veen en weide – terugkomen. De combinatie van landschap en bedrijventerrein. Een veenweidegebied in een stedelijk gebied, gelegen tussen woningen en bedrijven, kent een andere kwaliteit en uitvoering: het park. Een vernat veengebied, met een grote soortenrijkdom, vangt het Hollandse landschap in het stedelijk gebied: een modern landschaps- en stadspark.

De dijkzone bestaat uit wonen en kleine bedrijvigheid – kantoren en winkels. Net achter de dijk is een zone waar grootwinkelbedrijven en bouwmarkten ruimte krijgen.
In het veenweidepark staan de kantoren en woontorens vrij in de ruimte. Deze gebouwen zijn met hun vrije plek in het park een drager van de landschappelijke kwaliteit.
In het hart van het gebied liggen de 'gewone' bedrijven vermengd met de grootwinkelfuncties die de periferie kenmerken, bedrijven met een kleine hinderzone, een fors ruimtebeslag en een redelijke parkeerbehoefte. Deze bedrijven delen de ruimte echter met andere functies, functies met een ander 'tijdsslot': sport en recreatie. De ruimte op de gebouwen – op het dak – wordt gebruikt voor sportvelden, over de gebouwen heen ligt een hardloopbaan; meervoudig ruimtegebruik.
Omdat deze functies op andere tijden gebruikt worden dan de openingstijden van de bedrijven kan de parkeerruimte die in de parkeergebouwen en in de verlengde dijk is gecreëerd worden benut. Het meervoudig ruimtegebruik stopt niet bij het fysiek stapelen van functies.

De menging van functies biedt mogelijkheden voor de toekomst: we kunnen voor of achteruit. Alle volumes houden de mogelijkheid van meer wonen of meer werken open, er bestaat een goede basis voor een sterkere vervlechting met de stad en het landschap kan een plek krijgen in de stad actief als sport en spel gebied of passief als (noodzakelijk) stedelijk groen.
Deze combinatie van locaal en generiek, van functiemenging en landschap is een 'gouwegreep' een toekomstbestendige oplossing voor Gouda en de rest van Nederland.

Nat polderpark als inleiding tot het Groene Hart

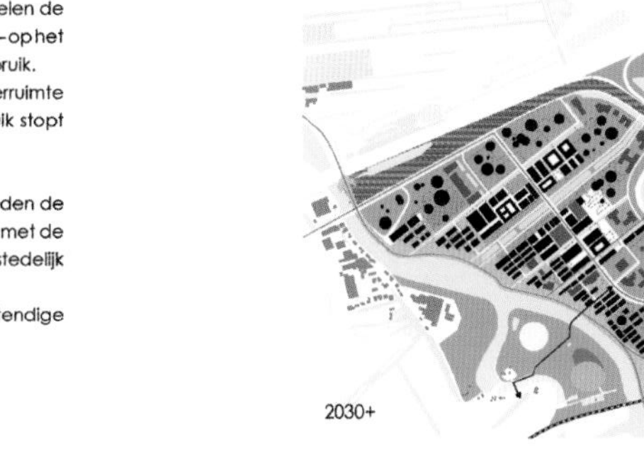

110 Mirakelsteeg | *Posad*

Participants : Posad-spatial Strategies
Partner : Schrijnen Groep
Project : the Neighborhood as a Spatial Enterprice
Typology : Urban Design/Rehabilitation

Location : Leiden, the Netherlands
Size of projectsite : 62,5 ha
Client : The Netherlands Architecture Fund, Housing corporation Portaal
Year : 2010 – 1st prize

Mirakelsteeg als ruimtelijke onderneming

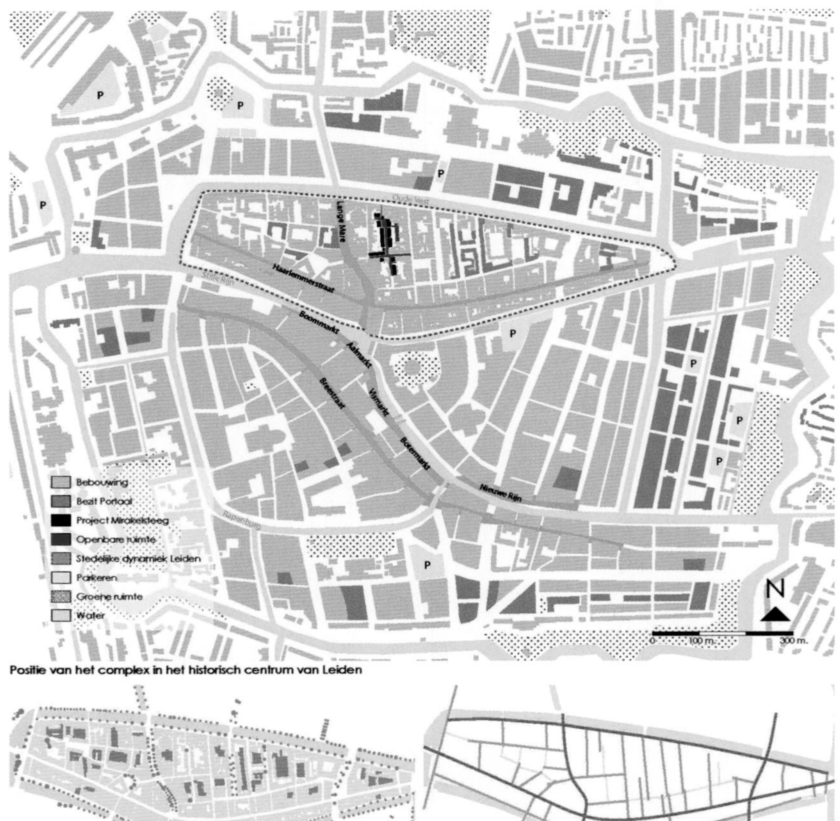

Positie van het complex in het historisch centrum van Leiden

Weinig groene ruimte in dit gedeelte van de stad

Space syntax - locatie zit onderaan in de hierarchie van het infrastructurele netwerk

In de periode van 1960-1990 heeft de enorme woningbouwproductie in Nederland op alle plekken binnen het stedelijk weefsel haar stempel achtergelaten. In Leiden was er onder de woningbouwverenigingen in deze periode geen groot enthousiasme tot het realiseren van nieuwbouwwoningen. De corporaties investeerden liever in de bestaande woningvoorraad en voerde op veel plekken ingrijpend onderhoud uit aan panden die reeds in beheer waren. De plekken in de binnenstad waar toch nieuwbouw is gepleegd waren dan ook veelal de plekken waar sloop en nieuwbouw de enige optie bleek; zo ook in de Mirakelsteeg en in de meeste gevallen waren die gebouwen enkel en alleen te gbruiken als woongebouwen. Hierdoor gebeuren er feitelijk nog maar twee dingen in het straatbeeld: wonen en parkeren.

Portaal
Portaal is eigenaar van tientallen kleinschalige complexen in de Leidse binnenstad. Nu, ruim voor het eind van de oorspronkelijke exploitatietermijn, horen deze complexen niet bepaald tot de mooiste en beste van de stad. Er zijn leefbaarheidsproblemen en er valt veel te zeggen voor bouwtechnische en energetische modernisering.

Aan de andere kant hebben deze complexen één bijzondere, onmiskenbare kwaliteit: hun ligging in het historische centrum van Leiden. Juist deze positie, in een van de dichts bevolkte steden van Zuid-Holland, kan een drijvende kracht zijn voor vernieuwing.

Door de potentie van de locatie maximaal te benutten, kan Portaal haar financiële positie, woningbezit en de aanliggende openbare ruimte verbeteren. Mits zij open staat voor maatwerk en combinaties van verbouwingen en kleinschalige herontwikkeling. Dit geldt vanzelfsprekend niet alleen voor de Mirakelsteeg, maar voor alle vergelijkbare locaties.

De ruimtelijke onderneming
Ruimtelijke ingrepen moeten volgens ons altijd een meervoudig effect hebben. In het geval van de Mirakelsteeg streven we onder meer naar een aantrekkelijkere straat, verlenging van de levensduur van de woningen, vermindering van leefbaarheidskosten en energetische duurzaamheid. En al deze doelen moeten wat ons betreft onder de streep tot een positief bedrijfsresultaat leiden.

Dit maakt de wijk tot een gezonde, ruimtelijke onderneming.

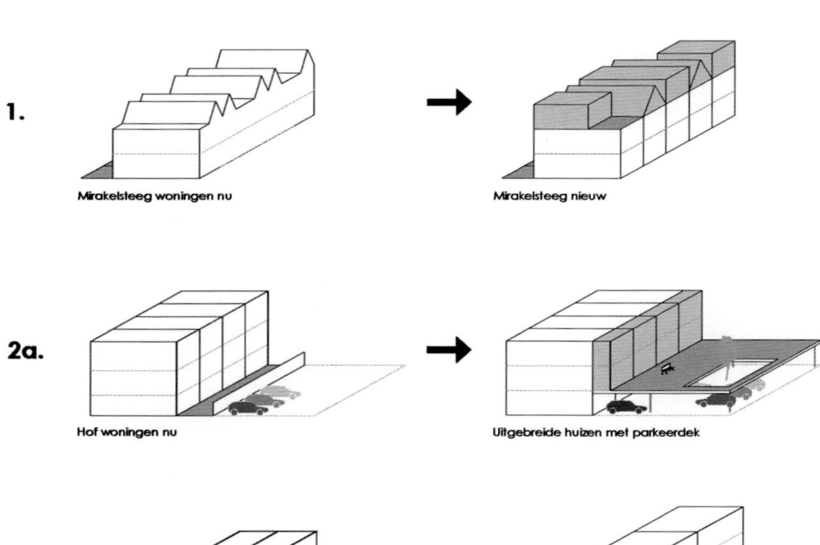

Mirakelsteeg woningen nu → Mirakelsteeg nieuw

Hof woningen nu → Uitgebreide huizen met parkeerdek

Mirakelsteeg huizen en garage nu → Het Mirakelblok

4.

Clarensteeg woningen nu → Buurtwinkels en appartementen in de Clarensteeg

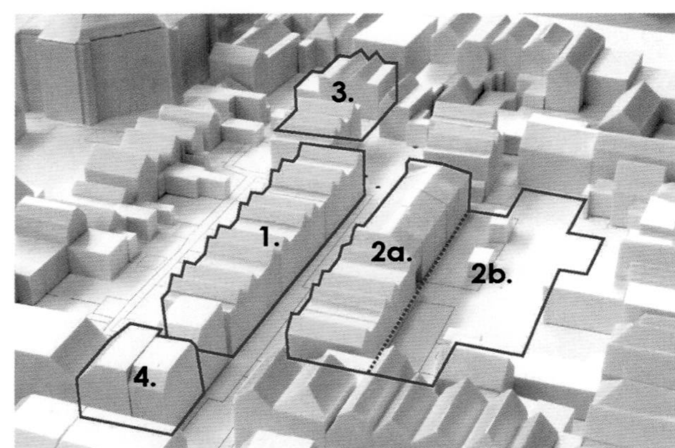

1. **Mirakelsteeg-west** **+ 430.000 €**
   - *Meer huuropbrengst door toename woonoppervlak*
   - *Betere Isolatie, dus beter energielabel*

2. **Mirakelsteeg-oost** **- 394.000 €**

2a. Praktijkwoningen
- *Groei huuropbrengst door toename woonoppervlak, grotere buitenruimte en parkeerplaats*
- *Van sociale huur naar markthuur*

2b. Parkeerdek
- *Van 11 ongure publieke parkeerplaatsen naar: 3 openbare, 9 gereserveerd voor huurwoningen en 13 in verkoop.*

3. **Het Mirakelblok** **+ 245.000 €**
   - *Offeren twee goed verhuurbare sociale woningen. Levert zes startersappartementen met parkeerplaats op. Inkomsten uit VON verkoop*

4. **Hoekpand** **- 50.000 €**
   - *Kostenpost ten behoeve van de totale kwaliteit en uitstraling Mirakelsteeg.*

5. **Puntensprokkel**
   - *Puntensprongen binnen 10 punten van de liberalisatiegrens zijn de moeite waard omdat ze binnen de oorspronkelijke exploitatietermijn (10-15 jaar) terug te verdienen zijn.*

Totaal **+ 231.000 €**

Problemen

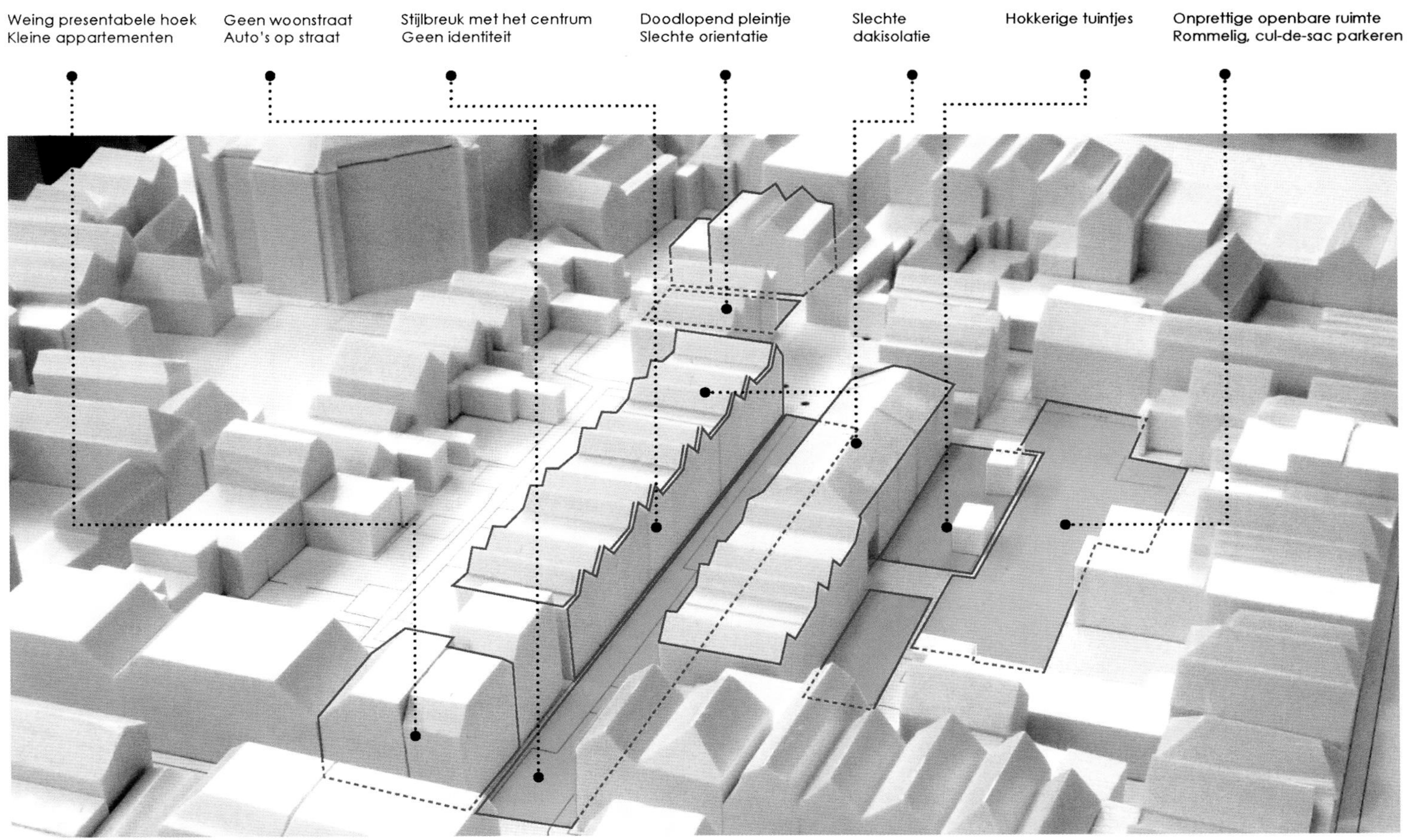
Weing presentabele hoek
Kleine appartementen
Geen woonstraat
Auto's op straat
Stijlbreuk met het centrum
Geen identiteit
Doodlopend pleintje
Slechte orientatie
Slechte
dakisolatie
Hokkerige tuintjes
Onprettige openbare ruimte
Rommelig, cul-de-sac parkeren

Oplossingen

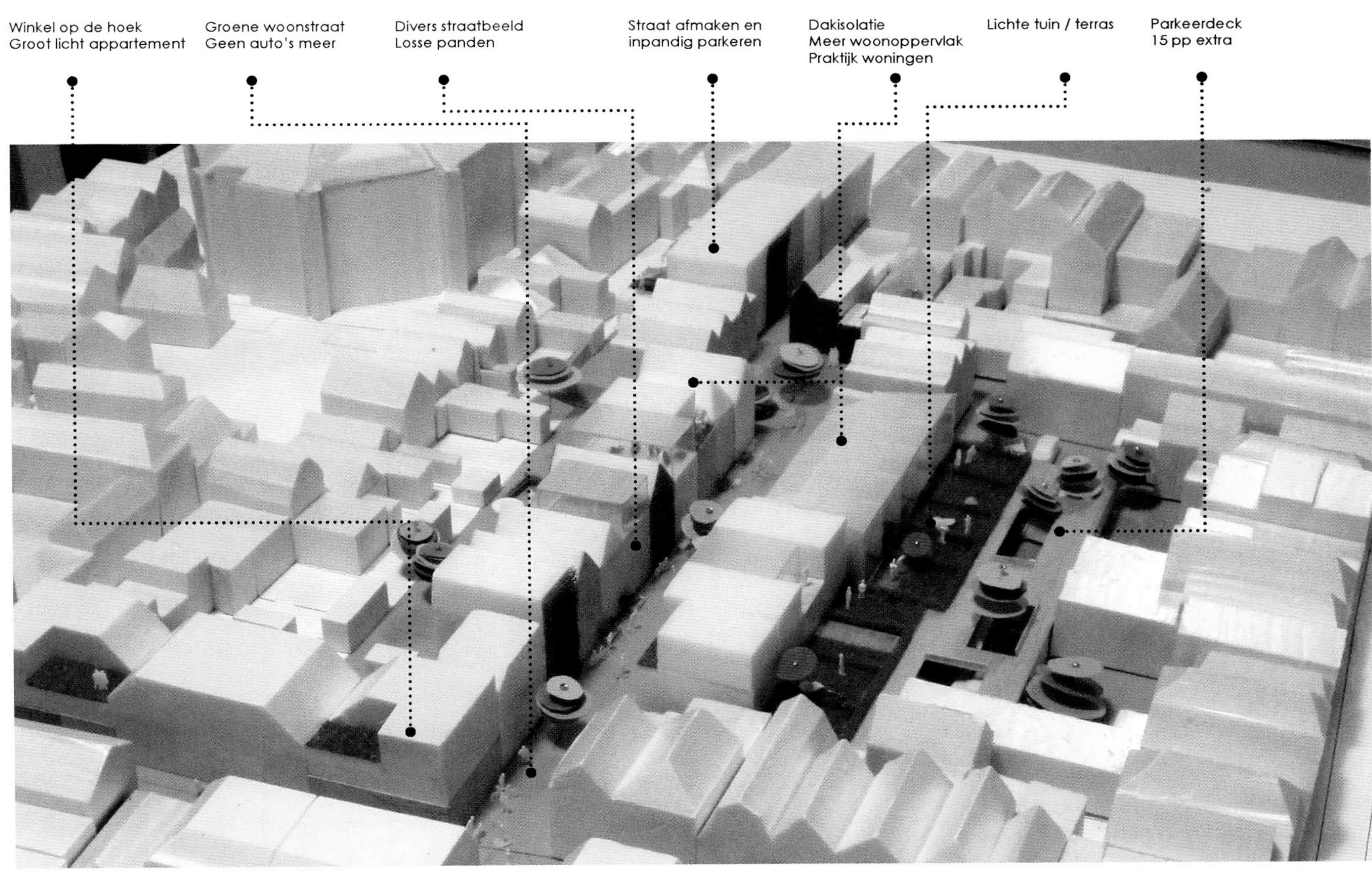
Winkel op de hoek
Groot licht appartement
Groene woonstraat
Geen auto's meer
Divers straatbeeld
Losse panden
Straat afmaken en
inpandig parkeren
Dakisolatie
Meer woonoppervlak
Praktijk woningen
Lichte tuin / terras
Parkeerdeck
15 pp extra

Mirakelblok — Op een strategische plek de straat afmaken

- Pleintje is op dit moment een kale en onprettige openbare ruimte.
- Door de herontwikkeling kan de straat afgemaakt worden.
- De garage van de buurman kan aansluitend op zijn eigen kavel teruggebracht worden.
- Alle appartementen hebben een eigen parkeerplaats op de begane grond, de dakterrassen kijken uit op de Marekerk

Mirakelblok doorsnede

Begane grond

Eerste verdieping

Zicht in de Mirakelsteeg vanaf de ingang op de Oude Vest.

Hoekpanden — De hoek van twee stegen wordt het middelpunt van de wijk

- Toevoegen programma straathoek geeft een fris gezicht aan de wijk en is belangrijk voor de andere ingrepen.
- Hoeken goed zichtbaar vanaf drukkere straten en kunnen zo de wijk ook programmatisch onderdeel maken van het centrum.
- De kleine donkere maisonettes worden getransformeerd tot lichte grote appartementen die uitkijken over de binnenstad.

Doorsnede huidig

Nieuwe doorsnede

Tweede verdieping nu

Tweede verdieping

Eerste verdieping nu

Eerste verdieping

Begane grond nu

Begane grond 1:200

Zicht op de hoek van de Clarensteeg en Mirakelsteeg.

Mirakelsteeg-west — Van parkeerstraat naar woonstraat in het centrum van Leiden

- Door de gevel op te delen per pand, ontstaat een beeld van losse panden die aansluit bij het historsch centrum.
- De verbetering van de dak- en gevelisolatie leidt tot een vergroening van het straatbeeld en een beter energielabel.
- Straat wordt nu gedomineerd door geparkeerde auto's. De indeling van de woningen is echter niet verkeerd en kan bij het oplossen van het parkeren leiden tot een betere koppeling tussen woning en straat.

Woning doorsnede nu

Nieuwe doorsnede

Tweede verdieping

Eerste verdieping nu

Eerste verdieping

Begane grond nu

Begane grond 1:200

Zicht in de Mirakelsteeg vanaf de Clarensteeg.

Parkeerdek — Wonen, werken, betere buitenruimte, een beter energielabel én meer parkeerplaatsen

- Het huidige hof is een onaantrekkelijke cul de sac. Het parkeerdek biedt oplossing: 15 extra parkeerplaatsen, tuin met meer licht en een betere relatie met omgeving.
- Het aanpassen van de woningplattegronden is hiervoor noodzakelijk: Door het koppelen van rugzakken aan de bestaande woningen ontstaan er praktijk- / werkruimten aan de straat. De grote woonverdiepingen hebben ook een betere en grotere buitenruimte op het dek.

Voorgestelde parkeersituatie 1:500

Tweede verdieping nu

Tweede verdieping

Eerste verdieping nu

Eerste verdieping

Begane grond nu

Begane grond 1:200

* De plattegronden van nr. 54 t/m 60 wijken af van getoonde plattegronden

Zicht over het parkeerdek in het binnenhof van de Mirakelsteeg.

Scape or no One – Doing Nothing – Nowhere | *Horhizon consortium*

Type : Film
Design : Eva Sommeregger

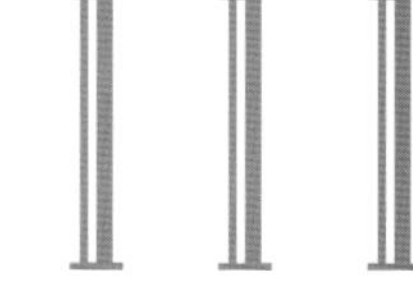

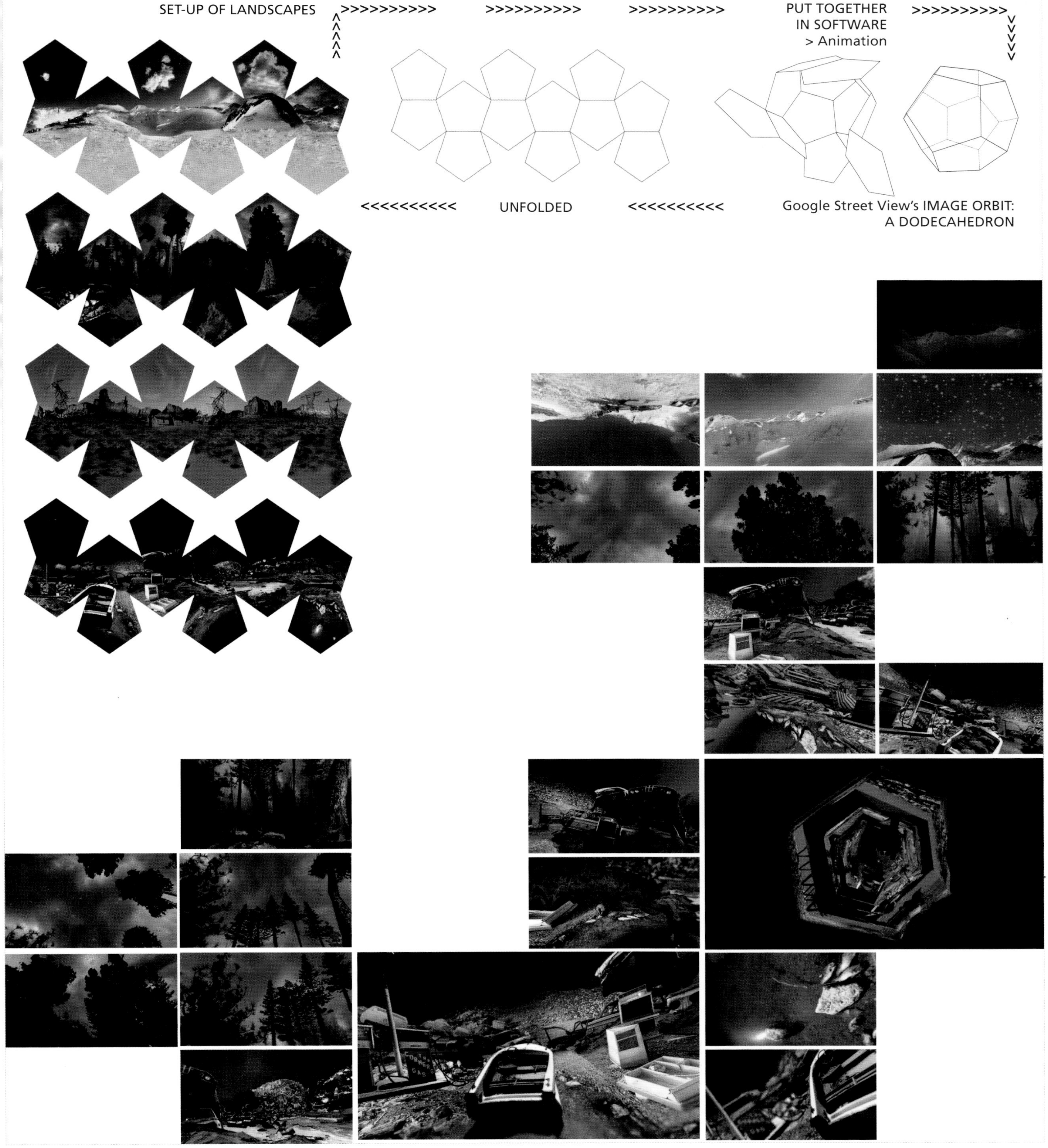

SET-UP OF LANDSCAPES ^^^^^ >>>>>>>>>> >>>>>>>>>> >>>>>>>>>>

PUT TOGETHER
IN SOFTWARE
> Animation

>>>>>>>>>>> vvvvv

<<<<<<<<<< UNFOLDED <<<<<<<<<<

Google Street View's IMAGE ORBIT:
A DODECAHEDRON

112

049821 | *AA & U For Architecture, Art and Urbanism*

Project Team : Socratis Stratis(Dr. architect, urbanist, assistant professor), Riccardo Urbano(architect)
Collaborators : Anastasia Angelidou(architect)

Support : Stavri Giannakou(architect), Savas Anastasiou(student of architecture), Vicky Theodorou(student of architecture), Filippo Gur(Student of Architecture)

049821

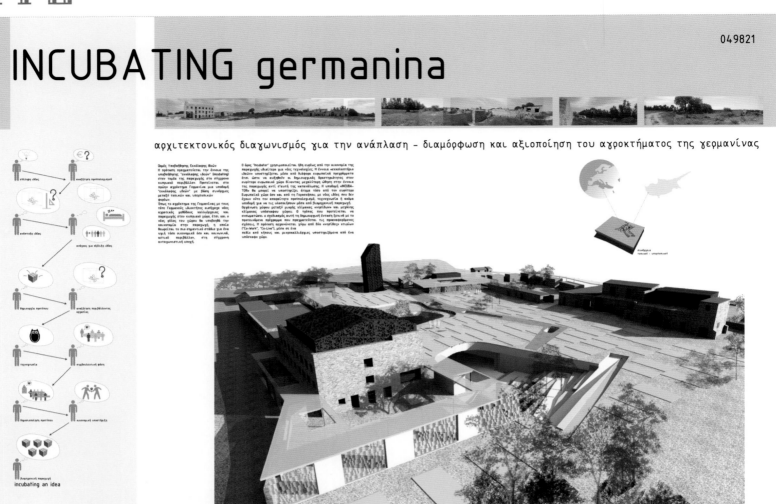

INCUBATING germanina

αρχιτεκτονικός διαγωνισμός για την ανάπλαση - διαμόρφωση και αξιοποίηση του αγροκτήματος της γερμανίνας

Δομές Υποβοήθησης Εκκόλαψης Ιδεών
Η πρόταση πραγματεύεται την έννοια της υποβοήθησης "εκκόλαψης ιδεών" (incubating) στον τομέα της παραγωγής στο σύγχρονο κυπριακό περιβάλλον. Προτείνεται στο πρώην αγρόκτημα Γερμανίνα μια υποδομή "εκκόλαψης ιδεών" με βάση συνέργιες μεταξύ τοπικών και υπερτοπικών φορέων.
Όπως το αγρόκτημα της Γερμανίνας με τους τότε Γερμανούς ιδιοκτήτες εισήγαγε νέες αγροτικές μεθόδους καλλιέργειας και παραγωγής στον κυπριακό χώρο, έτσι και ο νέος ρόλος του χώρου θα υποβοηθά την καινοτομία στην παραγωγή, η οποία θεωρείται το πιο σημαντικό στάδιο για ένα υγιή τόσο οικονομικά όσο και κοινωνικά, αστικό περιβάλλον, στη σύγχρονη ανταγωνιστική εποχή.

Ο όρος "Incubator" χρησιμοποιείται ήδη ευρέως από την οικονομία της παραγωγής ιδιαίτερα για νέες τεχνολογίες. Η έννοια «εκκολαπτήριο ιδεών» υποστηρίζεται μέσα από διάφορα ευρωπαϊκά προγράμματα έτσι ώστε να αυξηθούν οι δημιουργικές δραστηριότητες στον ευρύτερο ευρωπαϊκό χώρο δίνοντας μεγαλύτερη ώθηση στην έννοια της παραγωγής αντί σ'αυτή της κατανάλωσης. Η υποδομή «INCUBATOR» θα μπορεί να υποστηρίζει άτομα τόσο από τον ευρύτερο Ευρωπαϊκό χώρο όσο και από τη Γεροσκήπου, με νέες ιδέες που δεν έχουν ούτε τον απαραίτητο προϋπολογισμό, τεχνογνωσία ή ακόμα υποδομή για να τις υλοποιήσουν μέσα από βιομηχανική παραγωγή.
Οργάνωση χώρου: μεταξύ μικρής κλίμακας «νησίδων» και μεγάλης κλίμακας υπόσκαφου χώρου. Ο τρόπος που προτείνεται να ενσωματώσει ο σχεδιασμός αυτή τη δημιουργική ένταση ξεκινά με το προτεινόμενο πρόγραμμα που πραγματεύεται τις προαναφερόμενες σχέσεις. Η πρόταση οργανώνεται γύρω από δύο «νησίδες» κτιρίων ("Co-Work", "Co-Live"), μέσα σε ένα πεδίο από κήπους και μικροκαλλιέργειες υποστηριζόμενα από ένα υπόσκαφο χώρο.

incubating an idea

049821

Ράμπα κήπος για είσοδο στον υπόσκαφο χώρο

"Ιερός κήπος" Γερμανίνας

Μικρές καλλιέργειες

Τριανταφυλλώνας Γερμανίνας

Χώρος Στάθμευσης

ΝΗΣΙΔΑ "CO-WORK"

ΝΗΣΙΔΑ "CO-LIVE"

ΚΕΝΤΡΙΚΗ ΠΛΑΤΕΙΑ

προσβάσεις προς και από την περιοχή μελέτης

Χώρος Στάθμευσης

Βαθμιδωτός κήπος ως πρόσβαση στον υπόσκαφο χώρο (αμφιθεατρικός χώρος για εκδηλώσεις)

ΤΟΠΟΓΡΑΦΙΚΟ ΣΧΕΔΙΟ ΠΡΟΤΑΣΗΣ

προγραμματισμός νησίδων

ΤΟΜΗ Β - Β'

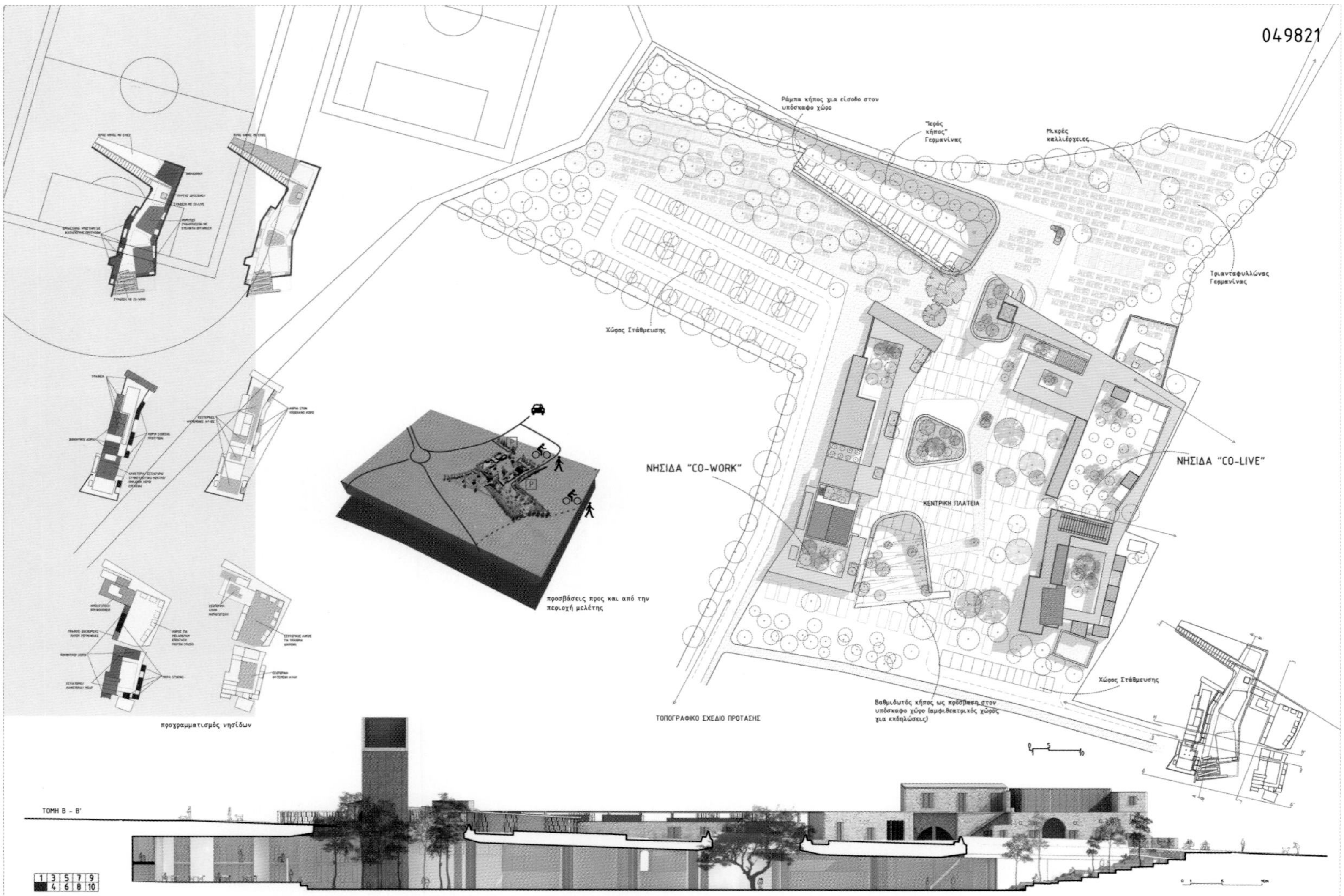

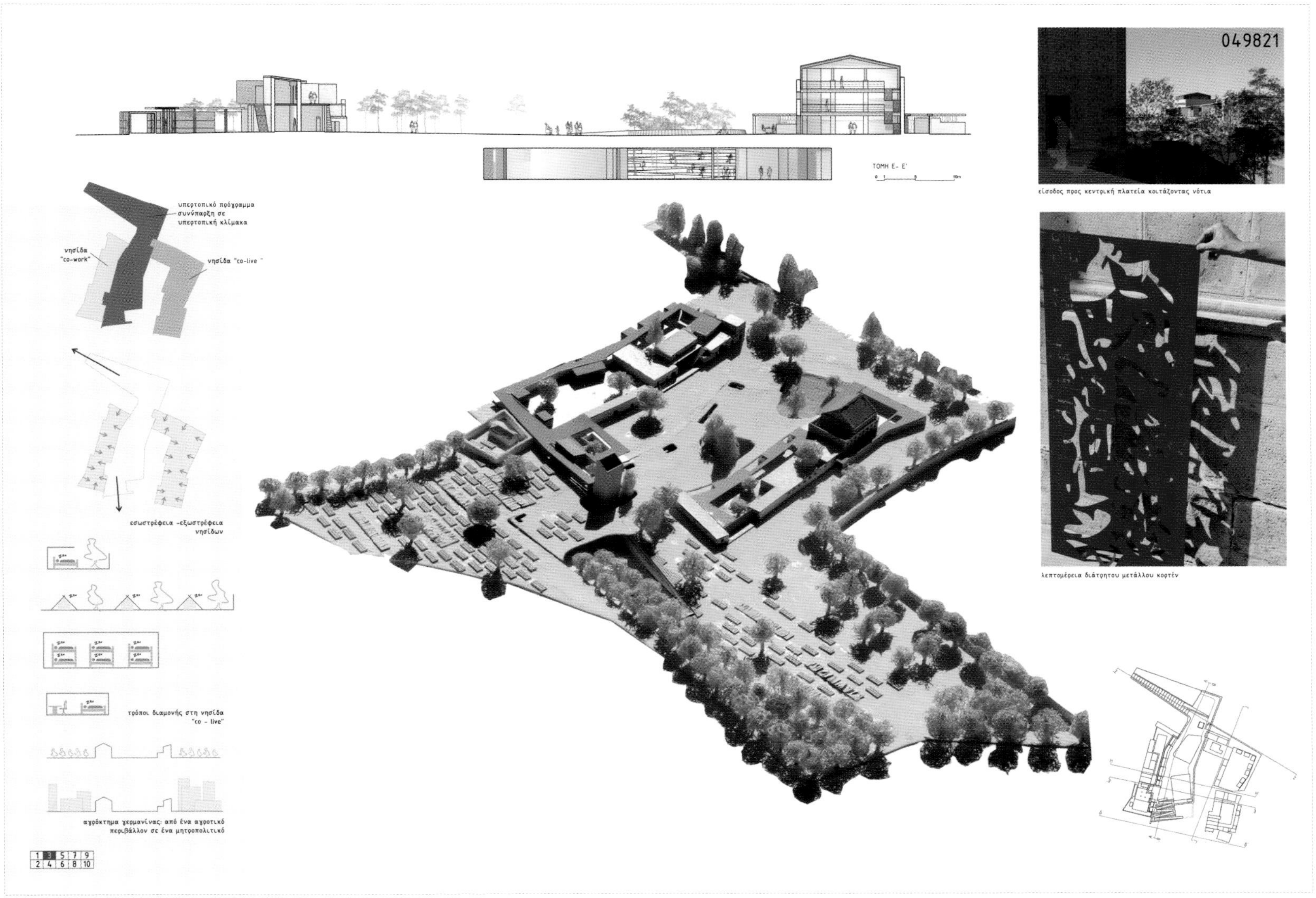

049821

ΤΟΜΗ Ε- Ε'

0 1 5 10m

είσοδος προς κεντρική πλατεία κοιτάζοντας νότια

υπερτοπικό πρόγραμμα
συνύπαρξη σε
υπερτοπική κλίμακα

νησίδα
"co-work"

νησίδα "co-live"

εσωστρέφεια -εξωστρέφεια
νησίδων

τρόποι διαμονής στη νησίδα
"co - live"

αγρόκτημα γερμανίνας: από ένα αγροτικό
περιβάλλον σε ένα μητροπολιτικό

λεπτομέρεια διάτρητου μετάλλου κορτέν

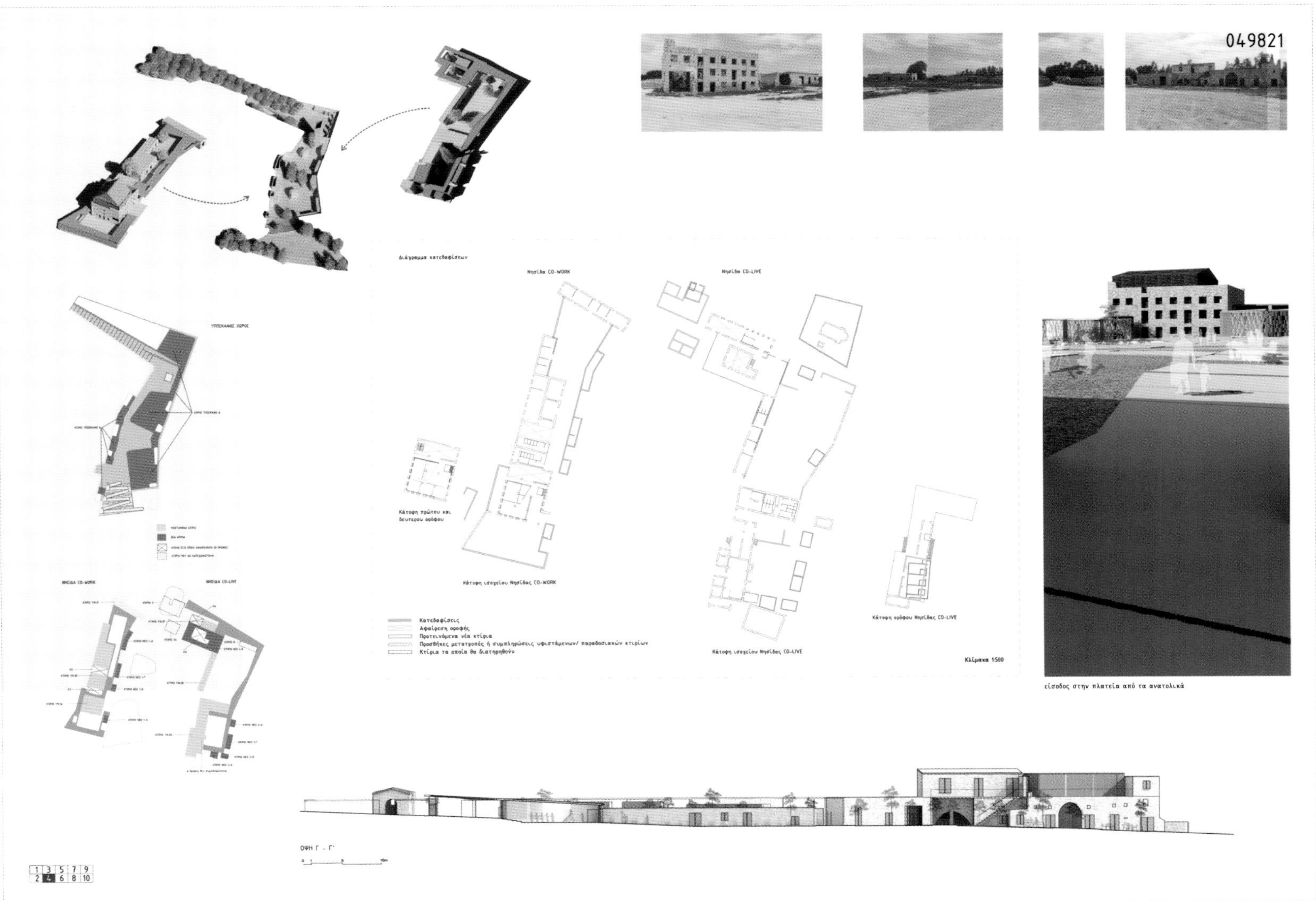

049821

διάγραμμα κατεδαφίσεων

Νησίδα CO-WORK

Νησίδα CO-LIVE

Κάτοψη πρώτου και
δευτερου ορόφου

Κάτοψη ισογείου Νησίδας CO-WORK

Κάτοψη ορόφου Νησίδας CO-LIVE

Κάτοψη ισογείου Νησίδας CO-LIVE

- Κατεδαφίσεις
- Αφαίρεση οροφής
- Προτεινόμενα νέα κτίρια
- Προσθήκες μετατροπές ή συμπληρώσεις υφιστάμενων/ παραδοσιακών κτιρίων
- Κτίρια τα οποία θα διατηρηθούν

Κλίμακα 1:500

είσοδος στην πλατεία από τα ανατολικά

ΟΨΗ Γ - Γ'

0 1 5 10m

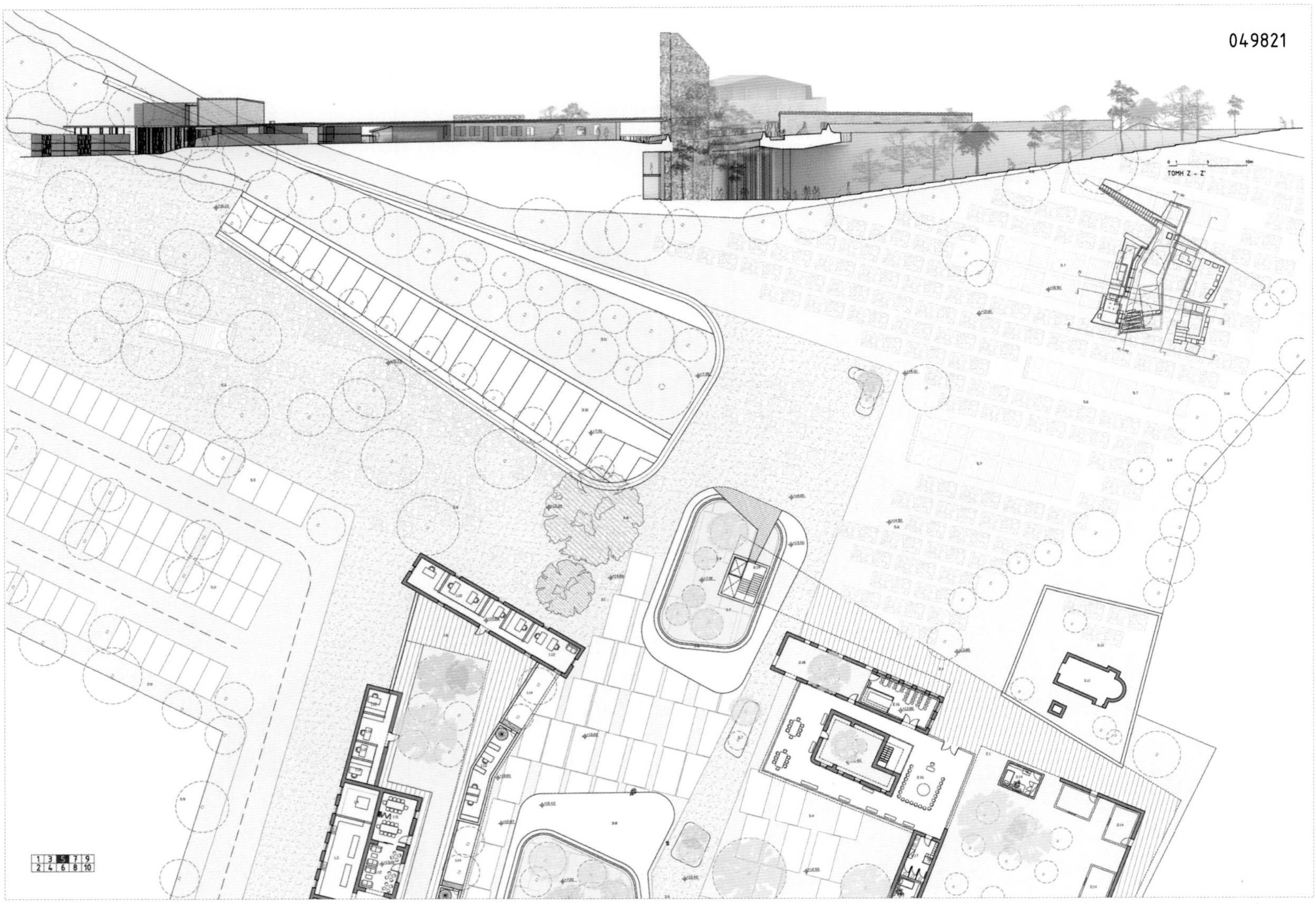

049821

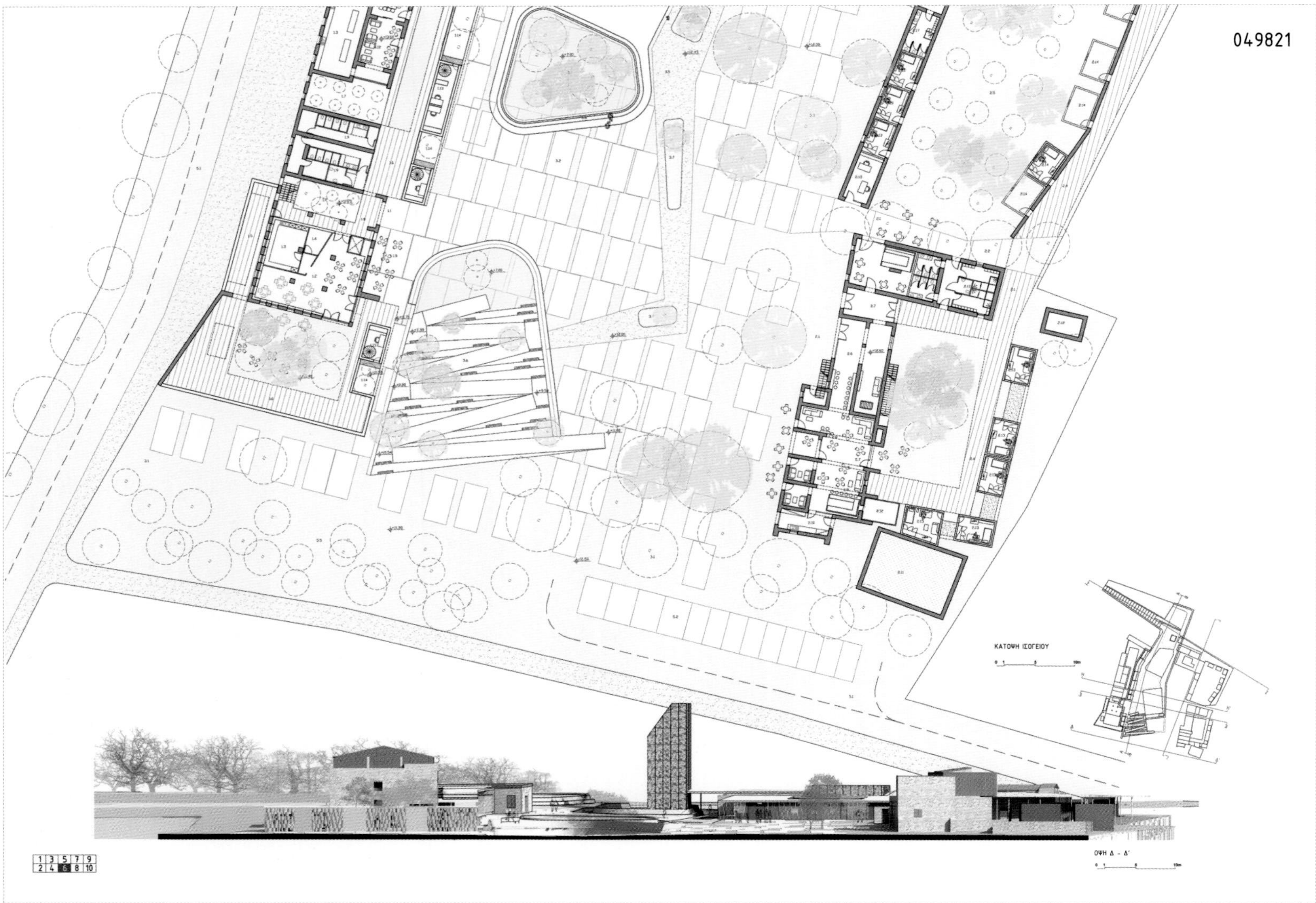

ΤΟΜΗ Ζ - Ζ'

1 3 5 7 9
2 4 6 8 10

049821

ΚΑΤΟΨΗ ΙΣΟΓΕΙΟΥ

ΟΨΗ Δ - Δ'

1 3 5 7 9
2 4 6 8 10

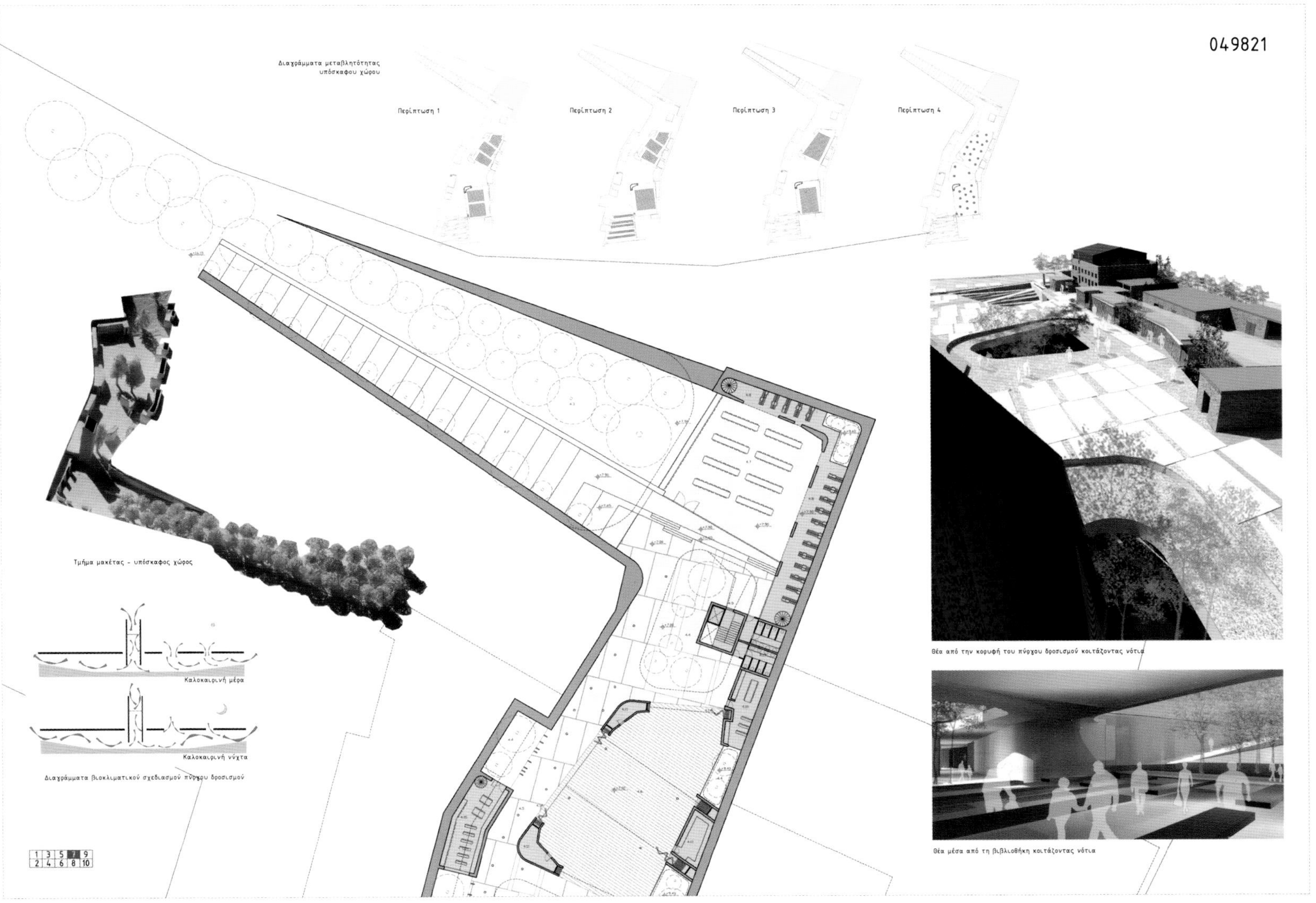

049821

Διαγράμματα μεταβλητότητας υπόσκαφου χώρου

Περίπτωση 1

Περίπτωση 2

Περίπτωση 3

Περίπτωση 4

Τμήμα μακέτας - υπόσκαφος χώρος

Καλοκαιρινή μέρα

Καλοκαιρινή νύχτα

Διαγράμματα βιοκλιματικού σχεδιασμού πύργου δροσισμού

Θέα από την κορυφή του πύργου δροσισμού κοιτάζοντας νότια

Θέα μέσα από τη βιβλιοθήκη κοιτάζοντας νότια

1	3	5	7	9
2	4	6	8	10

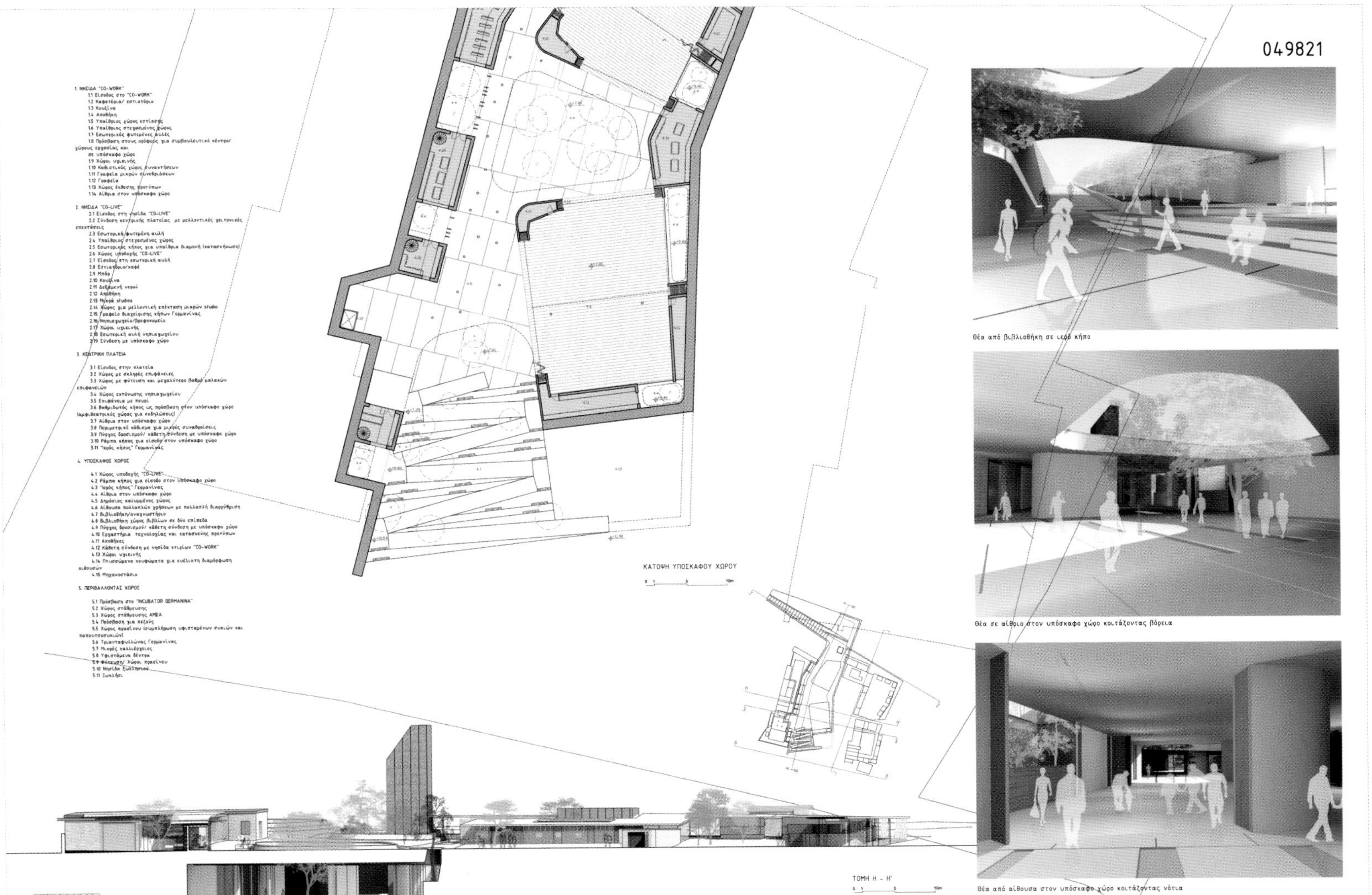

049821

1. ΝΗΣΙΔΑ "CO-WORK"
- 1.1 Είσοδος στο "CO-WORK"
- 1.2 Καφετέρια/ εστιατόριο
- 1.3 Κουζίνα
- 1.4 Αποθήκη
- 1.5 Υπαίθριος χώρος εστίασης
- 1.6 Υπαίθριος στεγασμένος χώρος
- 1.7 Εσωτερικές φυτεμένες αυλές
- 1.8 Πρόσβαση στους ορόφους για συμβουλευτικό κέντρο/ χώρους εργασίας και σε υπόσκαφο χώρο
- 1.9 Χώροι υγιεινής
- 1.10 Καθιστικός χώρος συναντήσεων
- 1.11 Γραφεία μικρών συνεδριάσεων
- 1.12 Γραφεία
- 1.13 Χώρος έκθεσης προτύπων
- 1.14 Αίθρια στον υπόσκαφο χώρο

2. ΝΗΣΙΔΑ "CO-LIVE"
- 2.1 Είσοδος στη νησίδα "CO-LIVE"
- 2.2 Σύνδεση κεντρικής πλατείας με μελλοντικές γειτονικές επεκτάσεις
- 2.3 Εσωτερική φυτεμένη αυλή
- 2.4 Υπαίθριος στεγασμένος χώρος
- 2.5 Εσωτερικός κήπος για υπαίθρια διαμονή (κατασκήνωση)
- 2.6 Χώρος υποδοχής "CO-LIVE"
- 2.7 Είσοδος στη εσωτερική αυλή
- 2.8 Εστιατόριο/καφέ
- 2.9 Μπάρ
- 2.10 Κουζίνα
- 2.11 Δεξαμενή νερού
- 2.12 Αποθήκη
- 2.13 Μικρά studios
- 2.14 Χώρος για μελλοντική επέκταση μικρών studio
- 2.15 Γραφείο διαχείρισης κήπων Γερμανίνας
- 2.16 Νηπιαγωγείο/Βρεφοκομείο
- 2.17 Χώροι υγιεινής
- 2.18 Εσωτερική αυλή νηπιαγωγείου
- 2.19 Σύνδεση με υπόσκαφο χώρο

3. ΚΕΝΤΡΙΚΗ ΠΛΑΤΕΙΑ
- 3.1 Είσοδος στην πλατεία
- 3.2 Χώρος με σκληρές επιφάνειες
- 3.3 Χώρος με φύτευση και μεγαλύτερο βαθμό μαλακών επιφανειών
- 3.4 Χώρος εκτόνωσης νηπιαγωγείου
- 3.5 Επιφάνεια με πουρί
- 3.6 Βαθμιδωτός κήπος ως πρόσβαση στον υπόσκαφο χώρο (αμφιθεατρικός χώρος για εκδηλώσεις)
- 3.7 Αίθρια στον υπόσκαφο χώρο
- 3.8 Περιμετρικό κάθισμα για μικρές συναθροίσεις
- 3.9 Πύργος δροσισμού/ κάθετη σύνδεση με υπόσκαφο χώρο
- 3.10 Ράμπα κήπος για είσοδο στον υπόσκαφο χώρο
- 3.11 "Ιερός κήπος" Γερμανίνας

4. ΥΠΟΣΚΑΦΟΣ ΧΩΡΟΣ
- 4.1 Χώρος υποδοχής "CO-LIVE"
- 4.2 Ράμπα κήπος για είσοδο στον υπόσκαφο χώρο
- 4.3 "Ιερός κήπος" Γερμανίνας
- 4.4 Αίθρια στον υπόσκαφο χώρο
- 4.5 Δημόσιος καλυμμένος χώρος
- 4.6 Αίθουσα πολλαπλών χρήσεων με πολλαπλή διαρρύθμιση
- 4.7 Βιβλιοθήκη/αναγνωστήριο
- 4.8 Βιβλιοθήκη χώρος βιβλίων σε δύο επίπεδα
- 4.9 Πύργος δροσισμού/ κάθετη σύνδεση με υπόσκαφο χώρο
- 4.10 Εργαστήρια τεχνολογίας και κατασκευής προτύπων
- 4.11 Αποθήκες
- 4.12 Κάθετη σύνδεση με νησίδα κτιρίων "CO-WORK"
- 4.13 Χώροι υγιεινής
- 4.14 Πτυσσόμενα κουφώματα για ευέλικτη διαμόρφωση αιθουσών
- 4.15 Μηχανοστάσιο

5. ΠΕΡΙΒΑΛΛΟΝΤΑΣ ΧΩΡΟΣ
- 5.1 Πρόσβαση στο "INCUBATOR GERMANINA"
- 5.2 Χώρος στάθμευσης
- 5.3 Χώρος στάθμευσης ΑΜΕΑ
- 5.4 Πρόσβαση για πεζούς
- 5.5 Χώρος πρασίνου (συμπλήρωση υφισταμένων συκιών και παπουτσοσυκιών)
- 5.6 Τριανταφυλλώνας Γερμανίνας
- 5.7 Μικρές καλλιέργειες
- 5.8 Υφιστάμενα δέντρα
- 5.9 Φύτευση/ Χώροι πρασίνου
- 5.10 Νησίδα ξωκλησιού
- 5.11 Ξωκλήσι

ΚΑΤΟΨΗ ΥΠΟΣΚΑΦΟΥ ΧΩΡΟΥ

Θέα από βιβλιοθήκη σε ιερό κήπο

Θέα σε αίθριο στον υπόσκαφο χώρο κοιτάζοντας βόρεια

ΤΟΜΗ Η - Η'

Θέα από αίθουσα στον υπόσκαφο χώρο κοιτάζοντας νότια

1	3	5	7	9
2	4	6	8	10

Διαμόρφωση "INCUBATING germanina" μέσα σε ένα πεδίο από κήπους. Η πορείες προς την κεντρική πλατεία φιλτράρονται μέσα από κήπους με θάμνους και δέντρα

Μικροκαλλιέργειες μέσα στους κήπους της Γερμανίνας

Ιερός Κήπος στους Κήπους της Γερμανίνας- κεκλιμένο επίπεδο προς υπόσκαφο χώρο

Καταφύγιο ηλιωκιωμένων ελιών υπό απειλή από συνεχείς οικοπεδοποιήσεις στο κυπριακό τοπίο

049821

Θέα από νηπιαγωγείο προς νοτιοδυτικά

049821

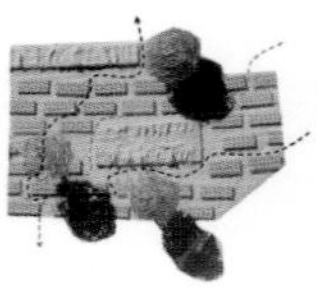

ΚΑΤΑΛΟΓΟΣ ΧΛΩΡΙΔΑΣ ΓΙΑ ΤΟΥΣ ΚΗΠΟΥΣ ΓΕΡΜΑΝΙΝΑΣ
(πηγή Τσιντίδης, Χατζηκυριάκου, Χριστοδούλου "Δέντρα και Θάμνοι στην Κύπρο"

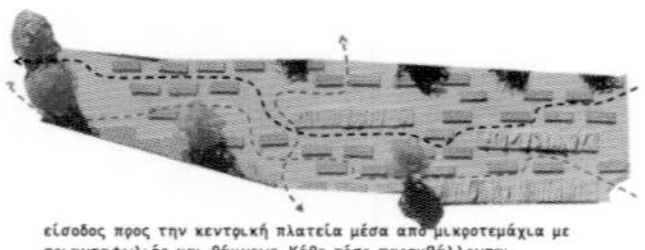

είσοδος προς την κεντρική πλατεία μέσα από μικροτεμάχια με τριανταφυλιές και θάμνους. Κάθε τόσο παρεμβάλλονται τεμάχια από μικροκαλλιέργιες.

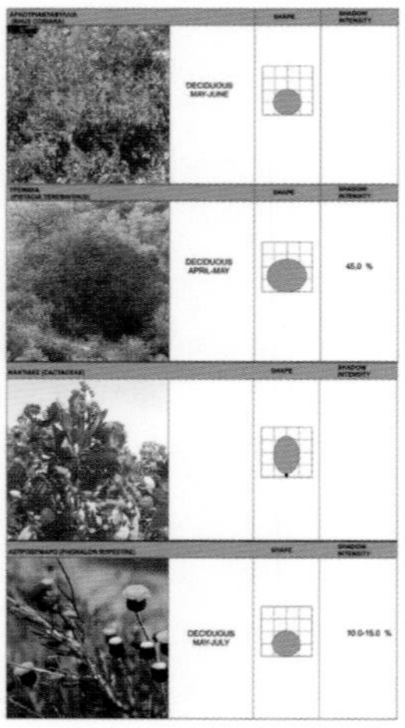

πολλαπλές πορείες μέσα από τους κήπους

Θέα σε αυλή στη νησίδα κτιρίων "Co-Live"- κοιτάζοντας νότια

Θέα σε αυλή στη νησίδα κτιρίων "Co-Work"- κοιτάζοντας νότια

Θέα από υπόσκαφο χώρο προς κερκιδωτό κήπο εισόδου

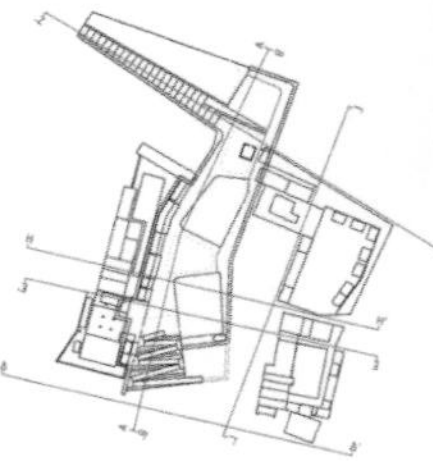

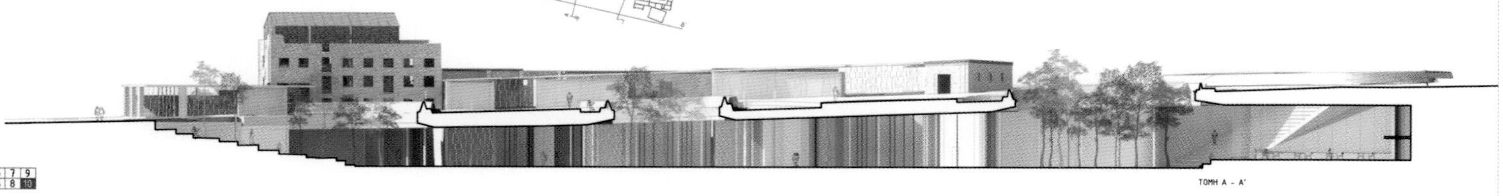

ΤΟΜΗ Α - Α'

1 3 5 7 9
2 4 6 8 10

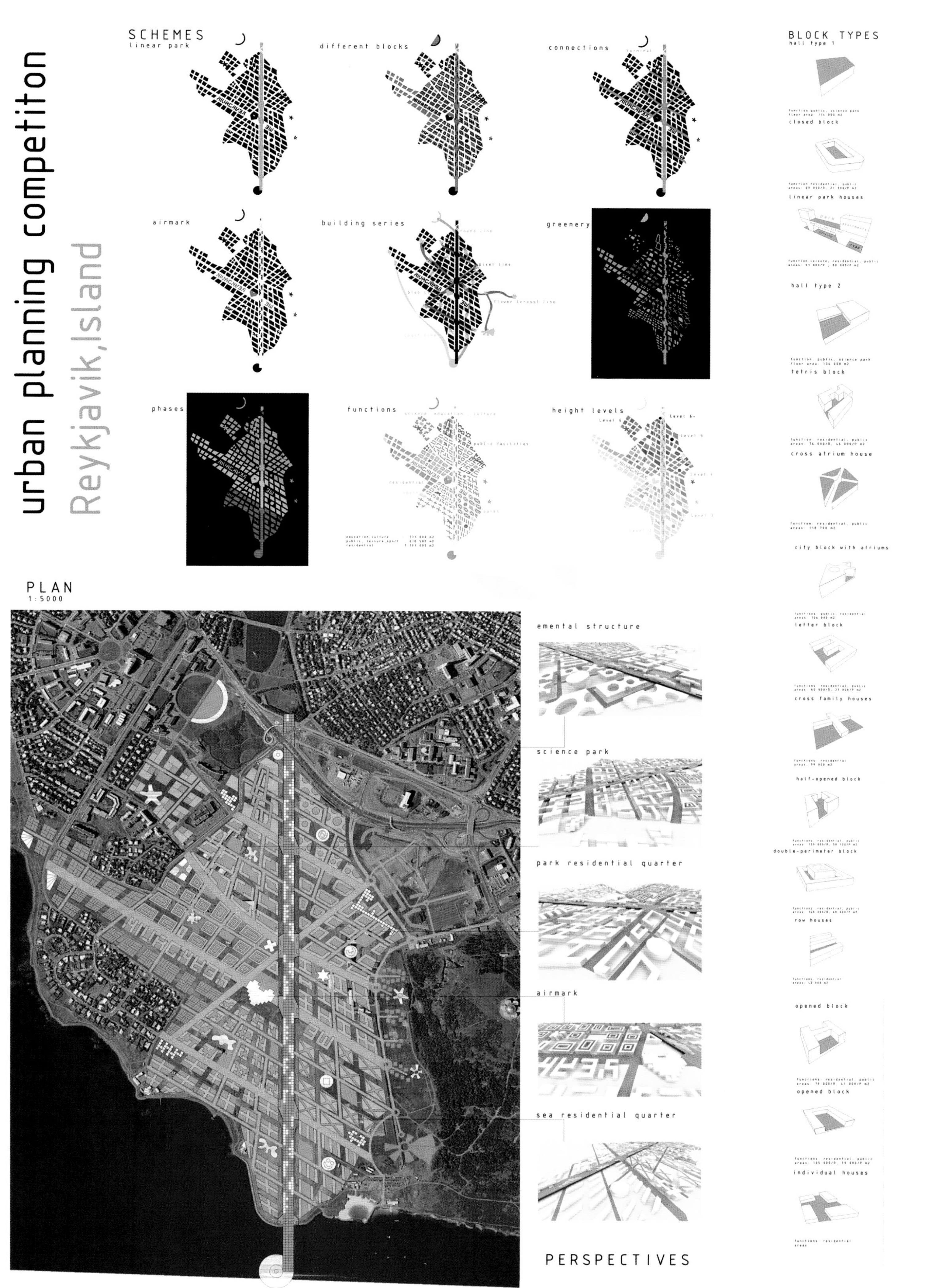
urban planning competiton
Reykjavik,Island
SCHEMES
linear park
different blocks
connections
airmark
building series
greenery
phases
functions
height levels
BLOCK TYPES
hall type 1
closed block
linear park houses
hall type 2
tetris block
cross atrium house
city block with atriums
letter block
cross family houses
half-opened block
double-perimeter block
row houses
opened block
opened block
individual houses
PLAN
1:5000
emental structure
science park
park residential quarter
airmark
sea residential quarter
PERSPECTIVES

114

394102 | *AA & U For Architecture, Art and Urbanism*

European Architectural Competition for the Redevelopment of Liopetri River Area, Cyprus(2nd phase)
Project Team : Socratis Stratis(Dr. Architect, Urbanist, Assistant Professor),
Christiana Ioannou(Architect), Christos Papastergiou(Architect)
Support : Students Of Architecture(Elena Gennari, Maria Prokopiou, Savia Palate, Chrisanthi Kostantinou, Costantinos Costantinou, Nearchos Costantinou), architect(Katerina Neophyt
Collaborators : Riccardo Urbano(architect, AA & U)

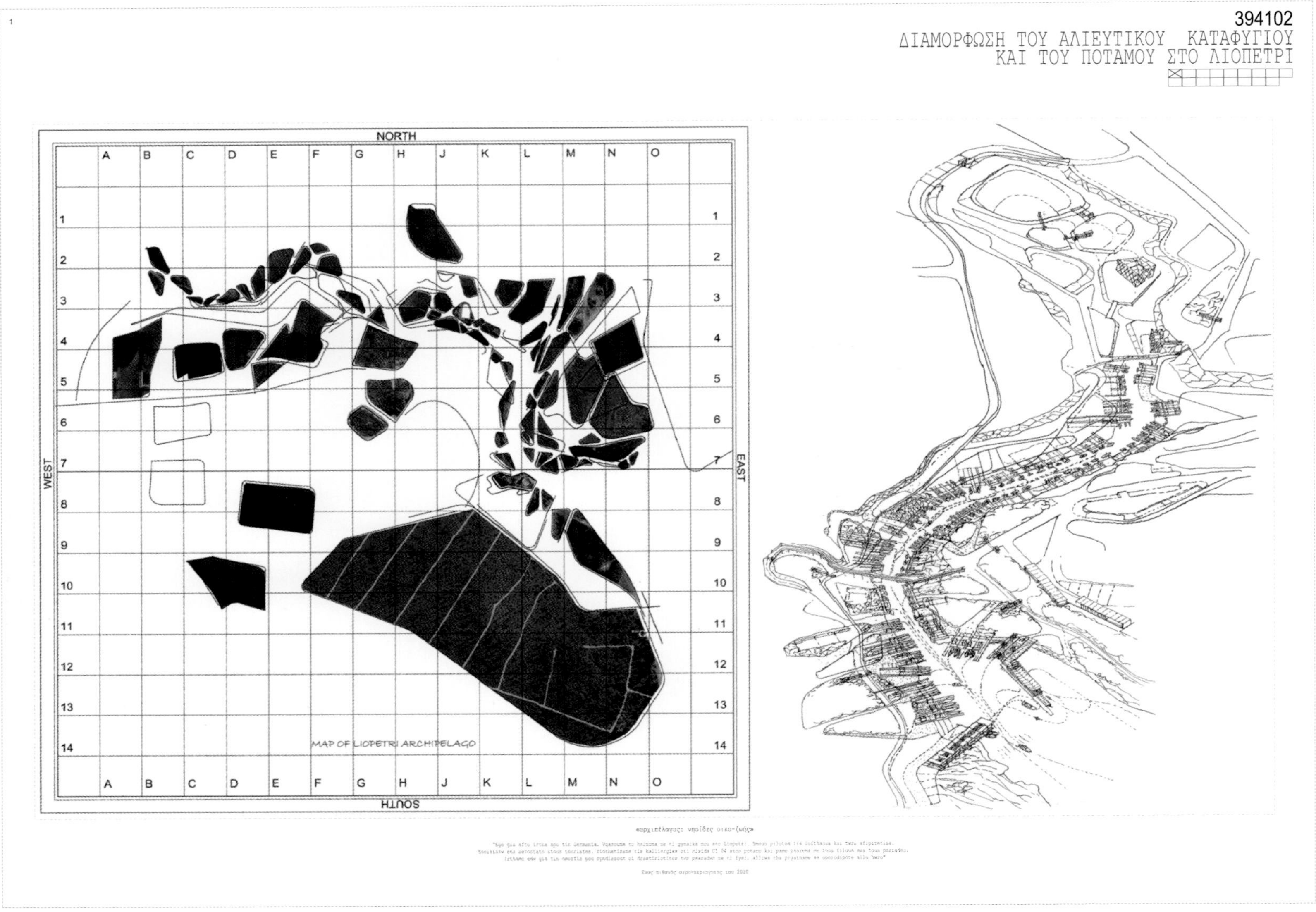

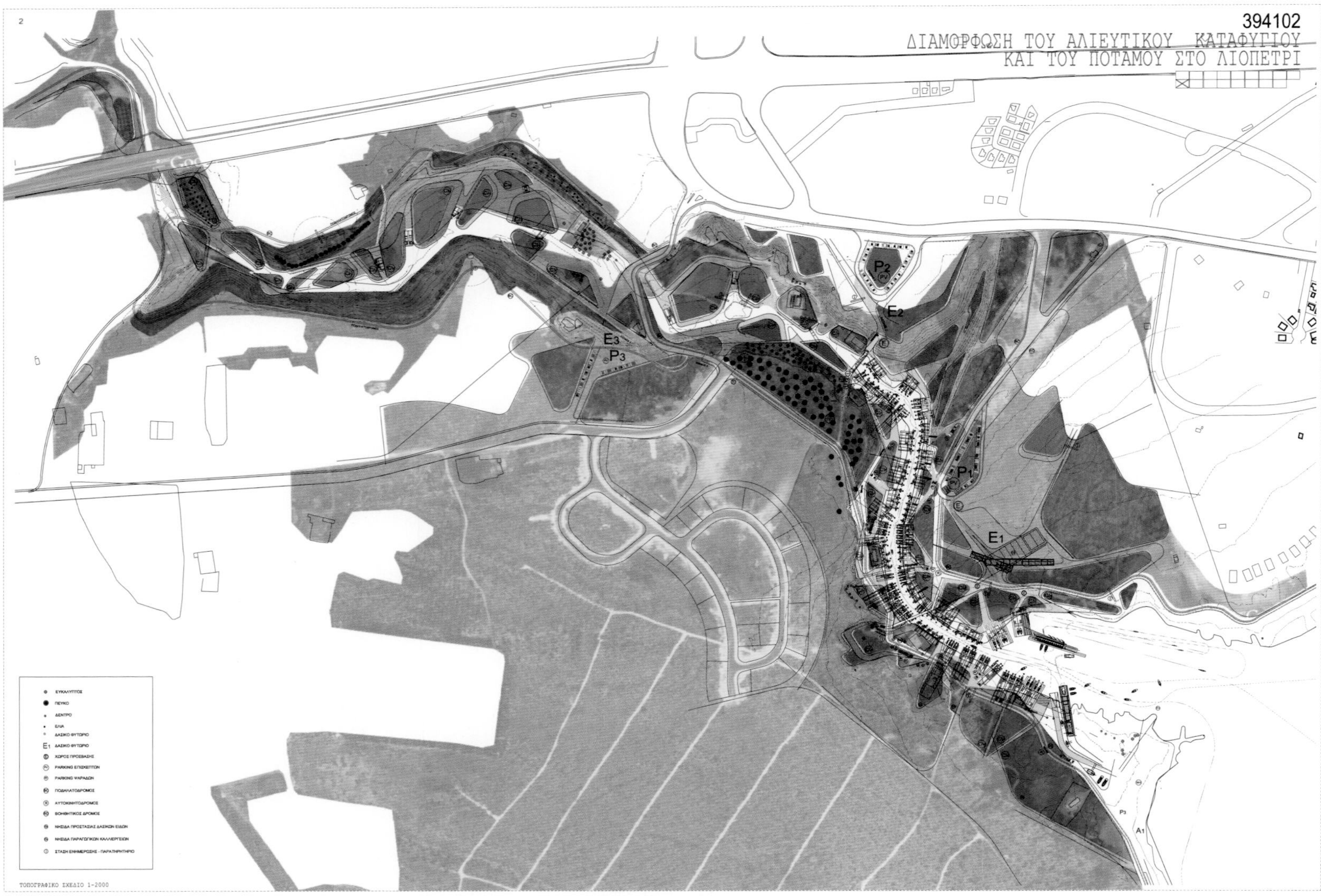

1

394102
ΔΙΑΜΟΡΦΩΣΗ ΤΟΥ ΑΛΙΕΥΤΙΚΟΥ ΚΑΤΑΦΥΓΙΟΥ
ΚΑΙ ΤΟΥ ΠΟΤΑΜΟΥ ΣΤΟ ΛΙΟΠΕΤΡΙ

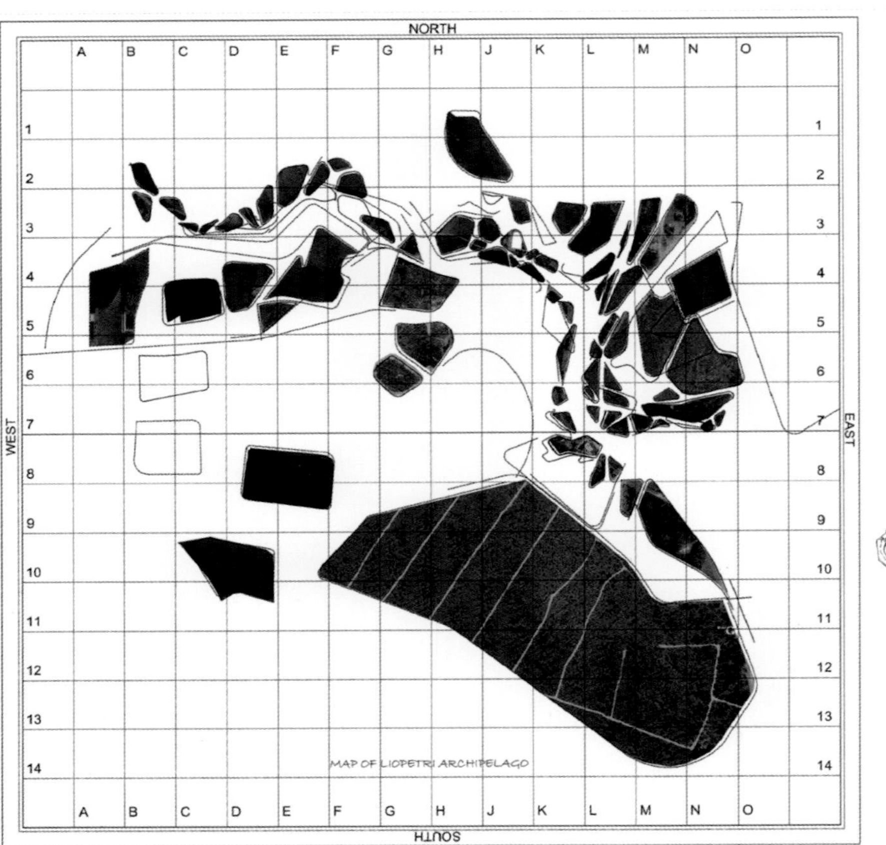

2

394102
ΔΙΑΜΟΡΦΩΣΗ ΤΟΥ ΑΛΙΕΥΤΙΚΟΥ ΚΑΤΑΦΥΓΙΟΥ
ΚΑΙ ΤΟΥ ΠΟΤΑΜΟΥ ΣΤΟ ΛΙΟΠΕΤΡΙ

P2 E2 E3 P3 P1 E1 P3 A1

ΤΟΠΟΓΡΑΦΙΚΟ ΣΧΕΔΙΟ 1:2000

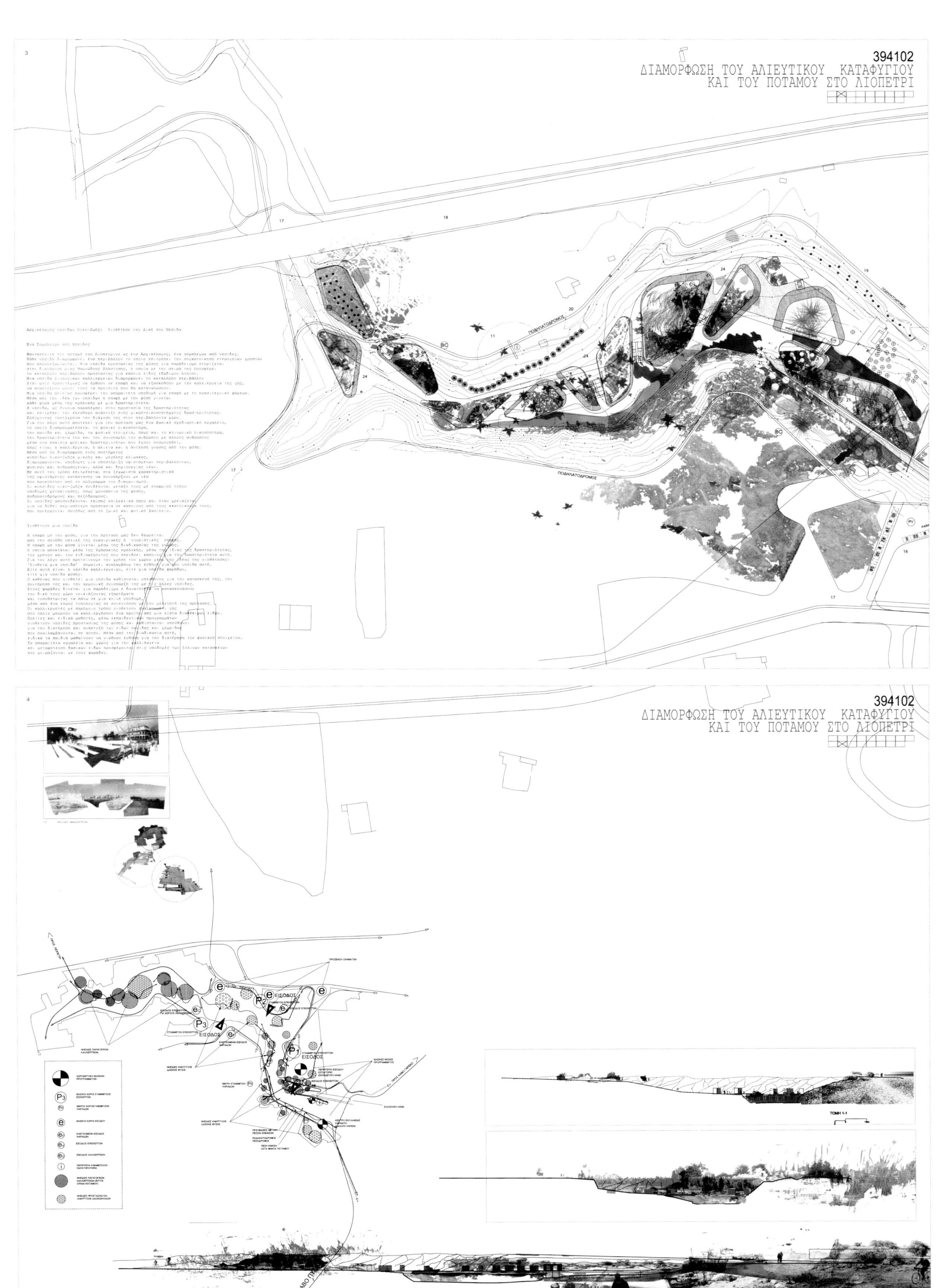

394102
ΔΙΑΜΟΡΦΩΣΗ ΤΟΥ ΑΛΙΕΥΤΙΚΟΥ ΚΑΤΑΦΥΓΙΟΥ
ΚΑΙ ΤΟΥ ΠΟΤΑΜΟΥ ΣΤΟ ΛΙΟΠΕΤΡΙ
ΠΟΔΗΛΑΤΟΔΡΟΜΟΣ
ΠΟΔΗΛΑΤΟΔΡΟΜΟΣ
394102
ΔΙΑΜΟΡΦΩΣΗ ΤΟΥ ΑΛΙΕΥΤΙΚΟΥ ΚΑΤΑΦΥΓΙΟΥ
ΚΑΙ ΤΟΥ ΠΟΤΑΜΟΥ ΣΤΟ ΛΙΟΠΕΤΡΙ
ΕΙΣΟΔΟΣ
ΕΙΣΟΔΟΣ
ΕΙΣΟΔΟΣ
ΤΟΜΗ 1-1
ΤΟΜΗ 4-4

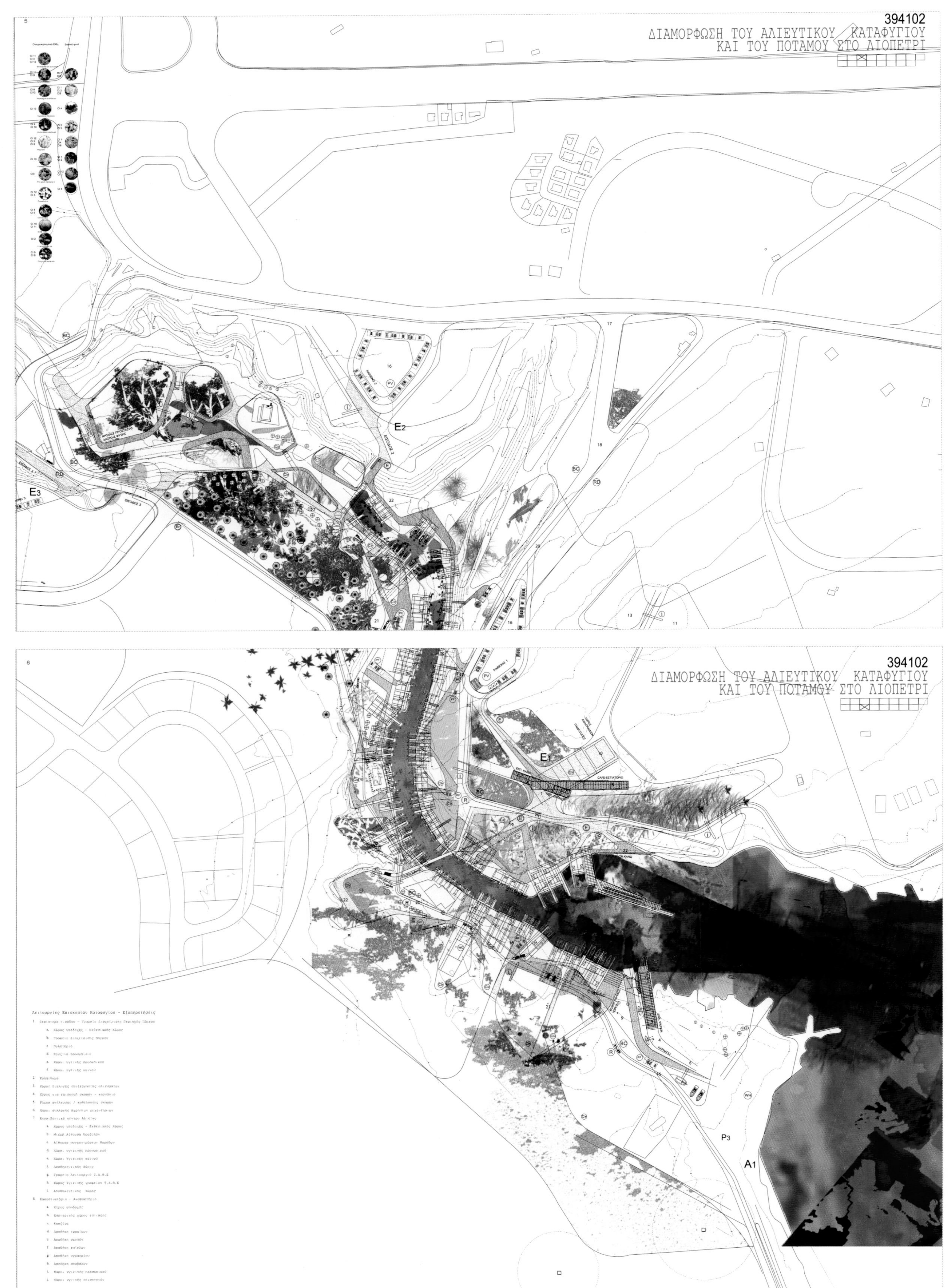

394102
ΔΙΑΜΟΡΦΩΣΗ ΤΟΥ ΑΛΙΕΥΤΙΚΟΥ ΚΑΤΑΦΥΓΙΟΥ
ΚΑΙ ΤΟΥ ΠΟΤΑΜΟΥ ΣΤΟ ΛΙΟΠΕΤΡΙ
E2
E3
394102
ΔΙΑΜΟΡΦΩΣΗ ΤΟΥ ΑΛΙΕΥΤΙΚΟΥ ΚΑΤΑΦΥΓΙΟΥ
ΚΑΙ ΤΟΥ ΠΟΤΑΜΟΥ ΣΤΟ ΛΙΟΠΕΤΡΙ
E1
P3
A1

7

394102

ΔΙΑΜΟΡΦΩΣΗ ΤΟΥ ΑΛΙΕΥΤΙΚΟΥ ΚΑΤΑΦΥΓΙΟΥ ΚΑΙ ΤΟΥ ΠΟΤΑΜΟΥ ΣΤΟ ΛΙΟΠΕΤΡΙ

1 Κρηπίδωμα
1.1 Κάθετες δημόσιες προσβάσεις προς το ποταμό
1.2 Παράλληλες δημόσιες προσβάσεις
1.3 Χώρος ψαράδων
1.4 Περιοχές με συμπυκνωμένο χώμα (compacted soil)
1.5 Περιοχές υποστήριξης οικοσυστημάτων Καταφυγίου & Πάρκου
2 Χώρος διαλογής επεξεργασίας αλιευμάτων
3 Χώρος για επισκευή σκαφών καρνάγιο
4 Ράμπα ανέλκυσης / καθέλκυσης σκαφών
5 Χώροι συλλογής άχρηστων μηχανέλαιων
6 Εκπαιδευτικό κέντρο Αλιείας
7 Στέγαστρο
7.1 Καθιστικοί χώροι
8 Χώρος στάθμευσης βάρκας για εκπαιδευτικές διαδρομές στον ποταμό και για πέρασμα στην απέναντι όχθη (στην εξέδρα αποθήκευσης κανώ)
9 Αίθουσα συγκεντρώσεων Ψαράδων
10 Γραφείο λειτουργού Τ.Α.Θ.Ε
11 Αποχωρητήρια Επισκεπτών Καταφυγίου
12 Υπαίθριος πολύ-λειτουργικός χώρος
13 Μετακίνηση και συντήρηση καραβιού που υπάρχει εγκατελειμμένο στο χώρο. Χρήση του ως τμήμα της εκπαιδευτικής διαδρομής
14 Εκπαιδευτική διαδρομή (η καθημερινότητα του καταφυγίου ως έκθεμα)
15 Πλατφόρμα αποθήκευσης κανώ (42 τεμάχια)
16 Παρατηρητήριο
17 Χώρος εξάσκησης αθλήματος

18 Νησίδες οικοζωής (ενίσχυση ενδημικής φύτευσης)

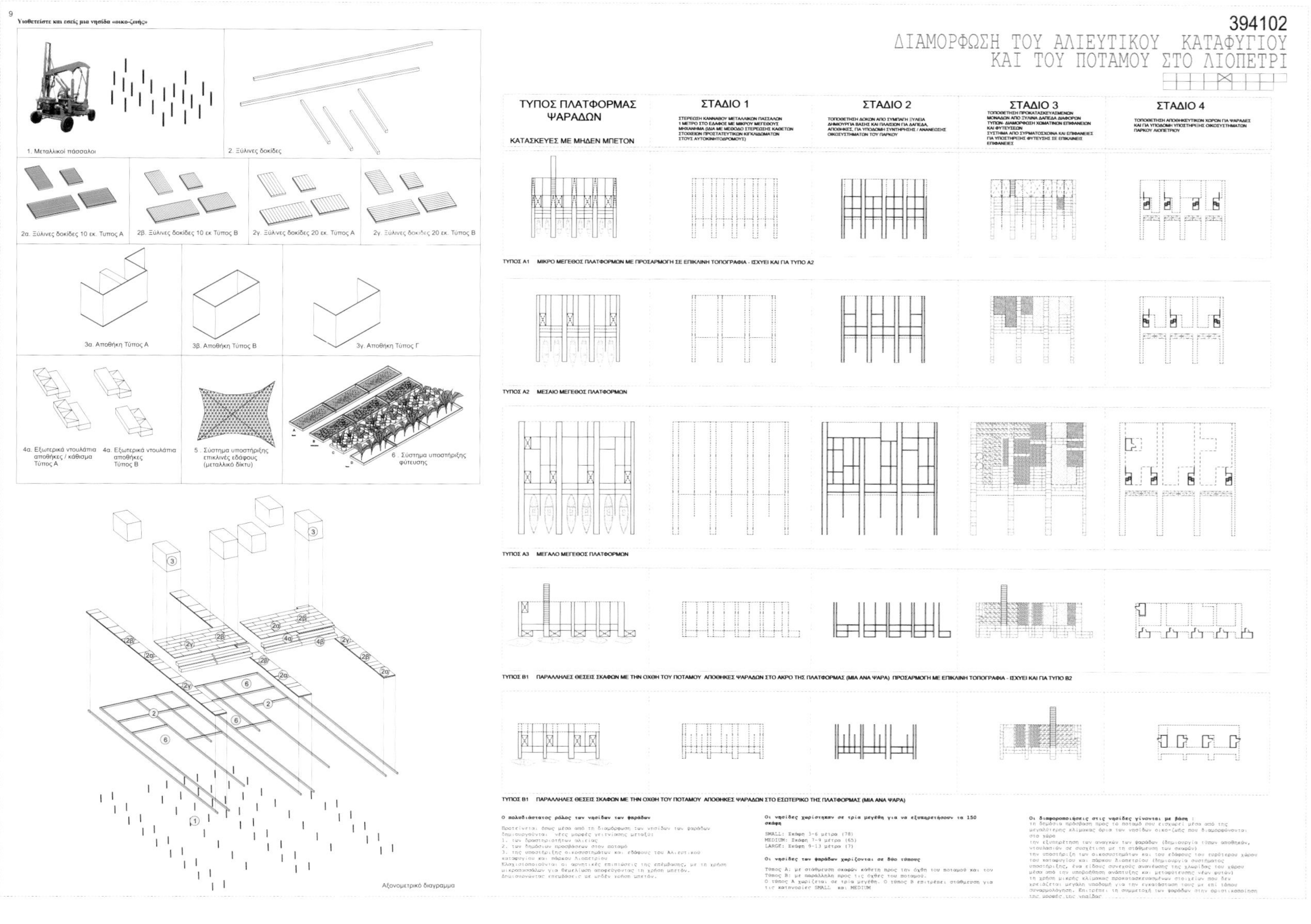

0 1 5 10m

9

Υιοθετείστε και εσείς μια νησίδα «οικο-ζωής»

1. Μεταλλικοί πάσσαλοι

2. Ξύλινες δοκίδες

2α. Ξύλινες δοκίδες 10 εκ. Τύπος Α

2β. Ξύλινες δοκίδες 10 εκ. Τύπος Β

2γ. Ξύλινες δοκίδες 20 εκ. Τύπος Α

2γ. Ξύλινες δοκίδες 20 εκ. Τύπος Β

3α. Αποθήκη Τύπος Α

3β. Αποθήκη Τύπος Β

3γ. Αποθήκη Τύπος Γ

4α. Εξωτερικά ντουλάπια αποθήκες / κάθισμα Τύπος Α

4α. Εξωτερικά ντουλάπια αποθήκες Τύπος Β

5 . Σύστημα υποστήριξης επικλινές εδάφους (μεταλλικό δίκτυ)

6 . Σύστημα υποστήριξης φύτευσης

Αξονομετρικό διάγραμμα

394102

ΔΙΑΜΟΡΦΩΣΗ ΤΟΥ ΑΛΙΕΥΤΙΚΟΥ ΚΑΤΑΦΥΓΙΟΥ ΚΑΙ ΤΟΥ ΠΟΤΑΜΟΥ ΣΤΟ ΛΙΟΠΕΤΡΙ

ΤΥΠΟΣ ΠΛΑΤΦΟΡΜΑΣ ΨΑΡΑΔΩΝ ΚΑΤΑΣΚΕΥΕΣ ΜΕ ΜΗΔΕΝ ΜΠΕΤΟΝ	ΣΤΑΔΙΟ 1	ΣΤΑΔΙΟ 2	ΣΤΑΔΙΟ 3	ΣΤΑΔΙΟ 4
	ΣΤΕΡΕΩΣΗ ΚΑΝΝΑΒΟΥ ΜΕΤΑΛΛΙΚΩΝ ΠΑΣΣΑΛΩΝ 1 ΜΕΤΡΟ ΣΤΟ ΕΔΑΦΟΣ ΜΕ ΜΙΚΡΟΥ ΜΕΓΕΘΟΥΣ ΜΗΧΑΝΗΜΑ (ΙΔΙΑ ΜΕ ΜΕΘΟΔΟ ΣΤΕΡΕΩΣΗΣ ΚΑΦΕΤΟΝ ΣΤΟΙΧΕΙΩΝ ΠΡΟΣΤΑΤΕΥΤΙΚΩΝ ΚΙΓΚΛΙΔΩΜΑΤΩΝ ΣΤΟΥΣ ΑΥΤΟΚΙΝΗΤΟΔΡΟΜΟΥΣ)	ΤΟΠΟΘΕΤΗΣΗ ΔΟΚΩΝ ΑΠΟ ΞΥΛΟ (ΞΥΛΕΙΑ ΔΗΜΙΟΥΡΓΙΑ ΒΑΣΗΣ ΚΑΙ ΠΛΑΙΣΙΩΝ ΓΙΑ ΔΑΠΕΔΑ, ΑΠΟΘΗΚΕΣ, ΓΙΑ ΥΠΟΔΟΜΗ ΣΥΝΤΗΡΗΣΗΣ / ΑΝΑΝΕΩΣΗΣ ΟΙΚΟΣΥΣΤΗΜΑΤΩΝ ΤΟΥ ΠΑΡΚΟΥ	ΤΟΠΟΘΕΤΗΣΗ ΠΡΟΚΑΤΑΣΚΕΥΑΣΜΕΝΩΝ ΜΟΝΑΔΩΝ ΑΠΟ ΞΥΛΙΝΑ ΔΑΠΕΔΑ ΔΙΑΦΟΡΩΝ ΤΥΠΩΝ- ΔΙΑΜΟΡΦΩΣΗ ΧΩΜΑΤΙΝΩΝ ΕΠΙΦΑΝΕΙΩΝ ΚΑΙ ΦΥΤΕΥΣΕΩΝ ΣΥΣΤΗΜΑ ΑΠΟ ΣΥΡΜΑΤΟΠΛΕΓΜΑ ΚΑΙ ΕΠΙΦΑΝΕΙΕΣ ΓΙΑ ΥΠΟΣΤΗΡΙΞΗ ΦΥΤΕΥΣΗΣ ΣΕ ΕΠΙΚΛΙΝΕΙΣ ΕΠΙΦΑΝΕΙΕΣ	ΤΟΠΟΘΕΤΗΣΗ ΑΠΟΘΗΚΕΥΤΙΚΩΝ ΧΩΡΩΝ ΓΙΑ ΨΑΡΑΔΕΣ ΚΑΙ ΓΙΑ ΥΠΟΔΟΜΗ ΥΠΟΣΤΗΡΙΞΗΣ ΟΙΚΟΣΥΣΤΗΜΑΤΩΝ ΠΑΡΚΟΥ ΛΙΟΠΕΤΡΟΥ

ΤΥΠΟΣ Α1 ΜΙΚΡΟ ΜΕΓΕΘΟΣ ΠΛΑΤΦΟΡΜΩΝ ΜΕ ΠΡΟΣΑΡΜΟΓΗ ΣΕ ΕΠΙΚΛΙΝΗ ΤΟΠΟΓΡΑΦΙΑ - ΙΣΧΥΕΙ ΚΑΙ ΓΙΑ ΤΥΠΟ Α2

ΤΥΠΟΣ Α2 ΜΕΣΑΙΟ ΜΕΓΕΘΟΣ ΠΛΑΤΦΟΡΜΩΝ

ΤΥΠΟΣ Α3 ΜΕΓΑΛΟ ΜΕΓΕΘΟΣ ΠΛΑΤΦΟΡΜΩΝ

ΤΥΠΟΣ Β1 ΠΑΡΑΛΛΗΛΕΣ ΘΕΣΕΙΣ ΣΚΑΦΩΝ ΜΕ ΤΗΝ ΟΧΘΗ ΤΟΥ ΠΟΤΑΜΟΥ ΑΠΟΘΗΚΕΣ ΨΑΡΑΔΩΝ ΣΤΟ ΑΚΡΟ ΤΗΣ ΠΛΑΤΦΟΡΜΑΣ (ΜΙΑ ΑΝΑ ΨΑΡΑ) ΠΡΟΣΑΡΜΟΓΗ ΜΕ ΕΠΙΚΛΙΝΗ ΤΟΠΟΓΡΑΦΙΑ - ΙΣΧΥΕΙ ΚΑΙ ΓΙΑ ΤΥΠΟ Β2

ΤΥΠΟΣ Β1 ΠΑΡΑΛΛΗΛΕΣ ΘΕΣΕΙΣ ΣΚΑΦΩΝ ΜΕ ΤΗΝ ΟΧΘΗ ΤΟΥ ΠΟΤΑΜΟΥ ΑΠΟΘΗΚΕΣ ΨΑΡΑΔΩΝ ΣΤΟ ΕΣΩΤΕΡΙΚΟ ΤΗΣ ΠΛΑΤΦΟΡΜΑΣ (ΜΙΑ ΑΝΑ ΨΑΡΑ)

Ο πολυδιάστατος ρόλος των νησίδων των ψαράδων

Οι νησίδες χωρίζονται σε τρία μεγέθη για να εξυπηρετήσουν τα 150 σκάφη

Οι νησίδες των ψαράδων χωρίζονται σε δύο τύπους

Οι διαμορφώσεις στις νησίδες γίνονται με βάση :

11

394102

ΚΑΙ ΤΟΥ ΠΟΤΑΜΟΥ ΣΤΟ ΛΙΟΠΕΤΡΙ

Βιώνοντας τη θαλασσινή διαδρομή της εισόδου του Πάρκου Ποταμού Λιοπετρίου

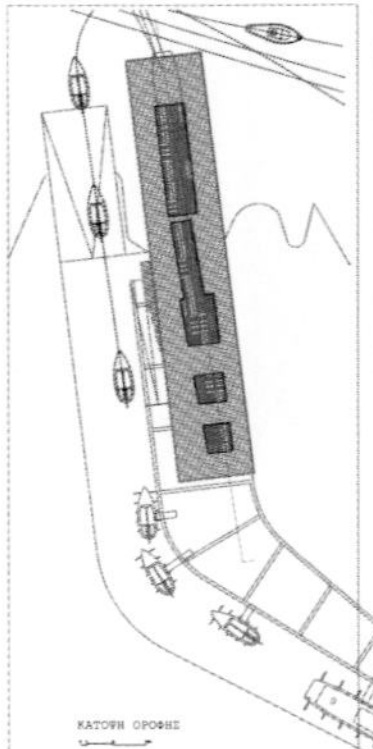

Θεωρείται σημαντική η θαλάσσια σύνδεση του Πάρκου ως είσοδος.
Η χωροθέτηση των υπολοίπων χρήσεων του προγράμματος γίνεται με τέτοιο τρόπο
ώστε να υποστηρίξουν αυτή τη λογική, ενδυναμώνοντας επίσης
τη λειτουργική και οπτική σύνδεση των δύο όχθων.
Το Εκπαιδευτικό Κέντρο Αλιείας οργανώνεται κάτω από ένα ξύλινο στέγαστρο
κατά μήκος της ράμπας ανέλκυσης και του καρνάγιου. Στο χερσαίο άκρο
του στεγάστρου σε επέκταση του καρνάγιου τοποθετείται ένα εγκαταλειμμένο
καράβι που βρίσκεται στο χώρο. Το καράβι συντηρείται για να γίνει μέρος
της εκπαιδευτικής διαδρομής,

Η γειτνίαση που δημιουργείται μεταξύ επισκεπτών του πάρκου
και των καθημερινών λειτουργιών του καταφυγίου έχει διπλό σκοπό.
Πρώτα επιτυγχάνεται ο εμπλουτισμός των εμπειριών των επισκεπτών που βιώνουν
τις διάφορες λειτουργίες και δεύτερο δίνεται συμβολική σημασία
σε καθημερινές χρήσεις που συνήθως τις βρίσκει κανείς στο πίσω μέρος,
όπως το καρνάγιο, ο χώρος διαλογής ψαριών κλπ. Ο τρόπος που οργανώνονται
οι χώροι κατά μήκος του στεγάστρου γίνεται για να επιτρέπει την απρόσκοπτη
χρήση του χώρου τόσο από τους ψαράδες όσο και από τους επισκέπτες.
Ο στεγασμένος εξωτερικός χώρος μετατρέπεται σε ένα ευχάριστο σκιασμένο χώρο
για όλους. Στο θαλάσσιο άκρο του στεγάστρου δημιουργείται υποδοχή
για τη στάθμευση πλεούμενου που θα συνδέει τόσο την περιοχή του καταφυγίου
με την ευρύτερη θαλάσσια περιοχή όσο και τις δύο πλευρές του ποταμού,
μεταφέροντας επισκέπτες στην πλατφόρμα πρακτικής εξάσκησης
και αποθήκευσης κανό,

ΚΑΤΟΨΗ ΟΡΟΦΗΣ

ΟΨΗ

ΤΟΜΗ

ΚΑΤΟΨΗ ΕΚΠΑΙΔΕΥΤΙΚΟΥ ΚΕΝΤΡΟΥ ΑΛΙΕΙΑΣ

14

394102

ΔΙΑΜΟΡΦΩΣΗ ΤΟΥ ΑΛΙΕΥΤΙΚΟΥ ΚΑΤΑΦΥΓΙΟΥ ΚΑΙ ΤΟΥ ΠΟΤΑΜΟΥ ΣΤΟ ΛΙΟΠΕΤΡΙ

ΠΑΡΑΤΗΡΗΤΗΡΙΟ ΠΟΥΛΙΩΝ/ΕΝΗΜΕΡΩΣΗ

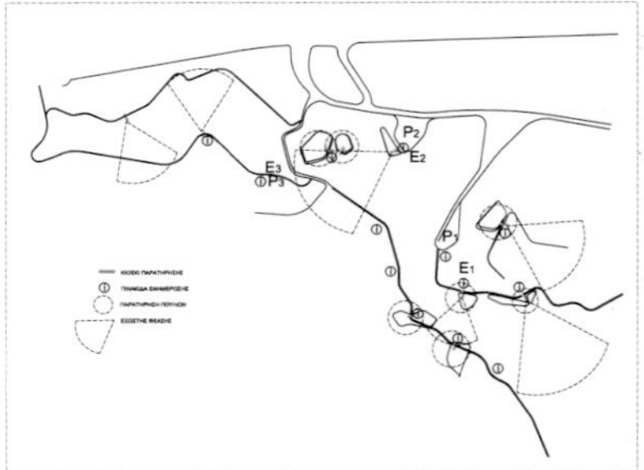

ΤΟΜΗ 1-50

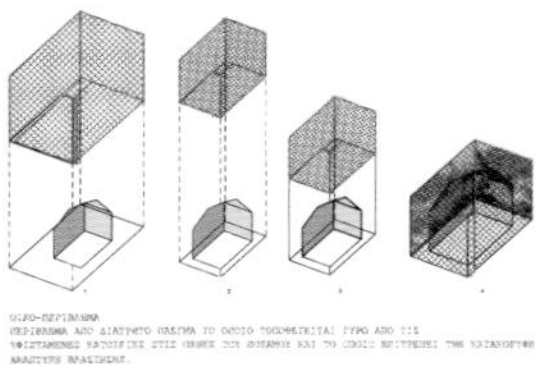

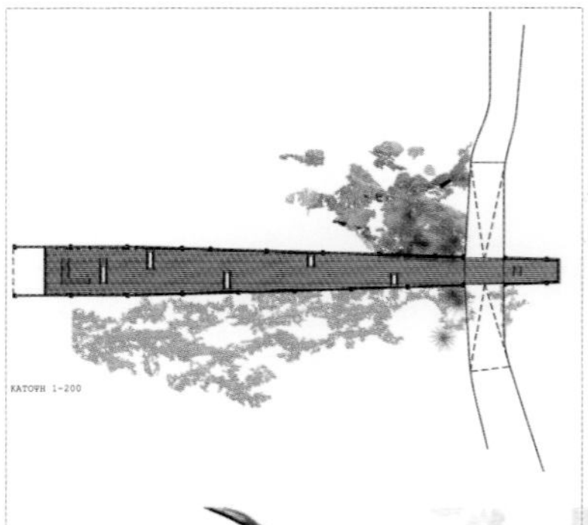

ΚΑΤΟΨΗ 1-200

ΤΟΜΗ 1-200

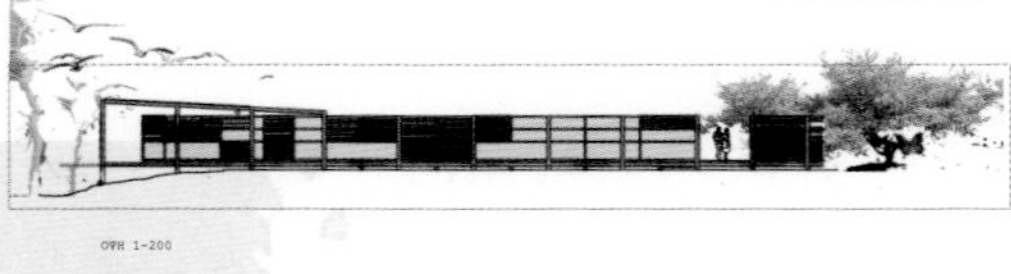

ΟΨΗ 1-200

Παρατηρητήριο

Το παρατηρητήριο αποτελεί γραμμική κατασκευή η οποία τοποθετείται κάθετα
σε προσβάσεις της περιοχής, όπως δρόμους ήπιας κυκλοφορίας, ποδηλατοδρόμους
και μονοπάτια της φύσης. Η κατασκευή χωρίζεται σε δυο μέρη.
Από την μια μεριά του μονοπατιού αποτελείται από διάδρομο πρόσβασης που καταλήγει
στο χώρο παρατήρησης, ο οποίος είναι προστατευμένος από επιδερμίδα αφήνοντας
χαραμάδες παρατήρησης, έτσι ώστε ο παρατηρητής να μην ενοχλεί τα πουλιά.
Με τον τρόπο αυτό το παρατηρητήριο μπορεί να διεισδύει σε θαμνώδεις νησίδες,
χωρίς να διαταράσσει το οικοσύστημα. Επίσης με τον ίδιο τρόπο οι κατασκευές αυτές
μπορούν να αποτελούν και χώρους θέασης τοποθετημένες σε κατάλληλες θέσεις.
Από την άλλη μεριά του μονοπατιού οι κατασκευές περιλαμβάνουν σημεία ενημέρωσης και στάσης,
είτε χημικές τουαλέτες ανά περίπτωση.
Στον χάρτη φαίνονται οι προτεινόμενες θέσεις των παρατηρητηρίων,
ανάλογα με το αν χρησιμεύουν για παρατήρηση πουλιών ή για θέαση, καθώς και τα σημεία ενημέρωσης

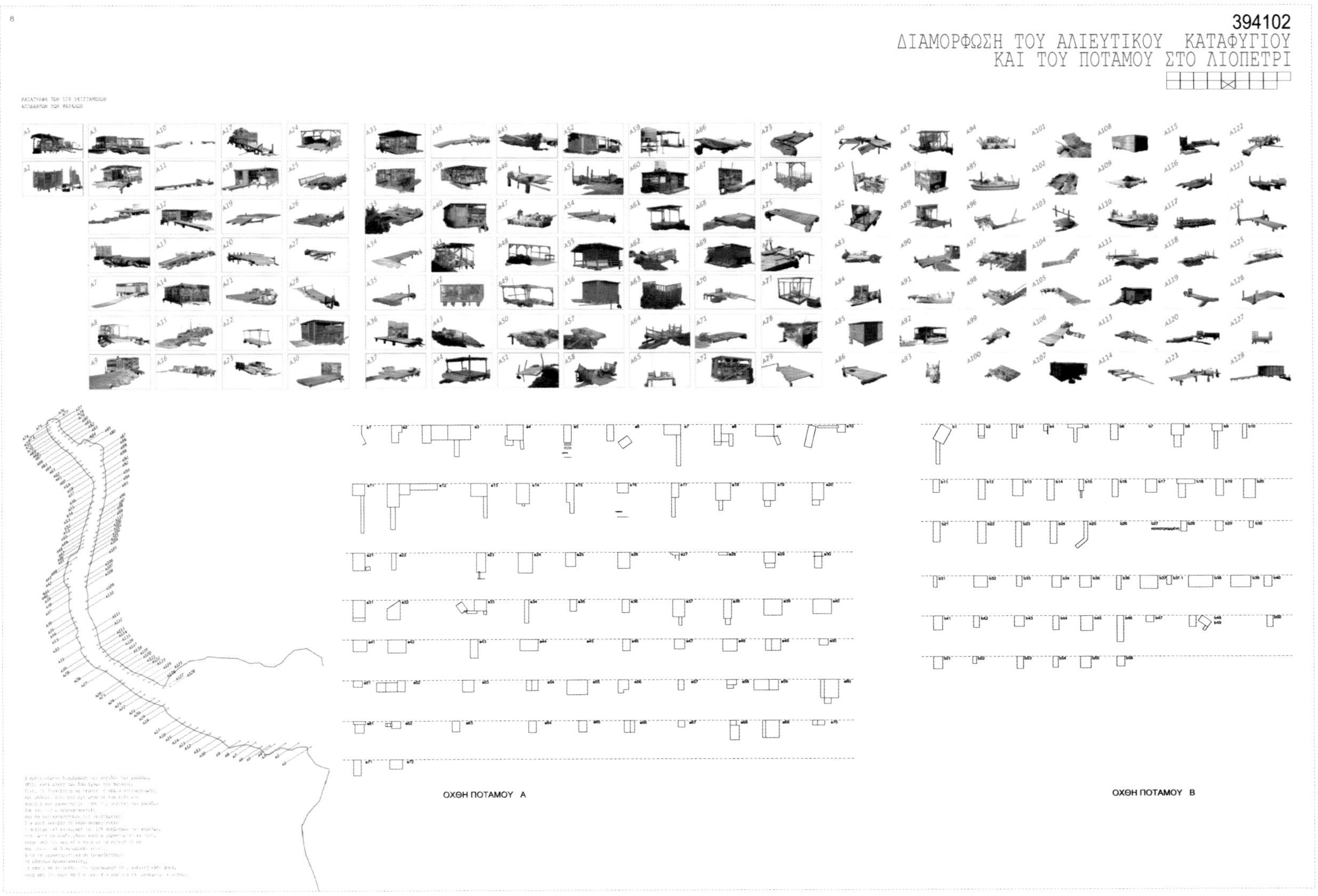

8

394102

ΔΙΑΜΟΡΦΩΣΗ ΤΟΥ ΑΛΙΕΥΤΙΚΟΥ ΚΑΤΑΦΥΓΙΟΥ ΚΑΙ ΤΟΥ ΠΟΤΑΜΟΥ ΣΤΟ ΛΙΟΠΕΤΡΙ

ΟΧΘΗ ΠΟΤΑΜΟΥ Α

ΟΧΘΗ ΠΟΤΑΜΟΥ Β

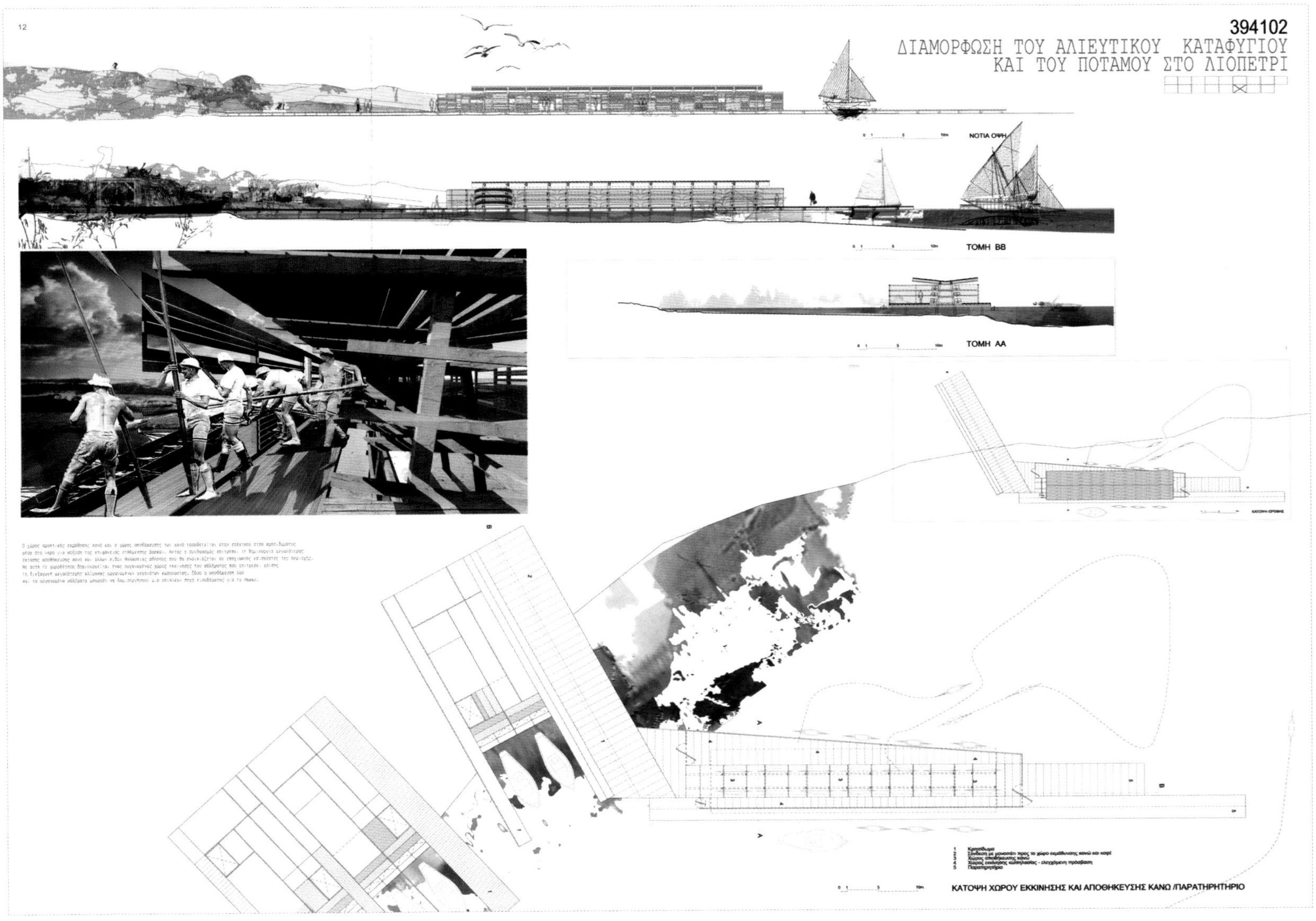

12

394102

ΔΙΑΜΟΡΦΩΣΗ ΤΟΥ ΑΛΙΕΥΤΙΚΟΥ ΚΑΤΑΦΥΓΙΟΥ ΚΑΙ ΤΟΥ ΠΟΤΑΜΟΥ ΣΤΟ ΛΙΟΠΕΤΡΙ

ΝΟΤΙΑ ΟΨΗ

ΤΟΜΗ ΒΒ

ΤΟΜΗ ΑΑ

ΚΑΤΟΨΗ ΧΩΡΟΥ ΕΚΚΙΝΗΣΗΣ ΚΑΙ ΑΠΟΘΗΚΕΥΣΗΣ ΚΑΝΩ /ΠΑΡΑΤΗΡΗΤΗΡΙΟ

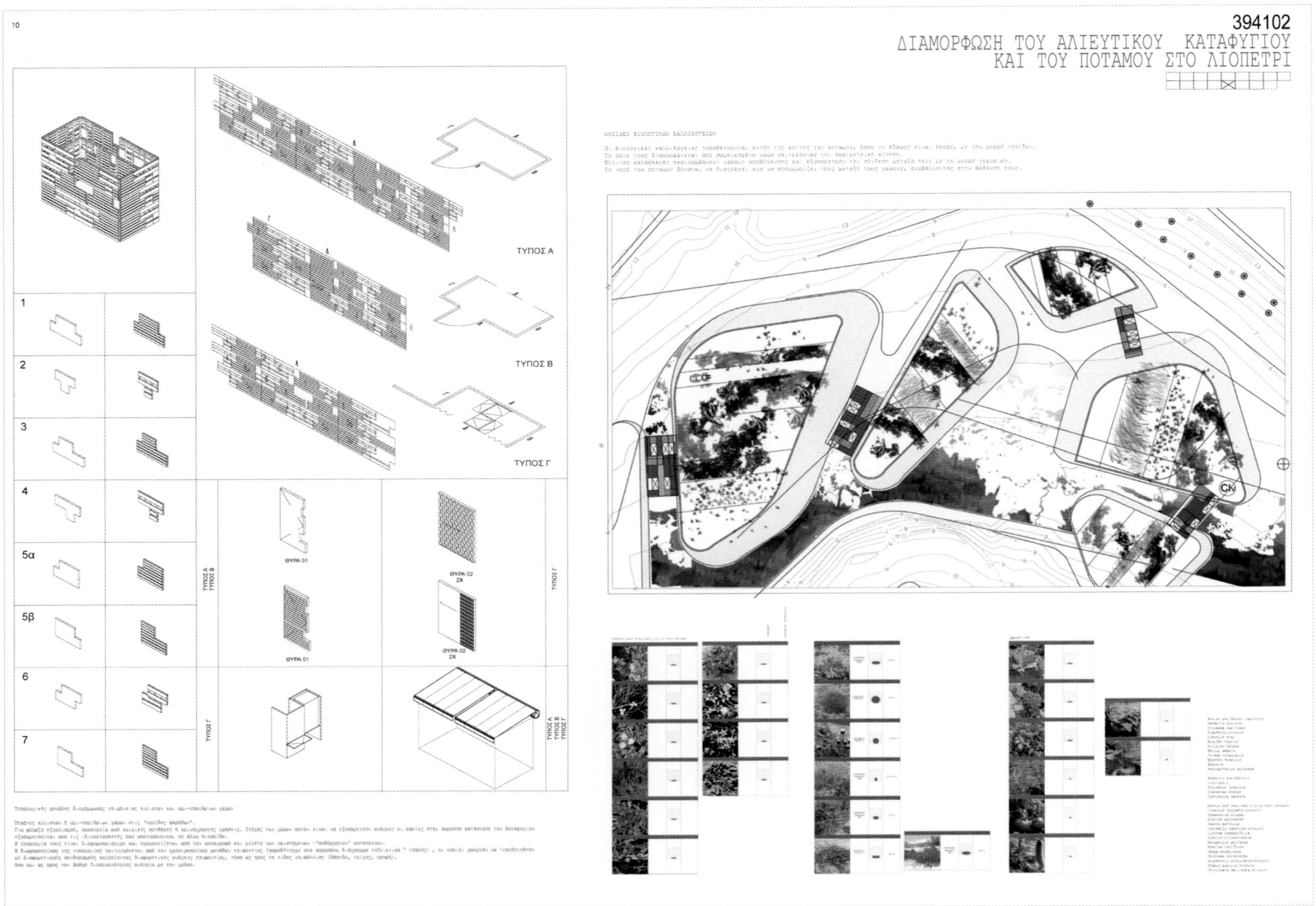

10

394102

ΔΙΑΜΟΡΦΩΣΗ ΤΟΥ ΑΛΙΕΥΤΙΚΟΥ ΚΑΤΑΦΥΓΙΟΥ ΚΑΙ ΤΟΥ ΠΟΤΑΜΟΥ ΣΤΟ ΛΙΟΠΕΤΡΙ

ΤΥΠΟΣ Α

ΤΥΠΟΣ Β

ΤΥΠΟΣ Γ

1

2

3

4

5α

5β

6

7

ΤΥΠΟΣ Α
ΤΥΠΟΣ Β

ΘΥΡΑ 01

ΘΥΡΑ 02
2Χ

ΘΥΡΑ 01

ΘΥΡΑ 02
2Χ

ΤΥΠΟΣ Γ

ΤΥΠΟΣ Γ

ΤΥΠΟΣ Α
ΤΥΠΟΣ Β
ΤΥΠΟΣ Γ

ΝΗΣΙΔΕΣ ΒΙΟΛΟΓΙΚΩΝ ΚΑΛΛΙΕΡΓΕΙΩΝ

Οι βιολογικές καλλιέργειες τοποθετούνται εντός της κοίτης του ποταμού, όπου το έδαφος είναι έφορο, με την μορφή νησίδων.
Τα όρια τους διαμορφώνεται από συμπιεσμένο χώμα επιτρέποντας την περιμετρική κίνηση.
Ξύλινες κατασκευές περιλαμβάνουν χώρους αποθήκευσης και εξυπηρετούν την σύνδεση μεταξύ τους με τη μορφή γεφυριών.
Το νερό του ποταμού δύναται να διατρέχει και να πλημμυρίζει τους μεταξύ τους χώρους, συμβάλλοντας στην άρδευση τους.

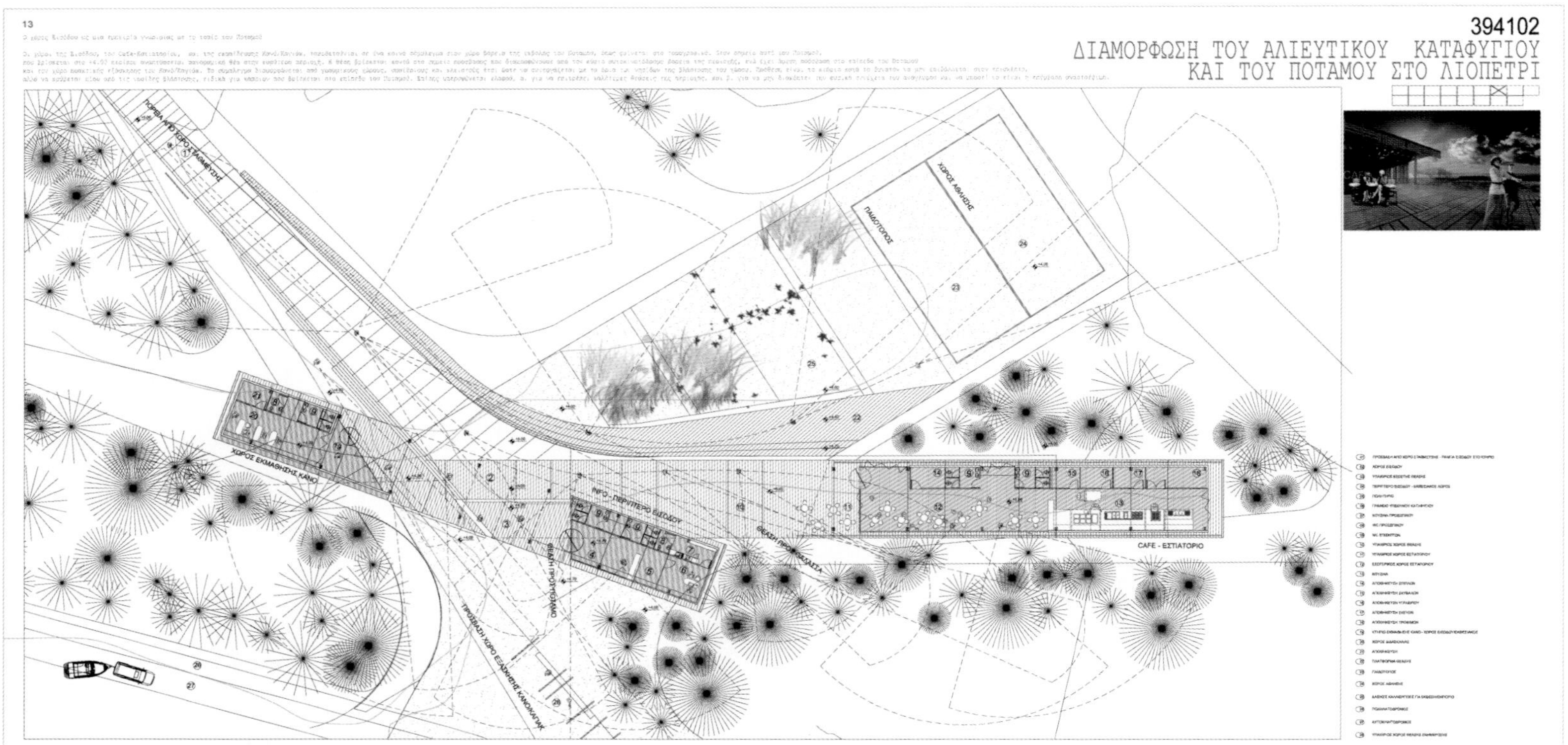

13

394102

ΔΙΑΜΟΡΦΩΣΗ ΤΟΥ ΑΛΙΕΥΤΙΚΟΥ ΚΑΤΑΦΥΓΙΟΥ ΚΑΙ ΤΟΥ ΠΟΤΑΜΟΥ ΣΤΟ ΛΙΟΠΕΤΡΙ

ΧΩΡΟΣ ΕΚΘΑΒΗΣΗΣ ΚΑΙΚΙ

CAFE - ΕΣΤΙΑΤΟΡΙΟ

ΤΟΜΗ 1-200

ΟΨΗ 1-200

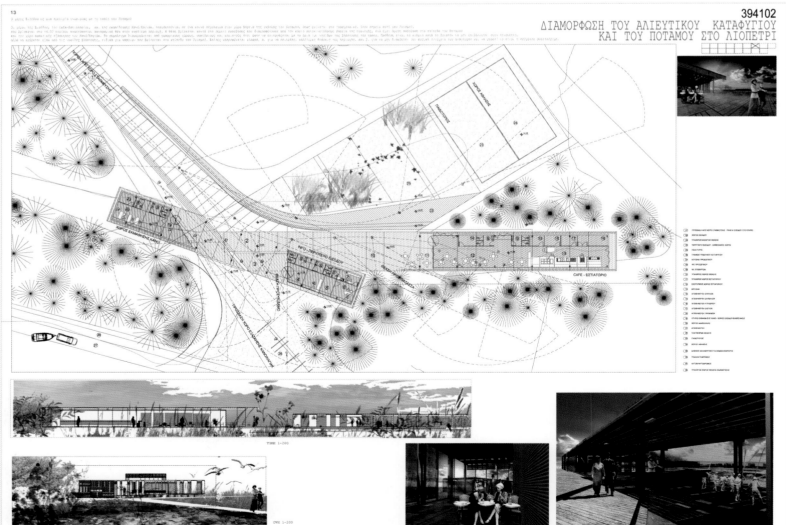

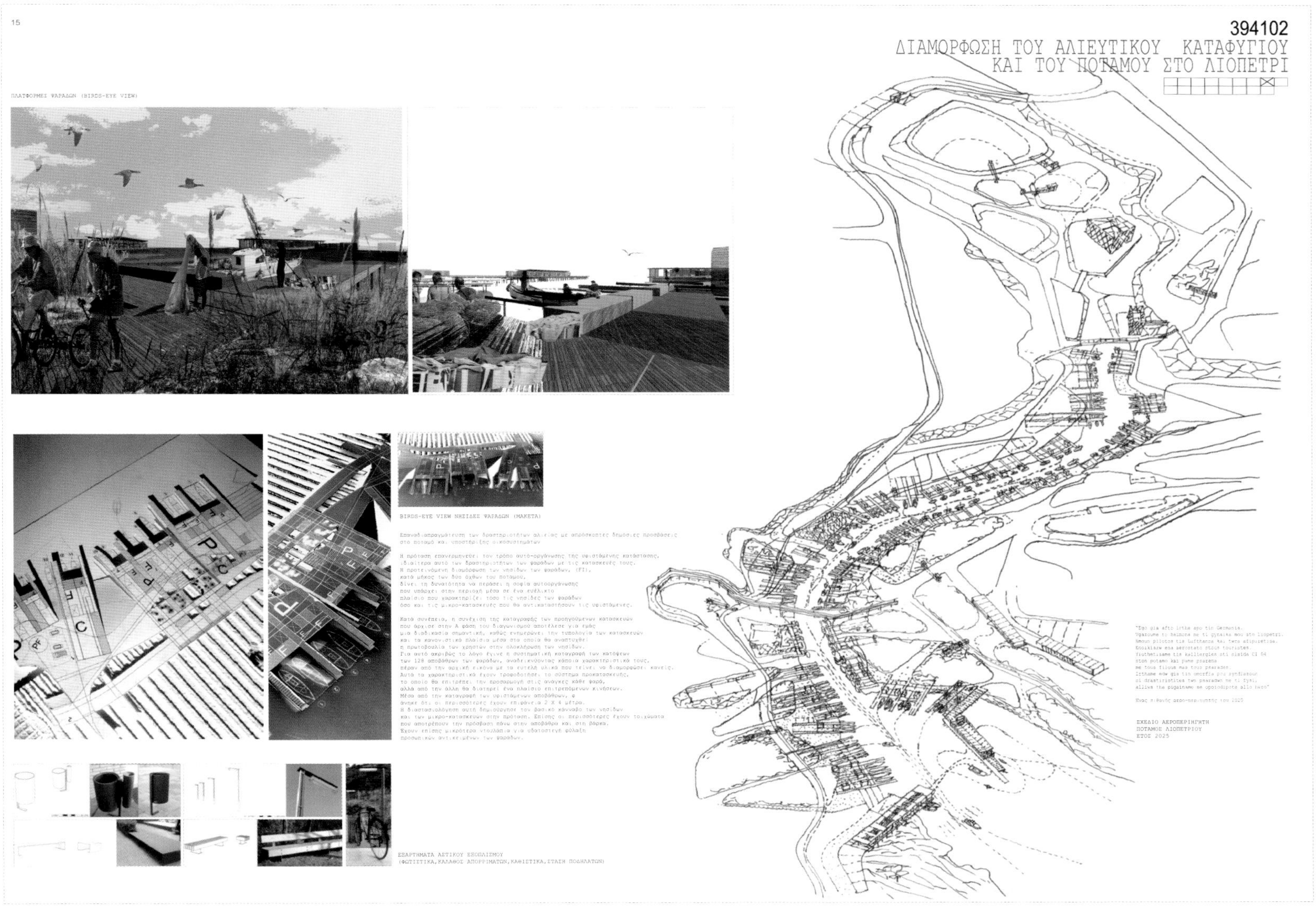

15

ΠΛΑΤΦΟΡΜΕΣ ΨΑΡΑΔΩΝ (BIRDS-EYE VIEW)

394102

ΔΙΑΜΟΡΦΩΣΗ ΤΟΥ ΑΛΙΕΥΤΙΚΟΥ ΚΑΤΑΦΥΓΙΟΥ ΚΑΙ ΤΟΥ ΠΟΤΑΜΟΥ ΣΤΟ ΛΙΟΠΕΤΡΙ

BIRDS-EYE VIEW ΝΗΣΙΔΕΣ ΨΑΡΑΔΩΝ (ΜΑΚΕΤΑ)

Επαναδιαπραγμάτευση των δραστηριοτήτων αλιείας με απρόσκοπτες δημόσιες προσβάσεις στο ποταμό και υποστήριξης οικοσυστημάτων

Η πρόταση επανερμηνεύει τον τρόπο αυτό-οργάνωσης της υφιστάμενης κατάστασης, ιδιαίτερα αυτό των δραστηριοτήτων των ψαράδων με τις κατασκευές τους. Η προτεινόμενη διαμόρφωση των νησίδων των ψαράδων, (FI), κατά μήκος των δύο όχθων του ποταμού, δίνει τη δυνατότητα να περάσει η σοφία αυτοοργάνωσης που υπάρχει στην περιοχή μέσα σε ένα ευέλικτο πλαίσιο που χαρακτηρίζει τόσο τις νησίδες των ψαράδων όσο και τις μικρο-κατασκευές που θα αντικαταστήσουν τις υφιστάμενες.

Κατά συνέπεια, η συνέχιση της καταγραφής των προηγούμενων κατασκευών που άρχισε στην Α φάση του διαγωνισμού αποτέλεσε για εμάς μια διαδικασία σημαντική, καθώς ενημερώνει την τυπολογία των κατασκευών και τα κανονιστικά πλαίσια μέσα στα οποία θα αναπτυχθεί η πρωτοβουλία των χρηστών στην ολοκλήρωση των νησίδων. Για αυτό ακριβώς το λόγο έγινε η συστηματική καταγραφή των κατόψεων των 128 αποβάθρων των ψαράδων, αναδεικνύοντας κάποια χαρακτηριστικά τους, πέραν από την αρχική εικόνα με τα ευτελή υλικά που τείνει να διαμορφώσει κανείς. Αυτά τα χαρακτηριστικά έχουν τροφοδοτήσει το σύστημα προκατασκευής, το οποίο θα επιτρέπει την προσαρμογή στις ανάγκες κάθε ψαρά, αλλά από την άλλη θα διατηρεί ένα πλαίσιο επιτρεπόμενων κινήσεων. Μέσα από την καταγραφή των υφιστάμενων αποβάθρων, φ άνηκε ότι οι περισσότερες έχουν επιφάνεια 2 Χ 4 μέτρα. Η διαστασιολόγηση αυτή δημιούργησε τον βασικό κάνναβο των νησίδων και των μικρο-κατασκευών στην πρόταση. Επίσης οι περισσότερες έχουν τοιχώματα που αποτρέπουν την πρόσβαση πάνω στην αποβάθρα και στη βάρκα. Έχουν επίσης μικρότερα ντουλάπια για υδατοστεγή φύλαξη προσωπικών αντικειμένων των ψαράδων.

"Ego gia afto irtha apo tin Germania.
Vgaroume to heimona me ti gynaika mou sto liopetri.
Hmoun pilotos tis Lufthansa kai twra afipiretisa.
Enoikiazw ena aerostato stous touristes.
Yiothetisame tis kalliergies sti nisida CI 04
ston potamo kai pame psarema
me tous filous mas tous psarades.
Irthame edw gia tin omorfia pou syndiazoun
oi drastiriotites twn psaradwn me ti fysi,
alliws tha pigainame se opoiodipote allo hwro"

Ενας πιθανός αερο-περιηγητής του 2025

ΣΧΕΔΙΟ ΑΕΡΟΠΕΡΙΗΓΗΤΗ
ΠΟΤΑΜΟΣ ΛΙΟΠΕΤΡΙΟΥ
ΕΤΟΣ 2025

ΕΞΑΡΤΗΜΑΤΑ ΑΣΤΙΚΟΥ ΕΞΟΠΛΙΣΜΟΥ
(ΦΩΤΙΣΤΙΚΑ, ΚΑΛΑΘΟΣ ΑΠΟΡΡΙΜΑΤΩΝ, ΚΑΘΙΣΤΙΚΑ, ΣΤΑΣΗ ΠΟΔΗΛΑΤΩΝ)

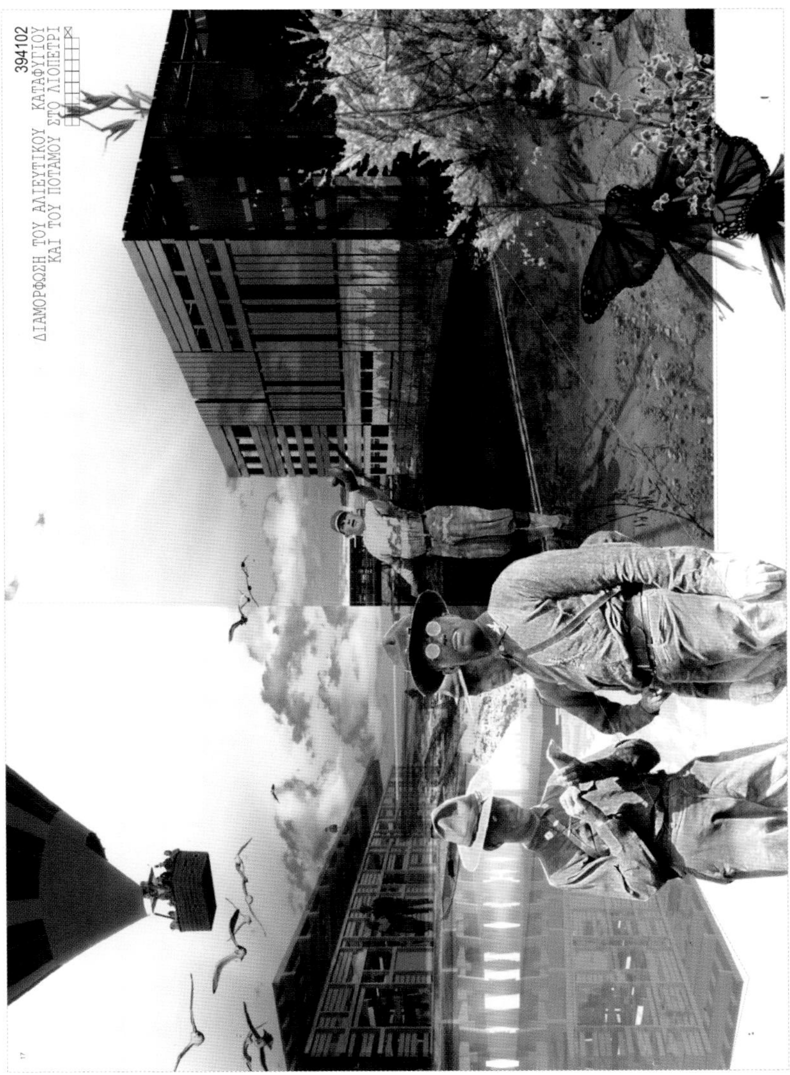

“ SIMPLIFY. IT MUST CONTAIN THE MOST IMPORTANT INFORMATION, HAVE A GOOD EYE PATH, AND ALWAYS HAVE HIERARCHY. ”

115 Cfpos Belgrade | *NABITO ARCHITECTS & PARTNERS*

Alessandra Faticanti – Roberto Ferlito and partners
Project : International Competition for the Construction of the Center For Promotion of Science, Belgrade, Republic of Serbia
Client : Ministry of Science and Technological Development of the Government of the Republic of Serbia
Project phase : International Competition, Final Stage
Estimate : € 22.818.070,00
Surface : 22.883,30 m²

Collaborators : Furio Sordini, Sebastiano Palumbo, Agita Putnina, Isidora Stecki, Sandra Stefanovic, Teo

PROJECT: INTERNATIONAL COMPETITION FOR THE CONSTRUCTION OF THE CENTER FOR PROMOTION OF SCIENCE, REPUBLIC OF SERBIA
AREA: 11.66 ha
BUILT SURFACE: 22.883,30 M2
UNDERGROUND BUILT SURFACE: 6.893 M2
WORKS: 22.818.070,00 €

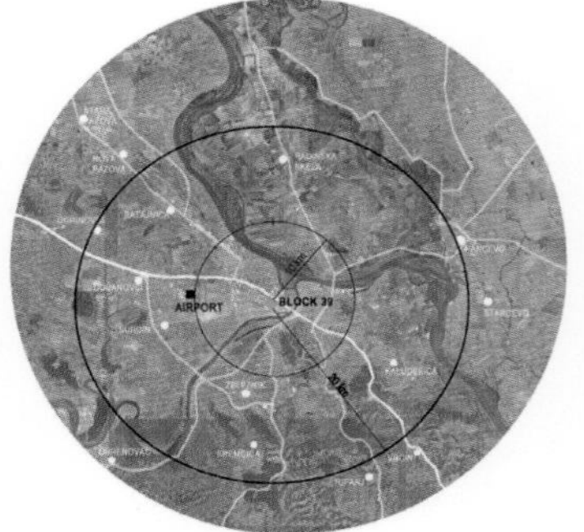

TERRITORIAL RELATIONSHIP

URBAN RELATIONSHIP

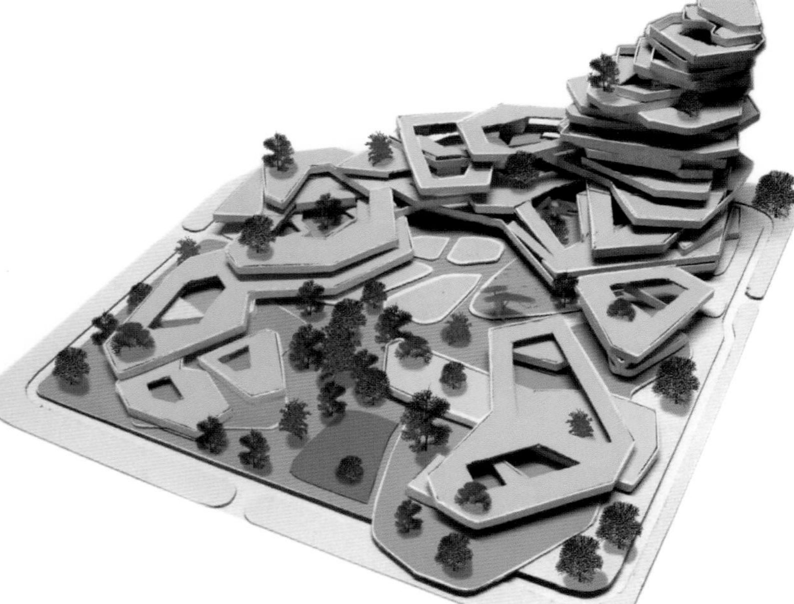

CYCLE OF BIODIVERSITY

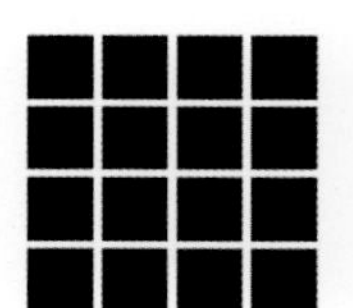

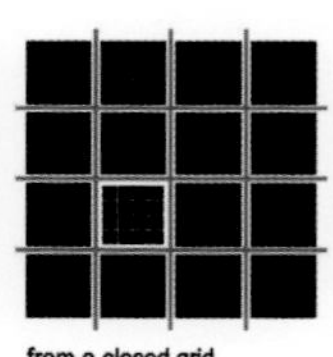

from a closed grid

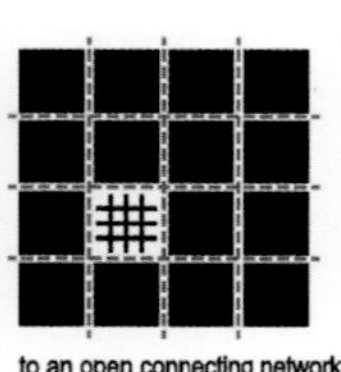

to an open connecting network

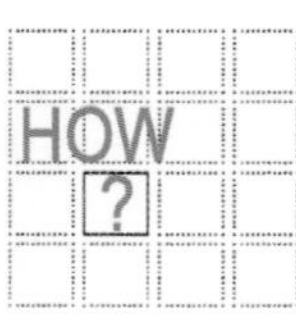

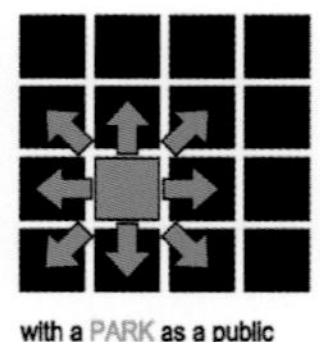

with a PARK as a public corridor of urban connections

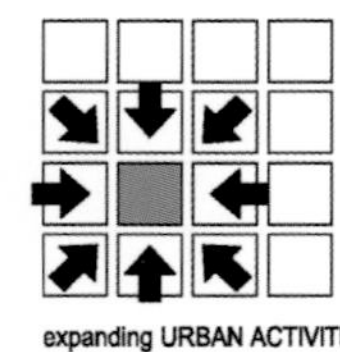

expanding URBAN ACTIVITIES into the park

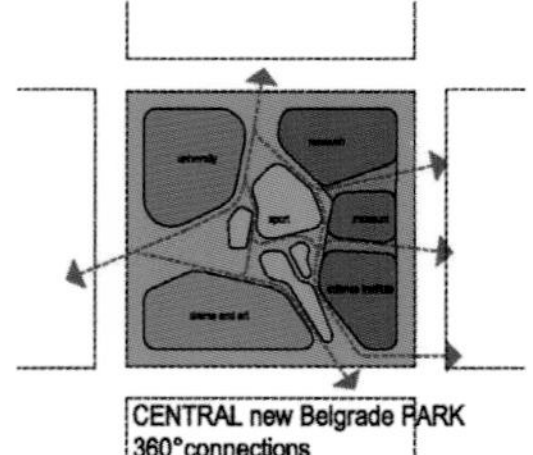

CENTRAL new Belgrade PARK 360°connections

3D VIEW ·F1·

3D VIEW ·F2·

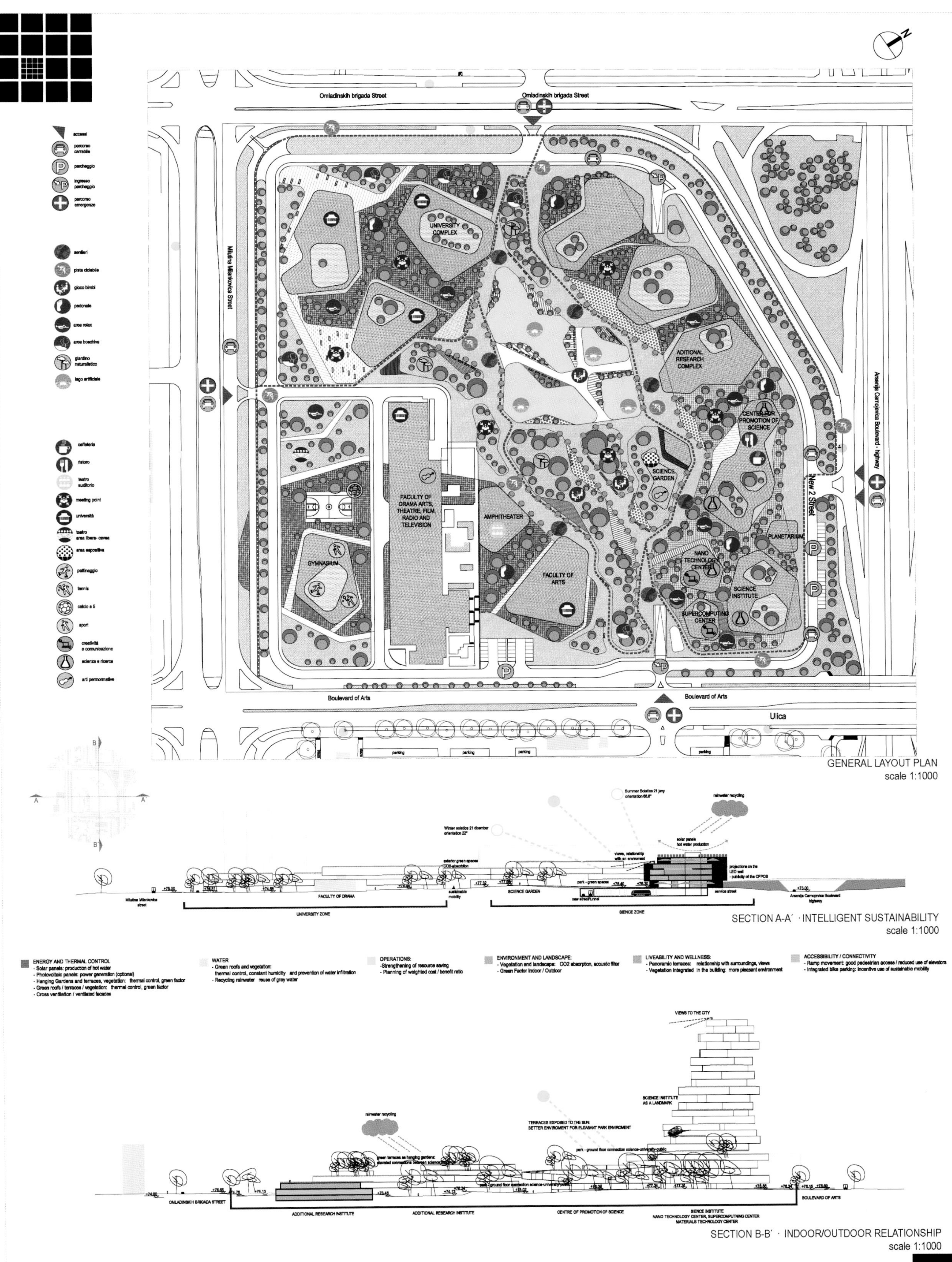
Omladinskih brigada Street
Milutina Milankovića Street
Arsenija Čarnojevića Boulevard - highway
New 2 Street
Boulevard of Arts
Ulica
UNIVERSITY COMPLEX
ADITIONAL RESEARCH COMPLEX
CENTER FOR PROMOTION OF SCIENCE
SCIENCE GARDEN
FACULTY OF DRAMA ARTS, THEATRE, FILM, RADIO AND TELEVISION
AMPHITHEATER
FACULTY OF ARTS
GYMNASIUM
PLANETARIUM
NANO TECHNOLOGY CENTER
SCIENCE INSTITUTE
SUPERCOMPUTING CENTER
GENERAL LAYOUT PLAN
scale 1:1000
SECTION A-A' · INTELLIGENT SUSTAINABILITY
scale 1:1000
UNIVERSITY ZONE
SIENCE ZONE
SECTION B-B' · INDOOR/OUTDOOR RELATIONSHIP
scale 1:1000
2
NEW BELGRADE CENTRAL PARK
Centre for Promotion of Science of the Republic of Serbia

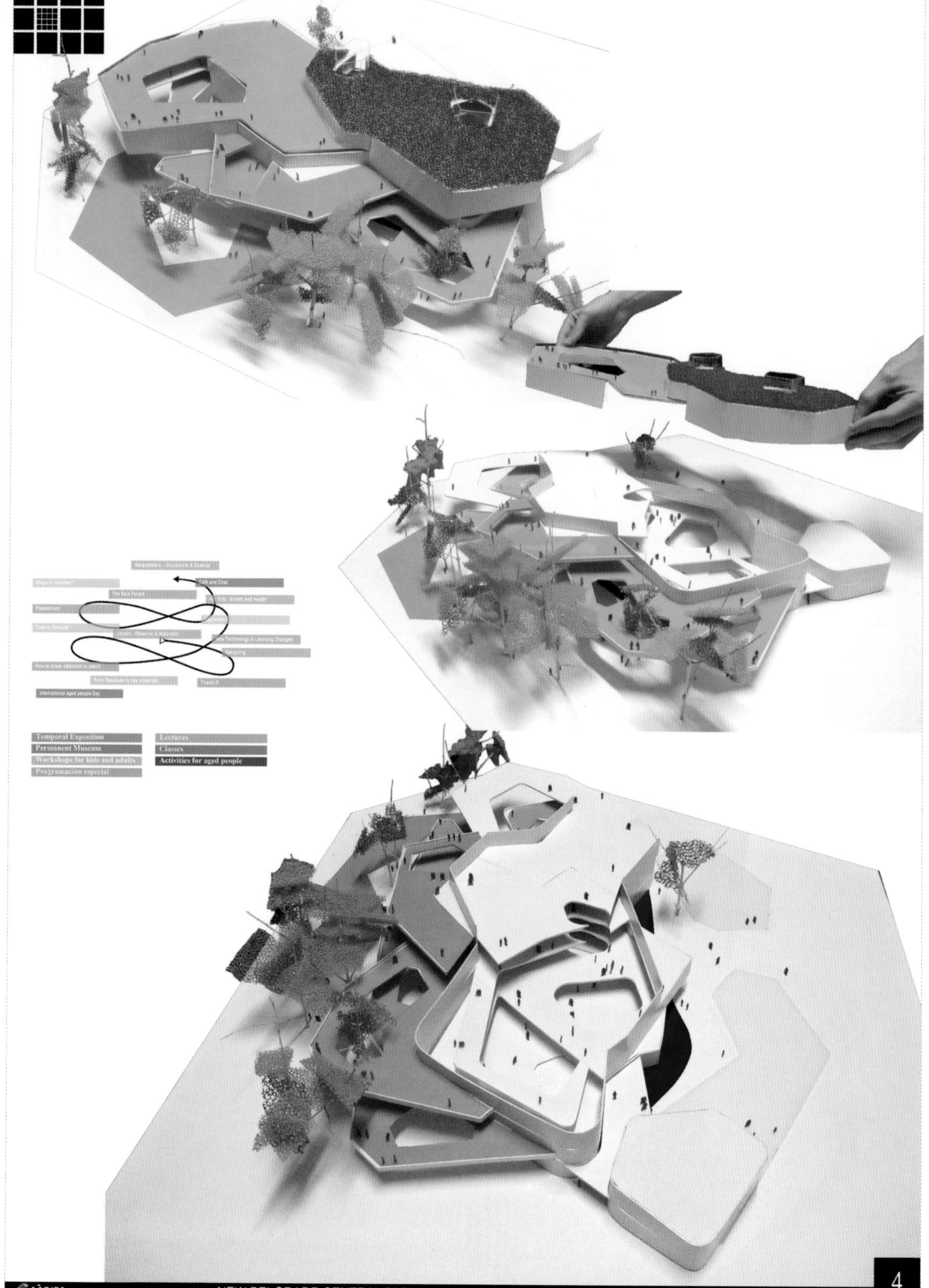

Temporal Exposition
Permanent Museum
Workshops for kids and adults
Programación especial
Lectures
Classes
Activities for aged people

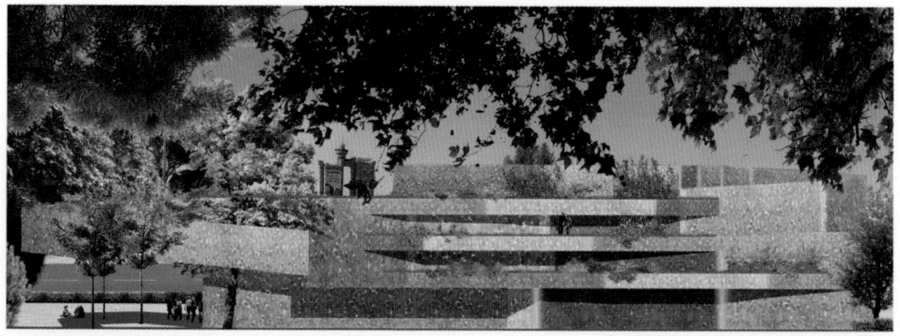

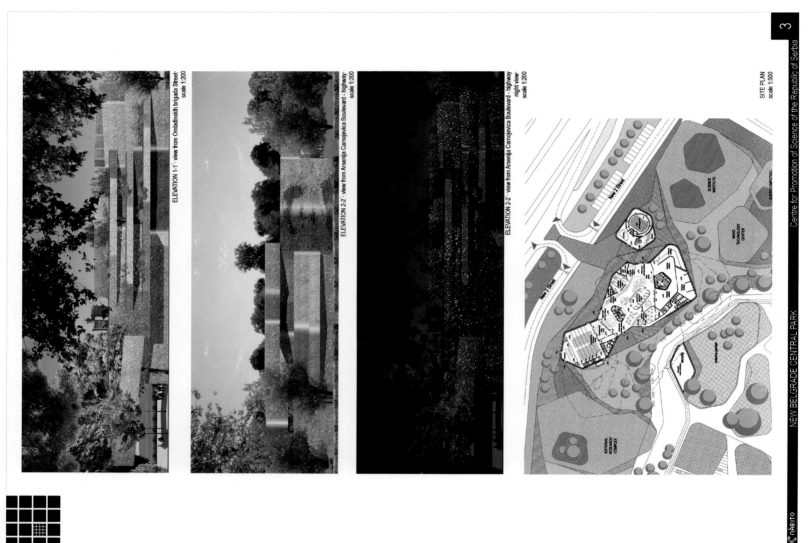

ELEVATION 1-1´· view from Omladinskih brigada Street· scale 1:200

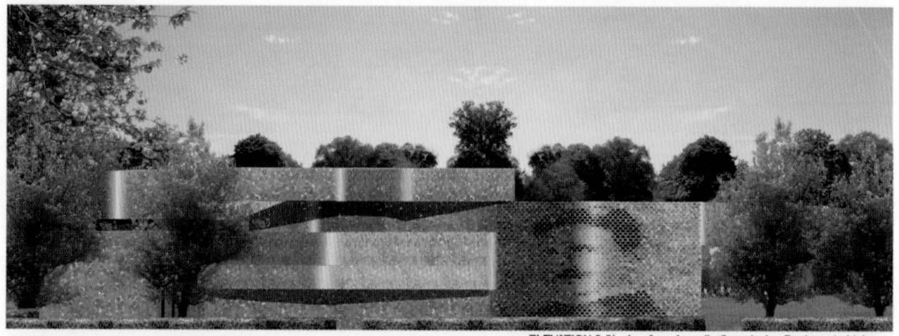

ELEVATION 2-2´· view from Arsenija Carnojevica Boulevard - highway· scale 1:200

ELEVATION 2-2´· view from Arsenija Carnojevica Boulevard - highway night view· scale 1:200

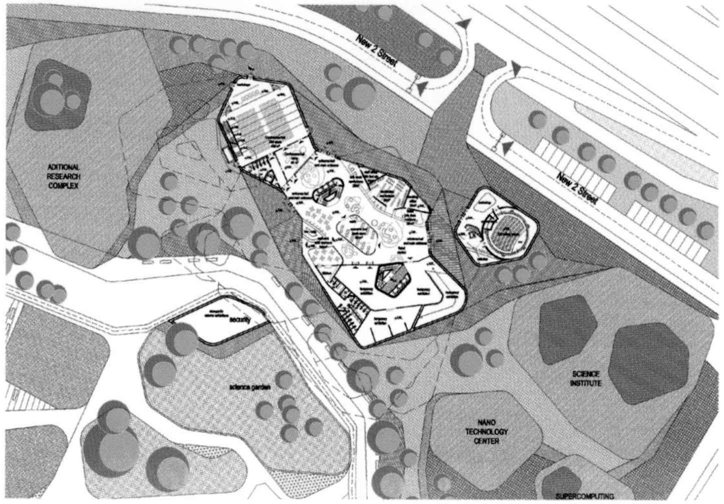

New 2 Street
ADITIONAL RESEARCH COMPLEX
SCIENCE INSTITUTE
NANO TECHNOLOGY CENTER
SUPERCOMPUTING

SITE PLAN scale 1:500

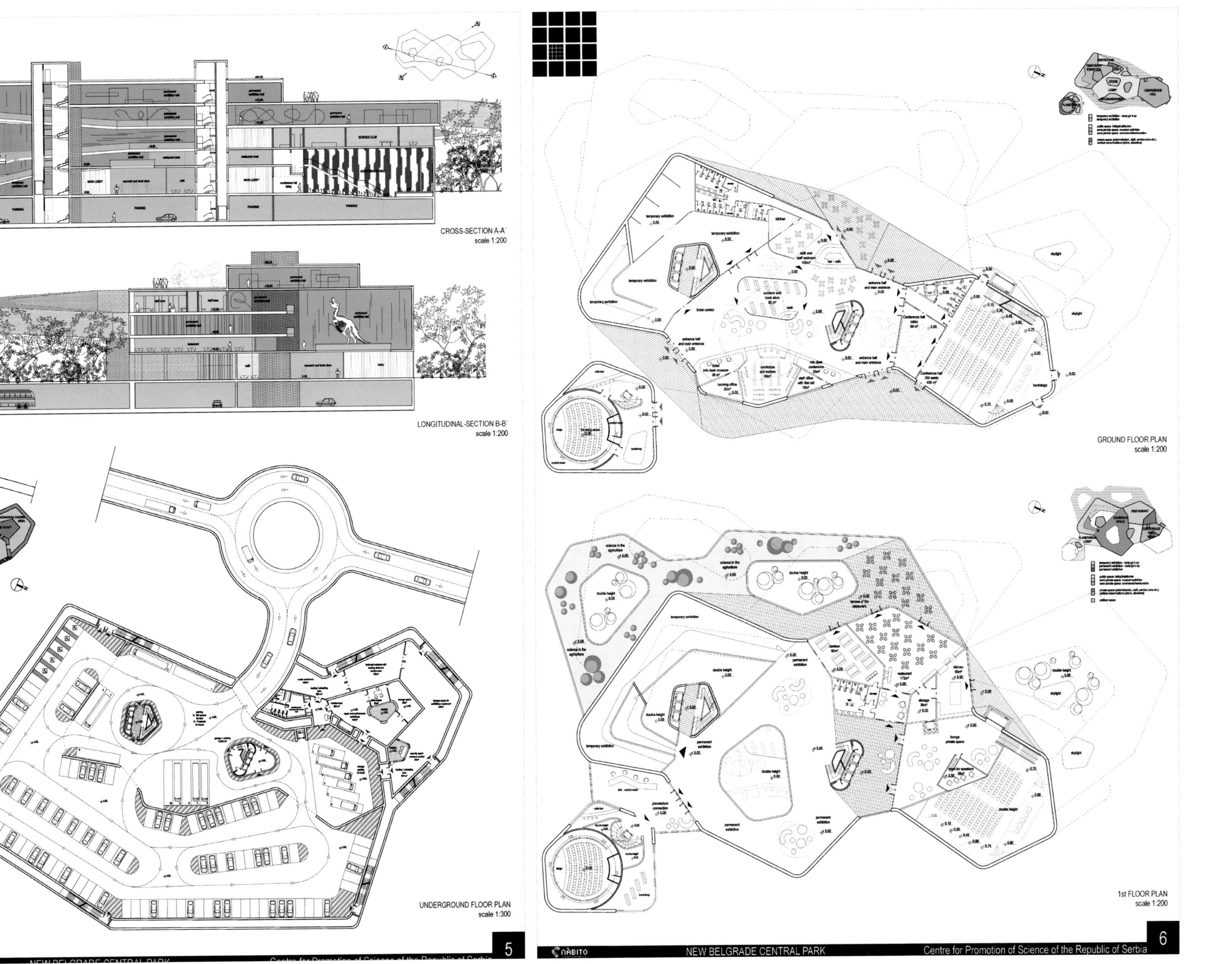

CROSS-SECTION A-A'
scale 1:200
LONGITUDINAL-SECTION B-B'
scale 1:200
UNDERGROUND FLOOR PLAN
scale 1:300
5
GROUND FLOOR PLAN
scale 1:200
1st FLOOR PLAN
scale 1:200
nābito
NEW BELGRADE CENTRAL PARK
Centre for Promotion of Science of the Republic of Serbia
6

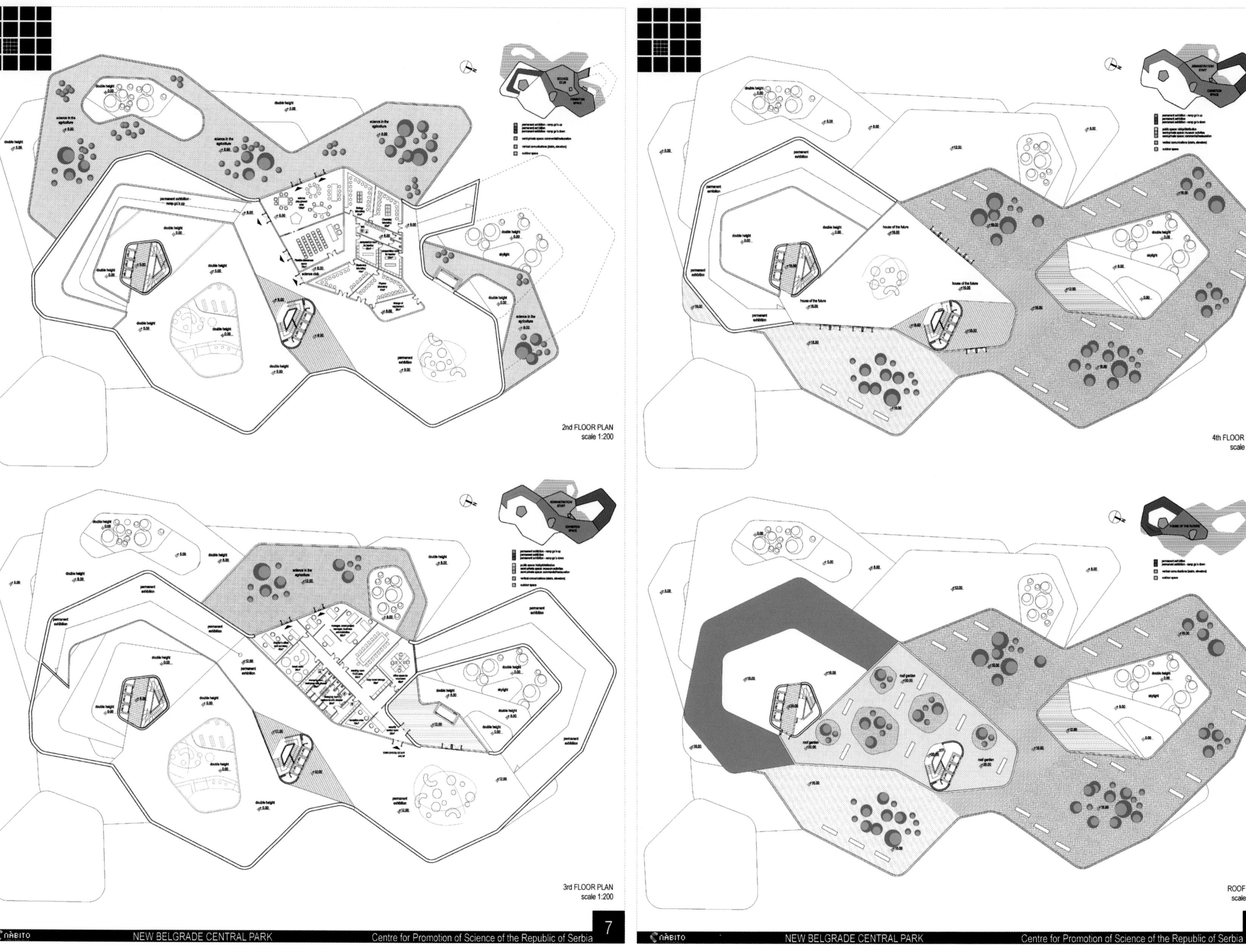
2nd FLOOR PLAN
scale 1:200
3rd FLOOR PLAN
scale 1:200
7
NÄBITO
NEW BELGRADE CENTRAL PARK
Centre for Promotion of Science of the Republic of Serbia
4th FLOOR PLAN
scale 1:200
ROOF PLAN
scale 1:200
8
NÄBITO
NEW BELGRADE CENTRAL PARK
Centre for Promotion of Science of the Republic of Serbia

Ex Fonderie Riunite | *modostudio*

116

Location : Modena, Italy
Client : Comune di Modena
Design Team : CCDP + Modostudio-Cibinel Laurenti
Martocchia architetti associati + Studio Cattinari

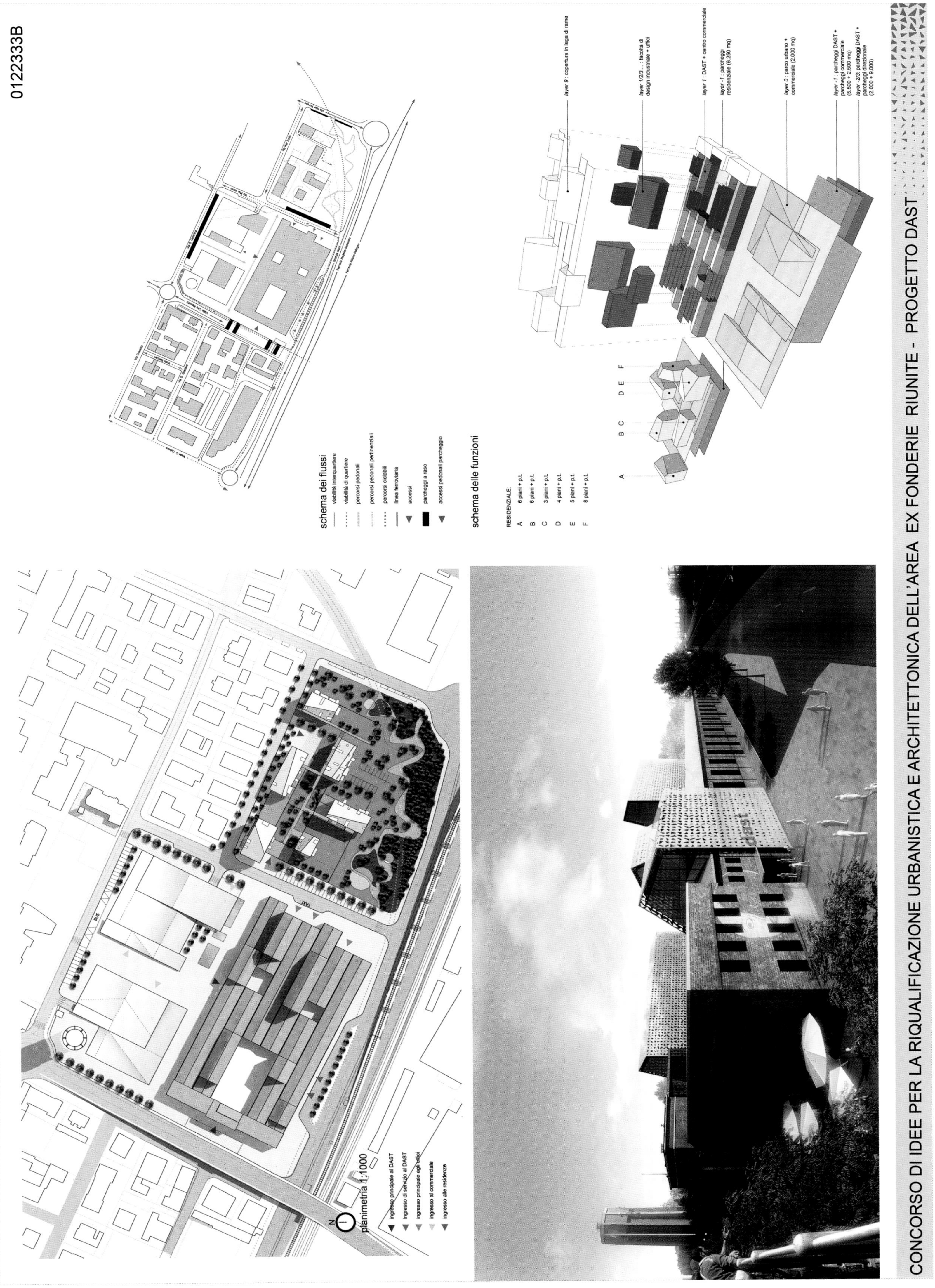

0122333B

schema dei flussi

schema delle funzioni

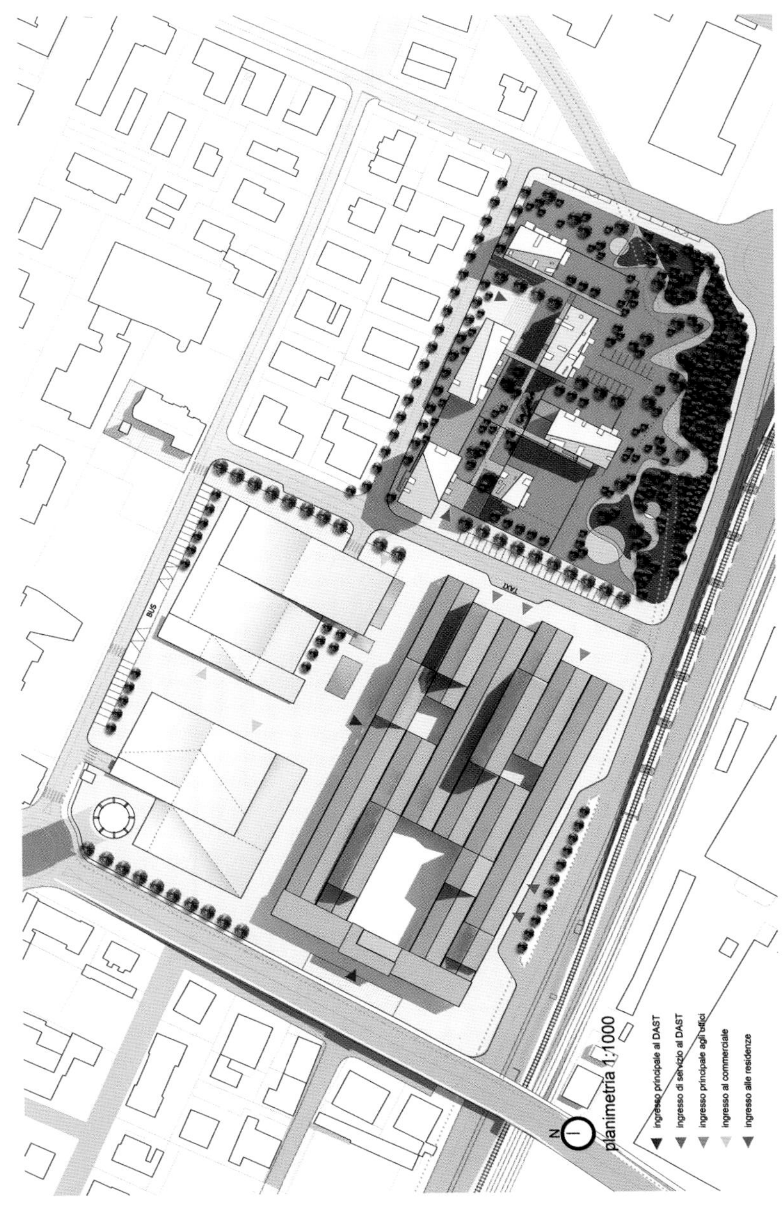

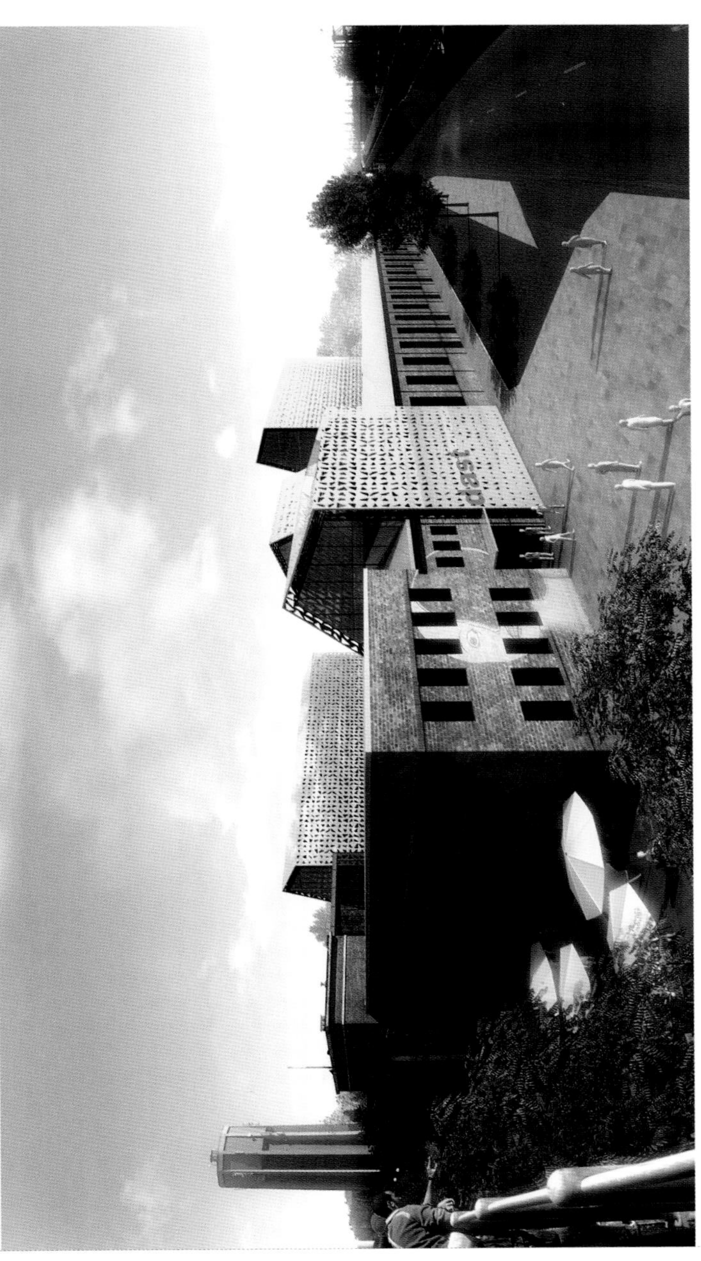

CONCORSO DI IDEE PER LA RIQUALIFICAZIONE URBANISTICA E ARCHITETTONICA DELL'AREA EX FONDERIE RIUNITE - PROGETTO DAST

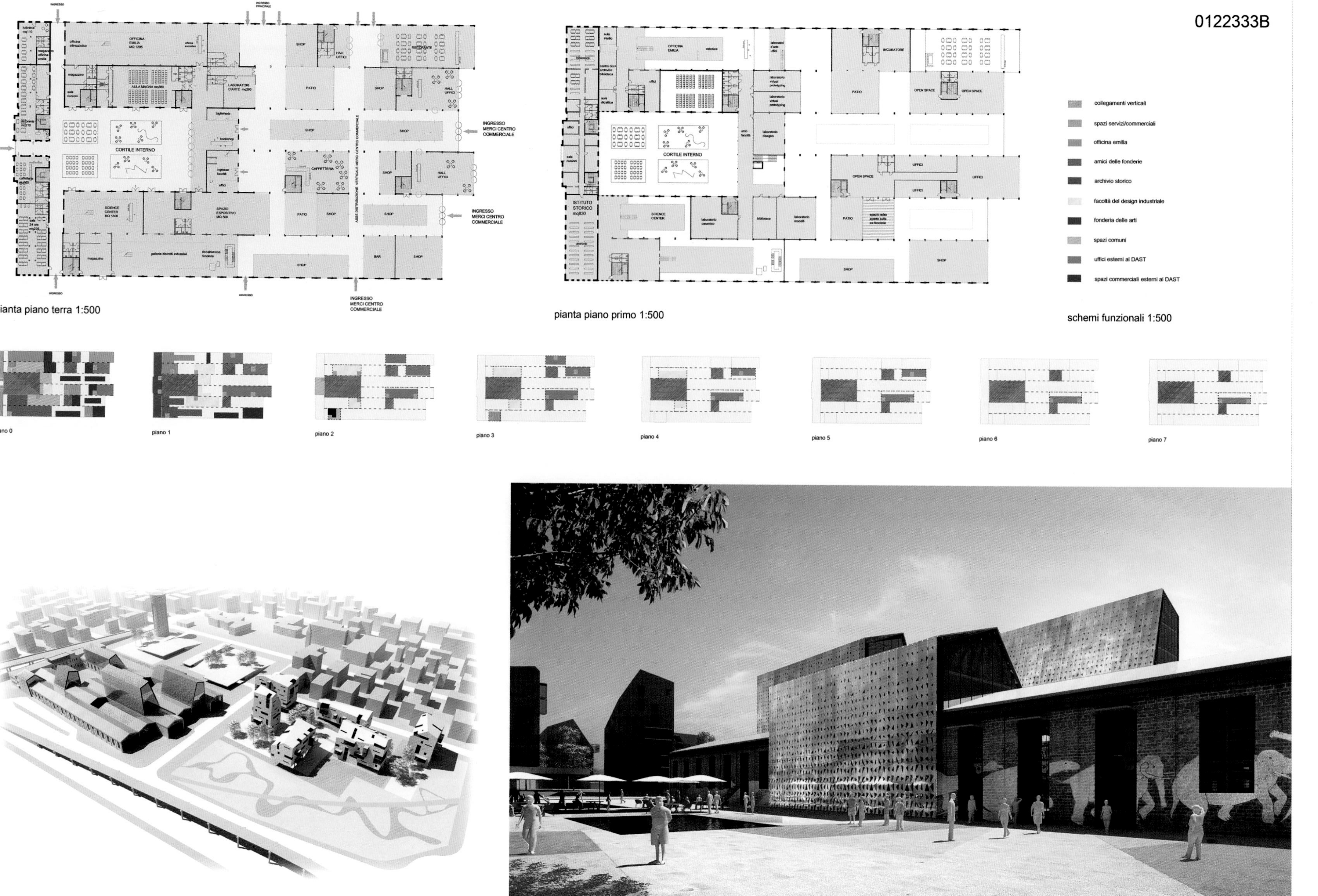
0122333B
pianta piano terra 1:500
pianta piano primo 1:500
schemi funzionali 1:500
collegamenti verticali
spazi servizi/commerciali
officina emilia
amici delle fonderie
archivio storico
facoltà del design industriale
fonderia delle arti
spazi comuni
uffici esterni al DAST
spazi commerciali esterni al DAST
piano 0
piano 1
piano 2
piano 3
piano 4
piano 5
piano 6
piano 7
CONCORSO DI IDEE PER LA RIQUALIFICAZIONE URBANISTICA E ARCHITETTONICA DELL'AREA EX FONDERIE RIUNITE - PROGETTO DAST

0122333B

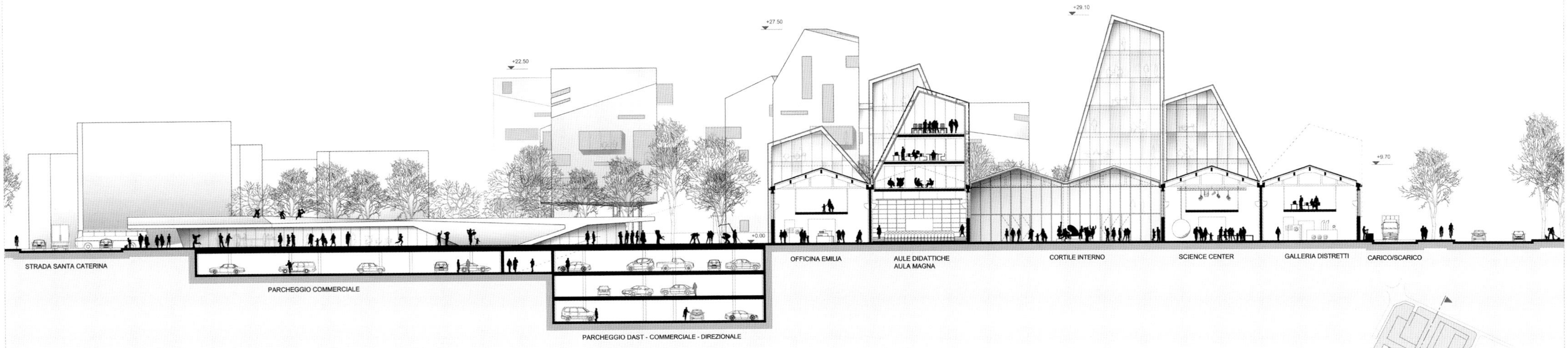

+22.50
+27.50
+29.10
+9.70
+0.00

STRADA SANTA CATERINA
PARCHEGGIO COMMERCIALE
PARCHEGGIO DAST - COMMERCIALE - DIREZIONALE
OFFICINA EMILIA
AULE DIDATTICHE
AULA MAGNA
CORTILE INTERNO
SCIENCE CENTER
GALLERIA DISTRETTI
CARICO/SCARICO

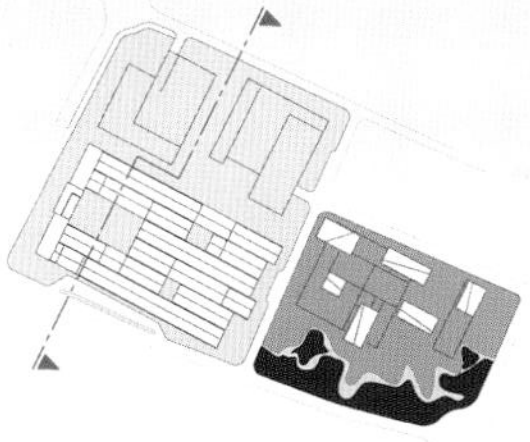

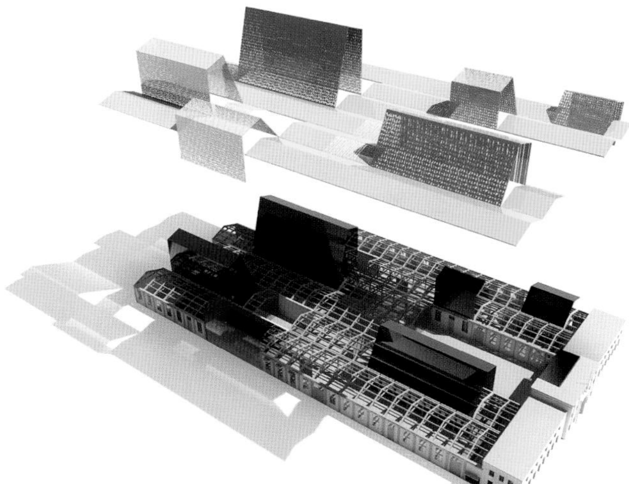

CONCORSO DI IDEE PER LA RIQUALIFICAZIONE URBANISTICA E ARCHITETTONICA DELL'AREA EX FONDERIE RIUNITE - PROGETTO DAST

117 The Eco Nest | *Geotectura*

Participants : Geotectura
Typology : Visitor Center
Location : Israel

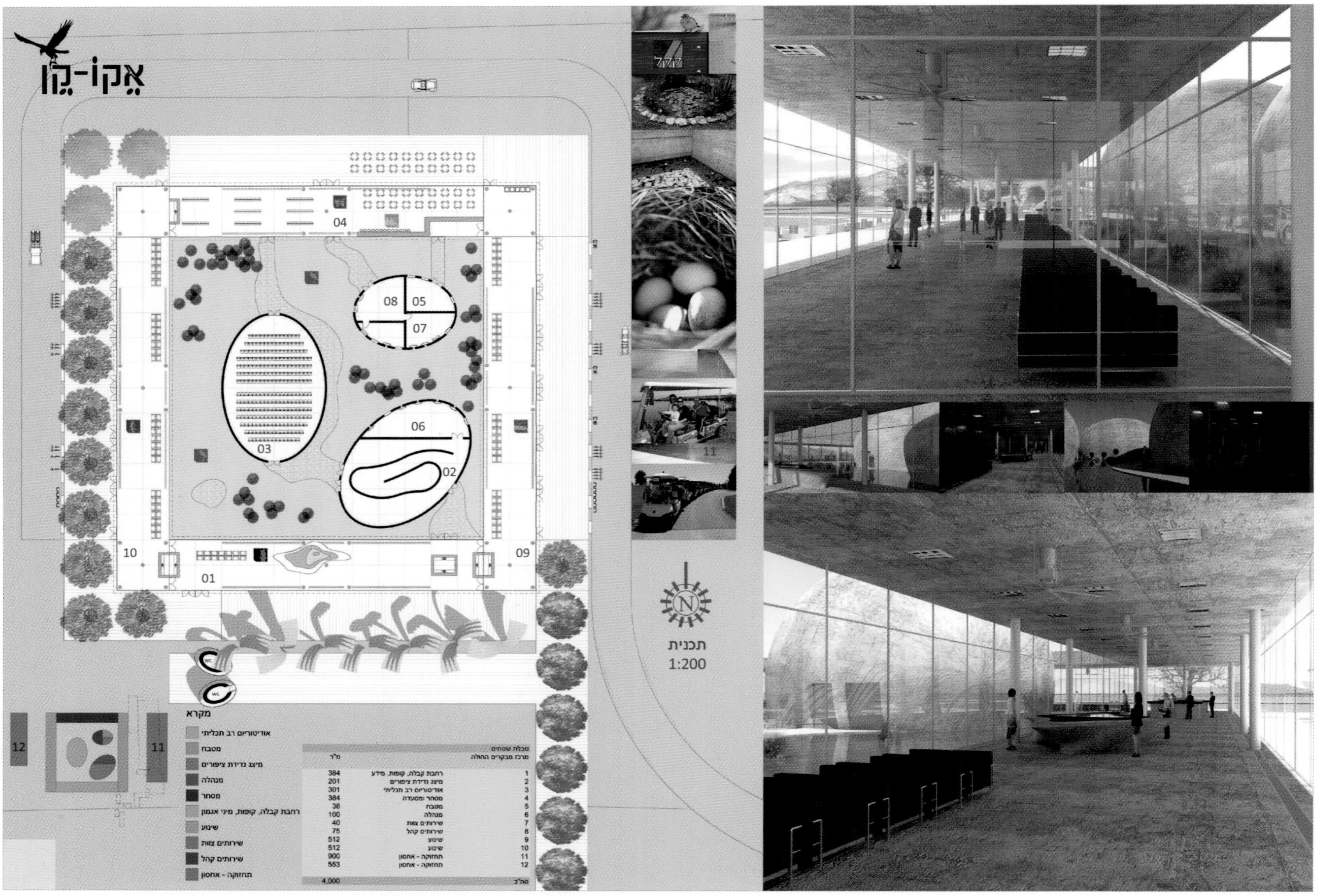

אקו-קן
חזית דרומית
1:200
חזית מערבית
1:200
חזית מזרחית
1:200
חזית צפונית
1:200
אקו-קן
תכנית גגות
1:1000
עומסים
שקיעות
מומנטים
הערכת עלויות
מרכז מבקרים החולה
דיפון וביסוס 500,000
עבודות שלד ופלדה 2,000,000
מעטפת 2,500,000
עבודות גמר 1,000,000
מערכות 1,000,000
גג ירוק 750,000
עבודות פיתוח 500,000
שונות 825,000
מע"מ 1,452,000
סה"כ 10,527,000
מתייחס לשטח של 2500 מ"ר!!
עלות למ"ר כולל מע"מ: 1050$

118 Community Centre Dobříš | *Vallo Sadovsky Architects*

Partner in Charge : Matúš Vallo, Oliver Sadovský
Participants : Branislav Husárik, Dušan Chupáč, Peter Janeček, Martin Lepej
Typology : Public building

Location : Dobříš, Czech Republic
Area : 1349 sqm

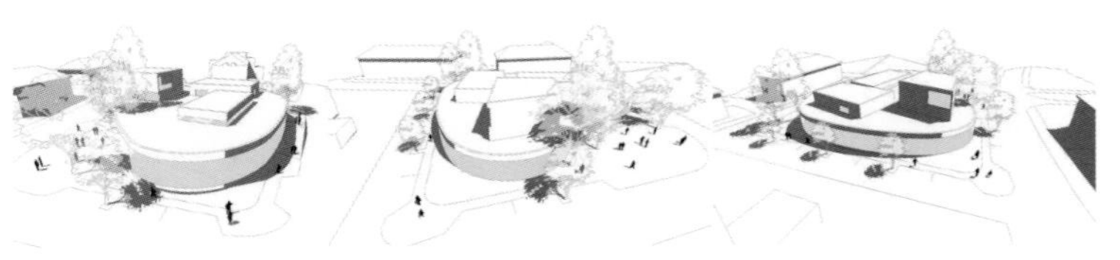

DEMOKRACE, TRANSPARENTNOST, FLEXIBILITA, DOSTUPNOST

Soutěž na Městský dům Dobříš nás zaujala z více důvodů. První byl ten, že se nám líbilo zadání a také nás zaujal způsob, jakým jsou obyvatelé zapojeni do dalšího rozvoje města. Máme pocit, že zadání vytvořili lidé, kteří budou dům opravdu využívat, cítili jsme opravdový zájem o vytvoření funkčního a otevřeného centra. Věříme, že vzdělání má být přístupné každému bez ohledu na věk nebo původ. Zároveň věříme, že setkávání se různých věkových skupin je důležité pro všechny. Chtěli bychom, aby se naše budova neobracela k nikomu zády. Má jasně ukazovat, co se v ní odehrává, má být sama o sobě přívětivá a lákavá pro možné návštěvníky. Nemá se podobat knihovně, ani domu kultury v takovém slova smyslu, v jakém je lidé znají a vnímají dnes. Chceme, aby to byl „obchodní dům" s INFORMACEMI, „nákupní centrum" SETKÁNÍ A KONTAKTŮ.
Tvar domu, jakož i jeho dispozice jasně definují dům bez zadní strany, stavbu, kterou je snadné pochopit a v dobrém slova smyslu „prokouknout". Usilovali jsme se ponechat většinu programu v přízemí a zabezpečit tak maximální dostupnost a možnost propojení. Na druhém poschodí se ve dvou objemech nachází administrativní část objektu, nebo počítačová učebna se studovnou. Hlavním prostorem v přízemí se stává multifunkční sál snadno propojitelný s prostorem kavárny, klubovnami nebo exteriérem, a dokonce i s knihovnou. **Flexibilita** a její nástroj **ZÁVĚS**/OPONA je jedním z hlavních nosných podmiňujících faktorů vzhledu interiéru: umožňují nám tvarovat prostor podle nutnosti, otevírat nebo zavírat, zmenšit nebo zvětšit, spojit nebo rozdělit. Prostor také zároveň zabarvují a změkčují. To všechno kvůli pohodlnému a příjemnému provozu na různých úrovních: klidné čtení knihy v plné knihovně, různé aktivity v jednom sálu, divadelní představení a samostatné fungování kluboven.
Myslíme si, že kvalitní architektura dokáže zlepšit život obyvatel města, pomoct k větší integraci a spojování různých skupin obyvatel, stejně jako najít nové návštěvníky tohoto centra.

PLOCHA POZEMKU.......2065 m2
ZASTAVANÁ PLOCHA.......1349 m2
UŽITNÁ PLOCHA CELKEM.......1538.3 m2
VOLNÝ VÝBĚR - POČET REGÁLŮ.......252 ks

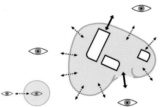

SITUACE ŠIRŠÍCH VZTAHŮ M 1:1000

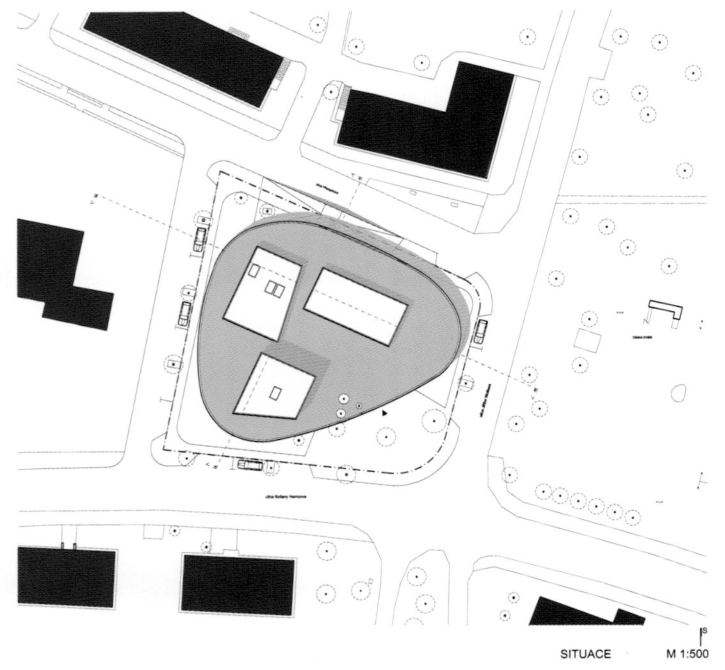

SITUACE M 1:500

OPTICKÉ PROPOJENÍ
ÚPLNÁ VIZUÁLNÍ KONTROLA ČINNOSTÍ V OBJEKTU Z ULIČNÍHO PROSTORU

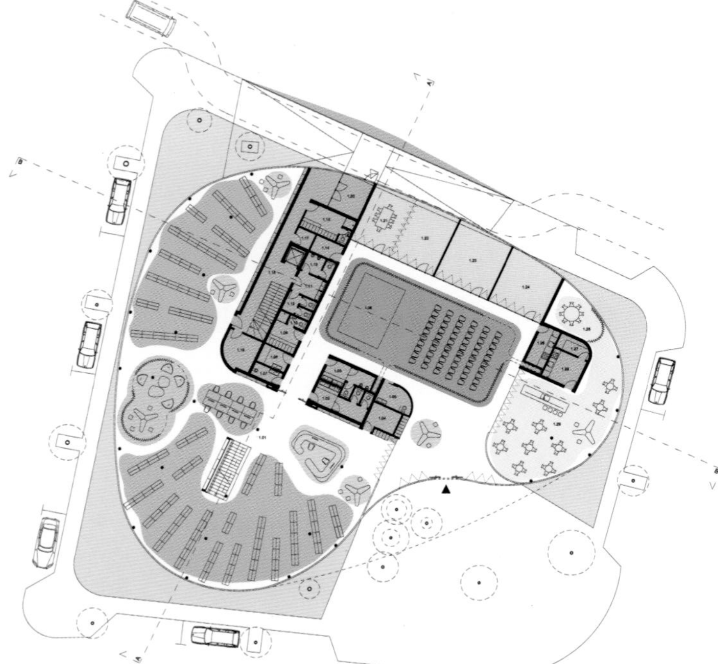

1.NP PŮDORYS M 1:250

FUNKČNÍ DELENÍ
KNIHOVNA - SÁL - UČEBNY - KAVÁRNA

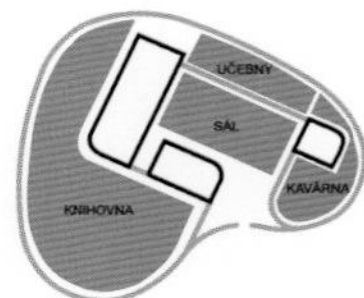

1.NP	PŮDORYS	M 1:250
1.01	Knihovna	567.2 m²
1.02	WC ženy	11.3 m²
1.03	WC muži	10.0 m²
1.04	Sklad	6.5 m²
1.05	WC imobilní	6.4 m²
1.06	Multifunkční sál	121.5 m²
1.07	Úklidová komora	3.4 m²
1.08	Prebalovňa	4.9 m²
1.09	Šatna účinkujících	7.1 m²
1.10	WC účinkující	1.5 m²
1.11	Předsíň	5.4 m²
1.12	WC ženy	4.9 m²
1.13	WC muži	4.7 m²
1.14	Sklad židlí	4.3 m²
1.15	Šatna	9.7 m²
1.16	WC šatna	1.4 m²
1.17	Serverovna	2.7 m²
1.18	Chodba	38.3 m²
1.19	Provozní sklad - MTZ	9.6 m²
1.20	Vchod pro zaměstnance	10.5 m²
1.21	Klubovna	21.9 m²
1.22	Učebna	24.9 m²
1.23	Učebna	30.2 m²
1.24	Učebna	27.0 m²
1.25	Salónek	17.4 m²
1.26	Kuchyňka	6.7 m²
1.27	Sklad	4.1 m²
1.28	Zázemí	9.1 m²
1.29	Kavárna	99.9 m²

SDÍLENÍ FUNKCÍ
MULTIFUNKČNÍ SÁL - NAMĚSTÍ

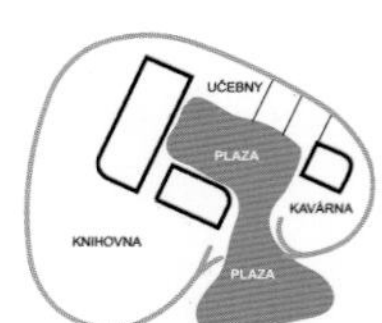

SDÍLENÍ FUNKCÍ
MULTIFUNKČNÍ SÁL - UČEBNY - KAVÁRNA - NÁMĚSTÍ

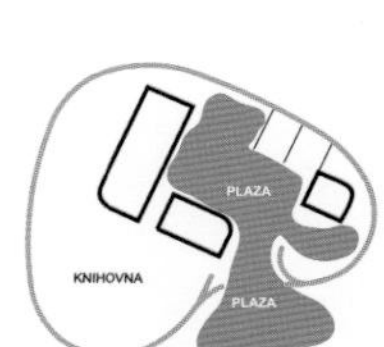

SDÍLENÍ FUNKCÍ
KNIHOVNA - MULTIFUNKČNÍ SÁL - UČEBNY - KAVÁRNA - NÁMĚSTÍ

Městský dům Dobříš

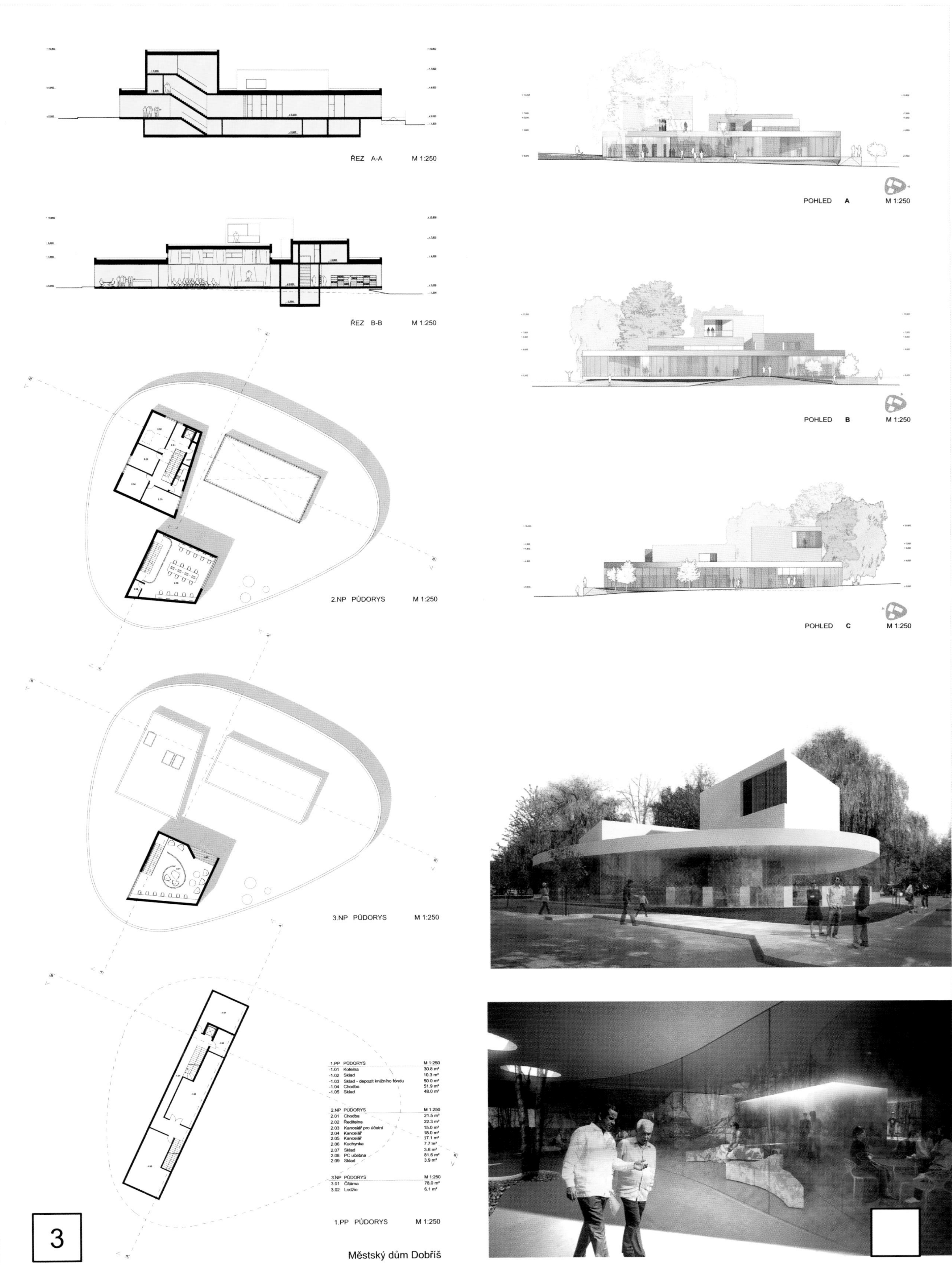
ŘEZ A-A M 1:250
POHLED A M 1:250
ŘEZ B-B M 1:250
POHLED B M 1:250
2.NP PŮDORYS M 1:250
POHLED C M 1:250
3.NP PŮDORYS M 1:250
1.PP PŮDORYS M 1:250
-1.01 Kotelna 30.8 m²
-1.02 Sklad 10.3 m²
-1.03 Sklad - depozit knižního fondu 50.0 m²
-1.04 Chodba 51.9 m²
-1.05 Sklad 48.0 m²
2.NP PŮDORYS M 1:250
2.01 Chodba 21.5 m²
2.02 Ředitelna 22.3 m²
2.03 Kancelář pro účetní 15.0 m²
2.04 Kancelář 18.0 m²
2.05 Kancelář 17.1 m²
2.06 Kuchynka 7.7 m²
2.07 Sklad 3.6 m²
2.08 PC učebna 81.6 m²
2.09 Sklad 3.9 m²
3.NP PŮDORYS M 1:250
3.01 Čítárna 78.0 m²
3.02 Lodžie 6.1 m²
1.PP PŮDORYS M 1:250
3
Městský dům Dobříš

119 Kites for Europe | *NABITO ARCHITECTS & PARTNERS*

Alessandra Faticanti – Roberto Ferlito and partners
Project : Renovation of Former Civil Hospital of Gorizia, Italy in the framework of the project "Spazio giovani alla frontiera"
Client : Municipality of Gorizia

Estimate : € 80.000.000,00
Collaborators : Furio Sordini, Sebastiano Palumbo, Agita Putnina, Isidora Stecki, Sandra Stefanovic

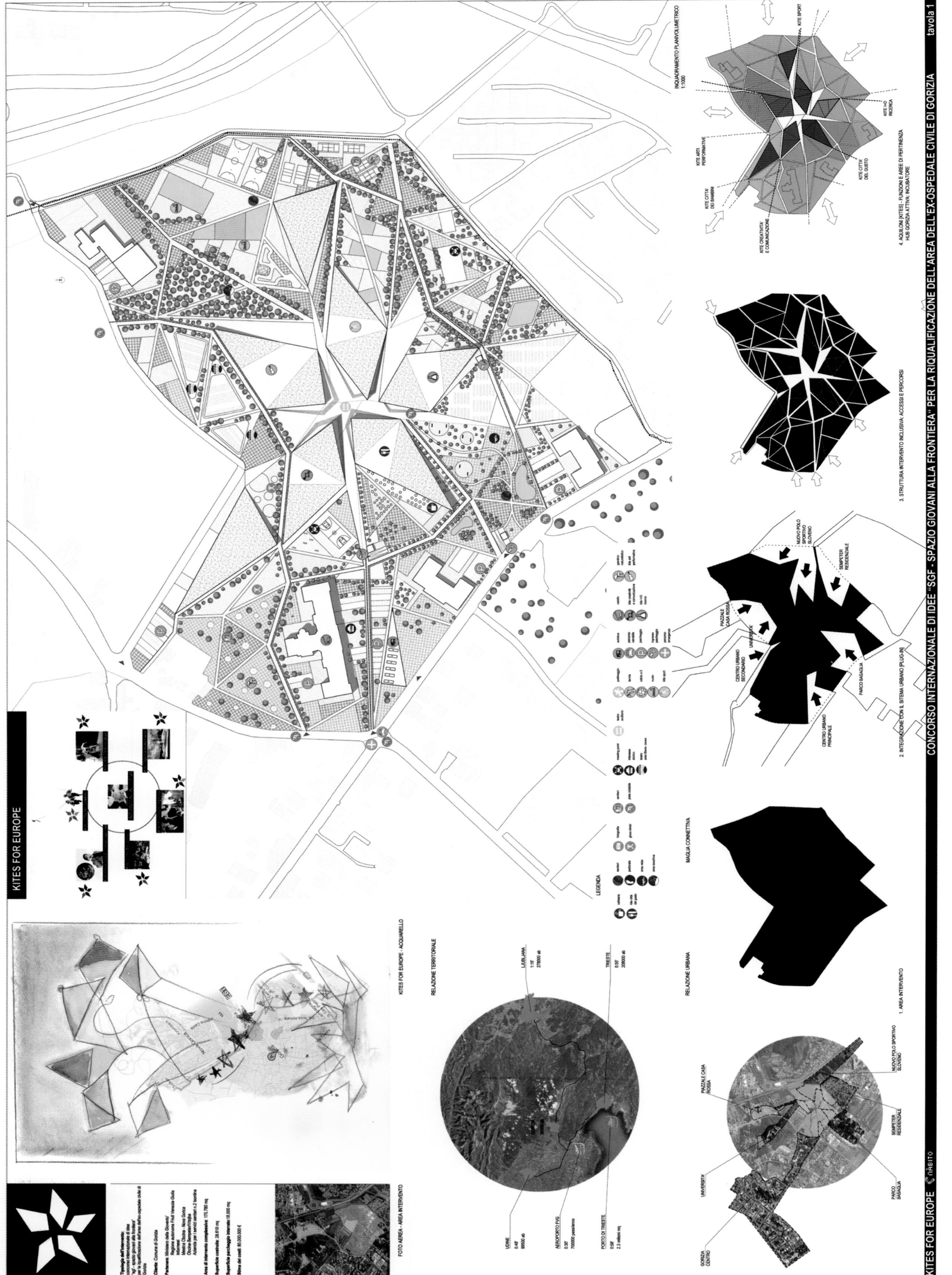

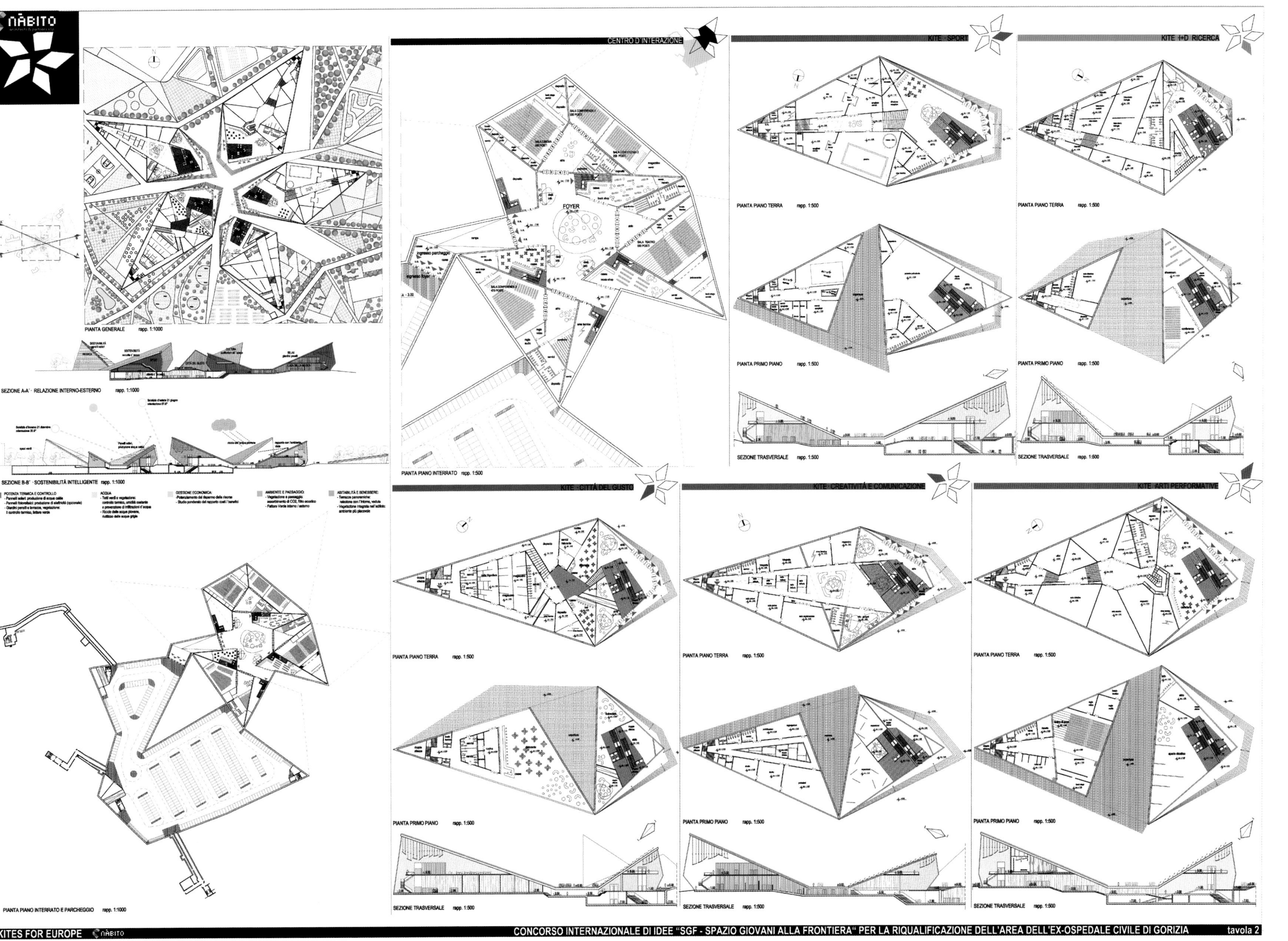

CENTRO D'INTERAZIONE
KITE: SPORT
KITE: I+D RICERCA
FOYER
PIANTA GENERALE rapp. 1:1000
SEZIONE A-A' - RELAZIONE INTERNO-ESTERNO rapp. 1:1000
SEZIONE B-B' - SOSTENIBILITÀ INTELLIGENTE rapp. 1:1000
PIANTA PIANO INTERRATO rapp. 1:500
PIANTA PIANO TERRA rapp. 1:500
PIANTA PRIMO PIANO rapp. 1:500
SEZIONE TRASVERSALE rapp. 1:500
KITE: CITTÀ DEL GUSTO
KITE: CREATIVITÀ E COMUNICAZIONE
KITE: ARTI PERFORMATIVE
PIANTA PIANO INTERRATO E PARCHEGGIO rapp. 1:1000
KITES FOR EUROPE
CONCORSO INTERNAZIONALE DI IDEE "SGF - SPAZIO GIOVANI ALLA FRONTIERA" PER LA RIQUALIFICAZIONE DELL'AREA DELL'EX-OSPEDALE CIVILE DI GORIZIA
tavola 2

COPERTURE Pubbliche
PRIMO LIVELLO -laboratori-
LIVELLO TERRA -fori interdisciplinari-
LIVELLO IPOGEO -interazione-
KITES FOR EUROPE
CONCORSO INTERNAZIONALE DI IDEE "SGF - SPAZIO GIOVANI ALLA FRONTIERA" PER LA RIQUALIFICAZIONE DELL'AREA DELL'EX-OSPEDALE CIVILE DI GORIZIA
tavola 3

Senj Squares | *3LHD*

120

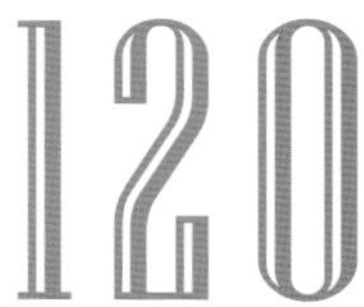

Collaborators : Vibor Granic
3D : Boris Goreta

Location : Senj, Croatia
Project Team : Sasa Begovic, Marko Dabrovic, Tatjana Grozdanic Begovic, Silvije Novak, Irena Mazer, Tomislav Soldo, Ida Ister

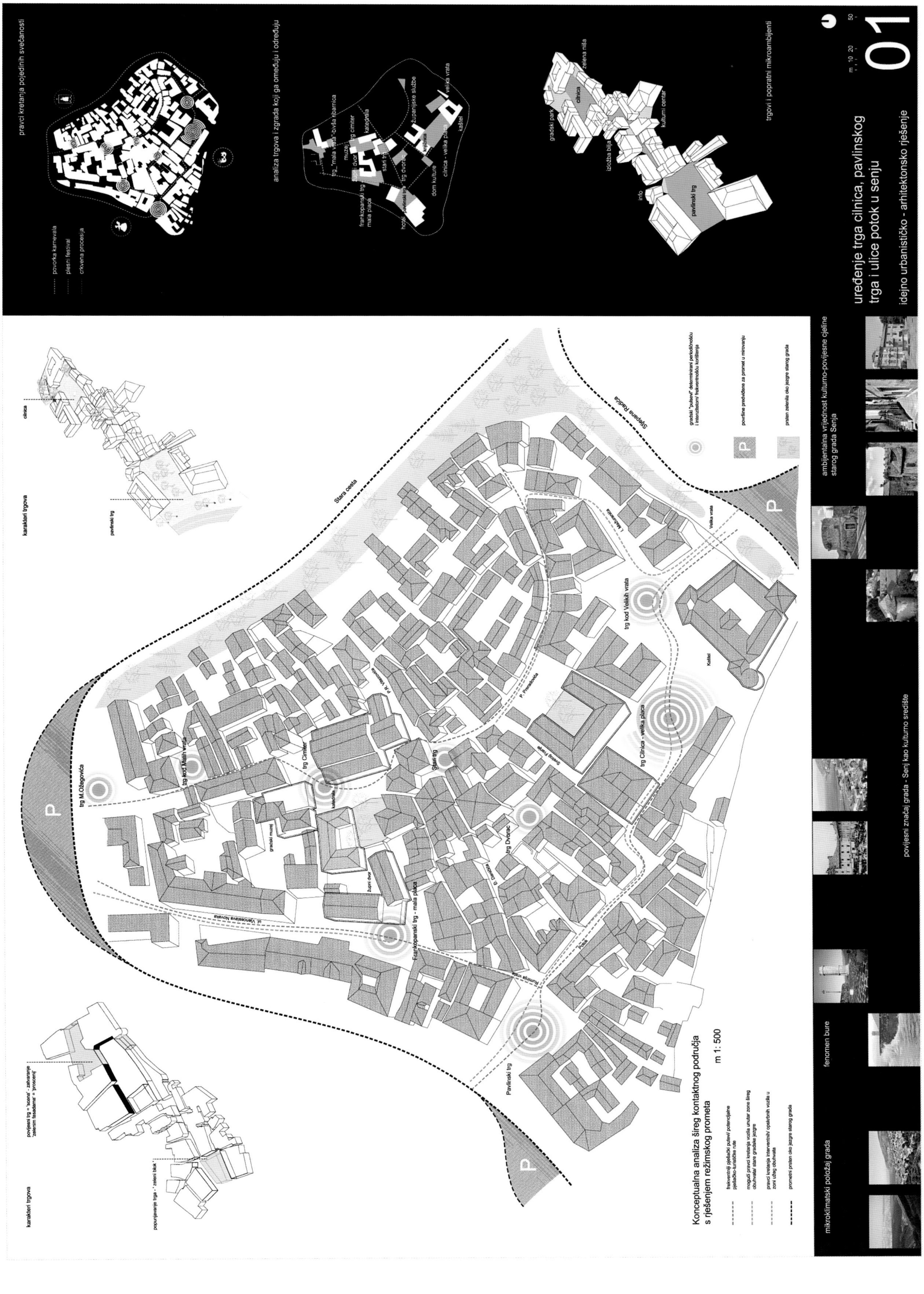

01
uređenje trga cilnica, pavlinskog trga i ulice potok u senju
idejno urbanističko - arhitektonsko rješenje
pravci kretanja pojedinih svečanosti
povorka karnevala
plesni festival
crkvena procesija
analiza trgova i zgrada koji ga omeđuju i određuju
trgovi i popratni mikroambijenti
Konceptualna analiza šireg kontaktnog područja s rješenjem režimskog prometa
m 1: 500
karakteri trgova
Stara cesta
Stjepana Radića
Kaštel
trg Cilnica - velika placa
trg kod Velikih vrata
Stari trg
trg Cimiter
trg kod Malih vrata
trg M.Ožegovića
trg Dvorac
Frankopanski trg - mala placa
Pavlinski trg
ambijentalna vrijednost kulturno-povijesne cjeline starog grada Senja
povijesni značaj grada - Senj kao kulturno središte
fenomen bure
mikroklimatski položaj grada

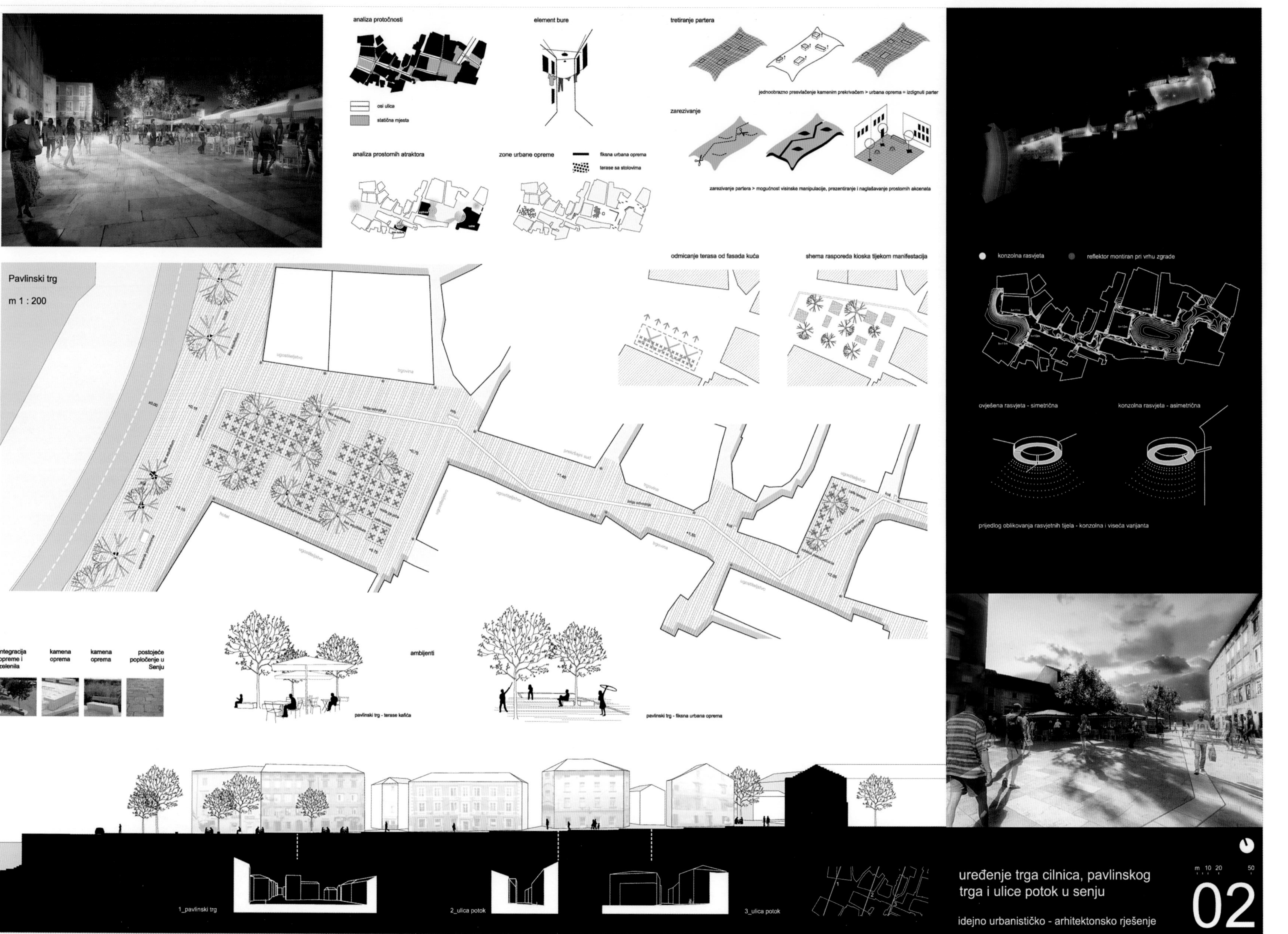

analiza protočnosti
osi ulica
statična mjesta
element bure
tretiranje partera
jednoobrazno presvlačenje kamenim prekrivačem > urbana oprema = izdignuti parter
zarezivanje
zarezivanje partera > mogućnost visinske manipulacije, prezentiranje i naglašavanje prostornih akcenata
analiza prostornih atraktora
zone urbane opreme
fiksna urbana oprema
terase sa stolovima
konzolna rasvjeta
reflektor montiran pri vrhu zgrade
ovješena rasvjeta - simetrična
konzolna rasvjeta - asimetrična
prijedlog oblikovanja rasvjetnih tijela - konzolna i viseća varijanta
Pavlinski trg
m 1 : 200
odmicanje terasa od fasada kuća
shema rasporeda kioska tijekom manifestacija
integracija opreme i zelenila
kamena oprema
kamena oprema
postojeće popločenje u Senju
ambijenti
pavlinski trg - terase kafića
pavlinski trg - fiksna urbana oprema
1_pavlinski trg
2_ulica potok
3_ulica potok
uređenje trga cilnica, pavlinskog trga i ulice potok u senju
idejno urbanističko - arhitektonsko rješenje
m 10 20 50
02

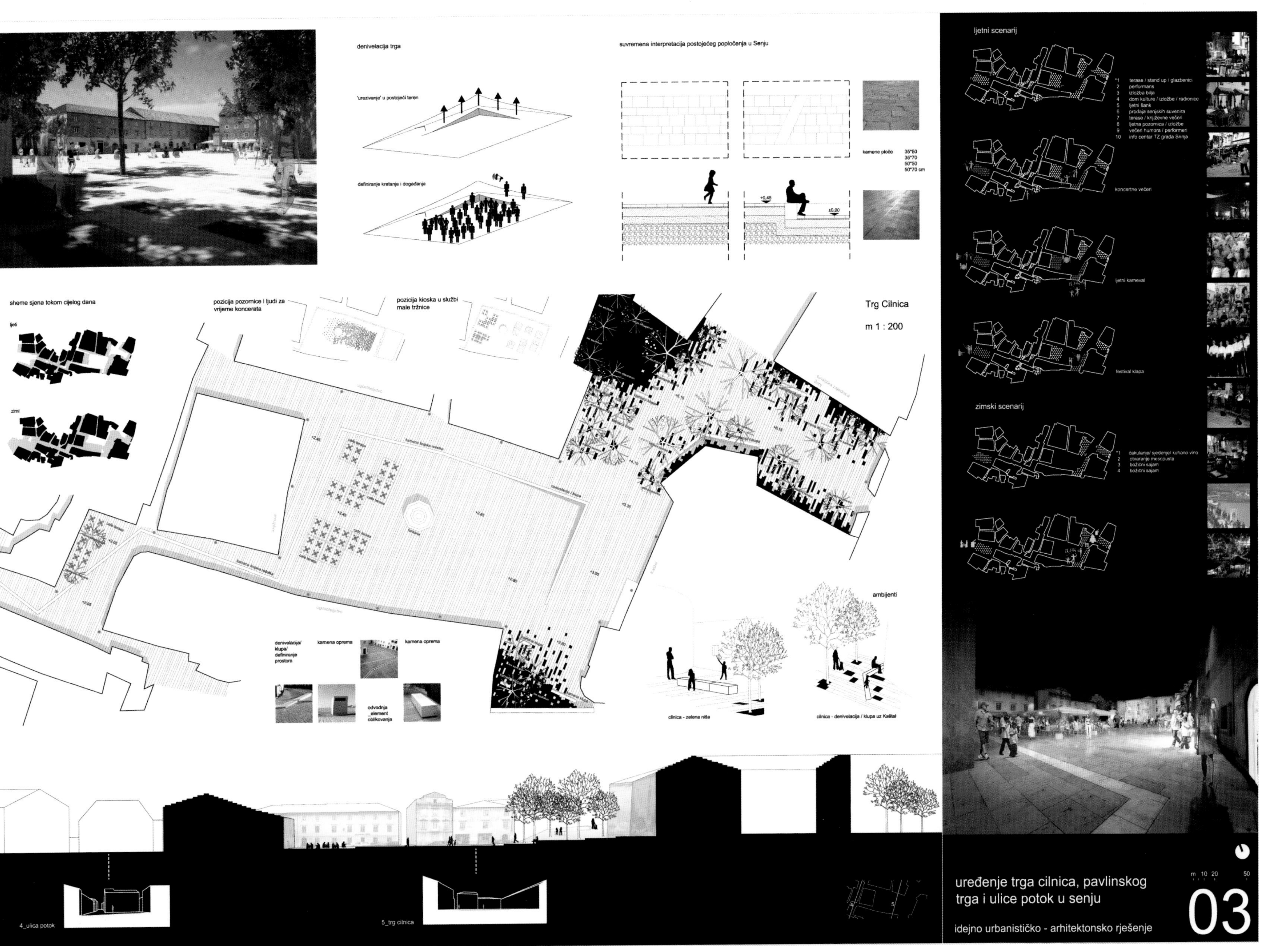
denivelacija trga
'urezivanje' u postojeći teren
definiranje kretanja i događanja
suvremena interpretacija postojećeg popločenja u Senju
+0,45
±0,00
kamene ploče
35*50
35*70
50*50
50*70 cm
ljetni scenarij
*1 terase / stand up / glazbenici
2 performans
3 izložba bilja
4 dom kulture / izložbe / radionice
5 ljetni šank
6 prodaja senjskih suvenira
7 terase / književne večeri
8 ljetna pozornica / izložbe
9 večeri humora / performeri
10 info centar TZ grada Senja
koncertne večeri
ljetni karneval
festival klapa
zimski scenarij
*1 čakulanje/ sjedenje/ kuhano vino
2 otvaranje mesopusta
3 božićni sajam
4 božićni sajam
sheme sjena tokom cijelog dana
ljeti
zimi
pozicija pozornice i ljudi za vrijeme koncerata
pozicija kioska u službi male tržnice
Trg Cilnica
m 1 : 200
denivelacija/ klupa/ definiranje prostora
kamena oprema
kamena oprema
odvodnja _element oblikovanja
ambijenti
cilnica - zelena niša
cilnica - denivelacija / klupa uz Kaštel
4_ulica potok
5_trg cilnica
uređenje trga cilnica, pavlinskog
trga i ulice potok u senju
idejno urbanističko - arhitektonsko rješenje
m 10 20 50
03

121 DER | *KLAIR Architecture*

Project Description : New City Hall
Location : Derinia, Cyprus
Design : KLAIR + Nenad Basic + Philippe Stanfield + D. Kypreotis Architects

ΠΑΓΚΥΠΡΙΟΣ ΑΡΧΙΤΕΚΤΟΝΙΚΟΣ ΔΙΑΓΩΝΙΣΜΟΣ ΓΙΑ ΤΗΝ ΑΝΕΓΕΡΣΗ ΝΕΟΥ ΔΗΜΟΤΙΚΟΥ ΜΕΓΑΡΟΥ ΔΕΡΥΝΕΙΑΣ 211296 1

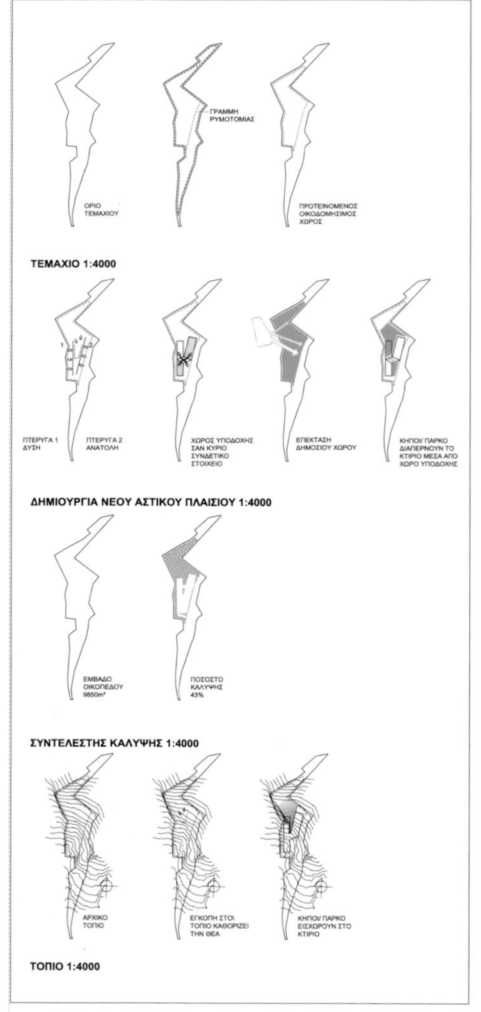

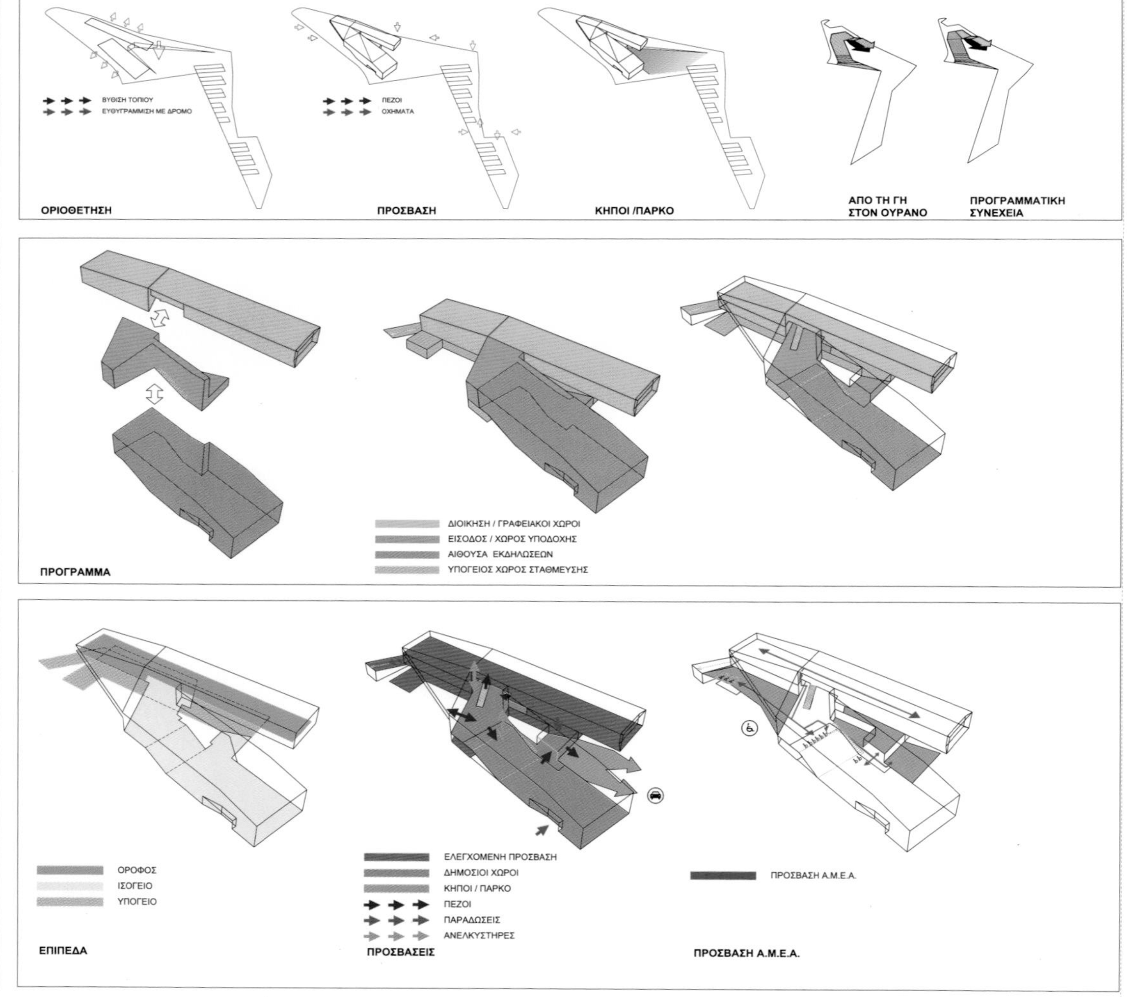

ΠΑΓΚΥΠΡΙΟΣ ΑΡΧΙΤΕΚΤΟΝΙΚΟΣ ΔΙΑΓΩΝΙΣΜΟΣ ΓΙΑ ΤΗΝ ΑΝΕΓΕΡΣΗ ΝΕΟΥ ΔΗΜΟΤΙΚΟΥ ΜΕΓΑΡΟΥ ΔΕΡΥΝΕΙΑΣ 211296 2

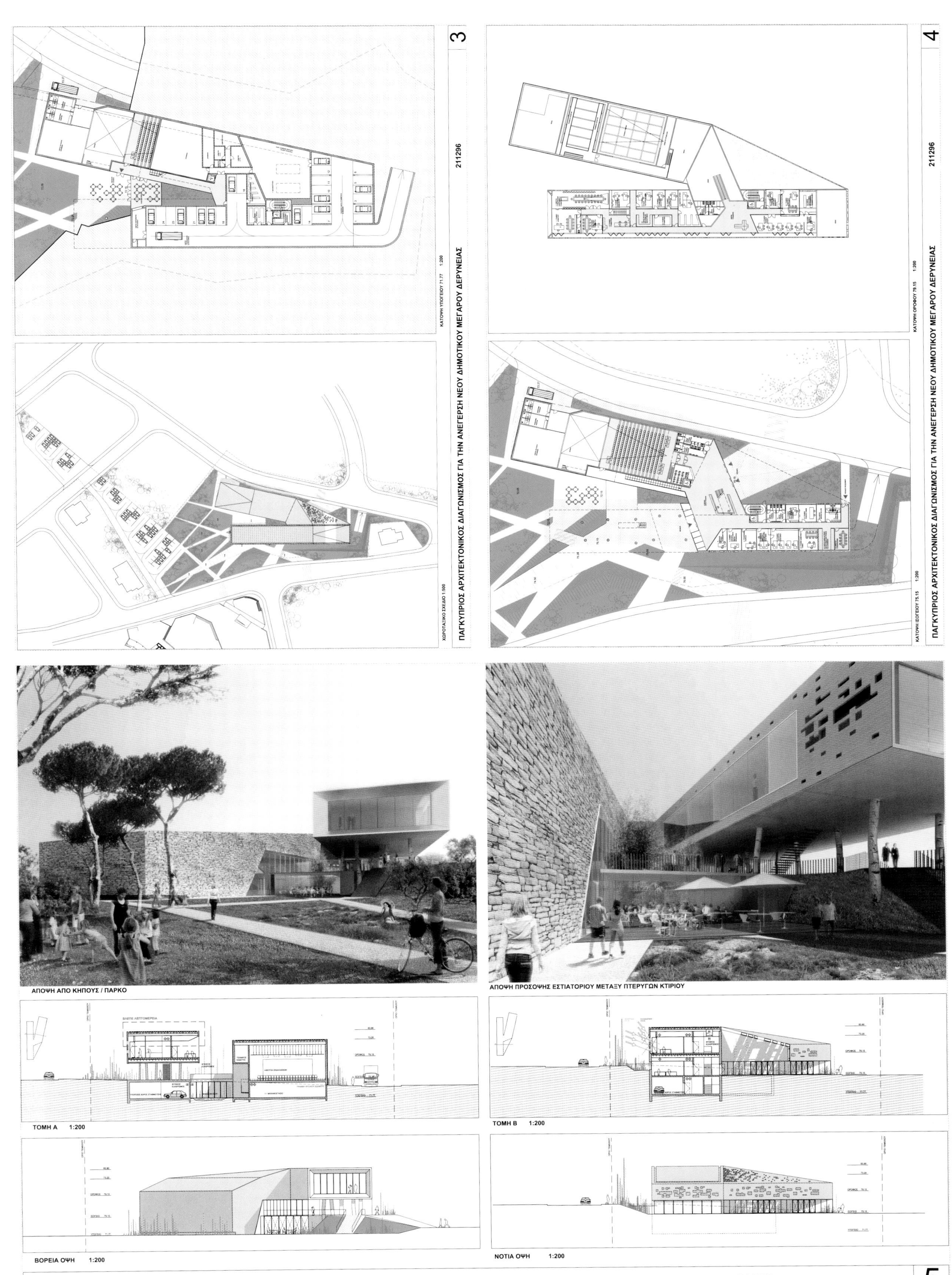
3
211296
ΚΑΤΟΨΗ ΥΠΟΓΕΙΟΥ 71.77 1:200
ΧΩΡΟΤΑΞΙΚΟ ΣΧΕΔΙΟ 1:500
ΠΑΓΚΥΠΡΙΟΣ ΑΡΧΙΤΕΚΤΟΝΙΚΟΣ ΔΙΑΓΩΝΙΣΜΟΣ ΓΙΑ ΤΗΝ ΑΝΕΓΕΡΣΗ ΝΕΟΥ ΔΗΜΟΤΙΚΟΥ ΜΕΓΑΡΟΥ ΔΕΡΥΝΕΙΑΣ
4
211296
ΚΑΤΟΨΗ ΟΡΟΦΟΥ 79.15 1:200
ΚΑΤΟΨΗ ΙΣΟΓΕΙΟΥ 75.15 1:200
ΠΑΓΚΥΠΡΙΟΣ ΑΡΧΙΤΕΚΤΟΝΙΚΟΣ ΔΙΑΓΩΝΙΣΜΟΣ ΓΙΑ ΤΗΝ ΑΝΕΓΕΡΣΗ ΝΕΟΥ ΔΗΜΟΤΙΚΟΥ ΜΕΓΑΡΟΥ ΔΕΡΥΝΕΙΑΣ
ΑΠΟΨΗ ΑΠΟ ΚΗΠΟΥΣ / ΠΑΡΚΟ
ΑΠΟΨΗ ΠΡΟΣΟΨΗΣ ΕΣΤΙΑΤΟΡΙΟΥ ΜΕΤΑΞΥ ΠΤΕΡΥΓΩΝ ΚΤΙΡΙΟΥ
ΤΟΜΗ Α 1:200
ΤΟΜΗ Β 1:200
ΒΟΡΕΙΑ ΟΨΗ 1:200
ΝΟΤΙΑ ΟΨΗ 1:200
ΠΑΓΚΥΠΡΙΟΣ ΑΡΧΙΤΕΚΤΟΝΙΚΟΣ ΔΙΑΓΩΝΙΣΜΟΣ ΓΙΑ ΤΗΝ ΑΝΕΓΕΡΣΗ ΝΕΟΥ ΔΗΜΟΤΙΚΟΥ ΜΕΓΑΡΟΥ ΔΕΡΥΝΕΙΑΣ
211296
5

ΑΠΟΨΗ ΕΙΣΟΔΟΥ ΑΠΟ ΝΟΤΟ

ΑΠΟΨΗ ΑΠΟ ΒΟΡΡΑ

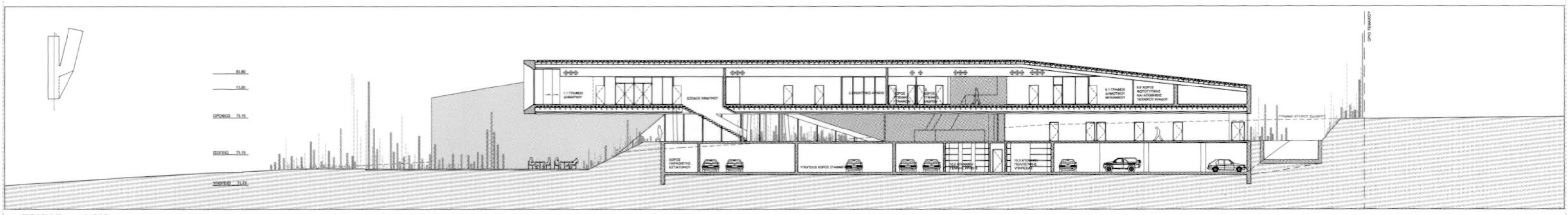

ΤΟΜΗ Γ 1:200

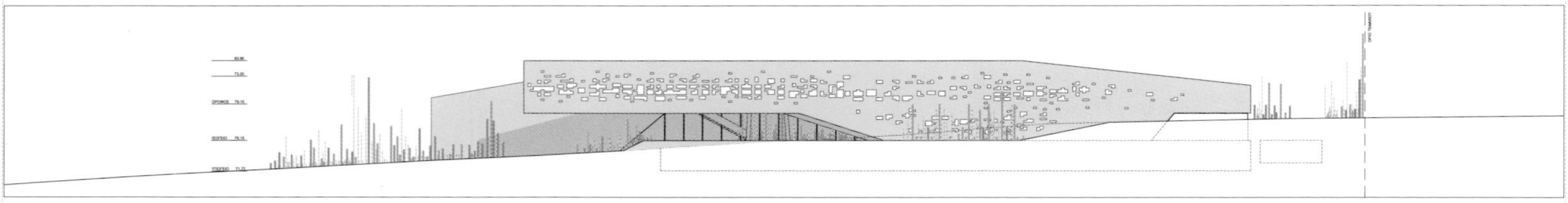

ΔΥΤΙΚΗ ΟΨΗ 1:200

ΠΑΓΚΥΠΡΙΟΣ ΑΡΧΙΤΕΚΤΟΝΙΚΟΣ ΔΙΑΓΩΝΙΣΜΟΣ ΓΙΑ ΤΗΝ ΑΝΕΓΕΡΣΗ ΝΕΟΥ ΔΗΜΟΤΙΚΟΥ ΜΕΓΑΡΟΥ ΔΕΡΥΝΕΙΑΣ 211296 6

ΑΠΟΨΗ ΧΩΡΟΥ ΥΠΟΔΟΧΗΣ

ΑΠΟΨΗ ΓΡΑΦΕΙΟΥ ΔΗΜΑΡΧΟΥ ΚΑΙ ΔΙΠΛΟΥ ΕΞΩΤΕΡΙΚΟΥ ΚΕΛΥΦΟΥΣ

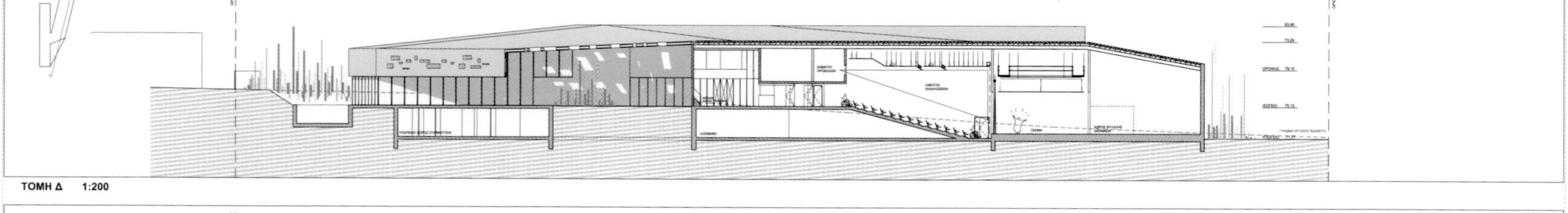

ΤΟΜΗ Δ 1:200

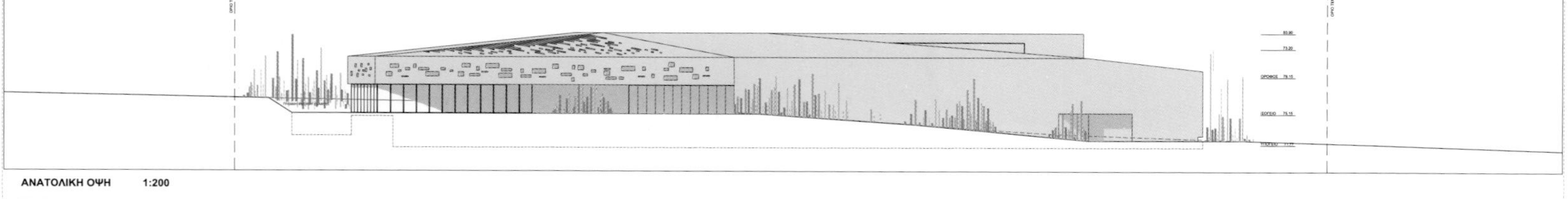

ΑΝΑΤΟΛΙΚΗ ΟΨΗ 1:200

ΠΑΓΚΥΠΡΙΟΣ ΑΡΧΙΤΕΚΤΟΝΙΚΟΣ ΔΙΑΓΩΝΙΣΜΟΣ ΓΙΑ ΤΗΝ ΑΝΕΓΕΡΣΗ ΝΕΟΥ ΔΗΜΟΤΙΚΟΥ ΜΕΓΑΡΟΥ ΔΕΡΥΝΕΙΑΣ 211296 7

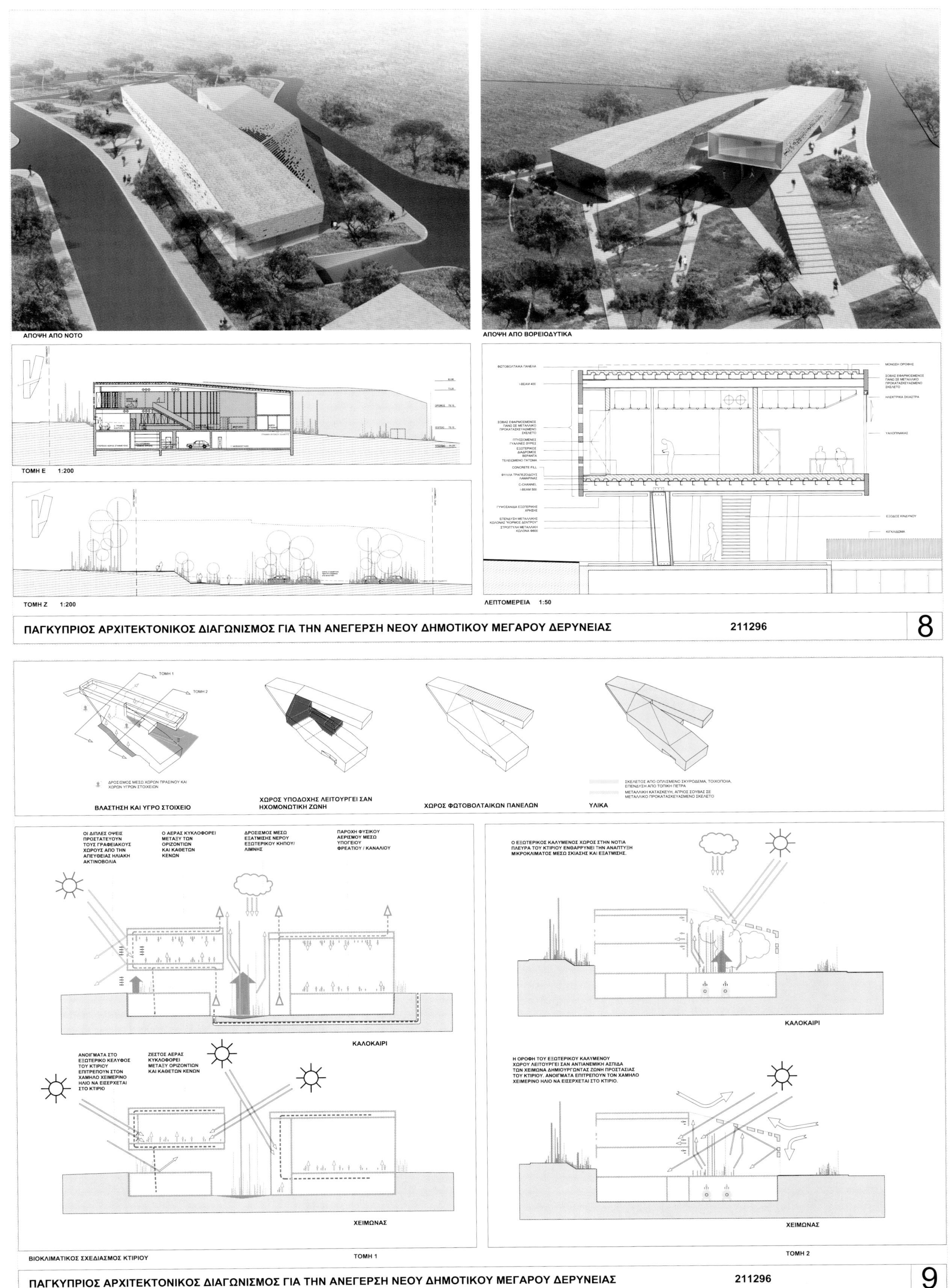
ΑΠΟΨΗ ΑΠΟ ΝΟΤΟ
ΑΠΟΨΗ ΑΠΟ ΒΟΡΕΙΟΔΥΤΙΚΑ
ΤΟΜΗ Ε 1:200
ΤΟΜΗ Ζ 1:200
ΛΕΠΤΟΜΕΡΕΙΑ 1:50
ΠΑΓΚΥΠΡΙΟΣ ΑΡΧΙΤΕΚΤΟΝΙΚΟΣ ΔΙΑΓΩΝΙΣΜΟΣ ΓΙΑ ΤΗΝ ΑΝΕΓΕΡΣΗ ΝΕΟΥ ΔΗΜΟΤΙΚΟΥ ΜΕΓΑΡΟΥ ΔΕΡΥΝΕΙΑΣ
211296
8
ΒΛΑΣΤΗΣΗ ΚΑΙ ΥΓΡΟ ΣΤΟΙΧΕΙΟ
ΧΩΡΟΣ ΥΠΟΔΟΧΗΣ ΛΕΙΤΟΥΡΓΕΙ ΣΑΝ ΗΧΟΜΟΝΩΤΙΚΗ ΖΩΝΗ
ΧΩΡΟΣ ΦΩΤΟΒΟΛΤΑΙΚΩΝ ΠΑΝΕΛΩΝ
ΥΛΙΚΑ
ΟΙ ΔΙΠΛΕΣ ΟΨΕΙΣ ΠΡΟΣΤΑΤΕΥΟΥΝ ΤΟΥΣ ΓΡΑΦΕΙΑΚΟΥΣ ΧΩΡΟΥΣ ΑΠΟ ΤΗΝ ΑΠΕΥΘΕΙΑΣ ΗΛΙΑΚΗ ΑΚΤΙΝΟΒΟΛΙΑ
Ο ΑΕΡΑΣ ΚΥΚΛΟΦΟΡΕΙ ΜΕΤΑΞΥ ΤΩΝ ΟΡΙΖΟΝΤΙΩΝ ΚΑΙ ΚΑΘΕΤΩΝ ΚΕΝΩΝ
ΔΡΟΣΙΣΜΟΣ ΜΕΣΩ ΕΞΑΤΜΙΣΗΣ ΝΕΡΟΥ ΕΞΩΤΕΡΙΚΟΥ ΚΗΠΟΥ/ ΛΙΜΝΗΣ
ΠΑΡΟΧΗ ΦΥΣΙΚΟΥ ΑΕΡΙΣΜΟΥ ΜΕΣΩ ΥΠΟΓΕΙΟΥ ΦΡΕΑΤΙΟΥ / ΚΑΝΑΛΙΟΥ
ΚΑΛΟΚΑΙΡΙ
ΑΝΟΙΓΜΑΤΑ ΣΤΟ ΕΞΩΤΕΡΙΚΟ ΚΕΛΥΦΟΣ ΤΟΥ ΚΤΙΡΙΟΥ ΕΠΙΤΡΕΠΟΥΝ ΣΤΟΝ ΧΑΜΗΛΟ ΧΕΙΜΕΡΙΝΟ ΗΛΙΟ ΝΑ ΕΙΣΕΡΧΕΤΑΙ ΣΤΟ ΚΤΙΡΙΟ
ΖΕΣΤΟΣ ΑΕΡΑΣ ΚΥΚΛΟΦΟΡΕΙ ΜΕΤΑΞΥ ΟΡΙΖΟΝΤΙΩΝ ΚΑΙ ΚΑΘΕΤΩΝ ΚΕΝΩΝ
ΧΕΙΜΩΝΑΣ
Ο ΕΞΩΤΕΡΙΚΟΣ ΚΑΛΥΜΕΝΟΣ ΧΩΡΟΣ ΣΤΗΝ ΝΟΤΙΑ ΠΛΕΥΡΑ ΤΟΥ ΚΤΙΡΙΟΥ ΕΝΘΑΡΡΥΝΕΙ ΤΗΝ ΑΝΑΠΤΥΞΗ ΜΙΚΡΟΚΛΙΜΑΤΟΣ ΜΕΣΩ ΣΚΙΑΣΗΣ ΚΑΙ ΕΞΑΤΜΙΣΗΣ.
ΚΑΛΟΚΑΙΡΙ
Η ΟΡΟΦΗ ΤΟΥ ΕΞΩΤΕΡΙΚΟΥ ΚΑΛΥΜΕΝΟΥ ΧΩΡΟΥ ΛΕΙΤΟΥΡΓΕΙ ΣΑΝ ΑΝΤΙΑΝΕΜΙΚΗ ΑΣΠΙΔΑ ΤΩΝ ΧΕΙΜΩΝΑ ΔΗΜΙΟΥΡΓΩΝΤΑΣ ΖΩΝΗ ΠΡΟΣΤΑΣΙΑΣ ΤΟΥ ΚΤΙΡΙΟΥ. ΑΝΟΙΓΜΑΤΑ ΕΠΙΤΡΕΠΟΥΝ ΤΟΝ ΧΑΜΗΛΟ ΧΕΙΜΕΡΙΝΟ ΗΛΙΟ ΝΑ ΕΙΣΕΡΧΕΤΑΙ ΣΤΟ ΚΤΙΡΙΟ.
ΧΕΙΜΩΝΑΣ
ΒΙΟΚΛΙΜΑΤΙΚΟΣ ΣΧΕΔΙΑΣΜΟΣ ΚΤΙΡΙΟΥ
ΤΟΜΗ 1
ΤΟΜΗ 2
ΠΑΓΚΥΠΡΙΟΣ ΑΡΧΙΤΕΚΤΟΝΙΚΟΣ ΔΙΑΓΩΝΙΣΜΟΣ ΓΙΑ ΤΗΝ ΑΝΕΓΕΡΣΗ ΝΕΟΥ ΔΗΜΟΤΙΚΟΥ ΜΕΓΑΡΟΥ ΔΕΡΥΝΕΙΑΣ
211296
9

122 A101 Urban Block | *b4architects*

Location : Moscow, Russia
Object : A101 Urban Block
Client : Masshtab Company
Area :14000 sqm

Program : Housing, Services, Commercial, Open Spaces
Project Team : Gianluca Evels & Stefania Papitto - B4architects With Sebastiano Maccarrone

P8E13M

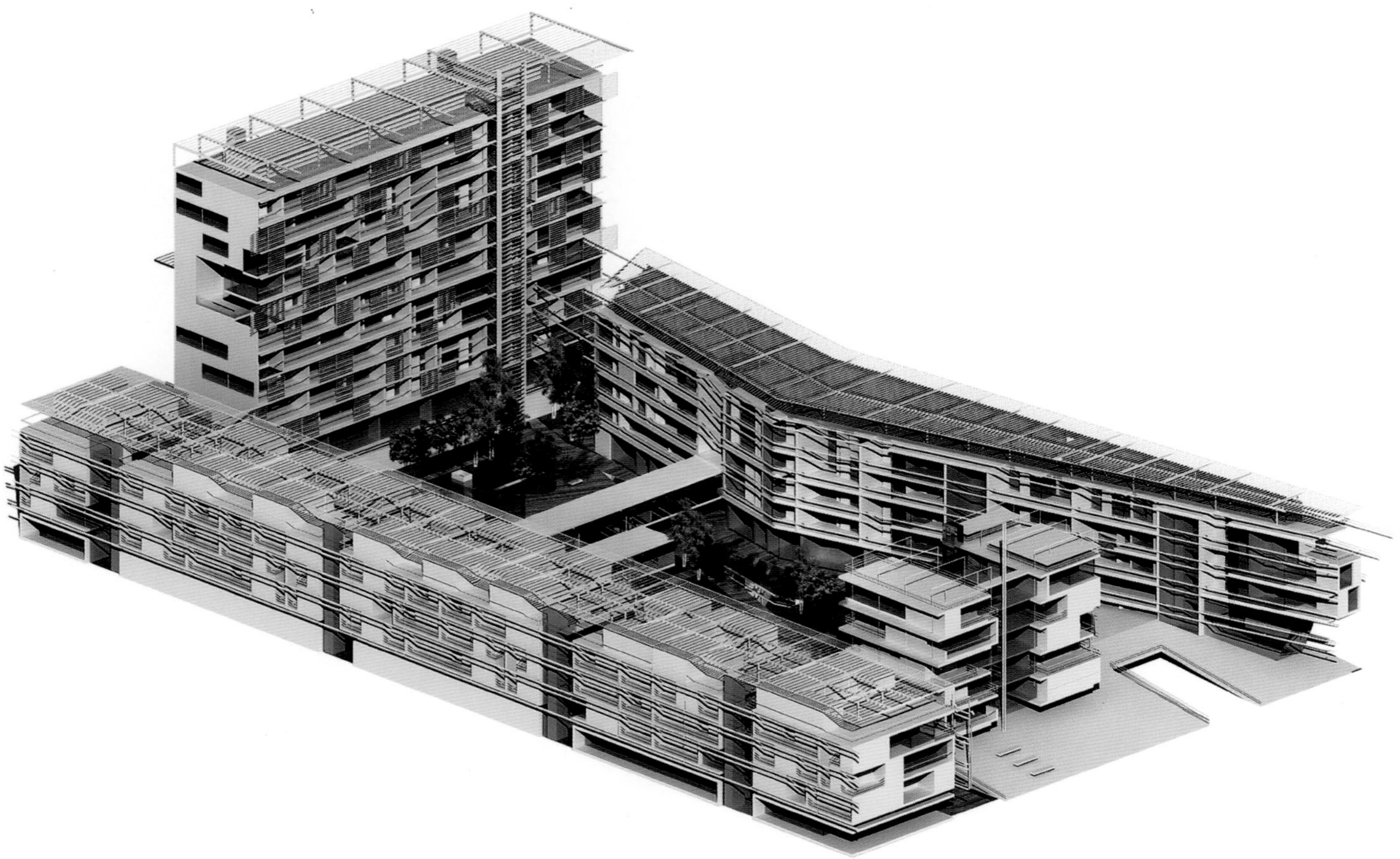

BE IN SUNSHINE

The city, the part of the landscape in which each individual identifies himself, is a world free of known limitations, which is based mainly on the relationship between the homes from which their inhabitants can have an idea of the world. The isotropic space of the board of the masterplan is accepted with the resulting a regular grid on plan and elevation on which some 'perturbations' are introduced: they can generate a place where people appreciates the complexity of contemporary life as aesthetic experience. On this watermark 17 variations are designed for the 4 housing typologies. These apartments are assembled with theoretically infinite number of combinations of starting. The result is a residential block that adapts itself to the variation of the context conditions and exposure to the sunlight. Common areas and distribution are designed as real public spaces where the rituals of the meeting need to be considered. The courtyard is a wide semi-public garden, with controlled accessibility, that, with all the green areas on the terrace, becomes an integrated system that involves every apartment. The project is a thoughtful making of spaces around the original archetype of fence, 'temenos' (τέμενος), an enclosing a space where can be possible to implement that innate sense of living of every human being.

A1

GROSS FLOOR AREA: 14.000 M^2
NET/GROSS FLOOR AREA RATIO: 0,87
FACADE/FLOOR AREA RATIO: 0,59
ENTRY CODE: P8E13M

low density - 14.000 sqm

possible development/alternative
high density - 28.000 sqm

sunlight
equinox

A1 low density, type1
B1 higt density, type1

A2 low density, type2

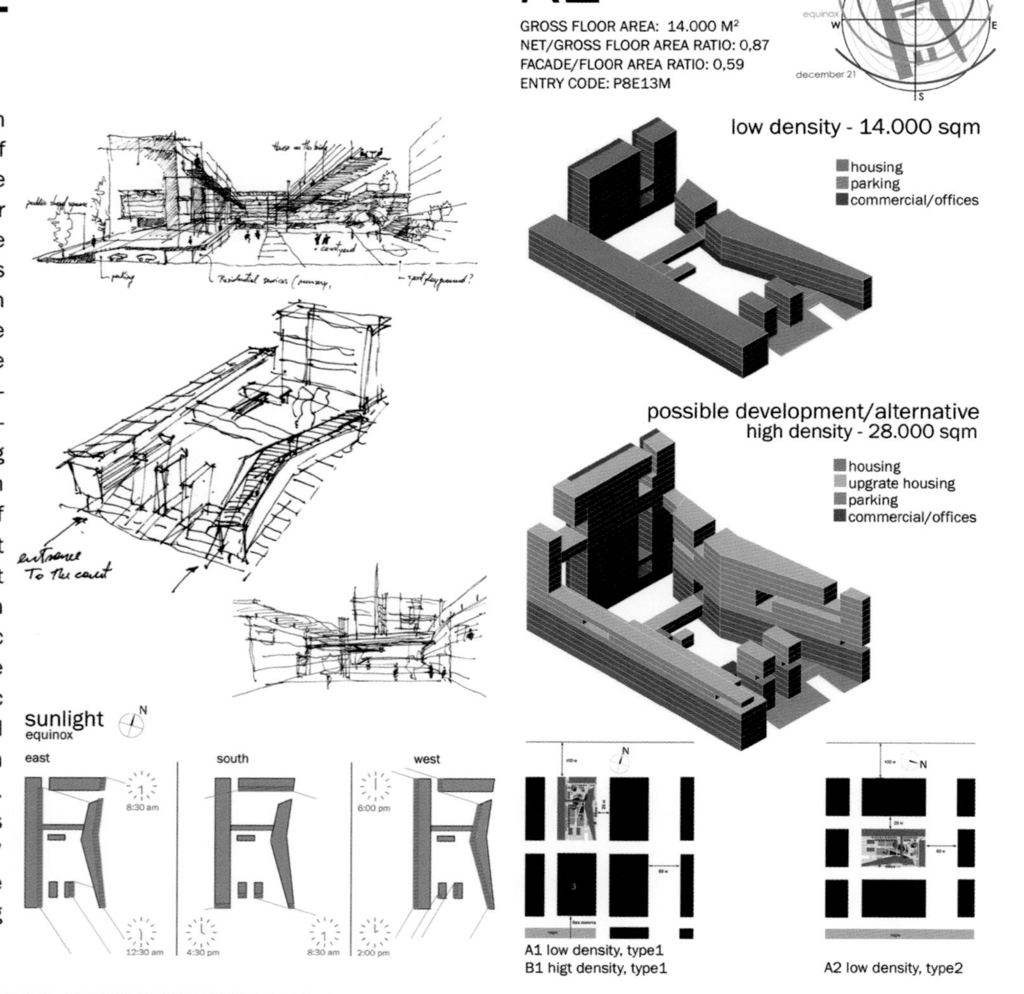

P8E13M

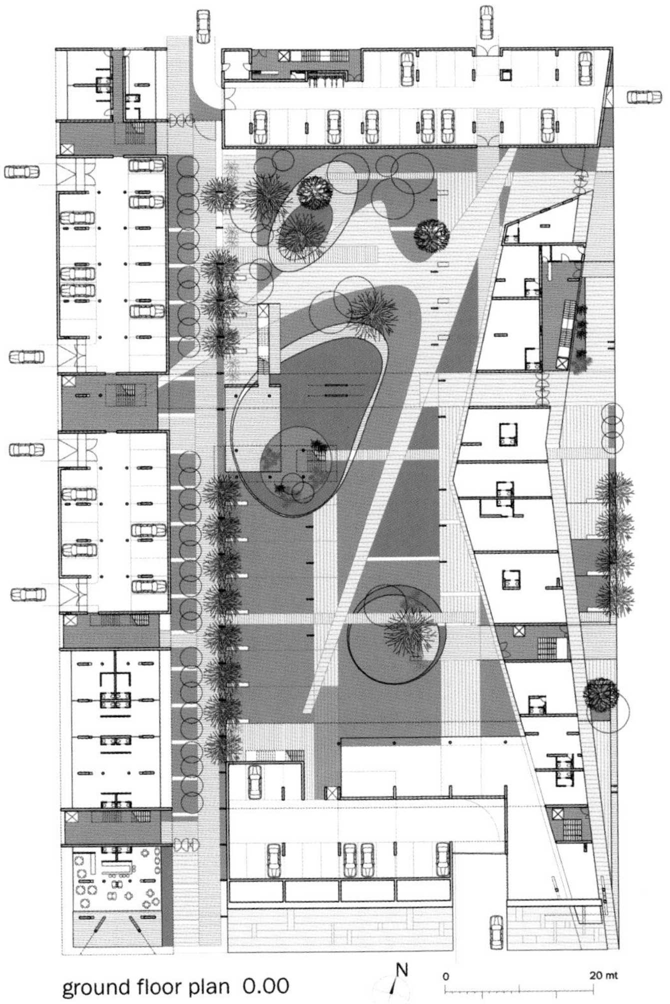

P8E13M

ground floor plan 0.00

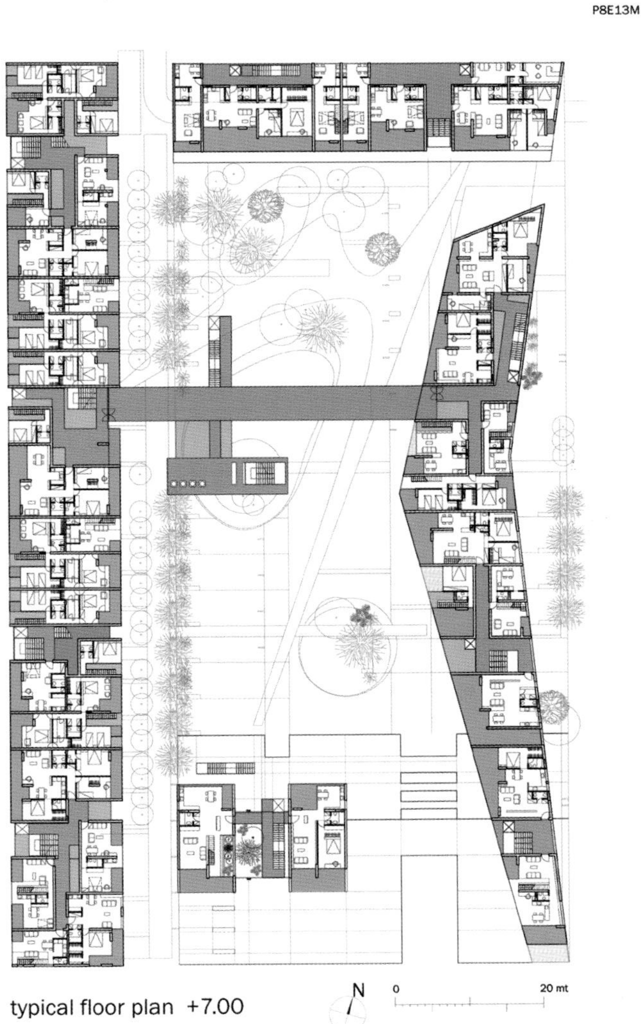

N

0 20 mt

typical floor plan +7.00

N

0 20 mt

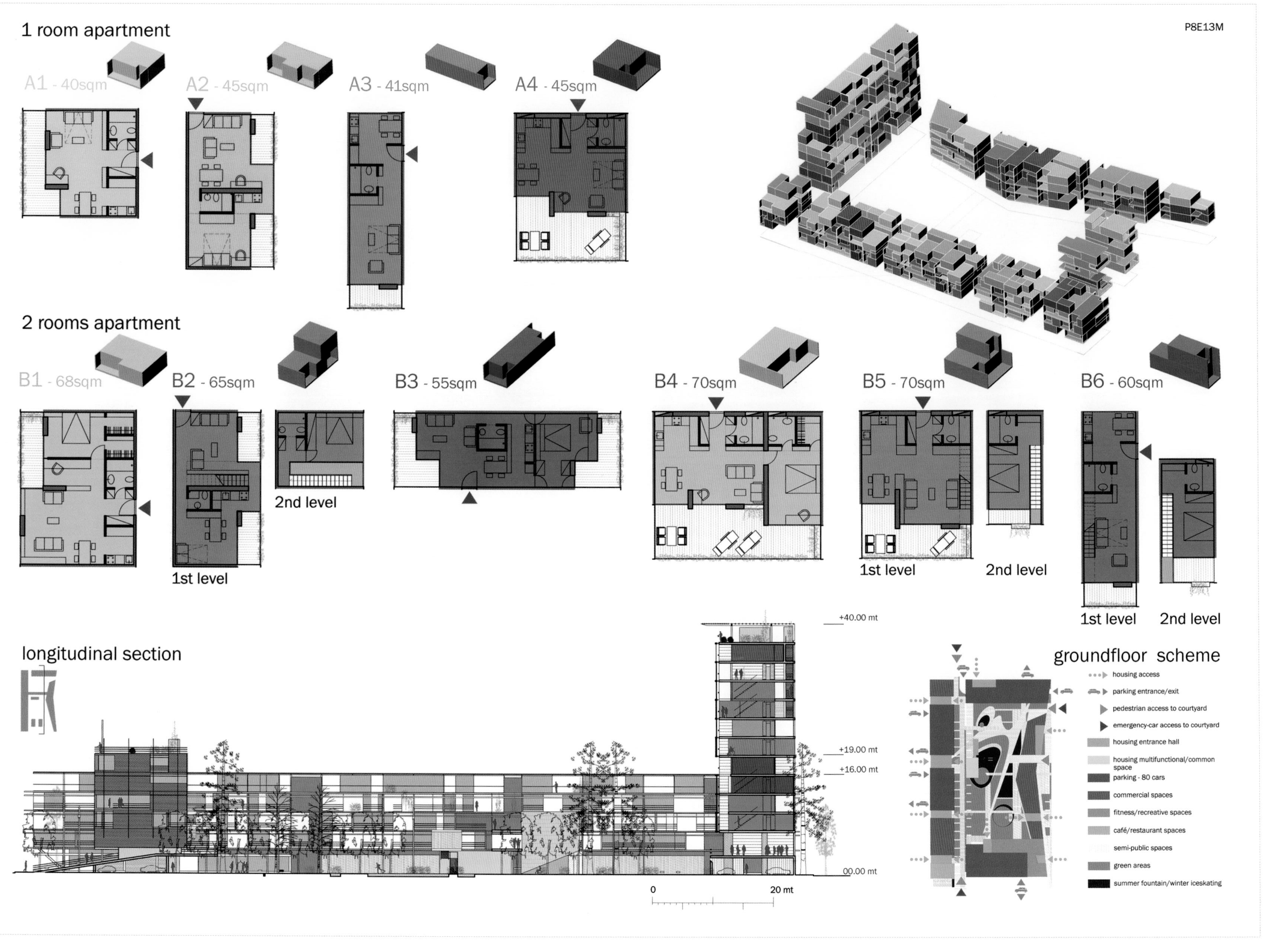
P8E13M
1 room apartment
A1 - 40sqm
A2 - 45sqm
A3 - 41sqm
A4 - 45sqm
2 rooms apartment
B1 - 68sqm
B2 - 65sqm
1st level
2nd level
B3 - 55sqm
B4 - 70sqm
B5 - 70sqm
1st level
2nd level
B6 - 60sqm
1st level
2nd level
longitudinal section
+40.00 mt
+19.00 mt
+16.00 mt
00.00 mt
0
20 mt
groundfloor scheme
housing access
parking entrance/exit
pedestrian access to courtyard
emergency-car access to courtyard
housing entrance hall
housing multifunctional/common space
parking - 80 cars
commercial spaces
fitness/recreative spaces
café/restaurant spaces
semi-public spaces
green areas
summer fountain/winter iceskating

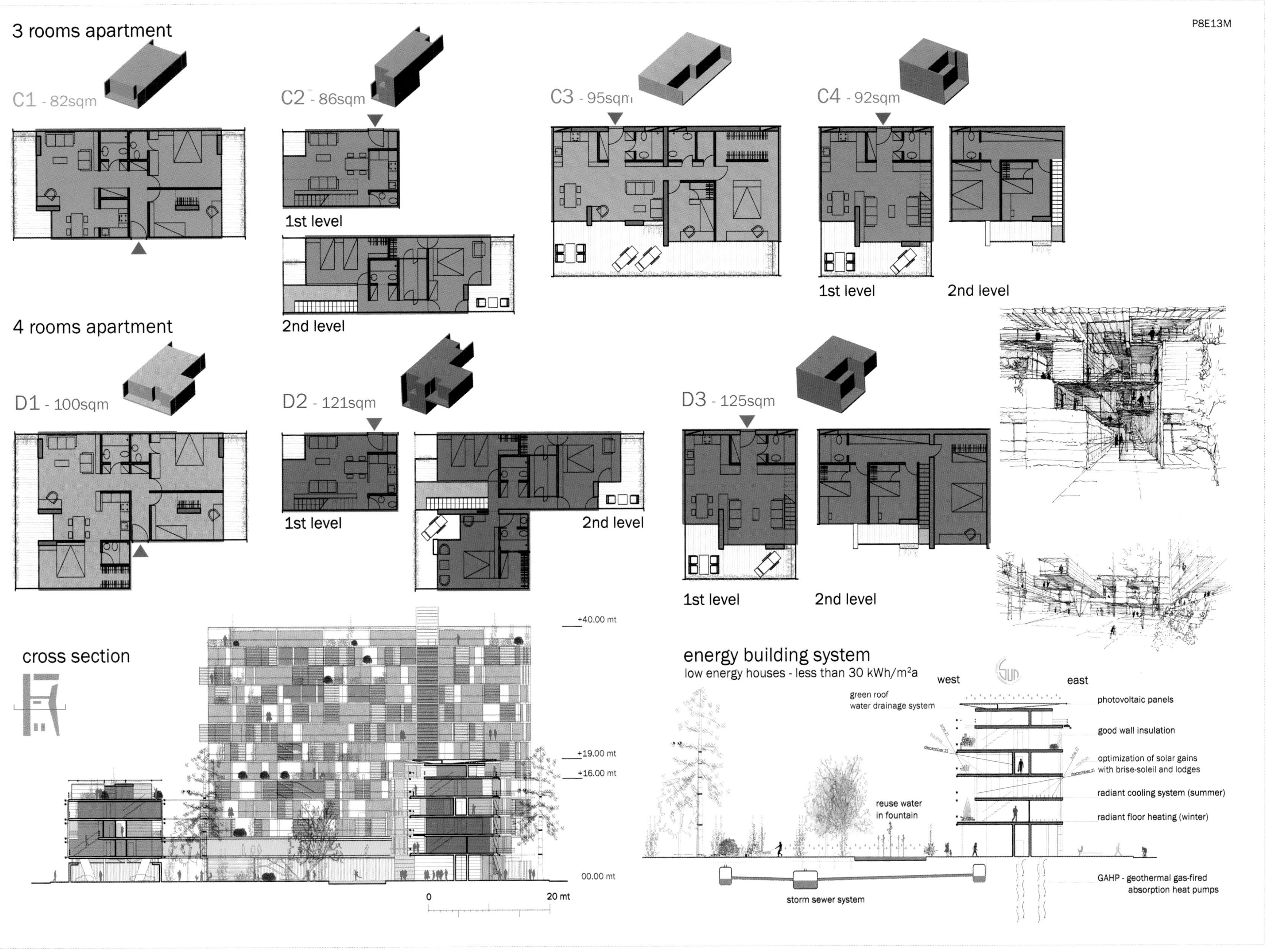
P8E13M
3 rooms apartment
C1 - 82sqm
C2 - 86sqm
1st level
2nd level
C3 - 95sqm
C4 - 92sqm
1st level
2nd level
4 rooms apartment
D1 - 100sqm
D2 - 121sqm
1st level
2nd level
D3 - 125sqm
1st level
2nd level
cross section
+40.00 mt
+19.00 mt
+16.00 mt
00.00 mt
0
20 mt
energy building system
low energy houses - less than 30 kWh/m²a
west
east
green roof
water drainage system
photovoltaic panels
good wall insulation
optimization of solar gains
with brise-soleil and lodges
radiant cooling system (summer)
radiant floor heating (winter)
reuse water
in fountain
storm sewer system
GAHP - geothermal gas-fired
absorption heat pumps

123 Alibaba | *XCOOP*

Type : Mix Use(Commercial, Office)
Size : 81.400m²
Location : Shenzhen(People Republic of China)
Year : 2011

CONCEPT DESIGN OF ALIBABA HEADQUARTERS IN SHENZHEN
阿里巴巴深圳大厦 设计概念方案

bird view 鸟瞰图

concept 概念图解

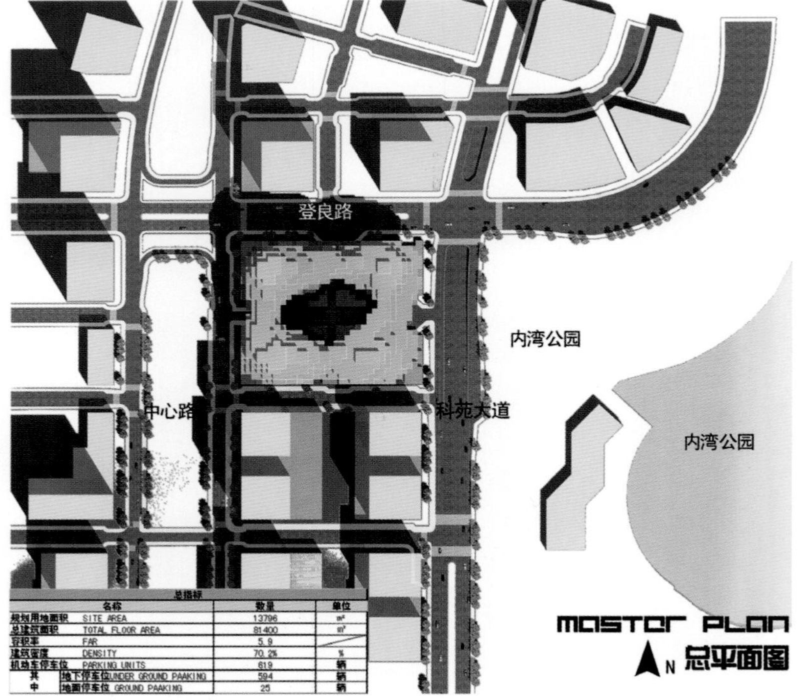

总指标			
名称		数量	单位
规划用地面积	SITE AREA	13796	m²
总建筑面积	TOTAL FLOOR AREA	81400	m²
容积率	FAR	5.9	
建筑密度	DENSITY	70.2%	%
机动车停车位	PARKING UNITS	619	辆
其中	地下停车位 UNDER GROUND PAAKING	594	辆
	地面停车位 GROUND PAAKING	25	辆

CONCEPT

GENESIS OF THE PROJECT:

The design of Alibaba's headquarter reflects the spirit of the Company: a multitude of individual enterprises projecting their dreams in a world of possibilities, based on shared values and with an outstanding regard to the common interest.

概念-起源

阿里巴巴总部的设计体现了其精神实质：为众多的中小企业提供一个可实现梦想、充满各种可能性的世界。在此，大家有共同的关注点，认同相同的价值。

While growing into a Business Cloud, the building liberates the ground for common use: the plinth is developed in the logic of a risen landscape. Its different levels are accessible to the community and provide a solid green connection between the different landscape's features around the site.
The floating Mass is organized to maximize views from the offices, the natural light and the ventilation of each working space.

升腾的"商务云"造型让地面可留作公共用途；裙房是升起来的景观，公众可到达不同高度的平台。这种处理可将基地周围不同特征的景观充分联系起来。飘浮的主体中，空间组织尽量将景观界面最大化，同时保证每个工作空间中自然光和通风的最优效果。

The building is designed to have a strong unitary identity while, at the same time, its structure allows for different organizations and subdivisions of the working space. Each floor plate can be integrated in one company or be split and leased to different ones.
建筑设计为有很强的单元特征，同时其结构允许办公空间不同的组织构架和划分。每层可以合在一起为一个公司所用，也可以分开来租给不同的公司。

section a-a A-A剖面图

CONCEPT DESIGN OF ALIBABA HEADQUARTERS IN SHENZHEN
阿里巴巴深圳大厦 设计概念方案

LANDSCAPE:

The masterplan of the Shenzhen bay focuses on the restoration of the ecosystem of the bay and the creation of modern park structures to enrich the lives of the citizens. Within this higher goal, the project plays a key role as a transition between the urban structures in the West towards the green and more natural areas towards the Shenzhen bay. Providing a pleasant public space for the urban residents, the building forms a contribution to the awareness of valuable green space within the city.

On a lower scale the building provides a green and slow traffic connection from the inner Sea and the natural area on the East and towards the urban linear park along the Zhong Xin Road on the West side. The building forms a magnet for people to walk trough, or to enjoy the view over the bay.

The plinth of the development is conceived as a risen landscape and allows flows of pedestrian to freely access the inner natural areas both at ground level and above. By minimizing the building substance on the ground and relocating it at higher levels, a significant amount of space is made free for public use: in the plinth area, retail and vegetation are working together in a synergy enhancing the possibility for a pleasant shopping experience. A diagonal pedestrian bridge makes it possible to make use of the public space without having to cross the branch road on street level.

景观

深圳湾的总体规划重点在于恢复生态系统，同时创造现代公园系统来丰富市民的生活。在这个较高的目标下，本项目在从城市西部向更自然的深圳湾区域过渡中扮演着关键的角色。在为城市居民提供舒适的公共空间的同时，建筑也充分体现了绿化空间在城市中的价值。

在较低的部分，建筑提供了从东面内海自然区域到西面沿中心路的线状城市公园之间绿色、轻缓的交通联系。建筑物吸引人们穿过其中，享受观赏湾区景色的乐趣。

裙房部分的构思源于"升起来的景观"，这样的设计业让人行流线可自由地到达内部，包括地面和上部的自然绿化区域。有相当数量的空间可让公众自由使用：裙房部分，商业以及绿化共同强化了愉快的购物体验。对角人行天桥让人们在使用公共空间时，不用穿过城市支路。

PLAN 平面图 1: 1000

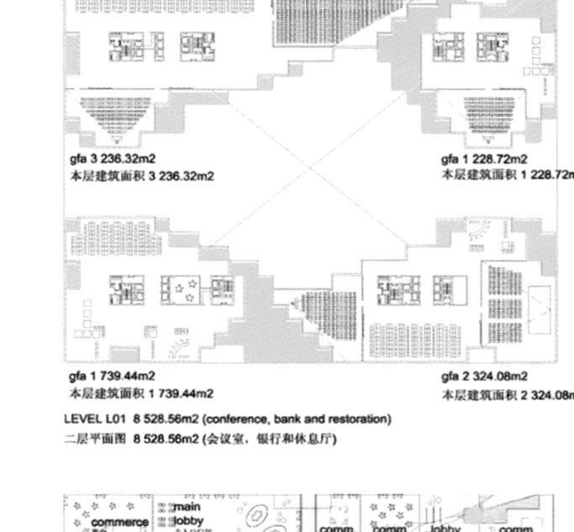

LEVEL L01 8 528.56m2 (conference, bank and restoration)
二层平面图 8 528.56m2 (会议室，银行和休息厅)

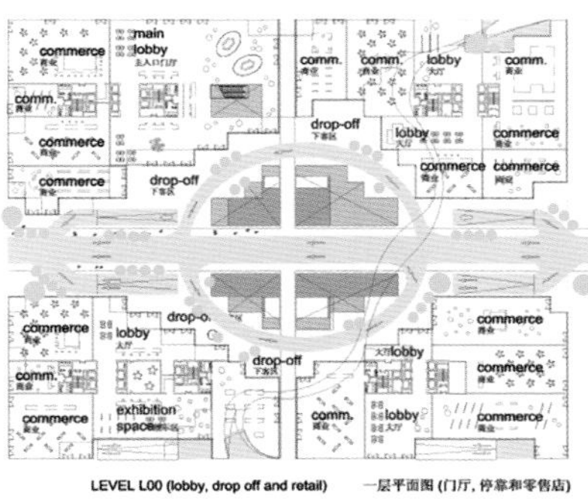

LEVEL L00 (lobby, drop off and retail) 一层平面图 (门厅，停靠和零售店)

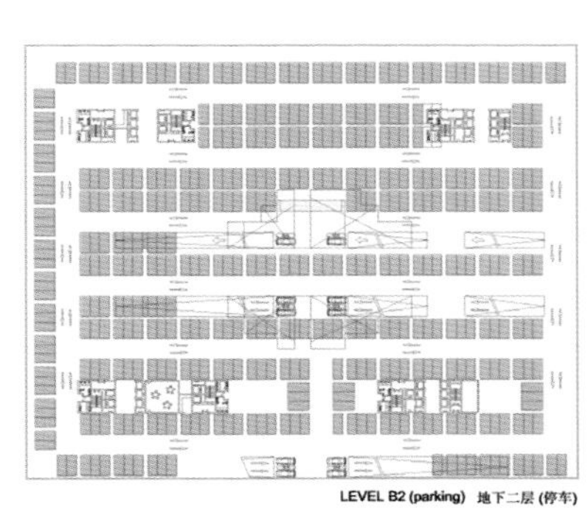

LEVEL B2 (parking) 地下二层 (停车)

LEVEL B1 (parking, retail and lobby) 地下一层 (停车，零售店和门厅)

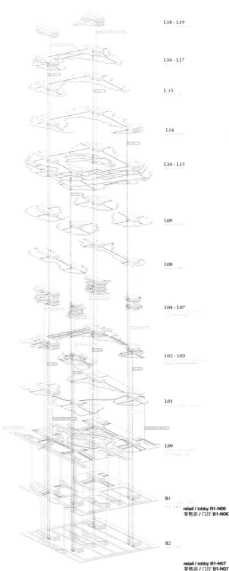

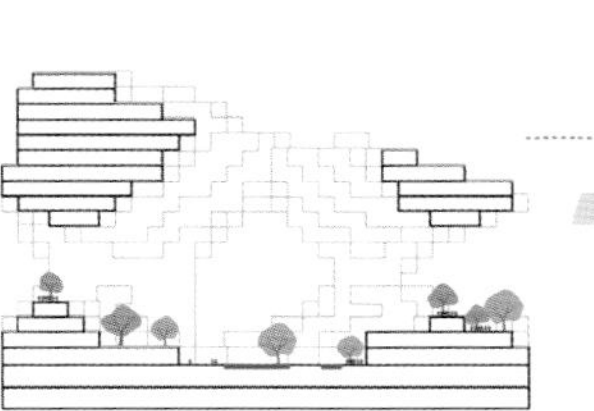

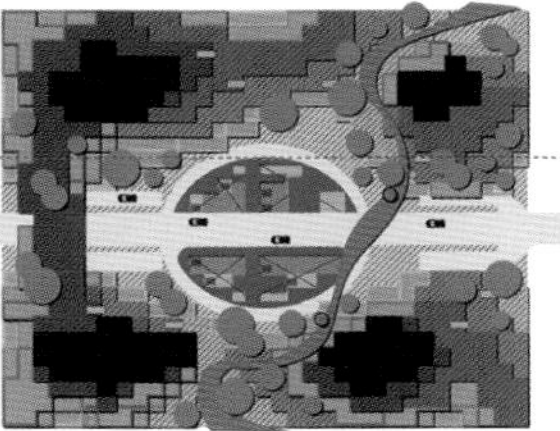

LANDSCAPE ANALYSIS 景观分析

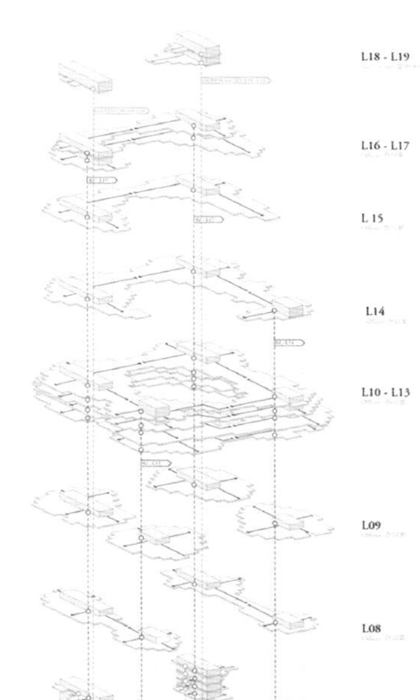

CIRCULATION 流线分析

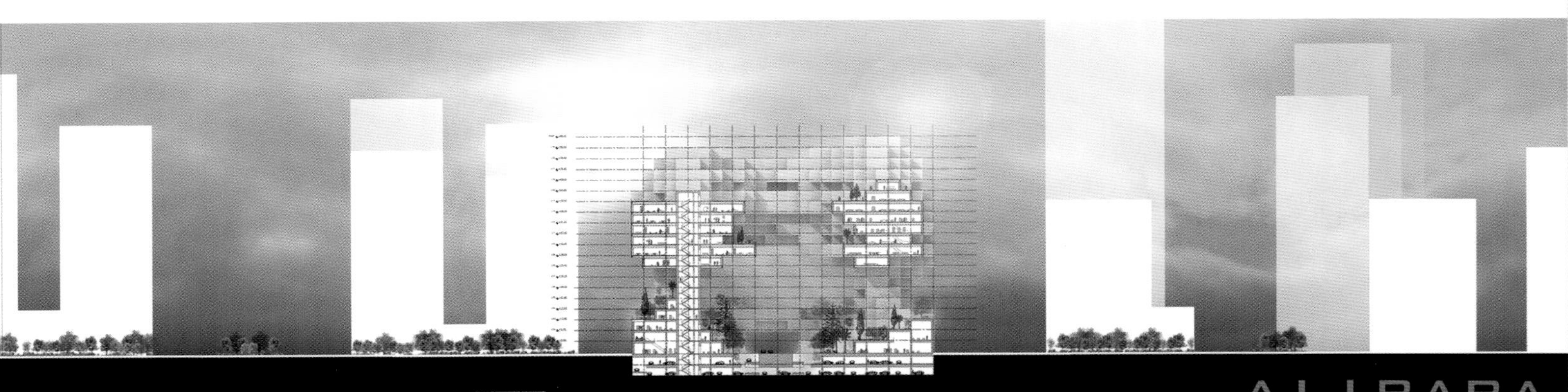

SECTION B-B B-B剖面图

CONCEPT DESIGN OF ALIBABA HEADQUARTERS IN SHENZHEN

阿里巴巴深圳大厦 设计概念方案

最幸福的员工

尽管构成建筑的簇群尺度和复杂性在增加，但它每个单元都保持了人性化的尺度，相互间可保持小范围的交流。

在支路周围设置了收集雨水的景观水池，给这片在半处于阴影中的公共空间宜人的氛围。在夏天可给该区域降温，对太阳光和灯光的反射也给公共空间和办公区在白天和晚上带来特殊的体验。
在建筑巨大的挖空部分，有露天的平台和空中花园给雇员提供互动、社交的机会。

基座区域展现了一种对于各种不同文化人群的欢迎姿态，同时象征着各种程序的集成。

阿里巴巴的员工可以很方便地在屋顶花园里参与各种活动并享受阳光生活。在这个中心位置，光与影、视觉与自然景观融合在一起，成为一个完美的、能够激发创造性的并对未来充满期待的场所。
员工的幸福指数对企业具有深远影响，进而改善个人的生活方式、幸福感、健康状况、积极性等，而一个独特新奇的建筑是达到这种效果最直接的方式。

THE HAPPIEST EMPLOYEE

Every single component gains from the union with the others: the more enterprises get together, the higher the business will fly.

Within the big void carving the building, there are open air terraces and sky gardens that offer moments of interaction and socialization to the employees.

Alibaba's employees are invited to join in and get creative through the simple act of participation on the bright life of the plinth. On this hub, light and shadow, views and nature all mix together providing the perfect place to generate ideas and positively look into the future.

Employee well-being affects a company's organization, overall: affecting a person's lifestyle, happiness, health and motivation in the working force by bringing in a curious and stimulating architecture is the simplest way to do this is to!

PLAN 平面图 1: 1000

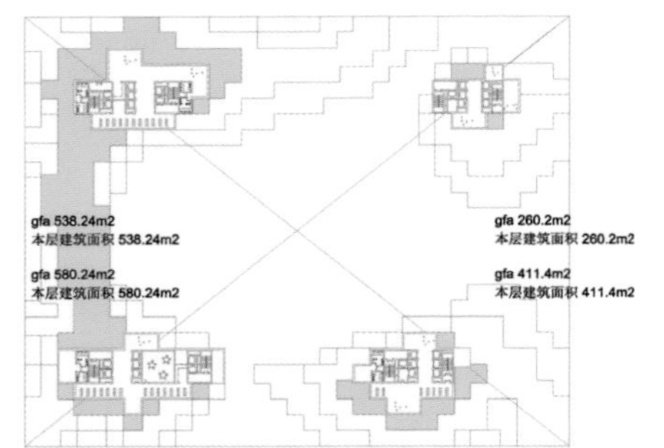

LEVEL L04 1 790.08m2 (additional facilities for employees)

五层平面图 1 790.08m2 (供员工使用的附加设施)

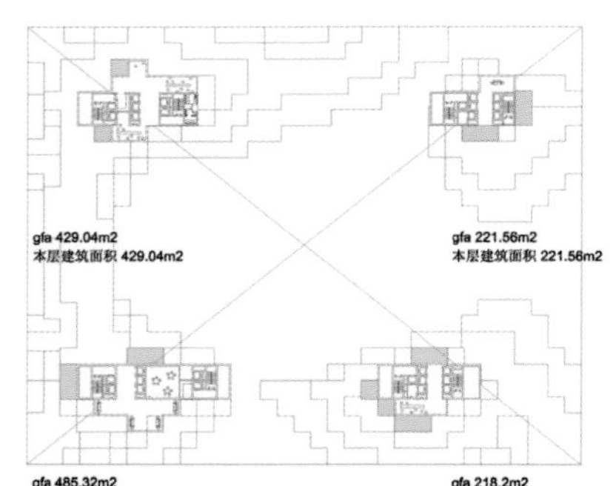

LEVEL L05 1 354.12m2 (additional facilities for employees)

六层平面图 1 354.12m2 (供员工使用的附加设施)

NORTH & SOUTH ELEVATION 北立面图和南立面图

ALIBABA

CONCEPT DESIGN OF ALIBABA HEADQUARTERS IN SHENZHEN
阿里巴巴深圳大厦 设计概念方案

PLAN 各层平面图 1: 3000

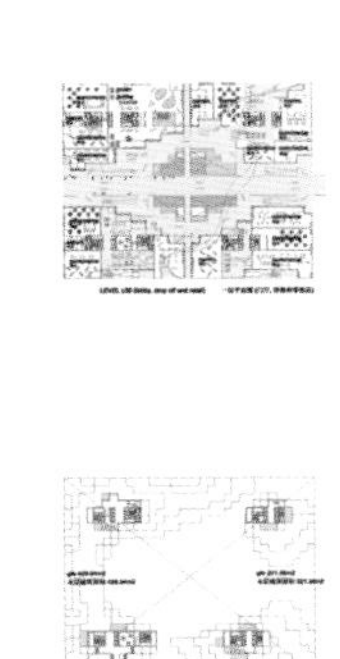
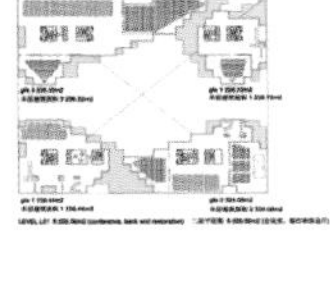

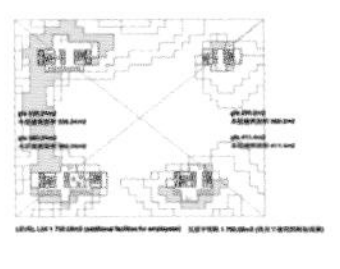

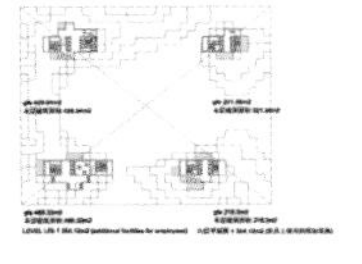
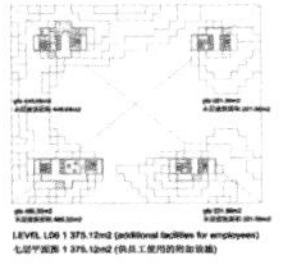
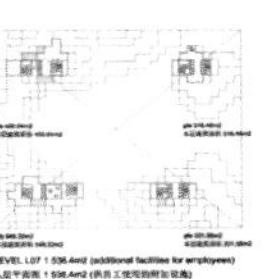

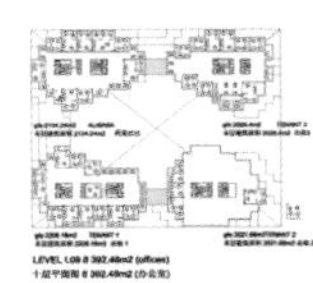

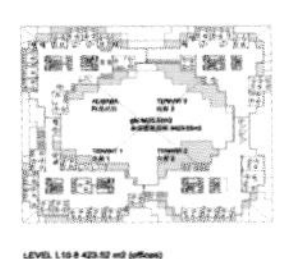
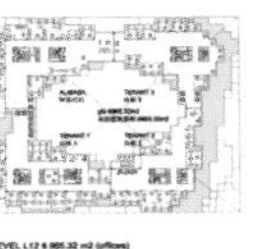
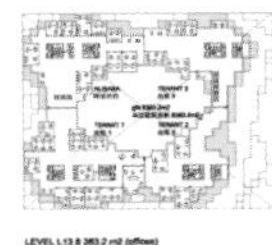
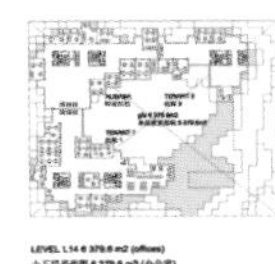
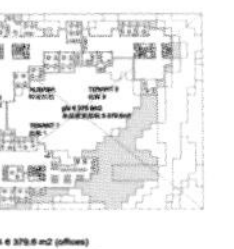

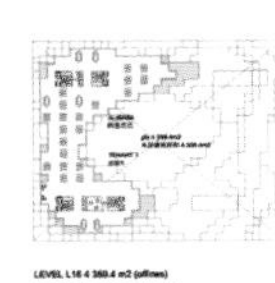
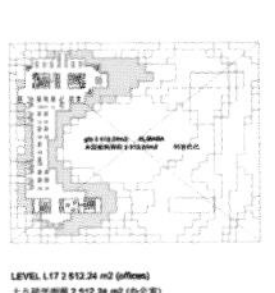
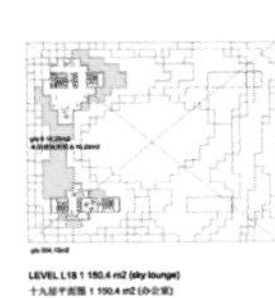
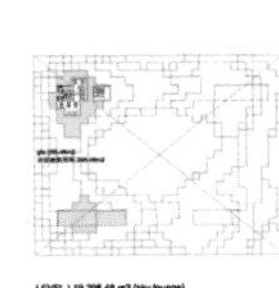

CONCLUSION:

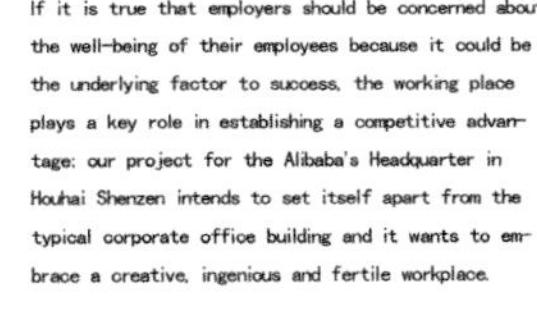

If it is true that employers should be concerned about the well-being of their employees because it could be the underlying factor to success, the working place plays a key role in establishing a competitive advantage: our project for the Alibaba's Headquarter in Houhai Shenzen intends to set itself apart from the typical corporate office building and it wants to embrace a creative, ingenious and fertile workplace.

结论:

关怀每一位员工的健康和幸福是一个企业成功的潜在因素，而工作环境的舒适程度又是其中最重要的环节：我们的设计宗旨就是为阿里巴巴的员工们创造一个不同于传统办公建筑的，更具有独特创造力的、充满活力办公环境。

WEST & EAST ELEVATION 东立面图和西立面图

ALIBABA

124 International Business Center | *Slot.*

Location : Armenia, Yerevan, Gai Avenue 14/3
Program : Business Center, Hotel, Swimming Pool, Apartments, Retail, Restaurants
Project Type : Open International Competition

Client : Avangard Motors LLC
Construction Area : 56,000m²

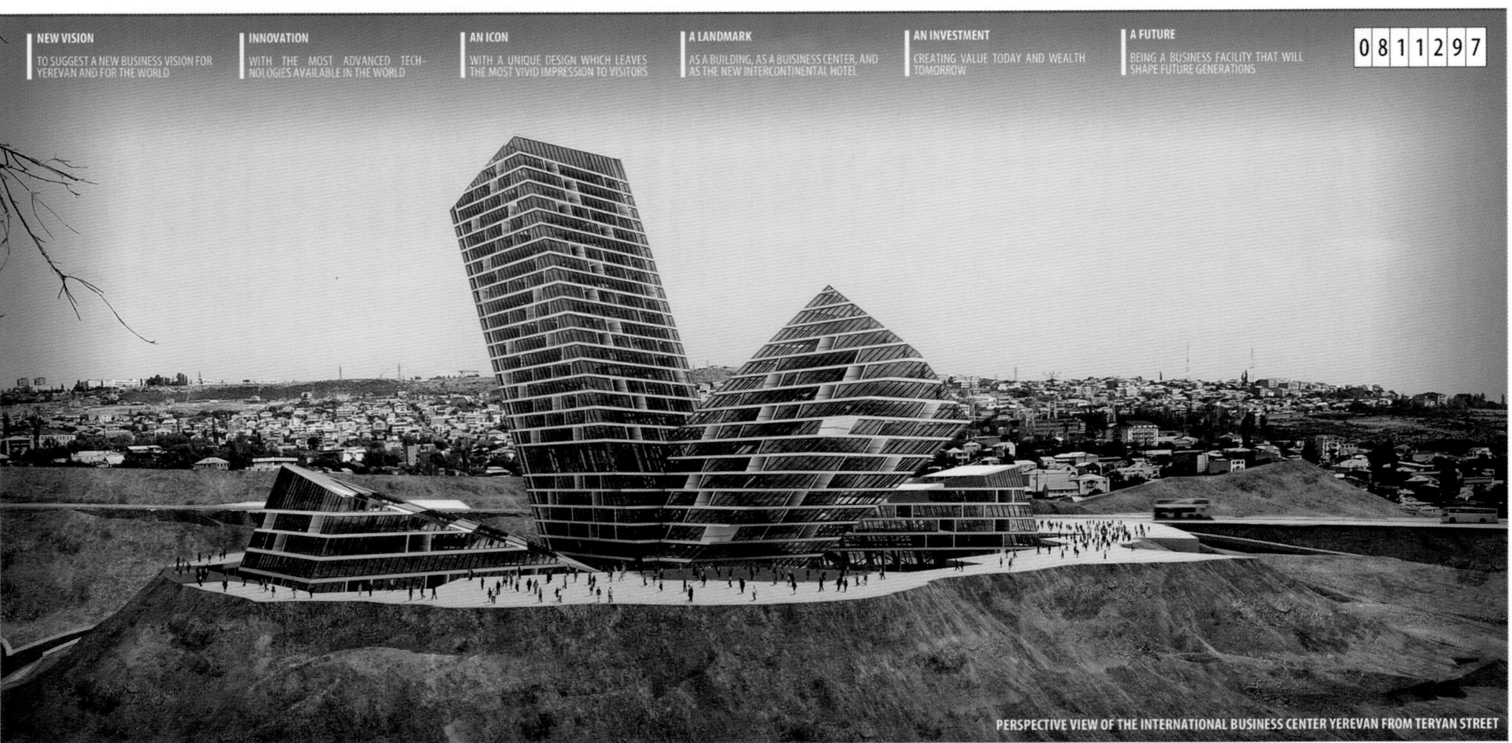

NEW VISION
TO SUGGEST A NEW BUSINESS VISION FOR YEREVAN AND FOR THE WORLD
INNOVATION
WITH THE MOST ADVANCED TECHNOLOGIES AVAILABLE IN THE WORLD
AN ICON
WITH A UNIQUE DESIGN WHICH LEAVES THE MOST VIVID IMPRESSION TO VISITORS
A LANDMARK
AS A BUILDING, AS A BUISINESS CENTER, AND AS THE NEW INTERCONTINENTAL HOTEL
AN INVESTMENT
CREATING VALUE TODAY AND WEALTH TOMORROW
A FUTURE
BEING A BUSINESS FACILITY THAT WILL SHAPE FUTURE GENERATIONS
0811297

PERSPECTIVE VIEW OF THE INTERNATIONAL BUSINESS CENTER YEREVAN FROM TERYAN STREET

CONCEPT DIAGRAMS

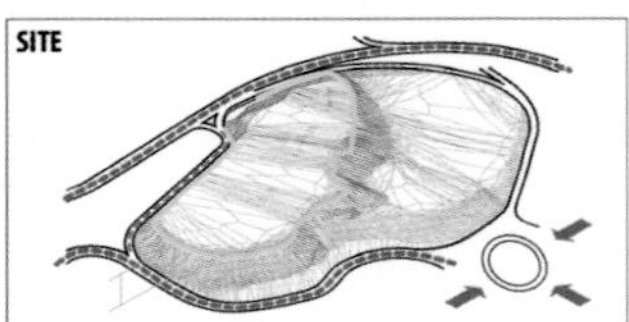

The site is located in the highest part of a plateau. The topography becomes an important element of the design solution.

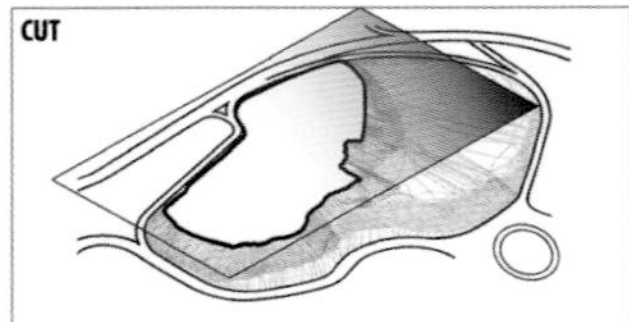

Locating an intermediate height, which can accomodate the program for accesses, the topography is cut horizontally.

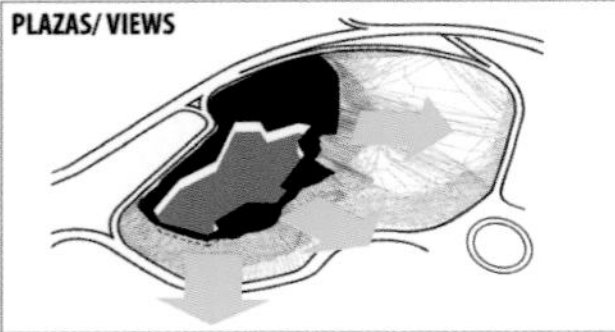

Two plazas are created by pressing the interior part of the plateau. The interior plaza becomes the heart of the building complex, while the exterior plaza convertes into a look-out terrace taking advantage of its elevation.

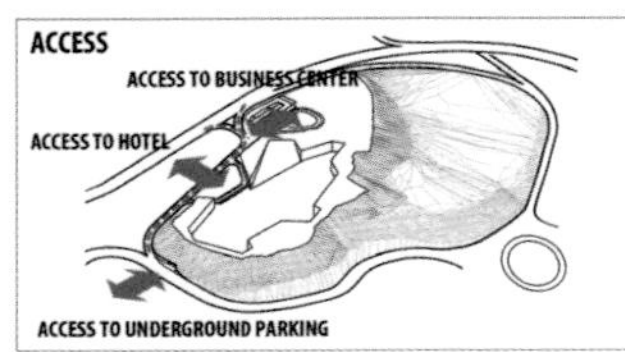

A secondary street penetrates the site at its back. This street provides access to the different programs on site.

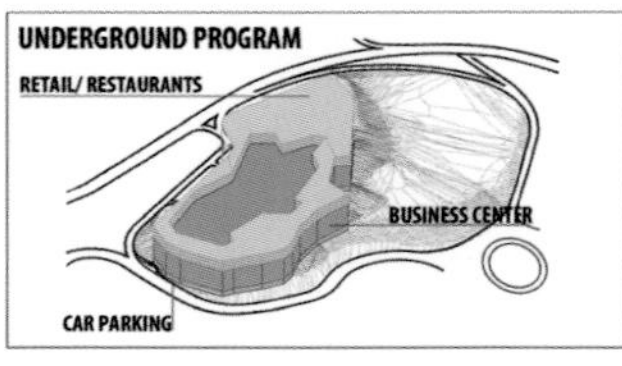

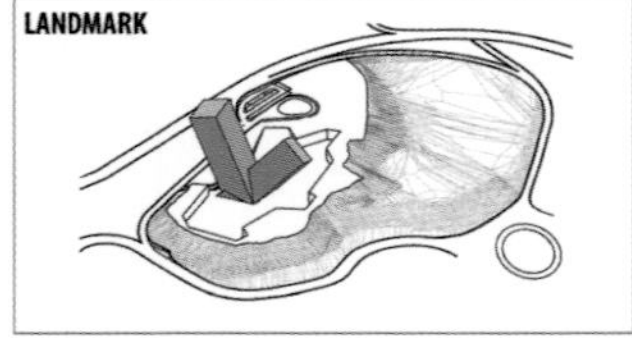

The hotel converts into the most dominant element of the building complex.

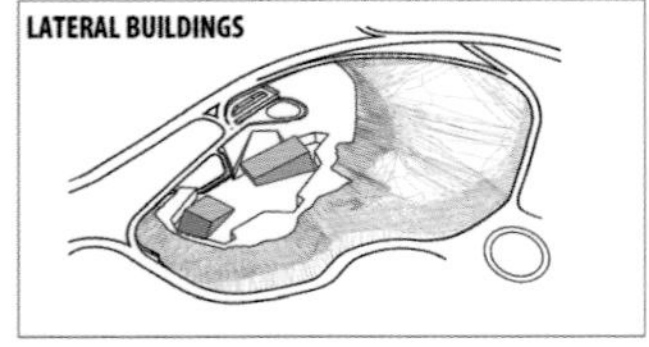

With the same formal expression, two lower volumes accomodate office space and apartments.

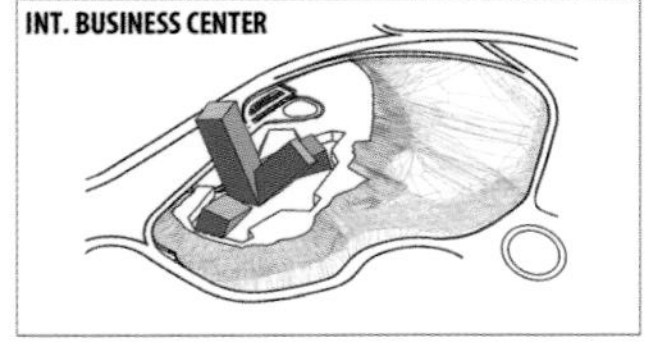

The International Business Center Yerevan evolutes from a topography to a plaza and from there to a landmark.

SITUATIONAL PLAN 1/1000

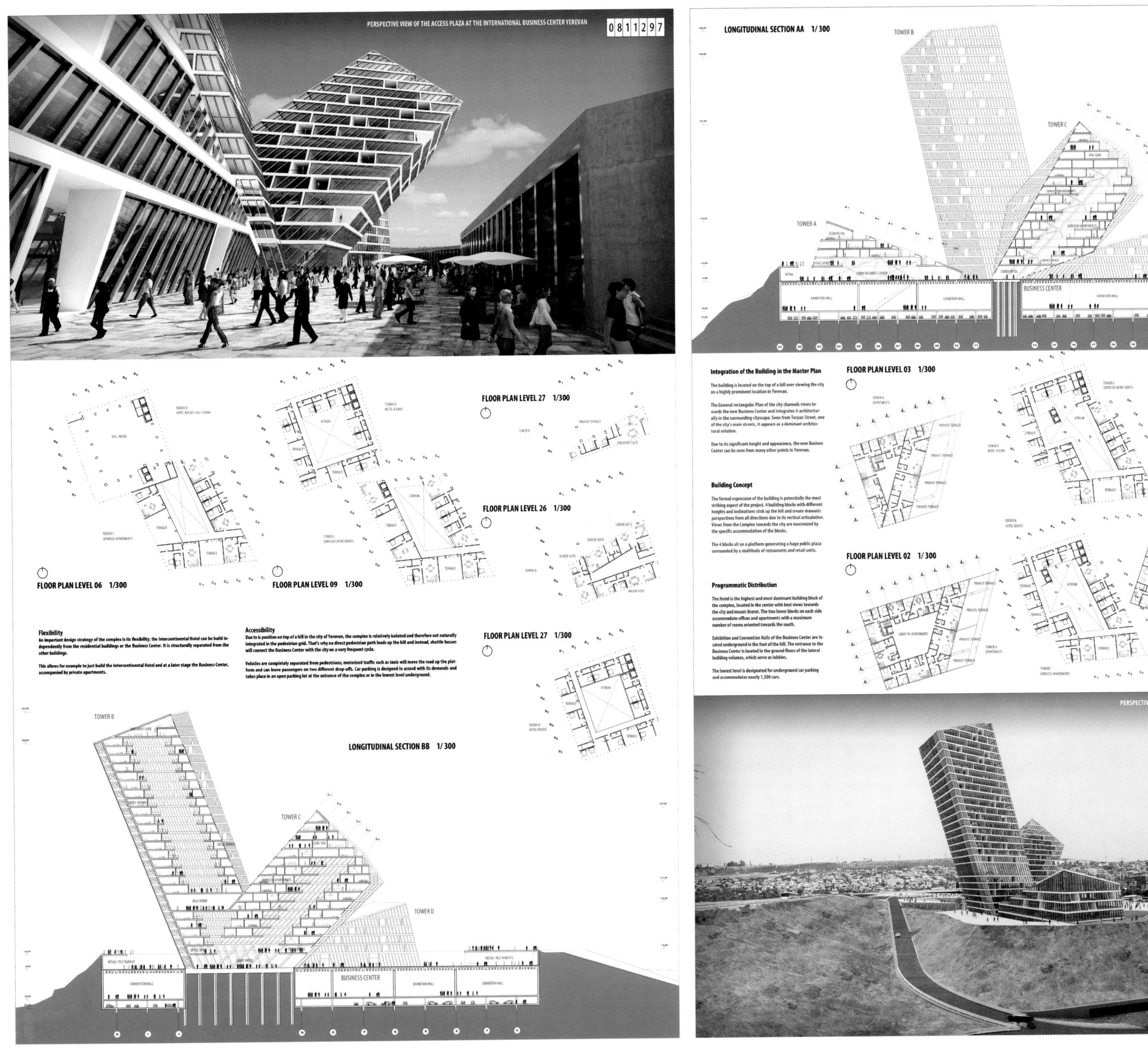
PERSPECTIVE VIEW OF THE ACCESS PLAZA AT THE INTERNATIONAL BUSINESS CENTER YEREVAN
0811297
FLOOR PLAN LEVEL 06 1/300
FLOOR PLAN LEVEL 09 1/300
FLOOR PLAN LEVEL 27 1/300
FLOOR PLAN LEVEL 26 1/300
FLOOR PLAN LEVEL 27 1/300
Flexibility
An important design strategy of the complex is its flexibility; the Intercontinental Hotel can be build independently from the residential buildings or the Business Center. It is structurally separated from the other buildings.
This allows for example to just build the Intercontinental Hotel and at a later stage the Business Center, accompanied by private apartments.
Accessibility
Due to is position on top of a hill in the city of Yerevan, the complex is relatively isolated and therefore not naturally integrated in the pedestrian grid. That's why no direct pedestrian path leads up the hill and instead, shuttle busses will connect the Business Center with the city on a very frequent cycle.
Vehicles are completely separated from pedestrians; motorized traffic such as taxis will move the road up the platform and can leave passengers on two different drop-offs. Car parking is designed in accord with its demands and takes place in an open parking lot at the entrance of the complex or in the lowest level underground.
LONGITUDINAL SECTION BB 1/300
TOWER B
TOWER C
TOWER D
BUSINESS CENTER
LONGITUDINAL SECTION AA 1/300
0811297
TOWER A
TOWER B
TOWER C
TOWER D
BUSINESS CENTER
Integration of the Building in the Master Plan
The building is located on the top of a hill over viewing the city on a highly prominent location in Yerevan.
The General rectangular Plan of the city channels views towards the new Business Center and integrates it architecturally in the surrounding cityscape. Seen from Teryan Street, one of the city's main streets, it appears as a dominant architectural solution.
Due to its significant height and appearance, the new Busines Center can be seen from many other points in Yerevan.
Building Concept
The formal expression of the building is potentially the most striking aspect of the project. 4 building blocks with different heights and inclinations stick up the hill and create dramatic perspectives from all directions due to its vertical articulation. Views from the Complex towards the city are maximized by the specific accommodation of the blocks.
The 4 blocks sit on a platform generating a huge public plaza surrounded by a multitude of restaurants and retail units.
Programmatic Distribution
The Hotel is the highest and most dominant building block of the complex, located in the center with best views towards the city and mount Ararat. The two lower blocks on each side accommodate offices and apartments with a maximum number of rooms oriented towards the south.
Exhibition and Convention Halls of the Business Center are located underground in the foot of the hill. The entrance to the Business Center is located in the ground floors of the lateral building volumes, which serve as lobbies.
The lowest level is designated for underground car parking and accommodates nearly 1,500 cars.
FLOOR PLAN LEVEL 03 1/300
FLOOR PLAN LEVEL 02 1/300
PERSPECTIVE VIEW OF THE INTERNATIONAL BUSINESS CENTER YEREVAN FROM SARALANJI STREET

0811297

PERSPECTIVE VIEW OF THE HOTEL LOBBY AT THE INTERNATIONAL BUSINESS CENTER YEREVAN

FUNCTIONAL DIAGRAMS

TOWER B
HOTEL
BALL ROOM
OFFICES
HOTEL LOBBY
TOWER C
AMENITIES OF HOTEL
SERVICED APARTMENTS
OFFICES
HOTEL LOBBY
HOTIZONTAL AND VERTICAL CIRCULATIONS
TOWER A
APARTMENTS
OFFICES
LOBBY BUSINESS CENTER
TOWER D
APARTMENTS
OFFICES
LOBBY BUSINESS CENTER

STRUCTURAL DIAGRAMS

STRESS DIAGRAM
TENSION OF BODIES IN NATURAL EQUILIBRIUM
TRANSFERENCE SLAB
PILOTS
MAIN STRUCTURE OF STEEL
TRANSFERENCE SLAB
PILOTS

STRUCTURAL DETAIL

FACADE STRUCTURE SELF-SUPPORTING
CANTILEVER OF STEEL
REINFORCED STRUCTURE
SECONDARY STEEL STRUCTURE
FLOOR SLAB
TRAPEZOIDAL SHEET
MAIN STRUCTURE OF STEEL VERTICAL
FLOOR FINISH
FACADE MOUNTING
GLASS
MAIN STRUCTURE OF STEEL HORIZONTAL
FACADE FRAMES

PERSPECTIVE VIEW OF THE INTERNATIONAL BUSINESS CENTER YEREVAN SEEN FROM BUS SHUTTLE TERMINAL IN THE EAST

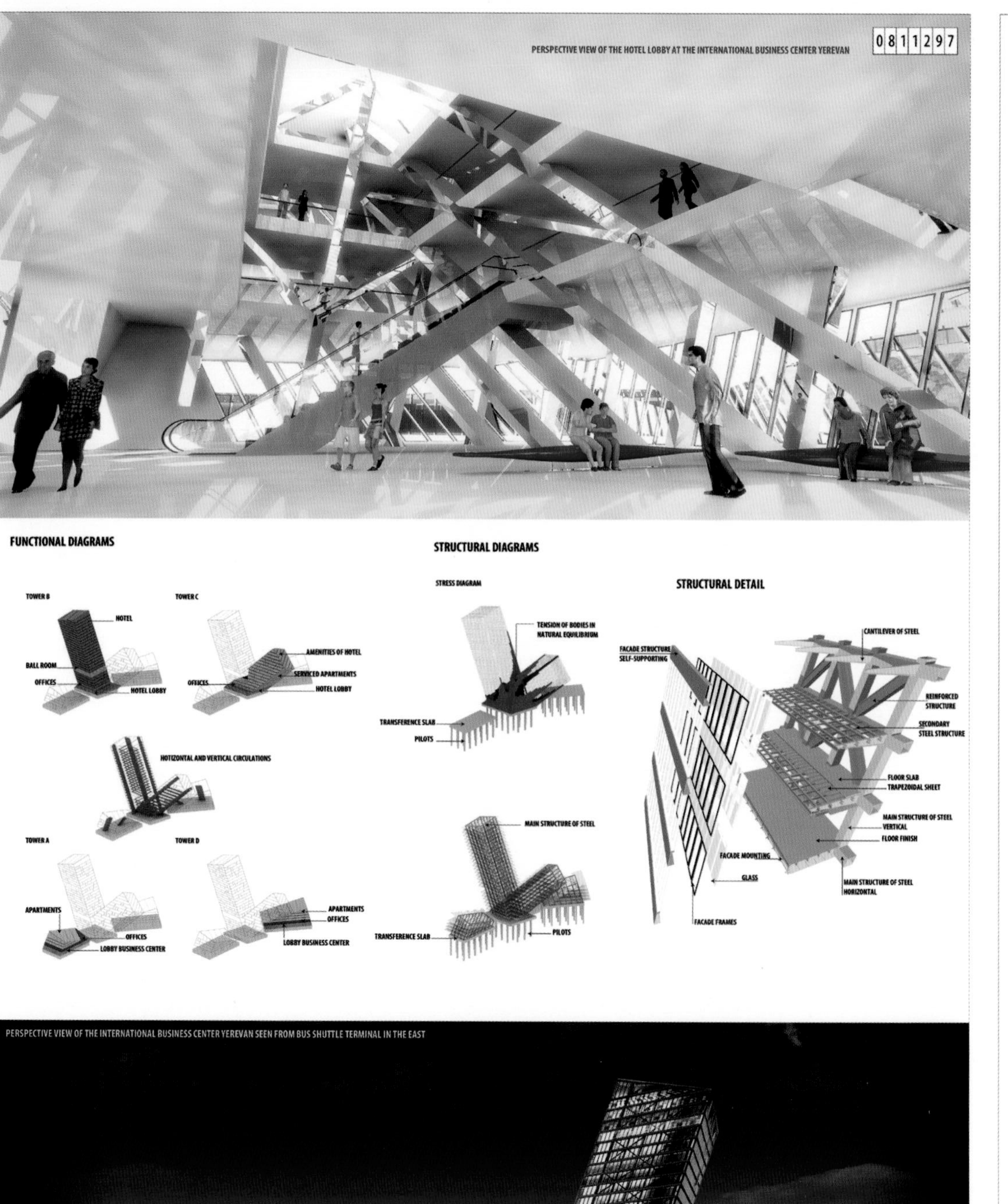

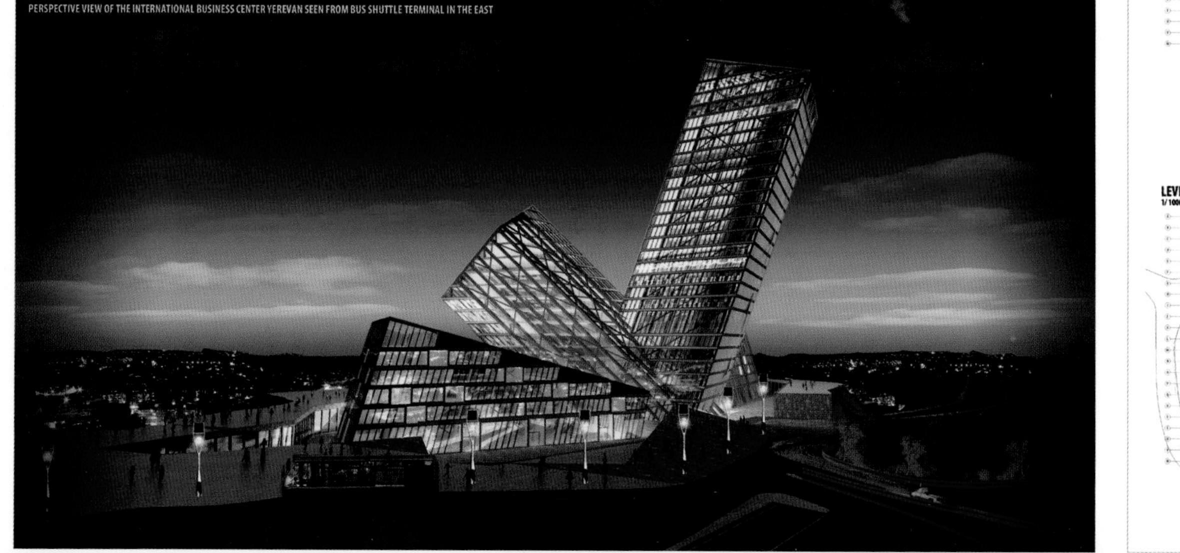

0811297

LEVEL 01 (0.00) 1/1000
LEVEL 00 (-6.00) 1/1000
LEVEL -01 (-18.00) 1/1000
LEVEL -02 (-21.50) 1/1000
LEVEL 14 (+45.50) 1/1000
LEVEL 13 (+42.00) 1/1000
LEVEL 12 (+38.50) 1/1000
LEVEL 11 (+35.00) 1/1000
LEVEL 10 (+31.50) 1/1000
LEVEL 09 (+28.00) 1/1000
LEVEL 08 (+24.50) 1/1000
LEVEL 07 (+21.00) 1/1000
LEVEL 06 (+17.50) 1/1000
LEVEL 05 (+14.00) 1/1000
LEVEL 04 (+10.50) 1/1000
LEVEL 03 (+7.00) 1/1000
LEVEL 02 (+3.50) 1/1000
LEVEL 27 (+91.00) 1/1000
LEVEL 26 (+87.50) 1/1000
LEVEL 25 (+84.00) 1/1000
LEVEL 24 (+80.50) 1/1000
LEVEL 23 (+77.00) 1/1000
LEVEL 22 (+73.50) 1/1000
LEVEL 21 (+70.00) 1/1000
LEVEL 20 (+66.50) 1/1000
LEVEL 19 (+63.00) 1/1000
LEVEL 18 (+59.50) 1/1000
LEVEL 17 (+56.00) 1/1000
LEVEL 16 (+52.50) 1/1000
LEVEL 15 (+49.00) 1/1000

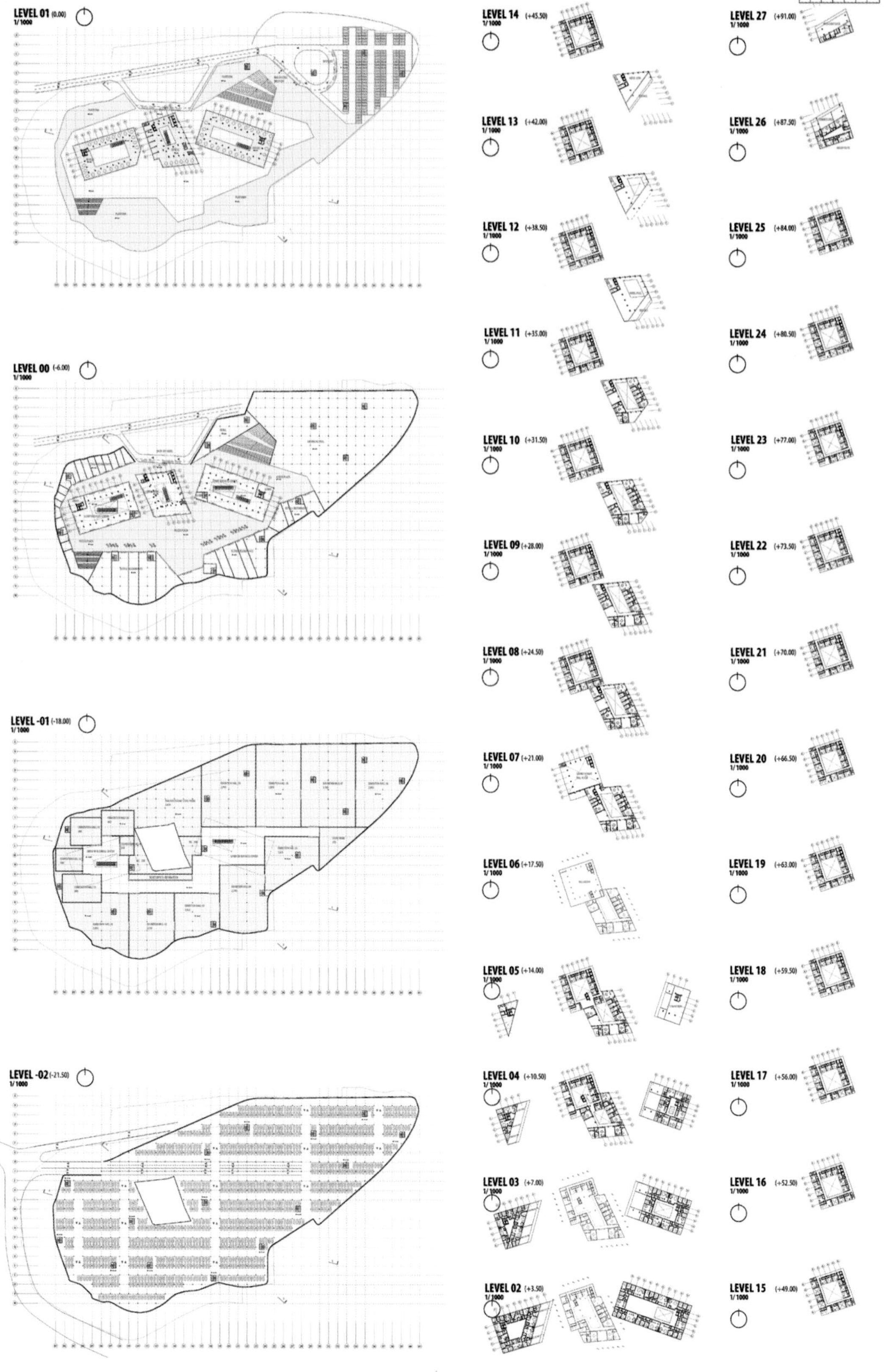

Lpailuohjeilma | *modostudio*

Design Team : Modostudio (Fabio Cibinel, Roberto Laurenti, Giorgio Martocchia, Irene Coppola) with Arkkitehtuura (Ville Tuura)

Location : Lohja, Finland
Client : Lohja Municipality
Type : International Competition - Purchase Prize

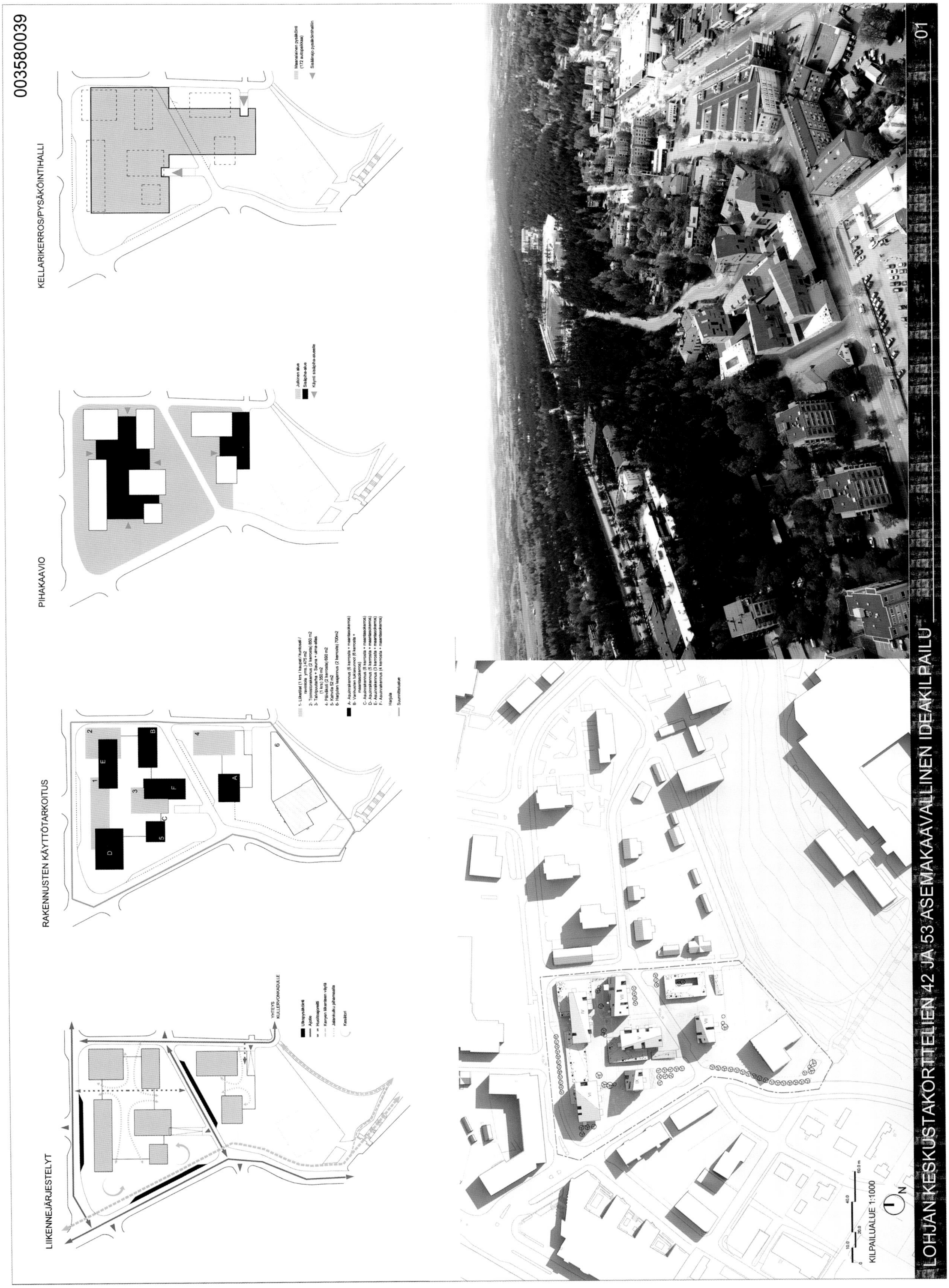

003580039

KELLARIKERROS/PYSÄKÖINTIHALLI

PIHAKAAVIO

RAKENNUSTEN KÄYTTÖTARKOITUS

LIIKENNEJÄRJESTELYT

KILPAILUALUE 1:1000

LOHJAN KESKUSTAKORTTELIEN 42 JA 53 ASEMAKAAVALLINEN IDEAKILPAILU 01

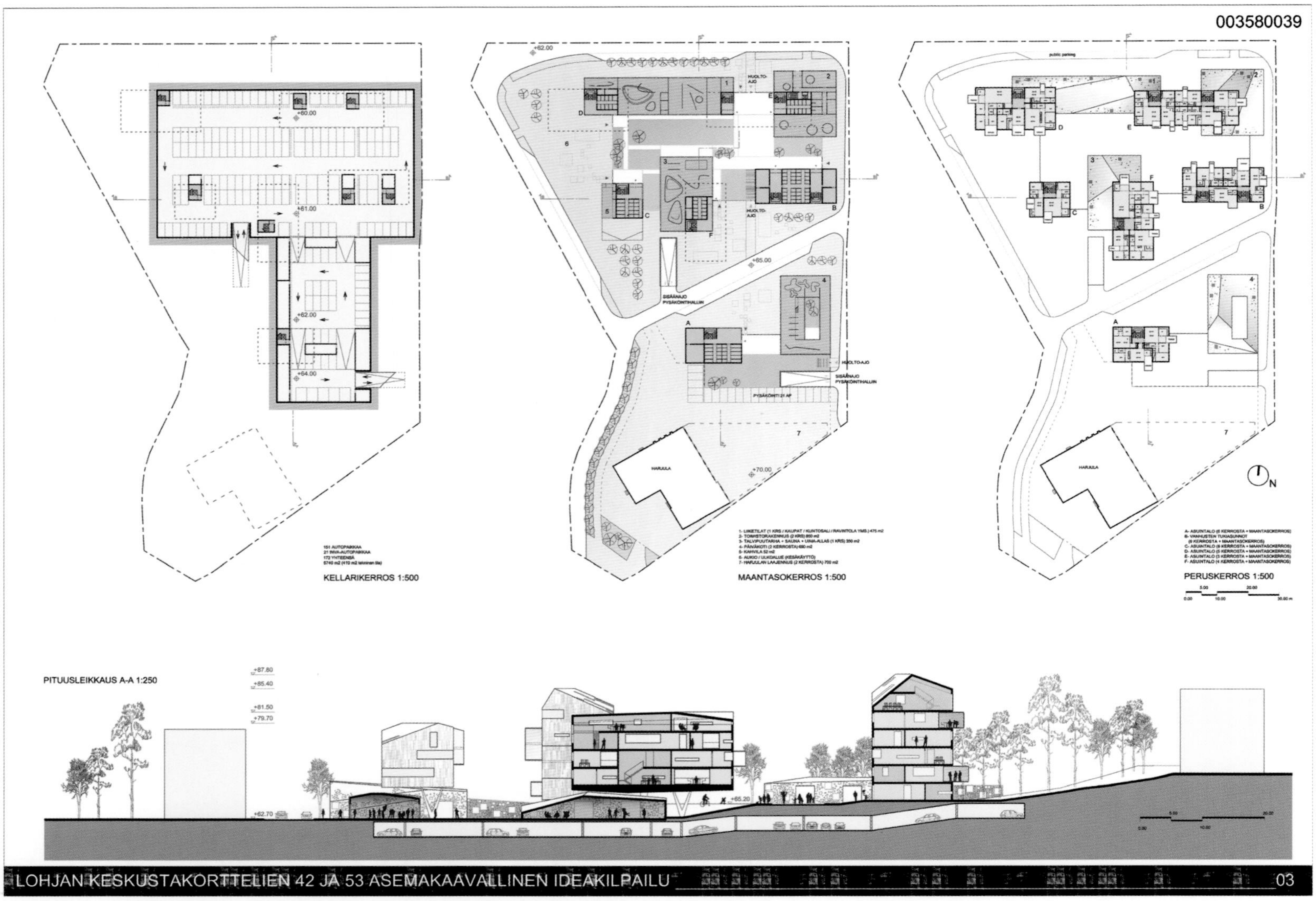
003580039
KELLARIKERROS 1:500
MAANTASOKERROS 1:500
PERUSKERROS 1:500
PITUUSLEIKKAUS A-A 1:250
LOHJAN KESKUSTAKORTTELIEN 42 JA 53 ASEMAKAAVALLINEN IDEAKILPAILU
03

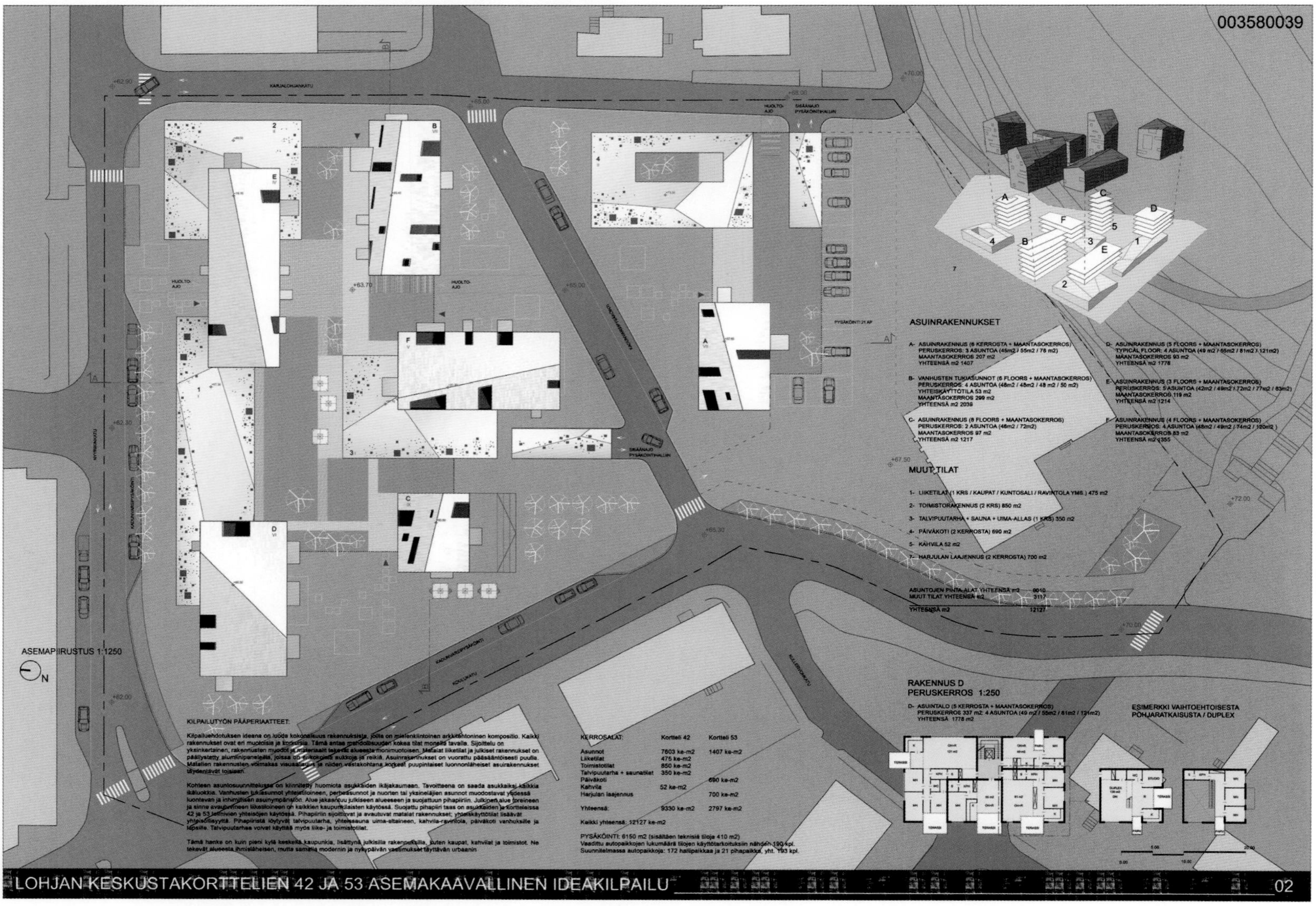
003580039
ASEMAPIIRUSTUS 1:1250
ASUINRAKENNUKSET
A- ASUINRAKENNUS (6 KERROSTA + MAANTASOKERROS)
PERUSKERROS: 3 ASUNTOA (45m2 / 55m2 / 78 m2)
MAANTASOKERROS 207 m2
YHTEENSÄ m2 1407
B- VANHUSTEN TUKIASUNNOT (6 FLOORS + MAANTASOKERROS)
PERUSKERROS: 4 ASUNTOA (48m2 / 48m2 / 48 m2 / 50 m2)
YHTEISKÄYTTÖTILA 53 m2
MAANTASOKERROS 299 m2
YHTEENSÄ m2 2039
C- ASUINRAKENNUS (8 FLOORS + MAANTASOKERROS)
PERUSKERROS: 2 ASUNTOA (46m2 / 72m2)
MAANTASOKERROS 97 m2
YHTEENSÄ m2 1217
D- ASUINRAKENNUS (5 FLOORS + MAANTASOKERROS)
TYPICAL FLOOR: 4 ASUNTOA (49 m2 / 55m2 / 81m2 / 121m2)
MAANTASOKERROS 93 m2
YHTEENSÄ m2 1778
E- ASUINRAKENNUS (3 FLOORS + MAANTASOKERROS)
PERUSKERROS: 5 ASUNTOA (42m2 / 49m2 / 72m2 / 77m2 / 83m2)
MAANTASOKERROS 119 m2
YHTEENSÄ m2 1214
F- ASUINRAKENNUS (4 FLOORS + MAANTASOKERROS)
PERUSKERROS: 4 ASUNTOA (48m2 / 49m2 / 74m2 / 120m2)
MAANTASOKERROS 83 m2
YHTEENSÄ m2 1355
MUUT TILAT
1- LIIKETILAT (1 KRS / KAUPAT / KUNTOSALI / RAVINTOLA YMS.) 475 m2
2- TOIMISTORAKENNUS (2 KRS) 850 m2
3- TALVIPUUTARHA + SAUNA + UIMA-ALLAS (1 KRS) 350 m2
4- PÄIVÄKOTI (2 KERROSTA) 690 m2
5- KAHVILA 52 m2
7- HARJULAN LAAJENNUS (2 KERROSTA) 700 m2
ASUNTOJEN PINTA-ALAT YHTEENSÄ m2 9010
MUUT TILAT YHTEENSÄ m2 3117
YHTEENSÄ m2 12127
RAKENNUS D
PERUSKERROS 1:250
D- ASUINTALO (5 KERROSTA + MAANTASOKERROS)
PERUSKERROS 337 m2: 4 ASUNTOA (49 m2 / 55m2 / 81m2 / 121m2)
YHTEENSÄ 1778 m2
ESIMERKKI VAIHTOEHTOISESTA
POHJARATKAISUSTA / DUPLEX
KILPAILUTYÖN PÄÄPERIAATTEET:
Kilpailuehdotuksen ideana on luoda kokonaisuus rakennuksista, joilla on mielenkiintoinen arkkitehtoninen kompositio. Kaikki rakennukset ovat eri muotoisia ja korkuisia. Tämä antaa mahdollisuuden kokea tilat monella tavalla. Sijoittelu on yksinkertainen, rakennusten muodot ja materiaalit tekevät alueesta monimuotoisen. Matalat liiketilat ja julkiset rakennukset on päällystetty alumiinipaneleilla, joissa on erikokoisia aukkoja ja reikiä. Asuinrakennukset on vuorattu pääsääntöisesti puulla. Matalien rakennusten voimakas visuaalisuus ja niiden vastakohtana korkeat puupintaiset luonnonläheiset asuirakennukset täydentävät toisiaan.
Kohteen asuntosuunnittelussa on kiinnitetty huomiota asukkaiden ikäjakaumaan. Tavoitteena on saada asukkaiksi kaikkia ikäluokkia. Vanhusten tukiasunnot yhteistiloineen, perheasunnot ja nuorten tai yksineläjien asunnot muodostavat yhdessä luontevan ja inhimillisen asuinympäristön. Alue jakaantuu julkiseen alueeseen ja suojattuun pihapiiriin. Julkinen alue toreineen ja sinne avautuvineen liiketiloineen on kaikkien kaupunkilaisten käytössä. Suojattu pihapiiri taas on asukkaiden ja kortteleissa 42 ja 53 toimivien yhteisöjen käytössä. Pihapiiriin sijoittuvat ja avautuvat matalat rakennukset; yhteiskäyttötilat lisäävät yhteisöllisyyttä. Pihapiiristä löytyvät talvipuutarha, yhteissauna uima-altaineen, kahvila-ravintola, päiväkoti vanhuksille ja lapsille. Talvipuutarhaa voivat käyttää myös liike- ja toimistotilat.
Tämä hanke on kuin pieni kylä keskellä kaupunkia, lisättynä julkisilla rakennuksilla, kuten kaupat, kahvilat ja toimistot. Ne tekevät alueesta ihmisläheisen, mutta samalla modernin ja nykypäivän vaatimukset täyttävän urbaanin
KERROSALAT: Kortteli 42 Kortteli 53
Asunnot 7603 ke-m2 1407 ke-m2
Liiketilat 475 ke-m2
Toimistotilat 850 ke-m2
Talvipuutarha + saunatilat 350 ke-m2
Päiväkoti 690 ke-m2
Kahvila 52 ke-m2
Harjulan laajennus 700 ke-m2
Yhteensä: 9330 ke-m2 2797 ke-m2
Kaikki yhteensä: 12127 ke-m2
PYSÄKÖINTI: 6150 m2 (sisältäen teknisiä tiloja 410 m2)
Vaadittu autopaikkojen lukumäärä tilojen käyttötarkoituksiin nähden 190 kpl.
Suunnitelmassa autopaikkoja: 172 hallipaikkaa ja 21 pihapaikkaa, yht. 193 kpl.
LOHJAN KESKUSTAKORTTELIEN 42 JA 53 ASEMAKAAVALLINEN IDEAKILPAILU
02

003580039

4

5

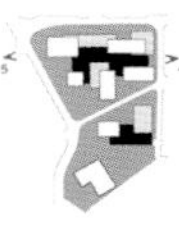

LOHJAN KESKUSTAKORTTELIEN 42 JA 53 ASEMAKAAVALLINEN IDEAKILPAILU 05

003580039

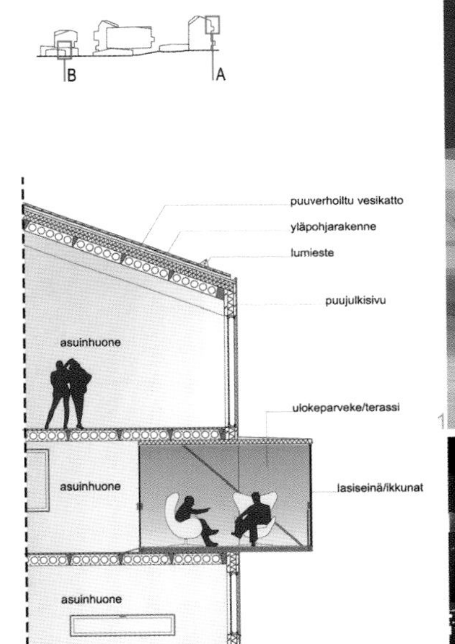

A Detaljileikkaus asuinrakennuksesta

1

2

3

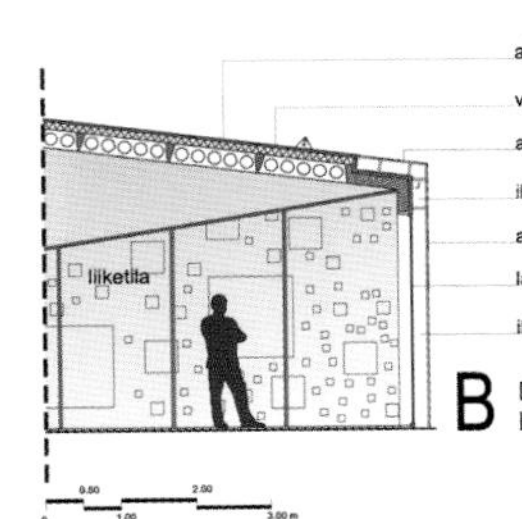

B Detaljileikkaus liiketilasta

POIKKILEIKKAUS B-B 1:250

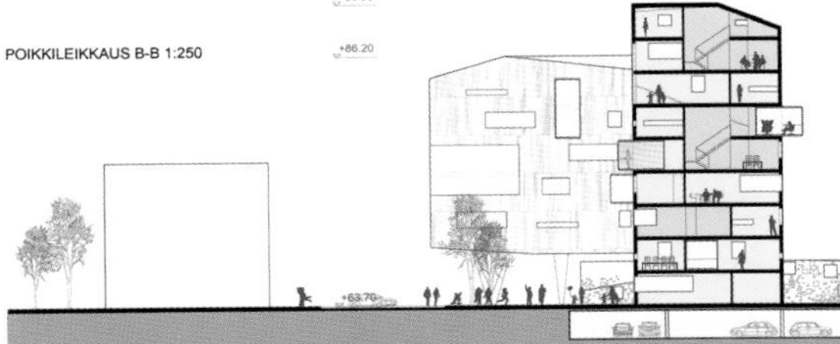

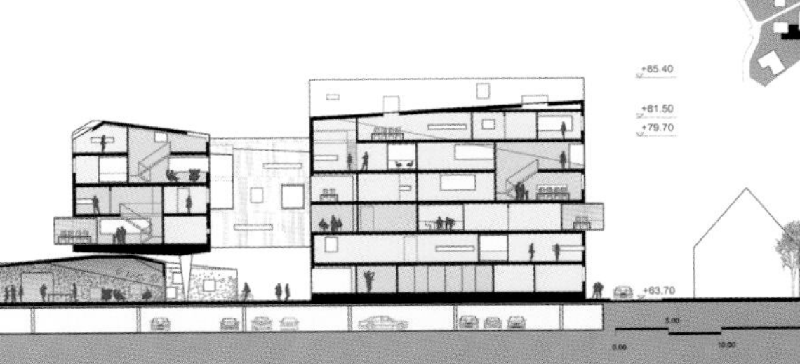

LOHJAN KESKUSTAKORTTELIEN 42 JA 53 ASEMAKAAVALLINEN IDEAKILPAILU 04

126 Masterplan Vienna | *Slot.*

Location : Austria, Vienna, Favoritenstrasse/ Wiener Guertel
Program : Housing, Retail, Offices, Educational Facilities, Recreational Spaces
Project Type : Open International Competition

Client : Oebb-Imobilienmanagement GmbH
Area : 8.9 ha

WETTBEWERB ENTWICKLUNGSGEBIET EGD

VOGELPERSPEKTIVE DES NEUEN STADTQUARTIERS

KONZEPTERKLÄRUNG

Städtisches Wachstum in Wellenform
Die Stadtentwicklung Wiens hat sich in konzentrischen Ringen vollzogen. Der erste Ring begrenzte das Stadtzentrum mit einer Stadtmauer. Im folgenden Ring bildeten sich die Vorstädte umgrenzt von einer zweite Stadtmauer.

Grüner Ring
Ursprünglich zu Verteidigungszwecken errichtet, bietet der „Glacis" heutzutage hohe städtische Qualitäten als Stadtpark.

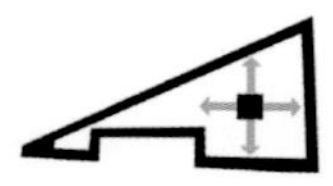

Wachstum nach außen
Die Stadtentwicklung Wiens dient uns als Beispiel für die Entwicklung des neuen Stadtviertels. Das zentrale Baufeld besteht aus Wohnungen und die Zusatzfunktionen befinden sich seinem Rand.

Durchlässiger Rand
Ein deutlich definierter Blockrand öffnet sich an einzelnen Stellen und verbindet das neue Stadtquartier mit dem Kontext.

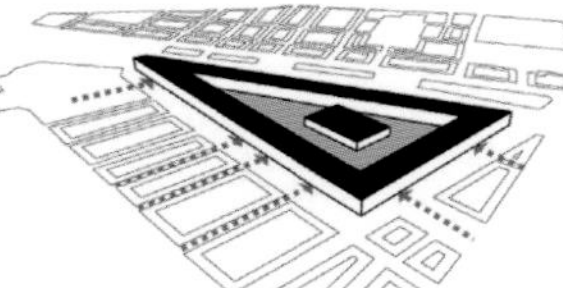

Städtische Verbindungen
Die vorhandenen städtischen Achsen aus dem Kontext werden aufgenommen. Somit wird der Blockrand zerschnitten und erlaubt Fußgängerverbindungen ins Innere.

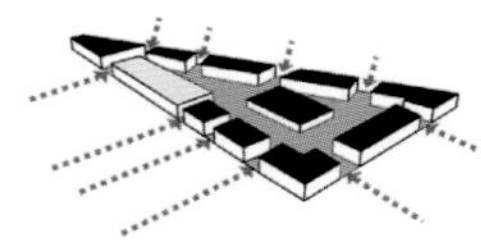

Die fragmentierte Stadtmauer
Mit der Durchlässigkeit des Blockrands und dem Grüngürtel welcher direkt dahinter entsteht, werden auf abstrakte Art und Weise die selben städtischen Charakteristika wiederholt, welcher der Stadt Wien eine hohe Lebensqualität gegeben haben.

Weitere Entwicklung
Entlang der zweiten Stadtmauer entsteht der „Gürtel", welcher sich insbesondere in den letzten Jahren stark entwickelt hat. Dort befindet sich auch das Wettbewerbsgebiet.

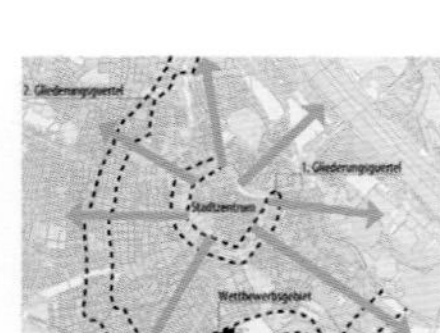
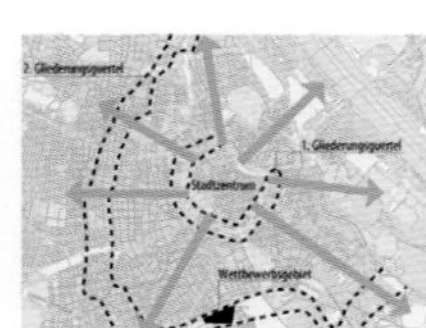

Zentrifugale Ausbreitung
Das Wachstum Wiens kann als ein Wachstum in Etappen interpretiert werden. Das Wachstum ging vom Zentrum aus und hat seine sich selbst gesetzten Grenzen schubweise überschritten.

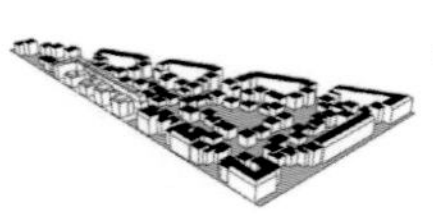

Auflösung des gründerzeitlichen Blockrands
Die sich ergebenden Volumen werden aufgelöst. In ihrem Innenhof entstehen Grünflächen mit unterschiedlichen Qualitäten.

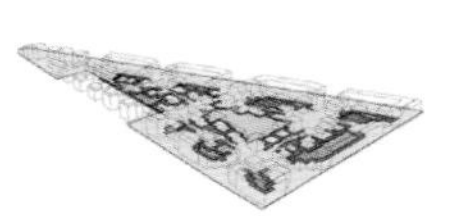

Bauvolumen
Die bauliche Dichte nimmt nach innen hin kontinuierlich ab. Somit ist das Innere des neuen Stadtviertels geschützt.

Grünflächen
Im Inneren entstehen Grünflächen privater, halb- öffentlicher und öffentlicher Natur, welche durch eine großzügige Fußgängerzone miteinander verbunden sind.

Schlussfolgerung
Ein Lösungsansatz mit geschichtlichen Bezügen, mit städtischem Charakter und in einem Maßstab, welcher sich am Fußgänger orientiert. Bestehend aus einem zentralen Wohnblock, welcher durch Grünflächen und Fußgängerzonen geschützt ist.

BEBAUUNGSKONZEPT

Ziel des Entwurfes ist die Erlangung eines städtebauliches Leitbildes, welches alle Qualitäten eines dichten und durchmischten Stadtviertels hat, bei gleichzeitig starker Durchgrünung und höchster Lebensqualität für seine Bewohner.

Dabei gilt es die anspruchsvolle städtebauliche Lage am Rand einer starken Barriere mit Trennwirkung (Eisenbahngleise) und die starken Lärm- und Emissionsbelastungen der umliegenden Strassen gleichermaßen zu berücksichtigen.

Von seinen Rändern betrachtet nimmt das Bebauungskonzept starken Bezug auf den städtischen Kontext der vorherrschenden Blockrandbebauung des zehnten, aber auch des vierten und fünften Bezirks Wiens. Eine 7-geschoßige Blockrandbebauung sorgt für eine hohe Dichte an den Rändern des neuen Stadtquartiers, und hält den Kern des Gebietes weitestgehend frei von Lärm und Umweltgiften.

Nach innen nimmt die bauliche Dichte kontinuierlich ab, es entsteht eine fußläufige Wohn- und Arbeitsatmosphäre mit hohen stadträumlichen Qualitäten und visuellen Sichtbeziehungen zwischen Straßenräumen und Innenhöfen.

Formal gesehen resultiert dies in einem starker Blockrand nach außen welcher sich nach innen hin mit Punkthaustypologien aufgelöst. Bestehende Strassen des Kontexts setzen sich in das neue Quartier fort.

Das Wettbewerbsgebiet teilt sich in 7 selbstständig entwickelbare Teilgebiete auf, 5 unabhängige Parzellen für Gewerbe und Wohnungen, die Schule und das zweite Technikgebäude. Diese Parzellen können von unterschiedlichen Investoren bebaut werden.

LEGENDE

- WIENER BAUORDNUNG, BAUKLASSE II
- WIENER BAUORDNUNG, BAUKLASSE III
- WIENER BAUORDNUNG, BAUKLASSE IV
- GESCHOSSANZAHL PRO GEBAEUDE
- BAULINIE
- BAUGRENZE
- ZUGAENGE
- OEFFENTLICHE GRUENFLAECHEN
- HALB-OEFFENTLICHE GRUENFLAECHEN
- PRIVATE GRUENFLAECHEN
- FREIRAUMAKTIVITAETEN

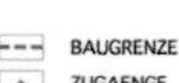

BEBAUUNGSPLAN 1/2000

AUFGELÖSTE STADTMAUER 770529

FREIRAUMKONZEPT

Der Entwurf berücksichtigt die Freiraumansprüche all seiner Benutzer. Prinzipiell besteht eine Aufteilung in drei unterschiedliche Freiraumklassen mit unterschiedlichen Öffentlichkeitsgraden:

-„Harte Plätze", definiert durch die öffentliche Freiräume welche sich durch die Übergänge zwischen den Baublöcken ergeben (der städtische Raum). Diese Plätze dienen als Aufenthalts- und Kommunikationsräume mit überwiegen kulturellem Angebote für alle Altersklassen.

- Eine nutzungsoffene Freifläche für temporäre Nutzungen aller Art mit öffentlichem Charakter im Zentrum des Wettbewerbsgebietes. Sportliche und gesellschaftliche Veranstaltungen von temporärem Charakter (z.B. das Grälzfest) können dort stattfinden.

- „Weiche Plätze", begrenzt durch die Bebauung innerhalb eines Baublocks als halböffentliche Plätze mit diversen Freiraumaktivitäten dienen als Freizeit- und Erholungsräume für die jeweils im Baublock lebenden und arbeitenden Personen.

Somit entsteht ein Stadtviertel mit einer attraktiven sozialen Infrastruktur und einer hohen Durchlässigkeit, welche das städtische Leben (charakterisiert durch differenzierte Freiräume unter Berücksichtigung all seiner Bewohner) im neuen Stadtteil besonders hervorhebt.

Grün ist zweifelsohne das dominierende Element im neuen Stadtviertel. Dieses Grün differenziert sich in öffentliches, halb- öffentliches und privates Grün.

Letzteres steht in direkter Verbindung mit den Wohntypologien. Erdgeschosswohnungen haben direkten Zugang zu einem privaten Garten vor oder hinter ihrer Wohnung. Die Wohnungen in den oberen Geschossen haben großzügige Terrassen und die Wohnungen im obersten Geschoss haben einen direkten Zugang zu ihrem privaten Garten auf dem Dach. So entsteht in seiner Gesamtheit ein Entwurf mit hohen landschaftsarchitektonischen Qualitäten.

Das Freiraumkonzept funktioniert unabhängig von den jeweiligen Bauphasen, da jeder Baublock seine halb- öffentlichen Freiflächen besitzt. Trotzdem ist das neue Stadtviertel erst mit seiner nutzungsoffenen Freifläche im Zentrum vollständig und deshalb sollte diese in der ersten Bauphase schon berücksichtigt werden. Alle notwendigen Ersatzplanzungen sind im neuen Stadtviertel integriert.

LEGENDE

FREIRAUM FUSSGAENGER/ RADFAHRER	OEFFENTLICHE GRUENFLAECHEN
HARTER PLATZ	HALB-OEFFENTLICHE GRUENFLAECHEN
NUTZUNGSNEUTRALER PLATZ	PRIVATE GRUENFLAECHEN
WEICHER PLATZ	FREIRAUMAKTIVITAETEN

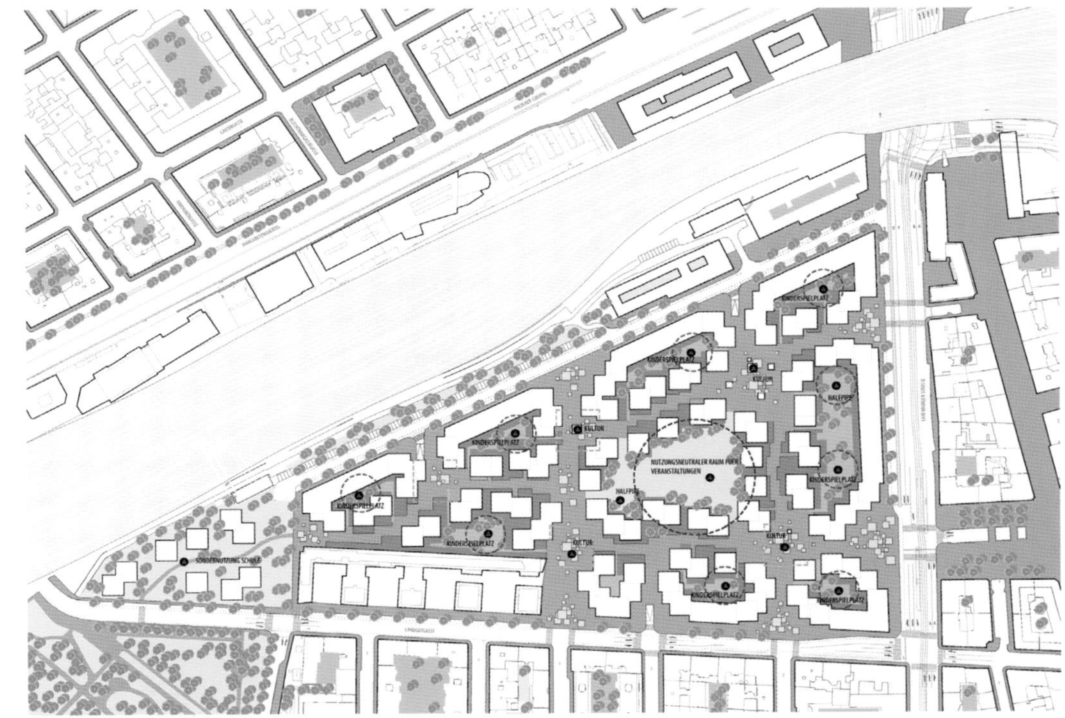

FREIRAUMPLAN 1/ 2000

REALISIERUNG IN BAUETAPPEN

PHASE 1

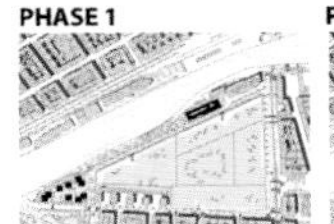

PHASE 2

PHASE 3

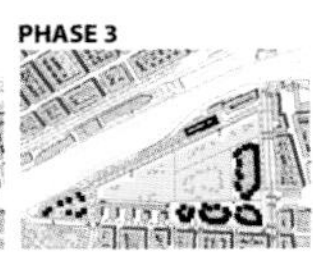

PHASE 4

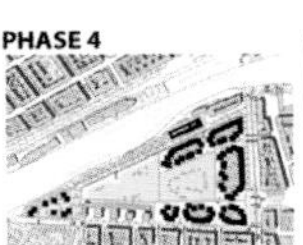

PHASE 5

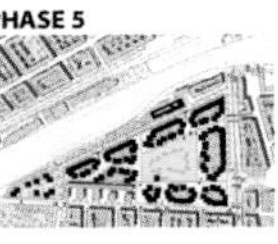

PHASE 6

WEICHER PLATZ

NUTZUNGSNEUTRALER PLATZ

HARTER PLATZ

INTEGRATION UND ANBINDUNG

Der neue Stadtteil nimmt Bezug auf die angrenzende Bebauung an der Landgut Gasse und der Laxenburger Strasse. Eine uniforme 7-geschossige Blockrandbebauung schirmt das Quartier vom Straßenlärm ab und öffnet sich an verschiedenen Stellen an welchen bestehende Strassen auf das Gebiet treffen (so zum Beispiel auch am Columbusplatz). Trotz der Blockrandbebauung ist das neue Stadtviertel auf diese Weise optimal an die Favoritenstrasse und den neuen Hauptbahnhof angeschlossen.

Im äußersten Westen des Wettbewerbsareals findet der Waldmüllerpark seine Fortsetzung ins neue Stadtviertel durch eine öffentliche Parkfläche in welcher sich auch die Schule befindet.

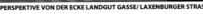

PERSPEKTIVE VON DER ECKE LANDGUT GASSE/ LAXENBURGER STRASSE

PERSPEKTIVE VON DER ECKE LANDGUTGASSE/ LAXENBURGER STRASSE

PERSPEKTIVE ENTLANG DER LANDGUT GASSE

WETTBEWERB ENTWICKLUNGSGEBIET EGD

PERSPEKTIVE VOM INNEREN DES NEUEN STADTQUARTIERS

FLÄCHENNUTZUNGSKONZEPT

Eine vielfältige Durchmischung der unterschiedlichen Nutzungen ist Grundbedingung für eine gut funktionierende Stadt welche fußläufige Distanzen und kurze Wege zum Ziel hat.

Unter Berücksichtigung dieses Grundsatzes ist eine gute Durchmischung von Wohnen und Gewerbe im neuen Stadtviertel vorgesehen welche sich wie folgt artikuliert:

Im Zentrum des Stadtviertels befindet sich ein Ring aus Wohnungen mit hohen Freiraum-Qualitäten welcher die nutzungsneutrale Grünfläche umschließt.

Dieser erste Ring wird gefolgt von einem zweiten mit höherer baulicher Dichte und vorwiegend Wohnnutzung mit gewerblichen Einheiten in den Erdgeschosszonen.

Der äußerste Ring ist schließlich der formelle Abschluss des neuen Quartiers und beherbergt zu 80 % Gewerbliche Nutzungen mit Einzelhandel in den Erdgeschosszonen, welcher sich zum vorhandenen Straßenraum orientiert.

Resultat ist ein ausgeglichenes Verhältnis von Wohnen und Arbeiten, welches einen nach außen orientierten geschlossenen Blockrand mit einem hohen Gewerbeanteil und ein nach innen orientiertes ruhiges Wohnviertel mit vereinzelter gewerblicher Nutzung in den Erdgeschosszonen zur Folge hat.

Im Westen des Wettbewerbsgebietes gegenüber des bestehenden Waldmüllerparks befindet sich die Schule auf einer Fläche von 10,000 Quadratmetern gruppieren sich Schulbauten in einem offenen Bebauungskonzept. Der Bauplatz der Schule ist gleichzeitig die Verlängerung des Waldmüllerparks ins neue Stadtquartier.

LEGENDE

WOHNNUTZUNG 100%	SCHULE
WOHNNUTZUNG MIT 5% GEWERBE	OEFFENTLICHE GRUENFLAECHEN
GEWERBENUTZUNG MIT 20% WOHNEN	HALB-OEFFENTLICHE GRUENFLAECHEN
EINZELHANDEL IM ERDGESCHOSS	PRIVATE GRUENFLAECHEN
	FREIRAUMAKTIVITAETEN

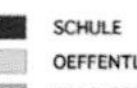

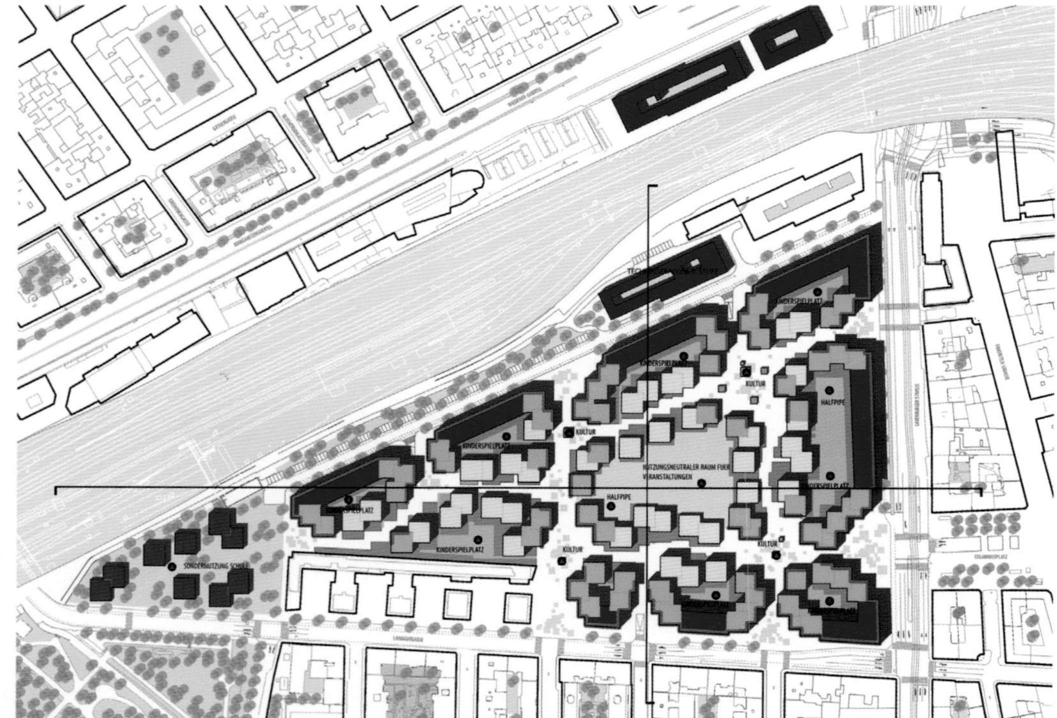

FLÄCHENNUTZUNGSPLAN 1/2000

HÖHENENTWICKLUNG

QUERSCHNITT 1/1500

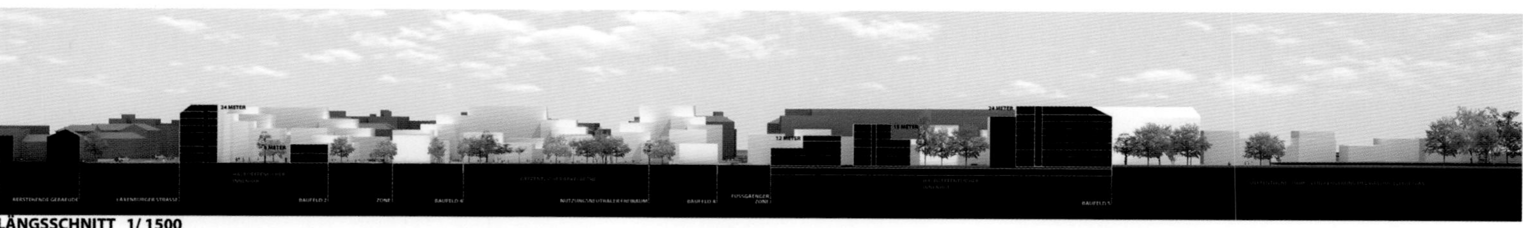

LÄNGSSCHNITT 1/1500

AUFGELÖSTE STADTMAUER 770529

VERKEHRSKONZEPT

Im Mittelpunkt des Verkehrskonzepts steht ein fußgängerorientiertes Stadtmodel mit kurzen Wegen und der Strasse als öffentlichem Aufenthaltsraum.

Mit Ausnahme einer Sammelstrasse im Norden des Wettbewerbsgebietes sind alle öffentlichen Räume autofrei abgesehen von Liefer- und unvermeidbarem Gelegenheitsverkehr. Der öffentliche Raum wird somit von Fußgängern und Radfahrern gleichermaßen genutzt und bietet höchste Aufenhaltsqalitäten. Ein dichtes barrierefreies Fuß- und Radwegnetz mit einer vielschichtigen Durchwegung durchzieht das neue Stadtquartier.

Der bestehende öffentliche Personennahverkehr erschließt das neue Stadtviertel bestens und somit sind keine weiteren Maßnahmen diesbezüglich notwendig.

Die Staßenverbreiterung im Bereich der Laxenburger Straße erlaubt einen großen Abstand zur bestehenden Bebauung und berücksichtigt somit den notwendigen Lichteinfall. Entlang der Landgut Gasse wird die Lücke im übergeordneten Radwegenetz geschlossen; außerdem wird der Einfüllpunkt im Bereich der Landgut Gasse um einen Häuserblock nach Osten verschoben.

Der Öbb-Bedienweg bleibt erhalten, wird jedoch nicht für die Erschließung des Wettbewerbsareals benutzt.

LEGENDE

- VERKEHRSSTRASSE
- UEBERGEORDNETE RADWEGEVERBINDUNG
- FUSS- UND RADWEGENETZ
- HALB-OEFFENTLICHES FUSS- UND RADWEGENETZ
- GRUENFLAECHEN
- ▲ ZUGANG ZUR PARKIERUNG IM UNTERGESCHOSS

PARKIERUNGSKONZEPT

Das Parkieren von Autos wird in Tiefgaragen unter jeder Bauparzelle gelöst. Es sind drei Zugänge zu den jeweiligen Tiefgaragen vorgesehen, von der Landgut Gasse im Süden, von der Laxenburger Strasse im Osten und von der neu geplanten Sammelstrasse im Norden. Außerdem besteht die Möglichkeit für Besucher, entlang der Landgut Gasse, der Laxenburger Strasse oder der neu geplanten Sammelstrasse im Norden auf Straßenniveau zu parken.

Es wäre wünschenswert, dieses neue Stadtquartier autofrei oder zumindest autoarm zu halten. In diesem Falle könnte auf die Tiefgaragen unter den Parzellen ganz verzichtet werden.

VERKEHRSPLAN 1/2000

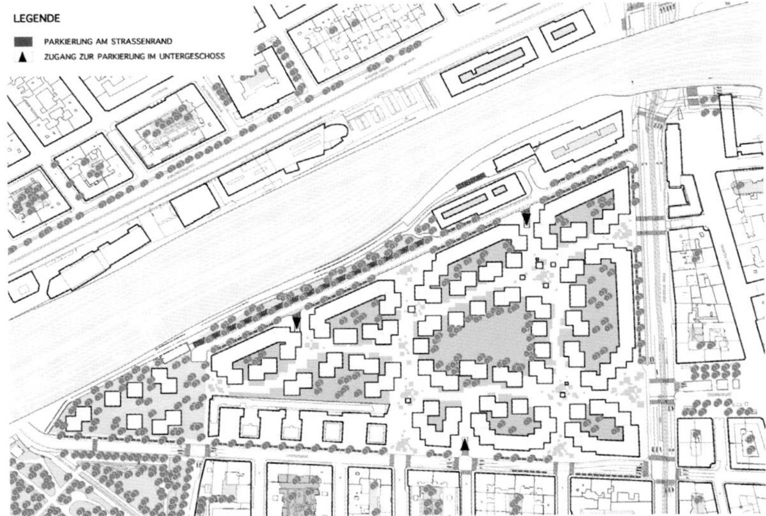

PARKIERUNGSPLAN IM ERDGESCHOSS 1/3000

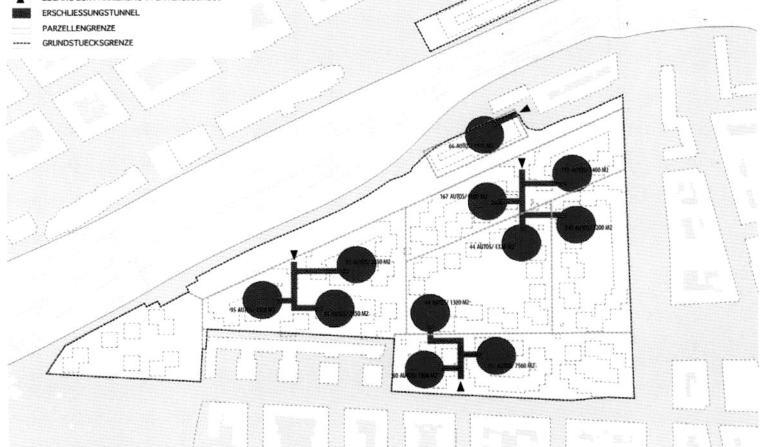

PARKIERUNGSPLAN IM UNTERGESCHOSS 1/3000

PERSPEKTIVE DES NUTZUNGSNEUTRALEN GRUNRAUMS IM ZENTRUM

127 Newark Gateway Project | *CJ Lom / Studio 8 Architects*

Design Team : CJ Lim/Studio 8 Architects with Jen Wang, Barry Cho, Pascal Bronner, Daniel Wang
Consultants : Techniker(structural engineers)

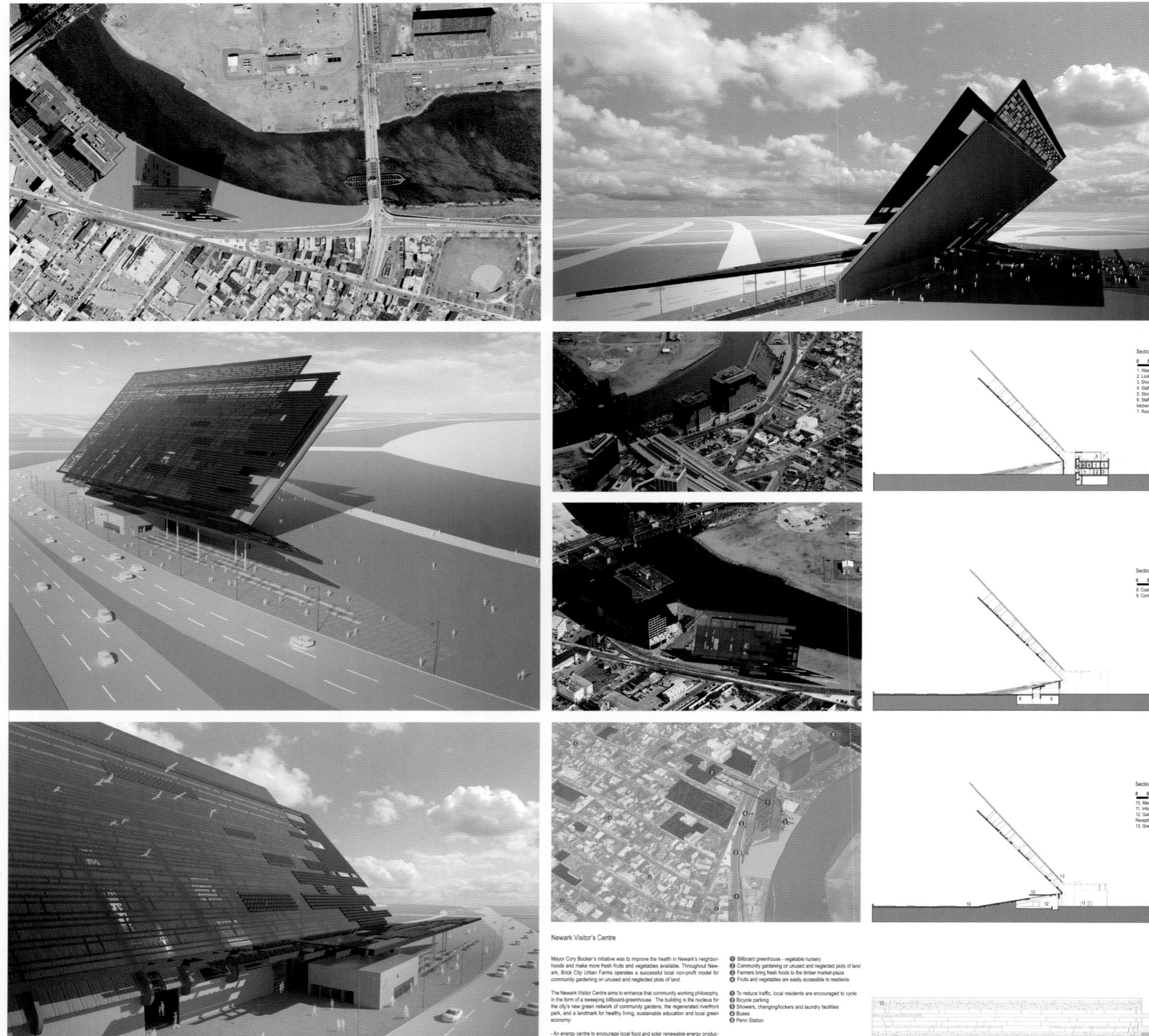

Newark Visitor's Centre
Mayor Cory Booker's initiative was to improve the health in Newark's neighborhoods and make more fresh fruits and vegetables available. Throughout Newark, Brick City Urban Farms operates a successful local non-profit model for community gardening on unused and neglected plots of land.
The Newark Visitor Centre aims to enhance that community working philosophy, in the form of a sweeping billboard-greenhouse. The building is the nucleus for the city's new green network of community gardens, the regenerated riverfront park, and a landmark for healthy living, sustainable education and local green economy:
- An energy centre to encourage local food and solar renewable energy production. The vegetable nursery within the billboard supplies seedlings to the community for their gardens. The structure is pixilated by solar cells.
- A transport hub for buses, trains and bicycles. To reduce traffic and parking problems, local residents are encouraged to cycle, especially to and from Penn Station. Within the NVC are bicycle parking, as well as showers, changing/lockers and laundry facilities for the sweaty cyclists. The exercise will make residents fitter, while reducing carbon footprint.
- A permanent forum for intercultural exchanges. Exhibition spaces, lecture theatre and information suite are to engage locals and visitors.
- A centre of excellence. Farmers bring fresh foods directly to the building, making fruits and vegetables easily accessible to residents. The timber market-plaza displays local pride.
The NVC will bring together the actions of hundreds of individuals investing their time, their energy, and their hopes in the future of the neighborhood.
1 Billboard greenhouse - vegetable nursery
2 Community gardening on unused and neglected plots of land
3 Farmers bring fresh foods to the timber market-plaza
4 Fruits and vegetables are easily accessible to residents
1 To reduce traffic, local residents are encouraged to cycle
2 Bicycle parking
3 Showers, changing/lockers and laundry facilities
4 Buses
5 Penn Station
Section DD 1:500
0 5m 10 20
13. Greenhouse roof
14. Reception area
15. Conference room
16. Auditorium
17. Permanent display area
18. Visitors' toilets
19. Newark City gift shop
20. Store room
21. Cafe
1 Billboard greenhouse - vegetable nursery
2 Solar Panels
3 Bicycle parking

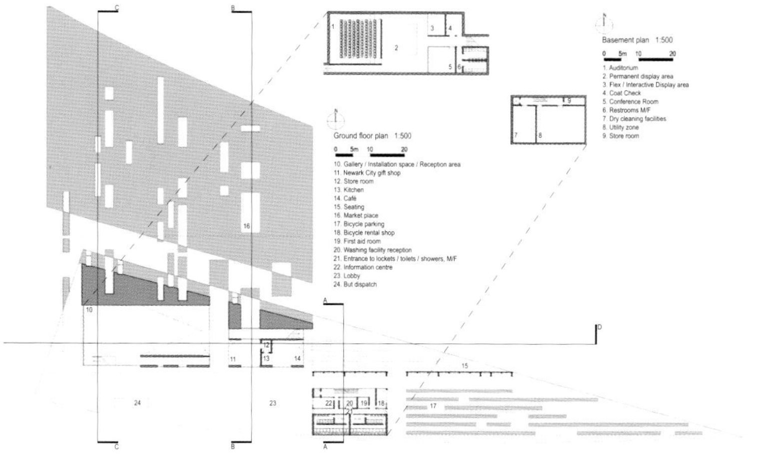

Basement plan 1:500

0 5m 10 20

1. Auditorium
2. Permanent display area
3. Flex / Interactive Display area
4. Coat Check
5. Conference Room
6. Restrooms M/F
7. Dry cleaning facilities
8. Utility zone
9. Store room

Ground floor plan 1:500

0 5m 10 20

10. Gallery / Installation space / Reception area
11. Newark City gift shop
12. Store room
13. Kitchen
14. Café
15. Seating
16. Market place
17. Bicycle parking
18. Bicycle rental shop
19. First aid room
20. Washing facility reception
21. Entrance to lockets / toilets / showers, M/F
22. Information centre
23. Lobby
24. But dispatch

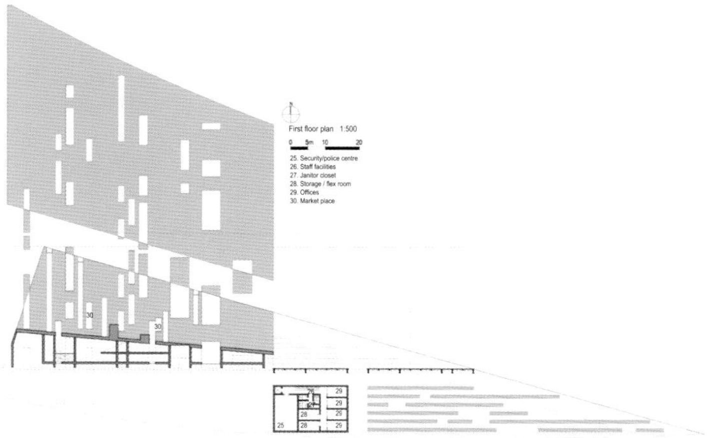

First floor plan 1:500

0 5m 10 20

25. Security/police centre
26. Staff facilities
27. Janitor closet
28. Storage / flex room
29. Offices
30. Market place

Second floor plan 1:500

0 5m 10 20

31. Staff break / workroom-kitchen
32. Roof garden

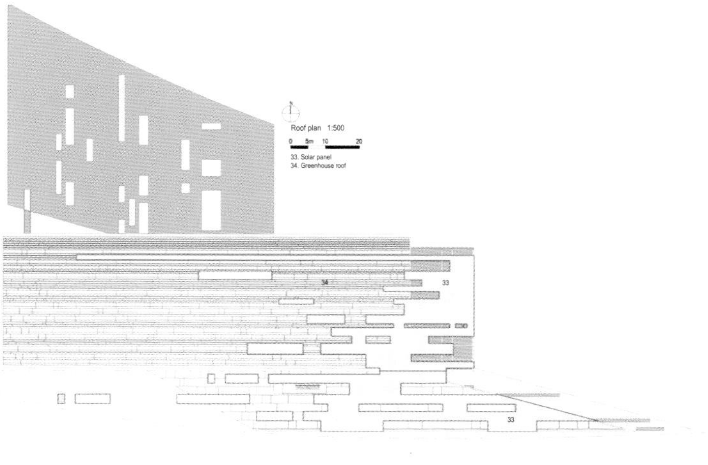

Roof plan 1:500

0 5m 10 20

33. Solar panel
34. Greenhouse roof

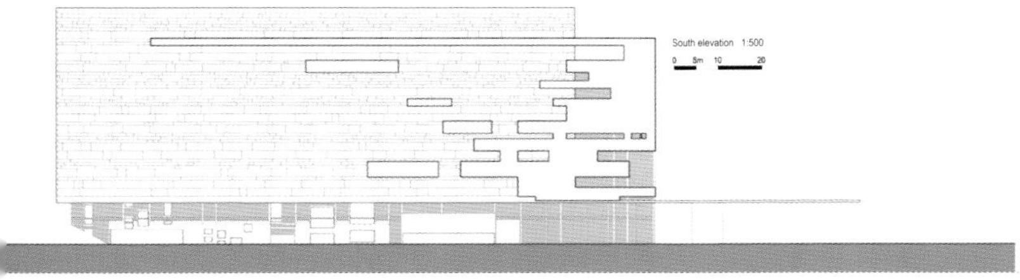

South elevation 1:500

0 5m 10 20

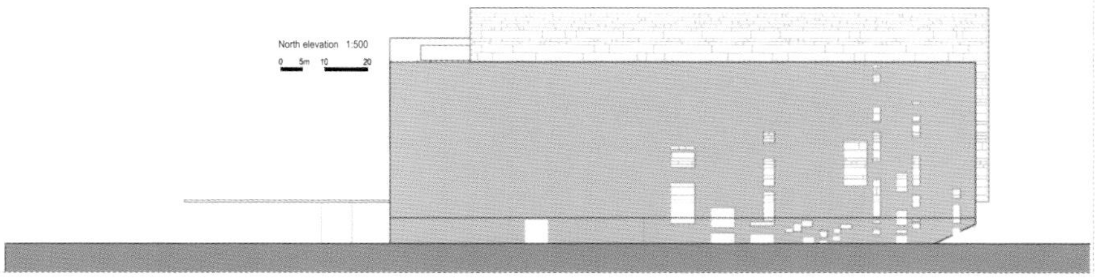

North elevation 1:500

0 5m 10 20

128 Quartier M Düsseldorf | *J. MAYER H. Architects*

Team : Juergen Mayer H., Max Reinhardt, Simon Kassner, Hugo Reis, Jan-Christoph Stockebrand
Investor : Lorac Investment Management, Luxemburg
Structure and facade planning : Knippers Helbig, Stuttgart
Climate and Energy Concept : Transsolar, Stuttgart
Traffic Consultant : GRI Gesellschaft für Gesamtverkehrsplanung, Berlin

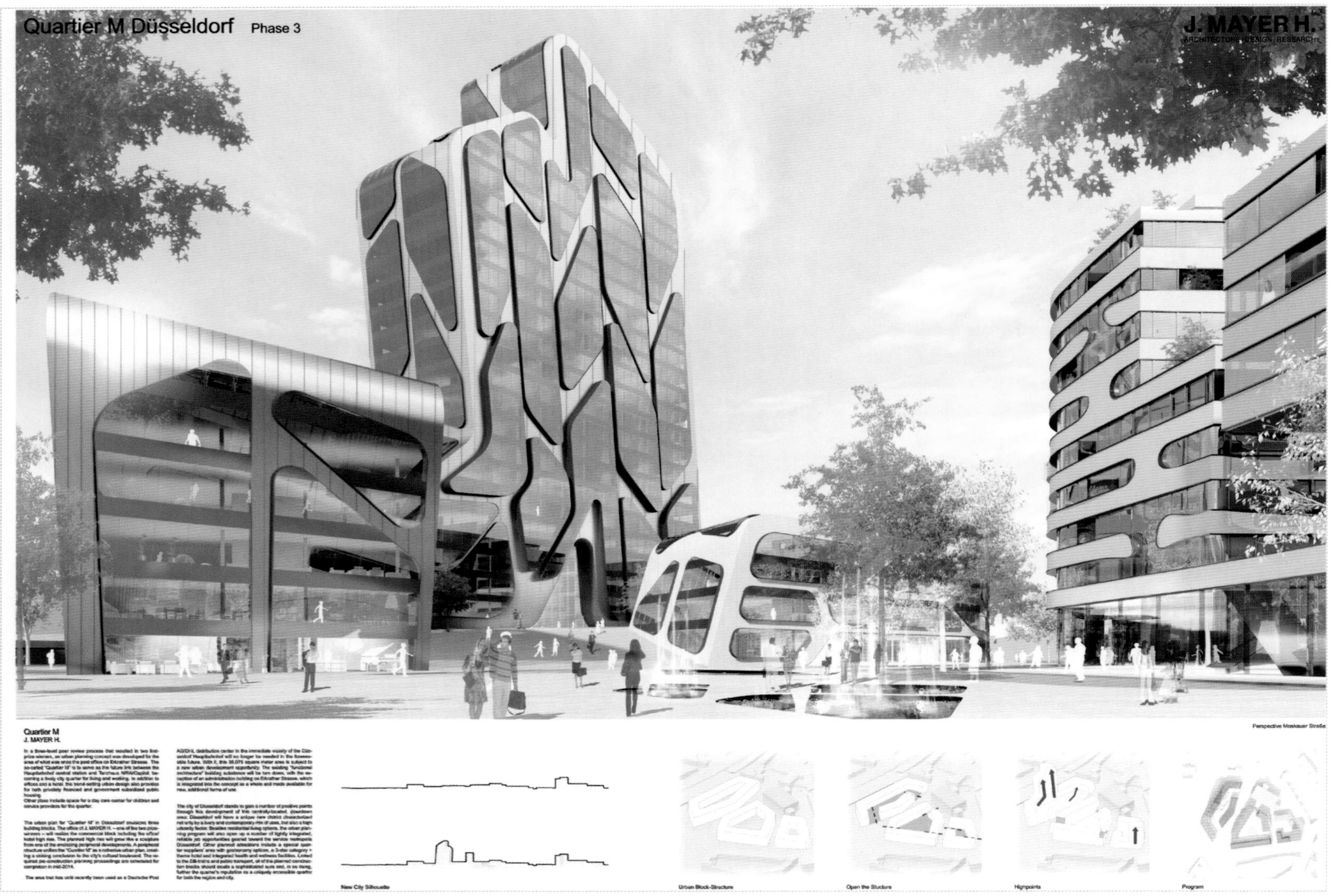

Quartier M Düsseldorf Phase 3

J. MAYER H.
ARCHITECTURE / DESIGN / RESEARCH

Quartier M
J. MAYER H.

Perspective Moskauer Straße

New City Silhouette

Urban Block-Structure

Open the Structure

Highpoints

Program

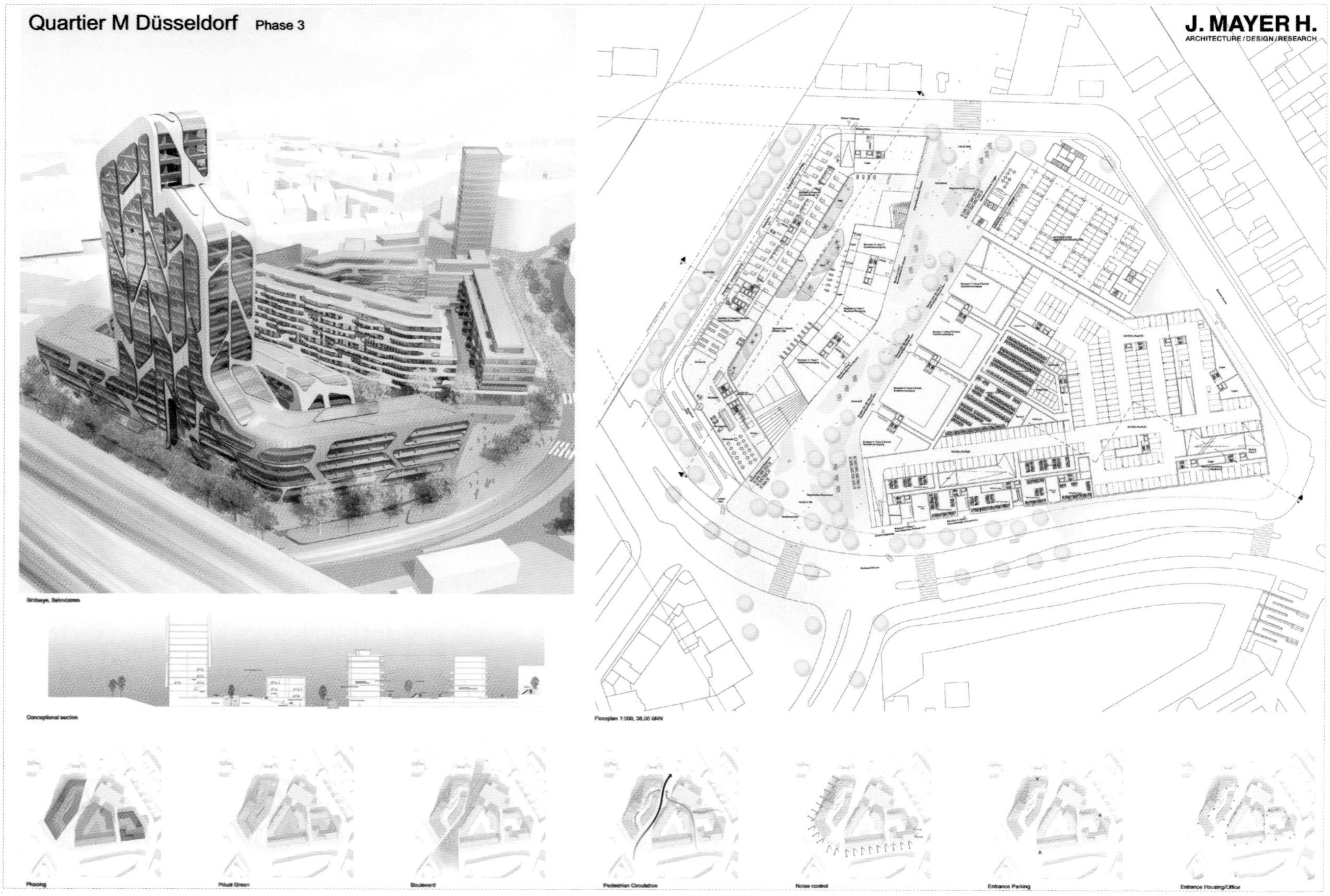

Quartier M Düsseldorf Phase 3

J. MAYER H.
ARCHITECTURE / DESIGN / RESEARCH

Conceptional section

Phasing

Privat Green

Boulevard

Pedestrian Circulation

Noise control

Entrance Parking

Entrance Housing/Office

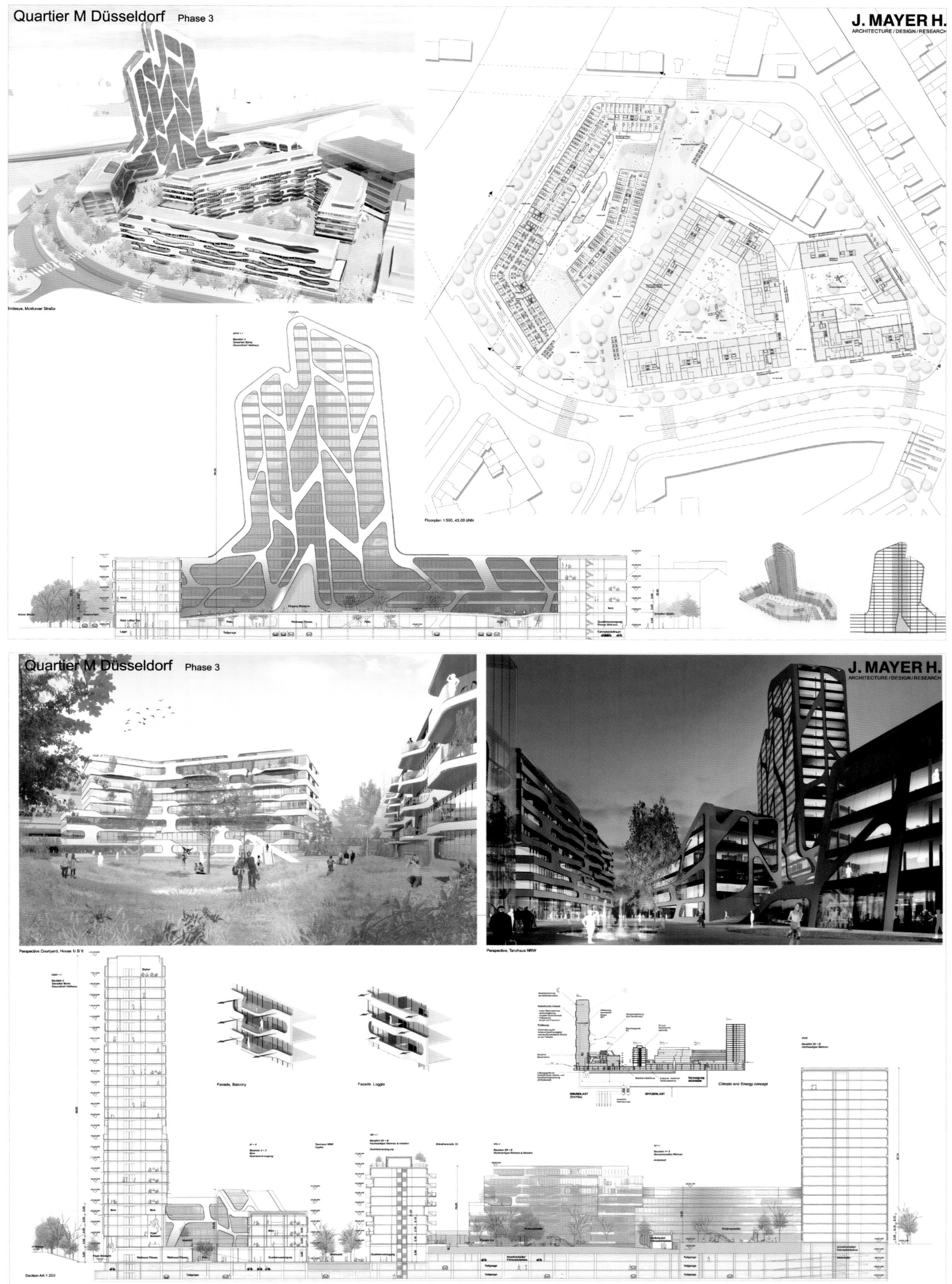

Quartier M Düsseldorf Phase 3
J. MAYER H.
ARCHITECTURE / DESIGN / RESEARCH
Floorplan 1:500, 43.00 üNN
Quartier M Düsseldorf Phase 3
J. MAYER H.
ARCHITECTURE / DESIGN / RESEARCH
Perspective Courtyard, House 1/ 5/ 6
Perspective, Tanzhaus NRW
Facade, Balcony
Facade, Loggia
Climate and Energy concept
Section AA 1:250

129 Amsterdam | *REC ARQUITECTURA*

Competition : Private Contest; Amsterdam/Holland
Team : Marcos Panteleón, Juan C. Zuñiga, Gerardo Recoder)

Chameleon Building is a sort of volume understood from different views, from the beginning point of the pier it can be seen as a tower, from the sea is configurated as the buildings at the shore, and finally from the future extension it stays parallel to the façade and the height.
The ground floor remains a glazed trade to float (elevated) the rest of the building and allows the continuity of the views from the pedestrian point.
The construction process it is thought to be built without leaving out of service the maritime transport.
It has shared spaces with views to the sea but above all a central space protected from the wind. The typologies work as one, two and one and a half level, with a distribution hall at the center and another perimetral one.

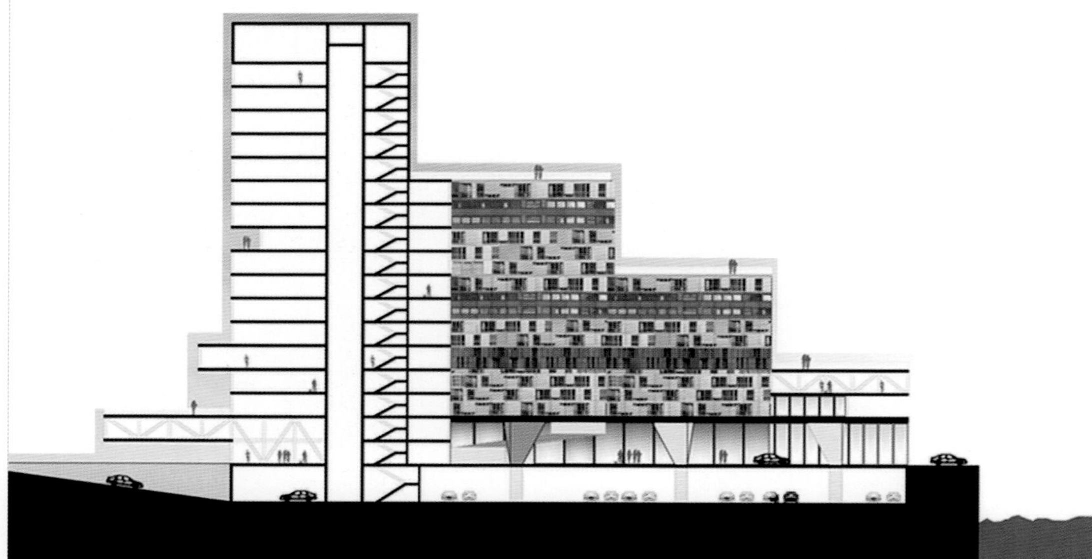

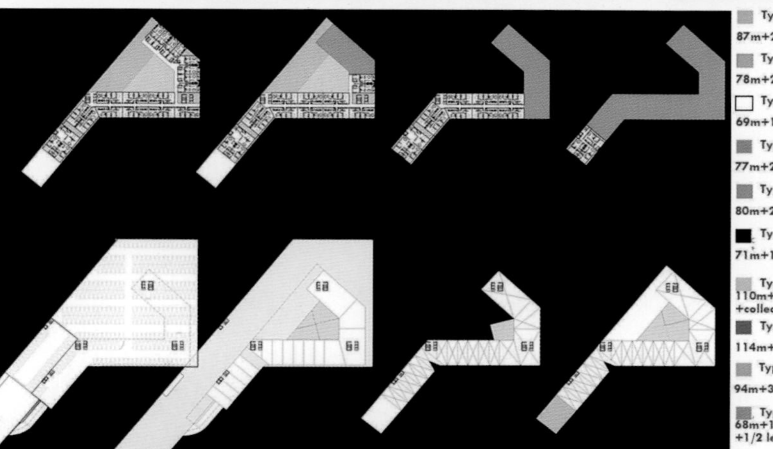

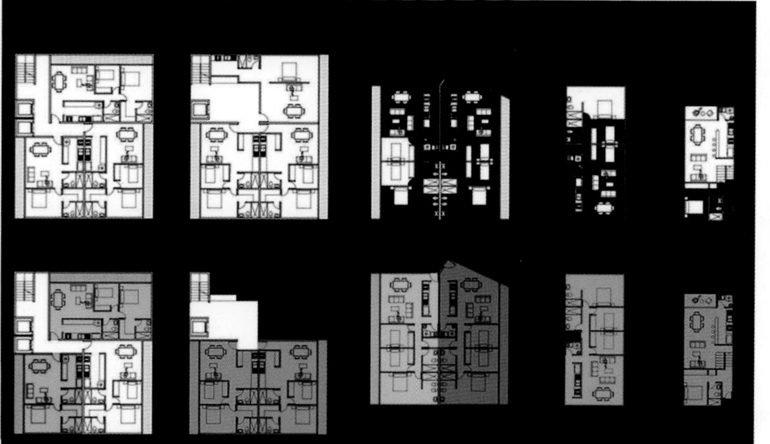

Second Act | *Jägnefält Milton*

Participants : Alex Boyea, Carl Jagnefalt, Konrad Milton, Hjalmar Wedholm

Time : July 2011

130

MO 457 MALMÖ

1

THE SECOND ACT

The ensemble, the instruments and the scenography is already in place. The stage is set for a great experience and all that is needed is a new choreography – less planned and more improvised.

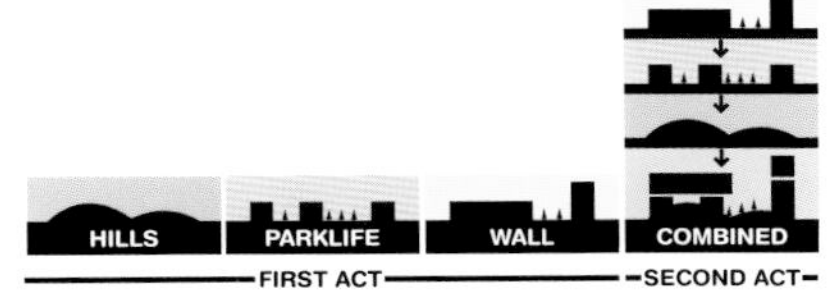

DIVERSE

By fusing Holma's existing, but currently separated, qualities of ribbon buildings, allotment gardens, undulating parks and deep parking garages the urban situation that arises will attract a diverse set of people and programs.

When Holma was built in the seventies it was planned as a rational orthogonal congregation of buildings set to contain 1500 dwellings. Now, forty years later, the tabula rasa is gone and Holma has become a rich fabric of ideas, customs, interactions and relationships. To plan an additional 1300 dwellings on the neighbouring site is not about increasing the density, its about adding potentials to the existing fabric. We propose a multitude of building forms that will house a diversity of both people and programs that will merge into the existing fabric and contribute to the whole of Holma.

The current Holma is characterized by its orthogonally organized ribbon buildings of three and eight floors. The suburban character with a lack of public and commercial programs remains even though Holma is no longer on the fringe of Malmö. The new development of Hyllie and its train station has suddenly put Holma not only in the middle of Malmö but also in close proximity to Copenhagen and its international airport. Our proposal is dealing with this rather delightful situation - a suburban "million programme" suddenly waking up in the middle of a city that almost over night has changed into a vibrating and diverse city full of confidence and opportunities.

By sticking to the existing planning typology with its rational orthogonal ribbon buildings the new development can more easily merge into the old. By adding layers of buildings, nature and public programs the new development will not only carry the genome from the old development, it will also insert potential in form of variation of people and their preferences. In the old homogenous development the plan was superior and each program had its specific place. We propose to stick to the plan but deviate from it in section. By doing so new urban situations will arise and the scale will be both smaller and bigger depending on how the volumes will interact both with each other and with the environment.

A building that has merged with the undulating landscape on top of the garage will be blessed with a private garden. While a building that is stacked on top of two others will provide a view of both the Danish strait and down town Malmö. The ground floors can house a variety of public and commercial programs since the people living in the floors above and in the proximity will have a more diverse set of preferences and also almost double the customer base.

Allotment gardens both on roof tops and on top of the garages will not only function as recreation but also contribute to the farmers market and to the daily dish.

The diversity of both different housing types and public and commercial programs is also a diversity of economies and of stakeholders. This will create a demand for additional, unforeseen services and programs utilising the untapped potential of the people already living in Holma.

VERSATILE

The city will continue to change. The new development will therefore be designed so it can adapt to new programmatic situations.

The old "million program" developments did not plan for change and therefore retrofitting the buildings to adapt to new situations becomes very costly. The result is either that nothing happens or that they are demolished - this is not only a waste of energy it is also a violation of peoples memories and emotional ties to their place. Holma is in this situation, but fortunately Holma is blessed with the project site that runs along the whole neighbourhood. If the new buildings are designed in a way where different programs can use the same space with little or no retrofitting this will not only save money and energy in the future, but it will also promote change and offer space for initiatives coming from the present Holma.

The 6x6x6 m grid is the starting point offering a structure that can expand in all dimensions – suitable for building depths of 12 m, floor to floor heights of 3 m and two parking spaces withing 6x3 m. The typical "million program" building was constructed of pre-cast load-bearing walls, concrete floor slabs and rigid cores. Those kind of heavy concrete structures consumes vast amount of energy and carbon dioxide. Steel is a better alternative; less carbon intensive, easier to recycle and faster to erect than concrete. Also, Malmö has a know-how of steel constructions since its history of ship building. Our proposal uses steel columns with autoclaved cellular concrete blocks for interior walls instead of pre-cast load-bearing walls. Bubble decks are used instead of heavy concrete floor slabs eliminating the need for beams between the columns. A steel exoskeleton is used for lateral stability instead of using the core. This makes its possible for the core to be moved out to the facade which gives both slender buildings and a more economical use of the layout. All in all, this structural concept will save resources and at the same time provide floor plans that can either be of a open floor plan type, suitable for offices and public programs or compartmentalised into housing, hotels and other smaller units.

The narrow floor plates of 12 m enables natural ventilation and enhances daylight which are key features to be able to provide different program uses over time. Common heating and cooling principles in the buildings further reduces the need for retrofitting in the future.

The facade glazing units of 1.5 x 3 m is interchangeable between different program uses and can also be replaced by future improvements in facade technology such as building integrated photovoltaics and improved insulation. Balconies can be inserted into the facade system and the balcony floor can be on the same level as the interior floor by using thin vacuum insulation panels for balcony slab insulation.

A interesting urban feature in todays Holma is the *Folkets hus* and the small stage that sits ontop of a underused parking garage. This *typology by improvisation* can be used as a urban strategy in the new development. The parking norm of 0.8 will result in vast areas of parking, but by placing the parking in covered spaces punctuated by courtyards those structures could both be used for parking and by small interventions partly turned into spaces for other programs such as workshops of different sizes, retail and public programs.

UNITED

The full potential of Holma is reached by channelling existing entrepreneurs and cultural life from the old development into the structures and infrastructure of the new development.

Today Holma is subdivided into three parts with two grocery stores in between. The northern third of the old Holma differs slightly from the two southern parts but on a whole the three part can be seen as one unit connected in north southern directions by bicycle and walking paths inside the area and roads for motor traffic on the perimeter. The new area runs along the eastern border of all three parts. Seen both from a socioeconomic and a spatial context the new development risks becoming a separate entity disconnected from the old Holma and could even enhance Holma's reputation, true or not, of a troubled suburb. If the street *Snödroppsgatan* along the western border of the site is widened and used for more intense traffic there is a risk for enhancing this barrier between new and old. We propose to give this street the same character as the bicycle and walking path in the park *Krokbäcksparken* and instead move the buses and the additional motor traffic to a street approximately following the existing one way street *Holmavångsvägen*. The area of risk free movement for kids will then be expanded into the new development and strengthen the social and spatial bonds in east-west directions between the two developments instead of the north-south directions that would separate new from old. This change of street use would also make it possible for new schools and services in the new development to serve both new and old Holma.

Currently all north bound traffic must drive all the way up to the northern entrance to enter Holma. We propose a new roundabout at the southern part of the street *Pildamsvägen* just north of the street *Annetorpsvägen*. The new entrance will be a focal point for both traffic and people providing good conditions for commercial and public programs such as markets, shops and the community centre – Folkets hus.

To further strengthen the east-west connections between new and old Holma we propose to utilize the underused parking garages situated inside the two existing sub centres. The two parking floors, one covered and one open on the top could be transformed into urban agriculture centres. The sub floor would be suitable for handling bio-waste decreasing the waste transport from Holma and instead turning it into useful soil and clean energy. The open top floor would provide the base for green houses enhancing the crop yield and nurturing plants for the allotment gardens in the new and old development.

The parking garages in the new development will house cars from both areas and as mentioned earlier will also provide flexible spaces for workshops etc. This character of small scale programs would provide an interesting counterweight to the large scale and mall-like character of the new development south of Holma and would enhance the *Holma spirit* to also include entrepreneurship and inventiveness. The green corridor that now is a separate area in the western part of Holma is extended to run atop of the garages to create a green loop running around the whole area enhancing the experience of a united Holma.

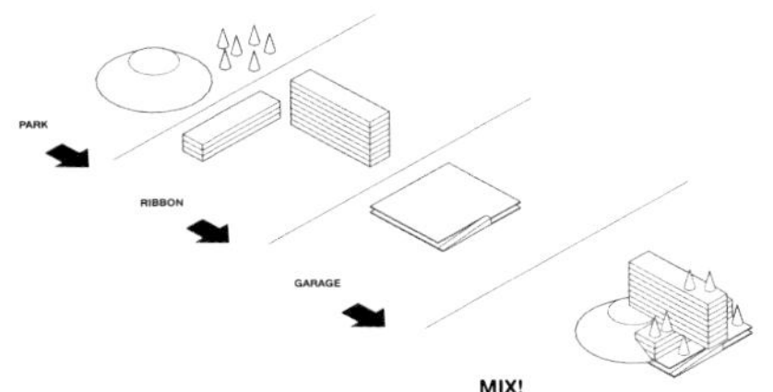

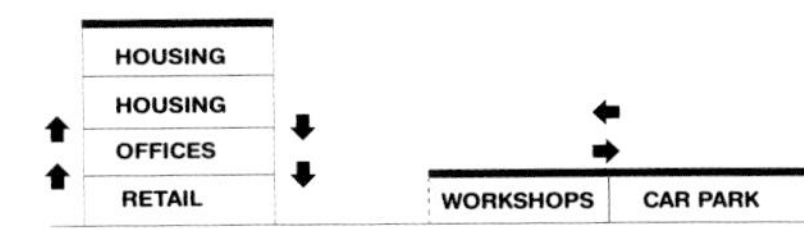

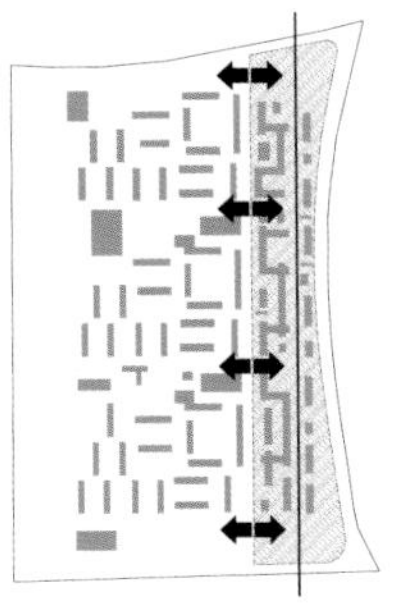

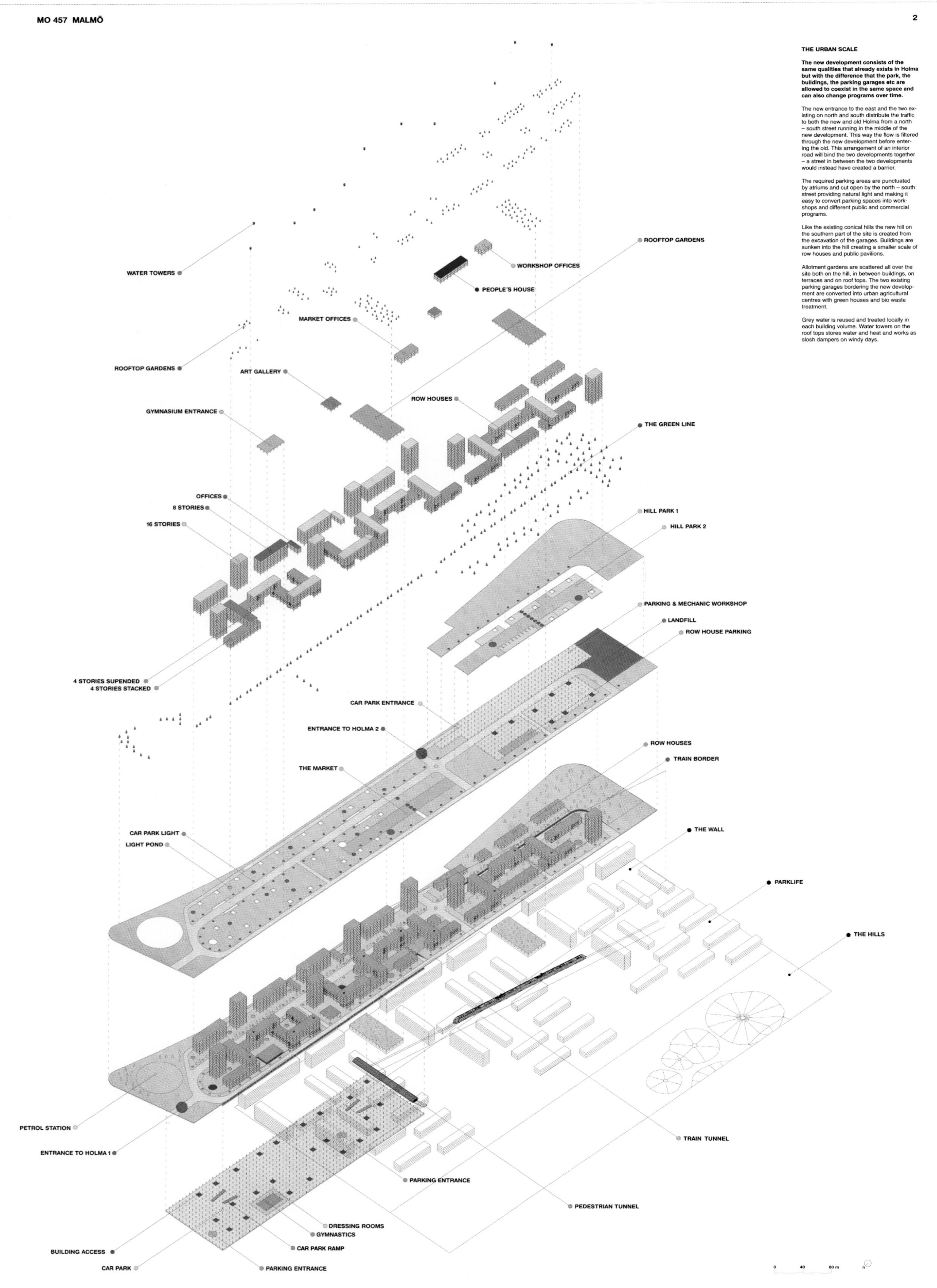

THE URBAN SCALE

The new development consists of the same qualities that already exists in Holma but with the difference that the park, the buildings, the parking garages etc are allowed to coexist in the same space and can also change programs over time.

The new entrance to the east and the two existing on north and south distribute the traffic to both the new and old Holma from a north – south street running in the middle of the new development. This way the flow is filtered through the new development before entering the old. This arrangement of an interior road will bind the two developments together – a street in between the two developments would instead have created a barrier.

The required parking areas are punctuated by atriums and cut open by the north – south street providing natural light and making it easy to convert parking spaces into workshops and different public and commercial programs.

Like the existing conical hills the new hill on the southern part of the site is created from the excavation of the garages. Buildings are sunken into the hill creating a smaller scale of row houses and public pavilions.

Allotment gardens are scattered all over the site both on the hill, in between buildings, on terraces and on roof tops. The two existing parking garages bordering the new development are converted into urban agricultural centres with green houses and bio waste treatment.

Grey water is reused and treated locally in each building volume. Water towers on the roof tops stores water and heat and works as slosh dampers on windy days.

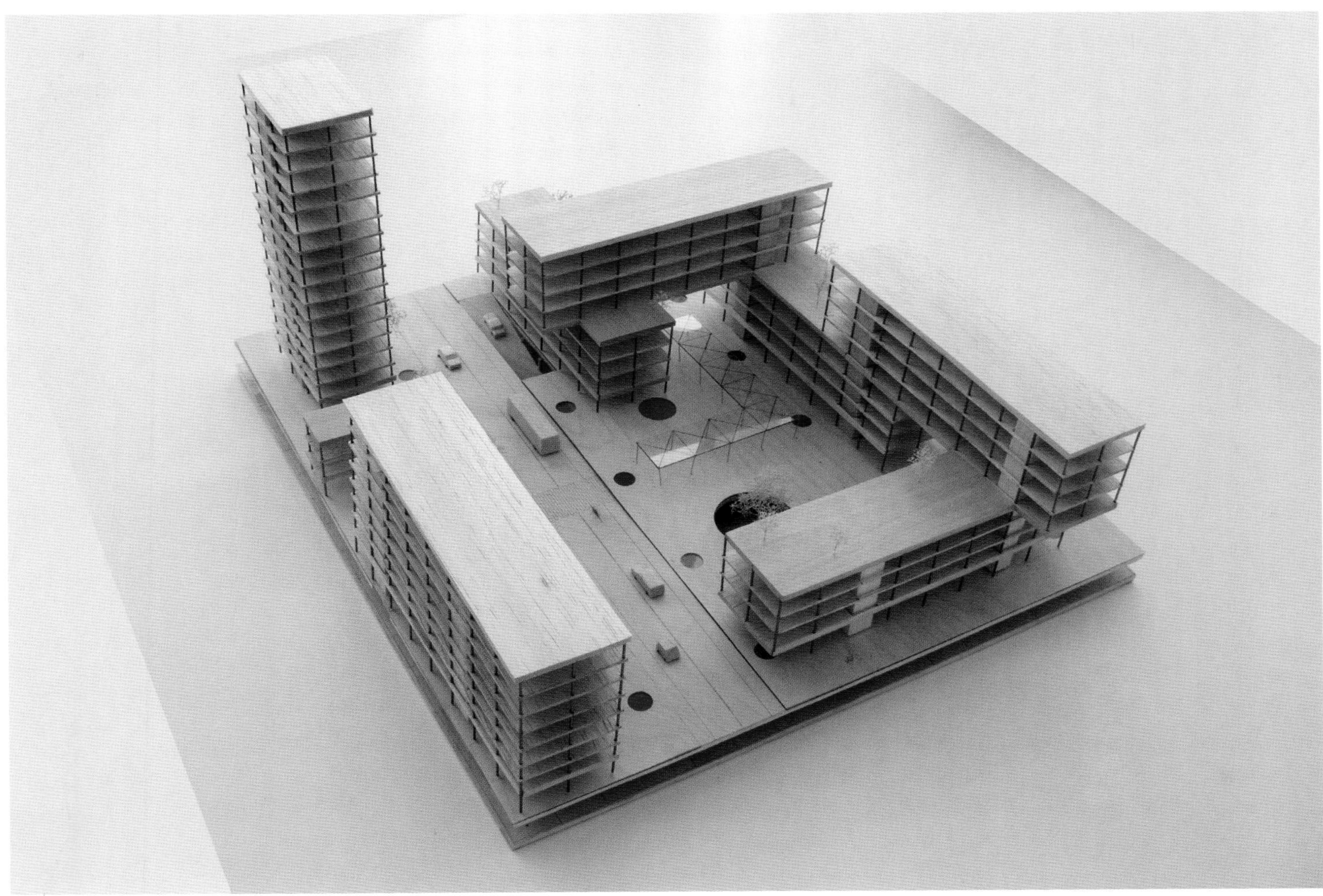

THE BUILDING SCALE

The proposal consist of different building typologies that are based on the same structural concept and building depth which creates endless possibilities of spatial and programmatic variations.

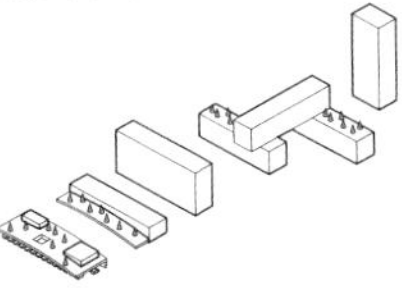

The cast of typologies. From the left:
- Ridge parking and pavilions
- Ridge side row house
- Ribbon house
- Stacked ribbon house
- Tower

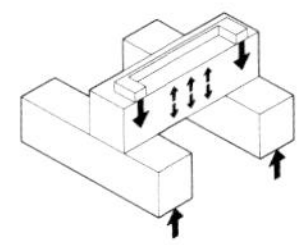

The floor slabs over the gaps are hanging in the roof beams connected to the core.

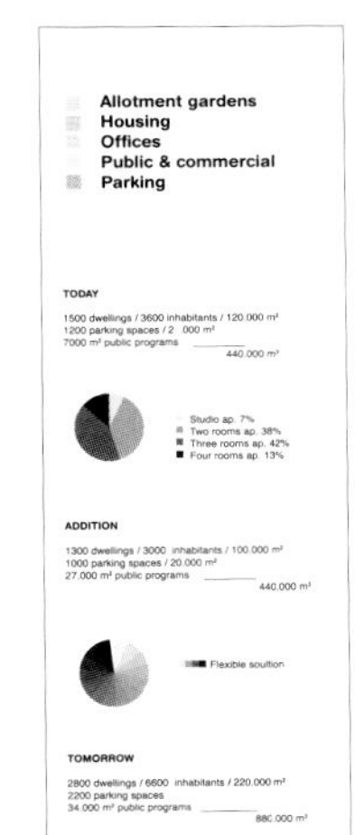

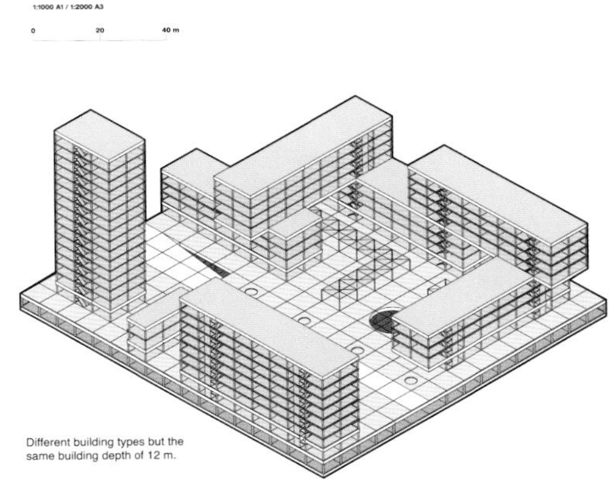

Different building types but the same building depth of 12 m.

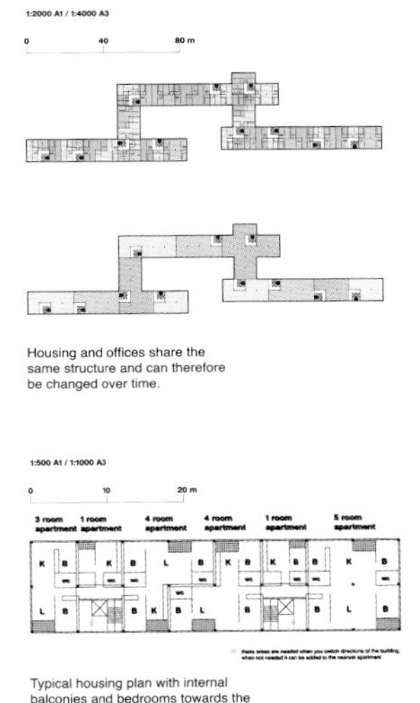

Housing and offices share the same structure and can therefore be changed over time.

Typical housing plan with internal balconies and bedrooms towards the silent side.

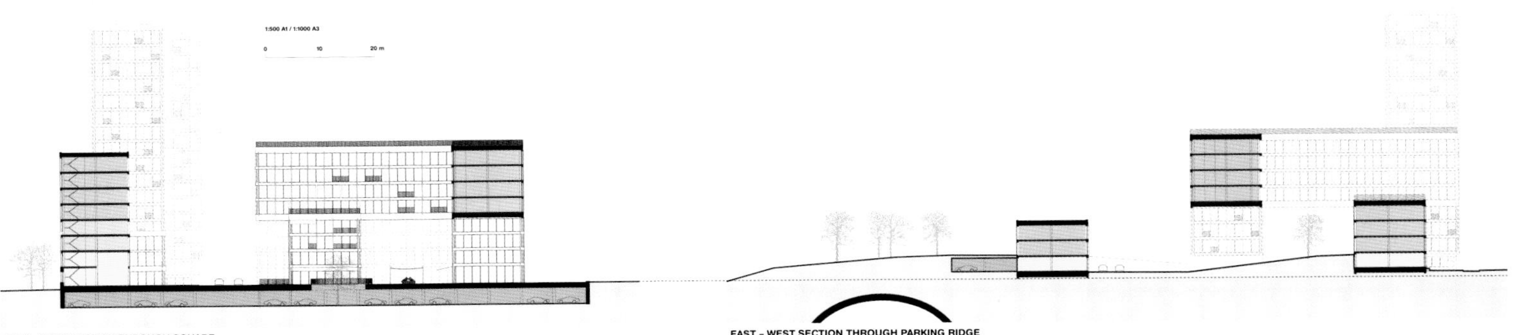

EAST – WEST SECTION THROUGH SQUARE

EAST – WEST SECTION THROUGH PARKING RIDGE

131

Sky Pier | *Jägnefält Milton*

Competition : The city of Galway and the Royal Institute of the Architects of Ireland Organized an Open International Competition to Design a Mixed Use Building
Award : 1st prize
Participants : Carl Jägnefält, Konrad Milton

THE SKY PIER – UNITY IN DUALITY

By using the same form but under two different conditions – horizontal and vertical – the concept of the open public space and the concept of the multiplied office space can coexist in the same shape of building.

When investigating the program three main areas becomes clear:
– Flexible spaces for exhibitions and retail.
– A seri of offices with the same areas.
– Public space connected to the water, the stage and the flexible spaces.
This implies that the flexible spaces and the public spaces should be well connected and that they both need spaces closely connected to the ground and with a generous footprint. On the other hand the office spaces are usually best suited for a stacked and multiplied solution. Still the Galway Harbour Company is seeking for a design that could unite this two different preferences in one building that also will contribute to the maritime and cultural image of the city.

Our proposed concept clearly states the unity in duality by using the same structural grid in both a horizontal condition where the exhibition and retail spaces are situated and a vertical conditions where the offices are stacked. The horizontal areas are pointing towards the city with its two long sides relating to the life on the pier on one side and the moored boats on the other. The vertical areas with mainly offices are facing the city on its one long side and the sea on the other offering an office space with both views. The result is a building that is not mediating between the two opposite preferences but instead, by flipping the direction of the building, creating a unity while maintaing the duality.

The flexible spaces for retail and exhibitions are situated on the ground level of the horizontal part of the building where the two main spaces can be compartmentalized within a 3 by 3 m grid and where the structural grid spans 6 meters both on the horizontal and the vertical plan.

The office spaces in the vertical part of the building are stacked and on the top are three floors that could serve both the offices as a conference area and the public as a sky bar with tourist information. The same structural grid of 6 by 6 m truss span provides a office gross floor area of 108 m^2. The vertical facade facing the city is glazed and has an external rasterized screen that provides privacy, yet offers a view when standing close to the windows. The raster has large openings in some places that mimics the horizontal roof landscape and at the same time provides spectacular variations in the facade – both for the viewers from the outside and from the inside. The vertical facade facing the sea does not need the privacy protection and are fully glazed making the whole office exposed to the visual impact of the ocean.

The junction of the horizontal and the vertical part of the building becomes the natural point for the stage and by making the roof of the horizontal part of the building accessible to the public the whole roof area can be used for out door spectator events. The stage could be made as an elevator thereby providing opportunities for different spectacles where the stage is first hidden (the view of the sea as a backdrop) and then raised from the ground floor or lowered from the roof. The same stage when resting on the ground floor will serve indoor events where the exhibition area is used for spectators.

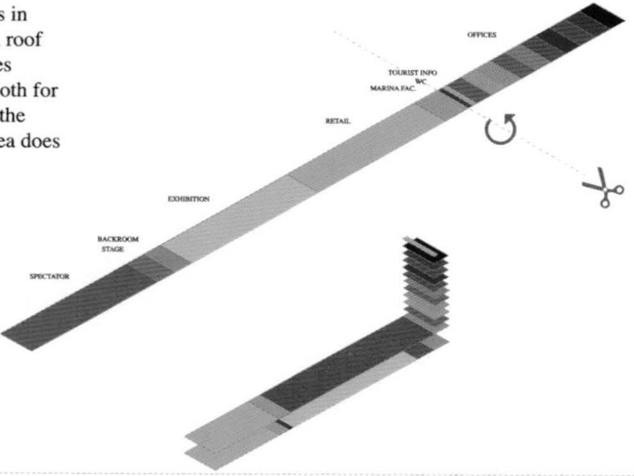

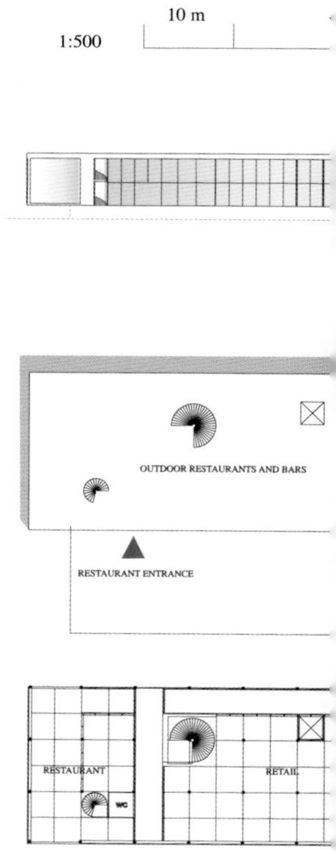

1:500
10 m

OUTDOOR RESTAURANTS AND BARS
RESTAURANT ENTRANCE
RESTAURANT
WC
RETAIL

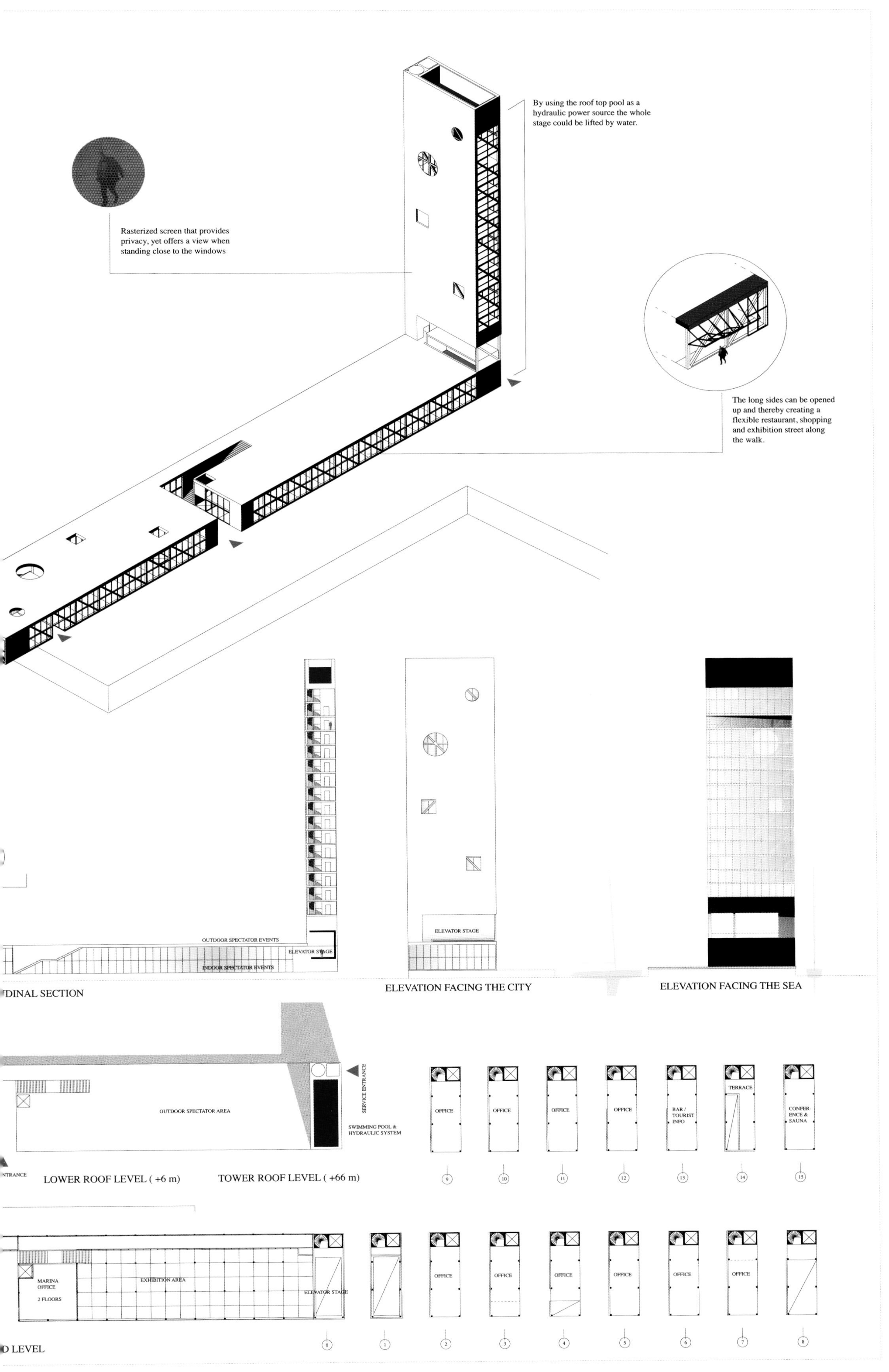
By using the roof top pool as a hydraulic power source the whole stage could be lifted by water.
Rasterized screen that provides privacy, yet offers a view when standing close to the windows
The long sides can be opened up and thereby creating a flexible restaurant, shopping and exhibition street along the walk.
OUTDOOR SPECTATOR EVENTS
ELEVATOR STAGE
INDOOR SPECTATOR EVENTS
DINAL SECTION
ELEVATOR STAGE
ELEVATION FACING THE CITY
ELEVATION FACING THE SEA
OUTDOOR SPECTATOR AREA
SERVICE ENTRANCE
SWIMMING POOL & HYDRAULIC SYSTEM
OFFICE
OFFICE
OFFICE
OFFICE
BAR / TOURIST INFO
TERRACE
CONFER-ENCE & SAUNA
NTRANCE
LOWER ROOF LEVEL (+6 m)
TOWER ROOF LEVEL (+66 m)
9
10
11
12
13
14
15
MARINA OFFICE
2 FLOORS
EXHIBITION AREA
ELEVATOR STAGE
OFFICE
OFFICE
OFFICE
OFFICE
OFFICE
OFFICE
D LEVEL
0
1
2
3
4
5
6
7
8

132 Villa Sapmi | *Jägnefält Milton*

Competition : The Finnish Association of Architects Organized an Open International Competition to Design Finlands Sami Parliament and Cultural Centre
Award : 3rd prize
Participants : Tobias Forsgren, Carl Jägnefält, Konrad Milton, Joacim Wahlstrom

VILLA SÁPMI *–Inari*

Competition entry
A familiar form taken to its extreme simplicity with an interior illuminated by its heart – a room and a fireplace extending all the way up to the ridge of the ceiling.

You will reach Villa Sápmi by walking through a meadow. The entrances sits in the middle of the long sides. The lobby and the library reaching all the way up to the ridge of the ceiling is illuminated by the sun during days and by the fireplace at nights. The northern part with the auditorium, stage and multipurpose hall is hovering among the pine trees. From the wooden deck on the ground floor to the assembly hall two floors up you can watch the river and take in the northern light. The restaurant in the south part opens up to the sun and faces an outdoor stage in the middle of the meadow. The sauna and its terrace at the top floor offers a view of the setting sun just above the tree line.

The shape and the wooden construction rests both in the landscape and in the culture, yet Villa Sápmi stands for something new, a symbol and a tool for the sami people.

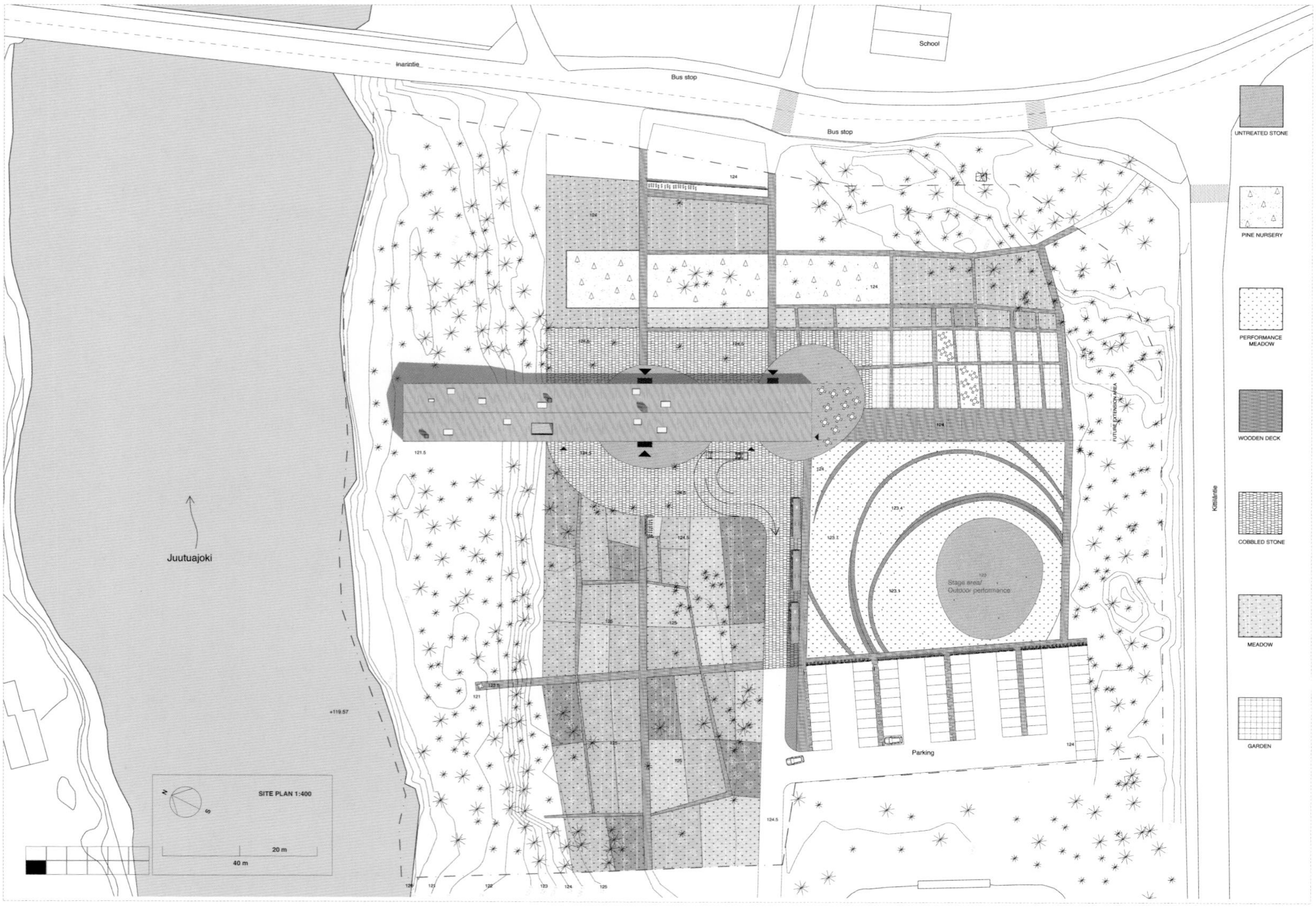

School
Inarintie
Bus stop
Bus stop
Juutuajoki
Stage area/ Outdoor performance
Parking
Kittiläntie
FUTURE EXTENSION AREA
SITE PLAN 1:400
20 m
40 m
UNTREATED STONE
PINE NURSERY
PERFORMANCE MEADOW
WOODEN DECK
COBBLED STONE
MEADOW
GARDEN

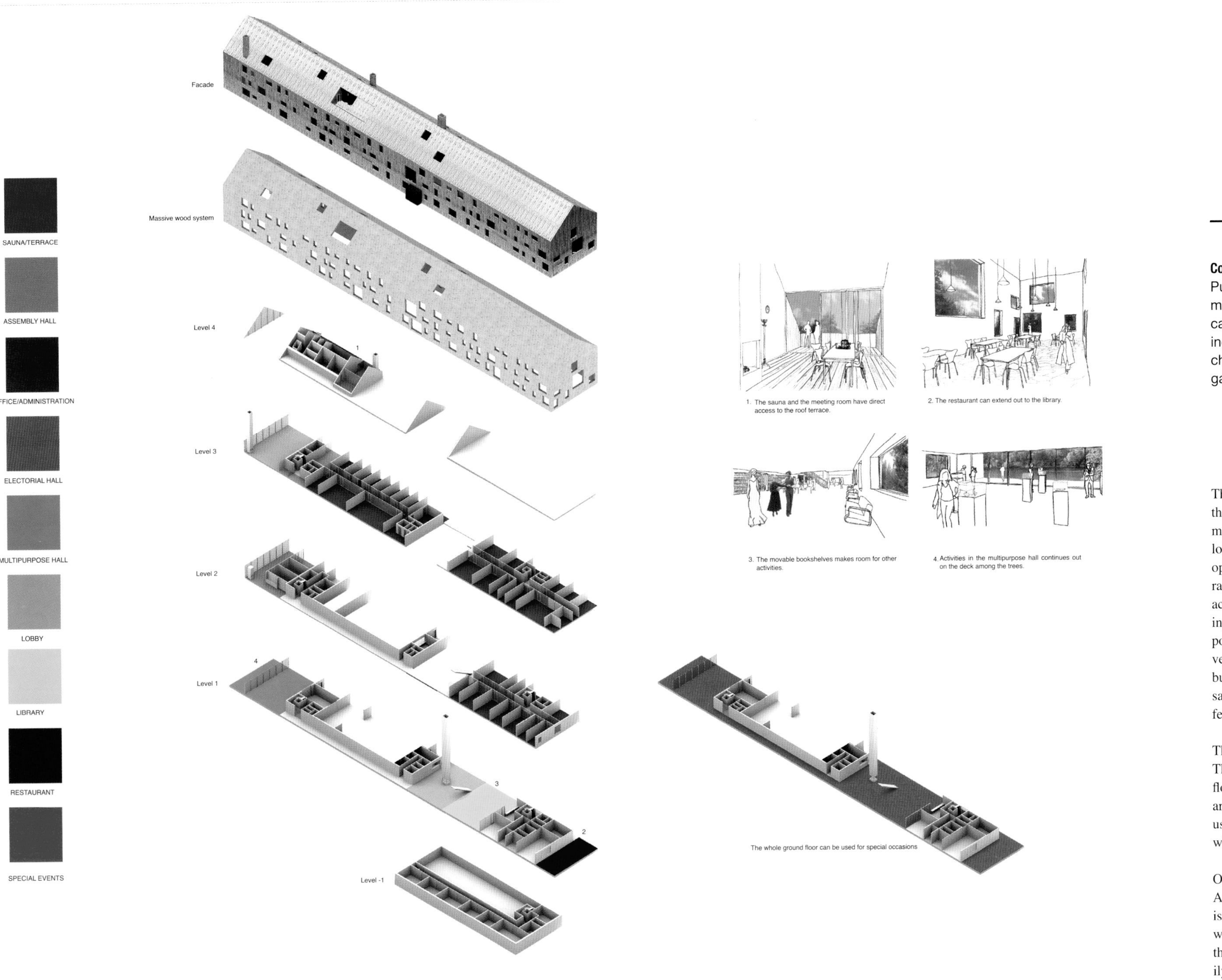

1. The sauna and the meeting room have direct access to the roof terrace.

2. The restaurant can extend out to the library.

3. The movable bookshelves makes room for other activities.

4. Activities in the multipurpose hall continues out on the deck among the trees.

The whole ground floor can be used for special occasions

–Usage

Concept
Public areas can be merged for specific occasions and the building structure encourages changes in plan and organizations.

The public part of the building – the library, the restaurant, the auditorium, stage and multipurpose hall – are all connected to the lobby. Sliding doors makes it possible to open up or close the areas, i.e., the restaurant can be closed without hindering other activities and the northern part of the building can be separated during stage work. It is possible to independently manage activities vertically through the northern part of the building – multipurpose hall, parliament, sauna and terrace – without mixing the different users.

The Library
The public part of the library is on the ground floor. By using movable bookshelves the area normally reserved for books can be used in larger gatherings that needs the whole ground floor.

Office and administration
An open but well defined office landscape is possible thanks to the building structure which needs a small amount of columns. In this way future changes are possible and easily done. The two elevator shafts that does not reach the attic can be extended upward without having to change the gabled roof.

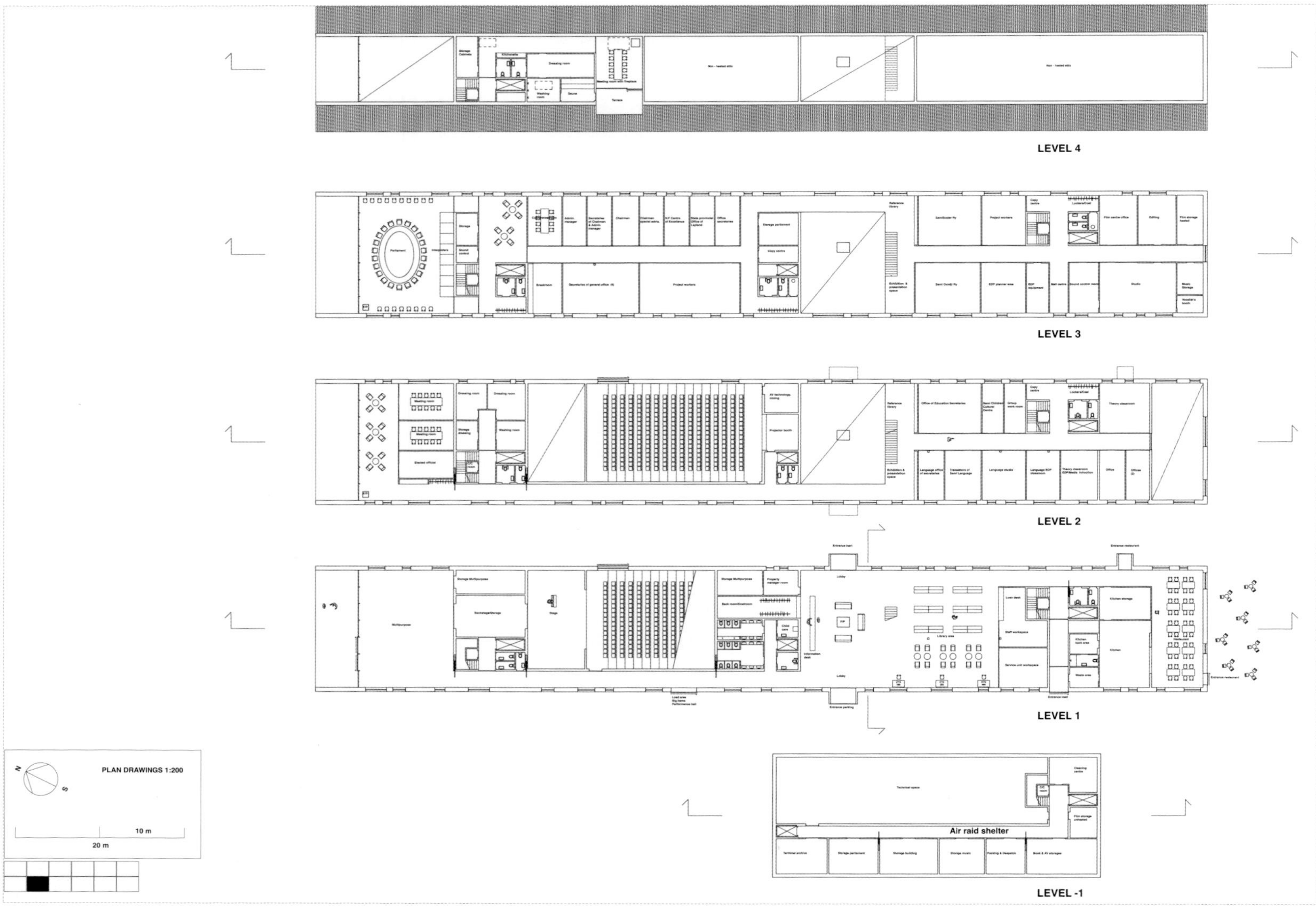

LEVEL 4

LEVEL 3

LEVEL 2

LEVEL 1

PLAN DRAWINGS 1:200

10 m

20 m

Air raid shelter

LEVEL -1

The Restaurant

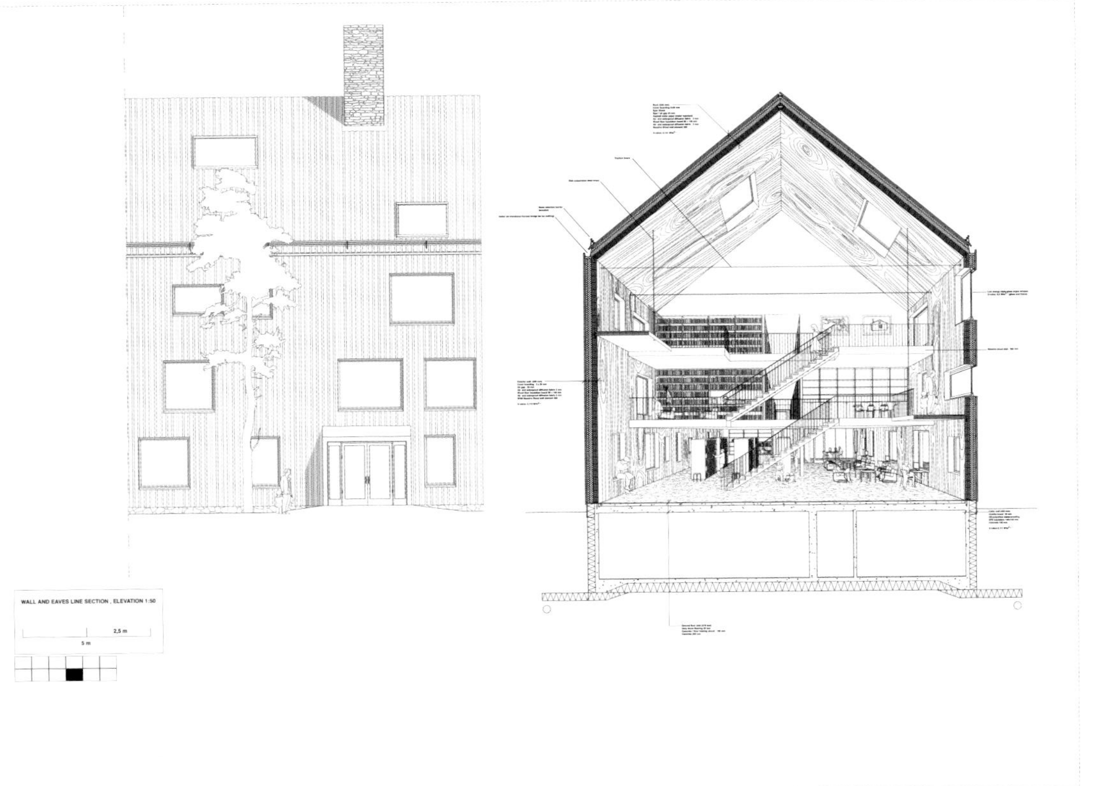

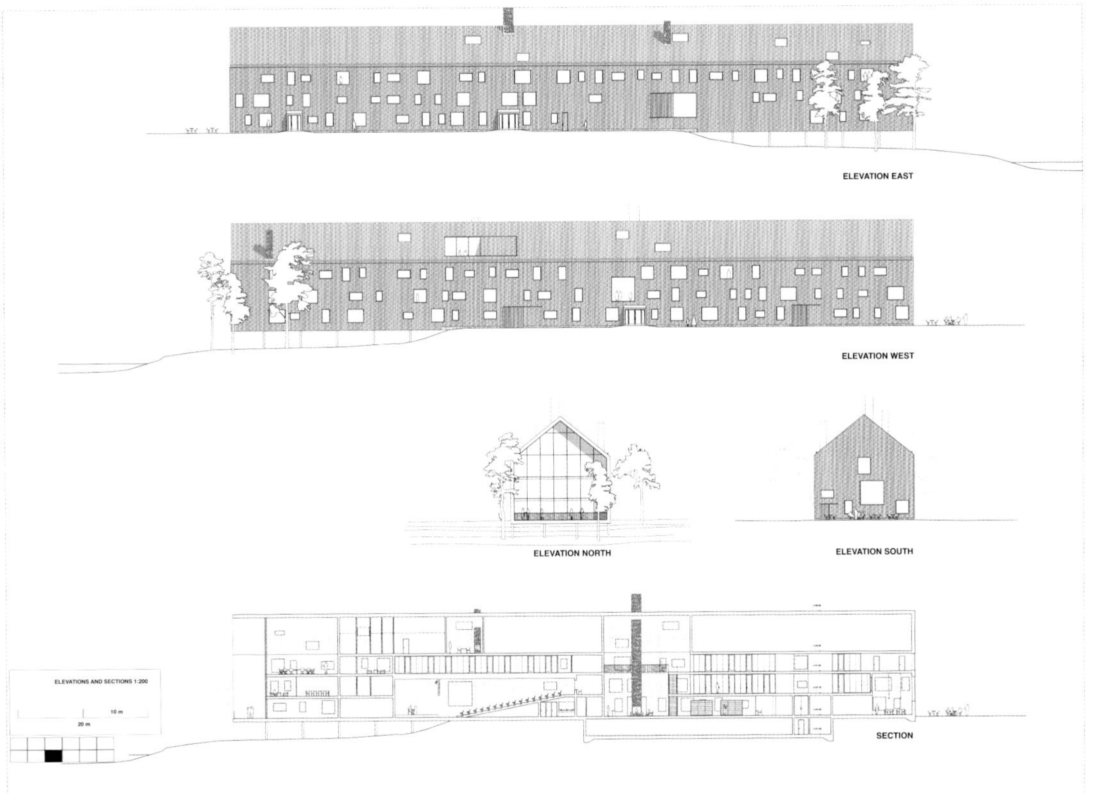

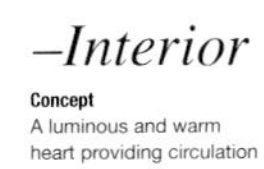

–Interior

Concept
A luminous and warm heart providing circulation close to its skin.

The experience of the outside inside the building is enhanced by the indigenous stones used both on outdoor surfaces and to cover the whole ground floor, the circulation running close to the outer walls and the gabled building form that is exposed in the interior spaces.

The lobby and its fireplace reaches all the way up to the ridge of the building. This space plays a central role in the building – it is here where people meet, greet or just bump into each other when passing through. Feel free to sit down in front of the fire with a book from the library.

The assembly hall in the northern part of the building will have a view over the river and the northern light – midnight sun in summer and aurora in winter.

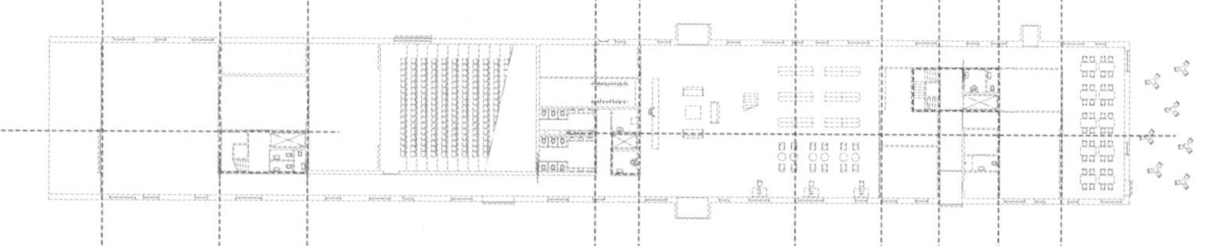

There are three elevator-and-staircase groups, stabilising the construction along the axis of the building.

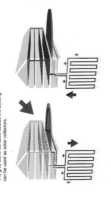

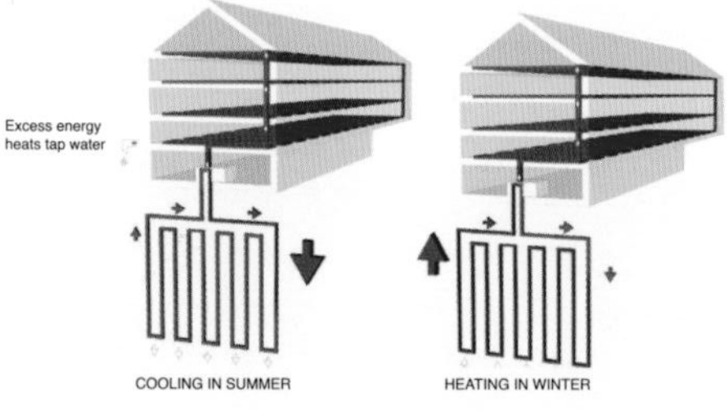

The grey stone surfaces outside the building can be used as solar collectors.

–Construction

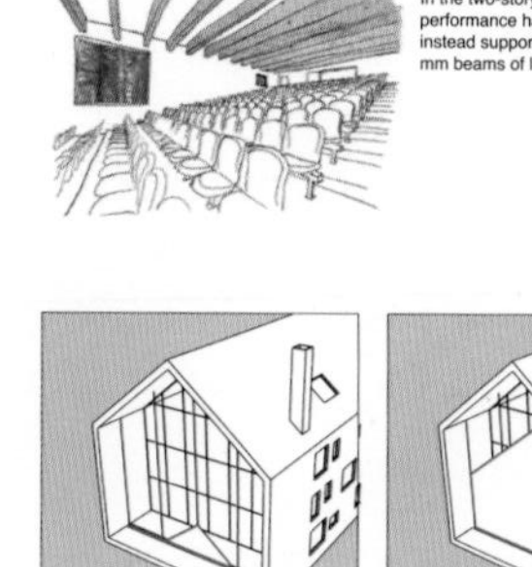

In the two-story high part of the performance hall, the ceiling is instead supported by 700x215 mm beams of laminated wood.

The northern glass façade can be covered by a large sail that is hoisted from below, reducing heat losses.

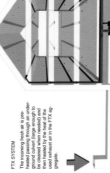

Preface

We want to work together with nature, not against it. Building in the arctic forest regions means having to cope with the real forces of nature. Their conditions are as tough as their beauty is breathtaking. We want our building to be a good co-player in this wild scene, strong and sturdy and at the same time humble and fair to its surroundings. This is the essence of the construction and energy concept.

The construction is very basic. A frame of massive wood elements are joined together to enclose the spaces inside. Exterior walls, roof and slabs. The frame is clad in vertical boarding wood. The building rests on a concrete platform and basement, a safe underground construction solution and a robust emergency shelter. The northern end pivoting out in the air towards the river is suported by massive wooden columns, a counterpart to the surounding pinetrees.

The interior slabs are supported by the exterior walls and by a grid of 200x200 mm wooden columns. In the two-story high part of the performance hall, the ceiling is instead supported by 700x215 mm beams of laminated wood. In the entrance hall and in the parliament, horisontal traction braces suspend the exterior walls. The upper walkways in the entrance hall space are also suspended in vertical steel bars from the ceiling. In the northern facade, window glass and slabs are supported by 60x140 mm wood profiles. There are three elevator-and-staircase groups, stabilising the construction along the axis of the building.

The essential element of the building is the loadbearing frame of massive wood. Bare towards the inside spaces, it lets the user or visitor experience the core of the construction immediately. It tells of life, nature and natural robustness. Wood is of course the obvious material of choice; traditional, natural, indigenous, plentiful on the site. Renewable and organic, it captures and stores carbon dioxide, thus reducing climate change. But is it also has great construction advantages, being able to "breathe" and buffer and transport vapour without problems as long as it isn't sealed, and with a great thermal capacity.

The MHM (Massive-Holz-Mauer) technique makes use of these inherent qualities and takes wooden construction to a new level. Timber boards are nailed together into solid wall and slab elements, which are then robotically sculpted to fit the design of the specific project with millimeter precision. This brings major benefits; production and on site assembly is fast, easy and inexpensive, and the wall can arrive prepared in detail with all sinkages and holes for installations etcetera. The irregular window compostion of Villa Sápmi is delivered automatically.

The solid wooden frame element contain thin air-space channels which improve their thermal insulation capacity. The wood itself will buffer heat over time and reduce temperature variation. It has been established that in massive wood buildings, heating energy use is lower than a U-value analysis would suggest; it is the thermal storage capacity of the solid wood that brings this unexpected result. The building will be kept warm in the winter and cool in summer.

As for moist and vapour; the massive wood elements have a large buffering capacity, are open for diffusion and will not rot or moulder as long as the moist is not locked inside them. They will dry out again, and the indoor climate is kept sound and healthy. The wall construction contains no plastic sealing and no glue. Fluid-water-proofing and airtightness in secured by using a gore-tex-like airtight, waterproof, but diffusion-open fabric (for example Bison).

The exterior walls and and roof are insulated with wood fiber insulation board; wood fiber that has been "boiled" until its inherent lignin is released and turn into an organic bonding agent which holds the board together. It has thermal properties equivalent to those of conventional thermal insulation, with a lambda value around 0,039.

The exterior walls and roof are clad in vertical boarding wood: either larch, which is tough enough to withstand outdoor conditions without any surface preparation, or, if a local species of wood is preferred, pine treated with copperas, which will age beautifully to wooden grey.

The gutters are hidden behind the boarding at the roof-base, to keep the shape of the building intact and free from nitty-gritty, and at the same time benefit from the heat transmission from the interior in order to melt ice and snow and avoid clogging up. The roof-wall meeting has been deliberately designed as a modest thermal bridge to secure this function.

Drawing on the benefits of the MHM pre-sculpting technique, the spouts are also hidden behind the boarding wood, somewhat countersink into the solid wood elements, benefitting from the transmission heat.

The roof construction is similar, expect that it is coated in asphalt roof paper underneath the spars, to ensure that water can run freely down the roof without ever getting into the core of the construction.

The bottom floor is paved with indigenous dark grey natural stone, of the same kind that is found in the big round shapes on the ground around the building. Underneath the surface of all four floors runs a floor heating circuit, giving comfortable heat to the floor and the space above it when needed (see below).

The northern glass façade can be covered by a large sail that is hoisted from below, reducing heat losses.

All windows are equipped with aluminium venetian blinds on the inside, that, when closed, also will reduce heat loss by radition.

Alltogether, this is a strong and sound construction made to suit the climate conditions of Inari, while providing an excellent, comfortable indoor climate.

MHM-system: production and on site assembly is fast, easy and inexpensive.

–Energy

Preface

Building an office and assembly building in an arctic climate is quite a challenge. Office buildings generally tend to have a need for cooling, because the people and equipment inside generate so much heat. On the other hand, in the far northern hemisphere the climate simply demands extensive heating in the winter. One has to consider this delicate balance.

FTX SYSTEM
The incoming fresh air is preheated passing through an underground culvert (large enough to be cleaned when needed) and then heated by the heat of the used exhaust air in the FTX aggregate.

Conventionally, buildings are equipped with both heating and cooling systems, burning oil or using electricity directly to heat, and using large amounts of electricity for the cooling systems, all of which results in large carbon dioxide emissions in the end.

Villa Sápmi has been designed to hit an equilibrium between the heat excess heat of the indoor activities and the cold of the outdoor climate. The building envelope is heavy, dense, energy-efficient and airtight, with low U-values and low-energy triple-glass windows. In a temperate climate zone it would have become severly over-heated by the excess heat of it's indoor activities, thus requiring massive cooling systems. However, in Inari, with a year average of -0,8 centigrades, heat losses through this building envelope will be on level that more or less evens out the internal heat loads.

Our energy calculations indicate that Villa Sápmi, in full use, will have a heating demand of about zero to fifteen kWh per squaremeter and year. In effect, however, this means that over the year, there will be variations with periods of both heating and cooling demand, like in any building. Instead of equipping the house with double climate systems that work against each other and use twice the energy, we would like to take care of the excess heat, store it, and use it later, when we need it.

This is achieved partly with the massive wood building frame, which in itself will absorb large amounts of energy and keep it until the surroundings are cooler. For greater cooling or heating needs, a water-pipe-circuit is built in above and below the slabs, where in the summer the water will absorb excess heat from the rooms, thus cooling them from above, and bring it to a heat-pump, that passes on the heat (not the water) to the tapwater boiler, thus making the useless heat useful producing hot water, saving lots of energy.

Further excess heat will be passed on from the heat pump down into a geothermal borehole storeage, that is drilled into the bedrock below the building. During the warm half of the year, heat will accumulate in the rock around the waterpipes. In the winter, the process is reversed, so that the heat is pumped back from the boreholes up into the circuit in floors of the building, warming the spaces from below. The heat is used and re-used.

A bonus feature, that might be applied, is the use of the great grey stone surfaces as solar collectors. A similar waterpipe circuit might be installed underneath their surface. In the summer, with two months of continuous daylight, the rock surface will gather substantial amounts of solar energy, that might in this way be taken care of and used for heating tap water or be stored in the bedrock for the winter.

Floor heating has the great advantage of using a very large surface for emitting energy, thus the surface does not need to be very much hotter than it's surroundings, which in turn allows the heat pump to run at low temperature and extremely efficiently. It may extract as much as five times as much energy from the water as it needs electricity to run.

The incoming fresh air is preheated passing through an underground culvert (large enough to be cleaned when needed) and then heated by the heat of the used exhaust air in the FTX aggregate. The windows can also be opened for natural ventilation in the summer.

Alltogether, this energy system, that relocates the energy to where and when it is best needed, is modern solution that requires a small amount of electricity to run. Our calculations point to a yearly average of 16,3 kWh per square meter for running pumps, heat pumps and heat exchangers. This should be compared to the 42,3 kWh per square meter that a regular office building of the same size and programme, but with conventional construction, would require. If we look at carbon dioxide emissions, all electricity use can be said to cause it, but while the electricity use of Villa Sápmi would cause about 7885 kg CO_2 emissions a year, the conventional building, heated with oil, would cause 38180 kg a year, or, heated with electricity directly, 121180 kg.

These are of course just calculation estimates, but it gives an idea how much more efficient Villa Sapmi is.Then we haven't taken into account the carbon dioxide that is allready captured and stored in the massive wood building frame. The electricity needed to run Villa Sápmis climate systems is just a small fraction of the average yearly production of a modern medium-size wind power-station in a decent position; that is, by investing in a single wind-power-station somewhere in the region (or elsewhere) in addition to the project, Villa Sápmi's carbon dioxide footprint would be zero. Or actually less.

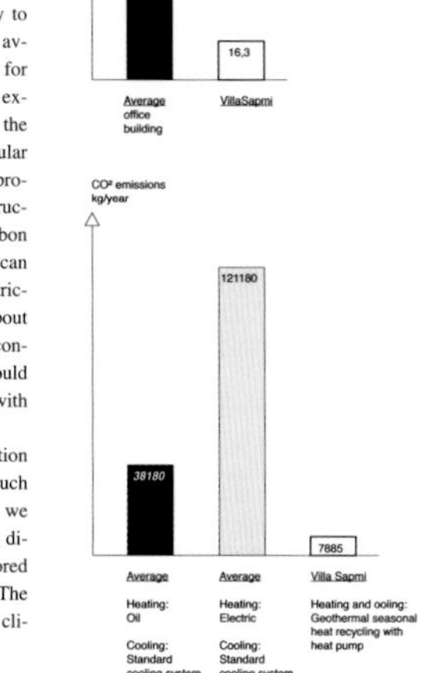

–Landscape

Concept
The site is reclaimed by nature turning a sterile sport field into a flowering meadow.

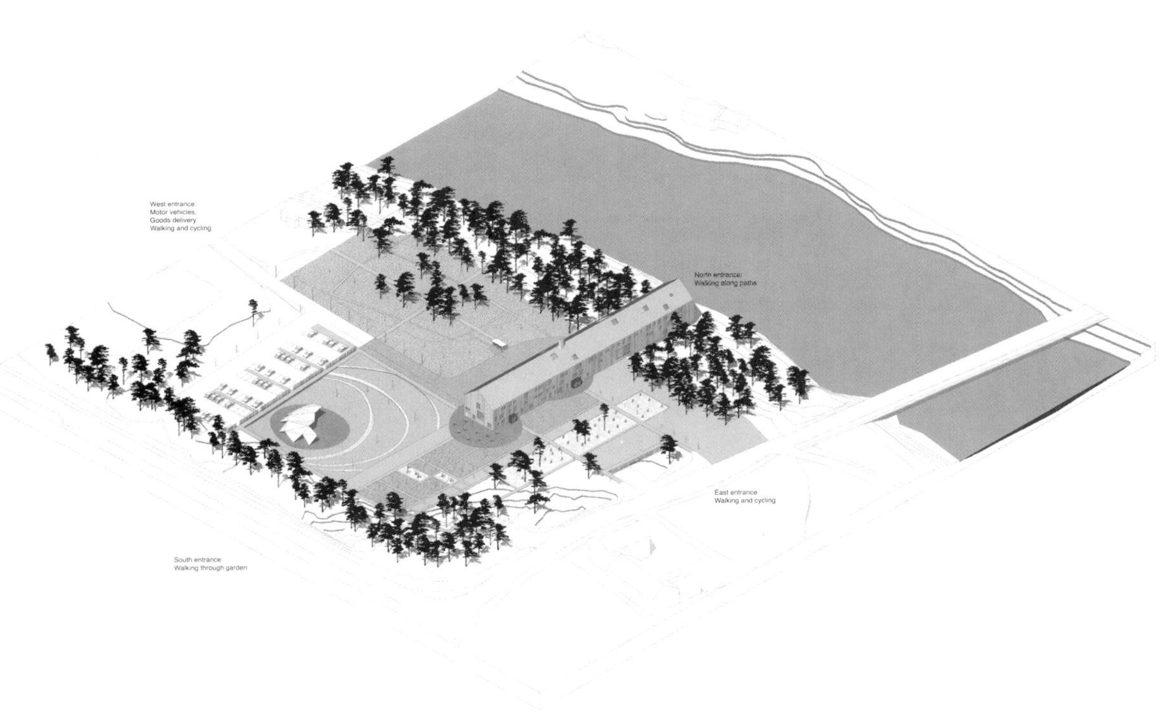

Villa Sápmi can be approached from all directions by foot and from the west by motor vehicles. The southern part of the site is dedicated to the outdoor stage, the restaurant and the kitchen garden. The northern part still belongs to the pine trees but plank walkways runs through the trees down to the river. The arctic park reassembling a meadow is covering the part of the site that before belonged to the sport field. Each flower exhibition area is reached by plank walkways. The position of the building on the site will give as small impact as possible on the existing pine trees and none of the old pine trees will be removed, but the trees that has to go will be replaced with new plants on the east side of the building in a gravel covered area in the shape of the buildings footprint. These baby pines, growing slowly, will form a monument over the greatness of their older relatives.

Plank walkways guides visitors in the arctic park.

New pines on a site big as the footprint of the building.

Meadow, pine groove and river are connected.

The outdoor performance area descends into the meadow.

133 DHPG Haus | *kadawittfeldarchitektur*

Participants : Gerhard Wittfeld, Klaus Kada, Kilian Kada, Astrid Dierkes, Julika Metz, Angie Müller
Partner : TGA: VIKA Ingenieur GmbH
Project : DHPG Haus

Typology : Office
Location : Bonn
Client : MKA Objekt GmbH in cooperation with Bundesstadt Bonn

kadawittfeldarchitektur

Lageplan M 1:500

Unser DHPG - Haus

DHPG ist ein multidisziplinäres Unternehmen aus 350 Rechtsanwälten, Steuerberatern und Wirtschaftsprüfern, das den Slogan „Wir beraten Sie persönlich" im Firmennamen trägt. Um diesem Anspruch gerecht zu werden, ist (neben dem gemeinsamen Auftritt Kunden gegenüber) vor allem die interdisziplinäre Vernetzung und die interne Kommunikation der unterschiedlichen Abteilungen des Hauses von besonderer Bedeutung.
Das neue DHPG- Haus sollte daher ein Bürogebäude sein, dessen Struktur und Organisation die „fünf Stufen der Kommunikation" eines Unternehmens abbilden kann.
Der unmittelbare Austausch unter Büronachbarn (1), die abteilungsinterne Vernetzung (2), die Kooperation mehrerer Abteilungen (3), das firmeninterne Networking (4) und schließlich die Repräsentation nach außen sind keineswegs abstrakte Begrifflichkeiten, sondern manifestieren sich tatsächlich in der Gestalt unseres Entwurfes.

Städtebau und Anbindung

Das Grundstück des DHPG Hauses liegt an prominenter Stelle direkt an der Marie- Kahle- Allee, die die Friedrich- Ebert- Allee (Diplomatenrennbahn) im Nord-Osten und die Oscar- Romero- Allee im Südwesten verbindet. Im Moment ist die Zufahrt zum Wettbewerbsgrundstück aus Nordosten sicher die bedeutsamere, allerdings wird die neue Haltestelle (ab 2014) des öffentlichen Personennahverkehrs an der Oscar- Romero- Allee auch höheren Zustrom aus nordwestlicher Richtung erzeugen.
Nicht nur die gute Lage an der Schnittstelle zweier Verkehrsachsen, auch die besonderen Gebäude in unmittelbarer Nachbarschaft sind prägende Elemente unseres städtebaulichen Zugangs. Aus großer Augenhöhe betrachtet, bilden das städtische Kunstmuseum, die Bundeskunsthalle und das Art- Quadrat Gebäude mit seinem Parkhaus eine Sequenz aus rechteckigen Solitären in Nord- Süd Richtung. Unser Ansatz ist nun, dieses Ensemble aus repräsentativen Kuben entlang einer „Diagonale" bis zum Sportpark Wasserland mit dem neuen DHPG Haus zu vervollständigen. Ein kompakter „Würfel" mit etwa 40m Kantenlänge besetzt als Kopfgebäude die nordwestliche Ecke des Grundstücks. Die prominente städtebauliche Lage macht einen Solitärbau absolut notwendig, da dieser zu allen Seiten präsent ist und somit keine Rückseiten entstehen können.
Aufgrund der kurzen Kantenlängen des Hauses ist sein Volumen auch gänzlich aus dem Blickwinkel Friedrich- Ebert- Alle einzusehen, ohne vom Gebäude der Postbank Data verdeckt zu werden.
Der weithin sichtbare, einprägsame Baukörper, der freundlich, einladend und zeitlos erscheint, besitzt seinen repräsentativen Haupteingang an der Marie- Kahle- Allee, während die Anlieferung und die Tiefgarageneinfahrt (63 Stellplätze) am Südost- Ende des Hauses an der Baunscheidtstrasse liegen.
Auch wenn das neue Gebäude seine Grundform eindeutig aus städtebaulichen Parametern ergründet, ist es vor allem (wie in der Einleitung erwähnt) konsequent von innen heraus nach Erkenntnissen aus der zeitgemäßen Kommunikations- Theorie und nach den speziellen Anforderungen des Nutzers entwickelt.

„Rotierende Kommunikationszonen"

Das Raumprogramm des DHPG- Hauses besteht im Wesentlichen aus zentralen Sonderflächen im Erdgeschoss, der Wirtschaftsprüfung und der Rechtsberatung im ersten Obergeschoß, der Steuerberatung im zweiten OG und der Insolvenzabteilung im dritten OG.
Natürlich dient die zentrale Sonderfläche im Erdgeschoß neben den Kundenkontakten, dem Konferenzbereich, der Innenverwaltung und der Lohnbuchhaltung der allgemeinen, abteilungsübergreifenden Kommunikation und dem firmeninternen Networking.
Dennoch steigert erst das viergeschossige, alle Etagen über einen Luftraum verbindende Atrium das Gemeinschaftsgefühl der geschossweise getrennten Abteilungen. Die drei Büro- Etagen, deren Zuschnitte auf moderne Bedürfnisse eines Kombibüros (ca. 13,50m) abgestimmt sind, wickeln sich um den lichtdurchfluteten Innenhof.
Der ringförmige Regelgrundriss der Büroetagen wird jeweils an einer Stirnseite „geöffnet", wobei sich der „Ring" in ein „U" verwandelt, welches die geforderte Nutzfläche abbildet. Der erschließungstechnisch optimale Ringschluss bleibt trotzdem erhalten, sodass überall kurze Wege entstehen.
Neben der Kombizone im Regelgrundriss der Bürogeschosse bietet dieser „offene" Bereich des „U"s mit seiner Außenterrasse und seiner je nach Bedarf bespielbaren Fläche einen Mehrwert für abteilungsübergreifende und abteilungsinterne Kommunikation.
Gleichzeitig gewährleistet dieses System um das Atrium rotierender Kommunikationsflächen ein flächenoptimiertes, flexibles Büro- Layout, ohne räumlich einzuengen.
Die drei Büroetagen sind darüber hinaus jeweils im Uhrzeigersinn zueinander um 90 Grad gedreht. Die somit versetzt zum Atrium angeordneten „Freiflächen" der U- Struktur bewirken im „Innenhof" ein atmosphärisch aufgeladenes, spannendes räumliches Wechselspiel aus offenen und geschlossenen Etagen, das sowohl freie Ausblicke in die Umgebung, als auch Einblicke in das Gebäudeinnere erlaubt.
Von außen sind die geschosshohen Öffnungen an der sonst homogenen Fassade als „Abbilder" der vernetzten, vertikalen Kommunikationszone im Innenraum abzulesen. Zusammen mit den gestaltprägenden Öffnungen an jeder Seite des DHPG- Würfels treten auch die bewusst durch Fugen getrennten Geschosse (bzw. Abteilungen) elegant in Erscheinung, um den Charakter des Hauses als dreidimensionales Logo des Unternehmens zu stärken.
Obwohl für Kunden des Hauses das Betreten der oberen Büroetagen nicht vorgesehen ist, erhält jeder Besucher über das Atrium Einblick in die Bürowelt des Unternehmens.
Wie erwähnt, befindet sich der großzügige und gedeckte Eingang leicht eingerückt in einer der Atriums-Öffnungen an der Marie- Kahle- Allee. Vom Eingangsbereich gelangt man direkt an den Empfangstresen und den Wartebereich.
Am verglasten Südende des Atriums befindet sich das Cafe mit Terrasse, die auch dem Konferenzbereich zur Verfügung steht.
Somit ist vom Eingang aus ein ungehinderter Blick durch den lichtdurchfluteten Innenhof bis zur Südterrasse möglich.
Die Konferenzzone mit allen zugeordneten Nebenräumen besetzt den westlichen Flügel des Erdgeschosses, während der Empfang, die Innenverwaltung und die Lohnbuchhaltung an der Ostseite des Atriums liegen. Zwei Kerne mit je einem Aufzug und einem Treppenraum sitzen diagonal versetzt an zwei Ecken des Innenhofes und versorgen die Büroetagen.

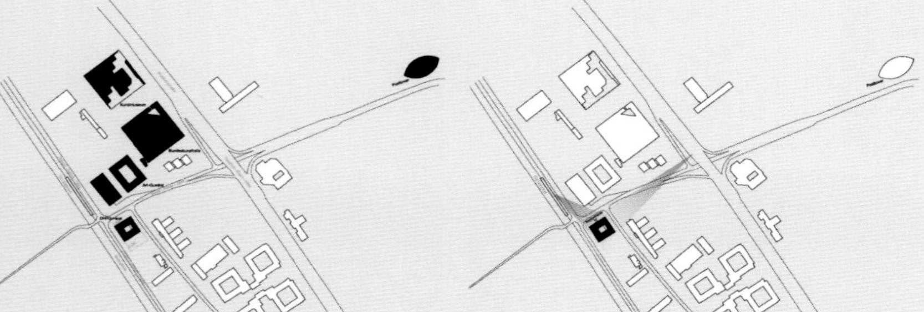

Solitär

Kopfgebäude

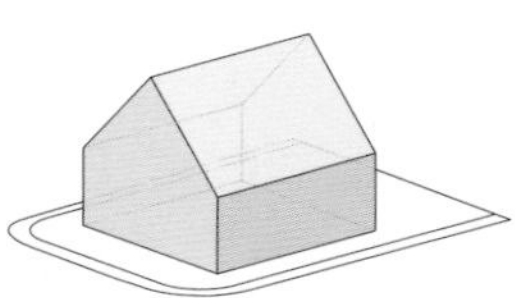

Das DHPG-Haus - „Wir beraten Sie persönlich"

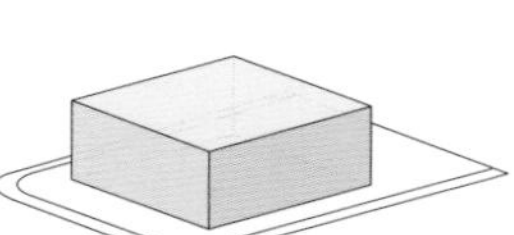

Der Solitär als Kopfgebäude

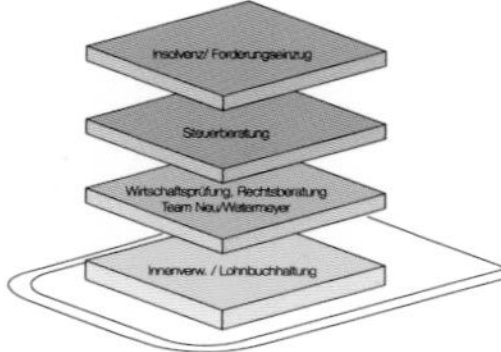

Programm

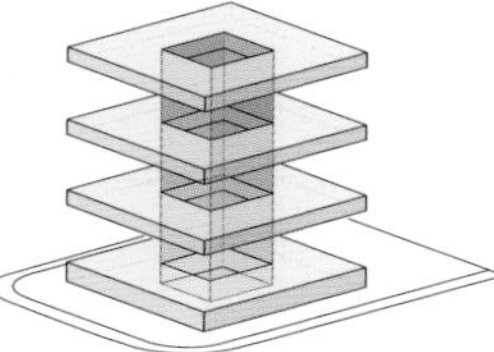

Allgemeine Kommunikation = Atrium

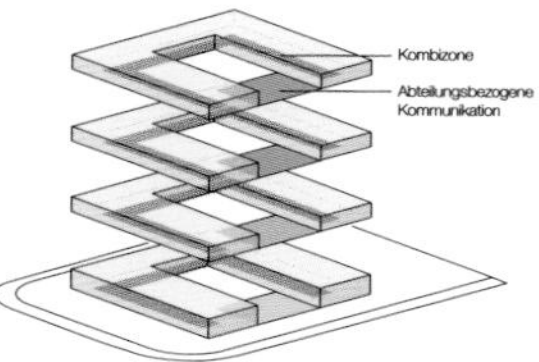

Abteilungsbezogene Kommunikation = U-Struktur

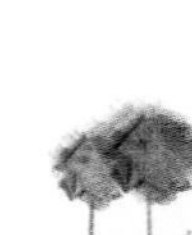

Ansicht Nord-West M 1:200

Ansicht Süd-Ost M 1:200

kadawittfeldarchitektur

Perspektive Marie-Kahle-Allee

Szenarien zur Nach- Verdichtung

„Nichts ist beständiger als der Wandel" H.Heine

Die drei U- förmigen Geschosse bilden als Kombitypologie die geforderte Nutzfläche der einzelnen Abteilungen und die anvisierte Mitarbeiterzahl von 150 Personen ab.
Schließlich kann aber über die offenen Freiflächen an zwei Seiten des Atriums in jedem Geschoß in zwei Schritten nachverdichtet werden (siehe Nachverdichtungsszenarien auf Plakaten).
Die „atmende" Struktur erlaubt auf unterschiedliche Arten die offene Atriums-Seite zu bestücken:
Beispielsweise sind an der Außenterrassen- Seite neben normalen Büros mit Kombizone auch größere Konferenzräume unterzubringen.
Nutzt man sämtliche zur Nachverdichtung geeigneten Flächen, kann man die Arbeitsplatzanzahl um 26 auf 176 erhöhen.

Fassaden, Materialität und Atriumdach

Die Fassaden des Gebäudes spiegeln die Struktur des Hauses und das entwurfsprägende Element der vertikal gestaffelten Atriumszonen wider.
So sind die vier übereinander gestapelten Abteilungen mithilfe der ausgeprägten Schattenfugen zwischen den Geschossen ablesbar. Die Fugen und die an jeder Gebäudeseite in unterschiedlicher Höhe auftretenden Terrassenöffnungen erzeugen das unverwechselbare Erscheinungsbild des Hauses, das zeitlos elegant und einladend wirkt.
Die Fugen und Öffnungen werden augenscheinlich, die Fassaden der Bürozonen wirken homogen transparent und zurückhaltend.
Grundsätzlich besteht die Oberfläche des Hauses aus einer großflächigen Dreischeibenisolierverglasung. Schmale, opake Drehflügelelemente ermöglichen die Lüftung. Diese undurchsichtigen Flügel aus eloxiertem Aluminium reduzieren den Glasanteil der Fassade auf energietechnisch sinnvolle 50 Prozent. Im Ausbauraster von 1,35m stehen 30 cm tiefe Aluminiumschwerter (in allen erdenklichen Farben ausführbar), deren Seitenflächen zu 50 Prozent gelocht sind. Sie reduzieren die Einstrahlung bei tiefstehender Sonne, können den Blendschutz (innen) ersetzen und Schall absorbieren. An den Ober- und Unterseiten durch Blechpaneele gerahmt, verleihen sie der Fassade optisch ansprechende Tiefe und den Räumen dahinter atmosphärisch angenehm gefilterte Lichtstimmungen.
Die Fassade besitzt darüber hinaus einen außenliegenden Sonnenschutz mit Tageslichtlenkung, der hinter den feststehenden Aluminiumschwertern geführt wird.
Die Verglasungen zum Atrium hin können als Einscheiben- Sicherheitsgläser ausgeführt werden und besitzen ebenfalls öffenbare Flügel, deren Rahmen filigran und dezent erscheinen.
Das Atriumdach besteht aus einer schlanken Stahl- Glaskonstruktion mit siebbedruckten Glasscheiben (Sonnenschutz) und einem außenliegenden, elektrisch betriebenen Sonnensegel mit Windwächter.

Konstruktion

Der Geschoßdecken- Aufbau entspricht dem „Goldbeck Fertigteilsystem" (Aufbauhöhe 675mm) im Stützen- Grundraster 2,70m (5,4/ 6,75/ 8,10m). Die Aussteifung der Decken erfolgt über die beiden Erschließungskerne. Um die Lasten in den relevanten Gebäudeöffnungen (offene Bereiche der U Struktur ohne Fassadenstützen) in Teilbereichen abzufangen, wird das Goldbeck System mit quer zu den Rippendecken eingelegten Stahlträgern (h = 40cm) kombiniert.

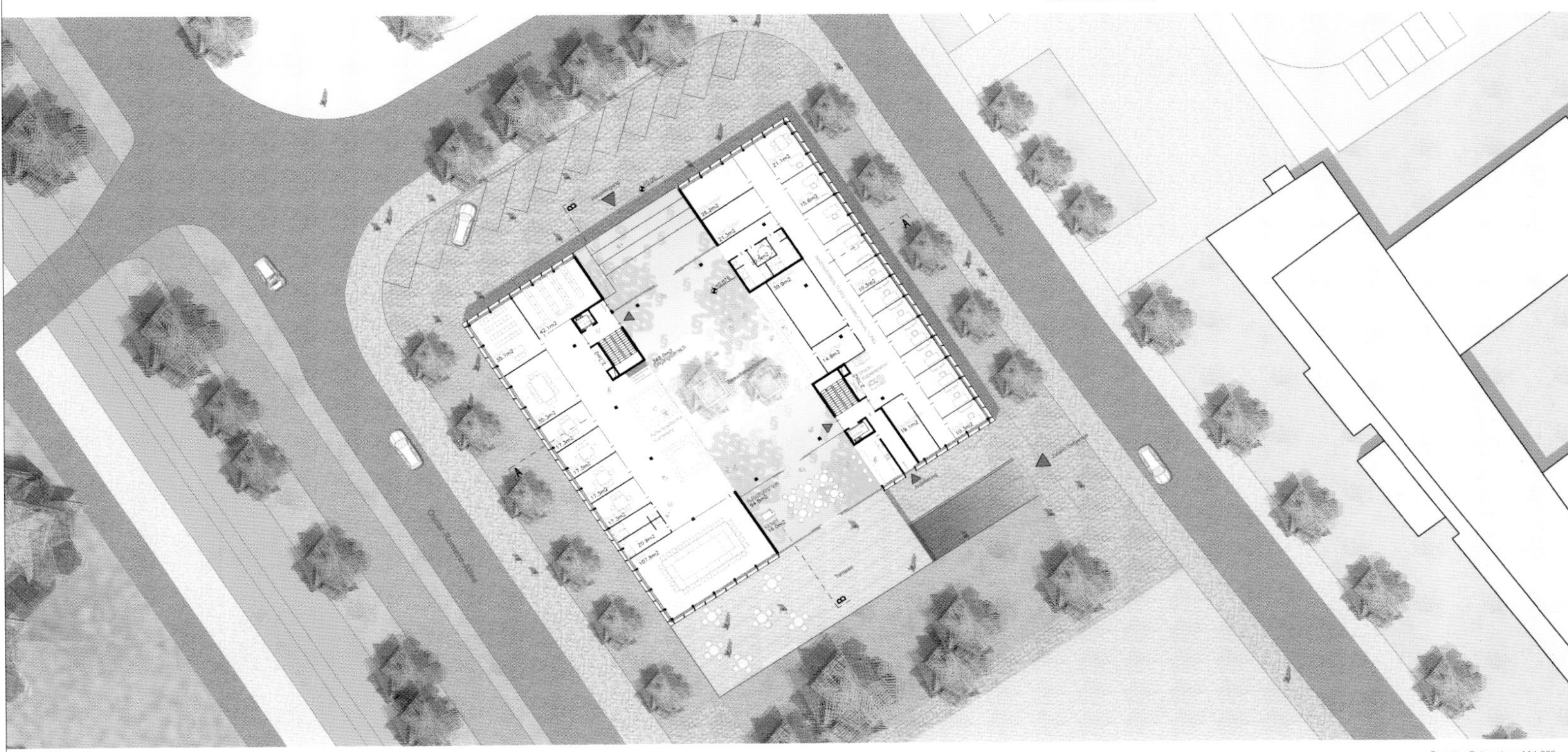

Grundriss Erdgeschoss M 1:200

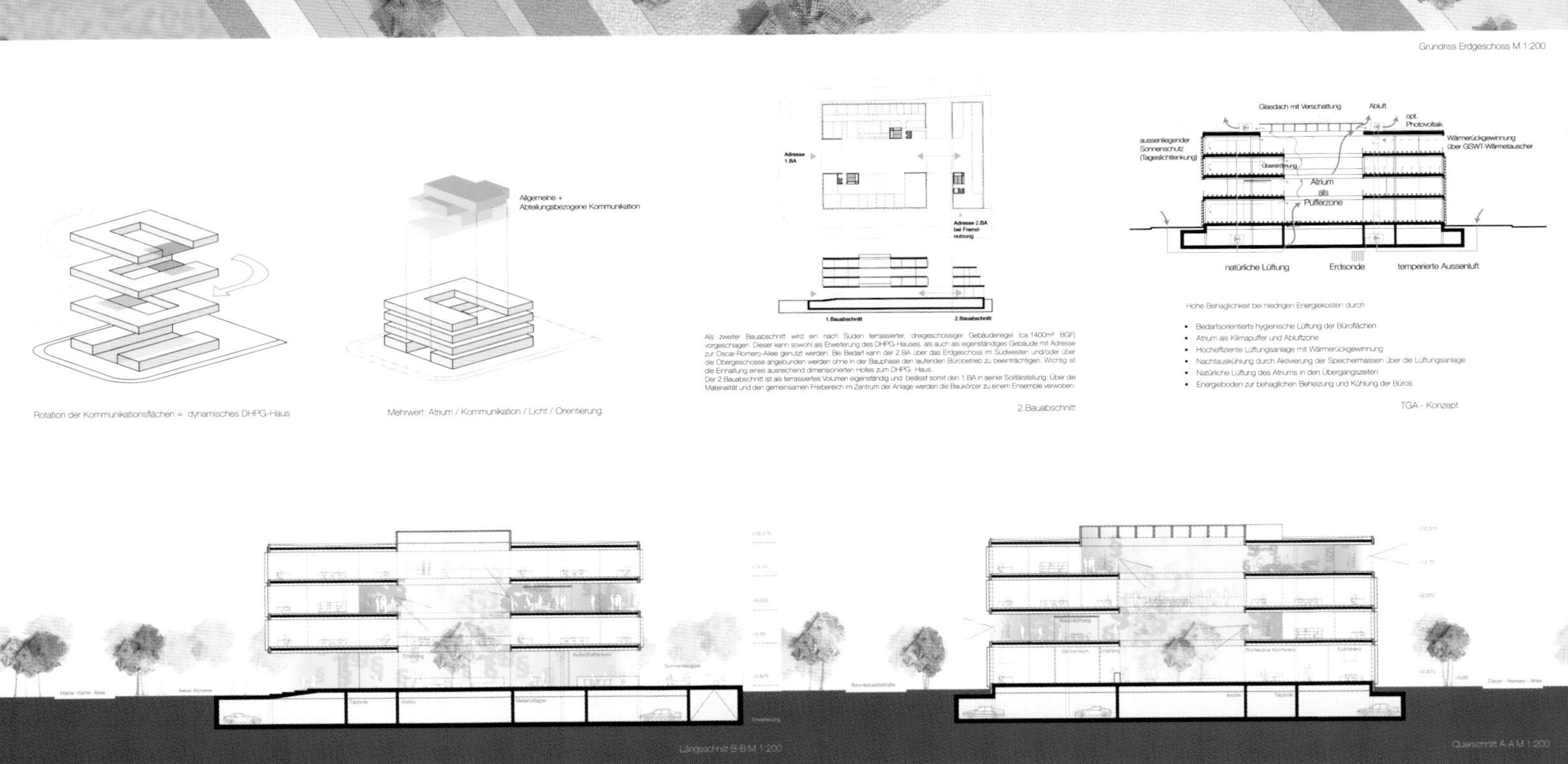

Rotation der Kommunikationsflächen = dynamisches DHPG-Haus

Mehrwert: Atrium / Kommunikation / Licht / Orientierung

Als zweiter Bauabschnitt wird ein nach Süden terrassierter, dreigeschossiger Gebäuderiegel (ca.1400m² BGF) vorgeschlagen. Dieser kann sowohl als Erweiterung des DHPG-Hauses, als auch als eigenständiges Gebäude mit Adresse zur Oscar-Romero-Allee genutzt werden. Bei Bedarf kann der 2.BA über das Erdgeschoss im Südwesten und/oder über die Obergeschosse angebunden werden ohne in der Bauphase den laufenden Bürobetrieb zu beeinträchtigen. Wichtig ist die Einhaltung eines ausreichend dimensionierten Hofes zum DHPG- Haus.
Der 2.Bauabschnitt ist als terrassiertes Volumen eigenständig und belässt somit den 1.BA in seiner Solitärstellung. Über die Materialität und den gemeinsamen Freibereich im Zentrum der Anlage werden die Baukörper zu einem Ensemble verwoben.

2.Bauabschnitt

Hohe Behaglichkeit bei niedrigen Energiekosten durch

- Bedarfsorientierte hygienische Lüftung der Büroflächen
- Atrium als Klimapuffer und Abluftzone
- Hocheffiziente Lüftungsanlage mit Wärmerückgewinnung
- Nachtauskühlung durch Aktivierung der Speichermassen über die Lüftungsanlage
- Natürliche Lüftung des Atriums in den Übergangszeiten
- Energieboden zur behaglichen Beheizung und Kühlung der Büros

TGA - Konzept

Längsschnitt B-B M 1:200

Querschnitt A-A M 1:200

kadawittfeldarchitektur

Grundriss 1.Obergeschoss M1:200

Nachverdichtungsszenario 1.Phase

Grundriss 2.Obergeschoss M1:200

Nachverdichtungsszenario 2.Phase
Variante 1

Grundriss 3.Obergeschoss M1:200

Grundriss Untergeschoss M1:200

Nachverdichtungsszenario 2.Phase
Variante 2
bei Nachverdichtung durch Kombizonenbüros auf allen drei Büroetagen entstehen 26 Arbeitsplätze mehr

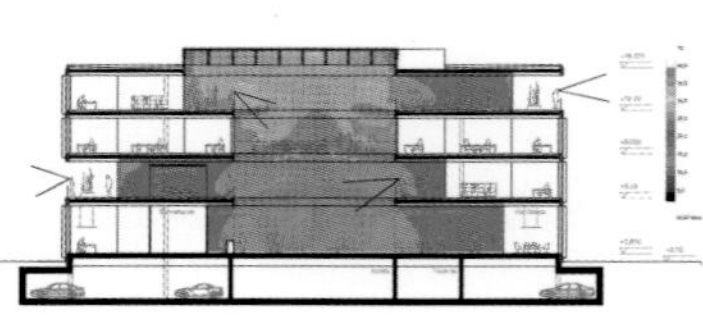

Atrium als Klimapuffer

Die Abluft strömt in das Atrium über und wird im oberen Bereich abgesaugt. Hierdurch wird ein effizientes System zur Luftführung und Wärmerückgewinnung geschaffen.
Selbst bei hohen Außentemperaturen von über 33°C wird ein Innenklima erreicht, welches höchsten Ansprüchen an die Behaglichkeit genügt.

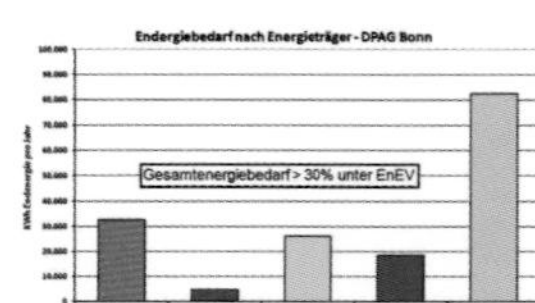

Energiebedarf nach Energieträger

Über die Optimierung von Gebäude und Anlagentechnik lässt sich der Energiebedarf der einzelnen Verbraucher soweit reduzieren, dass die gültige EnEV um mehr als 30% unterschritten wird.

Energiekonzept und Haustechnik
Integrales Energie- und Klimakonzept

Der sparsame Umgang mit begrenzten Ressourcen, wie fossilen Brennstoffen und Wasser, ist Maßgabe für jede nachhaltige Gebäudeentwicklung zur Optimierung der Life-Cycle-Costs und Reduzierung der Emission bis hin zum Nullemissionsgebäude.
Der Gebäudeentwurf realisiert einen hohen energetischen Standard. Der Energiekennwerte liegen um über 30% unter den aktuellen EnEV-Anforderungen. Über die hohe energetische Qualität der Fassade, die hygienische Lüftung, das behagliche Heiz- und Kühlsystem und eine hohe Tageslichtausnutzung wird ein behagliches Arbeitsumfeld geschaffen.

Raumbezogenes Klimakonzept
Bedarforientierte hygienische Lüftung

Zur Gewährleistung einer gleich bleibenden Luftqualität und Reduzierung des Energieverbrauches wird eine bedarfsorientierte hygienische Lüftung eingerichtet. Die Bemessung erfolgt über einen personenbezogenen Frischluftbedarf.
Die Zuluft wird über die Systemdecke in die Büroräume geführt, strömt von dort über Flur- und Nebenflächen in das Atrium. Das Atrium wirkt als Klimapuffer und Abluftzone. Im oberen Bereich des Atriums kann die Luft je nach Energiegehalt in die Wärmerückgewinnung der Lüftungsanlage gespeist oder als natürliche Lüftung direkt nach außen geführt werden. Über eine hocheffiziente Lüftungsanlage mit Wärmerückgewinnung im Gegenstromschichtwärmebetrieb (GSWT) kann ca. 90% der Wärme und Kälte der Abluft zurück gewonnen werden.

Nachtauskühlung

Über die Lüftungsanlage wird eine wirksame Nachtlüftung durch Aktivierung der Wärmespeicherfähigkeit der Raumumschließungsflächen und des Mobiliars aktiviert, womit eine spürbare Reduktion der maximalen sommerlichen Raumlufttemperaturen erreicht wird.

Natürliche Lüftung Atrium

Das Atrium kann in Abhängigkeit der Temperaturverhältnisse im Innen- und Außenbereich natürlich belüftet werden. Hierzu werden bodennah motorische Nachströmöffnungen vorgesehen, die in Verbindung mit der Entlüftung über das Atriumdach genügend Auftrieb schafft, um eine Durchströmung zu gewährleisten.

Natürliche Klimatisierung

Für einen effizienten Betrieb bieten sich Wärme- und Kälteverteilsysteme an, die mit niedrigen Vorlauftemperaturen im Heizfall und hohen Vorlauftemperaturen im Kühlfall betrieben werden können. Dies erhöht wesentlich den Wirkungsgrad der Anlage und damit die Wirtschaftlichkeit.
Eingesetzt wird ein Klimaboden. Im Winter kann in Verbindung mit der hochwertigen Fassade auf Zusatzheizkörper verzichtet, im Sommer kann der Klimaboden zur Kühlung der Büroräume genutzt werden. Durch dieses System werden in Verbindung mit der hygienischen Lüftung sehr behagliche Raumzustände erreicht.

Tageslichtnutzung

Eine äußere Verschattung mit lichtlenkenden Jalousien schafft eine hohe Tageslichtausnutzung. Dies reduziert den Bedarf an künstlicher Beleuchtung, spart Strom und schafft ein angenehmes Arbeitsumfeld.

CO_2-neutrale Energieerzeugung
Erdwärme/kälte-Nutzung

In Verbindung mit dem Klimaboden wird eine Erdwärmenutzung über eine Erdsondenanlage eingesetzt, die im Sommer zu großen Teilen ohne zusätzliche aktive Komponenten die Kühlung des Gebäudes gewährleistet und im Winter über eine Wärmepumpe ein hocheffizientes System zur Beheizung des Gebäudes bietet.
Option Fotovoltaik für eine CO_2-neutrales Gebäude
Durch den hohen Standard der Gebäudehülle, die effiziente Gebäudetechnik und die energiesparende Wärme- und Kälteerzeugung kann der Energiebedarf minimiert werden, so dass über eine Fotovoltaikanlage, die auf dem Dach des Gebäudes aufgestellt werden kann, ein Nullemissionsgebäude entsteht.

Perspektive Kommunikationsraum Atrium

MVRegensburg | *kadawittfeldarchitektur*

134

Tragwerksplanung : TSB Ingenieurgesellschaft mbH
Gebäude- und Energietechnik : PGS-Aachen Ingenieurbüro
Project : office building in Regensburg
Client : Mittelbayrischer Verlag KG

Participants : Gerhard Wittfeld, Klaus Kada, Kilian Kada, Astrid Dierkes, Julika Metz, Simon Kortemeier, Adrian Fischer, Dirk Zweering, Tim Danner, Andrea Blaschke, Student Maksim König Partner
Landschaftsarchitekt : ClubL94 LandschaftsArchitekten

Neubau eines Bürogebäudes für den Mittelbayerischen Verlag in Regensburg

mit städtebaulichem Ideenteil zur Gestaltung der angrenzenden Bauflächen

916458

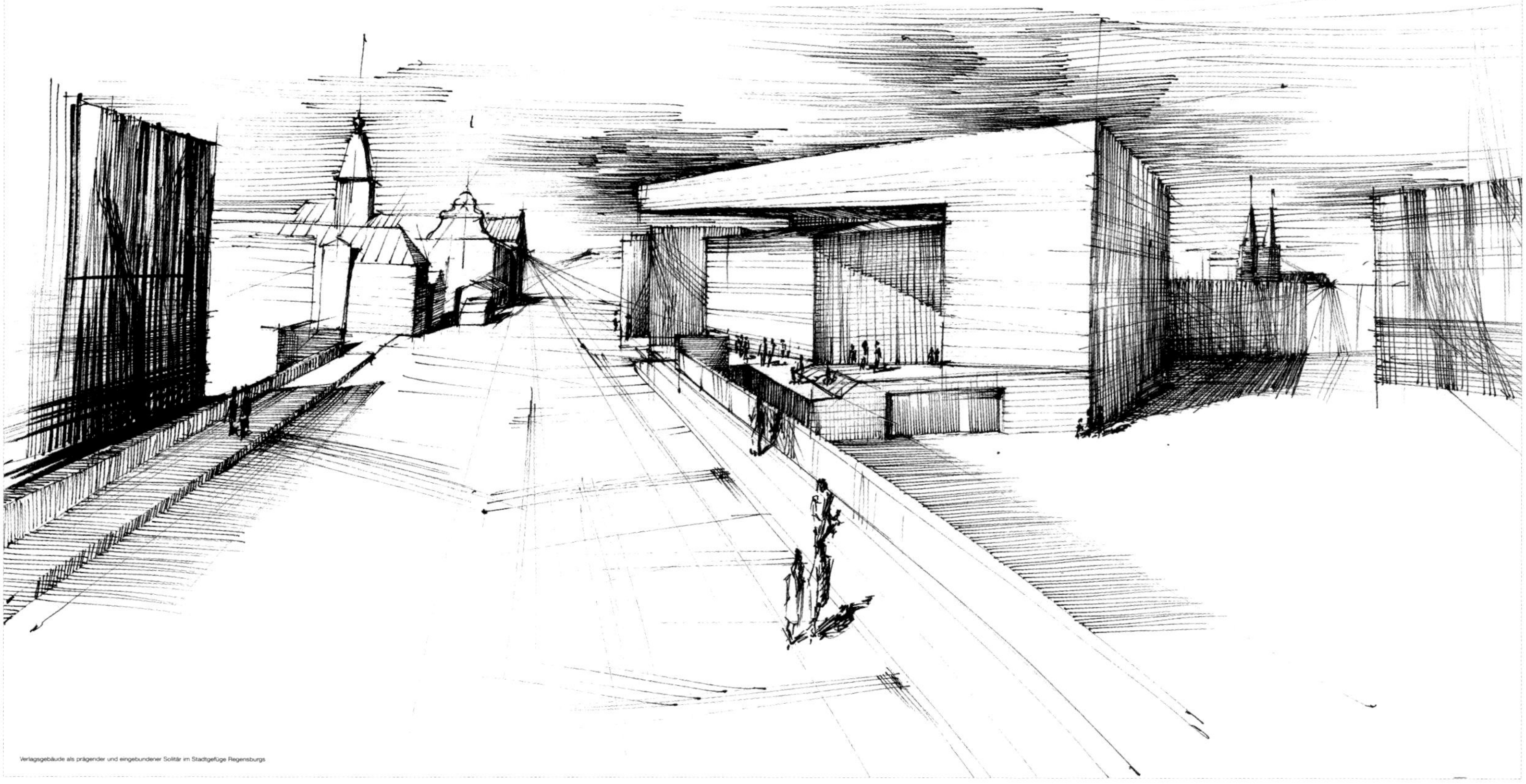

Verlagsgebäude als prägender und eingebundener Solitär im Stadtgefüge Regensburgs

„Raum geben"

916458

Städtebauliche Einbindung und Verknüpfung

Das Bearbeitungsfeld des Wettbewerbes für den Neubau des Mittelbayrischen Verlages liegt am östlichen Ende des „Stadtentwicklungsgebietes Innerer Westen" an der Kumpfmühler Brücke und ist laut Planungs- und Baureferat ein profilbildender Standort in der Pufferzone des Weltkulturerbes.

Das Verlagshaus und die neuen Gebäude (Baufelder 2-3) an der Bahn sollen nicht nur als prägendes Süd-Tor in die Stadt wahrgenommen werden, tatsächlich muss auch die Bahnhofstrasse an der Nordseite zwischen Brückenkopf und dem nahe gelegenen Regensburger Hauptbahnhof eine stadträumliche Aufwertung erfahren. Insbesondere der räumliche Charakter der Bahnhofstraße ist von großer Bedeutung.

Der großen Verantwortung einem städtebaulich wichtigen Ort am Rande der mittelalterlichen Stadt Regensburg und dem traditionsreichen Verlagshaus gegenüber, wollen wir mit großer Sorgfalt und Respekt in der Planung begegnen.

Der Mittelbayrische Verlag hat aufgrund seiner Geschichte die Berechtigung, besonders zu sein. Der wichtigen offenen Verbindung des Unternehmens zu seinen Lesern und Kunden tragen wir mit einem Gebäude von besonderer Stellung und einer Verzahnung des Stadtraumes mit den öffentlichen Zonen im Inneren des Hauses Rechnung.

Dies gelingt über eine deutliche Schrägstellung der Westfassade des Hauses in Richtung Osten, wodurch zur stark frequentierten Kumpfmühler Brücke hin ein teilweise gedeckter, großzügiger Vorplatz mit hoher Aufenthaltsqualität im Südlicht entsteht.

Dadurch bilden das neue Verlagshaus und der gegenüber liegende zukünftige Kopf-Bau (Bestandteil der Entwicklung West) im Westen der Brückenauffahrt ein Stadttor mit einer trichterförmigen Öffnung in die Altstadt.

Von der Brücke aus eintreffenden Passanten bleibt die schräggestellte Schauseite als breite, offene Geste besonders lange im Blickfeld. Gleichzeitig erscheint die Brückenauffahrt als Teil des großzügigen Vorplatz- Plateaus und definiert die neue Adresse am „Esser-Platz" des Mittelbayrischen Verlages.

Eine großzügige Freitreppe am östlichen Hang der Brückenböschung ermöglicht einen frühzeitigen Zugang von der erkerähnlichen, vorkragenden Aussichtskanzel der Kumpfmühler Brücke zum neuen Esser Platz. Im Westen des Plateaus befindet sich eine weitere Treppe, die der Öffentlichkeit eine Abkürzung auf den grünen Stadtboulevard an der Bahntrasse ermöglicht.

An der Nordseite des Grundstücks ist die parallel zur benachbarten Bebauung an der Bahnhofstrasse stehende Gebäudeseite so weit wie möglich nach Süden eingerückt, um ein breites Gehweg- Profil zu erzeugen und Kollisionen zwischen Radfahrern und aussteigenden Fahrgästen zu vermeiden.

Der Abbiegeradius der Kreuzung an der Kumpfmüler Strasse in die Bahnhofstrasse fällt durch das breite Profil wesentlich größer als bisher aus.

Die östliche Gebäudekante des Hauses ist schließlich nach Westen eingedreht, um von der Kumpfmühler Brücke aus freie Blicke auf die Spitzen des Regensburger Domes zu gewährleisten.

Letztendlich entsteht aus den oben genannten städtebaulichen Parametern ein kompaktes, in den Kontext eingebettetes Solitär-Gebäude ohne Rückseiten, dessen Projektion eine offene, dreieckige Grundform aufweist.

Das Haus besitzt vielmehr drei Schauseiten, was auch dem Straßenraum der Bahnhofstrasse im Westen Richtung Hauptbahnhof gut tut.

Nachdem wir vorschlagen, die Süd-Kanten der unabhängig voneinander zu errichtenden Gebäude der Baufelder zwei und drei an die Grenzen des Bearbeitungsgebietes an der Bahntrasse zu legen, eröffnet sich ein größerer Spielraum für die Gestaltung der Bahnhofstrasse, die den Charakter eines baumbestandenen Boulevards erhält.

An den mäandrierenden Baukörpern der Baufelder zwei und drei entsteht entlang der Bahnhofstrassen- Allee eine Sequenz aus attraktiven Plätzen; der Bahnhofstrassen- Boulevard, der den Abschnitt zwischen Verlagshaus und Hauptbahnhof stadträumlich angenehm prägen wird.

Das Erweiterungsgebäude auf Baufeld zwei stellt ein eigenständiges, unabhängig vom Haus des dritten Baufeldes zu errichtendes Gebäude dar. Bei der Bebauung des Baufeldes 3 kann an der Schmalseite von Gebäude 2 direkt angebaut werden, so dass der Charakter des Boulevards nicht zu offen Richtung Gleise ausfällt.

In der Folge leiten wir den an der Bahntrasse verlaufenden „Grünen Stadtboulevard" mit Geh- und Radweg auf Höhe der Ostseite des Verlagsgebäudes gemeinsam mit der indirekten Linksabbiegespur Im Güterbahnhof Richtung Norden in den Bahnhofstraßen- Boulevard, um diesen zu aktivieren, ohne auf einen bepflanzten Saum zwischen Bahntrasse und Baufeldern zwei und drei zu verzichten.

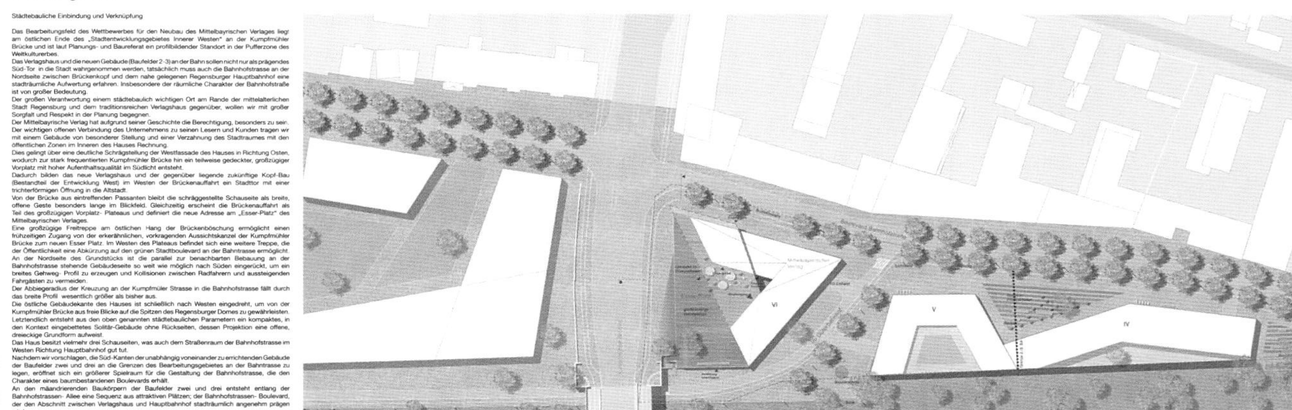

Lageplan Plangebiet M 1:500

Konzeption der Freianlagen

Situation
Die Neustrukturierungen des Standortes der Mittelbayerischen Verlag KG ermöglichen den Bau eines neuen Hauptgebäudes, welches die Bereiche Verlag, Redaktion und Verwaltung aufnehmen soll. Durch die Lage des neuen Haupthauses auf einem Grundstück im direkten Umfeld des ursprünglichen Standortes des Verlages wurde dem Wunsch nachgekommen, weiterhin in der Nähe der Regensburger Altstadt und somit im Bewusstsein der Stadtgesellschaft zu verbleiben.

Das Entwicklungsgebiet „Innerer Westen" wird mit dem östlich der Kumpfmühler Brücke gelegenen Wettbewerbsgebiet um einen wichtigen Baustein ergänzt. Die neue Adresse des Mittelbayerischen Verlages wird somit in Zukunft direkt an der Kumpfmühler Straße, einer wichtigen Einfahrt in den historischen Stadtkern Regensburg liegen und als Kopf des gesamten Entwicklungskonzeptes „Innerer Westen Regensburg" entlang der Eisenbahnlinie Nürnberg – München – Passau eine bedeutende Rolle spielen.

Konzept
Das Freiraumkonzept knüpft an das übergeordnete Grün- und Platzraumsystem an.

Ein neuer landschaftlicher Grünzug bildet einen grünen Puffer für das zukünftige Quartier entlang der Bahnlinie und schafft die Grünraumverbindung zu den Gärten und Parkanlagen des Grüngürtels um die Regensburger Altstadt. Der geplante, grüne Stadtboulevard in der Verlängerung der Ladehofstraße wird entlang der Bahnhofstraße bis zum Hauptbahnhof als Allee weitergeführt.

Desweiteren wird das neue Quartier „Innerer Westen" durch die Anordnung von Freiraumfugen und Plätzen entlang des Boulevards mit der nördlich gelegenen Innenstadt verknüpft.

Entwurf
Der Entwurf sieht vor, dem gesamten neuen Quartier einen homogenen und urbanen Charakter zu verleihen. Um den Zusammenhalt des Areals zu stärken wird ein einheitlicher Belag oder eine einheitliche Möblierung in den Außenanlagen vorgeschlagen. Die an den Neubauten entlang der Bahnhofstraße entstehenden Plätze werden mit großformatigen Betonplatten ausgebildet, die im umliegenden „Belags-Teppich" als Intarsien im Boden liegen.

Der Platz am Verlagshaus bildet die neue Adresse des Mittelbayerischen Verlags. Über eine großzügige Freitreppe wird der Besucher bereits von der Kumpfmühler Brücke aus auf das tiefer liegende Plateau gelangen und von dort aus auch die Möglichkeit haben, den neuen Grünzug zu erschließen.

Sowohl für die Angestellten als auch für die Besucher des Verlags wird auf dem Plateau ein attraktiver Freiraum entstehen. Pflanzschalen mit Oleander und Buxbäumen schaffen eine angenehme Aufenthaltsatmosphäre und Bänka laden zum Verweilen ein.

Schnitt AA M 1:500

Schnitt BB M 1:500

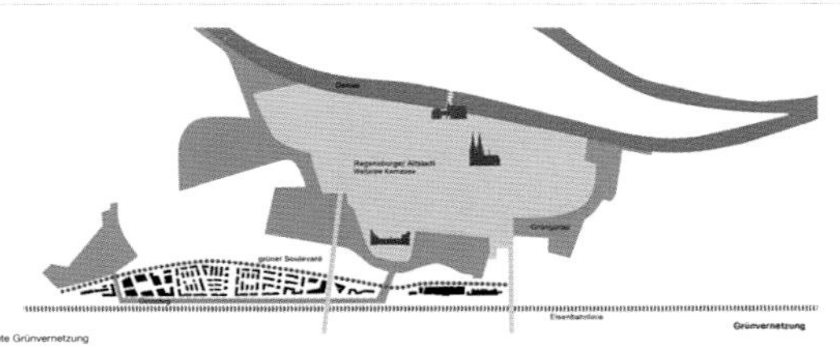

übergeordnete Grünvernetzung

Platzabfolge

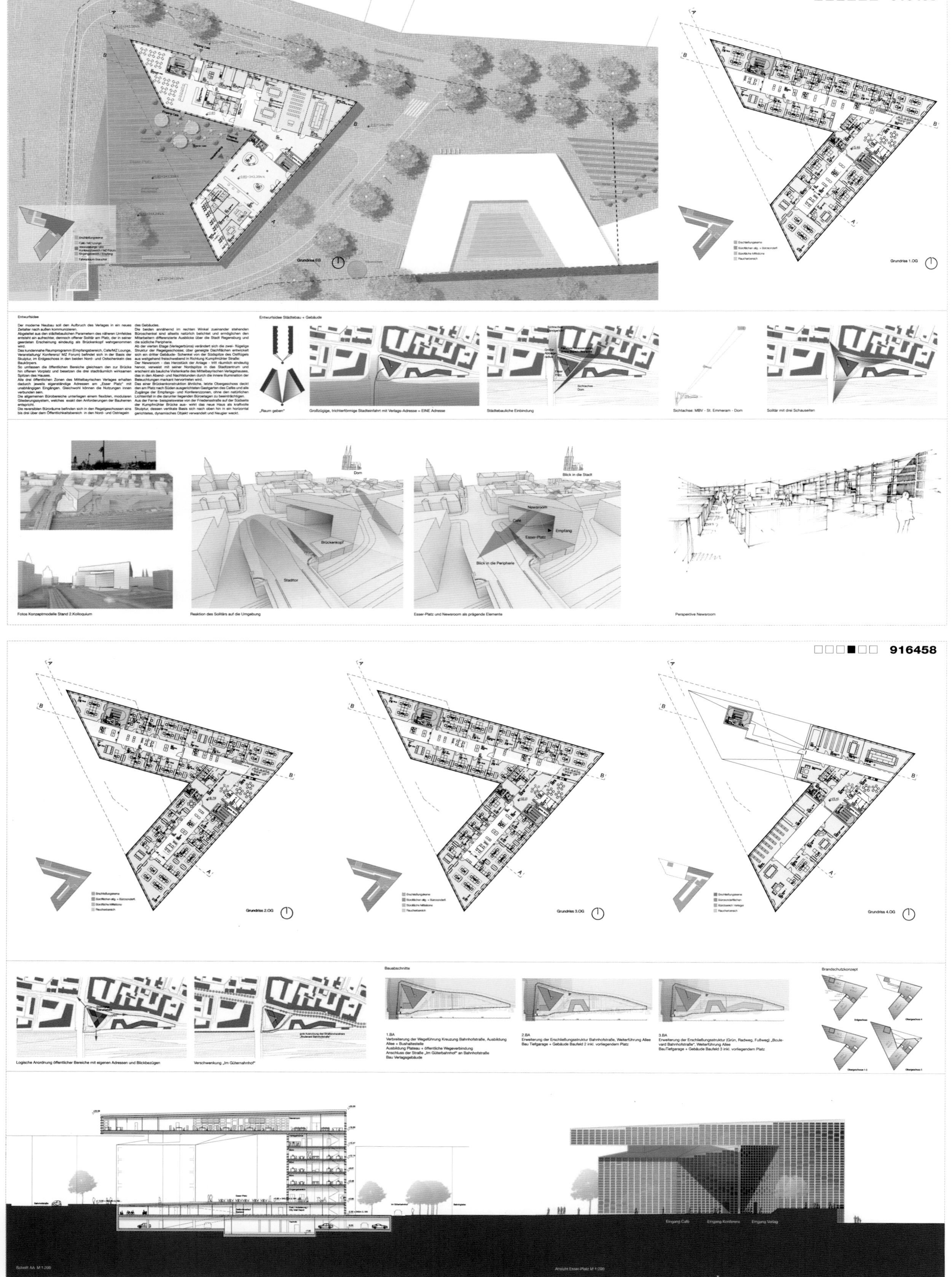
916458
Grundriss EG
Grundriss 1.OG
Entwurfsidee
Entwurfsidee Städtebau + Gebäude
„Raum geben"
Großzügige, trichterförmige Stadteinfahrt mit Verlags-Adresse = EINE Adresse
Städtebauliche Einbindung
Schlachse: MBV - St. Emmeram - Dom
Solitär mit drei Schauseiten
Dom
Brückenkopf
Stadttor
Blick in die Stadt
Newsroom
Café
Empfang
Esser-Platz
Blick in die Peripherie
Fotos Konzeptmodelle Stand 2.Kolloquium
Reaktion des Solitärs auf die Umgebung
Esser-Platz und Newsroom als prägende Elemente
Perspektive Newsroom
916458
Grundriss 2.OG
Grundriss 3.OG
Grundriss 4.OG
Logische Anordnung öffentlicher Bereiche mit eigenen Adressen und Blickbezügen
Verschwenkung „Im Güterbahnhof"
Bauabschnitte
1.BA
2.BA
3.BA
Brandschutzkonzept
Schnitt AA M 1:200
Ansicht Esser-Platz M 1:200
Eingang Café
Eingang Konferenz
Eingang Verlag

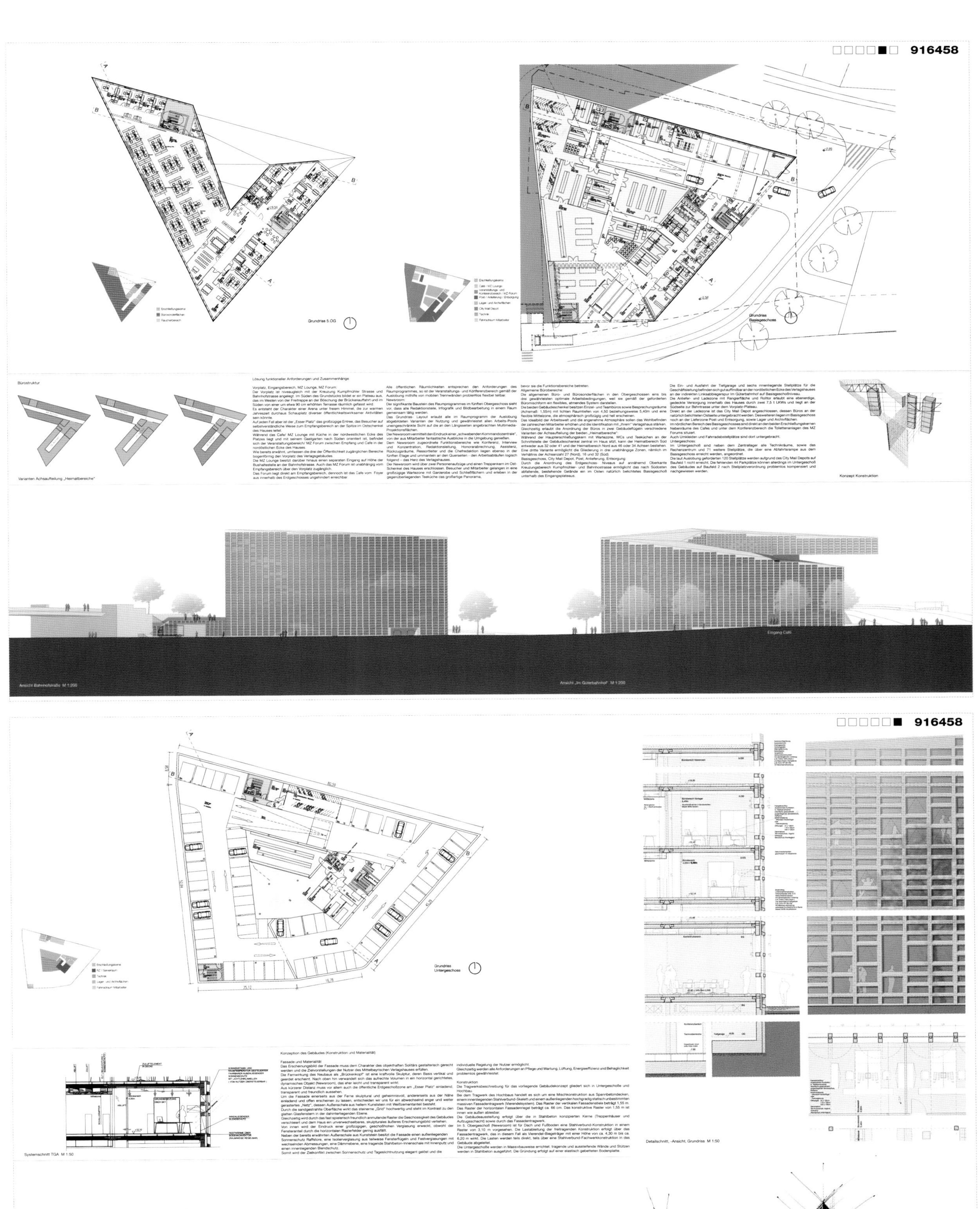
916458
Grundriss 5.OG
Grundriss Basisgeschoss
Ansicht Bahnhofstraße M 1:200
Ansicht „Im Güterbahnhof" M 1:200
Eingang Café
916458
Grundriss Untergeschoss
Systemschnitt TGA M 1:50
Detailschnitt, -Ansicht, Grundriss M 1:50
Ansicht Essen Platz M 1:200
Konzept Konstruktion
Varianten Achsaufteilung „Heimatbereiche"

135 Mönchengladbach Arcaden | *kadawittfeldarchitektur*

Participants : Gerhard Wittfeld, Klaus Kada, Kilian Kada, Johannes Müntinga, Julika Metz, Simon Kortemeier, Simona Czysch, Sascha Thomas
Project : Mönchengladbach Arcaden
Typology : Retail
Location : Mönchengladbach
Client : Mfi Grundstück GmbH & Co, Mönchengladbach Arcaden KG

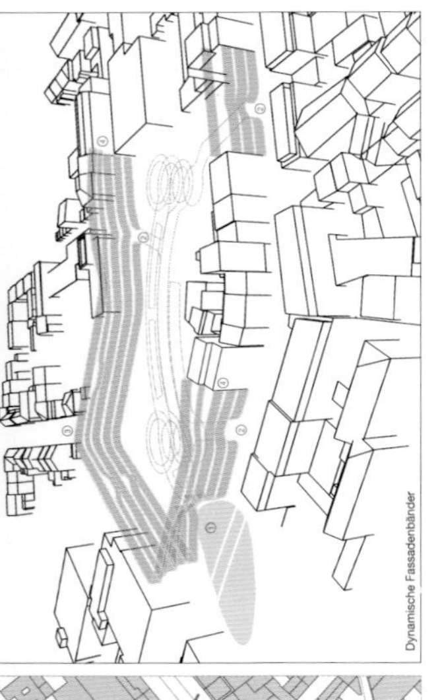

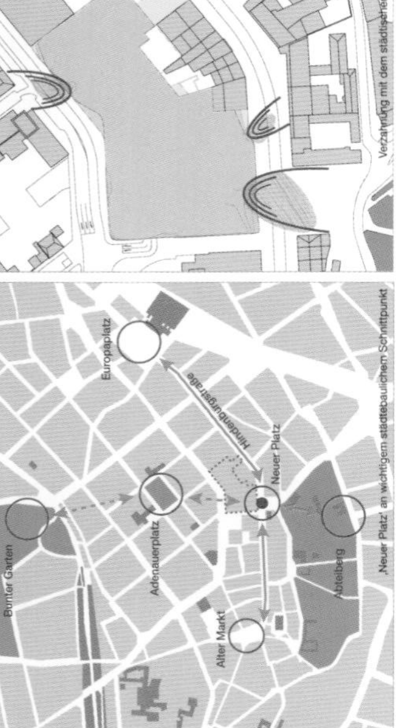

Nacht-Perspektive B | Hindenburgstraße

Perspektive D | Steinmetzstraße

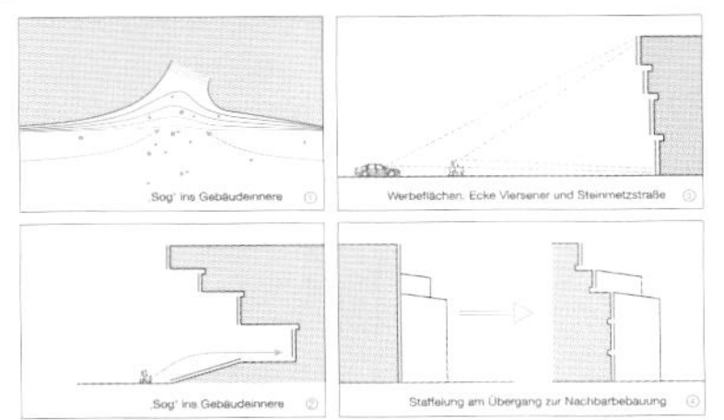

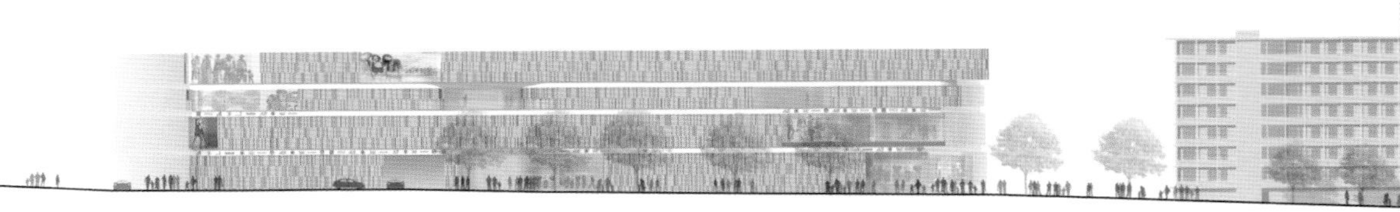
Ansicht West | 1:200

Architektur

Fassadengliederung

Eingänge

Anschluss an die Nachbarbebauung

Werbung

Nacht-Ansicht Nord | 1:200

Perspektive A | Hindenburgstraße

Perspektive C | Steinmetzstraße

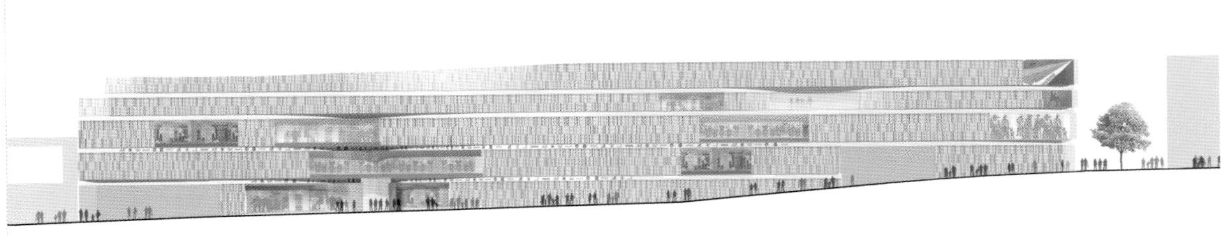
Ansicht Nord | 1:200

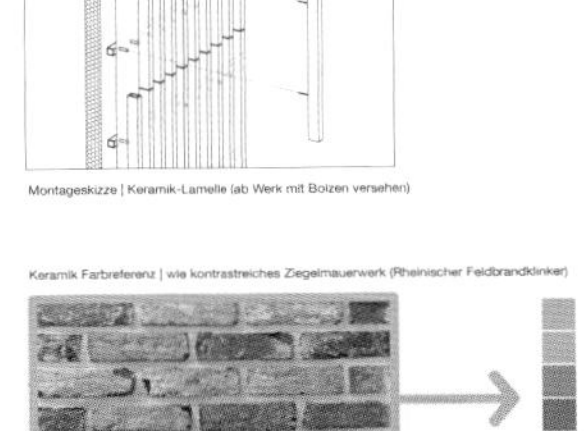
Montageskizze | Keramik-Lamelle (ab Werk mit Bolzen versehen)

Keramik Farbreferenz | wie kontrastreiches Ziegelmauerwerk (Rheinischer Feldbrandklinker)

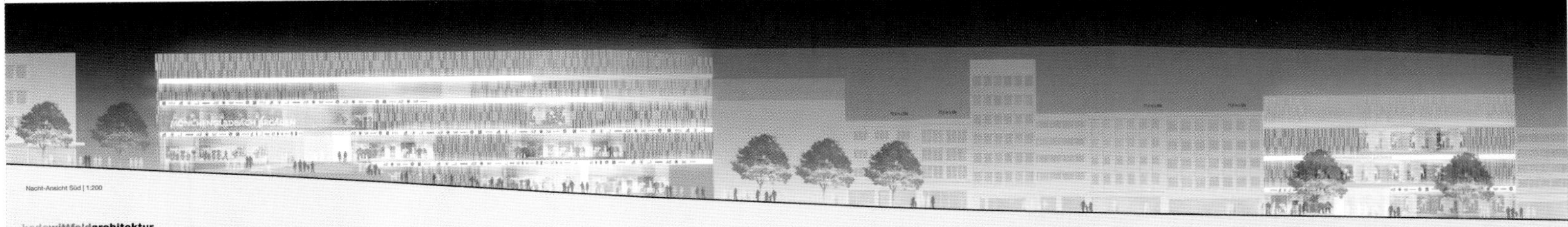

Nacht-Ansicht Süd | 1:200

kadawittfeldarchitektur

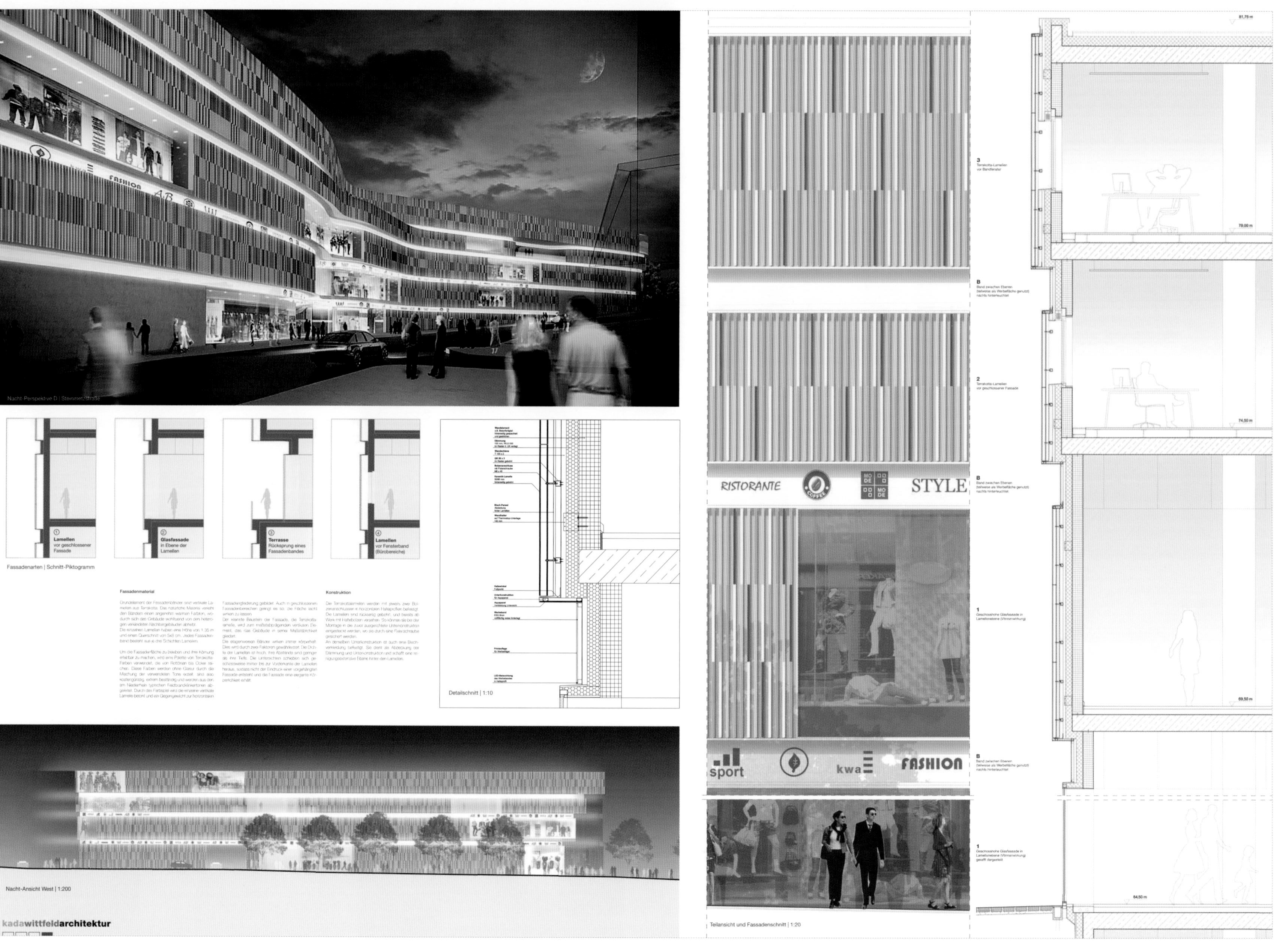
Nacht-Perspektive D | Steinmetzstraße
1 Lamellen vor geschlossener Fassade
2 Glasfassade in Ebene der Lamellen
3 Terrasse Rücksprung eines Fassadenbandes
4 Lamellen vor Fensterband (Bürobereiche)
Fassadenarten | Schnitt-Piktogramm
Fassadenmaterial
Konstruktion
Detailschnitt | 1:10
Nacht-Ansicht West | 1:200
kadawittfeldarchitektur
RISTORANTE
STYLE
sport
kwa
FASHION
Teilansicht und Fassadenschnitt | 1:20
81,75 m
79,00 m
74,50 m
69,50 m
64,50 m

Parachute Pavilion | *OCDC*

136

Project Team : Andy Ku, Kam Ku, Olivia Ku
Location : New York, USA
Typology : Mix-Use Retail / Office
Size : 558 m²

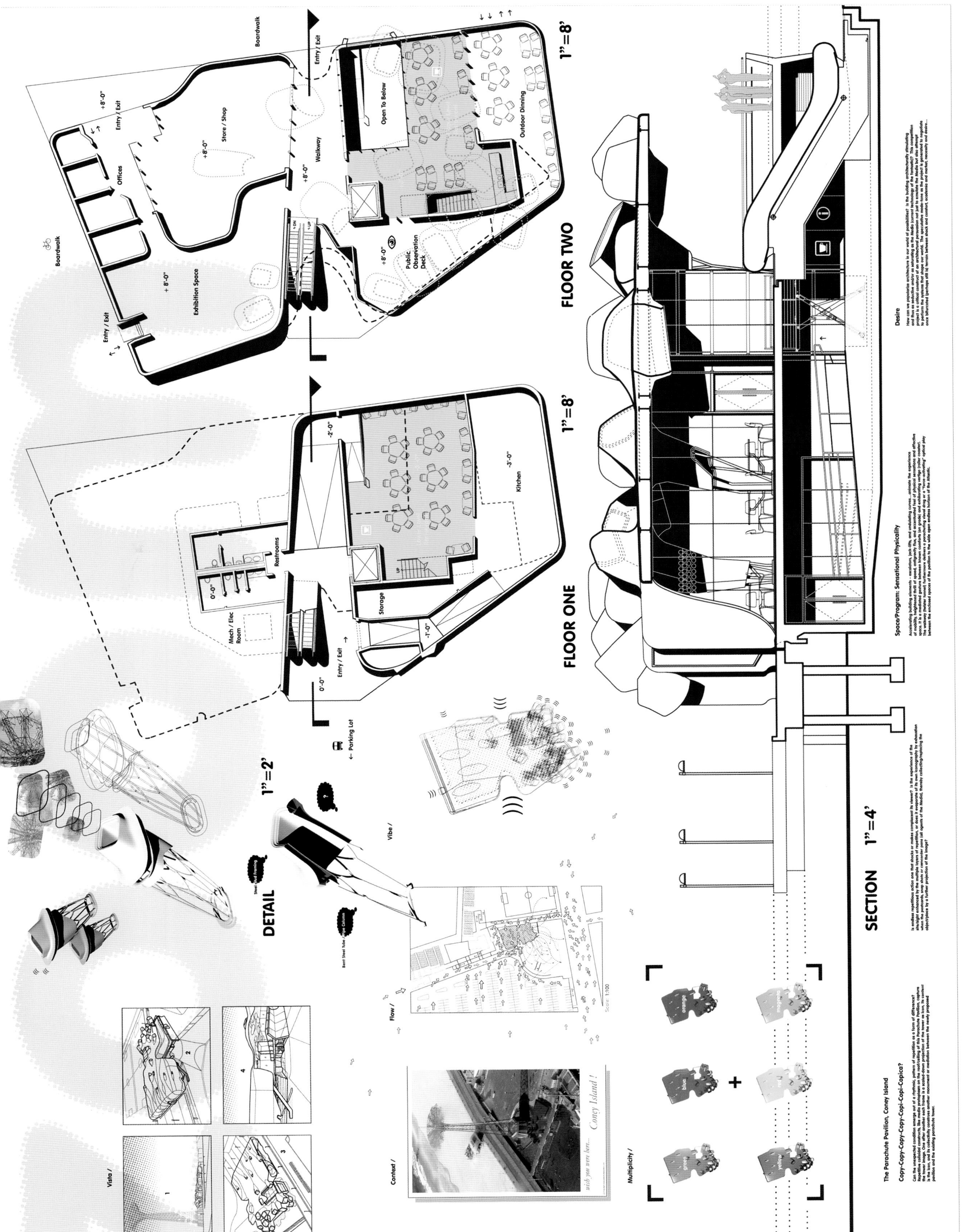

137 Thyssen Krupp | *kadawittfeldarchitektur*

Participants : Gerhard Wittfeld, Klaus Kada, Kilian Kada, Simon Kortemeier, Simona Czysch, Astrid Dierkes, Julika Metz, Johannes Müntinga, Andrea Blaschke Student Nisaan Uthayakumar Partner Statik/DGNB Werner Sobek Frankfurt GmbH & Co. KG Passivhaus Planer, LEED AP, DGNB Auditor Leiter WSF Greentech

Project : office building for ThyssenKrupp AG
Location : Berlin, Germany / Client : ThyssenKrupp AG

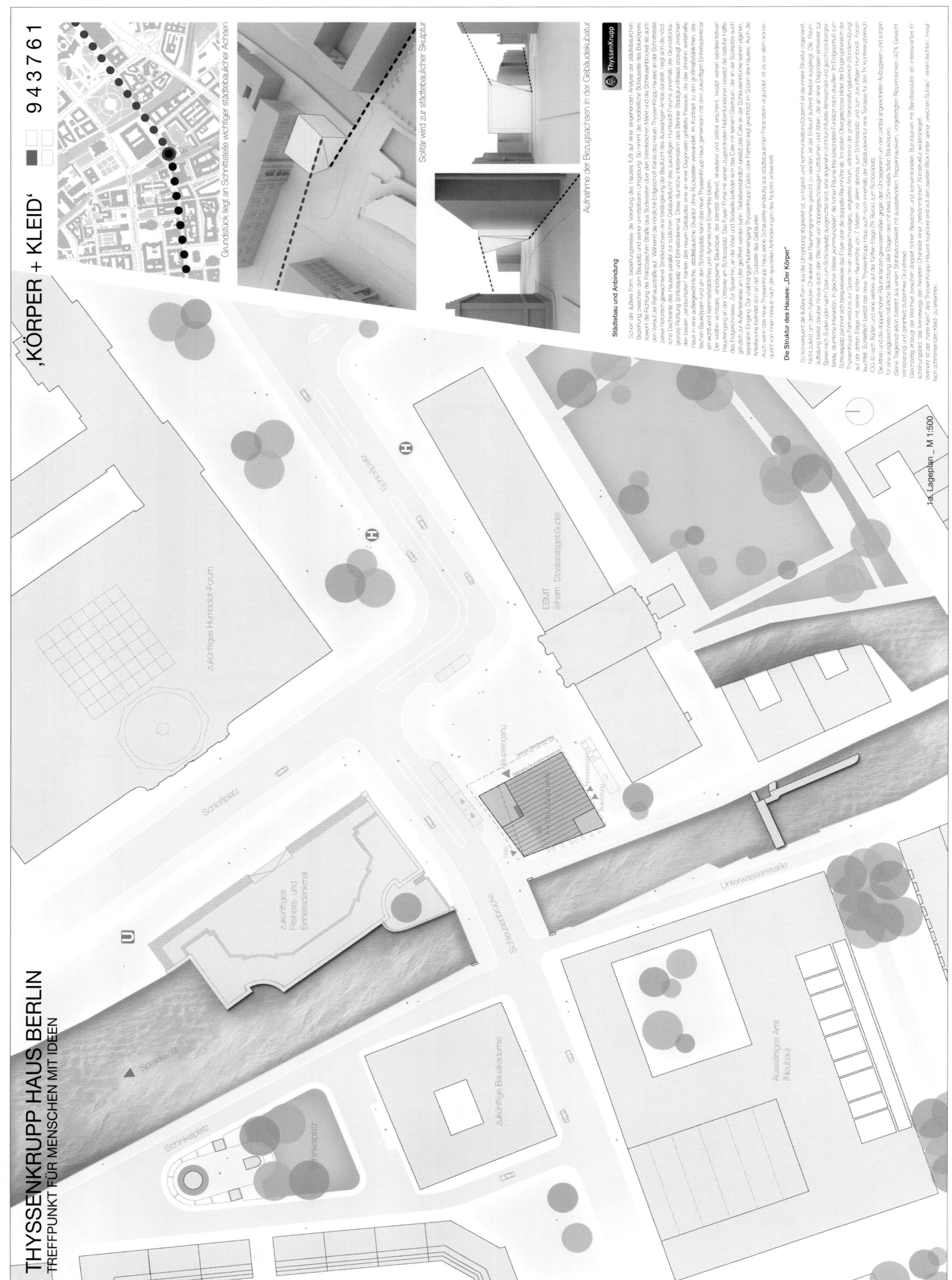

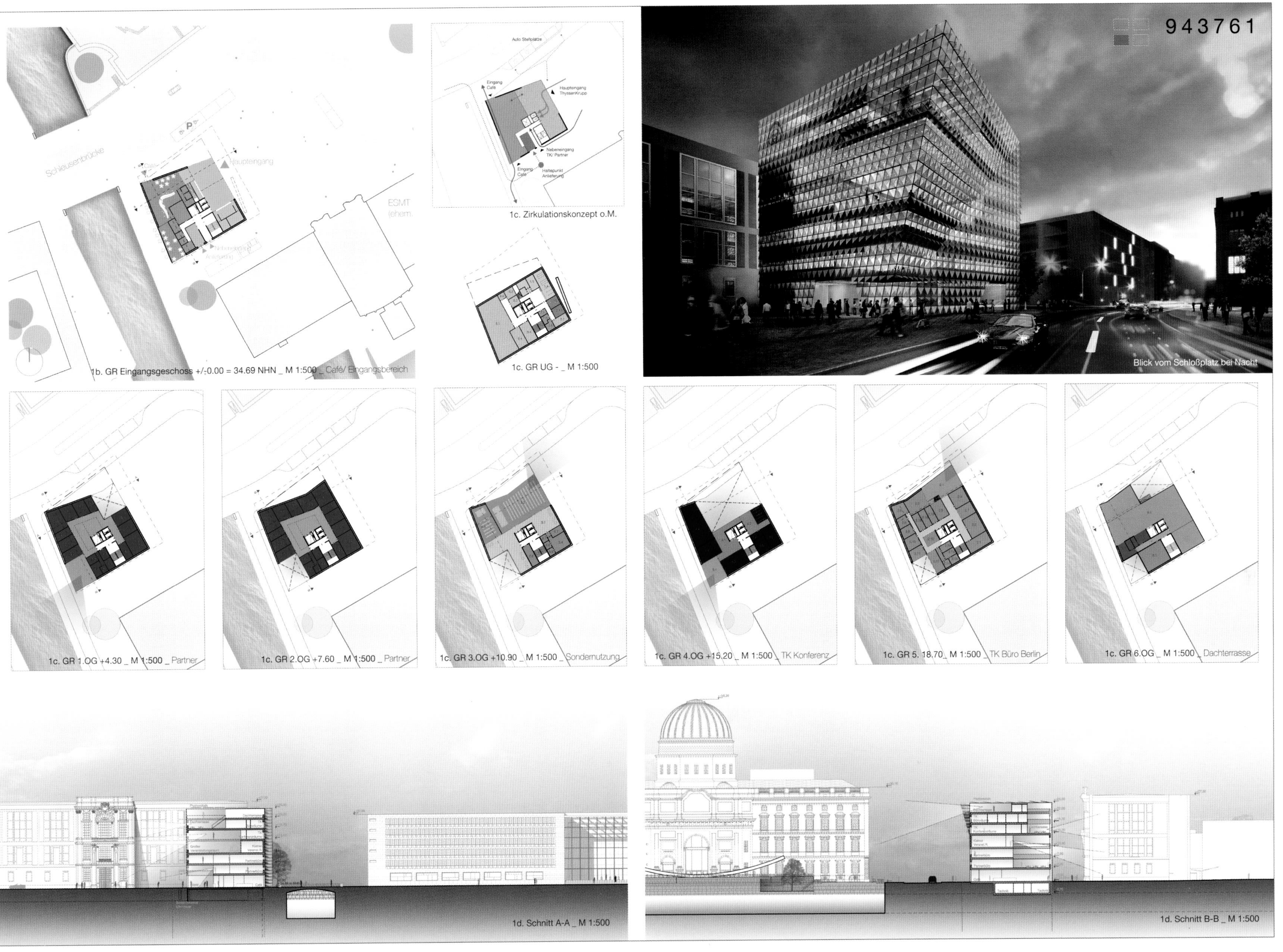
943761
Schleusenbrücke
Haupteingang
ESMT (ehem.
1b. GR Eingangsgeschoss +/-0.00 = 34.69 NHN _ M 1:500 _ Café/ Eingangsbereich
Auto Stellplätze
Eingang Café
Haupteingang ThyssenKrupp
Nebeneingang TK/ Partner
Haltepunkt Anlieferung
1c. Zirkulationskonzept o.M.
1c. GR UG - _ M 1:500
Blick vom Schloßplatz bei Nacht
1c. GR 1.OG +4.30 _ M 1:500 _ Partner
1c. GR 2.OG +7.60 _ M 1:500 _ Partner
1c. GR 3.OG +10.90 _ M 1:500 _ Sondernutzung
1c. GR 4.OG +15.20 _ M 1:500 _ TK Konferenz
1c. GR 5. 18.70_ M 1:500 _TK Büro Berlin
1c. GR 6.OG _ M 1:500 _ Dachterrasse
1d. Schnitt A-A _ M 1:500
1d. Schnitt B-B _ M 1:500

ehem. Staatsratsgebäude
Wettbewerbsgebiet
Schleusenbrücke
Unterwasser-
straße
Auswärtiges Amt (Neubau)
1e. Ansicht Nord _ M 1:500
ehem. Staatsratsgebäude
Wettbewerbsgebiet
Schlossplatz
zukünftige Bauakademie
1e. Ansicht Ost _ M 1:500
zukünftiges Humboldtforum
zukünftiges Freiheits- und Einheitsdenkmal
Schleusenbrücke
Wettbewerbsgebiet
ehem. Staatsratsgebäude
1e. Ansicht West _ M 1:500
943761
Blick vom Schloßplatz
Innenperspektive „Großer Veranstaltungsraum"

INNOVATION, TECHNOLOGIE UND FLEXIBILITÄT

‚KÖRPER + KLEID' 943761

1 ZIELE

„Wir entwickeln die Zukunft für Sie"

Klima-neutrales Gebäude

Die Primärenergiebilanz ergibt ein Plusenergiegebäude ohne CO_2 Emission = Klima-neutral

Primärenergiebilanz
BGF 4020 m²

Wärmebedarf	- 47 MWh/a
Kältebedarf	- 3 MWh/a
Beleuchtung	- 53 MWh/a
Lüftung	- 75 MWh/a
Verteilung	- 11 MWh/a
Verbrauch	- 188 MWh/a

Photovoltaik
540 m² Dach
Gewinn + 201 MWh/a

Die Energiebilanz ist positiv
Null CO_2 Emission

Hocheffizientes Heizen und Kühlen über Grundwasser - Wärmepumpe - Flächenheizung

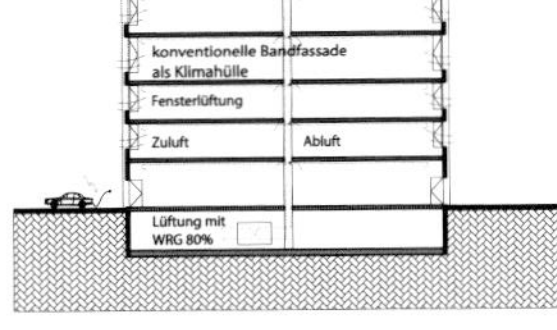
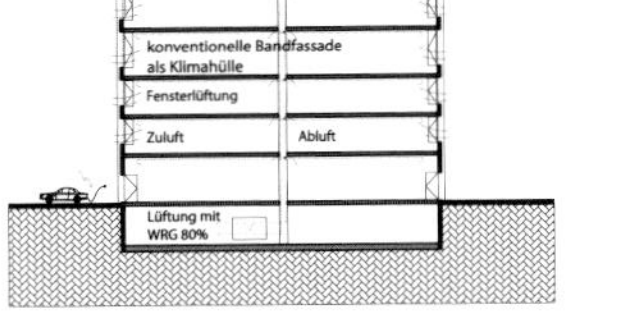

Hocheffiziente Lüftungsanlage mit 80% Wärmerückgewinnung

100 % rezyklierbares Gebäude

- Wiederverwendbarkeit aller verwendeten Bauteile
- Sortenreine Baustoffe
- Abbau und Wiederaufbau andernorts möglich

geringe Lebenszykluskosten (LCC)

Passivhaus-Standard wird angestrebt: geringere LCCs als EnEV Gebäude

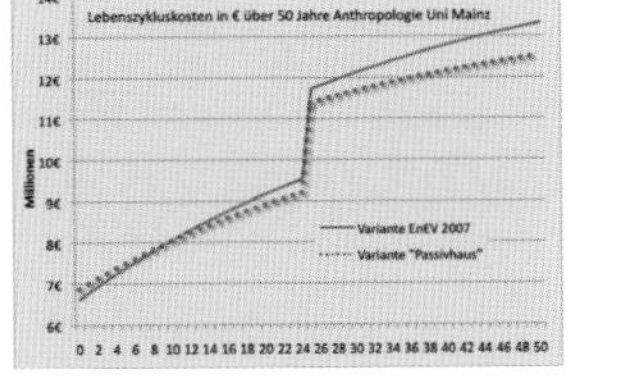

geringe Herstellungsenergie

- geringes Gewicht der Gebäudestruktur
- schnelle Montage durch Vorfertigung

Zertifizierungen Nachhaltiges Bauen

2 RÄUMLICHE INNOVATION

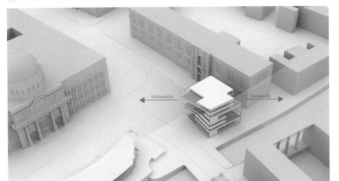

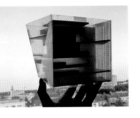

Ausblicke _ Lufträume (doppelte Raumhöhe) _ innenräumliche Vernetzung

Wechselspiel aus kommunizierenden Lufträumen.
Räumliche Verbindung aller Geschosse über Atrien.

3 FLEXIBILITÄT

NUTZUNGSSZENARIEN THYSSENKRUPP HAUS

1 getrennte, unabhängige Nutzung der Geschosse möglich

2 geschossübergreifende Nutzung („Veranstaltungsturm")

NUTZUNGSSZENARIEN PARTNER-BÜRO ETAGEN

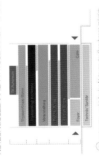

Ausstellung 1.OG · Veranstaltung 1.OG · Konferenz 1.OG
Ausstellung 2.OG · Veranstaltung 2.OG · Konferenz 2.OG

4 FASSADE

Corporate Design

Fassaden-Detail ‚HausKleid'

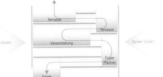

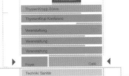

KONSTRUKTIONSPRINZIP DES ‚KLIMA-KLEIDES'

Außenliegender Sonnenschutz

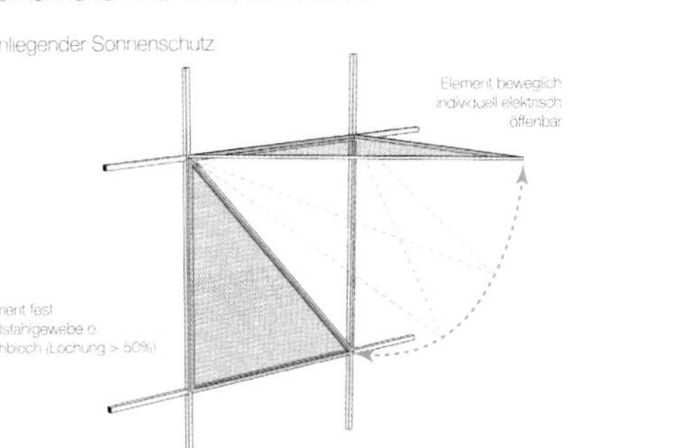

Prinzip Ausblick und Sonnenschutz

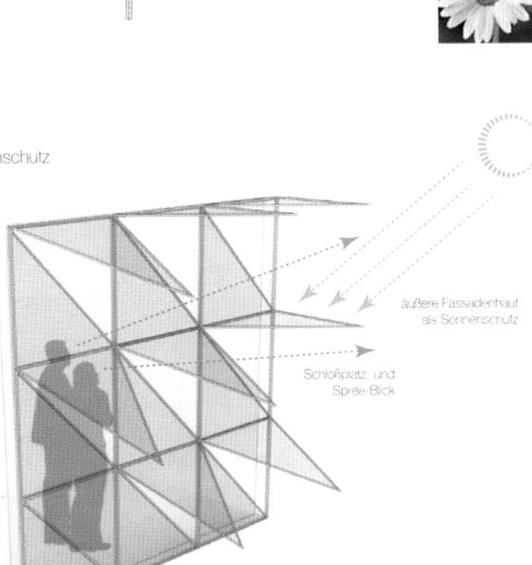

Fassade: „Das Klima-Kleid"

Ein hoher Tageslichtanteil im Gebäude spart Strom und erhöht die Zufriedenheit der Nutzer.

Dem gegenüber steht ein energietechnisch optimierter Verglasungsanteil an der Fassade von maximal 50%.

So ist der „Körper" des Gebäudes mit einer konventionellen, wirtschaftlichen Bandfassade als Klimahülle (vorgefertigte, vorgehängte, recyclebare Elemente) ausgestattet, deren Brüstungen und Stürze ein ausgewogenes Verhältnis zwischen opaken und verglasten Flächen erzielen. Schließlich ist aber dem „harten" Körper zusätzlich eine „weiche" Hülle vorgelagert, die in ihrer Erscheinung und Materialität inhaltlich eindeutig den Produkten des Konzerns zuzuordnen ist. Das Hauskleid aus Edelstahl soll den Geist des Unternehmens widerspiegeln und ein unverwechselbares Merkmal seines Corporate Designs darstellen.

Wie ein hochtechnologisches „Negligé" steuert die bewegliche „Haut" des Gebäudes die Sonneneinstrahlung und lenkt die Ausblicke der Nutzer. Das Fassadennetz basiert auf einem Rauten-Raster von etwa einem m², das in zwei Dreiecke aus Edelstahl (Lochblech mit mind. 50% Lochung, oder Edelstahl- Flechtwerk) unterteilt ist. Eine der beiden Dreiecksflächen kann individuell stufenlos elektrisch geöffnet bzw. geschlossen werden. Tagsüber erscheint die hochwertig glänzende Fassade des ThyssenKrupp Gebäudes daher eher homogen und geschlossen (ohne die Ausblicke der Nutzer zu beeinträchtigen), durch die stets unterschiedlich ausgerichteten Dreiecke aber sehr bewegt und abwechslungsreich.

Nachts, wenn alle beweglichen Elemente -einer sich öffnenden Blüte gleich- aufgerichtet stehen, erstrahlt der innere Körper mit seinen Veranstaltungsräumen in den typischen Farben der ThyssenKrupp- Palette.

Über dem Dachgeschoß schlagen wir eine, einer Pergola ähnliche Konstruktion aus Aluminiumprofilen vor, die den Besuchern der Terrassen Schatten spendet und auf etwa 500 m² Fotovoltaik- Paneele trägt.

1g. Liberoplan „Innovation und Technologie"

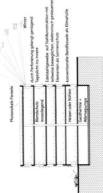

138 Sustainable Intersacalar Node | *NABITO ARCHITECTS & PARTNERS*

Alessandra Faticanti – Roberto Ferlito and Partners
International Competition "Europan 11" for a multifunctional complex
Housing, Commercial and Public space in Simrishamn, Sweden, 2011
Assigned Typology : Public / Client : Municipality of Simrishamn

Collaborators : Aldo Sollazzo, Daniel Güthler, Daniele Ceraudo, Alessandro Carabini, Furio Sordini, Federica Bufano, Lina Gronskyte

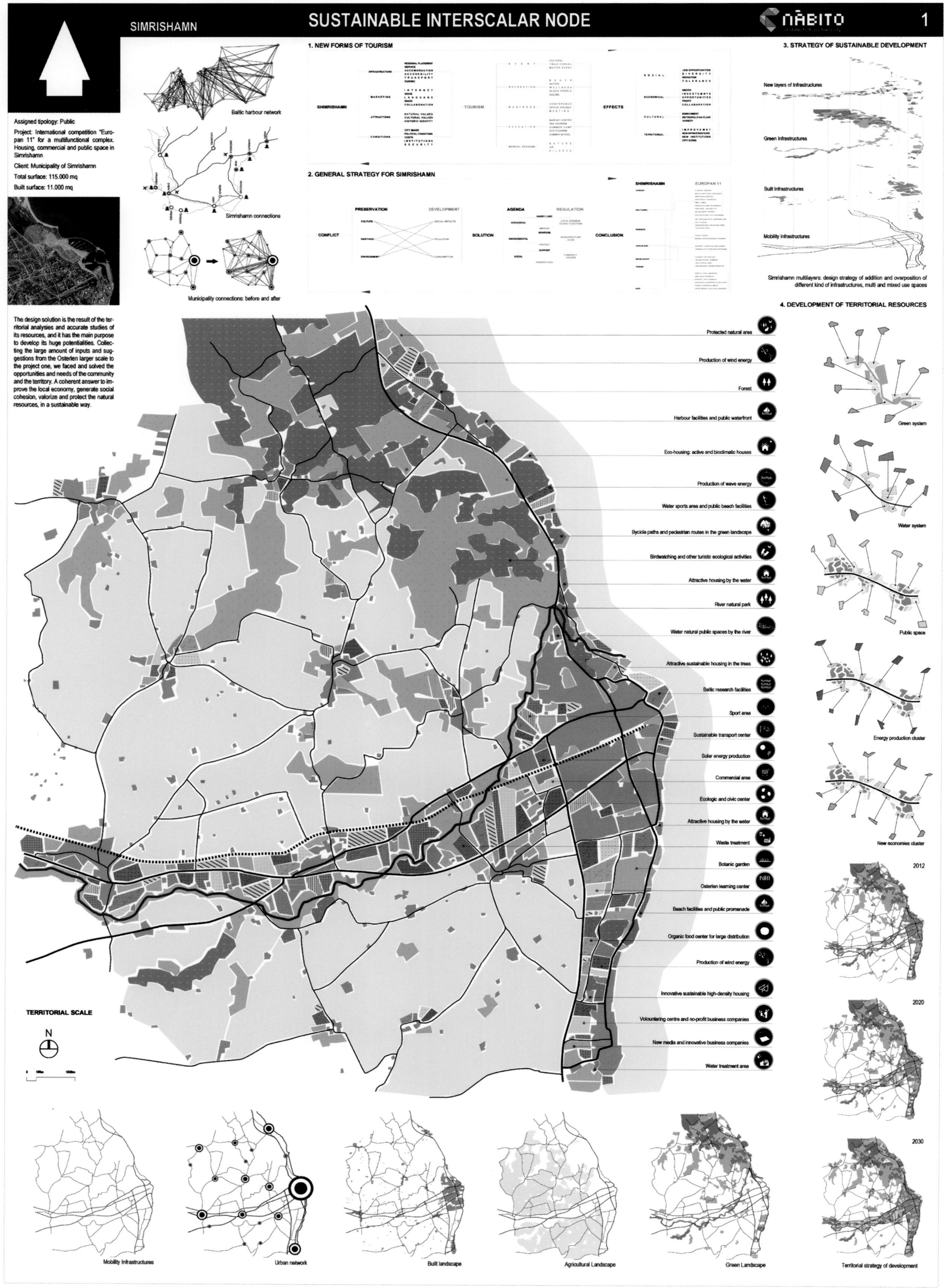

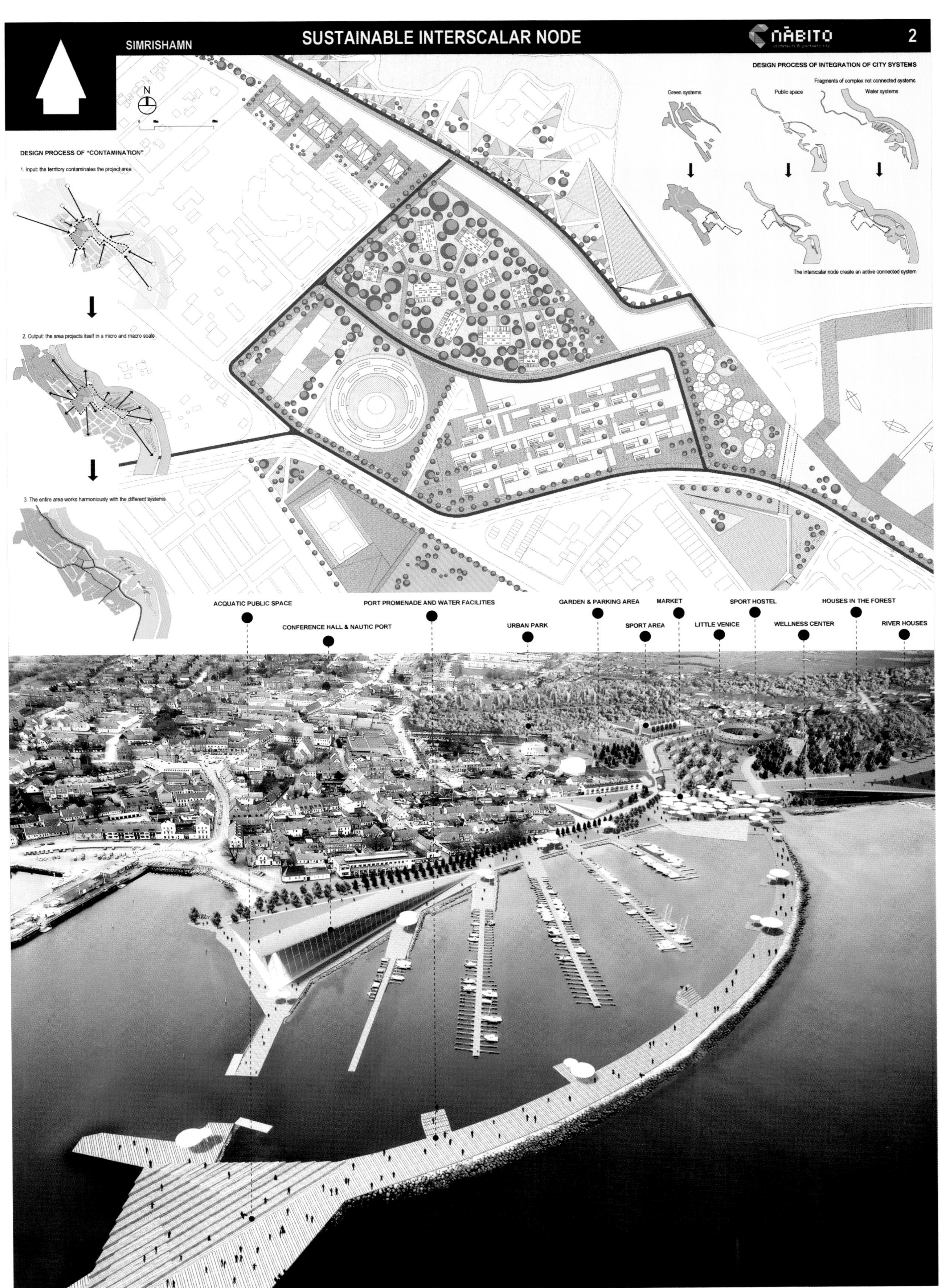
SIMRISHAMN
SUSTAINABLE INTERSCALAR NODE
2
DESIGN PROCESS OF "CONTAMINATION"
1. Input: the territory contaminates the project area
2. Output: the area projects itself in a micro and macro scale
3. The entire area works harmoniously with the different systems
DESIGN PROCESS OF INTEGRATION OF CITY SYSTEMS
Fragments of complex not connected systems
Green systems
Public space
Water systems
The interscalar node create an active connected system
ACQUATIC PUBLIC SPACE
CONFERENCE HALL & NAUTIC PORT
PORT PROMENADE AND WATER FACILITIES
URBAN PARK
GARDEN & PARKING AREA
SPORT AREA
MARKET
LITTLE VENICE
SPORT HOSTEL
WELLNESS CENTER
HOUSES IN THE FOREST
RIVER HOUSES

SIMRISHAMN
SUSTAINABLE INTERSCALAR NODE
NĀBITO
architects & partners slp
3
THE NEW SIMRISHAMN
Further we focused in detail on the site behind the harbour. The main idea to start from the existing in order to preserve the city's identity and improve the cultural, social and economical situation of Shimrishamn.
We create spots that relate to the qualities such as the house by the river, the houses in the forst which are placed around the exsting trees.
This concept is on the one hand sustainable as it preserves the exsiting infrastructure on the other hand is creates spots with a strong identity.
In terms of architecture this idea is realized aswell each cluster has its own housing type with a different shape.
However the building shape refer to the typical houses of Shimrishamn the maximum building height of 4 floors is considered aswell as the piched roof.
river houses
house in the forest
ring hostel
little Venice
N
HOUSE IN THE FOREST
1020 sqm in total
townhouses each 120 sqm
4 apartment s eac 70 sqm
running
skating
barbecue
cycling
lie
walking
RIVER HOUSES
1900 sqm in total
140 sqm per unit
swimming
fishing
sailing
water skating
running
lie
walking
barbecue
LITTLE VENICE
2100 sqm in total
100 sqm per unit
swimming
fishing
sailing
skating
running
lie
walking
barbecue
RING HOSTEL
football
cycling
socializing
running
skating
shopping
lie
walking
eating
2400 sqm
1200 sqm
Section C-C'
Section A-A'
Section B-B'

Business Centre Sopot | *3LHD*

Location : Zagreb, Croatia
T3D : Lukasz Gradzki

Project Team : Sasa Begovic, Tatjana Grozdanic Begovic, Marko Dabrovic, Silvije Novak, Tin Kavuric, Krunoslav Szorsen, Andrea Dujic

01 

ŠIRA SITUACIJA MJ 1_2000

POSLOVNI CENTAR SOPOT

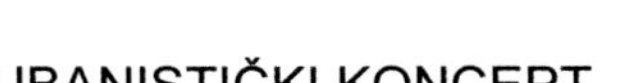

UBANISTIČKI KONCEPT

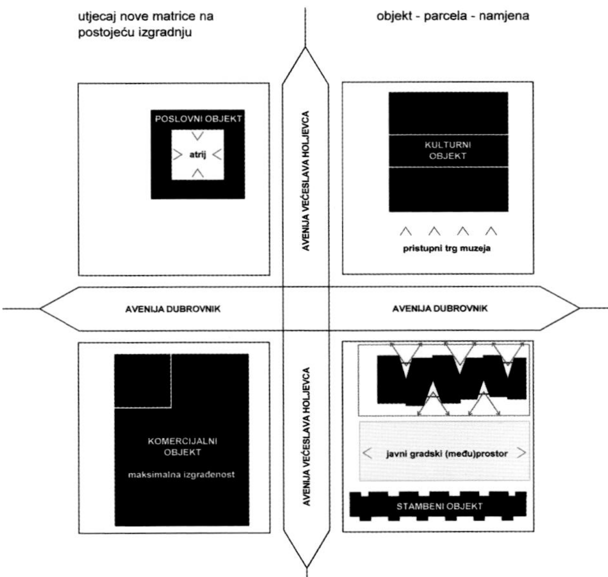

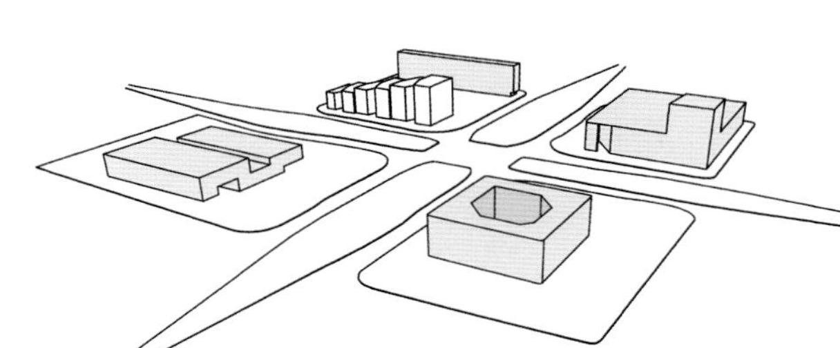

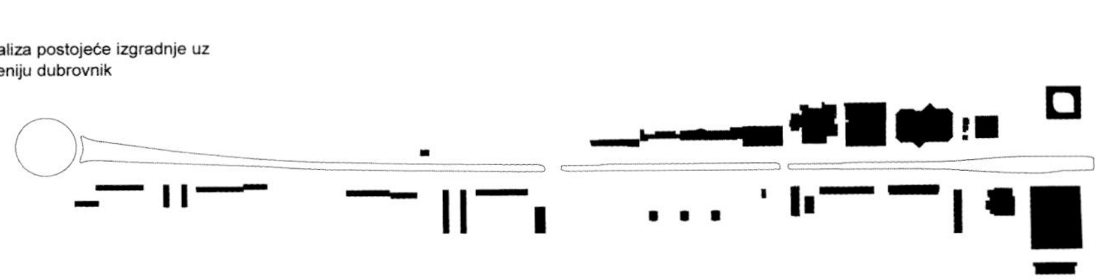

"ČETVRTI UGAO"

UŽA SITUACIJA NA KATASTRU MJ 1_1000

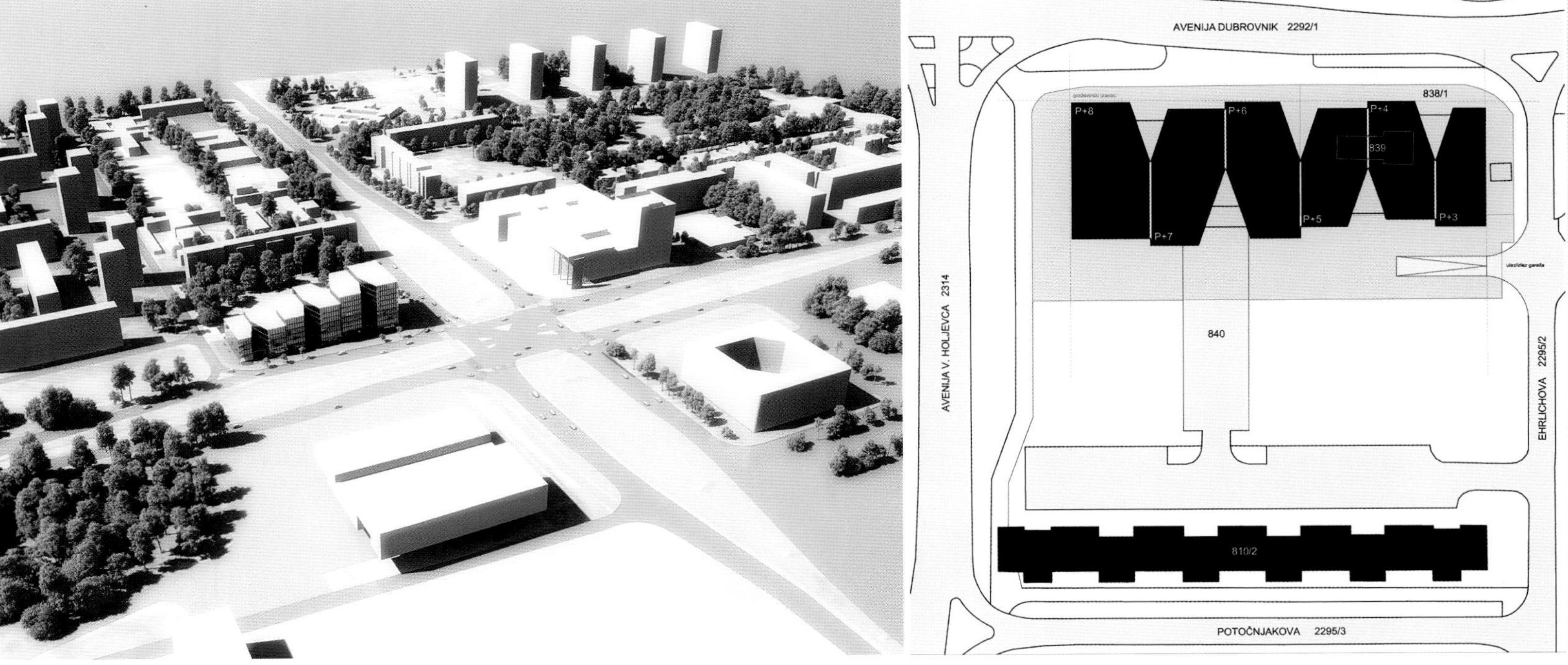

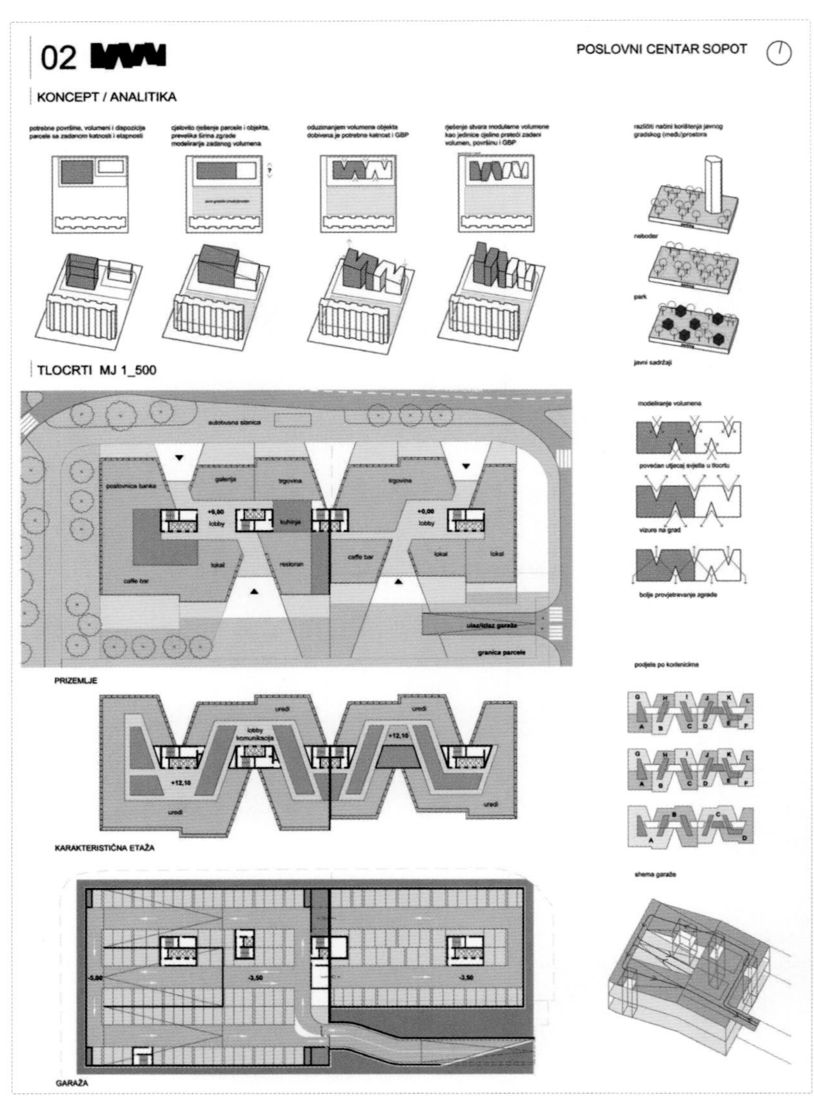
02
POSLOVNI CENTAR SOPOT
KONCEPT / ANALITIKA
TLOCRTI MJ 1_500
PRIZEMLJE
KARAKTERISTIČNA ETAŽA
GARAŽA

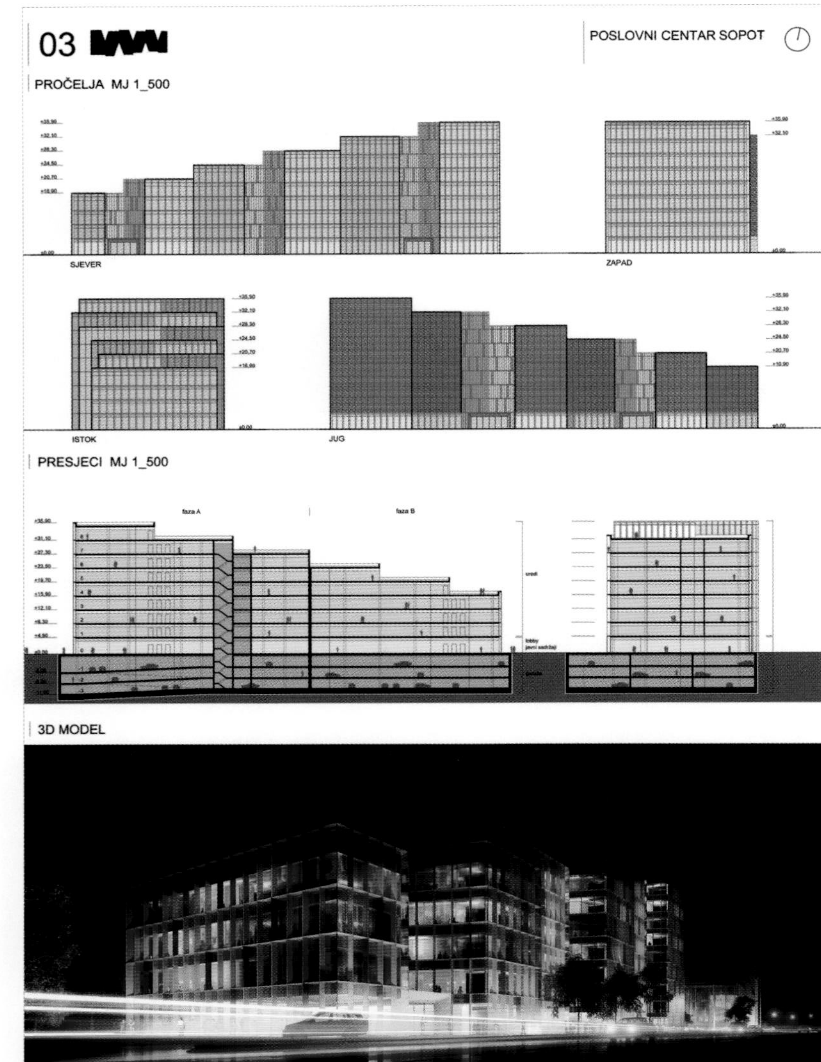
03
POSLOVNI CENTAR SOPOT
PROČELJA MJ 1_500
SJEVER
ZAPAD
ISTOK
JUG
PRESJECI MJ 1_500
3D MODEL

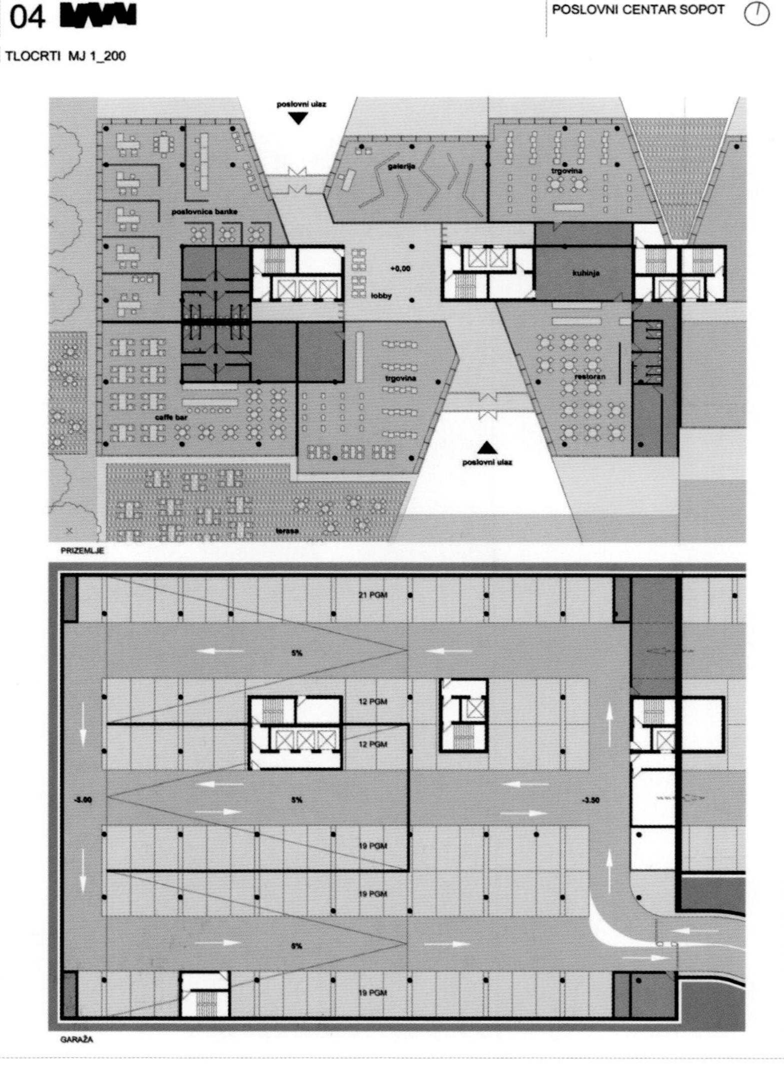
04
POSLOVNI CENTAR SOPOT
TLOCRTI MJ 1_200
poslovni ulaz
PRIZEMLJE
GARAŽA

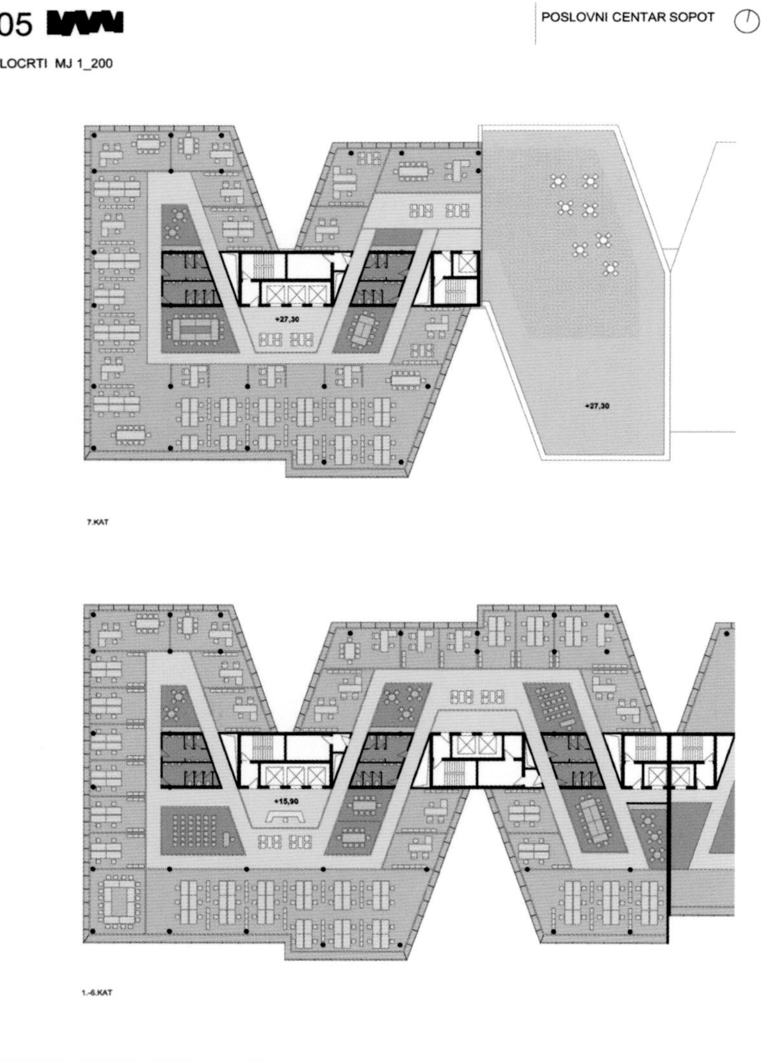
05
POSLOVNI CENTAR SOPOT
TLOCRTI MJ 1_200
7.KAT
1.-6.KAT

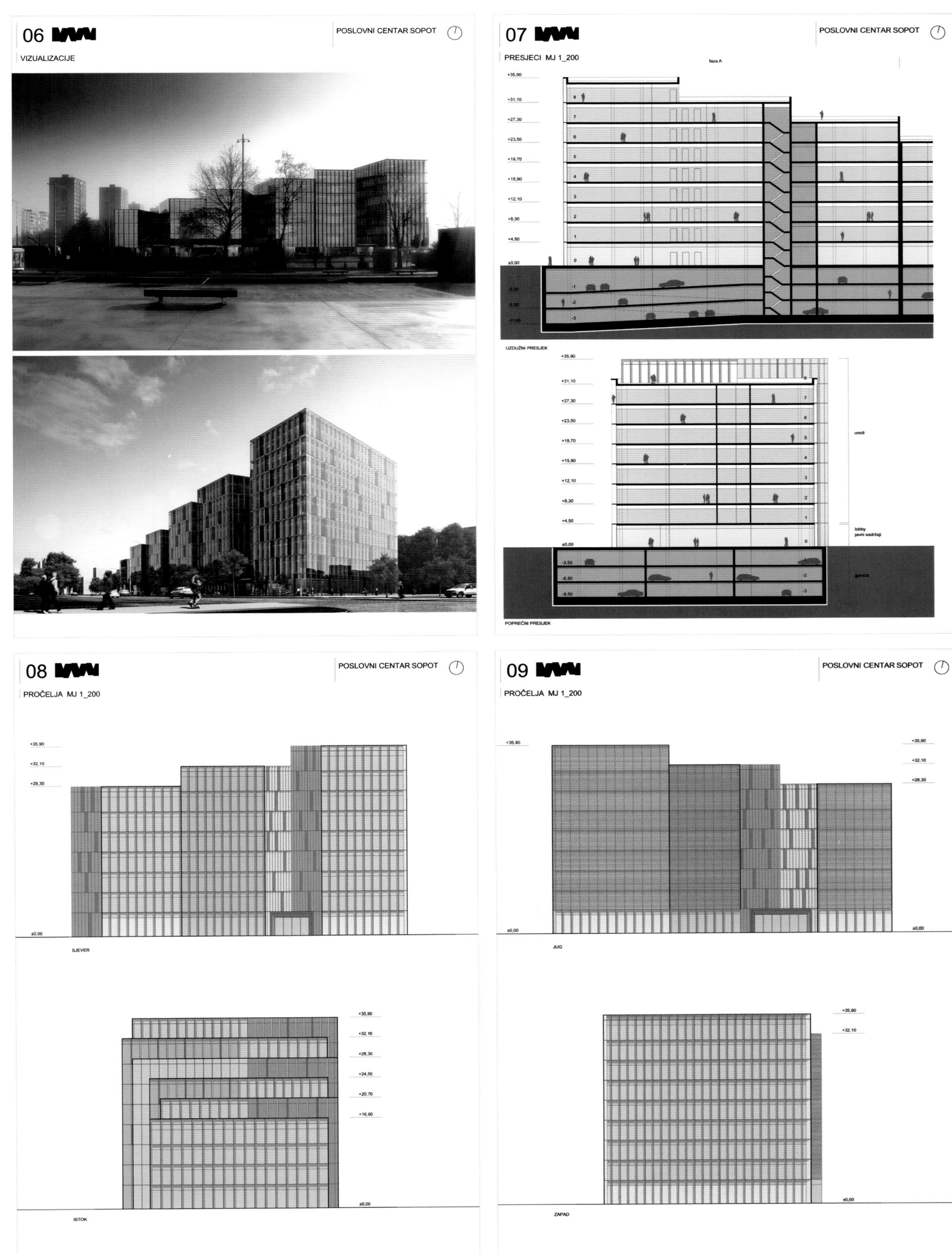
06
POSLOVNI CENTAR SOPOT
VIZUALIZACIJE
07
POSLOVNI CENTAR SOPOT
PRESJECI MJ 1_200
faza A
UZDUŽNI PRESJEK
uredi
lobby
javni sadržaji
garaža
POPREČNI PRESJEK
08
POSLOVNI CENTAR SOPOT
PROČELJA MJ 1_200
SJEVER
ISTOK
09
POSLOVNI CENTAR SOPOT
PROČELJA MJ 1_200
JUG
ZAPAD

140 Green Pavilion_Restaurant | *3LHD*

Location : Zagreb, Croatia
Type : Public, Culture, Education, Leisure, Housing
Client : University of Zagreb, Faculty of Agriculture and Forestry
Project Team : Sasa Begovic, Marko Dabrovic, Tatjana Grozdanic Begovic, Silvije Novak, Paula Kukuljica, Nevena Kuzmanic

Collaborators : Leon Lazaneo, Eugen Popovic, Anna Kocsis
3D : Boris Goreta

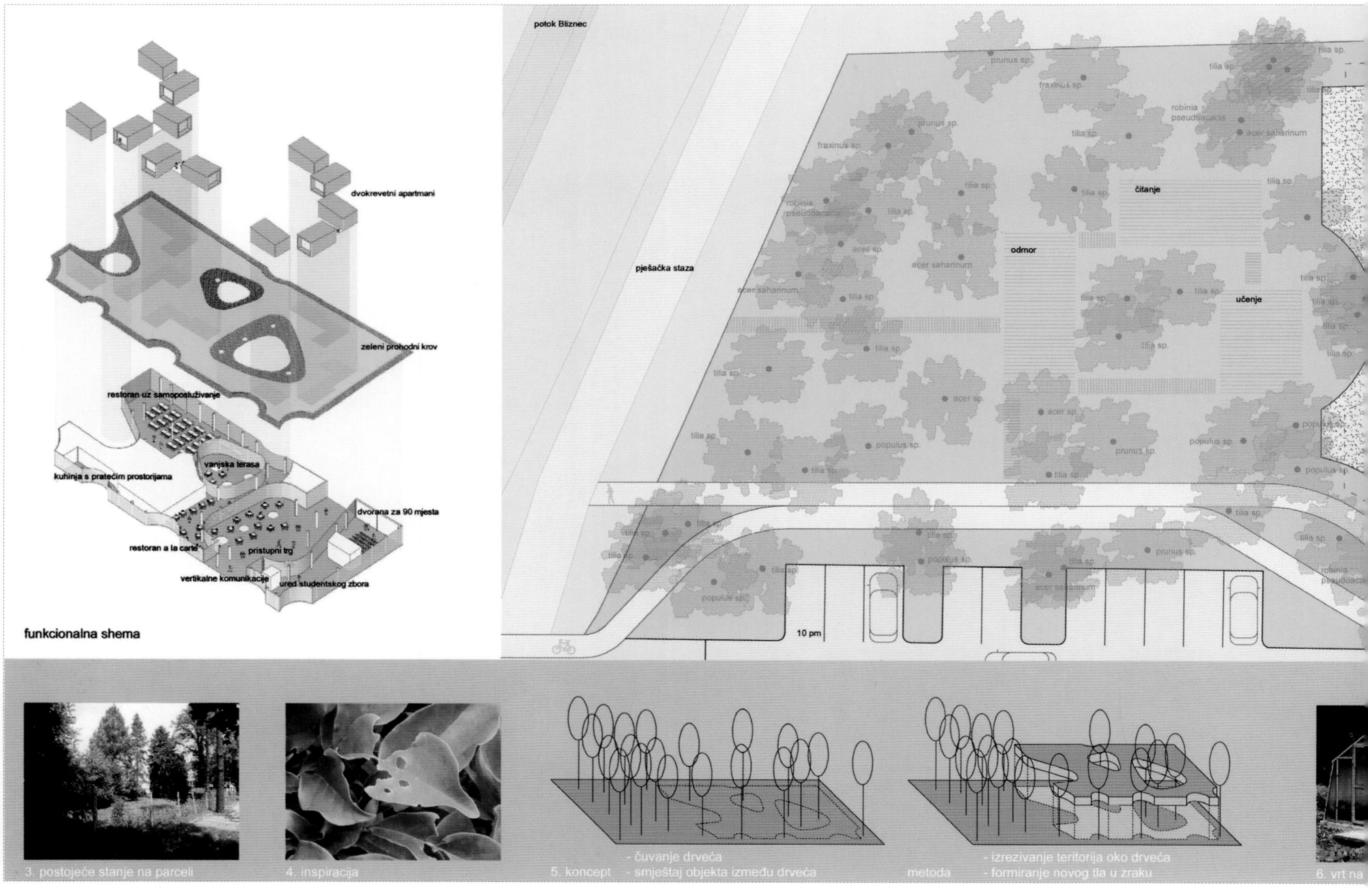

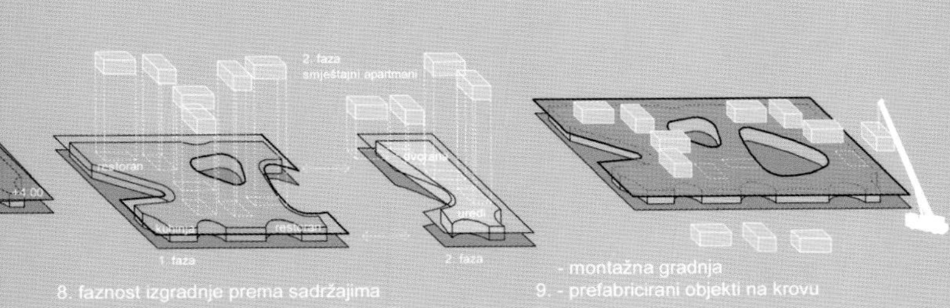

zeleni paviljon / restoran

idejno arhitektonsko rješenje

03

tlocrt kata
m 1/200

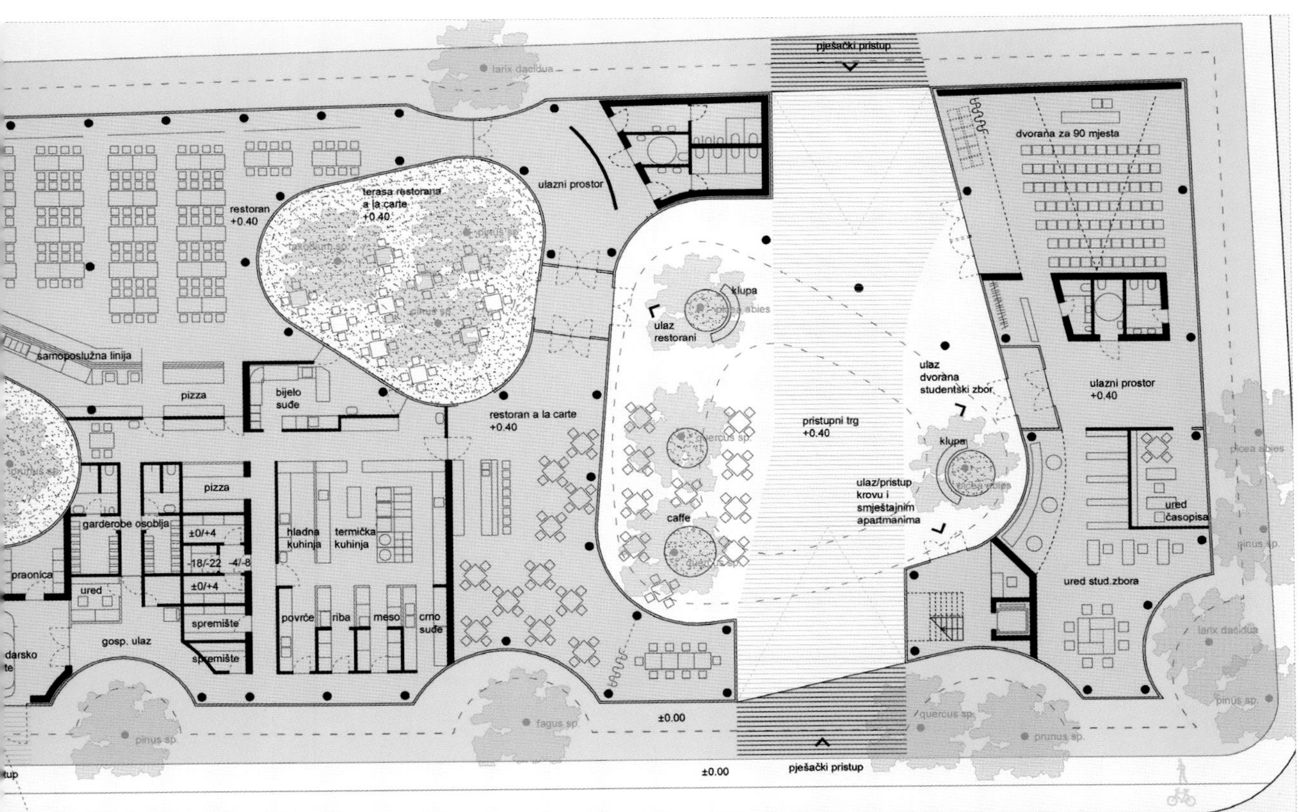

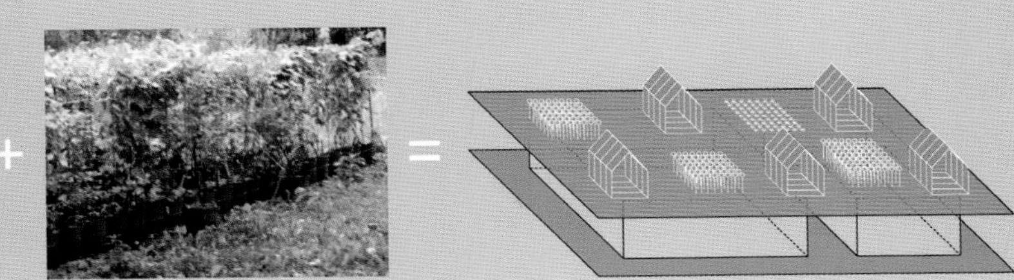

zeleni paviljon / restoran

idejno arhitektonsko rješenje

0

tlocrt prizemlja
m 1/200

zeleni paviljon / restoran
04
idejno arhitektonsko rješenje
presjek 1
m 1/200
10. zaštitna zona stabla

zeleni paviljon / restoran
07
idejno arhitektonsko rješenje
pročelje jug
m 1/200

zeleni paviljon / restoran 05

idejno arhitektonsko rješenje

presjeci 2, 3

m 1/200

zeleni paviljon / restoran 08

idejno arhitektonsko rješenje

pročelje istok

m 1/200

zeleni paviljon / restoran 09

idejno arhitektonsko rješenje

pročelje zapad

m 1/200

141 Wanda Wuhan Phase One | *Kokaistudios*

Chief Architect : Andrea Destefanis, Filippo Gabbiani, Peyron Pietro
Project Manager/Responsible : Li Wei
Design Team : Song Qing, Yao Yun, Chen Xi

Client : Wanda Wuhan
Location : Wuhan, China

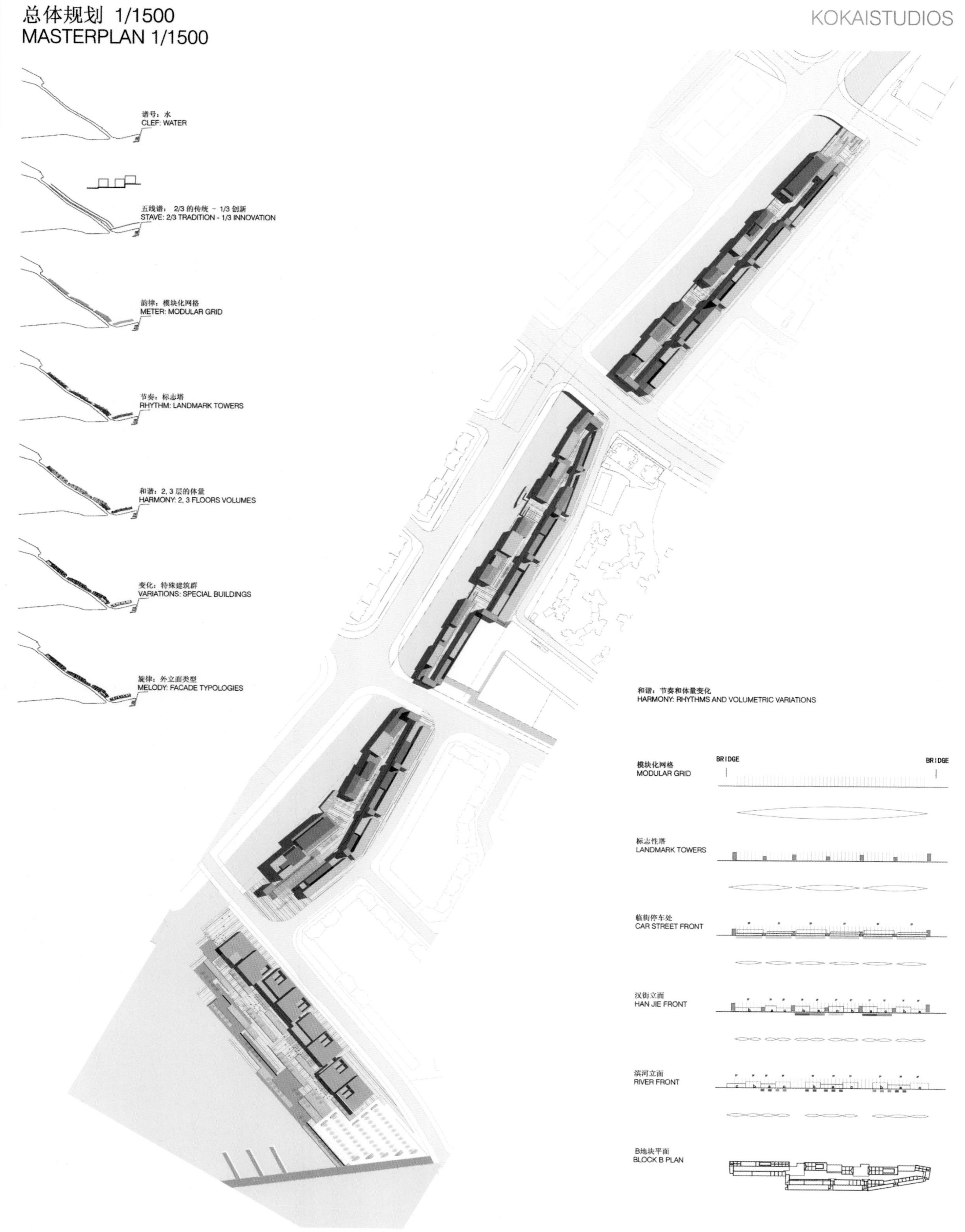

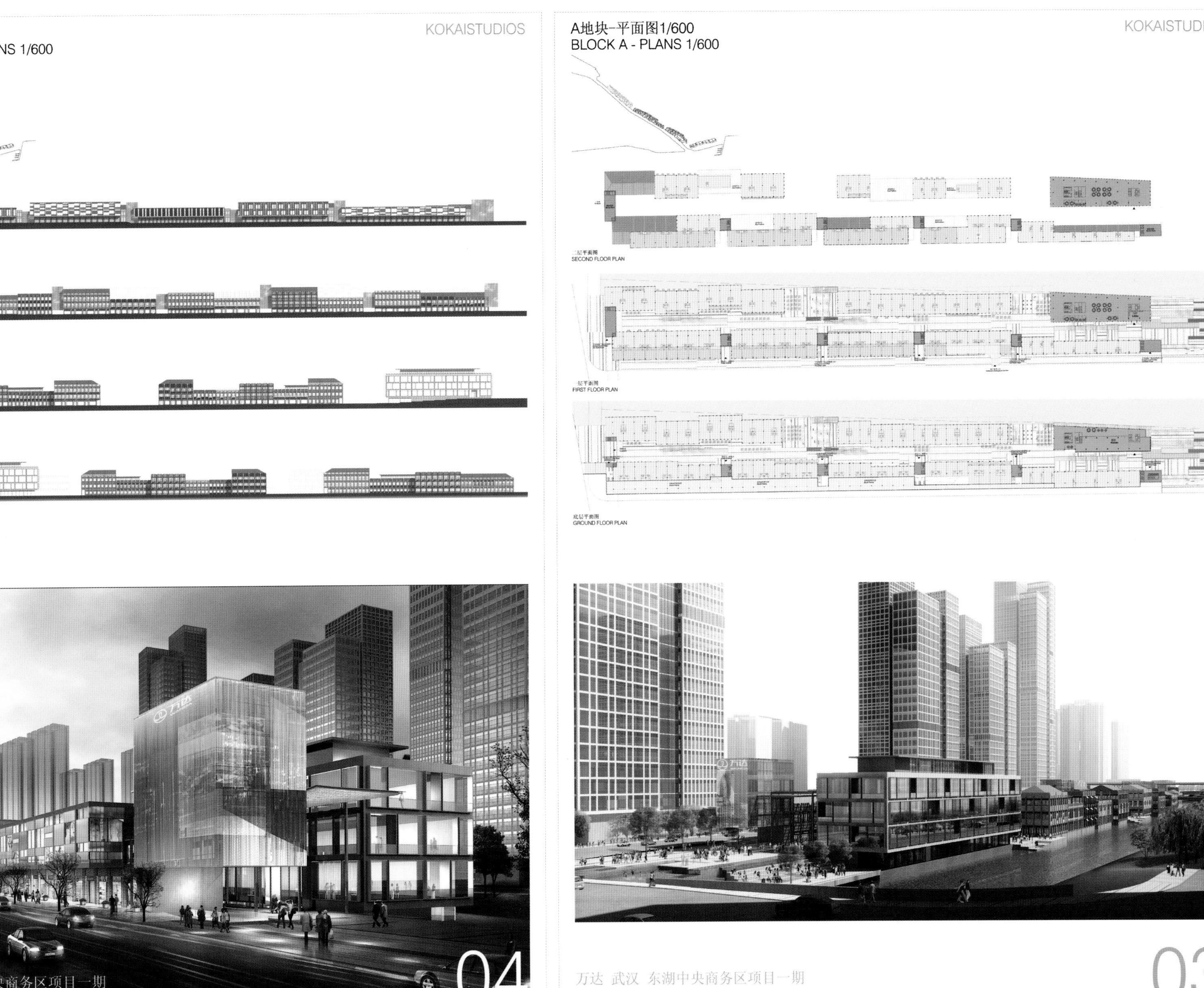
A地块-立面图1/600
BLOCK A - ELEVATIONS 1/600
KOKAISTUDIOS
ELEVATION ALONG CAR STREET
HAN JIE SOUTH FACADE
HAN JIE NORTH FACADE
FACADE ALONG CANAL
04
万达 武汉 东湖中央商务区项目一期
WANDA WUHAN PHASE 1 OF DONGHU CBD
A地块-平面图1/600
BLOCK A - PLANS 1/600
KOKAISTUDIOS
SECOND FLOOR PLAN
FIRST FLOOR PLAN
GROUND FLOOR PLAN
03
万达 武汉 东湖中央商务区项目一期
WANDA WUHAN PHASE 1 OF DONGHU CBD

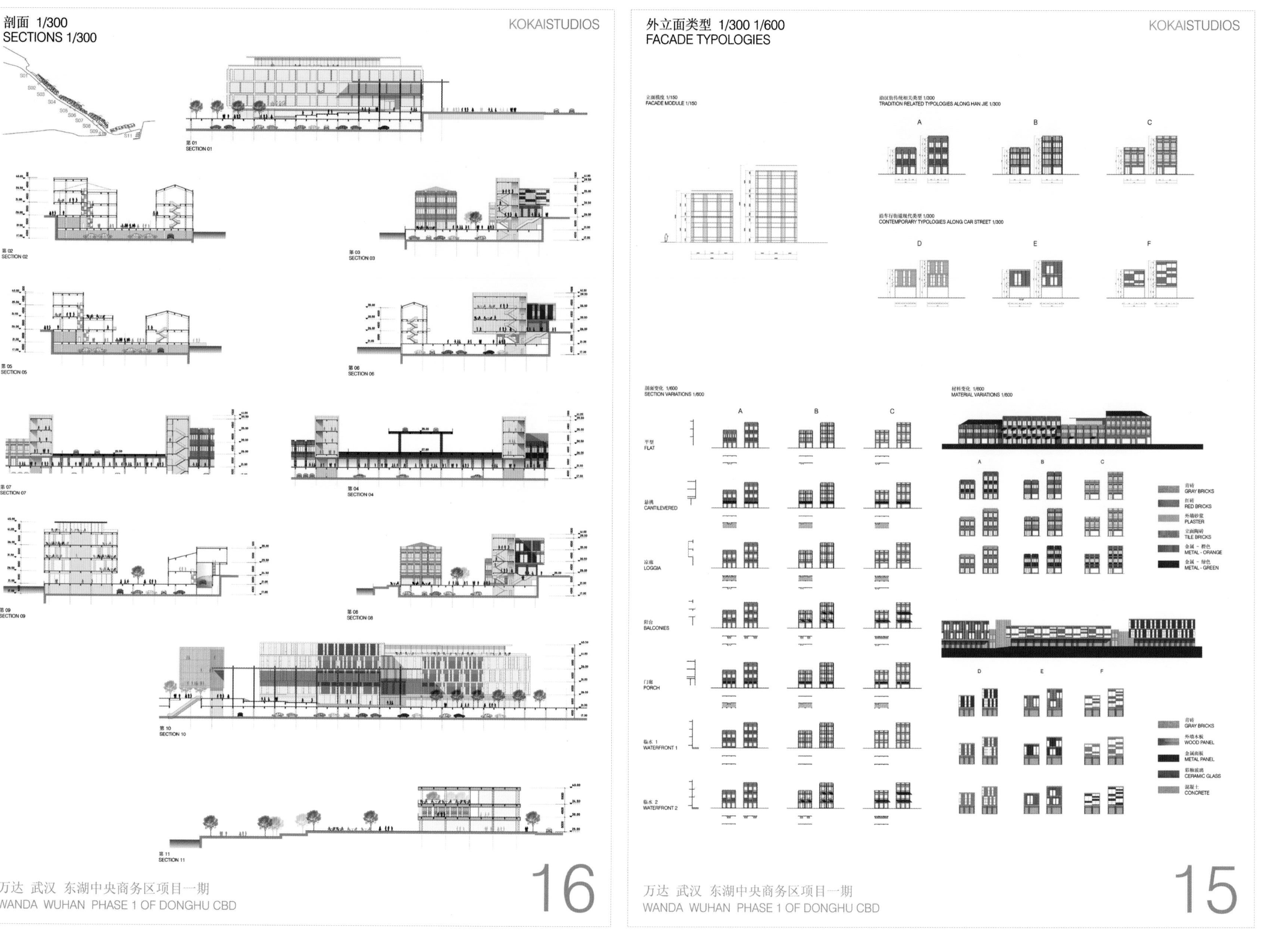
剖面 1/300
SECTIONS 1/300
KOKAISTUDIOS
第 01
SECTION 01
第 02
SECTION 02
第 03
SECTION 03
第 05
SECTION 05
第 06
SECTION 06
第 07
SECTION 07
第 04
SECTION 04
第 09
SECTION 09
第 08
SECTION 08
第 10
SECTION 10
第 11
SECTION 11
万达 武汉 东湖中央商务区项目一期
WANDA WUHAN PHASE 1 OF DONGHU CBD
16
外立面类型 1/300 1/600
FACADE TYPOLOGIES
KOKAISTUDIOS
立面模度 1/150
FACADE MODULE 1/150
沿汉街传统相关类型 1/300
TRADITION RELATED TYPOLOGIES ALONG HAN JIE 1/300
沿车行街道现代类型 1/300
CONTEMPORARY TYPOLOGIES ALONG CAR STREET 1/300
剖面变化 1/600
SECTION VARIATIONS 1/600
平型
FLAT
悬挑
CANTILEVERED
凉廊
LOGGIA
阳台
BALCONIES
门廊
PORCH
临水 1
WATERFRONT 1
临水 2
WATERFRONT 2
材料变化 1/600
MATERIAL VARIATIONS 1/600
青砖
GRAY BRICKS
红砖
RED BRICKS
外墙砂浆
PLASTER
立面陶砖
TILE BRICKS
金属 - 橙色
METAL - ORANGE
金属 - 绿色
METAL - GREEN
青砖
GRAY BRICKS
外墙木板
WOOD PANEL
金属面板
METAL PANEL
彩釉玻璃
CERAMIC GLASS
混凝土
CONCRETE
万达 武汉 东湖中央商务区项目一期
WANDA WUHAN PHASE 1 OF DONGHU CBD
15

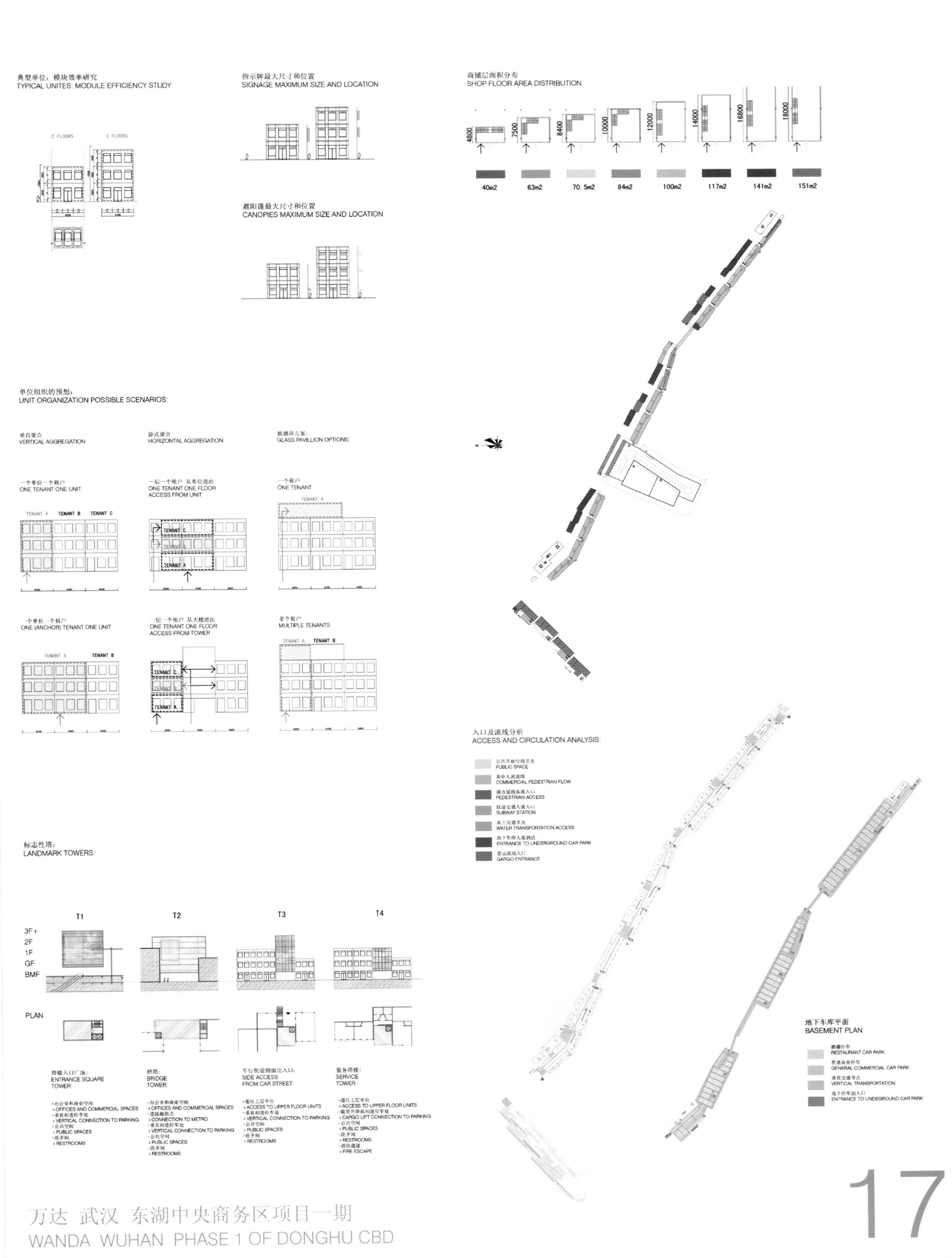
商业单位分析和可能性 1/300
COMMERCIAL UNITS ANALYSIS AND SCENARIOS 1/300
KOKAISTUDIOS
典型单位：模块效率研究
TYPICAL UNITES: MODULE EFFICIENCY STUDY
指示牌最大尺寸和位置
SIGNAGE MAXIMUM SIZE AND LOCATION
商铺层面积分布
SHOP FLOOR AREA DISTRIBUTION
40m2
63m2
70.5m2
84m2
100m2
117m2
141m2
151m2
遮阳篷最大尺寸和位置
CANOPIES MAXIMUM SIZE AND LOCATION
单位组织的预想：
UNIT ORGANIZATION POSSIBLE SCENARIOS:
VERTICAL AGGREGATION:
HORIZONTAL AGGREGATION
GLASS PAVILLION OPTIONS:
ONE TENANT ONE UNIT
ONE TENANT ONE FLOOR ACCESS FROM UNIT
ONE TENANT
ONE (ANCHOR) TENANT ONE UNIT
ONE TENANT ONE FLOOR ACCESS FROM TOWER
MULTIPLE TENANTS
入口及流线分析
ACCESS AND CIRCULATION ANALYSIS:
PUBLIC SPACE
COMMERCIAL PEDESTRIAN FLOW
PEDESTRIAN ACCESS
SUBWAY STATION
WATER TRANSPORTATION ACCESS
ENTRANCE TO UNDERGROUND CAR PARK
GARGO ENTRANCE
标志性塔：
LANDMARK TOWERS:
T1
T2
T3
T4
PLAN
ENTRANCE SQUARE TOWER
BRIDGE TOWER
SIDE ACCESS FROM CAR STREET
SERVICE TOWER
地下车库平面
BASEMENT PLAN
RESTAURANT CAR PARK
GENERAL COMMERCIAL CAR PARK
VERTICAL TRANSPORTATION
ENTRANCE TO UNDEGROUND CAR PARK
万达 武汉 东湖中央商务区项目一期
WANDA WUHAN PHASE 1 OF DONGHU CBD
17

142 Tian Fang Tower | *Kevin Kennon Architects*

Location : Eco-city, Tianjin, China
Program : Mixed-Use (Office, Retail And Shopping Mall)
System : Reinforced Concrete
Area : 11,5000 SQM
Height : 193m

AERIAL NIGHT VIEW

MASSING PROCESS

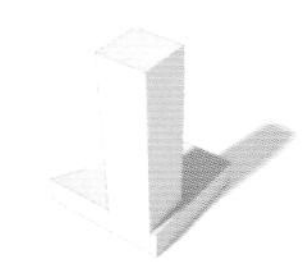

Tower at south end of site casts a shadow over the base

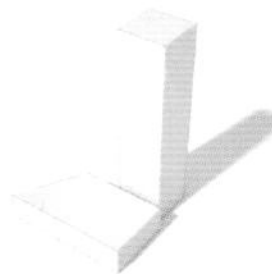

Tower moved to north end allows sunlight to reach all of base

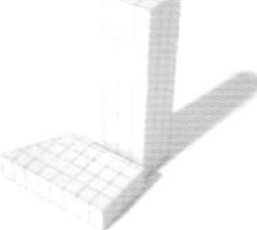

Bundling modules allow for maximum strength in poor soil conditions

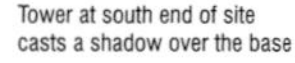

Modules shifted vertically allow sunlight deep into interior spaces

Rotated modules allow light and fresh air to penetrate deep into interior spaces

We examined the proposed site by questioning whether the tower, as currently zoned, is in the right location. How can we maximize the site by taking advantage of wind, sun, rain, as well as enhancing the micro-climate? The initial zoning diagrams placed the tower in the south and the retail base in the north. We conducted a study to determine if locating tower in the north is a feasible strategy since this would result in exposing the roof of the base to direct sunlight. Our environmental analysis proves that the tower can be located in the north with minimal detrimental impact. The roof of the base, with constant exposure to direct sunlight year round, is the perfect platform for solar panels.

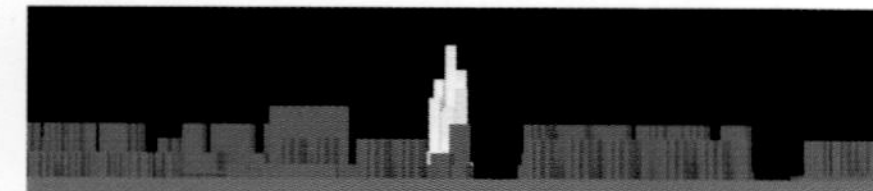

Initially, we looked at the tower shape as a simple rational box. We concluded that a mere box is not appropriate for the site. This will be the tallest tower in phase one of Eco-City. It will be visible from miles away especially from Tianjin to across the Hi river. The building should have a distinctive profile that has a significant impact on the skyline and serve as a unique landmark for Eco-City.

TIAN FANG TOWER

ECO-CITY_TIANJIN, CHINA

Location : Eco-city, Tianjin, China
Program : Mixed-use(office, retail and shopping mall)
System : Reinforced Concrete
Area : 11,5000 SQM
Height : 193m

The Biophilia Hypothesis describes the innate biological affinity we have to nature. This goes beyond mere sustainability. We are not simply discussing building systems, engineering protocol, or LEED certification, but rather every aspect of how we look at this building—from an intellectual, philosophical, and spiritual perspective—has been informed by the Biophilia hypothesis. We believe that architecture should directly respond to its environment by enhancing the connection between humans and nature. We have produced a design that not only incorporates sustainable engineering, but expands our dependence on nature beyond mere sustenance to include aesthetic, intellectual, and spiritual meaning. Our goal is to foster, even enhance, our innate biological affinity to life by creating a permeable architecture in which form and functions mimic nature.

SPACE DIAGRAM

ACTIVE ENERGY CONSERVATION STRATEGY

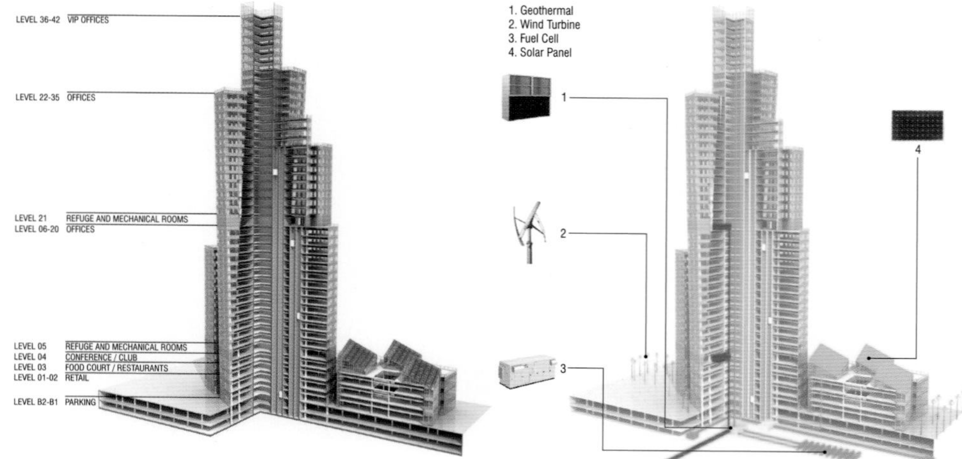

HVAC & DAYLIGHTING STRATEGY

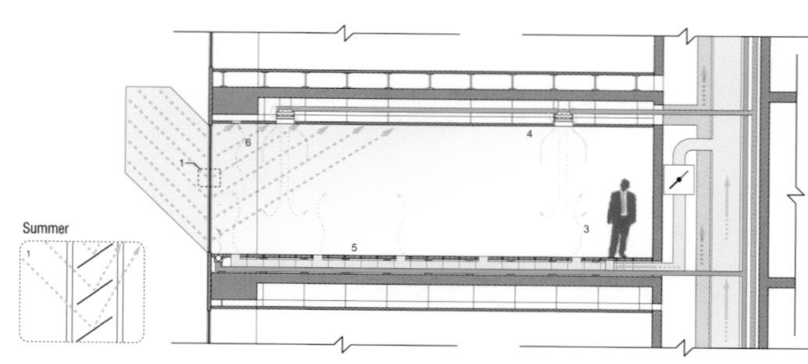

Conditioned Air
Exhaust Air
Chilled Water Loop
Hot Water or Steam
Sunlight

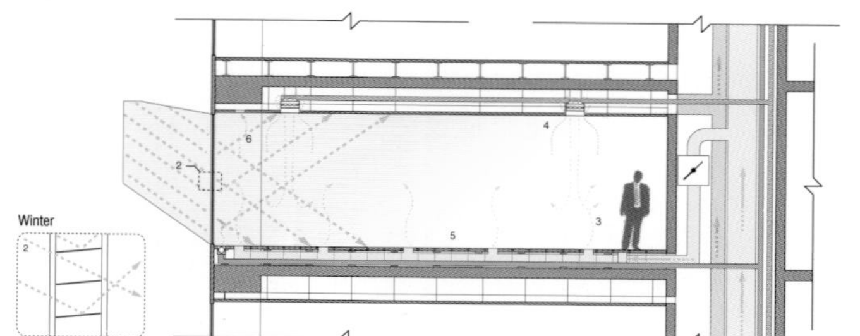

KEY NOTES

1. Louvered windows block harsh summer sunlight, avoiding direct solar gain.
2. Louvered windows allow in warm winter sunlight, allowing for solar warming.
3. Fresh air is introduced into the occupiable space.
4. In cooling mode, hot air naturally rises. Cooling beams cool the air and reintroduce it to the occupiable space.
5. In heating mode, a radiant flooring system in the raised access floor heats the occupiable space by allowing the heat to naturally rise by convection.
6. Stale air is exhausted from the room.

1. North View
2. Office Lobby

PASSIVE ENERGY CONSERVATION STRATEGY

1. Chilled Beam System : FlaktWoods Passive Chilled Beam
2. LED Lighting : Philips LED Lighting
3. Underfloor Air Distribution : Haworth TecCrete
4. Louvered Windows : Schott Glass & Okaflex Louvers

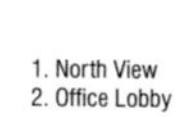

1 2 3 4

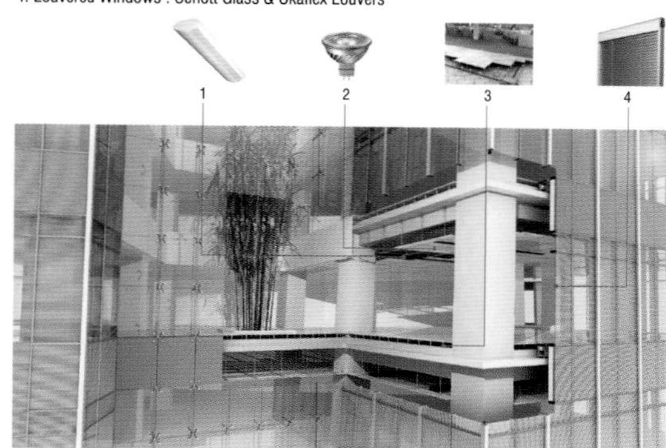

SECTIONS & ELEVATIONS

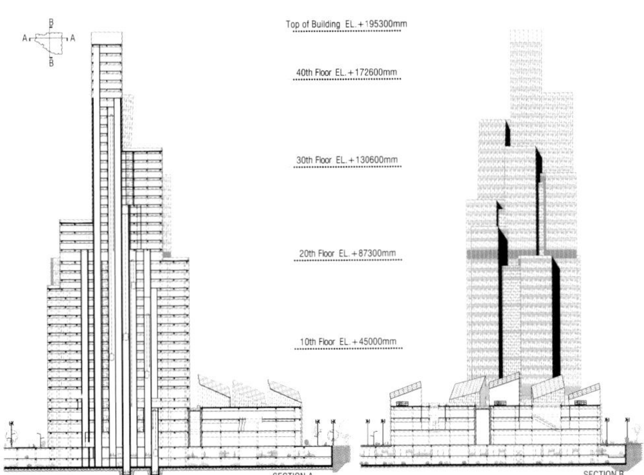

The division of the tower into nine square segments has the structural benefit of a bundled tube system. The bundled tube system further allows for each segment to act as structurally monolithic thereby eliminating costly transfer found in typical set back office towers.

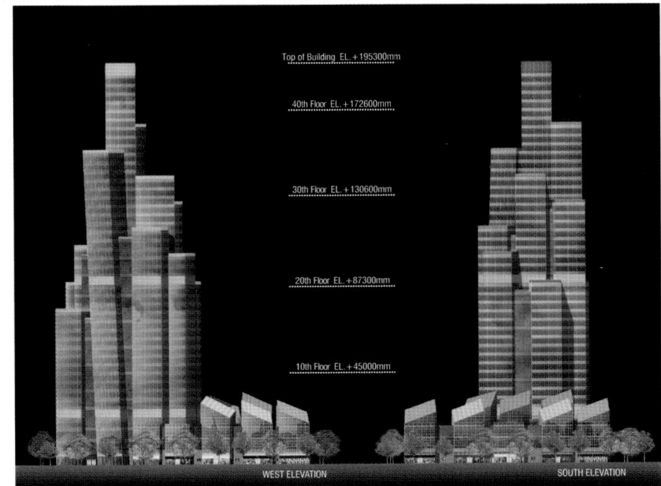

By breaking the tower into smaller parts we create a more human scale. By rotating and tilting the respective tower segments we can push the tower as far north as it can while respecting the initial six meter zoning set back.

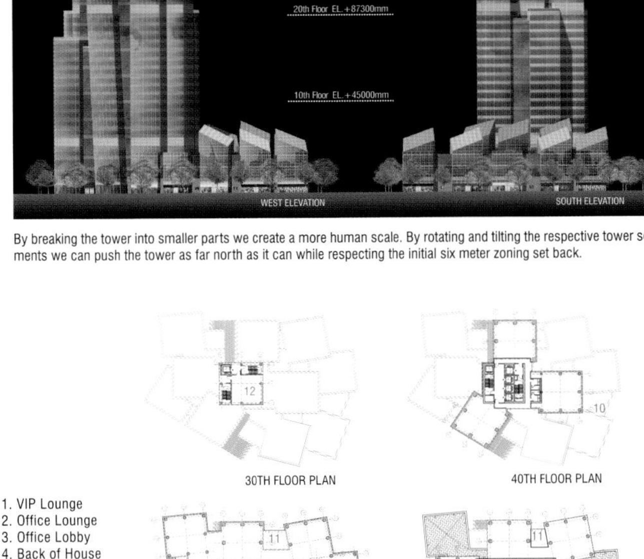

1. VIP Lounge
2. Office Lounge
3. Office Lobby
4. Back of House
5. VIP Lobby
6. Retail Lobby
7. Retail
8. Retail Center
9. Atrium
10. Office
11. Office Atrium
12. Penthouse Office

A square floor plan allows for only few corners which creates less surface area and less area for sunlight and fresh air to enter the interior. This floor plan only has 4 corners. Once the square floor plate is broken into 9 shifting modules, many more corners can be created, maximizing surface area, creating more corner offices, and allowing the maximum area for sunlight and fresh air to enter the interior. The Floor plan has 18 corners.

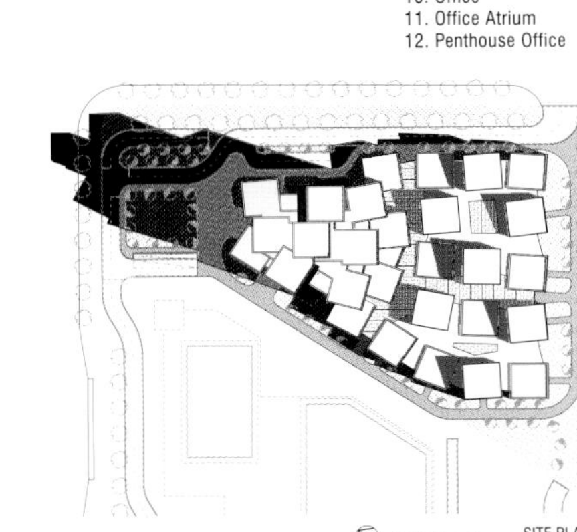

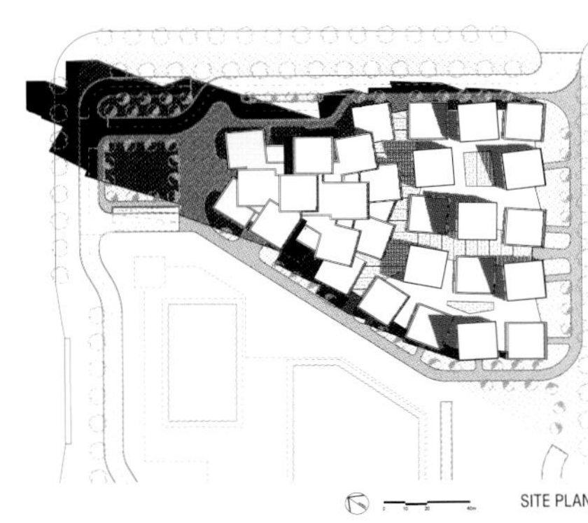

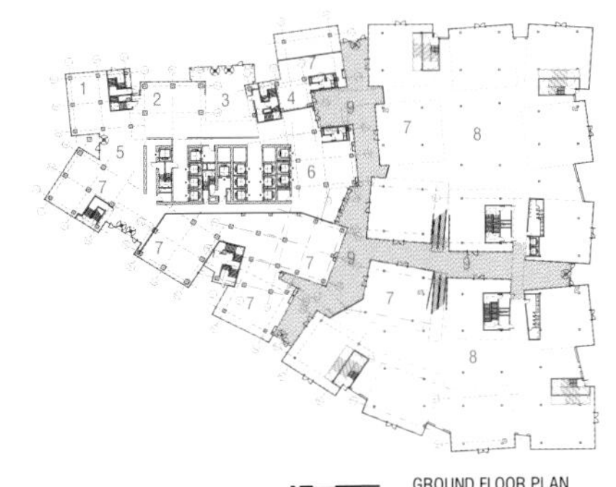

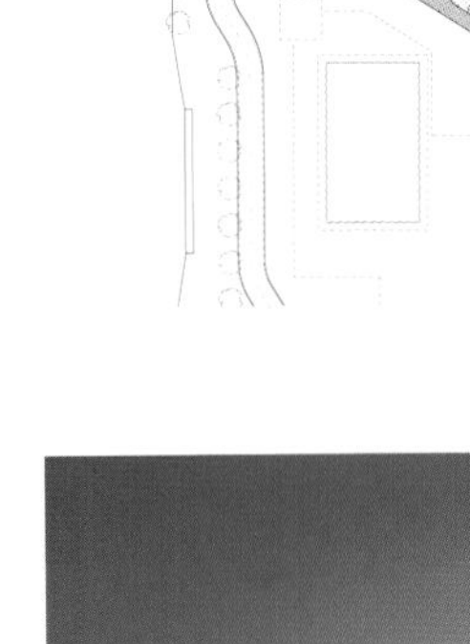

1. Office Atrium
2. Retail Center
3. Penthouse Office

BIOPHILIA EFFECT

The twisting, turning, and tilting of segments creates fissures that allow green atriums to permeate the tower. These atriums, which surround the tower, are staggered on every floor and have operable windows to allow fresh air to directly enter the interior. Further, our design strategy allows for the tower to open up on the south side like a fan thereby maximizing daylight and further allowing more green atriums along the façade.

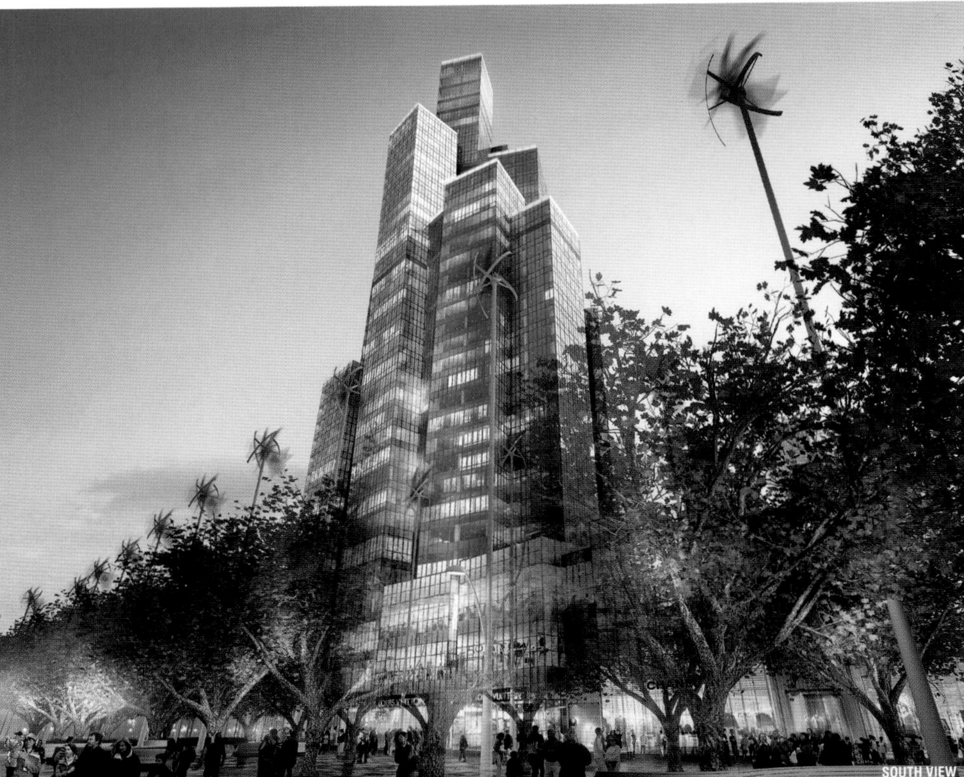

143 Ephemeral Structures | *Horhizon consortium*

Type : Civic
Design : Dietmar Koering, Tobias Klein

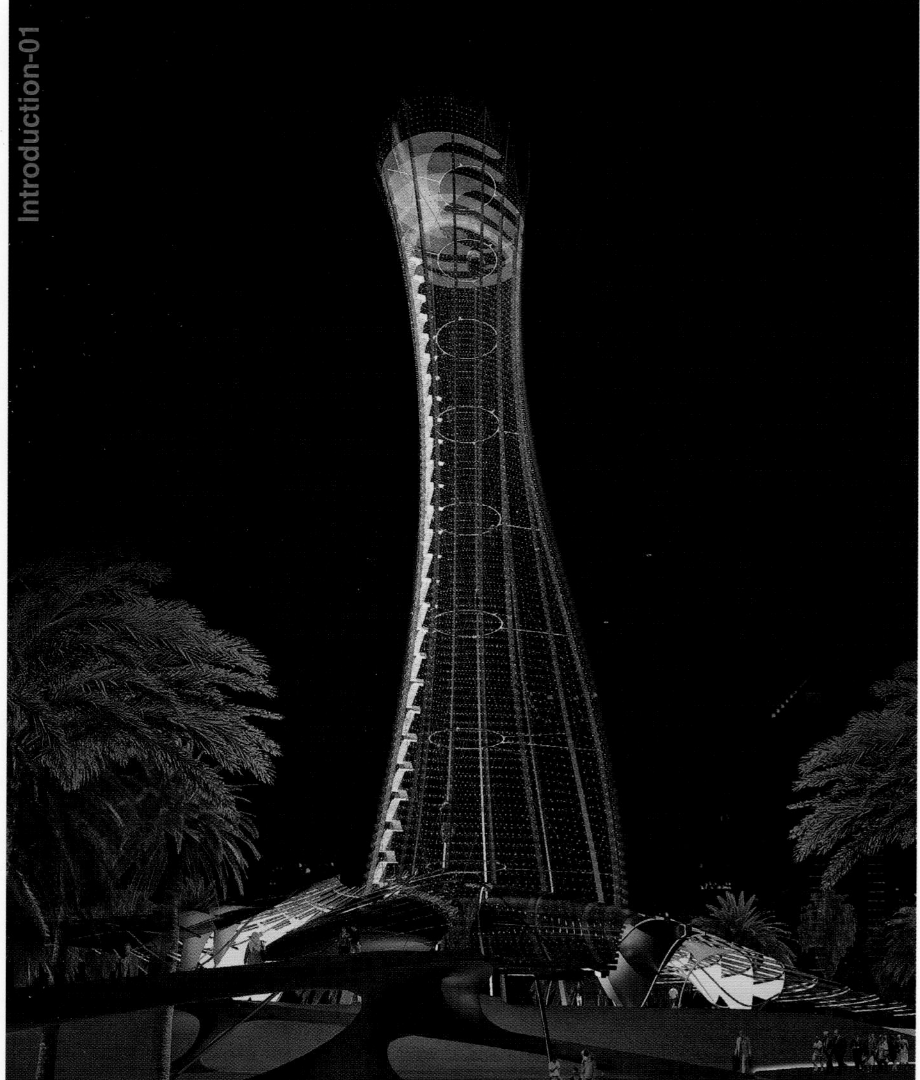

Stories of ephemeral structures

Introduction

These are some of the predicted stories, narratives that the landmark 'Ephemeral Structures' will evoke . They are simulated reactions of different user groups describing the various spaces and functions of the landmark. As the project is deeply embedded in the day and night cycle, these projected witness reports will start in the morning with the first towering impressions from a small child and range to a returning Business man and his reactions towards the glowing landmark at night. These stories attempt to construct the landmark of the people of Dubai as well as a landmark for the tourists and visitors.

8:00

For her it was the first time that she would go with her classmates to see the ***Ephemeral Structures.*** *A beautiful slim and elegant tower reflecting the morning sun. With its inbuilt nodal point LED's the tower was glittering in the light like the sparkle of a thousand diamonds. The school bus approached the building and entered into the ground level parking space. She could almost not see the entrance as it was carefully integrated within the Landscape. The base of the tower looked to her like giant airy cloth frozen in a moment. These petal-like shading elements allowed her to not enter the already strong sun, protecting her and creating a comfortable environment.*
She slowly approached the edge of the crater. Some of her friends had told her about the great experience of slowly seeing the meandering path spiraling in a vortex like movement down. She sat down at the edge looking up into the tower. She was dazzled by the repetitions, fractal arranged structures mirroring the gentle pathways leading into the deep . A gentle breeze came up from the bottom of the crater where she could just see the lake. She stood up and started her journey down the spiral to take the silvery elevator into the sky.

12:00

It was a great morning and his first time in the ***Ephemeral Structures****. A week ago his company decided to participate in this conference and now he actually was sitting in the conference rooms of the* ***Ephemeral Structures****. When he arrived a bit too early he decided not to take the silver shiny elevator suspended in the mid-air of the tower but to slowly descend into the cool air of the crater. Round by round, spiraling down he felt the heat of the midday disappear and replaced by a refreshing cool breeze. at mid-level he stopped and entered the conference facilities. At first he wondered whether he would miss windows, but his worries were unqualified and actually replaced by the gentle indirect light from the ground to ceiling openings to the crater. It was a comfortable indirect light that allowed digital projections to be played on the walls. He enjoyed the conference, secretly though looking forward to its end and the experience to go to the bottom of the spiral and then shooting up into the cafe to have a cool beverage in the end of the day overlooking Dubai.*

16:00

It was always heir dream to have holidays in Dubai. She landed a couple of ours ago and already from the airplane she and her newly wed husband tried to make out the position of the ***Ephemeral Structures*** *and although it was difficult to spot its ephemeral character by day she finally managed to see it. It was very hot this day and they did not regret a bit that they went directly to see the beauty and gracious posture of the* ***Ephemeral Structures****. It was cool and comfortable beneath its elegant petals. After a breathtaking descend to the bottom of the crater they finally entered the shiny lift. 220 meters of free ascending in an almost entire glass lift. It felt like flying, but a bit better as the repetitions of structure gave their flight a rhythm unachieved before. They arrived at the top holding hands and looking over the beautiful scenery of Dubai. The sun was setting in a stunning moment and all over sudden the light of thousands of LED was illuminating the night. A moment to remember.*

21:00

The flight attendance just announced the final landing approach to Dubai International airport. He was a bit nervous as he was not at home for a couple of years. He was working outside Dubai in New York and Europe but finally had the time to revisit the place of his upbringing, see his family and settle down in the place of his fathers. When he left the last he saw was the light of the ***Ephemeral Structures*** *shining metaphorically behind him and wishing him good luck on the adventures in foreign countries. And there it was again the airplane came through the clouds and the first thing he saw was the spectacular illumination of the* ***Ephemeral Structures****. Myriad of LED's where constantly shifting in colour producing an ever changing screen. He felt home again.*

ephemeral structures

TTDDI

Site

site concept

Firstly, site ,brief and concept inform a logical position , orientation and base form for the ephemeral landmark. Environmental vectors are influential and essential integrated in the design process and forming the base for design and ultimately define the structural, formal and programatic framework.

Form is then carved and sculpted with the narrative site context, engineered and optimised. The result is a highly narrative, ecological and clearly articulated form that responds to the environmental, cultural and emblematic site vectors. ***Ephemeral Structures*** is the attempt to create a soft yet dynamic and individual built response, resulting in an ephemeral constantly shifting structure.

infrastructure

Taking into account the complexity in programmatic and infrastructural terms, ephemeral structures utilizes consequently the existing infrastructural network and merely intersects them to serve the programatic needs for delivery of the Cafe and conference facilities.

The basic concept of the car infrastructure relies on the bypass and integration of the subterranean car-parking spaces situated beneath the ground level of the structure. This would allow visitors to enter the building in a gentle and elegant way providing them with an optimum level of comfort and protection from heat and direct sun light.

On the park internal pedestrian planning the proposal seeks again to naturally integrated the additional pathways within the exiting formal and functional planning of the park. The building integrates the flow of pedestrians on three levels, mimicring on a global level the bridged connection of the three park elements. The circulation in - as well external is designed under the premise of a maximised natural flow-rate, guaranteeing a comfortable but as well exiting exploration of the ephemeral structure.

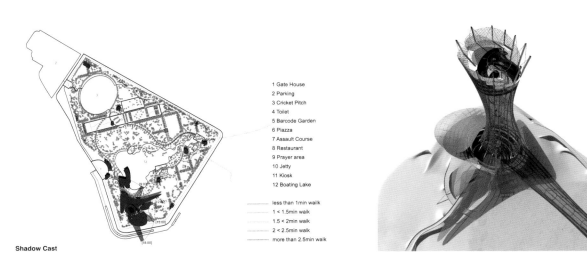

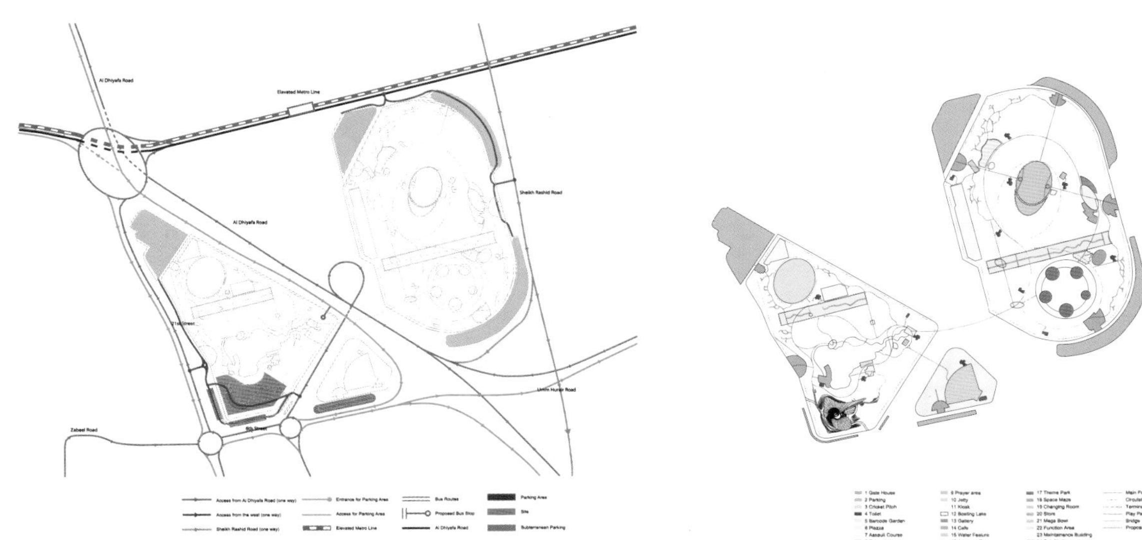

Traffic Circulation

Park Program

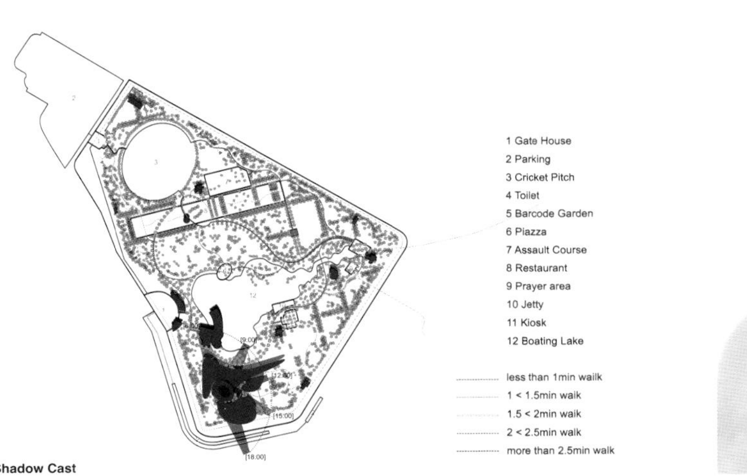

Shadow Cast

programmatic shadow

Shadow and the protection against the scorching heat and direct sunlight is essential to create any program in Dubai. Our design is heavily guide by the integration of the existing places of shadow in the park. We are visually linking the existing Cafe on the lake with the new design of the landmark. Additionally the 2 level high plinth is replaced by a light and airy leaf-like structures that helps to connect and bridge between the different shaded areas in the park.
The structure is based within a 50 m deep crater that additionally provides an excess of shaded surface area ready to be used by tourists, children and visitors.

ephemeral structures

TTDDI

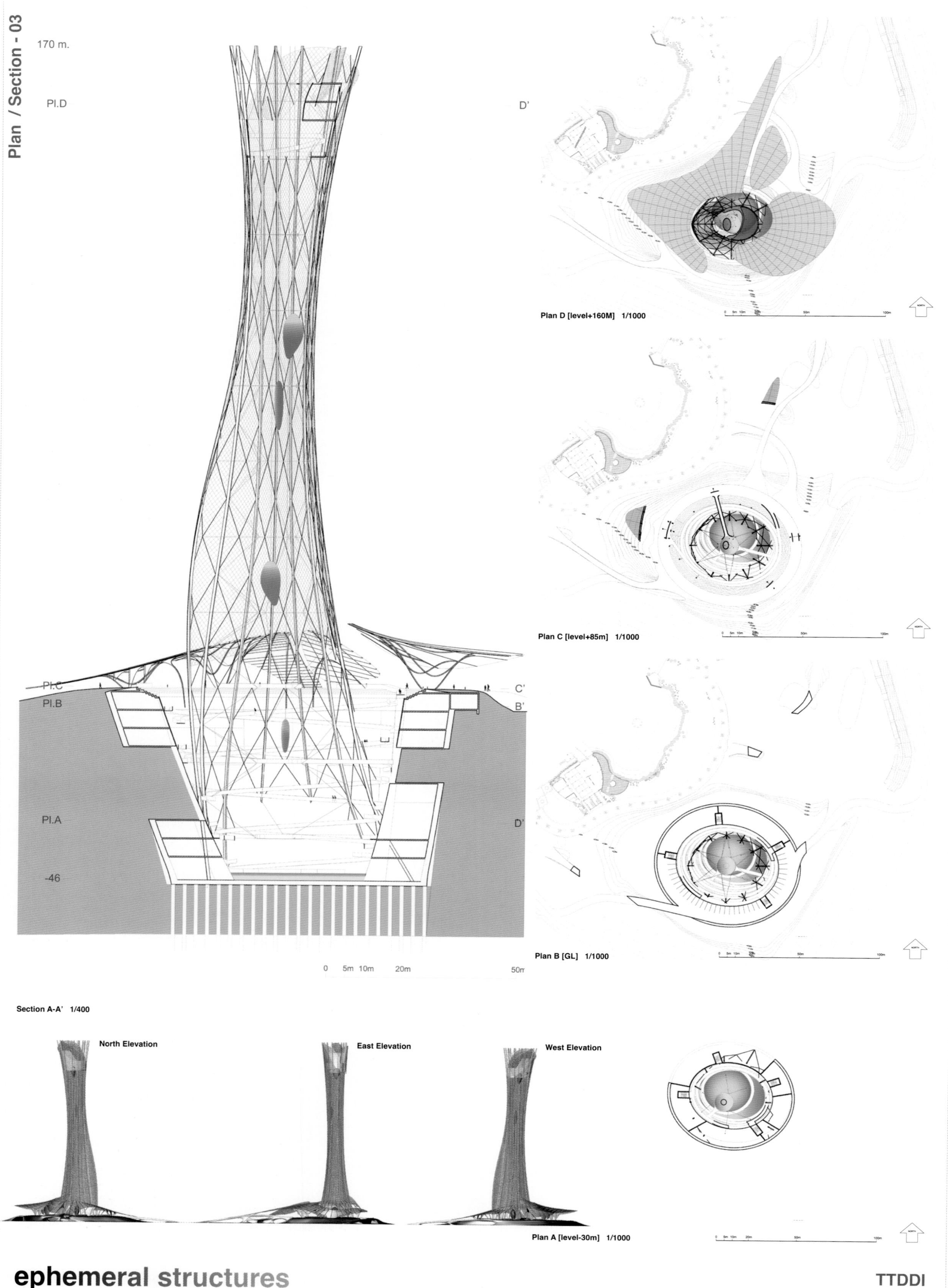
Plan / Section - 03
170 m.
Pl.D
D'
Pl.C
C'
Pl.B
B'
Pl.A
D'
-46
0 5m 10m 20m 50m
Section A-A' 1/400
Plan D [level+160M] 1/1000
Plan C [level+85m] 1/1000
Plan B [GL] 1/1000
North Elevation
East Elevation
West Elevation
Plan A [level-30m] 1/1000

Concept Strategies - 04

earth pipes

stack effect - Windtower

photovoltaic film

minimizing windload though open structure

climate response

Umbrellas
· provide shading
· positive stack effect

photovoltaics collect solar energy

fresh air

input for earthpipes next to lake for cooler and less dusty air

concrete functions as thermal mass

natural ventilation

fountain & vegetation generates positive mirco-climate

cool air drawn through earthpipes

Fountain

Strategies

environment

The environmental seed for this ambitious endeavor is to set up a smart system which has the ability to create a responsive, comfortable environment and reduces the carbon footprint. This is done through intensively using the "stack effect" to gain a positive climate through natural ventilation; photovoltaic panels for absorbing solar energy which also gives the possibility to control daylight and provide shading; to use thermal mass for natural cooling and a fountain plus vegetation to provide an ecological micro climate.
The design criteria to choose a tensegrity also influences positively the environment in reducing the amount of steel, which is normally needed for tall structures.

The cool climate within the building and the core is provided by fresh air which runs through earth pipes to cool the air. The feed-in nuzzles will be located next to the existing lake of the park, which enables that the warm air is already partly chilled through convection and evaporation. The natural airflow is generated by the stack effect and supported by the fountain at the bottom of the core, which creates a low pressure zone. The fountain also binds the dust and riches the air with water particles which leads to a positive and comfortable climate. A natural ventilation of the architectural program by windows can be done without any hesitation. The warm air under the umbrellas is used to create a positive pressure zone, which helps to use the opening on the top as a natural air exhaust by the natural climate response. The massive area on the umbrellas is clad with photovoltaic foil to absorb the solar energy. The solar foils are connected to the public net, which works as a battery storing the energy collected over the time of the day; this energy will be used at night to illuminate the LED façade in an ecological context.

The concrete walls and floors are used as thermal mass; they cool down the building at day time and provide it with heat at night if needed. Inside the core the walls are at particular areas mounted with "Biowall". This system enables that plants can grow vertically into a hydroponic-fed system. The benefits of this green walling include reduced thermal loading on buildings, water and air filtration, creation of urban ecological habitat, plus exciting and uplifting human urban environments.

Environmental Analysis

Gaussian Curvature Analysis

Vertical Menbers Curvature Analysis

Curvature analysis

Vertical Structure

Structural Menbers

Compression

Tension

Physical Study Models

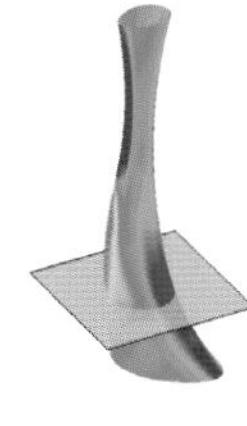

Gaussian Curvature Analysis

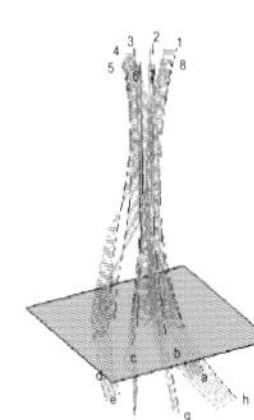

Vertical Menbers Curvature Analysis

Curvature analysis

Vertical Structure

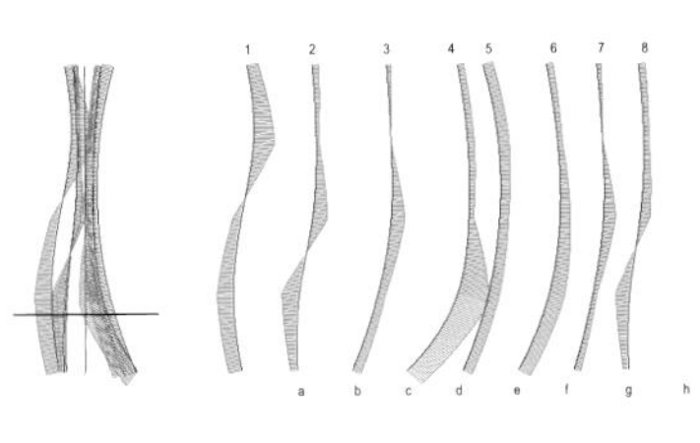

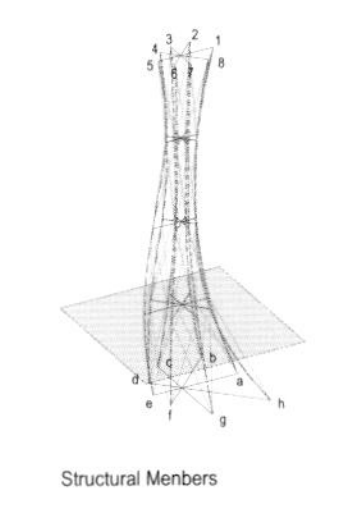

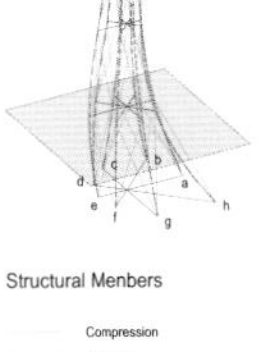

Structural Menbers

Compression

Tension

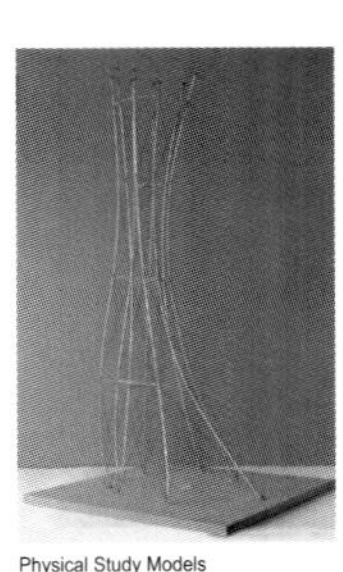

Physical Study Models

Structure Analysis

structure

The structure is light in its character, design and structure. ***Ephemeral structures*** provides an impeccable example of engineering and design merit. While environmental and climatic considerations have led to the subterranean shift in program, the over arching impression of the structural figurative character of the tower remains.

The main structural concept is based on the duality between tension and compression. Tensegrity is the exhibited strength that results "when push and pull have a win-win relationship with each other". Tension is continuous and compression discontinuous, such that continuous pull is balanced by equivalently discontinuous pushing forces.

Buckminster Fuller explained that these fundamental phenomena were not opposites, but complements that could always be found together. Tensegrity is the name for a synergy between co-existing pairs of fundamental physical laws; of push and pull, and compression and tension, or repulsion and attraction. Similar to the design concept between day and night the strutural concept lies on the tension and compression between the vertical structural elements and the flat surfaces on the cafe to spread the load and pre-tension the structure. The integrated rings in the elevator design keet the tension and pull back the primary elements.

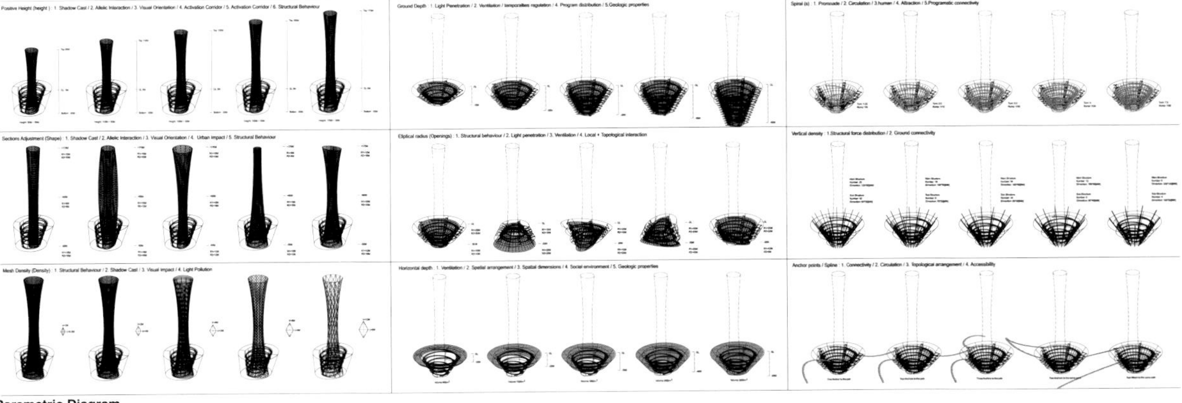

Parametric Diagram

parametric process

Throughout the design development of our structure we aimed for a learning process based approach which requires as such the capability of constant and rapid readjustment.

Using an instrumental parametric design toolbox helped to reconfigure effortless an in-process architecture, providing for a continuous perfect fine-tuning.

Our methodical approach focuses on design geometrical parameters which influence directly the project. We took decisions directly related to our design idea and concept, giving more or less importance to each parameter category. The connection and flow of influence between those categories will prioritise the formulation and importance of each case.

Moreover, within the parametric rules of geometry we have associated to it a layer of external data. This allows a further additional informational layer consisting of external properties such as structural dynamics, environmental conditions, sustainability, materialization or site specific and cultural sensibility, gaining as a consequence an integral parametric design setup.

As a result we do not have a final or finished single moment of our structures, but rather a smart architectural framework with an early implementation of inter-disciplinary design guidance hungry for a further multiple analysis-based process.

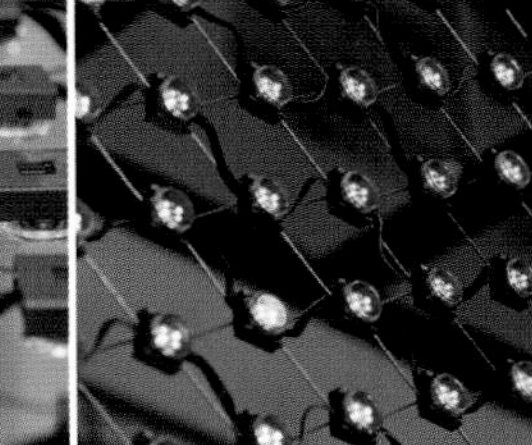

Mesh Stucture

net mesh

Throuout the day the energy of the sun is collected throught photovoltaic cells imprinted on the upper surface of the petal-like sun shaders. This energy is used in the night to illuminate the entire structure.

This structure transforms at night from the lightness of the day into an enlightened presence. A myriad of low energy LED create together a stunning display that generates its presence on the night skyline of Dubai. The LED s are networked together creating an impressive screen able to deliver information, film or advertisement. But furthermore this screen is a beacon visible from far creating an ever changing landmark.

The mesh net is made of stainless steel cables of different diameters as well as ferrules made of tinned copper or stainless steel. The ferrules are friction-pressed., and hence the mesh keeps its shape indefinitely and is effectively maintenance-free.
Even in a high-chloride or sulphurous atmosphere and the extreme tepera-tures and environmental conditions of Dubai, the material is highly corrosion-resistant. There are 54.000 LEDs, flexible and arranged on the nodal points to create the spectacular presence at night.

ephemeral structures

TTDDI

Program 01

Spaces

program

The spectacular structure of the ground space correlates to the tensegrity system of the towering structure. The use of light wave aluminum sets a counter point to the massive structure of the core itself. The central vortex explores and benefits from the blurring of the boundaries of the relation between nature and architecture based on spatial structures and natural forms. The result is achieved through computerized studies and is responsive to daylight.

Only people interacting with the landmark will fully enjoy a view from above of this unconventional setting for a contemporary landmark. The structure comes alive as a sculptural garden of avant-garde technology. After entering, visitors cross the peek of a little artificial hill, which has areas to sit and relax. This space can also be used for small performances and is distinguished by the boundary of a glass railing. From here the visitor decides whether to go via the lifts or to continue down wide spirals flanked with libraries, cafés, a conference center and terraces which leave space to rest and communicate. At night the openings for the architectural program act with their floor to ceiling windows as light emitters and invert the shadow strategy, while the tower comes alive as an animated LED skin. Overall the whole structure, the tower, spirals and core is reflected in a moving pattern, the fountain with its water surface. The whole space benefits from the cooler climate as well as from the indirect lighting conditions and creates a unique joyful space to experience in Dubai, far away from traffic and artificial air conditioning.

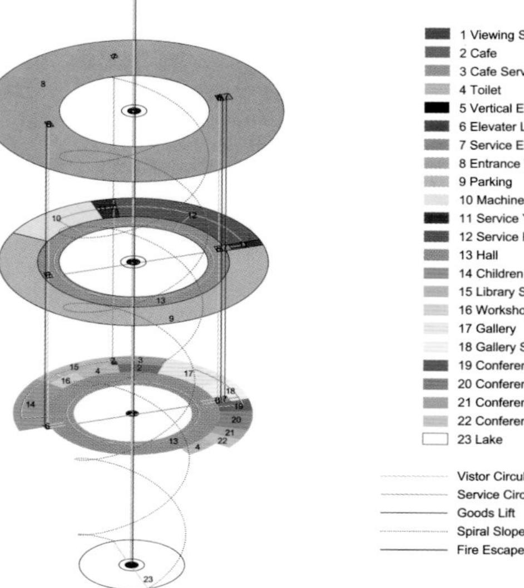

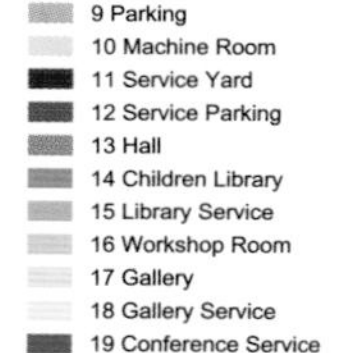

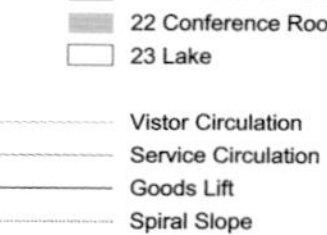

1 Viewing Space
2 Cafe
3 Cafe Service
4 Toilet
5 Vertical Elevater Lift and Staircase
6 Elevater Lift and Staircase
7 Service Elevater Lift and Staircase
8 Entrance Yard
9 Parking
10 Machine Room
11 Service Yard
12 Service Parking
13 Hall
14 Children Library
15 Library Service
16 Workshop Room
17 Gallery
18 Gallery Service
19 Conference Service
20 Conference Room1
21 Conference Room2
22 Conference Room3
23 Lake

Vistor Circulation
Service Circulation
Goods Lift
Spiral Slope
Fire Escape

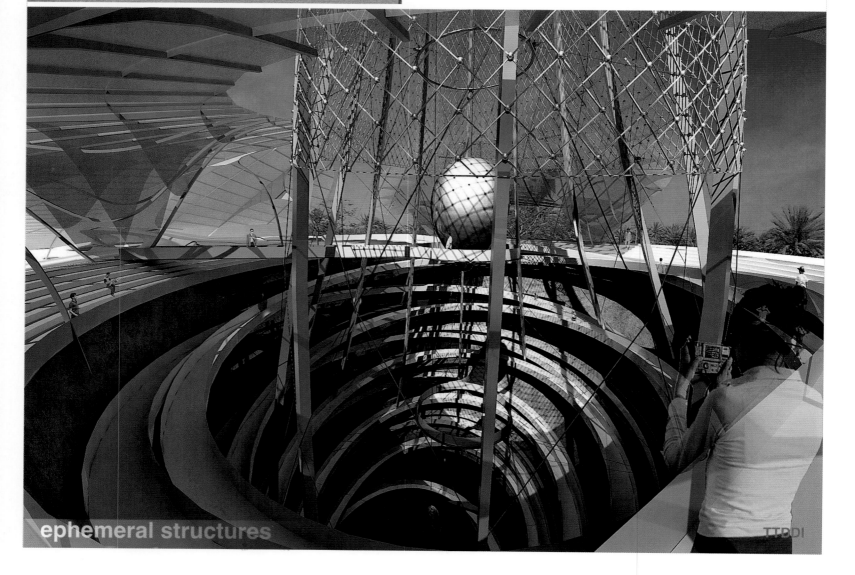

ephemeral structures

TTDDI

Kingscross Gasholder | *Horhizon consortium*

Team : Tobias Klein and Dietmar Koering with Paul Giencke
and Lucy Woods, Eleanor Dodman and Graham
Design : Dietmar Koering, Tobias Klein

Gasholder No.8 | The Urban Canopy

Gasholder

Trees

Secondary Landscape

Ground Floor

Site Footprint

Exploded Isometric diagram of elements

main pedestrian route

access to elementary school

drop off

existing infrastructure

secondary circulation

primary circulation path

Site Plan and Circulation Routes

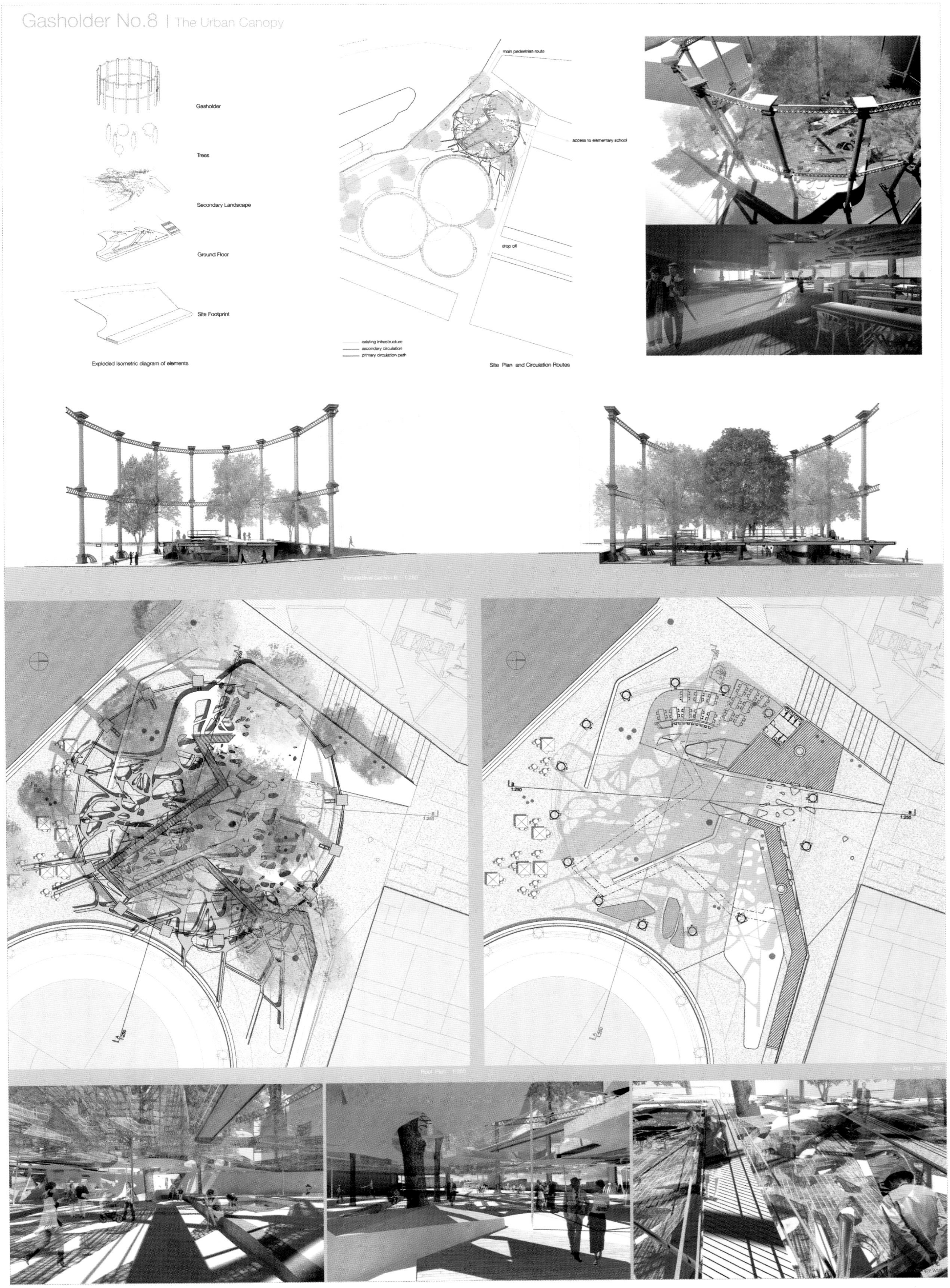

145

Narrating Embodiment | *Horhizon consortium*

Type : Architecture and film
Design : Tobias Klein, Eva Sommeregger

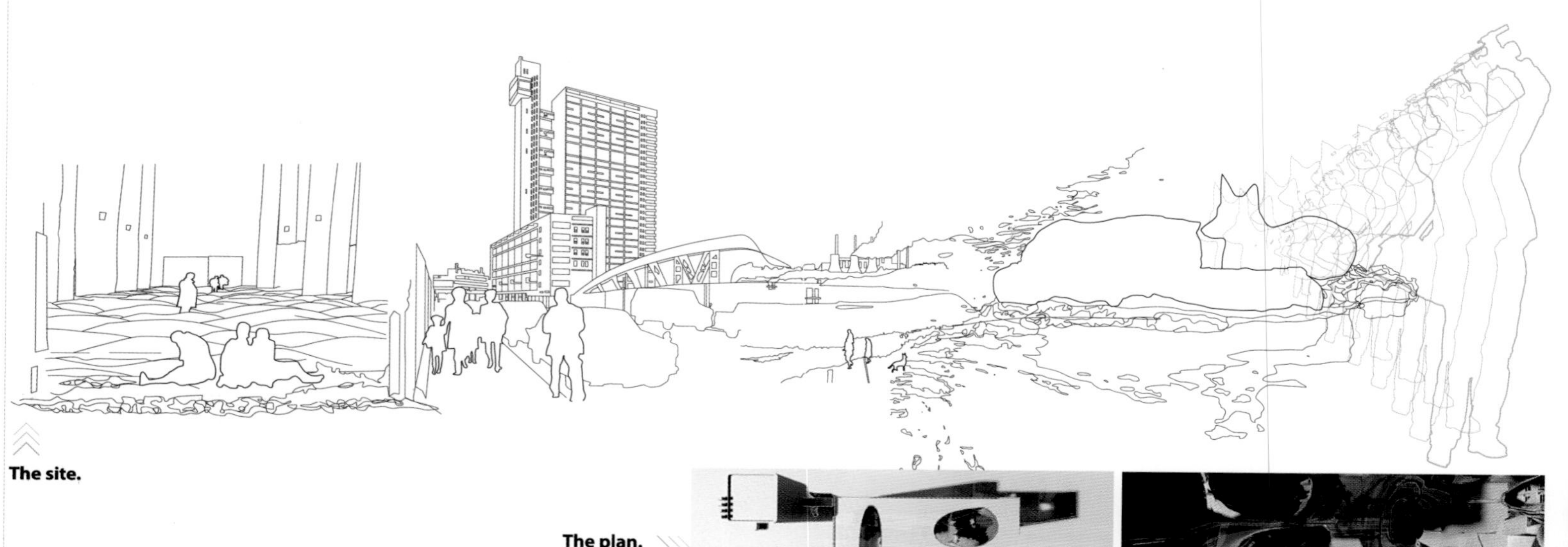

The site.

The plan.

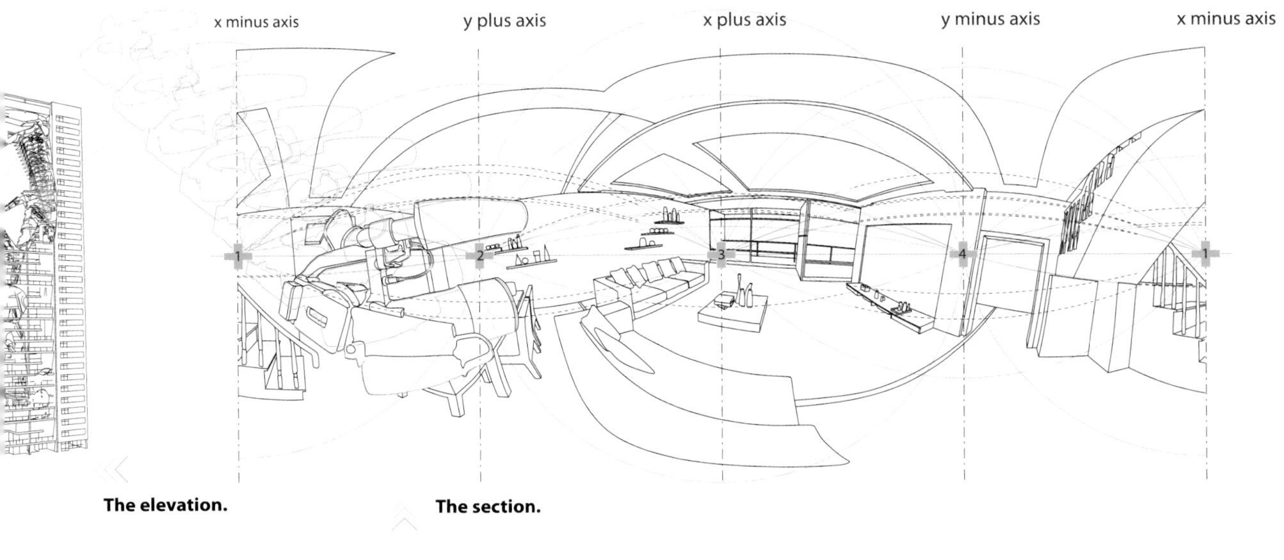

The elevation.

The section.

146

Orchid Tower | *Axi:Ome*

Principals in Charge : Heather Woofter and Sung Ho Kim
Project Designers : Catty Dan Zhang and Nick McFadden
Design Team : Rougu Liu, Daniel Katebini- Stengel, Yi Hou, Adam Novack, Steven Kim and Matt Hovarth

_ORCHID TOWER _ Taichung Taiwan_01

The orchid flower is a beautiful Taichung city icon with a rich and diverse ancient botanical history. The orchid is also a timely reference for a contemporary structural perspective on towers and a culturally significant form of environmental adaptability.

Contemporary Structure

The morphology of the orchid introduces variations of column structures and aerated root systems that are elegant embroideries. The delicate form sometimes shapes itself around found natural elements in a complex assembly of small parts. We liken the structural configuration of the Orchid Tower to a Miesian evolution. As Mies was expressing the thinness, lightness, and potential of steel material to transform our horizon into elegant reflective transparencies of form, the future direction of construction heightens strength to weight ratios to produce lighter structural members. These small parts work in collaboration to support the weight of dense vertical space. With population and natural resource issues ahead, exploration of vertical space structures is a critical question for architects today. Carbon fiber high performance materials, while primarily engaged in industrial products, are emerging as cost-effective pre-stressing materials, outweighing steel. The Orchid Tower is a high strength diaphanous veil of carbon fiber reinforced concrete expressing the future of lightweight materials able to sustain variations in form and structure.

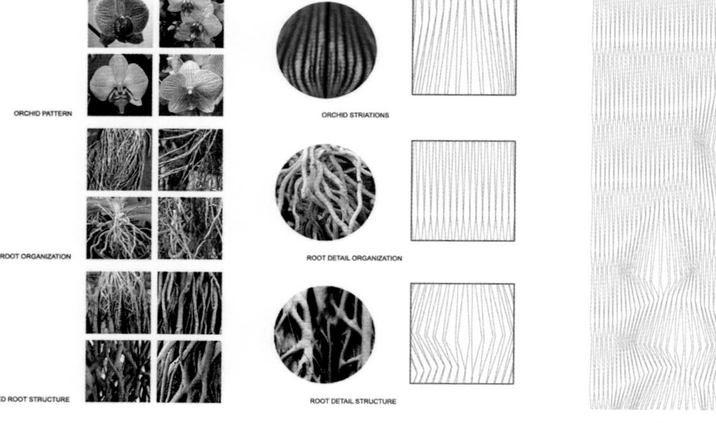

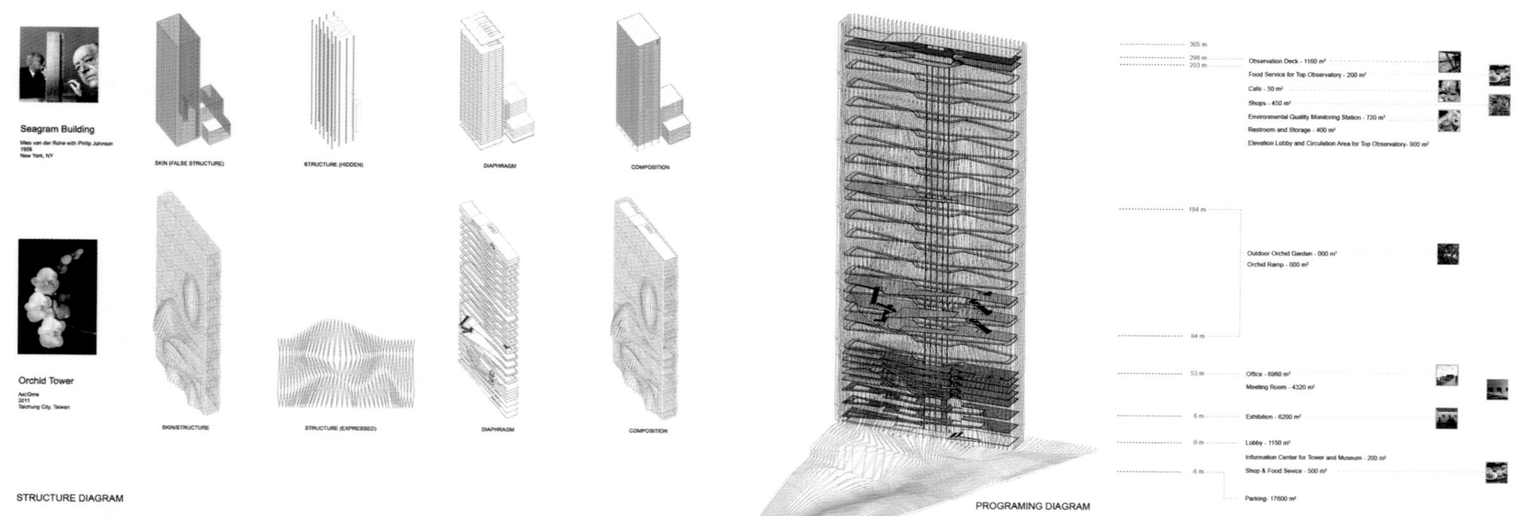

_ORCHID TOWER _ Taichung Taiwan_02

Environmental Adaptability

The orchid family is highly adaptable with one of the largest diversities of species and origins tracing back to pre-historic times. The industry in Taichung Taiwan is recognized as a global orchid industry and an essential component of the local economy. This proposal showcases both the production of the flower and the display of its beautiful form. A series of ramps and elevators connect bulbs of program, creating a promenade inhabited by orchids. Viewed from the interior and seen from the exterior through the structural façade, the vibrantly colored flowers are sustained through an aeroponic system. This network of misting lines occupies the gap in-between enclosed building spaces to create an open-air market. The nutrient rich-water recycles through the landscape in a productive feed loop, communicating the necessity for self-reliant systems occupying minimal ground territory. Suspended forms in vertical space express the thinness and lightness of the veil beyond and work with passive cooling strategies of air movement. As one enters through the wetland of horizontal ground surface into four levels of museum, the visitor is aware of likewise entering a botanical garden, traveling 1,000 feet into the air to observe the richly diverse environment of Taichung.

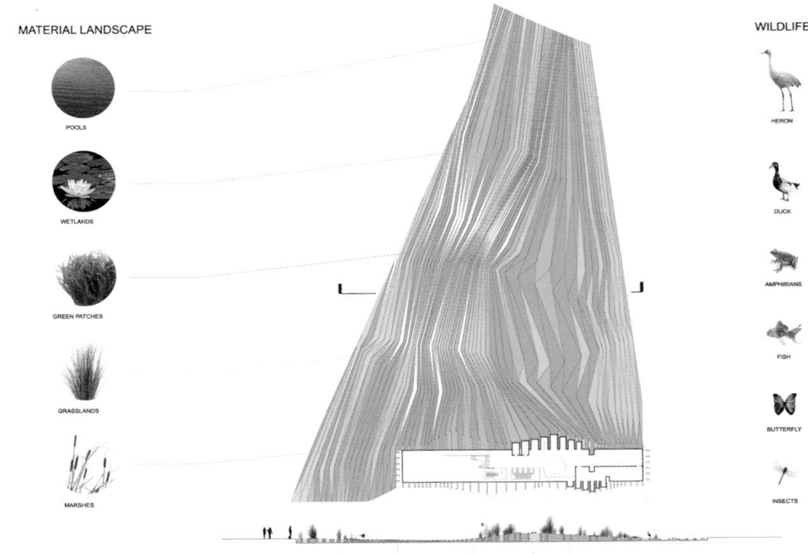

SITE MATERIAL DIAGRAM

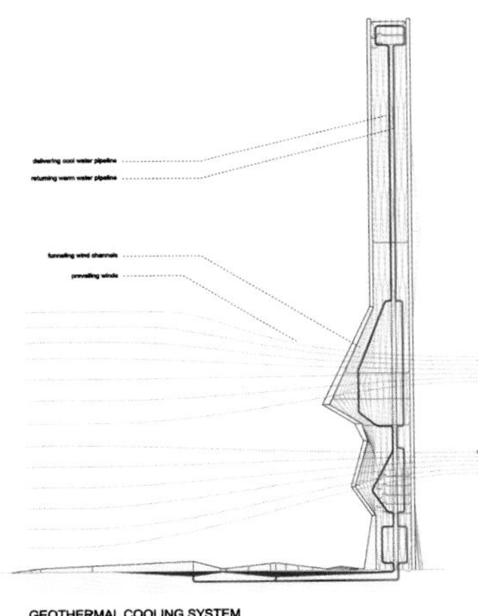

GEOTHERMAL COOLING SYSTEM

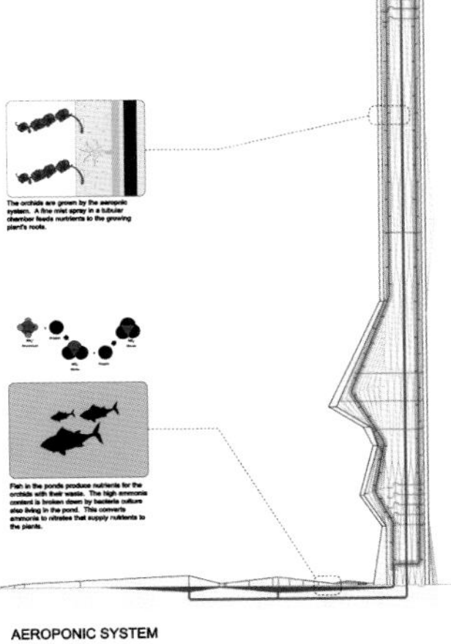

AEROPONIC SYSTEM

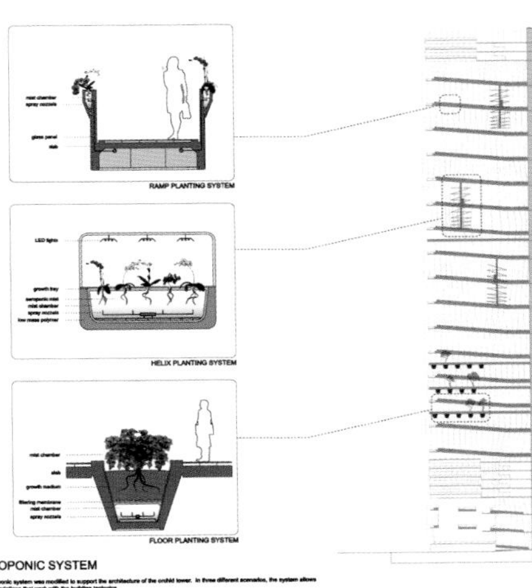

AEROPONIC SYSTEM

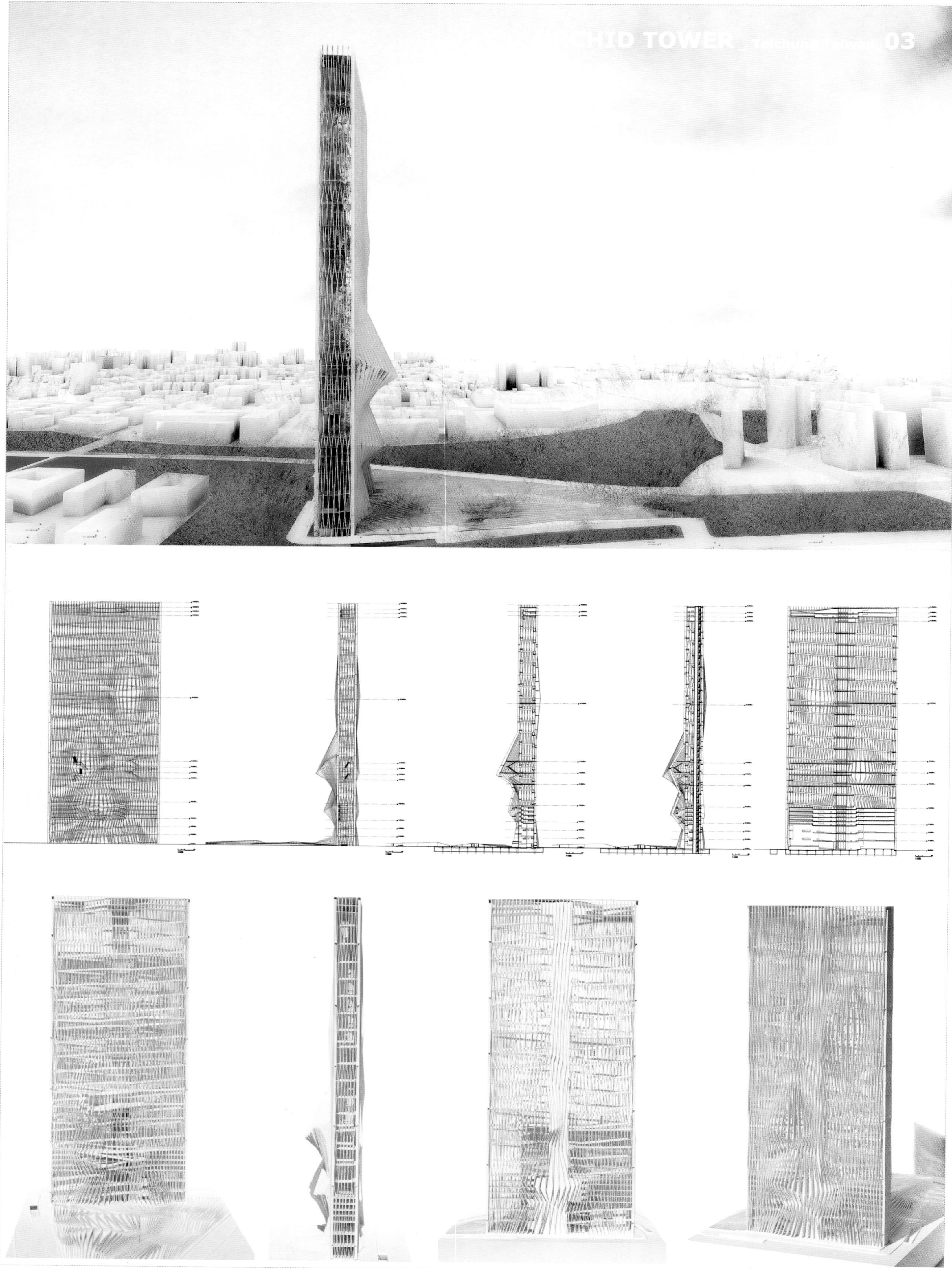

CHID TOWER
03

_ORCHID TOWER _ Taichung Taiwan_04

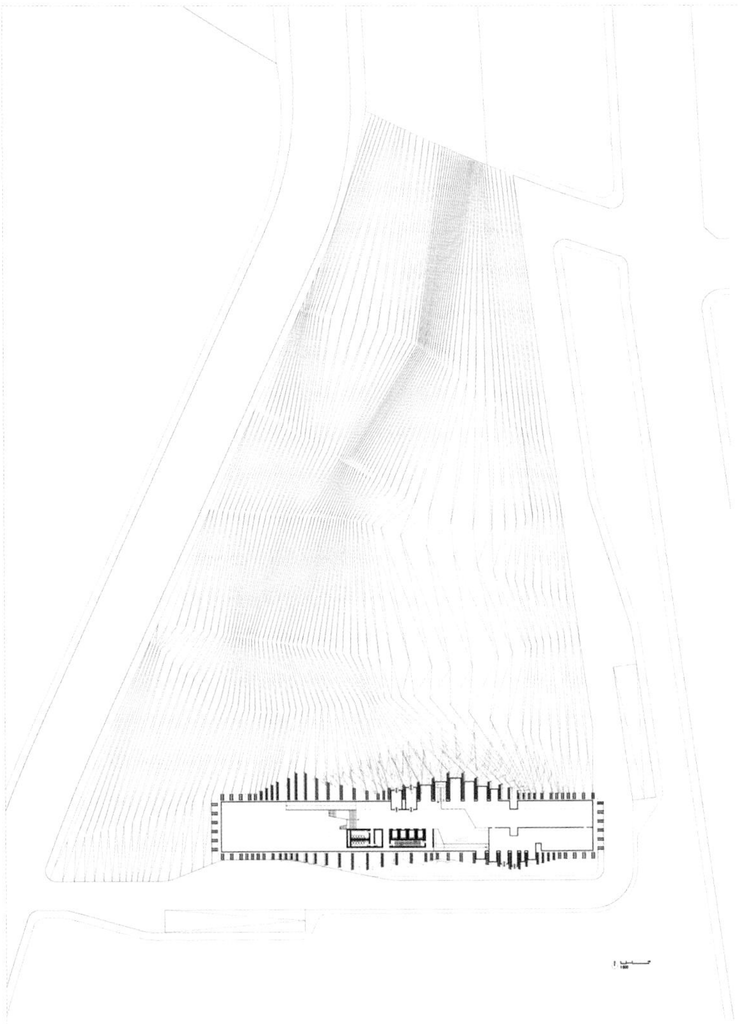

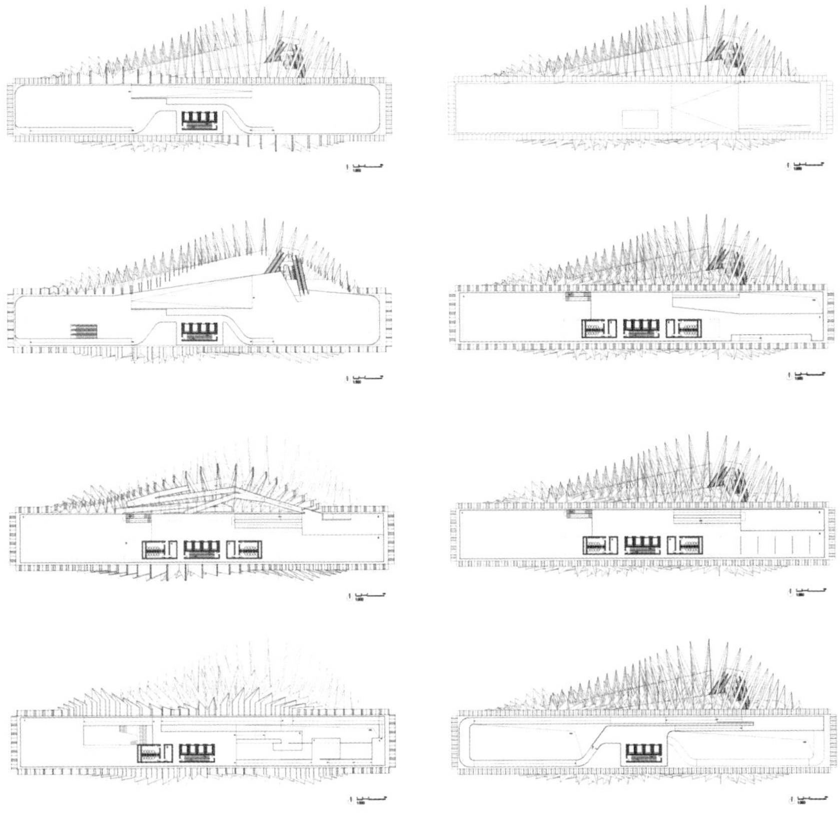

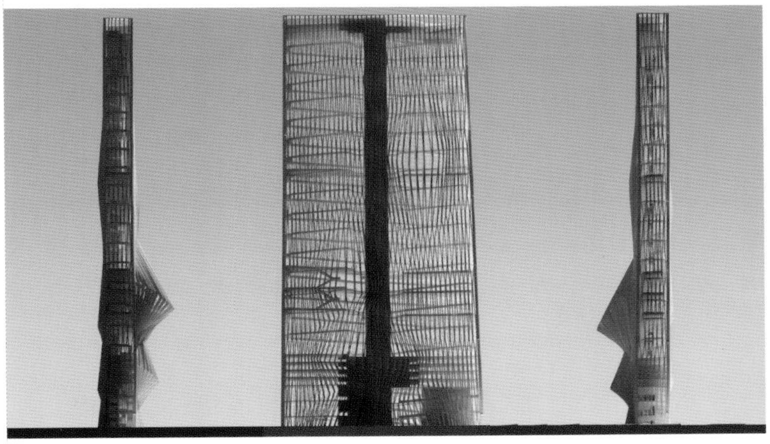

147 Linzertus | *gutiérrez-delafuente arquitectos*

Architects : Natalia Gutiérrez & Julio de la Fuente
Collaborators : Paul-Rouven Denz
Project : 2nd Prize International Competition Europan 11 Linz. "Opening up a Modernist Landmark"
Programme : Activation and Regeneration of the Tabakfabrik Industrial Complex Designed by Peter Behrens and Alexander Popp (1929-1935)
Location : Linz, Austria / Client : City of Linz, Europan

LINZ HR120

E11 LINZ 1
LINZERTUS

URBAN CONCEPTION

SITE PLAN

FROM ISLAND TO PERMEABLE LOCATION
- Opportunity to open the city on the North-East side
- Virtual and physical vectors = such permeable as possible
- Continuity of green structures from Danube Park to Gruberstraßer

1/10000 GROUNDFLOOR

TABAKFABRIK PLATZ, A NEW URBAN NODE
- New spot of public space with pedestrian scale and true city atmosphere
- Sculptural Power Station is used as the main public space actor
- Tabakfabrik Innenhof memories are absolutly preseved

1/10000 GROUNDFLOOR

LINZERTUS: LINZER "INSERTUS"

"INSERTUS" (Latin): FRAGMENT OF LIVE FLESH WHICH IS IMPLANTED IN ANY PART OF THE HUMAN BODY TO REPAIR AN INJURY.

"INSERTUS" (Latin): EIN STÜCK MENSCHLICHES GEWEBE, WELCHES AN JEGLICHEM ORT DES MENSCHLICHEN KÖRPERS IMPLANTIERT WERDEN KANN UM EINE VERLETZUNG ZU KURIEREN.

"LINZERTUS" (Europan 11): URBAN REGENERATION THERAPY COMPOSED OF SEVERAL PROGRAMATIC GRAFTS IN ORDER TO ACTIVATE THE TABAKFABRIK HISTORICAL BUILDINGS TO CREATE A NEW LIFE CYCLE IN THE NEIGHBORHOOD (UPDATING TABAKFABRIK). THIS PRECISION HEALING THERAPY WILL BE DONE OVER TIME, THROUGH A STEP-BY-STEP IMPLEMENTATION.

"LINZERTUS" (Europan 11): THERAPIE ZUR URBANEN REGENERIERUNG, BESTEHEND AUS UNTERSCHIEDLICHEN IMPLANTATEN UM DIE HISTORISCHEN BESTANDSGEBÄUDE DER TABAKFABRIK ZU AKTIVIEREN UND EINEN NEUEN LEBENSZYKLUS IN DER NACHBARSCHAFT ZU GENERIEREN (MODERNISIERUNG DER TABAKFABRIK). DIESER PRÄZISE HEILUNGSPROZESS WIRD ÜBER EINEN LÄNGEREN ZEITRAUM, MIT EINER SCHRITTWEISEN REALISIERUNG, DURCHGEFÜHRT.

A NEW CENTRALITY: TABAKFABRIK PLATZ

A NEW CENTRALITY IS CREATED UNDER THE NAME OF TABAKFABRIK PLATZ. THIS NEW URBAN ATTRACTOR, A NEW SPOT, IN THE INNENHOF AREA WILL REPRODUCE A TRUE CITY ATMOSPHERE, A LIVE PIECE OF CITY WHERE THE MAIN ACTORS ARE PEOPLE.
- FIRSTLY, THIS NEW PUBLIC SPACE HAS DOUBLE SCALE: THE NEIGHBOURS SCALE AND THE VISITORS SCALE. THE MIX OF PEOPLE IS ENSURED.
- SECONDLY, TWO KINDS OF PUBLIC SPACE ARE PROPOSED: OPEN PUBLIC SPACE IN THE INNENHOF AND COVERED PUBLIC SPACE IN LOSEHALLE IN RESPONSE TO THE LOCAL WEATHER PATTERNS TO ENCOURAGE PEOPLE TO USE THE PUBLIC SCENE.
- FINALLY, THREE KINDS OF PUBLIC SPACE MANAGEMENT ARE CREATED: PUBLIC-PUBLIC SPACE (MANAGED BY THE CITY OF LINZ), HYBRID SPACE (MANAGED BY NEIGHBOURS AND LOCAL ASSOCIATIONS) AND PRIVATE-PUBLIC SPACE (MANAGED BY PRIVATE OWNERS).

NEW LOCAL IDENTITY

THE INDUSTRIAL TABAKFABRIK MEMORY IS PRESERVED, BUT THERE IS NOTHING NOSTALGIC ABOUT THIS. ITS ARCHITECTURAL AIM IS PRESERVED IN ORDER TO TRANSFORM IT. THE TABAKFABRIK AREA FACES A NEW LIFE CYCLE WITH A COMPLETE MIXED USE PROGRAM. THE LINZ ECONOMY AND POPULATION ARE CHANGING FROM AN INDUSTRIAL TO A KNOWLEDGE AND CREATIVE SOCIETY, THE CHANGE IN THE AREA IS TAKING PLACE THROUGH A NEW IDENTITY. CREATIVE WORKERS AND YOUNG PEOPLE WITH NEW NEEDS WILL BE THE MAIN ACTORS IN THE CONVERSION. THEIR NEW NEEDS (HOUSING FOR NEW FORMS OF LIVE, WORK & LIVING SPACES, VARIED GASTRONOMY, TECHNO ENTERTAINMENT, INTELLECTUAL LEISURE) ARE AN OPPORTUNITY FOR CHANGE.

URBAN IDEAS: FROM ISLAND TO PERMEABLE LOCATION

NEW OPPORTUNITIES, POTENTIALS AND KEY VECTORS ARE BUILT AROUND THE HETEROGENEOUS URBAN CONTEXT WITH THE FOLLOWING TOPICS:
- FROM ISLAND TO PERMEABLE LOCATION: OPPORTUNITY TO OPEN THE CITY ON THE NORTH-EAST SIDE AND CREATE A NEW LAYER OF PUBLIC SPACE AS PERMEABLE AS POSSIBLE. OPPORTUNITY TO "BREAK" THE BIG SCALE OF THE COMPLEX FOLLOWING A NET OF VIRTUAL CONNECTIONS WITH THE DANUBE PARK IN THE NORTH,THE CURRENT INDUSTRIAL AREA IN THE EAST, THE HOUSING AREA IN THE SOUTH AND THE INNERCITY IN THE WEST SIDE.
- TABAKFABRIK PLATZ, A NEW URBAN NODE: A NEW SPOT OF PUBLIC SPACE WITH A PEDESTRIAN SCALE AND TRUE CITY ATMOSPHERE.
- NEW URBAN MOBILITY: PRIORITY FOR SOFT MOBILITIES AND CONNECTIONS WITH DANUBE PARK.
- SELECTION OF THE BEST AREAS FOR HOUSING: OPPORTUNITY TO EXPLORE NEW HOUSING TYPES IN THE APPROPIATE AREA.
- VIEWS OF THE DANUBE (TOWERS BETWEEN GAPS): OPPORTUNITY TO TAKE ADVANTAGE OF THE DANUBE AND RIVERSIDE VIEWS.
- IMPROVEMENT OF URBAN VISIBILITY: OPPORTUNITY TO CREATE A VIRTUAL GATE OF THE CITY IN THE NORTH-EAST ACCESS.

MIXED USE PROGRAM : COMPLETE LIFE CYCLE

A MIXED USE PROGRAM IS CREATED IN ORDER TO HAVE A COMPLETE LIFE CYCLE IN THE AREA. BECAUSE OF THE ECONOMICAL AND SOCIAL CHANGE IN THE AREA, THE MIXED USE PROGRAMS WILL BE FOCUSED ON CONTEMPORARY CULTURAL FIELDS OF PRODUCTION, CREATIVE AND PROGRESSIVE INDUSTRIES, EDUCATIONAL INSTITUTIONS, SOCIAL FACILITIES AND SPECIAL FORMS OF HOUSING (REGARDING THE VARIETY OF ECONOMY USES).

LINZER BLUE: NEW LOCAL AND STRONG IDENTITY

IN THE WAY OF CREATING A LOCAL AND STRONG IDENTITY, WE USE THE LOCAL COLOR IN A CONTEMPORARY WAY TO COHERE THE WHOLE COMPLEX. LINZER BLUE. IN THE TABAKFABRIK THERE ARE MANY SPACES WHERE THE MAIN FEATURE IS THE LINZER BLUE COLOR. WE PROPOSE A VARIETY OF ACTIONS OVER TIME IN SEVERAL PHASES TO REGENERATE AND ACTIVATE THE TABAKFABRIK COMPLEX, THEN THE LINZER BLUE WILL CREATE A HOMOGENEOUS IDENTITY WITH A HIGH DEGREE OF VISIBILITY AND A POSITIVE IMPACT ON THE SURROUNDING NEIGHBORHOODS.

THE NEW PROPOSED "PROGRAMATIC GRAFTS" WILL ANIMATE OLD BUILDINGS. AS A LOCAL REFERENCE TO THE CITY (INDUSTRIAL HERITAGE) AND THE COMPLEX, THESE "GRAFTS" WILL BE BUILT WITH A STELL SKELETON. THE "GRAFTS" WILL BE LIGHT AND PERMEABLE TO SHOW THE CITY THEIR NEW INTERIOR LIFE CYCLE.

THE MAIN FEATURE OF THE LINZER BLUE FACADES IS "DEMATERIALIZATION": BLUE BUILDINGS WITH A BLURRED SKYLINE. DURING THE NIGHT, THESE BLUE BUILDINGS WILL BE IMPRESSIVE URBAN LAMPS REINFORCING THE NEIGHBORHOOD TABAKFABRIK IDENTITY AND VISIBILITY.

STRATEGY OF POTENTIALS AND OPPORTUNITIES

THE "LINZERTUS" PROGRAMATIC STRATEGY IS BASED ON THE EXISTING SPATIAL AND PROGRAMATIC POTENTIALS AND OPPORTUNITIES. THE CURRENT URBAN, ECONOMICAL AND PSYCHOGEOGRAPHICAL SITUATION ARE ANALYSED TO TAKE ADVANTAGE OF THE LOCATION OPPORTUNITIES. THE FORMER AND PROTECTED TABAKFABRIK BUILDINGS AND THEIR SPATIAL CONDITIONS ARE STUDIED AND ALSO THE PHYSICAL AND VIRTUAL VECTORS SUCH AS ORIENTATION, CONNECTIONS, VIEWS, NOISE, SUN...ARE CAREFULLY STUDIED. FINALLY, THE PROGRAMATIC SITUATION APPEARS AS A RESULT OF ALL THESE "SIGNS".

THE NEW TABAKFABRIK LIFE CYCLE IS A COMPLETE LIFE CYCLE, WITH A REAL MIXED USE PROGRAM. A SPATIAL AND PROGRAMATIC GEOGRAPHY WITH QUALITIES IS CREATED TO GET SPECIFIC USES IN THE BEST CONDITIONS. INSTEAD OF A REGULAR MIXED USE PROGRAM, WE SUGGEST A PROGRAMATIC ATMOSPHERE. NOW WE HAVE TO TAKE CARE OF IT AND DEVELOPE IT STEP-BY-STEP.

ECO-LANDMARK : NEW SOCIAL ECO-CONSCIENCE

TAKING ADVANTAGE OF THE SCULPTURAL POWER PLANT AND CHIMNEY, WE VERTICALLY EXTEND THE CHIMNEY TO CREATE A NEW ECO-BLUE-LANDMARK WHICH DIALOGUES IN TERMS OF ENERGY WITH THE PAST AND THE FUTURE. THE OLD CHIMNEY WAS THE SYMBOL OF INDUSTRIAL ENERGY IN THE PAST, NOW, IT'S AN URBAN LANDMARK THAT SHOWS IN REAL TIME THE MANAGEMENT OF RESOURCES SUCH AS SOLAR, GEOTHERMAL, BIOMASS ENERGY, WASTED WATER, WEATHER FORECAST, ETC... IN ORDER TO CREATE A NEW ECO-CONSCIENCE IN THE DISTRICT, THE CITY AND THE REGION. IT'S AN ECO-INFORMATIONAL CHIMNEY. SUSTAINABILITY AS VISIBILITY OF ENERGY.

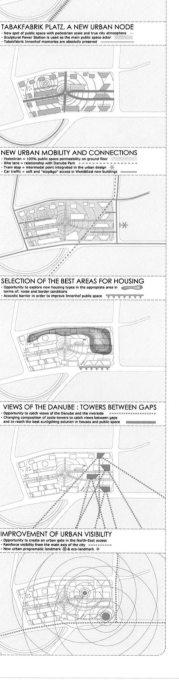

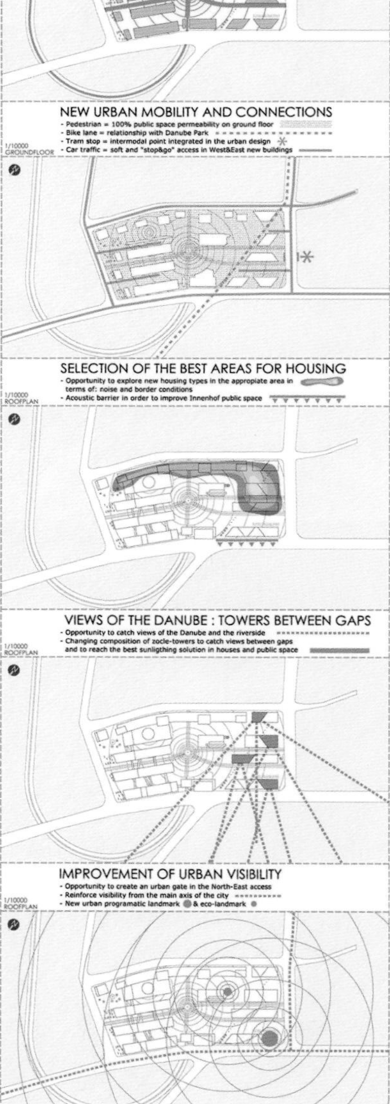
NEW URBAN MOBILITY AND CONNECTIONS
- Pedestrian = 100% public space permeability on ground floor
- Bike lane = relationship with Danube Park
- Tram stop = intermodal point integrated in the urban design
- Car traffic = soft and "stop&go" access in West&East new buildings
1/10000 GROUNDFLOOR
SELECTION OF THE BEST AREAS FOR HOUSING
- Opportunity to explore new housing types in the appropiate area in terms of: noise and border conditions
- Acoustic barrier in order to improve Innenhof public space
1/10000 ROOFPLAN
VIEWS OF THE DANUBE : TOWERS BETWEEN GAPS
- Opportunity to catch views of the Danube and the riverside
- Changing composition of zocle-towers to catch views between gaps and to reach the best sunligthing solution in houses and public space
1/10000 ROOFPLAN
IMPROVEMENT OF URBAN VISIBILITY
- Opportunity to create an urban gate in the North-East access
- Reinforce visibility from the main axis of the city
- New urban programatic landmark & eco-landmark
1/10000 ROOFPLAN

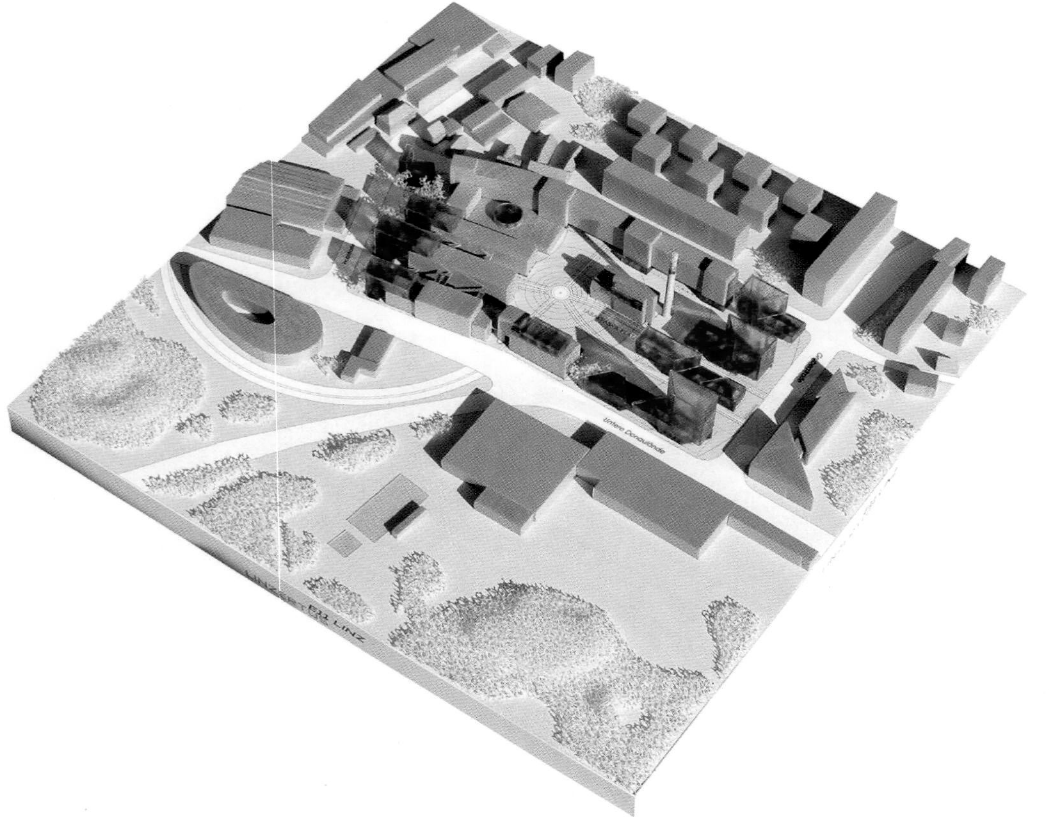

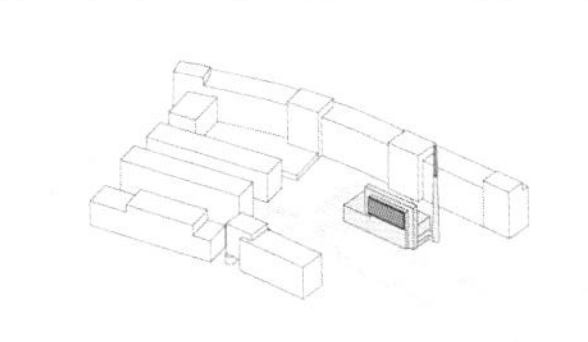

01. PHASE

POWER PLANT & NEW URBAN PUBLIC SPACE

SPATIAL & PROGRAMATIC POTENTIALS / OPPORTUNITIES

- The expressively designed Power Station is used like an industrial sculpture to lead the new urban identity of the area. Industrial heritage as main actor in public space with a "city atmosphere".
- Power Plant as an urban landmark will be the change's symbol: from isolation to social cohesion.
- The new extended chimney will dialogue with the past time and the future, and will be an urban interface between the city and the industrial area in the East. Also the new chimney will dialogue physically with the existing industrial chimneys in Eastern Linz.
- 2 scales: new public space with the backdrop of the Power Plant will be an urban attractor and, on the other hand, will have a positive impact in the surrounding neighborhoods thanks to the improved visibility and the high degree of permeability in terms of accessibility.
- The former footprints of the train tracks in the site are used to lead the urban design of public space, preserving the site industrial memories. Preserved space of "Innenhof" will be a new urban meeting point, a powerful new spot. A new urban node of activities called: Tabakfabrik Platz.

PROGRAMATIC SITUATIONS

- Public space in Tabakfabrik Platz. / Area: 1.5ha / Management: City of Linz, neighbours, pedestrians...
- Urban screen: information in real time, exhibitions, urban cinema, concerts, etc... urban attractor.
- Extended chimney of the Power Plant, with a new eco-blue-landmark which dialogue in terms of energy with the past and the future. The old Power Plant chimney, now, is a landmark that shows to people in live the management of resources (solar, geothermal, biomass energy, wasted water...) in order to create a new eco-conscience in the district, the city and the region. It's an eco-informational chimney.
- Tabakfabrik Museum (space and machines are preserved). / Area: 950m2 / Management: City of Linz.

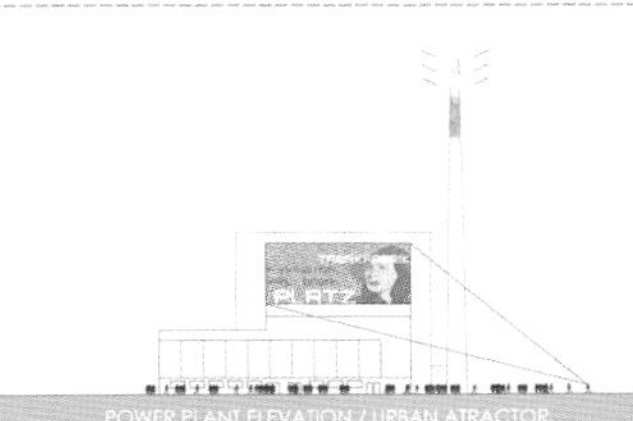

POWER PLANT ELEVATION / URBAN ATRACTOR

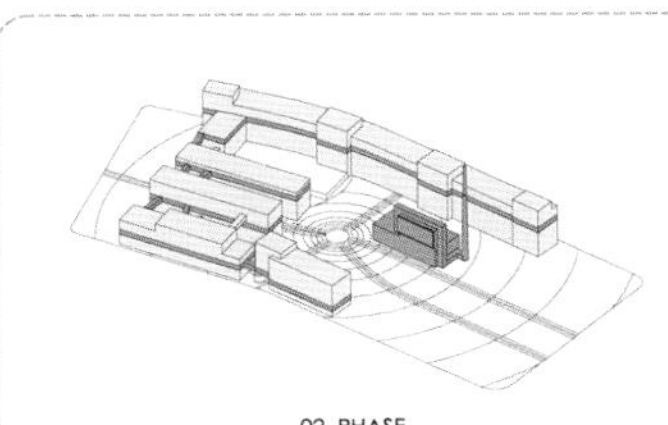

02. PHASE

TABAKFABRIK "3D PROMENADE" MUSEUM

SPATIAL & PROGRAMATIC POTENTIALS / OPPORTUNITIES

- Following the Monument Preservation policy,"... at least one storey must be preserved in its original condition...", a Tabakfabrik Museum is proposed in order to join all the Tabakfabrik complex.
- Tabakfabrik Museum will preserve one storey of each building from 1929-1935 project of Peter Behrens and Alexander Popp in original conditions to be visited. It will be the start point to create a new identity and a regional attractor.
- The Museum takes advantage of the spatial condition of the complex and the 3d relations between buildings because of the height connections through foot-bridges.
- A no-linear museum is created. It's a "promenade" Museum, a ride height tour. A different storey-level is preserved in each building creating a complete 3D experience around the complex.
- The Power Plant will be the start point of the tours and the virtual entrance to the museum.

PROGRAMATIC SITUATIONS

- Tabakfabrik Museum. / Area: 9.100m2 / Management: City of Linz.

Description of levels :

Power plant	/ Area: 950m2	/ Level: ground floor
Pipe tobacco factory	/ Area: 750m2	/ Level: first floor
Store room I	/ Area: 1.300m2	/ Level: second floor
Store room II	/ Area: 1.200m2	/ Level: third floor
Store room III	/ Area: 1.200m2	/ Level: fourth floor
Building I	/ Area: 3.700m2	/ Level: fifth floor

BAU I / BUILDING I
MAGAZIN III
MAGAZIN II
MAGAZIN I
BAU II / PIPE
KRAFTWERK

TABAKFABRIK MUSEUM LEVELS DIAGRAM

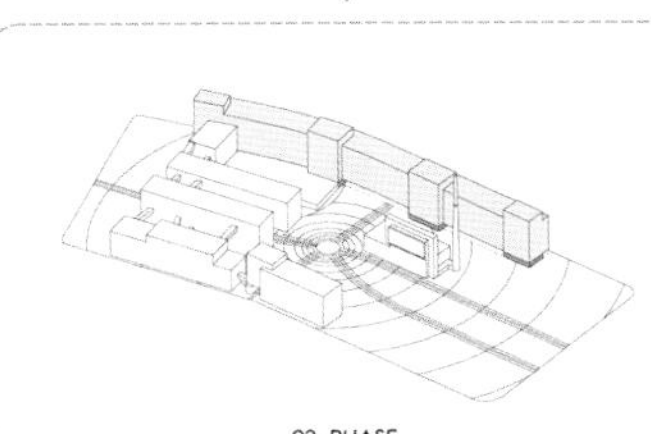

03. PHASE

LOFT LIVING SPACES IN BAU I / BUILDING I

SPATIAL & PROGRAMATIC POTENTIALS / OPPORTUNITIES

- The loft apartments program fits in the Building I, because of the spatial, constructive and urban features.
- Good location of the builiding in relation with the new housing fabric in the South (in the former hospital site), the residential district and inner city.
- Low noise levels, in the innenhof (new Tabakfabrik Platz) and in Ludlgasse.
- Good insulation:"...excellently insulated as tobacco was manufactured here..." and good natural lighting.
- Perfect spatial conditions because of the structure, the absence of interior walls.
- There are 4 existing cores, with stairs, lifts and installation pipes.
- Opportunity to explore new forms of housing with a industrial atmosphere, industrial finishing in loft apartments, for living or for living&working. Flexible loft type units.
- Opportunity to improve crossed urban connections in groundfloor (public space layer) in the North-South axis. A high degree of permeability is created thanks to new loft apartments common service programs which are permeable pavillions. The Building I is elevated and is floating on the public space.
- Opportunity to explore the "Le Corbusier - Unité d'habitation" type and its main features.

PROGRAMATIC SITUATIONS

- Loft living 70 units (living&working) / Area: 15.580m2 / Management: Rental aparts. (owner: City of Linz).

Description of types: Unité d'habitation type, green loggia type, mezzanine type, duplex type, tube type, luxury loft type, spa and water terrace type, penthouse-patio type, standard type.

Description of levels: (Linzer Unité d'habitation)
Permeable groundfloor with common service pavillions / Area: 1.580m2
Regular loft storeys / Area: 14.000m2
Common leisure program on the roof (sun and views) / Area: 2.000m2

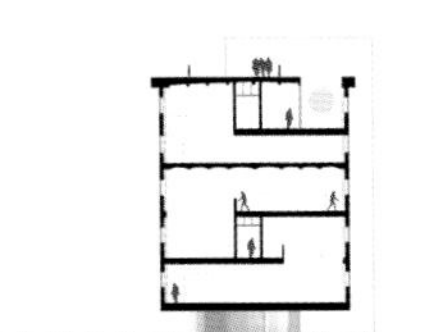

BAU I / LOFT LIVING SECTION

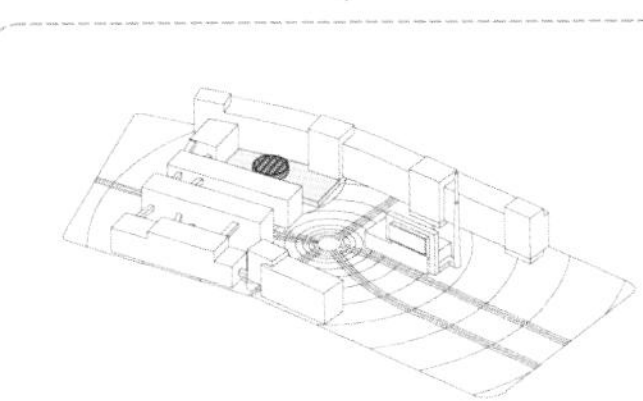

04. PHASE

MULTIPURPOSE & COVERED PUBLIC SPACE IN LÖSEHALLE

SPATIAL & PROGRAMATIC POTENTIALS / OPPORTUNITIES

- The Lösehalle (Break-up Hall) is a "...single storey hall largely free of pillars, the up to 5,30m-high. Rooms were originally naturally illuminated through the ceiling...". It's a opportunity to create a public multipurpose center because of the spatial conditions and the location.
- The Lösehalle is activated with a roof-graft, which is a big skylight cilinder that recovers the old condition of natural lighting from the ceiling.
- In continuity with the new node of public space called Tabakfabrik Platz, a new covered public space is created in the Lösehalle. It's a new secundary node of activities and an urban attractor for the district.
- Regarding to the local weather, a covered public space will encourage people to use the public scene and to maintain alive the "city atmosphere".
- The location of this space is an opportunity to create a permeable public space in the West-East axis. The boundaries of this space are blurred thanks to the lack of any envelope.
- Opportunity to create a programatic situation for demands of new young inhabitants with new leisure perspectives as a result of the postindustrial economical change in the city.

PROGRAMATIC SITUATIONS

- Multipurpose covered area / Area: 2.120m2 / Management: City of Linz & neighborhood associations

Description of uses: covered public space & multipurpose area for performances, concerts, exhibitions, public meetings, neighborhood associations activities, intellectual leisure and more indoor activities. The main space 5.3m-high free of pillars is supported by a strip of services, amenities and technical programs.

LÖSEHALLE / COVERED PUBLIC SPACE

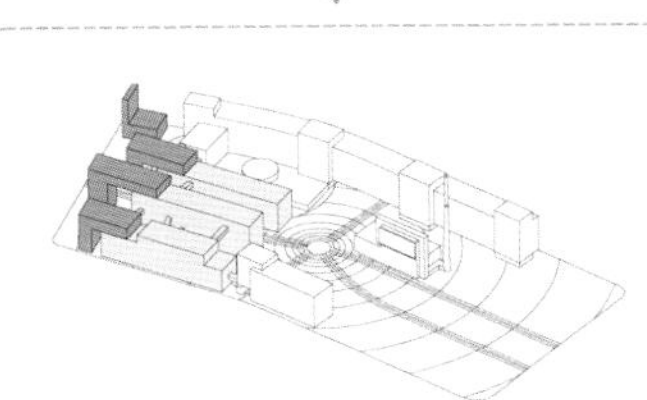

05. PHASE

WORKSHOP & LOFT ATELIER IN STORE ROOMS I, II, III

SPATIAL & PROGRAMATIC POTENTIALS / OPPORTUNITIES

- The Store Rooms spatial management takes advantage of its role as interface between the inner city-the new Tabakfabrik Platz and Eastern Linz. A high degree of permeability is created as far as possible, in order to produce urban continuity in the West-East axis, in the way to the future development towards the East.
- The new site-facade towards the East side of the city is created with informational-facades about the activities which happens in the Tabakfabrik complex. New info-society, new info-facades.
- Perhaps, the new indentiy of Linz, is coming with the postindustrial economical change. Population is changing to a knowledge and creative society, to a creative and progressive industry with a new kind of creative workers. New kind of worshops and loft atelier spaces will be created in the Store Rooms as an answer to the new contemporary cultural fields of production. These programs fit perfectly with the location and the spatial condition of the Store Rooms buildings.
- Opportunity to build a new, traslucent and continuous facade with natural light on the building long sides.
- Opportunity to build the new foot-bridges in glass between the Store Rooms.
- The former buildings are activate by programatic-grafts, with the new and necesary modern amenities.

PROGRAMATIC SITUATIONS

- Workshops and loft atelier spaces / Area: 15.800m2 / Management: Rental spaces (owner: City of Linz).

Description of uses: flexible workshops for cultural industry and creative companies, loft atelier spaces for artists, doctors, lawyers, architects, graphic designers..., seminars for classes of art, poetry, theatre..., space for an art center, radio studio, music practice rooms, spaces for temporary cultural fairs, contemporary gastronomy (specially in EG)
The programatic-grafts contain installations, stairs, lifts and common services.

MAGAZIN TYPE / LOFT & ATELIER SECTION

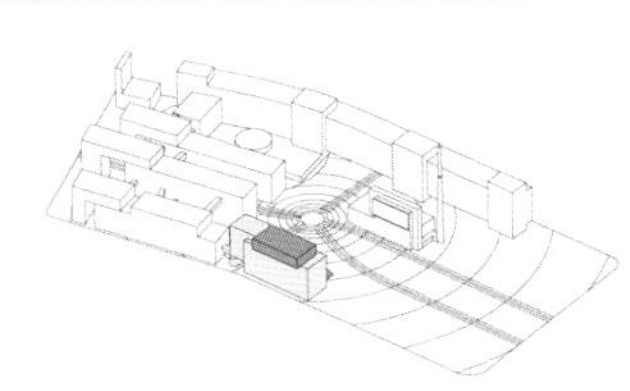

06. PHASE

SOCIAL FACILITIES IN PIPE TOBACCO FACTORY

SPATIAL & PROGRAMATIC POTENTIALS / OPPORTUNITIES

- The location of the Pipe Tobacco Factory, in a direct dialogue with the Power Plant and in a very strong relation with the new Tabakfabrik Platz is a opportunity to create a public and social program in continuity with the new urban node of public space.
- The contact with public space is resolved with a "carpet" of urban space which invites pedestrian to access.
- An internal-graft of vertical connections is built in continuity to the public space. It's a piece of public space that "runs" along the building until the rooftop to catch the best views.
- Finally, a rooftop-graft is create on the roof in order to create a multipurpose room for everybody and to catch the views of the Donau.
- Because of the noise, the building will be an introvert building and will be opened towards the Tabakfabrik Platz. Special mesures against the noise will be created in the Donaulände side.
- Opportunity to take advantage of the exisiting space which is illuminated in three sides.
- Opportunity to take advantage of the heatable condition of the building.

PROGRAMATIC SITUATIONS

- Social-cultural facilities & urban carpet & views catcher room / Area: 3.700m2 / Management: City of Linz

Description of uses: cultural and public leisure, social facilities.
"carpet" of public space in ground floor as an urban scene.
intergenerational uses crossing, to reach a social cohesion, thanks to mix programs such as childminders center, youth club, students area, workers club and senoir club.
public & multipurpose area on the rooftop (views catcher over Donau).

TABAKFABRIK PLATZ

BAU II / PUBLIC FACILITIES SECTION

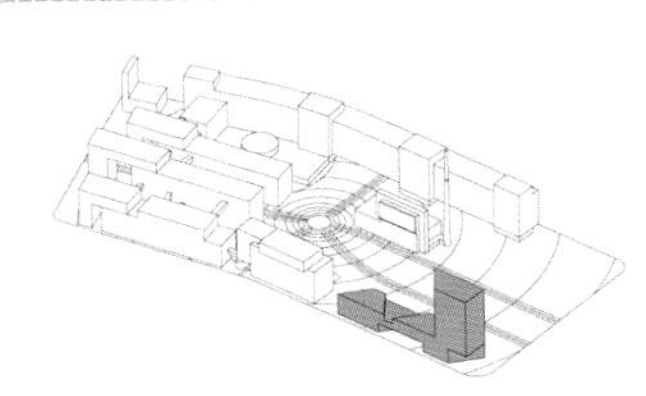

07. PHASE

NEW URBAN LANDMARK / HOTEL & CONVENTION CENTER

SPATIAL & PROGRAMATIC POTENTIALS / OPPORTUNITIES

- The tower as an answer to the lack of urban visibility of the area. The tower will be a new urban landmark. The tower is located in the most visible and representative point of the site, the North-West corner in the intersection of the main streets (Donaulände / Gruberstrasse).
- Because of the high levels of noise in this area of Donaulände, the new building works as an acoustic barrier. Then the Tabakfabrik Platz is a perfect space in terms of acoustic confort.
- High density in order to free the public space as much as possible.
- The location and shape of the zocle-tower creates a positive sunlight situation in the Tabakfabrik Platz.
- The tower as an opportunity to catch the views of the Donau. Thanks to the tower-shape, most of the rooms have nice views of the Park and the Donau.
- The program will have a regional and local positive impact. The restaurant and the convention center will attract new people to the district.

PROGRAMATIC SITUATIONS

- Hotel, convention center & rooftop restaurant views / Area: 8.400m2 / Management: Private owner.

Description of uses: Main entrance, foyer and common facilities / Area: 1.100m2
Convention center / Area: 2.500m2
Hotel, 90 beds with views over Donau / Area: 4.330m2
Rooftop restaurant with 360º views / Area: 470m2

NEW URBAN LANDMARK / HOTEL SECTION

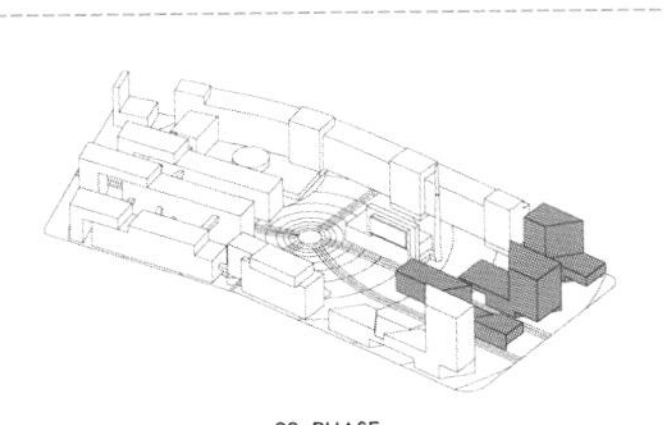

08. PHASE

3 BLOCKS & SOCLE-TOWER HOUSING TYPES

SPATIAL & PROGRAMATIC POTENTIALS / OPPORTUNITIES

- The three housing buildings take advantage of its role as interface between the inner city-the new Tabakfabrik Platz and Western Linz. A high degree of permeability as far as possible is created in order to produce urban continuity in the West-East axis. The new housing buildings are in continuity with the existing and consolidated urban fabric.
- The composition of the zocle-towers is changing, one each other, in order to improve the sunlight of the apartments and to allow to each tower to have views of the Donau. It´s a "between gaps" composition.
- High density in order to free the public space as much as possible.
- The location and shape of the buildings create a positive sunlight situation in the Tabakfabrik Platz.
- Linz population is changing to a knowledge and creative society. They demand a new kind of houses and forms of living. Then, a range of 3 different kinds, qualities and types of new housing blocks are proposed.
- The program of housing with commerce on ground floor, complete finally, a mixed use program in the Tabakfabrik Complex. The commerce program is understood as small shops for the neighborhood.

PROGRAMATIC SITUATIONS

- Housing and retail on ground floor / Area: 15.700m2 / Management: Private owners.

Description of blocks:
Housing block / zocle-tower 01 / Area: 4.500m2
24 regular quality, one storey type apartments from 90 to 140m2.
Housing block / zocle-tower 02 / Area: 7.000m2
30 hi-level quality, 2 storeys & green type apats. from 100 to 180 m2.
Housing block / zocle-tower 03 / Area: 4.200m2
38 low-budget quality, one storey & corridor type from 50 to 100m2.

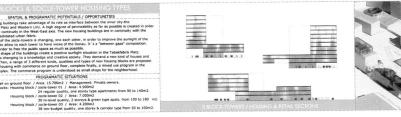

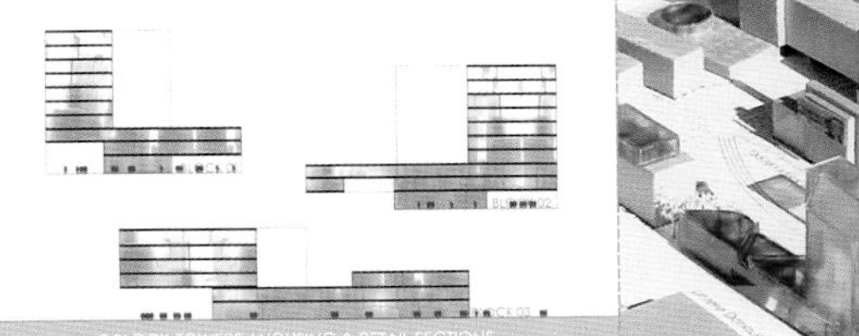

3 BLOCK-TOWERS / HOUSING & RETAIL SECTIONS

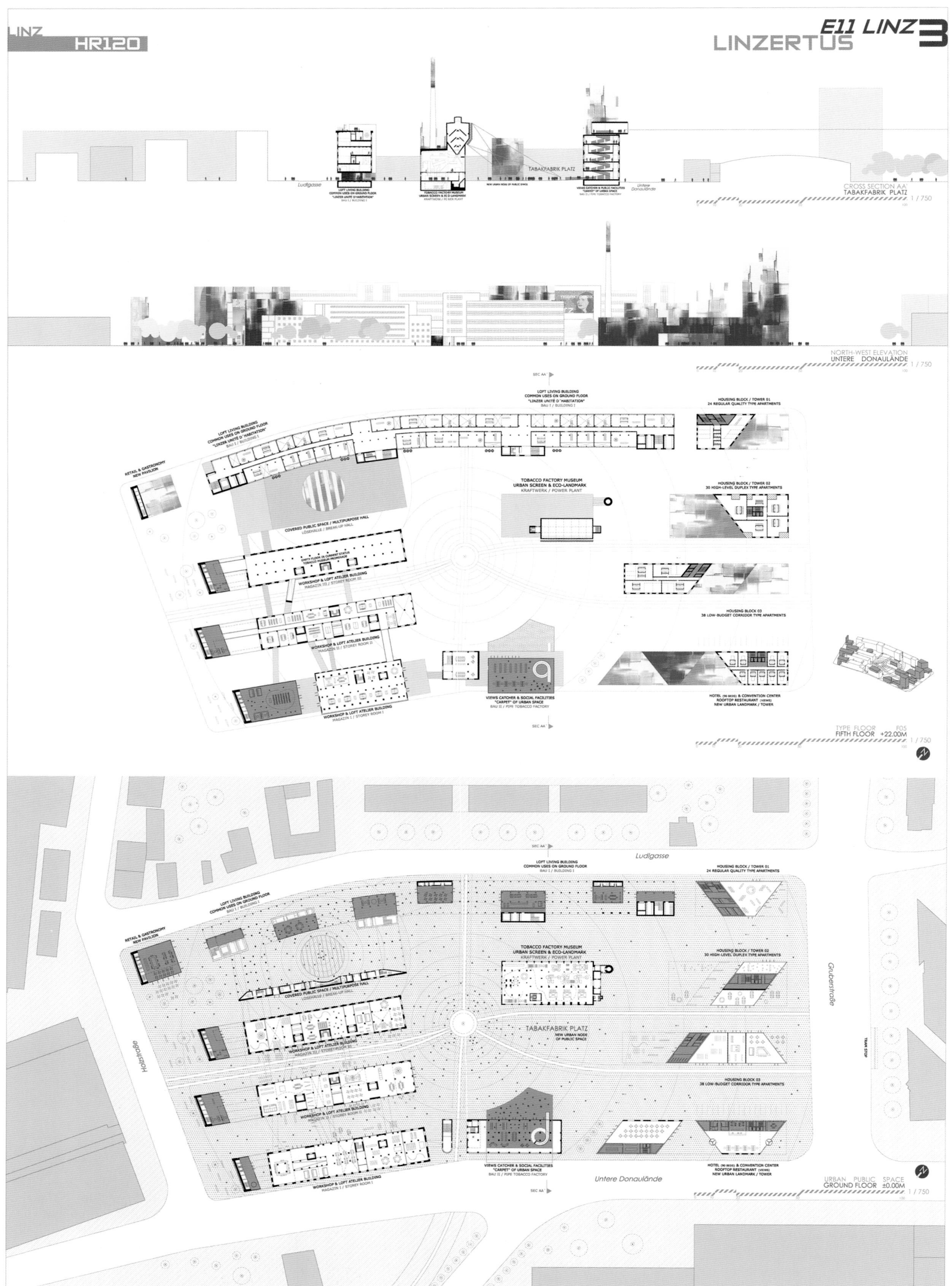
LINZ
HR120
E11 LINZ 3
LINZERTUS
Ludigasse
TABAKFABRIK PLATZ
Untere Donaulände
CROSS SECTION AA'
TABAKFABRIK PLATZ
1 / 750
NORTH-WEST ELEVATION
UNTERE DONAULÄNDE
1 / 750
LOFT LIVING BUILDING
COMMON USES ON GROUND FLOOR
"LINZER UNITÉ D'HABITATION"
BAU 1 / BUILDING I
HOUSING BLOCK / TOWER 01
24 REGULAR QUALITY TYPE APARTMENTS
RETAIL & GASTRONOMY
NEW PAVILION
TOBACCO FACTORY MUSEUM
URBAN SCREEN & ECO-LANDMARK
KRAFTWERK / POWER PLANT
HOUSING BLOCK / TOWER 02
30 HIGH-LEVEL DUPLEX TYPE APARTMENTS
COVERED PUBLIC SPACE / MULTIPURPOSE HALL
LÖSEHALLE / BREAK-UP HALL
WORKSHOP & LOFT ATELIER BUILDING
MAGAZIN III / STOREY ROOM III
HOUSING BLOCK 03
38 LOW-BUDGET CORRIDOR TYPE APARTMENTS
WORKSHOP & LOFT ATELIER BUILDING
MAGAZIN II / STOREY ROOM II
VIEWS CATCHER & SOCIAL FACILITIES
"CARPET" OF URBAN SPACE
BAU II / PIPE TOBACCO FACTORY
HOTEL & CONVENTION CENTER
ROOFTOP RESTAURANT (VIEWS)
NEW URBAN LANDMARK / TOWER
WORKSHOP & LOFT ATELIER BUILDING
MAGAZIN I / STOREY ROOM I
SEC AA'
TYPE FLOOR F05
FIFTH FLOOR +22.00M
1 / 750
Ludigasse
TABAKFABRIK PLATZ
NEW URBAN NODE
OF PUBLIC SPACE
Holzstraße
Gruberstraße
TRAM STOP
Untere Donaulände
URBAN PUBLIC SPACE
GROUND FLOOR ±0.00M
1 / 750

Unesco Delta City Competition Poster | *David Garcia Studio*

Location : Rotterdam, The Netherlands
Client : Unesco, Rotterdam City

Participants : David A. Garcia (Architect MAA), Frederik Allan, Ellemieke van Vliet
Project : Architectural Solutions to the Flood Risk Area of the Harbor in Rotterdam.
Typology : Landscaping, Residential Buildings with Additional Facilities

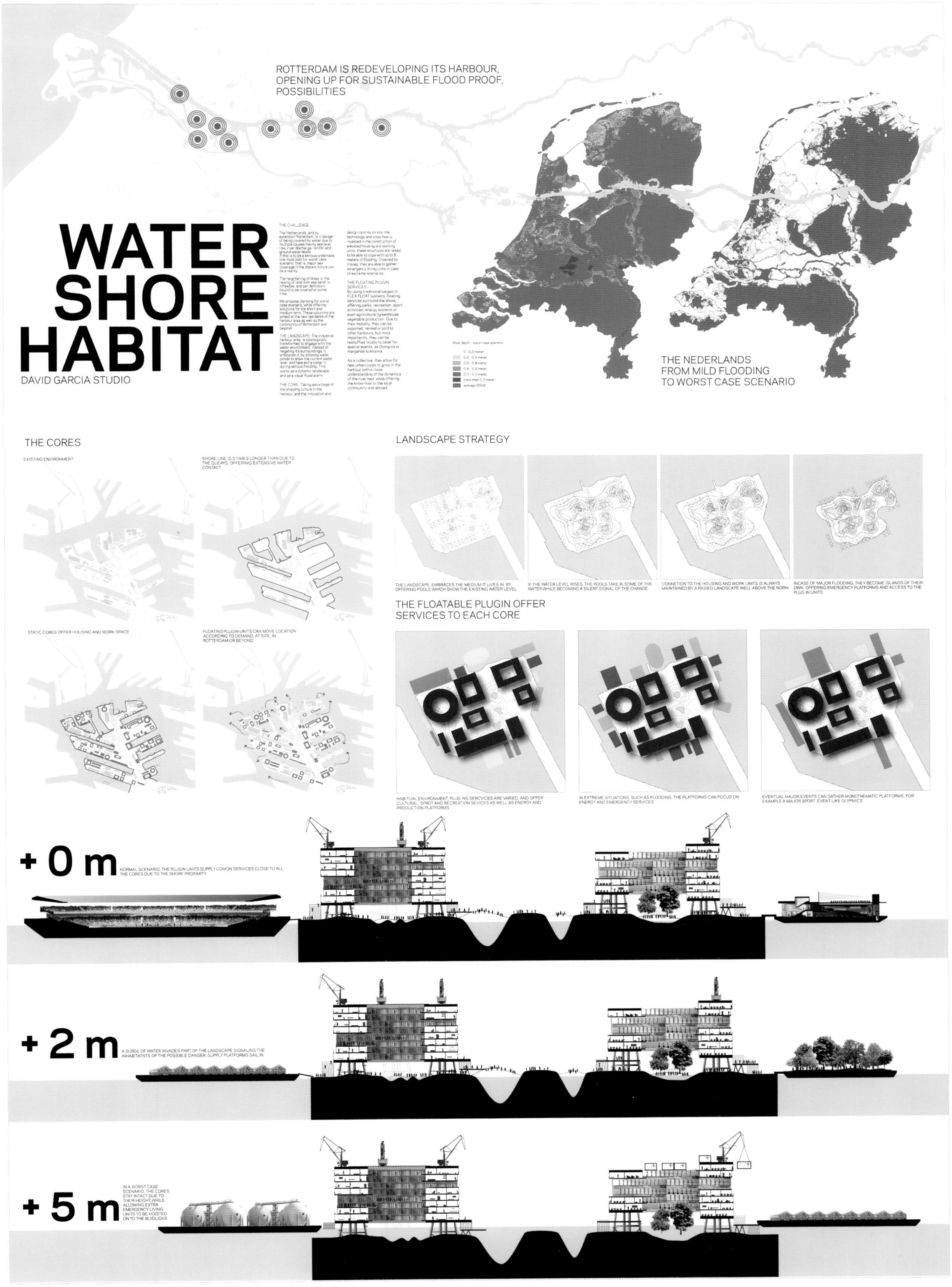

ROTTERDAM IS REDEVELOPING ITS HARBOUR, OPENING UP FOR SUSTAINABLE FLOOD PROOF, POSSIBILITIES

WATER SHORE HABITAT

DAVID GARCIA STUDIO

THE CHALLENGE

The Netherlands, and by extension Rotterdam, is in danger of being covered by water due to multiple causes mainly sea level rise, river discharge, rainfall and ground water levels.
If this is to be a serious undertake, one must plan for worst case scenario; that is, major sea coverage in the distant future can be a reality.

The heightening of dikes or the raising of land with sea sand, is inflexible, and per definition, bound to be covered at some time.

We propose planning for worst case scenario, while offering solutions for the short and medium term. These solutions are aimed at the new residents of the harbour area as well as the community of Rotterdam and beyond.

THE LANDSCAPE- The industrial harbour area, is topologically transformed to engage with the water environment. Instead of negating it's surroundings, it embraces it, by allowing water ponds to show the current water level, and take extra water in during serious flooding. This works as a dynamic landscape and as a visual flood alarm.

THE CORE - Taking advantage of the shipping culture in the harbour, and the innovation and design centres on site, the technology and know how is invested in the construction of elevated housing and working units, these structures are raised to be able to cope with up to 8 meters of flooding. Crowned by cranes, they are able to gather emergency living units in case of extreme scenarios.

THE FLOATING PLUGIN SERVICES -
By using traditional barges or FLEX FLOAT systems, floating services surround the shore, offering parks, recreation, sport activities, energy systems or even agricultural /greenhouse vegetable production. Due to their mobility, they can be exported, rented or sold to other harbours, but more importantly, they can be reshuffled locally to cater for special events, as Olympics or mergence scenarios.

As a collective, they allow for new urban cores to grow in the harbour with a close understanding of the dynamics of the river bed, while offering the know-how to the local community and abroad.

River depth - worst case scenario
0 - 0,2 meter
0,2 - 0,5 meter
0,5 - 0,8 meter
0,8 - 2,0 meter
2,0 - 5,0 meter
more then 5,0 meter
average 2008

THE NEDERLANDS FROM MILD FLOODING TO WORST CASE SCENARIO

THE CORES

EXISTING ENVIRONMENT

SHORE LINE IS 5 TIMES LONGER THAN DUE TO THE QUEAYS, OFFERINIG EXTENSIVE WATER CONTACT

STATIC CORES OFFER HOUSING AND WORK SPACE

FLOATING PLUGIN UNITS CAN MOVE LOCATION ACCORDING TO DEMAND, AT SITE, IN ROTTERDAM OR BEYOND

LANDSCAPE STRATEGY

THE LANDSCAPE EMBRACES THE MEDIUM IT LIVES IN, BY OFFERING POOLS WHICH SHOW THE EXISTING WATER LEVEL

IF THE WATER LEVEL RISES, THE POOLS TAKE IN SOME OF THE WATER WHILE BECOMING A SILENT SIGNAL OF THE CHANGE

CONNETION TO THE HOUSING AND WORK UNITS IS ALWAYS MAINTAINED BY A RASIED LANDSCAPE WELL ABOVE THE NORM

INCASE OF MAJOR FLOODING, THEY BECOME ISLANDS OF THEIR OWN, OFFERING EMERGENCY PLATFORMS AND ACCESS TO THE PLUG IN UNITS

THE FLOATABLE PLUGIN OFFER SERVICES TO EACH CORE

HABITUAL ENVIRONMENT, PLUG INS SERCVICES ARE VARIED, AND OFFER CULTURAL, SPROT AND RECREATION SEVICES AS WELL AS ENERGY AND PRODUCTION PLATFORMS

IN EXTREME SITUATIONS, SUCH AS FLOODING, THE PLATFORMS CAN FOCUS ON ENERGY AND EMERGENCY SERVICES

EVENTUAL MAJOR EVENTS CAN GATHER MONOTHEMATIC PLATFORMS, FOR EXAMPLE A MAJOR SPORT EVENT LIKE OLYPMICS

+ 0 m NORMAL SCENARIO, THE PLUGIN UNITS SUPPLY COMON SERVICES CLOSE TO ALL THE CORES DUE TO THE SHORE PROXIMITY

+ 2 m A SURGE OF WATER INVADES PART OF THE LANDSCAPE SIGNALING THE INHABITATNTS OF THE POSSIBLE DANGER. SUPPLY PLATFORMS SAIL IN

+ 5 m IN A WORST CASE SCENARIO, THE CORES STAY INTACT DUE TO THEIR HEIGHT, WHILE ALLOWING EXTRA EMERGENCY LIVING UNITS TO BE HOISTED ON TO THE BUIDLIGNS

Urban Sardinops | *gutiérrez-delafuente arquitectos*

Project : National Competition Plaza de la Baragaña de Candás Public space
Programme : Remodeling Plaza de la Baragaña Public Space in the Inner City of Candás
Location : Candás, Spain

Architects : Natalia Gutiérrez & Julio de la Fuente
Client : City of Candás

CONCURSO DE IDEAS PARA LA REURBANIZACION DE LA PLAZA DE LA BARAGANA

LEMA: SARDINOPS URBANA

MEMORIA / DESARROLLO CONCEPTUAL:

LA PROPUESTA SE CONCIBE COMO UN SUMATORIO DE DECISIONES QUE VAN CONFIGURANDO LA PLAZA DE LA BARAGAÑA BAJA VOLUMÉTRICA, PROGRAMÁTICA Y MATERIALMENTE.
ESTAS DECISIONES SE ARTICULAN ALREDEDOR DE TRES VARIABLES QUE INFORMAN EL PROYECTO, ESTAS VARIABLES QUE SE COMUNICAN ENTRE SI DURANTE EL PROCESO PROYECTUAL SON:
1/ LA CIUDAD: SE ESTUDIAN LAS CONEXIONES URBANAS Y LOS RECORRIDOS PEATONALES Y RODADOS, SE TRATA EL ESPACIO DE LA BARAGAÑA BAJA EN RELACIÓN A LOS USOS DE LOS OTROS ESPACIOS PÚBLICOS CERCANOS Y SE AHONDA EN LA CONCEPCIÓN TOPOGRÁFICA DE CANDÁS, "UNA VILLA EN SECCIÓN", PARA CONECTAR FÍSICA Y VISUALMENTE EL PAISAJE URBANO.
2/ VALORES INTRÍNSECOS DEL CONCEJO: NO SE TRATA DE IMPLANTAR UN ESPACIO PÚBLICO NUEVO SIN CONEXIONES CON LA CULTURA Y MEMORIA COLECTIVA LOCALES. ASÍ SE CREA UNA PLAZA REFERENCIANDO EL PASADO MARINERO , ASÍ COMO EL FOLCLORE POPULAR Y LA PROPIA FUNDACIÓN DEL CONCEJO. EN LA ELECCIÓN DE LA VEGETACIÓN TAMBIÉN SE TIENE ESPECIAL SENSIBILIDAD CON LA CULTURA LOCAL. SE ESTUDIAN LAS ACTIVIDADES REQUERIDAS POR LA POBLACIÓN SEGÚN LOS ESPACIOS PÚBLICOS EXISTENTES.
3/ MATERIALIDAD: SE REALIZA UN PROCESO PROYECTUAL DE GENERACIÓN DE LA PLAZA APOYADO EN LOS PUNTOS ANTERIORES Y SIGUIENDO UNA LÓGICA CONSTRUCTIVA Y ECONÓMICA APROPIADA PARA LA INTERVENCIÓN.
4/ SOSTENIBILIDAD: SE TOMAN SENCILLAS DECISIONES DURANTE EL PROCESO PROYECTUAL , DENOMINADAS DE LOW-COST, PERO QUE RESULTAN EFECTIVAS. NO SE TRATA DE OTRA COSA MÁS QUE DE APLICAR EL SENTIDO COMÚN.

P.SITUACIÓN 1/2000 — FOTO AÉREA DE EMPLAZAMIENTO ESCALA URBANA

1/ LA CIUDAD - CONTEXTO URBANO

1.1.- CONEXIONES URBANAS - SECUENCIA DE ESPACIOS PÚBLICOS URBANOS Y LAS CONEXIONES ENTRE ELLOS
1.2.- USOS Y CARACTERÍSTICAS DEL ESPACIO PÚBLICO - OFERTA COMPLETA DE DISITNTOS TIPOS DE ESPACIOS
1.3.- TOPOGRAFÍA CANDASINA - "UNA VILLA EN SECCIÓN" - CONTINUIDAD FÍSICA Y VISUAL DEL PAISAJE URBANO

1.1. - CONEXIONES URBANAS:
SE TOMA LA PLAZA DE LA BARAGAÑA BAJA COMO LA PIEDRA ANGULAR ,POR SU SITUACIÓN, DENTRO DEL TEJIDO URBANO DE CANDÁS. LA PLAZA ES UN LUGAR DE PASO ENTRE LOS DISTINTOS ESPACIOS PÚBLICOS, DE MANERA QUE DEBERÁ CONJUGAR ESA CARACTERÍSITCA EN SU CONCEPCIÓN. DE IGUAL MANERA ES UN LUGAR DE ENCUENTRO, EL CENTRO PSICOGEOGRÁFICO DE CANDÁS, EL CIERRE DE LA CALLE BRAULIO BUSTO, DEL MERCADILLO... ES LAS DOS COSAS A LA VEZ, UN LUGAR DE PASO OBLIGADO Y UN PUNTO DE ENCUENTRO Y ESTANCIA.
EN LA REURBANIZACIÓN SE CREA UN PUNTO DE ENCUENTRO E INFORMACIÓN EN LA ESQUINA SUR DE LA PLAZA Y SE TRATA TOPOGRÁFICAMENTE ESA VOCACIÓN DE LUGAR DE PASO.

1.2. - USOS Y CARACTERÍSTICAS DE LOS ESPACIOS PÚBLICOS Y LA PLAZA:
SE TRATA DE BUSCAR UNA ESCALA A LA PLAZA Y SU PROPIA IDENTIDAD PROGRAMÁTICA.
EL PARQUE LES CONSERVERES ES UN ESPACIO CAPAZ DE ACOGER GRANDES CONCENTRACIONES DE GENTE, ESPECTÁCULOS, ACTIVIDADES IMPROVISADAS, DADA SU ESCALA Y VOCACIÓN.
LA TRAMA IRREGULAR DEL CASCO ESTÁ JALONADA DE PEQUEÑAS PLAZAS DE USO ESTANCIAL DE CARÁCTER VECINAL.
LA CALLE BRAULIO BUSTO Y EL ENGANCHE CON EL PUERTO Y EL PASEO MARÍTIMO RESPONDE A OTRA TIPOLOGÍA DE ESPACIO PÚBLICO, DE CARÁCTER LINEAL.
LA SENDA VERDE COMPLETA UNA OFERTA INTERESANTE DE ESPACIO PÚBLICO.
FINALMENTE LA PLAZA DE LA BARAGAÑA, EN SU TOTALIDAD QUEDA COMO UN ESPACIO DE ENCUENTRO, DE PASO Y DE ESTANCIA A UNA ESCALA MENOR QUE LA QUE TIENE EN LA ACTUALIDAD LA PLAZA DE LA BARAGAÑA BAJA.

1.3. - USOS Y CARACTERÍSTICAS DE LOS ESPACIOS PÚBLICOS Y LA PLAZA:
SE CREA UNA PLAZA NUEVA A TRAVÉS DE LA TOPOGRAFÍA, DE LOS PLANOS FACETADOS , SIEMPRE RESPETANDO LA MÁXIMA PENDIENTE DEL 8% Y SITUÁNDO LAS ESCALERAS EN LOS LUGARES DONDE SUPONE LA ÚNICA SOLUCIÓN. CON ESTA TOPOGRAFÍA SE TRATA DE CONECTAR EL PAISAJE URBANO EN SECCIÓN, Y CREAR UN GRAN EJE VISUAL CON LA ESCALINATA J.G.PRENDES.

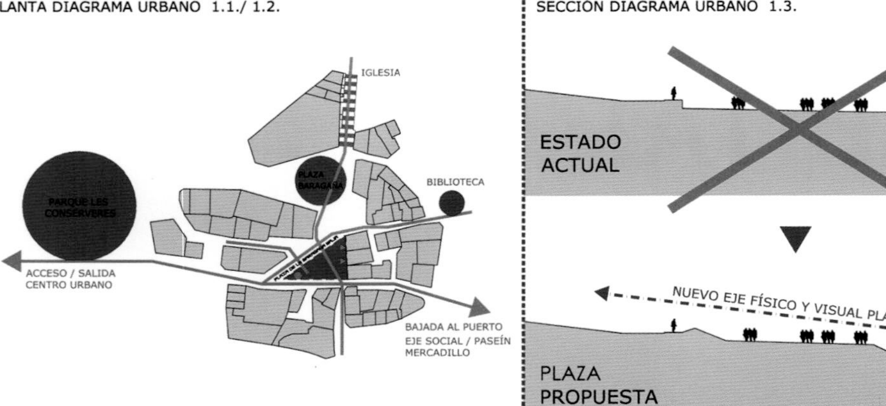

2/ VALORES INTRÍNSECOS CANDASINOS

2.1.- REFERENCIA AL PASADO MARINERO Y PESQUERO (INDUSTRIA CONSERVERA) ASÍ COMO AL FOLCLORE POPULAR Y A UNA DE LAS FIESTAS MÁS RECONOCIDAS COMO LA DE LA SARDINA. UNA SARDINA (SARDINOPS SAGAX SAGAX) HA SUBIDO DESDE EL PUERTO HASTA LA PLAZA DE LA BARAGAÑA BAJA ¡¡¡¡¡¡¡¡¡¡¡¡¡¡¡¡¡
2.2.- REFERENCIA FUNDACIONAL A LOS ORÍGENES DEL ESCUDO HERÁLDICO Y BLASÓN COMO ORIGEN DEL CONCEJO DE CARREÑO.
2.3.- REFERENCIA EN EL TRATAMIENTO DE ÁRBOLADO Y PLANTACIONES A ESPECIES AUTÓCTONAS Y ENRAIZADAS CULTURALMENTE EN LA REGIÓN.

2.1. UN SARDINOPS SAGAX SAGAX (SARDINA) HA SUBIDO DESDE EL PUERTO HASTA LA PLAZA DE LA BARAGAÑA BAJA ¡¡¡¡¡¡¡¡¡¡¡

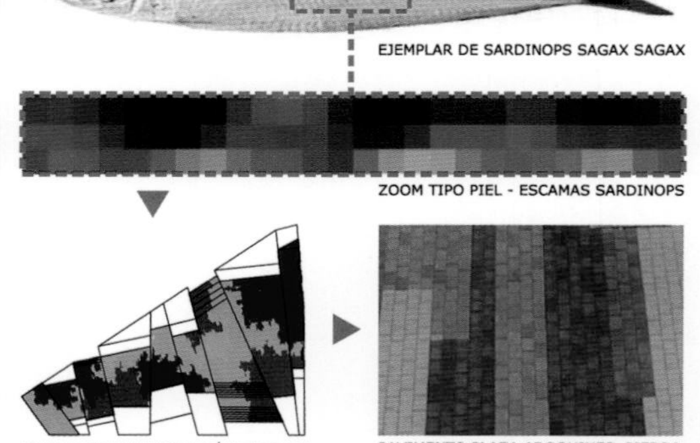

2.2. ORÍGENES DEL ESCUDO HERÁLDICO SEGÚN EL MANUSCRITO DE TIRSO DE AVILÉS....CUYO BLASÓN ES EL SIGUIENTE:

" EN ALTO CAMPO PINTADO
YO VI UN ÁGUILA REAL
TODA NEGRA Y PRINCIPAL,
Y POR SIETE ASPAS CERCADA
AMARILLAS SIN IGUAL.
LOS MONIZES DE CARREÑO
ESTAS ARMAS SON NOMBRADAS
POR ELLOS MUI BIEN GANADAS
EN BATALLAS QUE NO CUENTO
QUE FUERON BIEN AFAMADAS"

LA PLAZA ES FRAGMENTADA EN BANDAS CORRESPONDIENTES CADA UNA A UNA SECCIÓN TRANSVERSAL DISTINTA. EXISTEN 2 BANDAS DE CIRCULACIÓN Y 7 BANDAS DE ESPACIOS ESTANCIALES. EL NÚMERO 7 APARECE COMO REFERENCIA HISTÓRICO AL ORÍGEN FUNDACIONAL DEL CONCEJO. ES UNA UNIÓN DESCONTEXTUALIZADA CON EL PASADO.

2.3. EN EL TRATAMIENTO DEL ÁRBOLADO Y LAS PLANTACIONES DE LOS PARTERRES SE CUENTA CON EL CONTEXTO CANDASINO:

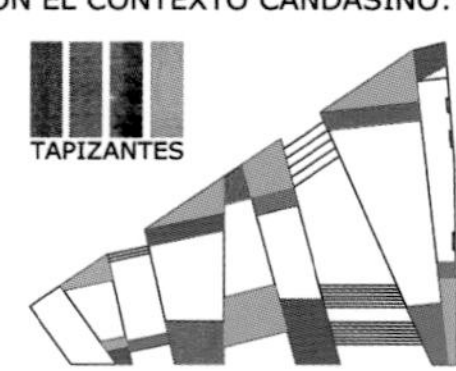

ARBOLADO:
-ARBOLADO EXISTENTE: SE DECIDE CONSERVAR LOS TRES MAGNOLIOS, (JÓVENES Y SANOS) UBICADOS EN LA PARTE INFERIOR DE LA PLAZA Y QUE SIRVEN COMO REMATE DE LA CALLE BRAULIO BUSTO Y COMO CIERRE VISUAL DEL MERCADILLO DE LOS SÁBADOS. SE CONSIDERA QUE ESTÁN YA ASUMIDOS POR LOS CANDASINOS DENTRO DEL PAISAJE URBANO DE LA PLAZA. ESTOS SERÁN INTEGRADOS EN LA REURBANIZACIÓN.
-ARBOLADO NUEVO: EN LA PARTE SUPERIOR DE LA PLAZA Y DIALOGANDO CON LOS TRES MAGNOLIOS, SE PLANTEAN TRES GRUPOS DE MANZANOS (MALUS COMMUNIS, EL MANZANO DE LA SIDRA). ESTE DIÁLOGO CIERRA UN FRAGMENTO DE LA PLAZA, DEJANDO LIBRE EL PERSEGUIDO EJE VISUAL TRANSVERSAL CON LA ESCALINATA DE CIERRE DEL PAISAJE URBANO. SE ELIGE EL MANZANO COMO REFERENCIA A LA CULTURA LOCAL Y COMO SÍMBOLO RECONOCIBLE DE LA PLAZA.

ESPECIES TAPIZANTES: SE DECIDE UTILIZAR CUATRO ESPECIES MUY COMUNES Y FACILMENTE RECONOCIBLES QUE HARÁN DE LA PLAZA UN LUGAR DE ESCALA DOMÉSTICA Y FAMILIAR, CASI COMO ESTAR EN EL JARDÍN DE UNA CASONA. ESTAS ESPECIES SON CÉSPED, ROMERO, ESPLIEGO Y ROSÁCEA. (VER MÁS EN CAPÍTULO VEGETACIÓN)

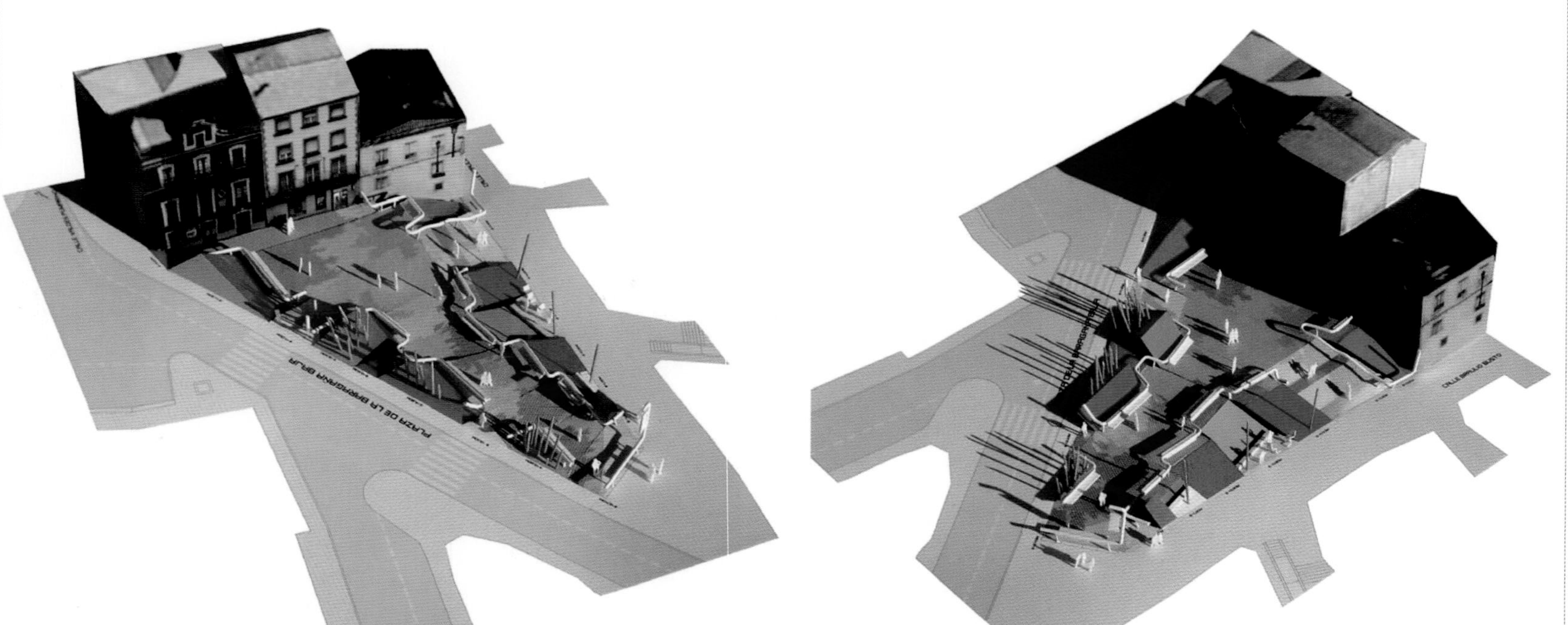

CONCURSO DE IDEAS PARA LA REURBANIZACION DE LA PLAZA DE LA BARAGANA

LEMA: SARDINOPS URBANA

3/ MATERIALIDAD DE LA PLAZA

3.1.- PROCESO DE GENERACIÓN: RESULTA UN PROCESO COMBINADO ENTRE CONDICIONANTES EXISTENTES Y DECISIONES PROYECTUALES. EL RESULTADO ES UNA SERIE DE RECORRIDOS IMPUESTOS POR EL ENTORNO URBANO QUE FUNCIONAN EN OPOSICIÓN A LOS LUGARES ESTANCIALES CREADOS.

3.2.- MATERIALIDAD: SE PROPONE UN PAVIMENTO CONTÍNUO (SARDINA URBANA) Y UNA SERIE DE PARTERRES Y ÁRBOLES QUE COMPONDRÁN EL PAISAJE URBANO.

3.3.- ELEMENTO "CONDUCTOR ESPACIAL": EXISTE UN ELEMENTO QUE UNIFICA TODOS LOS DISTINTOS ESPACIOS GENERADOS Y CONTIENE TODO EL PROGRAMA.

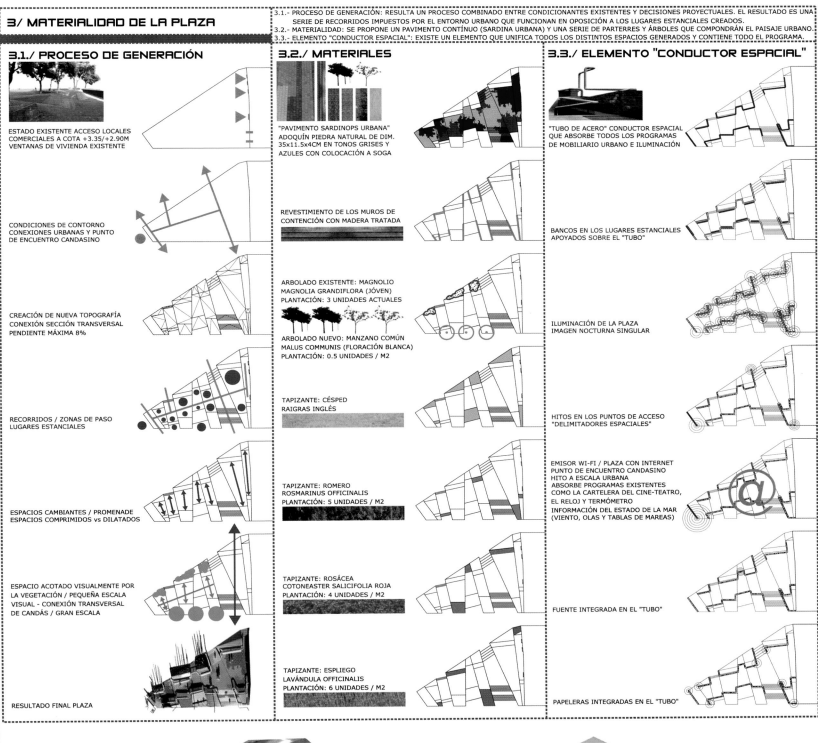

3.1./ PROCESO DE GENERACIÓN

ESTADO EXISTENTE ACCESO LOCALES COMERCIALES A COTA +3.35/+2.90M VENTANAS DE VIVIENDA EXISTENTE

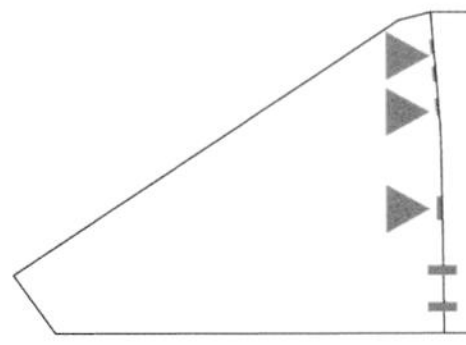

CONDICIONES DE CONTORNO CONEXIONES URBANAS Y PUNTO DE ENCUENTRO CANDASINO

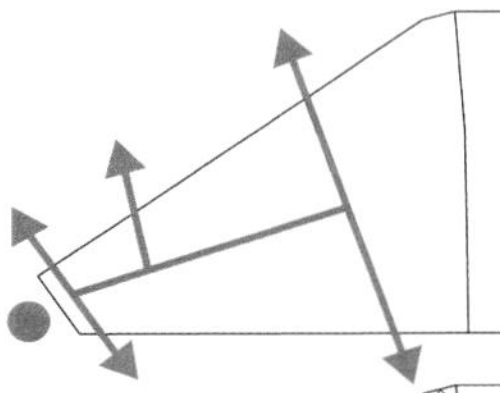

CREACIÓN DE NUEVA TOPOGRAFÍA CONEXIÓN SECCIÓN TRANSVERSAL PENDIENTE MÁXIMA 8%

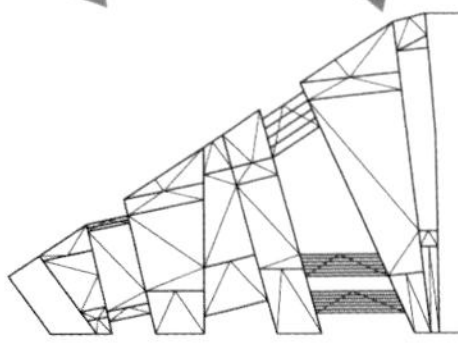

RECORRIDOS / ZONAS DE PASO LUGARES ESTANCIALES

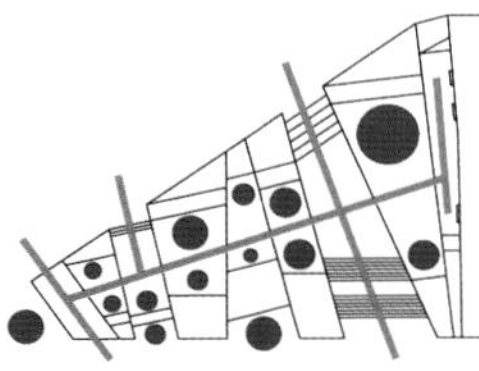

ESPACIOS CAMBIANTES / PROMENADE ESPACIOS COMPRIMIDOS vs DILATADOS

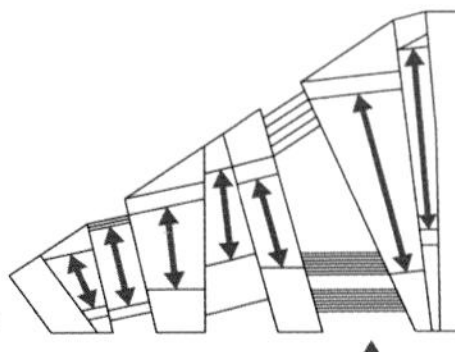

ESPACIO ACOTADO VISUALMENTE POR LA VEGETACIÓN / PEQUEÑA ESCALA VISUAL - CONEXIÓN TRANSVERSAL DE CANDÁS / GRAN ESCALA

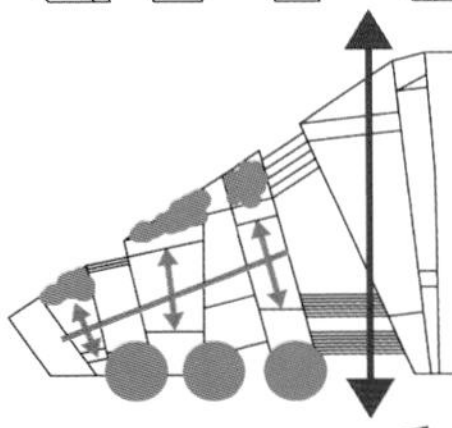

RESULTADO FINAL PLAZA

3.2./ MATERIALES

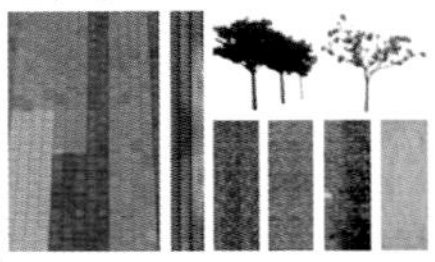

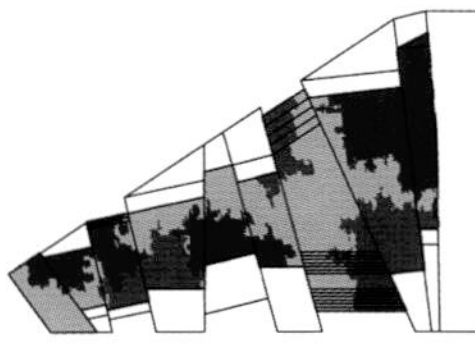

"PAVIMENTO SARDINOPS URBANA" ADOQUÍN PIEDRA NATURAL DE DIM. 35x11.5x4CM EN TONOS GRISES Y AZULES CON COLOCACIÓN A SOGA

REVESTIMIENTO DE LOS MUROS DE CONTENCIÓN CON MADERA TRATADA

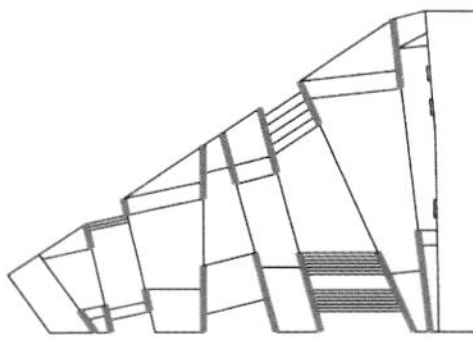

ARBOLADO EXISTENTE: MAGNOLIO MAGNOLIA GRANDIFLORA (JÓVEN) PLANTACIÓN: 3 UNIDADES ACTUALES

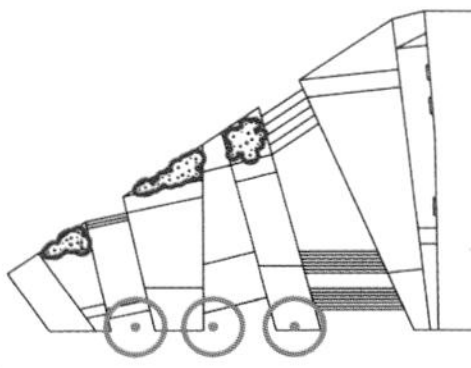

ARBOLADO NUEVO: MANZANO COMÚN MALUS COMMUNIS (FLORACIÓN BLANCA) PLANTACIÓN: 0.5 UNIDADES / M2

TAPIZANTE: CÉSPED RAIGRAS INGLÉS

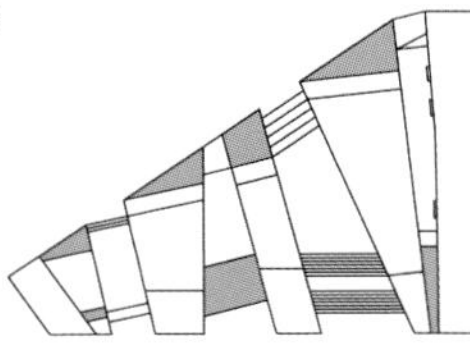

TAPIZANTE: ROMERO ROSMARINUS OFFICINALIS PLANTACIÓN: 5 UNIDADES / M2

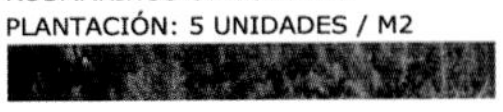

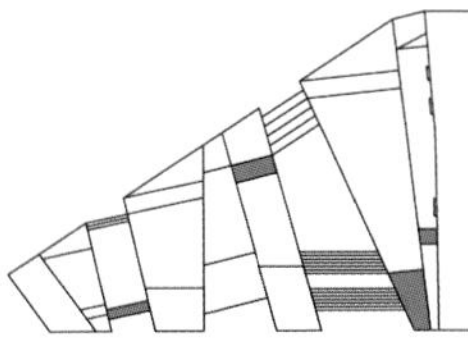

TAPIZANTE: ROSÁCEA COTONEASTER SALICIFOLIA ROJA PLANTACIÓN: 4 UNIDADES / M2

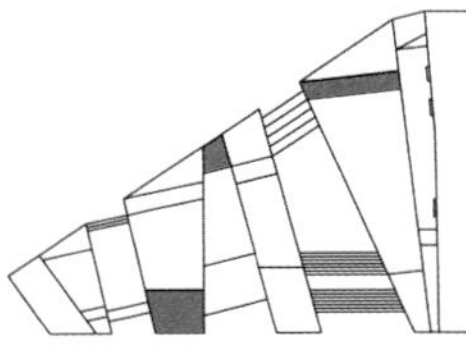

TAPIZANTE: ESPLIEGO LAVÁNDULA OFFICINALIS PLANTACIÓN: 6 UNIDADES / M2

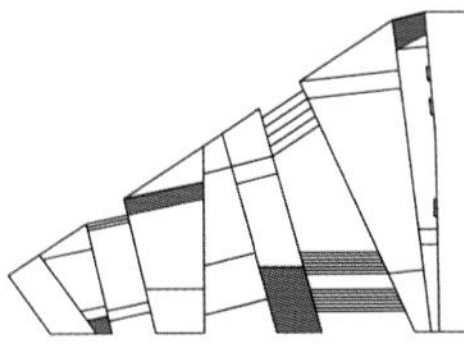

3.3./ ELEMENTO "CONDUCTOR ESPACIAL"

"TUBO DE ACERO" CONDUCTOR ESPACIAL QUE ABSORBE TODOS LOS PROGRAMAS DE MOBILIARIO URBANO E ILUMINACIÓN

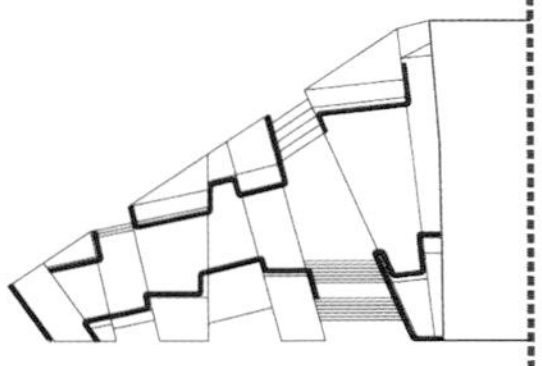

BANCOS EN LOS LUGARES ESTANCIALES APOYADOS SOBRE EL "TUBO"

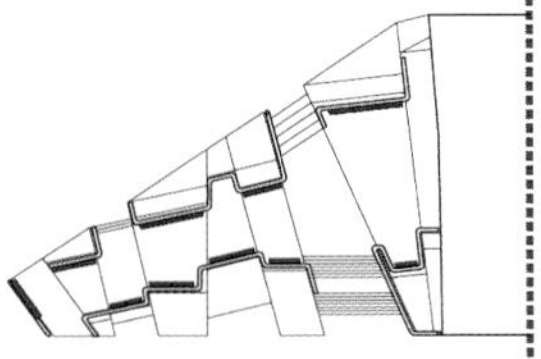

ILUMINACIÓN DE LA PLAZA IMAGEN NOCTURNA SINGULAR

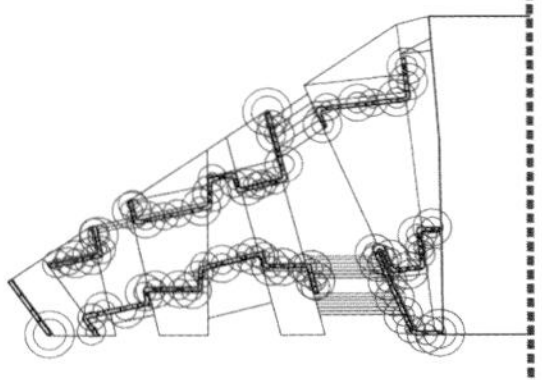

HITOS EN LOS PUNTOS DE ACCESO "DELIMITADORES ESPACIALES"

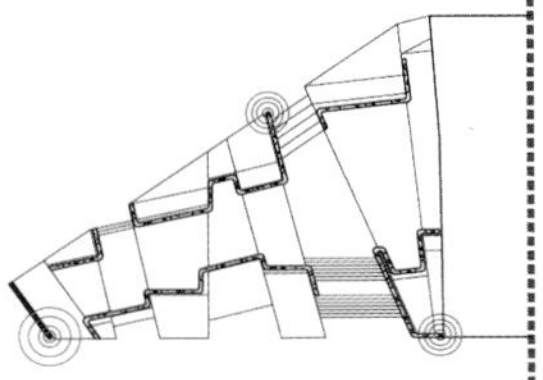

EMISOR WI-FI / PLAZA CON INTERNET PUNTO DE ENCUENTRO CANDASINO HITO A ESCALA URBANA ABSORBE PROGRAMAS EXISTENTES COMO LA CARTELERA DEL CINE-TEATRO, EL RELOJ Y TERMÓMETRO INFORMACIÓN DEL ESTADO DE LA MAR (VIENTO, OLAS Y TABLAS DE MAREAS)

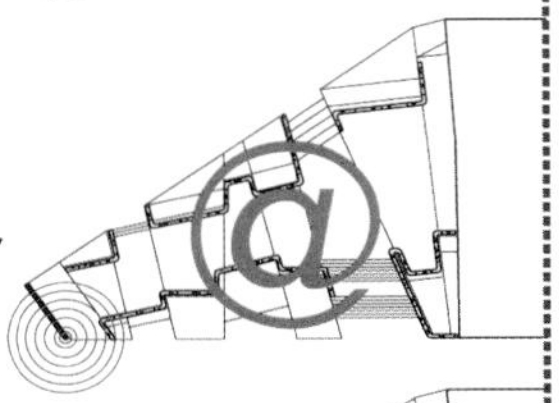

FUENTE INTEGRADA EN EL "TUBO"

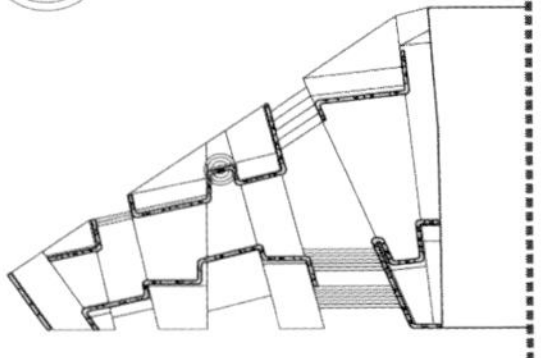

PAPELERAS INTEGRADAS EN EL "TUBO"

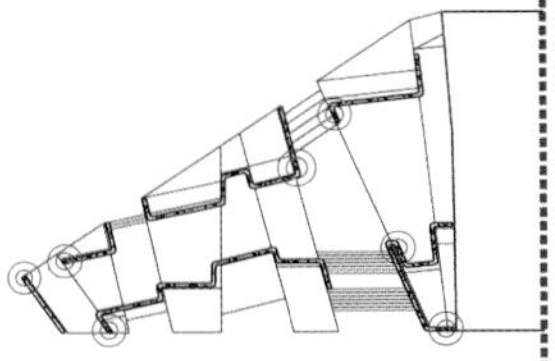

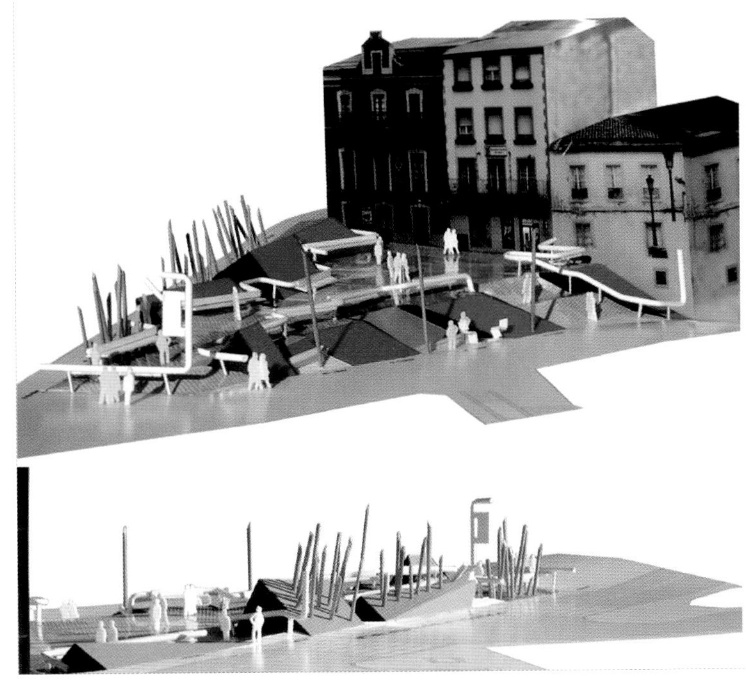

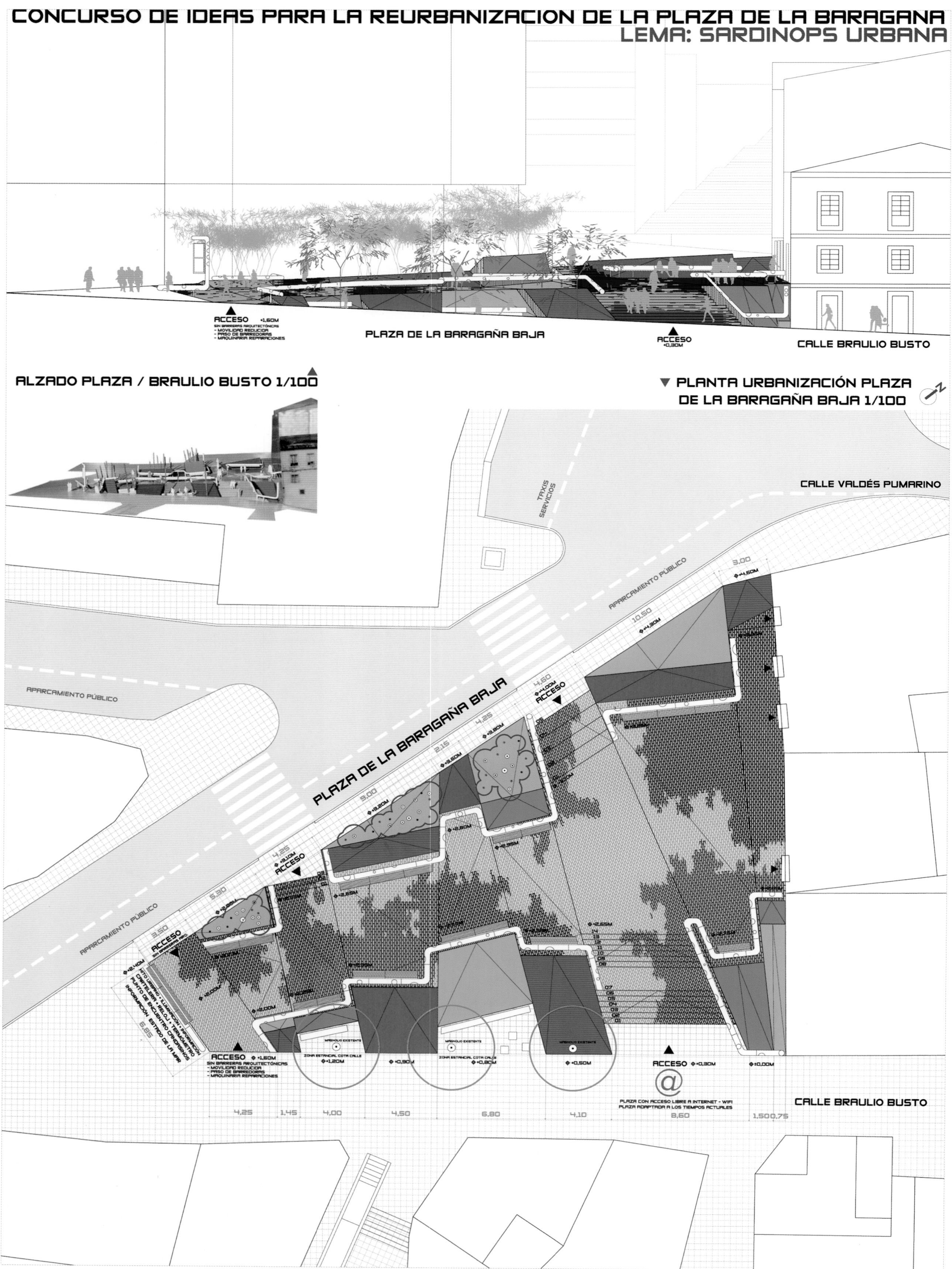
CONCURSO DE IDEAS PARA LA REURBANIZACION DE LA PLAZA DE LA BARAGANA
LEMA: SARDINOPS URBANA
ACCESO +1,60M
SIN BARRERAS ARQUITECTÓNICAS
- MOVILIDAD REDUCIDA
- PASO DE BARREDORAS
- MAQUINARIA REPARACIONES
PLAZA DE LA BARAGAÑA BAJA
ACCESO +0,30M
CALLE BRAULIO BUSTO
ALZADO PLAZA / BRAULIO BUSTO 1/100
PLANTA URBANIZACIÓN PLAZA DE LA BARAGAÑA BAJA 1/100
CALLE VALDÉS PUMARINO
TAXIS SERVICIOS
APARCAMIENTO PÚBLICO
PLAZA DE LA BARAGAÑA BAJA
ACCESO
MAGNOLIO EXISTENTE
ZONA ESTANCIAL COTA CALLE
ACCESO +1,60M
SIN BARRERAS ARQUITECTÓNICAS
- MOVILIDAD REDUCIDA
- PASO DE BARREDORAS
- MAQUINARIA REPARACIONES
ACCESO +0,30M
@
PLAZA CON ACCESO LIBRE A INTERNET - WIFI
PLAZA ADAPTADA A LOS TIEMPOS ACTUALES
CALLE BRAULIO BUSTO
4,25 1,45 4,00 4,50 6,80 4,10 8,60 1,50 0,75

CONCURSO DE IDEAS PARA LA REURBANIZACIÓN DE LA PLAZA DE LA BARAGANA

LEMA: SARDINOPS URBANA

06
03
05
01
04
02
SECC. TUBO E 1/10
01. TUBO DE ACERO Ø35CM e=5MM
02. SOPORTE DE PERFIL DE ACERO
03. PLETINAS INTERIORES DE REFUERZO
04. CONDUCCIÓN DE SERVICIOS
05. LUMINARIA PUNTUAL MÓDULO LED'S
06. PLETINA CIRCULAR ENGANCHE TRAMOS
REMATE DE PLAZA
01. PUNTO DE ENCUENTRO
02. BANCO / ESPERA
03. HITO A ESCALA URBANA
04. EMISOR INTERNET WIFI PLAZA ACCESO INTERNET
05. RELOJ
06. CARTELERA TEATRO / CINE
07. INFO. ESTADO DE LA MAR
7.1-TABLA DE MAREAS
7.2-OLAS Y VIENTO
08. TEMPERATURA Y HUMEDAD
ALZADO 1/50
13:45
CANDÁS

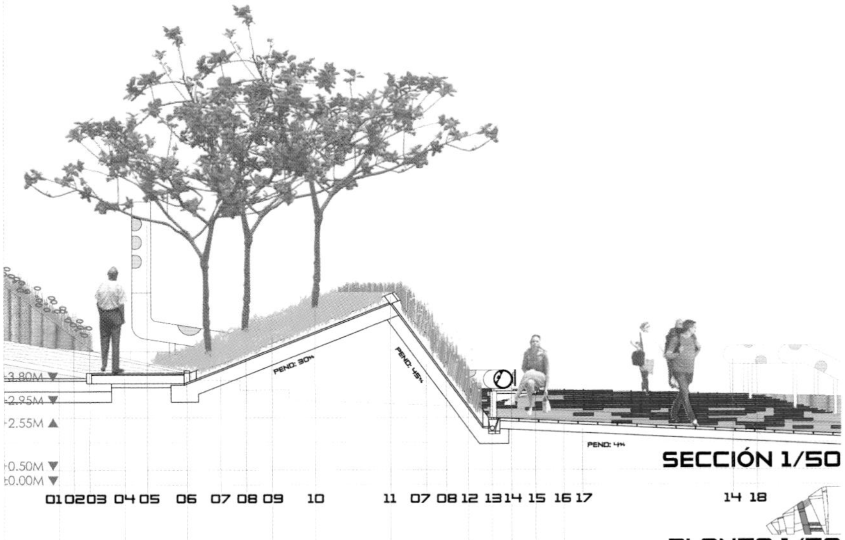

PEND: 30%
PEND: 45%
PEND: 4%
+3.80M
+2.95M
+2.55M
+0.50M
±0.00M
SECCIÓN 1/50
01 02 03 04 05 06 07 08 09 10 11 07 08 12 13 14 15 16 17 14 18

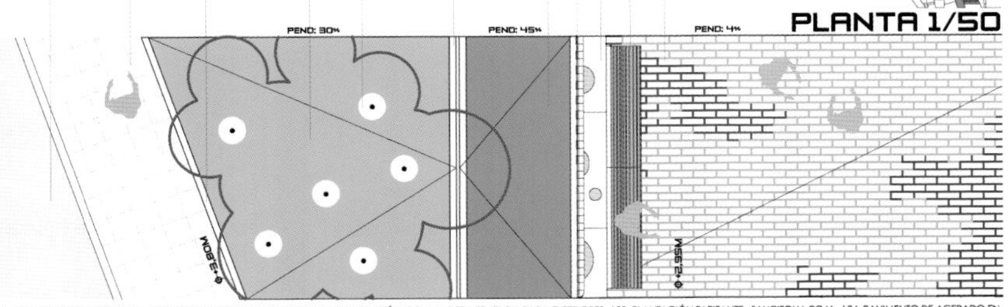

PLANTA 1/50
PEND: 30%
PEND: 45%
PEND: 4%
+3.80M
+2.55M

01. ASFALTADO VIAL EXISTENTE. / 02. REVESTIMIENTO DE LOS MUROS DE CONTENCIÓN CON MADERA TRATADA PARA EXTERIORES / 03. PLANTACIÓN TAPIZANTE : SALICIFOLIA ROJA / 04. PAVIMENTO DE ACERADO EN CONTINUIDAD CON EL ENTORNO / 05. ELEMENTO HITO CON LUMINARIA EN ACCESO NOROESTE / 06. PIEDRA DE BORDILLO EN PIEDRA NATURAL 12x16x10CM COMO REMATE INFERIOR / 07. SOLERA H.A. PEND.30% SOBRE TIERRA COMPACTADA SOBRE FIRME / 08. TIERRA VEGETAL + GEOTEXTIL / 09. PLANTACIÓN DE TAPIZANTES: CÉSPED RAIGRAS INGLÉS / 10. PLANTACIÓN ÁRBOLES: MANZANO COMÚN - MALUS COMMUNIS + FORMACIÓN DE ALCORQUE CON PLETINA METÁLICA / 11. REMATE SUPERIOR EN PIEDRA NATURAL 12x16x10CM / 12. PLANTACIÓN TAPIZANTES: ROMERO - ROAMANIRUS OFFICINALIS / 13. FORMACIÓN DE SUMIDERO LINEAL A BASE DE REJILLA DE FUNDICIÓN CONTINÚA A TUBO Ø 20 / 14. TUBO CONTÍNUO DE ACERO Ø35CM e=5MM / 15. BANCO DE MADERA INTEGRADO EN TUBO DE ACERO / 16. PAVIMENTO DE ADOQUINES DE PIEDRA NATURAL 35x11.5x4CM COLOCADO A SOGA EN TONOS GRISES Y AZULES - "SARDINOPS URBANA" / 17. BASE PARA EL ADOQUINADO DE ARENA DE MIGA + ARENA SELECCIONADA + RECEBADO DE JUNTAS CON ARENA CALIZA EN POLVO / 18. LUMINARIA PUNTUAL, A BASE DE MÓDULOS LED'S, INTEGRADA EN TUBO DE ACERO.

CATÁLOGO DE MOBILIARIO URBANO INTEGRADO EN EL "TUBO"

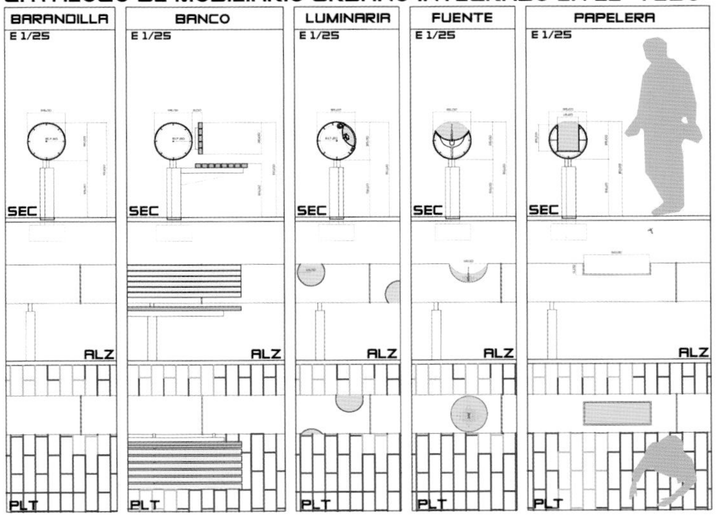

BARANDILLA
E 1/25
BANCO
E 1/25
LUMINARIA
E 1/25
FUENTE
E 1/25
PAPELERA
E 1/25
SEC
ALZ
PLT

4/ CRITERIOS DE SOSTENIBILIDAD

4.1.- CRITERIOS DE SOSTENIBILIDAD: SISTEMAS PASIVOS Y SISTEMAS ACTIVOS
4.2.- SISTEMAS PASIVOS: MANTENIMIENTO / SOLEAMIENTO / GESTIÓN DEL AGUA / VENTILACIÓN / VEGETACIÓN / CONDICIONES DE CONFORT
4.3.- SISTEMAS ACTIVOS: GESTIÓN ENERGÉTICA / GESTIÓN DEL AGUA (RIEGO)

4.1. / CRITERIO DE SOSTENIBILIDAD MIXTO:

EN EL PROYECTO SE DESARROLLAN EN PARALELO DOS CRITERIOS DE SOSTENIBILIDAD Y EFICIENCIA ENERGÉTICA:

-EL PRIMERO DE ELLOS RESPONDE A LAS MEDIDAS CLIMÁTICAS PASIVAS, QUE SON LAS DECISIONES PROYECTUALES Y DE DISEÑO QUE MEJORAN LA GESTIÓN ENERGÉTICA PARA CONSEGUIR LA SENSACIÓN DE CONFORT. ESTAS MEDIDAS SE PUEDEN CONSIDERAR COMO LOW-TECH, SON TRADICIONALES Y NO SUPONEN UN GASTO EXTRA. NO ES OTRA COSA QUE TENER UN POCO DE SENTIDO COMÚN EN ALGUNAS DECISIONES. ESTAS MEDIDAS AFECTAN AL MANTENIMIENTO, AL SOLEAMIENTO , A LA GESTIÓN DEL AGUA (DRENAJE DE PLUVIALES), A LA VENTILACIÓN Y LOS BARRIDOS DE AIRE, A LA VEGETACIÓN Y A LAS CONDICIONES DE CONFORT (HUMEDAD DEL AMBIENTE).

-EL SEGUNDO PAQUETE DE MEDIDAS RESPONDE A LAS MEDIDAS CLIMÁTICAS ACTIVAS, QUE SON LA INSTALACIÓN DE MECANISMOS RELACIONADOS CON EL APROVECHAMIENTO ENERGÉTICO Y LA GESTIÓN DEL AGUA. ESTAS INSTALACIONES SON ECONÓMICAMENTE VIABLES. ESTAS MEDIDAS AFECTAN PRINCIPALMENTE A LA GESTIÓN ENERGÉTICA Y DEL AGUA (PLUVIALES - RIEGO).

4.2. / SISTEMAS PASIVOS:

01/ MANTENIMIENTO:
-UTILIZACIÓN DE MATERIALES DE FÁCIL REPOSICIÓN Y CONSERVACIÓN.
-FÁCIL ACCESO PARA BARREDORAS Y MAQUINARIA DE MANTENIMIENTO.
-SISTEMA DE ILUMINACIÓN DE BAJO CONSUMO.

02/ SOLEAMIENTO:
-LA PLAZA ACTUAL POR SU ORIENTACIÓN, ENTORNO Y TIPO DE ARBOLADO TIENE UN CORRECTO CICLO DE SOLEAMIENTO, EL OBJETIVO ES NO ALTERARLO CON LA NUEVA REURBANIZACIÓN (Y EL NUEVO ARBOLADO).

03/ GESTIÓN DEL AGUA:
-SISTEMA DE DRENAJE SOSTENIBLE A BASE DE PAVIMENTOS PERMEABLES. ÁREAS PLANTACIÓN DE TAPIZANTES Y PAVIMENTACIÓN CON ADOQUINADO CON LAS JUNTAS DE ÁRIDO QUE PERMITE EL PASO DEL AGUA.

04/ VEGETACIÓN:
-SE GARANTIZA EL COMPORTAMIENTO CLIMÁTICO E HÍDRICO DE LAS ESPECIES SELECCIONADAS POR SER ESPECIES AUTÓCTONAS.

05/ CONDICIONES DE CONFORT / HUMEDAD:
-LAS TAPIZANTES ACTÚAN COMO REGULADORES DE LA HUMEDAD.

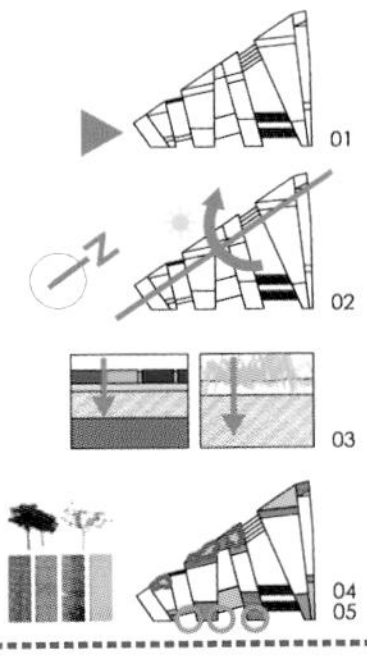

01
02
03
04
05

4.3. / SISTEMAS ACTIVOS:

01/ GESTIÓN ENERGÉTICA:
-LA PLAZA NO TIENE UN GRAN GASTO ENERGÉTICO, PERO LLEVANDO A CABO UNA ACTUACIÓN SOSTENIBLE EJEMPLAR EN ESTA MATERIA SE PUEDE CREAR CONCIENCIA . SE INSTALAN PANELES FOTOVOLTAICOS INTEGRADOS EN EL TUBO-BARANDILLA, EL EQUIVALENTE A ESA ENERGÍA CAPTURADA SERÍA EL GASTO DE ILUMIINACIÓN Y RIEGO.

02/ GESTIÓN DEL AGUA:
-SE TRATA DE APROVECHAR EL AGUA DE ESCORRENTÍA (ABUNDANTE DEBIDO A LA OROGRAFÍA DE CANDÁS) Y CONDUCIRLA POR LA RED DE DRENAJE HASTA UN ALJIBE ACUMULADOR SITUADO BAJO LA PLAZA, QUE JUNTO CON UN GRUPO DE PRESIÓN, SIRVE PARA EL SISTEMA DE RIEGO DE LAS ZONAS VERDES-ARBOLADO DE LA PLAZA.

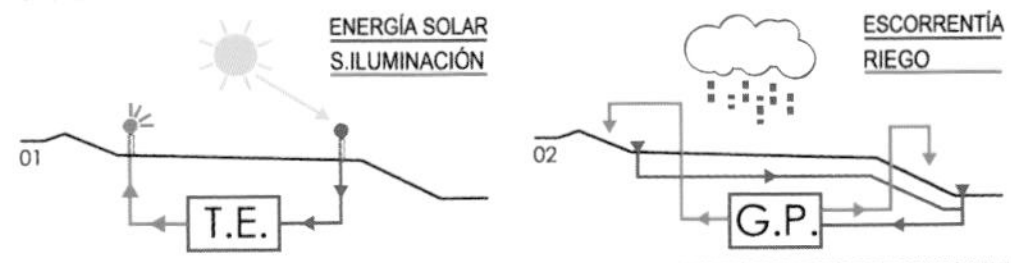

ENERGÍA SOLAR
S.ILUMINACIÓN
01
T.E.
ESCORRENTÍA
RIEGO
02
G.P.

AVANCE DE PRESUPUESTO

RESUMEN DE PRESUPUESTO POR CAPÍTULOS:

URBANIZACIÓN Y OBRA CIVIL	
ACTUACIONES PREVIAS	12.900,00 €
DEMOLICIONES / TIERRAS	18.900,00 €
ACONDICIONAMIENTO TERRENO	16.300,00 €
ESTRUCTURAS / CONTENCIÓN	25.500,00 €
IMPERMEABILIZACIONES	09.400,00 €
REVESTIMIENTOS	11.200,00 €
PAVIMENTACIÓN	37.500,00 €
INSTALACIONES	
SANEAMIENTO Y DRENAJE	08.000,00 €
RED AGUA Y RIEGO	10.700,00 €
INSTALACIÓN ELÉCTRICA	30.100,00 €
ALUMBRADO PÚBLICO	11.400,00 €
FUENTES / BEBEDEROS	03.200,00 €
TELECOMUNICACIONES	10.500,00 €
JARDINERÍA	
LABORES PREPARATORIAS	01.600,00 €
FORMACIÓN ARBOLADO / TAPIZANTES	04.800,00 €
MOBILIARIO URBANO	
MOBILIARIO URBANO	32.000,00 €
EQUIPAMIENTO URBANO	35.000,00 €
SEGURIDAD Y SALUD	15.000,00 €
CONTROL DE CALIDAD	06.000,00 €
TOTAL P.E.M	
PRESUPUESTO EJECUCIÓN MATERIAL	300.000,00 €

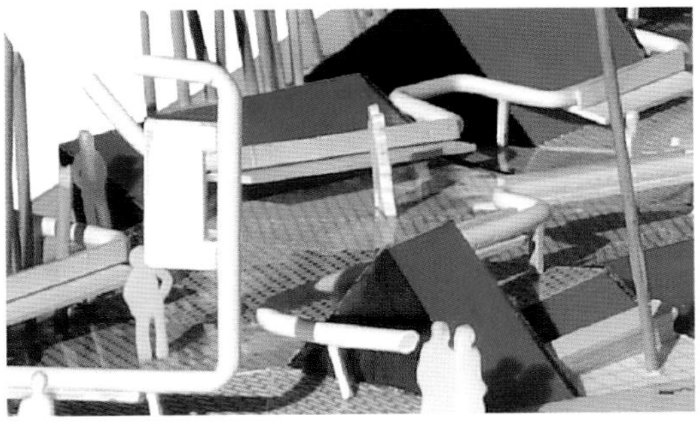

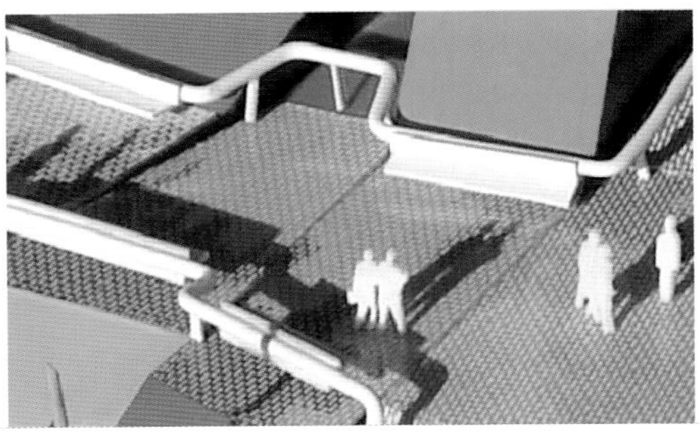

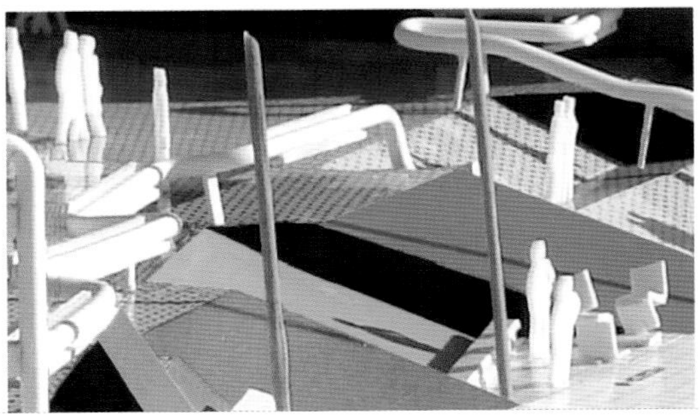

150

SHB Company Building | *franz zt gmbh*

Function : Offices and Laboratories
Competition : 2011
Location : Styria, Austria
Collaboration : Anna Gruber

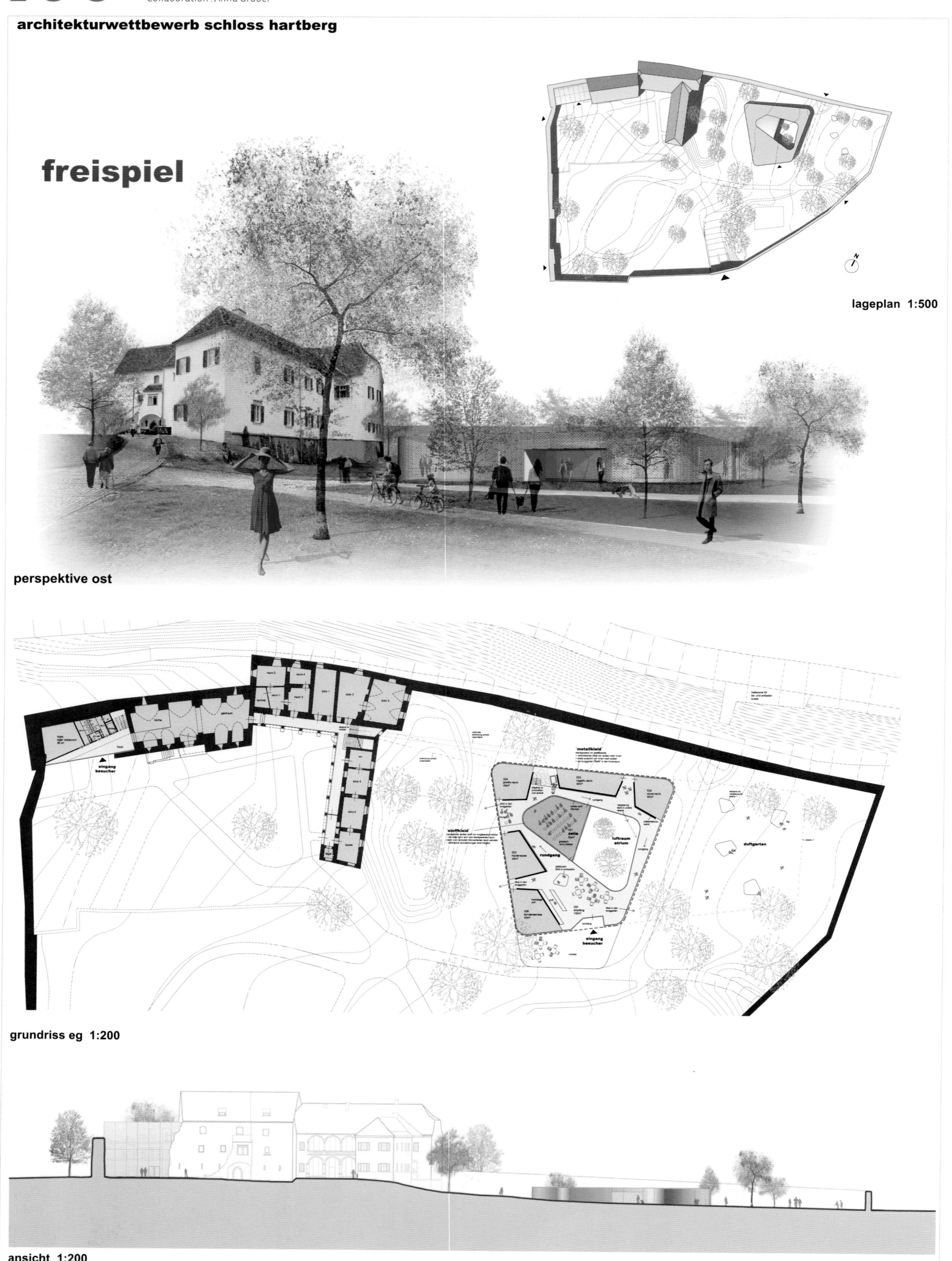

architekturwettbewerb schloss hartberg

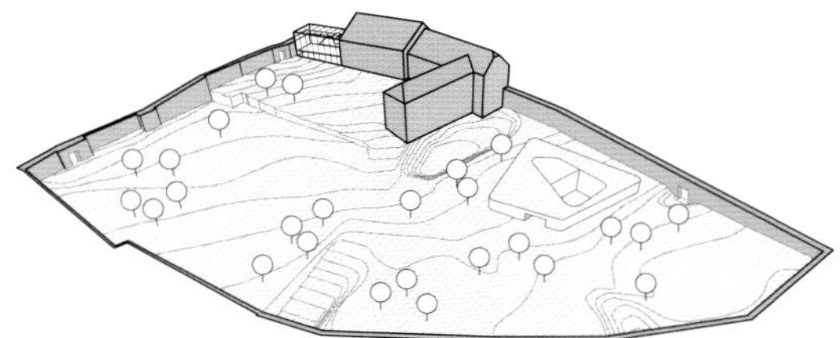

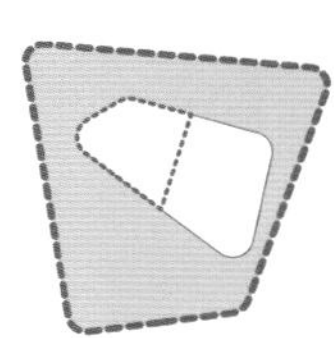

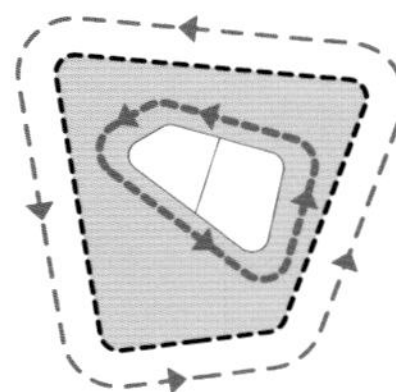

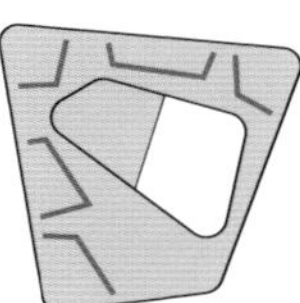

burgarten

der zubau west füllt die historische lücke mit einem transparenten körper. das skulpturale innenleben in sichtbeton setzt sich deutlich von den umfassenden mauern ab.

der zubau ost fügt sich als eigenständiger, flacher baukörper im burggarten ein. er ist so geformt und positioniert, daß ein freispielen von der historischen substanz möglich ist.

filter

ein "metallkleid" umhüllt das gebäude und weckt interesse. der filter zwischen burggarten und innenräumen ermöglicht unterschiedliche raumspannungen.

ein "stoffkleid" umhüllt die zelle im herzen des gebäudes. beweglicher textiler stoff an den wänden und der decke schafft maximale tranparenz oder auch absolute dunkelheit.

rundgang

fließende bewegungen innerhalb und ausserhalb des gebäudes. der rundgang sowohl im inneren als auch außen im burggarten formt das gebäude.

die besucher werden geleitet. die besichtigung der fa. rigana erfolgt direkt im inneren rundgang oder indirekt vom äusseren rundgang durch die verschleierte fassade

großraum

im erdgeschoß sitzt zentral die zelle mit dem anschließenden luftraum des atriums. es entsteht ein großraum, der langfristig frei bespielbar bleibt.

um diese zentrale mitte reihen sich die einzelnen funktionseinheiten. diese sind individuell formbar und füllen den raum wie große möbelstücke

perspektive zubau west

perspektive innenraum

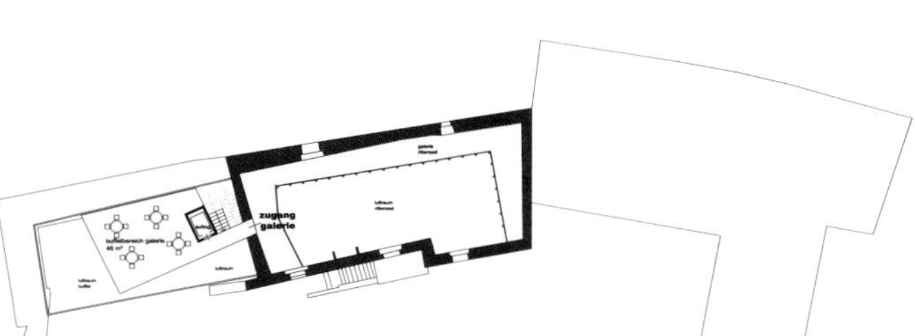

grundriss og2 1:200

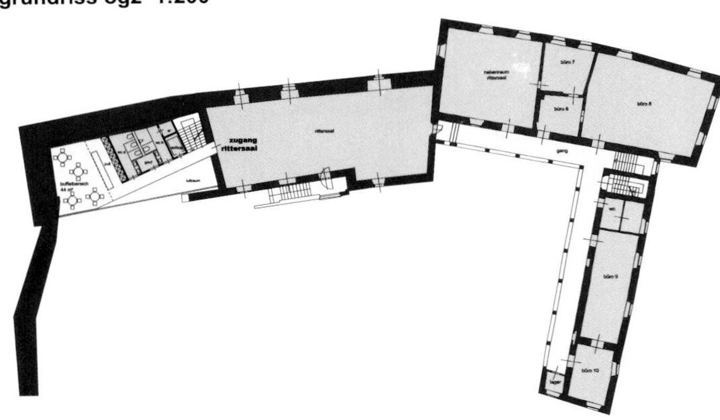

grundriss og1 1:200

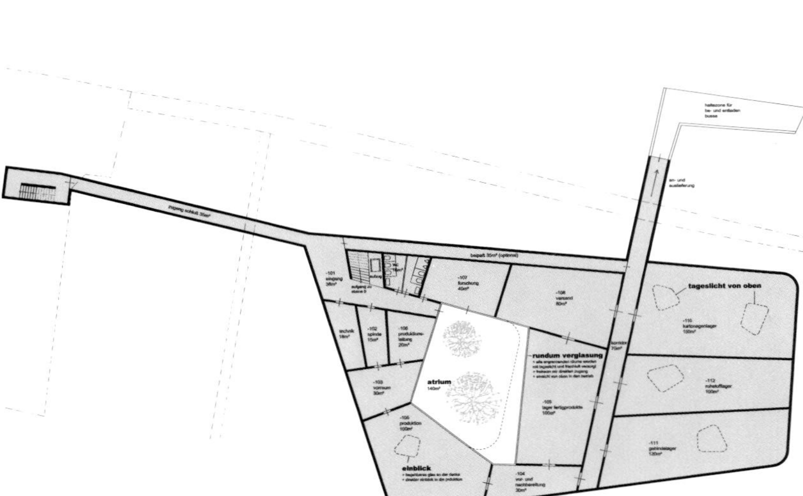

grundriss ug 1:200

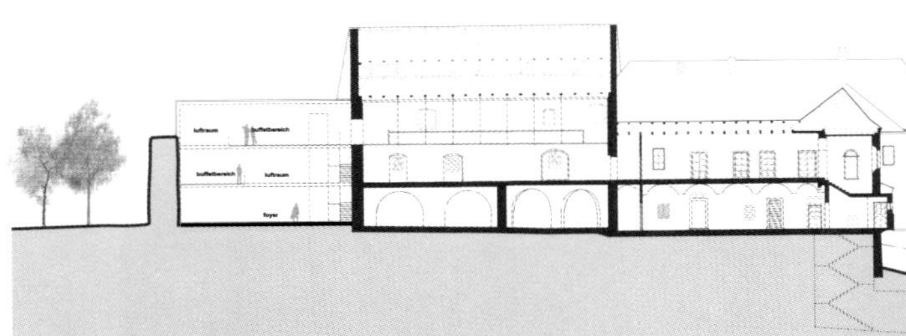

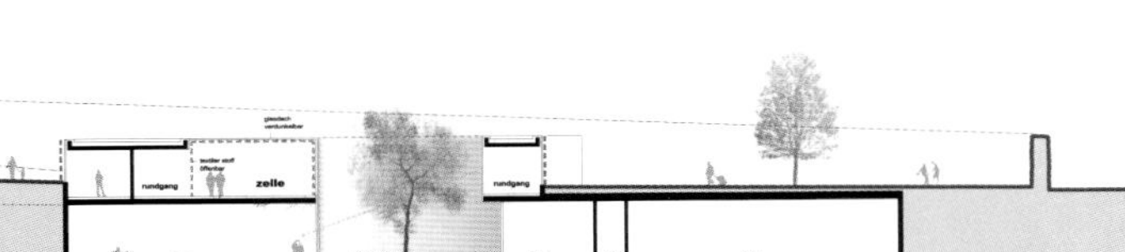

schnitt 1:200

151

City Municipality Ljubljana | *OFIS arhitekti*

Navigation : City Municipality Ljubljana, Slovenia
Location : Ljubljana, Slovenia
Type : Offices with Public Program
Client : City Municipality Ljubljana

Project Leaders : Rok Oman, Spela Videcnik
Project Team : Andrej Gregoric, Janez Martincic, Magdalena Lacka, Katja Aljaz

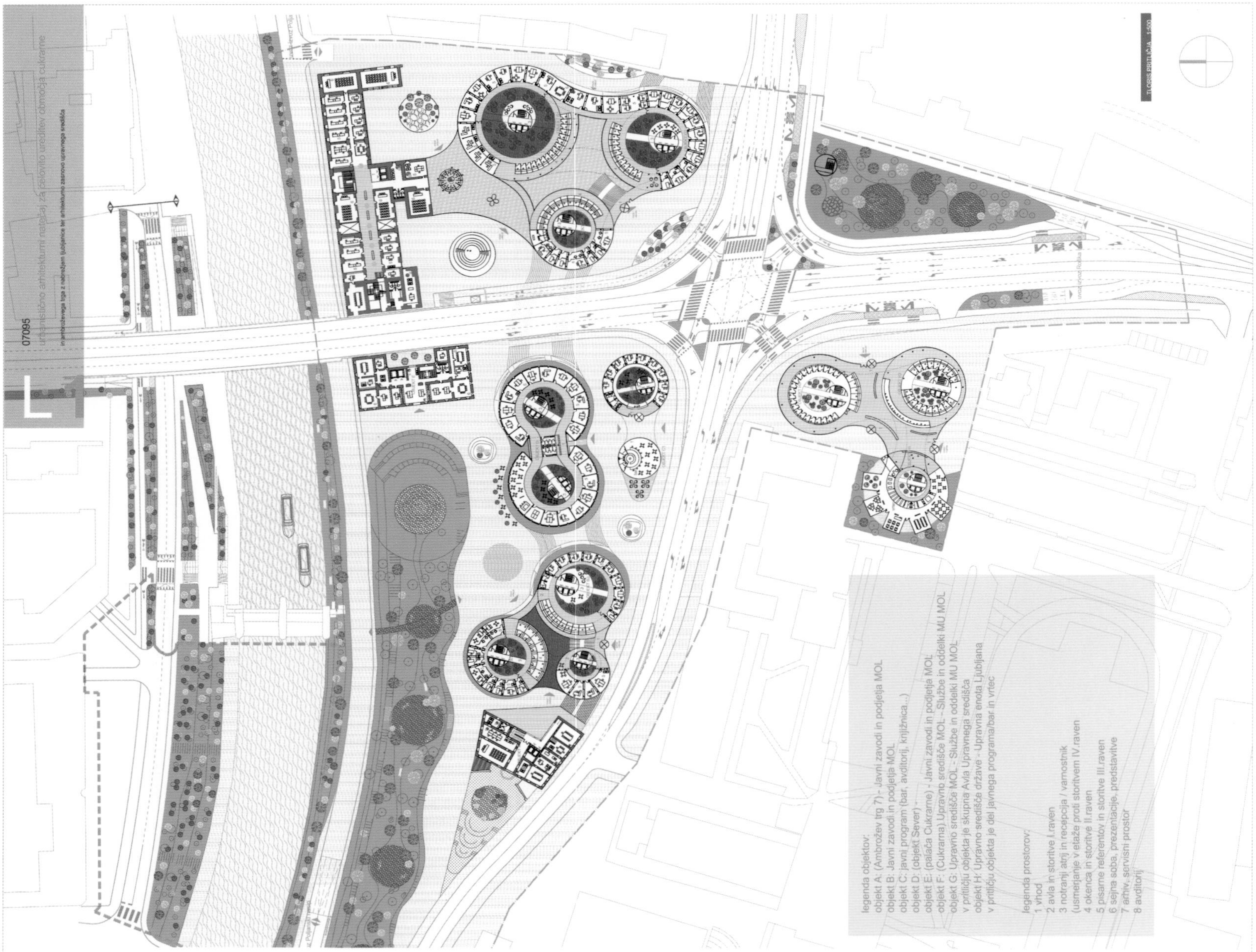

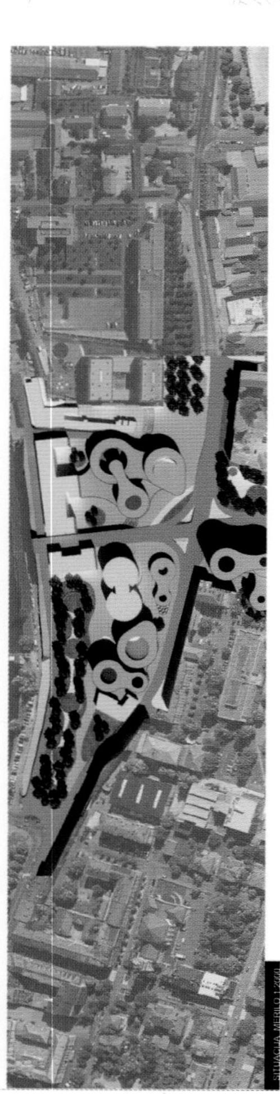

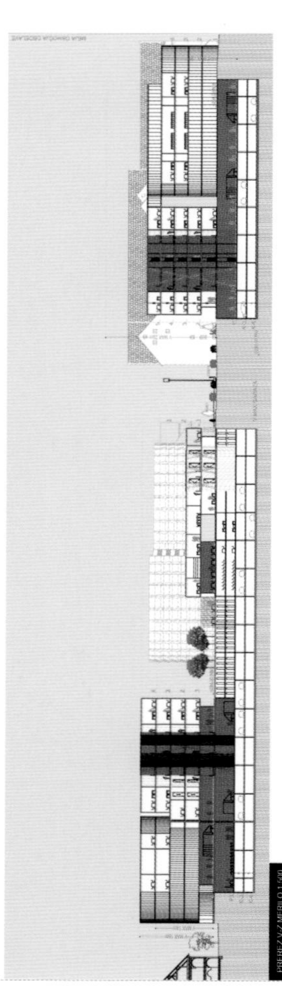

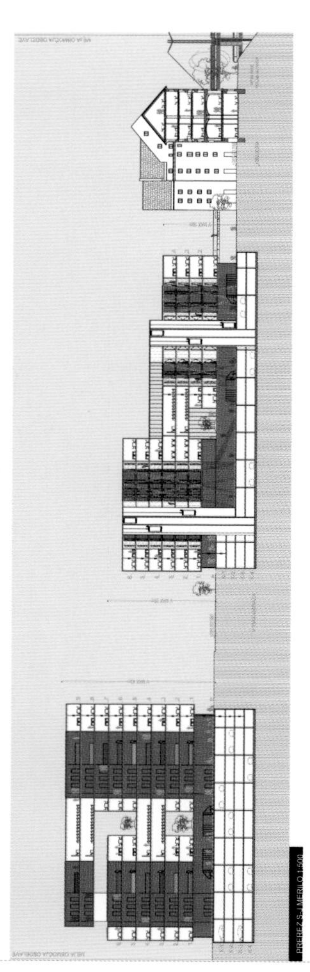

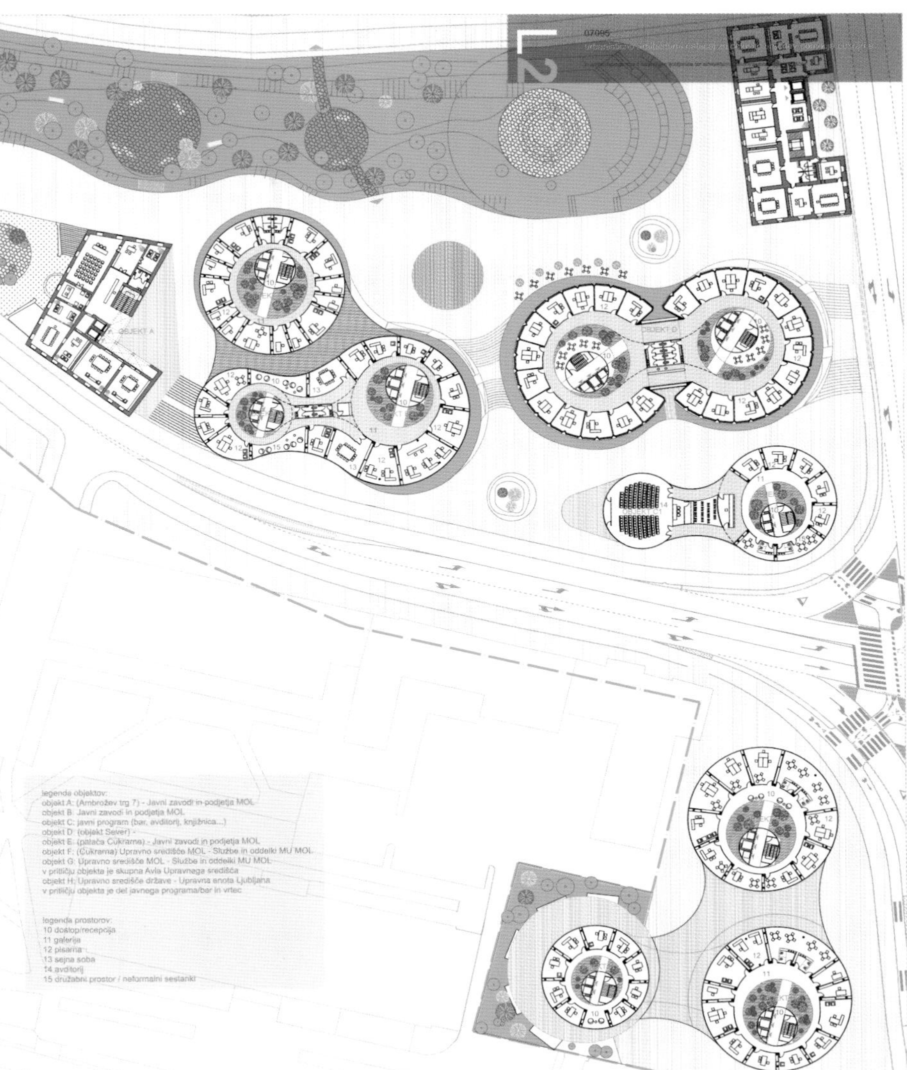
legenda objektov:
objekt A: (Ambrožev trg 7) - Javni zavodi in podjetja MOL
objekt B: Javni zavodi in podjetja MOL
objekt C: javni program (bar, avditorij, knjižnica...)
objekt D: (objekt Sever) -
objekt E: (palača Cukrarna) - Javni zavodi in podjetja MOL
objekt F: (Cukrarna) Upravno središče MOL - Službe in oddelki MU MOL
objekt G: Upravno središče MOL - Službe in oddelki MU MOL
v pritličju objekta je skupna Avla Upravnega središča
objekt H: Upravno središče države - Upravna enota Ljubljana
v pritličju objekta je del javnega programa/bar in vrtec
legenda prostorov:
10 dostop/recepcija
11 galerija
12 pisarna
13 sejna soba
14 avditorij
15 družabni prostor / neformalni sestanki

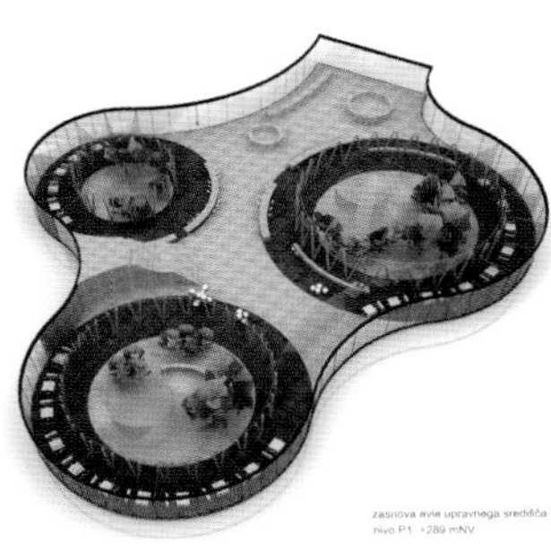

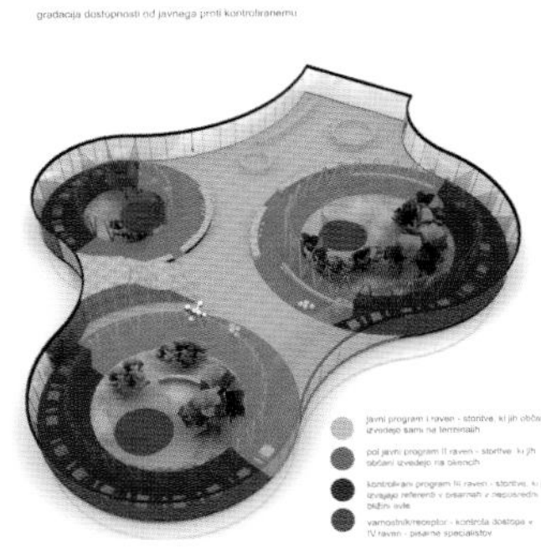

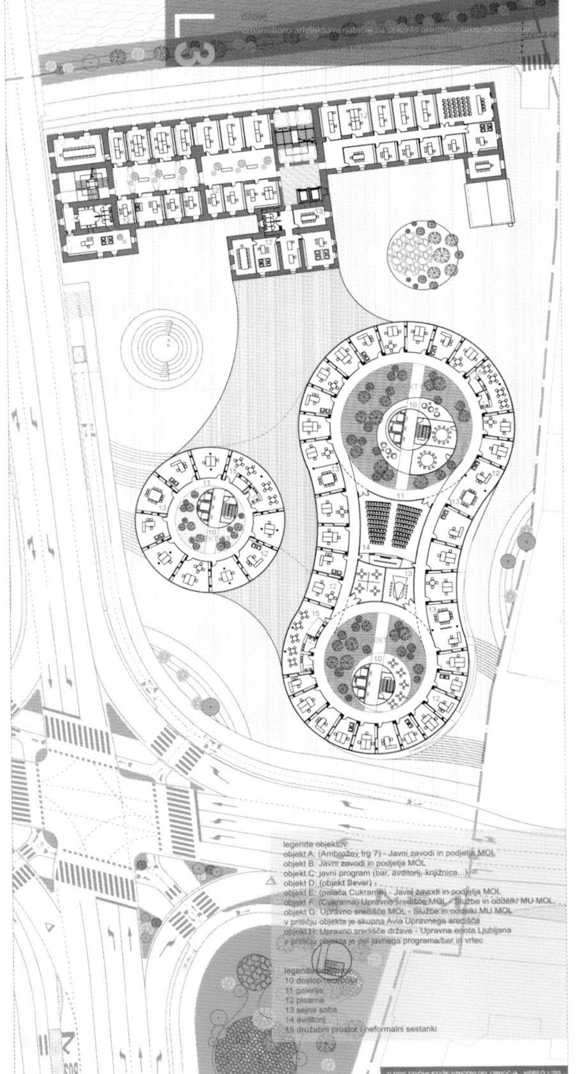

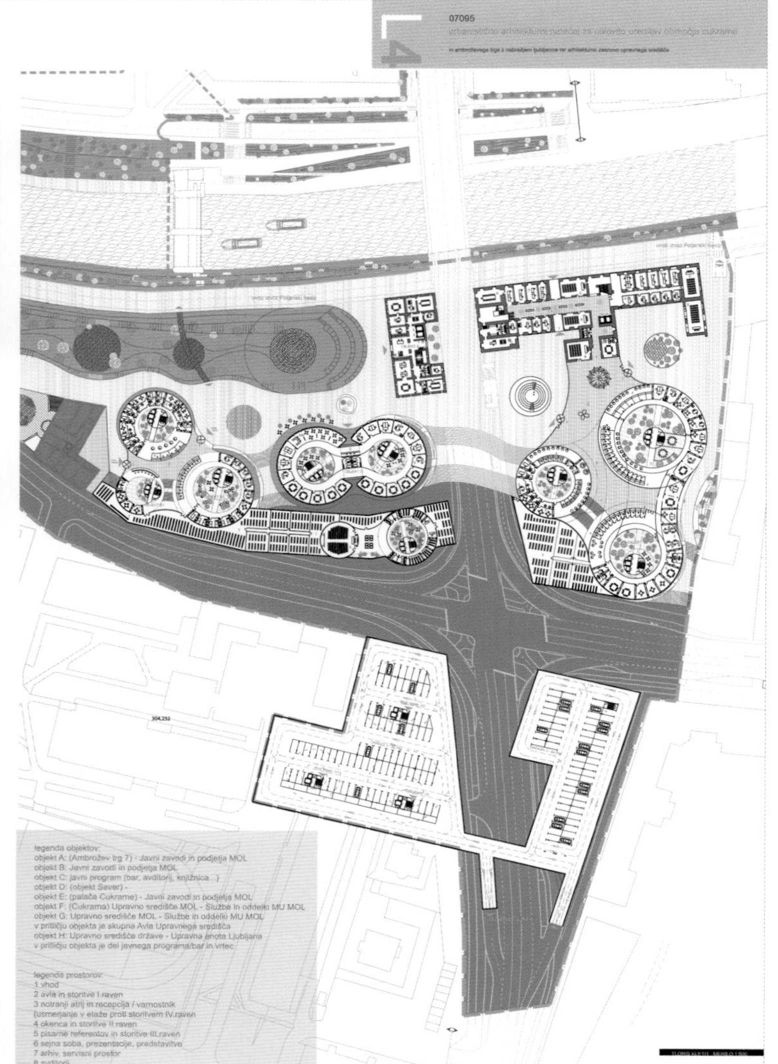
07095
urbanistično arhitekturni natečaj za celovito ureditev območja cukrarne
legenda objektov:
objekt A: (Ambrožev trg 7) - Javni zavodi in podjetja MOL
objekt B: Javni zavodi in podjetja MOL
objekt C: javni program (bar, avditorij, knjižnica...)
objekt D: (objekt Sever) -
objekt E: (palača Cukrarne) - Javni zavodi in podjetja MOL
objekt F: (Cukrarna) Upravno središče MOL - Službe in oddelki MU MOL
objekt G: Upravno središče MOL - Službe in oddelki MU MOL
v pritličju objekta je skupna Avla Upravnega središča
objekt H: Upravno središče države - Upravna enota Ljubljana
v pritličju objekta je del javnega programa/bar in vrtec
legenda prostorov:
1 vhod
2 avla in storitve I.raven
3 notranji atrij in recepcija / varnostnik
(usmerjanje v etaže proti storitvam IV.raven
4 okenca in storitve II raven
5 pisarne referentov in storitve III.raven
6 sejna soba, prezentacije, predstavitve
7 arhiv, servisni prostor
8 avditorij

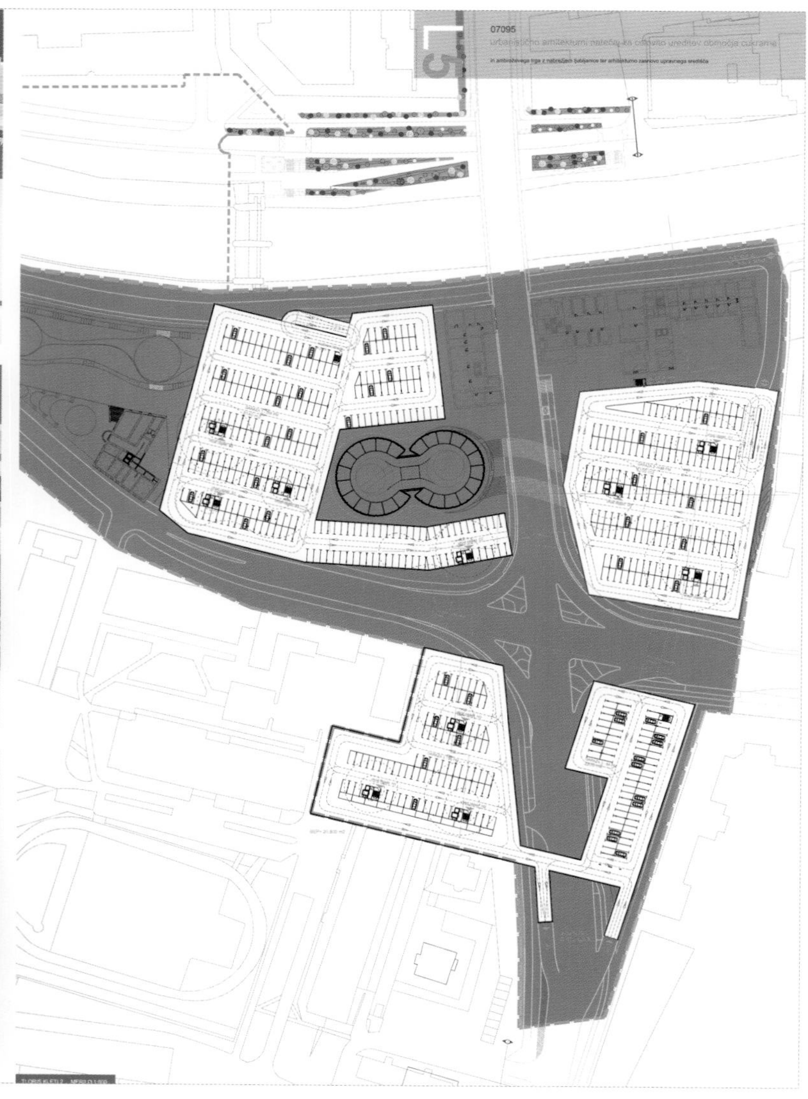
07095

L6

07095

urbanistično arhitekturni natečaj za celovito ureditev območja cukrarne

in ambroževega trga z nabrežjem ljubljanice ter arhitekturno zasnovo upravnega središča

AVLA UPRAVNEGA SREDIŠČA

POGLED NA DOSTOP V AVLO

POGLED NA JAVNI DEL - AVLA

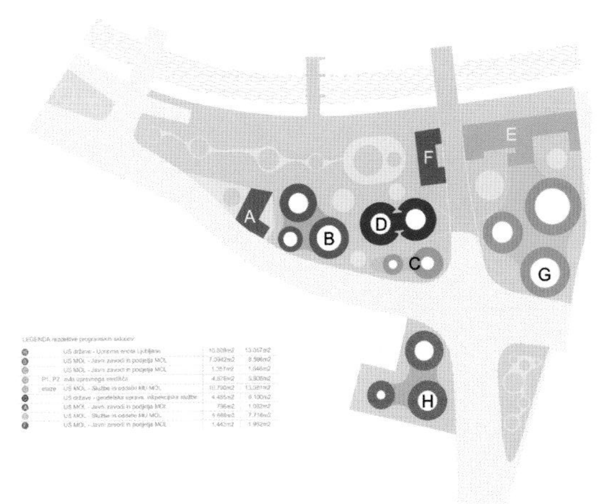

RAZPOREDITVE PROGRAMOV PO OBJEKTIH

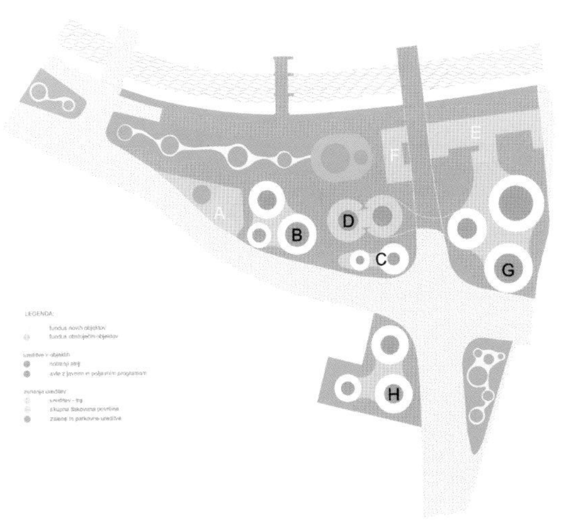

ZUNANJA UREDITEV IN NOTRANJI ATRIJ

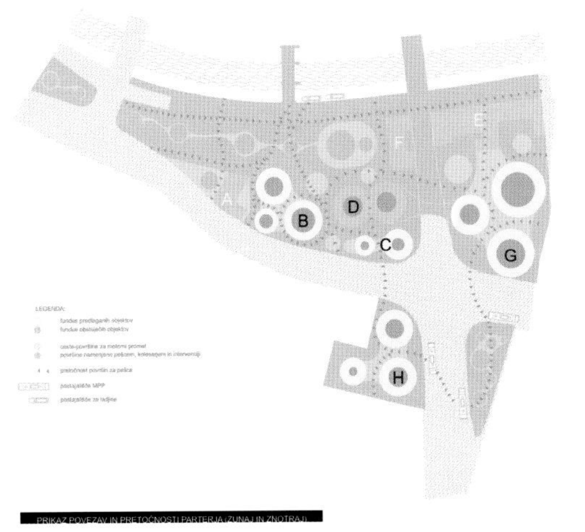

PRIKAZ POVEZAV IN PRETOČNOSTI PARTERJA (ZUNAJ IN ZNOTRAJ)

zasnova avle upravnega središča

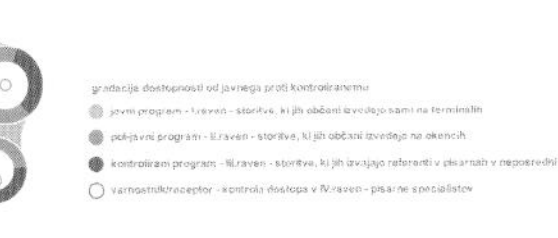

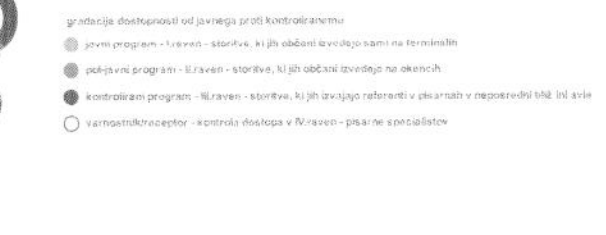

DIAGRAM KOMBINIRANJA ODDELKOV IN SLUŽB TER VZPOSTAVLJANJE SKUPNIH PROGRAMOV

2 / 1 3 →	pisarne oddelka 1,2 in 3 nimajo skupnega programa in medsebojno ne potrebujejo direktnih povezav
1U2U3 →	pisarne oddelka 1,2 in 3 potrebujejo skupni program (sejna soba, arhiv, prezentacijska soba, čajna kuhinja) in medsebojne direktne povezave, v etaži se vzpostavi most
1U3 →	pisarne oddelka 1 in 3 potrebujejo skupni program (sejna soba, arhiv, prezentacijska soba, čajna kuhinja) in medsebojne direktne povezave, v etaži se vzpostavi most
1U2 →	pisarne oddelka 1 in 2 potrebujejo skupni program (sejna soba, arhiv, prezentacijska soba, čajna kuhinja) in medsebojne direktne povezave, v etaži se vzpostavi most
2U3 →	pisarne oddelka 2 in 3 potrebujejo skupni program (sejna soba, arhiv, prezentacijska soba, čajna kuhinja) in medsebojne direktne povezave, v etaži se vzpostavi most

GRAFIČNI PRIKAZ NETO KVADRATUR PO POSAMEZNIH OBJEKTIH IN ETAŽAH:

	US MOL - službe in oddelki MU MOL		US MOL - Javni zavodi in podjetja MOL			US države - UE Ljubljana	Geodetska uprava in inšpekcijske službe	US pokrajine
objekt:	G	E	B	A	F	H	D	C
P1	3.011m2		1.285m2					517m2
P2	1.865m2	1.417m2	1.833m2	398m2	481m2	1.776m2	897m2	373m2
N.1	2.040m2	1.417m2	1.160m2	398m2	481m2	1.140m2	897m2	467m2
N.2	2.040m2	1.417m2	1.160m2		481m2	1.140m2	897m2	
N.3	2.191m2	1.417m2	1.139m2			1.452m2	897m2	
N.4	2.191m2		1.317m2			1.452m2	897m2	
N.5	1.508m2					904m2		
N.6	820m2					904m2		
N.7						483m2		
N.8						779m2		
N.9						779m2		
Σ	15.666m2	5.668m2	7.094m2	796m2	1.443m2	10.809m2	4.485m2	1.357m2
SUMMA NOVI OBJEKTI: 34.928m2								
SUMMA OBSTOJEČI OBJEKTI: 12.392m2								
SUMMA OBJEKTI: 47.318m2								

Avla US

152 TsuTsuTsu-Village | *Takashi Nishibori*

期間限定
災害避難
短期滞在
つつつ村

期間限定
災害避難
短期滞在
つつつ村

The aim of TsuTsuTsu-village:
Create individual space and shared space at the same time.
Connect villagers and local people in the area without asking anyone who comes.
Share the space with students, teachers and staff of the schools that are occupied.

Site criteria of TsuTsuTsu-village:
The grounds and gymnasiums of elementary and junior-high school are often used as shelter for disasters in Japan.
As for the proposal, we use elementary or junior-high school grounds, which are approximately 6000sqm, and, are able to include a 200m running truck.
We locate a plaza for a festival stage and bonfire in the center of the ground, and, arrange the shelters' -tent units- around it.

期間限定
災害避難
短期滞在
つつつ村
つどう・つながる・つぎへ

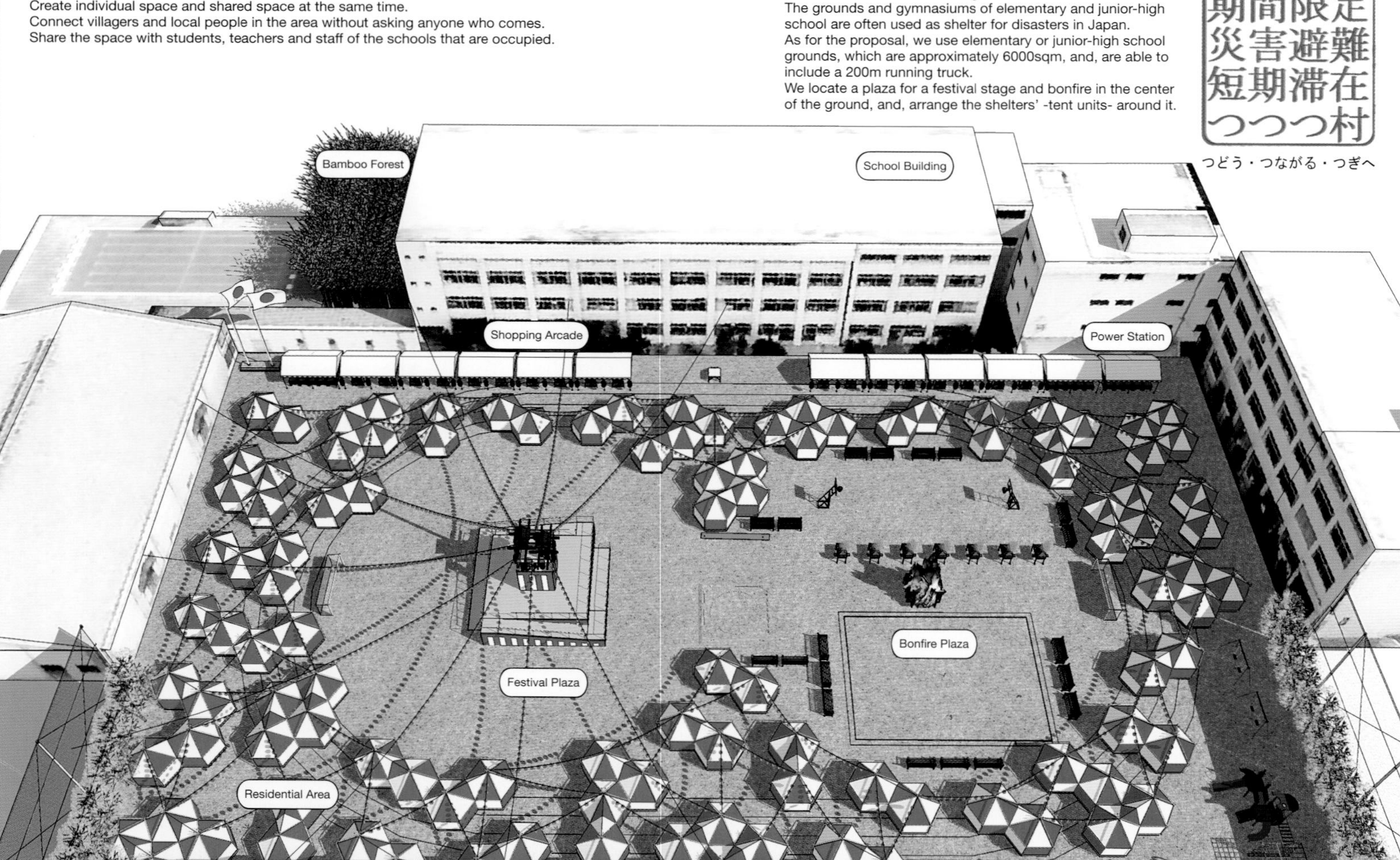

期間限定
災害避難
短期滞在
つつつ村

つどう・つながる・つぎへ

Formation of TsuTsuTsu-village 1 :
Nation : rent festival stage, booth, lantern, drum, portable shrine, etc

Formation of TsuTsuTsu-village 2 :
School : rent school equipment and furniture, share school facilities, raise a bamboo forest for preparation of resources for the structure of the tent

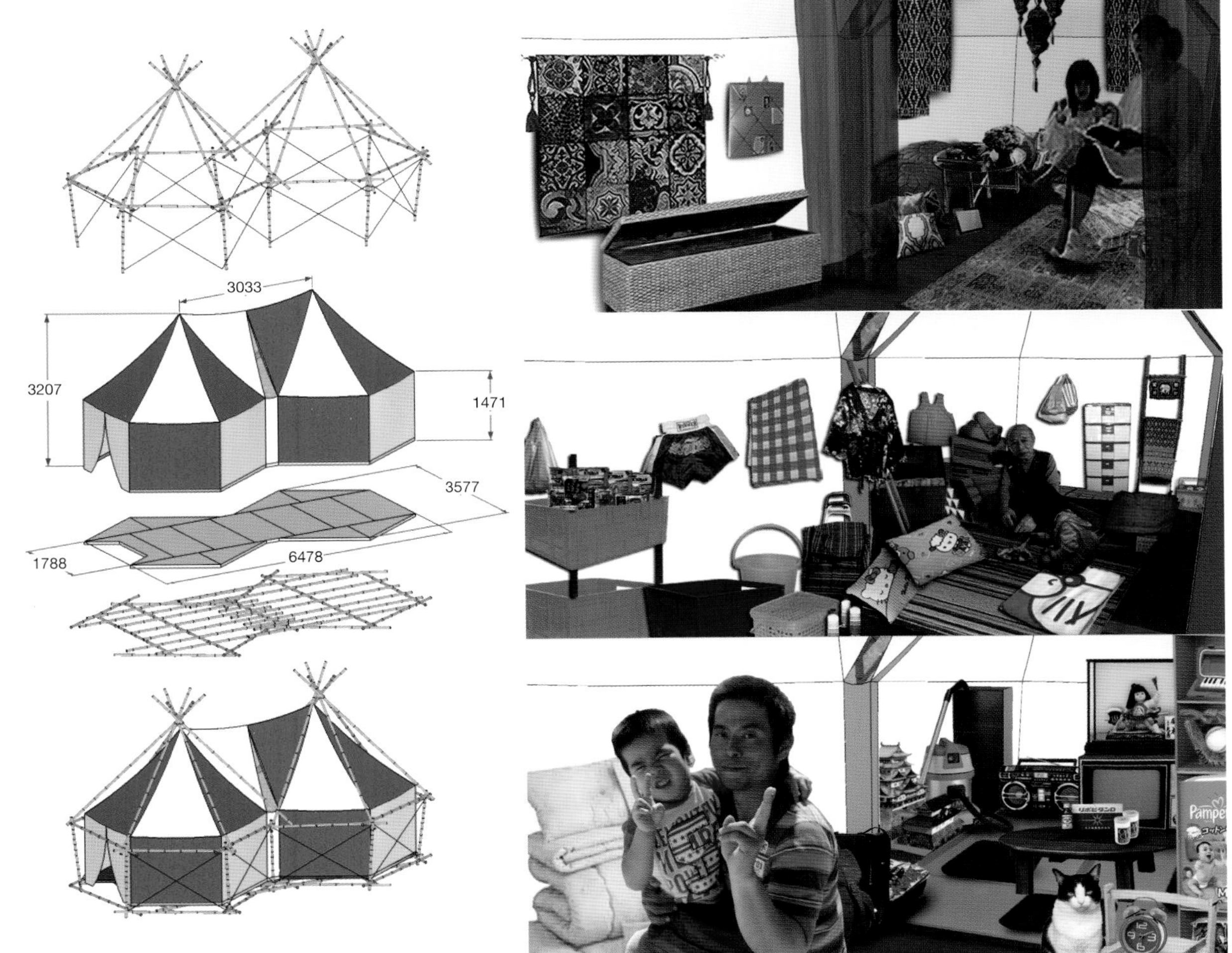

期間限定
災害避難
短期滞在
つつつ村

つどう・つながる・つぎへ

[Outline of residential unit]
Structure = nylon-rope tied bamboo structure
Exterior wall / roof material = prefabricated waterproof, fire resistant, highly insulated tent fabric (55.2sqm / unit)
Floor material = insulation filled panels x 11 (thickness = 54mm) (both sides coniferous plywood, size = 1820mm x 910mm x 12mm)
Height of floor = GL + 300mm
Window / Opening = translucent vinyl skylight, no opening (2placed at the center of tent)
Entrance = industrial zipper (lockable)
Floor area = apprx. 17.1sqm (10.2jyou-Japanese measurement-) / unit
Maximum height of unit = 3200mm

[Outline of village]
Entire ground : 6000sqm
Residential area : 2400sqm
(residential unit floor area total : 975sqm)
Plaza
(shared area) : 2400sqm
Shopping Arcade
(commercial area) : 800sqm
Recreation ground
(playground equipment) : 400sqm

Accommodation capacity / unit = 4-5 people
Number of units in TsuTsuTsu-village = 57 units (as for this example)
Maximum number of villagers = 285 people (as for this example)

Emergency shelter reference reading :
Calculate using international standard = 3.5sqm /per person

Formation of TsuTsuTsu-village 3 :
Government : prepare and store tent fabric, train and dispatch construction instructors

Formation of TsuTsuTsu-village 4 :
Overseas : send relief –various things are welcome-

Formation of Tsutsutsu-village 5 :
Villagers : create thevillage by themselves

153

eVolo 06 | *Marchi_Architectes*

Team : Architecture project(Adelaïde et Nicola Marchi[Marchi_Architectes]), 3D images(Jean François Marcheguet [Arte Factory])

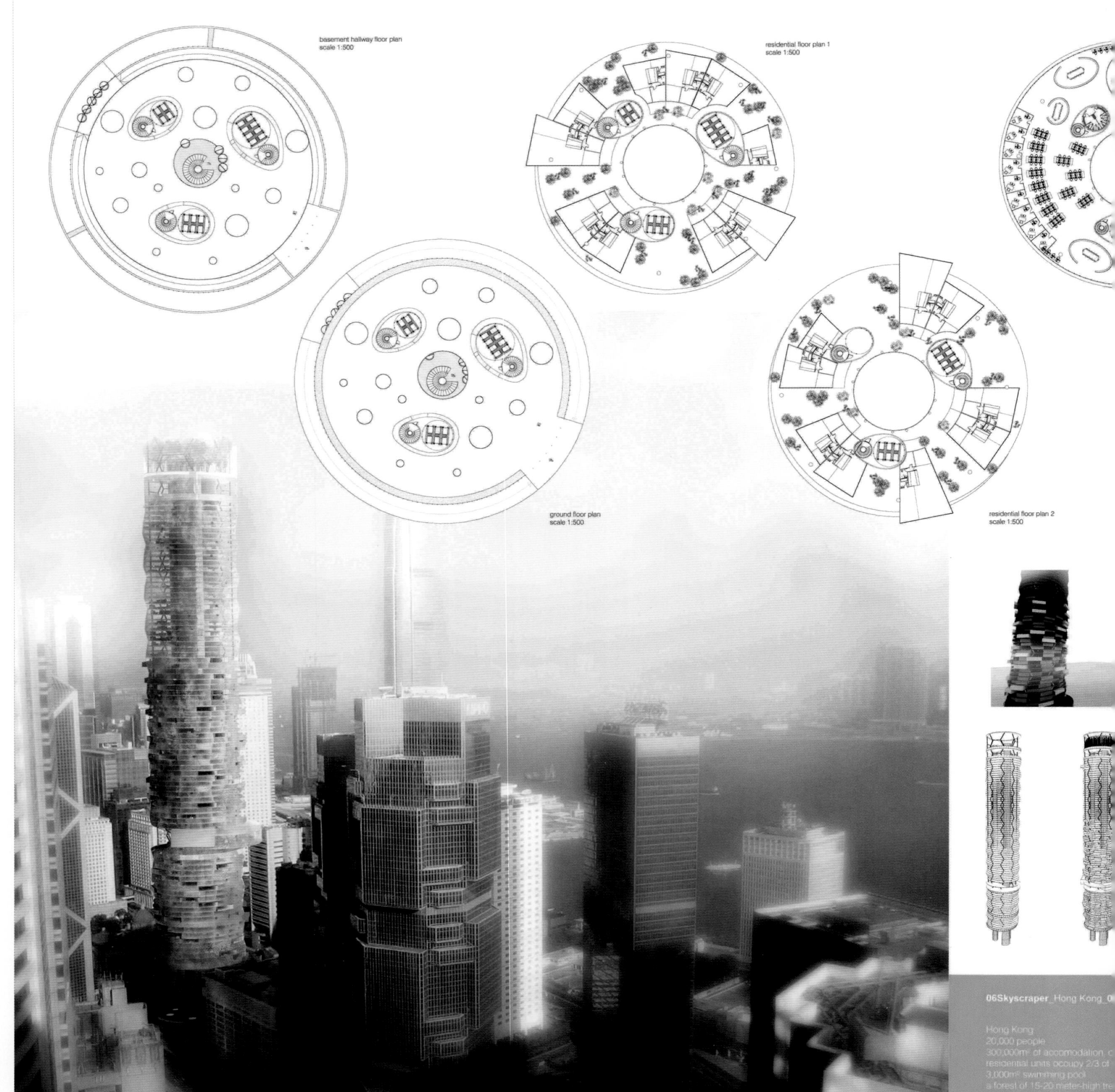

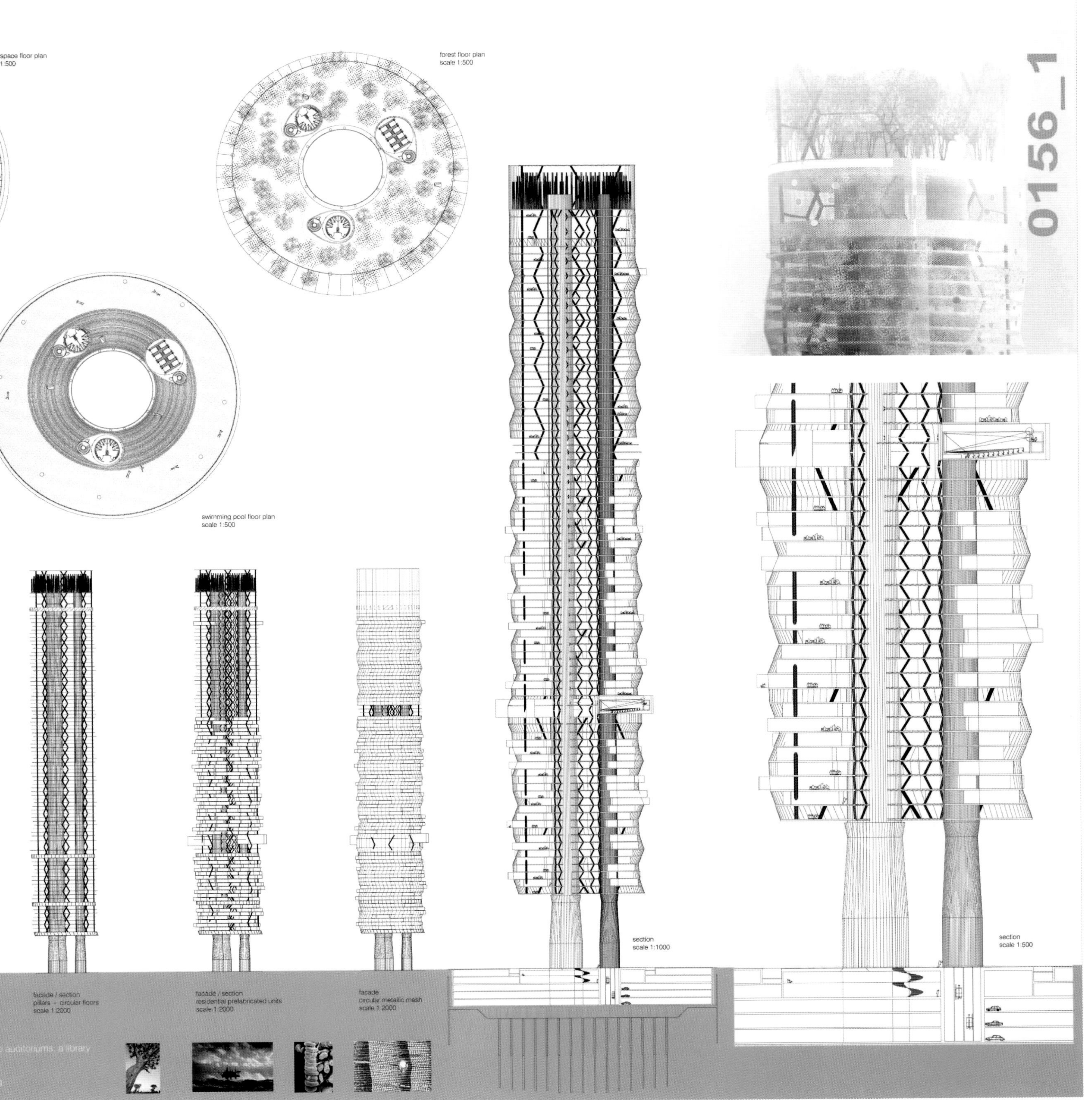

e space floor plan
le 1:500
forest floor plan
scale 1:500
0156_1
swimming pool floor plan
scale 1:500
section
scale 1:1000
section
scale 1:500
facade / section
pillars + circular floors
scale 1:2000
facade / section
residential prefabricated units
scale 1:2000
facade
circular metallic mesh
scale 1:2000
es auditoriums, a library

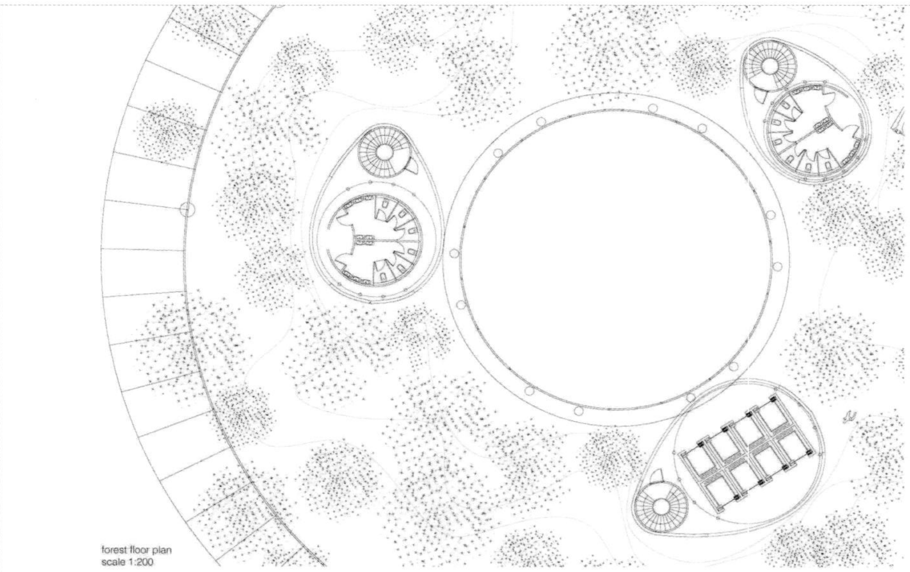

forest floor plan
scale 1:200

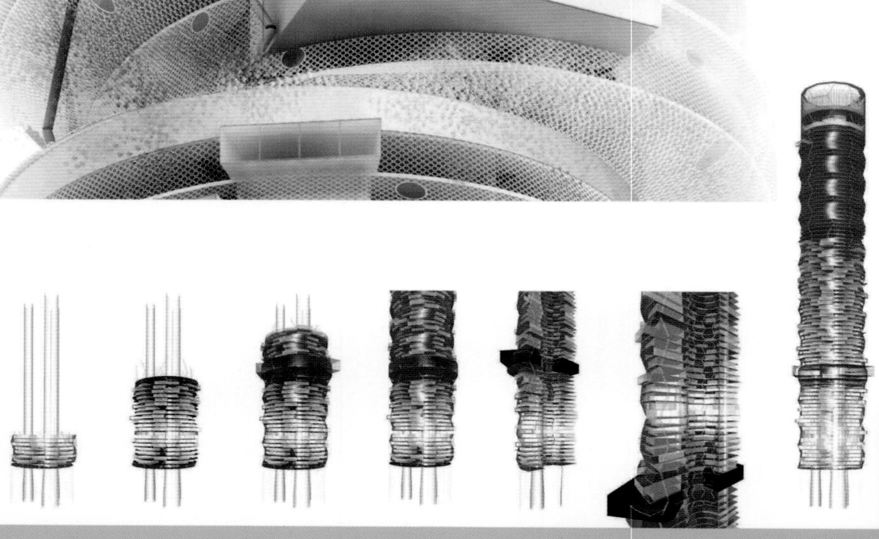

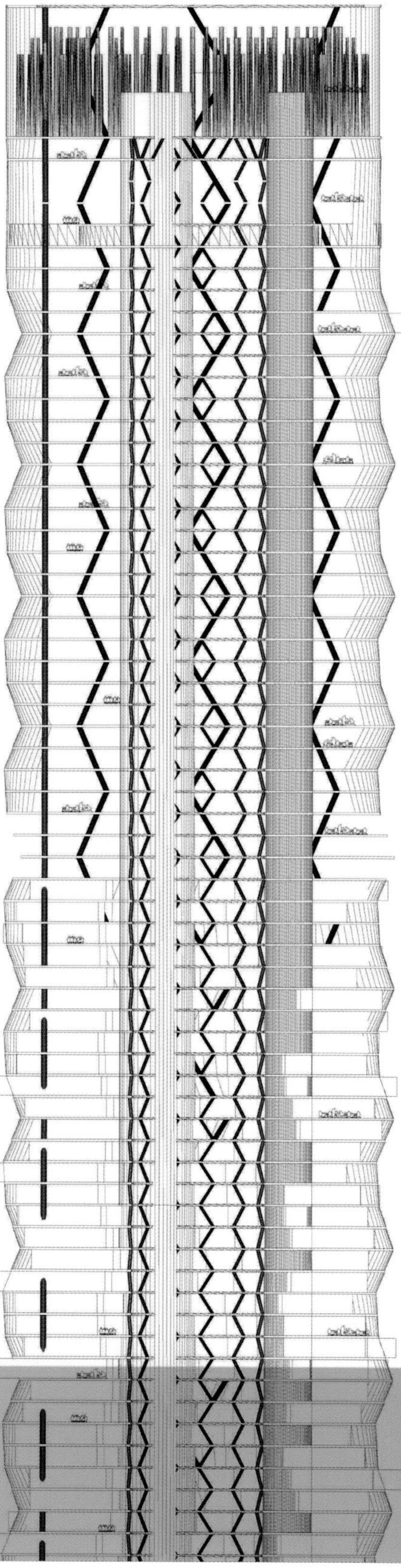

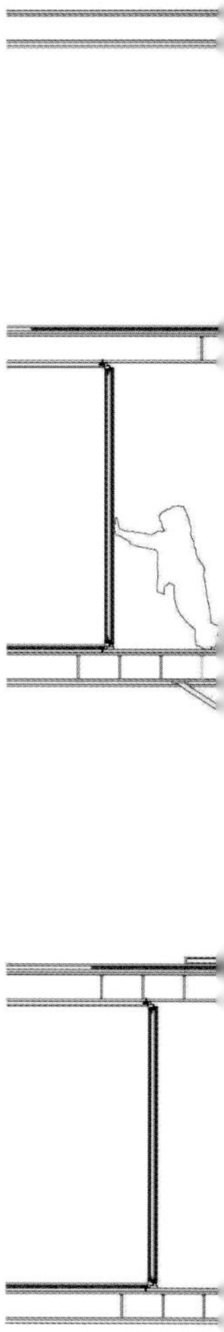

section circular metallic mesh wit
residential prefabricated units
scale 1:50

1 Residential units and self-con located in between the floor s These are entirely prefabricate adaptable to the demands of the user's requirements. Residential units are separate garden-spaces with wide view surroundings.
2 15mm thick circular metallic n diameter. This circular metallic with plants and solar panels a fashion and orientated approp
3 The circular solar panels gene providing natural shading. The numerous at the top of the tow preferentially on the eastern a to maximize production of sola latitude
4 The green screen modules, w 80mm thick and 50cm in diam for plants. When used in a ver the standard elements can be planting
5 Planting box: galvanized expa substrate for large plastic plan
6 PVC watering hose
7 Galvanized steel support struc

section
scale 1:500

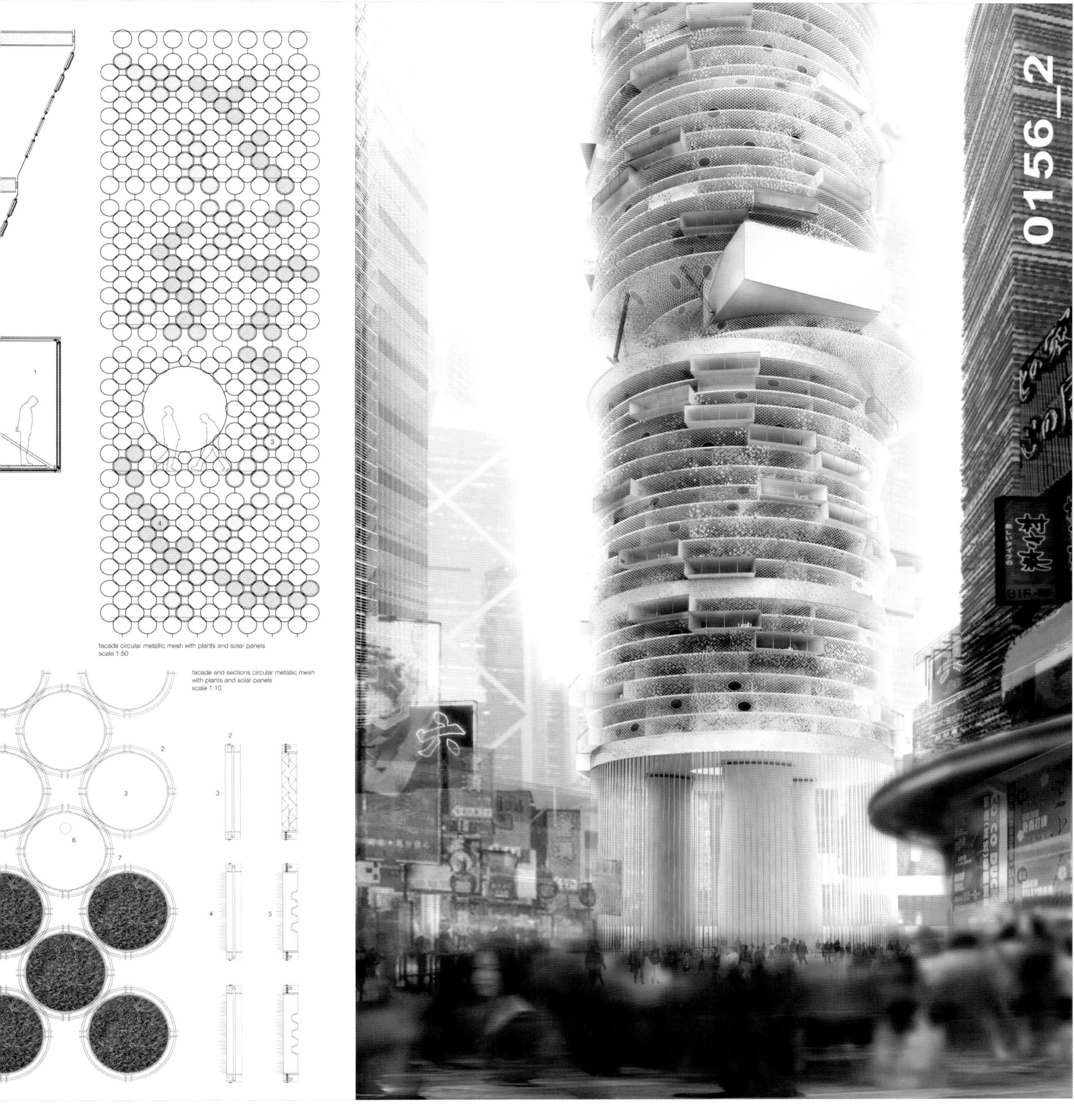
facade circular metallic mesh with plants and solar panels
scale 1:50
facade and sections circular metallic mesh
with plants and solar panels
scale 1:10
0156_2

154 110 Seconds Sociability | *AA&U For Architecture, Art and Urbanism*

European Architectural Competition for the Redevelopment of Former Football Stadium, Nicosia, Cyprus
Project Team : Socratis Stratis(Dr. architect, urbanist, assistant professor)
Collaborators : Riccardo Urbano(architect), Anastasia Angelidou(architect)
Support : Rui Santos(architect), Stavri Giannakou(architect), Savas Anastasiou(student of architecture), Filippo Gur(student of architecture)

110 SECONDS SOCIABILITY

ARCHITECTURAL COMPETITION FOR THE REDESIGN OF THE OLD "GSP" AREA, NICOSIA

The double chapter of the car

Urban Activating — Urban Discontinuing

15 km/h > u > 15 km/h

1.THEATRE LEVEL

1.1 Pedestrian wooden platform
1.2 Running track
1.3 Podium – seating area for open-air events
1.4 Roof garden
1.5 Roof terrace of the building
1.6 Old clock
1.7 Giant screen/s with audiovisual system for holding of events
1.8 Elevator

Generating a multiple sequence of shared spaces by the elevated running track, the Gates and the Sociability Booster Points

Extending the Theater entry level to an elevated running track

Inserting "Sociability Booster Points" (S.B.P) around the car elevators

Pulling the city with a terraced garden to a lower level

Creating "Gates" for alternative access to the square

V. Pavlou street

Afxentiou Avenue

Evagorou Avenue

PLAN OF THE THEATRE LEVEL
SCALE 1:500

The aim of this proposal has a double take. Firstly, it is to create frameworks for sociability in public space for the 1500 cars' motorists of the underground garage. In other words, to turn a rather passive practice of parking one's car within a massive underground parking, into an active practice of sociability on the grounds of the public space. The second take refers to the notion of reversibility. It is proposed that the proposal contains possible afterlives. This challenge becomes pertinent regarding the fact that a current policy about private cars in the city could be challenged in the next 10 or 20 years. Consequently, a former decision about concentrating 1500 cars at one spot, useful for current planning priorities, could become gradually obsolete. Containing possible afterlives could decrease investment risk. Both of the objectives want to enrich the debate around sustainability.

For this aim a major decision has been taken. To keep the parking users on the public space grounds by organizing the parking garage around 12 automatic parking units grouped in six blocks. Half of them are accessed from the "GSP" level (street) and the rest from the "Garden" level, (-6.00m). The latter is created by a big gesture at the south edge of the site by pushing the ground of the city to a lower level. The "Garden Level" is connected to the street level by a terraced garden and large inclined planes, supported by public program, vegetation and natural light.

CONVENTIONAL PARKING PLACE (FANEROMENI) FOR 200 CARS – ENTRY BY CAR

0:000 0:010 0:020 0:030 0:040 0:050 0:060 0:070 0:080 0:090 0:100 0:110 0:120 0:130 0:140 0:150

1	3	5	7	9
2	4	6	8	10

39224

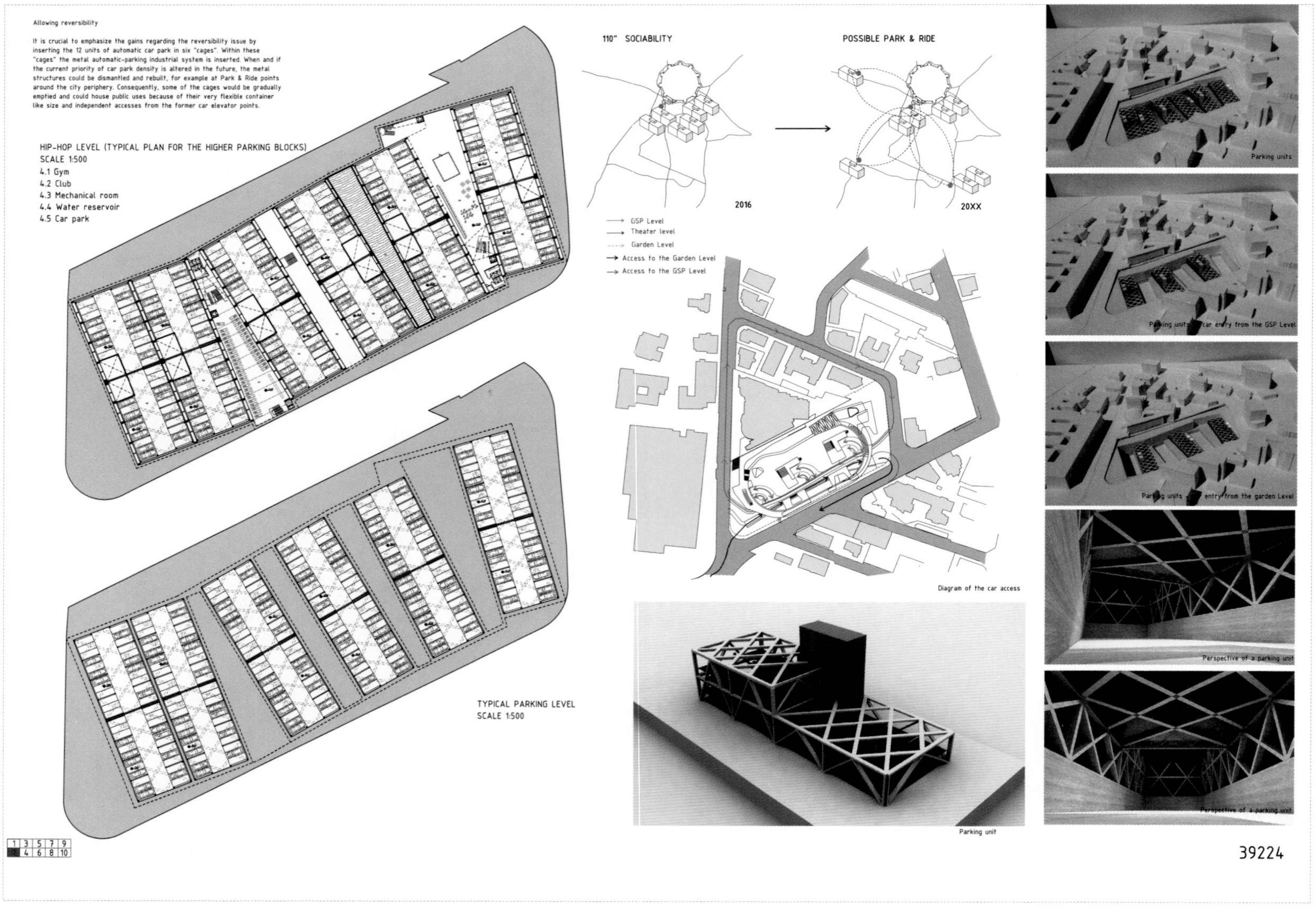

Allowing reversibility

It is crucial to emphasize the gains regarding the reversibility issue by inserting the 12 units of automatic car park in six "cages". Within these "cages" the metal automatic-parking industrial system is inserted. When and if the current priority of car park density is altered in the future, the metal structures could be dismantled and rebuilt, for example at Park & Ride points around the city periphery. Consequently, some of the cages would be gradually emptied and could house public uses because of their very flexible container like size and independent accesses from the former car elevator points.

HIP-HOP LEVEL (TYPICAL PLAN FOR THE HIGHER PARKING BLOCKS)
SCALE 1:500
4.1 Gym
4.2 Club
4.3 Mechanical room
4.4 Water reservoir
4.5 Car park

TYPICAL PARKING LEVEL
SCALE 1:500

110" SOCIABILITY — 2016

POSSIBLE PARK & RIDE — 20XX

GSP Level
Theater level
Garden Level
Access to the Garden Level
Access to the GSP Level

Diagram of the car access

Parking unit

Parking units

Parking units – car entry from the GSP Level

Parking units – entry from the garden Level

Perspective of a parking unit

Perspective of a parking unit

1	3	5	7	9
2	4	6	8	10

39224

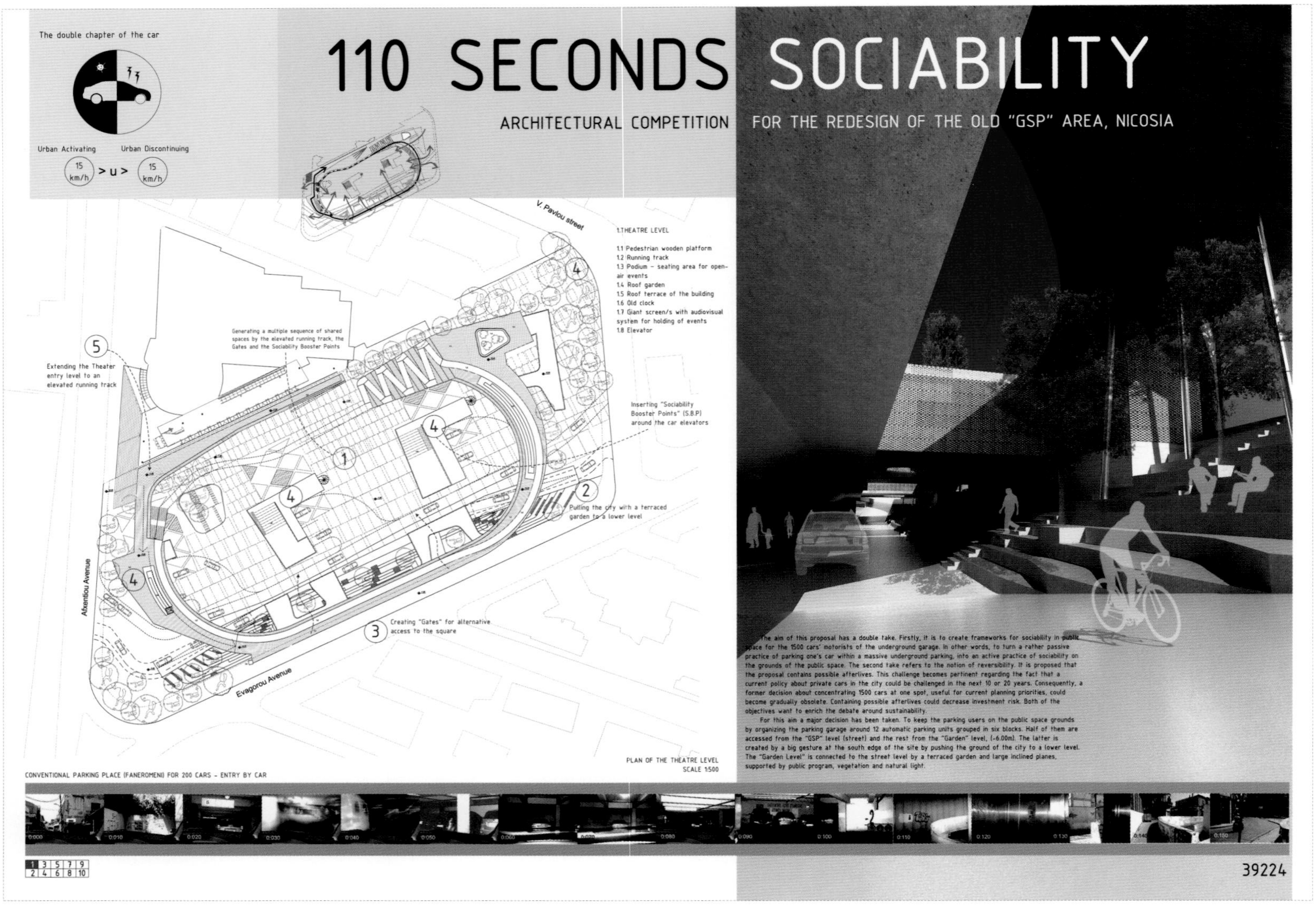

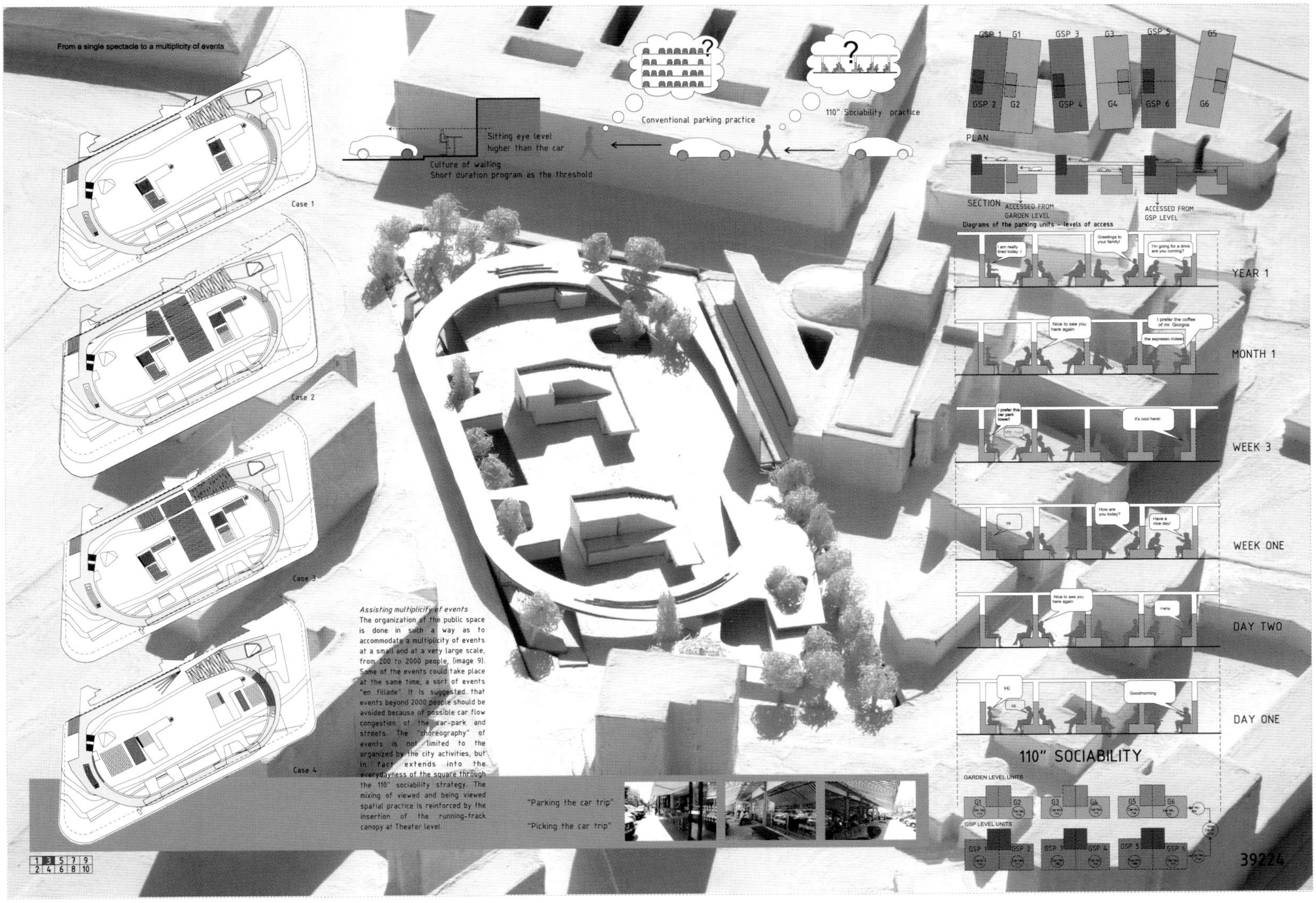

From a single spectacle to a multiplicity of events

Case 1

Case 2

Case 3

Case 4

Sitting eye level
higher than the car

Culture of waiting
Short duration program as the threshold

Conventional parking practice

110" Sociability practice

GSP 1 G1 GSP 3 G3 GSP 5 G5

GSP 2 G2 GSP 4 G4 GSP 6 G6

PLAN

SECTION

ACCESSED FROM GARDEN LEVEL

ACCESSED FROM GSP LEVEL

Diagrams of the parking units - levels of access

I am really tired today :/

Greetings to your family!

I'm going for a drink are you coming?

YEAR 1

Nice to see you here again

I prefer the coffee of mr. Giorgos

the espresso indeed

MONTH 1

I prefer this car park tower!

It's cool here!

WEEK 3

Hi

How are you today?

Have a nice day!

WEEK ONE

Nice to see you here again

Hello

DAY TWO

Hi

Hi

Goodmorning

DAY ONE

110" SOCIABILITY

GARDEN LEVEL UNITS

G1 G2 G3 G4 G5 G6

GSP LEVEL UNITS

GSP 1 GSP 2 GSP 3 GSP 4 GSP 5 GSP 6

Assisting multiplicity of events

The organization of the public space is done in such a way as to accommodate a multiplicity of events at a small and at a very large scale, from 200 to 2000 people, (image 9). Some of the events could take place at the same time, a sort of events "en fillade". It is suggested that events beyond 2000 people should be avoided because of possible car flow congestion of the car-park and streets. The "choreography" of events is not limited to the organized by the city activities, but in fact extends into the everydayness of the square through the 110" sociability strategy. The mixing of viewed and being viewed spatial practice is reinforced by the insertion of the running-track canopy at Theater level.

"Parking the car trip"

"Picking the car trip"

1	3	5	7	9
2	4	6	8	10

39224

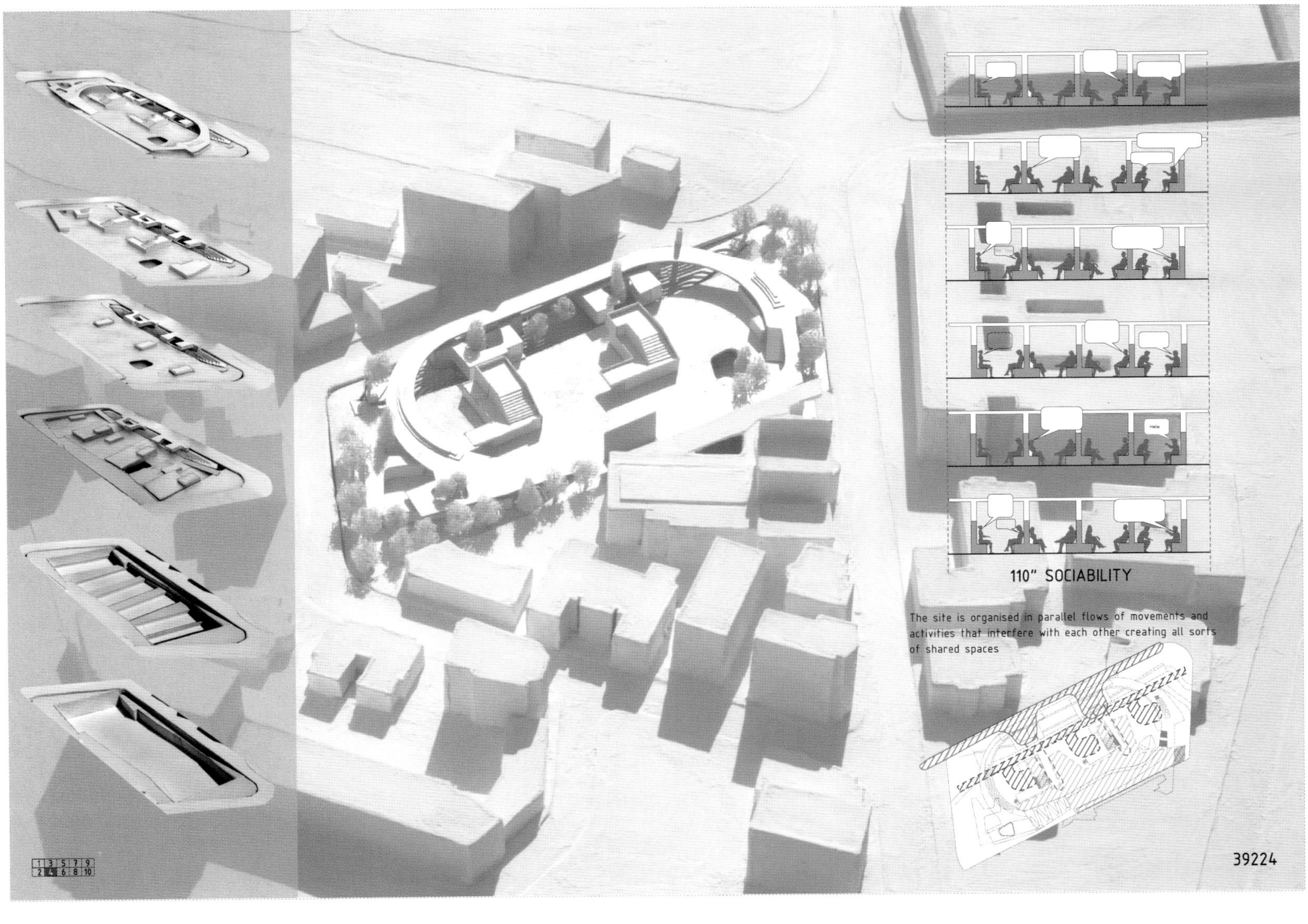

110" SOCIABILITY

The site is organised in parallel flows of movements and activities that interfere with each other creating all sorts of shared spaces

1	3	5	7	9
2	4	6	8	10

39224

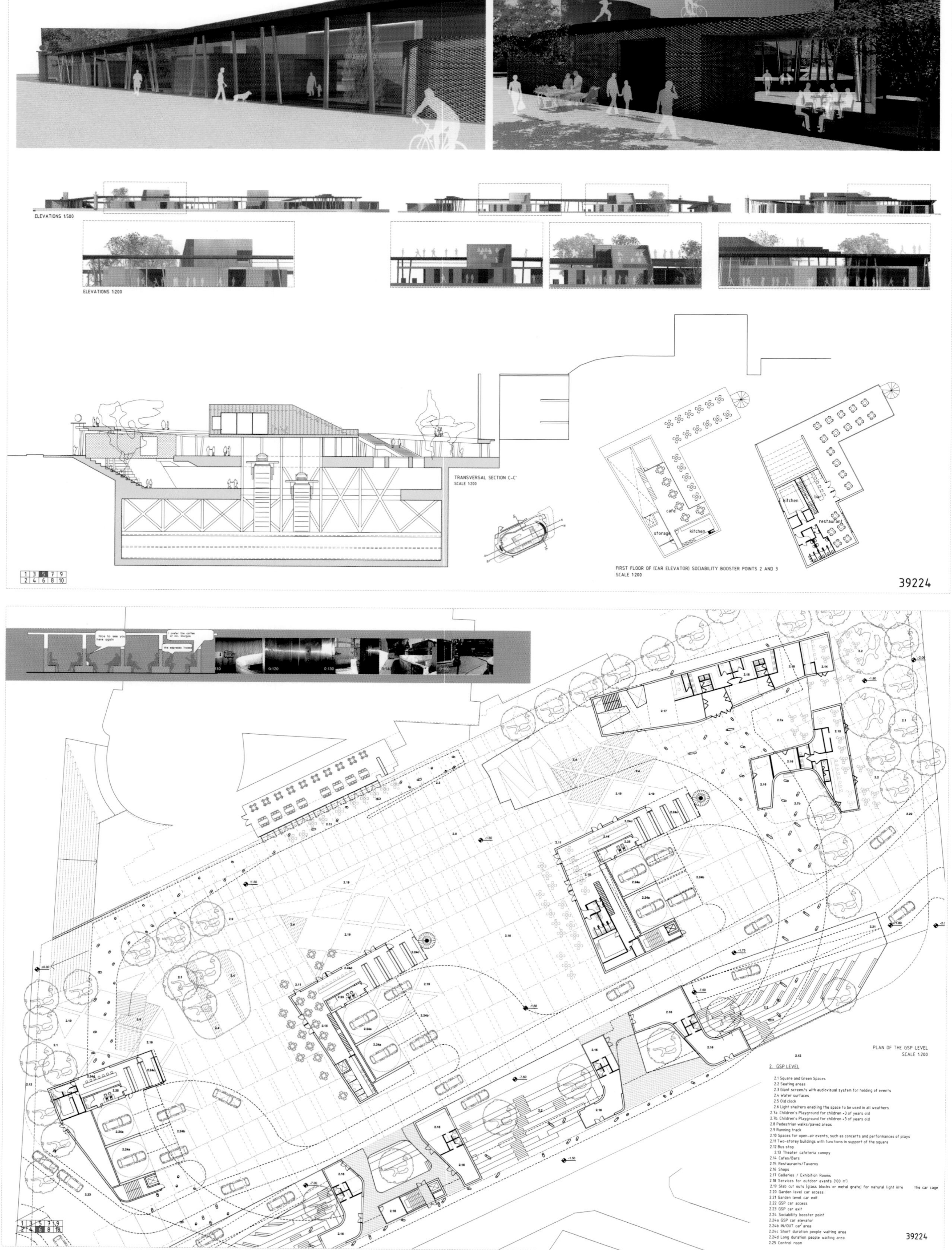

ELEVATIONS 1:500
ELEVATIONS 1:200
TRANSVERSAL SECTION C-C'
SCALE 1:200
cafe
storage
kitchen
kitchen
bar
restaurant
FIRST FLOOR OF (CAR ELEVATOR) SOCIABILITY BOOSTER POINTS 2 AND 3
SCALE 1:200
39224
PLAN OF THE GSP LEVEL
SCALE 1:200
2. GSP LEVEL
2.1 Square and Green Spaces
2.2 Seating areas
2.3 Giant screen/s with audiovisual system for holding of events
2.4 Water surfaces
2.5 Old clock
2.6 Light shelters enabling the space to be used in all weathers
2.7a Children's Playground for children >3 of years old
2.7b. Children's Playground for children <3 of years old
2.8 Pedestrian walks/paved areas
2.9 Running track
2.10 Spaces for open-air events, such as concerts and performances of plays
2.11 Two-storey buildings with functions in support of the square
2.12 Bus stop
2.13 Theater cafeteria canopy
2.14 Cafes/Bars
2.15 Restaurants/Taverns
2.16 Shops
2.17 Galleries / Exhibition Rooms
2.18 Services for outdoor events (100 m²)
2.19 Slab cut outs [glass blocks or metal grate] for natural light into the car cage
2.20 Garden level car access
2.21 Garden level car exit
2.22 GSP car access
2.23 GSP car exit
2.24 Sociability booster point
2.24a GSP car elevator
2.24b IN/OUT car area
2.24c Short duration people waiting area
2.24d Long duration people waiting area
2.25 Control room
39224

GSP LEVEL _ View from running track facing southwest.

GARDEN LEVEL _ View from gate's clusters.

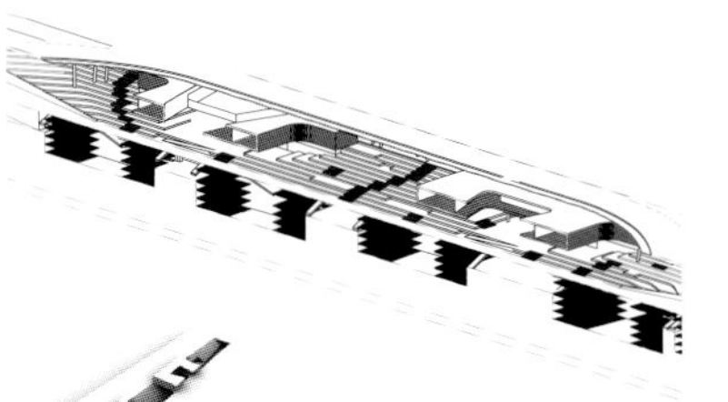

Axonometric section facing terrassed garden

PASSING-THROUGH GATES

The rest of the program is organized around "Gates", through which the users could pass in order to enter into the square, (image 8). The old-clock is located next to one of them, maintaining its former role. The edge of the square along Evagorou avenue acts as a registry for programmatic activities which then are directed towards "GSP", "Garden" and "hip-hop" levels, (located between the car-park "cages").

GARDEN LEVEL _ Arrival from south ramp.

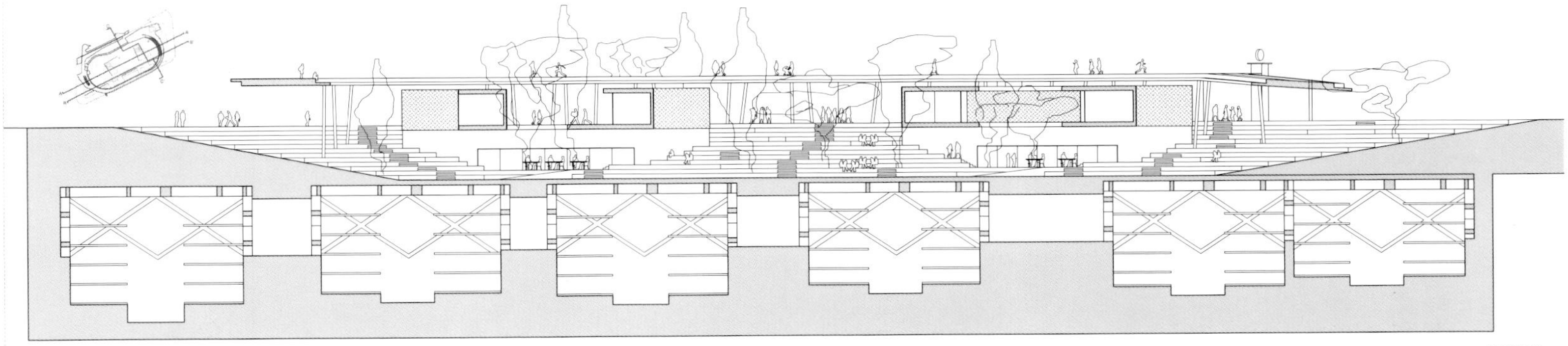

LONGITUDINAL SECTION B-B'
SCALE 1:200

39224

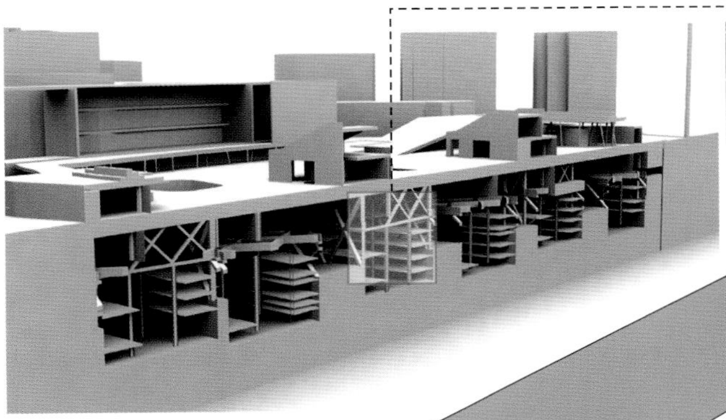

PLAN OF THE GARDEN LEVEL
SCALE 1:200

3. GARDEN LEVEL

3.1 Car park
3.2 Guard/Watchman's Room
3.3 Automatic Car wash
3.3a Office
3.3b Waiting Room
3.3c Store Room
3.3d Machine Room
3.4 Store rooms
3.5 Sociability booster point
3.5a GARDEN LEVEL car elevator
3.5b IN/OUT car area
3.5c Short duration people waiting area
3.5d Long duration people waiting area
3.6 Park and bike center
3.7 30' minutes car park
3.8a Men's Lavatories
3.8b Women's Lavatories
3.8c Storeroom
3.10 Cafes/Bars
3.11 Garden space
3.12 Access to gym
3.13 Access to club
3.14 Seating area

39224

The linear spaces between the concrete structured cages are ideal for uses such as gallery spaces, gym, and night-club. The view into the car-cages on both sides of the linear space gives a very unique character to those spaces. The automatic car parking process is viewed as a performance. During day time, natural light would filter through the car-cages by openings on their roofs.

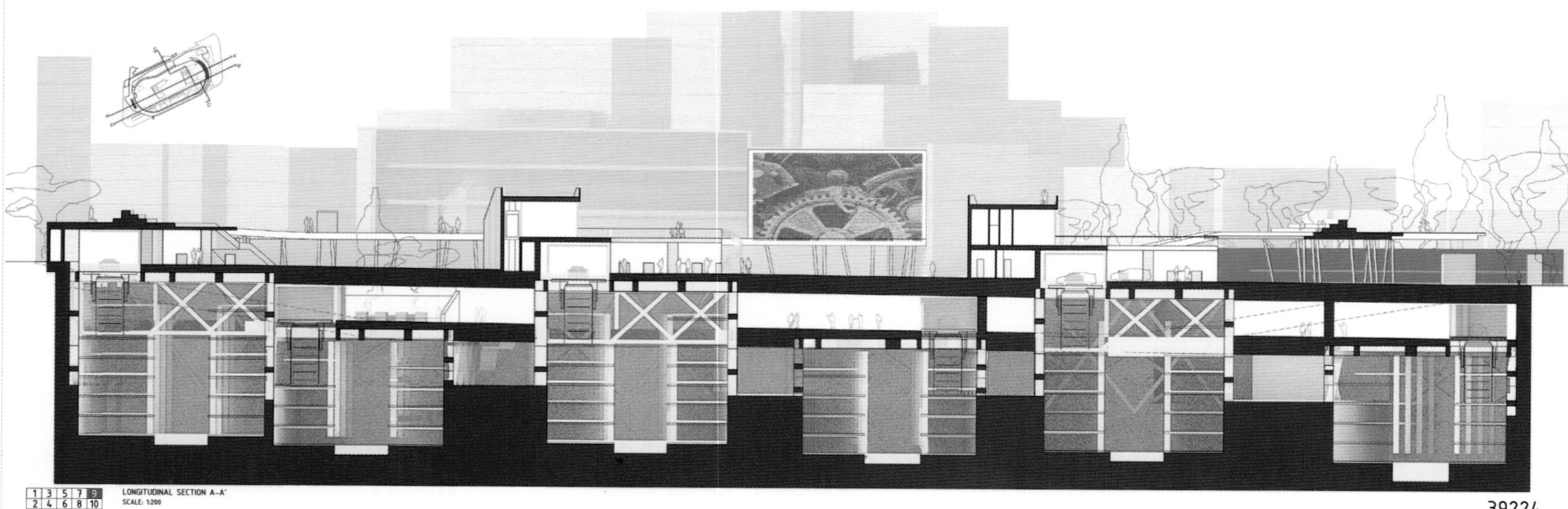

LONGITUDINAL SECTION A-A'
SCALE: 1:200

39224

Garden Level View looking towards Evagorou avenue from waiting area

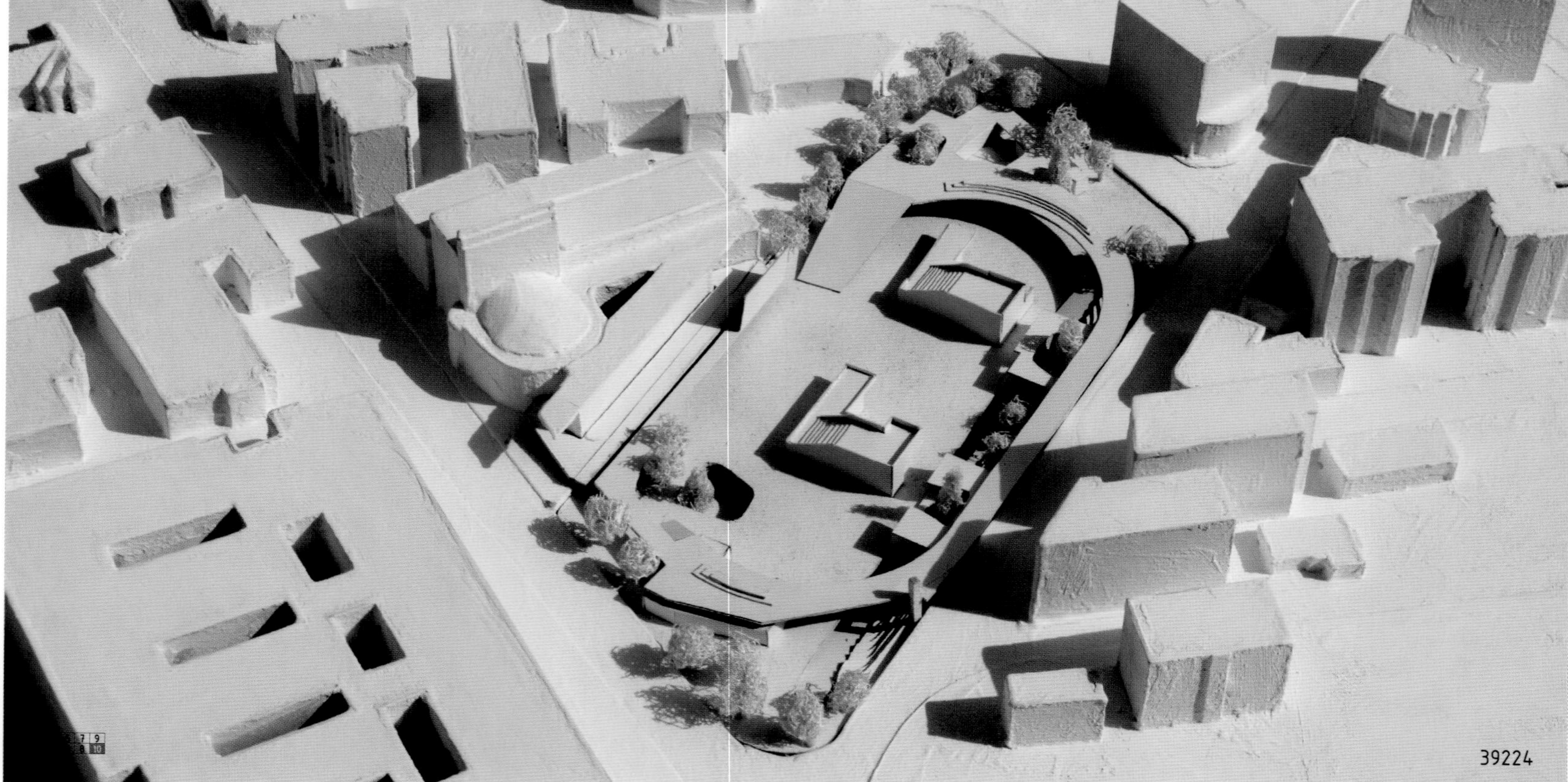

39224

Ramp up the 'Mun | *AQSO arquitectos office*

Typology : Cultural and Residential Building / Location : Dublin, Ireland
Built area (GFA) : 1760sqm / Client : Ballymun Regeneration Ltd.

Participants : Luis Aguirre Manso, Sergio Blanco Fernández, James Tendayi Matsuku, Juan José Cruz Martínez,
Collaborators : Dinah Zhang, Yang Shi, Yihang Zhang
Project : Multi-functional Cultural Center in Dublin

155

ig911
ramp up the 'mun

dublin 01

>> If site features are to be retained, how can this be achieved in a meaningful, sustainable manner that is of relevance to the project brief?

[- introducing our concept: the plaza!]

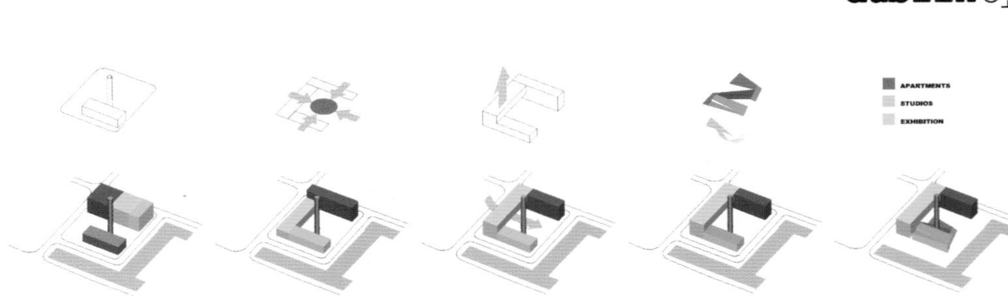

>> In addition to the brief's requirements, our proposal inserts an **urban plaza** into the site.
The plaza opens up the program around it, and positions the exhibitions, artist studios at a more civic and urban orientated level. Historically, plazas are the place for trade, for encounter, for chance **interaction**. Plazas have strong positive implications for social **synergy**, and these implications are carried through to the Boilerhouse site. The proposed plaza will create a center for the town, and a place where cultural **exchanges** can occur between artists, visitors and residents.

The plaza steps and slips into a series of ramps and surfaces to allow an **amphitheater atmosphere** where visitors and residents can gather, meeting, watch a street performance, observe passer by and enjoy public urban life.
The studio block is elevated to allow smooth transition from pedestrian path into the plaza through an **urban threshold**.

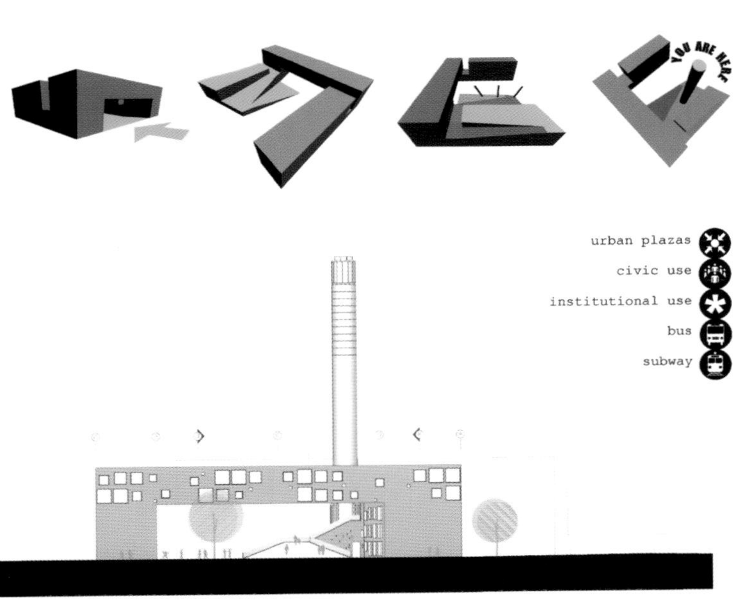

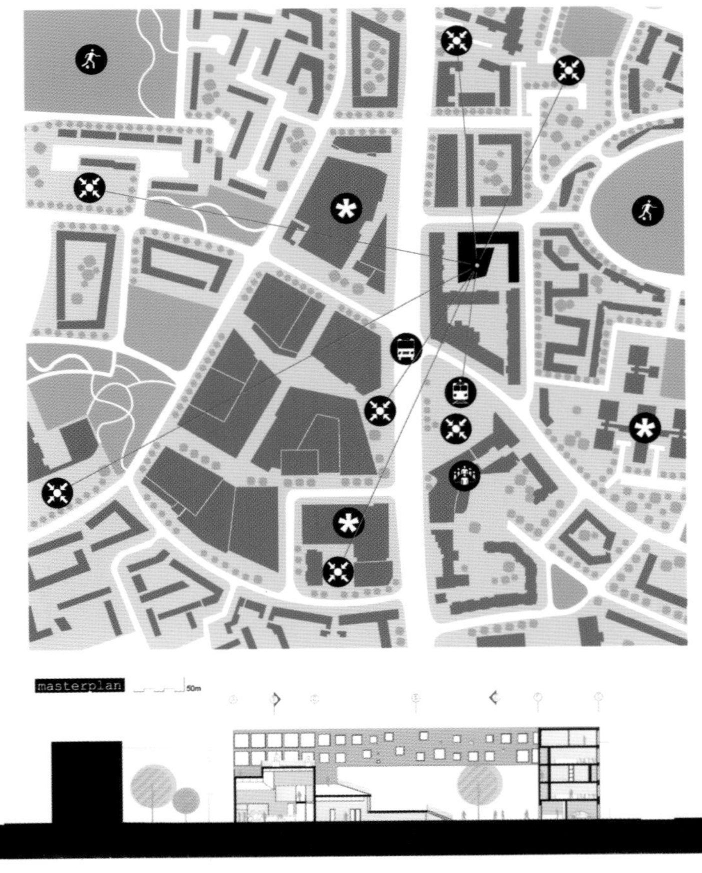

ig911

ramp up the 'mun

dublin 02

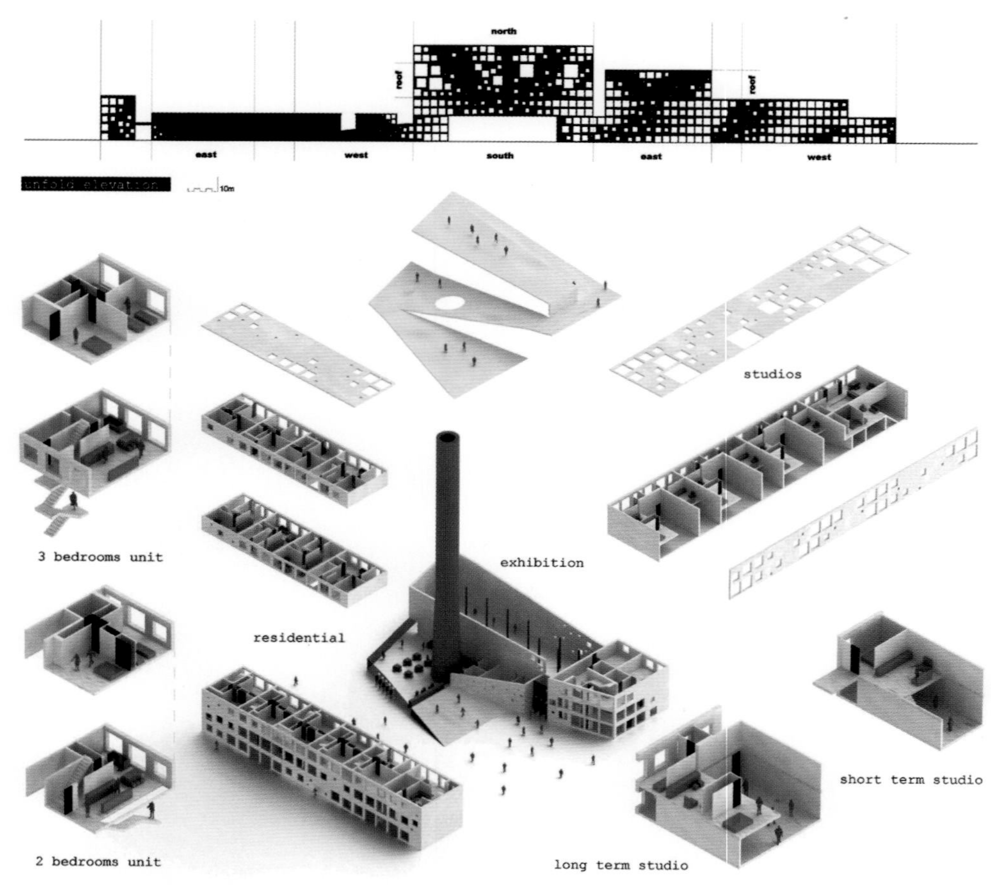

>> Especially in housing districts renovation, how can a better quality of life avoiding social exclusion be offered?

[- our way to understand the challenge: Boilerhouse to became a new cultural identity]

>> Ballymun's regeneration plan has gradually seen the introduction of a new town, parks, leisure facilities and other physical infrastructure which will increase the significance of Ballymun within Dublin's city fabric. Although investment efforts have improved urban quality in Ballymun, the Boilerhouse studios aim to provide something that is still missing in Ballymun, the project intents to create an identity that will give the town a unique sense of character and a new spirit.

>> In areas with a strong identity but with obsolete functions, how can spaces be adapted to a new dynamic of uses?

[- our strategy: keep the unique elements and understand the project as a precise intervention]

>> The old Boilerhouse will be transformed to house a new program. However, transformation of the building must be done sensitively with consideration to the existing fabric. This transformation will not create a completely new form, but rather, keep unique elements from the existing infrastructure in order to illuminate the distinctive qualities of the new additional buildings. The agenda of the project is to create links between Ballymun and Dublin city centre, between Ballymun and other national and international cultural communities. The project seeks to delve into the core of the urban problem and resolve it using small but precise interventions.

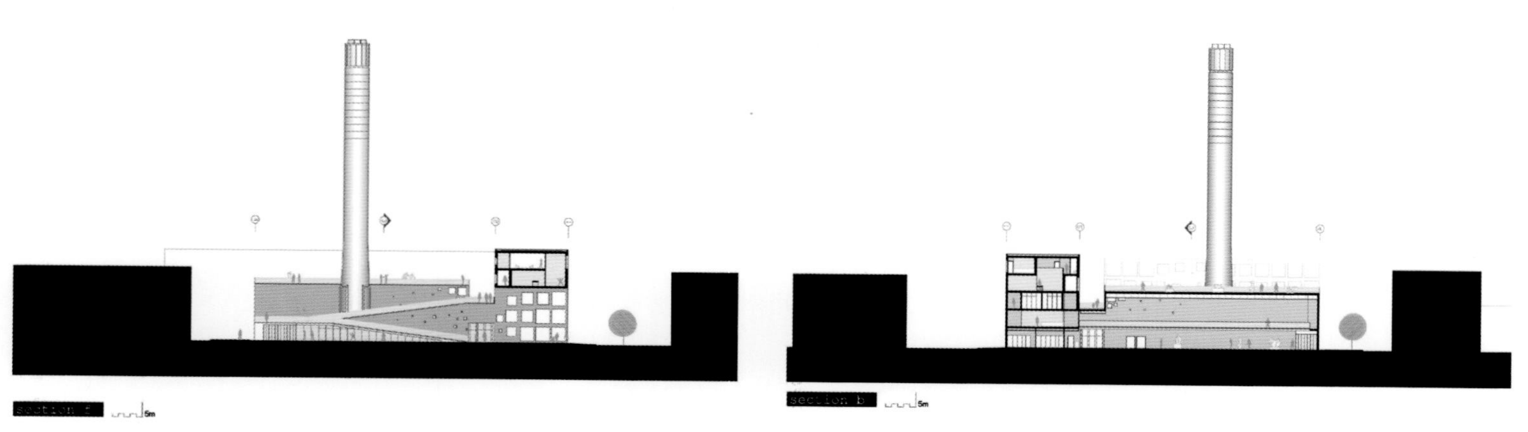

ig911

ramp up the 'mun

dublin 03

type A · type B · type C · apartments

type D · type B · type C · office

- parking
- coffee shop
- retail
- offices
- A
- B
- C apartment
- D
- T1
- T2 studio
- T3
- exhibition
- outdoor space
- workshop

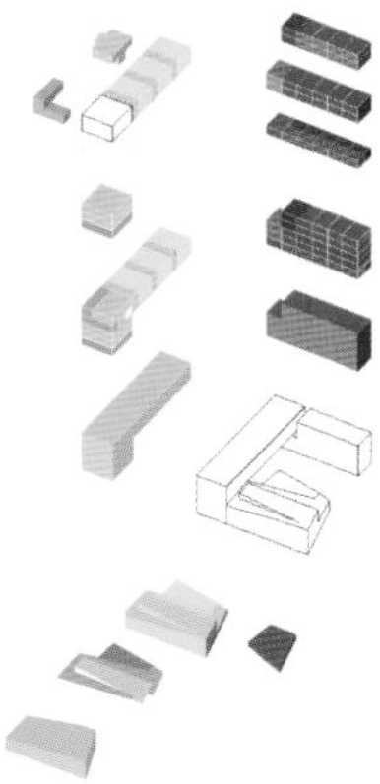

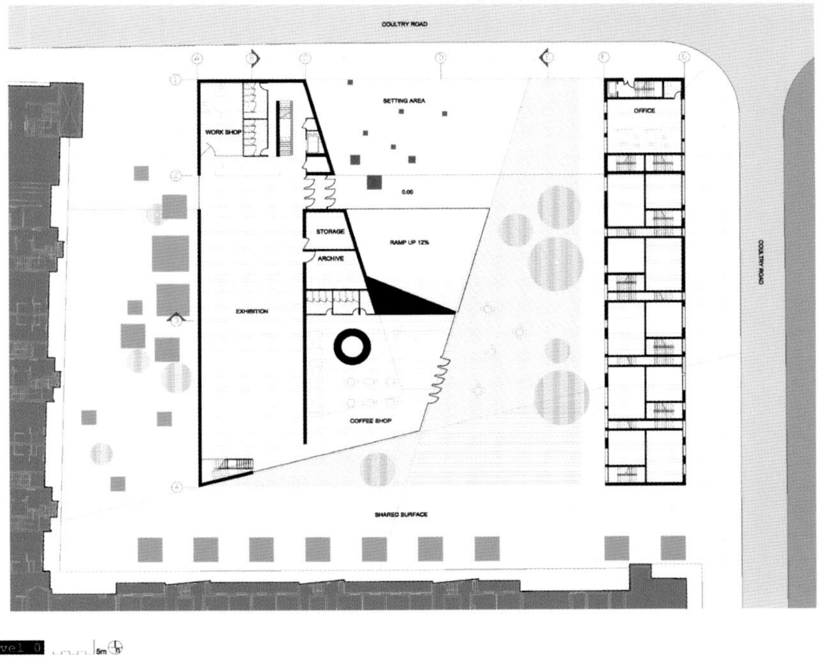

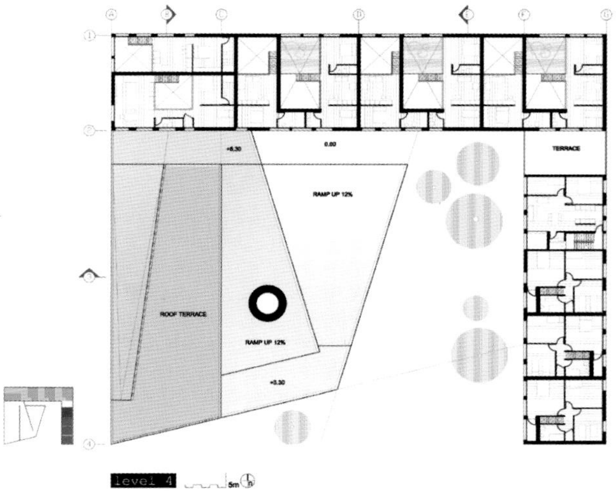

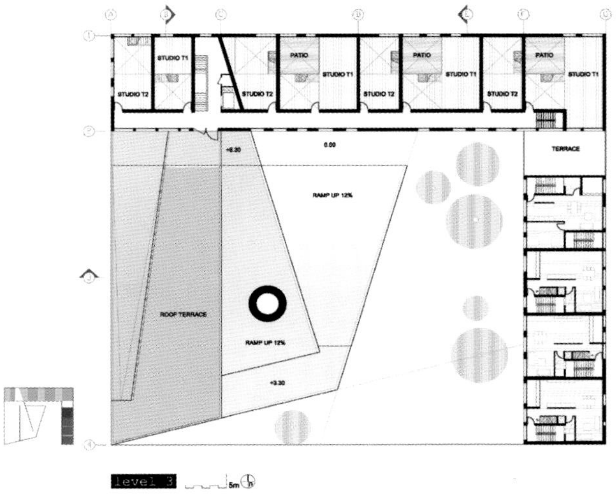

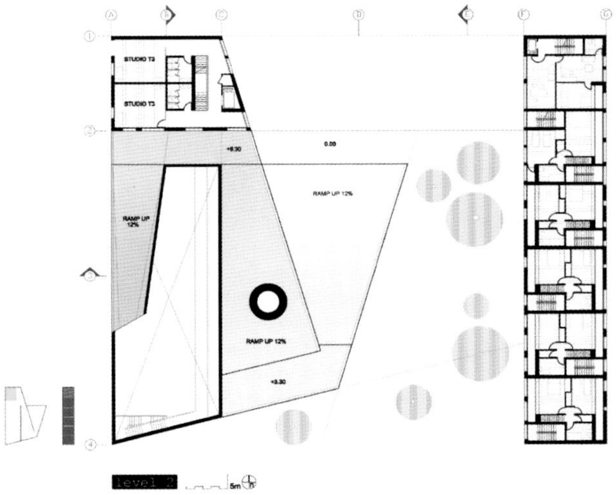

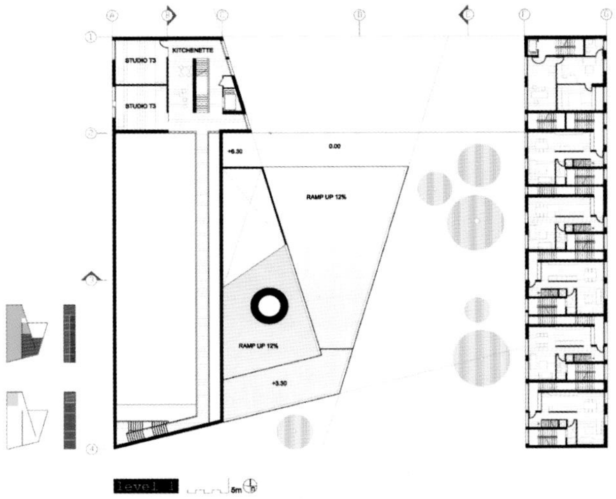

type 1 · type 2 · type 3 · studios

STUDIO · KITCHENETTE · STUDIO

type 1 · type 2 · type 3

PATIO · STUDIO · STUDIO

COULTRY ROAD

SETTING AREA · WORK SHOP · OFFICE · STORAGE · RAMP UP 12% · ARCHIVE · EXHIBITION · COFFEE SHOP · SHARED SURFACE · COULTRY ROAD

level 0 5m

TERRACE · RAMP UP 12% · ROOF TERRACE · RAMP UP 12% · +6.30 · 0.00 · +3.30

level 4 5m

STUDIO T1 · STUDIO T2 · PATIO · TERRACE · RAMP UP 12% · ROOF TERRACE · RAMP UP 12%

level 3 5m

STUDIO T3 · RAMP UP 12% · RAMP UP 12%

level 2 5m

STUDIO T3 · KITCHENETTE · RAMP UP 12% · RAMP UP 12%

level 1 5m

156 Woven Horizon | *CHA:COL*

WOVEN HORIZON
DEFINING AN URBAN LANDMARK
As one of the many suburban areas of the National Capital Region of Delhi still in expansion, Greater NOIDA finds itself in transition from an amorphous semi-agricultural landscape into an information technology corridor.
Given it's important historical relationship to the region, the Yamuna river has had a surprisingly diminished role in this rapid suburbanization enabled by the adjacent expressway enabled technology corridor. The location and program of this project therefore present a compelling opportunity to engage creative ideas.
The new Spiretec Tower is proposed to function as a woven surface that connects the riverfront with this corridor, yet also to define itself as a regional architectural landmark. The proposal attempts to organize a new Knowledge Centre using three critical components.
SITE SECTION 1:800
100 M HEIGHT LIMIT
THREADING THE YAMUNA
B4135Q
CONNECTING THE BIO STREETS
CREATING A CONTINOUS PARK
WEAVING THE LANDSCAPE
SITEPLAN 1:1000
THE PARK
The park's sculpted terrain will link the tower to the proposed IT blocks and bio streets by way of outdoor terraces and louvered promenades. A primary feature of the plan is the Green Avenue – a wide boulevard-like pedestrian street that runs east/west from the Yamuna riverfont to the entrance at the Plaza Gateway. This Avenue unlocks the entire site, connecting disparate elements, and is characterized by a dynamic mix of retail, cafes and wellness facilities along with 2 levels of below grade parking. While the commercially energized park base is designed for activity during the daytime, the convention center will host events at night, creating a vibrant 24-hour shopping and entertainment hub.
THE TOWER
The tower forms a major tectonic element to emphasize the other aspect of the project as landmark. Designed with a slight kink, it accentuates the base and emphasizes sightlines through an open corridor below and sky lobbies at two levels above. The lower 11 floors of residential, intentionally out of plumb from the upper 8 floors of hotel allow a differentiated volume that shifts in relation to the two constant vertical circulation cores. The bent tower form accommodates hotel and residential program areas along with a few floors of flexible office space.
THE SKIN
The 'second skin to the tower, referred to as the 'solar veil' is derived in part from the Indian saree. Designed as a screening device, oriented towards the southwest to reduce solar glare and maximize thermal efficiency for office, hotel and residential use, the 'solar veil' that wraps around the tower. The 'pixelated' glazed facade is designed for spectrally selective solar control.

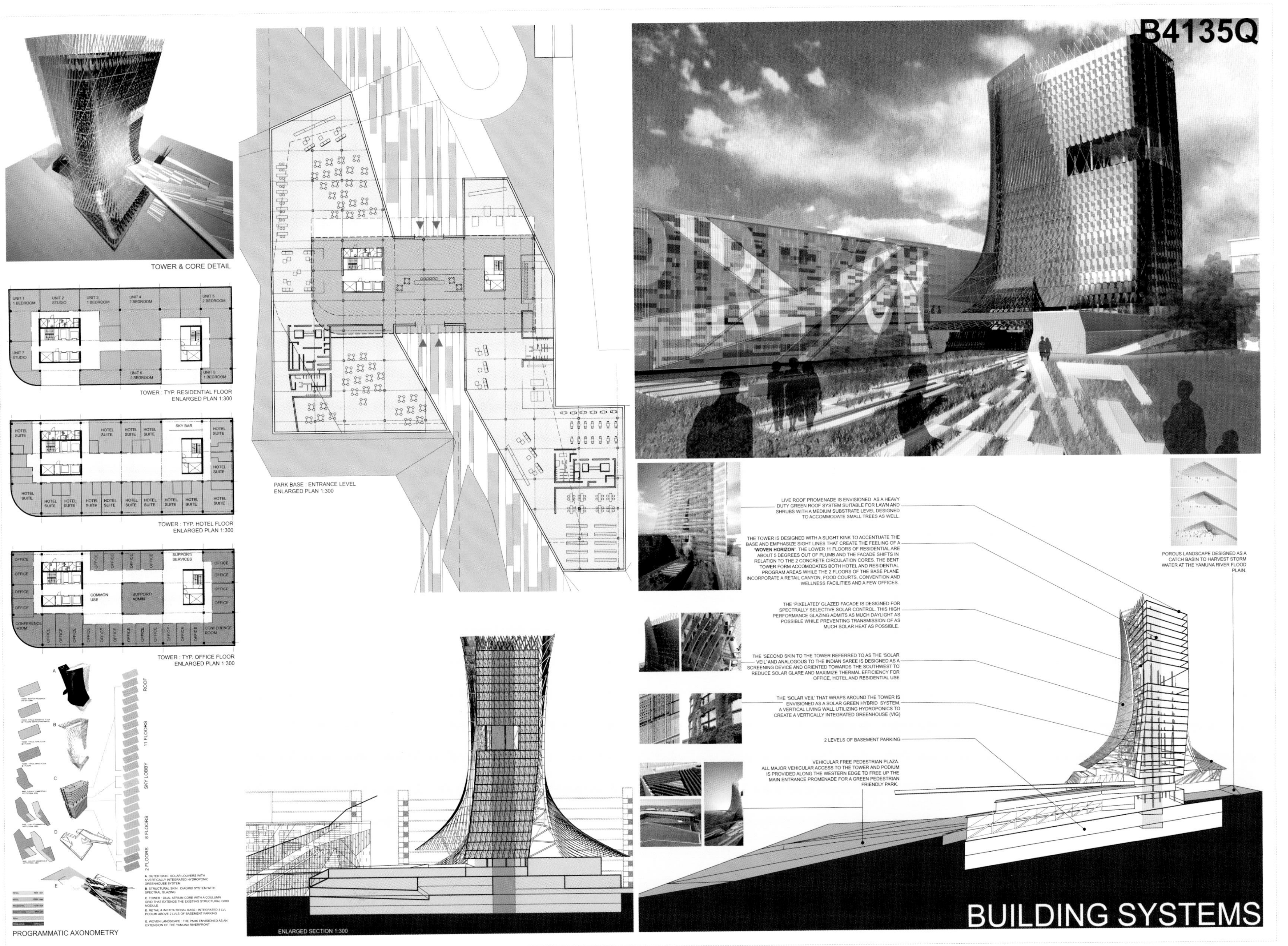

B4135Q
BUILDING SYSTEMS
TOWER & CORE DETAIL
UNIT 1 1 BEDROOM
UNIT 2 STUDIO
UNIT 3 1 BEDROOM
UNIT 4 2 BEDROOM
UNIT 5 2 BEDROOM
UNIT 7 STUDIO
UNIT 6 2 BEDROOM
UNIT 5 1 BEDROOM
TOWER : TYP. RESIDENTIAL FLOOR
ENLARGED PLAN 1:300
HOTEL SUITE
SKY BAR
TOWER : TYP. HOTEL FLOOR
ENLARGED PLAN 1:300
OFFICE
SUPPORT/ SERVICES
COMMON USE
SUPPORT/ ADMIN
CONFERENCE ROOM
TOWER : TYP. OFFICE FLOOR
ENLARGED PLAN 1:300
ROOF
11 FLOORS
SKY LOBBY
8 FLOORS
2 FLOORS
A. OUTER SKIN : SOLAR LOUVERS WITH A VERTICALLY INTEGRATED HYDROPONIC GREENHOUSE SYSTEM
B. STRUCTURAL SKIN : DIAGRID SYSTEM WITH SPECTRAL GLAZING
C. TOWER : DUAL ATRIUM CORE WITH A COULUMN GRID THAT EXTENDS THE EXISTING STRUCTURAL GRID MODULE
D. RETAIL & INSTITUTIONAL BASE : INTEGRATED 3 LVL PODIUM ABOVE 2 LVLS OF BASEMENT PARKING
E. WOVEN LANDSCAPE : THE PARK ENVISIONED AS AN EXTENSION OF THE YAMUNA RIVERFRONT
PROGRAMMATIC AXONOMETRY
PARK BASE : ENTRANCE LEVEL
ENLARGED PLAN 1:300
ENLARGED SECTION 1:300
LIVE ROOF PROMENADE IS ENVISIONED AS A HEAVY DUTY GREEN ROOF SYSTEM SUITABLE FOR LAWN AND SHRUBS WITH A MEDIUM SUBSTRATE LEVEL DESIGNED TO ACCOMMODATE SMALL TREES AS WELL.
THE TOWER IS DESIGNED WITH A SLIGHT KINK TO ACCENTUATE THE BASE AND EMPHASIZE SIGHT LINES THAT CREATE THE FEELING OF A 'WOVEN HORIZON'. THE LOWER 11 FLOORS OF RESIDENTIAL ARE ABOUT 5 DEGREES OUT OF PLUMB AND THE FACADE SHIFTS IN RELATION TO THE 2 CONCRETE CIRCULATION CORES. THE BENT TOWER FORM ACCOMODATES BOTH HOTEL AND RESIDENTIAL PROGRAM AREAS WHILE THE 2 FLOORS OF THE BASE PLANE INCORPORATE A RETAIL CANYON, FOOD COURTS, CONVENTION AND WELLNESS FACILITIES AND A FEW OFFICES.
THE 'PIXELATED' GLAZED FACADE IS DESIGNED FOR SPECTRALLY SELECTIVE SOLAR CONTROL. THIS HIGH PERFORMANCE GLAZING ADMITS AS MUCH DAYLIGHT AS POSSIBLE WHILE PREVENTING TRANSMISSION OF AS MUCH SOLAR HEAT AS POSSIBLE.
THE 'SECOND SKIN TO THE TOWER REFERRED TO AS THE 'SOLAR VEIL' AND ANALOGOUS TO THE INDIAN SAREE IS DESIGNED AS A SCREENING DEVICE AND ORIENTED TOWARDS THE SOUTHWEST TO REDUCE SOLAR GLARE AND MAXIMIZE THERMAL EFFICIENCY FOR OFFICE, HOTEL AND RESIDENTIAL USE
THE 'SOLAR VEIL' THAT WRAPS AROUND THE TOWER IS ENVISIONED AS A SOLAR GREEN HYBRID SYSTEM. A VERTICAL LIVING WALL UTILIZING HYDROPONICS TO CREATE A VERTICALLY INTEGRATED GREENHOUSE (VIG)
2 LEVELS OF BASEMENT PARKING
VEHICULAR FREE PEDESTRIAN PLAZA. ALL MAJOR VEHICULAR ACCESS TO THE TOWER AND PODIUM IS PROVIDED ALONG THE WESTERN EDGE TO FREE UP THE MAIN ENTRANCE PROMENADE FOR A GREEN PEDESTRIAN FRIENDLY PARK.
POROUS LANDSCAPE DESIGNED AS A CATCH BASIN TO HARVEST STORM WATER AT THE YAMUNA RIVER FLOOD PLAIN.

051508

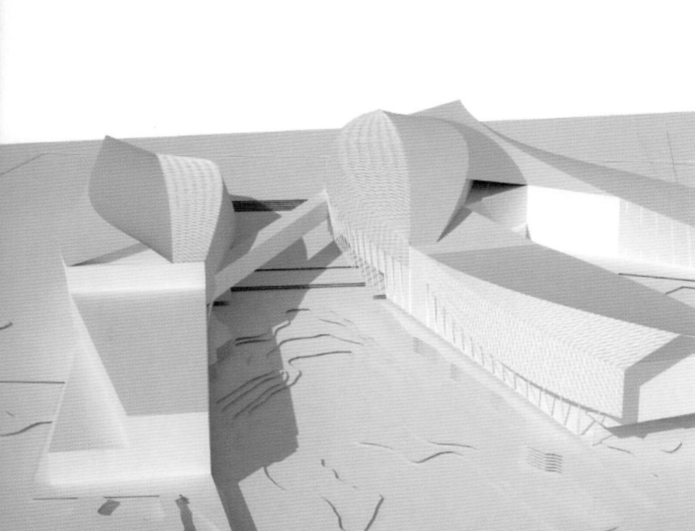

PARENTHESIS ( )

BRACKETING THE RAVINE

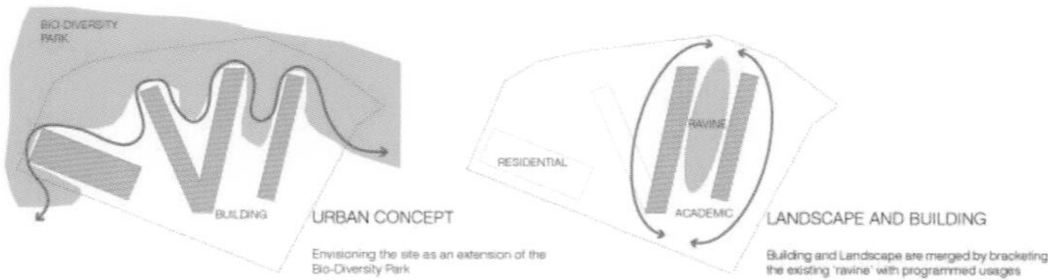

URBAN CONCEPT

Envisioning the site as an extension of the Bio-Diversity Park

LANDSCAPE AND BUILDING

Building and Landscape are merged by bracketing the existing 'ravine' with programmed usages

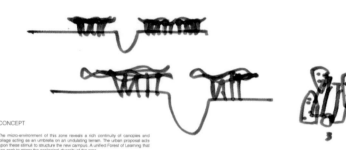

CONCEPT

The micro-environment of this zone reveals a rich continuity of canopies and foliage acting as an umbrella on an undulating terrain. The urban proposal acts upon these stimuli to structure the new campus. A unified Forest of Learning that can seek to mirror the ecological diversity of the area.

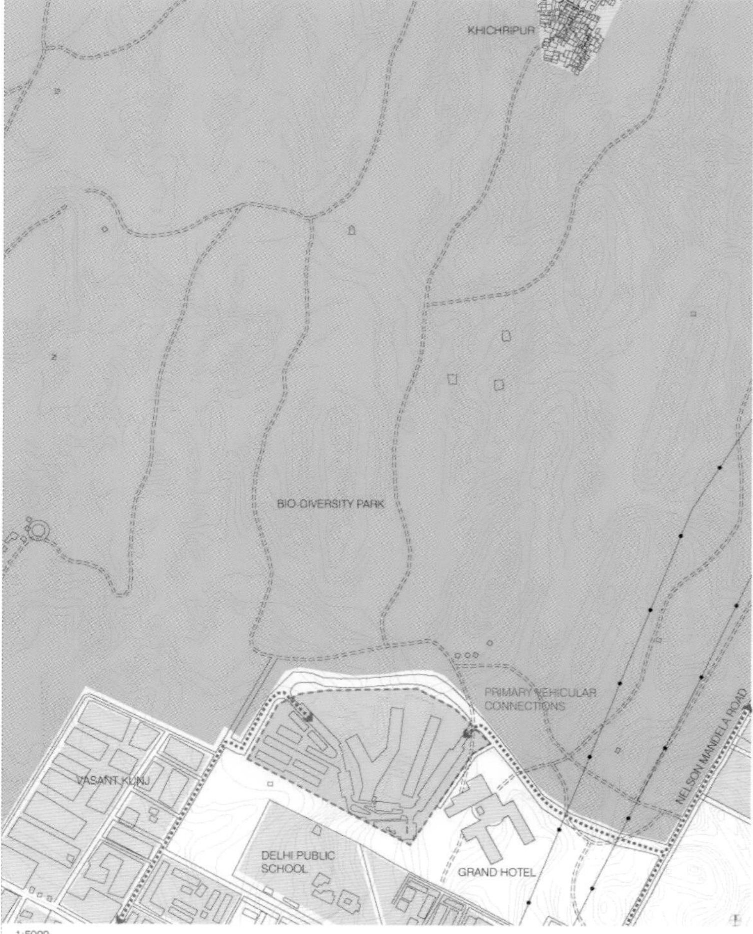

1:5000

PARENTHESIS is seen as a project that strategically embeds program on the site to connect the surrounding area into a new whole, blending built and natural environments

A PLACE FOR KNOWLEDGE

The New School of Planning and Architecture presents an opportunity to not only relocate an institution, but indeed to redefine it. Learning, research and training constitute the traditional framework of a University. In the 21st century however, exchange, collaboration, experimentation and cross-pollination are equally critical to a school.

India is fortunate to have a rich history in this arena. Taxila and Nalanda for example, were pathbreaking in the formal structuring of education.

This proposal therefore, seeks to draw upon both the traditional and the contemporary, to re-imagine the New School of Planning and Architecture.

THE SITE

The Site is characterized by the South Central Ridge to the North, Residential Development to the South and major Commercial and Institutional buildings to the East and West. The Ridge has been designated as a Bio-Diversity Park that will act as an ecological corridor and help harvest rainwater. The terrain of the area is fairly undulated and rocky and is characterized by a diverse arrangement of water systems and vegetative patterns that are perfect for recharging groundwater and growing rich flora.

The site has been exploited to create programmatic usages that allow the ridge to weave in and help transition between landscape and the urban fabric.

ORGANIZATION OF PROGRAM

The Site is diagonally sliced by a feeder road that helps unify the Academic and Residential zones. This single feeder road also connects to the main service lane. Residential program is located to the West of the road, a private zone and Academic program to the East, a public zone.

The Academic program is further divided into Undergraduate and Post-Graduate blocks. The Ravine becomes a primary armature. An organizational strategy is defined by 'bracketing' this ravine.

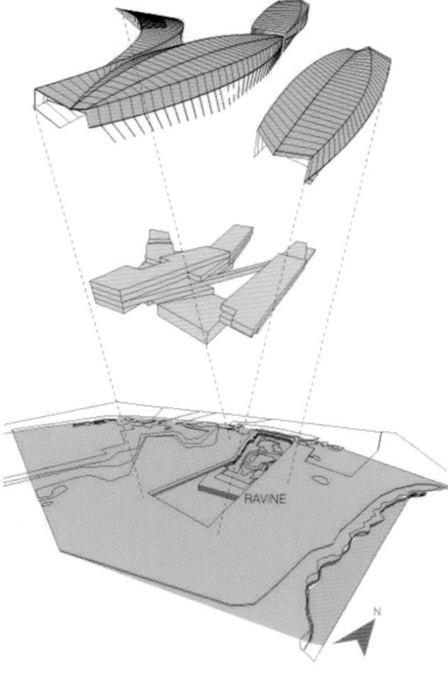

18m

1. CONCEPT

051508
EXISTING CONDITIONS
Maximizing preservation of the micro-environment by creating distinct Landscape Zones
HISTORIC PRECEDENTS
Reinterpreting historic prototypes of Stepped Wells and Ghats to structure open spaces and dovetail them with adjacent built form
TYPICAL FEATURES
Creating a landscape hierarchy to enrich proposed zones and to preserve the existing character of the Ridge. Tree, Canopy, Scrub types have been derived from categories mentioned in the Yamuna Biodiversity Plan.
BRACKETING THE RAVINE BLENDING BUILT & NATURAL ENVIRONMENTS
ESTABLISHING TERRAIN
Preserving major on-site vegetation and conserving existing trees and canopy cover
RETAINING TERRAIN
Identifying major ridge lines & seasonal water bodies to
Develop circulation connectors and harvest zones
CONSTRUCTING TERRAIN
Embedding built form into graded terrain and flanking the 'ravine' with program to create zones of learning, gathering and dwelling
FOREST
FISHBOWL
WALL
PLATEAU
FOUR LANDSCAPE ZONES
ROAD 30M ROW
32M WIDE GREEN STRIP
SERVICE ROAD 16.5M ROW
Based on the Yamuna Bio Diversity Plan this zone is classified as 'Tropical dry deciduous forest'
TROPICAL DRY DECUDUOUS FOREST ECOSYSTEM WITH SAL AS A DOMINANT SPECIES
Top canopy – Shorea robusta, Diospros melanoxylon, Putranjiva roxburghii
Middle storey – Erythrina indica, Cassia fistula, Albizia sp., Sterculia urens
Shrub layer – Carissa spinarum, Zizyphus oenoplea, Nyctanthus arbortristis
Herbs & Grasses – Chloris, Eragrostis, Fimbristylis ferruginea, Indigofera tinctoria
Climbers – Smilax zeylanica, Clittoria turnatea, Marsdenia, Cocculus hirsutus
TROPICAL DRY DECIDUOUS FOREST WITH TEAK AS A DOMINANT SPECIES
Top Canopy – Tectona grandis, Butea monosperma, Sterculia urens, Terminalia chebula
Middle storey – Emblica officinalis, Bauhina variegata, Cochlospermum religiosum
Shrub layer – Gardenia turgida, Randia dumetorum, Grewia asiatica
Herbs & Grasses – Barleria prionitis, Bothriochloa pertusa, Dicanthium Hetropogo
Climbers – Abrus pulchellus, Cocculus hirsutus
FOREST
FISHBOWL
PLATEAU
HOTEL GRAND HYATT
DELHI PUBLIC SCHOOL VASANT KUNJ
TYPOLOGIES
GENERATED LANDSCAPE 1 : 1000
2. LANDSCAPE

051508

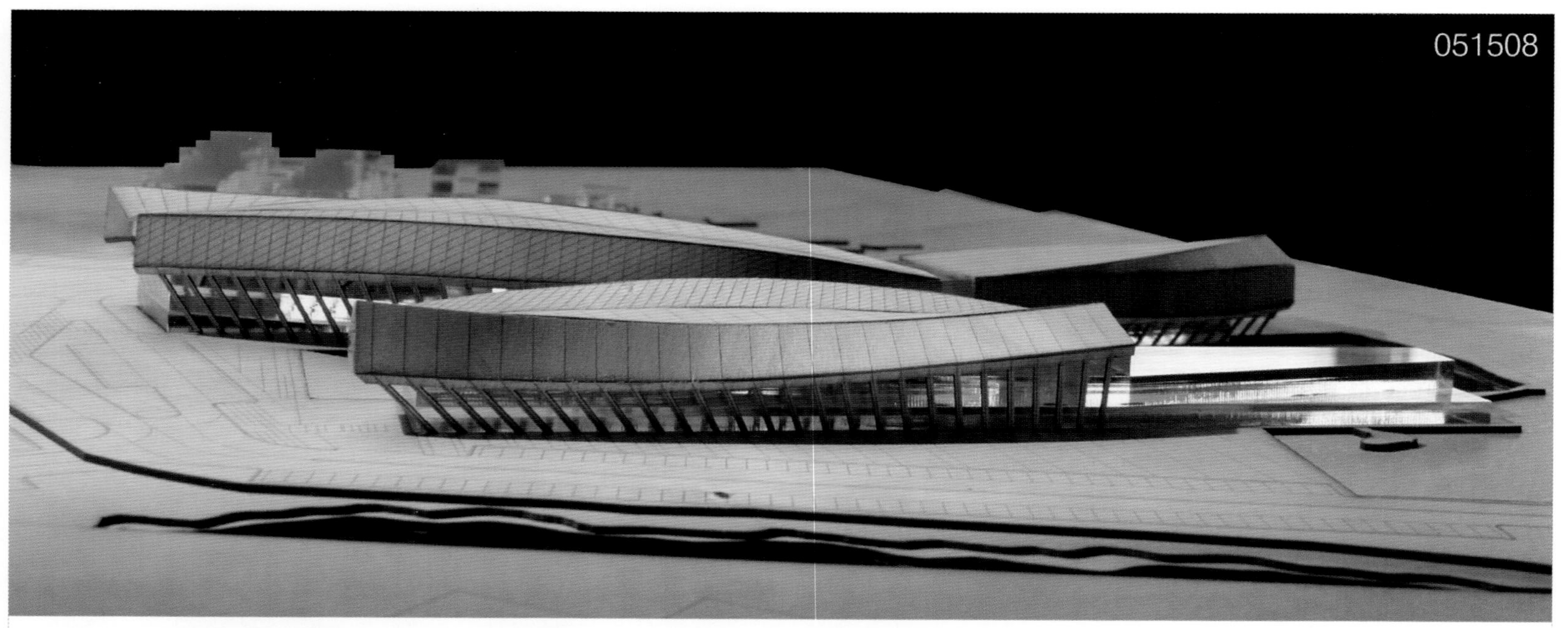

BRACKETING THE RAVINE BLENDING BUILT & NATURAL ENVIRONMENTS

SCALED PROGRAM TABULATION

UNDER-GRADUATE ARCHITECTURE – 8 578 SQM
UNDER-GRADUATE PLANNING – 2 338 SQM
POST-GRADUATE DEPARTMENTS – 9,958 SQM
COMMON FACILITIES – 6,235 SQM
ADMINISTRATION /MAINTAINANCE – 1,306 SQM
RESIDENTIAL PROGRAM – 16,290 SQM
RECREATIONAL PROGRAM – 1,892 SQM
0 10
50
100M

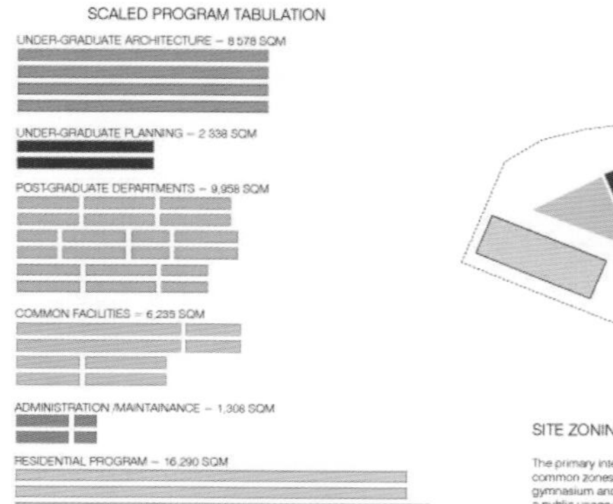

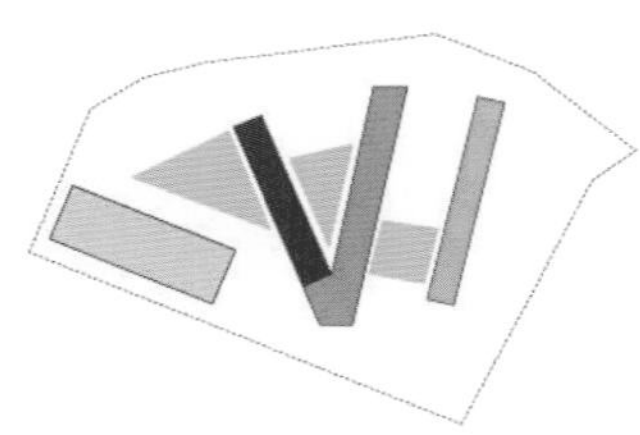

SITE ZONING RATIONALE

The primary intent of program distribution is the creation of common zones that separate and unify the site. The library, gymnasium and theatre, for example are each an example of a public usage that encourages merging and mingling of otherwise distinct program zones.
Common areas are therefore publicly accessible for research, events and conferences in addition to internal institutional use.

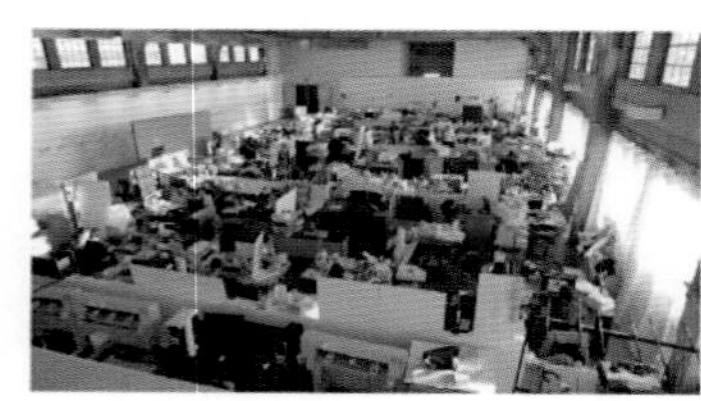

STUDIO MODULES

The Architectural academic block is entirely predicated on unit modules that enable a typical studio to be subdivided into further faculty-student units, thereby encouraging leaner teacher-student ratios without sacrificing on the unified space needed for creative collaboration.

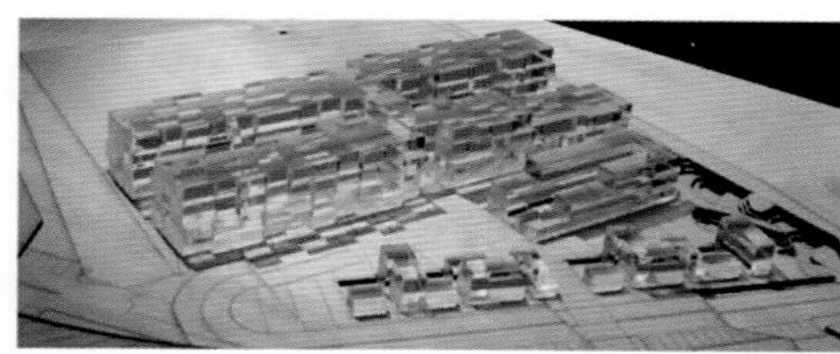

HOUSING MODULES

Dormitories are planned along unit modules. Each module acts as a formal generator in addition to optimizing the underlying 8.5m x 8.5m grid. Guest houses are designed as volumes with garden courtyards between units.
The strict comb-like articulation and cubic volumes accentuate the planar quality of the facades in contrast to the more organically shaped academic zone.

PROGRAM DISTRIBUTION

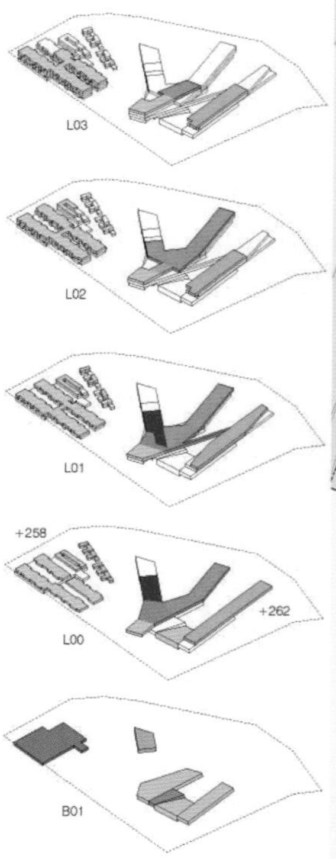

L03
L02
L01
+258
+262
L00
B01

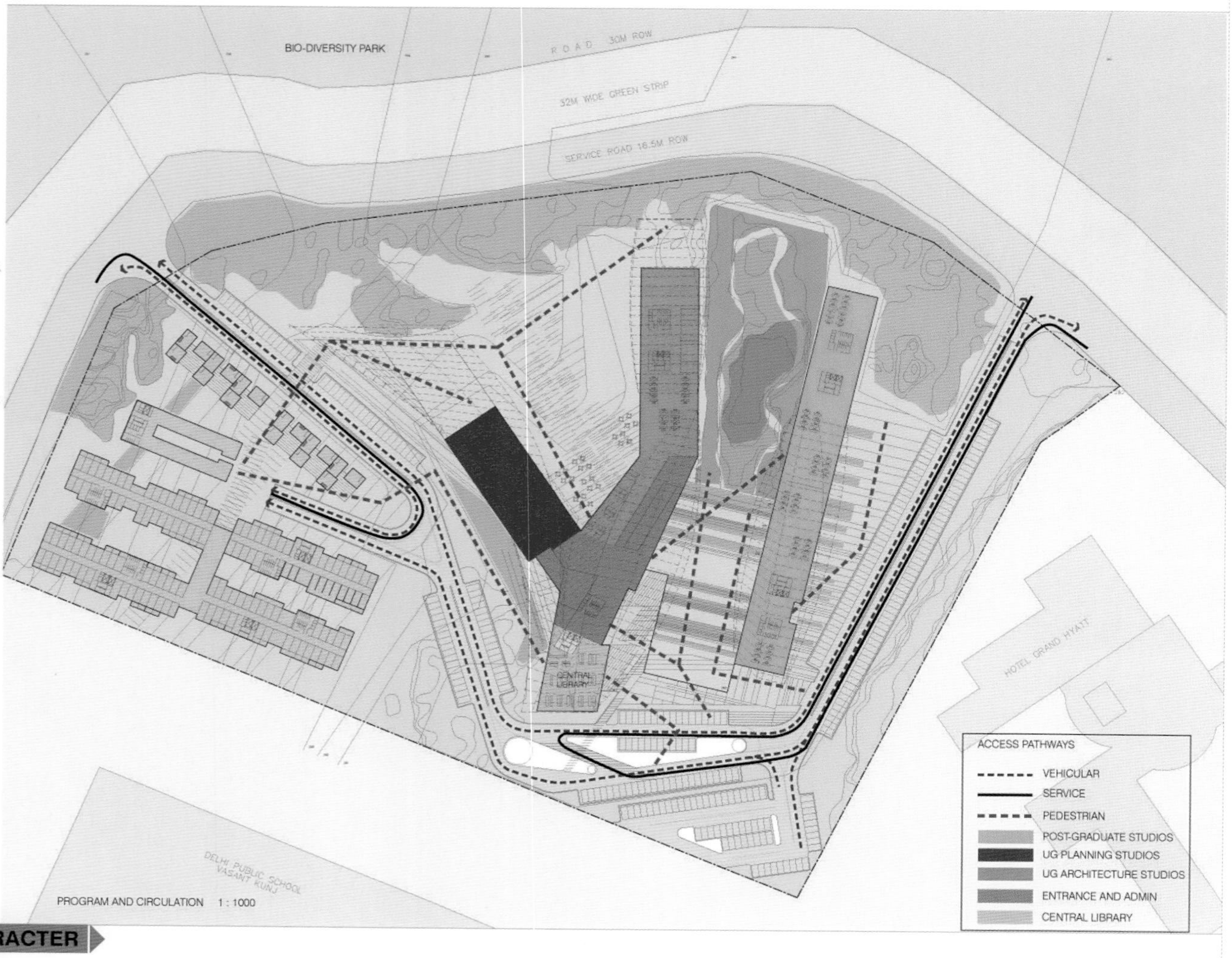

BIO-DIVERSITY PARK
ROAD 30M ROW
30M WIDE GREEN STRIP
SERVICE ROAD 16.5M ROW
CENTRAL LIBRARY
HOTEL GRAND HYATT
DELHI PUBLIC SCHOOL VASANT KUNJ
ACCESS PATHWAYS
VEHICULAR
SERVICE
PEDESTRIAN
POST-GRADUATE STUDIOS
UG PLANNING STUDIOS
UG ARCHITECTURE STUDIOS
ENTRANCE AND ADMIN
CENTRAL LIBRARY

PROGRAM AND CIRCULATION 1 : 1000

3. ARCHITECTURAL CHARACTER

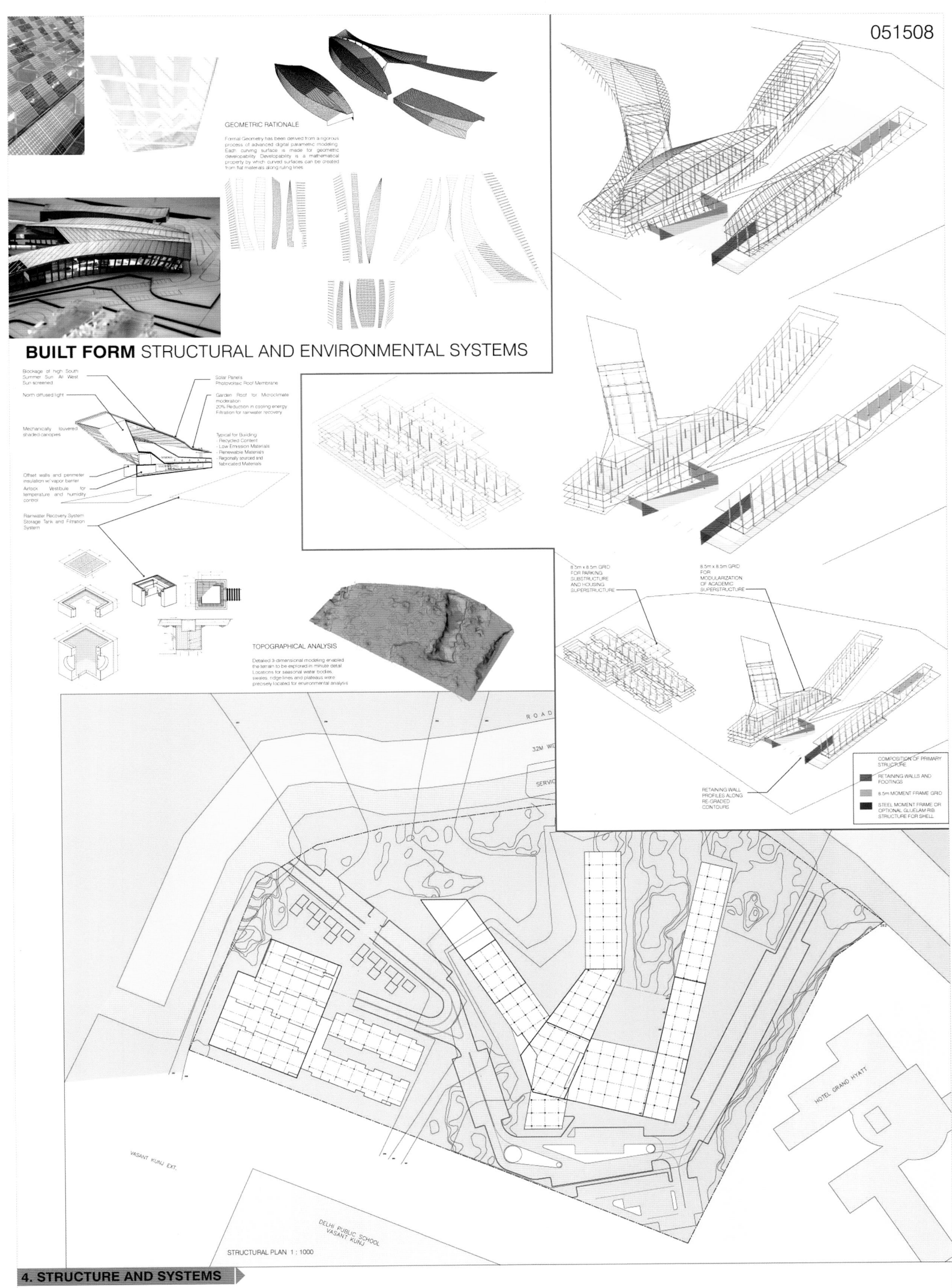

051508
GEOMETRIC RATIONALE
BUILT FORM STRUCTURAL AND ENVIRONMENTAL SYSTEMS
TOPOGRAPHICAL ANALYSIS
COMPOSITION OF PRIMARY STRUCTURE
RETAINING WALLS AND FOOTINGS
8.5m MOMENT FRAME GRID
STEEL MOMENT FRAME OR OPTIONAL GLUELAM RIB STRUCTURE FOR SHELL
RETAINING WALL PROFILES ALONG RE-GRADED CONTOURS
HOTEL GRAND HYATT
VASANT KUNJ EXT.
DELHI PUBLIC SCHOOL VASANT KUNJ
STRUCTURAL PLAN 1 : 1000

4. STRUCTURE AND SYSTEMS

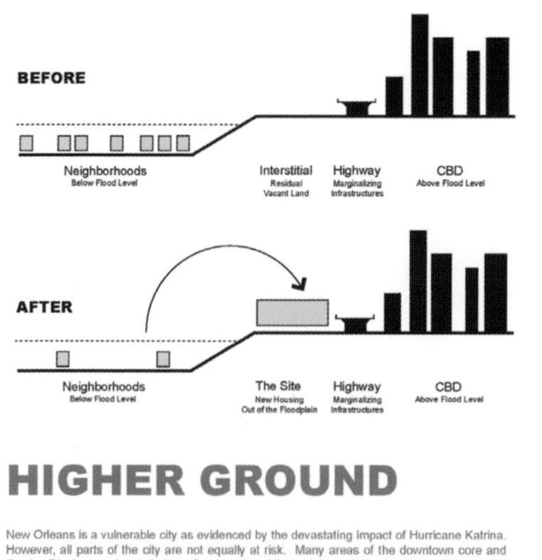

HIGHER GROUND

New Orleans is a vulnerable city as evidenced by the devastating impact of Hurricane Katrina. However, all parts of the city are not equally at risk. Many areas of the downtown core and Garden District are elevated above flood levels, while out-lying neighborhoods (such as the 9th Ward) are in the crosshairs of floodwaters. Along these lines, Katrina dealt an unequal blow to the citizens of New Orleans

Immediately following the disaster, some argued that New Orleans shouldn't be rebuilt. As insensitive as this position may be to established communities with rich histories, social networks and memories – it is difficult to imagine resettling the city with the same vulnerabilities it has always had knowing what we know since Katrina.

Historically New Orleans has been characterized by two major densities – downtown high rises (largely commercial office), and low-rise single-family residential development further out in the neighborhoods. Some mid-century housing projects and the French Quarter reveal some hints at a mid scale, but neither demonstrate a prototypical housing solution for the city.

Our proposal looks to reshuffle New Orleans in order to make a safer more equitable city for all of its population. Analysis of flood maps reveal that there is substantial downtown territory above the flood elevation that lies vacant or under-developed. This area includes the competition site. We believe that this is an unexploited opportunity to provide new housing options to people living in low-lying neighborhoods to remain in the city – safely out of harms way. We also envision this new mid-rise prototype as an invitation to the 100,000 residents who have been unable to return to New Orleans to-date and could be offered a more walkable, high-amenity urban core location rather than a dangerous, low-lying location further out. This new mid-rise density could begin to define a new layer of urban fabric that could help evolve a greater proportion of New Orleans into a walkable, mixed-use vibrant city.

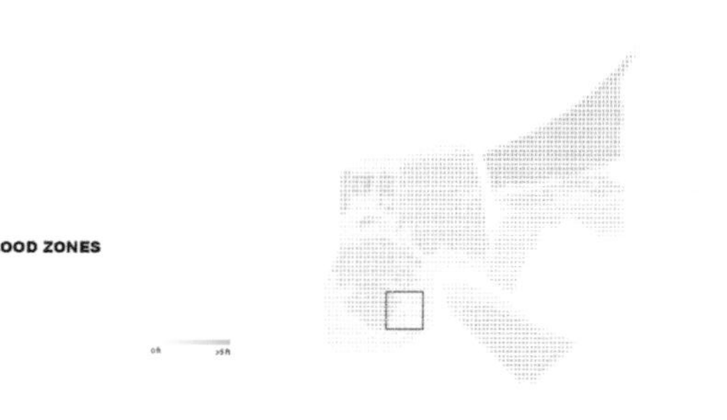

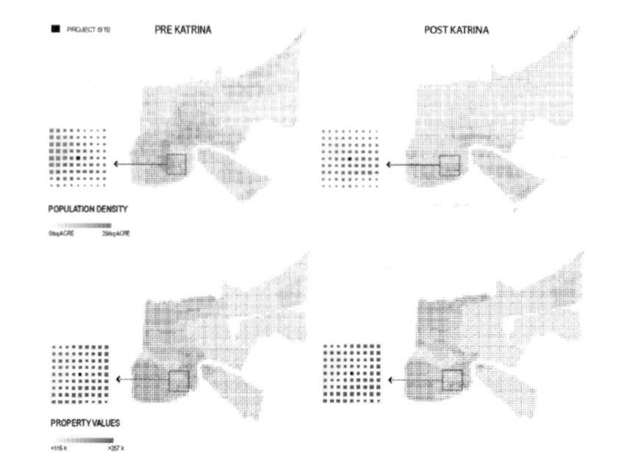

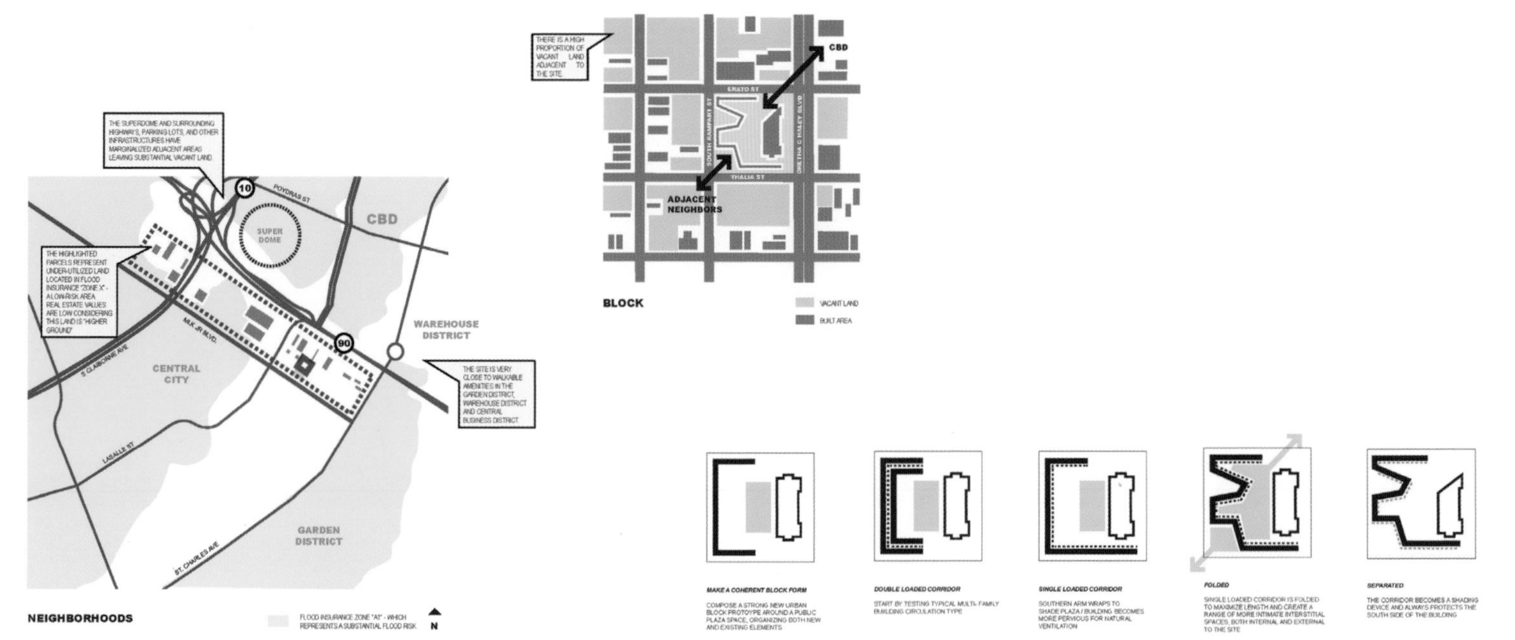

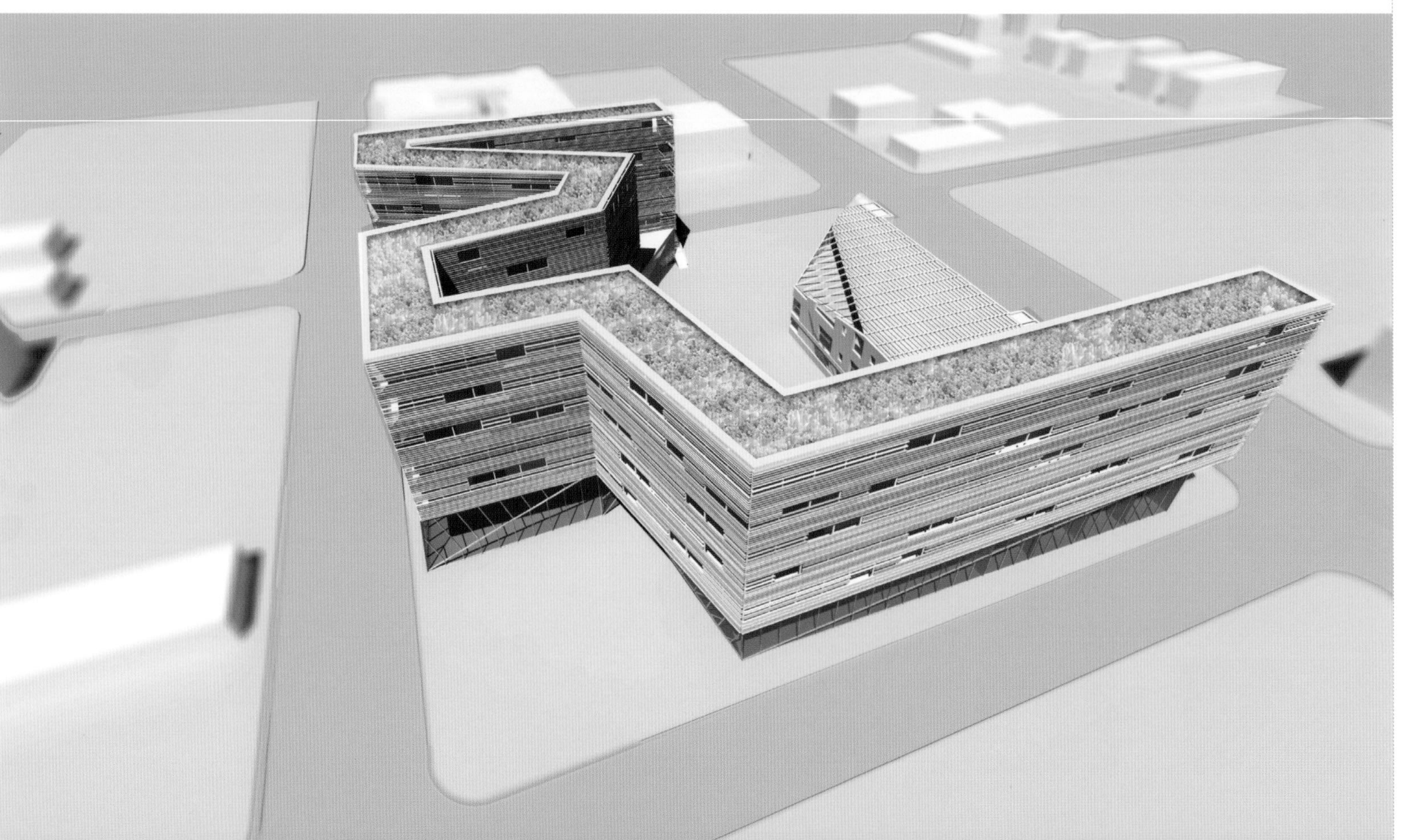

DESIGN INTENT

Our approach is equal parts urban planning, community-making, and green building. We see the solution as a prototype that can infiltrate those marginalized zones of the city, plagued by vacant land, which are well positioned above the flood plain. The plan integates existing fragments of urban fabric (the former school building) into a whole block configuration that strengthens the walkable, mixed-use, urban characteristics of New Orleans.

Rather than a conventional double loaded corridor building, we have proposed a single loaded building with an unconditioned circulation spine that also serves as a massive shading device. The plan figure undulates to maximize the perimeter and density of housing units. This creates an indoor/outdoor hallway that mediating access to light, inviting natural ventilation and encouraging mini-communities to emerge along the corridors.

Our scheme proposes a radical re-activation of the former school building into community-oriented amenities such as social clinics, daycare and recreational facilities meant to serve the immediate residents. The idea of this new block development approach is to integrate existing buildings with new developments in a mutually beneficial manner. We have cut and removed a piece of the building to help reinforce the urban connection to the northeast. We replace that cut with a glass curtainwall to show the new activity in the re-commissioned building to the city at-large. The badly damaged roof is replaced with a delicate roof trellis that becomes a shading device for the building as well as an environmental mediator with PV panels and a green roof.

COLOR AND TEXTURE

VERNACULAR NEW ORLEANS ARCHITECTURE INSPIRED THE COLORFUL SCREEN ELEMENT OF OUR PROPOSAL / IT IS BOTH VISUALLY "LOCAL" AS WELL AS ENVIRIONMENTALLY FUNCTIONAL

NORTH EAST

NORTH WEST

SOUTH WEST

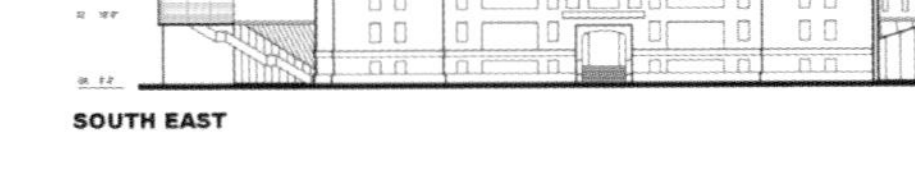

SOUTH EAST

BUILDING ELEVATIONS 1"=32'

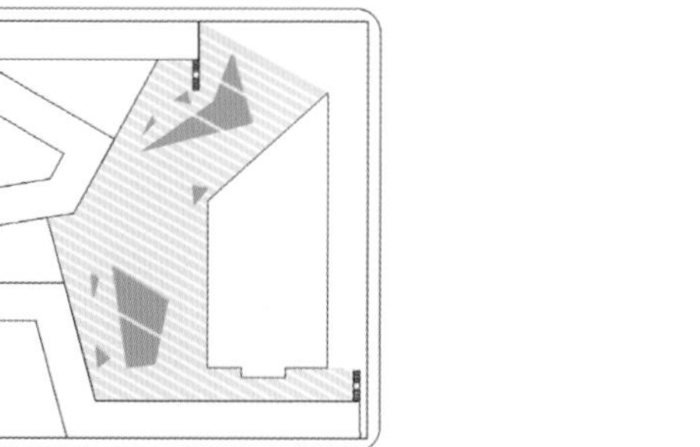

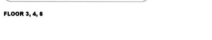

ROOF PLAN

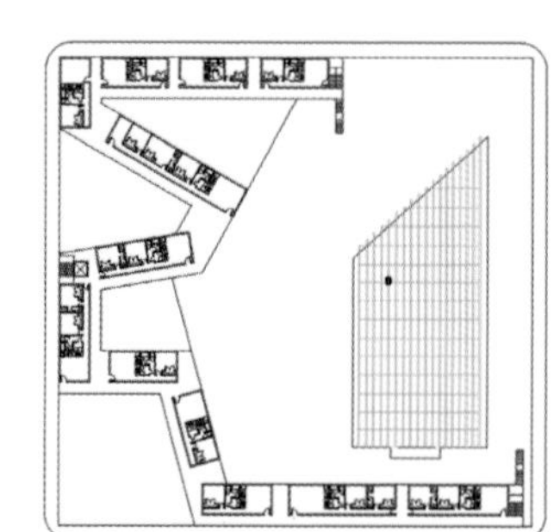

FLOOR 3, 4, 6

FLOOR 2, 5

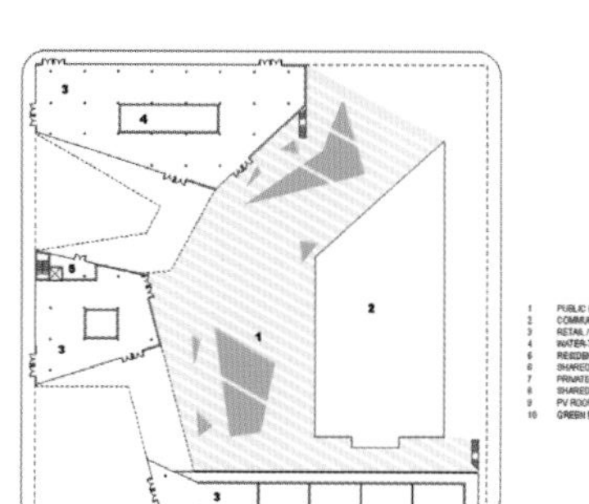

FLOOR 1

BUILDING FLOOR PLANS 1"=50'

UNIT FLOOR PLANS 1"=8'

PROGRAM STATISTICS

Community Services / Rec (in former school)	30,000 SF
Commercial / Retail	14,900 SF
Residential Units (5 stories above retail)	77,000 SF (total)
Break down by unit type	(33) 1BR @ approx 670 SF/ ea (24) 2BR @ approx 950 SF/ ea (3) 3BR @ approx 1,400 SF/ ea
Common Terraces (level 2)	4,500 SF
Plaza (public)	21,000 SF

SUSTAINABILITY

Our approach to sustainability is wide-ranging and operates at several levels:

URBAN

New Orleans was forever changed by Hurricane Katrina and needs to aggressively seize new opportunities. With 100,000 residents still displaced across the world and throngs of tourists, investors, and business people drawn to the city on a regular basis, there are new possibilities for making the city walkable, compact, and therefore efficient. By situating higher density close to the city center and making new mixed-use communities, New Orleans becomes a lower-energy, more sustainable urban center.

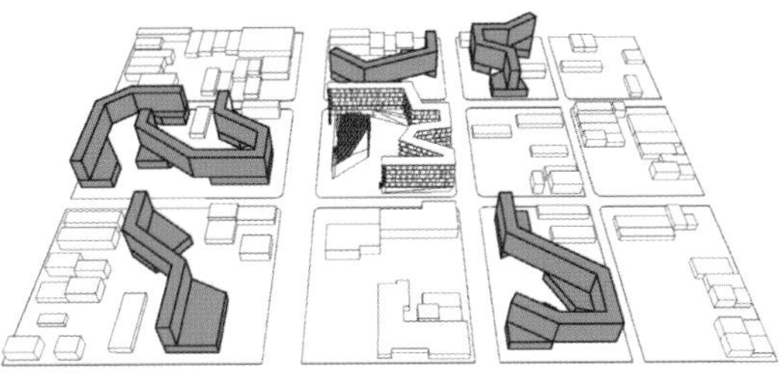

GREEN BUILDING

Buildings can consume much less energy by simply making smart decisions. Our design process is equal parts site planning, building massing, orientation, and smart construction and systems as a strategy for a low-energy project. We believe that green buildings make communities affordable and sustainable by reducing energy bills. The shaded, circulation spine demonstrates a synthesis of program, materiality, and image into a single move that addresses multiple layers of community building while also providing a powerful green building element. That spine acts as a vertical chimney to passively encourage cooled air to permeate the circulation spaces and are invited through the units by way of individually controlled operable windows and dampers.

Mechanical cooling is the major energy consumer in New Orleans. By our calculations seven gallons of water are produced per hour during the cooling season from condensate. We propose to harvest this resource and provide a major graywater reserve for the building.

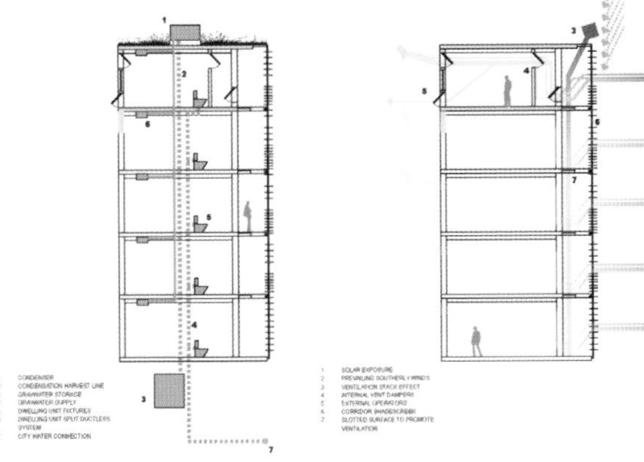

FEEDBACK

Buildings can use less energy in two ways. They can utilize green building technology and sensitive design strategies to fundamentally consume less energy. High performance envelopes and high efficiency equipment are both proven ways to achieve this goal. However, the modification of the behavior of the occupants is another strategy that can lead to significant reduction in energy use. We propose a smartphone app that would allow residents to receive alerts to remind them when the temperature and humidity are ideal for window opening, and when it's time to change their HVAC filters, etc. The app can perform micro-commissioning through a series of real-time weather calibrated prompts to help modify behavior through time.

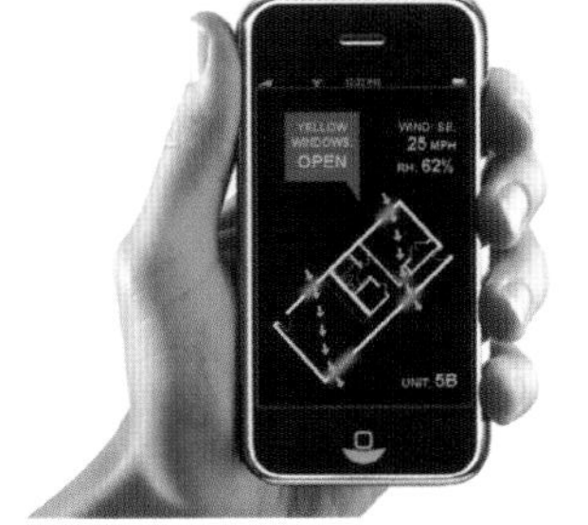

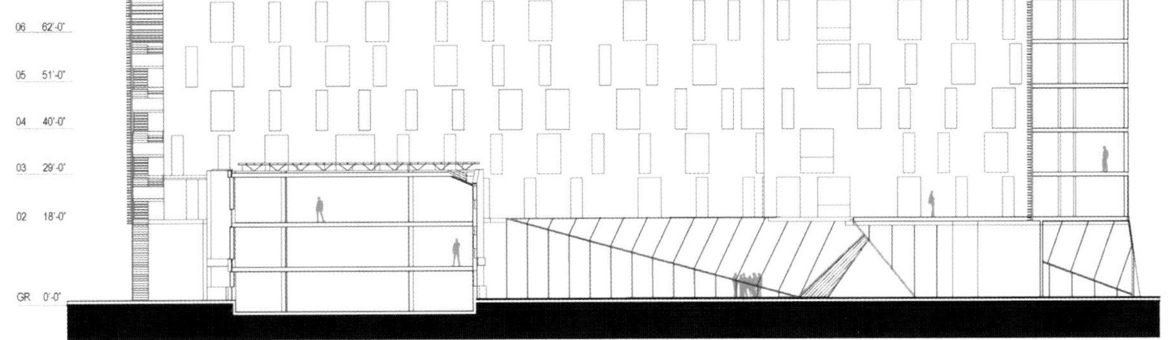

BUILDING SECTION 1/16" = 1'

159 Cheongna City Tower | *IaN+*

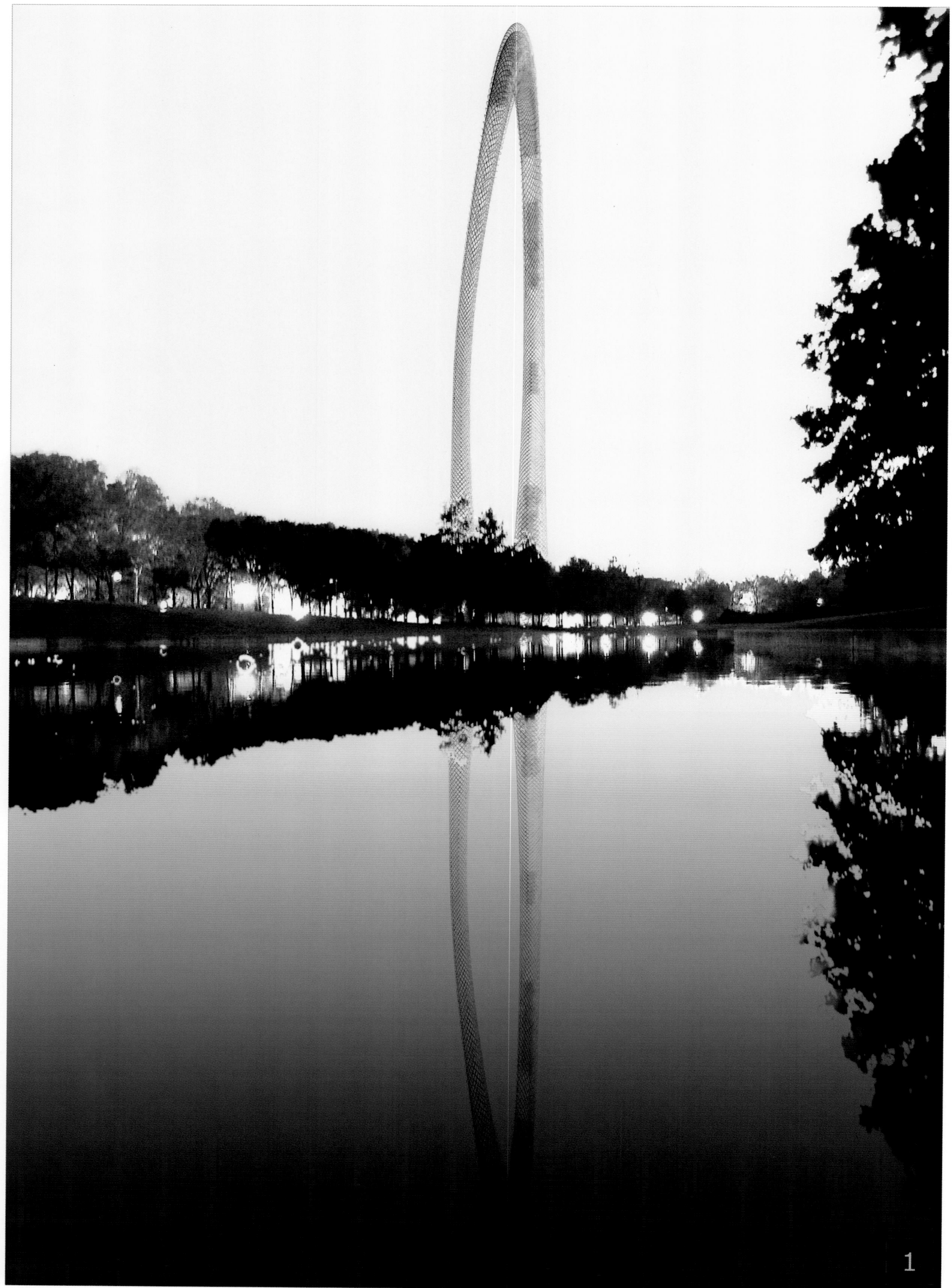
1

CHEONGNA CITY TOWER > OPEN WINDOW TO THE WORLD

A landmark for the new identity of Incheon

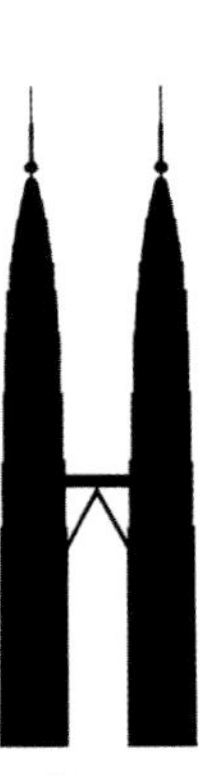

The Arch, a sign bridging History and Nature

In history Arches have always been a clear icon associated to the tradition and glory of the different places.

Monumental "city gates" were the threshold among "inside-outside", the door whose beauty and magnitude would symbolize the importance of the place you were about to enter; Triumphal Arches were an evolution of the city-gates, being at first very simple symbolic temporary gateways to the city, and later evolved into really intricate and elaborated architecture to celebrate a victory in war or a ruler.

The form of the arch also reflects many examples found in nature. As the building bridges the strip of water the bisects the island, it recalls the natural stone arches that are carved out over millenia by water and wind. The open, interlocking structure soaring overhead is suggestive of the canopy of tall trees that reach towards each other from either side of a country road. The fluid lines are derived from the geometries of plant life and the shapes given to the earth by the forces of water, wind, and time. The tower doesn't merely sit on the site - it appears to have been extracted from it, pulled out of the ground to reach skywards, and then descending back again to reconnect to the gardens and find its union with the earth. As in nature, there is an easy balance of form and character struck between environment, function, and tectonics.

Cheongna City Tower

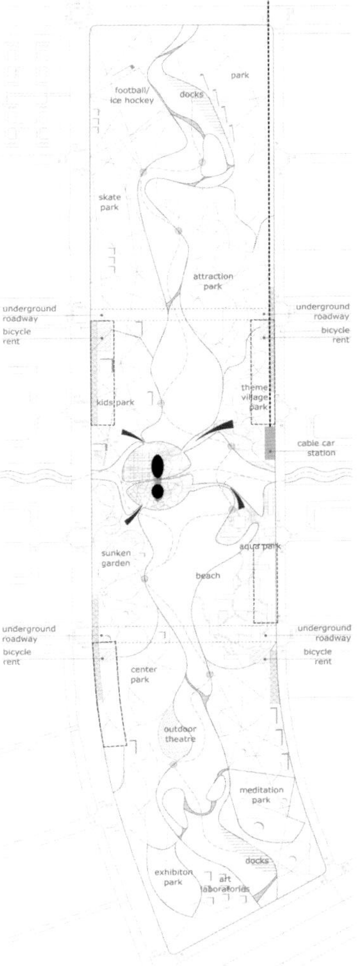

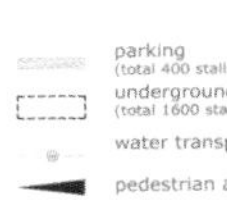

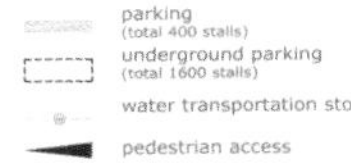

Master plan
scale 1:5000

Vertical Park within the Tower

The open weave of the tower's structure, peeling off to flow into the lines of the gardens and waterfront, formally connect the tower to its site. To augment this connection between building and landscape, we propose the tower to act as a soaring vertical garden, bringing the surrounding park first inside its boundaries and then pulling them high into the air. This treatment of green space not only further blurs the division between interior and exterior (a blurring initiated by the weaving structure of the tower, the alternating patterns of enclosed spaces and open terraces, the large expanses of the tower that are open-air, and the transparent, shimmering quality of the enclosing facade) but also completes a connection between the larger scale of the city of Cheongna. The canals and parks that flow through the city open up to become the expansive gardens and lake of Crystal Park, which in turn flow into the tower island and then up into the building itself. The experience of the tower thus becomes that of being enveloped by green and luminous nature, even while standing in the observatory deck 425 meters above the earth.

Open window to the sky

The new observation tower establishes a monumental dialogue with its surroundings through a prominent vertical element. In function, the creation of an observatory tower and related amusement-leisure facilities gives new meaning to the relationship between the landscape, visitors, and the City of Incheon.

As a formal reference to the relationship with Nature, an open window to the sky, the tower's form captures the essence of the poetical bond between matter and void, becoming an iconic beacon in the area. Similar to monuments such as the St. Louis Arch, the Cheongna City Tower's gentle sculptural form is a distinguished presence within the surrounding landscape and skyline.

The project transforms the existing parcel in front of the canal into a lively landscaped piazza open to leisure and amusement activities, strengthening the connection to the adjacent public park and canals through a system of bridges branching from the tower's roots.

2

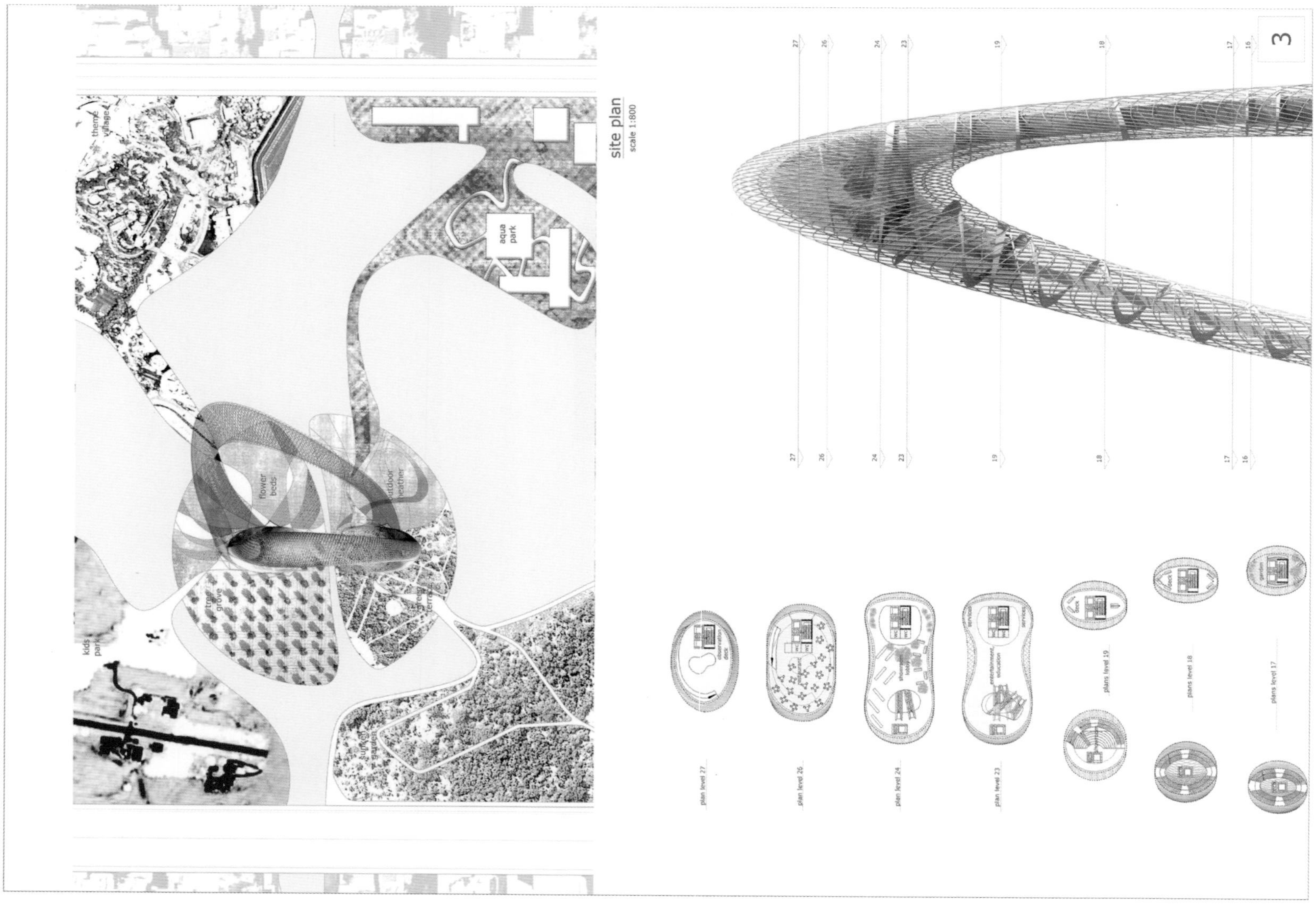

section detail 2
scale 1:400

section detail 1
scale 1:400

section detail 2
observation deck
restaurant
kitchen
services
showroom
lobby
entertainment
cafe/bar
services
lounge
deck
lounge
services
observation deck
observation deck
indoor garden
observation deck
indoor garden
lounges
jumping
indoor garden
services
administration
indoor garden
bar, cafe/
observation deck
outdoor garden
lounge
administration

section detail 1
indoor garden
exhibition hall
exhibition hall
book shop
souvenir/
gift shop
garden
lounge
indoor garden
lounge
services
technical level

section
scale 1:800

4

kids park
theme village
tree grove
flower beds
outdoor weather
green terrace
aqua park

site plan
scale 1:800

plan level 27
plan level 26
plan level 24
plan level 23
plans level 19
plans level 18
plans level 17

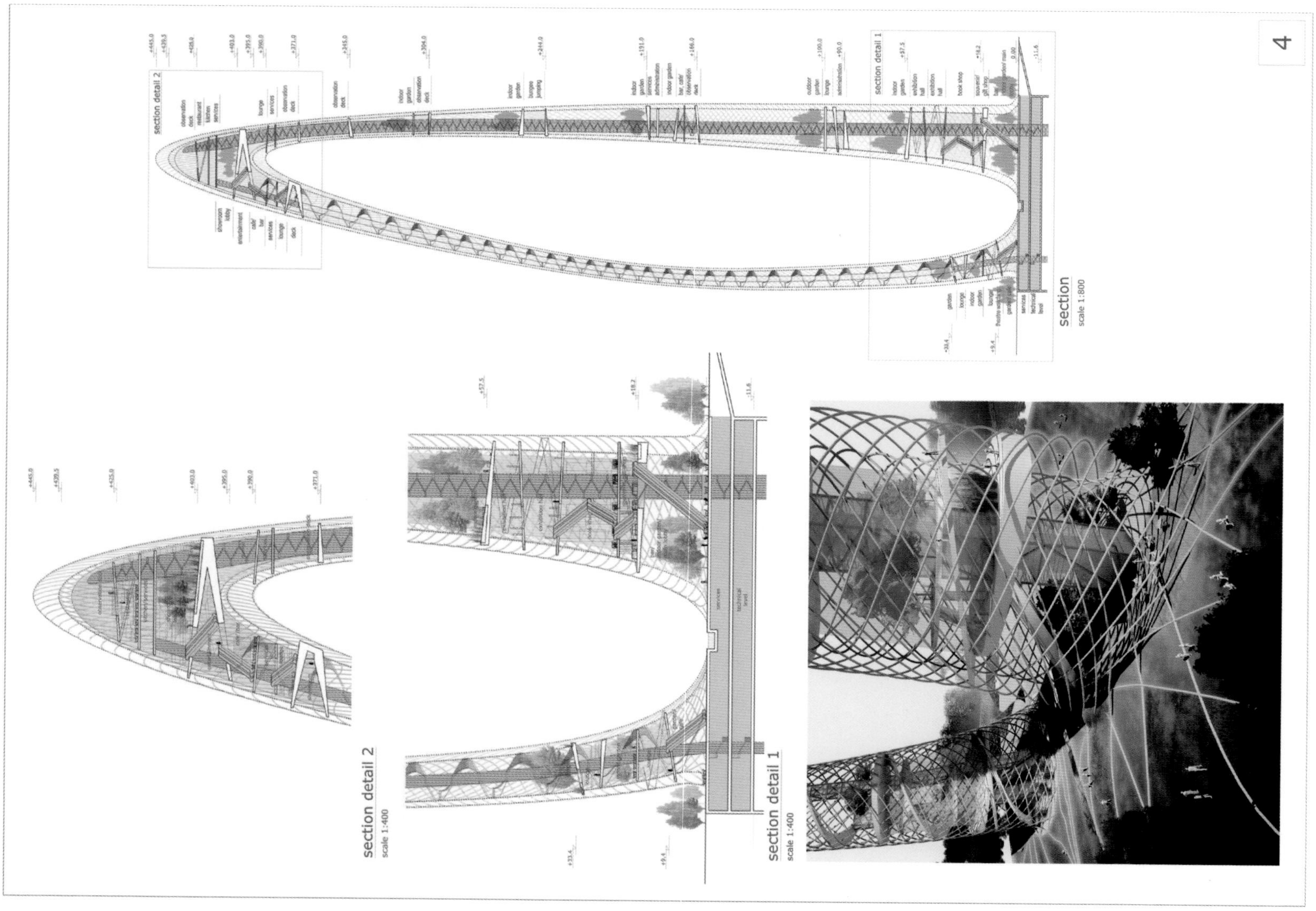

3

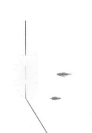

The Arch as a urban beacon

We admire what German conceptual artist Joseph Beuys said: "By producing art we lend our conscience to the things of the world. So they become our conscience." That's what we are trying to do - we try to lend our conscience to all materials here and we feel very responsible for the outcome of this project. An object is chosen because it can perform in a certain way and because we are looking for a certain performance. Forms are generated by particular circumstances and therefore become unique.
In shaping the Cheongna City Tower we addressed the issue of a strongly iconic shape, highly technically calculated but that would try to achieve an integration with nature. As a formal reference the intertwined braches in a wood, and the effect of light cutting through it, we tried to turn it into architecture.

The structural system

The tower doesn't merely sit on the site - it appears to have been extracted from it, pulled out of the ground to reach skywards, and then descending back again to reconnect to the gardens and find its union with the earth. As in nature, there is an easy balance of form and character struck between environment, function, and tectonics.
Foundations: the foundations will be constituted by deep structures like foundation bed and foundation poles, and the correct typology will be chosen on the basis of an in-depth geological investigations.
Those structures will have to be suitable to bear the load generated both by the static and dynamic components that are released to the ground.
Elevation structures: from a structural point of view we estimate the construction of a properly rigid configuration to absorb both the static and the stationary dynamic forces; to get to this result we calculated an elevation structure that is mainly composed by three elements:

1. Prestressed concrete internal core
2. High resistence steel doble mesh
3. Steel floor slabs with stiffening function
4. Foundation poles anchored to rocky layers

The "Fogging system"

As an integral part of its environment, the building is equipped formally, functionally, and technologically to be a benefit to the site. The summer climate of Incheon is quite hot, and the building is fitted with appropriate technology to create an inviting, comfortable space for its visitors, both inside the tower and in the gardens in its immediate vicinity. In order to provide visitors with ambient comfort, we propose to use a thermo-environmental controlling device, which works through a "fogging system" hidden and integrated within the building structure.
The "fogging systems" carries out four main functions:

1. Climate controlling > ambient comfort
2. Landscape integration > blurs tower with the lake
3. Green mantainance > gardens irrigation system
4. Pollution control > fights the suspended dust specks

The intertwined skin

We admire what German conceptual artist Joseph Beuys said: "By producing art we lend our conscience to the things of the world. So they become our conscience." That's what we are trying to do - we try to lend our conscience to all materials here and we feel very responsible for the outcome of this project.
In shaping the Cheongna City Tower we addressed the issue of a strongly iconic shape, highly technically calculated but that would try to achieve an integration with nature.
The form of the twisting, weaving structure of the tower is derived from the fluid, organic forms that are found in nature, especially in plant life. The connection of the structure to the ground is riminiscent of the roots of a tree; the sinuous lines of the lakefront and gardens are concentrated inside the island that acts as the focal point for the entire surrounding city, and pulled skyward, wrapping together to form the enclosure for the building. This actual, formal connection draws visitors from every part of the park and allows the tower to be relevant at both the iconic scale of the skyline and at the personal level of the pedestrian.

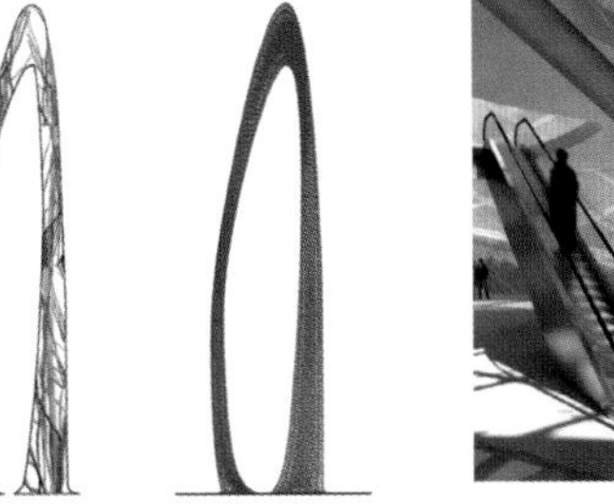

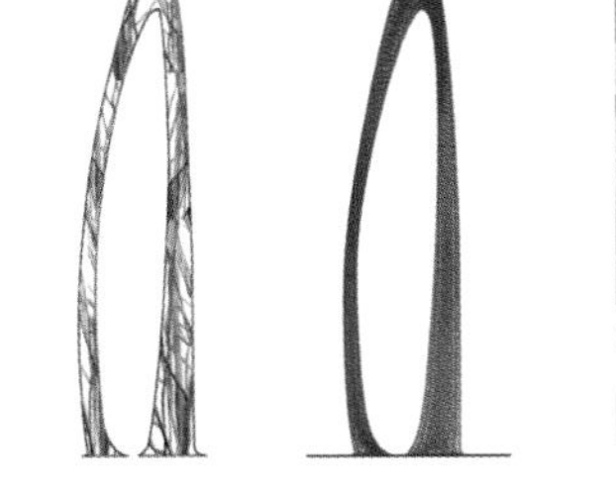

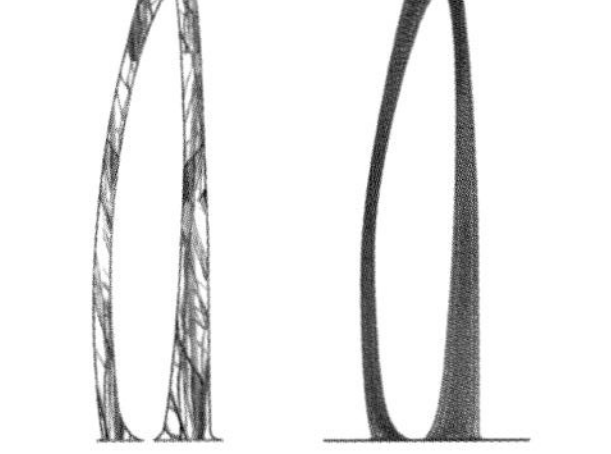

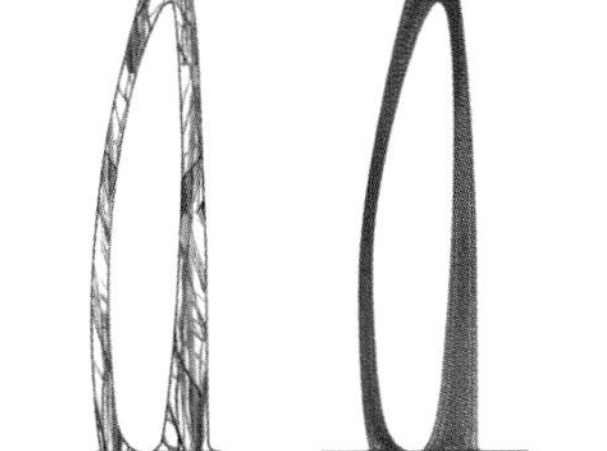

5

plans level 16

plans level 15

plans level 14

plans level 10

plans level 9

plans level 8

plans level 7

plans level 5

plans level 3

plans level 2

plans level 1

plans level 0

floor plans
scale 1:400

elevation
scale 1:400

6

Maribor | *IaN+*

I EPK-DRAVA RIVER 2012 0 10 50 100 88578 / 3

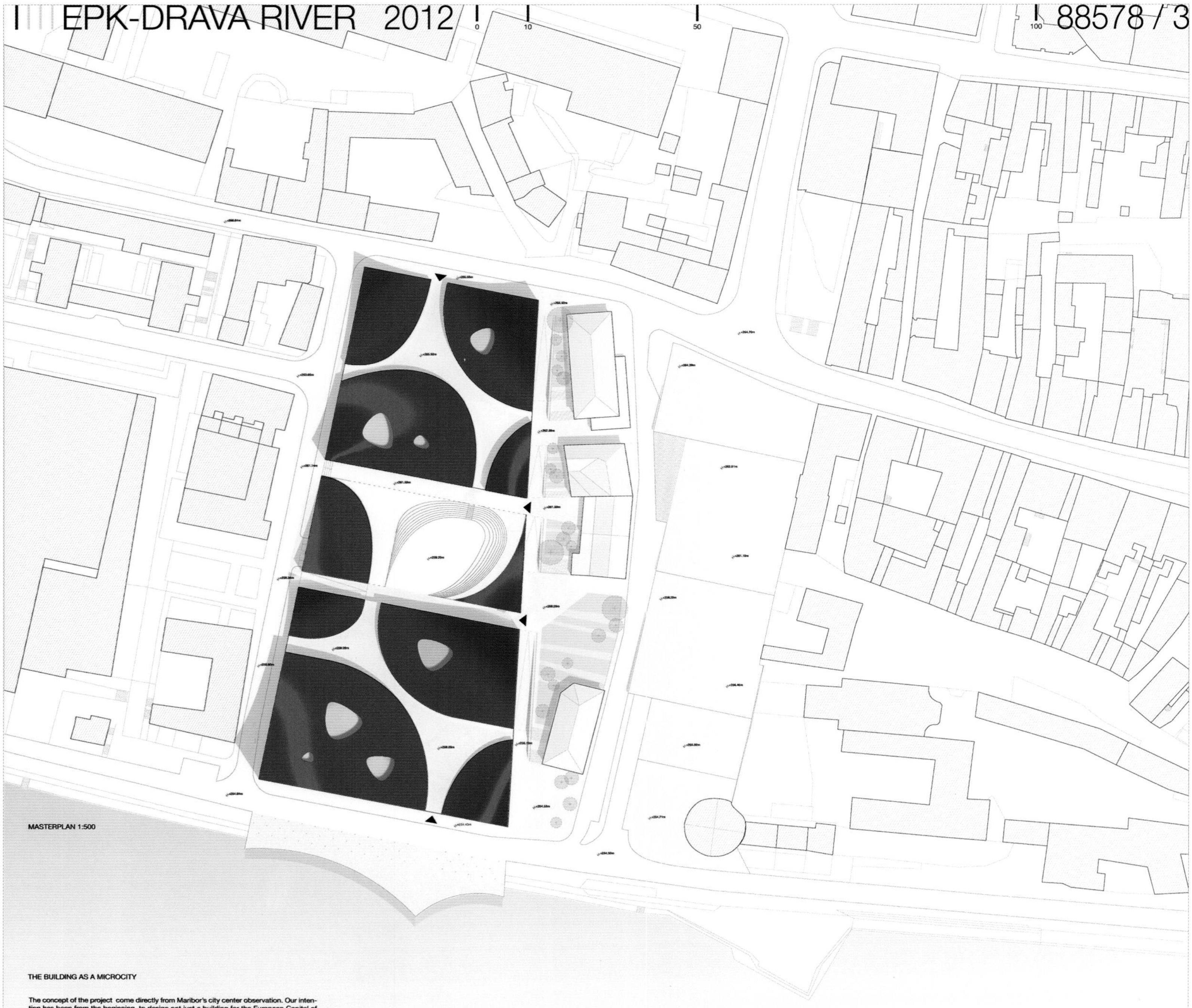

MASTERPLAN 1:500

THE BUILDING AS A MICROCITY

The concept of the project come directly from Maribor's city center observation. Our intention has been from the beginning to design not just a building for the European Capital of Culture 2012 but a space that belongs to the city, a new part of the city where the star is the building together with the streets, little squares, widdenings and so on: a space where the social life will take place.
The concept of a micro city with close and open spaces will perfectly integrate the new part of the city with the old one even solving the different height (due to the city's topography) through ramps and stairs.

The Complex is divided into different volumes: from the smallest ones at the end of the site to the highest one (central gallery activities) in front of the river. The particular shingles wants to characterized the Maribor sky line with a concave reinterpretation of the traditional red roofs.

The site position, directly after the end of the pedestrian riverside, give a strong quality to the fragmented building concept since there will be a lot of permeability in between the plot and the river front and will of course give new life even to this part of the river side.

The New Maribor Art Gallery will, for sure, bring new life even to the river side, which is now not perceive as a livable and pleasant space because of no actractive functions are placed around it. The different volumes of the Complex will instead create new connections throug activities and urban functions.

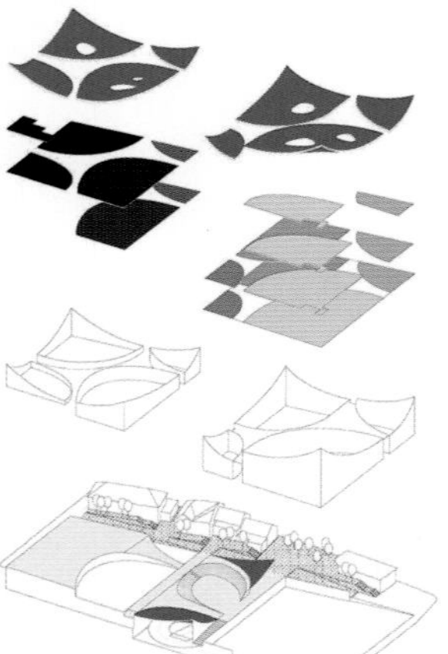

ROOFS

FUNCTIONAL UNITS

BUILDING SKIN

EQUIPPED GROUND

MICROCITY'S ELEMENTS

1. open external space
2. green relaxing area
3. exhibition space
4. management
5. library + gallery shop + coffee
6.infocenter + cloackroom
7. architectural center + restaurant
8. club + coffe room
1. creative industry center
1. residential apartments
1. exhibition space

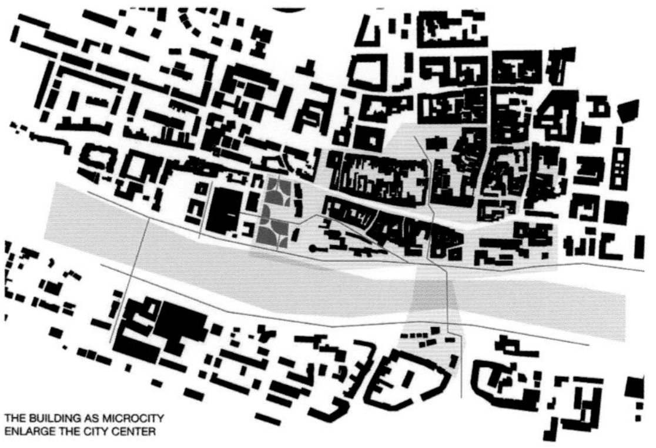

THE BUILDING AS MICROCITY
ENLARGE THE CITY CENTER

microcity
car-free area
main pedestrian connections

EPK-DRAVA RIVER 2012

0 5 10 50

88578 / 3

	LIST OF ROOMS AND SPACES	PROPOSED (m2)	YOURS (m2)
1.	NEW UGM	8580	9264,0
1.1.	EXHIBITION SPACE	4000	3953,0
1.2.	CITY DAILY ROOM	750	1180,0
1.3.	EDUCATION WORKSHOPS	100	181,0
1.4.	LIBRARY AND ARCHIVE	600	677,0
1.5.	RESIDENTIAL APARTMENTS	150	219,0
1.6.	LECTURE ROOM	400	401,0
1.7.	DEPOSITORIES	1650	1783,0
1.8.	TECHNICAL WORKSHOPS	370	321,0
1.9.	MANAGEMENT	300	300,0
1.10.	SERVICE ROOMS	260	249,0
2.	CHILDREN'S MUSEUM	700	657,0
2.1.	DAILY CARE CENTRE	180	176,0
2.2.	HOUSE OF EXPERIMENTS	100	102,0
2.3.	MULTIPURPOSE ROOM	250	225,0
2.4.	EDUCATOR'S ROOM	40	33,0
2.5.	SERVICE ROOMS	130	121,0
3.	CREATIVE INDUSTRY CENTRE	1200	1049,0
3.1.	STUDIOS	750	537,0
3.2.	RESIDENTIAL APARTMENT FOR ARTIST	200	249,0
3.3.	MULTIPURPOSE SPACE	70	76,0
3.4.	SERVICE ROOMS	180	187,0
4.	ARCHITECTURAL CENTRE	500	500,0
4.1.	EXHIBITION SPACE	375	370,0
4.2.	SERVICE ROOMS	125	130,0
5.	CATERING AREA	650	832,0
5.1.	RESTAURANT	280	355,0
5.2.	COFFEEROOM	150	224,0
5.3.	CLUB	130	136,0
5.4.	SERVICE ROOMS	90	117,0
6.	VERTICAL AND HORIZONTAL COMMUNICATION	1800	1896,0
7.	TECHNICAL ROOMS	250	321,0
7.1.	CENTRAL SURVEILLANCE SYSTEM	20	49,0
7.2.	ELECTRO SPACE	30	51,0
7.3.	BOILER ROOMS	50	62,0
7.4.	AIR-CONDITIONING MACHINE ROOMS	150	159,0
8.	GARAGE	1500	2135,0
	TOTAL NEW UGM	15180	16654,0

LEGEND

1. exhibition space
2. management
   - 2.1. PR, marketing
   - 2.2. curators and educators
   - 2.3. secretariat + waiting room
3. library and shop area
   - 3.1. library
   - 3.2. gallery shop
   - 3.3. coffeeroom
4. city daily room
   - 4.1. multipurpose entrance hall
   - 4.2. info center
   - 4.3. cloackroom
5. creative industry center
   - 5.1. studios
   - 5.2. multipurpose space

5.3. tea room

6. club
7. children's museum
   - 7.1. multipurpose room
   - 7.2. educators room
   - 7.3. storage
   - 7.4. care unit
   - 7.5. house of experiments
8. residences
   - 8.1. atelier
   - 8.2. residential apartments for artists
   - 8.3. residential apartments for UGM's employers
9. open external spaces
   - 9.1. scene for gallery events
   - 9.2. catering terrace

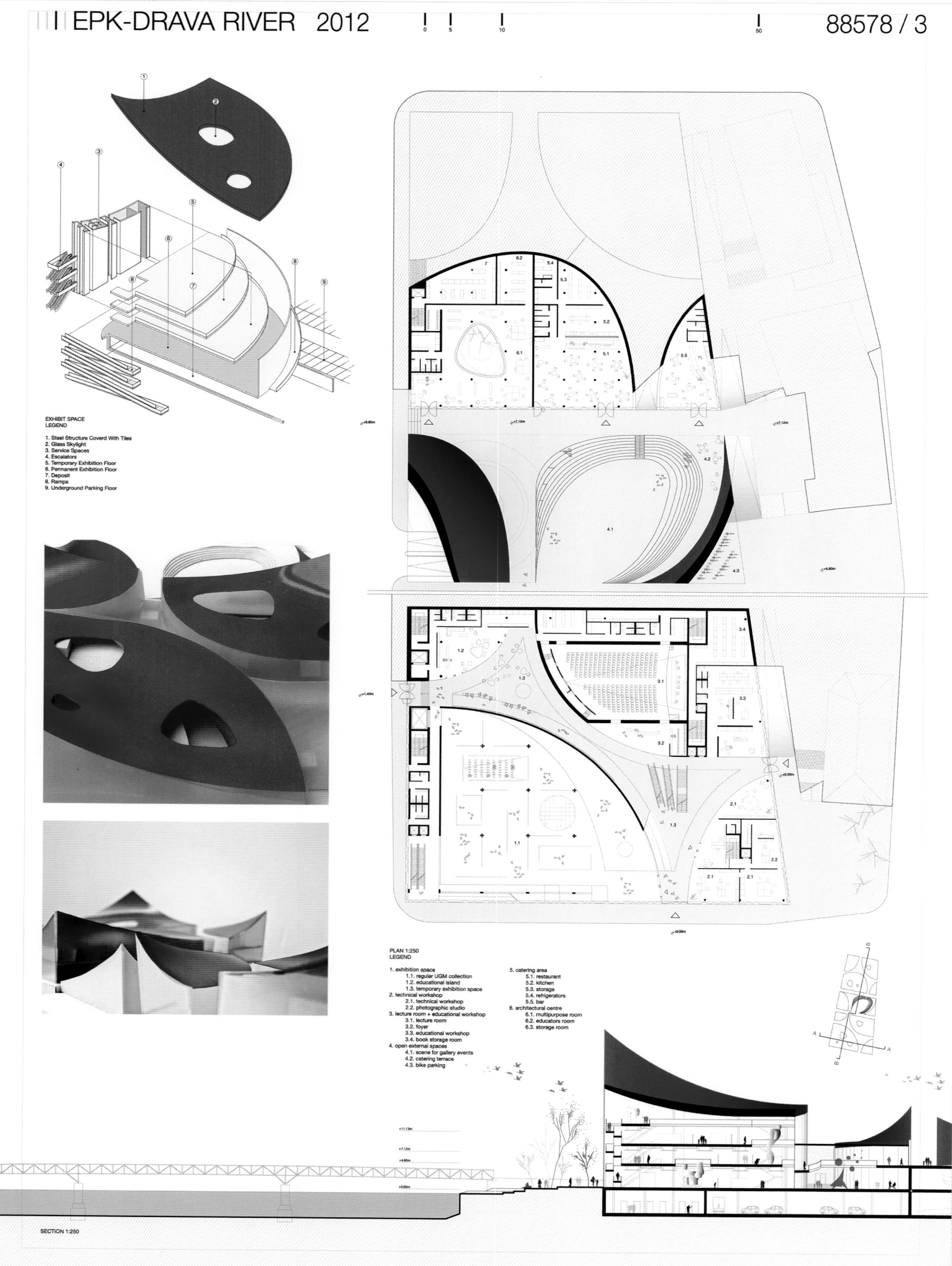
EPK-DRAVA RIVER 2012
0
5
10
50
88578 / 3
EXHIBIT SPACE
LEGEND
1. Steel Structure Coverd With Tiles
2. Glass Skylight
3. Service Spaces
4. Escalators
5. Temporary Exhibition Floor
6. Permanent Exhibition Floor
7. Deposit
8. Ramps
9. Underground Parking Floor
PLAN 1:250
LEGEND
1. exhibition space
1.1. regular UGM collection
1.2. educational island
1.3. temporary exhibition space
2. technical workshop
2.1. technical workshop
2.2. photographic studio
3. lecture room + educational workshop
3.1. lecture room
3.2. foyer
3.3. educational workshop
3.4. book storage room
4. open external spaces
4.1. scene for gallery events
4.2. catering terrace
4.3. bike parking
5. catering area
5.1. restaurant
5.2. kitchen
5.3. storage
5.4. refrigerators
5.5. bar
6. architectural centre
6.1. multipurpose room
6.2. educators room
6.3. storage room
+11.13m
+7.12m
+4.80m
±0.00m
SECTION 1:250

EPK-DRAVA RIVER 2012

0 5 10 50

88578 / 3

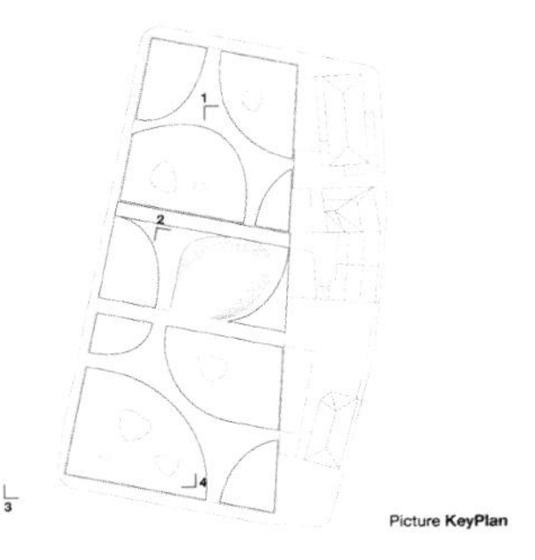
Picture KeyPlan

New UGM: a big flexible urban loft.

The central square: the main public space which will host the coolest cultural events.

New UGM: the simbol of the Capital of Culture 2012.

The buildings together with the streets, squares, outdoor galleries and widdenings: space for the social life.

New UGM: reinterpretation of the traditional and historical skyline.

4
2 3
5 1

161 Mixed-Use Building Konventná Street | *Vallo Sadovsky Architects*

Partner in Charge : Matúš Vallo, Oliver Sadovský
Participants : Branislav Husárik, Dušan Chupá, Peter Jane ek
Typology : Mixed-use building
Location : Bratislava, Slovakia

Area : 5270 sqm
Year : 2011

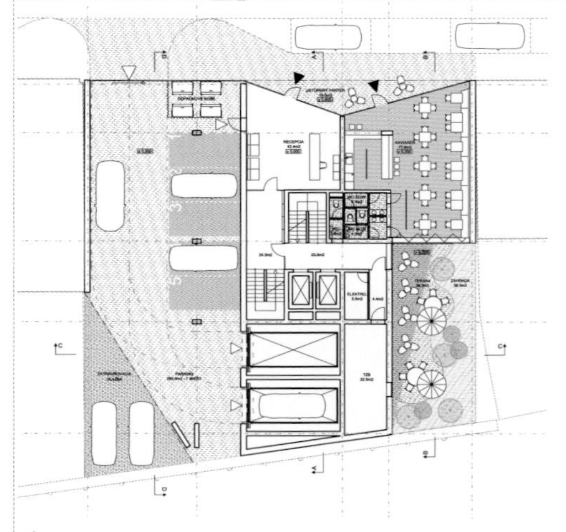

PÔDORYS 1.NP

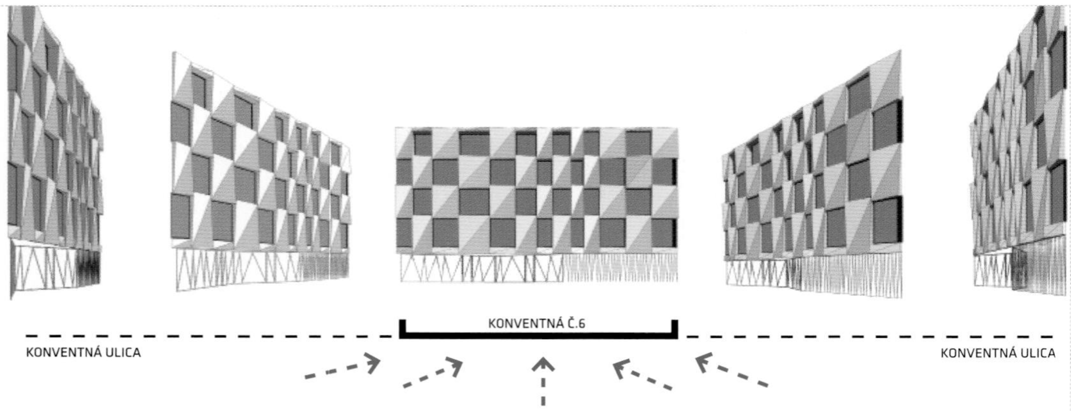

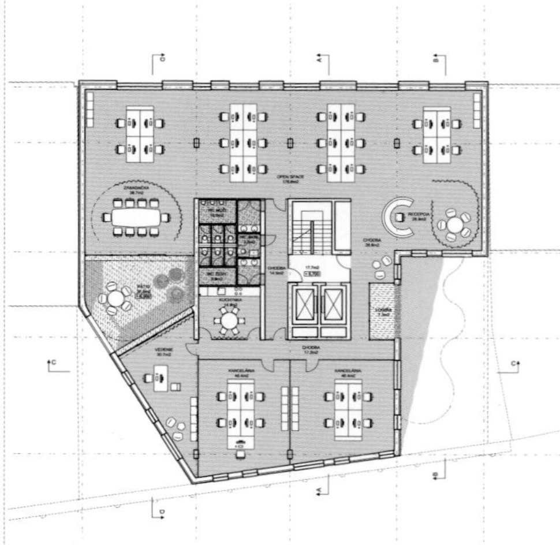

PÔDORYS 3.NP

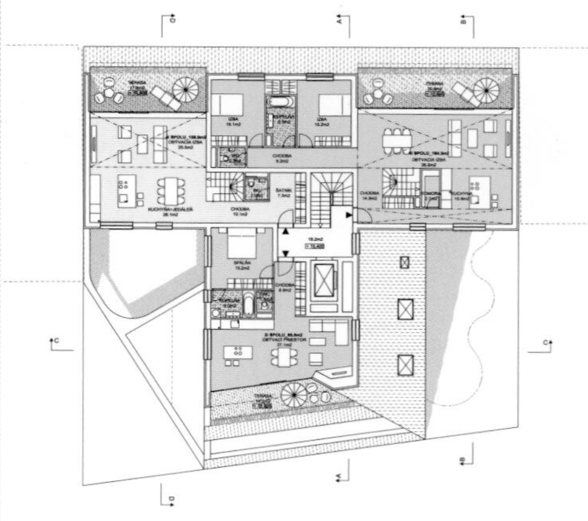

PÔDORYS 5.NP

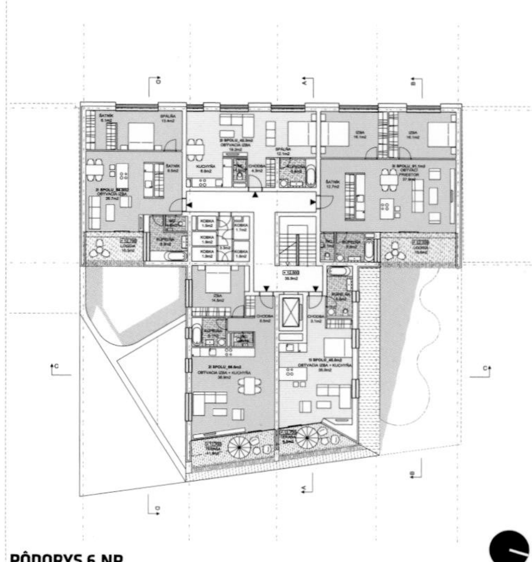

PÔDORYS 6.NP

KONVENTNÁ Č.6

KONVENTNÁ ULICA

KONVENTNÁ ULICA

SCHÉMA - PLASTICITA FASÁDY V ZÁVISLOSTI OD UHLU POHĽADU

PREDNÁ FASÁDA BUDOVY JE HLAVNÝ KOMUNIKAČNÝ ELEMENT NOVÉHO MESTSKÉHO PRVKU. JEJ PÔSOBENIE SME ROZDELILI NA DVA HLAVNÉ SMERY.
PRVÝ, KTORÝ PREDSTAVUJE ČELNÝ POHĽAD NA BUDOVU A KTORÝ KOMUNIKUJE NAJMÄ S BUDOVOU OPROTI PREDSTAVUJE VEĽMI JASNÝ A GEOMETRICKY JEDNODUCHÝ POHĽAD. ŽIADNYM SPÔSOBOM NEMÁ BUDOVE OPROTI KONKUROVAŤ, NEMÁ RUŠIŤ JEJ OBYVATEĽOV S KTORÝMI BUDE V SILNOM OPTICKOM KONTAKTE, MÁ BYŤ PRE ŇU LEN POKOJNÉ A JEDNOZNAČNÉ POZADIE.
DRUHÝ SMER JE TEN AKO BUDOVA KOMUNIKUJE S ULICOU, TENTO POHĽAD JE DEFINOVANÝ NAJMÄ BOČNÝMI PRIEHĽADMI. V TOMTO PRÍPADE, VĎAKA ŠPECIFICKÉMU TVARU FASÁDNYCH PANELOV, BUDOVA TROCHU ODVÁŽNEJŠIE OPTICKY " VYSTUPUJE " DO ULICE, STÁVA SA AKÝMSI LÁKADLOM A POKORNE ALE ISTO SA ODDEĽUJE OD ZVYŠKU ULICE.

POHĽAD D - DO PÁTIA ZO ZASADAČKY NA 3.NP

POHĽAD C - TERASA KAVIARNE V PARTERI

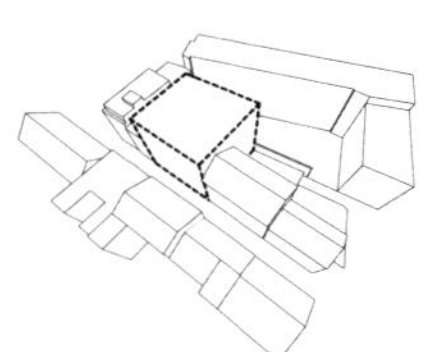

1
MAXIMÁLNA HMOTA OBJEKTU

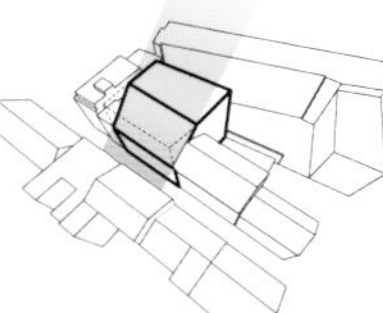

2
EKVIVALENTNÝ UHOL TIENENIA 42°

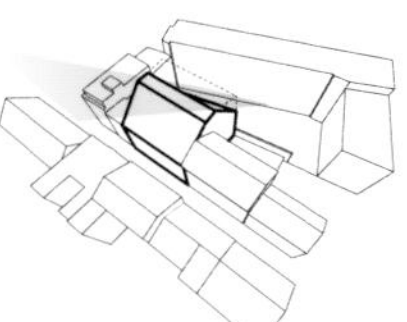

3
EKVIVALENTNÝ UHOL TIENENIA 42°

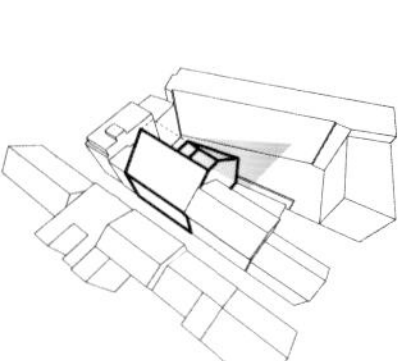

4
EKVIVALENTNÝ UHOL TIENENIA 42°

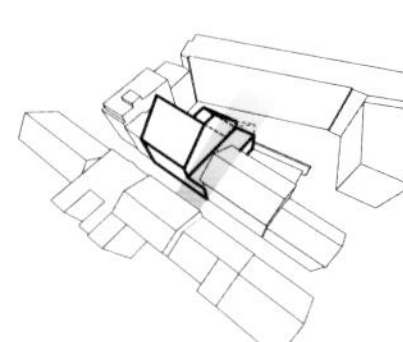

5
POŽIADAVKA NA PRESLNENIE BYTOV NA KONVENTNEJ 7

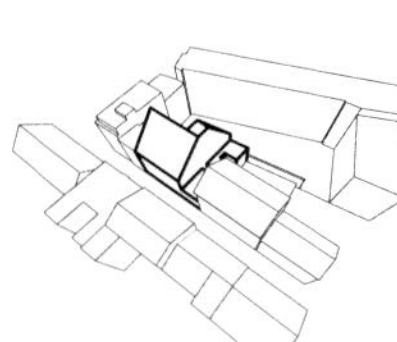

6
VÝSLEDNÁ HMOTA OBJEKTU

POHĽAD B - TERASY BYTOV V J-ČASTI, ZO STRANY VNÚTROBLOKU

POLYFUNKČNÁ BUDOVA KONVENTNÁ 6

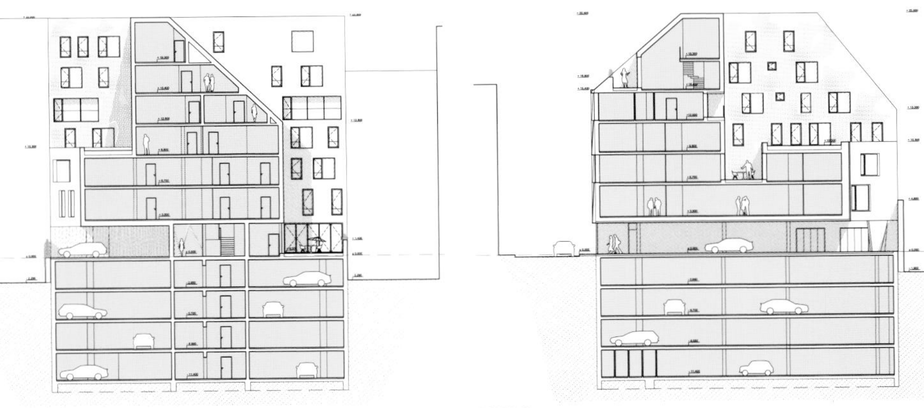

REZ C-C

REZ D-D

POHĽAD Z VNÚTROBLOKU

POHĽAD ULIČNÝ

162 Dubai | *2:pm architectures*

Project : International Competition for an Iconic Building
Location : Dubai (UAE)
Design Team : 2:pm architectures + Dauphins (arch)

08 026 // 1/5
Dubaï, tall emblem structure in Za'abeel Park :
ELEMENT, Six rays in the sky
This architectural emblem for Dubai may not be reduced to a mere solitary element, something unchanging and infertile, to a mere piece of sculpture or a vulgar tower. Its symbolic power lies in the diversity it offers us, for its parts come together to form a meaningful whole, a complex entity, changing and adapting with each passing year. It is a lofty structure, rising high above the ground, composed of six tall columns, each of which entertains intimate bonds with the inherent identity of the city.
The site on which the project is planned pays humble tribute to the oasis, and the ground is remodelled as if under the effect of tectonic movement, opening up a deep gash in the earth some 4 metres deep. This trench is designed to play home to a palm grove, providing a pleasant breathing space within the city's dense urban fabric, offering visitors a moment of calm respite. The vegetation is to be protected by a concrete mesh with apertures of variable gauge, allowing air and light to flood into the calm oasis sheltering below and for the trees to grow upwards through it. From street level, only the tops of the palm trees are visible.
Through the mesh, six architectural columns reach up for the sky. The first is dedicated to science. Standing some 90 m proud, it is clad in photovoltaic panels, a water harvesting system, sails to harness wind energy and a double wind turbine. The whole complex can be powered by the energy generated by this one building alone. The second is dedicated to culture. Reaching 100m into the sky, it is cased in mirrors and sports a loudspeaker system. It is destined to become Dubai's cultural mouthpiece. The mirrors reflect back the city's image and the loud speakers accompany this with sounds of city life going on in key places (the airport, Burj Dubai, the port, the historical centre...).
The third column explores the notion of flux. Some 120m tall, it comprises a vast screen across which a rising torrent of figures and data pours, quantifying the flow of people through strategic areas of the city.
The fourth element represents the economy. A network of luminous diodes emits light of changing colour and intensity, reflecting fluctuations on the stock exchange and within the economy. The column comprises 17 rings, each representing a major company, and varying in colour to the rhythm of its changing fortunes on the markets.
The fifth structure is in harmony with the climate. It is a living entity, its outer skin dilating as the air temperature rises. Once the temperature reaches a given level, a fine mist issues from this living being, producing a cool cloud of vapour which refreshes the whole vicinity.
The last column represents time; it is Dubai's timepiece and is composed of a rising series of rings of varying dimensions, sheathed in a fine golden mesh. Each circular disk represents a unit of time (seconds, minutes, hours... centuries even), revolving at their own pace ad infinitum.
REFERENCE
SCIENCE
CULTURE
FLUX
ECONOMY
CLIMATE
TIME
The fault is created by accentuating existing undulations in site topography, thus serving to highlight and explore the natural character of the land. Relief becomes an essential tool for generating a variety of landscapes down by the lake. The site's 'identity' becomes more clearly voiced.
Our main aim is to shape a new territory and create homogeneous links between it and the surrounding context. Only a contextual approach to design allows for harmonious bonds to be established between the local site and the global megalopolis within which it is situated.
The new site must be pleasant for people to live and work in. This can be achieved by creating a well-ventilated skin beneath which a microclimate may be sustained. Palm trees provide shade from the sun and foster vegetation beneath them. The lower level becomes a magnificent park, a luxuriant oasis for the public to enjoy.
The columns symbolise the identity of Dubai and entertain intimate connections with the surrounding environment. Their presence is deployed over the mesh above the park and light slips down from each building through its apertures to the ground below, creating a sense of spectacular height.
For the public (inhabitants of Dubai, workers, or tourists) the project will allow for a deeper understanding of the city, conveying to them the true identity of Dubai at any given moment. Understanding Dubai, reading Dubai, appreciating Dubai, enjoying Dubai is our motto.

08 026 // 2/5

This emblematic architectural complex is at once a pleasant urban oasis in the heart of the city and a vital force, reaching up for the sky. Each section of the architectural structure houses a specific function (auditorium, children's library, bar) and each is oriented in a meaningful direction – Mecca, Burj Dubai and the airport. Access to each level may be gained by escalators, inviting the visitor on a journey up through the clouds. Gentle slopes lead down to the oasis below. The concrete mesh filters the sunlight, moderating its intensity. Our aim is to create a verdant area in which to take a stroll or meet up with friends. Above the concrete framework, the palm trees peep out, providing a green rooftop and shade below. The buildings span its whole length and breadth, reaching upwards in concord like tall columns of light.

GROUND PLAN SCALE 1/500"

VIEW FROM 6 STREET

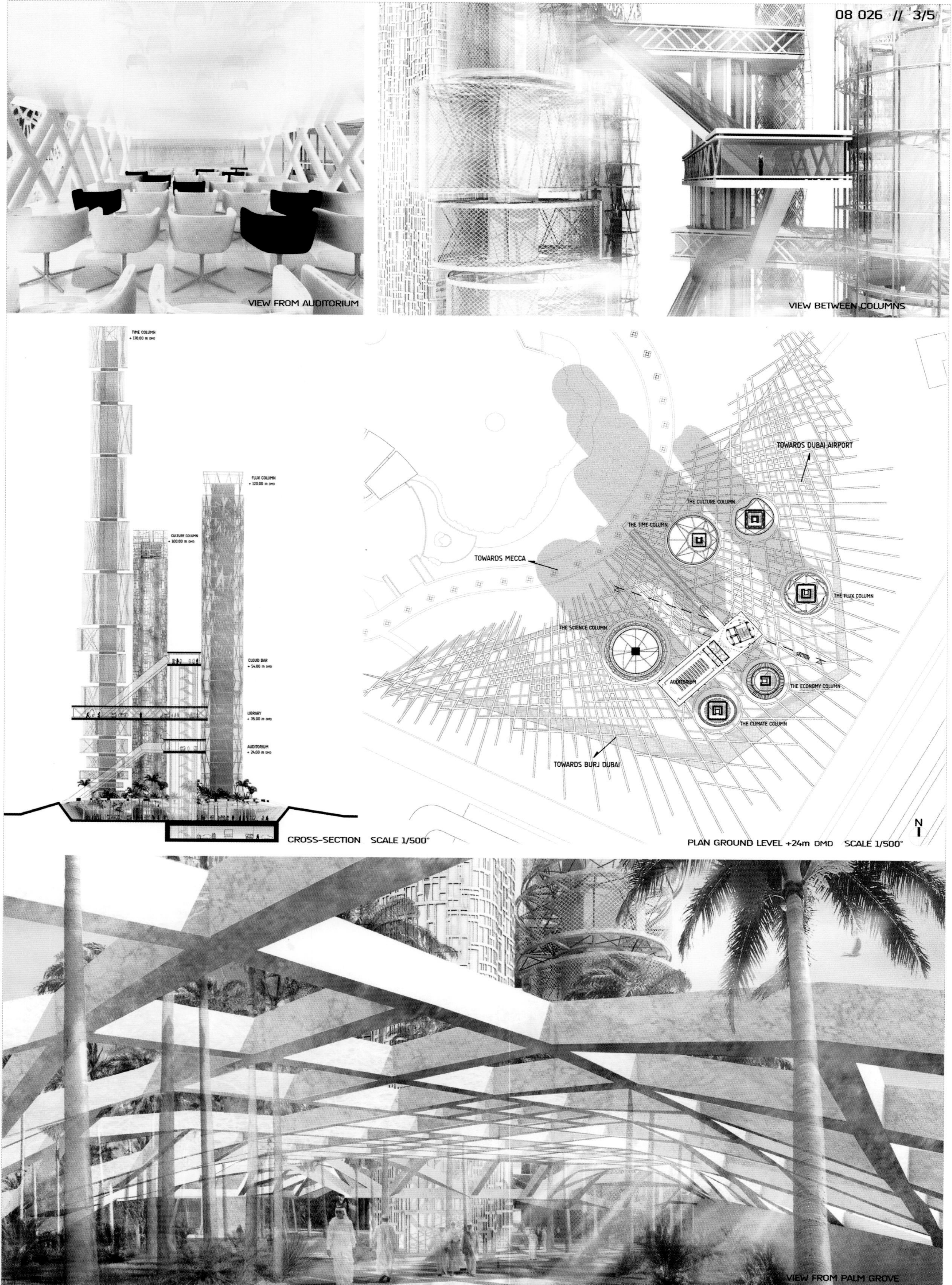

08 026 // 3/5
VIEW FROM AUDITORIUM
VIEW BETWEEN COLUMNS
TIME COLUMN
FLUX COLUMN
CULTURE COLUMN
CLOUD BAR
LIBRARY
AUDITORIUM
CROSS-SECTION SCALE 1/500"
TOWARDS DUBAI AIRPORT
THE CULTURE COLUMN
THE TIME COLUMN
TOWARDS MECCA
THE FLUX COLUMN
THE SCIENCE COLUMN
AUDITORIUM
THE ECONOMY COLUMN
THE CLIMATE COLUMN
TOWARDS BURJ DUBAI
N
PLAN GROUND LEVEL +24m DMD SCALE 1/500"
VIEW FROM PALM GROVE

08 026 // 4/5

THE SCIENCE COLUMN

+ 90.00 m

This might be the smallest of the columns, but it has the capacity to supply the whole site with energy. It embodies the future of science to come, particularly in the field of sustainable development. Its architectural composition is divided into three parts, comprising a series of rings over a metal framework. The lower part is cased in photovoltaic panels and has a water harvesting system. Above this, wind traps are designed to capture the humidity in the air and a double wind turbine produces the energy required to power the whole complex. The site is thus endowed with an efficient and fully autonomous energy production system.

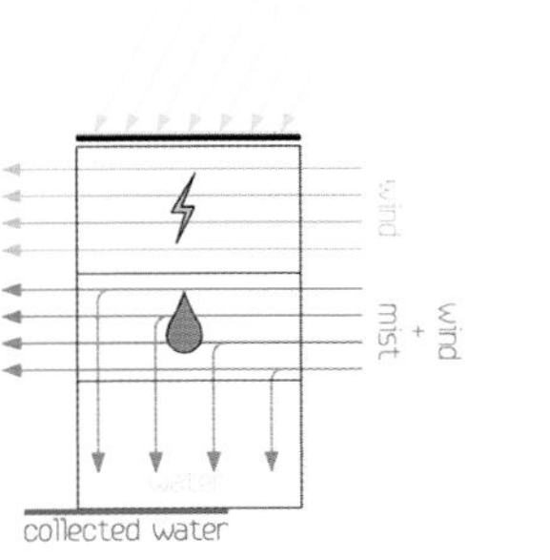

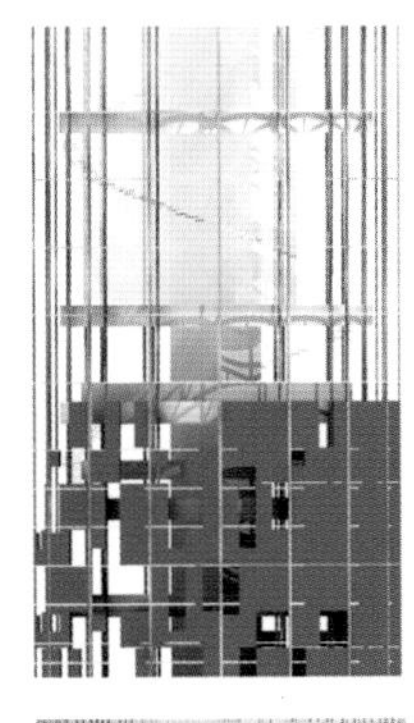

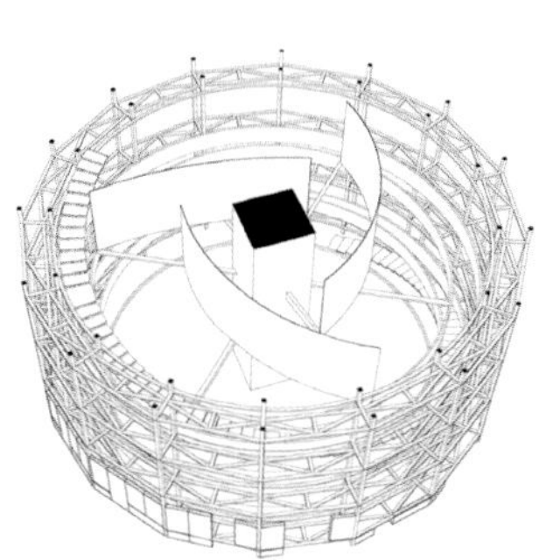

THE CULTURE COLUMN

+ 100.00 m

The soul of Dubai is captured and reflected in the mirrors of this column. The visitor catches a glimpse of their own reflection and the glimmering silhouette of the city in the distance. Like a mirage, Dubai is reflected in the full splendour of its elevation. People going about their everyday business appear reflected across the outside case, and beneath the mirrors lie loud speakers, softly transmitting the hustle and bustle of life going on in emblematic sites across the city. The hum of the city comes alive for us, and the sights and sounds this building captures and relays back offer new insight into life in Dubai. It reflects the plurality of the people who live and work in this city in full expansion and brimming with exciting new developments.

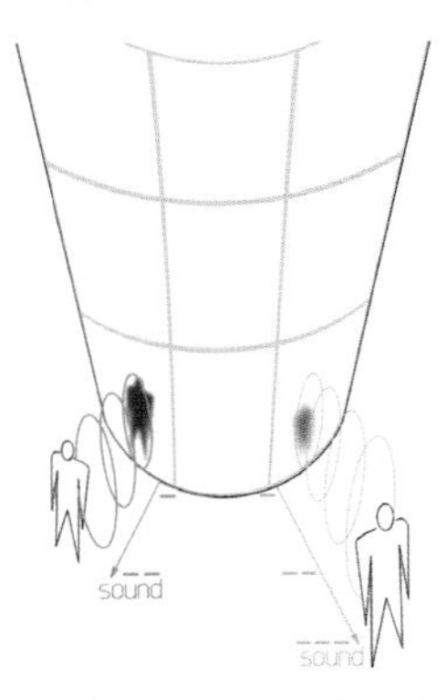

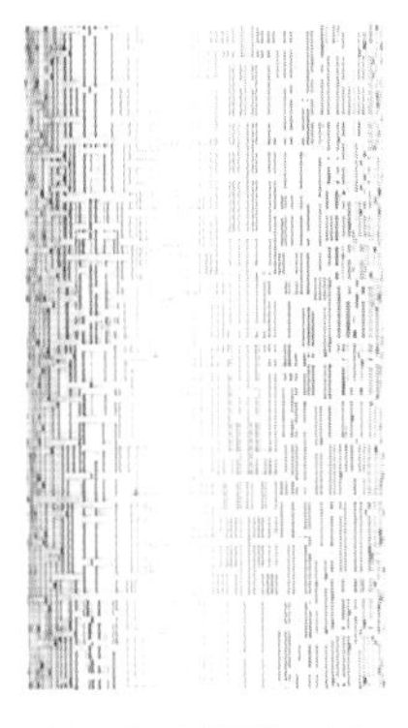

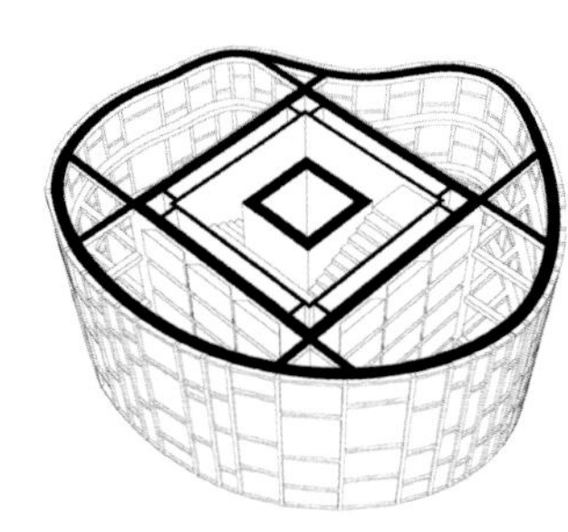

THE FLUX COLUMN

+ 120.00 m

This is the mathematical face of the city. A cylindrical screen pours out a rising torrent of figures, each corresponding to the number of people or vehicles coming in and out of the city in specific areas, like the airport or port. The visitor to the building sees their own impact and presence immediately reflected in the statistics. The closer visitors draw and the greater their number, the larger the figures become. The building reflects the ebb and flow of life in the city, people coming and going, as the numbers travel up the screen and evaporate into the sky above Dubai.

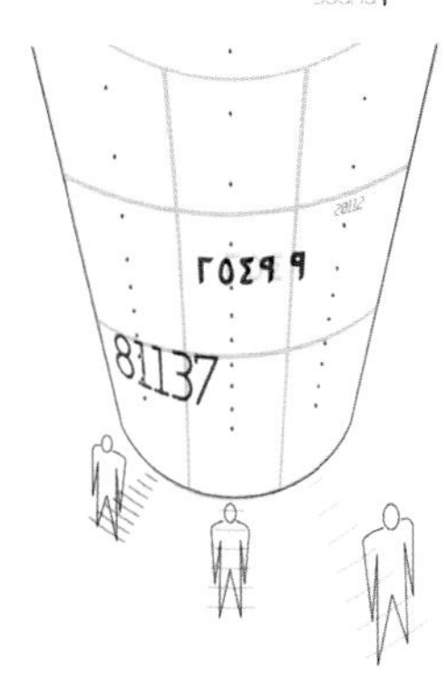

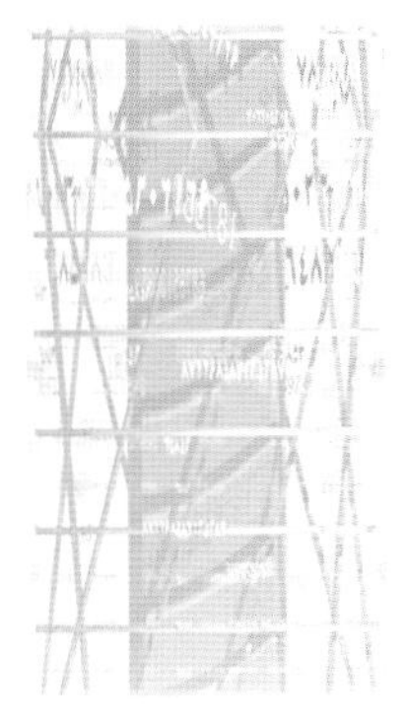

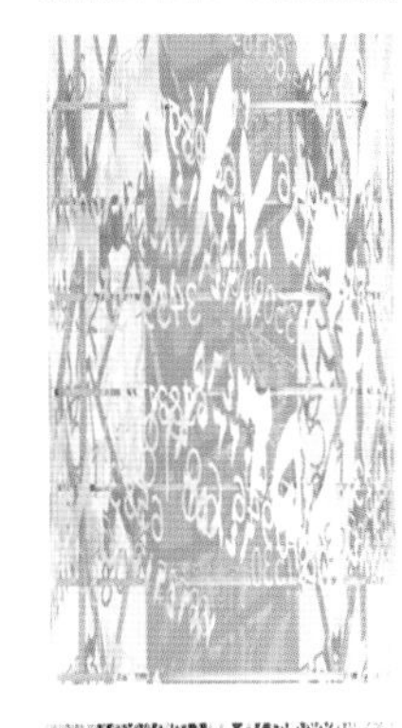

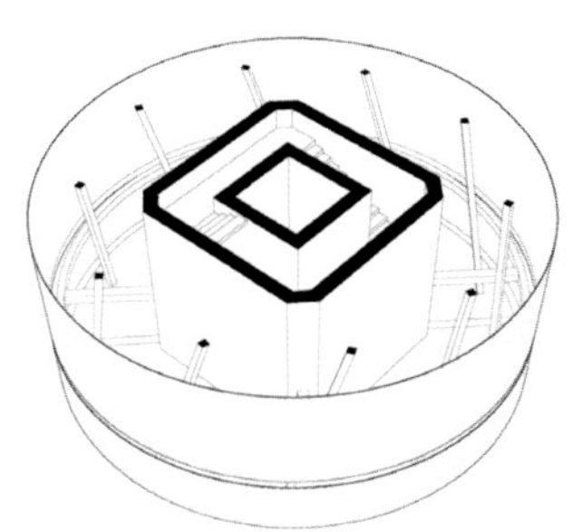

THE ECONOMY COLUMN

+ 130.00 m

This column is an indicator of Dubai's wealth. A network of luminous diodes of varying colour and intensity encircle the building's concrete core, reflecting fluctuations on the stock exchange and within the economy. Three main values are given - the stock market index, GDP and takings in various shops. The rings correspond to Dubai's foremost businesses and change colour to reflect their changing fortunes on the markets.

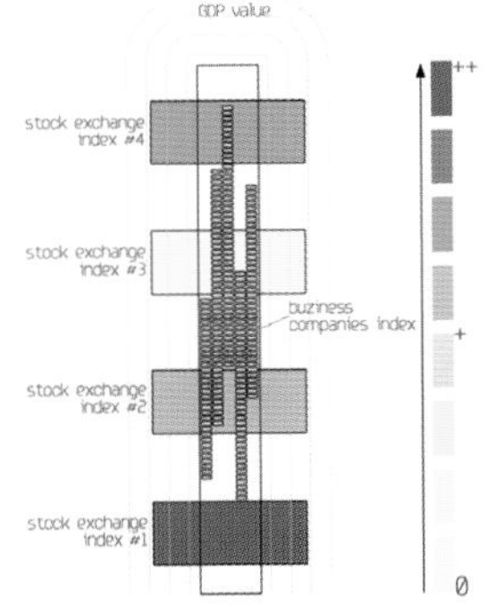

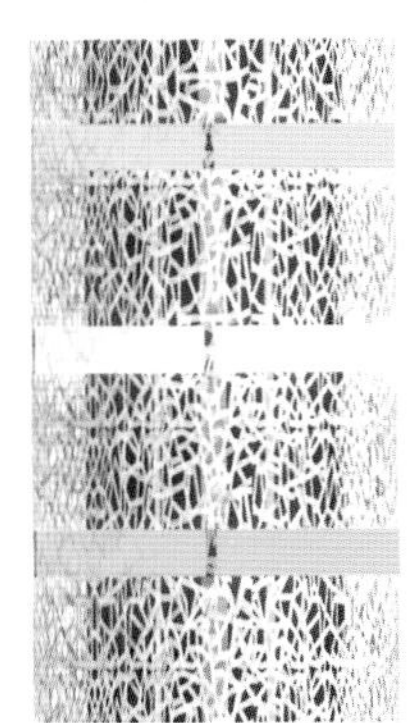

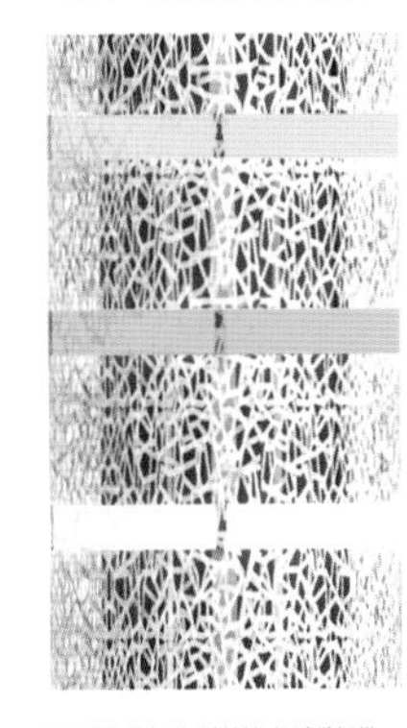

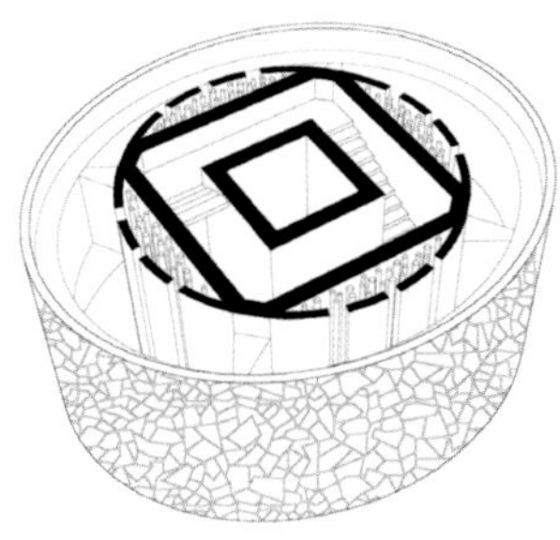

THE CLIMATE COLUMN

+ 140.00 m

The Climate Column is a living, breathing organism, clad in a metal mesh of the utmost delicacy. This skin changes to adapt to variations in air temperature.
If the temperature rises, it dilates. If the heat becomes sufficiently intense, the skin dilates to such an extent that a cloud of water vapour rises from it. This mist cools the mesh and returns the skin to its initial shape. The whole area is pleasantly refreshed by this cool breath of air. The climate becomes an explicit phenomenon, made tangibly perceptible by the dilation of the skin and cloud of mist.

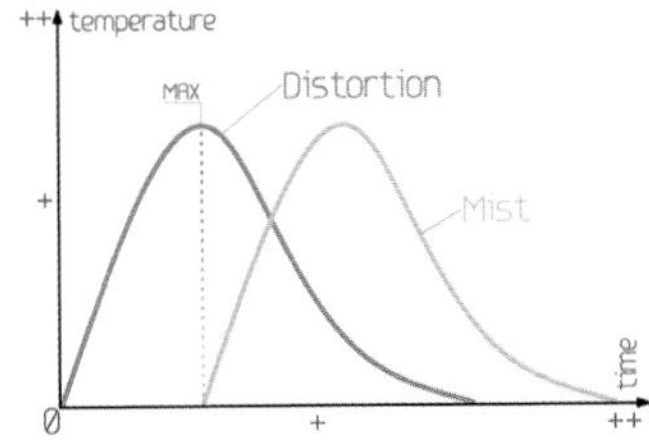
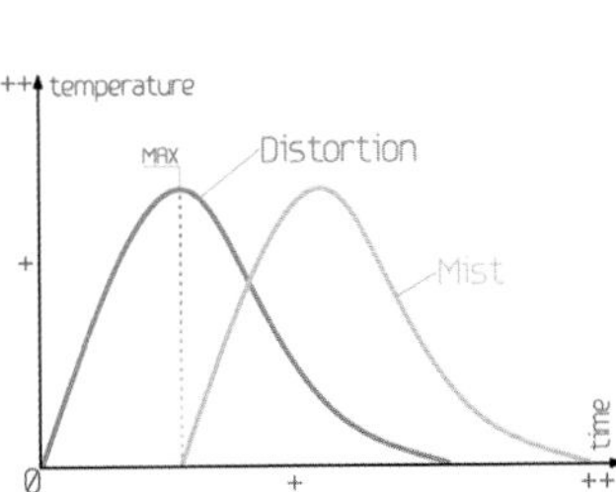

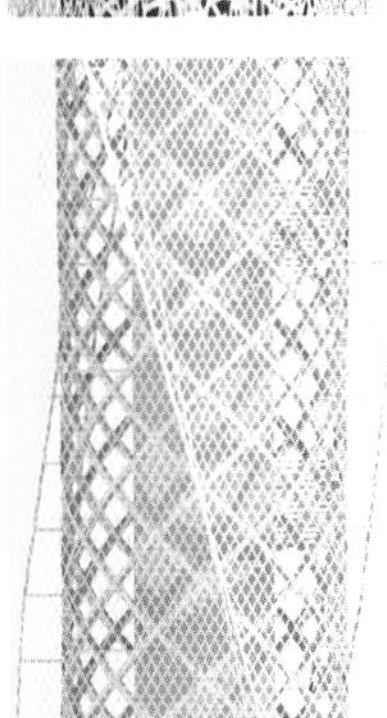

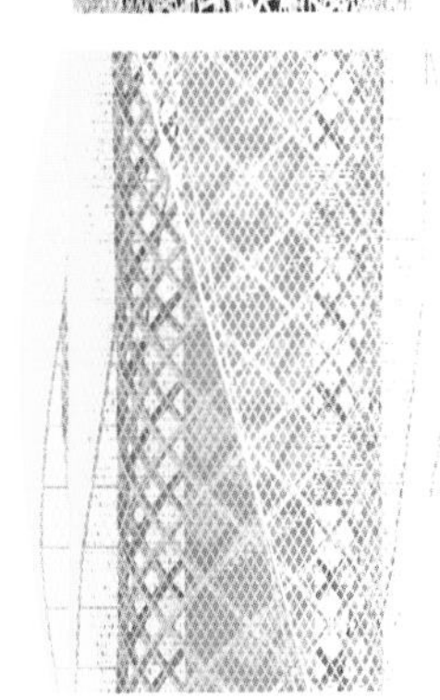

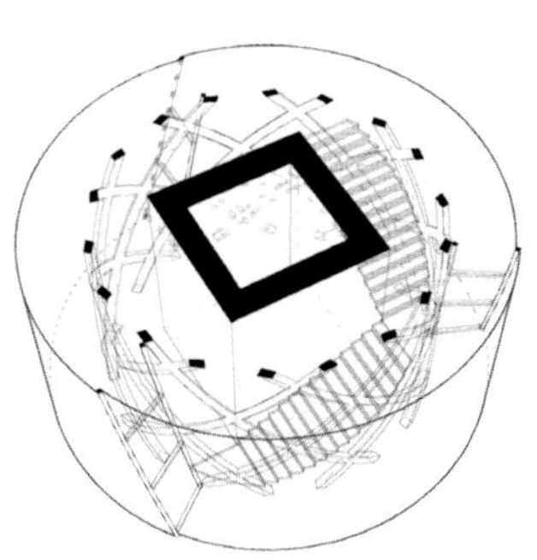

THE TIME COLUMN

+ 170.00 m

The Time Column is the tallest of all. It is the site's timepiece and symbolises the course of time. Each ring represents an individual unit of time and revolves at its own pace. Seconds, minutes, hours, days, months and years each have their own ring, each turning to mark the slow advance of time. The column hoists its summit high into the sky above the city, its base turning slow as a snail upon its millennium ring, the summit revolving far more swiftly as the minutes tick by. A fine golden mesh sheathes the whole like delicate lace, filtering the sunlight and veiling the time discs. The column reflects passing time in Dubai and allows each one of us find our temporal bearings.

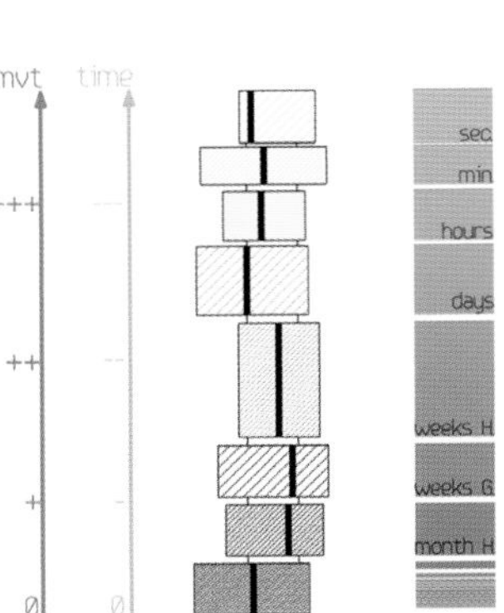

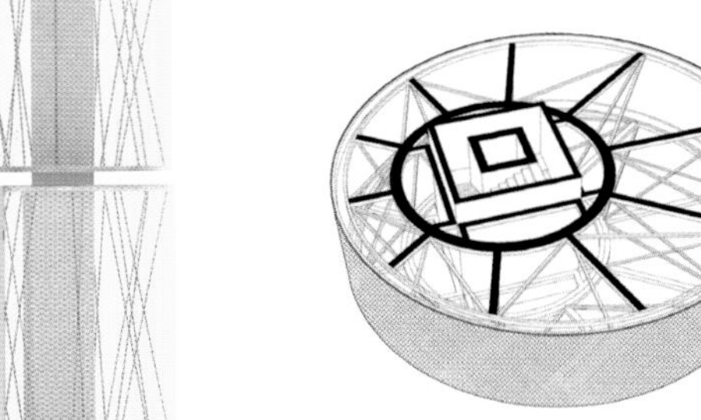

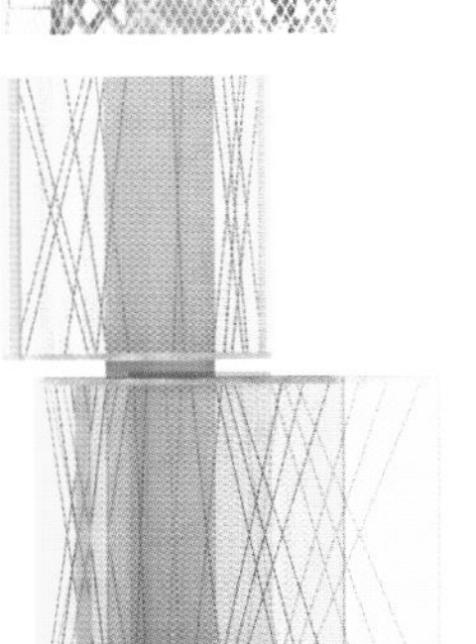

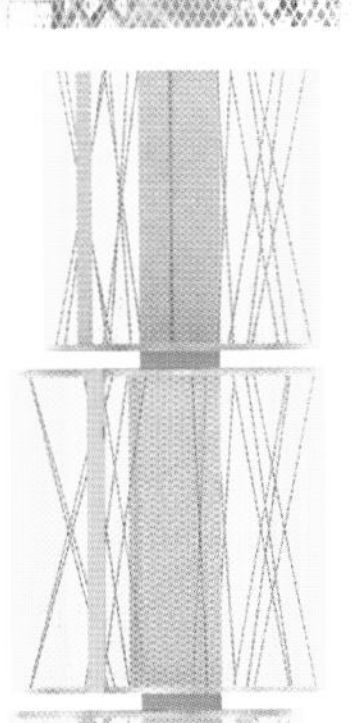

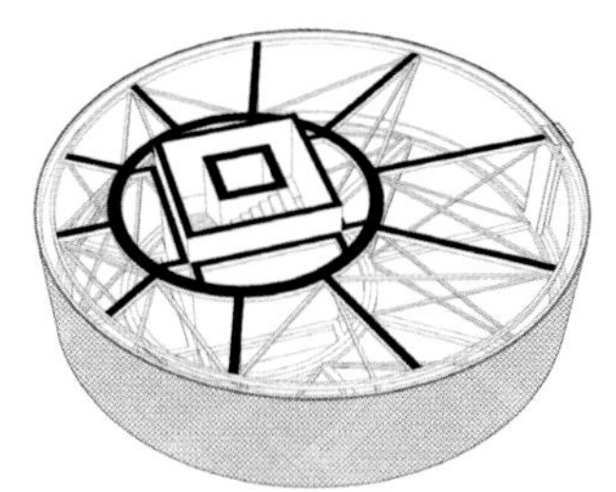

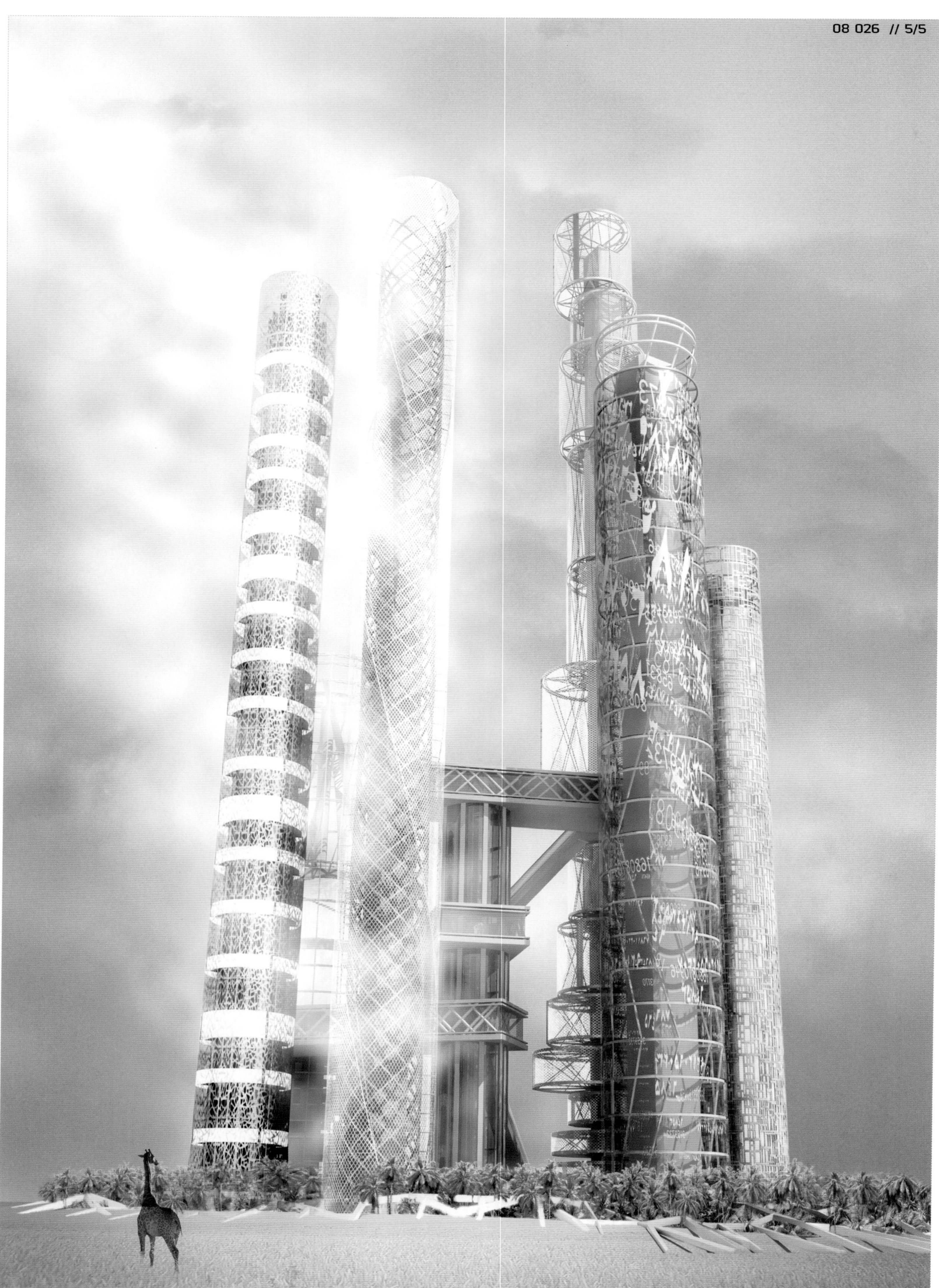
08 026 // 5/5

FIS-SST Office Building | *ZALEWSKI ARCHITECTURE GROUP*

Year : 2011, prize - Honourable Mention in Category Building of the Year 2011 in Competition : "Architecture of the Year in Silesia Region"

Participants : Krzysztof Zalewski, Grzegorz Zi Bik, Dorota Knia ewska
Project : Office building for FIS-SST company
Location : Gliwice, Poland
Client : FIS-SST Sp. z o. o

ODDZIAŁ KATOWICE

16. EDYCJA KONKURSU
ARCHITEKTURA ROKU WOJEWÓDZTWA ŚLĄSKIEGO
nominacja do nagrody
BUDYNEK BIUROWY FIS-SST
ZALEWSKI ARCHITECTURE GROUP

Śląsk przechodzi metamorfozę. Oddech przemysłu coraz słabiej wyczuwany, ale ciągle rzeczywisty, pozostawia ślady w przestrzeni regionu. Ślady te stają się początkiem zmiany: kierunków rozwoju, przestrzeni, mentalności, kultury - wreszcie architektury.

Przykładem takiej wielopłaszczyznowej zmiany jest Centrum Edukacji i Biznesu „Nowe Gliwice", które tworzy się na obszarach pozostałych po likwidacji Kopalni Węgla Kamiennego „Gliwice" funkcjonującej w tym miejscu końca XX wieku. Intencją Agencji Rozwoju Lokalnego - założyciela Centrum - była zmiana negatywnych konotacji związanych ze zdegradowanym terenem kopalni i zastąpienie ich obrazem miejsca, które tworzy sprzyjające warunki dla rozwoju firm nowoczesnych technologii.

Tu właśnie, pomiędzy odnowionymi budynkami kopalni a wyrobiskową hałdą zlokalizowany został budynek biurowy firmy FIS-SST i jako pierwszy budynek zrealizowany na terenie Centrum stał się inspiracją dla dalszych pozytywnych zmian i kolejnych inwestycji.

Sąsiedztwo budynków kopalni oraz hałdy, a także profil firmy Inwestora zajmującej się zaawansowanymi technologiami IT oraz ograniczony budżet stały się inspiracją dla kreacji minimalistycznej w wyrazie architektury i rygorystycznego potraktowania budowlanych rozwiązań obiektu - zaprojektowano obiekt "low-tech" o oszczędnej estetyce i zdyscyplinowanych rozwiązaniach wewnętrznych. Ograniczone koszty realizacji zostały tu potraktowane jako inspiracja do poszukiwania rozwiązań „skrojonych na miarę", zapewniających jednocześnie komfort pracy i użytkowania jak i wysoką estetykę i jakość architektury.

Wizerunek obiektu chętnie wykorzystywany jako wizytówka pozytywnych przemian przez Miasto Gliwice, dla którego biurowiec jest jednym z narzędzi promocji pod hasłem „Stare Miasto – Nowy Świat". W rezultacie rozpoznawalność architektury zaowocowała promocją firmy, przyczyniła się do rehabilitacji terenów poprzemysłowych i sprzyja ich dalszemu rozwojowi.

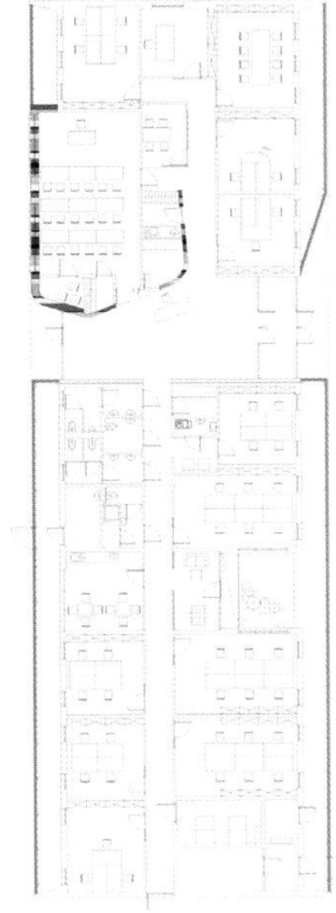

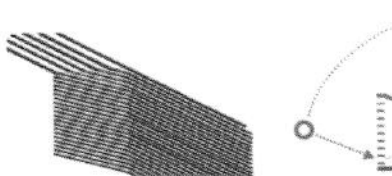

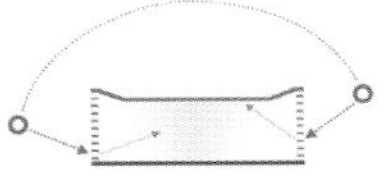

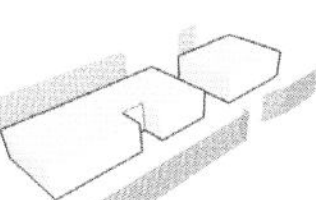

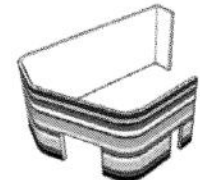

164

Edil Tomarchio | *modostudio*

Location : Aci Sant'Antonio - Italy
Client : Edil Tomarchio
Fase – Phase : Architectural Competition | Second Prize

Area : 14.950 sqm
Construction budget : € 7,982,000,00

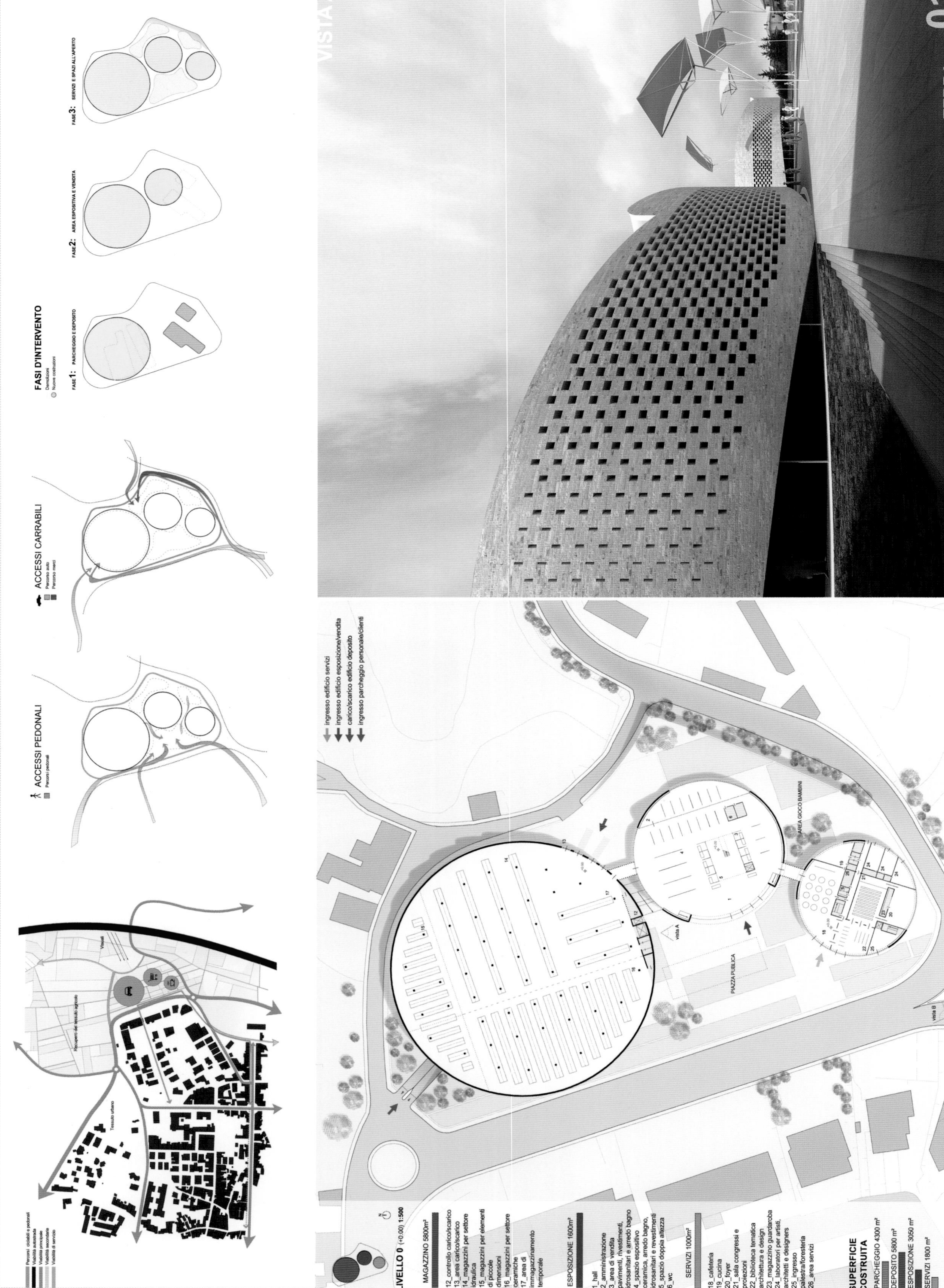

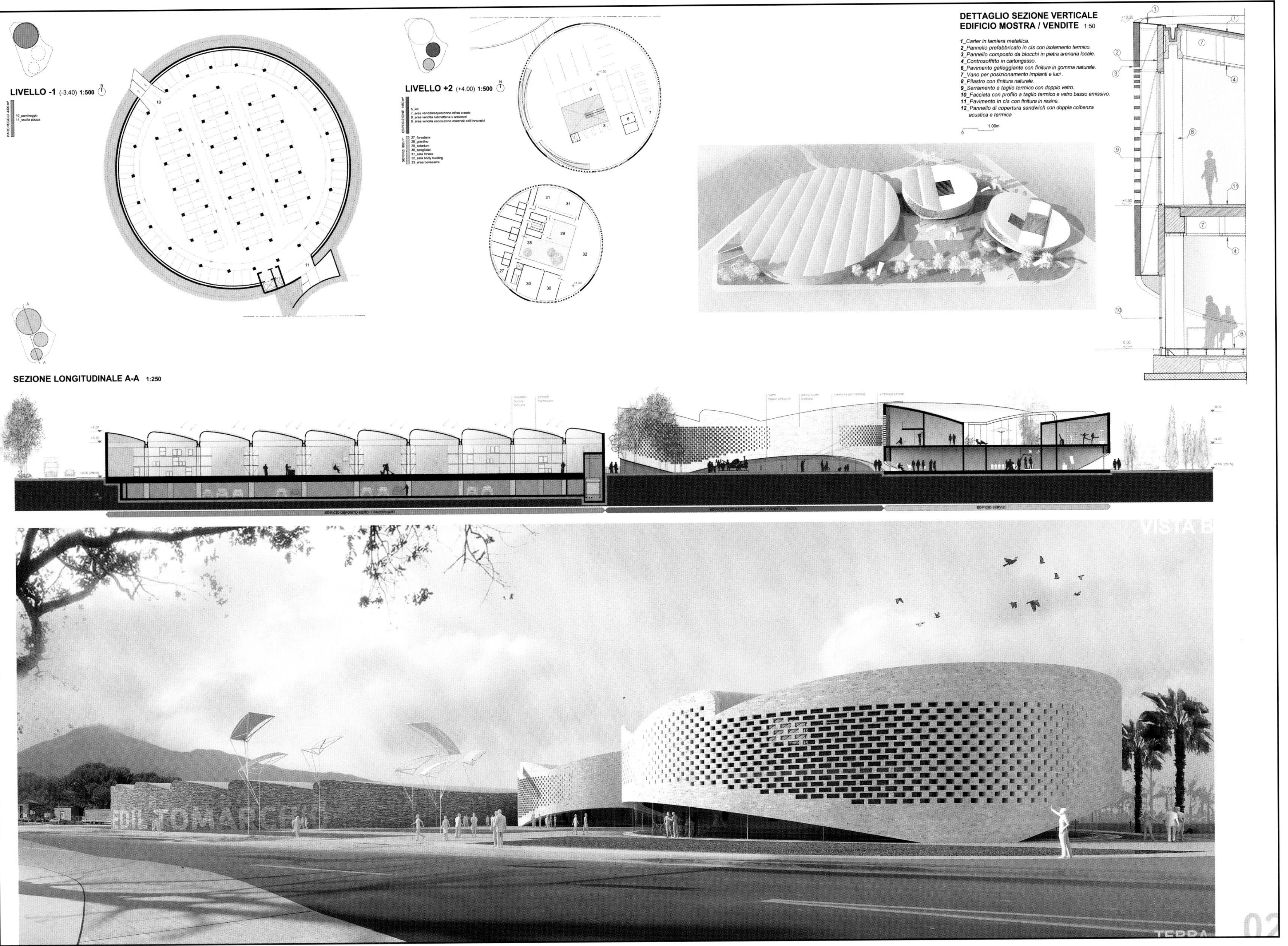
LIVELLO -1 (-3.40) 1:500
LIVELLO +2 (+4.00) 1:500
DETTAGLIO SEZIONE VERTICALE
EDIFICIO MOSTRA / VENDITE 1:50
1_Carter in lamiera metallica.
2_Pannello prefabbricato in cls con isolamento termico.
3_Pannello composto da blocchi in pietra arenaria locale.
4_Controsoffitto in cartongesso.
6_Pavimento galleggiante con finitura in gomma naturale.
7_Vano per posizionamento impianti e luci.
8_Pilastro con finitura naturale.
9_Serramento a taglio termico con doppio vetro.
10_Facciata con profilo a taglio termico e vetro basso emissivo.
11_Pavimento in cls con finitura in resina.
12_Pannello di copertura sandwich con doppia coibenza acustica e termica
SEZIONE LONGITUDINALE A-A 1:250
VISTA B
EDIL TOMARCHIO
TERRA
02

165 Urban Block | *Donner Sorcinelli Architecture*

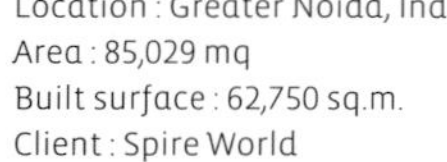

Location : Greater Noida, India
Area : 85,029 mq
Built surface : 62,750 sq.m.
Client : Spire World

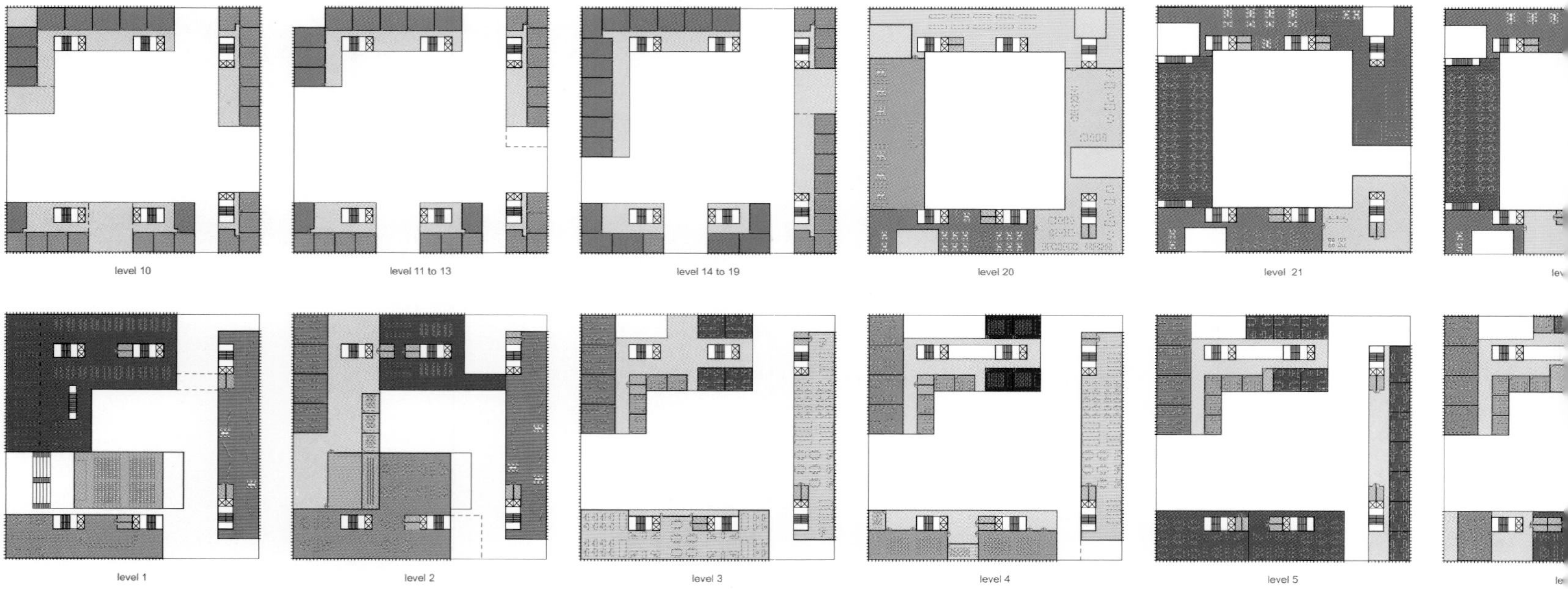

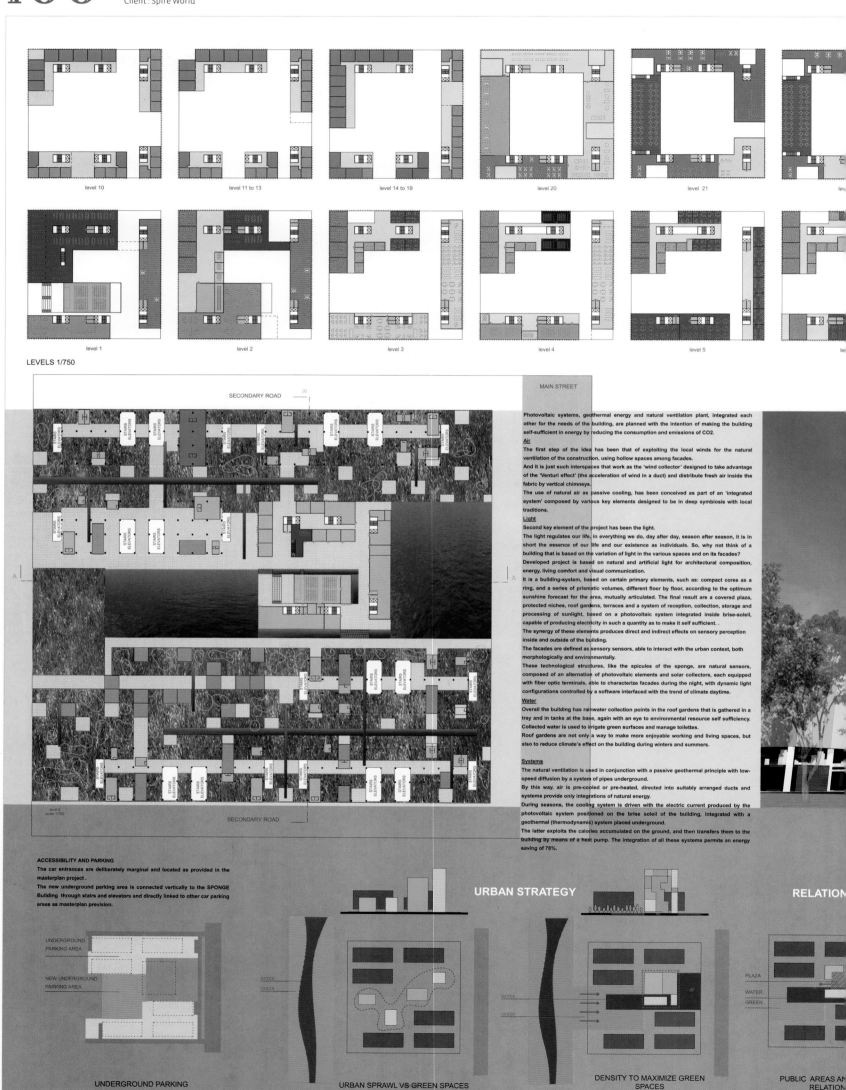

level 10 · level 11 to 13 · level 14 to 19 · level 20 · level 21

level 1 · level 2 · level 3 · level 4 · level 5

LEVELS 1/750

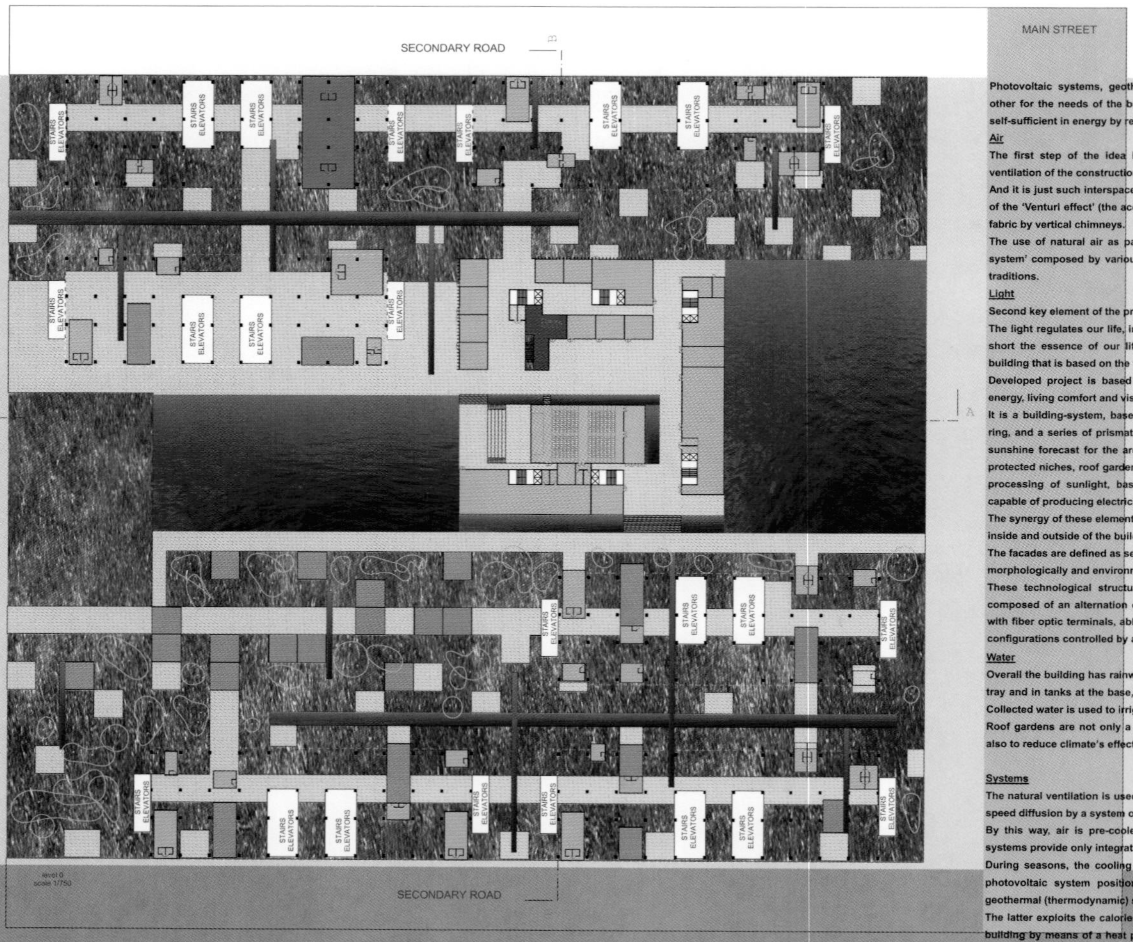

SECONDARY ROAD

MAIN STREET

Photovoltaic systems, geothermal energy and natural ventilation plant, integrated each other for the needs of the building, are planned with the intention of making the building self-sufficient in energy by reducing the consumption and emissions of CO_2.

Air

The first step of the idea has been that of exploiting the local winds for the natural ventilation of the construction, using hollow spaces among facades.

And it is just such interspaces that work as the 'wind collector' designed to take advantage of the 'Venturi effect' (the acceleration of wind in a duct) and distribute fresh air inside the fabric by vertical chimneys.

The use of natural air as passive cooling, has been conceived as part of an 'integrated system' composed by various key elements designed to be in deep symbiosis with local traditions.

Light

Second key element of the project has been the light.

The light regulates our life, in everything we do, day after day, season after season, it is in short the essence of our life and our existence as individuals. So, why not think of a building that is based on the variation of light in the various spaces and on its facades?

Developed project is based on natural and artificial light for architectural composition, energy, living comfort and visual communication.

It is a building-system, based on certain primary elements, such as: compact cores as a ring, and a series of prismatic volumes, different floor by floor, according to the optimum sunshine forecast for the area, mutually articulated. The final result are a covered plaza, protected niches, roof gardens, terraces and a system of reception, collection, storage and processing of sunlight, based on a photovoltaic system integrated inside brise-soleil, capable of producing electricity in such a quantity as to make it self sufficient. .

The synergy of these elements produces direct and indirect effects on sensory perception inside and outside of the building.

The facades are defined as sensory sensors, able to interact with the urban context, both morphologically and environmentally.

These technological structures, like the spicules of the sponge, are natural sensors, composed of an alternation of photovoltaic elements and solar collectors, each equipped with fiber optic terminals, able to characterize facades during the night, with dynamic light configurations controlled by a software interfaced with the trend of climate daytime.

Water

Overall the building has rainwater collection points in the roof gardens that is gathered in a tray and in tanks at the base, again with an eye to environmental resource self sufficiency. Collected water is used to irrigate green surfaces and manage toilettes.

Roof gardens are not only a way to make more enjoyable working and living spaces, but also to reduce climate's effect on the building during winters and summers.

Systems

The natural ventilation is used in conjunction with a passive geothermal principle with low-speed diffusion by a system of pipes underground.

By this way, air is pre-cooled or pre-heated, directed into suitably arranged ducts and systems provide only integrations of natural energy.

During seasons, the cooling system is driven with the electric current produced by the photovoltaic system positioned on the brise soleil of the building, integrated with a geothermal (thermodynamic) system placed underground.

The latter exploits the calories accumulated on the ground, and then transfers them to the building by means of a heat pump. The integration of all these systems permits an energy saving of 78%.

level 0
scale 1/750

SECONDARY ROAD

ACCESSIBILITY AND PARKING

The car entrances are deliberately marginal and located as provided in the masterplan project .

The new underground parking area is connected vertically to the SPONGE Building through stairs and elevators and directly linked to other car parking areas as masterplan prevision.

UNDERGROUND PARKING AREA

NEW UNDERGROUND PARKING AREA

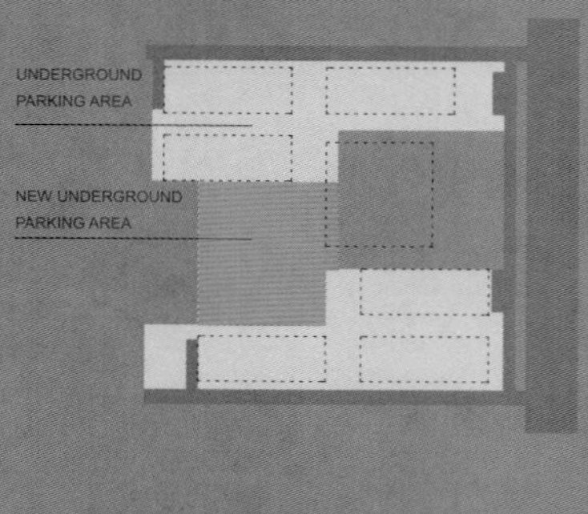

UNDERGROUND PARKING

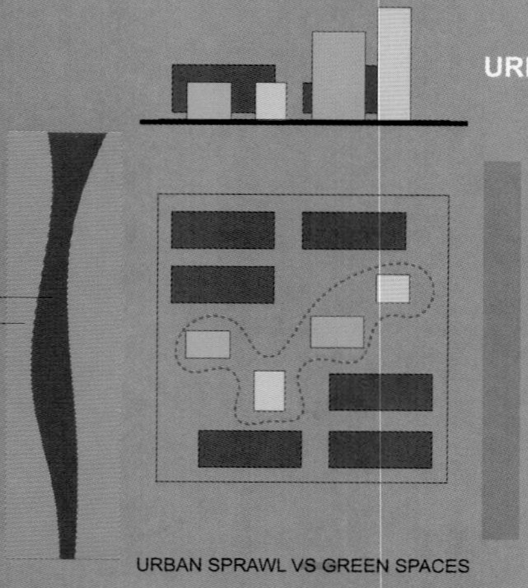

URBAN STRATEGY

URBAN SPRAWL VS GREEN SPACES

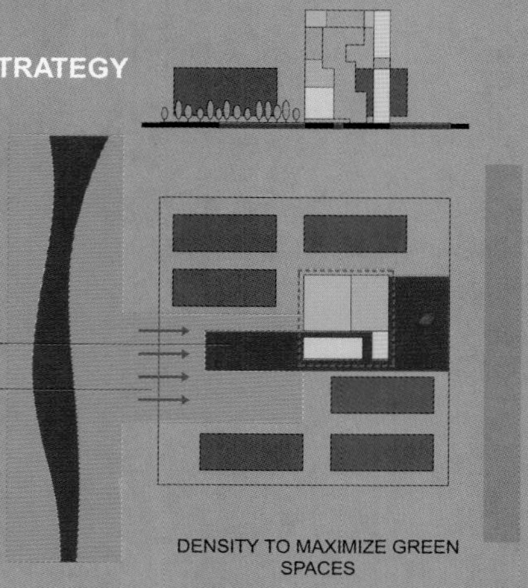

DENSITY TO MAXIMIZE GREEN SPACES

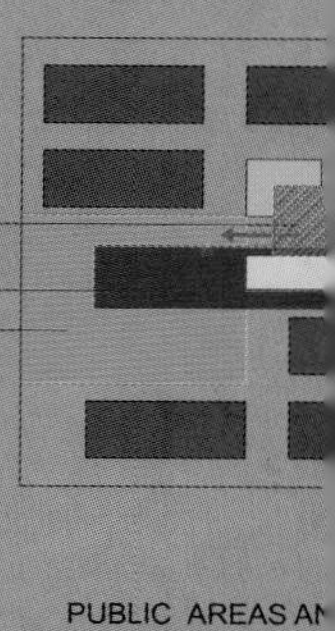

RELATION

PLAZA
WATER
GREEN

PUBLIC AREAS AN RELATION

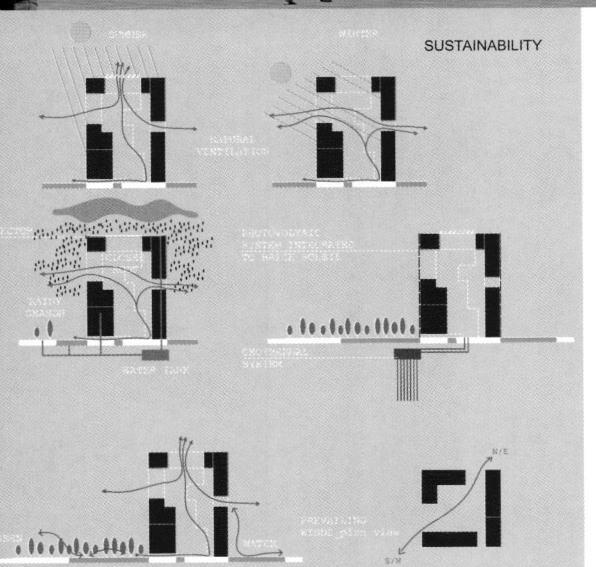

ENERGY SPONGE

The 'Energy Sponge' concept not only refers to the exploitation of natural ventilation for the wellness of its dwellers and visitors, but also to the absorption - just as a sponge - of the different though complementary energies present in nature (aeolian, solar and geothermal). For this reason, the figurative result is the direct consequence of mixing vernacular habits with natural ecosystems, integral to local traditions of constructing, made of passive cooling, green roofs and sustainable technologies.

Cause of its cultural specificity in the globalized world, the city needs an unique interpretation of its recognizable landmarks.

The figurative element from which the project evolved, should contain within itself, not just symbolism associated with the current international vision, but also a deep relationship with the cultural identity of this city.

Building mass, with its formal intrinsic tension, seems suited to represent its specific internal dynamism, born from the functional program and sustainable solutions, based on various related steps.

Natural resources are part of a strategy that aims towards real sustainability and from this point of view water, green and sunlight are integral parts of the structure.

Particular shape of the building has led to the development of a strong sculptural form, as main figure.

The result is an asymmetrical and atypical fabric, just like a SPONGE, with a strong iconographic impact and universal symbolism.

The sculptural final mass is characterized by dominant figurative elements, where the plasticity, the essentiality and the dynamism of forms, mark both the appearance that the functional composition, in keeping with the nature of the surrounding urban structure.

The asymmetrical shape, will permit, with the passing of seasons and according to the points of view, to perceive the building in a different and unique way, making this vision a unique experience at sensory level.

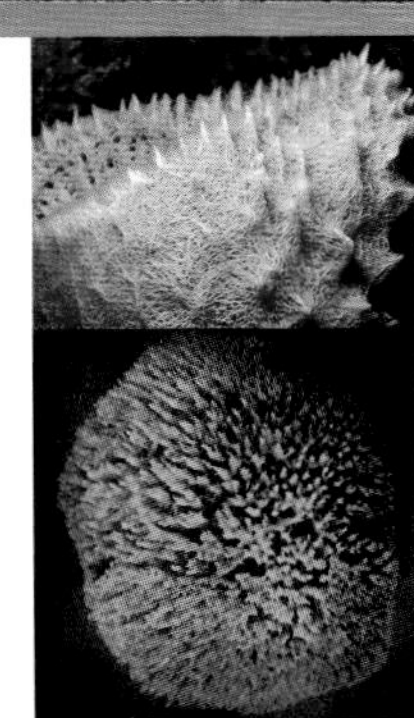

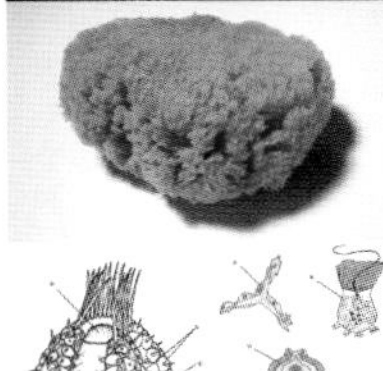

FUNCTIONAL PROGRAM

The commercial and institutional podium, based on two levels, thanks to its shape and open geometry, welcomes visitors along the pedestrian path, while various entrances, located on three sides of the internal square, permits to separate flows and maintain privacy for offices and apartments on upper levels.

The ring core have been provided with toilets for each level, lifts, technical rooms and the main corridor, maintaining functional flexibility of interior spaces.

Last levels provides hotel facilities, rooms and pool, where city's skyline will be the catalyst scenic element.

The morphology of the green roofs enable not only to bring dynamism to the classic monolithic structure of this type of building, but also to enjoy the scenic views, the landscape and the surrounding city, always different in different directions, and so unique for this reason.

Open and closed spaces interact each other and with the landscape in a dynamic and interactive way, by creating selective views.

The building, so conceived, has been treated not as one mass, but as a "system of aggregates", flexible and therefore easily adaptable to local functional conditions.

OUTDOOR SPACES

The outdoor spaces are designed as integrated into the overall design of the ground level, and constitute an element of continuity f
The new network of pedestrian path is linked to the design of the SPONGE building as to the other fabrics, for an easier circulatio
The green park areas, based on Vastu Shastra concept, are places of socialization and therefore the heart of the outdoor spaces, p
seating and lighting furnitures, food courts and small shops.

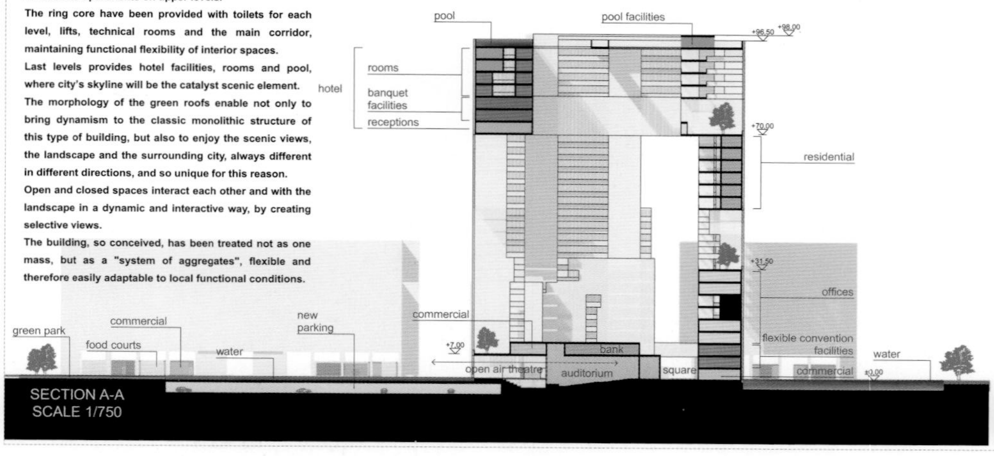

SECTION A-A
SCALE 1/750

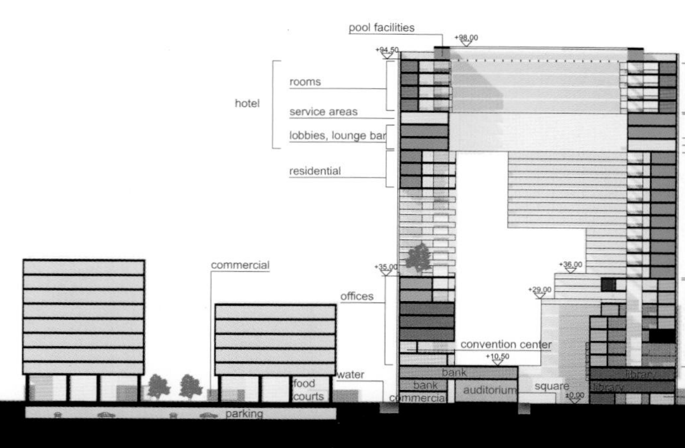

S5367U

THE SQUARE

The 'Energy Sponge' internal square is a public space conceived as an AGORA', where people can meet together, discuss, simply shopping or can reach the auditorium, with the open air theatre, the library and exposition areas, offices, etc.
Public functions are mixed with commercial activities and during all seasons people can live this place thanks to the double configuration of the roof.
In fact, the upper window holes can be closed during rainy season to protect the square itself and opened in sunny days.
These facades and roof holes are the base to exploit the natural ventilation inside the building and the square itself, during all the year.

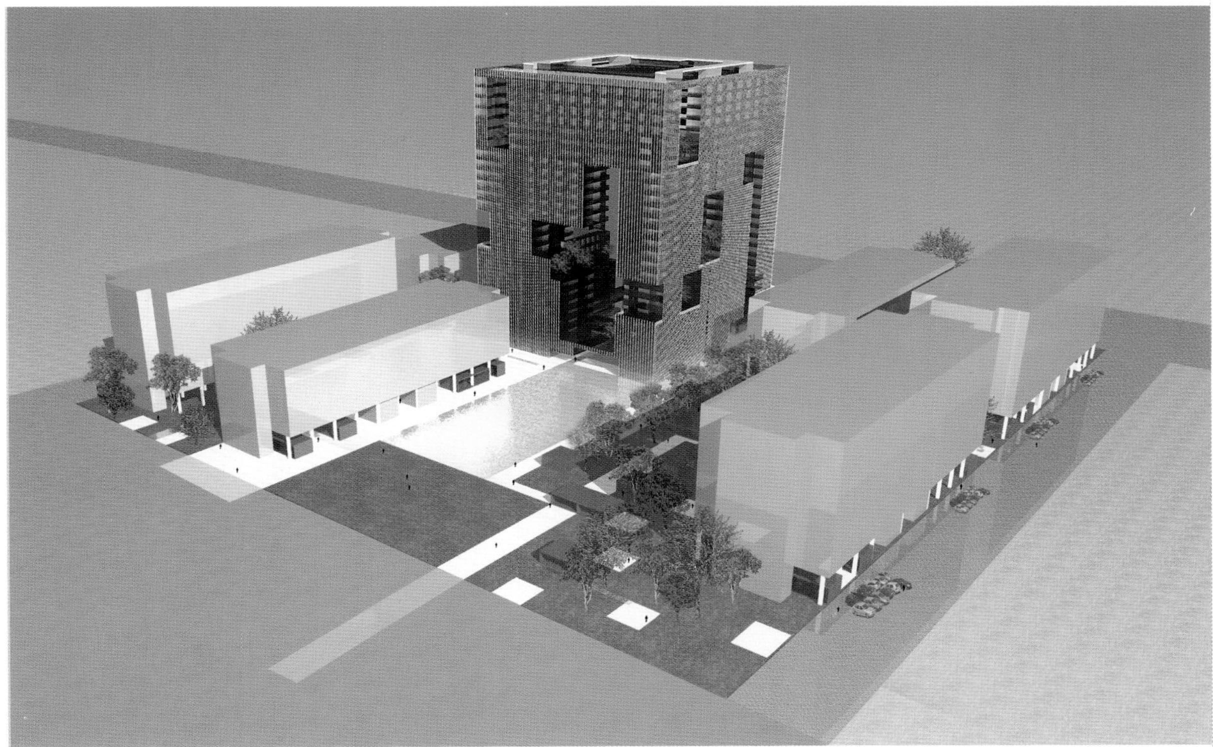

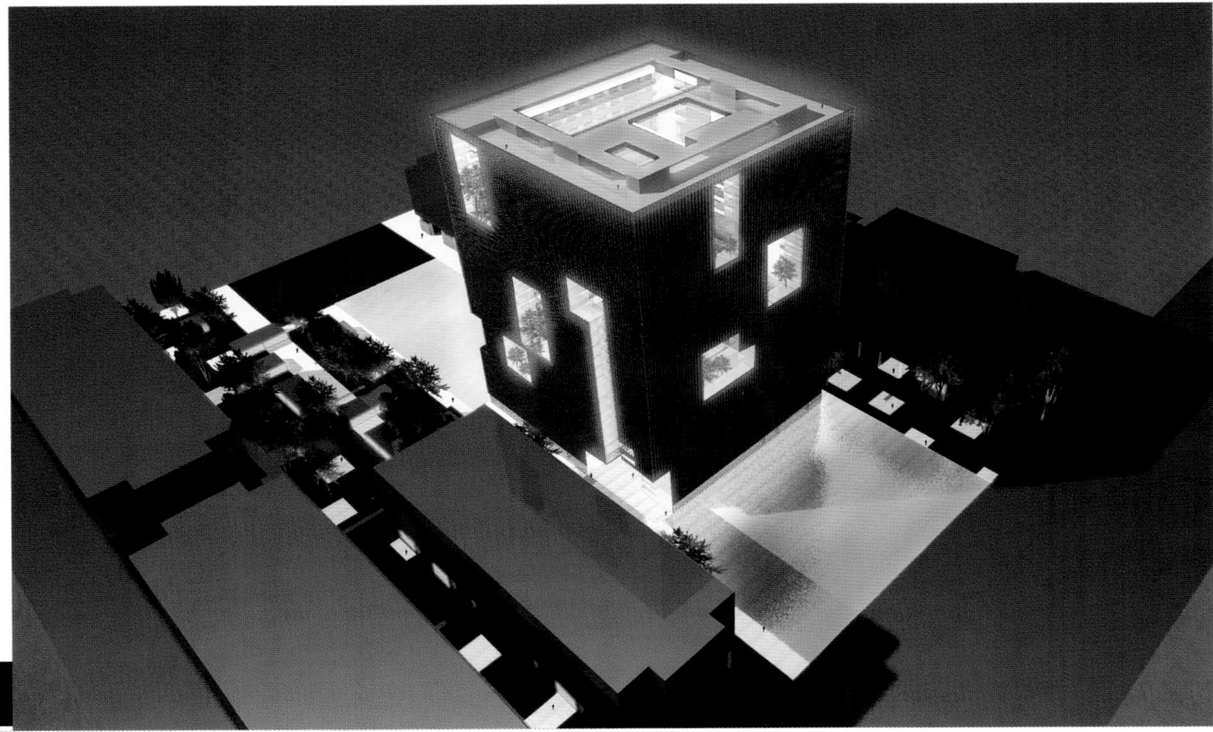

SECTION B-B
SCALE 1/750

166 Watermark Shaping | *b4architects*

Client : Municipality of Mora, Europan
Site area : 15ha
Program : Housing, Public Space, Urban Park, Travel Centre
Project team : Gianluca Evels & Stefania Papitto - b4architects with Francesco Fazzio Architect

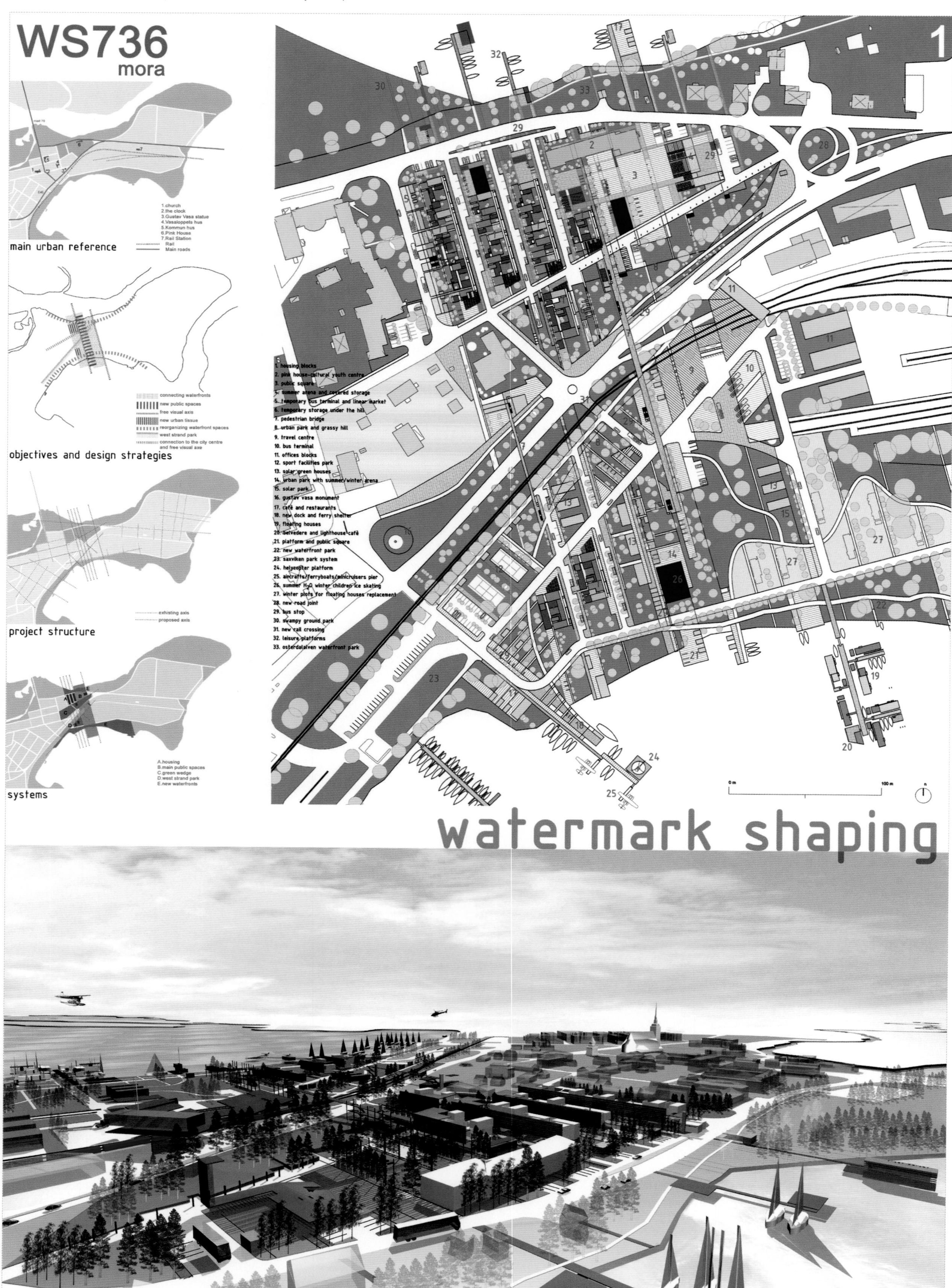

WS736
mora
2
public squares
pedestrian pathway
pedestrian bridge
byke route
byke point/parking
summer swimming areas
winter skiing areas
kayak rental
winter ice-skate
summer waterplay ground
summer arena
free visual axes
public system
pink house-cultural youth centre
housing
public services
travel centre
floating housing
floating housing-winter periode
temporary storage
greenhouses
kiosk/commercial
restaurant/cafè/retail
marina services
exhisting building
building system
lakefront
rail
main
local
residential flow
node-junction
level-crossing
bus station
new travel centre
parking
exhisting parking
car rental/sharing
TAXI taxi parking
bus stop
mooring wharf
residential mooring wharf
cruise station
mooring wharf
helicopter
aircraft
natural barrier noises
traffic flows
main public square
forest
park
urban park
residential green
exhisting urban green
playgroung areas
winter ice/summer water
solar park
coastal park
green system
cross section
0
50
100 m
watermark shaping

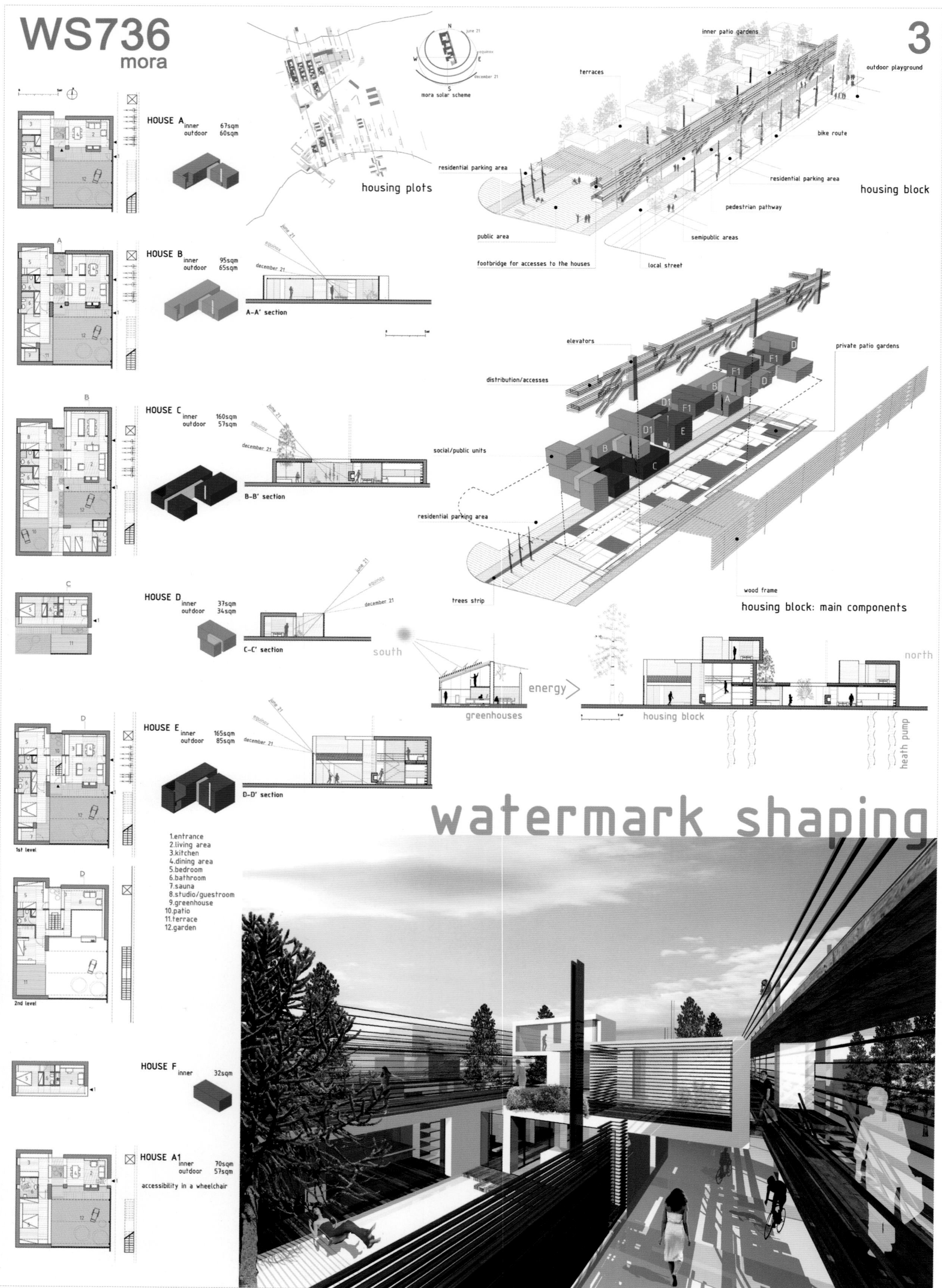
WS736
mora
3
HOUSE A inner 67sqm outdoor 60sqm
HOUSE B inner 95sqm outdoor 65sqm
HOUSE C inner 160sqm outdoor 57sqm
HOUSE D inner 37sqm outdoor 34sqm
HOUSE E inner 165sqm outdoor 85sqm
HOUSE F inner 32sqm
HOUSE A1 inner 70sqm outdoor 57sqm
accessibility in a wheelchair
1st level
2nd level
1.entrance
2.living area
3.kitchen
4.dining area
5.bedroom
6.bathroom
7.sauna
8.studio/guestroom
9.greenhouse
10.patio
11.terrace
12.garden
mora solar scheme
june 21
equinox
december 21
housing plots
A-A' section
B-B' section
C-C' section
D-D' section
inner patio gardens
terraces
outdoor playground
bike route
residential parking area
housing block
pedestrian pathway
public area
semipublic areas
footbridge for accesses to the houses
local street
elevators
private patio gardens
distribution/accesses
social/public units
wood frame
trees strip
housing block: main components
south
north
energy
greenhouses
housing block
heath pump
watermark shaping

Client : University of Zagreb
Project : 2010-2011
Type : public competition
Project team : Saša Begović, Marko Dabrović, Tatjana Grozdanić Begović, Silvije Novak, Eugen Popović, Leon Lazaneo, Anna Kocsis, Krunoslav Szorsen
3D : Josip Miklec

Project number : 191
City : Zagreb
Country : Croatia
Program : education, urbanism

Kampus Borongaj
01

Situacija šire zone_tlocrt krova 1:5000
— Wider area Masterplan_roof top view

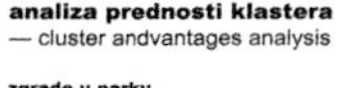

analiza prednosti klastera
— cluster andvantages analysis

zgrade u parku
— buildings integrated in park

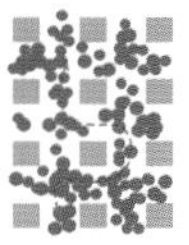

gustoća/urbanost ×
dense/urbanity
optimalne udaljenosti ×
optimal distances
veze kroz zelenilo ✓
green links
faznost ×
phasing

gusti klaster
— dense cluster

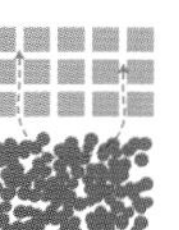

gustoća/urbanost ✓
dense/urbanity
optimalne udaljenosti ✓
optimal distances
veze kroz zelenilo ×
green links
faznost ×
phasing

multiplikacija klastera
— clusters multiplication

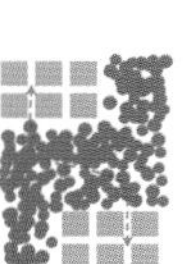

gustoća/urbanost ✓
dense/urbanity
optimalne udaljenosti ✓
optimal distances
veze kroz zelenilo ✓
green links
faznost ✓
phasing

odnos prema kontekstu grada
— relation to city

interakcija/odnos izgrađeno/neizgrađeno
— relationship built/unbuilt

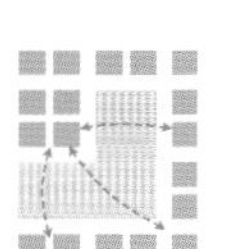

segment zelene potkove
— part of Zagreb green horseshoe

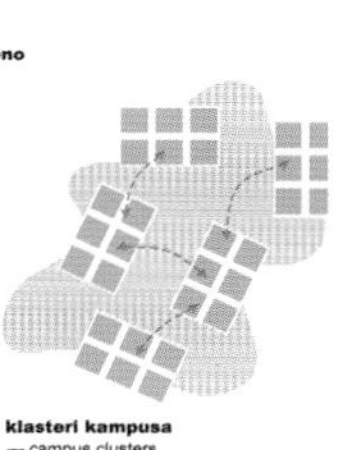

klasteri kampusa
— campus clusters

shema šireg prometa
— traffic scheme

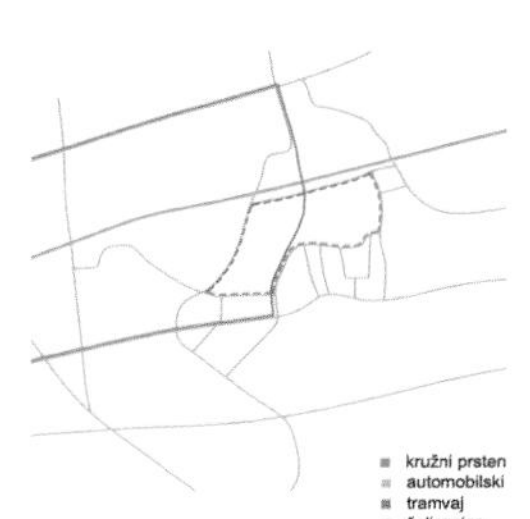

koncept ekološkog koridora
— ecological corridor concept

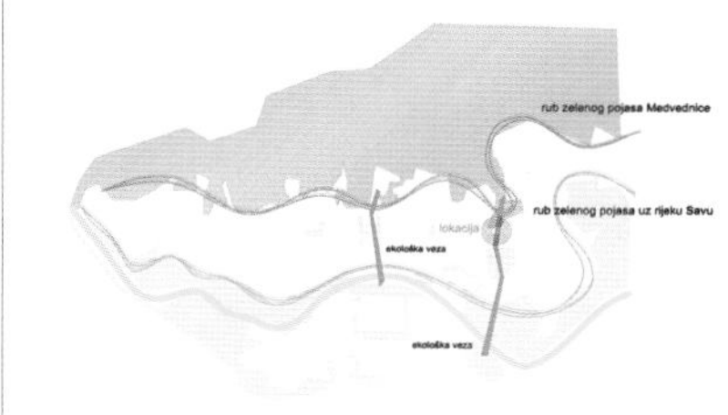

utjecaj i zaštita od vjetra
— wind impact and protection

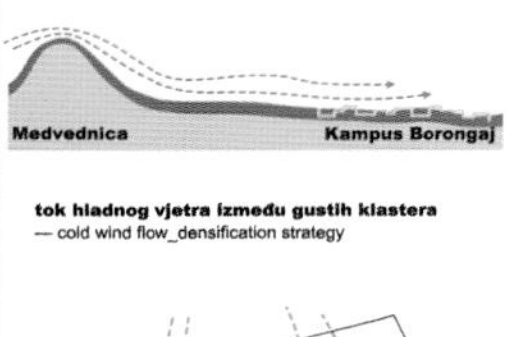

tok hladnog vjetra između gustih klastera
— cold wind flow_densification strategy

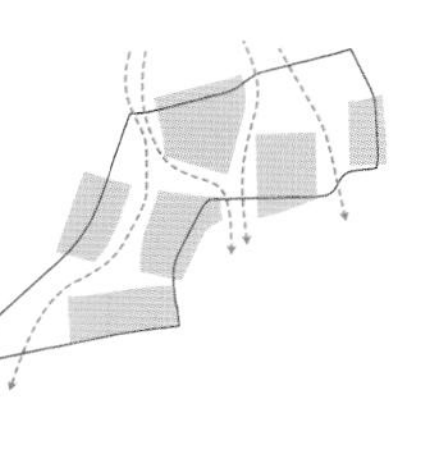

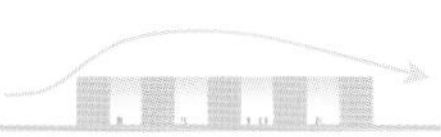

vjetar prelazi gusti klaster
— wind sheltering, densification strategy

utjecaj i zaštita od sunca
— insolation impact and protection

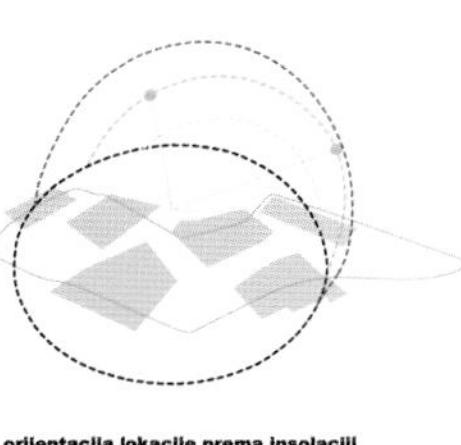

orijentacija lokacije prema insolaciji
— site orientation

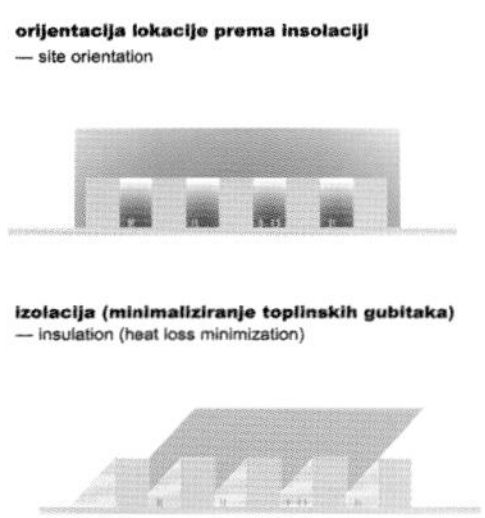

izolacija (minimaliziranje toplinskih gubitaka)
— insulation (heat loss minimization)

minimaliziranje pregrijavanja
— overheating minimization

shema ekološkog koridora
— ecological corridor scheme

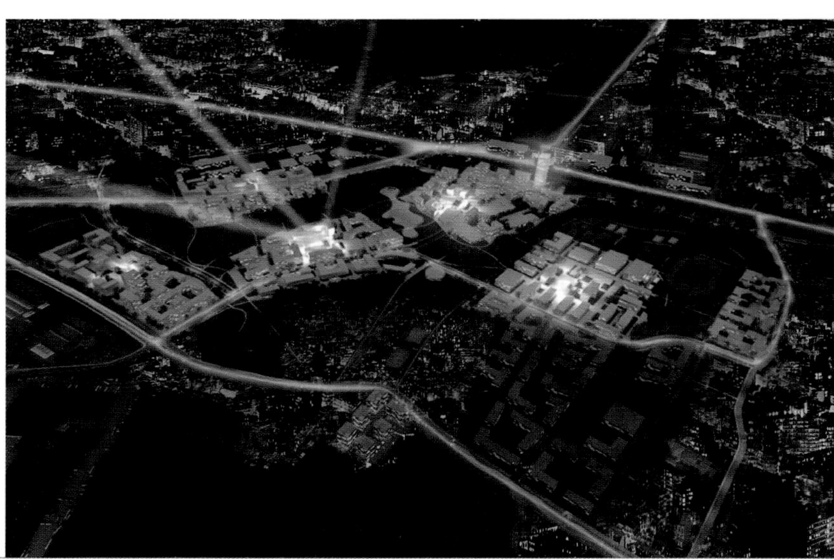

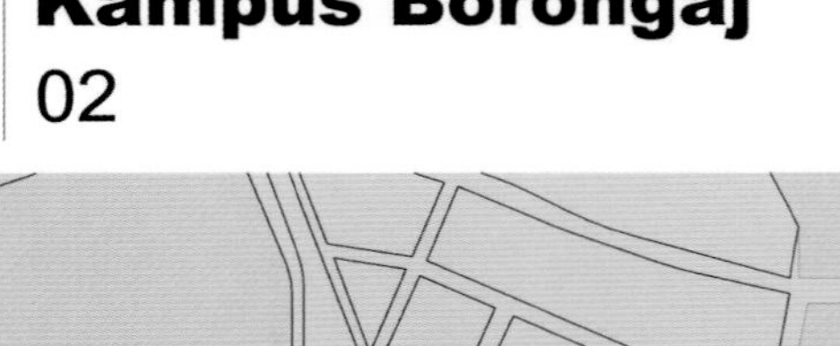

Kampus Borongaj
02

Situacija uže zone_tlocrt krova 1:2000
— Masterplan_roof top view

definiranje klastera
— clusters determination

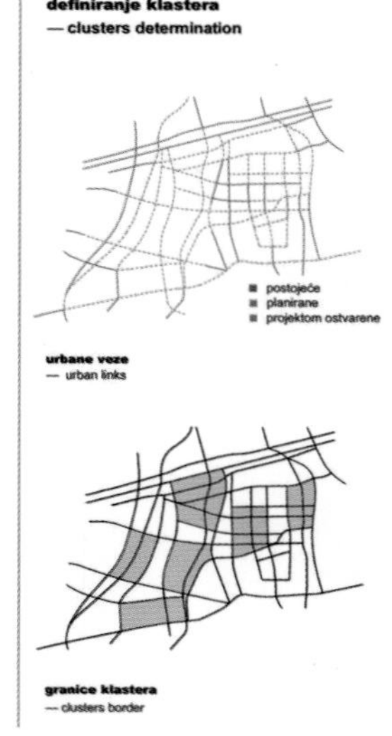

urbane veze
— urban links

granice klastera
— clusters border

odnos klasteri - urbani kontekst
— clusters relationship to urban context

integracija sa postojećim urbanim strukturama, formiranje uličnih pročelja
— integration with existing urban structures, streets facades formation

kontinuitet veza sa gradskim zelenim zonama
— continuous green connections

prometno povezivanje klastera
— traffic links between clusters

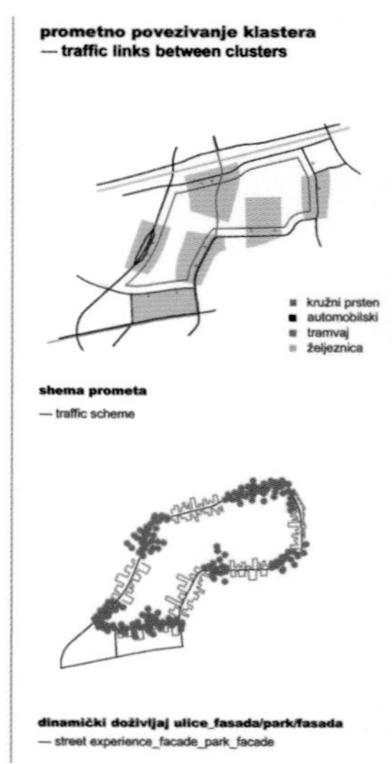

shema prometa
— traffic scheme

dinamički doživljaj ulice_fasada/park/fasada
— street experience_facade_park_facade

Kampus Borongaj
03

Situacija uže zone_tlocrt prizemlja 1:2000
— Masterplan_Ground floor

jezero
palube uz jezero za boravak na suncu
postojeća prirodna visoka vegetacija
zaštitno visoko zelenilo
dekorativno zelenilo
pasivno korištenje travnjaka
aktivno korištenje travnjaka + manifestacije
aktivno korištenje travnjaka + rekreacija
vidikovac
točka sa zanimljivom vizurom

zoniranje funkcija
— zoning

zgrade fakulteta
tehnološki park
gl. zajednički akademski sadržaji
gl. zajednički sadržaji (kantina, kongresni centar)
sportski sadržaji
studentski domovi
dodatni smještaj
upravne zgrade na nivou znanstvenog kampusa
upravne zgrade upravne zgrade
predloženi sadržaji izvan obuhvata
trigeneracijska energana

pješačke udaljenosti od centara gravitacije
— walking distance from the center of gravity

r=250m

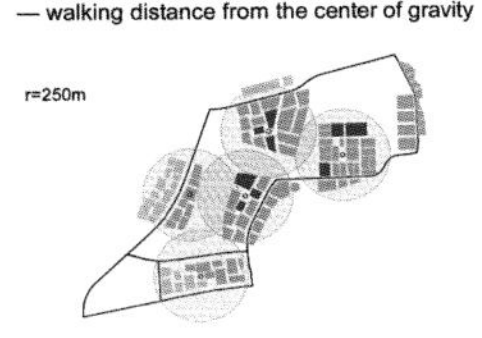

presjek sjever-jug 1:2000
— north-south section

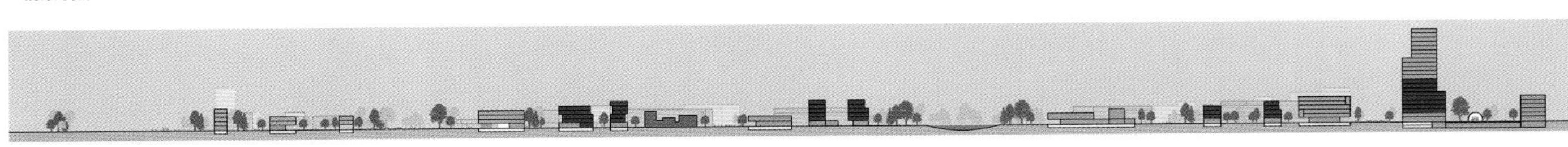

koridori ulica 1:500
— street section

section 1

section 2

section 4

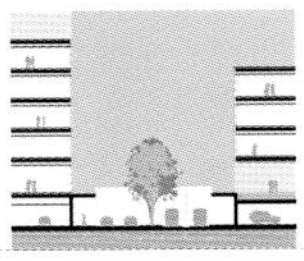

section 5

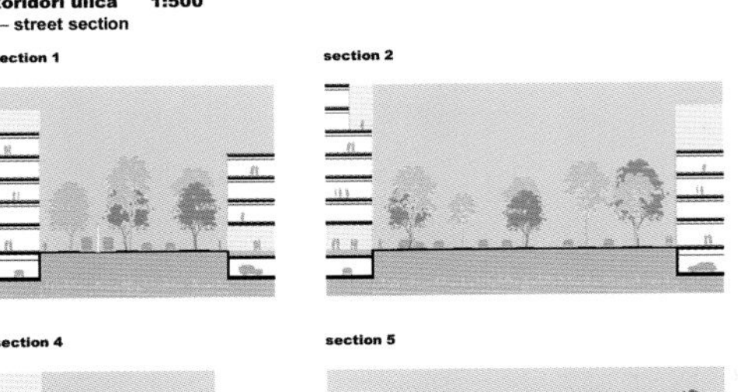

section 3

Kampus Borongaj
04

Shema fakultetskog i stambenog sklopa_tlocrt prizemlja i karakteristične etaže 1:500
— Scheme of college and dorm_ground floor and typical floor

prizemlje
— ground floor

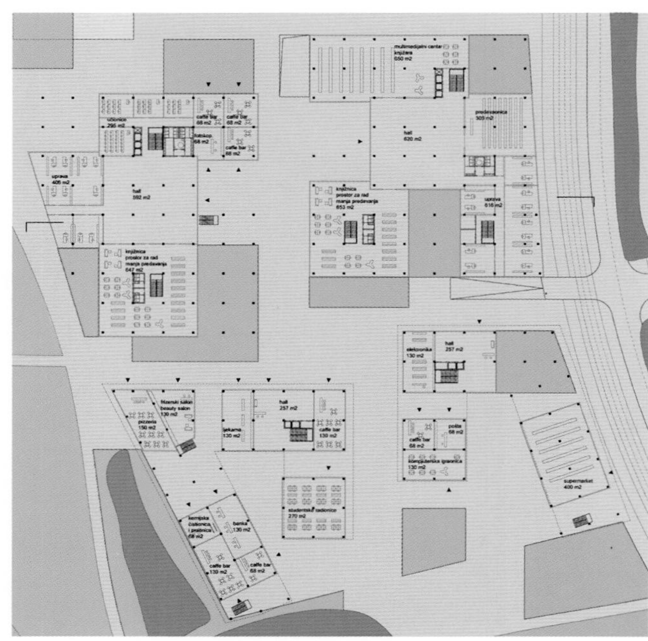

karakteristična etaža
— typical floor

organizacija klastera
— cluster organization

dinamika komunikacija / usporavanje vjetra
— communications dynamics / slowdown wind

granica obuhvata
— plot boundary

zadana granica kampusa
nova granica kampusa
granica obuhvata

presjek 1:500
— section

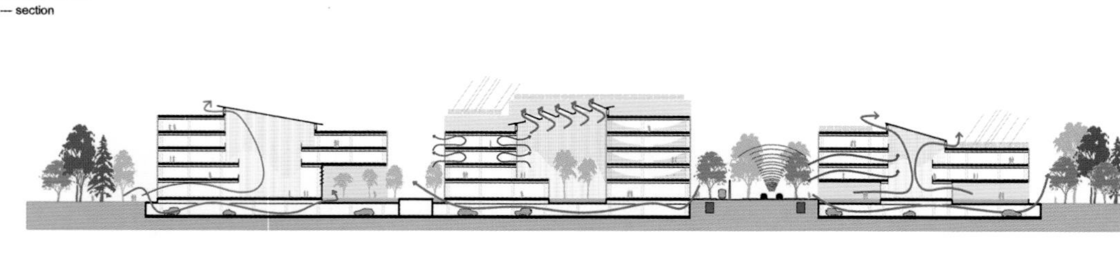

ispreplitanje sadržaja
— mix use

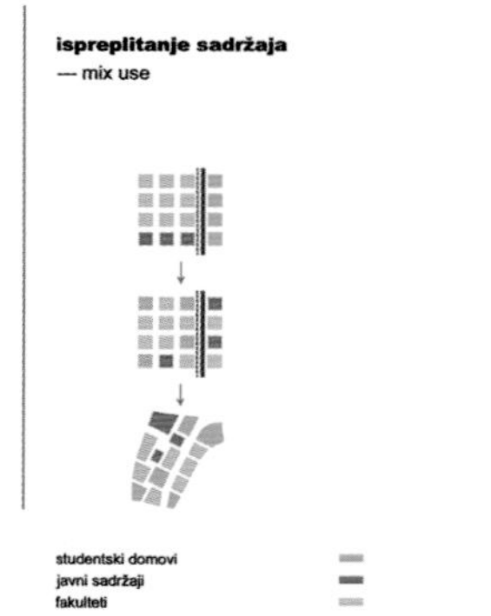

studentski domovi
javni sadržaji
fakulteti

odnos postojeće/novo
— relation existing/new

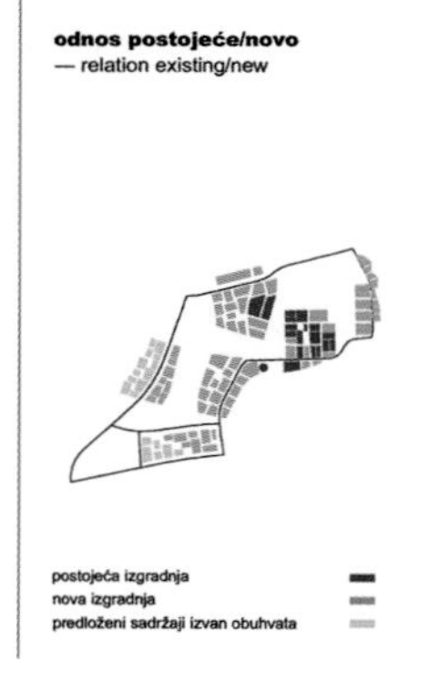

postojeća izgradnja
nova izgradnja
predloženi sadržaji izvan obuhvata

faznost
— stages

prva faza
— first stage

druga faza
— second stage

treća faza
— third stage

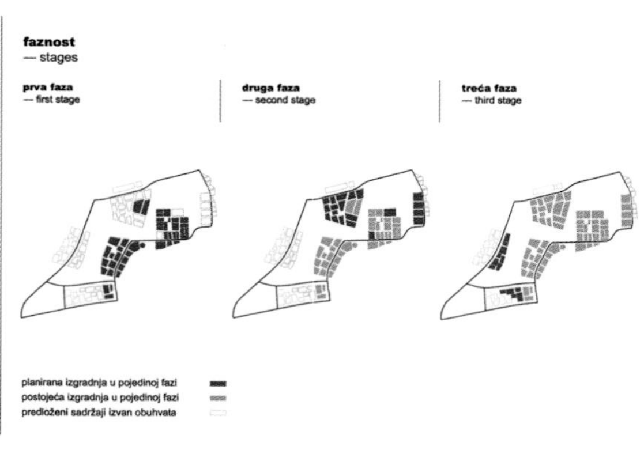

planirana izgradnja u pojedinoj fazi
postojeća izgradnja u pojedinoj fazi
predloženi sadržaji izvan obuhvata

tlocrt podzemne etaže karakterističnog klastera 1:2000
— typical cluster underground floor

shema sustava podzemnog parkiranja
— underground parking scheme

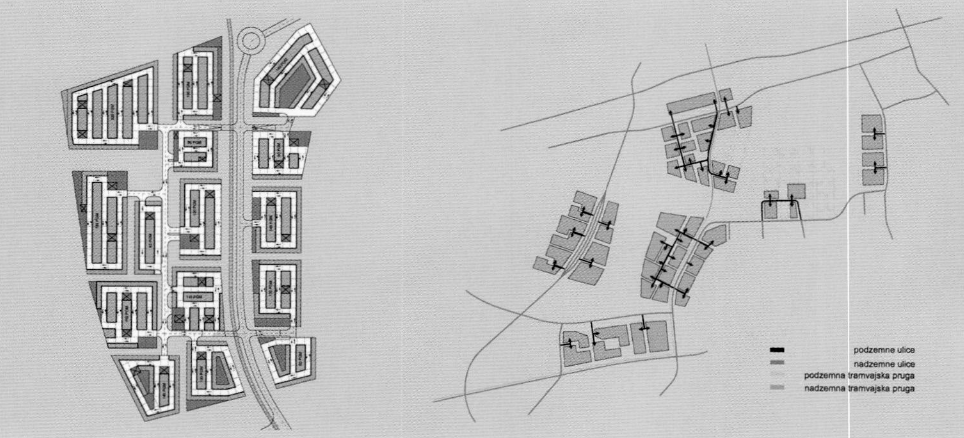

Kampus Borongaj
05

Ciljevi
— Targets

0 emisije plinova
— Carbon Emissions

60% redukcija vode
— 60% Potable Water Use Reduction

nula CO2 emisija
— zero CO2 Emissions Transport

Recikliranje 90% otpada
— Recyce 90% Waste

Zaštita staništa
— Protect Habitats

Promocija bioraznolikosti
— Promote Biodiversity

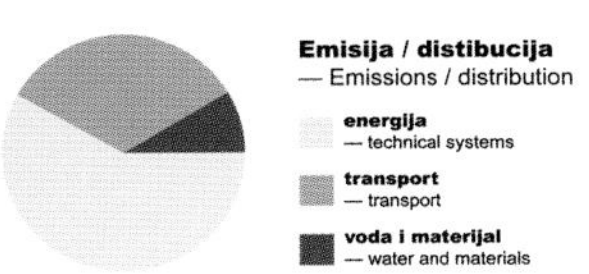

Metodologija
— Metodology

Dizajn metodologija u 4 koraka
— 4-Step Design Methodology

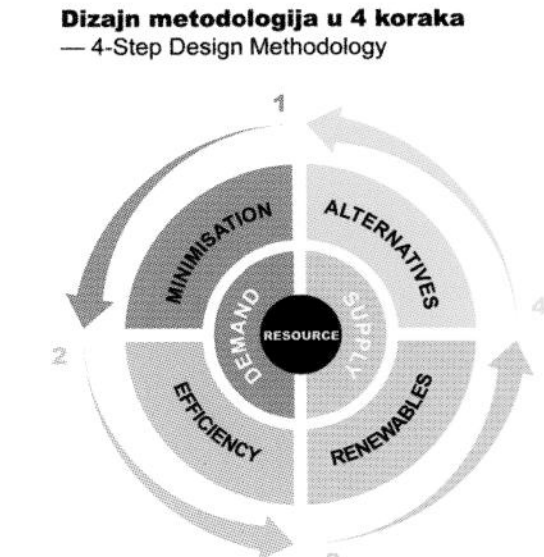

Minimizacija resursa
— Resources Minimization

Emisija CO2
— CO2 emissions

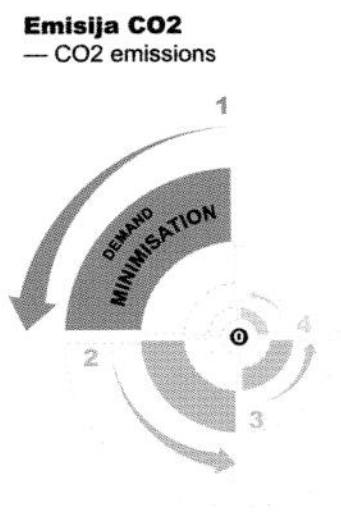

Klima
— Climate

Analiza vjetrova
— Wind analyses

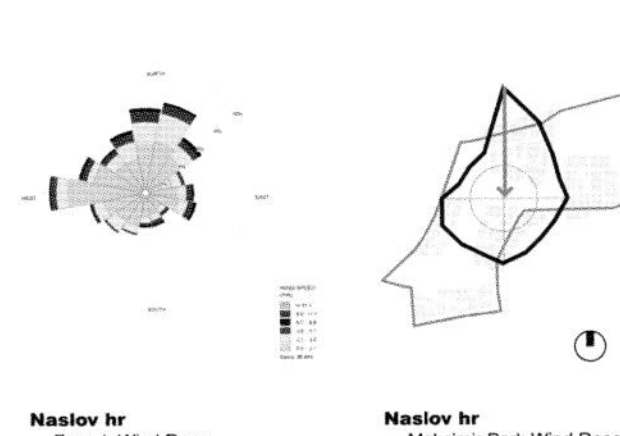

Naslov hr
— Zagreb Wind Rose

Naslov hr
— Maksimir Park Wind Rose

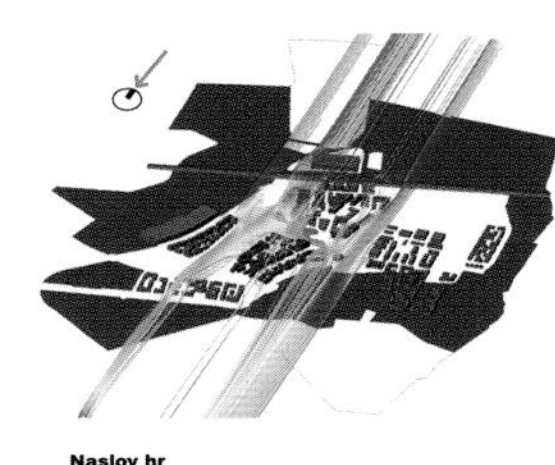

Naslov hr
— Predominant Northernly Wind Flow Simulation

Sunce
— Sun path

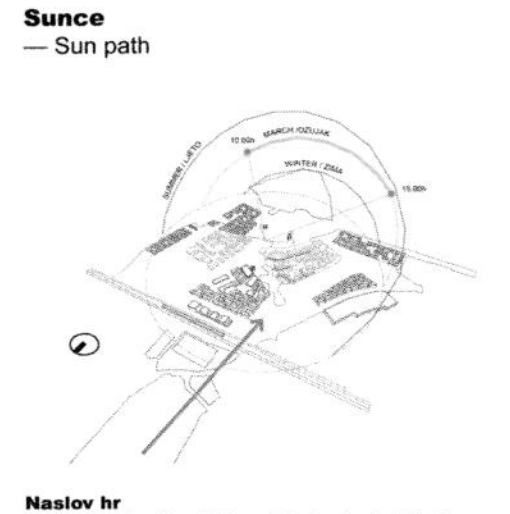

Naslov hr
— Site Overlay (Sun Path and Predominated Wind)

Energetski koncept — Energy concept and CO2 emissions

HR naslov
— Smart grid

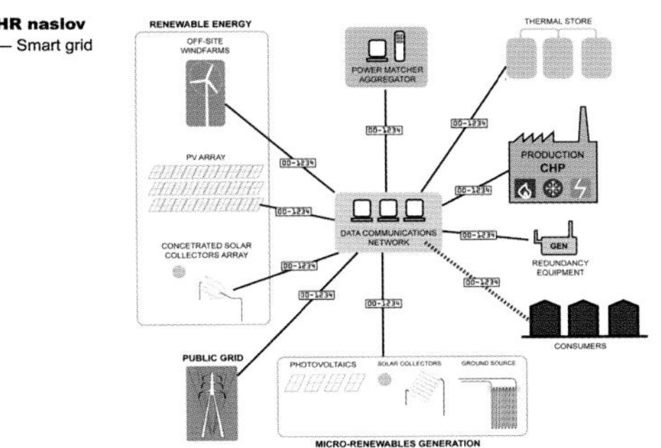

HR naslov
— Borongaj Masterplan

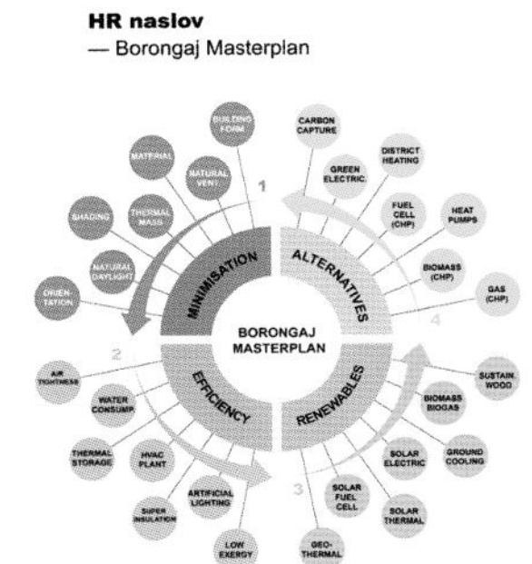

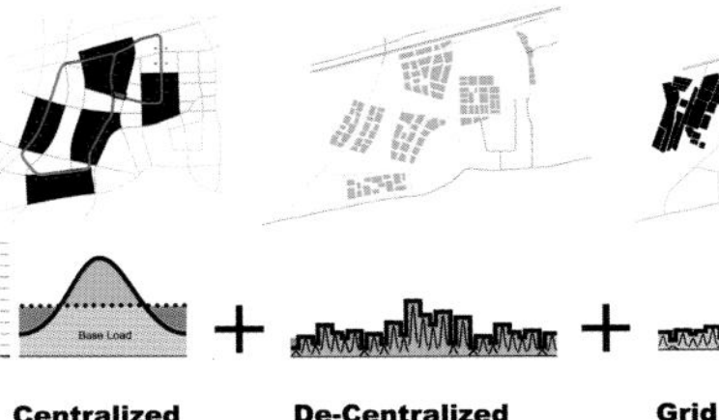

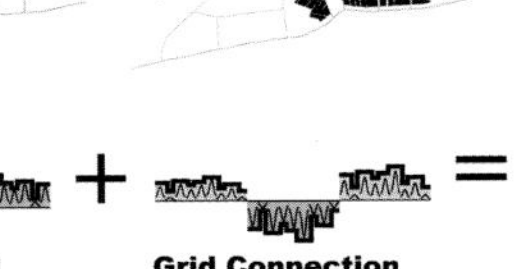

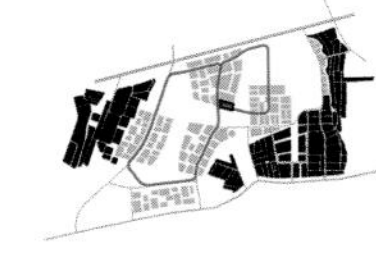

Centralized
- Economies of Scale
- Load Profiles Matching
- (Equipment Optimization)
- Equipment Underutilization

De-Centralized
- Every Building is Energy Generator
- Minimized Trasmisson Losses
- Equipment Oversizing

Grid Connection
- Redundancy & Backup
- Security of Supply
- Variable Demand

Hybrid Option
- Load Matching & Balancing
- Better Equipment Sizing (Capital Savings)
- Renewables Energy Storage (Export Surplus & Import from Grid When Generation Insufficient)
- Network Resilience
- Security of Supply (Redundancy)
- Minimized Energy & Maintence (operational) Costs

HR naslov / Hr naslov
— Energy Center Options / Phasing

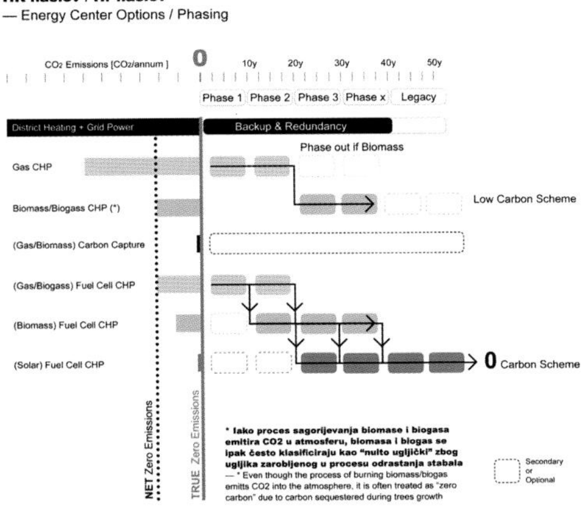

* Iako proces sagorijevanja biomase i biogasa emitira CO2 u atmosferu, biomasa i biogas se ipak često klasificiraju kao "nulto ugljični" zbog ugljika zarobljenog u procesu odrastanja stabala
— * Even though the process of burning biomass/biogas emitts CO2 into the atmosphere, it is often treated as "zero carbon" due to carbon sequestered during trees growth

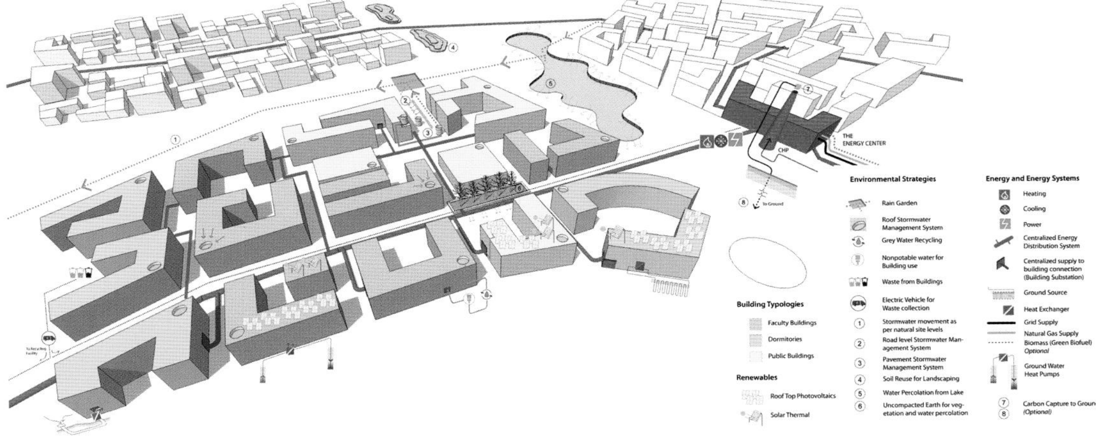

Voda
— Water

Minimizacija potrošnje pitke vode
Kontroliranje oborinske vode
— Minimize Potable Water Use
Storwater Management

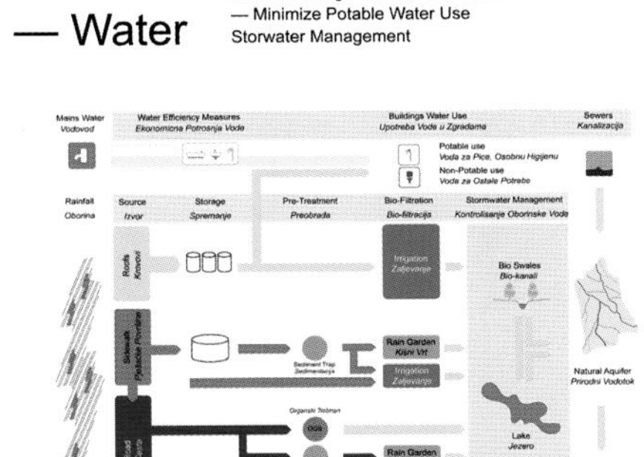

Transport
— Transport

Vozila za nultom emisijom ugljika
— Introduce Zero Emissions Vehicles

Promovirati hodanje i biciklirarnje
— Promote Walking and Cycling

Veza sa čvorovima za masovni prijevoz
— Linkage to Mass Transportation

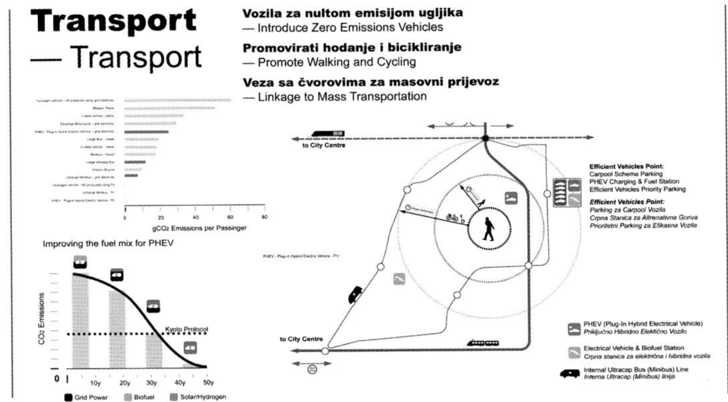

Odpad i materijal
— Waste and Materials

Minimiziranje i recikliranje građevinskog materijala
Recikliranje (u operativnoj fazi objekta)
Odgovorna politika nabave robe (ISO 14001)
Upotreba lokalnih građevinskih materijala
Građevinski materijali sa velikim recikliranim sadržajem
— Construction Waste Minimization and Reuse
— Recycling
— Responsible Procurement Policies (ISO 14001)
— Local Construction Materials
— High Recycled Content of Construction Materials

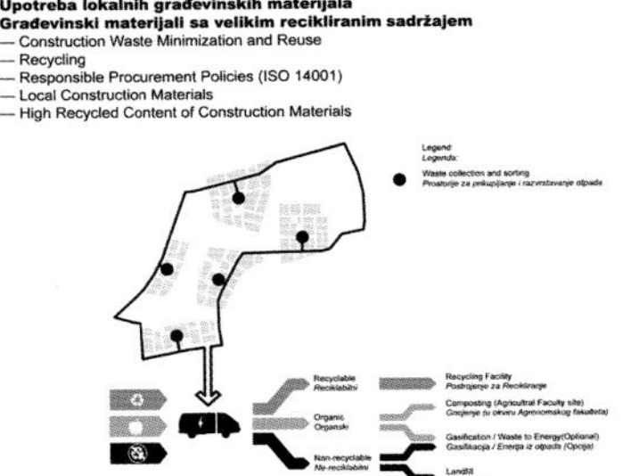

168

Bezalel | *Alessandro Console Studio*

Competition : A new Campus for Bezalel in the Center of Jerusalem International Architecture Competition
Promoter : Bezalel Academy of Art and Design
Location : Jerusalem - Israel / Tipology : University
Team Leader : Alessandro Console

Project Team : Gina Oliva, Giuditta Benedetti, Andrea Canale, Alessio Cancellieri

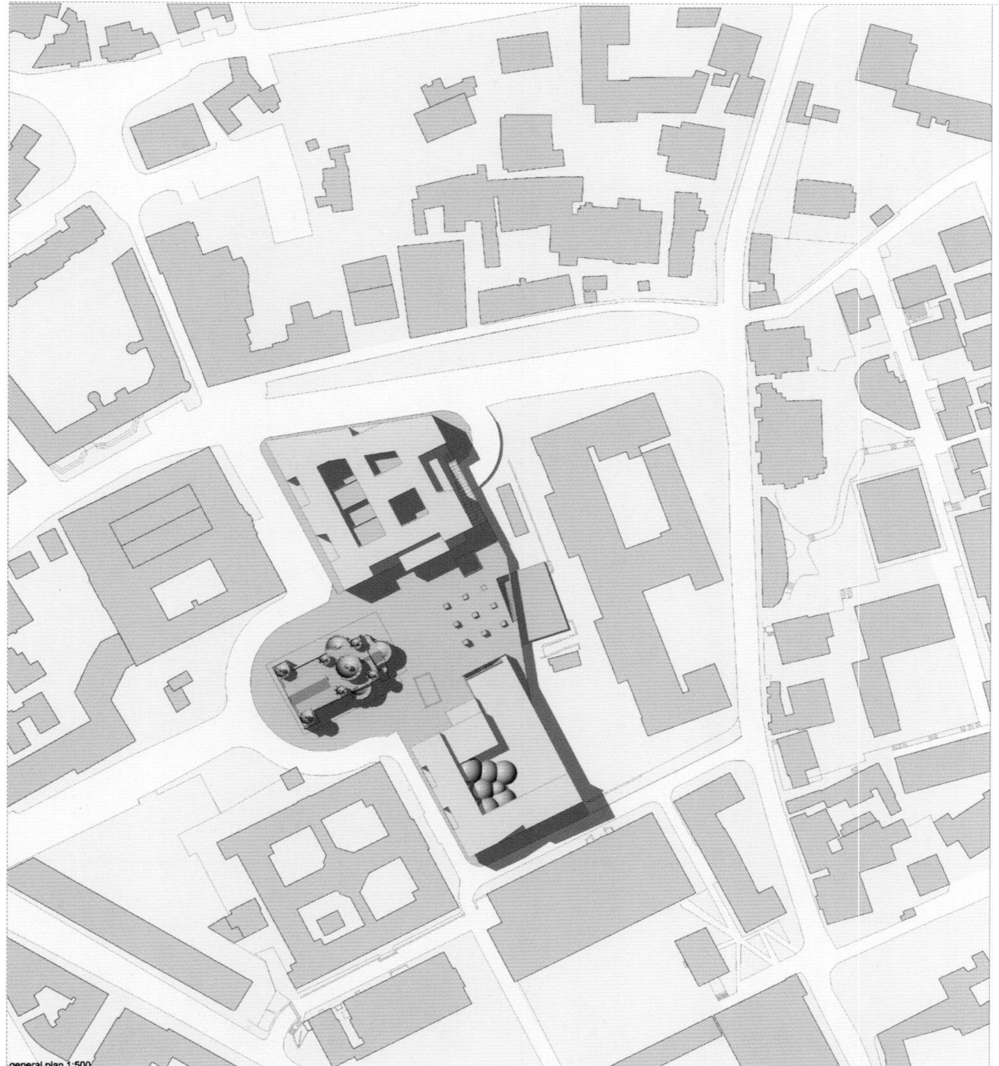
general plan 1:500

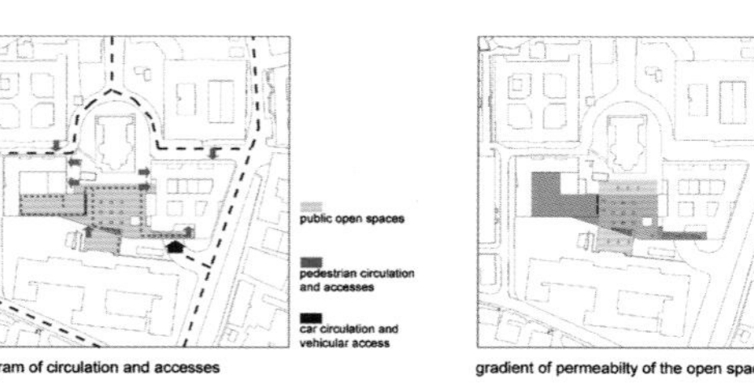

diagram of circulation and accesses

gradient of permeabilty of the open spaces

The city of Jerusalem has always been a place where ethnic groups and cultures, very different among each other, exist at the same time: it is considered a symbolic city for the three main monotheistic religions, that find in it the indisputable references of their identity (the Crying Wall, the Gold Dome Mosque, the Holy Sepulchre, etc.).
Starting from this considerations regarding the character and the peculiarity of this very special city, our project for the Bezalel Academy of Arts & Design was developed through a careful estimation both of the urban context's specific aspects (the Russian Compound), and of the strategies to develop its potential.
The project consists of a basement that starts from the lowest part of the site up to the church level; from this block, two lateral volumes, considered as parts of a single element, rise, redefining the streets aspects and becoming the real urban wings that frame and enhance the church's sight from the center of the city.
This two elements descend from the same matrix, but nevertheless they have very different characters.
From the church side they both appear more compact and unitary: here two angular accesses to the building are provided at 0.00 level.
From the opposite side, instead, they show a different but complementary aspect: on the left, there is an open and stratified block, defined by the assembly of various volumes and a complex geometry (the system of domes that forms the roof of the auditorium); on the right, a block - into which excavated parts generate a spatial system of courts - is eroded along its surfaces, preservating in any case, the enclosed and unitary aspect.
The aim, therefore, is to create an articulate skyline through the combination of various elements that coexist without denying the identity of each part and enhancing their own potential: an attempt to translate the Jerusalem's peculiar plurality of confessions in a strategy to build the architectural form.
The formal distinction between the two volumes is strictly related to the functional and distributive strategy chosen for the Bezalel Campus: the first one hosts the departments without special requirements, in the other one there are the departments with special requirements and all the related spaces.
Thought each block has also a distinct access, the users' freedom of flows is granted thanks to the continuity of the basement: this part is the main entrance from the lower level and hosts the common and service spaces for all the departments, the management offices and the car parking.
Along the north-south axe, the volumes face each other along the sides of the empty open space behind the church: this space becomes a real public square, independent even though it remains a dialectical part of the project and an inner urban space spreading to the lateral volumes. From the lowest level of the project area, it is possible to reach the square, articulated by a series of cubic elements. These ones characterize the spatial environment of the square and allow the natural and zenithal lighting of the canteen, located directly under the square. Then, from the square it is possible to enter directly in the campus through its most public parts (coffee, shops, etc.) or else to take a system of stairs and ramps that allows the users to reach the level +4.00 of the block, on one side and, on the other side, the roof terrace on top of the gymnasium, that faces the city.
The imagine of the whole building is articulated, compact and materic at once.
The facades of the building are mostly covered by local stone slabs, (with the same colour and tonality of the surrounding buildings) that are alternated with glass walls, distributed in a measured and strategic way in the lower levels, especially in the access areas, and on the surfaces of the internal courts.
On the surface of the stone panels (assembled and connected to the external walls with a dry system), is reproduced a continuous pattern consisting of a succession of key words referred to the activities carried out in the campus: within each slab some of these words are a simple bas-relief, that emphasize the three-dimensionality of the facade, some, instead, are true holes that allow an adequate and peculiar lighting of the internal spaces. The stone panels are a contemporary translation of the oriental tradition of the building skin considered as a complex system of textures that guarantee an indirect illumination of the internal spaces.
Significantly, these key words are written in three languages, (Hebrew, Arabic and English) corresponding to the three main groups that live in Jerusalem, and represent the metaphor of the coexisting cultures, as it should be for any cultural institution.

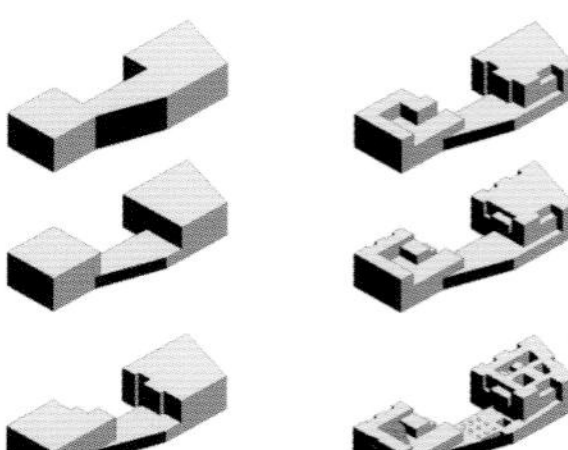

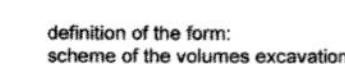
definition of the form:
scheme of the volumes excavation

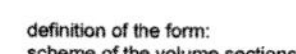
definition of the form:
scheme of the volume sections

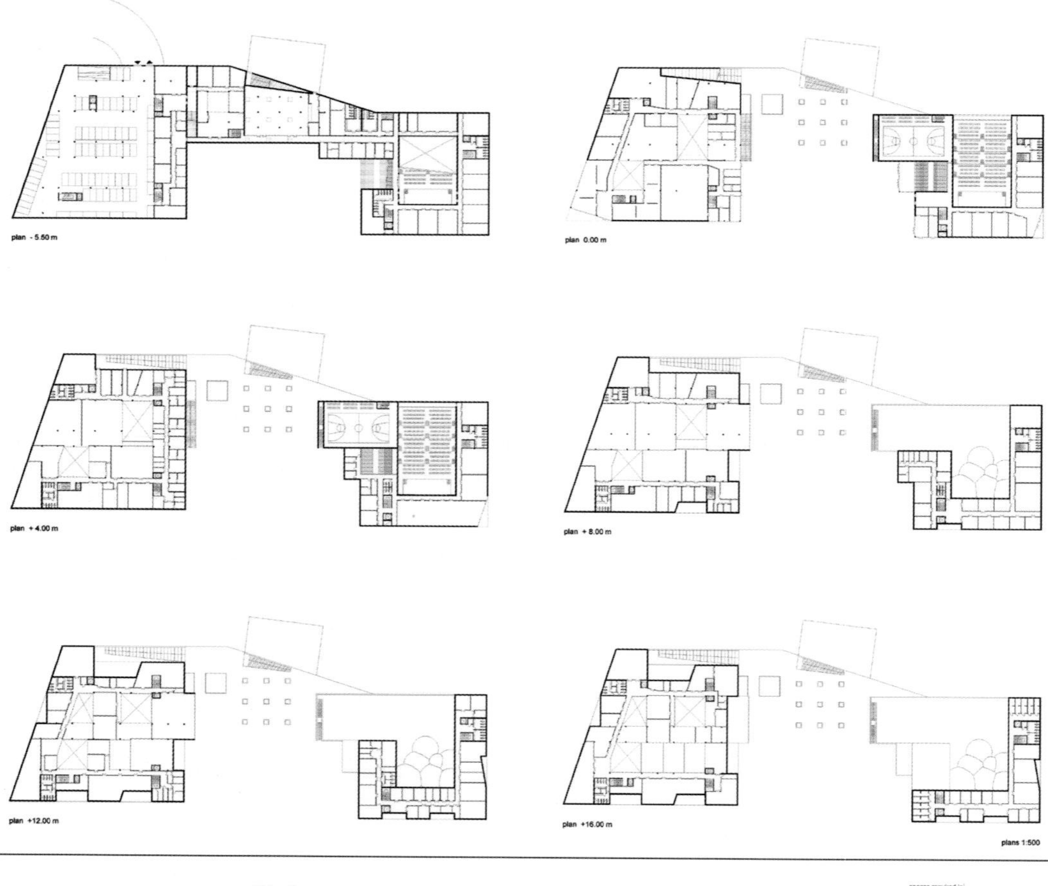

plans 1:500

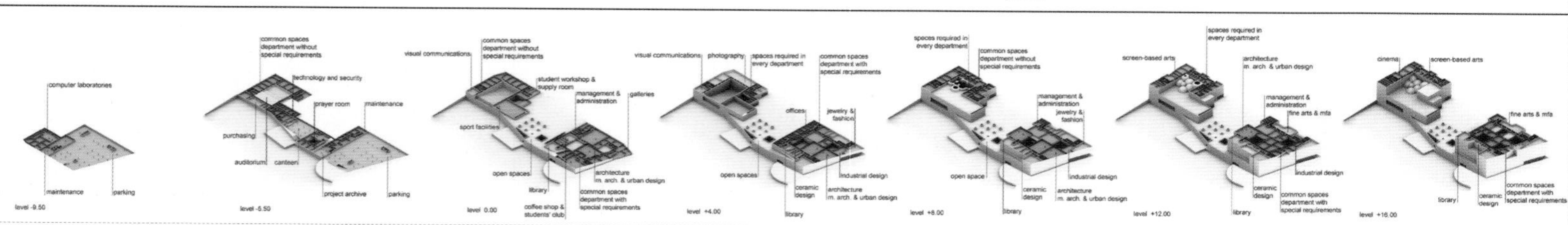

sequence of stone panels in facade

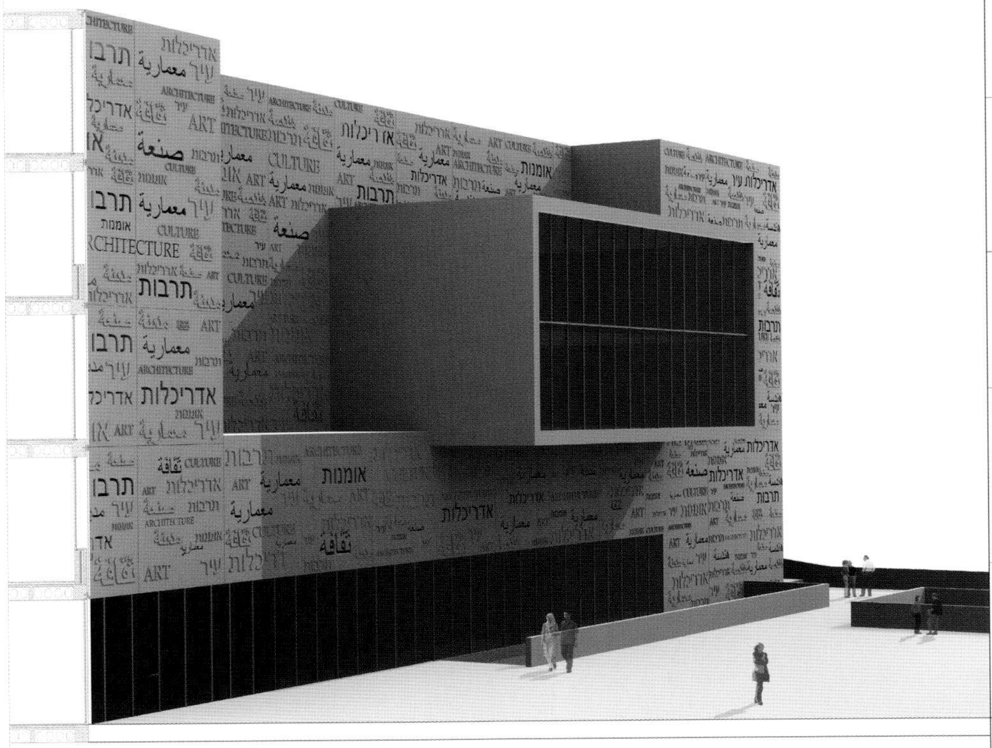

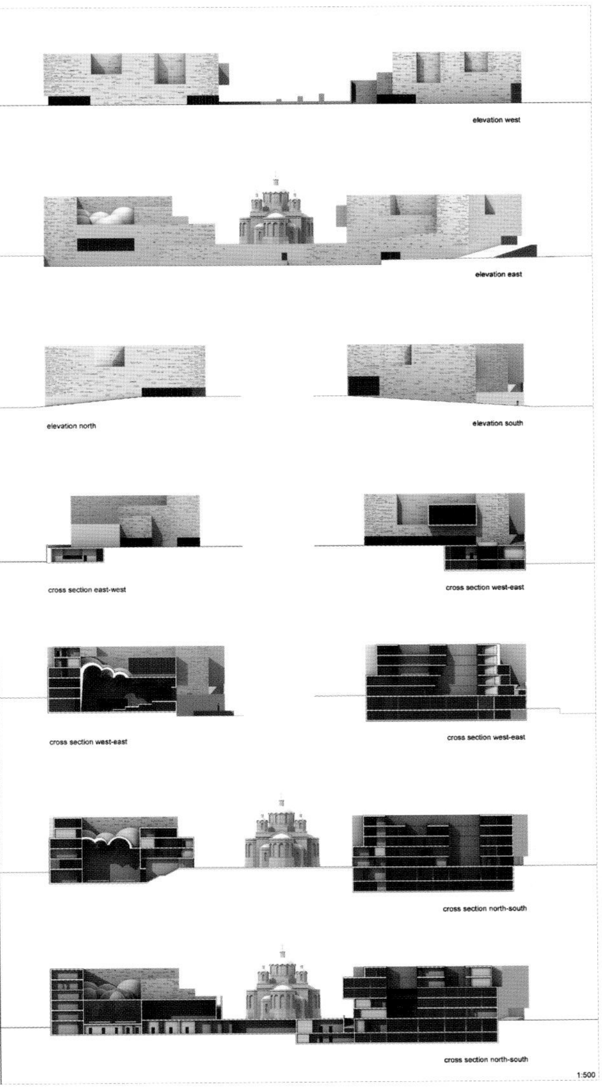

elevation west

elevation east

elevation north

elevation south

cross section east-west

cross section west-east

cross section west-east

cross section west-east

cross section north-south

cross section north-south

1:500

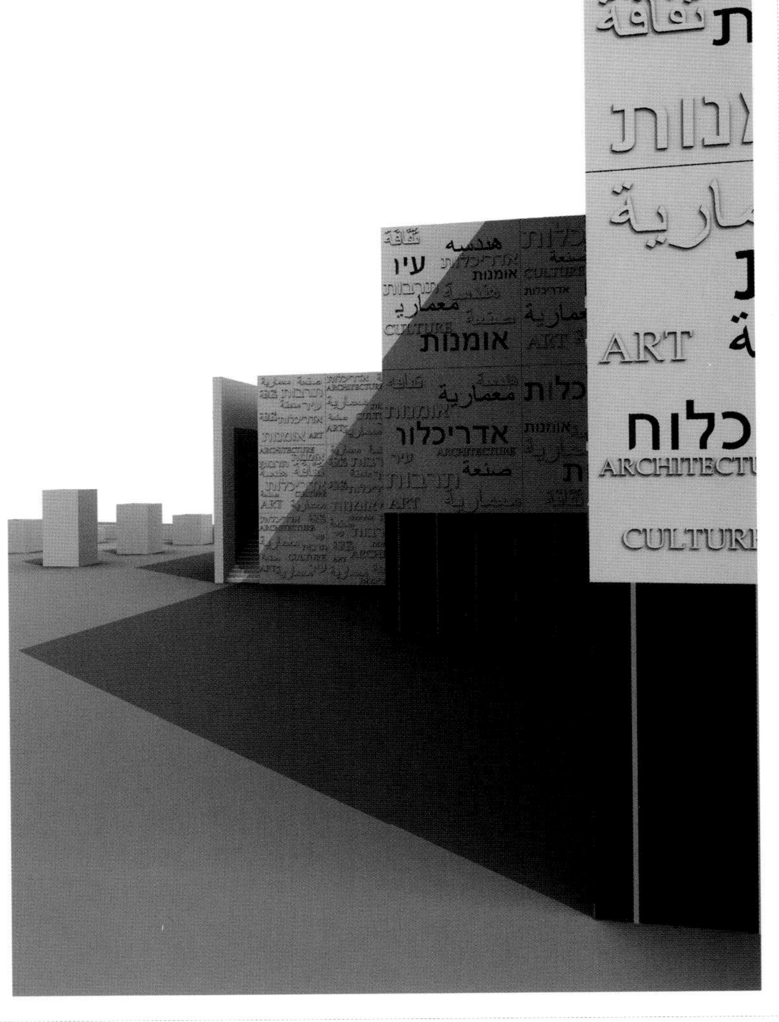

169 Kinder Garten | *b4architects*

Location : Sluderno(BZ) –Italy
Object : Nursery School and Music Practice Room Building
Client : Municipalità of Sluderno

Area : 7000 sqm / Programme : Nursery / Music Practice Room / Public Park
Project Team : gianluca evels & stefania papitto - b4architects

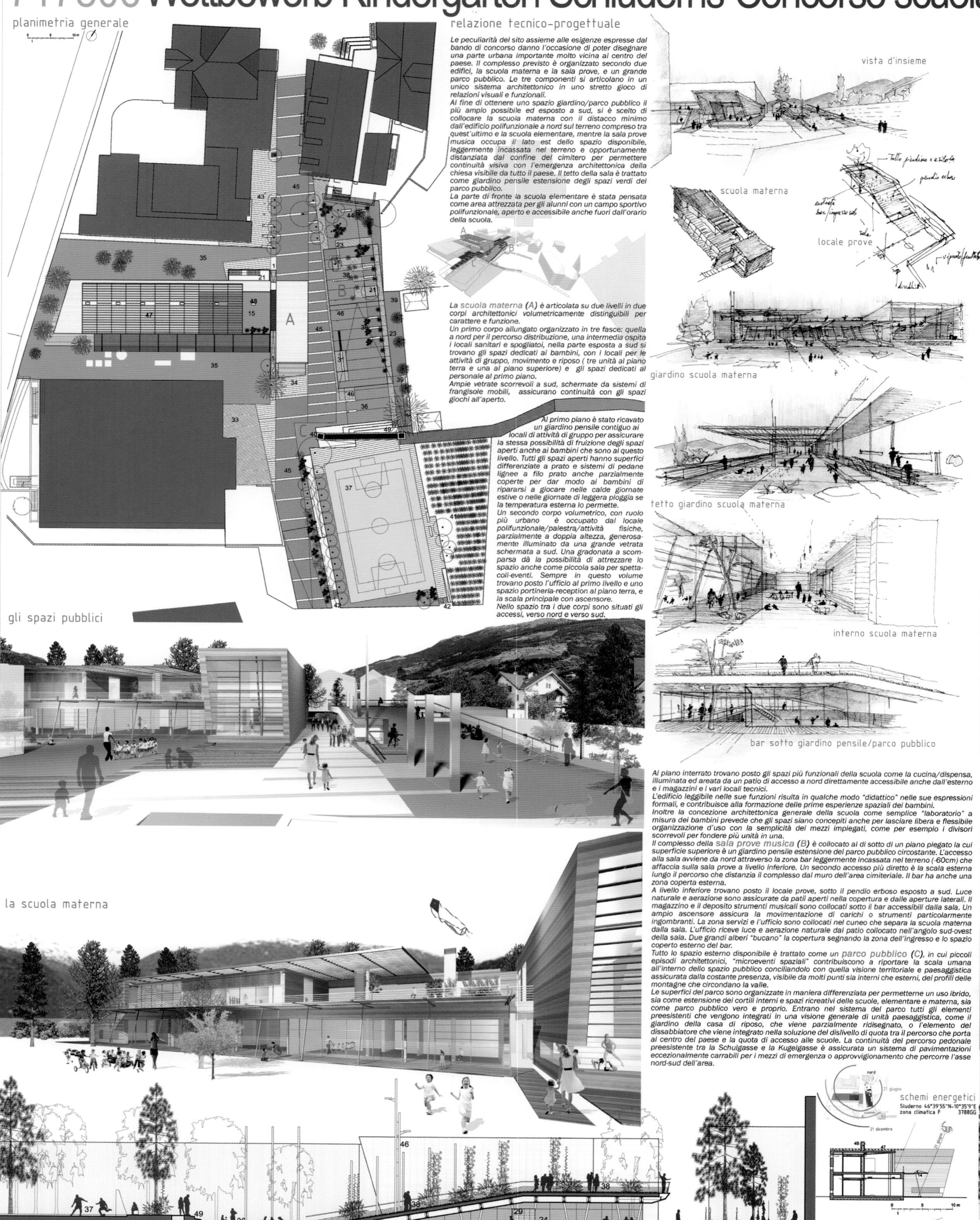

717806 Wettbewerb Kindergarten Schluderns-Concorso scuola
planimetria generale
relazione tecnico-progettuale
Le peculiarità del sito assieme alle esigenze espresse dal bando di concorso danno l'occasione di poter disegnare una parte urbana importante molto vicina al centro del paese. Il complesso previsto è organizzato secondo due edifici, la scuola materna e la sala prove, e un grande parco pubblico. Le tre componenti si articolano in un unico sistema architettonico in uno stretto gioco di relazioni visuali e funzionali.
Al fine di ottenere uno spazio giardino/parco pubblico il più ampio possibile ed esposto a sud, si è scelto di collocare la scuola materna con il distacco minimo dall'edificio polifunzionale a nord sul terreno compreso tra quest'ultimo e la scuola elementare, mentre la sala prove musica occupa il lato est dello spazio disponibile, leggermente incassata nel terreno e opportunamente distanziata dal confine del cimitero per permettere continuità visiva con l'emergenza architettonica della chiesa visibile da tutto il paese. Il tetto della sala è trattato come giardino pensile estensione degli spazi verdi del parco pubblico.
La parte di fronte la scuola elementare è stata pensata come area attrezzata per gli alunni con un campo sportivo polifunzionale, aperto e accessibile anche fuori dall'orario della scuola.
La scuola materna (A) è articolata su due livelli in due corpi architettonici volumetricamente distinguibili per carattere e funzione.
Un primo corpo allungato organizzato in tre fasce: quella a nord per il percorso distribuzione, una intermedia ospita i locali sanitari e spogliatoi, nella parte esposta a sud si trovano gli spazi dedicati ai bambini, con i locali per le attività di gruppo, movimento e riposo (tre unità al piano terra e una al piano superiore) e gli spazi dedicati al personale al primo piano.
Ampie vetrate scorrevoli a sud, schermate da sistemi di frangisole mobili, assicurano continuità con gli spazi giochi all'aperto.
Al primo piano è stato ricavato un giardino pensile contiguo ai locali di attività di gruppo per assicurare la stessa possibilità di fruizione degli spazi aperti anche ai bambini che sono al questo livello. Tutti gli spazi aperti hanno superfici differenziate a prato e sistemi di pedane lignee a filo prato anche parzialmente coperte per dar modo ai bambini di ripararsi a giocare nelle calde giornate estive o nelle giornate di leggera pioggia se la temperatura esterna lo permette.
Un secondo corpo volumetrico, con ruolo più urbano è occupato dal locale polifunzionale/palestra/attività fisiche, parzialmente a doppia altezza, generosamente illuminato da una grande vetrata schermata a sud. Una gradonata a scomparsa dà la possibilità di attrezzare lo spazio anche come piccola sala per spettacoli-eventi. Sempre in questo volume trovano posto l'ufficio al primo livello e uno spazio portineria-reception al piano terra, e la scala principale con ascensore.
Nello spazio tra i due corpi sono situati gli accessi, verso nord e verso sud.
vista d'insieme
scuola materna
locale prove
giardino scuola materna
tetto giardino scuola materna
interno scuola materna
bar sotto giardino pensile/parco pubblico
gli spazi pubblici
la scuola materna
Al piano interrato trovano posto gli spazi più funzionali della scuola come la cucina/dispensa, illuminata ed areata da un patio di accesso a nord direttamente accessibile anche dall'esterno e i magazzini e i vari locali tecnici.
L'edificio leggibile nelle sue funzioni risulta in qualche modo "didattico" nelle sue espressioni formali, e contribuisce alla formazione delle prime esperienze spaziali dei bambini.
Inoltre la concezione architettonica generale della scuola come semplice "laboratorio" a misura dei bambini prevede che gli spazi siano concepiti anche per lasciare libera e flessibile organizzazione d'uso con la semplicità dei mezzi impiegati, come per esempio i divisori scorrevoli per fondere più unità in una.
Il complesso della sala prove musica (B) è collocato al di sotto di un piano piegato la cui superficie superiore è un giardino pensile estensione del parco pubblico circostante. L'accesso alla sala avviene da nord attraverso la zona bar leggermente incassata nel terreno (-60cm) che affaccia sulla sala prove a livello inferiore. Un secondo accesso più diretto è la scala esterna lungo il percorso che distanzia il complesso dal muro dell'area cimiteriale. Il bar ha anche una zona coperta esterna.
A livello inferiore trovano posto il locale prove, sotto il pendio erboso esposto a sud. Luce naturale e aerazione sono assicurate da patii aperti nella copertura e dalle aperture laterali. Il magazzino e il deposito strumenti musicali sono collocati sotto il bar accessibili dalla sala. Un ampio ascensore assicura la movimentazione di carichi o strumenti particolarmente ingombranti. La zona servizi e l'ufficio sono collocati nel cuneo che separa la scuola materna dalla sala. L'ufficio riceve luce e aerazione naturale dal patio collocato nell'angolo sud-ovest della sala. Due grandi alberi "bucano" la copertura segnando la zona dell'ingresso e lo spazio coperto esterno del bar.
Tutto lo spazio esterno disponibile è trattato come un parco pubblico (C), in cui piccoli episodi architettonici, "microeventi spaziali" contribuiscono a riportare la scala umana all'interno dello spazio pubblico conciliandolo con quella visione territoriale e paesaggistica assicurata dalla costante presenza, visibile da molti punti sia interni che esterni, dei profili delle montagne che circondano la valle.
Le superfici del parco sono organizzate in maniera differenziata per permetterne un uso ibrido, sia come estensione dei cortili interni e spazi ricreativi delle scuole, elementare e materna, sia come parco pubblico vero e proprio. Entrano nel sistema del parco tutti gli elementi preesistenti che vengono integrati in una visione generale di unità paesaggistica, come il giardino della casa di riposo, che viene parzialmente ridisegnato, o l'elemento del dissabbiatore che viene integrato nella soluzione del dislivello di quota tra il percorso che porta al centro del paese e la quota di accesso alle scuole. La continuità del percorso pedonale preesistente tra la Schulgasse e la Kugelgasse è assicurata un sistema di pavimentazioni eccezionalmente carrabili per i mezzi di emergenza o approvvigionamento che percorre l'asse nord-sud dell'area.
schemi energetici
Sluderno 46°39'55"N-10°35'9"E
zona climatica F 3788GG
nord
21 giugno
21 dicembre
sezione C-C'

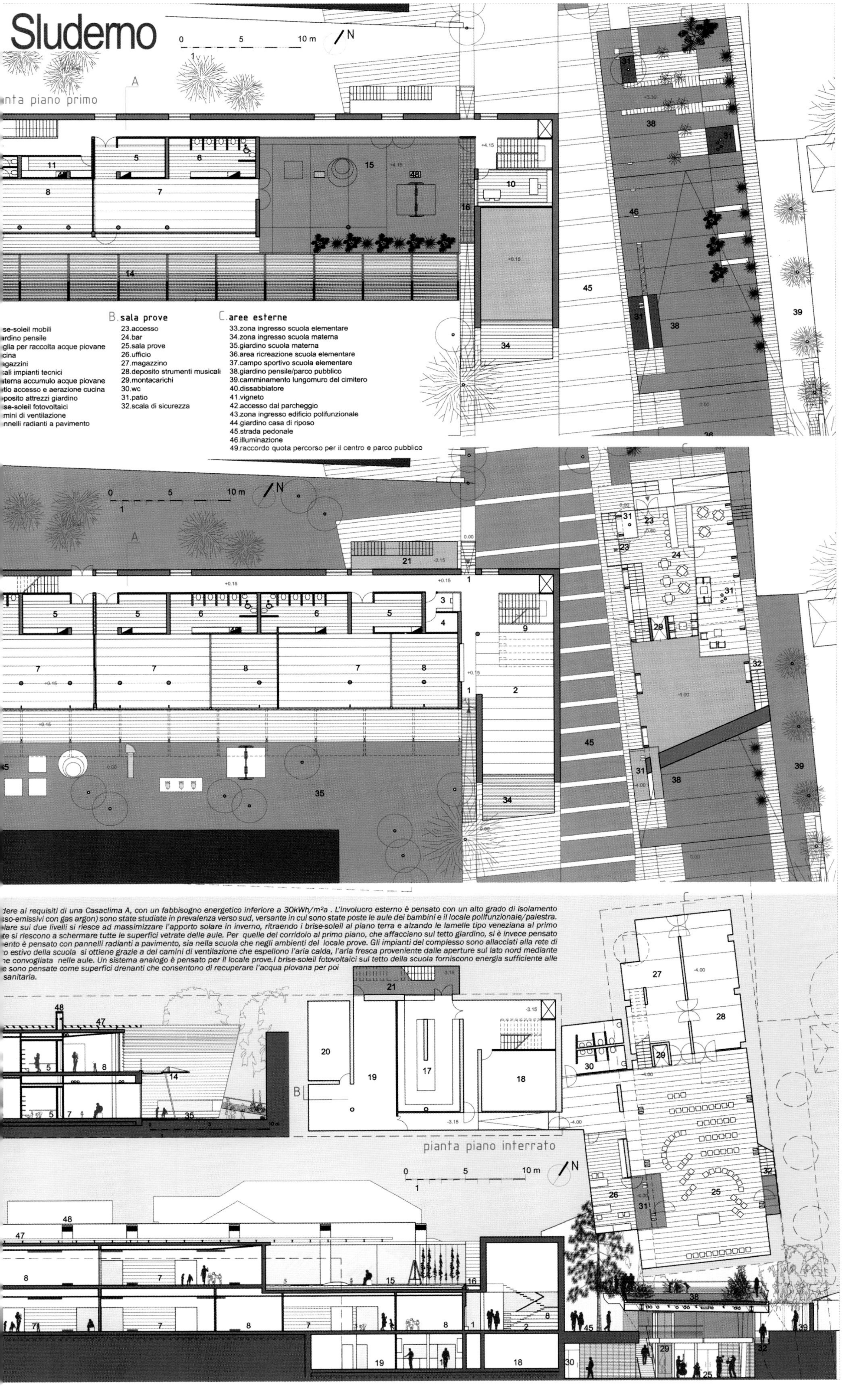
Sluderno
0 5 10 m N
1
nta piano primo
B. sala prove
23.accesso
24.bar
25.sala prove
26.ufficio
27.magazzino
28.deposito strumenti musicali
29.montacarichi
30.wc
31.patio
32.scala di sicurezza
C. aree esterne
33.zona ingresso scuola elementare
34.zona ingresso scuola materna
35.giardino scuola materna
36.area ricreazione scuola elementare
37.campo sportivo scuola elementare
38.giardino pensile/parco pubblico
39.camminamento lungomuro del cimitero
40.dissabbiatore
41.vigneto
42.accesso dal parcheggio
43.zona ingresso edificio polifunzionale
44.giardino casa di riposo
45.strada pedonale
46.illuminazione
49.raccordo quota percorso per il centro e parco pubblico
se-soleil mobili
ardino pensile
glia per raccolta acque piovane
cina
agazzini
cali impianti tecnici
sterna accumulo acque piovane
tio accesso e aerazione cucina
posito attrezzi giardino
se-soleil fotovoltaici
mini di ventilazione
nnelli radianti a pavimento
dere ai requisiti di una Casaclima A, con un fabbisogno energetico inferiore a 30kWh/m²a . L'involucro esterno è pensato con un alto grado di isolamento
sso-emissivi con gas argon) sono state studiate in prevalenza verso sud, versante in cui sono state poste le aule dei bambini e il locale polifunzionale/palestra.
lare sui due livelli si riesce ad massimizzare l'apporto solare in inverno, ritraendo i brise-soleil al piano terra e alzando le lamelle tipo veneziana al primo
te si riescono a schermare tutte le superfici vetrate delle aule. Per quelle del corridoio al primo piano, che affacciano sul tetto giardino, si è invece pensato
ento è pensato con pannelli radianti a pavimento, sia nella scuola che negli ambienti del locale prove. Gli impianti del complesso sono allacciati alla rete di
o estivo della scuola si ottiene grazie a dei camini di ventilazione che espellono l'aria calda, l'aria fresca proveniente dalle aperture sul lato nord mediante
ne convogliata nelle aule. Un sistema analogo è pensato per il locale prove.I brise-soleil fotovoltaici sul tetto della scuola forniscono energia sufficiente alle
e sono pensate come superfici drenanti che consentono di recuperare l'acqua piovana per poi
sanitaria.
pianta piano interrato

170 Paraparvulos | *gutiérrez-delafuente arquitectos*

Project : Finalist VII Young Architects National Competition 07 Kindergarten Spain
Program : Kindergarten in Las Tablas, Madrid
Location : Madrid, Spain

Client : City of Madrid
Architects : Natalia Gutiérrez & Julio de la Fuente

VII CONCURSO NACIONAL DE IDEAS PARA JÓVENES ARQUITECTOS DEL DISTRITO DE FUENCARRAL - EL PARDO
ESCUELA DE EDUCACIÓN INFANTIL EN LA PARCELA B-25 LAS TABLAS

PLANTA DE SITUACIÓN 1/3000

LA CIUDAD / CONDICIONES DE CONTORNO:

-SOLEAMIENTO: las condiciones óptimas de soleamiento para el patio de juegos y las aulas, nos llevan a analizar las sombras arrojadas por los edificios colindantes en esas orientaciones. como resultado se obtiene la única zona viable de ocupación de la parcela. zona "X".
-ACCESOS: el tráfico rodado de la vía principal, situada al norte de la parcela se considera de gran intensidad en el futuro, así que dado el área de acción de la edificación por la anterior variable , los acceso se organizan desde el vial sureste, con una carga de tráfico y escala más adecuada.
-CONDOMINIO NIÑOS: la gran escala de la parcela difiere mucho de la escala del patio de juegos infantiles, así que la estrategia es crear un espacio para los niños del que se puedan apropiar y sentirlo suyo, su condominio, entendido desde la posesión. ese condominio estará acotado por una pequeña operación topográfica y de arbolado. el resto de la parcela, a efectos de los niños, será "el mundo exterior", se tratará como un bosque urbano, silvestre, que pueda ser usado por los vecinos de forma convenida.

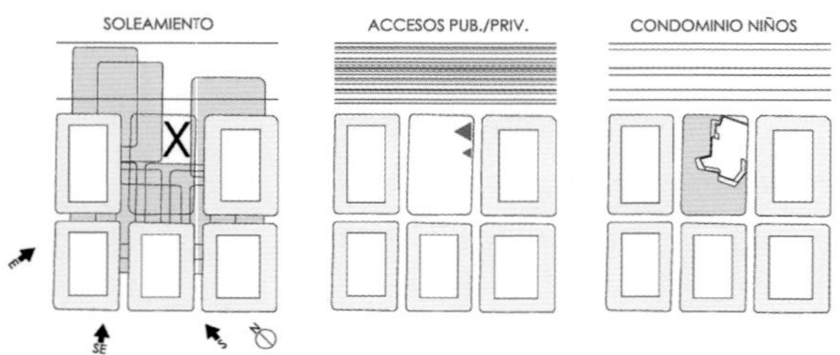

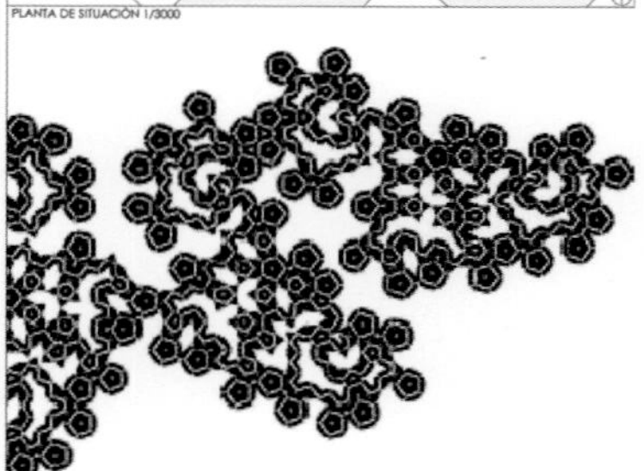

"ROSARIO AXIOMÁTICO" 1999 - TÉCNICA MIXTA EN TELA
AUTOR: MAURO MACHADO

CREACIÓN DE UN SISTEMA / GEOMETRÍA:

- la búqueda de una escuela infantil que sea abierta, flexible a futuros cambios y no lineal, lleva a considerar la creación de un sistema isomórfico, casi como un juego de formas geométricas (profesor Fröbel) donde los niños lo usan y se apropian de él, descubriéndolo de forma intuitiva y ayudados por el color. con esta estrategia se huye de un esquema tipológico de pasillo-aula , que parece tan ajeno a los niños (ya tendrán tiempo de pasillos...).
- la tipología planteada arranca de una forma simple, "un cristal" pentagonal, que seriado y sometido a una serie de operaciones geométricas y con unas leyes marcadas derivadas del cumplimiento del programa, nos da como resultado la escuela infantil deseada.
- las zonas de niños y mayores están "cosidas" por un espacio intersticial, heterogéneo, con diferentes cualidades espaciales según se recorre y que además de hacer funcionar el programa, está abierto a la improvisación, a los juegos los días de lluvia, a conocer otros niños....un jardín interior...y amarillo¡¡¡.
- el sistema desarrollado conlleva una solución estructural óptima. se trata de una estructura muraria, sencilla, económica y adecuada para el desarrollo horizontal del programa.

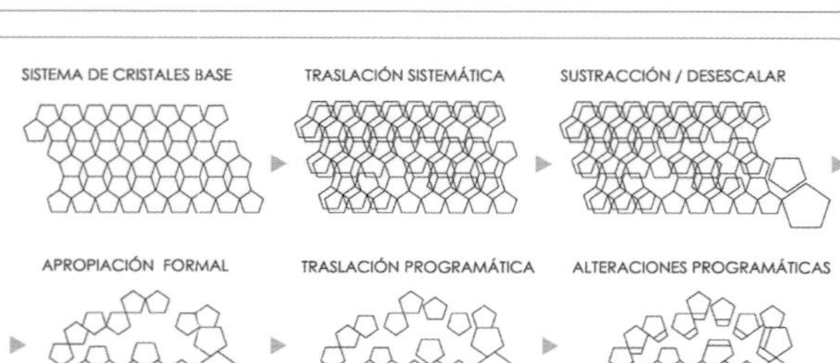

LEMA: PARAPARVULOS

MEMORIA PARAPARVULOS:
"LA CIUDAD Y EL PROFESOR FRÖBEL" :

-la escala de la parcela y las condiciones de contorno de su ubicación son las primeras variables con la que se trabaja, sobre estas decisiones arranca la propuesta (ver "la ciudad / condiciones de contorno").

- en 1816 el profesor Fröbel funda su primera escuela para niños, el primer kindergarten. para ello ideó una nueva metodología que iba creando en los niños una relación comprensiva con el mundo exterior. uno de los llamados "dones" o leccioens sucesivas, consistía en el trabajo con formas geométricas básicas, creando complejidad a través de patrones o leyes. estos "dones" se apoyaban en las formas de la naturaleza, las del conocimiento y las de la belleza.
el método se extendió por toda europa hacia 1940.
en la propuesta de escuela infantil se busca una tipología apropiada y la huida de un esquema tan ajeno a los niños como es el de volúmenes lineales de pasillo-aula.
así el sistema propuesto arranca de una de las lecciones de Fröbel, apoyado en una forma sencilla pentagonal se construye una entidad compleja a través de leyes sencillas.
(ver : "creación de un sistema / geometría").

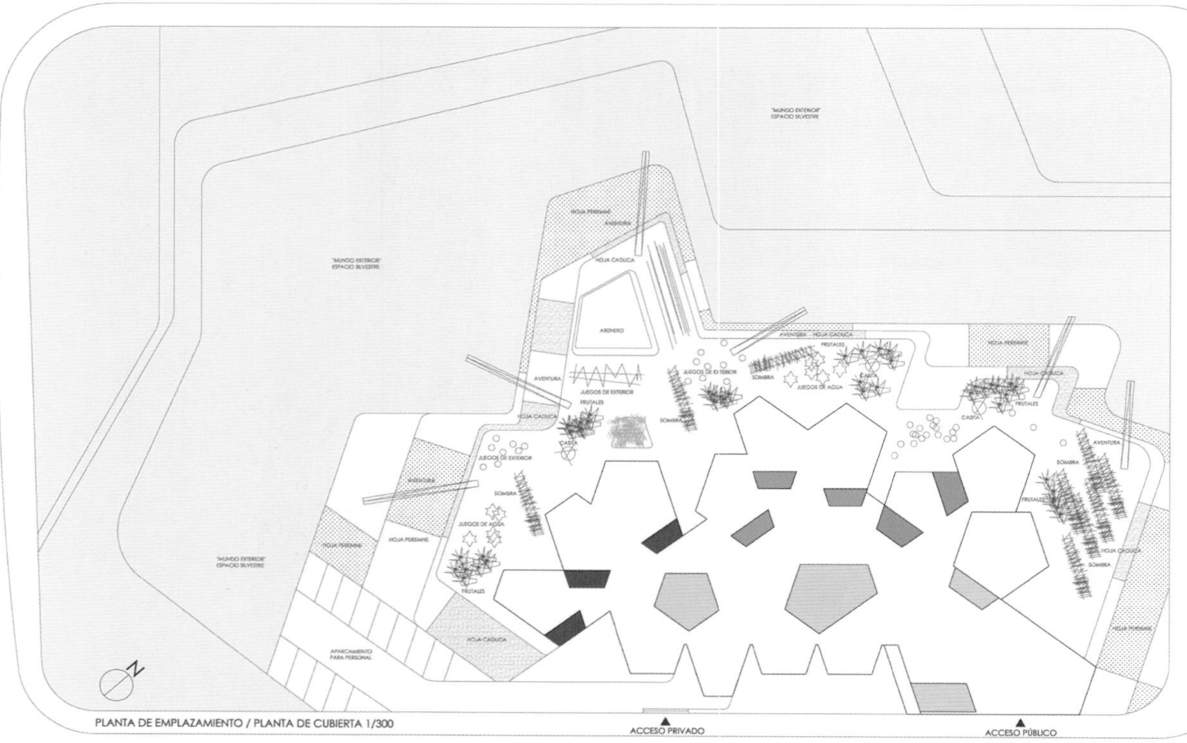

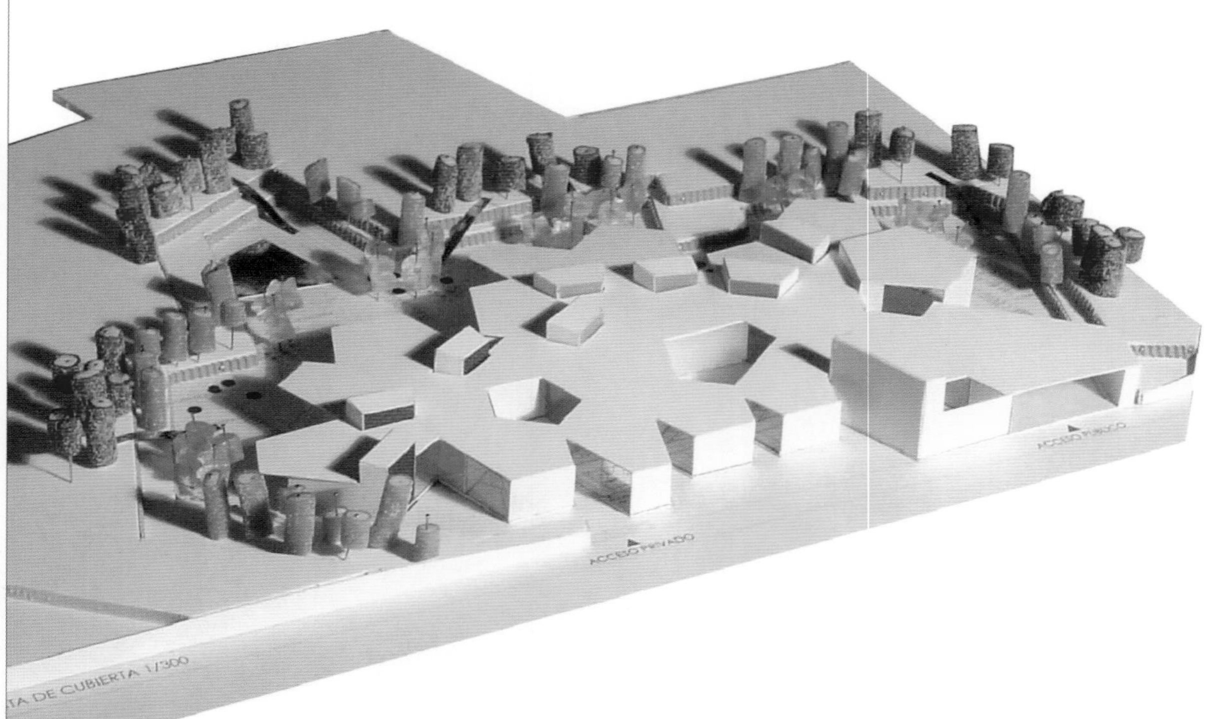

1/2

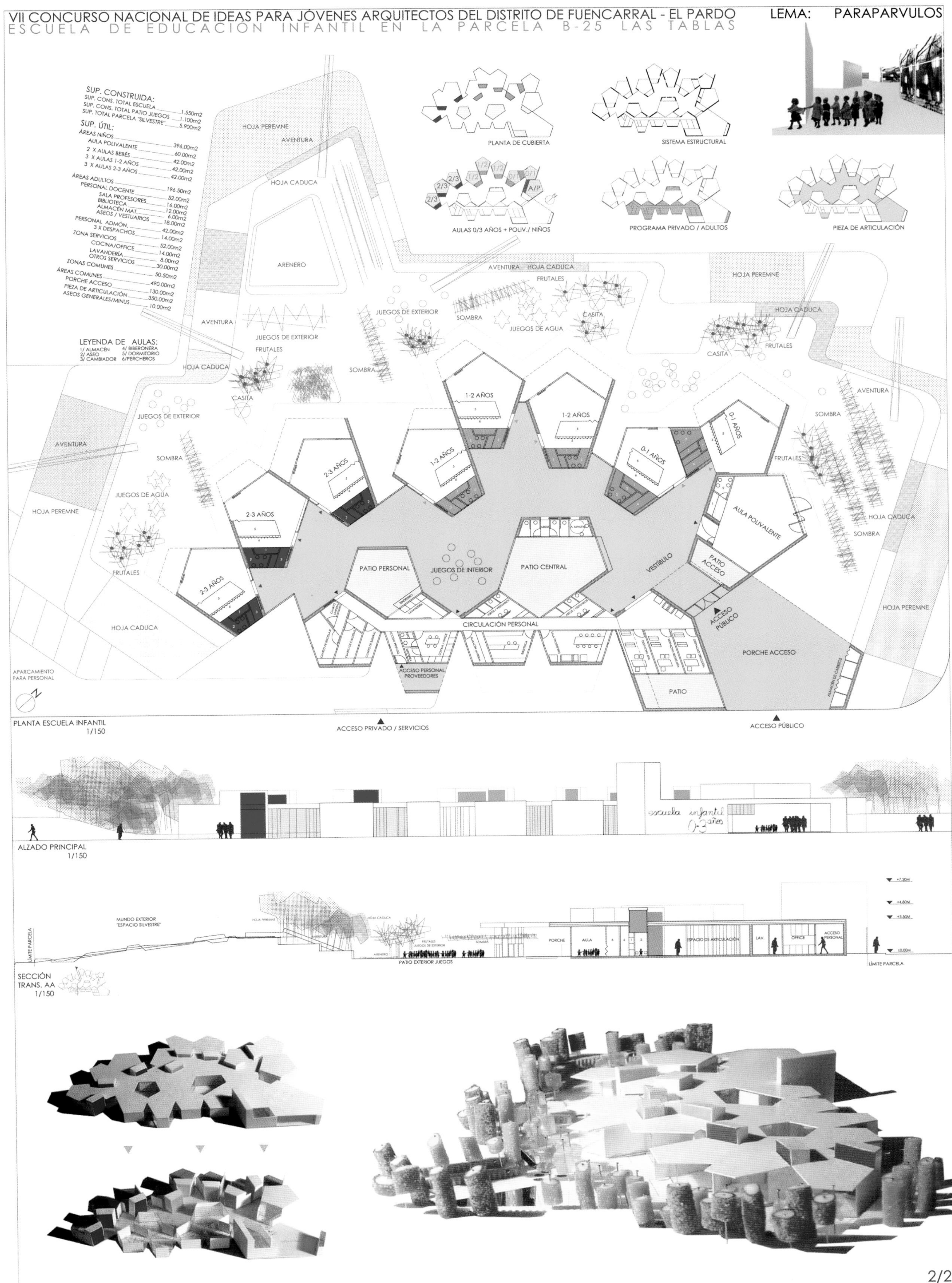
VII CONCURSO NACIONAL DE IDEAS PARA JÓVENES ARQUITECTOS DEL DISTRITO DE FUENCARRAL - EL PARDO
ESCUELA DE EDUCACIÓN INFANTIL EN LA PARCELA B-25 LAS TABLAS
LEMA: PARAPARVULOS
SUP. CONSTRUIDA:
SUP. CONS. TOTAL ESCUELA 1.550m2
SUP. CONS. TOTAL PATIO JUEGOS 1.100m2
SUP. TOTAL PARCELA "SILVESTRE" 5.900m2
SUP. ÚTIL:
ÁREAS NIÑOS
AULA POLIVALENTE 396.00m2
2 X AULAS BEBÉS 60.00m2
3 X AULAS 1-2 AÑOS 42.00m2
3 X AULAS 2-3 AÑOS 42.00m2
42.00m2
ÁREAS ADULTOS
PERSONAL DOCENTE 196.50m2
SALA PROFESORES 52.00m2
BIBLIOTECA 16.00m2
ALMACÉN MAT. 12.00m2
ASEOS / VESTUARIOS 6.00m2
18.00m2
PERSONAL ADMÓN.
3 X DESPACHOS 42.00m2
ZONA SERVICIOS 14.00m2
COCINA/OFFICE 52.00m2
LAVANDERÍA 14.00m2
OTROS SERVICIOS 8.00m2
ZONAS COMUNES 30.00m2
ÁREAS COMUNES 50.50m2
PORCHE ACCESO 490.00m2
PIEZA DE ARTICULACIÓN 130.00m2
ASEOS GENERALES/MINUS. 350.00m2
10.00m2
LEYENDA DE AULAS:
1/ ALMACÉN 4/ BIBERONERA
2/ ASEO 5/ DORMITORIO
3/ CAMBIADOR 6/PERCHEROS
PLANTA DE CUBIERTA
SISTEMA ESTRUCTURAL
AULAS 0/3 AÑOS + POLIV./ NIÑOS
PROGRAMA PRIVADO / ADULTOS
PIEZA DE ARTICULACIÓN
HOJA PEREMNE
AVENTURA
HOJA CADUCA
ARENERO
JUEGOS DE EXTERIOR
FRUTALES
SOMBRA
JUEGOS DE AGUA
CASITA
1-2 AÑOS
2-3 AÑOS
0-1 AÑOS
AULA POLIVALENTE
PATIO PERSONAL
JUEGOS DE INTERIOR
PATIO CENTRAL
VESTÍBULO
PATIO ACCESO
ACCESO PÚBLICO
CIRCULACIÓN PERSONAL
ACCESO PERSONAL PROVEEDORES
PORCHE ACCESO
PATIO
APARCAMIENTO PARA PERSONAL
PLANTA ESCUELA INFANTIL
1/150
ACCESO PRIVADO / SERVICIOS
ACCESO PÚBLICO
escuela infantil 0-3 años
ALZADO PRINCIPAL
1/150
MUNDO EXTERIOR "ESPACIO SILVESTRE"
LÍMITE PARCELA
PATIO EXTERIOR JUEGOS
PORCHE
AULA
ESPACIO DE ARTICULACIÓN
LAV.
OFFICE
ACCESO PERSONAL
SECCIÓN TRANS. AA
1/150
2/2

171

S87 Kindergarten | *franz zt gmb*

Function : Kindergarten
Competition : 2010
Location : Vienna, Austria
Collaboration : Anna Gruber

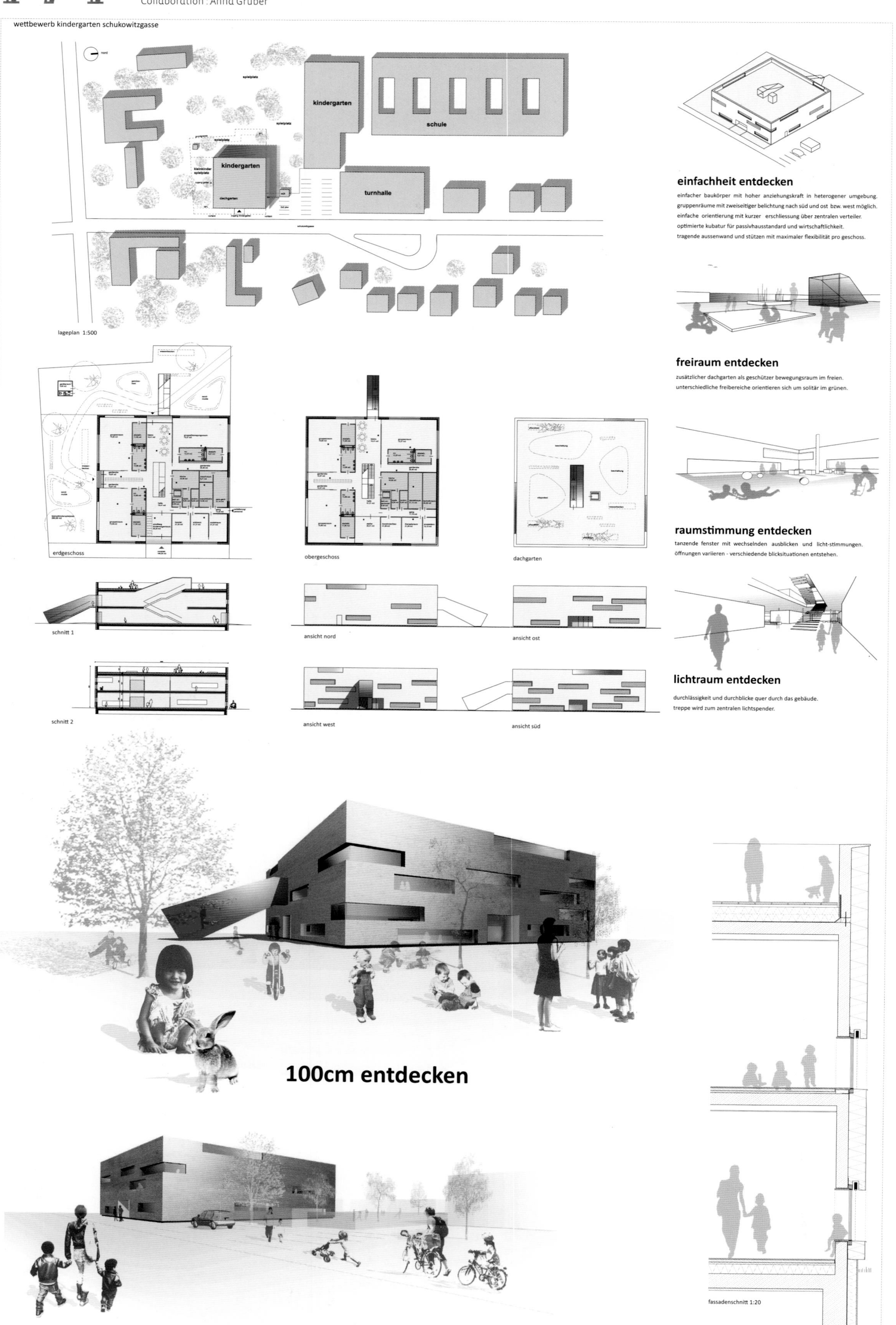

wettbewerb kindergarten schukowitzgasse
kindergarten
schule
kindergarten
turnhalle
lageplan 1:500
einfachheit entdecken
einfacher baukörper mit hoher anziehungskraft in heterogener umgebung.
gruppenräume mit zweiseitiger belichtung nach süd und ost bzw. west möglich.
einfache orientierung mit kurzer erschliessung über zentralen verteiler.
optimierte kubatur für passivhausstandard und wirtschaftlichkeit.
tragende aussenwand und stützen mit maximaler flexibilität pro geschoss.
freiraum entdecken
zusätzlicher dachgarten als geschützer bewegungsraum im freien.
unterschiedliche freibereiche orientieren sich um solitär im grünen.
raumstimmung entdecken
tanzende fenster mit wechselnden ausblicken und licht-stimmungen.
öffnungen variieren - verschiedende blicksituationen entstehen.
lichtraum entdecken
durchlässigkeit und durchblicke quer durch das gebäude.
treppe wird zum zentralen lichtspender.
erdgeschoss
obergeschoss
dachgarten
schnitt 1
ansicht nord
ansicht ost
schnitt 2
ansicht west
ansicht süd
100cm entdecken
fassadenschnitt 1:20

172

Project Description : Nursery
Location : Lancy, Switzerland
Design : KLAIR
Status of project : Competition Entry 2011

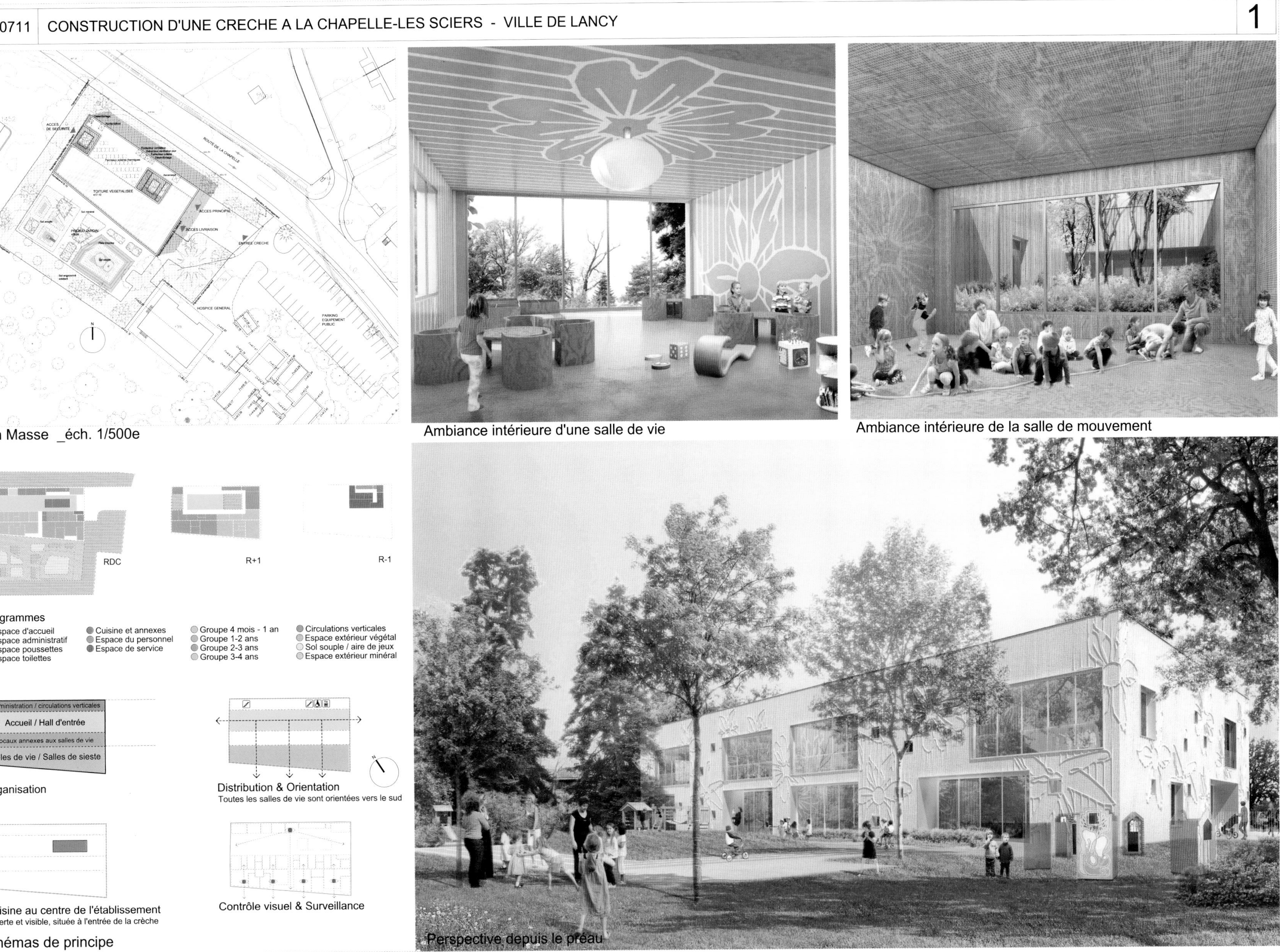

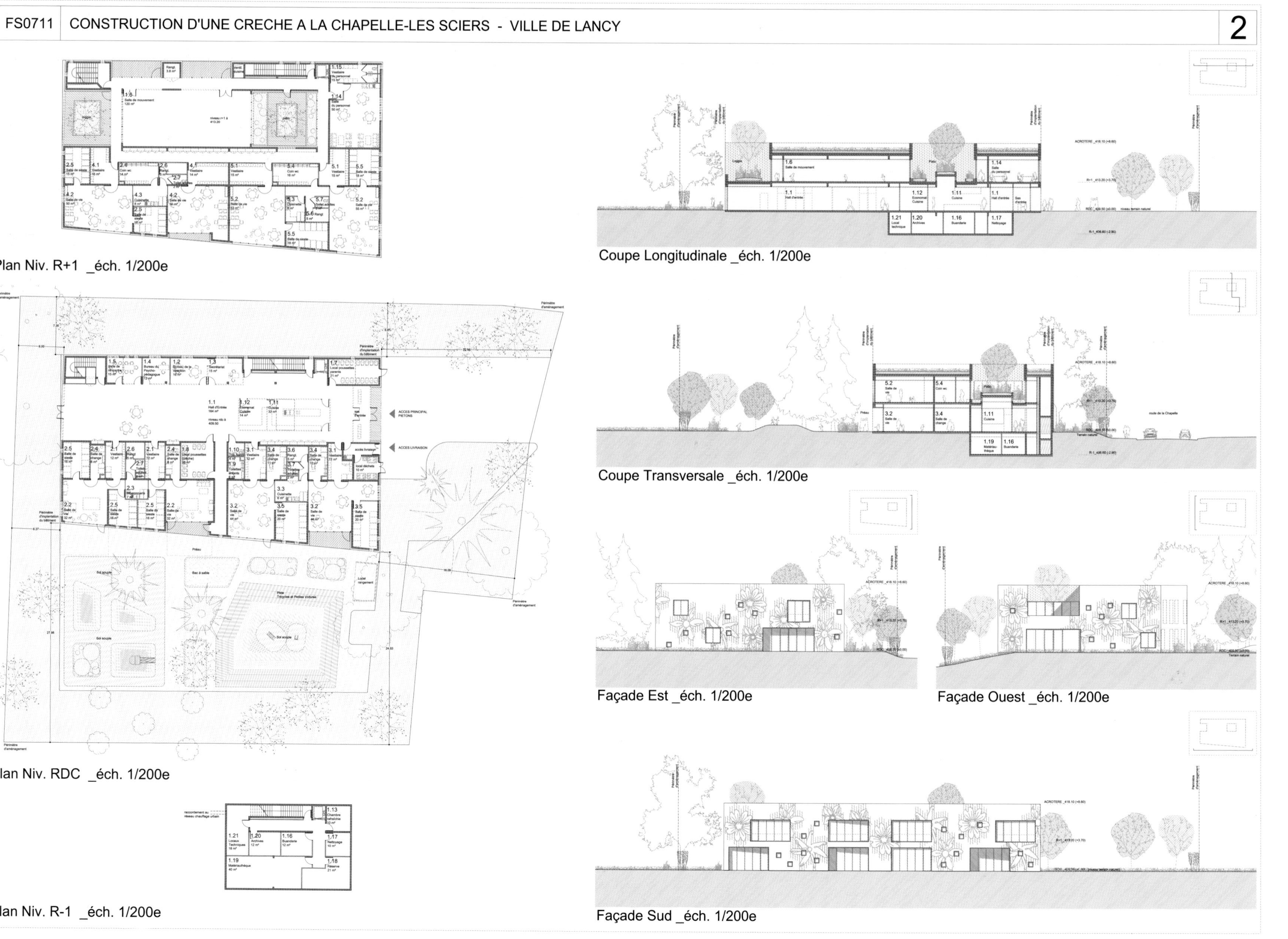
FS0711
CONSTRUCTION D'UNE CRECHE A LA CHAPELLE-LES SCIERS - VILLE DE LANCY
2
Plan Niv. R+1 _éch. 1/200e
Plan Niv. RDC _éch. 1/200e
Plan Niv. R-1 _éch. 1/200e
Coupe Longitudinale _éch. 1/200e
Coupe Transversale _éch. 1/200e
Façade Est _éch. 1/200e
Façade Ouest _éch. 1/200e
Façade Sud _éch. 1/200e

FS0711 CONSTRUCTION D'UNE CRECHE A LA CHAPELLE-LES SCIERS - VILLE DE LANCY **3**

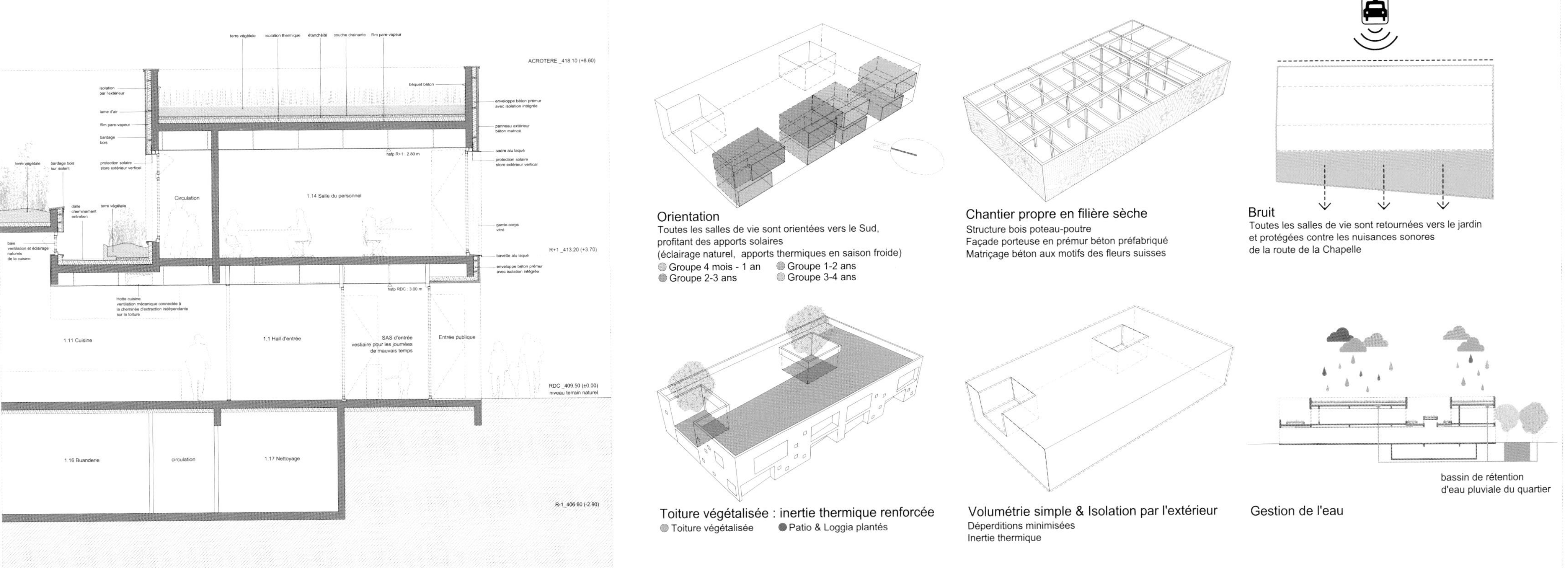

Coupe verticale de principe _éch. 1/50e

Orientation
Toutes les salles de vie sont orientées vers le Sud, profitant des apports solaires (éclairage naturel, apports thermiques en saison froide)
Groupe 4 mois - 1 an
Groupe 2-3 ans
Groupe 1-2 ans
Groupe 3-4 ans

Chantier propre en filière sèche
Structure bois poteau-poutre
Façade porteuse en prémur béton préfabriqué
Matriçage béton aux motifs des fleurs suisses

Bruit
Toutes les salles de vie sont retournées vers le jardin et protégées contre les nuisances sonores de la route de la Chapelle

Toiture végétalisée : inertie thermique renforcée
Toiture végétalisée
Patio & Loggia plantés

Volumétrie simple & Isolation par l'extérieur
Déperditions minimisées
Inertie thermique

bassin de rétention d'eau pluviale du quartier

Gestion de l'eau

niveau R+1

niveau RDC

Ventilation naturelle
hall traversant, patio et loggia

Pour une architecture en connivence avec la nature.

Le projet s'insère dans un jardin arboré de riches végétations existantes, un environnement qui représente déjà une grande qualité en tant qu'espace vert mais aussi un fort potentiel pour devenir le cadre d'une crèche. **Les enfants pourront s'éveiller en étroit contact avec la nature** dès leur 1er âge dans un contexte exceptionnel.

Pour laisser exprimer la nature, nous proposons **une architecture simple avec une fonctionnalité claire**. Nos réflexions portent avant tout sur la pertinence d'un concept global, du programme fonctionnel, sur l'organisation intérieur et sa relation avec l'extérieur :
Sur cette base, **des solutions simples et durables** sont développées.

Toutes les salles de vie des enfants sont **orientées vers le jardin au Sud**, **déconnectées des contingences (nuisance sonore, regard direct, pollution d'air...) de la route de la chapelle** située au Nord.
Les feuillages des végétations du jardin forment de la protection solaire dès les premiers beaux jours. Les salles de vie bénéficient des apports solaires (éclairage naturel, apports thermiques en saison froide). Une grande toiture végétalisée, un patio et une loggia viennent renforcer ce lien étroit entre le bâti et la nature.

Le hall d'accueil traversant permet l'organisation des fêtes et de petites manifestations, et en même temps de distribuer les différents corps fonctionnels. Le vide structure les programmes de façon très fluide.
Ouverte et visible de tous les côtés, **la cuisine est placée au cœur de l'établissement**, près de l'entrée, pour accompagner les orientations pédagogiques souhaitées.
Les couloirs sont doublés par de **généreux espaces pour le rangement**.

L'organisation simple des plans permettra une grande flexibilité pour faire face aux éventuelles évolutions programmatiques.

Aménagement extérieur
Sol revêtement minéral
Espaces verts / sol perméable
Terrain de jeux / sol souple
Piste tricycles & petites voitures

Connivence avec la nature
Arbres existants de haute tige conservés
Arbres plantés
Espaces verts engazonnés

Principes environnementaux

TO BE CONTINUED